CRITICAL

AND

MISCELLANEOUS

ESSAYS.

BY THOMAS CARLYLE,

AUTHOR OF THE HISTORY OF THE FRENCH REVOLUTION.

A NEW EDITION,

COMPLETE IN ONE VOLUME.

PHILADELPHIA:

A. HART, LATE CAREY & HART,

No. 126 CHESTNUT STREET.

1852.

Printed by T. K. & P. G. Collins.

ADVERTISEMENT.

The Publishers introduce the present edition of Mr. Carlyle's Essays with the following note from the American Editor of the First Edition.

Messrs. Carey & Hart,

Gentlemen:—I have to signify to his American readers, Mr. Carlyle's concurrence in this new edition of his Essays, and his expressed satisfaction in the author's share of pecuniary benefit which your justice and liberality have secured to him in anticipation of the sale. With every hope for the success of your enterprise, I am your obedient servant,

R. W. Emerson.

Concord, June, 1845.

CONTENTS.

CONTENTS.

CARLYLE'S

MISCELLANEOUS WRITINGS.

JEAN PAUL FRIEDRICH RICHTER.

[Edinburgh Review, 1827.]

Dr. Johnson, it is said, when he first heard of Boswell's intention to write a life of him, announced, with decision enough, that, if he thought Boswell really meant to *write his* life, he would prevent it by *taking Boswell's!* That great authors should actually employ this preventive against bad biographers is a thing we would by no means recommend; but the truth is, that, rich as we are in biography, a well-written life is almost as rare as a well-spent one; and there are certainly many more men whose history deserves to be recorded than persons willing and able to furnish the record. But great men, like the old Egyptian kings, must all be tried after death, before they can be embalmed: and what, in truth, are these "Sketches," "Anas," "Conversations," "Voices," and the like, but the votes and pleadings of the ill-informed advocates, and jurors, and judges, from whose conflict, however, we shall in the end have a true verdict? The worst of it is at the first; for weak eyes are precisely the fondest of glittering objects. And, accordingly, no sooner does a great man depart, and leave his character as public property, than a crowd of little men rushes towards it. There they are gathered together, blinking up to it with such vision as they have, scanning it from afar, hovering round it this way and that, each cunningly endeavouring, by all arts, to catch some reflex of it in the little mirror of himself; though, many times, this mirror is so twisted with convexities and concavities, and, indeed, so extremely small in size, that to expect any true image, or any image whatever from it, is out of the question.

Richter was much better-natured than Johnson; and took many provoking things with the spirit of a humorist and philosopher; nor can we think that so good a man, even had he foreseen this work of Doering's, would have gone the length of assassinating him for it. Doering is a person we have known for several years, as a compiler, and translator, and ballad-monger, whose grand enterprise, however, is his *Gallery of Weimar Authors;* a series of strange little biographies, beginning with Schiller, and already extending over Wieland and Herder,—now comprehending, probably by conquest, Klopstock also, and lastly, by a sort of *droit d'aubaine*, Jean Paul Friedrich Richter, neither of whom belonged to Weimar. Authors, it must be admitted, are happier than the old painter with his cocks: for they write, naturally and without fear of ridicule or offence, the name and description of their work on the title-page; and thenceforth the purport and tendency of each volume remains indisputable. Doering is sometimes lucky in this privilege; for his manner of composition, being so peculiar, might now and then occasion difficulty, but for this precaution. His biographies he works up simply enough. He first ascertains, from the Leipzig *Conversationslexicon* or Jörden's *Poetical Lexicon*, Flögel, or Koch, or other such *Compendium* or *Handbook*, the date and place of the proposed individual's birth, his parentage, trade, appointments, and the titles of his works; (the date of his death you already know from the newspapers;) this serves as a foundation for the edifice. He then goes through his writings, and all other writings where he or his pursuits are treated of, and whenever he finds a passage with his name in it, he cuts it out, and carries it away. In this manner a mass of materials is collected, and the building now proceeds apace. Stone is laid on the top of stone, just as it comes to hand; a trowel or two of biographic mortar, if perfectly convenient, being perhaps spread in here and there, by way of cement; and so the strangest pile suddenly arises; amorphous, pointing every way but to the zenith,—here a block of granite, there a mass of pipe-clay; till the whole finishes, when the materials are finished,—and you leave it standing to posterity, like some miniature Stonehenge, a perfect architectural enigma.

To speak without figure, this mode of life-writing has its disadvantages. For one thing, the composition cannot well be what the critics call harmonious; and, indeed, Herr Doering's transitions are often abrupt enough. His hero

---

* *Jean Paul Friedrich Richter's Leben, nebst Characteristik seiner Werke; von Heinrich Doering.* (Jean Paul Friedrich Richter's Life, with a Sketch of his Works; by Heinrich Doering.) Gotha. Hennings, 1826. 12mo. pp. 208.

changes his object and occupation from page to page, often from sentence to sentence, in the most unaccountable way; a pleasure journey, and a sickness of fifteen years, are despatched with equal brevity; in a moment you find him married, and the father of three fine children. He dies no less suddenly;—he is studying as usual, writing poetry, receiving visits, full of life and business, when instantly some paragraph opens under him, like one of the trapdoors in the *Vision of Mirza*, and he drops, without note of preparation, into the shades below. Perhaps, indeed, not for ever: we have instances of his rising after the funeral, and winding up his affairs. The time has been, that when the brains were out the man would die; but Doering orders these matters differently.

We beg leave to say, however, that we really have no private pique against Doering: on the contrary, we are regular purchasers of his ware; and it gives us true pleasure to see his spirits so much improved since we first met him. In the *Life of Schiller*, his state did seem rather unprosperous: he wore a timorous, submissive, and downcast aspect, as if like Sterne's Ass, he were saying, "Don't thrash me;—but if you will, you may!" Now, however, comforted by considerable sale, and praise from this and the other *Literaturblatt*, which has commended his diligence, his fidelity, and, strange to say, his method, he advances with erect countenance and firm hoof, and even recalcitrates contemptuously against such as do him offence. *Glück auf dem Weg!* is the worst we wish him.

Of his *Life of Richter*, these preliminary observations may be our excuse for saying but little. He brags much, in his preface, that it is all true and genuine; for Richter's widow, it seems, had, by public advertisement, cautioned the world against it; another biography, partly by the illustrious deceased himself, partly by Otto, his oldest friend and the appointed editor of his works, being actually in preparation. This rouses the indignant spirit of Doering, and he stoutly asseverates, that, his documents being altogether authentic, this biography is *no* pseudo-biography. With greater truth he might have asseverated that it was no biography at all. Well are he and Hennings of Gotha aware that this thing of shreds and patches has been vamped together for sale only. Except a few letters to Kunz, the Bamberg bookseller, which turn mainly on the purchase of spectacles, and the journeyings and freightage of two boxes that used to pass and repass between Richter and Kunz's circulating library; with three or four notes of similar importance, and chiefly to other booksellers, there are no biographical documents here, which were not open to all Europe as well as to Heinrich Doering. Indeed, very nearly one-half of the *Life* is occupied with a description of the funeral and its appendages,—how the "sixty torches, with a number of lanterns and pitchpans," were arranged; how this patrician or professor followed that, through Friedrich-street, Chancery-street, and other streets of Bayreuth; and how at last the torches all went out, as Doctor Gabler and Doctor Spatzier were perorating (decidedly in bombast) over the grave. Then, it seems, there were meetings held in various parts of Germany, to solemnize the memory of Richter; among the rest, one in the Museum of Frankfort on the Maine; where a Doctor Börne speaks another long speech, if possible in still more decided bombast. Next come threnodies from all the four winds, mostly on very splay-footed metre. The whole of which is here snatched from the kind oblivion of the newspapers, and "lives in Settle's numbers one day more."

We have too much reverence for the name of Richter to think of laughing over these unhappy threnodies and panegyrists; some of whom far exceed any thing we English can exhibit in the epicedial style. They rather testify, however maladroitly, that the Germans have felt their loss,—which, indeed, is one to Europe at large; they even affect us with a certain melancholy feeling, when we consider how a heavenly voice must become mute, and nothing be heard in its stead but the whoop of quite earthly voices, lamenting, or pretending to lament. Far from us be all remembrance of Doering and Company, while we speak of Richter! But his own works give us some glimpses into his singular and noble nature; and to our readers a few words on this man, certainly one of the most remarkable of his age, will not seem thrown away.

Except by name, Jean Paul Friedrich Richter is little known out of Germany. The only thing connected with him, we think, that has reached this country, is his saying, imported by Madame de Staël, and thankfully pocketed by most newspaper critics: "Providence has given to the French the empire of the land, to the English that of the sea, to the Germans that of—the air!" Of this last element, indeed, his own genius might easily seem to have been a denizen: so fantastic, many-coloured, far-grasping, every way perplexed and extraordinary in his mode of writing, that to translate him is next to impossible; nay, a dictionary of his works has actually been in part published for the use of German readers! These things have restricted his sphere of action, and may long restrict it to his own country: but there, in return, he is a favourite of the first class; studied through all his intricacies with trustful admiration, and a love which tolerates much. During the last forty years, he has been continually before the public, in various capacities, and growing generally in esteem with all ranks of critics; till, at length, his gainsayers have been either silenced or convinced; and Jean Paul, at first reckoned half-mad, has long ago vindicated his singularities to nearly universal satisfaction, and now combines popularity with real depth of endowment, in perhaps a greater degree than any other writer; being second in the latter point to scarcely more than one of his contemporaries, and in the former second to none.

The biography of so distinguished a person could scarcely fail to be interesting, especially his autobiography; which, accordingly, we wait for, and may in time submit to our readers, if it seem worthy: meanwhile, the history of his life, so far as outward events characterize it, may be stated in few words. He was born at Wunsiedel in Bayreuth, in March, 1763. His father was a subaltern teacher in the *Gymnasium* of the place, and was afterwards promoted to be clergyman at Schwarzbach on the Saale. Richter's early education was of the scantiest sort; but his fine faculties and unwearied diligence supplied every defect. Unable to purchase books, he borrowed what he could come at, and transcribed from them, often great part of their contents,—a habit of excerpting, which continued with him through life, and influenced, in more than one way, his mode of writing and study. To the last, he was an insatiable and universal reader; so that his extracts accumulated on his hands, "till they filled whole chests." In 1780, he went to the University of Leipzig; with the highest character, in spite of the impediments which he had struggled with, for talent and acquirement. Like his father, he was destined for Theology; from which, however, his vagrant genius soon diverged into Poetry and Philosophy, to the neglect, and, ere long, to the final abandonment, of his appointed profession. Not well knowing what to do, he now accepted a tutorship in some family of rank; then he had pupils in his own house,—which, however, like his way of life, he often changed; for by this time he had become an author, and, in his wanderings over Germany, was putting forth,—now here, now there,—the strangest books, with the strangest titles: For instance,—*Greenland Lawsuits*;—*Biographical Recreations under the Cranium of a Giantess*;—*Selection from the Papers of the Devil*;—and the like. In these indescribable performances, the splendid faculties of the writer, luxuriating as they seemed in utter riot, could not be disputed; nor, with all its extravagance, the fundamental strength, honesty, and tenderness of his nature. Genius will reconcile men to much. By degrees, Jean Paul began to be considered not a strange, crackbrained mixture of enthusiast and buffoon, but a man of infinite humour, sensibility, force, and penetration. His writings procured him friends and fame; and at length a wife and a settled provision. With Caroline Mayer, his good spouse, and a pension (in 1802) from the King of Bavaria, he settled in Bayreuth, the capital of his native province; where he lived thenceforth, diligent and celebrated in many new departments of literature; and died on the 14th of November, 1825, loved as well as admired by all his countrymen, and most by those who had known him most intimately.

A huge, irregular man, both in mind and person, (for his portrait is quite a physiognomical study,) full of fire, strength, and impetuosity, Richter seems, at the same time, to have been, in the highest degree, mild, simple-hearted, humane. He was fond of conversation, and might well shine in it: he talked, as he wrote, in a style of his own, full of wild strength and charms, to which his natural Bayreuth accent often gave additional effect. Yet he loved retirement, the country, and all natural things; from his youth upwards, he himself tells us, he may almost be said to have lived in the open air; it was among groves and meadows that he studied,—often that he wrote. Even in the streets of Bayreuth, we have heard, he was seldom seen without a flower in his breast. A man of quiet tastes, and warm, compassionate affections! His friends he must have loved as few do. Of his poor and humble mother he often speaks by allusion, and never without reverence and overflowing tenderness. "Unhappy is the man," says he, "for whom his own mother has not made all other mothers venerable!" and elsewhere:—"O thou who hast still a father and a mother, thank God for it in the day when thy soul is full of joyful tears, and needs a bosom wherein to shed them!"—We quote the following sentences from Doering, almost the only memorable thing he has written in this volume:—

"Richter's studying or sitting apartment offered, about this time, (1793,) a true and beautiful emblem of his simple and noble way of thought, which comprehended at once the high and the low. Whilst his mother, who then lived with him, busily pursued her household work, occupying herself about stove and dresser, Jean Paul was sitting in a corner of the same room, at a simple writing-desk, with few or no books about him, but merely with one or two drawers containing excerpts and manuscripts. The jingle of the household operations seemed not at all to disturb him, any more than did the cooing of the pigeons, which fluttered to and fro in the chamber,—a place, indeed, of considerable size."—P. 8.

Our venerable Hooker, we remember, also enjoyed "the jingle of household operations," and the more questionable jingle of shrewd tongues to boot, while he wrote; but the good thrifty mother, and the cooing pigeons, were wanting. Richter came afterwards to live in finer mansions, and had the great and learned for associates; but the gentle feelings of those days abode with him: through life he was the same substantial, determinate, yet meek and tolerating man. It is seldom that so much rugged energy can be so blandly attempered;—that so much vehemence and so much softness will go together.

The expected edition of Richter's works is to be in sixty volumes: and they are no less multifarious than extensive; embracing subjects of all sorts, from the highest problems of transcendental philosophy, and the most passionate poetical delineations, to *Golden Rules for the Weather-Prophet*, and instructions in the *Art of Falling Asleep*. His chief productions are novels: the *Unsichtbare Loge* (Invisible Lodge); *Flegeljahre* (Wild-Oats); *Life of Fixlein*; the *Jubelsenior* (Parson in Jubilee); *Schmelzle's Journey to Flätz*; *Katzenberger's Journey to the Bath*; *Life of Fibel*; with many lighter pieces; and two works of a higher order, *Hesperus* and *Titan*, the largest and the best of his novels. It was the former that first (in 1795) introduced him into decisive and universal estimation with his countrymen: the latter he himself, with the most judicious of his critics, regarded as his master-piece. But the name Novelist, as we in England must understand it, would ill describe so vast and discursive a genius: for, with all his grotesque, tumultuous pleasantry, Richter is a man of a truly earnest, nay, high and solemn character and seldom writes without a meaning far beyond the sphere of common romancers. *Hesperus* and *Titan* themselves, though in form nothing more than "novels of real life," as the Minerva Press would say, have solid metal enough in them to furnish whole circulating libaries, were it beaten into the usual filigree; and much which, attenuate it as we might, no quarterly subscriber could well carry with him. Amusement is often, in part almost always, a mean with Richter; rarely or never his highest end. His thoughts, his feelings, the creations of his spirit, walk before us imbodied under wondrous shapes, in motley and ever-fluctuating groups; but his essential character, however he disguise it, is that of a Philosopher and moral Poet, whose study has been human nature, whose delight and best endeavour are with all that is beautiful, and tender, and mysteriously sublime, in the fate or history of man. This is the purport of his writings, whether their form be that of fiction or of truth; the spirit that pervades and ennobles his delineations of common life, his wild wayward dreams, allegories, and shadowy imaginings, no less than his disquisitions of a nature directly scientific.

But in this latter province also, Richter has accomplished much. His *Vorschule der Aesthetik* (Introduction to Æsthetics*) is a work on poetic art, based on principles of no ordinary depth and compass, abounding in noble views, and, notwithstanding its frolicsome exuberance, in sound and subtile criticism; esteemed even in Germany, where criticism has long been treated of as a science, and by such persons as Winkelmann, Kant, Herder, and the Schlegels. Of this work we could speak long, did our limits allow. We fear it might astonish many an honest brother of our craft, were he to read it; and altogether perplex and dash his maturest counsels, if he chanced to understand it.—Richter has also written on education, a work entitled *Levana;* distinguished by keen practical sagacity, as well as generous sentiment, and a certain sober magnificence of speculation; the whole presented in that singular style which characterizes the man. Germany is rich in works on Education; richer at present than any other country: it is there only that some echo of the Lockes and Miltons, speaking of this high matter, may still be heard; and speaking of it in the language of our own time, with insight into the actual wants, advantages, perils, and prospects of this age. Among writers on this subject, Richter holds a high place; if we look chiefly at his tendency and aims, perhaps the highest.—The *Clavis Fichtiana* is a ludicrous performance, known to us only by report; but Richter is said to possess the merit, while he laughs at Fichte, of understanding him; a merit among Fichte's critics, which seems to be one of the rarest. Report also, we regret to say, is all that we know of the *Campaner Thal*, a Discourse on the Immortality of the Soul; one of Richter's beloved topics, or rather the life of his whole philosophy, glimpses of which look forth on us from almost every one of his writings. He died while engaged, under recent and almost total blindness, in enlarging and remodelling this *Campaner Thal:* the unfinished manuscript was borne upon his coffin to the burial vault; and Klopstock's hymn, *Auferstehen wirst du*, "Thou shalt arise, my soul," can seldom have been sung with more appropriate application than over the grave of Jean Paul.

We defy the most careless or prejudiced reader to peruse these works without an impression of something splendid, wonderful, and daring. But they require to be studied as well as read, and this with no ordinary patience, if the reader, especially the foreign reader, wishes to comprehend rightly either their truth or their want of truth. Tried by many an accepted standard, Richter would be speedily enough disposed of; pronounced a mystic, a German dreamer, a rash and presumptuous innovator; and so consigned, with equanimity, perhaps with a certain jubilee, to the Limbo appointed for all such wind-bags and deceptions. Originality is a thing we constantly clamour for, and constantly quarrel with; as if, observes our author himself, any originality but our own could be expected to content us! In fact, all strange things are apt, without fault of theirs, to estrange us at first view, and unhappily scarcely any thing is perfectly plain, but what is also perfectly common. The current coin of the realm passes into all hands; and be it gold, silver, copper, is acceptable and of known value: but with new ingots, with foreign bars, and medals of Corinthian brass, the case is widely different.

There are few writers with whom deliberation and careful distrust of first impressions are more necessary than with Richter. He is a phenomenon from the very surface; he presents himself with a professed and determined singularity: his language itself is a stone of stumbling to the critic; to critics of the grammarian species, an unpardonable, often an insuperable, rock of offence. Not that he is ignorant of grammar, or disdains the sciences of spelling and parsing; but he exercises both in a certain latitudinarian spirit; deals with astonishing liberality in parentheses, dashes, and subsidiary clauses; invents hundreds of new words, alters old ones, or by hyphen, chains, pairs, and packs them together into most jarring combination; in short, produces sentences of the most heterogeneous, lumbering, interminable kind. Figures without limit indeed the whole is one tissue of metaphors, and similes, and allusions to all the provinces of Earth, Sea, and Air, interlaced with epigrammatic breaks, vehement bursts, or sardonic turns, interjections, quips, puns, and even oaths! A perfect Indian jungle it seems; a boundless, unparalleled imbroglio; nothing on all sides but darkness, dissonance, confusion worse confounded! Then the style of the whole corresponds, in perplexity and extravagance, with that of the parts. Every work, be it in fiction or serious treatise, is embaled in some fantastic wrappage, some mad narrative accounting for its appearance, and connecting it with the author, who generally becomes a per-

* From *αἰσθάνομαι, to feel.* A word invented by Baumgarten, (some eighty years ago,) to express generally the *Science of the Fine Arts*; and now in universal use among the Germans. Perhaps we also might as well adopt it; at least if any such *science* should ever arise among us.

son of the drama himself, before all is over. He has a whole imaginary geography of Europe in his novels; the cities of Flachsenfingen, Haarhaar, Scheerau, and so forth, with their princes, and privy-councillors, and serene highnesses; most of whom, odd enough fellows every way, are Richter's private acquaintances, talk with him of state matters, (in the purest Tory dialect,) and often incite him to get on with his writing. No story proceeds without the most erratic digressions, and voluminous tagrags rolling after it in many a snaky twine. Ever and anon there occurs some "Extra-leaf," with its satirical petition, programme, or other wonderful intercalation, no mortal can foresee on what. It is, indeed, a mighty maze; and often the panting reader toils after him in vain, or, baffled and spent, indignantly stops short, and retires perhaps for ever.

All this, we must admit, is true of Richter; but much more is true also. Let us not turn from him after the first cursory glance, and imagine we have settled his account by the words Rhapsody and Affectation. They are cheap words we allow, and of sovereign potency; we should see, therefore, that they be not rashly applied. Many things in Richter accord ill with such a theory. There are rays of the keenest truth, nay, steady pillars of scientific light rising through this chaos: Is it in fact a chaos, or may it be that our eyes are not of infinite vision, and have only missed the plan? Few rhapsodists are men of science, of solid learning, of rigorous study, and accurate, extensive, nay, universal knowledge; as he is. With regard to affectation, also, there is much to be said. The essence of affectation is that it be *assumed:* the character is, as it were, forcibly crushed into some foreign mould, in the hope of being thereby reshaped and beautified; the unhappy man persuades himself that he is in truth a new and wonderfully engaging creature, and so he moves about with a conscious air, though every movement betrays not symmetry, but dislocation. This it is to be affected, to walk in a vain show. But the strangeness alone is no proof of the vanity. Many men that move smoothly in the old established railways of custom will be found to have their affectation; and perhaps here and there some divergent genius be accused of it unjustly. The *show*, though common, may not cease to be *vain;* nor become so for being uncommon. Before we censure a man for seeming what he is not, we should be sure that we know what he *is*. As to Richter in particular, we think it but fair to observe, that strange and tumultuous as he is, there is a certain benign composure visible in his writings; a mercy, a gladness, a reverence, united in such harmony, as we cannot but think bespeaks not a false, but a genuine state of mind; not a feverish and morbid, but a healthy and robust state.

The secret of the matter, perhaps, is that Richter requires more study than most readers care to give; for, as we approach more closely, many things grow clearer. In the man's own sphere there is consistency; the farther we advance into it, we see confusion more and more unfold itself into order till at last, viewed from its proper centre, his intellectual universe, no longer a distorted, incoherent series of air-landscapes, coalesces into compact expansion; a vast, magnificent, and variegated scene; full, indeed, of wondrous products, and rude, it may be, and irregular; but gorgeous, and varied, and ample; gay with the richest verdure and foliage, and glittering in the brightest and kindest sun.

Richter has been called an intellectual Colossus; and in truth it is still somewhat in this light that we view him. His faculties are all of gigantic mould; cumbrous, awkward in their movements; large and splendid rather than harmonious or beautiful; yet joined in living union, and of force and compass altogether extraordinary. He has an intellect vehement, rugged, irresistible; crushing in pieces the hardest problems; piercing into the most hidden combinations of things, and grasping the most distant: an imagination vague, sombre, splendid, or appalling; brooding over the abysses of Being; wandering through Infinitude, and summoning before us, in its dim religious light, shapes of brilliancy, solemnity, or terror: a fancy of exuberance literally unexampled; for it pours its treasures with a lavishness which knows no limit, hanging, like the sun, a jewel on every grass-blade, and sowing the earth at large with orient pearl. But deeper than all these lies Humour, the ruling quality with Richter; as it were the central fire that pervades and vivifies his whole being. He is a humorist from his inmost soul; he thinks as a humorist, he feels, imagines, acts as a humorist: Sport is the element in which his nature lives and works. A tumultuous element for such a nature, and wild work he makes in it! A Titan in his sport as in his earnestness, he oversteps all bound, and riots without law or measure. He heaps Pelion upon Ossa, and hurls the universe together and asunder like a case of playthings. The Moon "bombards" the Earth, being a rebellious satellite; Mars "preaches" to the other planets very singular doctrine; nay, we have Time and Space themselves playing fantastic tricks: it is an infinite masquerade; all Nature is gone forth mumming in the strangest guises.

Yet the anarchy is not without its purpose; these vizards are not mere hollow masks; but there are living faces beneath them, and this mumming has its significance. Richter is a man of mirth, but he seldom or never condescends to be a merry-andrew. Nay, in spite of its extravagance, we should say that his humour is of all his gifts intrinsically the finest and most genuine. It has such witching turns; there is something in it so capricious, so quaint, so heartfelt. From his Cyclopean workshop, and its fuliginous limbecs, and huge unwieldy machinery, the little shrivelled, twisted figure comes forth at last, so perfect and so living, to be for ever laughed at and for ever loved! Wayward as he seems, he works not without forethought; like Rubens, by a single stroke, he can change a laughing face into a sad one. But in his smile itself, a touching pathos may lie hidden, a pity too deep for tears. He is a man of feeling, in the noblest sense of that word; for he loves all living with the heart of a brother; his soul rushes forth, in sympathy with gladness and sorrow, with goodness or grandeur, over all creation. Every gentle and generous affection, every thrill of mercy, every glow of nobleness, awakens in his bosom a response, nay, strikes his spirit into harmony; a wild music as of wind-harps, floating round us in fitful swells, but soft sometimes, and pure and soul-entrancing as the song of angels! Aversion itself with him is not hatred; he despises much, but justly, with tolerance also, with placidity, and even a sort of love. Love, in fact, is the atmosphere he breathes in, the medium through which he looks. His is the spirit which gives life and beauty to whatever it embraces. Inanimate Nature itself is no longer an insensible assemblage of colours and perfumes, but a mysterious Presence, with which he communes in unutterable sympathies. We might call him, as he once called Herder, "a Priest of Nature, a mild Bramin," wandering amid spicy groves, and under benignant skies. The infinite Night with her solemn aspects, Day, and the sweet approach of Even and Morn, are full of meaning for him. He loves the green Earth with her streams and forests, her flowery leas and eternal skies; loves her with a sort of passion, in all her vicissitudes of light and shade; his spirit revels in her grandeur and charms; expands like the breeze over wood and lawn, over glade and dingle, stealing and giving odours.

It has sometimes been made a wonder that things so discordant should go together; that men of humour are often likewise men of sensibility. But the wonder should rather be to see them divided; to find true genial humour dwelling in a mind that was coarse or callous. The essence of humour is sensibility; warm, tender fellow-feeling with all forms of existence. Nay, we may say that unless seasoned and purified by humour, sensibility is apt to run wild; will readily corrupt into disease, falsehood, or, in one word, sentimentality. Witness Rousseau, Zimmermann, in some points also St. Pierre: to say nothing of living instances; or of the Kotzebues, and other pale hosts of wobegone mourners, whose wailings, like the howl of an Irish wake, from time to time cleft the general ear. The last perfection of our faculties, says Schiller with a truth far deeper than it seems, is that their activity, without ceasing to be sure and earnest, become *sport*. True humour is sensibility, in the most catholic and deepest sense; but it is this *sport* of sensibility; wholesome and perfect therefore; as it were, the playful teasing fondness of a mother to her child.

That faculty of irony, of caricature, which often passes by the name of humour, but consists chiefly in a certain superficial distortion or reversal of objects, and ends at best in laughter, bears no resemblance to the humour of Richter. A shallow endowment this; and often more a habit than an endowment. It is but a poor fraction of humour; or rather, it is the body to which the soul is wanting; any life it has being false, artificial, and irrational. True humour springs not more from the head than from the heart; it is not contempt, its essence is love; it issues not in laughter, but in still smiles, which lie far deeper. It is a sort of inverse sublimity; exalting, as it were, into our affections what is below us, while sublimity draws down into our affections what is above us. The former is scarcely less precious or heart-affecting than the latter; perhaps it is still rarer, and, as a test of genius, still more decisive. It is, in fact, the bloom and perfume, the purest effluence of a deep, fine, and loving nature; a nature in harmony with itself, reconciled to the world and its stintedness and contradiction, nay, finding in this very contradiction new elements of beauty as well as goodness. Among our own writers, Shakspeare in this as in all other provinces, must have his place: yet not the first; his humour is heartfelt, exuberant, warm, but seldom the tenderest or most subtile. Swift inclines more to simple irony; yet he had genuine humour too, and of no unloving sort, though cased, like Ben Jonson's, in a most bitter and caustic rind. Sterne follows next; our last specimen of humour, and, with all his faults, our best; our finest, if not our strongest, for *Yorick*, and *Corporal Trim*, and *Uncle Toby*, have yet no brother but in *Don Quixote*, far as he lies above them. Cervantes is indeed the purest of all humourists; so gentle and genial, so full, yet so ethereal, is his humour, and in such accordance with itself and his whole noble nature. The Italian mind is said to abound in humour; yet their classics seem to give us no right emblem of it: except, perhaps, in Ariosto, there appears little in their current poetry that reaches the region of true humour. In France, since the days of Montaigne, it seems to be nearly extinct. Voltaire, much as he dealt in ridicule, never rises into humour; and even with Molière, it is far more an affair of the understanding than of the character.

That in this point, Richter excels all German authors, is saying much for him, and may be said truly. Lessing has humour,—of a sharp, rigid, substantial, and on the whole, genial sort: yet the ruling bias of his mind is to logic. So likewise has Wieland, though much diluted by the general *loquacity* of his nature, and impoverished still farther by the influences of a cold, meagre, French skepticism. Among the Ramlers, Gellerts, Hagedorns, of Frederick the Second's time, we find abundance, and delicate in kind too, of that light matter which the French call pleasantry; but little or nothing that deserves the name of humour. In the present age, however, there is Goethe, with a rich true vein; and this sublimated, as it were, to an essence, and blended in still union with his whole mind. Tieck also, among his many fine susceptibilities, is not without a warm keen sense for the ridiculous; and a humour rising, though by short fits, and from a much lower atmosphere, to be poetic. But of all these men, there is none that, in depth, copiousness, and intensity of humour, can be compared with Jean Paul. He alone exists in humour; lives, moves, and has his being in it. With him it is not so much united to his other qualities, of intellect, fancy, imagination, moral feeling, as these are united to it; or rather unite themselves to it, and grow under its warmth, as in their proper temperature and climate. Not as if we meant to assert that his humour is in all cases perfectly natural and pure; nay, that it is not often extravagant, untrue, or even absurd: but still, on the whole, the core and life of it are genuine, subtile, spiritual. Not without reason have his panegyrists named him *Jean Paul der Einzige*,—"Jean Paul the Only:" in one sense or the other, either as praise or censure, his critics also must adopt this epithet; for surely, in the whole circle of literature, we look in vain for his parallel. Unite the sportfulness of Rabellais, and the best sensibility of Sterne, with the earnestness, and, even in slight portions, the sublimity of Milton; and and let the mosaic brain of old Burton give forth the workings of this strange union, with the pen of Jeremy Bentham!

To say how, with so peculiar a natural endowment, Richter should have shaped his mind by culture, is much harder than to say that he has shaped it wrong. Of affectation we will neither altogether clear him, nor very loudly pronounce him guilty. That his manner of writing is singular, nay, in fact, a wild complicated Arabesque, no one can deny. But the true question is,—how nearly does this manner of writing represent his real manner of thinking and existing? With what degree of freedom does it allow this particular form of being to manifest itself; or what fetters and perversions does it lay on such manifestation? For the great law of culture is: Let each become all that he was created capable of being; expand, if possible, to his full growth; resisting all impediments, casting off all foreign, especially all noxious adhesions; and show himself at length in his own shape and stature, be these what they may. There is no uniform of excellence, either in physical or spiritual nature: all *genuine* things are what they ought to be. The reindeer is good and beautiful, so likewise is the elephant. In literature it is the same: "every man," says Lessing, "has his own style, like his own nose." True, there are noses of wonderful dimensions; but no nose can justly be amputated by the public,—not even the nose of Slawkenbergius himself: so it *be* a real nose, and no wooden one, put on for deception's sake and mere show.

To speak in grave language, Lessing means, and we agree with him, that the outward style is to be judged of by the inward qualities of the spirit which it is employed to body forth; that, without prejudice to critical propriety, well understood, the former may vary into many shapes as the latter varies; that, in short, the grand point for a writer is not to be of this or that external make and fashion, but, in every fashion, to be genuine, vigorous, alive,—alive with his whole being, consciously, and for beneficent results.

Tried by this test, we imagine Richter's wild manner will be found less imperfect than many a very tame one. To the man it may not be unsuitable. In that singular form, there is a fire, a splendour, a benign energy, which persuades us into tolerance, nay into love, of much that might otherwise offend. Above all, this man, alloyed with imperfections as he may be, is consistent and coherent: he is at one with himself; he knows his aims, and pursues them in sincerity of heart, joyfully, and with undivided will. A harmonious development of being, the first and last object of all true culture, has therefore been attained; if not completely, at least more completely than in one of a thousand ordinary men. Nor let us forget, that in such a nature, it was not of easy attainment; that where much was to be developed, some imperfection should be forgiven. It is true, the beaten paths of literature lead the safeliest to the goal; and the talent pleases us most, which submits to shine with new gracefulness through old forms. Nor is the noblest and most peculiar mind too noble or peculiar for working by prescribed laws: Sophocles, Shakspeare, Cervantes, and in Richter's own age, Goethe, how little did they innovate on the given forms of composition, how much in the spirit they breathed into them! All this is true; and Richter must lose of our esteem in proportion. Much, however, will remain; and why should we quarrel with the high, because it is not the highest? Richter's worst faults are nearly allied to his best merits; being chiefly exuberance of good, irregular squandering of wealth, a dazzling with excess of true light. These things may be pardoned the more readily, as they are little likely to be imitated.

On the whole, Genius has privileges of its own; it selects an orbit for itself; and be this never so eccentric, if it is indeed a celestial orbit, we mere star-gazers must at last compose ourselves; must cease to cavil at it, and begin to observe it, and calculate its laws. That Richter is a new planet in the intellectual heavens, we dare not affirm; an atmospheric meteor he is not wholly; perhaps a comet, that, though with long aberrations, and shrouded in a nebulous veil, has yet its place in the empyrean.

Of Richter's individual works, of his opinions, his general philosophy of life, we have no room left us to speak. Regarding his novels, we may say, that, except in some few instances, and those chiefly of the shorter class, they are not what, in strict language, we can term unities: with much *callida junctura* of parts, it is rare that any of them leaves on us the impression of a perfect, homogeneous, indivisible whole A true work of art requires to be *fused* in the mind of its creator, and as it were, poured forth (from his imagination, though not from his pen) at one simultaneous gush. Richter's works do not always bear sufficient marks of having been in *fusion;* yet neither are they merely *riveted* together: to say the least, they have been *welded.* A similar remark applies to many of his characters; indeed, more or less, to all of them, except such as are entirely humourous, or have a large dash of humour. In this latter province, certainly he is at home; a true poet, a maker: his *Siebenkäs*, his *Schmelzle*, even his *Fibel* and *Fixlein* are living figures. But in heroic personages, passionate, massive, overpowering as he is, we have scarcely ever a complete ideal; art has not attained to the concealment of itself. With his heroines again he is more successful; they are often true heroines, though perhaps with too little variety of character; bustling, buxom mothers and housewives, with all the caprices, perversities, and warm, generous helpfulness of women; or white, half-angelic creatures, meek, still, long-suffering, high-minded, of tenderest affections, and hearts crushed yet uncomplaining. Supernatural figures he has not attempted; and wisely, for he cannot write without belief. Yet many times he exhibits an imagination of a singularity, nay, on the whole, of a truth and grandeur, unexampled elsewhere. In his *dreams* there is a mystic complexity, a gloom, and amid the dim, gigantic, half-ghastly shadows, gleamings of a wizard splendour, which almost recall to us the visions of Ezekiel. By readers who have studied the *Dream in the New-year's Eve* we shall not be mistaken.

Richter's Philosophy, a matter of no ordinary interest, both as it agrees with the common philosophy of Germany, and disagrees with it, must not be touched on for the present. One only observation we shall make: it is not mechanical, or skeptical; it springs not from the forum or the laboratory, but from the depths of the human spirit; and yields as its fairest product a noble system of morality, and the firmest conviction of religion. In this latter point we reckon him peculiarly worthy of study. To a careless reader he might seem the wildest of infidels; for nothing can exceed the freedom with which he bandies to and fro the dogmas of religion, nay, sometimes, the highest objects of Christian reverence. There are passages of this sort, which will occur to every reader of Richter; but which, not to fall into the error we have already blamed in Madame de Staël, we shall refrain from quoting. More light is in the following: "Or," inquires he, in his usual abrupt way, (Note to *Schmelzle's Journey*,) "Or are all your Mosques, Episcopal Churches, Pagodas, Chapels of Ease, Tabernacles, and Pantheons, any thing else but the Ethnic Fore-court of the Invisible Temple and its Holy of Holies?" Yet, independently of all dogmas, nay, perhaps in spite of many, Richter is, in the highest sense of the word, religious. A reverence, not a self-interested fear, but a noble reverence for the spirit of all goodness, forms the crown and glory of his culture. The fiery elements of his nature have been purified under holy influences, and chastened by a principle of mercy and humility into peace and well-doing. An intense and continual faith in man's immortality and native grandeur accompanies him; from amid the vortices of life he looks up to a heavenly loadstar; the solution of what is visible and transient, he finds in what is invisible and eternal. He has doubted, he denies, yet he believes. "When, in your last hour," says he, (*Levana*, p. 251,) "when, in your last hour, (think of this,) all faculty in the broken spirit shall fade away and die into inanity,—imagination, thought, effort, enjoyment,—then at last will the night-flower of Belief alone continue blooming, and refresh with its perfumes in the last darkness."

To reconcile these seeming contradictions, to explain the grounds, the manner, the congruity of Richter's belief, cannot be attempted here. We recommend him to the study, the tolerance, and even the praise, of all men who have inquired into this highest of questions with a right spirit; inquired with the martyr fearlessness, but also with the martyr reverence, of men that love Truth, and will not accept a lie. A frank, fearless, honest, yet truly spiritual faith is of all things the rarest in our time.

Of writings which, though with many reservations, we have praised so much, our hesitating readers may demand some specimen. To unbelievers, unhappily, we have none of a convincing sort to give. Ask us not to represent the Peruvian forests by three twigs plucked from them; or the cataracts of the Nile by a handful of its water! To those, meanwhile, who will look on twigs as mere dissevered twigs, and a handful of water as only so many drops, we present the following. It is a summer Sunday night; Jean Paul is taking leave of the Hukelum Parson and his wife; like him we have long laughed at them or wept for them; like him, also, we are sad to part from them.

"We were all of us too deeply moved. We at last tore ourselves asunder from repeated embraces; my friend retired with the soul whom he loves. I remained alone behind with the Night.

"And I walked without aim through woods, through valleys, and over brooks, and through sleeping villages, to enjoy the great Night, like a Day. I walked, and still looked, like the magnet, to the region of midnight, to strengthen my heart at the gleaming twilight, at this upstretching aurora of a morning beneath our feet. White night-butterflies flitted, white blossoms fluttered, white stars fell, and the white snow-powder hung silvery in the high Shadow of the Earth, which reaches beyond the Moon, and which is our Night. Then began the Æolian Harp of the Creation to tremble and to sound, blown on from above; and my immortal Soul was a string in this harp.—The heart of a brother, everlasting Man, swelled under the everlasting heaven, as the seas swell under the sun and under the moon.—The distant village clocks struck midnight, mingling, as it were, with the ever-pealing tone of ancient Eternity.—The limbs of my buried ones touched cold on my soul, and drove away its blots, as dead hands heal eruptions of the skin. —I walked silently through little hamlets, and close by their outer church-yards, where crumbled upcast coffin-boards were glimmering, while the once bright eyes that had lain in them were mouldered into gray ashes. Cold thought! clutch not like a cold spectre at my heart: I look up to the starry sky, and an everlasting chain stretches thither, and over, and below; and all is Life and Warmth, and Light, and all is Godlike or God...

"Towards morning, I described thy late lights, little city of my dwelling, which I belong to on this side the grave; I returned to the Earth; and in thy steeples, behind the by-advanced great midnight, it struck half-past two: about this hour, in 1794, Mars went down in the west, and the Moon rose in the east; and my soul desired, in grief for the noble warlike blood which is still streaming on the blossoms of spring: 'Ah, retire, bloody War, like red Mars: and thou, still Peace, come forth like the mild divided Moon!'"—End of *Quintus Fixlein*.

Such, seen through no uncoloured medium, but in dim remoteness, and sketched in hurried, transitory outline, are some features of Jean Paul Friedrich Richter and his works. Germany has long loved him; to England also he must one day become known; for a man of this magnitude belongs not to one people, but to the world. What our countrymen may decide of him, still more what may be his fortune with posterity, we will not try to foretell. Time has a contracting influence on many a wide-spread fame; yet of Richter we will say, that he may survive much. There is in him that which does not die; that Beauty and Earnestness of soul, that spirit of Humanity, of Love and mild Wisdom, over which the vicissitudes of mode have no sway. This is that excellence of the inmost nature which alone confers immortality on writings; that charm which still, under every defacement, binds us to the pages of our own Hookers, and Taylors, and Brownes, when their way of thought has long ceased to be ours, and the most valued of their merely intellectual opinions have passed away, as ours too must do, with the circumstances and events in which they took their shape or rise. To men of a right mind, there may long be in Richter much that has attraction and value. In the moral desert of vulgar Literature, with its sandy wastes, and parched, bitter, and too often poisonous shrubs, the writings of this man will rise in their irregular luxuriance, like a cluster of date-trees, with its greensward and well of water, to refresh the pilgrim, in the sultry solitude, with nourishment and shade.

STATE OF GERMAN LITERATURE.*

[Edinburgh Review, 1827.]

These two books, notwithstanding their diversity of title, are properly parts of one and the same; the "Outlines," though of prior date in regard to publication, having now assumed the character of sequel and conclusion to the larger work,—of fourth volume to the other three. It is designed, of course, for the home market; yet the foreign student also will find in it a safe and valuable help, and, in spite of its imperfections, should receive it with thankfulness and good-will. Doubtless we might have wished for a keener discriminative and descriptive talent, and perhaps for a somewhat more catholic spirit, in the writer of such a history: but in their absence we have still much to praise. Horn's literary creed would, on the whole, we believe, be acknowledged by his countryman as the true one; and this, though it is chiefly from one immovable station that he can survey his subject, he seems heartily anxious to apply with candour and tolerance. Another improvement might have been a deeper principle of arrangement, a firmer grouping into periods and schools; for, as it stands, the work is more a critical sketch of German Poets, than a history of German Poetry.

Let us not quarrel, however, with our author; his merits as a literary historian are plain, and by no means inconsiderable. Without rivalling the almost frightful laboriousness of Bouterwek or Eichhorn, he gives creditable proofs of research and general information, and possesses a lightness in composition, to which neither of these erudite persons can well pretend. Undoubtedly he has a flowing pen, and is at home in this province; not only a speaker of the word, indeed, but a doer of the work; having written, besides his great variety of tracts and treatises, biographical, philosophical, and critical, several very deserving works of a poetic sort. He is not, it must be owned, a very strong man, but he is nimble and orderly, and goes through his work with a certain gayety of heart; nay, at times, with a frolicsome alacrity which might even require to be pardoned. His character seems full of susceptibility; perhaps too much so for its natural vigour. His novels, accordingly, to judge from the few we have read of them, verge towards the sentimental. In the present work, in like manner, he has adopted nearly all the best ideas of his contemporaries, but with something of an undue vehemence; and he advocates the cause of religion, integrity, and true poetic taste with great heartiness and vivacity, were it not that too often his zeal outruns his prudence and insight. Thus, for instance, he declares repeatedly, in so many words, that no mortal can be a poet unless he is a Christian. The meaning here is very good; but why this phraseology? Is it not inviting the simple-minded (not to speak of scoffers, whom Horn very justly contemns,) to ask, when Homer subscribed the Thirty-nine Articles? or whether Sadi and Hafiz were really of the Bishop of Peterborough's opinion? Again, he talks too often of "representing the Infinite in the Finite," of expressing the unspeakable, and such high matters. In fact, Horn's style, though extremely readable, has one great fault; it is, to speak it in a single word, an affected style. His stream of meaning, uniformly clear and wholesome in itself, will not flow quietly along its channel; but is ever and anon spurting up into epigram and antithetic jets. Playful he is, and kindly, and we do believe, honest-hearted; but there is a certain snappishness in him, a frisking abruptness; and then his sport is more a perpetual

* 1. *Die Poesie und Beredsamkeit der Deutschen, von Luthers Zeit bis zur Gegenwart. Dargestellt von Franz Horn.* (The Poetry and Oratory of the Germans, from Luther's Time to the Present. Exhibited by Franz Horn.) Berlin, 1822—1824. 3 vols. 8vo.

2. *Umrisse zur Geschichte und Kritik der schönen Literatur Deutschlands während der Jahre*, 1790—1818. (Outlines for the History and Criticism of Polite Literature in Germany, during the years 1790—1818.) By Franz Horn. Berlin, 1819, 8vo.

giggle, than any dignified smile, or even any sufficient laugh with gravity succeeding it. This sentence is among the best we recollect of him, and will partly illustrate what we mean. We submit it, for the sake of its import likewise, to all superfine speculators on the Reformation, in their future contrasts of Luther and Erasmus. "Erasmus," says Horn, "belongs to that species of writers who have all the desire in the world to build God Almighty a magnificent church,—at the same time, however, not giving the Devil any offence; to whom, accordingly, they set up a neat little chapel close by, where you can offer him some touch of sacrifice at a time, and practise a quiet household devotion for him without disturbance." In this style of "witty and conceited mirth," considerable part of the book is written.

But our chief business at present is not with Franz Horn, or his book; of whom accordingly, recommending his labours to all inquisitive students of German, and himself to good estimation with all good men, we must here take leave. We have a word or two to say on that strange literature itself; concerning which our readers probably feel more curious to learn what it is, than with what skill it has been judged of.

Above a century ago, the Père Bouhours propounded to himself the pregnant question: *Si un Allemand peut avoir de l'esprit?* Had the Père Bouhours bethought him of what country Kepler and Leibnitz were, or who it was that gave to mankind the three great elements of modern civilization, Gunpowder, Printing, and the Protestant Religion, it might have thrown light on his inquiry. Had he known the *Nibelungen Lied;* and where *Reinecke Fuchs*, and *Faust*, and the *Ship of Fools*, and four-fifths of all the popular mythology, humour, and romance, to be found in Europe in the sixteenth and seventeenth centuries, took its rise; had he read a page or two of Ulrich Hutten, Opitz, Paul Flemming, Logau, or even Lohenstein and Hoffmanns-waldau, all of whom had already lived and written in his day; had the Père Bouhours taken this trouble, who knows but he might have found, with whatever amazement, that a German *could* actually have a little *esprit*, or perhaps even something better? No such trouble was requisite for the Père Bouhours. Motion *in vacuo* is well known to be speedier and surer than through a resisting medium, especially to imponderous bodies; and so the light Jesuit, unimpeded by facts or principles of any kind, failed not to reach his conclusion; and, in a comfortable frame of mind, to decide negatively, that a German could *not* have any literary talent.

Thus did the Père Bouhours evince that he had "a pleasant wit;" but in the end he has paid dear for it. The French, themselves, have long since begun to know something of the Germans, and something also of their own critical Daniel; and now it is by this one *untimely* joke that the hapless Jesuit is doomed to live; for the blessing of full oblivion is denied him, and so he hangs suspended in his own noose, over the dusky pool which he struggles toward, but for a great while will not reach. Might his fate but serve as a warning to kindred men of wit, in regard to this and so many other subjects! For surely the pleasure of despising, at all times and in itself a dangerous luxury, is much safer *after* the toil of examining than before it.

We differ from the Père Bouhours in this matter, and must endeavour to discuss it differently. There is, in fact, much in the present aspect of German Literature, not only deserving notice but deep consideration from all thinking men, and far too complex for being handled in the way of epigram. It is always advantageous to think justly of our neighbours; nay, in mere common honesty, it is a duty; and, like every other duty, brings its own reward. Perhaps at the present era this duty is more essential than ever; an era of such promise and such threatening, when so many elements of good and evil are everywhere in conflict, and human society is, as it were, struggling to body itself forth anew, and so many *coloured rays* are springing up in this quarter and in that, which only by their union can produce *pure light*. Happily, too, though still a difficult, it is no longer an impossible duty; for the commerce in material things has paved roads for commerce in things spiritual, and a true thought, or a noble creation, passes lightly to us from the remotest countries, provided only our minds be open to receive it. This, indeed, is a rigorous proviso, and a great obstacle lies in it; one which to many must be insurmountable, yet which it is the chief glory of social culture to surmount. For if a man who mistakes his own contracted individuality for the type of human nature, and deals with whatever contradicts *him*, as if it contradicted *this*, is but a pedant, and without true wisdom, be he furnished with partial equipments as he may,—what better shall we think of a nation that, in like manner, isolates itself from foreign influence, regards its own modes as so many laws of nature, and rejects all that is different as unworthy even of examination?

Of this narrow and perverted condition, the French, down almost to our own times, have afforded a remarkable and instructive example; as indeed of late they have been often enough upbraidingly reminded, and are now themselves, in a manlier spirit, beginning to admit. That our countrymen have at any time erred much in this point, cannot, we think, truly be alleged against them. Neither shall we say, with some passionate admirers of Germany, that to the Germans in particular they have been unjust. It is true, the literature and character of that country, which, within the last half century, have been more worthy perhaps than any other of our study and regard, are still very generally unknown to us, or, what is worse, misknown: but for this there are not wanting less offensive reasons. That the false and tawdry ware, which was in all hands, should reach us before the chaste and truly excellent, which it required some excellence to recognise; that Kotzebue's insanity should have spread faster, by some fifty years, than Lessing's wisdom; that Kant's Philosophy should stand in the back-ground as a dreary and abortive dream, and Gall's Craniology be held out to us from every booth as a reality;—

all this lay in the nature of the case. That many readers should draw conclusions from imperfect premises, and by the imports judge too hastily of the stock imported from, was likewise natural. No unfair bias, no unwise indisposition, that we are aware of, has ever been at work in the matter; perhaps, at worst, a degree of indolence, a blamable incuriosity to all products of foreign genius: for what more do we know of recent Spanish or Italian literature than of German; of Grossi and Manzoni, of Campomanes or Jovellanos, than of Tieck and Richter? Wherever German art, in those forms of it which need no interpreter, has addressed us immediately, our recognition of it has been prompt and hearty; from Dürer to Mengs, from Händel to Weber and Beethoven, we have welcomed the painters and musicians of Germany, not only to our praise, but to our affections and beneficence. Nor, if in their literature we have been more backward, is the literature itself without blame. Two centuries ago, translations from the German were comparatively frequent in England: Luther's *Table-Talk* is still a venerable classic in our language; nay Jacob Boehme has found a place among us, and this not as a dead letter, but as a living apostle to a still living sect of our religionists. In the next century, indeed, translation ceased; but then it was, in a great measure, because there was little worth translating. The horrors of the Thirty Years' War, followed by the conquests and conflagrations of Louis the Fourteenth, had desolated the country; French influence, extending from the courts of princes to the closets of the learned, lay like a baleful incubus over the far nobler mind of Germany; and all true nationality vanished from its literature, or was heard only in faint tones, which lived in the hearts of the people, but could not reach with any effect to the ears of foreigners.* And now that the genius of the country has awaked in its old strength, our attention to it has certainly awakened also; and if we yet know little or nothing of the Germans, it is not because we wilfully do them wrong, but, in good part, because they are somewhat difficult to know.

In fact prepossessions of all sorts naturally enough find their place here. A country which has no national literature, or literature too insignificant to force its way abroad, must always be, to its neighbours, at least in every important spiritual respect, an unknown and misestimated country. Its towns may figure on our maps; its revenues, population, manufactures, political connections, may be recorded in statistical books; but the character of the people has no symbol and no voice; we cannot know them by speech and discourse, but only mere sight and outward observation of their manners and procedure. Now, if both sight and speech, if both travellers and native literature, are found but ineffectual in this respect, how incalculably more so the former alone! To seize a character, even that of one man, in its life and secret mechanism, requires a philosopher; to delineate it with truth and impressiveness, is a work for a poet. How then shall one or two sleek clerical tutors, with here and there a tedium-stricken esquire, or speculative half-pay captain, give us views on such a subject? How shall a man, to whom all characters of individual men are like sealed books, of which he sees only the title and the covers, decipher from his four-wheeled vehicle, and depict to us, the character of a nation? He courageously depicts his own optical delusions; notes this to be incomprehensible, that other to be insignificant; much to be good, much to be bad, and most of all indifferent; and so, with a few flowing strokes, completes a picture which, though it may not even resemble any possible object, his countrymen are to take for a national portrait. Nor is the fraud so readily detected: for the character of a people has such complexity of aspect, that even the honest observer knows not always, not perhaps after long inspection, what to determine regarding it. From his, only accidental, point of view, the figure stands before him like the tracings on veined marble,—a mass of mere random lines, and tints, and entangled strokes, out of which a lively fancy may shape almost *any* image. But the image he brings along with him is always the readiest; this is tried, it answers as well as another; and a second voucher now testifies its correctness. Thus each, in confident tones, though it may be with a secret misgiving, repeats his precursor; the hundred times repeated comes in the end to be

* Not that the Germans were idle; or altogether engaged, as we too loosely suppose, in the work of commentary and lexicography. On the contrary, they rhymed and romanced with due vigour as to quantity; only the quality was bad. Two facts on this head may deserve mention: In the year 1749, there were found, in the library of one virtuoso, no fewer than 300 volumes of devotional poetry, containing, says Horn, "a treasure of 33,712 German hymns;" and, much about the same period, one of Gottsched's scholars had amassed as many as 1500 German novels, all of the 17th century. The hymns we understand to be much better than the novels, or rather, perhaps, the novels to be much worse than the hymns. Neither was critical study neglected, nor indeed honest endeavour on all hands to attain improvement: witness the strange books from time to time put forth, and the still stranger institutions established for this purpose. Among the former we have the "Poetical Funnel," (*Poetische Trichter*,) manufactured at Nürnberg in 1650, and professing, within six hours, to pour in the whole essence of this difficult art into the most unfurnished head. Nürnberg also was the chief seat of the famous *Meistersänger* and their *Sängerzünfte*, or Singer-guilds, in which poetry was taught and practised like any other handicraft, and this by sober and well-meaning men, chiefly artisans, who could not understand why labour, which manufactured so many things, should not also manufacture another. Of these tuneful guild-brethren, Hans Sachs, by trade a shoemaker, is greatly the most noted and most notable. His father was a tailor; he himself learned the mystery of song under one Nunnebeck, a weaver. He was an adherent of his great contemporary Luther, who has even deigned to acknowledge his services in the cause of Reformation: how diligent a labourer Sachs must have been, will appear from the fact, that, in his 74th year, (1568,) on examining his stock for publication, he found that he had written 6048 poetical pieces, among which were 208 tragedies and comedies; and this, besides having all along kept house, like an honest Nürnberg burgher, by assiduous and sufficient shoemaking! Hans is not without genius, and a shrewd irony; and above all, the most gay, childlike, yet devout and solid character. A man neither to be despised nor patronized, but left standing on his own basis, as a singular product, and a still legible symbol, and clear mirror, of the time and country where he lived His best piece known to us, and many are well worth perusing, is the *Fastnachtsspiel* (Shrovetide Farce) of the *Narrenschneiden*, where the Doctor cures a bloated and lethargic patient by cutting out half a dozen *Fools* from his interior!

believed; the foreign nation is now once for all understood, decided on, and registered accordingly; and dunce the thousandth writes of it like dunce the first.

With the aid of literary and intellectual intercourse, much of this falsehood may, no doubt, be corrected: yet even here, sound judgment is far from easy; and most national characters are still, as Hume long ago complained, the product rather of popular prejudice than of philosophic insight. That the Germans, in particular, have by no means escaped such misrepresentation, nay, perhaps, have had more than the common share of it, cannot, in their circumstances, surprise us. From the time of Optiz and Flemming, to those of Klopstock and Lessing,—that is, from the early part of the seventeenth to the middle of the eighteenth century,—they had scarcely any literature known abroad, or deserving to be known: their political condition, during this same period, was oppressive and every way unfortunate externally; and at home, the nation, split into so many factions and petty states, had lost all feeling of itself as of a nation; and its energies in arts as in arms were manifested only in detail, too often in collision, and always under foreign influence. The French, at once their plunderers and their scoffers, described them to the rest of Europe as a semi-barbarous people; which comfortable fact the rest of Europe was willing enough to take on their word. During the greater part of the last century, the Germans, in our intellectual survey of the world, were quietly omitted; a vague contemptuous ignorance prevailed respecting them; it was a Cimmerian land, where, if a few sparks did glimmer, it was but so as to testify their own existence, too feebly to enlighten *us*.* The Germans passed for apprentices in all provinces of art; and many foreign craftsmen scarcely allowed them so much.

Madame de Staël's book has done away with this; all Europe is now aware that the Germans are something; something independent and apart from others; nay, something deep, imposing, and, if not admirable, wonderful. What that something is, indeed, is still undecided; for this gifted lady's *Allemagne*, in doing much to excite curiosity, has still done little to satisfy or even direct it. We can no longer make ignorance a boast, but we are yet far from having acquired right knowledge; and cavillers, excluded from contemptuous negation, have found a resource in almost as contemptuous assertion. Translators are the same faithless and stolid race that they have ever been: the particle of gold they bring us over is hidden from all but the most patient eye, among shiploads of yellow sand and sulphur. Gentle Dulness too, in this as in all other things, still loves her joke. The Germans, though much more attended to, are perhaps not less mistaken than before.

Doubtless, however, there is in this increased attention a progress towards the truth; which it is only investigation and discussion that can help us to find. The study of German literature has already taken such firm root among us, and its spreading so visibly, that by and by, as we believe, the true character of it must and will become known. A result, which is to bring us into closer and friendlier union with forty millions of civilized men, cannot surely be otherwise than desirable. If they have precious truth to impart, we shall receive it as the highest of all gifts; if error, we shall not only reject it, but explain it and trace out its origin, and so help our brethren also to reject it. In either point of view, and for all profitable purposes of national intercourse, correct knowledge is the first and indispensable preliminary.

Meanwhile, errors of all sorts prevail on this subject: even among men of sense and liberality we have found so much hallucination, so many groundless or half-grounded objections to German literature, that the tone in which a multitude of other men speak of it cannot appear extraordinary. To much of this, even a slight knowledge of the Germans would furnish a sufficient answer. But we have thought it might be useful were the chief of these objections marshalled in distinct order, and examined with what degree of light and fairness is at our disposal. In attempting this, we are vain enough, for reasons already stated, to fancy ourselves discharging what is in some sort a national duty. It is unworthy of one great people to think falsely of another; it is unjust, and therefore unworthy. Of the injury it does to ourselves we do not speak, for that is an inferior consideration: yet surely if the grand principle of free intercourse is so profitable in material commerce, much more must it be in the commerce of the mind, the products of which are thereby not so much transported out of one country into another, as multiplied over all, for the benefit of all, and without loss to any. If that man is a benefactor to the world who causes two ears of corn to grow where only one grew before, much more is he a benefactor who causes two truths to grow up together in harmony and mutual confirmation, where before only one stood solitary, and, on that side at least, intolerant and hostile.

In dealing with the host of objections which front us on this subject, we think it may be convenient to range them under two principal heads. The first, as respects chiefly unsoundness or imperfection of sentiment; an error which may in general be denominated *Bad Taste*. The second, as respects chiefly a wrong condition of intellect; an error which may be designated by the general title of *Mysticism*. Both of these, no doubt, are partly connected; and each, in some degree, springs from and returns into the other: yet, for present purposes, the divisions may be precise enough.

First, then, of the first: It is objected that the Germans have a radically bad taste. This

---

* So late as the year 1811, we find, from *Pinkerton's Geography*, the sole representative of German literature to be Gottshed, (with his name wrong spelt,) "who first introduced a more refined style."—Gottsched has been dead the greater part of the century; and, for the last fifty years, ranks among the Germans somewhat as Prynne or Alexander Ross does among ourselves. A man of a cold, rigid, perseverant character, who mistook himself for a poet and the perfection of critics, and had skill to pass current during the greater part of his literary life for such. On the strength of his Boileau and Batteux, he long reigned supreme: but it was like Night, in rayless majesty, and over a slumbering people. They awoke, before his death, and hurled him, perhaps too indignantly, into his native Abyss

is a deep-rooted objection, which assumes many forms, and extends through many ramifications. Among men of less acquaintance with the subject of German taste, or of taste in general, the spirit of the accusation seems to be somewhat as follows: That the Germans, with much natural susceptibility, are still in a rather coarse and uncultivated state of mind; displaying, with the energy and other virtues of a rude people, many of their vices also; in particular, a certain wild and headlong temper, which seizes on all things too hastily and impetuously; weeps, storms, loves, hates, too fiercely and vociferously; delighting in coarse excitements, such as flaring contrasts, vulgar horrors, and all sorts of showy exaggeration. Their literature, in particular, is thought to dwell with peculiar complacency among wizards and ruined towers, with mailed knights, secret tribunals, monks, spectres, and banditti; on the other hand, there is an undue love of moonlight, and mossy fountains, and the moral sublime: then we have descriptions of things which should not be described; a general want of tact; nay, often hollowness, and want of sense. In short, the German Muse comports herself, it is said, like a passionate, and rather fascinating, but tumultuous, uninstructed, and but half-civilized Muse. A *belle sauvage* at best, we can only love her with a sort of supercilious tolerance; often she tears a passion to rags; and, in her tumid vehemence, struts without meaning, and to the offence of all literary decorum.

Now, in all this there is a certain degree of truth. If any man will insist upon taking Heinse's *Ardinghello*, and Miller's *Siegwart*, and the works of Veit Weber the younger, and, above all, the everlasting Kotzebue, as his specimens of German literature, he may establish many things. Black Forests, and the glories of Lubberland; sensuality and horror, the spectre nun, and the charmed moonshine, shall not be wanting. Boisterous outlaws, also, with huge whiskers, and the most cat-o'-mountain aspect; tear-stained sentimentalists, the grimmest man-haters, ghosts, and the like suspicious characters, will be found in abundance. We are little read in this bowl-and-dagger department; but we do understand it to have been at one time rather diligently cultivated; though at present it seems to be mostly relinquished as unproductive. Other forms of Unreason have taken its place; which in their turn must yield to still other forms; for it is the nature of this goddess to descend in frequent *avatars* among men. Perhaps not less than five hundred volumes of such stuff could still be collected from the book-stalls of Germany. By which truly we may learn that there is in that country a class of unwise men and unwise women; that many readers there labour under a degree of ignorance and mental vacancy, and read not actively but passively, not to learn but to be amused. But is this fact so very new to us? Or what should we think of a German critic that selected his specimens of British literature from the *Castle Spectre*, Mr. Lewis's *Monk*, or even the *Mysteries of Udolpho*, and *Frankenstein or the Modern Prometheus?* Or would he judge rightly of our dramatic taste, if he took his extracts from Mr. Egan's *Tom and Jerry;* and told his readers, as he might truly do, that *no* play had ever enjoyed such currency on the English stage as this most classic performance? We think not. In like manner, till some author of acknowledged merit shall so write among the Germans, and be approved of by critics of acknowledged merit among them, or at least secure for himself some permanency of favour among the million, we can prove nothing by such instances. That there is so perverse an author, or so blind a critic, in the whole compass of German literature, we have no hesitation in denying.

But farther: among men of deeper views, and with regard to works of really standard character, we find, though not the same, a similar objection repeated. Goethe's *Wilhelm Meister*, it is said, and *Faust*, are full of bad taste also. With respect to the taste in which they are written, we shall have occasion to say somewhat hereafter: meanwhile, we may be permitted to remark that the objection would have more force, did it seem to originate from a more mature consideration of the subject. We have heard few English criticisms of such works, in which the first condition of an approach to accuracy was complied with;—a transposition of the critic into the author's point of vision, a survey of the author's means and objects as they lay before himself, and a just trial of these by rules of universal application. *Faust*, for instance, passes with many of us for a mere tale of sorcery and art-magic: but it would scarcely be more unwise to consider *Hamlet* as depending for its main interest on the ghost that walks in it, than to regard *Faust* as a production of this sort. For the present, therefore, this objection may be set aside; or at least may be considered not as an assertion, but an inquiry, the answer to which may turn out rather that the German taste is different from ours, than that it is worse. Nay, with regard even to difference, we should scarcely reckon it to be of great moment. Two nations that agree in estimating Shakspeare as the highest of all poets, can differ in no essential principle, if they understood one another, that relates to poetry.

Nevertheless, this opinion of our opponents has attained a certain degree of consistency with itself; one thing is thought to throw light on another; nay, a quiet little theory has been propounded to explain the whole phenomenon. The cause of this bad taste, we are assured, lies in the condition of the German authors. These, it seems, are generally very poor; the ceremonial law of the country excludes them from all society with the great; they cannot acquire the polish of drawing-rooms, but must live in mean houses, and therefore write and think in a mean style.

Apart from the truth of these assumptions, and in respect of the theory itself, we confess there is something in the face of it that afflicts us. Is it then so certain that taste and riches are dissolubly connected? that truth of feeling must ever be preceded by weight of purse, and the eyes be dim for universal and eternal Beauty, till they have long rested on gilt walls and costly furniture? To the great body of mankind this were heavy news; for, of the thousand, scarcely one is rich, or connected with the rich; nine hundred and ninety-nine have always been poor, and must always be so. We take the liberty of questioning the whole postulate. We think that, for acquiring true poetic taste, riches, or association with the rich, are distinctly among the minor requisites; that, in fact, they have little or no concern with the matter. This we shall now endeavour to make probable.

Taste, if it mean any thing but a paltry connoisseurship, must mean a general susceptibility to truth and nobleness; a sense to discern, and a heart to love and reverence, all beauty, order, goodness, wheresoever, or in whatsoever forms and accompaniments they are to be seen. This surely implies, as its chief condition, not any given external rank or situation, but a finely gifted mind, purified into harmony with itself, into keenness and justness of vision; above all, kindled into love and generous admiration. Is culture of this sort found exclusively among the higher ranks? We believe it proceeds less from without than within, in every rank. The charms of Nature, the majesty of Man, the infinite loveliness of Truth and Virtue, are not hidden from the eye of the poor; but from the eye of the vain, the corrupted, and self-seeking, be he poor or rich. In all ages, the humble Minstrel, a mendicant, and lord of nothing but his harp and his own free soul, had intimations of those glories, while to the proud Baron in his barbaric halls they were unknown. Nor is there still any aristocratic monopoly of judgment more than of genius: And as to that *Science of Negation*, which is taught peculiarly by men of professed elegance, we confess we hold it rather cheap. It is a necessary, but decidedly a subordinate accomplishment: nay, if it be rated as the highest, it becomes a ruinous vice. This is an old truth; yet ever needing new application and enforcement. Let us know what to love, and we shall know also what to reject; what to affirm, and we shall know also what to deny: but it is dangerous to *begin* with denial, and fatal to end with it. To deny is easy; nothing is sooner learnt or more generally practised: as matters go, we need no man of polish to teach it; but rather, if possible, a hundred men of wisdom to show us its limits, and teach us its reverse.

Such is our hypothesis of the case: But how stands it with the facts? Are the fineness and truth of sense manifested by the artist found, in most instances, to be proportionate to his wealth and elevation of acquaintance? Are they found to have any perceptible relation either with the one or the other? We imagine not. Whose taste in painting, for instance, is truer and finer than Claude Lorraine's? And was not he a poor colour-grinder; outwardly, the meanest of menials? Where, again, we might ask, lay Shakspeare's rent-roll; and what generous peer took him by the hand and unfolded to him the "open secret" of the Universe; teaching him that this was beautiful, and that not so? Was he not a peasant by birth, and by fortune something lower; and was it not thought much, even in the height of his reputation, that Southampton allowed him equal patronage with the zanies, jugglers, and bearwards of the time? Yet compare his taste, even as it respects the negative side of things; for in regard to the positive, and far higher side, it admits no comparison with any other mortal's,—compare it, for instance, with the taste of Beaumont and Fletcher, his contemporaries, men of rank and education, and of fine genius like himself. Tried even by the nice, fastidious, and in great part false, and artificial delicacy of modern times, how stands it with the two parties: with the gay triumphant men of fashion, and the poor vagrant link-boy? Does the latter sin against, we shall not say taste, but etiquette, as the former do? For one line, for one word, which some Chesterfield might wish blotted from the first, are there not in the others whole pages and scenes which, with palpitating heart, he would hurry into deepest night? This, too, observe, respects not their genius, but their culture; not their appropriation of beauties, but their rejection of deformities, by supposition, the grand and peculiar result of high breeding! Surely, in such instances, even that humble supposition is ill borne out.

The truth of the matter seems to be, that with the culture of a genuine poet, thinker, or other aspirant to fame, the influence of rank has no exclusive or even special concern. For men of action, for senators, public speakers, political writers, the case may be different; but of such we speak not at present. Neither do we speak of imitators, and the crowd of mediocre men, to whom fashionable life sometimes gives an external inoffensiveness, often compensated by a frigid malignity of character. We speak of men, who, from amid the perplexed and conflicting elements of their everyday existence, are to form themselves into harmony and wisdom, and show forth the same wisdom to others that exist along with them. To such a man, high life, as it is called, will be a province of human life certainly, but nothing more. He will study to deal with it as he deals with all forms of mortal being; to do it justice, and to draw instruction from it: but his light will come from a loftier region, or he wanders for ever in darkness; dwindles into a man of *vers de société*, or attains at best to be a Walpole or a Caylus. Still less can we think that he is to be viewed as a hireling; that his excellence will be regulated by his pay. "Sufficiently provided for from within, he has need of little from without:" food and raiment, and an unviolated home, will be given him in the rudest land; and with these, while the kind earth is round him, and the everlasting heaven is over him, the world has little more that it can give. Is he poor? So also were Homer and Socrates; so was Samuel Johnson; so was John Milton. Shall we reproach him with his poverty, and infer that, because he is poor, he must likewise be worthless? God forbid that the time should ever come when he too shall esteem riches the synonyme of good! The spirit of Mammon has a wide empire; but it cannot, and must not, be worshipped in the Holy of Holies. Nay, does not the heart of every genuine disciple of literature, however mean his sphere, instinctively deny this principle, as applicable either to himself or another? Is it not rather true, as D'Alembert has said, that for every man of letters, who deserves that name, the motto and the watchword will be Freedom, Truth, and even this same Poverty? and that if he fear the last, the two first can never be made sure to him?

We have stated these things, to bring the question somewhat nearer its real basis; not for the sake of the Germans, who nowise need the admission of them. The German authors are not poor; neither are they excluded from association with the wealthy and well-born. On the contrary, we scruple not to say, that, in both these respects, they are considerably better situated than our own. Their booksellers, it is true, cannot pay as ours do; yet, there as here, a man lives by his writings; and, to compare *Jorden* with *Johnson* and *D'Israeli*, somewhat better there than here. No case like our own noble Otway's has met us in their biographies; Boyces and Chattertons are much rarer in German, than in English history. But farther, and what is far more important: From the number of universities, libraries, collections of art, museums, and other literary or scientific institutions of a public or private nature, we question whether the chance, which a meritorious man of letters has before him, of obtaining some permanent appointment, some independent civic existence, is not a hundred to one in favour of the German, compared with the Englishman. This is a weighty item, and indeed the weightiest of all; for it will be granted, that, for the votary of literature, the relation of entire dependence on the merchants of literature, is, at best, and however liberal the terms, a highly questionable one. It tempts him daily and hourly to sink from an artist into a manufacturer; nay, so precarious, fluctuating, and every way unsatisfactory must his civic and economic concerns become, that too many of his class cannot even attain the praise of common honesty as manufacturers. There is, no doubt, a spirit of martyrdom, as we have asserted, which can sustain this too: but few indeed have the spirit of martyrs; and that state of matters is the safest which requires it least. The German authors, moreover, to their credit be it spoken, seem to set less store by wealth than many of ours. There have been prudent, quiet men among them, who actually appeared not to want more wealth,—whom wealth could not tempt, either to this hand or that, from their pre-appointed aims. Neither must we think so hardly of the German nobility as to believe them insensible to genius, or of opinion that a patent from the Lion King is so superior to "a patent direct from Almighty God." A fair proportion of the German authors are themselves men of rank: we mention only, as of our own time, and notable in other respects, the two Stolbergs and Novalis. Let us not be unjust to this class of persons. It is a poor error to figure them as wrapt up in ceremonial stateliness, avoiding the most gifted man of a lower station; and, for their own supercilious triviality, themselves avoided by all truly gifted men. On the whole, we should change our notion of the German nobleman: that ancient, thirsty, thickheaded, sixteen-quartered Baron, who still hovers in our minds, never did exist in such perfection, and is now as extinct as our own Squire Western. His descendant is a man of other culture, other aims, and other habits. We question whether there is an aristocracy in Europe, which, taken as a whole, both in a public and private capacity, more honours art and literature, and does more both in public and private to encourage them. Excluded from society! What, we would ask, was Wieland's, Schiller's, Herder's, Johannes Müller's society? Has not Goethe, by birth a Frankfort burgher, been, since his twenty-sixth year, the companion, not of nobles but of princes, and for half his life a minister of state? And is not this man, unrivalled in so many far deeper qualities, known also and felt to be unrivalled in nobleness of breeding and bearing; fit not to learn of princes, in this respect, but by the example of his daily life to teach them?

We hear much of the munificent spirit displayed among the better classes in England; their high estimation of the arts, and generous patronage of the artist. We rejoice to hear it; we hope it is true, and will become truer and truer. We hope that a great change has taken place among these classes, since the time when Bishop Burnet could write of them,—"They are for the most part the *worst* instructed, and the *least* knowing, of any of their rank I ever went among!" Nevertheless, let us arrogate to ourselves no exclusive praise in this particular. Other nations can appreciate the arts, and cherish their cultivators, as well as we. Nay, while learning from us in many other matters, we suspect the Germans might even teach us somewhat in regard to this. At all events, the pity, which certain of our authors express for the civil condition of their brethren in that country, is, from such a quarter, a superfluous feeling. Nowhere, let us rest assured, is genius more devoutly honoured than there, by all ranks of men, from peasants and burghers up to legislators and kings. It was but last year that the Diet of the Empire passed an act in favour of one individual poet: the final edition of Goethe's works was guarantied to be protected against commercial injury in every state of Germany; and special assurances to that effect were sent him, in the kindest terms, from all the Authorities there assembled, some of them the highest in his country or in Europe. Nay, even while we write, are not the newspapers recording a visit from the Sovereign of Bavaria in person, to the same venerable man; a mere ceremony, perhaps, but one which almost recalls to us the era of the antique Sages and the Grecian Kings?

This hypothesis, therefore, it would seem, is not supported by facts, and so returns to its original elements. The causes it alleges are impossible: but, what is still more fatal, the effect it proposes to account for has, in reality, no existence. We venture to deny that the Germans are defective in taste; even as a nation, as a public, taking one thing with another, we imagine they may stand comparison with any of their neighbours; as writers, as critics, they may decidedly court it. True, there is a mass of dulness, awkwardness, and false susceptibility in the lower regions of their literature: but is not bad taste endemical in such regions of every literature under the sun? Pure Stupidity, indeed, is of a quiet nature, and content to be merely stupid. But seldom do we find it pure; seldom unadulterated with some tincture of ambition, which drives it into new and strange metamorphoses. Here it has assumed a contemptuous trenchant air, intended to represent superior tact, and a sort of all-wisdom; there a truculent atrabilious scowl, which is to stand for passionate strength: now we have an outpouring of tumid fervour; now a fruitless, asthmatic hunting after wit and humour. Grave or gay, enthusiastic or derisive, admiring or despising, the dull man would be something which he is not and cannot be. Shall we confess, that, of these too common extremes, we reckon the German error considerably the more harmless, and, in our day, by far the more curable? Of unwise admiration much may be hoped, for much good is really in it: but unwise contempt is itself a negation; nothing comes of it, for it *is* nothing.

To judge of a national taste, however, we must raise our view from its transitory modes to its perennial models; from the mass of vulgar writers, who blaze out and are extinguished with the popular delusion which they flatter, to those few who are admitted to shine with a pure and lasting lustre; to whom, by common consent, the eyes of the people are turned, as to its lodestar and celestial luminaries. Among German writers of this stamp, we would ask any candid reader of them, let him be of what country or what creed he might, whether bad taste struck him as a prevailing characteristic. Was Wieland's taste uncultivated? Taste, we should say, and taste of the very species which a disciple of the Negative School would call the highest, formed the great object of his life; the perfection he unweariedly endeavoured after, and, more than any other perfection, has attained. The most fastidious Frenchman might read him, with admiration of his merely French qualities. And is not Klopstock, with his clear enthusiasm, his azure purity, and heavenly, if still somewhat cold and lunar light, a man of taste? His *Messias* reminds us oftener of no other poets than of Virgil and Racine. But it is to Lessing that an Englishman would turn with the readiest affection. We cannot but wonder that more of this man is not known among us; or that the knowledge of him has not done more to remove such misconceptions. Among all the writers of the eighteenth century, we will not except even Diderot and David Hume, there is not one of a more compact and rigid intellectual structure; who more distinctly knows what he is aiming at, or with more gracefulness, vigour, and precision sets it forth to his readers. He thinks with the clearness and piercing sharpness of the most expert logician: but a genial fire pervades him, a wit, a heartiness, a general richness and fineness of nature, to which most logicians are strangers. He is a skeptic in many things, but the noblest of skeptics; a mild, manly, half-careless enthusiasm struggles through his indignant unbelief: he stands before us like a toilworn, but unwearied and heroic champion, earning not the conquest but the battle; as indeed himself admits to us, that "it is not the finding of truth, but the honest search for it, that profits." We confess, we should be entirely at a loss for the literary creed of that man who reckoned Lessing other than a thoroughly cultivated writer; nay entitled to rank, in this particular, with the most distinguished writers of any existing nation. As a poet, as a critic, philosopher, or controversialist, his style will be found precisely such as we of England are accustomed to admire most; brief, nervous, vivid; yet quiet, without glitter or antithesis; idiomatic, pure without purism, transparent, yet full of character and reflex hues of meaning. "Every sentence," says Horn, and justly, "is like a phalanx;" not a word wrong placed, not a word that could be spared; and it forms itself so calmy and lightly, and stands in its completeness, so gay, yet so impregnable! As a poet he contemptuously denied himself all merit; but his readers have not taken him at his word: here, too, a similar felicity of style attends him; his plays, his *Minna von Barnhelm*, his *Emilie Galotti*, his *Nathan der Weise*, have a genuine and graceful poetic life; yet no works known to us in any language are purer from exaggeration, or any appearance of falsehood. They are pictures, we might say painted not in colours, but in crayons; yet a strange attraction lies in them; for the figures are grouped into the finest attitudes, and true and spirit-speaking in every line. It is with his style chiefly that we have to do here; yet we must add, that the matter of his works is not less meritorious. His Criticism and philosophic or religious Skepticism were of a higher mood than had yet been heard in Europe, still more in Germany: his *Dramaturgie* first exploded the pretensions of the French theatre, and, with irresistible conviction, made Shakspeare known to his countrymen; preparing the way for a brighter era in their literature, the chief men of which still thankfully look back to Lessing as their patriarch. His *Laocoon*, with its deep glances into the philosophy of Art, his *Dialogues of Free-masons*, a work of far higher import than its title indicates, may yet teach many things to most of us, which we know not, and ought to know.

With Lessing and Klopstock might be joined, in this respect, nearly, every one, we do not say of their distinguished, but even of their tolerated contemporaries. The two Jacobis, known more or less in all countries, are little known here, if they are accused of wanting literary taste. These are men, whether as thinkers or poets, to be regarded and admired for their mild and lofty wisdom, the devoutness, the benignity and calm grandeur of their philosophical views. In such, it were strange if among so many high merits, this lower one of a just and elegant style, which is indeed their natural and even necessary product, had been wanting. We recommend the elder Jacobi no less for his clearness than for his depth; of the younger, it may be enough in this point of view to say, that the chief praisers of his earlier poetry were the French. Neither are Hamann and Mendelsohn, who could meditate deep thoughts, defective in the power of uttering them with propriety. The *Phædon* of the latter, in its chaste precision and simplicity of style, may almost remind us of Xenophon: Socrates, to our mind, has spoken in no modern language so like Socrates, as here, by the lips of this wise and cultivated Jew.*

Among the poets and more popular writers of the time, the case is the same: Utz, Gellert, Cramer, Ramler, Kleist, Hagedorn, Rabener, Gleim, and a multitude of lesser men, whatever excellences they might want, certainly are not chargeable with bad taste. Nay, perhaps of all writers they are the least chargeable with it: a certain clear, light, unaffected elegance, of a higher nature than French elegance, it might be, yet to the exclusion of all very deep or genial qualities, was the excellence they strove after, and, for the most part, in a fair measure attained. They resemble English writers of the same, or perhaps an earlier period, more than any other foreigners: apart from Pope, whose influence is visible enough, Beattie, Logan, Wilkie, Glover, unknown perhaps to any of them, might otherwise have almost seemed their models. Goldsmith also would rank among them; perhaps, in regard to true poetic genius, at their head, for none of them has left us a *Vicar of Wakefield;* though, in regard to judgment, knowledge, general talent, his place would scarcely be so high.

The same thing holds, in general, and with fewer drawbacks, of the somewhat later and more energetic race, denominated the *Göttingen School*, in contradistinction from the *Saxon*, to which Rabener, Cramer, and Gellert directly belonged, and most of those others indirectly. Hölty, Bürger, the two Stolbergs, are men whom Bossu might measure with his scale and compasses as strictly as he pleased. Of Herder, Schiller, Goethe, we speak not here: they are men of another stature and form of movement, whom Bossu's scale and compasses could not measure without difficulty, or rather not at all. To say that such men wrote with taste of this sort, were saying little; for this forms not the apex, but the basis, in their conception of style; a quality not to be paraded as an excellence, but to be understood as indispensable, as there by necessity, and like a thing of course.

In truth, for it must be spoken out, our opponents are so widely astray in this matter, that their views of it are not only dim and perplexed, but altogether imaginary and delusive. It is proposed to School the Germans in the Alphabet of taste; and the Germans are already busied with their Accidence! Far from being behind other nations in the practice or science of Criticism, it is a fact, for which we fearlessly refer to all competent judges, that they are distinctly, and even considerably, in advance. We state what is already known to a great part of Europe to be true. Criticism has assumed a new form in Germany; it proceeds on other principles, and proposes to itself a higher aim. The grand question is not now a question concerning the qualities of diction, the coherence of metaphors, the fitness of sentiments, the general logical truth, in a work of art, as it was some half century ago among most critics. Neither is it a question mainly of a psychological sort, to be answered by discovering and delineating the peculiar nature of the poet from his poetry, as is usual with the best of our own critics at present; but it is, not indeed exclusively, but inclusively of those two other questions, properly and ultimately a question on the essence and peculiar life of the poetry itself. The first of these questions, as we see it answered, for instance, in the criticisms of Johnson and Kames, relates, strictly speaking, to the *garment* of poetry; the second, indeed, to its *body* and material existence, a much higher point; but only the last to its *soul* and spiritual existence, by which alone can the body, in its movements and phases, be *informed* with significance and rational life. The problem is not now to determine by what mechanism Addison composed sentences, and struck out similitudes, but by what far finer and more mysterious mechanism Shakspeare organized his dramas, and gave life and individuality to his Ariel and his Hamlet. Wherein lies that life; how have they attained that shape and individuality? Whence comes that empyrean fire, which irradiates their whole being, and pierces, at least in starry gleams, like a diviner thing, into all hearts? Are these dramas of his not verisimilar only, but true; nay, truer than reality itself, since the essence of unmixed reality is bodied forth in them under more expressive symbols? What is this unity of theirs; and can our deeper inspection discern it to be indivisible, and existing by necessity, because each work springs, as it were, from the general elements of all Thought, and grows up therefrom, into form and expansion, by its own growth? Not only who was the poet, and how did he compose; but what and how was the poem, and why was it a poem and not rhymed eloquence, creation and not figured passion? These are the questions for the critic. Criticism stands like an interpreter between the inspired and the uninspired; between the prophet and those who hear the melody of his words, and catch some glimpse of their material meaning, but understand not their deeper import. She pretends to open for us this deeper import; to clear our sense that it may discern the pure brightness of this eternal Beauty, and recognise it as heavenly, under all forms where it looks forth, and reject, as

* The history of Mendelsohn is interesting in itself, and full of encouragement to all lovers of self-improvement. At thirteen he was a wandering Jewish beggar, without health, without home, almost without a language, for the jargon of broken Hebrew and provincial German which he spoke could scarcely be called one. At middle age, he could write this *Phædon;* was a man of wealth and breeding, and ranked among the teachers of his age. Like Pope, he abode by his original creed, though often solicited to change it: indeed, the grand problem of his life was to better the inward and outward condition of his own ill-fated people; for whom he actually accomplished much benefit. He was a mild, shrewd, and worthy man; and might well love *Phædon* and Socrates, for his own character was Socratic. He was a friend of Lessing's: indeed a pupil; for Lessing having accidentally met him at chess, recognised the spirit that lay struggling under such incumbrances, and generously undertook to help him. By teaching the poor Jew a little Greek he disenchanted him from the Talmud and the Rabbins. The two were afterwards co-labourers in Nicolai's *Deutsche Bibliothek*, the first German *Review* of any character; which, however, in the hands of Nicolai himself, it subsequently lost. Mendelsohn's Works have mostly been translated into French.

of the earth earthy, all forms, be their material splendour what it may, where no gleaming of that other shines through.

This is the task of Criticism, as the Germans understand it. And how do they accomplish this task? By a vague declamation clothed in gorgeous mystic phraseology? By vehement tumultuous anthems to the poet and his poetry; by epithets and laudatory similitudes drawn from Tartarus and Elysium, and all intermediate terrors and glories; whereby, in truth, it is rendered clear both that the poet is an extremely great poet, and also that the critic's allotment of understanding, overflowed by these Pythian raptures, has unhappily melted into deliquium? Nowise in this manner do the Germans proceed: but by rigorous scientific inquiry; by appeal to principles which, whether correct or not, have been deduced patiently, and by long investigation, from the highest and calmest regions of Philosophy. For this finer portion of their Criticism is now also embodied in systems; and standing, so far as these reach, coherent, distinct, and methodical, no less than, on their much shallower foundation, the systems of Boileau and Blair. That this new Criticism is a complete, much more a certain science, we are far from meaning to affirm: the *æsthetic* theories of Kant, Herder, Schiller, Goethe, Richter, vary in external aspect, according to the varied habits of the individual; and can at best only be regarded as approximations to the truth, or modifications of it; each critic representing it as it harmonizes more or less perfectly with the other intellectual persuasions of his own mind, and of different classes of minds that resemble his. Nor can we here undertake to inquire what degree of such approximation to the truth there is in each or all of these writers; or in Tieck and the two Schlegels, who, especially the latter, have laboured so meritoriously in reconciling these various opinions; and so successfully in impressing and diffusing the best spirit of them, first in their own country, and now also in several others. Thus much, however, we will say: That we reckon the mere circumstance of such a science being in existence, a ground of the highest consideration, and worthy the best attention of all inquiring men. For we should err widely, if we thought that this new tendency of critical science pertains to Germany alone. It is a European tendency, and springs from the general condition of intellect in Europe. We ourselves have all, for the last thirty years, more or less distinctly felt the necessity of such a science: witness the neglect into which our Blairs and Bossus have silently fallen; our increased and increasing admiration, not only of Shakspeare, but of all his contemporaries, and of all who breathe any portion of his spirit; our controversy whether Pope was a poet; and so much vague effort on the part of our best critics, everywhere, to express some still unexpressed idea concerning the nature of true poetry; as if they felt in their hearts that a pure glory, nay, a divineness, belonged to it, for which they had as yet no name, and no intellectual form. But in Italy too, in France itself, the same thing is visible. Their grand controversy, so hotly urged, between the *Classicists* and the *Romanticists*, in which the Schlegels are assumed, much too loosely, on all hands, as the patrons and generalissimos of the latter, shows us sufficiently what spirit is at work in that long stagnant literature. Doubtless this turbid fermentation of the elements will at length settle into clearness, both there, and here, as in Germany it has already in a great measure done; and perhaps a more serene and genial poetic day is everywhere to be expected with some confidence. How much the example of the Germans may have to teach us in this particular, needs no farther exposition.

The authors and first promulgators of this new critical doctrine, were at one time contemptuously named the *New School;* nor was it till after a war of all the few good heads in the nation, with all the many bad ones, had ended as such wars must ever do,* that these critical principles were generally adopted; and their assertors found to be no *School* or new heretical Sect, but the ancient primitive Catholic Communion, of which all sects that had any living light in them were but members and subordinate modes. It is, indeed, the most sacred article of this creed to preach and practise universal tolerance. Every literature of the world has been cultivated by the Germans; and to every literature they have studied to give due honour. Shakspeare and Homer, no doubt, occupy alone the loftiest station in the poetical Olympus; but there is space for all true Singers, out of every age and clime. Ferdusi and the primeval Mythologists of Hindostan, live in brotherly union with the Troubadours and ancient Story-tellers of the West. The wayward mystic gloom of Calderon, the lurid fire of Dante, the auroral light of Tasso, the clear icy glitter of Racine, all are acknowledged and reverenced: nay, in the celestial fore-court an abode has been appointed for the Gressets and Delilles, that no spark of inspiration, no tone of mental music, might remain unrecognised. The Germans study foreign nations in a spirit which deserves to be oftener imitated. It is their honest endeavour to understand each with its own peculiarities, in its own special manner of existing; not that they may praise it, or censure it, or attempt to alter it, but simply that they may see this manner of existing as the nation itself sees it, and so participate in whatever worth or beauty it has brought into being. Of all literatures, accordingly, the German has the best as well as the most translations; men like Goethe, Schiller, Wieland, Schlegel, Tieck, have not disdained this task. Of Shakspeare there are three entire versions admitted to be good; and we know not how

* It began in Schiller's *Musenalmanach* for 1793. The *Xenien*, (a series of philosophic epigrams jointly by Schiller and Goethe,) descended there unexpectedly, like a flood of ethereal fire, on the German literary world; quickening all that was noble into new life, but visiting the ancient empire of Dulness with astonishment and unknown pangs. The agitation was extreme: scarcely since the age of Luther, has there been such stir and strife in the intellect of Germany; indeed, scarcely since that age, has there been a controversy, if we consider its ultimate bearings on the best and noblest interests of mankind, so important as this, which, for the time, seemed only to turn on metaphysical subtilties, and matters of mere elgance. Its farther applications became apparent by degrees.

many partial, or considered as bad. In their criticisms of him we ourselves have long ago admitted, that no such clear judgment or hearty appreciation of his merits had ever been exhibited by any critic of our own.

To attempt stating in separate aphorisms the doctrines of this new poetical system, would, in such space as is now allowed us, be to ensure them of misapprehension. The science of Criticism, as the Germans practise it, is no study of an hour; for it springs from the depths of thought, and remotely or immediately connects itself with the subtilest problems of all philosophy. One characteristic of it we may state, the obvious parent of many others. Poetic beauty, in its pure essence, is not, by this theory, as by all our theories, from Hume's to Alison's, derived from any thing external, or of merely intellectual origin; not from association, or any reflex or reminiscence of mere sensations; nor from natural love, either of imitation, of similarity in dissimilarity, of excitement by contrast, or of seeing difficulties overcome. On the contrary, it is assumed as underived; not borrowing its existence from such sources, but as lending to most of these their significance and principal charm for the mind. It dwells, and is born in the inmost Spirit of Man, united to all love of Virtue, to all true belief in God; or rather, it is one with this love and this belief, another phase of the same highest principle in the mysterious infinitude of the human Soul. To apprehend this beauty of poetry, in its full and purest brightness, is not easy, but difficult; thousands on thousands eagerly read poems, and attain not the smallest taste of it; yet to all uncorrupted hearts, some effulgences of this heavenly glory are here and there revealed; and to apprehend it clearly and wholly, to acquire and maintain a sense and heart that sees and worships it, is the last perfection of all humane culture. With mere readers for amusement, therefore, this Criticism has, and can have, nothing to do; these find their amusement, in less or greater measure, and the nature of Poetry remains for ever hidden from them in the deepest concealment. On all hands, there is no truce given to the hypothesis, that the ultimate object of the poet is to please. Sensation, even of the finest and most rapturous sort, is not the end but the means. Art is to be loved, not because of its effects, but because of itself; not because it is useful for spiritual pleasure, or even for moral culture, but because it is Art, and the highest in man, and the soul of all Beauty. To inquire after its *utility*, would be like inquiring after the *utility* of a God, or what to the Germans would sound stranger than it does to us, the *utility* of Virtue and Religion. On these particulars, the authenticity of which we might verify, not so much by citation of individual passages, as by reference to the scope and spirit of whole treatises, we must for the present leave our readers to their own reflections. Might we advise them, it would be to inquire farther, and, if possible, to see the matter with their own eyes.

Meanwhile, that all this must tend, among the Germans, to raise the general standard of Art, and of what an Artist ought to be in his own esteem and that of others, will be readily inferred. The character of a Poet does, accordingly, stand higher with the Germans than with most nations. That he is a man of integrity as a man; of zeal and honest diligence in his art, and of true manly feeling towards all men, is of course presupposed. Of persons that are not so, but employ their gifts, in rhyme or otherwise, for brutish or malignant purposes, it is understood that such lie without the limits of Criticism, being subjects not for the judge of Art, but for the judge of Police. But even with regard to the fair tradesman, who offers his talent in open market, to do work of a harmless and acceptable sort for hire,—with regard to this person also, their opinion is very low. The "Bread-artist," as they call him, can gain no reverence for himself from these men. "Unhappy mortal!" says the mild but lofty-minded Schiller, "Unhappy mortal! that, with Science and Art, the noblest of all instruments, effectest and attemptest nothing more than the day-drudge with the meanest; that in the domain of perfect freedom, bearest about in thee the spirit of a Slave!" Nay, to the genuine Poet, they deny even the privilege of regarding what so many cherish, under the title of their "fame," as the best and highest of all. Hear Schiller again:

"The Artist, it is true, is the son of his age; but pity for him if he is its pupil, or even its favourite! Let some beneficent divinity snatch him, when a suckling, from the breast of his mother, and nurse him with the milk of a better time, that he may ripen to his full stature beneath a distant Grecian sky. And having grown to manhood, let him return a foreign shape, into his century; not, however, to delight it by his presence, but dreadful, like the son of Agamemnon, to purify it. The matter of his works he will take from the present, but their form he will derive from a nobler time; nay, from beyond all time, from the absolute unchanging unity of his own nature. Here, from the pure æther of his spiritual essence, flows down the Fountain of Beauty, uncontaminated by the pollutions of ages and generations, which roll to and fro in their turbid vortex far beneath it. His matter, Caprice can dishonour, as she has ennobled it; but the chaste form is withdrawn from her mutations. The Roman of the first century had long bent the knee before his Cæsars, when the statues of Rome were still standing erect; the temples continued holy to the eye, when their gods had long been a laughing-stock; and the abominations of a Nero and a Commodus were silently rebuked by the style of the edifice, which lent them its concealment. Man has lost his dignity, but Art has saved it, and preserved it for him in expressive marbles. Truth still lives in fiction, and from the copy the original will be restored.

"But how is the Artist to guard himself from the corruptions of his time, which on every side assail him? By despising its decisions. Let him look upwards to his dignity and the law, not downwards to his happiness and his wants. Free alike from the vain activity that longs to impress its traces on the fleeting instant, and from the querulous spirit of enthusiasm that measures by the scale of perfection the meagre product of reality, let him leave to mere Understanding, which is here at home, the province of the actual; while *he* strives, by uniting the possible with the necessary, to produce the ideal. This let him imprint and express in fiction and truth; imprint it in the sport of his imagination and the earnest of his actions; imprint it in all sensible and spiritual forms, and cast it silently into everlasting time."*

Still higher are Fichte's notions on this subject; or rather expressed in higher terms, for the central principle is the same both in the philosopher and the poet. According to Fichte, there is a "Divine Idea" pervading the visible Universe; which visible Universe is indeed but its symbol and sensible manifestation, having in itself no meaning, or even true existence independent of it. To the mass of men this Divine Idea of the world lies hidden: yet to discern it, to seize it, and live wholly in it, is the condition of all genuine virtue, knowledge, freedom; and the end, therefore, of all spiritual effort in every age. Literary Men are the appointed interpreters of this Divine Idea; a perpetual priesthood, we might say, standing forth, generation after generation, as the dispensers and living types of God's everlasting wisdom, to show it and imbody it in their writings and actions, in such particular form as their own particular times require it in. For each age, by the law of its nature, is different from every other age, and demands a different representation of this Divine Idea, the essence of which is the same in all; so that the literary man of one century is only by mediation and re-interpretation applicable to the wants of another. But in every century, every man who labours, be it in what province he may, to teach others, must first have possessed himself of this Divine Idea, or, at least, be with his whole heart and his whole soul striving after it. If, without possessing it or striving after it, he abide diligently by some material practical department of knowledge, he may indeed still be (says Fichte, in his usual rugged way,) a "useful hodman;" but should he attempt to deal with the Whole, and to become an architect, he is, in strictness of language, "Nothing;"—"he is an ambiguous mongrel between the possessor of the Idea, and the man ho feels himself solidly supported and carried on by the common Reality of things; in his fruitless endeavour after the Idea, he has neglected to acquire the craft of taking part in this Reality; and so hovers between two worlds, without pertaining to either." Elsewhere he adds:

"There is still, from another point of view, another division in our notion of the Literary Man, and one to us of immediate application. Namely, either the Literary Man has already laid hold of the whole Divine Idea, in so far as it can be comprehended by man, or perhaps of a special portion of this its comprehensible part,—which truly is not possible without at least a clear oversight of the whole,—he has already laid hold of it, penetrated, and made it entirely clear to himself, so that it has become a possession recallable at all times in the same shape to his view, and a component part of his personality: in that case he is a completed and equipt Literary Man, a man who *has* studied. Or else, he is still struggling and striving to make the Idea in general, or that particular portion and point of it, from which onwards he for his part means to penetrate the whole,—entirely clear to himself; detached sparkles of light already spring forth on him from all sides, and disclose a higher world before him; but they do not yet unite themselves into an indivisible whole; they vanish from his view as capriciously as they came; he cannot yet bring them under obedience to his freedom; in that case he is a progressing and self-unfolding literary man, a Student. That it be actually the Idea, which is possessed or striven after, is common to both. Should the striving aim merely at the outward form, and the letter of learned culture, there is then produced, when the circle is gone round, the completed, when it is not gone round, the progressing, Bungler (*Stümper*). The latter is more tolerable than the former; for there is still room to hope that, in continuing his travel, he may at some future point be seized by the Idea; but of the first all hope is over."*

From this bold and lofty principle the duties of the Literary man are deduced with scientific precision; and stated, in all their sacredness and grandeur, with an austere brevity more impressive than any rhetoric. Fichte's metaphysical theory may be called in question, and readily enough misapprehended; but the sublime stoicism of his sentiments will find some response in many a heart. We must add the conclusion of his first Discourse, as a farther illustration of his manner:

"In disquisitions of the sort like ours of today, which all the rest, too, must resemble, the generality are wont to censure: First, their severity; very often on the good-natured supposition that the speaker is not aware how much his rigour must displease us; that we have but frankly to let him know this, and then doubtless he will reconsider himself, and soften his statements. Thus, we said above, that a man who, after literary culture, had not arrived at knowledge of the Divine Idea, or did not strive towards it, was in strict speech Nothing; and farther down, we said that he was a Bungler. This is in a style of those unmerciful expressions by which philosophers give such offence.—Now looking away from the present case, that we may front the maxim in its general shape, I remind you that this species of character, without decisive force to renounce all respect for Truth, seeks merely to bargain and cheapen something out of her, whereby itself on easier terms may attain to some consideration. But truth, which once for all is as she is, and cannot alter aught of her nature, goes on her way; and there remains for her, in regard to those who desire her not simply because she is true, nothing else but to leave them standing as if they had never addressed her.

"Then farther, discourses of this sort are wont

* *Ueber die Aesthetische Erziehung des Menschen.* (On the Æsthetic Education of Man.)

* *Ueber das Wesen des Gelehrten;* (On the Nature of the Literary Man;) a Course of Lectures delivered at Jena, in 1805.

to be censured as unintelligible. Thus I figure to myself,—nowise you, Gentlemen, but some completed Literary Man of the second species, whose eye the disquisition here entered upon chanced to meet, as coming forward, doubting this way and that, and at last reflectively exclaiming: 'The Idea, the Divine Idea, that which lies at the bottom of Appearance: what pray may *this* mean?' Of such a questioner I would inquire in turn: 'What pray may this question mean?'—Investigate it strictly, it means in most cases nothing more than this, 'Under what other names and in what other formulas, do I already know this same thing, which thou expressest by so strange and to me so unknown a symbol?' And to this again in most cases the only suitable reply were, 'Thou knowest this thing not at all, neither under this, nor under any other name; and wouldst thou arrive at the knowledge of it, thou must even now begin at the beginning to make study thereof; and then, most fitly, under that name by which it is first presented to thee!'"

With such a notion of the Artist, it were a strange inconsistency did Criticism show itself unscientific or lax in estimating the products of his Art. For light on this point, we might refer to the writings of almost any individual among the German critics: take, for instance, the *Charakteristiken* of the two Schlegels, a work too of their younger years; and say whether in depth, clearness, minute and patient fidelity, these *Characters* have often been surpassed, or the import and poetic worth of so many poets and poems more vividly and accurately brought to view. As an instance of a much higher kind, we might refer to Goethe's criticism of *Hamlet* in his *Wilhelm Meister*. This truly is what may be called the poetry of criticism; for it is in some sort also a creative art; aiming, at least, to reproduce under a different shape the existing product of the poet; painting to the intellect what already lay painted to the heart and the imagination. Nor is it over poetry alone that criticism watches with such loving strictness: the mimic, the pictorial, the musical arts, all modes of representing or addressing the highest nature of man, are acknowledged as younger sisters of Poetry, and fostered with the like care. Winkelmann's *History of Plastic Art* is known by repute to all readers: and of those who know it by inspection, many may have wondered why such a work has not been added to our own literature, to instruct our own statuaries and painters. On this subject of the plastic arts, we cannot withhold the following little sketch of Goethe's, as a specimen of pictorial criticism in what we consider a superior style. It is of an imaginary landscape-painter, and his views of Swiss scenery; it will bear to be studied minutely, for there is no word without its meaning:

"He succeeds in representing the cheerful repose of lake prospects, where houses in friendly approximation, imaging themselves in the clear wave, seem as if bathing in its depths; shores encircled with green hills, behind which rise forest mountains, and icy peaks of glaciers. The tone of colouring in such scenes is gay, mirthfully clear; the distances as if overflowed with softening vapour, which from watered hollows and river valleys mounts up grayer and mistier, and indicates their windings. No less is the master's art to be praised in views from valleys lying nearer the high Alpine ranges, where declivities slope down, luxuriantly overgrown, and fresh streams roll hastily along by the foot of rocks.

"With exquisite skill, in the deep shady trees of the foreground, he gives the distinctive character of the several species, satisfying us in the form of the whole, as in the structure of the branches, and the details of the leaves; no less so in the fresh green with its manifold shadings, where soft airs appear as if fanning us with benignant breath, and the lights as if thereby put in motion.

"In the middle-ground, his lively green tone grows fainter by degrees; and at last, on the more distant mountain-tops, passing into weak violet, weds itself with the blue of the sky. But our artist is above all happy in his paintings of high Alpine regions; in seizing the simple greatness and stillness of their character; the wide pastures on the slopes, where dark solitary firs stand forth from the grassy carpet; and from high cliffs, foaming brooks rush down. Whether he relieves his pasturages with grazing cattle, or the narrow winding rocky path with mules and laden pack-horses, he paints all with equal truth and richness; still, introduced in the proper place, and not in too great copiousness, they decorate and enliven these scenes, without interrupting, without lessening their peaceful solitude. The execution testifies a master's hand; easy, with a few sure strokes, and yet complete. In his later pieces, he employed glittering English permanent-colours on paper: these pictures, accordingly, are of preëminently blooming tone; cheerful, yet, at the same time, strong and sated.

"His views of deep mountain chasms, where, round and round, nothing fronts us but dead rock, where, in the abyss, overspanned by its bold arch, the wild stream rages, are, indeed, of less attraction than the former: yet their truth excites us; we admire the great effect of the whole, produced at so little cost, by a few expressive strokes, and masses of local colours.

"With no less accuracy of character can he represent the regions of the topmost Alpine ranges, where neither tree nor shrub any more appears; but only amid the rocky teeth and snow summits, a few sunny spots clothe themselves with a soft sward. Beautiful, and balmy and inviting as he colours these spots, he has here wisely forborne to introduce grazing herds; for these regions give food only to the chamois, and a perilous employment to the wild-hay-men."*

We have extracted this passage from *Wilhelm Meister's Wanderjahre*, Goethe's last Novel. The perusal of his whole Works would show, among many other more important facts, that Criticism also is a science of which he is master; that if ever any man had studied Art in all its branches and bearings, from its origin in

---

* The poor wild-hay-man of the Rigiberg,
Whose trade is, on the brow of the abyss,
To mow the common grass from nooks and shelves,
To which the cattle dare not climb.

SCHILLER'S *Wilhelm Tell*.

the depths of the creative spirit, to its minutest finish on the canvas of the painter, on the lips of the poet, or under the finger of the musician, he was that man. A nation which appreciates such studies, nay, requires and rewards them, cannot, wherever its defects may lie, be defective in judgment of the arts.

But a weightier question still remains. What has been the fruit of this its high and just judgment on these matters? What has criticism profited it, to the bringing forth of good works? How do its poems and its poets correspond with so lofty a standard? We answer, that on this point also, Germany may rather court investigation than fear it. There are poets in that country who belong to a nobler class than most nations have to show in these days; a class entirely unknown to some nations; and, for the last two centuries, rare in all. We have no hesitation in stating, that we see in certain of the best German poets, and those too of our own time, something which associates them, remotely or nearly we say not, but which does associate them with the Masters of Art, the Saints of Poetry, long since departed, and, as we thought, without successors, from the earth; but canonized in the hearts of all generations, and yet living to all by the memory of what they did and were. Glances we do seem to find of that ethereal glory, which looks on us in its full brightness from the *Transfiguration* of Rafaelle, from the *Tempest* of Shakspeare; and in broken, but purest and still heart-piercing beams, struggling through the gloom of long ages, from the tragedies of Sophocles and the weather-worn sculptures of the Parthenon. This is that heavenly spirit, which, best seen in the aerial embodiment of poetry, but spreading likewise over all the thoughts and actions of an age, has given us Surreys, Sydneys, Raleighs in court and camp, Cecils in policy, Hookers in divinity, Bacons in philosophy, and Shakspeares and Spensers in song. All hearts that know this, know it to be the highest; and that, in poetry or elsewhere, it alone is true and imperishable. In affirming that any vestige, however feeble, of this divine spirit, is discernible in German poetry, we are aware that we place it above the existing poetry of any other nation.

To prove this bold assertion, logical arguments were at all times unavailing; and, in the present circumstances of the case, more than usually so. Neither will any extract or specimen help us; for it is not in parts, but in whole poems, that the spirit of a true poet is to be seen. We can, therefore, only name such men as Tieck, Richter, Herder, Schiller, and, above all, Goethe; and ask any reader who has learned to admire wisely our own literature of Queen Elizabeth's age, to peruse these writers also; to study them till he feels that he has understood them, and justly estimated both their light and darkness; and then to pronounce whether it is not, in some degree, as we have said. Are there not tones here of that old melody? Are there not glimpses of that serene soul, that calm harmonious strength, that smiling earnestness, that Love and Faith and Humanity of nature? Do these foreign contemporaries of ours still exhibit, in their characters as men, something of that sterling nobleness, that union of majesty with meekness, which we must ever venerate in those our spiritual fathers? And do their works, in the new form of this century, show forth that old nobleness, not consistent only, with the science, the precision, the skepticism of these days, but wedded to them, incorporated with them, and shining through them like their life and soul? Might it in truth almost seem to us, in reading the prose of Goethe, as if we were reading that of Milton; and of Milton writing with the culture of this time; combining French clearness with old English depth? And of his poetry may it indeed be said that it *is* poetry, and yet the poetry of our own generation; an ideal world, and yet the world we even now live in? —These questions we must leave candid and studious inquirers to answer for themselves; premising only, that the secret is not to be found on the surface; that the first reply is likely to be in the negative, but with inquirers of this sort, by no means likely to be the final one.

To ourselves, we confess, it has long so appeared. The poetry of Goethe, for instance, we reckon to be Poetry, sometimes in the very highest sense of that word; yet it is no reminiscence, but something actually present and before us; no looking back into an antique Fairy-land, divided by impassable abysses from the real world as it lies about us and within us; but a looking round upon that real world itself, now rendered holier to our eyes, and once more become a solemn temple, where the spirit of Beauty still dwells, and, under new emblems, to be worshipped as of old. With Goethe, the mythologies of bygone days pass only for what they are; we have no witchcraft or magic in the common acceptation; and spirits no longer bring with them airs from heaven or blasts from hell; for Pandemonium and the steadfast Empyrean have faded away, since the opinions which they symbolized no longer are. Neither does he bring his heroes from remote Oriental climates, or periods of Chivalry, or any section either of Atlantis or the Age of Gold? feeling that the reflex of these things is cold and faint, and only hangs like a cloud-picture in the distance, beautiful but delusive, and which even the simplest know to be delusion. The end of Poetry is higher; she must dwell in Reality, and become manifest to men in the forms among which they live and move. And this is what we prize in Goethe, and more or less in Schiller and the rest; all of whom, each in his own way, are writers of a similar aim. The coldest skeptic, the most callous worldling, sees not the actual aspects of life more sharply than they are here delineated: the nineteenth century stands before us, in all its contradiction and perplexity; barren, mean, and baleful, as we have all known it; yet here no longer mean or barren, but enamelled into beauty in the poet's spirit; for its secret significance is laid open, and thus, as it were, the life-giving fire that slumbers in it is called forth, and flowers and foliage, as of old, are springing on its bleakest wildernesses, and overmantling its sternest cliffs. For these men have not only the clear eye, but the loving heart. They have penetrated into the mystery of Nature; after long trial they have been initiated: and, to unwearied endeavour, Art has at last yielded her secret; and thus can the Spirit of our Age, imbodied in fair imaginations, look forth on us, earnest and full of meaning, from their works. As the first and indispensable condition of good poets, they are wise and good men: much they have seen and suffered, and they have conquered all this, and made it all their own; they have known life in its heights and depths, and mastered it in both, and can teach others what it is, and how to lead it rightly. Their minds are as a mirror to us, where the perplexed image of our own being is reflected back in soft and clear interpretation. Here mirth and gravity are blended together; wit rests on deep devout wisdom, as the greensward with its flowers must rest on the rock, whose foundations reach downward to the centre. In a word, they are believers; but their faith is no sallow plant of darkness; it is green and flowery, for it grows in the sunlight. And this faith is the doctrine they have to teach us, the sense which, under every noble and graceful form, it is their endeavour to set forth:

As all nature's thousand changes
But one changeless God proclaim,
So in Art's wide kingdoms ranges
One sole meaning, still the same;
This is Truth, eternal Reason,
Which from Beauty takes its dress,
And, serene through time and season,
Stands for aye in loveliness.

Such indeed is the end of Poetry at all times; yet in no recent literature known to us, except the German, has it been so far attained; nay, perhaps, so much as consciously and steadfastly attempted.

The reader feels that if this our opinion be in any measure true, it is a truth of no ordinary moment. It concerns not this writer or that; but it opens to us new views on the fortune of spiritual culture with ourselves and all nations. Have we not heard gifted men complaining that Poetry had passed away without return; that creative imagination consorted not with vigour of intellect, and that in the cold light of science there was no longer room for faith in things unseen? The old simplicity of heart was gone; earnest emotions must no longer be expressed in earnest symbols; beauty must recede into elegance, devoutness of character be replaced by clearness of thought, and grave wisdom by shrewdness and *persiflage.* Such things we have heard, but hesitated to believe them. If the poetry of the Germans, and this not by theory but by example, have proved, or even begun to prove, the contrary, it will deserve far higher encomiums than any we have passed upon it.

In fact, the past and present aspect of German literature illustrates the literature of England in more than one way. Its history keeps pace with that of ours; for so closely are all European communities connected, that the phases of mind in any one country, so far as these represent its general circumstances and intellectual position, are but modified repetitions of its phases in every other. We hinted above, that the Saxon School corresponded with what might be called the Scotch: Cramer was not unlike our Blair; Von Cronegk might be compared with Michael Bruce; and Rabener and Gellert with Beattie and Logan. To this mild and cultivated period, there succeeded, as with us, a partial abandonment of poetry, in favour of political and philosophical Illumination. Then was the time, when hot war was declared against Prejudice of all sorts; Utility was set up for the universal measure of mental as well as material value; poetry, except of an economical and preceptorial character, was found to be the product of a rude age; and religious enthusiasm was but derangement in the biliary organs. Then did the Prices and Condorcets of Germany indulge in day-dreams of perfectibility; a new social order was to bring back the Saturnian era to the world; and philosophers sat on their sunny Pisgah, looking back over dark savage deserts, and forward into a land flowing with milk and honey.

This period also passed away, with its good and its evil; of which chiefly the latter seems to be remembered; for we scarcely ever find the affair alluded to, except in terms of contempt, by the title *Aufklärerey* (Illuminationism); and its partisans, in subsequent satirical controversies, received the nickname of *Philistern* (Philistines), which the few scattered remnants of them still bear, both in writing and speech. Poetry arose again, and in a new and singular shape. The *Sorrows of Werter, Goetz von Berlichingen,* and *The Robbers,* may stand as patriarchs and representatives of three separate classes, which, commingled in various proportions, or separately coexisting, now with the preponderance of this, now of that, occupied the whole popular literature of Germany, till near the end of the last century. These were the Sentimentalists, the Chivalry-play-writers, and other gorgeous and outrageous persons; as a whole, now pleasantly denominated the *Kraftmänner,* literally, Power-men. They dealt in skeptical lamentation, mysterious enthusiasm, frenzy and suicide: they recurred with fondness to the Feudal Ages, delineating many a battlemented keep, and swart buff-belted man-at-arms; for in reflection as in action, they studied to be strong, vehement, rapidly effective; of battle-tumult, love-madness, heroism, and despair, there was no end. This literary period is called the *Sturm-und-Drang-Zeit,* the Storm-and-Stress Period; for great indeed was the wo and fury of these Power-men. Beauty, to their mind, seemed synonymous with Strength. All passion was poetical, so it were but fierce enough. Their head moral virtue was Pride: their *beau idéal* of manhood was some transcript of Milton's Devil. Often they inverted Bolingbroke's plan, and instead of "patronizing Providence," did directly the opposite; raging with extreme animation against Fate in general, because it enthralled free virtue; and with clenched hands, or sounding shields, hurling defiance towards the vault of heaven.

These Power-men are gone too; and, with few exceptions, save the three originals above named, their works have already followed them. The application of all this to our own literature is too obvious to require much exposition. Have we not also had our Powermen? And will not, as in Germany, to us likewise a milder, a clearer, and a truer time come round? Our Byron was, in his youth, but what Schiller and Goethe had been in theirs: yet the author of *Werter* wrote *Iphigenie* and *Torquato Tasso;* and he who began with *The Robbers* ended with *Wilhelm Tell.* With longer life, all things were to have been hoped for from Byron: for he loved truth in his inmost heart, and would have discovered at last that his Corsairs and Harolds were not true. It was otherwise appointed: but with one man all hope does not die. If this way is the right one, we too shall find it. The poetry of Germany, meanwhile, we cannot but regard as well deserving to be studied, in this as in other points of view: it is distinctly an advance beyond any other known to us; whether on the right path or not, may be still uncertain; but a path selected by Schillers and Goethes, and vindicated by Schlegels and Tiecks, is surely worth serious examination. For the rest, need we add that it is study for self-instruction, nowise for purposes of imitation, that we recommend? Among the deadliest of poetical sins is imitation; for if every man must have his own way of expressing it, much more every nation. But of danger on that side, in the country of Shakspeare and Milton, there seems little to be feared.

We come now to the second grand objection against German literature, its *mysticism.* In treating of a subject itself so vague and dim, it were well if we tried, in the first place, to settle, with more accuracy, what each of the two contending parties really means to say or to contradict regarding it. Mysticism is a word in the mouths of all: yet, of the hundred, perhaps not one has ever asked himself what this opprobrious epithet properly signified in his mind; or where the boundary between true Science and this Land of Chimeras was to be laid down. Examined strictly, *mystical,* in most cases, will turn out to be merely synonymous with *not understood.* Yet surely there may be haste and oversight here; for it is well known, that, to the understanding of any thing, *two* conditions are equally required; *intelligibility* in the thing itself being no whit more indispensable than *intelligence* in the examiner of it. "I am bound to find you in reasons, Sir," said Johnson, "but not in brains;" a speech of the most shocking unpoliteness, yet truly enough expressing the state of the case.

It may throw some light on this question, if we remind our readers of the following fact. In the field of human investigation, there are objects of two sorts: First, the *visible,* including not only such as are material, and may be seen by the bodily eye; but all such, likewise, as may be represented in a *shape,* before the mind's eye, or in any way pictured there: And, secondly, the *invisible,* or such as are not only unseen by human eyes, but as cannot be seen by any eye; not objects of sense at all; not capable, in short, of being *pictured* or imaged in the mind, or in any way represented by a *shape* either without the mind or within it. If any man shall here turn upon us, and assert that there are no such invisible objects; that whatever cannot be so pictured or imagined (meaning *imaged*) is nothing, and the science that relates to it nothing; we shall regret the circumstance. We shall request him, however, to consider seriously and deeply within himself what he means simply by these two words, GOD and his own SOUL; and whether he finds that visible shape and true existence are here also one and the same? If he still persist in denial, we have nothing for it, but to wish him good speed on his own separate path of inquiry; and he and we will agree to differ on this subject of mysticism, as on so many more important ones.

Now, whoever has a material and visible object to treat, be it of natural Science, Political Philosophy, or any such externally and sensibly existing department, may represent it to his own mind, and convey it to the minds of others, as it were, by a direct diagram, more complex indeed than a geometrical diagram, but still with the same sort of precision; and provided his diagram be *complete,* and the *same* both to himself and his reader, he may reason of it, and discuss it, with the clearness, and, in some sort, the certainty of geometry itself. If he do not so reason of it, this must be for want of comprehension to image out the *whole* of it, or of distinctness to convey the *same* whole to his reader: the diagrams of the two are different; the conclusions of the one diverge from those of the other, and the obscurity here, provided the reader be a man of sound judgment and due attentiveness, results from incapacity on the part of the writer. In such a case, the latter is justly regarded as a man of imperfect intellect; he grasps more than he can carry; he confuses what, with ordinary faculty, might be rendered clear; he is not a mystic, but, what is much worse, a dunce. Another matter it is, however, when the object to be treated of belongs to the invisible and immaterial class; cannot be pictured out even by the writer himself, much less, in ordinary symbols, set before the reader. In this case, it is evident, the difficulties of comprehension are increased an hundred-fold. Here it will require long, patient, and skilful effort, both from the writer and the reader, before the two can so much as speak together; before the former can make known to the latter, not *how* the matter stands, but even *what* the matter *is,* which they have to investigate in concert. He must devise new means of explanation, describe conditions of mind in which this invisible idea arises, the false persuasions that eclipse it, the false shows that may be mistaken for it, the glimpses of it that appear elsewhere; in short, strive by a thousand well-devised methods, to guide his reader up to the perception of it; in all which, moreover, the reader must faithfully and toilsomely co-operate with him, if any fruit is to come of their mutual endeavour. Should the latter take up his ground too early, and affirm to himself that now he has seized what he still has not seized; that this and nothing else is the thing aimed at by his teacher, the consequences are plain enough: disunion, darkness, and contradiction between the two; the writer has written for another man, and this reader, after long provocation, quarrels with him finally, and quits him as a *mystic*.

Nevertheless, after all these limitations, we shall not hesitate to admit, that there is in the German mind a tendency to mysticism, properly so called; as perhaps there is, unless carefully guarded against, in all minds tempered like theirs. It is a fault; but one hardly separable from the excellencies we admire most in them. A simple, tender, and devout nature, seized by some touch of divine Truth, and of this perhaps under some rude enough symbol, is wrapt with it into a whirlwind of unutterable thoughts; wild gleams of splendour dart to and fro in the eye of the seer, but the vision will not abide with him, and yet he feels that its light is light from heaven, and precious to him beyond all price. A simple nature, a George Fox, or a Jacob Boehme, ignorant of all the ways of men, of the dialect in which they speak, or the forms by which they think, is labouring with a poetic, a religious idea, which, like all such ideas, must express itself by word and act, or consume the heart it dwells in. Yet how shall he speak, how shall he pour forth into other souls, that of which his own soul is full even to bursting? He cannot speak to us; he knows not *our* state, and cannot make known to us his own. His words are an inexplicable rhapsody, a speech in an unknown tongue. Whether there is meaning in it to the speaker himself, and how much or how true, we shall never ascertain; for it is not in the language of men, but of one man who had not learned the language of men; and, with himself, the key to its full interpretation was lost from amongst us. These are mystics; men who either know not clearly their own meaning, or at least cannot put it forth in formulas of thought, whereby others, with whatever difficulty, may apprehend it. Was their meaning clear to themselves, gleams of it will yet shine through, how ignorantly and unconsciously soever it may have been delivered; was it still wavering and obscure, no science could have delivered it wisely. In either case, much more in the last, they merit and obtain the name of mystics. To scoffers they are a ready and cheap prey; but sober persons understand that pure evil is as unknown in this lower Universe as pure good; and that even in mystics, of an honest and deep-feeling heart, there may be much to reverence, and of the rest more to pity than to mock.

But it is not to apologize for Boehme, or Novalis, or the school of Theosophus and Flood, that we have here undertaken. Neither is it on such persons that the charge of mysticism brought against the Germans mainly rests. Boehme is little known among us; Novalis, much as he deserves knowing, not at all; nor is it understood, that, in their own country, these men rank higher than they do, or might do, with ourselves. The chief mystics in Germany, it would appear, are the Transcendental Philosophers, Kant, Fichte, and Schelling! With these is the chosen seat of mysticism, these are its "tenebrific constellation," from which it "doth ray out darkness" over the earth. Among a certain class of thinkers, does a frantic exaggeration in sentiment, a crude fever-dream in opinion, any where break forth, it is directly labelled as Kantism; and the moon-struck speculator is, for the time, silenced and put to shame by this epithet. For often, in such circles, Kant's Philosophy is not only an absurdity, but a wickedness and a horror; the pious and peaceful sage of Königsberg passes for a sort of Necromancer and Blackartist in Metaphysics; his doctrine is a region of boundless baleful gloom, too cunningly broken here and there by splendours of unholy fire; spectres and tempting demons people it; and, hovering over fathomless abysses, hang gay and gorgeous air-castles, into which the hapless traveller is seduced to enter, and so sinks to rise no more.

If any thing in the history of Philosophy could surprise us, it might well be this. Perhaps among all the metaphysical writers of the eighteenth century, including Hume and Hartley themselves, there is not one that so ill meets the conditions of a mystic as this same Immanuel Kant. A quit, vigilant, clear-sighted man, who had become distinguished to the world in mathematics before he attempted philosophy; who, in his writings generally, on this and other subjects, is perhaps characterized by no quality so much as precisely by the distinctness of his conceptions, and the sequence and iron strictness with which he reasons. To our own minds, in the little that we know of him, he has more than once recalled Father Boscovich in Natural Philosophy; so piercing, yet so sure; so concise, so still, so simple; with such clearness and composure does he mould the complicacy of his subject and so firm, sharp, and definite are the results he evolves from it.* Right or wrong as his hypothesis may be, no one that knows him will suspect that he himself had not seen it, and seen over it; had not meditated it with calmness and deep thought, and studied throughout to expound it with scientific rigor. Neither, as we often hear, is there any superhuman faculty required to follow him. We venture to assure such of our readers as are in any measure used to metaphysical study, that the *Kritik der reinen Vernunft* is by no means the hardest task they have tried. It is true, there is an unknown and forbidding terminology to be mastered; but is not this the case also with Chemistry, and Astronomy, and all other sciences that deserve the name of science? It is true, a careless or unprepared reader will find Kant's writing a riddle; but will a reader of this sort make much of Newton's *Principia*, or D'Alembert's *Calculus of Variations?* He will make nothing of them; perhaps less than nothing; for if he trust to his own judgment, he will pronounce them madness. Yet if the Philosophy of Mind is any philosophy at all, Physics and Mathematics must be plain subjects compared with it. But these latter are happy, not only in the fixedness and simplicity of their methods, but also in the universal acknowledgment of their

* We have heard that the Latin Translation of his works is unintelligible, the Translator himself not having understood it; also that Villers is no safe guide in the study of him. Neither Villers nor those Latin works are known to us.

claim to that prior and continual intensity of application, without which all progress in any science is impossible; though more than one may be attempted without it; and blamed, because without it they will yield no result.

The truth is, German Philosophy differs not more widely from ours in the substance of its doctrines, than in its manner of communicating them. The class of disquisitions, named *Kamin-Philosophie* (Parlor-fire Philosophy) in Germany, is there held in little estimation. No right treatise on any thing, it is believed, least of all on the nature of the human mind, can be profitably read, unless the reader himself co-operates: the blessing of half-sleep in such cases is denied him; he must be alert, and strain every faculty, or it profits nothing. Philosophy, with these men, pretends to be a Science, nay, the living principle and soul of all Sciences, and must be treated and studied scientifically, or not studied and treated at all. Its doctrines should be present with every cultivated writer; its spirit should pervade every piece of composition, how slight or popular soever; but to treat itself popularly would be a degradation and an impossibility. Philosophy dwells aloft in the Temple of Science, the divinity of its inmost shrine: her dictates descend among men, but she herself descends not; whoso would behold her, must climb with long and laborious effort; nay, still linger in the forecourt, till manifold trial have proved him worthy of admission into the interior solemnities.

It is the false notion prevalent respecting the objects aimed at, and the purposed manner of attaining them, in German Philosophy, that causes, in great part, this disappointment of our attempts to study it, and the evil report which the disappointed naturally enough bring back with them. Let the reader believe us, the Critical Philosophers, whatever they may be, are no mystics, and have no fellowship with mystics. What a mystic is, we have said above. But Kant, Fichte, and Schelling, are men of cool judgment, and determinate energetic character; men of science and profound and universal investigation; nowhere does the world, in all its bearings, spiritual or material, theoretic or practical, lie pictured in clearer or truer colours, than in such heads as these. We have heard Kant estimated as a spiritual brother of Boehme; as justly might we take Sir Isaac Newton for a spiritual brother of Count Swedenborg, and Laplace's *Mechanism of the Heavens* for a peristyle to the *Vision of the New Jerusalem*. That this is no extravagant comparison, we appeal to any man acquainted with any single volume of Kant's writings. Neither, though Schelling's system differs still more widely from ours, can we reckon Schelling a mystic. He is a man evidently of deep insight into individual things; speaks wisely, and reasons with the nicest accuracy, on all matters where we understand his data. Fairer might it be in us to say that we had not yet appreciated his truth, and *therefore* could not appreciate his error. But above all, the mysticism of Fichte might astonish us. The cold, colossal, adamantine spirit, standing erect and clear, like a Cato Major among degenerate men: fit to have been the teacher of the Stoa, and to have discoursed of Beauty and Virtue in the groves of Academe! Our reader has seen some words of Fichte's: are these like words of a mystic? We state Fichte's character, as it is known and admitted by men of all parties among the Germans, when we say that so robust an intellect, a soul so calm, so lofty, massive, and immovable, has not mingled in philosophical discussion since the time of Luther. We figure his motionless look, had he heard this charge of mysticism! For the man rises before us, amid contradiction and debate, like a granite mountain amid clouds and wind. Ridicule, of the best that could be commanded, has been already tried against him; but it could not avail. What was the wit of a thousand wits to him? The cry of a thousand choughs assaulting that old cliff of granite: seen from the summit, these, as they winged the midway air, showed scarce so gross as beetles, and their cry was seldom even audible. Fichte's opinions may be true or false; but his character, as a thinker, can be slightly valued only by such as know it ill; and as a man, approved by action and suffering, in his life and in his death, he ranks with a class of men who were common only in better ages than ours.

The Critical Philosophy has been regarded by persons of approved judgment, and nowise directly implicated in the furthering of it, as distinctly the greatest intellectual achievement of the century in which it came to light. August Wilhelm Schlegel has stated in plain terms his belief, that, in respect of its probable influence on the moral culture of Europe, it stands on a line with the Reformation. We mention Schlegel as a man whose opinion has a known value among ourselves. But the worth of Kant's philosophy is not to be gathered from votes alone. The noble system of morality, the purer theology, the lofty views of man's nature derived from it; nay, perhaps, the very discussion of such matters, to which it gave so strong an impetus, have told with remarkable and beneficial influence on the whole spiritual character of Germany. No writer of any importance in that country, be he acquainted or not with the Critical Philosophy, but breathes a spirit of devoutness and elevation more or less directly drawn from it. Such men as Goethe and Schiller cannot exist without effect in any literature or in any century: but if one circumstance more than another has contributed to forward their endeavours, and introduce that higher tone into the literature of Germany, it has been this philosopical system; to which, in wisely believing its results, or even in wisely denying them, all that was lofty and pure in the genius of poetry, or the reason of man, so readily allied itself.

That such a system must in the end become known among ourselves, as it is already becoming known in France and Italy, and over all Europe, no one acquainted in any measure with the character of this matter, and the character of England, will hesitate to predict. Doubtless it will be studied here, and by heads adequate to do it justice: it will be investigated duly and thoroughly, and settled in our minds on the footing which belongs to it, and where thenceforth it must continue. Respecting the degrees of truth and error which will then be found to exist in Kant's system, or in the modifications it has since received, and is still receiving, we desire to be understood as making no estimate, and little qualified to make any. We would have it studied and known, on general grounds; because even the errors of such men are instructive; and because, without a large admixture of truth, no error *can* exist under such combinations, and become diffused so widely. To judge of it we pretend not: we are still inquirers in the mere outskirts of the matter; and it is but inquiry that we wish to see promoted.

Meanwhile, as an advance or first step towards this, we may state something of what has most struck ourselves as characterizing Kant's system; as distinguishing it from every other known to us; and chiefly from the Metaphysical philosophy which is taught in Britain, or rather which *was* taught; for, on looking round, we see not that there is any such Philosophy in existence at the present day.* The Kantist, in direct contradiction to Locke and all his followers, both of the French, and English or Scotch school, commences from within, and proceeds outwards; instead of commencing from without, and, with various precautions and hesitations, endeavouring to proceed inwards. The ultimate aim of all Philosophy must be to interpret appearances,—from the given symbol to ascertain the thing. Now the first step towards this, the aim of what may be called Primary or Critical Philosophy, must be to find some indubitable principle; to fix ourselves on some unchangeable basis: to discover what the Germans call the *Urwahr*, the Primitive Truth, the necessarily, absolutely, and eternally *True*. This necessarily True, this absolute basis of Truth, Locke silently, and Reid and his followers with more tumult, find in a certain modified Experience, and evidence of Sense, in the universal and natural persuasions of all men. Not so the Germans: they deny that there is here any absolute Truth, or that any Philosophy whatever can be built on such a basis; nay, they go the length of asserting, that such an appeal even to the universal persuasions of mankind, gather them with what precautions you may, amounts to a total abdication of Philosophy, strictly so called, and renders not only its further progress, but its very existence, impossible. What, they would say, have the persuasions, or instinctive beliefs, or whatever they are called, of men, to do in this matter? Is it not the object of Philosophy to enlighten, and rectify, and many times directly contradict these very beliefs. Take, for instance, the voice of all generations of men on the subject of Astronomy. Will there, out of any age or climate, be one dissentient against the *fact* of the Sun's going round the Earth? Can any evidence be clearer, is there any persuasion more universal, any belief more instinctive? And yet the sun moves no hairsbreadth; but stands in the centre of his Planets, let us vote as we please. So is it likewise with our evidence for an external independent existence of Matter, and, in general, with our whole argument against Hume; whose reasonings, from the premises admitted both by him and us, the Germans affirm to be rigorously consistent and legitimate, and, on these premises, altogether uncontroverted and incontrovertible. British Philosophy, since the time of Hume, appears to them nothing more than a "laborious and unsuccessful striving to build dike after dike in front of our Churches and Judgment-halls, and so turn back from them the deluge of Skepticism, with which that extraordinary writer overflowed us, and still threatens to destroy whatever we value most." This is Schlegel's meaning: his words are not before us.

The Germans take up the matter differently, and would assail Hume, not in his outworks, but in the centre of his citadel. They deny his first principle, that Sense is the only inlet of Knowledge, that Experience is the primary ground of Belief. Their Primitive Truth, however, they seek, not historically and by experiment, in the universal persuasions of men, but by intuition, in the deepest and purest nature of Man. Instead of attempting, which they consider vain, to prove the existence of God, Virtue, an immaterial Soul, by inferences drawn, as the conclusion of all Philosophy, from the world of sense, they find these things written as the beginning of all Philosophy, in obscured but ineffaceable characters, within our inmost being; and themselves first affording any certainty and clear meaning to that very world of sense, by which we endeavour to demonstrate them. God *is*, nay, alone *is*, for with like emphasis we cannot say that any thing else is. This is the Absolute, the Primitively True, which the philosopher seeks. Endeavouring, by logical argument, to prove the existence of God, a Kantist might say, would be like taking out a candle to look for the sun; nay, gaze steadily into your candle-light, and the sun himself may be invisible. To open the inward eye to the sight of this Primitively True; or, rather, we might call it, to clear off the Obscurations of sense, which eclipse this truth within us, so that we may

* The name of Dugald Stewart is a name venerable to all Europe, and to none more dear and venerable than to ourselves. Nevertheless his writings are not a philosophy, but a making ready for one. He does not enter on the field to till it, he only encompasses it with fences, invites cultivators, and drives away intruders; often (fallen on evil days) he is reduced to long arguments with passers by, to prove that it *is* a field, that this so highly prized domain of his is, in truth, soil and substance, not clouds and shadow. We regard his discussions on the nature of philosophic Language, and his unwearied efforts to set forth and guard against its fallacies, as worthy of all acknowledgment; as indeed forming the greatest, perhaps the only true improvement, which Philosophy has received among us in our age. It is only to a superficial observer that the import of these discussions can seem trivial: rightly understood they give sufficient and final answer to Hartley's and Darwin's and all other possible forms of Materialism, the grand Idolatry, as we may rightly call it, by which, in all times, the true Worship, that of the invisible, has been polluted and withstood. Mr. Stewart has written warmly against Kant; but it would surprise him to find how much of a Kantist he himself essentially is. Has not the whole scope of his labours been to reconcile what a Kantist would call his Understanding with his Reason; a noble, but still too fruitless effort to overarch the chasm which, for all minds but his own, separates his Science from his Religion? We regard the assiduous study of his Works, as the best preparation of studying those of Kant.

see it, and believe it not only to be true, but the foundation and essence of all other truth, may, in such language as we are here using, be said to be the problem of Critical Philosophy.

In this point of view, Kant's system may be thought to have a remote affinity to those of Malebranche and Descartes. But if they in some measure agree as to their aim, there is the widest difference as to the means. We state what to ourselves has long appeared the grand characteristic of Kant's Philosophy, when we mention his distinction, seldom perhaps expressed so broadly, but uniformly implied, between Understanding and Reason (*Verstand* and *Vernunft*). To most of our readers this may seem a distinction without a difference; nevertheless, to the Kantists it is by no means such. They believe that both Understanding and Reason are organs, or rather, we should say, modes of operation, by which the mind discovers truth; but they think that their manner of proceeding is essentially different: that their provinces are separable and distinguishable, nay, that it is of the last importance to separate and distinguish them. Reason, the Kantists say, is of a higher nature than Understanding; it works by more subtle methods, on higher objects, and requires a far finer culture for its development, indeed in many men it is never developed at all; but its results are no less certain, nay, rather, they are much more so; for Reason discerns Truth itself, the absolutely and primitively *True;* while Understanding discerns only *relations*, and cannot decide without *if*. The proper province of Understanding is all, strictly speaking, *real*, practical, and material knowledge, Mathematics, Physics, Political Economy, the adaptation of means to ends in the whole business of life. In this province it is the strength and universal implement of the mind: an indispensable servant, without which, indeed, existence itself would be impossible. Let it not step beyond this province, however, not usurp the province of Reason, which it is appointed to obey, and cannot rule over without ruin to the whole spiritual man. Should Understanding attempt to prove the existence of God, it ends, if thorough-going and consistent with itself, in Atheism, or a faint possible Theism, which scarcely differs from this: should it speculate of Virtue, it ends in *Utility*, making Prudence and a sufficiently cunning love of Self the highest good. Consult Understanding about the Beauty of Poetry, and it asks, where is this Beauty? or discovers it at length in rhythms and fitnesses, and male and female rhymes. Witness also its everlasting paradoxes on Necessity and the Freedom of the Will; its ominous silence on the end and meaning of man; and the enigma which, under such inspection, the whole purport of existence becomes.

Nevertheless, say the Kantists, there is a truth in these things. Virtue is Virtue, and not prudence; not less surely than the angle in a semicircle is a right angle, and no trapezium: Shakspeare is a Poet, and Boileau is none think of it as you may: Neither is it more certain that I myself exist, than that God exists, infinite, eternal, invisible, the same yesterday, to-day, and for ever. To discern these truths is the province of Reason, which therefore is to be cultivated as the highest faculty in man. Not by logic and argument does it work; yet surely and clearly may it be taught to work: and its domain lies in that higher region whither logic and argument cannot reach; in that holier region, where Poetry, and Virtue, and Divinity abide, in whose presence Understanding wavers and recoils, dazzled into utter darkness by that "sea of light," at once the fountain and the termination of all true knowledge.

Will the Kantists forgive us for the loose and popular manner in which we must here speak of these things, to bring them in any measure before the eyes of our readers?—It may illustrate this distinction still farther, if we say, that, in the opinion of a Kantist, the French are of all European nations the most gifted with Understanding, and the most destitute of Reason;* that David Hume had no forecast of this latter, and that Shakspeare and Luther dwelt perennially in its purest sphere.

Of the vast, nay, in these days boundless, importance of this distinction, could it be scientifically established, we need remind no thinking man. For the rest, far be it from the reader to suppose that this same Reason is but a new appearance, under another name, of our own old "Wholesome Prejudice," so well known to most of us! Prejudice, wholesome or unwholesome, is a personage for whom the German Philosophers disclaim all shadow of respect; nor do the vehement among them hide their deep disdain for all and sundry who fight under her flag. Truth is to be loved purely and solely because it is true. With moral, political, religious considerations, high and dear as they may otherwise be, the Philosopher, as such, has no concern. To look at them would but perplex him, and distract his vision from the task in his hands. Calmly he constructs his theorem, as the Geometer does his, without hope or fear, save that he may or may not find the solution; and stands in the middle, by the one, it may be, accused as an Infidel, by the other as an Enthusiast and a Mystic, till the tumult ceases, and what was true is and continues true to the end of all time.

Such are some of the high and momentous questions treated of, by calm, earnest, and deeply meditative men, in this system of Philosophy, which to the wiser minds among us is still unknown, and by the unwiser is spoken of and regarded as their nature requires. The profoundness, subtilty, extent of investigation, which the answer of these questions presupposes, need not be farther pointed out. With the truth or falsehood of the system, we have here, as already stated, no concern; our aim has been, so far as might be done, to show it as it appeared to us; and to ask such of our readers as pursue these studies, whether this also

* Schelling has said as much or more, (*Methode des Academischen Studium*, pp. 105—111,) in terms which we could wish we had space to transcribe.

is not worthy of some study. The reply, we must now leave to themselves.

As an appendage to the charge of Mysticism brought against the Germans, there is often added the seemingly incongruous one of Irreligion. On this point also we had much to say; but must for the present decline it. Meanwhile, let the reader be assured, that to the charge of Irreligion, as to so many others, the Germans will plead not guilty. On the contrary, they will not scruple to assert that their literature is, in a positive sense, religious; nay, perhaps to maintain, that if ever neighbouring nations are to recover that pure and high spirit of devotion, the loss of which, however we may disguise it or pretend to overlook it, can be hidden from no observant mind, it must be by travelling, if not on the same path, at least in the same direction, in which the Germans have already begun to travel. We shall add, that the Religion of Germany is a subject not for slight but for deep study, and, if we mistake not, may in some degree reward the deepest.

Here, however, we must close our examination or defence. We have spoken freely, because we felt distinctly, and thought the matter worthy of being stated, and more fully inquired into. Farther than this, we have no quarrel for the Germans; we would have justice done them, as to all men and all things; but for their literature or character we profess no sectarian or exclusive preference. We think their recent Poetry, indeed, superior to the recent Poetry of any other nation; but taken as a whole, inferior to that of several; inferior not to our own only, but to that of Italy, nay, perhaps to that of Spain. Their Philosophy, too, must still be regarded as uncertain; at best only the beginning of better things. But surely even this is not to be neglected. A little light is precious in great darkness: nor, amid the myriads of Poetasters and *Philosophes*, are Poets and Philosophers so numerous that we should reject such, when they speak to us in the hard, but manly, deep, and expressive tones of that old Saxon speech, which is also our mother-tongue.

We confess the present aspect of spiritual Europe might fill a melancholic observer with doubt and foreboding. It is mournful to see so many noble, tender, and high-aspiring minds deserted of that religious light which once guided all such: standing sorrowful on the scene of past convulsions and controversies, as on a scene blackened and burnt up with fire; mourning in the darkness, because there is desolation, and no home for the soul; or what is worse, pitching tents among the ashes, and kindling weak earthly lamps which we are to take for stars. This darkness is but transitory obscuration: these ashes are the soil of future herbage and richer harvests. Religion, Poetry, is not dead; it will never die. Its dwelling and birthplace is in the soul of man, and it is eternal as the being of man. In any point of Space, in any section of Time, let there be a living Man: and there is an Infinitude above him and beneath him, and an eternity encompasses him on this hand and on that; and tones of Sphere-music, and tidings from loftier worlds, will flit round him, if he can but listen, and visit him with holy influences, even in the thickest press of trivialities, or the din of busiest life. Happy the man, happy the nation that can hear these tidings; that has them written in fit characters, legible to every eye, and the solemn import of them present at all moments to every heart! That there is, in these days, no nation so happy, is too clear; but that all nations, and ourselves in the van, are, with more or less discernment of its nature, struggling towards this happiness, is the hope and the glory of our time. To us, as to others, success, at a distant or a nearer day, cannot be uncertain. Meanwhile, the first condition of success is, that, in striving honestly ourselves, we honestly acknowledge the striving of our neighbour; that with a Will unwearied in seeking Truth, we have a Sense open for it, wheresoever and howsoever it may arise.

LIFE AND WRITINGS OF WERNER.

[Foreign Review, 1828.]

If the charm of fame consisted, as Horace has mistakenly declared, "in being pointed at with the finger, and having it said, This is he!" few writers of the present age could boast of more fame than Werner. It has been the unhappy fortune of this man to stand for a long period incessantly before the world, in a far stronger light than naturally belonged to him, or could exhibit him to advantage. Twenty years ago he was a man of considerable note, which has ever since been degenerating into notoriety. The mystic dramatist, the skeptical enthusiast, was known and partly esteemed by all students of poetry; Madame de Staël, we recollect, allows him an entire chapter in her "Allemagne." It was a much coarser curiosity, and in a much wider circle, which the

* 1. *Lebens-Abriss Friedrich Ludwig Zacharias Werners. Von dem Herausgeber von Hoffmanns Leban und Nachlass.*) Sketch of the Life of Frederic Ludwig Zacharias Werner. By the Editor of "Hoffmann's Life and Remains.") Berlin, 1823.

2. *Die Söhne des Thals.* (The Sons of the Valley.) A Dramatic Poem. Part I. *Die Templer auf Cypern.* (The Templars in Cyprus.) Part II. *Die Kreuzesbrüder.* (The Brethren of the Cross.) Berlin, 1801, 1802.

3. *Das Kreuz an der Ostsee.* (The Cross on the Baltic.) A Tragedy. Berlin, 1806.

4. *Martin Luther, oder Die Weihe der Kraft.* (Martin Luther, or the Consecration of Strength.) A Tragedy. Berlin, 1807.

5. *Die Mutter der Makkabäer.* (The Mother of the Maccabees.) A Tragedy. Vienna, 1820.

dissipated man, by successive indecorums, occasioned; till at last the convert to Popery, the preaching zealot, came to figure in all newspapers; and some picture of him was required for all heads that would not sit blank and mute in the topic of every coffeehouse and *æsthetic tea*. In dim heads, that is, in the great majority, the picture was, of course, perverted into a strange bugbear, and the original decisively enough condemned; but even the few, who might see him in his true shape, felt too well that nothing loud could be said in his behalf; that, with so many mournful blemishes, if extenuation could not avail, no complete defence was to be attempted.

At the same time, it is not the history of a mere literary profligate that we have here to do with. Of men whom fine talents cannot teach the humblest prudence, whose high feeling, unexpressed in noble action, must lie smouldering with baser admixtures in their own bosom, till their existence, assaulted from without and from within, becomes a burnt and blackened ruin, to be sighed over by the few, and stared at, or trampled on, by the many,—there is unhappily no want in any country; nor can the unnatural union of genius with depravity and degradation have such charms for our readers, that we should go abroad in quest of it, or in any case to dwell on it, otherwise than with reluctance. Werner is something more than this: a gifted spirit, struggling earnestly amid the new, complex, tumultuous influences of his time and country, but without force to body himself forth from amongst them; a keen adventurous swimmer, aiming towards high and distant landmarks, but too weakly in so rough a sea, for the currents drive him far astray, and he sinks at last in the waves, attaining little for himself, and leaving little, save the memory of his failure, to others. A glance over his history may not be unprofitable; if the man himself can less interest us, the ocean of German, of European Opinion, still rolls in wild eddies to and fro; and with its movements and refluxes, indicated in the history of such men, every one of us is concerned.

Our materials for this survey are deficient, not so much in quantity as quality. The "Life," now known to be by Hitzig of Berlin, seems a very honest, unpresuming performance; but, on the other hand, it is much too fragmentary and discursive for our wants; the features of the man are nowhere united into a portrait, but left for the reader to unite as he may; a task which, to most readers, will be hard enough: for the work, short in compass, is more than proportionally short in details of facts; and Werner's history, much as an intimate friend must have known of it, still lies before us, in great part, dark and unintelligible. For what he has done we should doubtless thank our Author; yet it seems a pity, that, in this instance, he had not done more and better. A singular chance made him, at the same time, companion of both Hoffmann and Werner, perhaps the two most showy, heterogeneous, and misinterpretable writers of his day; nor shall we deny, that, in performing a friend's duty to their memory, he has done truth also a service. His "Life of Hoffmann," pretending to no artfulness of arrangement, is redundant, rather than defective, in minuteness; but there, at least, the means of a correct judgment are brought within our reach, and the work, as usual with Hitzig, bears marks of the utmost fairness; and of an accuracy which we might almost call professional: for the author, it would seem, is a legal functionary of long standing, and now of respectable rank; and he examines and records, with a certain notarial strictness too rare in compilations of this sort. So far as Hoffmann is concerned, therefore, we have reason to be satisfied. In regard to Werner, however, we cannot say so much: here we should certainly have wished for more facts, though it had been with fewer consequences drawn from them; were these somewhat chaotic expositions of Werner's character exchanged for simple particulars of his walk and conversation, the result would be much surer, and, especially to foreigners, much more complete and luminous. As it is, from repeated perusals of this biography, we have failed to gather any very clear notion of the man; nor with, perhaps, more study of his writings than, on other grounds, they might have merited, does his manner of existence still stand out to us with that distinct cohesion which puts an end to doubt. Our view of him the reader will accept as an approximation, and be content to wonder with us, and charitably pause where we cannot altogether interpret.

Werner was born at Königsberg, in East Prussia, on the 18th of November, 1768. His father was Professor of History and Eloquence in the University there; and further, in virtue of this office, Dramatic Censor, which latter circumstance procured young Werner almost daily opportunity of visiting the theatre, and so gave him, as he says, a greater acquaintance with the mechanism of the stage than even most players are possessed of. A strong taste for the drama it probably enough gave him; but this skill in stage mechanism may be questioned, for often in his own plays no such skill, but rather the want of it, is evinced.

The Professor and Censor, of whom we hear nothing in blame or praise, died in the fourteenth year of his son, and the boy now fell to the sole charge of his mother, a woman whom he seems to have loved warmly, but whose guardianship could scarcely be the best for him. Werner himself speaks of her in earnest commendation, as of a pure, high-minded, and heavily-afflicted being. Hoffmann, however, adds, that she was hypochondriacal, and generally quite delirious, imagining herself to be the Virgin Mary, and her son to be the promised Shiloh! Hoffmann had opportunity enough, of knowing; for it is a curious fact that these two singular persons were brought up under the same roof, though, at this time, by reason of their difference of age, Werner being eight years older, they had little or no acquaintance. What a nervous and melancholic parent was, Hoffmann, by another unhappy coincidence had also full occasion to know: his own mother parted from her husband, lay helpless and broken-hearted for the last seventeen years of her life, and the first seventeen of his; a source of painful influences, which he used to trace through the whole of his own character; as to the like cause he imputed the primary perversion of Werner's. How far his views on this point were accurate or exaggerated, we have no means of judging.

Of Werner's early years the biographer says little or nothing. We learn only that, about the usual age, he matriculated in the Königsberg University, intending to qualify himself for the business of a lawyer; and with his professional studies united, or attempted to unite, the study of philosophy under Kant. His college-life is characterized by a single, but too expressive word: "It is said," observes Hitzig, "to have been very dissolute." His progress in metaphysics, as in all branches of learning, might thus be expected to be small; indeed, at no period of his life can he, even in the language of panegyric, be called a man of culture or solid information on any subject. Nevertheless, he contrived, in his twenty-first year, to publish a little volume of "Poems," apparently in very tolerable magazine metre, and after some "roamings" over Germany, having loitered for a while at Berlin, and longer at Dresden, he betook himself to more serious business, applied for admittance and promotion as a Prussian man of law; the employment which young jurists look for in that country being chiefly in the hands of government: consisting, indeed, of appointments in the various judicial or administrative Boards by which the Provinces are managed. In 1793, Werner accordingly was made *Kammersecretär* (Exchequer Secretary;) a subaltern office, which he held successively in several stations, and last and longest in Warsaw, where Hitzig, a young man following the same profession, first became acquainted with him in 1799.

What the purport or result of Werner's "roamings" may have been, or how he had demeaned himself in office or out of it, we are nowhere informed; but it is an ominous circumstance that, even at this period, in his thirtieth year, he had divorced *two* wives, the last at least by mutual consent, and was looking out for a third! Hitzig, with whom he seems to have formed a prompt and close intimacy, gives us no full picture of him under any of his aspects: yet we can see, that his life, as naturally it might, already wore somewhat of a shattered appearance in his own eyes, that he was broken in character, in spirit, perhaps in bodily constitution; and, contenting himself with the transient gratifications of so gay a city, and so tolerable an appointment, had renounced all steady and rational hope either of being happy or of deserving to be so. Of unsteady and irrational hopes, however, he had still abundance. The fine enthusiasm of his nature, undestroyed by so many external perplexities, nay, to which, perhaps, these very perplexities had given fresh and undue excitement, glowed forth in strange many-coloured brightness, from amid the wreck of his fortunes, and led him into wild worlds of speculation, the more vehemently, that the real world of action and duty had become so unmanageable in his hands.

Werner's early publication had sunk, after a brief provincial life, into merited oblivion; in fact, he had then only been a rhymer, and was now, for the first time, beginning to be a poet. We have one of those youthful pieces transcribed in this volume, and certainly it exhibits a curious contrast with his subsequent writings, both in form and spirit. In form, because, unlike the first fruits of a genius, it is cold and correct: while his later works, without exception, are fervid, extravagant, and full of gross blemishes. In spirit no less, because, treating of his favourite theme, Religion, it treats of it harshly and skeptically; being, indeed, little more than a metrical version of common Utilitarian Freethinking, as it may be found (without metre) in most taverns and debating-societies. Werner's intermediate secret history might form a strange chapter in psychology: for now, it is clear, his French skepticism had got overlaid with wondrous theosophic garniture; his mind was full of visions and cloudy glories, and no occupation pleased him better than to controvert, in generous inquiring minds, that very unbelief which he appears to have once entertained in his own. From Hitzig's account of the matter, this seems to have formed the strongest link of *his* intercourse with Werner. The latter was his senior by ten years of time, and by more than ten years of unhappy experience; the grand questions of Immortality, of Fate, Free-will, Fore-knowledge absolute, were in continual agitation between them; and Hitzig still remembers with gratitude these earnest warnings against irregularity of life, and so many ardent and not ineffectual endeavours to awaken in the passionate temperament of youth a glow of purer and enlightening fire.

"Some leagues from Warsaw," says the Biographer, "enchantingly embosomed in a thick wood, close by the high banks of the Vistula, lies the Cameldulensian Abbey of Bielany, inhabited by a class of monks, who in strictness of discipline yield only to those of La Trappe. To this cloistral solitude Werner was wont to repair with his friend, every fine Saturday of the summer of 1800, so soon as their occupations in the city were over. In defect of any formal inn, the two used to bivouac in the forest, or at best to sleep under a temporary tent. The Sunday was then spent in the open air; in roving about the woods; sailing on the river, and the like; till late night recalled them to the city. On such occasions, the younger of the party had ample room to unfold his whole heart before his more mature and settled companion; to advance his doubts and objections against many theories, which Werner was already cherishing: and so, by exciting him with contradiction, to cause him to make them clearer to himself."

Week after week, these discussions were carefully resumed from the point where they had been left: indeed, to Werner, it would seem, this controversy had unusual attractions; for he was now busy composing a Poem, intended principally to convince the world of those very truths which he was striving to impress on his friend; and to which the world, as might be expected, was likely to give a similar reception. The character, or at least the way of thought, attributed to Robert d'Heredon, the Scottish Templar, in the *Sons of the Valley*, was borrowed, it appears, as if by regular instalments, from these conferences with Hitzig; the result of the one Sunday being duly entered in dramatic form during the week; then audited on the Sunday following; and so forming the text for further disquisition. "Blissful days," adds Hitzig, "pure and innocent, which doubtless Werner also ever held in pleased remembrance!"

The *Söhne des Thals*, composed in this rather questionable fashion, was in due time forthcoming; the First Part in 1801, the Second about a year afterwards. It is a drama, or rather two dramas, unrivalled at least in one particular, in length; each Part being a play of six acts, and the whole amounting to somewhat more than eight hundred small octavo pages! To attempt any analysis of such a work would but fatigue our readers to little purpose: it is, as might be anticipated, of a most loose and formless structure: expanding on all sides into vague boundlessness, and, on the whole, resembling not so much a poem as the rude materials of one. The subject is the destruction of the Templar Order; an event which has been dramatized more than once, but on which, notwithstanding, Werner, we suppose, may boast of being entirely original. The fate of Jacques Molay, and his brethren, acts here but like a little leaven; and lucky were we, could it leaven the lump; but it lies buried under such a mass of Mystical theology, Masonic mummery, Cabalistic tradition, and Rosicrucian philosophy, as no power could work into dramatic union. The incidents are few, and of little interest; interrupted continually by flaring shows and long-winded speculations; for Werner's besetting sin, that of loquacity, is here in decided action; and so we wander, in aimless windings, through scene after scene of gorgeousness or gloom; till at last the whole rises before us like a wild phantasmagoria; cloud heaped on cloud, painted indeed here and there with prismatic hues, but representing nothing, or at least not the subject, but the author.

In this last point of view, however, as a picture of himself, independently of other considerations, this play of Werner's may still have a certain value for us. The strange chaotic nature of the man is displayed in it: his skepticism and theosophy; his audacity, yet intrinsic weakness of character; his baffled longings, but still ardent endeavours after Truth and Good; his search for them in far journeyings, not on the beaten highways, but through the pathless infinitude of Thought. To call it a work of art would be a misapplication of names: it is little more than a rhapsodic effusion; the outpouring of a passionate and mystic soul, only half knowing what it utters, and not ruling its own movements, but ruled by them. It is fair to add that such also, in a great measure, was Werner's own view of the matter: most likely the utterance of these things gave him such relief, that, crude as they were, he could not suppress them. For it ought to be remembered, that in this performance one condition, at least, of genuine inspiration is not wanting: Werner evidently thinks that in these his ultramundane excursions he has found truth; he has something positive to set forth, and he feels himself as if bound on a high and holy mission in preaching it to his fellow-men.

To explain with any minuteness the articles of Werner's creed, as it was now fashioned, and is here exhibited, would be a task perhaps too hard for us, and, at all events, unprofitable in proportion to its difficulty. We have found some separable passages, in which, under dark symbolical figures, he has himself shadowed forth a vague likeness of it: these we shall now submit to the reader, with such expositions as we gather from the context, or as German readers, from the usual tone of speculation in that country, are naturally enabled to supply. This may, at the same time, convey as fair a notion of the work itself, with its tawdry splendours, and tumid grandiloquence, and mere playhouse thunder and lightning, as by any other plan our limits would admit.

Let the reader fancy himself in the island of Cyprus, where the Order of the Templars still subsists, though the heads of it are already summoned before the French King and Pope Clement; which summons they are now, not without dreary enough forebodings, preparing to obey. The purport of this First Part, so far as it has any dramatic purport, is to paint the situation, outward and inward, of that once pious and heroic, and still magnificent and powerful body. It is entitled *The Templars in Cyprus;* but why it should also be called *The Sons of the Valley* does not so well appear; for the Brotherhood of the *Valley* has yet scarcely come into activity, and only hovers before us in glimpses, of so enigmatic a sort, that we know not fully so much as whether these its *Sons* are of flesh and blood like ourselves, or of some spiritual nature, or of something intermediate, and altogether nondescript. For the rest, it is a series of spectacles and dissertations; the action cannot so much be said to advance as to revolve. On this occasion the Templars are admitting two new members; the acolytes have already passed their preliminary trials; this is the chief and final one:—

ACT FIFTH.—SCENE FIRST.

Midnight. Interior of the Temple Church. Backwards, a deep perspective of Altars and Gothic Pillars. On the right-hand side of the foreground, a little Chapel; and in this an Altar with the figure of St. Sebastian. The scene is lighted very dimly by a single Lamp which hangs before the Altar.

* * * * * *

ADALBERT (*dressed in white, without mantle or doublet; groping his way in the dark.*)

Was it not at the Altar of Sebastian
That I was bid to wait for the unknown?
Here should it be; but darkness with her veil
Inwraps the figures.

(*Advancing to the Altar.*)

Here is the fifth pillar!
Yes, this is he, the Sainted.—How the glimmer
Of that faint lamp falls on his fading eye!—
Ah, it is not the spears o' th' Saracens,
It is the pangs of hopeless love that burning
Transfix thy heart, poor Comrade!—O my Agnes,
May not thy spirit, in this earnest hour,
Be looking on? Art hovering in that moon-beam
Which struggles through the painted window, and dies
Amid the cloister's gloom? Or linger'st thou

Behind these pillars, which, ominous and black,
Look down on me, like horrors of the Past
Upon the Present; and hidest thy gentle form,
Lest with thy paleness thou too much affright me?
Hide not thyself, pale shadow of my Agnes,
Thou affrightest not thy lover.—Hush!—
Hark! Was there not a rustling?—Father! You?

PHILIP (*rushing in with wild looks.*)

Yes, Adalbert!—But time is precious!—Come,
My son, my one sole Adalbert, come with me!

ADALBERT.

What would you, father, in this solemn hour?

PHILIP.

This hour, or never!
(*Leading* ADALBERT *to the Altar.*)
Hither!—Know'st thou *him?*

ADALBERT.

'T is Saint Sebastian.

PHILIP.

Because he would not
Renounce his faith, a tyrant had him murder'd,
(*Points to his head.*)
These furrows, too, the rage of tyrants ploughed
In thy old father's face. My son, my first-born child,
In this great hour I do conjure thee! Wilt thou,
Wilt thou obey me?

ADALBERT.

Be it just, I will!

PHILIP.

Then swear, in this great hour, in this dread presence,
Here by thy father's head made early gray,
By the remembrance of thy mother's agony,
And by the ravished blossom of thy Agnes,
Against the Tyranny which sacrificed us,
Inexpiable, bloody, everlasting hate!

ADALBERT.

Ha! *This* the All-avenger spoke through thee!—
Yes! Bloody shall my Agnes' death-torch burn
In Philip's heart; I swear it!

PHILIP (*with increasing vehemence.*)

And if thou break
This oath, and if thou reconcile thee to him,
Or let his golden chains, his gifts, his prayers,
His dying-moan itself, avert thy dagger
When th' hour of vengeance comes,—shall this gray head,
Thy mother's wail, the last sigh of thy Agnes,
Accuse thee at the bar of the Eternal?

ADALBERT.

So be it, if I break my oath!

PHILIP.

Then man thee!—
(*Looking up, then shrinking together as with dazzled eyes.*)
Ha! was not that his lightning?—Fare thee well!
I hear the footstep of the Dreaded!—Firm!—
Remember me, remember this stern midnight!
(*Retires hastily.*)

ADALBERT (*alone.*)

Yes, Grayhead, whom the beckoning of the Lord
Sent hither to awake me out of craven sleep,
I will remember thee and this stern midnight,
And my Agnes' spirit shall have vengeance!

Enter an ARMED MAN. (*He is mailed from head to foot in black harness; his visor is closed.*)

ARMED MAN.

Pray!
(ADALBERT *kneels.*)
Bare thyself!
(*He strips him to the girdle and raises him.*)
Look on the ground, and follow!

(*He leads him into the back-ground to a trap door, on the right. He descends first himself; and when* ADALBERT *has followed him, it closes.*)

SCENE SECOND.

Cemetery of the Templars, under the Church. The scene is lighted only by a Lamp which hangs down from the vault. Around are Tombstones of deceased Knights, marked with Crosses and sculptured Bones. In the back-ground, two colossal Skeletons holding between them a large white Book, marked with a red Cross; from the under end of the Book hangs a long black curtain. The Book, of which only the cover is visible, has an inscription in black ciphers. The Skeleton on the right holds in its right hand a naked drawn sword; that on the left holds in its left hand a Palm turned downwards. On the right side of the foreground, stands a black Coffin open; on the left, a similar one with the body of a Templar in full dress of his Order; on both Coffins are inscriptions in white ciphers. On each side, nearer the back-ground, are seen the lowest steps of the stairs, which lead up into the Temple Church above the vault.

ARMED MAN (*not yet visible; above on the right-hand stairs.*)

Dreaded! Is the grave laid open?

CONCEALED VOICES.

Yea!

ARMED MAN (*who after a pause shows himself on the stairs.*)

Shall he behold the Tombs o' th' fathers?

CONCEALED VOICES.

Yea!

(ARMED MAN *with drawn sword leads* ADALBERT *carefully down the steps, on the right hand.*)

ARMED MAN (*to* ADALBERT.)

Look down! 'Tis on thy life!
(*Leads him to the open Coffin.*)
What seest thou?

ADALBERT.

An open empty Coffin.

ARMED MAN.

'T is the house
Where thou one day shalt dwell. Canst read th' inscription?

ADALBERT.

No.

ARMED MAN.

Hear it, then; "Thy wages, Sin, is Death."
(*Leads him to the opposite Coffin where the Body is lying.*)
Look down! 'T is on thy life!—What seest thou?
(*Shows the Coffin.*)

ADALBERT.

A Coffin with a Corpse.

ARMED MAN.

He is thy Brother,
One day thou art as he.—Canst read the inscription?

ADALBERT

No.

ARMED MAN.

Hear: "Corruption is the name of Life."
Now look around; go forward,—move, and act!—
(*He pushes him towards the back-ground of the stage.*)

ADALBERT (*observing the Book.*)

Ha! Here the Book of Ordination!—Seems
(*Approaching.*)
As if th' inscription on it might be read.
(*He reads it.*)
"Knock four times on the ground,
Thou shalt behold thy loved one."
O Heavens! And may I see thee, sainted Agnes?
(*Hastening close to the Book.*)
My bosom yearns for thee!—

(*With the following words, he stamps four times on the ground.*)

One,—Two,—Three,—Four!—

(*The Curtain hanging from the Book rolls rapidly up, and covers it. A colossal Devil's-head appears between the two Skeletons: its form is horrible; it is gilt; has a huge golden Crown, a Heart of the same in its Brow; rolling flaming Eyes: Serpents instead of Hair: golden Chains round its neck, which is visible to the breast: and a golden Cross, yet not a Crucifix, which rises over its right shoulder, as if crushing it down. The whole Bust rests on four gilt Dragon's feet. At sight of it,* ADALBERT *starts back in horror, and exclaims:*)

Defend us!

ARMED MAN.

Dreaded, may he hear it?

CONCEALED VOICES.

Yea!

ARMED MAN (*touches the Curtain with his sword: it rolls down over the Devil's-head, concealing it again; and above, as before, appears the Book, but now opened, with white colossal leaves and red characters. The* ARMED MAN, *pointing constantly to the Book with his Sword, and therewith turning the leaves, addresses* ADALBERT, *who stands on the other side of the Book, and nearer the foreground.*)

List to the Story of the Fallen Master.

(*He reads the following from the Book: yet not standing before it but on one side, at some paces distance, and whilst he reads, turning the leaves with his sword.*)

"So now when the foundation-stone was laid,
The Lord called forth the Master, Baffometus,
And said to him: Go and complete my Temple!
But in his heart the Master thought: What boots it
Building thee a temple? and took the stones,
And built himself a dwelling, and what stones
Were left he gave for filthy gold and silver.
Now after forty moons the Lord returned,
And spake: Where is my temple, Baffometus?
The Master said: I had to build myself
A dwelling: grant me other forty weeks.
And after forty weeks, the Lord returns,
And asks: where is my temple, Baffometus?
He said: There were no stones (but he had sold them
For filthy gold;) so wait yet forty days.
In forty days thereafter came the Lord,
And cried: Where is my temple, Baffometus?
Then like a mill-stone fell it on his soul
How he for lucre had betrayed his Lord;
But yet to other sin the Fiend did tempt him,
And he answered, saying: Give me forty hours!
And when the forty hours were gone, the Lord
Came down in wrath: My Temple, Baffometus?
Then fell he quaking on his face, and cried
For mercy; but the Lord was wroth, and said:
Since thou hast cozened me with empty lies,
And those the stones I lent thee for my Temple
Hast sold them for a purse of filthy gold,
Lo, I will cast thee forth, and with the Mammon
Will chastise thee, until a Saviour rise
Of thy own seed, who shall redeem thy trespass.
Then did the Lord lift up the purse of Gold;
And shook the gold into a melting-pot,
And set the melting-pot upon the Sun,
So that the metal fused into a fluid mass.
And then he dipt a finger in the same,
And, straightway touching Baffometus,
Anoints him on the chin and brow and cheeks.
Then was the face of Baffometus changed:
His eye-balls rolled like fire-flames,
His nose became a crooked vulture's bill,
The tongue hung bloody from his throat; the flesh
Went from his hollow cheeks; and of his hair
Grew snakes, and of the snakes grew Devil's-horns.
Again the Lord put forth his finger with the gold
And pressed it upon Baffometus' heart;
Whereby the heart did bleed and wither up,
And all his members bled and withered up,
And fell away, the one and then the other.
At last his back itself sunk into ashes:
The head alone continued gilt and living;
And instead of back, grew dragon's-talons,
Which destroyed all life from off the Earth.
Then from the ground the Lord took up the heart,
Which, as he touched it, also grew of gold,
And placed it on the brow of Baffometus;
And of the other metal in the pot
He made for him a burning crown of gold,
And crushed it on his serpent-hair, so that
Ev'n to the bone and brain, the circlet scorched him.
And round the neck he twisted golden chains,
Which strangled him and pressed his breath together.
What in the pot remained he poured upon the ground.
Athwart, along, and there it formed a cross;
The which he lifted and laid upon his neck,
And bent him that he could not raise his head.
Two Deaths moreover he appointed warders
To guard him: Death of Life, and Death of Hope.
The sword of the first he sees not but it smites him;
The other's Palm he sees, but it escapes him.
So languishes the outcast Baffometus
Four thousand years and four-and-forty moons,
Till once a Saviour rise from his own seed,
Redeem his trespass, and deliver him."

(*To* ADALBERT.)

This is the Story of the Fallen Master.

(*With his sword he touches the Curtain, which now as before rolls up over the book: so that the* HEAD *under it again becomes visible, in its former shape.*)

ADALBERT (*looking at the* HEAD.)

Hah, what a hideous shape!

HEAD (*with a hollow voice.*)

Deliver me!

ARMED MAN.

Dreaded! Shall the work begin?

CONCEALED VOICES.

Yea!

ARMED MAN (*to* ADALBERT.)

Take the Neckband
Away! (*Pointing to the* HEAD.)

ADALBERT.

I dare not!

HEAD (*with a still more piteous tone.*)

O, deliver me!

ADALBERT (*taking off the chains.*)

Poor fallen one!

ARMED MAN.

Now lift the Crown from 's head!

ADALBERT

It seems so heavy!

ARMED MAN.

Touch it, it grows light.

ADALBERT (*taking off the Crown, and casting it, as he did the chains, on the ground.*)

ARMED MAN.

Now take the golden heart from off his brow!

ADALBERT.

It seems to burn!

ARMED MAN.

Thou errest; ice is warmer.

ADALBERT (*taking the Heart from the Brow.*)

Hah! shivering frost!

ARMED MAN.

Take from his back the Cross,
And throw it from thee!—

ADALBERT.

How! the Saviour's token?

HEAD.

Deliver, O deliver me!

ARMED MAN.

This Cross
Is not thy Master's, not that bloody one:
Its counterfeit is this: throw 't from thee!

ADALBERT (*taking it from the Bust, and laying it softly on the ground.*)

The Cross of the Good Lord that died for me?

ARMED MAN.

Thou shalt no more believe in one that died;
Thou shalt henceforth believe in one that liveth
And never dies!—Obey, and question not,—
Step over it!

ADALBERT.

Take pity on me!

ARMED MAN (*threatening him with his sword.*)

Step!

ADALBERT.

I do 't with shuddering—
(*Steps over, and then looks up to the* HEAD *which raises itself, as if freed from a load.*)
How the figure rises
And looks in gladness!

ARMED MAN.

Him whom thou hast served
Till now, deny!

ADALBERT (*horror-struck.*)

Deny the Lord my God?

ARMED MAN.

Thy God 'tis not: the Idol of this world!
Deny him, or—
(*Pressing on him with the Sword in a threatening posture.*)
—thou diest!

ADALBERT.

I deny!

ARMED MAN (*pointing to the Head with his Sword.*)

Go to the Fallen!—Kiss his lips!—

—And so on through many other sulphurous pages! How much of this mummery is copied from the actual practice of the Templars we know not with certainty; nor what precisely either they or Werner intended, by this marvellous "Story of the Fallen Master," to shadow forth. At first view, one might take it for an allegory, couched in masonic language,—and truly no flattering allegory,—of the Catholic Church; and this trampling on the Cross, which is said to have been actually enjoined on every Templar at his initiation, to be a type of his secret behest to undermine that Institution, and redeem the spirit of Religion from the state of thraldom and distortion under which it was there held. It is known at least, and was well known to Werner, that the heads of the Templars entertained views, both on religion and politics, which they did not think meet for communicating to their age, and only imparted by degrees, and under mysterious adumbrations, to the wiser of their own Order. They had even publicly resisted, and succeeded in thwarting, some iniquitous measures of Philippe Auguste, the French King, in regard to his coinage; and this, while it secured them the love of the people, was one great cause, perhaps second only to their wealth, of the hatred which that sovereign bore them, and of the savage doom which he at last executed on the whole body.

But on these secret principles of theirs, as on Werner's manner of conceiving them, we are only enabled to guess; for Werner, too, has an esoteric doctrine, which he does not promulgate, except in dark Sybilline enigmas, to the unitiated. As we are here seeking chiefly for his religious creed, which forms, in truth, with its changes, the main thread whereby his wayward, desultory existence attains any unity or even coherence in our thoughts, we may quote another passage from the same First Part of this rhapsody; which, at the same time, will afford us a glimpse of his favourite hero, Robert d'Heredon, lately the darling of the Templars, but now, for some momentary infraction of their rules, cast into prison, and expecting death, or, at best, exclusion from the Order. Gottfried is another Templar, in all points the reverse of Robert.

ACT FOURTH. SCENE FIRST.

(*Prison; at the wall a Table.* ROBERT, *without sword, cap, or mantle, sits downcast on one side of it:* GOTTFRIED, *who keeps watch by him, sitting at the other.*)

GOTTFRIED.

But how could'st thou so far forget thyself?
Thou wert our pride, the Master's friend and favourite!

ROBERT.

I did it, thou perceivest!

GOTTFRIED.

How could a word
Of the old surly Hugo so provoke thee?

ROBERT.

Ask not!—Man's being is a spider-web:
The passionate flash o' th' soul—comes not of him;
It is the breath of that dark Genius,
Which whirls invisible along the threads:
A servant of eternal Destiny,
It purifies them from the vulgar dust,
Which earthward strives to press the net:
But Fate gives sign; the breath becomes a whirlwind
And in a moment rends to shreds the thing
We thought was woven for Eternity.

GOTTFRIED.

Yet each man shapes his destiny himself.

ROBERT.

Small soul! Dost thou too know it? Has the story
Of Force and free Volition, that, defying
The corporal Atoms and Annihilation,
Methodic guides the car of Destiny,
Come down to *thee?* Dream'st thou, poor Nothingness,
That thou, and like of thee, and ten times better
Than thou or I, can lead the wheel of Fate
One hair's-breadth from its everlasting track?
I too have had such dreams: but fearfully
Have I been shook from sleep; and they are fled!—
Look at our Order: has it spared its thousands
Of noblest lives, the victims of its Purpose;
And has it gained this Purpose; can it gain it?
Look at our noble Molay's silvered hair:
The fruit of watchful nights and stormful days,
And of the broken yet still burning heart!
That mighty heart!—Through sixty battling years,
'T has beat in pain for nothing: his creation
Remains the vision of his own great soul;
It dies with him; and one day shall the pilgrim
Ask where his dust is lying, and not learn!

GOTTFRIED (*yawning.*)

But then the Christian has the joy of Heaven
For recompense: in his flesh he shall see God.

ROBERT.

In his flesh?—Now fair befal the journey!
Wilt stow it in behind, by way of luggage,
When the Angel comes to coach thee into Glory?
Mind also that the memory of those fair hours
When dinner smoked before thee, or thou usedst
To dress thy nag, or scour thy rusty harness,
And such like noble business be not left behind!—
Ha! self-deceiving bipeds, is it not enough
The carcass should at every step oppress,
Imprison you; that toothache, headache,
Gout,—who knows what all,—at every moment,
Degrades the god of Earth into a beast;
But you would take this villanous mingle,
The coarser dross of all the elements,
Which, by the Light-beam from on high that visits
And dwells in it, but baser shows its baseness,—
Take this, and all the freaks which, bubble-like,
Spring forth o' th' blood, and which by such fair names
You call,—along with you into your Heaven?—
Well, be it so! much good may't—

(*As his eye, by chance, lights on Gottfried, who meanwhile has fallen asleep*)

—Sound already?
There is a race for whom all serves as—pillow,
Even rattling chains are but a lullaby.

This Robert d'Heredon, whose preaching has here such a narcotic virtue, is destined ultimately for a higher office than to rattle his chains by way of lullaby. He is ejected from the Order; not, however, with disgrace and in anger, but in sad feeling of necessity, and with tears and blessings from his brethren; and the messenger of the *Valley*, a strange, ambiguous, little sylph-like maiden, gives him obscure encouragement, before his departure, to possess his soul in patience; seeing, if he can learn the grand secret of Renunciation, his course is not ended, but only opening on a fairer scene. Robert knows not well what to make of this; but sails for his native Hebrides, in darkness and contrition, as one who can do no other.

In the end of the Second Part, which is represented as divided from the First by an interval of seven years, Robert is again summoned forth; and the whole surprising secret of his mission, and of the *Valley* which appoints it for him, is disclosed. This *Friedenthal* (Valley of Peace), it now appears, is an immense secret association, which has its chief seat somewhere about the roots of Mount Carmel, if we mistake not; but, comprehending in its ramifications the best heads and hearts of every country, extends over the whole civilized world; and has, in particular, a strong body of adherents in Paris, and indeed a subterraneous, but seemingly very commodious suite of rooms, under the Carmelite Monastery of that city. Here sit in solemn conclave the heads of the Establishment; directing from their lodge, in deepest concealment, the principal movements of the kingdom: for William of Paris, Archbishop of Sens, being of their number, the king and his other ministers, fancying within themselves the utmost freedom of action, are nothing more than puppets in the hands of this all-powerful Brotherhood, which watches, like a sort of Fate, over the interests of mankind, and by mysterious agencies, forwards, we suppose, "the cause of civil and religious liberty over all the world." It is they that have doomed the Templars; and, without malice or pity, are sending their leaders to the dungeon and the stake. That knightly Order, once a favourite minister of good, has now degenerated from its purity, and come to mistake its purpose, having taken up politics and a sort of radical reform; and so must now be broken and reshaped, like a worn implement, which can no longer do its appointed work.

Such a magnificent "Society for the Suppression of Vice" may well be supposed to walk by the most philosophical principles. These *Friedenthalers*, in fact, profess to be a sort of Invisible Church; preserving in vestal purity the sacred fire of religion, which burns with more or less fuliginous admixture in the worship of every people, but only with its clear sidereal lustre in the recesses of the *Valley*. They are Bramins on the Ganges, Bonzes on the Hoangho, Monks on the Seine. They addict themselves to contemplation, and the subtilest study; have penetrated far into the mysteries of spiritual and physical nature; they command the deep-hidden virtues of plant and mineral; and their sages can discriminate the eye of the mind from its sensual instruments, and behold, without type or material embodyment, the essence of Being. Their activity is all-comprehending and unerringly calculated: they rule over the world by the authority of wisdom over ignorance.

In the Fifth Act of the Second Part, we are at length, after many a hint and significant note of preparation, introduced to the privacies of this philosophical *Sainte Hermandad.* A strange Delphic cave this of theirs, under the very pavements of Paris! There are brazen folding doors, and concealed voices, and sphinxes, and naptha-lamps, and all manner of wondrous furniture. It seems, moreover, to be a sort of gala evening with them; for the "Old Man of Carmel, in eremite garb, with a long beard reaching to his girdle," is for a moment discovered "reading in a deep monotonous voice." The "Strong Ones," meanwhile, are out in quest of Robert d'Heredon; who, by cunning practices, has been enticed from his Hebridean solitude, in the hope of saving Molay, and is even now to be initiated, and equipped for his task. After a due allowance of pompous ceremonial, Robert is at last ushered in, or rather dragged in; for it appears that he has made a stout debate, not submitting to the customary form of being *ducked*,—an essential preliminary, it would seem,—till compelled by the direst necessity. He is in a truly Highland anger, as is natural: but by various manipulations and solacements, he is reduced to reason again, finding, indeed, the fruitlessness of any thing else; for when lance and sword and free space are given him, and he makes a thrust at Adam of Valincourt, the master of the ceremonies, it is to no purpose: the old man has a torpedo quality in him, which benumbs the stoutest arm; and no death issues from the baffled sword-point, but only a small spark of electric fire. With his Scottish prudence, Robert, under these circumstances, cannot but perceive that quietness is best. The people hand him, in succession, the "Cup of Strength," the "Cup of Beauty," and the "Cup of Wisdom;" liquors brewed, if we may judge from their effect, with the highest stretch of Rosicrucian art; and which must have gone far to disgust Robert d'Heredon with his natural *usquebaugh*, however excellent, had that fierce drink been in use then. He rages in a fine frenzy; dies away in raptures; and then, at last, "considers what he wanted and what he wants." Now is the time for Adam of Valincourt to strike in with an interminable exposition of the "objects of the society." To not unwilling, but still cautious ears, he unbosoms himself, in mystic wise, with extreme copiousness; turning aside objections like a veteran disputant, and leading his apt and courageous pupil, by signs and wonders, as well as by logic, deeper and deeper into the secrets of theosophic and thaumaturgic science. A little glimpse of this our readers may share with us; though we fear the allegory will seem to most of them but a hollow nut. Nevertheless, it is an allegory—of its sort; and we can profess to have translated with entire fidelity.

* * * * * *

ADAM.

Thy riddle by a second will be solved,

(*He leads him to the Sphinx.*)

Behold this Sphinx! Half-beast, half-angel, both
Combined in one, it is an emblem to thee
Of th' ancient Mother, Nature, herself a riddle,
And only by a deeper to be master'd.
Eternal clearness in th' eternal Ferment:
This is the riddle of Existence:—read it,—
Propose that other to her, and she serves thee!

(*The door on the right hand opens, and, in the space behind it appears, as before, the* OLD MAN OF CARMEL, *sitting at a Table, and reading in a large Volume. The deep strokes of a Bell are heard.*)

OLD MAN OF CARMEL (*reading with a loud but still monotonous voice.*)

"And when the Lord saw Phosphoros"—

ROBERT (*interrupting him.*)

Ha! Again
A story as of Baffometus?

ADAM.

Not so.
That tale of theirs was but some poor distortion
Of th' outmost image of our sanctuary.—
Keep silence here; and see thou interrupt not,
By too bold cavilling, this mystery.

OLD MAN (*reading.*)

"And when the Lord saw Phosphoros his pride,
Being wroth thereat, he cast him forth,
And shut him in a prison called LIFE;
And gave him for a Garment, earth and water,
And bound him straitly in four Azure Chains,
And pour'd for him the bitter Cup of Fire.
The Lord moreover spake: Because thou hast forgotten
My will I yield thee to the Element,
And thou shalt be his slave, and have no longer
Remembrance of thy birthplace or my name.
And sithence thou hast sinn'd against me by
Thy prideful Thought of being One and Somewhat,
I leave with thee that thought to be thy whip,
And this thy weakness for a Bit and Bridle;
Till once a Saviour from the waters rise,
Who shall again baptize thee in my bosom,
That so thou may'st be Nought and All.
"And when the Lord had spoken, he drew back
As in a mighty rushing; and the Element
Rose up round Phosphoros, and tower'd itself
Aloft to Heav'n; and he lay stunn'd beneath it.
"But when his first-born Sister saw his pain,
Her heart was full of sorrow, and she turn'd her
To the Lord; and with veil'd face, thus spake Mylitta:*
Pity my Brother, and let me console him!
"Then did the Lord in pity rend asunder
A little chink in Phosphoros his dungeon,
That so he might behold his Sister's face:
And when she silent peep'd into his Prison,
She left with him a Mirror for his solace,
And when he look'd therein, his earthly Garment
Pressed him less; and, like the gleam of morning,
Some faint remembrance of his Birthplace dawn'd
"But yet the Azure Chains she could not break,
The bitter Cup of Fire not take from him.
Therefore she pray'd to Mythras, to her Father,
To save his younger-born: and Mythras went
Up to the footstool of the Lord, and said:
Take pity on my Son!—Then said the Lord;
Have I not sent Mylitta that he may
Behold his Birthplace?—Wherefore Mythras answer'd:
What profits it? The chains she cannot break,
The bitter Cup of Fire not take from him.
So will I, said the Lord, the Salt be given him.
That so the bitter Cup of Fire be softened;
But yet the Azure Chains must lie on him
Till once a Saviour rise from out the Waters.—
And when the Salt was laid on Phosphor's tongue
The Fire's piercing ceased; but th' Element
Congeal'd the Salt to Ice, and Phosphoros
Lay there benumb'd, and had not power to move.
But Isis saw him, and thus spake the mother:
"Thou who art Father, Strength and Word and Light:
Shall he my last-born grandchild lie for ever
In pain, the down-press'd thrall of his rude Brother?
Then had the Lord compassion, and he sent him
The Herald of the Saviour from the Waters;
The cup of Fluidness, and in the Cup
The drops of Sadness and the drops of Longing.
And then the Ice was thawed, the Fire grew cool,
And Phosphoros again had room to breathe.
But yet the earthy Garment cumber'd him,
The Azure chains still gall'd, and the Remembrance
Of the Name, the Lord's, which he had lost, was wanting.
"Then the Mother's heart was moved with pity,
She beckoned the Son to her, and said:
Thou who art more than I, and yet my nursling,

*Mylitta, in the old Persian mysteries, was the name of the Moon; *Mythras* that of the Sun.

Put on this Robe of Earth, and show thyself
To fallen Phosphoros bound in the dungeon,
And open him that dungeon's narrow cover.
Then said the Word: It shall be so! and sent
His messenger DISEASE; she broke the roof
Of Phosphor's Prison, so that once again
The Fount of Light he saw: the Element
Was dazzled blind; but Phosphor knew his Father.
And when the Word, in Earth, came to the Prison,
The Element address'd him as his like;
But Phosphoros look'd up to him, and said:
Thou art sent hither to redeem from Sin,
Yet art thou not the Saviour from the Waters.—
Then spake the Word: The Saviour from the Waters
I surely am not; yet when thou hast drunk
The Cup of Fluidness, I will Redeem thee.
Then Phosphor drank the Cup of Fluidness,
Of Longing, and of Sadness; and his Garment
Did drop sweet drops; wherewith the Messenger
Of the Word wash'd all his Garment, till its folds
And stiffness vanish'd, and it 'gan grow light.
And when the Prison LIFE she touch'd, straightway
It wax'd thin and lucid like to crystal.
But yet the Azure Chains she could not break.—
Then did the Word vouchsafe him the Cup of Faith,
And having drunk it, Phosphoros look'd up,
And saw the Saviour standing in the Waters.
Both hands the Captive stretch'd to grasp that Saviour;
But he fled.
"So Phosphoros was grieved in heart:
But yet the Word spake comfort, giving him
The Pillow *Patience*, there to lay his head.
And having rested, he rais'd his head, and said:
Wilt thou redeem me from the Prison too?
Then said the Word: Wait yet in peace seven moons,
It may be nine, until thy hour shall come.
And Phosphor answer'd, Lord, thy will be done!
"Which when the mother Isis saw, it grieved her;
She called the Rainbow up, and said to him:
Go thou and tell the Word that he forgive
The Captive these seven moons! And Rainbow flew
Where he was sent; and as he shook his wings
There dropt from them, the *Oil of Purity*:
And this the Word did gather in a Cup,
And cleansed with it the Sinner's head and bosom.
Then passing forth into his Father's Garden,
He breathed upon the ground, and there arose
A flow'ret out of it, like milk and rose-bloom;
Which having wetted with the dew of Rapture,
He crown'd therewith the Captive's brow; then grasp'd him
With his right hand, the Rainbow with the left;
Mylitta likewise with the Mirror came,
And Phosphoros looked into it, and saw
Wrote on the Azure of Infinity
The long-forgotten NAME, and the REMEMBRANCE
OF HIS BIRTHPLACE, gleaming as in light of gold.
"Then fell there as if scales from Phosphor's eyes,
He left the Thought of being One and Somewhat,
His nature melted in the mighty All;
Like sighings from above came balmy healing,
So that his heart for very bliss was bursting.
For Chains and Garment cumber'd him no more:
The Garment he had changed to royal purple,
And of his Chains were fashion'd glancing jewels.
"True, still the Saviour from the Waters tarried;
Yet came the Spirit over him; the Lord
Turn'd towards him a gracious countenance,
And Isis held him in her mother-arms.
"This is the last Evangile.

(The door closes, and again conceals the OLD MAN OF CARMEL.)

The purport of this enigma Robert confesses that he does not "wholly" understand; an admission in which, we suspect, most of our readers, and the Old Man of Carmel himself, were he candid, might be inclined to agree with him. Sometimes, in the deeper consideration which translators are bound to bestow on such extravagances, we have fancied we could discern in this apologue some glimmerings of meaning, scattered here and there like weak lamps in the darkness; not enough to interpret the riddle, but to show that by possibility it might have an interpretation,—was a typical vision, with a certain degree of significance in the wild mind of the poet, not an inane fever-dream. Might not Phosphoros, for example, indicate generally the spiritual essence of a man, and this story be an emblem of his history? He longs to be "One and Somewhat;" that is, he labours under the very common complaint of *egotism;* cannot, in the grandeur of Beauty and Virtue, forget his own so beautiful and virtuous *Self;* but, amid the glories of the majestic All, is still haunted and blinded by some shadow of his own little *Me.* For this reason he is punished; imprisoned in the "Element" (of a material body,) and has the "four Azure Chains" (the four principles of matter) bound round him; so that he can neither think nor act, except in a foreign medium, and under conditions that confuse him. The "Cup of Fire" is given him; perhaps, the rude, barbarous passion and cruelty natural to all uncultivated tribes? But, at length, he beholds the "Moon;" begins to have some sight and love of material Nature; and, looking into her "Mirror," forms to himself, under gross emblems, a theogony and sort of mythologic poetry; in which, if he cannot behold the "Name," and has forgotten his own "Birthplace," both of which are blotted out and hidden by the "Element," he finds some spiritual solace, and breathes more freely. Still, however, the "Cup of Fire" tortures him; till the "Salt" (intellectual culture?) is vouchsafed; which, indeed, calms the raging of that furious bloodthirstiness and warlike strife, but leaves him, as mere culture of the understanding may be supposed to do, frozen into irreligion and moral inactivity, and farther from the "Name" and his "Own Original" than ever. Then is the "Cup of Fluidness" a more merciful disposition? and intended, with "the Drops of Sadness and the Drops of Longing," to shadow forth that wo-struck, desolate, yet softer and devouter state in which mankind displayed itself at the coming of the "Word," at the first promulgation of the Christian religion? Is the "Rainbow" the modern poetry of Europe, the Chivalry, the new form of Stoicism, the whole *romantic* feeling of these later days? But who or what the "*Heiland aus den Wassern*" (Saviour from the Waters) may be, we need not hide our entire ignorance; this being apparently a secret of the *Valley*, which Robert d'Heredon, and Werner, and men of like gifts, are in due time to show the world, but unhappily have not yet succeeded in bringing to light. Perhaps, indeed, our whole interpretation may be thought little better than lost labour; a reading of what was only scrawled and flourished, not written; a shaping of gay castles and metallic palaces from the sunset clouds, which, though mountain-like, and purple and golden of hue, and towered together as if by Cyclopean arms, are but dyed vapour.

Adam of Valincourt continues his exposition in the most liberal way; but, through many pages of metrical lecturing, he does little to satisfy us. What was more to his purpose, he partly succeeds in satisfying Robert d'Heredon; who, after due preparation,—Molay being burnt like a martyr, under the most promising omens, and the Pope and the King of France struck dead, or nearly so,—sets out to found the order of St. Andrews in his own country, that of Calatrava in Spain, and other knightly Missions of the *Heiland aus den Wassern* elsewhere; and thus, to the great satisfaction of all parties, the *Sons of the Valley* terminates, "positively for the last time."

Our reader may have already convinced himself that in this strange phantasmagoria there are not wanting indications of very high poetic talent. We see a mind of great depth, if not of sufficient strength; struggling with objects which, though it cannot master them, are essentially of richest significance. Had the writer only kept his piece till the ninth year; meditating it with true diligence and unwearied will! But the weak Werner was not a man for such things: he must reap the harvest on the morrow after seed-day, and so stands before us at last, as a man capable of much, only not of bringing aught to perfection.

Of his natural dramatic genius, this work, ill-concocted as it is, affords no unfavourable specimen; and may, indeed, have justified expectations which were never realized. It is true, he cannot yet give form and animation to a character, in the genuine poetic sense; we do not *see* any of his *dramatis personæ*, but only hear of them: yet, in some cases his endeavour, though imperfect, is by no means abortive; and here, for instance, Jacques Molay, Philip Adalbert, Hugo, and the like, though not living men, have still as much life as many a buff-and-scarlet Sebastian or Barbarossa, whom we find swaggering, for years, with acceptance, on the boards. Of his spiritual beings, whom in most of his plays he introduces too profusely, we cannot speak in commendation: they are of a mongrel nature, neither rightly dead nor alive; in fact, they sometimes glide about like real, though rather singular mortals, through the whole piece; and only vanish as ghosts in the fifth act. But, on the other hand, in contriving theatrical incidents and sentiments; in scenic shows, and all manner of gorgeous, frightful, or astonishing machinery, Werner exhibits a copious invention, and strong though untutored feeling. Doubtless, it is all crude enough; all illuminated by an impure, barbaric splendour; not the soft, peaceful brightness of sunlight, but the red, resinous glare of playhouse torches. Werner, however, was still young; and had he been of a right spirit, all that was impure and crude might in time have become ripe and clear; and a poet of no ordinary excellence would have been moulded out of him.

But as matters stood, this was by no means the thing Werner had most at heart. It is not the degree of poetic talent manifested in the *Sons of the Valley* that he prizes, but the religious truth shadowed forth in it. To judge from the parables of Baffometus and Phosphoros, our readers may be disposed to hold his revelations on this subject rather cheap. Nevertheless, taking up the character of *Vates* in its widest sense, Werner earnestly desires not only to be a poet, but a prophet; and, indeed, looks upon his merits in the former province as altogether subservient to his higher purposes in the latter. We have a series of the most confused and long-winded letters to Hitzig, who had now removed to Berlin; setting forth, with a singular simplicity, the mighty projects Werner was cherishing on this head. He thinks that there ought to be a new Creed promulgated, a new Body of Religionists established; and that, for this purpose, not writing, but actual preaching, can avail. He detests common Protestantism, under which he seems to mean a sort of Socinianism, or diluted French Infidelity; he talks of Jacob Bœhme, and Luther, and Schleiermacher, and a new Trinity of "Art, Religion, and Love." All this should be sounded in the ears of men, and in a loud voice, that so their torpid slumber, the harbinger of spiritual death, may be driven away. With the utmost gravity he commissions his correspondent to wait upon Schlegel, Tieck, and others of a like spirit, and see whether they will not join him. For his own share in the matter, he is totally indifferent; will serve in the meanest capacity, and rejoice with his whole heart, if, in zeal and ability as poets and preachers, not some only, but every one, should infinitely outstrip him. We suppose, he had dropped the thought of being "One and Somewhat;" and now wished, rapt away by this divine purpose, to be "Nought and All."

On the *Heiland aus den Wassern* this correspondence throws no further light: what the new Creed specially was, which Werner felt so eager to plant and propagate, we nowhere learn with any distinctness. Probably, he might himself have been rather at a loss to explain it in brief compass. His theogony, we suspect, was still very much *in posse;* and perhaps only the moral part of this system could stand before him with some degree of clearness. On this latter point, indeed, he is determined enough; well assured of his dogmas, and apparently waiting but for some proper vehicle in which to convey them to the minds of men. His fundamental principle of morals we have seen in part already: it does not exclusively or primarily belong to himself; being little more than that high tenet of entire Self-forgetfulness, that "merging of the *Me* in the *Idea;*" a principle which reigns both in Stoical and Christian ethics, and is at this day common, in theory, among all German philosophers, especially of the Transcendental class. Werner has adopted this principle with his whole heart and his whole soul, as the indispensable condition of all Virtue. He believes it, we should say, intensely, and without compromise, exaggerating rather than softening or concealing its peculiarities. He will not have Happiness, under any form, to be the real or chief end of man; this is but love of enjoyment, disguise it as we like; a more complex and sometimes more respectable species of hunger, he would say to be admitted as an indestructible element in human nature, but nowise to be recognised as the highest; on the contrary, to be resisted and incessantly warred with, till it become obedient to love of God, which is only, in the truest sense, love of Goodness, and the germ of which lies deep in the inmost nature of man; of authority superior to all sensitive impulses; forming, in fact, the grand law of his being, as subjection to it forms the first and last condition of spiritual health. He thinks that to propose a reward for virtue is to render virtue impossible. He warmly seconds Schleiermacher in declaring that even the hope of Immortality is a consideration unfit to be introduced into religion, and tending only to pervert it, and impair its sacredness. Strange as this may seem, Werner is firmly convinced of its importance; and has even enforced it specifically in a passage of his *Söhne des Thals*, which he is at the pains to cite and expound in his correspondence with Hitzig. Here is another fraction of that wondrous dialogue between Robert d'Heredon and Adam of Valincourt, in the cavern of the *Valley:*

* * * * * *

ROBERT.

And Death,—so dawns it on me,—Death perhaps,
The doom that leaves nought of this *Me* remaining,
May be perhaps the Symbol of that Self-denial,—
Perhaps still more,——perhaps,—I have it, friend!—
That cripplish Immortality,—think'st not?—
Which but spins forth our paltry *Me*, so thin
And pitiful, into Infinitude,
That too must *die*?—This shallow Self of ours,
We are not nail'd to it eternally?
We can, we must be free of it, and then
Uncumber'd wanton in the Force of All!

ADAM (*calling joyfully into the interior of the Cavern.*)

Brethren, he has renounced! Himself has found it!
Oh! praised be Light! He sees! The North is saved!

CONCEALED VOICES *of the old men of the Valley.*

Hail and joy to thee, thou Strong One;
Force to thee from above, and Light!
Complete,—complete the work!

ADAM (*embracing Robert.*)

Come to my heart!—&c. &c.

Such was the spirit of that new Faith, which, symbolized under mythuses of Baffometus and Phosphoros, and "Saviours from the Waters," and "Trinities of Art, Religion, and Love," and to be preached abroad by the aid of Schleiermacher, and what was then called the *New Poetical School*, Werner seriously purposed, like another Luther, to cast forth, as good seed, among the ruins of decayed and down-trodden Protestantism! Whether Hitzig was still young enough to attempt executing his commission, and applying to Schlegel and Tieck for help; and if so, in what gestures of speechless astonishment, or what peals of inextinguishable laughter they answered him, we are not informed. One thing, however, is clear: that a man with so unbridled an imagination, joined to so weak an understanding, and so broken a volition; who had plunged so deep into Theosophy, and still hovered so near the surface in all practical knowledge of men and their affairs; who, shattered and degraded in his own private character, could meditate such apostolic enterprises, was a man likely, if he lived long, to play fantastic tricks in abundance; and, at least, in his religious history, to set the world a-wondering. Conversion, not to Popery, but, if it so chanced, to Braminism, was a thing nowise to be thought impossible.

Nevertheless, let his missionary zeal have justice from us! It does seem to have been grounded on no wicked or even illaudable motive: to all appearance, he not only believed what he professed, but thought it of the highest moment that others should believe it. And if the proselytizing spirit, which dwells in all men, be allowed exercise even when it only assaults what it reckons Errors, still more should this be so, when it proclaims what it reckons Truth, and fancies itself not taking from us what in our eyes may be good, but adding thereto what is better.

Meanwhile, Werner was not so absorbed in spiritual schemes, that he altogether overlooked his own merely temporal comfort. In contempt of former failures, he was now courting for himself a third wife, "a young Poless of the highest personal attractions;" and this under difficulties which would have appalled an ordinary wooer: for the two had no language in common; he not understanding three words of Polish, she not one of German. Nevertheless, nothing daunted by this circumstance, nay, perhaps discerning in it an assurance against many a sorrowful curtain lecture, he prosecuted his suit, we suppose by signs and dumb-show, with such ardour, that he quite gained the fair mute; wedded her in 1801; and soon after, in her company quitted Warsaw for Königsberg, where the helpless state of his mother required immediate attention. It is from Königsberg that most of his missionary epistles to Hitzig are written; the latter, as we have hinted above, being now stationed, by his official appointment, in Berlin. The sad duty of watching over his crazed, forsaken, and dying mother, Werner appears to have discharged with true filial assiduity: for three years she lingered in the most painful state, under his nursing; and her death, in 1804, seems notwithstanding to have filled him with the deepest sorrow. This is an extract of his letter to Hitzig on that mournful occasion:

"I know not whether thou hast heard that on the 24th of February, (the same day when our excellent Mnioch died in Warsaw,) my mother departed here, in my arms. My Friend! God knocks with an iron hammer at our hearts; and we are duller than stone, if we do not feel it; and madder than mad, if we think it shame to cast ourselves into the dust before the All-powerful, and let our whole so highly miserable Self be annihilated in the sentiment of His infinite greatness and long-suffering. I wish I had words to paint how inexpressibly pitiful my *Söhne des Thals* appeared to me in that hour, when, after eighteen years of neglect, I again went to partake in the Communion! This death of my mother,—the pure, royal poet-and-martyr spirit, who for eight years had lain continually on a sick-bed, and suffered unspeakable things,—affected me, (much as, for her sake and my own, I could not but wish it with altogether agonizing feelings.) Ah, Friend, how heavy do my youthful faults lie on me! How much would I give to have my mother—(though both I and my wife have of late times lived wholly for her, and had much to endure on her account)—how much would I give to have her back to me but one week, that I might disburden my heavy-laden heart with tears of repentance! My beloved Friend, give thou no grief to thy parents! ah, no earthly voice can awaken the dead! God and Parents, that is the first concern; *all* else is secondary."

This affection for his mother forms, as it were, a little island of light and verdure in Werner's history, where, amid so much that is dark and desolate, one feels it pleasant to linger. Here was at least one duty, perhaps, indeed, the only one, which, in a wayward, wasted life, he discharged with fidelity: from his conduct towards this one hapless being, we may, perhaps, still learn that his heart, however perverted by circumstances, was not incapable of true, disinterested love. A rich heart by Nature; but unwisely squandering its riches, and attaining to a pure union only with this one heart; for it seems doubtful whether he ever loved another! His poor mother, while alive, was the haven of all his earthly voyagings; and, in after years, from amid far scenes, and crushing perplexities, he often looks back to her grave with a feeling to which all bosoms must respond.* The date of her decease became a memorable era in his mind; as may appear from the title which he gave, long afterwards, to one of his most popular and tragical productions, *Die Vier-und-zwanzigste Februar* (The Twenty-fourth of February.)

After this event, which left him in possession of a small but competent fortune, Werner returned with his wife to his post at Warsaw. By this time, Hitzig, too, had been sent back, and to a higher post: he was now married likewise; and the two wives, he says, soon became as intimate as their husbands. In a little while Hoffmann joined them; a colleague in Hitzig's office, and by him ere long introduced to Werner, and the other circle of Prussian men of law, who, in this foreign capital, formed each other's chief society; and, of course, cleave to one another more closely than they might have done elsewhere. Hoffmann does not seem to have loved Werner; as, indeed, he was at all times rather shy in his attachments; and, to his quick eye, and more rigid, fastidious feeling, the lofty theory and low selfish practice, the general diffuseness, nay, incoherence of character, the pedantry and solemn affectation, too visible in the man, could nowise be hidden. Nevertheless, he feels and acknowledges the frequent charm of his conversation: for Werner many times could be frank and simple; and the true humour and abandonment with which he often launched forth into bland satire on his friends, and still oftener on himself, atoned for many of his whims and weaknesses. Probably the two could not have lived together by themselves: but in a circle of common men, where these touchy elements were attempered by a fair addition of wholesome insensibilities and formalities, they even relished one another; and, indeed, the whole social union seems to have stood on no undesirable footing. For the rest, Warsaw itself was, at this time, a gay, picturesque, and stirring city; full of resources for spending life in pleasant occupation, either wisely or unwisely.*

It was here, that, in 1805, Werner's *Kreuz an der Ostsee* (Cross on the Baltic) was written: a sort of half-operatic performance, for which Hoffmann, who to his gifts as a writer added perhaps still higher attainments, both as a musician and a painter, composed the accompaniment. He complains that, in this matter, Werner was very ill to please. A ridiculous scene, at the first reading of the piece, the same shrewd wag has recorded in his *Serapions-Bruder*; Hitzig assures us that it is literally true, and that Hoffmann himself was the main actor in the business.

"Our Poet had invited a few friends, to read to them, in manuscript, his *Kreuz an der Ostsee*, of which they already knew some fragments that had raised their expectations to the highest stretch. Planted, as usual, in the middle of the circle, at a little miniature table, on which two clear lights, stuck in high candlesticks, were burning, sat the poet: he had drawn the manuscript from his breast; the huge snuff-box, the blue-checked handkerchief, aptly reminding you of Baltic muslin, as in use for petticoats and other indispensable things, lay arranged in order before him.—Deep silence on all sides!—Not a breath heard!—The poet cuts one of those unparalleled, ever-memorable, altogether indescribable faces you have seen in him, and begins.—Now you recollect, at the rising of the curtain, the Prussians are assembled on the coast of the Baltic, fishing amber, and com-

* See, for example, the Preface to his *Mutter der Makkabäer*, written at Vienna, in 1819. The tone of still, but deep and heartfelt sadness, which runs through the whole of this piece, cannot be communicated in extracts. We quote only a half stanza, which, except in prose, we shall not venture to translate:

Ich, dem der Liebe Kosen
Und alle Freudenrosen,
Beym ersten Schaufeltosen
Am Muttergrab' entflohn.—

"I, for whom the caresses of love and all roses of joy withered away, as the first shovel with its mould sounded on the coffin of my mother."

* Hitzig has thus described the first aspect it presented to Hoffmann: "Streets of stately breadth, formed of palaces in the finest Italian style, and wooden huts which threatened every moment to rush down over the heads of their inmates; in these edifices, Asiatic pomp combined in strange union with Greenland squalor. An ever-moving population, forming the sharpest contrasts, as in a perpetual masquerade: long-bearded Jews; monks in the garb of every order; here veiled and deeply-shrouded nuns of strictest discipline, walking, self-secluded and apart: there flights of young Polesses, in silk mantles of the brightest colours, talking and promenading over broad squares. The venerable ancient Polish noble, with moustaches, caftan, girdle, sabre, and red or yellow boots: the new generation equipt to the utmost pitch as Parisian *Incroyables*; with Turks, Greeks, Russians, Italians, Frenchmen, in ever-changing throng. Add to this a police of inconceivable tolerance, disturbing no popular sport; so that little puppet-theatres, apes, camels, dancing bears, practised incessantly in open spaces and streets; while the most elegant equipages, and the poorest pedestrian bearers of burden, stood gazing at them. Further, a theatre in the national language; a good French company; an Italian opera; German players of at least a very passable sort; masked-balls on a quite original but highly entertaining plan; places for pleasure-excursions all round the city," &c. &c.—*Hoffmann's Leben und Nachlass*, b. i. p. 287.

mence by calling on the god who presides over this vocation.—So—begins:

Bangputtis! Bangputtis! Bangputtis!

—Brief pause!—Incipient stare in the audience!—and from a fellow in the corner comes a small clear voice: 'My dearest, most valued friend! my best of poets! If thy whole dear opera is written in that cursed language, no soul of us knows a syllable of it; and I beg, in the Devil's name, thou wouldst rather have the goodness to translate it first!' "*

Of this *Kreuz an der Ostsee* our limits will permit us to say but little. It is still a fragment; the Second Part, which was often promised, and, we believe, partly written, having never yet been published. In some respects, it appears to us the best of Werner's dramas: there is a decisive coherence in the plot, such as we seldom find with him; and a firmness, a rugged nervous brevity in the dialogue, which is equally rare. Here, too, the mystic dreamy agencies, which, as in most of his pieces, he has interwoven with the action, harmonize more than usually with the spirit of the whole. It is a wild subject, and this helps to give it a corresponding wildness of locality. The first planting of Christianity among the Prussians, by the Teutonic Knights, leads us back of itself into dim ages of antiquity, of superstitious barbarism, and stern apostolic zeal: it is a scene hanging, as it were, in half-ghastly *chiaroscuro*, on a ground of primeval Night: where the Cross and St. Adalbert come in contact with the Sacred Oak and the Idols of Romova, we are not surprised that spectral shapes peer forth on us from the gloom.

In the constructing and depicting of characters, Werner, indeed, is still little better than a mannerist: his persons, differing in external figure, differ too slightly in inward nature; and no one of them comes forward on us with a rightly visible or living air. Yet, in scenes and incidents, in what may be called the general costume of his subject, he has here attained a really superior excellence. The savage Prussians, with their amber-fishing, their bear-hunting, their bloody idolatry, and stormful untutored energy, are brought vividly into view; no less so the Polish Court of Plozk, and the German Crusaders, in their bridal-feasts and battles, as they live and move, here placed on the verge of Heathendom, as it were, the vanguard of Light in conflict with the kingdoms of Darkness. The nocturnal assault on Plozk by the Prussians, where the handful of Teutonic Knights is overpowered, but the city saved from ruin by the miraculous interposition of the "Harper," who now proves to be the spirit of St. Adalbert; this, with the scene which follows it, on the Island of the Vistula, where the dawn slowly breaks over doings of wo and horrid cruelty, but of wo and cruelty atoned for by immortal hope,—belongs undoubtedly to Werner's most successful efforts. With much that is questionable, much that is merely common, there are intermingled touches from the true Land of Wonders; indeed, the whole is overspread with a certain dim religious light, in which its many pettinesses and exaggerations are softened into something which at least resembles poetic harmony. We give this drama a high praise, when we say that more than once it has reminded us of Calderon.

The "Cross on the Baltic" had been bespoke by Iffland for the Berlin theatre; but the complex machinery of the piece, the "little flames" springing, at intervals, from the heads of certain characters, and the other supernatural ware with which it is replenished, were found to transcend the capabilities of any merely terrestrial stage. Iffland, the best actor in Germany, was himself a dramatist, and a man of talent, but in all points differing from Werner, as a stage-machinist may differ from a man with the *second-sight*. Hoffmann chuckles in secret over the perplexities in which the shrewd prosaic manager and playwright must have found himself, when he came to the "little flames." Nothing remained but to write back a refusal, full of admiration and expostulation: and Iffland wrote one which, says Hoffmann, "passes for a master-piece of theatrical diplomacy."

In this one respect, at least, Werner's next play was happier, for it actually crossed the "Stygian marsh" of green-room hesitations, and reached, though in a maimed state, the Elysium of the boards; and this to the great joy, as it proved, both of Iffland and all other parties interested. We allude to the *Martin Luther, oder die Weihe der Kraft*, (Martin Luther, or the Consecration of Strength,) Werner's most popular performance, which came out at Berlin in 1807, and soon spread over all Germany, Catholic as well as protestant, being acted, it would seem, even in Vienna, to overflowing and delighted audiences.

If instant acceptance, therefore, were a measure of dramatic merit, this play should rank high among that class of works. Nevertheless, to judge from our own impressions, the sober reader of *Martin Luther* will be far from finding in it such excellence. It cannot be named among the best dramas: it is not even the best of Werner's. There is, indeed, much scenic exhibition, many a "fervid sentiment," as the newspapers have it; nay, with all its mixture of coarseness, here and there a glimpse of genuine dramatic inspiration; but, as a whole, the work sorely disappoints us; it is of so loose and mixed a structure and falls asunder in our thoughts, like the iron and clay in the Chaldean's Dream. There is an interest, perhaps of no trivial sort, awakened in the First Act; but, unhappily, it goes on declining, till, in the Fifth, an ill-natured critic might almost say, it expires. The story is too wide for Werner's dramatic lens to gather into a focus; besides, the reader brings with him an image of it, too fixed for being so boldly metamorphosed, and too high and august for being ornamented with tinsel and gilt pasteboard. Accordingly, the Diet of Worms, plentifully furnished as it is with sceptres and armorial shields, continues a much grander scene in History, than it is here in Fiction. Neither, with regard to the persons of the play, excepting those of Luther and Catharine, the Nun whom he weds, can we find much scope

* Hoffmann's *Serapions-Brüder*, b. iv. s. 240.

for praise. Nay, our praise even of these two must have many limitations. Catharine, though carefully enough depicted, is, in fact, little more than a common tragedy-queen, with the storminess, the love, and other stage-heroism, which belong prescriptively to that class of dignitaries. With regard to Luther himself, it is evident that Werner has put forth his whole strength in this delineation; and, trying him by common standards, we are far from saying that he has failed. Doubtless it is, in some respects, a significant and even sublime delineation: yet must we ask whether it is Luther, the Luther of History, or even the Luther proper for this drama; and not rather some ideal portraiture of Zacharias Werner himself? Is not this Luther, with his too assiduous flute-playing, his trances of three days, his visions of the Devil, (at whom, to the sorrow of the housemaid, he resolutely throws his huge ink-bottle,) by much too spasmodic and brainsick a personage? We cannot but question the dramatic beauty, whatever it may be in history, of that three days' trance; the hero must before this have been in want of mere victuals; and there, as he sits deaf and dumb, with his eyes sightless, yet fixed and staring, are we not tempted less to admire, than to send in all haste for some officer of the Humane Society?—Seriously, we cannot but regret that these and other such blemishes had not been avoided, and the character, worked into chasteness and purity, been presented to us in the simple grandeur which essentially belongs to it. For, censure as we may, it were blindness to deny that this figure of Luther has in it features of an austere loveliness, a mild, yet awful beauty: undoubtedly a figure rising from the depths of the poet's soul; and, marred as it is with such adhesions, piercing at times into the depths of ours! Among so many poetical sins, it forms the chief redeeming virtue, and truly were almost in itself a sort of atonement.

As for the other characters, they need not detain us long. Of Charles the Fifth, by far the most ambitious,—meant, indeed, as the counterpoise of Luther,—we may say, without hesitation, that he is a failure. An empty Gascon this; bragging of his power, and honour, and the like, in a style which Charles, even in his nineteenth year, could never have used. "One God, one Charles," is no speech for an emperor; and, besides, is borrowed from some panegyrist of a Spanish opera-singer. Neither can we fall in with Charles, when he tells us, that "he fears nothing,—not even God." We humbly think he must be mistaken. With the old Miners, again, with Hans Luther and his Wife, the Reformer's parents, there is more reason to be satisfied; yet in Werner's hands simplicity is always apt, in such cases, to become too simple, and these honest peasants, like the honest Hugo in the "Sons of the Valley," are *very* garrulous.

This drama of "Martin Luther" is named likewise the "Consecration of Strength;" that is, we suppose, the purifying of this great theologian from all remnants of earthly passion, into a clear heavenly zeal; an operation which is brought about, strangely enough, by two half-ghosts and one whole ghost,—a little fairy girl, Catharine's servant, who impersonates Faith; a little fairy youth, Luther's servant, who represents Art; and the "Spirit of Cotta's wife," an honest housekeeper, but defunct many years before, who stands for Purity. These three supernaturals hover about in very whimsical wise, cultivating flowers, playing on flutes, and singing dirge-like epithalamiums over unsound sleepers: we cannot see how aught of this is to "consecrate strength;" or, indeed, what such jack-o'-lantern personages have in the least to do with so grave a business. If the author intended by such machinery to elevate his subject from the Common, and unite it with the higher region of the Infinite and the Invisible, we cannot think that his contrivance has succeeded, or was worthy to succeed. These half-allegorical, half-corporeal beings yield no contentment anywhere: Abstract Ideas, however they may put on fleshly garments, are a class of characters whom we cannot sympathize with or delight in. Besides, how can this mere imbodyment of an allegory be supposed to act on the rugged materials of life, and elevate into ideal grandeur the doings of real men, that live and move amid the actual pressure of worldly things? At best, it can stand but like a *hand in the margin:* it is not *performing* the task proposed, but only telling us that it was meant to be performed. To our feelings, this entire episode runs like straggling bindweed through the whole growth of the piece, not so much uniting as encumbering and choking up what it meets with; in itself, perhaps, a green and rather pretty weed; yet here superfluous, and, like any other weed, deserving only to be altogether cut away.

Our general opinion of "Martin Luther," it would seem, therefore, corresponds ill with that of the "overflowing and delighted audiences" over all Germany. We believe, however, that now, in its twentieth year, the work may be somewhat more calmly judged of even there. As a classical drama it could never pass with any critic; nor, on the other hand, shall we ourselves deny that, in the lower sphere of a popular spectacle, its attractions are manifold. We find it, what, more or less, we find all Werner's pieces to be, a splendid, sparkling mass; yet not of pure metal, but of many-coloured scoria, not unmingled with metal; and must regret, as ever, that it had not been refined in a stronger furnace, and kept in the crucible till the true *silver-gleam,* glancing from it, had shown that the process was complete.

Werner's dramatic popularity could not remain without influence on him, more especially as he was now in the very centre of its brilliancy, having changed his residence from Warsaw to Berlin, some time before his *Weihe der Kraft* was acted, or indeed written. Von Schrötter, one of the state-ministers, a man harmonizing with Werner in his "zeal both for religion and freemasonry," had been persuaded by some friends to appoint him his secretary. Werner naturally rejoiced in such promotion; yet, combined with his theatrical success, it perhaps, in the long run, did him more harm than good. He might now, for the first time, be said to see the busy and influential world with his own eyes: but to draw future instruction from it, or even to guide himself in its present complexities, he was little qualified. He took a shorter method: "he plunged into the vortex of society," says Hitzig, with brief expressiveness; became acquainted, indeed, with Fichte, Johannes Müller and other excellent men, but united himself also, and with closer partiality, to players, play-lovers, and a long list of jovial, admiring, but highly unprofitable companions. His religious schemes, perhaps, rebutted by collision with actual life, lay dormant for the time, or mingled in strange union with wine-vapours, and the "feast of reason, and the flow of soul." The result of all this might, in some measure, be foreseen. In eight weeks, for example, Werner had parted with his wife. It was not to be expected, he writes, that she should be happy with him. "I am no bad man," continues he, with considerable candour; "yet a weakling in many respects, (for God strengthens me also in several,) fretful, capricious, greedy, impure. Thou knowest me! Still, immersed in my fantasies, in my occupation: so that here, what with playhouses, what with social parties, she had no manner of enjoyment with me. *She* is innocent. I, too, perhaps, for can I pledge myself that I am so?" These repeated divorces of Werner's at length convinced him that he had no talent for managing wives; indeed, we subsequently find him, more than once, arguing in dissuasion of marriage altogether. To our readers one other consideration may occur: astonishment at the state of marriage-law, and the strange footing this "sacrament" must stand on throughout Protestant Germany. For a Christian man, at least not a Mohammedan, to leave *three* widows behind him, certainly wears a peculiar aspect. Perhaps it is saying much for German morality, that so absurd a system has not, by the disorders resulting from it, already brought about its own abrogation.

Of Werner's further proceedings in Berlin, except by implication, we have little notice. After the arrival of the French armies, his secretaryship ceased; and now wifeless and placeless, in the summer of 1807, "he felt himself," he says, "authorized by Fate to indulge his taste for pilgriming." Indulge it accordingly he did; for he wandered to and fro many years, nay, we may almost say to the end of his life, like a perfect Bedouin. The various stages and occurrences of his travels, he has himself recorded in a paper, furnished by him for his own *Name*, in some Biographical Dictionary. Hitzig quotes great part of it, but it is too long and too meagre for being quoted here. Werner was at Prague, Vienna, Munich, —everywhere received with open arms; "saw at Jena, in December, 1807, for the first time, the most universal and the clearest man of his age, (the man whose like no one that has seen him will ever see again,) the great, nay, only GOETHE; and, under his introduction, the pattern of German princes," (the Duke of Weimar;) and then, "after three ever-memorable months in this society, beheld at Berlin the triumphant entry of the pattern of European tyrants" (Napoleon.) On the summit of the Rigi, at sunrise, he became acquainted with the Crown-Prince, King of Bavaria; was by him introduced to the Swiss festival at Interlacken, and to the most "intellectual lady of our time, the Baroness de Staël;" and must beg to be credited when, after sufficient individual experience, he can declare, that the heart of this high and noble woman was at least as great as her genius. Coppet, for a while, was his head quarters, but he went to Paris, to Weimar,* again to Switzerland; in short, trudged and hurried hither and thither, inconstant as an *ignis fatuus*, and restless as the Wandering Jew.

On his mood of mind during all this period, Werner gives us no direct information; but so unquiet an outward life betokens of itself no inward repose; and when we, from other lights, gain a transient glimpse into the wayfarer's thoughts, they seem still more fluctuating than his footsteps. His project of a New Religion was by this time abandoned: Hitzig thinks his closer survey of life at Berlin had taught him the impracticability of such chimeras. Nevertheless, the subject of Religion, in one shape or another, nay, of propagating it in new purity by teaching and preaching, had nowise vanished from his meditations. On the contrary, we can perceive that it still formed the master-principle of his soul, "the pillar of cloud by day, and the pillar of fire by night," which guided him, so far as he had any guidance, in the pathless desert of his now solitary, barren, and cheerless existence. What his special opinions or prospects on the matter had, at this period, become, we nowhere learn; except, indeed, negatively,—for if he has not yet found the new, he still cordially enough detests the old. All his admiration of Luther cannot reconcile him to modern Lutheranism. This he regards but as another and more hideous impersonation of the Utilitarian spirit of the age, nay, as the last triumph of Infidelity, which has now dressed itself in priestly garb, and even mounted the pulpit, to preach, in heavenly symbols, a doctrine which is altogether of the earth. A curious passage from his preface to the "Cross on the Baltic" we may quote, by way of illustration. After speaking of St. Adalbert's miracles, and how his body, when purchased from the heathen for its weight in gold, became light as gossamer, he proceeds:

"Though these things may be justly doubted; yet *one* miracle cannot be denied him, the miracle, namely, that after his death he has extorted from this Spirit of Protestantism against Strength in general,—which now replaced the old heathen and catholic Spirit of Persecution, and weighs almost as much as Adalbert's body, —the admission, that he knew what he wanted; was what he wished to be; was so wholly; and therefore must have been a man, at all points diametrically opposite both to that Protestantism, and to the culture of our day." In a Note, he adds: "There is another Protestantism,

* It was here that Hitzig saw him, for the last time, in 1809, found admittance, through his means, to a court festival in honour of Bernadotte; and he still recollects, with gratification, "the lordly spectacle of Goethe and that sovereign standing front to front, engaged in the liveliest conversation."

however, which constitutes in Conduct, what Art is in Speculation, and which I reverence so highly, that I even place it above Art, as Conduct is above Speculation at all times. But in this, St. Adalbert and St. Luther are—colleagues: and if God, which I daily pray for, should awaken Luther to us *before* the Last Day, the *first* task he would find, in respect of that degenerate and spurious Protestantism, would be, in his somewhat rugged manner, to —*protest* against it."

A similar, or perhaps still more reckless temper, is to be traced elsewhere, in passages of a gay, as well as grave character. This is the conclusion of a letter from Vienna, in 1807

"We have Tragedies here which contain so many edifying maxims, that you might use them instead of *Jesus Sirach*, and have them read from beginning to end in the Berlin Sunday-schools. Comedies, likewise, absolutely bursting with household felicity and nobleness of mind. The genuine Kasperl is dead, and Schikander gone his ways; but here, too, Bigotry and Superstition are attacked in enlightened Journals with such profit, that the people care less for Popery than even you in Berlin do; and prize, for instance, the *Weihe der Kraft*, which has also been declaimed in Regensburg and Munich to thronging audiences,—chiefly for the multitude of liberal Protestant opinions therein brought to light; and regard the author, all his struggling to the contrary unheeded, as a secret *Illuminatus*, or at worst an amiable Enthusiast. In a word, Vienna is determined, without loss of time, to overtake Berlin in the career of improvement; and when I recollect that Berlin, on her side, carries Porsten's *Hymn-book* with her, in her reticule, to the shows in the *Thiergarten;* and that the ray of Christiano-catholico-platonic Faith pierces deeper and deeper into your (already by nature very deep) Privy-councillor Mamsell,—I almost fancy that Germany is one great madhouse; and could find in my heart to pack up my goods, and set off for Italy to-morrow morning;—not, indeed, that I might work there, where follies enough are to be had too; but that, amid ruins and flowers, I might forget all things, and myself in the first place."—*Lebens-Abriss*, s. 70.

To Italy accordingly he went, though with rather different objects, and not quite so soon as on the morrow. In the course of his wanderings, a munificent ecclesiastical Prince, the Fürst Primas von Dalberg, had settled a yearly pension on him; so that now he felt still more at liberty to go whither he listed. In the course of a second visit to Coppet, and which lasted four months, Madame de Staël encouraged and assisted him to execute his favourite project; he set out, through Turin and Florence, and "on the 9th of December, 1809, saw, for the first time, the capital of the world!" Of his proceedings here, much as we should desire to have minute details, no information is given in this narrative; and Hitzig seems to know, by a letter, merely, that "he knelt with streaming eyes over the graves of St. Peter and St. Paul." This little phrase says much. Werner appears likewise to have assisted at certain "Spiritual Exercitations" (*Geistliche Uebungen;*) a new invention set on foot at Rome for quickening the devotion of the faithful, consisting, so far as we can gather, in a sort of fasting-and-prayer meetings, conducted on the most rigorous principles, the considerable band of devotees being bound over to strict silence, and secluded for several days, with conventual care, from every sort of intercourse with the world. The effect of these Exercitations, Werner elsewhere declares, was edifying to an extreme degree; at parting on the threshold of their holy tabernacle, all the brethren "embraced each other, as if intoxicated with divine joy; and each confessed to the other, that throughout these precious days he had been, as it were, in heaven; and now, strengthened as by a soul-purifying bath, was but loath to venture back into the cold week-day world." The next step from these Tabor-feasts, if, indeed, it had not preceded them, was a decisive one: "On the 19th of April, 1811, Werner had grace given him to return to the Faith of his fathers, the Catholic!"

Here, then, the "crowning mercy" had at length arrived! This passing of the Rubicon determined the whole remainder of Werner's life, which had henceforth the merit, at least, of entire consistency. He forthwith set about the professional study of Theology; then being perfected in this, he left Italy in 1813, taking care, however, by the road, "to supplicate, and certainly not in vain, the help of the Gracious Mother at Loretto; and after due preparation, under the superintendence of his patron, the Prince Archbishop von Dalberg, had himself ordained a Priest at Aschaffenburg, in June, 1814. Next, from Aschaffenburg he hastened to Vienna; and there, with all his might, began preaching; his first auditory being the Congress of the Holy Alliance, which had then just begun its venerable sessions. "The novelty and strangeness," he says, "nay, originality of his appearance, secured him an extraordinary concourse of hearers." He was, indeed, a man worth hearing and seeing; for his name, noised abroad in many-sounding peals, was filling all Germany from the hut to the palace. This, he thinks, might have affected his head; but he "had a trust in God, which bore him through." Neither did he seem anywise anxious to still this clamour of his judges, least of all to propitiate his detractors: for already, before arriving at Vienna, he had published, as a pendant to his "Martin Luther, or the Consecration of Strength," a pamphlet, in doggrel metre, entitled the "Consecration of Weakness," wherein he proclaims himself to the whole world as an honest seeker and finder of truth, and takes occasion to revoke his old "Trinity," of art, religion, and love; love having now turned out to be a dangerous ingredient in such mixtures. The writing of this *Weihe der Unkraft* was reckoned by many a bold but injudicious measure,—a throwing down of the gauntlet when the lists were full of tumultuous foes, and the knight was but weak, and his cause, at best, of the most questionable sort. To reports, and calumnies, and criticisms, and vituperations, there was no limit.

What remains of this strange eventful history may be summed up in few words. Werner accepted no special charge in the Church; but continued a private and secular Priest; preaching diligently, but only where he himself saw good; oftenest at Vienna, but in summer over all parts of Austria, in Styria, Carinthia, and even Venice. Everywhere, he says, the opinions of his hearers were "violently divided." At one time, he thought of becoming Monk, and had actually entered on a sort of noviciate; but he quitted the establishment rather suddenly, and, as he is reported to have said, "for reasons known only to God and himself." By degrees, his health grew very weak; yet he still laboured hard both in public and private; writing or revising poems, devotional or dramatic; preaching, and officiating as father-confessor, in which last capacity he is said to have been in great request. Of his poetical productions during this period, there is none of any moment known to us, except the *Mother of the Maccabees* (1819); a tragedy of careful structure, and apparently in high favour with the author, but which, notwithstanding, need not detain us long. In our view, it is the worst of all his pieces; a pale, bloodless, indeed quite ghost-like affair; for a cold breath as from a sepulchre chills the heart in perusing it: there is no passion or interest, but a certain wo-struck martyr zeal, or rather frenzy, and this not so much storming as shrieking; not loud and resolute, but shrill, hysterical, and bleared with ineffectual tears. To read it may well sadden us: it is a convulsive fit, whose uncontrollable writhings indicate, not strength, but the last decay of it.*

Werner was, in fact, drawing to his latter end: his health had long been ruined; especially of later years, he had suffered much from disorders of the lungs. In 1817, he was thought to be dangerously ill; and afterwards, in 1822, when a journey to the Baths partly restored him; though he himself still felt that his term was near, and spoke and acted like a man that was shortly to depart. In January, 1823, he was evidently dying: his affairs he had already settled; much of his time he spent in prayer; was constantly cheerful, at intervals even gay. "His death," says Hitzig, "was especially mild. On the eleventh day of his disorder, he felt himself, particularly towards evening, as if altogether light and well; so that he would hardly consent to have any one to watch with him. The servant whose turn it was did watch, however; he had sat down by the bedside between two and three next morning, (the 17th,) and continued there a considerable while, in the belief that his patient was asleep. Surprised, however, that no breathing was to be heard, he hastily aroused the household, and it was found that Werner had already passed away."

In imitation, it is thought, of Lipsius, he bequeathed his Pen to the treasury of the Virgin at Mariazell, "as a chief instrument of his aberrations, his sins, and his repentance." He was honourably interred at Enzersdorf on the Hill, where a simple inscription, composed by himself, begs the wanderer to "pray charitably for his poor soul;" and expresses a trembling hope that, as to Mary Magdalen, "because she loved much," so to him also, "much may be forgiven."

We have thus, in hurried movement, travelled over Zacharias Werner's Life and Works; noting down from the former such particulars as seemed most characteristic; and gleaning from the latter some more curious passages, less indeed with a view to their intrinsic excellence, than to their fitness for illustrating the man. These scattered indications we must now leave our readers to interpret each for himself: each will adjust them into that combination which shall best harmonize with his own way of thought. As a writer, Werner's character will occasion little difficulty. A richly gifted nature; but never wisely guided, or resolutely applied: a loving heart; an intellect subtile and inquisitive, if not always clear and strong; a gorgeous, deep, and bold imagination; a true, nay, keen and burning sympathy with all high, all tender and holy things;—here lay the main elements of no common poet; save only that one was still wanting,—the force to cultivate them, and mould them into pure union. But they have remained uncultivated, disunited, too often struggling in wild disorder: his poetry, like his life, is still not so much an edifice as a quarry. Werner had cast a look into perhaps the very deepest region of the Wonderful; but he had not learned to live there: he was yet no denizen of that mysterious land: and, in his visions, its splendour is strangely mingled and overclouded with the flame or smoke of mere earthly fire. Of his dramas we have already spoken; and with much to praise, found always more to censure. In his rhymed pieces, his shorter, more didactic poems, we are better satisfied: here, in the rude, jolting vehicle of a certain Sternhold-and-Hopkins metre, we often find a strain of true pathos, and a deep, though quaint significance. His prose, again, is among the worst known to us: degraded with silliness; diffuse, nay, tautological, yet obscure and vague; contorted into endless involutions; a misshapen, lumbering, complected coil, well nigh inexplicable in its entanglements, and seldom worth the trouble of unravelling. He does not move *through* his subject, and arrange it, and rule over it; for the most part, he but welters in it, and laboriously tumbles it, and at last sinks under it.

As a man, the ill-fated Werner can still less content us. His feverish, inconstant, and wasted life we have already looked at. Hitzig, his determined well-wisher, admits that in practice he was selfish, wearying out his best friends by the most barefaced importunities; a man of no dignity; avaricious, greedy, sensual, at times obscene; in discourse, with all his

* Of his *Attila*, (1808,) his *Vier-und-zwanzigste Februar*, (1809,) his *Cunegunde*, (1814,) and various other pieces written in his wanderings, we have not room to speak. It is the less necessary, as the *Attila* and *Twenty-fourth of February*, by much the best of these, have already been forcibly, and, on the whole, fairly characterized by Madame de Staël. Of the last-named little work we might say, with double emphasis, *Nec pueros coram populo Medea trucidet*: it has a deep and genuine tragic interest, were it not so painfully protracted into the regions of pure horror. Werner's *Sermons*, his *Hymns*, his *Preface to Thomas à Kempis, &c.*, are entirely unknown to us.

humour and heartiness, apt to be intolerably long-winded; and of a maladroitness, a blank ineptitude, which exposed him to incessant ridicule and manifold mystifications from people of the world. Nevertheless, under all this rubbish, contends the friendly Biographer, there dwelt, for those who could look more narrowly, a spirit, marred indeed in its beauty, and languishing in painful conscious oppression, yet never wholly forgetful of its original nobleness. Werner's soul was made for affection; and often as, under his too rude collisions with external things, it was struck into harshness and dissonance, there was a tone which spoke of melody, even in its jarrings. A kind, a sad, and heartfelt remembrance of his friends seems never to have quitted him: to the last he ceased not from warm love to men at large; nay, to awaken in them, with such knowledge as he had, a sense for what was best and highest, may be said to have formed the earnest, though weak and unstable aim of his whole existence. The truth is, his defects as a writer were also his defects as a man: he was feeble, and without volition; in life, as in poetry, his endowments fell into confusion; his character relaxed itself on all sides into incoherent expansion; his activity became gigantic endeavour, followed by most dwarfish performance.

The grand incident of his life, his adoption of the Roman Catholic religion, is one on which we need not heap further censure; for already, as appears to us, it is rather liable to be too harshly than too leniently dealt with. There is a feeling in the popular mind, which, in well-meant hatred of inconsistency, perhaps in general too sweepingly condemns such changes. Werner, it should be recollected, *had* at all periods of his life *a* religion; nay, he hungered and thirsted after truth in this matter, as after the highest good of man; a fact which of itself must, in this respect, set him far above the most consistent of mere unbelievers,—in whose barren and callous soul consistency, perhaps, is no such brilliant virtue. We pardon genial weather for its changes; but the steadiest of all climates is that of Greenland. Further, we must say that, strange as it may seem, in Werner's whole conduct, both before and after his conversion, there is not visible the slightest trace of insincerity. On the whole, there are fewer genuine renegades than men are apt to imagine. Surely, indeed, that must be a nature of extreme baseness, who feels that, in worldly good, he *can* gain by such a step. Is the contempt, the execration of all that have known and loved us, and of millions that have never known us, to be weighed against a mess of pottage, or a piece of money? We hope there are not many, even in the rank of sharpers, that would think so. But for Werner there was no gain in any way; nay, rather certainty of loss. He enjoyed or sought no patronage; with his own resources he was already independent though poor, and on a footing of good esteem with all that was most estimable in his country. His little pension, conferred on him, at a prior date, by a Catholic Prince, was not continued after his conversion, except by the Duke of Weimar, a Protestant. He became a mark for calumny; the defenceless butt at which every callow witling made his proof-shot; his character was more deformed and mangled than that of any other man. What had he to gain? Insult and persecution; and with these, as candour bids us believe, the approving voice of his own conscience. To judge from his writings, he was far from repenting of the change he had made; his Catholic faith evidently stands in his own mind as the first blessing of his life; and he clings to it as to the anchor of his soul. Scarcely more than once (in the Preface to his *Mutter der Makkabäer*) does he allude to the legions of falsehoods that were in circulation against him; and it is in a spirit which, without entirely concealing the querulousness of nature, nowise fails in the meekness and endurance which became him as a Christian. Here is a fragment of another Paper, published since his death, as it was meant to be; which exhibits him in a still clearer light. The reader may condemn, or what will be better, pity and sympathize with him; but the structure of this strange piece surely bespeaks any thing but insincerity. We translate it with all its breaks and fantastic crotchets, as it stands before us:

"Testamentary Inscription, from Friedrich Ludwig Zacharias Werner, a son," &c.—(here follows a statement of his parentage and birth, with vacant spaces for the date of his death,)—"of the following lines, submitted to all such as have more or less felt any friendly interest in his unworthy person, with the request to take warning by his example, and charitably to remember the poor soul of the writer before God, in prayer and good deeds.

"Begun at Florence, on the 24th of September, about eight in the evening, amid the still distant sound of approaching thunder. Concluded, when and where God will!

"Motto, Device, and Watchword in Death: *Remittuntur ei peccata multa, quoniam dilexit multum! ! !—Lucas, Caput* vii. *v.* 47.

"N. B. Most humbly and earnestly, and in the name of God, does the Author of this Writing beg, of such honest persons as may find it, to submit the same in any suitable way to public examination.

"*Fecisti nos, Domine, ad Te, et irrequietum est cor nostrum, donec requiescat in Te.—S. Augustinus.*

"*Per multa dispergitur, et hic illucque quærit* (*cor*) *ubi requiescere possit, et nihil invenit quod ei sufficiat, donec ad ipsum* (*sc. Deum*) *redeat.—S. Bernardus.*

"In the name of God the Father, Son, and Holy Ghost, Amen!

"The thunder came hither, and is still rolling, though now at a distance.—The name of the Lord be praised! Hallelujah!—I begin:

"This Paper must needs be brief; because the appointed term for my life itself may already be near at hand. There are not wanting examples of important and unimportant men, who have left behind them in writing the defence, or even sometimes the accusation, of their earthly life. Without estimating such procedure, I am not minded to imitate it. With trembling I reflect that I myself shall first learn in its whole terrific compass what properly I was, when these lines shall be read by men; that is to say, in a point of Time which for me will be no Time; in a condition wherein all experience will for me be too late!

Rex tremendæ majestatis,
Qui salvandos salvas gratis,
Salva me, fons pietatis!!!

But if I do, till that day when All shall be laid open, draw a veil over my past life, it is not merely out of false shame that I so order it; for though not free from this vice also, I would willingly make known my guilt to all and every one whom my voice might reach, could I hope, by such confession, to atone for what I have done; or thereby to save a single soul from perdition. There are two motives, however, which forbid me to make such an open personal revelation after death: the *one*, because the unclosing of a pestilential grave may be dangerous to the health of the uninfected looker-on; the *other*, because in my writings, (which may God forgive me!) amid a wilderness of poisonous weeds and garbage, there may also be here and there a medicinal herb lying scattered, from which poor patients, to whom it might be useful, would start back with shuddering, did they know the pestiferous soil on which it grew.

"So much, however, in regard to those good creatures as they call themselves, namely, to those feeble weaklings who brag of what they designate their good hearts,—so much must I say before God, that such a heart alone, when it is not checked and regulated by forethought and steadfastness, is not only incapable of saving its possessor from destruction, but it is rather certain to hurry him, full speed, into that abyss, where I have been, whence I—perhaps?!!!—by God's grace am snatched, and from which may God mercifully preserve every reader of these lines."—*Werner's Letzte Lebenstagen*, (quoted by Hitzig, p. 80.)

"All this is melancholy enough; but it is not like the writing of a hypocrite or repentant apostate. To Protestantism, above all things, Werner shows no thought of returning. In allusion to a rumour, which had spread, of his having given up Catholicism, he says (in the *Preface* already quoted):

"A stupid falsehood I must reckon it; since, according to my deepest conviction, it is as impossible that a soul in Bliss should return back into the Grave, as that a man, who, like me, after a life of error and search has found the priceless jewel of Truth, should, I will not say, give up the same, but hesitate to sacrifice for it blood and life, nay, many things perhaps far dearer, with joyful heart, when the one good cause is concerned."

And elsewhere in a private letter:

"I not only assure thee, but I beg of thee to assure all men, if God should ever so withdraw the light of his grace from me, that I ceased to be a Catholic, I would a thousand times sooner join myself to Judaism, or to the Bramins on the Ganges: but to that shallowest, driest, most contradictory, inanest Inanity of Protestantism, *never, never, never!*"

Here, perhaps, there is a touch of priestly, of almost feminine vehemence; for it is to a Protestant and an old friend that he writes: but the conclusion of his *Preface* shows him in a better light. Speaking of Second Parts, and regretting that so many of his works were unfinished, he adds:

"But what specially comforts me is the prospect of—our general Second Part; where, even in the first Scene, *this* consolation, that there *all* our works will be known, may not indeed prove solacing *for us all*: but where, through the strength of Him that alone completes all works, it will be granted to those whom He has saved, not only to know each other, but even to know Him, as by Him they are known! —With my trust in Christ, whom I have not yet won, I regard, with the Teacher of the Gentiles, all things but dross that I may win Him; and to him, cordially and lovingly do I, in life or at death, commit you all, my beloved Friends and my beloved Enemies!"

On the whole, we cannot think it doubtful that Werner's belief was real and heartfelt. But how then, our wondering readers may inquire, if his belief was real and not pretended, *how* then did he believe? He, who scoffs in infidel style at the truths of Protestantism, by what alchemy did he succeed in tempering into credibility the harder and bulkier dogmas of Popery? Of Popery, too, the frauds and gross corruptions of which he has so fiercely exposed in his *Martin Luther!* and this, moreover, without cancelling, or even softening his vituperations, long after his conversion, in the very last edition of that drama? To this question, we are far from pretending to have any answer that altogether satisfies ourselves, much less that shall altogether satisfy others. Meanwhile, there are two considerations which throw light on the difficulty for us: these, as some step, or at least, attempt towards a solution of it, we shall not withhold. The *first* lies in Werner's individual character and mode of life. Not only was he born a *mystic*, not only had he lived from of old amid freemasonry, and all manner of cabalistic and other traditionary chimeras; he was also, and had long been what is emphatically called *dissolute*; a word which has now lost somewhat of its original force; but which, as applied here, is still more just and significant in its etymological, than in its common acception. He was a man *dissolute*; that is, by a long course of vicious indulgences, enervated and *loosened asunder.* Everywhere in Werner's life and actions, we discern a mind relaxed from its proper tension; no longer capable of effort and toilsome resolute vigilance; but floating almost passively with the current of its impulses, in languid, imaginative, Asiatic reverie. That such a man should discriminate, with sharp, fearless logic, between beloved errors and unwelcome truths, was not to be expected. His belief is likely to have been *persuasion* rather than *conviction*, both as it related to Religion, and to other subjects. What, or how much a man in this way may bring himself to *believe*, with such force and distinctness as he honestly and usually calls *belief*, there is no predicting.

But *another* consideration, which we think should nowise be omitted, is the general state of religious opinion in Germany, especially among such minds as Werner was most apt to take for his examplars. To this complex and highly interesting subject, we can for the present do nothing more than allude. So much, however, we may say: It is a common theory among the Germans, that every Creed, every Form of worship, is a *form* merely; the mortal and everchanging *body*, in which the immortal and unchanging *spirit* of Religion is, with more or less completeness, expressed to the material eye, and made manifest and influential among the doings of men. It is thus, for instance, that Johannes Müller, in his *Universal History*, professes to consider the Mosaic Law, the creed of Mahomet, nay, Luther's Reformation; and, in short, all other systems of Faith; which he scruples not to designate, without special praise or censure, simply as *Vorstellungsarten*, "modes of Representation." We could report equally singular things of Schelling and others, belonging to the philosophic class; nay of Herder, a Protestant clergyman, and even bearing high authority in the Church. Now, it is clear, in a country where such opinions are openly and generally professed, a change of religious creed must be comparatively a slight matter. Conversions to Catholicism are accordingly by no means unknown among the Germans: Friedrich Schlegel, and the younger Count von Stolberg, men, as we should think, of vigorous intellect, and of character above suspicion, were colleagues, or rather precursors, of Werner in this adventure; and, indeed, formed part of his acquaintance at Vienna. It is but, they would pay perhaps, as if a melodist, inspired with harmony of inward music, should choose this instrument in preference to that, for giving voice to it: the inward inspiration is the grand concern; and to express it, the "deep majestic solemn organ" of the Unchangeable Church may be better fitted than the "scrannel pipe" of a withered, trivial, Arian Protestantism. That Werner, still more that Schlegel and Stolberg, could, on the strength of such hypotheses, put off or put on their religious creed, like a new suit of apparel, we are far from asserting; they are men of earnest hearts, and seem to have a deep feeling of devotion: but it should be remembered, that what forms the groundwork of their religion, is professedly not Demonstration but Faith; and so pliant a theory could not but help to soften the transition from the former to the latter. That some such principle, in one shape or another, lurked in Werner's mind, we think we can perceive from several indications; among others, from the Prologue to his last tragedy, where, mysteriously enough, under the emblem of a Phœnix, he seems to be shadowing forth the history of his own Faith; and represents himself even then as merely "climbing the *tree*, where the pinions of his Phœnix last *vanished*;" but not hoping to regain that blissful vision, till his eyes shall have been opened by death.

On the whole, we must not pretend to understand Werner, or expound him with scientific rigour: acting many times with only half consciousness, he was always, in some degree, an enigma to himself, and may well be obscure to us. Above all, there are mysteries and unsounded abysses in every human heart; and that is but a questionable philosophy which undertakes so readily to explain them. Religious belief especially, at least when it seems heartfelt and well-intentioned, is no subject for harsh or even irreverent investigation. He is a wise man that, having such a belief, knows and sees clearly the grounds of it in himself: and those, we imagine, who have explored with strictest scrutiny the secret of their own bosoms, will be least apt to rush with intolerant violence into that of other men's.

"The good Werner," says Jean Paul, "fell, like our more vigorous Hoffmann, into the poetical fermenting vat (*Gährbottich*) of our time, where all Literatures, Freedoms, Tastes, and Untastes are foaming through each other: and where all is to be found, excepting truth, diligence, and the polish of the file. Both would have come forth clearer had they studied in Lessing's day."* We cannot justify Werner: yet let him be condemned with pity! And well were it could each of us apply to himself those words, which Hitzig, in his friendly indignation, would "thunder in the ears" of many a German gainsayer: *Take thou the beam out of thine own eye; then shalt thou see clearly to take the mote out of thy brother's.*

* Letter to Hitzig, in *Jean Paul's Leben*, by Doering.

GOETHE'S HELENA.*

[FOREIGN REVIEW, 1828.]

NOVALIS has rather tauntingly asserted of Goethe, that the grand law of his being is to conclude whatsoever he undertakes; that, let, him engage in any task, no matter what its difficulties or how small its worth, he cannot quit it till he has mastered its whole secret, finished it, and made the result of it his own. This, surely, whatever Novalis might think, is a quality of which it is far safer to have too much than too little; and if, in a friendlier spirit, we admit that it does strikingly belong to Goethe, these his present occupations will not seem out of harmony with the rest of his life; but rather it may be regarded as a singular constancy of fortune, which now allows him, after completing so many single enterprizes, to adjust deliberately the details and combination of the whole; and thus, in perfecting his individual works, to put the last hand to the highest of all his works, his own literary character, and leave the impress of it to posterity in that form and accompaniment which he himself reckons fittest. For the last two years, as many of our readers may know, the venerable Poet has been employed in a patient and thorough revisal of all his Writings; an edition of which, designated as the "complete and final" one, was commenced in 1827, under external encouragements of the most flattering sort, and with arrangements for private co-operation, which, as we learn, have secured the constant progress of the work "against every accident." The first *Lieferung*, of five volumes, is now in our hands; a second of like extent, we understand to be already on its way hither; and thus by regular "Deliveries," from half-year to half-year, the whole Forty Volumes are to be completed in 1831.

To the lover of German literature, or of literature in general, this undertaking will not be indifferent: considering, as he must do, the works of Goethe to be among the most important which Germany for some centuries has sent forth, he will value their correctness and completeness for its own sake; and not the less, as forming the conclusion of a long process to which the last step was still wanting; whereby he may not only enjoy the result, but instruct himself by following so great a master through the changes which led to it. We can now add, that, to the mere book-collector also, the business promises to be satisfactory. This Edition, avoiding any attempt at splendour or unnecessary decoration, ranks, nevertheless, in regard to accuracy, convenience, and true, simple elegance, among the best specimens of German typography. The cost, too, seems moderate; so that, on every account, we doubt not but that these tasteful volumes will spread far and wide in their own country, and by and by, we may hope, be met with here in many a British library.

Hitherto, in the First Portion, we have found little or no alteration of what was already known; but, in return, some changes of arrangement; and, what is more important, some additions of heretofore unpublished poems; in particular, a piece entitled "*Helena, a classico-romantic Phantasmagoria*," which occupies some eighty pages of Volume Fourth. It is to this piece that we now propose directing the attention of our readers. Such of these, as have studied *Helena* for themselves, must have felt how little calculated it is, either intrinsically or by its extrinsic relations and allusions, to be rendered very interesting or even very intelligible to the English public, and may incline to augur ill of our enterprise. Indeed, to our own eyes it already looks dubious enough. But the dainty little "Phantasmagoria," it would appear, has become a subject of diligent and truly wonderful speculation to our German neighbours; of which, also, some vague rumours seem now to have reached this country, and these likely enough to awaken on all hands a curiosity,* which, whether intelligent or idle, it were a kind of good deed to allay. In a Journal of this sort, what little light on such a matter is at our disposal may naturally be looked for.

Helena, like many of Goethe's works, by no means carries its significance written on its forehead, so that he who runs may read; but, on the contrary, it is enveloped in a certain mystery, under coy disguises, which, to hasty readers, may not be only offensively obscure, but altogether provoking and impenetrable. Neither is this any new thing with Goethe. Often has he produced compositions, both in prose and verse, which bring critic and commentator into straits, or even to a total nonplus. Some we have, wholly parabolic; some half-literal, half-parabolic; these latter are occasionally studied, by dull heads, in the literal sense alone; and not only studied, but condemned: for, in truth, the outward meaning seems unsatisfactory enough, were it not that ever and anon we are reminded of a cunning, manifold meaning which lies hidden under it; and incited by capricious beckonings to evolve this, more and more completely, from its quaint concealment.

Did we believe that Goethe adopted this mode of writing as a vulgar lure, to confer on his poems the interest which might belong to

* *Goethe's Sämmtliche Werke. Vollständige Ausgabe letzter Hand.* (Goethe's Collective Works. Complete Edition, with his final Corrections.) First Portion, vols. i—v. 16mo and 8vo. Cotta: Stuttgard & Tübingen. 1827.

* See, for instance, the "Athenæum," No. vii., where an article stands headed with these words: FAUST, HELEN OF TROY, AND LORD BYRON.

so many charades, we should hold it a very poor proceeding. Of this most readers of Goethe will know that he is incapable. Such juggleries, and uncertain anglings for distinction, are a class of accomplishments to which he has never made any pretension. The truth is, this style has, in many cases, its own appropriateness. Certainly, in all matters of Business and Science, in all expositions of fact or argument, clearness and ready comprehensibility are a great, often an indispensable, object. Nor is there any man better aware of this principle than Goethe, or who more rigorously adheres to it, or more happily exemplifies it, wherever it seems applicable. But in this, as in many other respects, Science and Poetry, having separate purposes, may have each its several law. If an artist has conceived his subject in the secret shrine of his own mind, and knows, with a knowledge beyond all power of cavil, that it is true and pure, he may choose his own manner of exhibiting it, and will generally be the fittest to choose it well. One degree of light, he may find, will beseem one delineation; quite a different degree of light another. The Face of Agamemnon was not painted but hidden in the old Picture; the Veiled Figure at Sais was the most expressive in the Temple. In fact, the grand point is to *have* a meaning, a genuine, deep, and noble one; the proper form for embodying this, the form best suited to the subject and to the author, will gather round it almost of its own accord. We profess ourselves unfriendly to no mode of communicating Truth; which we rejoice to meet with in all shapes, from that of the child's Catechism to the deepest poetical Allegory. Nay, the Allegory itself may sometimes be the truest part of the matter. John Bunyan, we hope, is nowise our best theologian; neither, unhappily, is theology our most attractive science; yet, which of our compends and treatises, nay, which of our romances and poems, lives in such mild sunshine as the good old *Pilgrim's Progress*, in the memory of so many men?

Under Goethe's management, this style of composition has often a singular charm. The reader is kept on the alert, ever conscious of his own active co-operation; light breaks on him, and clearer and clearer vision, by degrees; till at last the whole lovely Shape comes forth, definite, it may be, and bright with heavenly radiance, or fading, on this side and that, into vague expressive mystery; but true in both cases, and beautiful with nameless enchantments, as the poet's own eye may have beheld it. We love it the more for the labour it has given us; we almost feel as if we ourselves had assisted in its creation. And herein lies the highest merit of a piece, and the proper art of reading it. We have not *read* an author till we have seen his object, whatever it may be, as *he* saw it. It is a matter of reasoning, and has he reasoned stupidly and falsely? We should understand the circumstances which to his mind made it seem true, or persuaded him to write it, knowing that it was not so. In any other way we do him injustice if we judge him. Is it of poetry? His words are so many symbols, to which we ourselves must furnish the interpretation; or they remain, as in all prosaic minds the words of poetry ever do, a dead letter: indications they are, barren in themselves, but by following which, we also may reach, or approach, that Hill of Vision where the poet stood, beholding the glorious scene which it is the purport of his poem to show others. A reposing state, in which the Hill were brought under us, not we obliged to mount it, might, indeed, for the present be more convenient; but, in the end, it could not be equally satisfying. Continuance of passive pleasure, it should never be forgotten, is here, as under all conditions of mortal existence, an impossibility. Everywhere in life, the true question is, not what we *gain*, but what we *do:* so also in intellectual matters, in conversation, in reading, which is more precise and careful conversation, it is not what we *receive*, but what we are made to *give*, that chiefly contents and profits us. True, the mass of readers will object; because, like the mass of men, they are too indolent. But if any one affect, not the active and watchful, but the passive and somnolent line of study, are there not writers, expressly fashioned for him, enough and to spare? It is but the smaller number of books that become more instructive by a second perusal: the great majority are as perfectly plain as perfect triteness can make them. Yet, if time is precious, no book that will not improve by repeated readings deserves to be read at all. And were there an artist of a right spirit; a man of wisdom, conscious of his high vocation, of whom we could know beforehand that he had not written without purpose and earnest meditation, that he knew what he had written, and had imbodied in it, more or less, the creations of a deep and noble soul,—should we not draw near to him reverently, as disciples to a master; and what task could there be more profitable than to read him as we have described, to study him even to his minutest meanings? For, were not this to think as he had thought, to see with his gifted eyes, to make the very mood and feeling of his great and rich mind the mood also of our poor and little one? It is under the consciousness of some such mutual relation that Goethe writes, and his countrymen now reckon themselves bound to read him; a relation singular, we might say solitary, in the present time; but which it is ever necessary to bear in mind in estimating his literary procedure.

To justify it in this particular, much more might be said, were it our chief business at present. But what mainly concerns us here, is, to know that such, justified or not, is the poet's manner of writing; which also must prescribe for us a correspondent manner of studying him, if we study him at all. For the rest, on this latter point he nowhere expresses any undue anxiety. His works have invariably been sent forth without preface, without note or comment of any kind; but left, sometimes plain and direct, sometimes dim and typical, in what degree of clearness or obscurity he himself may have judged best, to be scanned, and glossed, and censured, and distorted, as might please the innumerable multitude of critics; to whose verdict he has been, for a great part of his life, accused of listening with unwarrantable composure. *Helena* is no exception to that practice, but rather among the strong instances of it. This *Interlude to Faust* presents itself abruptly, under a character not a little enigmatic; so that, at first view, we know not well what to make of it; and only after repeated perusals, will the scattered glimmerings of significance begin to coalesce into continuous light, and the whole, in any measure, rise before us with that greater or less degree of coherence which it may have had in the mind of the poet. Nay, after all, no perfect clearness may be attained, but only various approximations to it; hints and half glances of a meaning, which is still shrouded in vagueness; nay, to the just picturing of which this very vagueness was essential. For the whole piece has a dream-like character; and, in these cases, no prudent soothsayer will be altogether confident. To our readers we must now endeavour, so far as possible, to show both the dream and its interpretation: the former as it stands written before us; the latter from our own private conjecture alone; for of those strange German comments we yet know nothing, except by the faintest hearsay.

Helena forms part of a continuation to *Faust;* but, happily for our present undertaking, its connection with the latter work is much looser than might have been expected. We say, happily; because *Faust*, though considerably talked of in England, appears still to be nowise known. We have made it our duty to inspect the English translation of *Faust,* as well as the Extracts which accompany Retzsch's Outlines; and various disquisitions and animadversions, vituperative or laudatory, grounded on these two works; but, unfortunately, have found there no cause to alter the above persuasion. *Faust* is emphatically a work of Art; a work matured in the mysterious depths of a vast and wonderful mind; and bodied forth with that truth and curious felicity of composition, in which this man is generally admitted to have no living rival. To reconstruct such a work in another language; to show it in its hard yet graceful strength; with those slight witching traits of pathos or of sarcasm, those glimpses of solemnity or terror, and so many reflexes and evanescent echoes of meaning, which connect it in strange union with the whole Infinite of thought,—were business for a man of different powers than has yet attempted German translation among us. In fact, *Faust* is to be read not once but many times, if we would understand it: every line, every word has its purport; and only in such minute inspection will the essential significance of the poem display itself. Perhaps it is even chiefly by following these fainter traces and tokens, that the true point of vision for the whole is discovered to us; and we stand at last in the proper scene of Faust; a wild and wondrous region, where, in pale light, the primeval Shapes of Chaos, —as it were, the Foundations of Being itself,—seem to loom forth, dim and huge, in the vague Immensity around us; and the life and nature of man, with its brief interests, its misery and sin, its mad passion and poor frivolity, struts and frets its hour, encompassed and overlooked by that stupendous All, of which it forms an indissoluble though so mean a fraction. He who would study all this must for a long time, we are afraid, be content to study it in the original.

But our English criticisms of *Faust* have been of a still more unedifying sort. Let any man fancy the *Œdipus Tyrannus* discovered for the first time, translated from an unknown Greek manuscript, by some ready-writing manufacturer, and "brought out" at Drury Lane, with new music, made as "apothecaries make new mixtures, by pouring out of one vessel into another!" Then read the theatrical report in the morning Papers, and the Magazines of next month. Was not the whole affair rather "heavy?" How indifferent did the audience sit; how little use was made of the handkerchief, except by such as took snuff! Did not Œdipus somewhat remind us of a blubbering schoolboy, and Jocasta of a decayed milliner? Confess that the plot was monstrous; nay, considering the marriage-law of England, highly immoral. On the whole, what a singular deficiency of *taste* must this Sophocles have laboured under! But probably he was excluded from the "society of the influential classes:" for, after all, the man is not without indications of genius: had *we* had the training of him,—And so on, through all the variations of the critical cornpipe.

So might it have fared with the ancient Grecian; for so has it fared with the only modern that writes in a Grecian spirit. This treatment of *Faust* may deserve to be mentioned, for various reasons; not to be lamented over, because, as in much more important instances, it is inevitable, and lies in the nature of the case. Besides, a better state of things is evidently enough coming round. By and by, the labours, poetical and intellectual, of the Germans, as of other nations, will appear before us in their true shape; and *Faust*, among the rest, will have justice done it. For ourselves, it were unwise presumption, at any time, to pretend opening the full poetical significance of *Faust;* nor is this the place for making such an attempt. Present purposes will be answered if we can point out some general features and bearings of the piece; such as to exhibit its relation with *Helena;* by what contrivances this latter has been intercalated into it, and how far the strange picture and the strange framing it is inclosed in correspond.

The story of Faust forms one of the most remarkable productions of the Middle Ages; or rather, it is the most striking embodiment of a highly remarkable belief, which originated or prevailed in those ages. Considered strictly, it may take the rank of a Christian mythus, in the same sense as the story of Prometheus, of Titan, and the like, are Pagan ones; and to our keener inspection, it will disclose a no less impressive or characteristic aspect of the same human nature,—here bright, joyful, self-confident, smiling even in its sternness; there deep, meditative, awe-struck, austere,—in which both they and it took their rise. To us, in these days, it is not easy to estimate how this story of Faust, invested with its magic and infernal horrors, must have harrowed up the souls of a rude and earnest people, in an age when its dialect was not yet obsolete, and such contracts with the principle of Evil were thought not only credible in general, but possible to every individual auditor who here shuddered at the mention of them. The day of Magic has gone by; Witchcraft has been put a stop to by act of parliament. But the mysterious relations which it emblemed still continue; the Soul of Man still fights with the dark influences of Ignorance, Misery, and Sin; still lacerates itself, like a captive bird, against the iron limits which Necessity has drawn round it; still follows False Shows, seeking peace and good on paths where no peace or good is to be found. In this sense, *Faust* may still be considered as true; nay, as a truth of the most impressive sort, and one which will always remain true. To body forth, in modern symbols, a feeling so old and deep-rooted in our whole European way of thought, were a task not unworthy of the highest poetical genius. In Germany, accordingly, it has several times been attempted, and with very various success. Klinger has produced a Romance of *Faust*, full of rugged sense, and here and there not without considerable strength of delineation; yet, on the whole, of an essentially unpoetical character; dead, or living with only a mechanical life; coarse, almost gross, and, to our minds, far too redolent of pitch and bitumen. Maler Müller's *Faust*, which is a Drama, must be regarded as a much more genial performance, so far as it goes; the secondary characters, the Jews and rakish Students, often remind us of our own Fords and Marlowes. His main persons, however, Faust and the Devil, are but inadequately conceived; Faust is little more than self-willed, supercilious, and, alas, insolvent; the Devils, above all, are savage, long-winded, and insufferably noisy. Besides, the piece has been left in a fragmentary state; it can nowise pass as the best work of Müller's.* Klingemann's Faust, which also is (or lately *was*) a Drama, we have never seen; and have only heard of it as of a tawdry and hollow article, suited for immediate use, and immediate oblivion.

Goethe, we believe, was the first who tried this subject; and is, on all hands, considered as by far the most successful. His manner of treating it appears to us, so far as we can understand it, peculiarly just and happy. He retains the supernatural vesture of the story, but retains it with the consciousness, on his and our part, that it is a chimera. His art-magic comes forth in doubtful twilight; vague in its outline; interwoven everywhere with light sarcasm; nowise as a real Object, but as a real Shadow of an Object, which is also real, yet lies beyond our horizon, and, except in its shadows, cannot itself be seen. Nothing were simpler than to look into this poem for a new "Satan's Invisible World displayed," or any effort to excite the skeptical minds of these days by goblins, wizards, and other infernal ware. Such enterprises belong to artists of a different species: Goethe's Devil is a cultivated personage, and acquainted with the modern sciences; sneers at witchcraft and the black-art, even while employing them, as heartily as any member of the French Institute; for he is a *philosophe*, and doubts most things, nay, half disbelieves even his own existence. It is not without a cunning effort that all this is managed; but managed, in a considerable degree, it is; for a world of magic is opened to us which, we might almost say, we feel to be at once true and not true.

In fact, Mephistopheles comes before us, not arrayed in the terrors of Cocytus and Phlegethon, but in the natural indelible deformity of Wickedness; he is the Devil, not of Superstition, but of Knowledge. Here is no cloven foot, or horns and tail: he himself informs us that, during the late march of intellect, the very Devil has participated in the spirit of the age, and laid these appendages aside. Doubtless, Mephistopheles "has the manners of a gentleman;" he "knows the world;" nothing can exceed the easy tact with which he manages himself; his wit and sarcasm are unlimited; the cool heartfelt contempt with which he despises all things, human and divine, might make the fortune of half a dozen "fellows about town." Yet, withal, he is a devil in very deed; a genuine Son of Night. He calls himself the Denier, and this truly is his name; for, as Voltaire did with historical doubt, so does he with all moral appearances; settles them with a *N'en croyez rien.* The shrewd, all-informed intellect he has, is an attorney intellect; it can contradict, but it cannot affirm. With lynx vision, he descries at a glance the ridiculous, the unsuitable, the bad; but for the solemn, the noble, the worthy, he is blind as his ancient Mother. Thus does he go along, qualifying, confuting, despising; on all hands detecting the false, but without force to bring forth, or even to discern, any glimpse of the true. Poor Devil! what truth should there be for him? To see Falsehood is his only truth: falsehood and evil are the rule, truth and good the exception which confirms it. He can believe in nothing, but in his own self-conceit, and in the indestructible baseness, folly, and hypocrisy of men. For him, virtue

* Frederic Müller (more commonly called *Maler*, or *Painter* Müller) is here, so far as we know, named for the first time to English readers. Nevertheless, in any solid study of German literature, this author must take precedence of many hundreds whose reputation has travelled faster. But Müller has been unfortunate in his own country, as well as here. At an early age, meeting with no success as a poet, he quitted that art for painting; and retired, perhaps in disgust, into Italy; where also but little preferment seems to have awaited him. His writings, after almost half a century of neglect, were at length brought into sight and general estimation by Ludwig Tieck; at a time when the author might indeed say, that he was "old and could not enjoy it, solitary and could not impart it," but not, unhappily, that he was "known and did not want it," for his fine genius had yet made for itself no free way amid so many obstructions, and still continued unrewarded and unrecognised. His paintings, chiefly of still-life and animals, are said to possess a true though no very extraordinary merit: but of his poetry we will venture to assert that it bespeaks a genuine feeling and talent, nay, rises at times even into the higher regions of Art. His *Adam's Awakening*, his *Satyr Mopsus*, his *Nusskernen* (Nutshelling), informed as they are with simple kindly strength, with clear vision, and love of nature, are incomparably the best German or, indeed, modern Idyls; his "Genoveva" will still stand reading, even with that of Tieck. These things are now acknowledged among the Germans; but to Müller the acknowledgment is of no avail. He died some two years ago at Rome, where he seems to have subsisted latterly as a sort of picture-cicerone.

is some bubble of the blood: "it stands written on his face that he never loved a living soul." Nay, he cannot even hate: at Faust himself he has no grudge; he merely tempts him by way of experiment, to pass the time scientifically. Such a combination of perfect Understanding with perfect Selfishness, of logical Life with moral Death; so universal a denier, both in heart and head,—is undoubtedly a child of Darkness, an emissary of the primeval Nothing: and coming forward, as he does, like a person of breeding, and without any flavour of Brimstone, may stand here, in his merely spiritual deformity, at once potent, dangerous, and contemptible, as the best and only genuine Devil of these latter times.

In strong contrast with this impersonation of modern worldly-mindedness, stands Faust himself, by nature the antagonist of it, but destined also to be its victim. If Mephistopheles represent the spirit of Denial, Faust may represent that of Inquiry and Endeavour: the two are, by necessity, in conflict; the light and the darkness of man's life and mind. Intrinsically, Faust is a noble being, though no wise one. His desires are towards the high and true; nay, with a whirlwind impetuosity he rushes forth over the Universe to grasp all excellence; his heart yearns towards the infinite and the invisible: only that he knows not the conditions under which alone this is to be attained. Confiding in his feeling of himself, he has started with the tacit persuasions, so natural to all men, that *he* at least, however it may fare with others, shall and must be *happy;* a deep-seated, though only half-conscious conviction lurks in him, that wherever he is not successful, fortune has dealt with him *unjustly.* His purposes are fair, nay, generous: why should he not prosper in them? For in all his lofty aspirings, his strivings after truth and more than human greatness of mind, it has never struck him to inquire how he, the striver, was warranted for such enterprises; with what faculty Nature had equipped him; within what limits she had hemmed him in; by what right *he* pretended to be happy, or could, some short space ago, have pretended to *be* at all. Experience, indeed, will teach him, for "Experience is the best of schoolmasters; only the school-fees are heavy." As yet, too, disappointment, which fronts him on every hand, rather maddens than instructs. Faust has spent his youth and manhood, not as others do in the sunny crowded paths of profit, or among the rosy bowers of pleasure, but darkly and alone in the search of Truth: is it fit that Truth should now hide herself, and his sleepless pilgrimage towards Knowledge and Vision end in the pale shadow of Doubt? To his dream of a glorious higher happiness, all earthly happiness has been sacrificed; friendship, love, the social rewards of ambition were cheerfully cast aside, for his eye and his heart were bent on a region of clear and supreme good; and now, in its stead, he finds isolation, silence, and despair. What solace remains? Virtue once promised to be her own reward; but because she does not pay him in the current coin of worldly enjoyment, he reckons her too a delusion; and, like Brutus, reproaches as a shadow, what he once worshipped as a substance. Whither shall he now tend? For his loadstars have gone out one by one; and as the darkness fell, the strong and steady wind has changed into a fierce and aimless tornado. Faust calls himself a monster, "without object, yet without rest." The vehement, keen, and stormful nature of the man is stung into fury, as he thinks of all he has endured and lost; he broods in gloomy meditation, and, like Bellerophon, wanders apart, "eating his own heart;" or bursting into fiery paroxysms, curses man's whole existence as a mockery; curses hope, and faith, and joy, and care, and what is worst, "curses patience more than all the rest." Had his weak arm the power, he could smite the Universe asunder, as at the crack of Doom, and hurl his own vexed being along with it into the silence of Annihilation.

Thus Faust is a man who has quitted the ways of vulgar men, without light to guide him on a better way. No longer restricted by the sympathies, the common interests and common persuasions by which the mass of mortals, each individually ignorant, nay, it may be, stolid, and altogether blind as to the proper aim of life, are yet held together, and like stones in the channel of a torrent, by their very multitude and mutal collision, are made to move with some regularity,—he is still but a slave; the slave of impulses, which are stronger, not truer or better, and the more unsafe that they are solitary. He sees the vulgar of mankind happy; but happy only in their baseness. Himself he feels to be peculiar; the victim of a strange, an unexampled destiny; not as other men, he is "*with* them, not *of* them." There is misery here; nay, as Goethe has elsewhere wisely remarked, the beginning of madness itself. It is only in the sentiment of companionship that men feel safe and assured: to all doubts and mysterious "questionings of destiny," their sole satisfying answer is, *Others do and suffer the like.* Were it not for this, the dullest day-drudge of Mammon might think himself into unspeakable abysses of despair; for he, too, is "fearfully and wonderfully made;" Infinitude and Incomprehensibility surround him on this hand and that; and the vague spectre Death, silent and sure as Time, is advancing at all moments to sweep him away for ever. But he answers, *Others do and suffer the like;* and plods along without misgivings. Were there but One Man in the world, he would be a terror to himself; and the highest man not less so than the lowest. Now it is as this One Man that Faust regards himself; he is divided from his fellows; cannot answer with them, *Others do the like;* and yet, why or how he specially is to *do* or *suffer* will nowhere reveal itself. For he is still "in the gall of bitterness;" Pride and an entire uncompromising, though secret love of Self, are still the mainsprings of his conduct. Knowledge with him is precious only because it is power; even virtue he would love chiefly as a finer sort of sensuality, and because it was *his* virtue. A ravenous hunger for enjoyment haunts him everywhere; the stinted allotments of earthly life are as a mockery to him: to the iron law of Force h will not yield, for his heart, though torn, is yet unweakened, and till Humility shall open his eyes, the soft law of Wisdom will be hidden from him.

To invest a man of this character with supernatural powers is but enabling him to repeat his error on a larger scale, to play the same false game with a deeper and more ruinous stake. Go where he may, he will "find himself again in a conditional world;" widen his sphere as he pleases, he will find it again encircled by the empire of Necessity; the gay island of Existence is again but a fraction of the ancient realm of Night. Were he all-wise and all-powerful, perhaps he might be contented and virtuous; scarcely otherwise. (The poorest human soul is infinite in wishes, and the infinite Universe was not made for one, but for all.) Vain were it for Faust, by heaping height on height, to struggle towards infinitude; while to that law of Self-denial, by which alone man's narrow destiny may become an infinitude within itself, he is still a stranger. Such, however, is his attempt: not indeed incited by hope, but goaded on by despair, he unites himself with the Fiend, as with a stronger though a wicked agency; reckless of all issues, if so were that by these means the craving of his heart might be stayed, and the dark secret of Destiny unravelled or forgotten.

It is this conflicting union of the higher nature of the soul with the lower elements of human life; of Faust, the son of Light and Free-will, with the influences of Doubt, Denial, and Obstruction, or Mephistopheles, who is the symbol and spokesman of these, that the poet has here proposed to delineate. A high problem; and of which the solution is yet far from completed; nay, perhaps, in a poetical sense, is not, strictly speaking, capable of completion. For it is to be remarked that, in this contract with the Prince of Darkness, little or no mention or allusion is made to a Future Life; whereby it might seem as if the action was not intended, in the manner of the old Legend, to terminate in Faust's perdition;* but rather as if an altogether different end must be provided for him. Faust, indeed, wild and wilful as he is, cannot be regarded as a wicked, much less as an utterly reprobate man: we do not reckon him ill-intentioned, but misguided and miserable; he falls into crime, not by purpose, but by accident and blindness. To send him to the Pit of Wo, to render such a character the eternal slave of Mephistopheles, would look like making darkness triumphant over light, blind force over erring reason; or, at best, were cutting the Gordian knot, not loosing it. If we mistake not, Goethe's *Faust* will have a finer moral than the old nursery-tale, or the other plays and tales that have been founded on it. Our seared and blighted, yet still noble Faust, will not end in the madness of horror, but in Peace grounded on better Knowledge. Whence that Knowledge is to come, what higher and freer world of Art or Religion may be hovering in the mind of the poet, we will not try to surmise: perhaps in bright aerial emblematic glimpses, he may yet show it us, transient and afar off, yet clear with orient beauty, as a Land of Wonders, and new Poetic Heaven.

With regard to that part of the work already finished, we must here say little more. *Faust*, as it yet stands, is, indeed, only a stating of the difficulty; but a stating of it wisely, truly, and with deepest poetic emphasis. For how many living hearts, even now imprisoned in the perplexities of Doubt, do these wild piercing tones of Faust, his withering agonies and fiery desperation, "speak the word they have long been waiting to hear!" A nameless pain had long brooded over the soul: here, by some light touch, it starts into form and voice; we see it and know it, and see that another also knew it. This *Faust* is as a mystic Oracle for the mind; a Dodona grove, where the oaks and fountains prophesy to us of our destiny, and murmur unearthly secrets.

How all this is managed, and the poem so curiously fashioned; how the clearest insight is combined with the keenest feeling, and the noblest and wildest imagination; by what soft and skilful finishing these so heterogeneous elements are blended in fine harmony, and the dark world of spirits, with its merely metaphysical entities, plays like a chequering of strange mysterious shadows among the palpable objects of material life; and the whole, firm in its details, and sharp and solid as reality, yet hangs before us melting on all sides into air, and free, and light, as the baseless fabric of a vision; all this the reader can learn fully nowhere but, by long study, in the work itself. The general scope and spirit of it we have now endeavoured to sketch: the few incidents on which, with the aid of much dialogue and exposition, these have been brought out, are perhaps already known to most readers, and, at all events, need not be minutely recapitulated here. Mephistopheles has promised to himself that he will lead Faust "through the bustling inanity of life," but that its pleasures shall tempt and not satisfy him; "food shall hover before his eager lips, but he shall beg for nourishment in vain." Hitherto they have travelled but a short way together; yet, so far, the Denier has kept his engagement well. Faust, endowed with all earthly, and many more than earthly advantages, is still no nearer contentment; nay, after a brief season of marred and uncertain joy, he finds himself sunk into deeper wretchedness than ever. Margaret, an innocent girl whom he loves, but has betrayed, is doomed to die, and already crazed in brain, less for her own errors than for his: in a scene of true pathos, he would fain persuade her to escape with him, by the aid of Mephistopheles, from prison; but in the instinct of her heart she finds an invincible aversion to the Fiend; she chooses death and ignominy, rather than life and love, if of his giving. At her final refusal, Mephistopheles proclaims that "she is judged," a "voice from Above" that "she is saved;" the action terminates; Faust and Mephistopheles vanish from our sight, as into boundless Space.

And now, after so long a preface, we arrive at *Helena*, the "Classico-romantic Phantasmagoria," where these Adventurers, strangely altered by travel, and in altogether different costume, have again risen into sight. Our long preface was not needless, for *Faust* and *Helena*, though separated by some wide and marvellous interval, are nowise disconnected. The characters may have changed by absence; Faust is no longer the same bitter and tempestuous man, but appears in chivalrous composure, with a silent energy, a grave, and, as it were, commanding ardour. Mephistopheles alone may retain somewhat of his old spiteful shrewdness: but still the past state of these personages must illustrate the present; and only by what we remember of them, can we try to interpret what we see. In fact, the style of *Helena* is altogether new: quiet, simple, joyful; passing by a short gradation from Classic dignity into Romantic pomp; it has everywhere a full and sunny tone of colouring; resembles not a tragedy, but a gay gorgeous mask. Neither is Faust's former history alluded to, or any explanation given us of occurrences that may have intervened. It is a light scene, divided by chasms and unknown distance from that other country of gloom. Nevertheless, the latter still frowns in the back-ground; nay, rises aloft, shutting out further view, and our gay vision attains a new significance as it is painted on that canvas of storm.

We question whether it ever occurred to any English reader of Faust, that the work needed a continuation, or even admitted one. To the Germans, however, in their deeper study of a favourite poem, which also they have full means of studying, this has long been no secret; and such as have seen with what zeal most German readers cherish *Faust*, and how the younger of them will recite whole scenes of it, with a vehemence resembling that of Gil Blas and his *Figures Hibernoises*, in the streets of Oviedo, may estimate the interest excited in that country by the following Notice from the Author, published last year in his *Kunst und Alterthum*.

"*Helena. Interlude in Faust.*

"Faust's character, in the elevation to which latter refinement, working on the old rude Tradition, has raised it, represents a man who, feeling impatient and imprisoned within the limits of mere earthly existence, regards the possession of the highest knowledge, the enjoyment of the fairest blessings, as insufficient even in the slightest degree to satisfy his longing: a spirit, accordingly, which, struggling out on all sides, ever returns the more unhappy.

"This form of mind is so accordant with our modern disposition, that various persons of ability have been induced to undertake the treatment of such a subject. My manner of attempting it obtained approval: distinguished men considered the matter, and commented on my performance; all which I thankfully observed. At the same time I could not but wonder that none of those who undertook a continuation and completion of my Fragment, had lighted on the thought, which seemed so obvious, that the composition of a Second Part must necessarily elevate itself altogether away from the hampered sphere of the First, and conduct a man of such a nature into higher regions, under worthier circumstances.

"How I, for my part, had determined to essay this, lay silently before my own mind, from time to time exciting me to some progress; while, from all and each, I carefully guarded my secret, still in hope of bringing the work to the wished-for issue. Now, however, I must no longer keep back; or, in publishing my collective Endeavours, conceal any further secret from the world; to which, on the contrary, I feel myself bound to submit my whole labours, even though in a fragmentary state.

"Accordingly I have resolved that the above-named Piece, a smaller drama, complete within itself, but pertaining to the Second Part of *Faust*, shall be forthwith presented in the First Portion of my Works.

"The wide chasm between that well-known dolorous conclusion of the first part, and the entrance of an antique Grecian Heroine, is not yet overarched; meanwhile, as a preamble, my readers will accept what follows:

"The old Legend tells us, and the Puppet-play fails not to introduce the scene, that Faust, in his imperious pride of heart, required from Mephistopheles the love of the fair Helena of Greece; in which demand the other, after some reluctance, gratified him. Not to overlook so important a concern in our work, was a duty for us; and how we have endeavoured to discharge it, will be seen in this Interlude. But what may have furnished the proximate occasion of such an occurrence, and how, after manifold hindrances, our old magical Craftsman can have found means to bring back the individual Helena, in person, out of Orcus into Life, must, in this stage of the business, remain undiscovered. For the present, it is enough if our reader will admit that the real Helena may step forth, on antique tragedy-cothurnus, before her primitive abode in Sparta. We then request him to observe in what way and manner Faust will presume to court favour from this royal all-famous Beauty of the world."

To manage so unexampled a courtship will be admitted to be no easy task; for the mad hero's prayer must here be fulfilled to its largest extent, before the business can proceed a step; and the gods, it is certain, are not in the habit of annihilating time and space, even to "make two lovers happy." Our Marlowe was not ignorant of this mysterious *liaison* of Faust's: however, he slurs it over briefly, and without fronting the difficulty; Helena merely flits across the scene as an airy pageant, without speech or personality, and makes the love-sick philosopher "immortal by a kiss." Probably there are not many that would grudge Faust such immortality; we at least nowise envy him: for who does not see that this, in all human probability, is no real Helena, but only some hollow phantasm attired in her shape, while the true Daughter of Leda still dwells afar off in the inane kingdoms of Dis, and heeds not and hears not the most potent invocations of black-art? Another matter it is to call forth the frail fair one in very deed; not in form only, but in soul and life, the *same* Helena whom the Son of Atreus wedded, and for whose sake Ilion ceased to be. For Faust must behold this Wonder, not as she seemed, but as she was; and at his unearthly desire, the Past shall become Present; and the antique Time must be new-created, and give back its persons and circumstances, though so long since reingulphed in the silence of the blank by-gone Eternity! However, Mephistopheles is a cunning genius; and will not start at common obstacles. Perhaps, indeed, he is Metaphysician enough to know that Time and Space are but quiddities, not entities; *forms* of the human soul, Laws of Thought, which to us appear independent existences, but, out of our brains, have no existence whatever; in which case the whole nodus may be more of a logical cobweb, than any actual material perplexity. Let us see how he unravels it, or cuts it.

The scene is Greece; not our poor oppressed Otteman Morea, but the old heroic Hellas; for the sun again shines on Sparta, and "Tyndarus' high House" stands here bright, massive, and entire, among its mountains, as when Menelaus revisited it, wearied with his ten years of warfare, and eight of sea-roving. Helena appears in front of the Palace, with a Chorus of captive Trojan maidens. These are but Shades, we know, summoned from the deep realms of Hades, and imbodied for the nonce: but the Conjurer has so managed it, that they themselves have no consciousness of this their true and highly precarious state of existence: the intermediate three thousand years have been obliterated, or compressed into a point; and these fair figures, on revisiting the upper air, entertain not the slightest suspicion that they had ever left it, or, indeed, that any thing special had happened; save only that they had just disembarked from the Spartan ships, and been sent forward by Menelaus to provide for his reception, which is shortly to follow. All these indispensable preliminaries, it would appear, Mephistopheles has arranged with considerable success. Of the poor Shades, and their entire ignorance, he is so sure that he would not scruple to cross-question them on this very point, so ticklish for his whole enterprise; nay, cannot forbear, now and then, throwing out malicious hints to mystify Helena herself, and raise the strangest doubts as to her personal identity. Thus on one occasion, as we shall see, he reminds her of a scandal which had gone abroad of her being a *double* personage, of her living with King Proteus in Egypt at the very time when she lived with Beau Paris in Troy; and, what is more extraordinary still, of her having been dead, and married to Achilles afterwards in the Island of Leuce! Helena admits that it is the most inexplicable thing on earth; can only conjecture that "she a Vision was joined to him a vision;" and then sinks into a reverie, or swoon, in the arms of the Chorus. In this way, can the nether-world Scapin sport with the perplexed Beauty; and by sly practice make her show us the secret, which is unknown to herself!

For the present, however, there is no thought of such scruples. Helena and her maidens, far from doubting that they are real authentic denizens of this world, feel themselves in a deep embarrassment about its concerns. From the dialogue, in long Alexandrines, or choral Recitative, we soon gather that matters wear a threatening aspect. Helena salutes her paternal and nuptial mansion in such style as may beseem an erring wife, returned from so eventful an elopement; alludes with charitable lenience to her frailty; which, indeed, it would seem, was nothing but the merest accident, for she had simply gone to pay her vows, "according to sacred wont," in the temple of Cytherea, when the "Phrygian robber" seized her; and further informs us that the Immortals still foreshow to her a dubious future:

For seldom, in our swift ship, did my husband deign
To look on me; and word of comfort spake he none.
As if a-brooding mischief, there he silent sat;
Until, when steered into Eurotas' bending bay,
The first ships with their prows but kissed the land,
He rose, and said, as by the voice of gods inspired:
Here will I that my warriors, troop by troop, disbark;
I muster them, in battle-order, on the ocean strand.
But thou, go forward, up Eurotas' sacred bank,
Guiding the steeds along the flower-besprinkled space,
Till thou arrive on the fair plain where Lacedæmon,
Erewhile a broad fruit-bearing field, has piled its roofs
Amid the mountains, and sends up the smoke of hearths.
Then enter thou the high-towered Palace; call the Maids
I left at parting, and the wise old Stewardess:
With her inspect the Treasures which thy father left,
And I, in war or peace still adding, have heaped up.
Thou findest all in order standing; for it is
The prince's privilege to see, at his return,
Each household item as it was, and where it was;
For of himself the slave hath power to alter nought.

It appears, moreover, that Manelaus has given her directions to prepare for a solemn Sacrifice: the ewers, the pateras, the altar, the axe, dry wood, are all to be in readiness, only of the victim there was no mention; a circumstance from which Helena fails not to draw some rather alarming surmises. However, reflecting that all issues rest with the higher Powers, and that, in any case, irresolution and procrastination will avail her nothing, she at length determines on this grand enterprise of entering the palace, to make a general review and enters accordingly. But long before any such business could have been finished, she hastily returns with a frustrated, nay, terrified aspect; much to the astonishment of her Chorus, who pressingly inquire the cause.

HELENA (*who has left the door-leaves open, agitated.*)

Beseems not that Jove's daughter shrink with common fright,
Nor by the brief cold touch of Fear be chill'd and stunned.
Yet the Horror, which ascending, in the womb of Night,
From deeps of Chaos, rolls itself together many-shaped,
Like glowing Clouds from out the mountain's fire-throat,
In threatening ghastliness, may shake even heroes' hearts.
So have the Stygian here to-day appointed me
A welcome to my native Mansion, such that fain
From the oft-trod, long-wished-for threshold, like a guest
That has took leave, I would withdraw my steps, for ay
But no! Retreated have I to the light, nor shall
Ye farther force me, angry Powers, be who ye may,
New expiations will I use; then purified,
The blaze of the Hearth may greet the Mistress as the Lord.

PANTHALIS *the* CHORAGE.*

Discover, noble queen, to us thy handmaidens,
That wait by thee in love, what misery has befallen

* Leader of the Chorus.

HELENA.

What I have seen, ye too with your own eyes shall see,
If Night have not already sucked her Phantoms back
To the abysses of her wonder-bearing breast.
Yet, would ye know this thing, I tell it you in words.
When bent on present duty, yet with anxious thought,
I solemnly set foot in these high royal Halls,
The silent, vacant passages astounded me;
For tread of hasty footsteps nowhere met the ear,
Nor bustle as of busy menial-work the eye.
No maid comes forth to me, no Stewardess, such as
Still wont with friendly welcome to salute all guests,
But as, alone advancing, I approach the Hearth,
There, by the ashy remnant of dim outburnt coals,
Sits, crouching on the ground, up-muffled, some huge Crone;
Not as in sleep she sat, but as in drowsy muse.
With ordering voice I bid her rise; nought doubting 't was
The Stewardess the King, at parting hence, had left.
But, heedless, shrunk together, sits she motionless;
And as I chid, at last outstretched her lean right arm,
As if she beckoned me from hall and hearth away.
I turn indignant from her, and hasten out forthwith
Towards the steps whereon aloft the Thalamos
Adorned rises; and near by it the Treasure-room;
When lo! the Wonder starts abruptly from the floor;
Imperious, barring my advance, displays herself
In haggard stature, hollow bloodshot eyes; a shape
Of hideous strangeness, to perplex all sight and thought.
But I discourse to the air: for words in vain attempt
To body forth to sight the form that dwells in us.
There see herself! She ventures forward to the light!
Here we are masters till our Lord and King shall come.
The ghastly births of Night, Apollo, beauty's friend,
Disperses back to their abysses, or subdues.

(PHORCYAS *enters on the threshold, between the door-posts.*)

CHORUS.

Much have I seen, and strange, though the ringlets
Youthful and thick still wave round my temples:
Terrors a many, war and its horrors
Witnessed I once in Ilion's night,
When it fell
Thorough the clanging, cloud-covered din of
Onrushing warriors, heard I th' Immortals
Shouting in anger, heard I Bellona's
Iron-toned voice resound from without
City-wards.

Ah! the city yet stood; with its
Bulwarks; Illion safely yet
Towered; but spreading from house over
House, the flame did begirdle us;
Sea-like, red, loud, and billowy;
Hither, thither, as tempest-floods,
Over the death-circled city.

Flying, saw I, through heat and through
Gloom and glare of that fire-ocean,
Shapes of Gods in their wrathfulness,
Stalking grim, fierce, and terrible,
Giant-high, through the luridly
Flame-dyed dusk of that vapour.

Did I see it, or was it but
Terror of heart that fashioned
Forms so affrighting? Know can I
Never: but here that I view this
Horrible Thing with my own eyes,
This of a surety believe I:
Yea, I could clutch 't in my fingers
Did not, from Shape so dangerous,
Fear at a distance keep me.

Which of old Phorcys'
Daughters then art thou?
For I compare thee to
That generation.
Art thou belike, of the Graiæ,
Gray-born, one eye, and one tooth
Using alternate,
Child or descendant?

Darest thou, Haggard,
Close by such beauty,
'Fore the divine glance of
Phœbus, display thee?
But display as it pleases thee;
For the ugly he heedeth not,
As his bright eye yet never did
Look on a shadow.

But as mortals, alas for it!
Law of destiny burdens us
With the unspeakable eye-sorrow
Which such a sight, unblessed, detestable,
Doth in lovers of beauty awaken.

Nay then, hear, since thou shamelessly
Com'st forth fronting us, hear only
Curses, hear all manner of threatenings,
Out of the scornful lips of the happier
That were made by the Deities.

PHORCYAS.

Old is the saw, but high and true remains its sense,
That Shame and Beauty ne'er, together hand in hand,
Were seen pursue their journey over the earth's green path.
Deep rooted dwells an ancient hatred in these two;
So that wherever, on their way, one haps to meet
The other, each on its adversary turns his back:
Then hastens forth the faster on its separate road;
Shame all in sorrow, Beauty pert and light of mood;
Till the hollow night of Orcus catches it at length,
If age and wrinkles have not tamed it long before.
So you, ye wantons, wafted hither from strange lands,
I find in tumult, like the cranes' hoarse jingling flight,
That over our heads, in long-drawn cloud, sends down
Its creaking gabble, and tempts the silent wanderer that he look
Aloft at them a moment: but they go their way,
And he goes his; so also will it be with us.

Who then are ye? that here in Bacchanalian-wise,
Like drunk ones ye dare uproar at this Palace-gate?
Who then are ye that at the Stewardess of the King's House
Ye howl, as at the moon the crabbed brood of dogs?
Think ye 'tis hid from me what manner of thing ye are?
Ye war-begotten, fight-bred, feather-headed crew!
Lascivious crew, seducing as seduced, that waste,
In rioting, alike the soldier's and the burgher's strength!
Here seeing you gathered, seems as a cicada-swarm
Had lighted, covering the herbage of the fields.
Consumers ye of other's thrift, ye greedy-mouthed
Quick squanderers of fruits men gain by tedious toil;
Cracked market-ware, stol'n, bought, and bartered troop of slaves!

We have thought it right to give so much of these singular expositions and altercations, in the words, as far as might be, of the parties themselves; happy, could we, in any measure, have transfused the broad, yet rich and chaste simplicity of these long iambics; or imitated the tone as we have done the metre, of that choral song; its rude earnestness, and tortuous, awkward-looking, artless strength, as we have done its dactyls and anapæsts. The task was no easy one; and we remain, as might have been expected, little contented with our efforts; having, indeed, nothing to boast of, except a sincere fidelity to the original. If the reader, through such distortion, can obtain any glimpse of *Helena* itself, he will not only pardon us, but thank us. To our own minds, at least, there is everywhere a strange, piquant, quite peculiar, charm in these imitations of the old Grecian style; a dash of the ridiculous, if we might say so, is blended with the sublime, yet blended with it softly, and only to temper its austerity: for often, so graphic is the delinea tion, we could almost feel as if a vista were opened through the long gloomy distance of ages, and we with our modern eyes and modern levity, beheld afar off, in clear light, the very figures of that old grave time; saw them again living in their old antiquarian costume and environment, and heard them audibly discourse in a dialect which had long been dead. Of all this no man is more master than Goethe; as a modern-antique, his *Iphigenie* must be considered unrivalled in poetry. A similar, thoroughly classical spirit will be found in this First Part of *Helena;* yet the manner of the two pieces is essentially different. Here, we should say, we are more reminded of Sophocles, perhaps of Æschylus, than of Euripides: it is more rugged, copious, energetic, inartificial; a still more ancient style. How very primitive, for instance, are Helena and Phorcyas in their whole deportment here! How frank and downright in speech; above all, how minute and specific; no glimpse of "philosophical culture;" no such thing as a "general idea;" thus, every different object seems a new unknown one, and requires to be separately stated. In like manner, what can be more honest and edifying than the chant of the Chorus? With what inimitable *naïveté* they recur to the sack of Troy, and endeavour to convince themselves that they do actually see this "horrible Thing;" then lament the law of Destiny which dooms them to such "unspeakable eye-sorrow;" and, finally, break forth into sheer cursing; to all which, Phorcyas answers in the like free and plain-spoken fashion.

But to our story. This hard-tempered and so dreadfully ugly old lady, the reader cannot help suspecting, at first sight, to be some cousin-german of Mephistopheles, or, indeed, that great Actor of all Work himself; which latter suspicion the devilish nature of the beldame, by degrees, confirms into a moral certainty. There is a sarcastic malice in the "wise old Stewardess" which cannot be mistaken. Meanwhile the Chorus and the beldame indulge still further in mutual abuse; she upbraiding them with their giddiness and wanton disposition; they chanting unabatedly her extreme deficiency in personal charms. Helena, however, interposes; and the old Gorgon, pretending that she has not till now recognised the stranger to be her mistress, smooths herself into gentleness, affects the greatest humanity, and even appeals to her for protection against the insolence of these young ones. But wicked Phorcyas is only waiting her opportunity; still neither unwilling to wound, nor afraid to strike. Helena, to expel some unpleasant vapours of doubt, is reviewing her past history, in concert with Phorcyas; and observes that the latter had been appointed Stewardess by Menelaus, on his return from his Cretan expedition to Sparta. No sooner is Sparta mentioned, than the crone, with an officious air of helping out the story, adds:

Which thou forsookest, Ilion's tower-encircled town
Preferring, and the unexhausted joys of Love.

HELENA.

Remind me not of joys; an all too heavy wo's
Infinitude soon follow'd, crushing breast and heart.

PHORCYAS.

But I have heard thou livest on earth a double life;
In Ilion seen, and seen the while in Egypt too.

HELENA.

Confound not so the weakness of my weary sense;
Here even, who or what I am, I know it not.

PHORCYAS.

Then I have heard how, from the hollow Realm of Shades,
Achilles, too, did fervently unite himself to thee;
Thy earlier love reclaiming, spite of all Fate's laws.

HELENA.

To him the Vision, I a Vision joined myself:
It was a dream, the very words may teach us this.
But I am faint; and to myself a Vision grow.
(*Sinks into the arms of one division of the Chorus.*)

CHORUS.

Silence! silence!
Evil-eyed, evil-tongued, thou!
Thro' so shrivelled-up, one-tooth'd a
Mouth, what good can come from that
Throat of horrors detestable—

—In which style they continue musically rating her, till "Helena has recovered, and again stands in the middle of the Chorus;" when Phorcyas, with the most wheedling air, hastens to greet her, in a new sort of verse, as if nothing whatever had happened:

PHORCYAS.

Issues forth from passing cloud the sun of this bright day;
If when veil'd she so could charm us, now her beams in splendour blind.
As the world doth look before thee, in such gentle wise thou look'st.
Let them call me so unlovely, what is lovely know I well.

HELENA.

Come so wavering from the Void which in that faintness circled me,
Glad I were to rest again, a space: so weary are my limbs.
Yet it well becometh queens, all mortals it becometh well,
To possess their hearts in patience, and await what can betide.

PHORCYAS.

Whilst thou standest in thy greatness, in thy beauty here,
Says thy look that thou commandest: what command'st thou? Speak it out.

HELENA.

To conclude your quarrel's idle loitering be prepared:
Haste, arrange the Sacrifice, the King commanded me.

PHORCYAS.

All is ready in the Palace, bowl and tripod, sharp-ground axe;
For besprinkling, for befuming: now the Victim let us see.

HELENA.

This the King appointed not.

PHORCYAS.

Spoke not of this? O word of wo!

HELENA.

What strange sorrow overpowers thee?

PHORCYAS.

Queen, 'tis thou he meant.

HELENA.

PHORCYAS.

And these.

CHORUS.

O wo! O wo!

PHORCYAS

Thou fallest by the axe's stroke.

HELENA.

Horrible, yet look'd for: hapless I!

PHORCYAS.

Inevitable seems it me.

CHORUS.

Ah, and us? What will become of us?

PHORCYAS.

She dies a noble death:
Ye, on the high Beam within that bears the rafters and the roof,
As in birding-time so many woodlarks, in a row, shall sprawl.

(HELENA *and* CHORUS *stand astounded and terror-struck; in expressive, well-concerted grouping.*)

PHORCYAS.

Poor spectres!—All like frozen statues thêre ye stand,
In fright to leave the Day which not belongs to you.
No man or spectre, more than you, is fond to quit
The Upper Light; yet rescue, respite finds not one:
All know it, all believe it, few delight in it.
Enough, 't is over with you! And so let's to work.

How the cursed old beldame enjoys the agony of these poor Shades: nay, we suspect, she is laughing in her sleeve at the very classicism of this drama, which she herself has contrived, and is even now helping to enact! Observe, she has quitted her octameter trochaics again, and taken to plain blank verse; a sign, perhaps, that she is getting weary of the whole classical concern! But however this may be, she now claps her hands; whereupon certain distorted dwarf figures appear at the door, and with great speed and agility, at her order, bring forth the sacrificial apparatus; on which she fails not to descant demonstratively, explaining the purpose of the several articles as they are successively fitted up before her. Here is the "gold-horned" altar, the "axe glittering over its silver edge:" then there must be "water-urns to wash the black blood's defilement," and a "precious mat," to kneel on, for the victim is to be beheaded queenlike. On all hands, mortal horror! But Phorcyas hints darkly that there is still a way of escape left; this, of course, every one is in deepest eagerness to learn. Here, one would think, she might for once come to the point without digression; but Phorcyas has her own way of stating a fact. She thus commences:

PHORCYAS.

Whoso, collecting store of wealth, at home abides
To parget in due season his high dwelling's walls,
And prudent guard his roof from inroad of the rain,
With him, through long still years of life, it shall be well.
But he who lightly, in his folly, bent to rove,
O'ersteps with wand'ring foot his threshold's sacred line,
Will find, at his return, the ancient place, indeed
Still there, but else all alter'd, if not overthrown.

HELENA.

Why these trite saws? Thou wert to teach us, not reprove.

PHORCYAS.

Historical it is, is nowise a reproof.
Sea-roving, steer'd King Menelaus, brisk from bay to bay;
Descended on all ports and isles, a plundering foe,
And still came back with booty, which yet moulders here
Then by the walls of Ilion spent he ten long years;
How many in his homeward voyage were hard to know.
But all this while how stands it here with Tyndarus'
High house? How stands it with his own domains around?

HELENA.

Is love of railing, then, so interwoven with thee,
That thus, except to chide, thou canst not move thy lips?

PHORCYAS.

So many years forsaken stood the mountain glen;
Which, north from Sparta, towards the higher land ascends
Behind Taygetus; where, as yet a merry brook,
Eurotas gurgles on, and then, along our Vale,
In sep'rate streams abroad outflowing feeds your Swans.
There, backwards in the rocky hills, a daring race
Have fix'd themselves, forth issuing from Cimmerian Night;
An inexpugnable stronghold have piled aloft,
From which they harry land and people as they please.

HELENA.

How could they? All impossible it seems to me.

PHORCYAS.

Enough of time they had! 'tis haply twenty years.

HELENA.

Is One the Master? Are there Robbers many? leagued?

PHORCYAS.

Not Robbers these: yet many, and the Master One.
Of him I say no ill, though hither too he came.
What might not he have took? yet did content himself
With some small Present, so he called it, Tribute, not.

HELENA.

How looks he?

PHORCYAS.

Nowise ill! To me he pleasant look'd.
A jocund, gallant, hardy, handsome man it is,
And rational in speech, as of the Greeks are few.
We call the folk Barbarian; yet I question much
If one there be so cruel, as at Ilion
Full many of our best heroes man-devouring were.
I do respect his greatness, and confide in him.
And for his Tower! This with your own eyes ye should see:
Another thing it is than clumsy boulder-work,
Such as our Fathers, nothing scrupling, huddled up,
Cyclopean, and like Cyclops-builders, one rude crag
On other rude crags tumbling: in that Tow'r of theirs
'T is plumb and level all, and done by square and rule.
Look on it from without! Heav'nward it soars on high,
So strait, so tight of joint, and mirror-smooth as steel:
To clamber there—Nay, even your very Thought slides down,
And then, within, such courts, broad spaces, all around,
With masonry encompass'd of every sort and use
There have ye arches, archlets, pillars, pillarlets,
Balconies, galleries, for looking out and in,
And coats of arms.

CHORUS.

Of arms? What mean'st thou?

PHORCYAS.

Ajax bore
A twisted Snake on his shield, as ye yourselves have seen.
The Seven also before Thebes bore carved work
Each on his Shield; devices rich and full of Sense:
There saw ye moon and stars of the nightly heaven's vault,
And goddesses, and heroes, ladders, torches, swords,
And dangerous tools, such as in storm o'erfall good towns.
Escutcheons of like sort our heroes also bear:

There see ye lions, eagles, claws besides and bills,
The buffalo-horns, and wings, and roses, peacock's tails;
And bandelets, gold and black and silver, blue and red.
Such like are there uphung in Halls, row after row;
In halls, so large, so lofty, boundless as the World;
There might ye dance!

CHORUS.

Ha! Tell us, are there dancers there?

PHORCYAS.

The best on earth! A golden-haired, fresh, younker band,
They breathe of youth; Paris alone so breathed when to
Our Queen he came too near.

HELENA.

Thou quite dost lose
The tenor of thy story: say me thy last word.

PHORCYAS.

Thyself wilt say it: say in earnest audibly, Yes!
Next moment, I surround thee with that Tow'r.

The step is questionable: for is not this Phorcyas a person of the most suspicious character; or rather, is it not certain that she is a Turk in grain, and will almost, of a surety, go how it may, turn good into bad? And yet, what is to be done? A trumpet, said to be that of Menelaus, sounds in the distance; at which the Chorus shrink together in increased terror. Phorcyas coldly reminds them of Deiphobus, with his slit nose, as a small token of Menelaus' turn of thinking on these matters; supposes, however, that there is now nothing for it but to wait the issue, and die with propriety. Helena has no wish to die either with propriety or impropriety; she pronounces, though with a faltering resolve, the definitive Yes. A burst of joy breaks from the Chorus; thick fog rises all round; in the midst of which, as we learn from their wild tremulous chant, they feel themselves hurried through the air: Eurotas is swept from sight, and the cry of its Swans fades ominously away in the distance; for now, as we suppose, "Tyndarus' high House," with all its appendages, is rushing back into the depths of the Past; old *Lacedæmon* has again become new *Misetra*; only Taygetus, with another name, remains unchanged; and the King of Rivers feeds among his sedges quite a different race of Swans than those of Leda! The mist is passing away, but yet, to the horror of the Chorus, no clear daylight returns. Dim masses rise round them: Phorcyas has vanished. Is it a castle? Is it a cavern? They find themselves in the "Interior Court of the Tower, surrounded with rich fantastic buildings of the middle ages!"

If, hitherto, we have moved along, with considerable convenience, over ground singular enough, indeed, yet, the nature of it once understood, affording firm footing and no unpleasant scenery, we come now to a strange mixed element, in which it seems as if neither walking, swimming, nor even flying, could rightly avail us. We have cheerfully admitted, and honestly believed, that Helena and her Chorus were Shades; but now they appear to be changing into mere Ideas, mere Metaphors, or poetic Thoughts! Faust, too, for *he*, as every one sees, must be lord of this Fortress, is a much altered man since we last met him. Nay, sometimes we could fancy he were only *acting a part* on this occasion; were a mere mummer, representing not so much his own natural *personality*, as some shadow and impersonation of his *history;* not so much his own Faustship, as the tradition of Faust's adventures, and the Genius of the People among whom this took its rise. For, indeed, he has strange gifts of flying through the air, and living, in apparent friendship and contentment, with mere Eidolons; and, being excessively reserved withal, he becomes not a little enigmatic. In fact, our whole "Interlude" changes its character at this point: the Greek style passes abruptly into the Spanish; at one bound we have left the *Seven before Thebes*, and got into the *Vida es Sueño*. The action, too, becomes more and more typical; or rather, we should say, half-typical; for it will neither hold rightly together as allegory nor as matter of fact.

Thus do we see ourselves hesitating on the verge of a wondrous region, "neither sea nor good dry land;" full of shapes and musical tones, but all dim, fluctuating, unsubstantial, chaotic. Danger there is that the critic may require "both oar and sail;" nay, it will be well if, like that other great Traveller, he meet not some vast vacuity, where, all unawares,

Fluttering his pennons vain, plumb down he drop
Ten thousand fathom deep . . . .

and so keep falling till

The strong rebuff of some tumultuous cloud,
Instinct with fire and nitre, hurry him
As many miles aloft . . . .

—Meaning, probably, that he is to be "blown up" by nonplused and justly exasperated Review-reviewers!—Nevertheless, unappalled by these possibilities, we venture forward into this impalpable Limbo; and must endeavour to render such account of the "sensible species," and "ghosts of defunct bodies," we may meet there, as shall be moderately satisfactory to the reader.

In the little notice from the Author, quoted above, we were bid specially to observe in what way and manner Faust would presume to court this World's-beauty. We must say, his style of gallantry seems to us of the most chivalrous and high-flown description, if, indeed, it is not a little *euphuistic.* In their own eyes, Helena and her Chorus, encircled in this Gothic Court, appear, for some minutes, no better than captives; but, suddenly issuing from galleries and portals, and descending the stairs in stately procession, are seen a numerous suite of Pages, whose gay habiliments and red downy cheeks are greatly admired by the Chorus: these bear with them a throne and canopy, with footstools and cushions, and every other necessary apparatus of royalty; the portable machine, as we gather from the Chorus, is soon put together, and Helena, being reverently beckoned into the same, is thus forthwith constituted Sovereign of the whole Establishment. To herself such royalty still seems a little dubious; but no sooner have the Pages, in long train, fairly descended, than "Faust appears above, on the stairs, in knightly court-dress of the middle ages, and with deliberate dignity comes down," astonishing the poor "feather-headed" Chorus with the gracefulness of his deportment and his more than human beauty. He leads with him a culprit in fetters; and, by way of introduction, explains to Helena that this man, Lynceus, has deserved death by his misconduct; but that to her, as Queen of the Castle, must appertain the right of dooming or of pardoning him. The crime of Lynceus is, indeed, of an extraordinary nature: he was Warder of the Tower; but now, though gifted, as his name imports, with the keenest vision, he has failed in warning Faust that so august a visitor was approaching, and thus occasioned the most dreadful breach of politeness. Lynceus pleads guilty: quick-sighted as a lynx, in usual cases, he has been blinded with excess of light, in this instance. While looking towards the orient at the "course of morning," he noticed "a sun rise wonderfully in the south," and, all his senses taken captive by such surpassing beauty, he no longer knew his right hand from his left, or could move a limb, or utter a word, to announce her arrival. Under these peculiar circumstances, Helena sees room for extending the royal prerogative; and, after expressing unfeigned regret at this so fatal influence of her charms over the whole male sex, dismisses the Warder with a reprieve. We must beg our readers to keep an eye on this Innamorato; for there may be meaning in him. Here is the pleading, which produced so fine an effect given in his own words:

Let me kneel and let me view her,
Let me live, or let me die,
Slave to this high woman, truer
Than a bondsman born, am I.

Watching o'er the course of morning,
Eastward, as I mark it run,
Rose there, all the sky adorning,
Strangely in the South a sun.

Draws my look towards those places,
Not the valley, not the height,
Not the earth's or heaven's spaces;
She alone the queen of light.

Eyesight truly hath been lent me,
Like the lynx on highest tree;
Boots not; for amaze hath shent me:
Do I dream, or do I see?

Knew I aught? or could I ever
Think of tow'r or bolted gate?
Vapours waver, vapours sever,
Such a goddess comes in state!

Eye and heart I must surrender
Drown'd as in a radiant sea;
That high creature with her splendour
Blinding all hath blinded me.

I forgot the warder's duty;
Trumpet, challenge, word of call:
Chain me, threaten: sure this beauty
Stills thy anger, saves her thrall.

Save him accordingly she did; but no sooner is he dismissed, and Faust has made a remark on the multitude of "arrows" which she is darting forth on all sides, than Lynceus returns in a still madder humour. "Re-enter Lynceus with a chest, and men carrying other chests behind him."

LYNCEUS.

Thou see'st me, Queen, again advance,
The wealthy begs of thee one glance;
He look'd at thee, and feels e'er since
As beggar poor, and rich as prince.

What was I erst? What am I grown?
What have I meant, or done, or known?
What boots the sharpest force of eyes?
Back from thy throne it baffled flies.

From Eastward marching came we on,
And soon the West was lost and won;
A long broad army forth we pass'd,
The foremost knew not of the last.

The first did fall, the second stood,
The third hew'd in with falchion good;
And still the next had prowess more,
Forgot the thousands slain before.

We stormed along, we rushed apace,
The masters we from place to place.
And where I lordly ruled to-day,
To-morrow another did rob and slay.

We look; our choice was quickly made;
This snatch'd with him the fairest Maid,
That seized the Steer for burden bent,
The horses all and sundry went.

But I did love apart to spy
The rarest things could meet the eye:
Whate'er in others' hands I saw,
That was for me but chaff and straw.

For treasures did I keep a look,
My keen eyes pierced to every nook;
Into all pockets I could see,
Transparent each strong-box to me.

And heaps of gold I gained this way,
And precious Stones of clearest ray:
Now where's the Diamond meet to shine?
'Tis meet alone for breast like thine.

So let the Pearl from depths of sea,
In curious stringlets wave on thee:
The Ruby for some covert seeks,
'Tis paled by redness of thy cheeks.

And so the richest treasure's brought
Before thy throne, as best it ought;
Beneath thy feet here let me lay
The fruit of many a bloody fray.

So many chests we now do bear;
More chests I have, and finer ware:
Think me but to be near thee worth
Whole treasure-vaults I empty forth.

For scarcely art thou hither sent,
All hearts and wills to thee are bent;
Our riches, reason, strength, we must
Before the loveliest lay as dust.

All this I reckon'd great, and mine,
Now small I reckon it, and thine.
I thought it worthy, high, and good;
'Tis naught, poor, and misunderstood.

So dwindles what my glory was,
A heap of mown and wither'd grass:
What worth it had, and now does lack,
O, with one kind look, give it back!

FAUST.

Away! away: take back the bold-earn'd load,
Not blamed indeed, but also not rewarded.
Her's is already whatsoe'er our Tower
Of costliness conceals. Go heap me treasures
On treasures, yet with Order; let the blaze
Of Pomp unspeakable appear; the ceilings

Gem-fretted, shine like skies; a Paradise
Of lifeless life create. Before her feet
Unfolding quick, let flow'ry carpet roll
Itself from flow'ry carpet, that her step
May light on softness, and her eye meet nought
But splendour blinding only not the Gods.

LYNCEUS.

Small is what our Lord doth say;
Servants do it; 'tis but play:
For o'er all we do or dream
Will this Beauty reign supreme.
Is not all our host grown tame?
Every sword is blunt and lame.
To a form of such a mould
Sun himself is dull and cold:
To the richness of that face,
What is beauty, what is grace,
Loveliness we saw or thought?
All is empty, all is nought.

And herewith *exit* Lynceus, and we see no more of him! We have said that we thought there might be method in this madness. In fact, the allegorical, or at least fantastical and figurative, character of the whole action is growing more and more decided every moment. Helena, we must conjecture, is, in the course of this her real historical intrigue with Faust, to present, at the same time, some dim adumbration of Grecian Art, and its flight to the Northern Nations, when driven by stress of War from its own country. Faust's Tower will, in this case, afford not only a convenient station for *lifting black-mail* over the neighbouring district, but a cunning, though vague and fluctuating, emblem of the Product of Teutonic Mind; the Science, Art, Institutions of the Northmen, of whose Spirit and Genius he himself may in some degree become the representative. In this way, the extravagant homage and admiration paid to Helena are not without their meaning. The manner of her arrival, enveloped as she was in thick clouds, and frightened onwards by hostile trumpets, may also have more or less propriety. And who is Lynceus, the mad Watchman? We cannot but suspect him of being a Schoolman Philosopher, or School Philosophy itself, in disguise; and that this wonderful "march" of his has a covert allusion to the great "march of intellect," which did march in those old ages, though only at "ordinary time." We observe, the military, one after the other, all fell; for discoverers, like other men, must die; but "still the next had prowess more," and forgot the thousands that had sunk in clearing the way for him. However, Lynceus, in his love of plunder, did not take "the fairest maid," nor "the steer" fit for burden, but rather jewels and other rare articles of value; in which quest his high power of eyesight proved of great service to him. Better had it been, perhaps, to have done as others did, and seized "the fairest maid," or even the "steer" fit for burden, or one of the "horses" which were in such request: for, when he quitted practical Science and the philosophy of Life, and addicted himself to curious subtilties and Metaphysical crotchets, what did it avail him? At the first glance of the Grecian beauty, he found that it was "naught, poor, and misunderstood." His extraordinary obscuration of vision on Helena's approach; his narrow escape from death, on that account, at the hands of Faust; his pardon by the fair Greek; his subsequent magnanimous offer to her, and discourse with his master on the subject,—might give rise to various considerations. But we must not loiter, questioning the strange Shadows of that strange country, who, besides, are apt to mystify one. Our nearest business is to get across it: we again proceed.

Whoever or whatever Faust and Helena may be, they are evidently fast rising into high favour with each other; as, indeed, from so generous a gallant, and so fair a dame, was to be anticipated. She invites him to sit with her on the throne, so instantaneously acquired by force of her charms; to which graceful proposal he, after kissing her hand in knightly wise, fails not to accede. The courtship now advances apace. Helena admires the dialect of Lynceus, and how "one word seemed to kiss the other," for the Warder, as we saw, speaks in doggerel; and she cannot but wish that she also had some such talent. Faust assures her that nothing is more easy than this same practice of rhyme: it is but speaking right from the heart, and the rest follows of course. Withal, he proposes that they should make a trial of it themselves. The experiment succeeds to mutual satisfaction: for not only can they two build the lofty rhyme, in concert, with all convenience, but, in the course of a page or two of such crambo, many love-tokens come to light; nay, we find by the Chorus, that the wooing has well nigh reached a happy end: at least, the two are "sitting near and nearer each other,—shoulder on shoulder, knee by knee, hand in hand, they are swaying over the throne's upcushioned lordliness;" which, surely, are promising symptoms.

Such ill-timed dalliance is abruptly disturbed by the entrance of Phorcyas, now, as ever, a messenger of evil, with malignant tidings that Menelaus is at hand, with his whole force, to Storm the Castle, and ferociously avenge his new injuries. An immense "explosion of signals from the towers, of trumpets, clarions, military music, and the march of numerous armies," confirms the news. Faust however, treats the matter coolly; chides the unceremonious trepidation of Phorcyas, and summons his men of war; who accordingly enter, steel-clad, in military pomp, and quitting their battalions, gather round him to take his orders. In a wild Pindaric ode, delivered with due emphasis, he directs them not so much how they are to conquer Menelaus, whom doubtless he knows to be a sort of dream, as how they are respectively to manage and partition the Country, they shall hereby acquire. Germanus is to have "the bays of Corinth;" while "Achaia, with its hundred dells," is recommended to the care of Goth; the host of the Franks must go towards Elis; Messene is to be the Saxon's share; and Normann is to clear the seas, and make Argolis great. Sparta, however, is to continue the territory of Helena, and be queen and patroness of these inferior Dukedoms. In all this, are we to trace some faint changeful shadow of the National Character, and respective Intellectual Performance of the several European tribes? Or, perhaps, of the real History of the Middle Ages; the irruption of the northern swarms, issuing, like Faust and his air-warriors, "from Cimmerian Night," and spreading over so many fair regions? Perhaps of both, and of more; perhaps properly of neither: for the whole has a chameleon character, changing hue as we look on it. However, be this as it may, the Chorus cannot sufficiently admire Faust's strategic faculty; and the troops march off, without speech indeed, but evidently in the highest spirits. He himself concludes with another rapid dithyrambic, describing the Peninsula of Greece, or rather, perhaps, typically the Region of true Poesy, "kissed by the sea-waters," and "knit to the last mountain-branch" of the firm land. There is a wild glowing fire in these two odes; a musical indistinctness, yet enveloping a rugged, keen sense, which, were the gift of rhyme so common as Faust thinks it, we should have pleasure in presenting to our readers. Again and again, we think of Calderon and his *Life a Dream.*

Faust, as he resumes his seat by Helena, observes that "she is sprung from the highest gods, and belongs to the first world alone. It is not meet that bolted towers should encircle her; and near by Sparta, over the hills, "Arcadia blooms in eternal strength of youth, a blissful abode for them two." "Let thrones pass into groves; Arcadianly free be such felicity!" No sooner said, than done. Our Fortress, we suppose, rushes asunder like a Palace of Air, for, "*the scene altogether changes. A series of Grottoes now are shut in by close Bowers. Shady Grove, to the foot of the Rocks which encircle the place. Faust and Helena are not seen. The Chorus, scattered around, lie sleeping.*"

In Arcadia, the business grows wilder than ever. Phorcyas, who has now become wonderfully civil, and, notwithstanding her ugliness, stands on the best footing with the poor light-headed Cicada-Swarm of a Chorus, awakes them to hear and see the wonders that have happened so shortly. It appears, too, that there are certain "Bearded Ones" (we suspect, Devils) waiting with anxiety, "sitting watchful there below," to see the issue of this extraordinary transaction; but of these Phorcyas gives her silly woman no hint whatever. She tells them, in glib phrase, what great things are in the wind. Faust and Helena have been happier than mortals in these grottoes. Phorcyas, who was in waiting, gradually glided away, seeking "roots, moss, and rinds," on household duty bent, and so "they two remained alone."

CHORUS.

Talk'st as if within those grottoes lay whole tracts of country,
Wood and meadow, rivers, lakes: what tales thou palm'st on us!

PHORCYAS.

Sure enough, ye foolish creatures! These are unexplored recesses;
Hall runs out on hall, spaces there on spaces: these I musing traced.
But at once re-echoes from within a peal of laughter:
Peeping in, what is it? Leaps a boy from mother's breast to Father's,
From the Father to the Mother: such a fondling, such a dandling,
Foolish Love's caressing, teasing; cry of jest, and shriek of pleasure,
In their turn do stun me quite.
Naked, without wings a Genius, Faun in humour without coarseness,
Springs he sportful on the ground; but the ground reverberating,
Darts him up to airy heights; and at the third, the second gambol,
Touches he the vaulted Roof.

Frightened cries the Mother: Bound away, away, and as thou pleasest,
But, my Son, beware of Flying; wings nor power of flight are thine.
And the Father thus advises: in the Earth resides the virtue
Which so fast doth send thee upwards; touch but with thy toe the surface,
Like the earth-born old Antæus, straightway thou art strong again.
And so skips he, hither, thither, on these jagged rocks; from summit
Still to summit, all about, like stricken ball rebounding, springs.

But at once in cleft of some rude cavern sinking as he vanished,
And so seems it we have lost him. Mother mourning, Father cheers her,
Shrug my shoulders I, and look about me. But again, behold, what vision!
Are there treasures lying here concealed? There he is again, and garments
Glittering, flower-bestriped has on.

Tassels waver from his arms, about his bosom flutter breastknots,
In his hand the golden Lyre; wholly like a little Phœbus,
Steps he light of heart upon the beetling cliffs: astonished stand we,
And the Parents, in their rapture, fly into each other's arms.
For what glittering 's that about his head? Were hard to say what glitters,
Whether Jewels and gold, or Flame of all-subduing strength of soul.
And with such a bearing moves he, in himself this boy announces
Future Master of all Beauty, whom the Melodies Eternal
Do inform through every fibre; and forthwith so shall ye hear him,
And forthwith so shall ye see him, to your uttermost amazement.

The Chorus suggest, in their simplicity, that this elastic little urchin may have some relationship to the "Son of Maia," who, in old times, whisked himself so nimbly out of his swaddling clothes, and stole the "Sea-ruler's trident" and "Hephæstos' tongs," and various other articles before he was well span-long. But Phorcyas declares all this to be superannuated fable, unfit for modern uses. And now, "*a beautiful, purely melodious music of stringed instruments resounds from the Cave. All listen, and soon appear deeply moved. It continues playing in full tone;*" while Euphorion, in person, makes his appearance, "*in the costume above described;*" larger of stature, but no less frolicsome and tuneful.

Our readers are aware that this Euphorion, the offspring of Northern Character wedded to Grecian Culture, frisks it here not without reference to Modern Poesy, which had a birth so precisely similar. Sorry are we that we cannot follow him through these fine warblings and trippings on the light fantastic toe: to our ears there is a quick, pure, small-toned music in them, as perhaps of elfin bells when the Queen of Faery rides by moonlight. It is, in truth, a graceful emblematic dance, this little life of Euphorion; full of meanings and half-meanings. The history of Poetry, traits of individual Poets; the Troubadours, the Three Italians; glimpses of all things, full vision of nothing! Euphorion grows rapidly, and passes from one pursuit to another. Quitting his boyish gambols, he takes to dancing and romping with the Chorus; and this in a style of tumult which rather dissatisfies Faust. The wildest and coyest of these damsels he seizes with avowed intent of snatching a kiss; but, alas, she resists, and still more singular, "*flashes up in flame into the air:*" inviting him, perhaps in mockery, to follow her, and "catch his vanished purpose." Euphorion shakes off the remnants of the flame, and now, in a wilder humour, mounts on the crags, begins to talk of courage and battle; higher and higher he rises, till the Chorus see him on the topmost cliff, shining "in harness as for victory;" and yet, though at such a distance, they still hear his tones, neither is his figure diminished in their eyes; which indeed, as they observe, always is, and should be, the case with "sacred Poesy," though it mounts heavenward, farther and farther, till it "glitter like the fairest star." But Euphorion's life-dance is near ending. From his high peak, he catches the sound of war, and fires at it, and longs to mix in it, let Chorus, and Mother, and Father say what they will.

EUPHORION.

And hear ye thunders on the ocean,
And thunders roll from tower and wall,
And host with host in fierce commotion,
See mixing at the trumpet's call:
And to die in strife
Is the law of life,
That is certain once for all.

HELENA, FAUST, *and* CHORUS.

What a horror! spoken madly!
Wilt thou die? then what must I?

EUPHORION.

Shall I view it, safe and gladly?
No! to share it will I hie.

HELENA, FAUST, *and* CHORUS.

Fatal are such haughty things,
War is for the stout.

EUPHORION.

Ha!—and a pair of wings
Folds itself out!
Thither! I must! I must!
'T is my hest to fly!

(*He casts himself into the air: his Garments support him for a moment; his Head radiates, a Train of Light follows him.*)

CHORUS.

Icarus! earth and dust!
O, wo! thou mount'st too high.

(*A beautiful Youth rushes down at the feet of the Parents; you fancy you recognise in the dead a well-known Form;* but the bodily part instantly disappears; the gold Crownlet mounts like a comet to the sky, Coat, Mantle, and Lyre, are left lying.*)

HELENA *and* FAUST.

Joy soon changes to wo,
And mirth to heaviest moan.

EUPHORION'S *voice* (*from beneath.*)

Let me not to realms below
Descend, O mother, alone!

The prayer is soon granted. The Chorus chant a dirge over his remains, and then:

HELENA (*to* FAUST.)

A sad old saying proves itself again in me,
Good hap with beauty hath no long abode.
So with love's Band is life's asunder rent:
Lamenting both, I clasp thee in my arms
Once more, and bid thee painfully farewell.
Persephoneia take my boy, and with him me.

(*She embraces Faust; her Body melts away; Garment and Veil remain in his arms.*)

PHORCYAS (*to* FAUST.)

Hold fast, what now alone remains to thee
That Garment quit not. They are tugging there,
These Demons at the skirt of it; would fain
To the Nether Kingdoms take it down. Hold fast!
The goddess is it not, whom thou hast lost,
Yet godlike is it. See thou use aright
The priceless high bequest, and soar aloft:
'T will lift thee away above the common world,
Far up to Æther, so thou canst endure.
We meet again, far, very far from hence.

(HELENA'S *Garments unfold into Clouds, encircle* FAUST; *raise him aloft and float away with him.*)

(PHORCYAS *picks up* EUPHORION'S *Coat, Mantle, and Lyre from the Ground, comes forward into the Proscenium, holds these Remains aloft, and says:*)

Well, fairly found be happily won!
'T is true, the Flame is lost and gone:
But well for us we have still this stuff!
A gala-dress to dub our poets of merit,
And make guild-brethren snarl and cuff;
And can't they borrow the Body and Spirit
At least, I'll lend them Clothes enough.
(*Sits down in the Proscenium at the foot of a pillar.*)

The rest of the personages are now speedily disposed of. Panthalis, the Leader of the Chorus, and the only one of them who has shown any glimmerings of Reason, or of aught beyond mere sensitive life, mere love of Pleasure and fear of Pain, proposes that, being now delivered from the soul-confusing spell of the "Thessalian Hag," they should forthwith return to Hades, to bear Helena company. But none will volunteer with her; so she goes herself. The Chorus have lost their taste for Asphodel Meadows, and playing so subordinate a part in Orcus: they prefer abiding in the Light of Day, though, indeed, under rather peculiar circumstances; being no longer "Persons," they say, but a kind of Occult Qualities, as we conjecture, and Poetic Inspirations, residing in various natural objects. Thus, one division become a sort of invisible Hamadryads, and have their being in Trees, and their joy in the various movements, beauties

* It is perhaps in reference to this phrase, that certain sagacious critics among the Germans have hit upon the wonderful discovery of Euphorion being—Lord Byron! A fact, if it is one, which curiously verifies the author's prediction in this passage. But unhappily, while we fancy that we recognise in the dead a well-known form, "the bodily part instantly disappears;" and the keenest critic finds that he can see no deeper into a millstone than another man. Some *allusion* to our English Poet there is, or may be, here and in the page that precedes, and the page that follows; but Euphorion is no image of any person: least of all, one would think, of George Lord Byron.

and products of trees. A second change into Echoes; a third, into the Spirit of Brooks; and a fourth take up their abode in Vineyards, and delight in the manufacture of Wine. No sooner have these several parties made up their minds, than the *Curtain falls;* and Phorcyas "*in the Proscenium rises in gigantic size; but steps down from her cothurni, lays her Mask and Veil aside, and shows herself as* MEPHISTOPHELES, *in order, so far as may be necessary, to comment on the piece, by way of Epilogue.*"

Such is *Helena* the *interlude in Faust.* We have all the desire in the world to hear Mephisto's Epilogue: but far be it from us to take the word out of so gifted a mouth! In the way of commentary on *Helena*, we ourselves have little more to add. The reader sees, in general, that Faust is to save himself from the straits and fetters of Worldly Life in the loftier regions of Art, or in that temper of mind by which alone those regions can be reached, and permanently dwelt in. Further, also, that this doctrine is to be stated emblematically and parabolically; so that it might seem as if, in Goethe's hands, the History of Faust, commencing among the realities of every-day existence, superadding to these certain spiritual agencies, and passing into a more aerial character as it proceeds, may fade away, at its termination, into a phantasmagoric region, where symbol and thing signified are no longer clearly distinguished; and thus the final result be curiously and significantly indicated, rather than directly exhibited. With regard to the special purport of Euphorion, Lynceus, and the rest, we have nothing more to say at present; nay, perhaps we may have already said too much. For it must not be forgotten by the commentator, and will not, of a surety, be forgotten by Mephistopheles, whenever he may please to deliver his Epilogue, that *Helena* is not an Allegory, but a Phantasmagory; not a type of one thing, but a vague, fluctuating, fitful adumbration of many. This is no Picture painted on canvas, with mere material colours, and steadfastly abiding our scrutiny; but rather it is like the Smoke of a Wizard's Cauldron, in which as we gaze on its flickering tints and wild splendours, thousands of strangest shapes unfold themselves, yet no one will abide with us; and thus, as Goethe says elsewhere, "we are reminded of Nothing and of All."

Properly speaking, *Helena* is what the Germans call a *Mährchen* (Fabulous Tale), a species of fiction they have particularly excelled in, and of which Goethe has already produced more than one distinguished specimen. Some day we purpose to translate for our readers, that little piece of his, deserving to be named, as it is, "THE *Mährchen*," and which we must agree with a great critic in reckoning the "Tale of all Tales." As to the composition of this *Helena*, we cannot but perceive it to be deeply-studied, appropriate, and successful. It is wonderful with what fidelity the Classical style is maintained throughout the earlier part of the poem; how skilfully it is at once united to the Romantic style of the latter part, and made to re-appear, at intervals, to the end. And then the small half-secret touches of sarcasm, the curious little traits by which we get a peep behind the curtain! Figure, for instance, that so transient allusion to these "Bearded Ones sitting watchful there below," and then their tugging at Helena's Mantle to pull it down with them. By such light hints does Mephistopheles point out our Whereabout; and ever and anon remind us, that not on the firm earth, but on the wide and airy Deep, has he spread his strange pavilion, where, in magic light, so many wonders are displayed to us.

Had we chanced to find that Goethe, in other instances, had ever written one line without meaning, or many lines without a deep and true meaning, we should not have thought this little cloud-picture worthy of such minute development, or such careful study. In that case, too, we should never have seen the true *Helena* of Goethe, but some false one of our own too indolent imagination; for this Drama, as it grows clearer, grows also more beautiful and complete; and the third, the fourth perusal of it pleases far better than the first. Few living artists would deserve such faith from us; but few also would so well reward it.

On the general relation of *Helena* to *Faust*, and the degree of fitness of the one for the other, it were premature to speak more expressly at present. We have learned, on authority which we may justly reckon the best, that Goethe is even now engaged in preparing the entire Second Part of Faust, into which this Helena passes as a component part. With the third *Lieferung* of his Works, we understand, the beginning of that Second Part is to be published: we shall then, if need be, feel more qualified to speak.

For the present, therefore, we take leave of *Helena* and *Faust*, and of their Author: but with regard to the latter, our task is nowise ended; indeed, as yet, hardly begun, for it is not in the province of the *Mährchen*, that Goethe will ever become most interesting to English readers. But, like his own Euphorion, though he rises aloft into Æther, he derives, Antæus-like, his strength from the earth. The dullest plodder has not more practical understanding, or a sounder or more quiet character, than this most aerial and imaginative of poets. We hold Goethe to be the Foreigner, at this era, who, of all others, the best, and the best by many degrees, deserves our study and appreciation. What help we individually can give in such a matter, we shall consider it a duty and a pleasure to have in readiness. We purpose to return, in our next Number, to the consideration of his Works and Character in general.

GOETHE.*

[FOREIGN REVIEW, 1828.]

IT is not on this "Second Portion" of Goethe's works, which at any rate contains nothing new to us, that we mean at present to dwell. In our last Number, we engaged to make some survey of his writings and character in general; and must now endeavour, with such insight as we have, to fulfil that promise.

We have already said that we reckoned this no unimportant subject; and few of Goethe's readers can need to be reminded that it is no easy one. We hope also that our pretensions in regard to it are not exorbitant; the sum of our aims being nowise to solve so deep and pregnant an inquiry, but only to show that an inquiry of such a sort lies ready for solution; courts the attention of thinking men among us, nay, merits a thorough investigation, and must sooner or later obtain it. Goethe's literary history appears to us a matter, beyond most others, of rich, subtile, and manifold significance; which will require and reward the best study of the best heads, and to the right exposition of which not one but many judgments will be necessary.

However, we need not linger, preluding on our own inability, and magnifying the difficulties we have so courageously volunteered to front. Considering the highly complex aspect which such a mind of itself presents to us; and, still more, taking into account the state of English opinion in respect of it, there certainly seem few literary questions of our time so perplexed, dubious, perhaps hazardous, as this of the character of Goethe; but few also on which a well-founded, or even a sincere, word would be more likely to profit. For our countrymen, at no time indisposed to foreign excellence, but at all times cautious of foreign singularity, have heard much of Goethe; but heard, for the most part, what excited and perplexed rather than instructed them. Vague rumors of the man have, for more than half a century, been humming through our ears: from time to time, we have even seen some distorted, mutilated transcript of his own thoughts, which, all obscure and hieroglyphical as it might often seem, failed not to emit here and there a ray of keenest and purest sense; travellers also are still running to and fro, importing the opinions or, at worst, the gossip of foreign countries: so that, by one means or another, many of us have come to understand, that considerably the most distinguished poet and thinker of his age is called Goethe, and lives at Weimar, and must, to all appearance, be an extremely surprising character: but here, unhappily, our knowledge almost terminates; and still must Curiosity, must ingenuous love of Information and mere passive Wonder alike inquire: What manner of man *is* this? How shall we interpret, how shall we even see him? What is his spiritual structure, what at least are the outward form and features of his mind? Has he any real poetic worth; and if so, how much; how much to his own people, how much to us?

Reviewers, of great and of small character, have manfully endeavoured to satisfy the British world on these points: but which of us could believe their report? Did it not rather become apparent, as we reflected on the matter, that this Goethe of theirs was not the real man, nay, could not be any real man whatever? For what, after all, were their portraits of him but copies, with some retouchings and ornamental appendages, of our grand English original Picture of the German generically?—In itself such a piece of art, as national portraits, under like circumstances, are wont to be; and resembling Goethe, as some unusually expressive Sign of the Saracen's Head may resemble the present Sultan of Constantinople!

Did we imagine that much information, or any very deep sagacity were required for avoiding such mistakes, it would ill become us to step forward on this occasion. But surely it is given to every man, if he will but take heed, to know so much as whether or not he *knows*. And nothing can be plainer to us than that if, in the present business, we can report *aught* from our own personal vision and clear hearty belief, it will be a useful novelty in the discussion of it. Let the reader be patient with us then; and according as he finds that we speak honestly and earnestly, or loosely and dishonestly, consider our statement, or dismiss it as unworthy of consideration.

Viewed in his merely external relations, Goethe exhibits an appearance such as seldom occurs in the history of letters, and indeed, from the nature of the case, can seldom occur. A man, who, in early life, rising almost at a single bound into the highest reputation over all Europe; by gradual advances, fixing himself more and more firmly in the reverence of his countrymen, ascends silently through many vicissitudes to the supreme intellectual place among them; and now, after half a century, distinguished by convulsions, political, moral, and poetical, still reigns, full of years and honours, with a soft undisputed sway; still labouring in his vocation, still forwarding, as with knightly benignity, whatever can profit the culture of his nation: such a man might justly attract our notice, were it only by the singularity of his fortune. Supremacies of

* *Goethe's Sämmtliche Werke. Vollständige Ausgabe letzter Hand.* (Goethe's Collective Works. Complete Edition, with his final Corrections.) *Zweite Lieferung, Bde.* vi.—x. Cotta: Stuttgard and Tübingen. 1827.

this sort are rare in modern times; so universal, and of such continuance, they are almost unexampled. For the age of the Prophets and Theologic Doctors had long since passed away; and now it is by much slighter, by transient and mere earthly ties, that bodies of men connect themselves with a man. The wisest, most melodious voice cannot in these days pass for a divine one; the word Inspiration still lingers, but only in the shape of a poetic figure, from which the once earnest, awful, and soul-subduing sense has vanished without return. The polity of Literature is called a Republic; oftener it is an Anarchy, where, by strength or fortune, favourite after favourite rises into splendour and authority, but like Masaniello, while judging the people, is on the third day deposed and shot. Nay, few such adventurers can attain even this painful pre-eminence; for at most, it is clear, any given age can have but one first man; many ages have only a crowd of secondary men, each of whom is first in his own eyes: and seldom, at best, can the "Single Person" long keep his station at the head of this wild commonwealth; most sovereigns are never universally acknowledged, least of all in their lifetimes; few of the acknowledged can reign peaceably to the end.

Of such a perpetual dictatorship Voltaire among the French gives the last European instance; but even with him it was perhaps a much less striking affair. Voltaire reigned over a sect, less as their lawgiver than as their general; for he was at bitter enmity with the great numerical majority of his nation, by whom his services, far from being acknowledged as benefits, were execrated as abominations. But Goethe's object has, at all times, been rather to unite than to divide; and though he has not scrupled, as occasion served, to speak forth his convictions distinctly enough on many delicate topics, and seems, in general, to have paid little court to the prejudices or private feelings of any man or body of men, we see not at present that his merits are anywhere disputed, his intellectual endeavours controverted, or his person regarded otherwise than with affection and respect. In later years, too, the advanced age of the poet has invested him with another sort of dignity; and the admiration to which his great qualities give him claim, is tempered into a milder, grateful feeling, almost as of sons and grandsons to their common father. Dissentients, no doubt, there are and must be; but, apparently, their cause is not pleaded in words: no man of the smallest note speaks on that side; or at most, such men may question, not the worth of Goethe, but the cant and idle affectation with which, in many quarters, this must be promulgated and bepraised. Certainly there is not, probably there never was, in any European country, a writer who, with so cunning a style, and so deep, so abstruse a sense, ever found so many readers. For, from the peasant to the king, from the callow dilettante and innamorato, to the grave transcendental philosopher, men of all degrees and dispositions are familiar with the writings of Goethe: each studies them with affection, with a faith which, "where it cannot unriddle, learns to trust;" each takes with him what he is adequate to carry, and departs thankful for his own allotments. Two of Goethe's intensest admirers are Schelling of Munich, and a worthy friend of ours in Berlin; one of these among the deepest men in Europe, the other among the shallowest.

All this is, no doubt, singular enough; and a proper understanding of it would throw light on many things. Whatever we may think of Goethe's ascendency, the existence of it remains a highly curious fact; and to trace its history, to discover by what steps such influence has been attained, and how so long preserved, were no trivial or unprofitable inquiry. It would be worth while to see so strange a man for his own sake; and here we should see, not only the man himself, and his own progress and spiritual development, but the progress also of his nation; and this at no sluggish or even quiet era, but in times marked by strange revolutions of opinions, by angry controversies, high enthusiasm, novelty of enterprise, and doubtless, in many respects, by rapid advancement: for that the Germans have been, and still are, restlessly struggling forward, with honest unwearied effort, sometimes with enviable success, no one, who knows them, will deny; and as little, that in every province of Literature, of Art, and humane accomplishment, the influence, often the direct guidance of Goethe may be recognised. The history of his mind is, in fact, at the same time, the history of German culture in his day; for whatever excellence this individual might realize has sooner or later been acknowledged and appropriated by his country; and the title of *Musagetes*, which his admirers give him, is perhaps, in sober strictness, not unmerited. Be it for good or for evil, there is certainly no German, since the days of Luther, whose life can occupy so large a space in the intellectual history of that people.

In this point of view, were it in no other, Goethe's *Dichtung und Wahrheit*, so soon as it is completed, may deserve to be reckoned one of his most interesting works. We speak not of its literary merits, though in that respect, too, we must say that few Autobiographies have come in our way, where so difficult a matter was so successfully handled; where perfect knowledge could be found united so kindly with perfect tolerance; and a personal narrative, moving along in soft clearness, showed us a man, and the objects that environed him, under an aspect so verisimilar, yet so lovely, with an air dignified and earnest, yet graceful, cheerful, even gay: a story as of a Patriarch to his children; such indeed, as few men can be called upon to relate, and few, if called upon, could relate so well. What would we give for such an Autobiography of Shakspeare, of Milton, even of Pope or Swift! *Dichtung und Wahrheit* has been censured considerably in England; but not, we are inclined to believe, with any insight into its proper meaning. The misfortune of the work among us was, that we did not know the narrator *before* his narrative; and could not judge what sort of narrative he was bound to give, in these circumstances, or whether he was bound to give any at all. We say nothing of his situation; heard only the sound of his voice; and hearing it, never doubted that he must be perorating in official garments from the rostrum, instead of speaking trustfully by the fireside. For the chief ground of offence seemed to be, that the story was not noble enough; that it entered on details of too poor and private a nature; verged here and there towards garrulity; was not, in one word, written in the style of what we call a *gentleman.* Whether it might be written in the style of a *man*, and how far these two styles might be compatible, and what might be their relative worth and preferableness, was a deeper question, to which apparently no heed had been given. Yet herein lay the very cream of the matter; for Goethe was not writing to "persons of quality" in England, but to persons of heart and head in Europe: a somewhat different problem perhaps, and requiring a somewhat different solution. As to this ignobleness and freedom of detail, especially, we may say, that, to a German, few accusations could appear more surprising than this, which, with us, constitutes the head and front of his offending. Goethe, in his own country, far from being accused of undue familiarity towards his readers, had, up to that date, been labouring under precisely the opposite charge. It was his stateliness, his reserve, his indifference, his contempt for the public, that were censured. Strange, almost inexplicable, as many of his works might appear; loud, sorrowful, and altogether stolid as might be the criticisms they underwent, no word of explanation could be wrung from him; he had never even deigned to write a preface. And in later and juster days, when the study of Poetry came to be prosecuted in another spirit, and it was found that Goethe was standing, not like a culprit to plead for himself before the literary *plebeians*, but like a higher teacher and preacher, speaking for truth, to whom both *plebeians* and *patricians* were bound to give all ear, the outward difficulty of interpreting his works began indeed to vanish; but enough still remained, nay, increased curiosity had given rise to new difficulties, and deeper inquiries. Not only *what* were these works, but *how* did they originate, became questions for the critic. Yet several of Goethe's chief productions, and, of his smaller poems, nearly the whole, seemed so intimately interwoven with his private history, that without some knowledge of this, no answer to such questions could be given. Nay, commentaries have been written on single pieces of his, endeavouring, by way of guess, to supply this deficiency.* We can thus judge whether, to the Germans, such minuteness of exposition in this *Dichtung und Wahrheit* may have seemed a sin. Few readers of Goethe, we believe, but would wish rather to see it extended than curtailed.

It is our duty also to remark, if any one be still unaware of it, that the *Memoirs of Goethe*, published some years ago in London, can have no real concern with this autobiography. The rage of hunger is an excuse for much; otherwise that German translator, whom indignant Reviewers have proved to know *no* German, were a highly reprehensible man. His work, it appears, is done from the French, and shows subtractions, and, what is worse, additions. But the unhappy Dragoman has already been chastised, perhaps too sharply. If warring with the reefs and breakers and cross eddies of Life, he still hover on this side the shadow of Night, and any word of ours might reach him, we would rather say: Courage, Brother! Grow honest, and times will mend!

It would appear, then, that for inquirers into Foreign Literature, for all men, anxious to see and understand the European world as it lies around them, a great problem is presented in this Goethe; a singular, highly significant phenomenon, and now, also, means more or less complete for ascertaining its significance. A man of wonderful, nay unexampled reputation and intellectual influence among forty millions of reflective, serious, and cultivated men, invites us to study him; and to determine for ourselves whether and how far such influence has been salutary, such reputation merited. That this call will one day be answered, that Goethe will be seen and judged of in his real character among us, appears certain enough. His name, long familiar everywhere, has now awakened the attention of critics in all European countries to his works: he is studied wherever true study exists; eagerly studied even in France; nay, some considerable knowledge of his nature and spiritual importance seems already to prevail there.

For ourselves, meanwhile, in giving all due weight to so curious an exhibition of opinion, it is doubtless our part, at the same time, to beware that we do not give it too much. This universal sentiment of admiration is wonderful, is interesting enough; but it must not lead us astray. We English stand as yet without the sphere of it; neither will we plunge blindly in, but enter considerately, or, if we see good, keep aloof from it altogether. Fame, we may understand, is no sure test of merit, but only a probability of such: it is an accident, not a property, of a man; like light, it can give little or nothing, but at most may show what is given; often, it is but a false glare, dazzling the eyes of the vulgar, lending by casual, extrinsic splendour the brightness and manifold glance of the diamond to the pebbles of no value. A man is in all cases simply *the* man, of the same intrinsic worth and weakness, whether his worth and weakness lie hidden in the depths of his own consciousness, or be betrumpeted and beshouted from end to end of the habitable globe. These are plain truths, which no one should lose sight of; though, whether in love or in anger, for praise or for condemnation, most of us are too apt to forget them. But least of all can it become the critic to "follow a multitude to do evil," even when that evil is excess of admiration; on the contrary, it will behove him to lift up his voice, how feeble soever, how unheeded soever, against the common delusion; from which, if

* See, in particular, Dr. Kannengiesser *Ueber Goethe's Hausreise in Winter*, 1820.

* Witness *Le Tasse, Drame par Duval*, and the Criticisms on it. See also the Essays in the *Globe*. Nos 55, 64, (1826.)

he can save, or help to save, any mortal, his endeavours will have been repaid.

With these things in some measure before us, we must remind our readers of another influence at work in this affair, and one acting, as we think, in the contrary direction. That pitiful enough desire for "originality," which lurks and acts in all minds, will rather, we imagine, lead the critic of Foreign Literature to adopt the negative than the affirmative with regard to Goethe. If a writer, indeed, feel that he is writing for England alone, invisibly and inaudibly to the rest of the Earth, the temptations may be pretty equally balanced; if he write for some small conclave, which he mistakenly thinks the representative of England, they may sway this way or that, as it chances. But writing in such isolated spirit is no longer possible. Traffic, with its swift ships, is uniting all nations into one; Europe at large is becoming more and more one public: and in this public, the voices for Goethe, compared with those against him, are in the proportion, as we reckon them, both as to the number and value, of perhaps a hundred to one. We take in, not Germany alone, but France and Italy; not the Schlegels and Schellings, but the Manzonis and de Staëls. The bias of originality, therefore, may lie to the side of the censure: and whoever among us shall step forward, with such knowledge as our common critics have of Goethe, to enlighten the European public, by contradiction in this matter, displays a heroism, which, in estimating his other merits, ought nowise to be forgotten.

Our own view of the case coincides, we confess, in some degree with that of the majority. We reckon that Goethe's fame has, to a considerable extent, been deserved; that his influence has been of high benefit to his own country; nay more, that it promises to be of benefit to us, and to all other nations. The essential grounds of this opinion, which to explain minutely were a long, indeed boundless task, we may state without many words. We find, then, in Goethe, an Artist, in the high and ancient meaning of that term; in the meaning which it may have borne long ago among the masters of Italian painting, and the fathers of Poetry in England; we say that we trace in the creations of this man, belonging in every sense to our own time, some touches of that old, divine spirit, which had long passed away from among us, nay, which, as has often been laboriously demonstrated, was not to return to this world any more.

Or perhaps we come nearer our meaning, if we say that in Goethe we discover by far the most striking instance, in our time, of a writer who is, in strict speech, what Philosophy can call a Man. He is neither noble nor plebeian, neither liberal nor servile, nor infidel, nor devotee; but the best excellence of *all* these, joined in pure union; "a clear and universal *Man.*" Goethe's poetry is no separate faculty, no mental handicraft; but the voice of the whole harmonious manhood: nay it is the very harmony, the living and life-giving harmony of that rich manhood which forms his poetry. All good men may be called poets in act, or in word; all good poets are so in both. But Goethe besides appears to us a person of that deep endowment, and gifted vision, of that experience also and sympathy in the ways of all men, which qualify him to stand forth, not only as the literary ornament, but in many respects too as the Teacher and exemplar of his age. For, to say nothing of his natural gifts, he has cultivated himself and his art, he has studied how to live and write, with a fidelity, an unwearied earnestness, of which there is no other living instance; of which, among British poets especially, Wordsworth alone offers any resemblance. And this in our view is the result: To our minds, in these soft, melodious imaginations of his, there is embodied the Wisdom which is proper to this time; the beautiful, the religious Wisdom, which may still, with something of its old impressiveness, speak to the whole soul; still, in these hard, unbelieving, utilitarian days, reveal to us glimpses of the Unseen but not unreal World, that so the Actual and the Ideal may again meet together, and clear Knowledge be again wedded to Religion, in the life and business of men.

Such is our conviction or persuasion with regard to the poetry of Goethe. Could we demonstrate this opinion to be true, could we even exhibit it with that degree of clearness and consistency which it has attained in our own thoughts, Goethe were, on our part, sufficiently recommended to the best attention of all thinking men. But, unhappily, it is not a subject susceptible of demonstration: the merits and characteristics of a Poet are not to be set forth by logic; but to be gathered by personal, and as, in this case, it must be, by deep and careful inspection of his works. Nay, Goethe's world is every way so different from ours; it costs us such effort, we have so much to remember and so much to forget, before we can transfer ourselves in any measure into his peculiar point of vision, that a right study of him, for an Englishman, even of ingenuous, open, inquisitive mind, becomes unusually difficult; for a fixed, decided, contemptuous Englishman, next to impossible. To a reader of the first class, helps may be given, explanations will remove many a difficulty; beauties that lay hidden may be made apparent; and directions, adapted to his actual position, will at length guide him into the proper track for such an inquiry. All this, however, must be a work of progression and detail. To do our part in it, from time to time, must rank among the best duties of an English Foreign Review. Meanwhile, our present endeavour limits itself within far narrower bounds. We cannot aim to make Goethe known, but only to prove that he is worthy of being known; at most, to point out, as it were afar off, the path by which some knowledge of him may be obtained. A slight glance at his general literary character and procedure, and one or two of his chief productions, which throw light on these, must for the present suffice.

A French diplomatic personage, contemplating Goethe's physiognomy, is said to have observed: *Voilà un homme qui a eu beaucoup de chagrins.* A truer version of the matter, Goethe himself seems to think, would have been: Here is a man who has struggled toughly; who has *es sich recht sauer werden lassen.* Goethe's life, whether as a writer and thinker, or as a living, active man, has indeed been a life of effort, of earnest toilsome endeavour after all excellence. Accordingly, his intellectual progress, his spiritual and moral history, as it may be gathered from his successive works, furnishes, with us, no small portion of the pleasure and profit we derive from perusing them. Participating deeply in all the influences of his age, he has from the first, at every new epoch, stood forth to elucidate the new circumstances of the time: to offer the instruction, the solace, which that time required. His literary life divides itself into two portions widely different in character: the products of the first, once so new and original, have long, either directly or through the thousand, thousand imitations of them, been familiar to us; with the products of the second, equally original, and, in our day, far more precious, we are yet little acquainted. These two classes of works stand curiously related with each other; at first view, in strong contradiction, yet, in truth, connected together by the strictest sequence. For Goethe has not only suffered and mourned in bitter agony under the spiritual perplexities of his time; but he has also mastered these, he is above them, and has shown others how to rise above them. At one time, we found him in darkness, and now, he is in light; he was once an Unbeliever; and now he is a Believer; and he believes, moreover, not by denying his unbelief, but by following it out; not by stopping short, still less turning back, in his inquiries, but by resolutely prosecuting them. This, it appears to us, is a case of singular interest, and rarely exemplified, if at all, elsewhere, in these our days. How has this man, to whom the world once offered nothing but blackness, denial, and despair, attained to that better vision which now shows it to him, not tolerable only, but full of solemnity and loveliness? How has the belief of a Saint been united in this high and true mind with the clearness of a Skeptic; the devout spirit of a Fenelon made to blend in soft harmony with the gayety, the sarcasm, the shrewdness of a Voltaire?

Goethe's two earliest works are *Goetz von Berlichingen* and *The Sorrows of Werter*. The boundless influence and popularity they gained, both at home and abroad, is well known. It was they that established almost at once his literary fame in his own country; and even determined his subsequent private history, for they brought him into contact with the Duke of Weimar; in connection with whom, the Poet, engaged in manifold duties, political as well as literary, has lived for fifty-four years, and still, in honourable retirement, continues to live.* Their effects over Europe at large were not less striking than in Germany.

"It would be difficult," observes a writer on this subject, "to name two books which have exercised a deeper influence on the subsequent literature of Europe than these two performances of a young author; his first-fruits, the produce of his twenty-fourth year. *Werter* appeared to seize the hearts of men in all quarters of the world, and to utter for them the word which they had long been waiting to hear. As usually happens, too, this same word, once uttered, was soon abundantly repeated; spoken in all dialects, and chanted through all notes of the gamut, till the sound of it had grown a weariness rather than a pleasure. Skeptical sentimentality, view-hunting, love, friendship, suicide, and desperation, became the staple of literary ware; and though the epidemic, after a long course of years, subsided in Germany, it reappeared with various modifications in other countries, and everywhere abundant traces of its good and bad effects are still to be discerned. The fortune of *Berlichingen with the Iron Hand*, though less sudden, was by no means less exalted. In his own country, *Goetz*, though he now stands solitary and childless, became the parent of an innumerable progeny, of chivalry plays, feudal delineations, and poetico-antiquarian performances; which, though long ago deceased, made noise enough in their day and generation: and with ourselves, his influence has been perhaps still more remarkable. Sir Walter Scott's first literary enterprise was a translation of *Goetz von Berlichingen;* and, if genius could be communicated like instruction, we might call this work of Goethe's the prime cause of *Marmion* and the *Lady of the Lake*, with all that has followed from the same creative hand. Truly, a grain of seed that has lighted on the right soil! For if not firmer and fairer, it has grown to be taller and broader than any other tree; and all the nations of the earth are still yearly gathering of its fruit.

"But overlooking these spiritual genealogies, which bring little certainty and little profit, it may be sufficient to observe of *Berlichingen* and *Werter*, that they stand prominent among the causes, or at the very least, among the signals of a great change in modern literature. The former directed men's attention with a new force to the picturesque effects of the Past; and the latter, for the first time, attempted the more accurate delineation of a class of feelings deeply important to modern minds, but for which our elder poetry offered no exponent, and perhaps could offer none, because they are feelings that arise from Passion incapable of being converted into Action, and belong chiefly to an age as indolent, cultivated, and unbelieving as our own. This, notwithstanding the dash of falsehood which may exist in *Werter* itself, and the boundless delirium of extravagance which it called forth in others, is a high praise which cannot justly be denied it. The English reader ought also to understand that our current version of *Werter* is mutilated and inaccurate: it comes to us through the all-subduing medium of the French, shorn of its caustic strength, with its melancholy rendered maudlin, its hero reduced from the stately gloom of a broken-hearted poet to the tearful wrangling of a dyspeptic tailor."*

To the same dark, wayward mood, which, in *Werter*, pours itself forth in bitter wailings

* Since the above was written, that worthy Prince, worthy, we have understood, in all respects, exemplary in whatever concerned Literature and the Arts, has been called suddenly away. He died on his road from Berlin, near Torgau, on the 24th of June.

* German Romance, vol. iv. pp. 5—7.

over human life; and, in *Berlichingen*, appears as a fond and sad looking back into the Past, belong various other productions of Goethe's; for example, the *Mitschuldigen*, and the first idea of *Faust*, which, however, was not realized in actual composition, till a calmer period of his history. Of this early "harsh and crude," yet fervid and genial period, *Werter* may stand here as the representative; and, viewed in its external and internal relation, will help to illustrate both the writer and the public he was writing for.

At the present day, it would be difficult for us, satisfied, nay, sated to nausea, as we have been with the doctrines of Sentimentality, to estimate the boundless interest which *Werter* must have excited when first given to the world. It was then new in all senses; it was wonderful, yet wished for, both in its own country and in every other. The literature of Germany had as yet but partially awakened from its long torpor: deep learning, deep reflection, have at no time been wanting there: but the creative spirit had for above a century been almost extinct. Of late, however, the Ramlers, Rabeners, Gellerts, had attained to no inconsiderable polish of style; Klopstock's *Messias* had called forth the admiration, and perhaps still more the pride, of the country, as a piece of art; a high enthusiasm was abroad; Lessing had roused the minds of men to a deeper and truer interest in literature, had even decidedly begun to introduce a heartier, warmer, and more expressive style. The Germans were on the alert; in expectation, or at least in full readiness for some far bolder impulse; waiting for the Poet that might speak to them from the heart to the heart. It was in Goethe that such a Poet was to be given them.

Nay, the literature of other countries, placid self-satisfied as they might seem, was in an equally expectant condition. Everywhere, as in Germany, there was polish and languor, external glitter and internal vacuity; it was not fire, but a picture of fire, at which no soul could be warmed. Literature had sunk from its former vocation: it no longer held the mirror up to nature; no longer reflected, in many-coloured expressive symbols, the actual passions, the hopes, sorrows, joys of Living men; but dwelt in a remote conventional world, in *Castles of Otranto*, in *Epigoniads* and *Leonidases*, among clear, metallic heroes, and white, high, stainless beauties, in whom the drapery and elocution were nowise the least important qualities. Men thought it right that the heart should swell into magnanimity with Caractacus and Cato, and melt into sorrow with many an Eliza and Adelaide; but the heart was in no haste either to swell or to melt. Some pulses of heroical sentiment, a few *un*natural tears might, with conscientious readers, be actually squeezed forth on such occasions: but they came only from the surface of the mind; nay, had the conscientious man considered of the matter, he would have found that they ought not to have come at all. Our only English poet of the period was Goldsmith; a pure, clear, genuine spirit, had he been of depth or strength sufficient: his *Vicar of Wakefield* remains the best of all modern Idyls; but it is and was nothing more. And consider our leading writers; consider the poetry of Gray, and the prose of Johnson. The first a laborious mosaic, through the hard, stiff lineaments of which little life or true grace could be expected to look: real feeling, and all freedom of expressing it, are sacrificed to pomp, to cold splendour; for vigour we have a certain mouthing vehemence, too elegant indeed to be tumid, yet essentially foreign to the heart, and seen to extend no deeper than the mere voice and gesture. Were it not for his *Letters*, which are full of warm, exuberant power, we might almost doubt whether Gray was a man of genius; nay, was a living man at all, and not rather some thousand-times more cunningly devised poetical turning-loom, than that of Swift's Philosophers in Laputa. Johnson's prose is true, indeed, and sound, and full of practical sense: few men have seen more clearly into the motives, the interests, the whole walk and conversation of the living busy world as it lay before him; but farther than this busy, and, to most of us, rather prosaic world, he seldom looked: his instruction is for men of business, and in regard to matters of business alone. Prudence is the highest Virtue he can inculcate; and for that finer portion of our nature, that portion of it which belongs essentially to Literature strictly so called; where our highest feelings, our best joys and keenest sorrows, our Doubt, our Love, our Religion reside, he has no word to utter; no remedy, no counsel to give us in our straits; or at most, if, like poor Boswell, the patient is importunate, will answer: "My dear Sir, endeavour to clear your mind of Cant."

The turn which Philosophical speculation had taken in the preceding age corresponded with this tendency, and enhanced its narcotic influences; or was, indeed, properly speaking, the root they had sprung from. Locke, himself, a clear, humble-minded, patient, reverent, nay, religious man, had paved the way for banishing religion from the world. Mind, by being modelled in men's imaginations into a Shape, a Visibility; and reasoned of as if it had been some composite, divisible and reunitable substance, some finer chemical salt, or curious piece of logical joinery,—began to lose its immaterial, mysterious, divine though invisible character: it was tacitly figured as something that might, were our organs fine enough, be *seen*. Yet who had ever seen it? Who could ever see it? Thus by degrees it passed into a Doubt, a Relation, some faint possibility; and at last into a highly-probable Nonentity. Following Locke's footsteps, the French had discovered that "as the stomach secretes Chyle, so does the brain secrete Thought." And what then was Religion, what was Poetry, what was all high and heroic feeling? Chiefly a delusion; often a false and pernicious one. Poetry, indeed, was still to be preserved; because Poetry was a useful thing: men needed amusement, and loved to amuse themselves with Poetry: the playhouse was a pretty lounge of an evening; then there were so many precepts, satirical, didactic, so much more impressive for the rhyme; to say nothing of your occasional verses, birth-day odes, epithalamiums, epicediums, by which "the dream of existence may be so highly sweetened and embellished." Nay, does not Poetry, acting on the imaginations of men, excite them to daring purposes; sometimes, as in the case of Tyrtæus, to fight better; in which wise may it not rank as a useful stimulant to man, along with Opium and Scotch Whisky, the manufacture of which is allowed by law? In Heaven's name, then, let Poetry be preserved.

With Religion, however, it fared somewhat worse. In the eyes of Voltaire and his disciples, Religion was a superfluity, indeed a nuisance. Here, it is true, his followers have since found that he went too far; that Religion, being a great sanction to civil morality, is of use for keeping society in order, at least the lower classes, who have not the feeling of Honour in due force; and therefore, as a considerable help to the Constable and Hangman, *ought* decidedly to be kept up. But such toleration is the fruit only of later days. In those times, there was no question but how to get rid of it, root and branch, the sooner the better. A gleam of zeal, nay, we will call it, however basely alloyed, a glow of real enthusiasm and love of truth, may have animated the minds of these men, as they looked abroad on the pestilent jungle of Superstition, and hoped to clear the earth of it for ever. This little glow, so alloyed, so contaminated with pride and other poor or bad admixtures, was the last which thinking men were to experience in Europe for a time. So is it always in regard to Religious Belief, how degraded and defaced soever: the delight of the Destroyer and Denier is no pure delight, and must soon pass away. With bold, with skilful hand, Voltaire set his torch to the jungle: it blazed aloft to heaven; and the flame exhilarated and comforted the incendiaries; but, unhappily, such comfort could not continue. Ere long this flame, with its cheerful light and heat, was gone: the jungle, it is true, had been consumed; but, with its entanglements, its shelter and spots of verdure also; and the black, chill, ashy swamp, left in its stead, seemed for the time a greater evil than the other.

In such a state of painful obstruction, extending itself everywhere over Europe, and already master of Germany, lay the general mind, when Goethe first appeared in Literature. Whatever belonged to the finer nature of man had withered under the Harmattan breath of Doubt, or passed away in the conflagration of open Infidelity; and now, where the Tree of Life once bloomed and brought fruit of goodliest savour, there was only barrenness and desolation. To such as could find sufficient interest in the day-labour and day-wages of earthly existence; in the resources of the five bodily Senses, and of Vanity, the only mental sense which yet flourished, which flourished indeed with gigantic vigour, matters were still not so bad. Such men helped themselves forward, as they will generally do; and found the world, if not an altogether proper sphere, (for every man, disguise it as he may, has a *soul* in him,) at least a tolerable enough place; where, by one item and another, some comfort, or show of comfort, might from time to time be got up, and these few years, especially since they were so few, be spent without much murmuring. But to men afflicted with the "malady of Thought," some devoutness of temper was an inevitable heritage: to such the noisy forum of the world could appear but an empty, altogether insufficient concern; and the whole scene of life had become hopeless enough. Unhappily, such feelings are yet by no means so infrequent with ourselves, that we need stop here to depict them. That state of Unbelief from which the Germans do seem to be in some measure delivered, still presses with incubus force on the greater part of Europe; and nation after nation, each in its own way, feels that the first of all moral problems is how to cast it off, or how to rise above it. Governments naturally attempt the first expedient; Philosophers, in general, the second.

The poet, says Schiller, is a citizen not only of his country, but of his time. Whatever occupies and interests men in general, will interest him still more. That nameless Unrest, the blind struggle of a soul in bondage, that high, sad, longing Discontent, which was agitating every bosom, had driven Goethe almost to despair. All felt it; he alone could give it voice. And here lies the secret of his popularity; in his deep, susceptive heart, he felt a thousand times more keenly what every one was feeling; with the creative gift which belonged to him as a poet, he bodied it forth into visible shape, gave it a local habitation and a name; and so made himself the spokesman of his generation. *Werter* is but the cry of that dim, rooted pain, under which all thoughtful men of a certain age were languishing: it paints the misery, it passionately utters the complaint; and heart and voice, all over Europe, loudly and at once respond to it. True, it prescribes no remedy; for that was a far different, far harder enterprise, to which other years and a higher culture were required; but even this utterance of the pain, even this little, for the present, is ardently grasped at, and with eager sympathy appropriated in every bosom. If Byron's life-weariness, his moody melancholy, and mad, stormful indignation, borne on the tones of a wild and quite artless melody, could pierce so deep into many a British heart, now that the whole matter is no longer new,—is indeed old and trite,—we may judge with what vehement acceptance this *Werter* must have been welcomed, coming as it did like a voice from unknown regions, the first thrilling peal of that impassioned dirge, which, in country after country, men's ears have listened to, till they were deaf to all else. For *Werter*, infusing itself into the core and whole spirit of Literature, gave birth to a race of Sentimentalists, who have raged and wailed in every part of the world; till better light dawned on them, or at worst exhausted Nature laid herself to sleep, and it was discovered that lamenting was an unproductive labour. These funereal choristers, in Germany, a loud, haggard, tumultuous, as well as tearful class, were named the *Kraftmänner*, or Power-men; but have all long since, like sick children, cried themselves to rest. Byron was our English Sentimentalist and Power-man; the strongest of his kind in Europe; the wildest, the gloomiest, and it may be hoped, the last. For what good is it to "whine, put finger i' the eye, and sob," in such a case? Still more, to snarl and snap in malignant wise, "like dog distract, or a monkey sick?" Why should we quarrel with our existence, here as it lies before us, our field and inheritance, to make or to mar, for better or for worse; in which, too, so many noblest men have, ever from the beginning, warring with the very evils we war with, both made and been what will be venerated to all time?

What shapest thou here at the World? 'Tis shapen long ago;
The Maker shaped it, and thought it were best even so.
Thy lot is appointed, go follow its hest;
Thy journey's begun, thou must move and not rest;
For sorrow and care cannot alter thy case,
And running, not raging, will win thee the race.

Meanwhile, of the philosophy which reigns in *Werter*, and which it has been our lot to hear so often repeated elsewhere, we may here produce a short specimen. The following passage will serve our turn; and be, if we mistake not, new to the mere English reader.

"That the life of man is but a dream, has come into many a head; and with me, too, some feeling of that sort is ever at work. When I look upon the limits within which man's powers of action and inquiry are hemmed in; when I see how all effort issues simply in procuring supply for wants, which again have no object but continuing this poor existence of ours; and then, that all satisfaction on certain points of inquiry is but a dreaming resignation, while you paint, with many-coloured figures and gay prospects, the walls you sit imprisoned by,—all this, Wilhelm, makes me dumb. I return to my own heart, and find there such a world! Yet a world too, more in forecast and dim desire, than in vision and living power. And then all swims before my mind's eye; and so I smile, and again go dreaming on as others do.

"That children know not what they want, all conscientious tutors and education-philosophers have long been agreed: but that full-grown men, as well as children, stagger to and fro along this earth; like these, not knowing whence they come or whither they go; aiming, just as little, after true objects: governed just as well by biscuit, cakes, and birch-rods: this is what no one likes to believe; and yet, it seems to me, the fact is lying under our very nose.

"I will confess to thee, for I know what thou wouldst say to me on this point, that those are the happiest, who, like children, live from one day to the other, carrying their dolls about with them, to dress and undress; gliding, also, with the highest respect, before the drawer where mamma has locked the gingerbread: and, when they do get the wished-for morsel, devouring it with puffed-out cheeks, and crying, More!—These are the fortunate of the earth. Well is it likewise with those who can label their rag-gathering employments, or perhaps their passions, with pompous titles, and represent them to mankind as gigantic undertakings for its welfare and salvation. Happy the man who can live in such wise! But he who, in his humility, observes where all this issues, who sees how featly any small thriving citizen can trim his patch of garden into a Paradise, and with what unbroken heart even the unhappy crawls along under his burden, and all are alike ardent to see the light of this sun but one minute longer:—yes, he is silent, and he too forms his world out of himself, and he too is happy because he is a man. And then, hemmed in as he is, he ever keeps in his heart the sweet feeling of freedom, and that this dungeon—can be left when he likes." *

What Goethe's own temper and habit of thought must have been, while the materials of such a work were forming themselves within his heart, might be in some degree conjectured, and he has himself informed us. We quote the following passage from his *Dichtung und Wahrheit*. The writing of *Werter*, it would seem, vindicating so gloomy, almost desperate a state of mind in the author, was at the same time a symptom, indeed a cause, of his now having got delivered from such melancholy. Far from recommending suicide to others, as *Werter* has often been accused of doing, it was the first proof that Goethe himself had abandoned these "hypochondriacal crotchets:" the imaginary "Sorrows" had helped to free him from many real ones.

"Such weariness of life," he says, "has its physical and spiritual causes; those we shall leave to the Doctor, these to the Moralist, for investigation; and in this so trite matter, touch only on the main point, when that phenomenon expresses itself most distinctly. All pleasure in life is founded on the regular return of external things. The alternations of day and night, of the seasons, of the blossoms and fruits, and whatever else meets us from epoch to epoch with the offer and command of enjoyment,—these are the essential springs of earthly existence. The more open we are to such enjoyments, the happier we feel ourselves; but, should the vicissitude of these appearances come and go without our taking interest in it, should such benignant invitations address themselves to us in vain, then follows the greatest misery, the heaviest malady; one grows to view life as a sickening burden. We have heard of the Englishman who hanged himself, to be no more troubled with daily putting off and on his clothes. I knew an honest gardener, the overseer of some extensive pleasure-grounds, who once splenetically exclaimed: Shall I see these clouds for ever passing, then, from east to west? It is told of one of our most distinguished men,† that he viewed with dissatisfaction the spring again growing green, and wished that, by way of change, it would for once be red. These are specially the symptoms of life-weariness,

**Leiden des jüngen Werther. Am 22 May.*

†Lessing, we believe: but perhaps it was less the greenness of spring that vexed him than Jacobi's too lyric admiration of it.—Ed.

which not seldom issues in suicide, and, at this time, among men of meditative, secluded character, was more frequent than might be supposed.

"Nothing, however, will sooner induce this feeling of satiety than the return of love. The first love, it is said justly, is the only one; for in the second, and by the second, the highest significance of love is in fact lost. That idea of infinitude, of everlasting endurance, which supports and bears it aloft, is destroyed; it seems transient, like all that returns. * * *

"Further, a young man soon comes to find, if not in himself, at least in others, that moral epochs have their course, as well as the seasons. The favour of the great, the protection of the powerful, the help of the active, the good-will of the many, the love of the few, all fluctuates up and down; so that we cannot hold it fast, any more than we can hold sun, moon, and stars. And yet these things are not mere natural events: such blessings flee away from us, by our own blame or that of others, by accident or destiny; but they flee away, they fluctuate, and we are never sure of them.

"But what most pains the young man of sensibility is the incessant return of our faults: for how long is it before we learn, that in cultivating our virtues, we nourish our faults along with them? The former rests on the latter, as on their roots; and these ramify themselves in secret as strongly and as wide as those others in the open light. Now, as we for the most part practise our virtues with forethought and will, but by our faults are overtaken unexpectedly, the former seldom give us much joy, the latter are continually giving us sorrow and distress. Indeed, here lies the subtilest difficulty in Self-knowledge, the difficulty which almost renders it impossible. But figure, in addition to all this, the heat of youthful blood, an imagination easily fascinated and paralyzed by individual objects; further, the wavering commotions of the day, and you will find that an impatient striving to free one's self from such a pressure was no unnatural state.

"However, these gloomy contemplations, which, if a man yield to them, will lead him to boundless lengths, could not have so decidedly developed themselves in our young German minds, had not some outward cause excited and forwarded us in this sorrowful employment. Such a cause existed for us in the Literature, especially the Poetical Literature, of England, the great qualities of which are accompanied by a certain earnest melancholy, which it imparts to every one that occupies himself with it.

* * * * * *

"In such an element, with such an environment of circumstances, with studies and tastes of this sort, harassed by unsatisfied desires, externally nowhere called forth to important action; with the sole prospect of dragging on a languid, spiritless, mere civic life, we had recurred, in our disconsolate pride, to the thought that life, when it no longer suited one, might be cast aside at pleasure; and had helped ourselves hereby, stintedly enough, over the crosses and tediums of the time. These sentiments were so universal, that *Werter*, on this very account, could produce the greatest effect; striking in everywhere with the dominant humour, and representing the interior of a sickly, youthful heart, in a visible and palpable shape. How accurately the English have known this sorrow, might be seen from these few significant lines, written before the appearance of *Werter*:

> To griefs congenial prone
> More wounds than nature gave he knew,
> While misery's form his fancy drew
> In dark ideal hues, and horrors not its own.*

"Self-murder is an occurrence in men's affairs, which, how much soever it may have already been discussed and commented upon, excites an interest in every mortal; and, at every new era, must be discussed again. Montesquieu confers on his heroes and great men the right of putting themselves to death when they see good; observing, that it must stand at the will of every one to conclude the Fifth Act of his Tragedy whenever he thinks best. Here, however, our business lies not with persons who, in activity, have led an important life, who have spent their days for some mighty empire, or for the cause of freedom: and whom one may forbear to censure, when, seeing the high ideal purpose which had inspired them vanish from the earth, they meditate pursuing it to that other undiscovered country. Our business here is with persons to whom, properly for want of activity, and in the peacefullest condition imaginable, life has, nevertheless, by their exorbitant requisitions on themselves, become a burden. As I myself was in this predicament, and know best what pain I suffered in it, what efforts it cost me to escape from it, I shall not hide the speculations, I from time to time considerately prosecuted, as to the various modes of death one had to choose from.

"It is something so unnatural for a man to break loose from himself, not only to hurt, but to annihilate himself, that he for the most part catches at means of a mechanical sort for putting his purpose in execution. When Ajax falls on his sword, it is the weight of his body that performs this service for him. When the warrior adjures his armour-bearer to slay him, rather than that he come into the hands of the enemy, this is likewise an external force which he secures for himself; only a moral instead of a physical one. Women seek in the water a cooling for their desperation; and the highly mechanical means of pistol-shooting insures a quick act with the smallest effort. Hanging is a death one mentions unwillingly, because it is an ignoble one. In England it may happen more readily than elsewhere, because from youth upwards you there see that punishment frequent without being specially ignominious. By poison, by opening of veins, men aim but at parting slowly from life; and the most refined the speediest, the most painless death, by means of an asp, was worthy of a Queen, who had spent her life in pomp and luxurious pleasure. All these, however, are external helps

* So in the original.

are enemies, with which a man, that he may fight against himself, makes league.

"When I considered these various methods, and, further, looked abroad over history, I could find among all suicides no one that had gone about this deed with such greatness and freedom of spirit as the Emperor Otho. This man, beaten indeed as a general, yet nowise reduced to extremities, determines for the good of the Empire, which already in some measure belonged to him, and for the saving of so many thousands, to leave the world. With his friends he passes a gay, festive night, and next morning it is found that with his own hand he has plunged a sharp dagger into his heart. This sole act seemed to me worthy of imitation; and I convinced myself that whoever could not proceed herein as Otho had done, was not entitled to resolve on renouncing life. By this conviction, I saved myself from the purpose, or indeed, more properly speaking, from the whim, of suicide, which in those fair peaceful times had insinuated itself into the mind of indolent youth. Among a considerable collection of arms, I possessed a costly well-ground dagger. This I laid down nightly beside my bed; and before extinguishing the light, I tried whether I could succeed in sending the sharp point an inch or two deep into my breast. But as I truly never could succeed, I at last took to laughing at myself; threw away all these hypochondriacal crotchets, and determined to live. To do this with cheerfulness, however, I required to have some poetical task given me, wherein all that I had felt, thought, or dreamed on this weighty business, might be spoken forth. With such view, I endeavoured to collect the elements which for a year or two had been floating about in me; I represented to myself the circumstances which had most oppressed and afflicted me; but nothing of all this would take form; there was wanting an incident, a fable, in which I might imbody it.

"All at once I hear tidings of Jerusalem's death; and directly following the general rumour, came the most precise and circumstantial description of the business; and in this instant the plan of *Werter* was invented; the whole shot together from all sides, and became a solid mass; as the water in the vessel, which already stood on the point of freezing, is by the slightest motion changed at once into firm ice."*

A wide, and every way most important, interval divides *Werter*, with its skeptical philosophy, and "hypochondriacal crotchets," from Goethe's next novel, *Wilhelm Meister's Apprenticeship*, published some twenty years afterwards. This work belongs, in all senses, to the second and sounder period of Goethe's life, and may indeed serve as the fullest, if perhaps not the purest, impress of it; being written with due forethought, at various times, during a period of no less than ten years. Considered as a piece of Art, there were much to be said on *Meister;* all which, however, lies beyond our present purpose. We are here looking at the work chiefly as a document for the writer's history; and in this point of view, it certainly seems, as contrasted with its more popular precursor, to deserve our best attention: for the problem which had been stated in *Werter*, with despair of its solution, is here solved. The lofty enthusiasm, which, wandering wildly over the universe, found no resting place, has here reached its appointed home; and lives in harmony with what long appeared to threaten it with annihilation. Anarchy has now become Peace; the once gloomy and perturbed spirit is now serene, cheerfully vigorous, and rich in good fruits. Neither, which is most important of all, has this Peace been attained by a surrender to Necessity, or any compact with Delusion; a seeming blessing, such as years and dispiritment will of themselves bring to most men, and which is indeed no blessing, since even continued battle is better than destruction or captivity; and peace of this sort is like that of Galgacus's Romans, who "called it peace when they had made a desert." Here the ardent, high aspiring youth has grown into the calmest man, yet with increase and not loss of ardour, and with aspirations higher as well as clearer. For he has conquered his unbelief; the Ideal has been built on the actual; no longer floats vaguely in darkness and regions of dreams, but rests in light, on the firm ground of human interest and business, as in its true scene, on its true basis.

It is wonderful to see with what softness the skepticism of Jarno, the commercial spirit of Werner, the reposing, polished manhood of Lothario and the Uncle, the unearthly enthusiasm of the Harper, the gay, animal vivacity of Philina, the mystic, ethereal, almost spiritual nature of Mignon, are blended together in this work; how justice is done to each, how each lives freely in his proper element, in his proper form; and how, as Wilhelm himself, the mild-hearted, all-hoping, all-believing Wilhelm, struggles forward towards his world of Art through these curiously complected influences, all this unites itself into a multifarious, yet so harmonious Whole, as into a clear poëtic mirror, where man's life and business in this age, his passions and purposes, the highest equally with the lowest, are imaged back to us in beautiful significance. Poetry and Prose are no longer at variance, for the poet's eyes are opened: he sees the changes of many-coloured existence, and sees the loveliness and deep purport which lies hidden under the very meanest of them; hidden to the vulgar sight, but clear to the poet's; because the "open secret," is no longer a secret to him, and he knows that the Universe is *full* of goodness; that whatever has being has beauty.

Apart from its literary merits or demerits, such is the temper of mind we trace in Goethe's *Meister*, and, more or less expressly exhibited, in all his later works. We reckon it a rare phenomenon, this temper; and worthy, in our times, if it do exist, of best study from all inquiring men. How has such a temper been attained in this so lofty and impetuous mind, once, too, dark, desolate, and full of doubt, more than any other? How may we, each of us in his several sphere, attain it, or strengthen

* *Dichtung und Wahrheit*, b. iii. s. 200—213.

it, for ourselves? These are questions, this last is a question, in which no one is unconcerned.

To answer these questions, to begin the answer of them, would lead us very far beyond our present limits. It is not, as we believe, without long, sedulous study, without learning much, and unlearning much, that, for any man, the answer of such questions is even to be hoped. Meanwhile, as regards Goethe, there is one feature of the business which, to us, throws considerable light on his moral persuasions, and will not, in investigating the secret of them, be overlooked. We allude to the spirit in which he cultivates his Art; the noble, disinterested, almost religious love with which he looks on Art in general, and strives towards it as towards the sure, highest, nay, only good. We extract one passage from *Wilhelm Meister*: it may pass for a piece of fine declamation, but not in that light do we offer it here. Strange, unaccountable as the thing may seem, we have actually evidence before our mind that Goethe believes in such doctrines, nay, has, in some sort, lived and endeavoured to direct his conduct by them.

"'Look at men,' continues Wilhelm, 'how they struggle after happiness and satisfaction! Their wishes, their toil, their gold, are ever hunting restlessly; and after what? After that which the Poet has received from nature; the right enjoyment of the world: the feeling of himself in others; the harmonious conjunction of many things that will seldom go together.

"'What is it that keeps men in continual discontent and agitation? It is that they cannot make realities correspond with their conceptions, that enjoyment steals away from among their hands, that the wished-for comes too late, and nothing reached and acquired produces on the heart the effect which their longing for it at a distance led them to anticipate. Now fate has exalted the Poet above all this, as if he were a god. He views the conflicting tumult of the passions; sees families and kingdoms raging in aimless commotion; sees those perplexed enigmas of misunderstanding, which often a single syllable would explain, occasioning convulsions unutterably baleful. He has a fellow-feeling of the mournful and the joyful in the fate of all mortals. When the man of the world is devoting his days to wasting melancholy for some deep disappointment; or, in the ebullience of joy, is going out to meet his happy destiny, the lightly-moved and all-conceiving spirit of the Poet steps forth, like the sun from night to day, and with soft transition tunes his harp to joy or wo. From his heart, its native soil, springs the fair flower of Wisdom; and if others while waking dream, and are pained with fantastic delusions from their every sense, he passes the dream of life like one awake, and the strangest event is to him nothing, save a part of the past and of the future. And thus the Poet is a teacher, a prophet, a friend of gods and men. How! Thou wouldst have him descend from his height to some paltry occupation? He who is fashioned, like a bird, to hover round the world, to nestle on the lofty summits, to feed on flowers and fruits, exchanging gaily one bough for another, *he* ought also to work at the plough like an ox; like a dog to train himself to the harness and draught; or, perhaps, tied up in a chain, to guard a farm-yard by his barking?'

"Werner, it may well be supposed, had listened with the greatest surprise. 'All true,' he rejoined, 'if men were but made like birds; and, though they neither spun nor weaved, could spend peaceful days in perpetual enjoyment; if, at the approach of winter, they could as easily betake themselves to distant regions; could retire before scarcity, and fortify themselves against frost.'

"'Poets have lived so,' exclaimed Wilhelm, 'in times when true nobleness was better reverenced; and so should they ever live. Sufficiently provided for within, they had need of little from without; the gift of imparting lofty emotions, and glorious images to men, in melodies and words that charmed the ear, and fixed themselves inseparably on whatever they might touch, of old enraptured the world, and served the gifted as a rich inheritance. At the courts of kings, at the tables of the great, under the windows of the fair, the sound of them was heard, while the ear and the soul were shut for all beside; and men felt, as we do when delight comes over us, and we pause with rapture if, among the dingles we are crossing, the voice of the nightingale starts out, touching and strong. They found a home in every habitation of the world, and the lowliness of their condition but exalted them the more. The hero listened to their songs, and the Conqueror of the Earth did reverence to a Poet; for he felt that, without poets, his own wild and vast existence would pass away like a whirlwind, and be forgotten for ever. The lover wished that he could feel his longings and his joys so variedly and so harmoniously as the Poet's inspired lips had skill to show them forth; and even the rich man could not of himself discern such costliness in his idol grandeurs, as when they were presented to him shining in the splendour of the Poet's spirit, sensible to all worth, and ennobling all. Nay, if thou wilt have it, who but the Poet was it that first formed Gods for us; that exalted us to them, and brought them down to us?'"*

For a man of Goethe's talent to write many such pieces of rhetoric, setting forth the dignity of poets, and their innate independence on external circumstances, could be no very hard task: accordingly, we find such sentiments again and again expressed, sometimes with still more gracefulness, still clearer emphasis, in his various writings. But to adopt these sentiments into his sober practical persuasion; in any measure to feel and believe that such was still, and must always be, the high vocation of the poet; on this ground of universal humanity, of ancient and now almost forgotten nobleness, to take his stand, even in these trivial, jeering, withered, unbelieving days; and through all their complex, dispiriting, mean, yet tumultuous influences, to "make his light shine before men," that it might beautify even our "rag-gathering age" with some beams of that mild, divine splendour, which had long

* *Wilhelm Meister's Apprenticeship*, book ii. chap. 2.

left us—the very possibility of which was denied; heartily and in earnest to meditate all this, was no common proceeding; to bring it into practice, especially in such a life as his has been, was among the highest and hardest enterprises, which any man whatever could engage in. We reckon this a greater novelty, than all the novelties which as a mere writer he ever put forth, whether for praise or censure. We have taken it upon us to say that if such *is*, in any sense, the state of the case with regard to Goethe, he deserves not mere approval as a pleasing poet and sweet singer; but deep, grateful study, observance, imitation, as a Moralist and Philosopher. If there be any *probability* that such is the state of the case, we cannot but reckon it a matter well worthy of being inquired into. And it is for this only that we are here pleading and arguing.

On the literary merit and meaning of *Wilhelm Meister* we have already said that we must not enter at present. The book has been translated into English; it underwent the usual judgment from our Reviews and Magazines; was to some a stone of stumbling, to others foolishness, to most an object of wonder. On the whole, it passed smoothly through the critical Assaying-house, for the Assayers have Christian dispositions, and very little time; so *Meister* was ranked, without umbrage, among the legal coin of the Minerva Press; and allowed to circulate as copper currency among the rest. That in so quick a process, a German *Freidrich d'or* might not slip through unnoticed among new and equally brilliant British brass Farthings, there is no warranting. For our critics can now criticise *impromptu*, which, though far the readiest, is nowise the surest plan. *Meister* is the mature product of the first genius in our times; and must, one would think, be different, in various respects, from the immature products of geniuses who are far from the first, and whose works spring from the brain in as many weeks as Goethe's cost him years.

Nevertheless, we quarrel with no man's verdict; for Time, which tries all things, will try this also, and bring to light the truth, both as regards criticism and the thing criticised; or sink both into final darkness, which likewise will be the truth as regards them. But there is one censure which we must advert to for a moment, so singular does it seem to us. *Meister*, it appears, is a "vulgar" work; no "gentleman," we hear in certain circles, could have written it; few real gentlemen, it is insinuated, can like to read it; no real lady, unless possessed of considerable courage, should profess having read it at all. Of Goethe's "gentility" we shall leave all men to speak that have any, even the faintest knowledge of him; and with regard to the gentility of his readers, state only the following fact. Most of us have heard of the late Queen of Prussia, and know whether or not she was genteel enough, and of real ladyhood: nay, if we must prove every thing, her character can be read in the *Life of Napoleon*, by Sir Walter Scott, who passes for a judge of those matters. And yet this is what we find written in the *Kunst und Alterthum* for 1824.*

* Band v. s. 8.

"Books, too, have their past happiness, which no chance can take away:

> *Wer nie sein Brod mit Thränen ass,*
> *Wer nicht die kummervollen Nächte*
> *Auf seinem Bette weinend sass,*
> *Der kennt euch nicht, ihr himmlischen Mächte.* *

"These heart-broken lines a highly noble-minded, venerated Queen repeated in the cruelest exile, when cast forth to boundless misery. She made herself familiar with the Book in which these words, with many other painful experiences, are communicated, and drew from it a melancholy consolation. This influence, stretching of itself into boundless time, what is there that can obliterate?"

Here are strange diversities of taste; "national discrepancies" enough, had we time to investigate them! Nevertheless, wishing each party to retain his own special persuasions, so far as they are honest, and adapted to his intellectual position, national or individual, we cannot but believe that there is an inward and essential Truth in Art; a Truth far deeper than the dictates of mere Mode, and which, could we pierce through these dictates, would be true for all nations and all men. To arrive at this Truth, distant from every one at first, approachable by most, attainable by some small number, is the end and aim of all real study of Poetry. For such a purpose, among others, the comparison of English with foreign judgment, on works that will bear judging, forms no unprofitable help. Some day, we may translate Friedrich Schlegel's Essay on *Meister*, by way of contrast to our English animadversions on that subject. Schlegel's praise, whatever ours might do, rises sufficiently high: neither does he seem, during twenty years, to have repented of what he said; for we observe in the edition of his works, at present publishing, he repeats the whole *Character*, and even appends to it, in a separate sketch, some new assurances and elucidations.

It may deserve to be mentioned here that *Meister*, at its first appearance in Germany, was received very much as it has been in England. Goethe's known character, indeed, precluded indifference there; but otherwise it was much the same. The whole guild of criticism was thrown into perplexity, into sorrow; everywhere was dissatisfaction open or concealed. Official duty impelling them to speak, some said one thing, some another; all felt in secret that they knew not what to say. Till the appearance of Schlegel's *Character*, no word, that we have seen, of the smallest chance to be decisive, or indeed to last beyond the day, had been uttered regarding it. Some regretted that the fire of *Werter* was so wonderfully abated; whisperings there might be about "lowness," "heaviness;" some spake forth boldly in behalf of suffering "virtue." Novalis was not among the speakers, but he censured the work in secret, and this for a reason which to us will seem the strangest; for its being, as we should say, a Benthamite work! Many are the bitter aphorisms we find, among his Frag-

* Who never ate his bread in sorrow;
Who never spent the darksome hours
Weeping and watching for the morrow,
He knows you not, ye unseen Powers.
Wilhelm Meister, book ii. chap. 13.

ments, directed against *Meister* for its prosaic, mechanical, economical, cold-hearted, altogether Utilitarian character. We English again call Goethe a mystic: so difficult is it to please all parties! But the good, deep, nobl Novalis made the fairest amends; for notwithstanding all this, Tieck tells us, if we remember rightly, he regularly perused *Meister* twice a year.

On a somewhat different ground, proceeded quite another sort of assault from one Pustkucher of Quedlinburg. Herr Pustkucher felt afflicted, it would seem, at the want of Patriotism and Religion too manifest in *Meister;* and determined to take what vengeance he could. By way of sequel to the *Apprenticeship,* Goethe had announced his *Wilhelm Meisters Wanderjahre,** as in a state of preparation; but the book still lingered: whereupon, in the interim, forth comes this Pustkucher with a pseudo-*Wanderjahre* of his own; satirizing, according to ability, the spirit and principles of the *Apprenticeship.* We have seen an epigram on Pustkucker and his *Wanderjahre,* attributed, with what justice we know not, to Goethe himself; whether it is his or not, it is written in his name; and seems to express accurately enough for such a purpose the relation between the parties,—in language which we had rather not translate:

Will denn von Quedlinburg aus
Ein neuer Wanderer traben?
Hat doch die Wallfisch seine Laus,
Muss auch die meine haben.

So much for Pustkucher, and the rest. The true *Wanderjahre* has at length appeared: the first volume has been before the world since 1821. This fragment, for it still continues such, is in our view one of the most perfect pieces of composition that Goethe has ever produced. We have heard something of his being at present engaged in extending or completing it: what the whole may in his hands become, we are anxious to see; but the *Wanderjahre,* even in its actual state, can hardly be called unfinished, as a piece of writing; it coheres so beautifully within itself; and yet we see not whence the wonderous landscape came, or whither it is stretching; but it hangs before us as a fairy region, hiding its borders on this side in light sunny clouds, fading away on that into the infinite azure: already, we might almost say, it gives us the notion of a *completed fragment,* or the state in which a fragment, not meant for completion, might be left.

But apart from its environment, and considered merely in itself, this *Wanderjahre* seems to us a most estimable work. There is, in truth, a singular gracefulness in it; a high, melodious Wisdom; so light is it, yet so earnest; so calm, so gay, yet so strong and deep for the purest spirit of all Art rests over it and breathes through it; "mild Wisdom is wedded in living union to Harmony divine;" the Thought of the Sage is melted, we might say, and incorporated in the liquid music of the Poet. "It is called a Romance," observes the English Translator; "but it treats not of romance characters or subjects; it has less relation to Fielding's *Tom Jones,* than to Spenser's *Faëry Queen.*" We have not forgotten what is due to Spenser; yet, perhaps, beside his immortal allegory this *Wanderjahre* may, in fact, not unfairly be named; and with this advantage, that it is an allegory, not of the Seventeenth century, but of the Nineteenth; a picture full of expressiveness, of what men are striving for, and ought to strive for in these actual days. "The scene," we are further told, "is not laid on this firm earth; but in a fair Utopia of Art and Science and free Activity; the figures, light and aëriform, come unlooked for, and melt away abruptly, like the pageants of Prospero, in his Enchanted Island." We venture to add, that, like Prospero's Island, this too is drawn from the inward depths, the purest sphere of poetic inspiration: ever, as we read it, the images of old Italian Art flit before us; the gay tints of Titian; the quaint grace of Domenichino; sometimes the clear, yet unfathomable depth of Rafaelle; and whatever else we have known or dreamed of in that rich old genial world.

As it is Goethe's moral sentiments, and cul ture as a man, that we have made our chief object in this survey, we would fain give some adequate specimen of the *Wanderjahre,* where, as appears to us, these are to be traced in their last degree of clearness and completeness. But to do this, to find a specimen that should be adequate, were difficult, or rather impossible. How shall we divide what is in itself one and indivisible? How shall the fraction of a complex picture give us any idea of the so beautiful whole? Nevertheless, we shall refer our readers to the Tenth and Eleventh Chapters of the *Wanderjahre;* where in poetic and symbolic style, they will find a sketch of the nature, objects, and present ground of Religious Belief, which, if they have ever reflected duly on that matter, will hardly fail to interest them. They will find these chapters, if we mistake not, worthy of deep consideration; for this is the merit of Goethe: his maxims will bear study, nay, they require it, and improve by it more and more. They come from the depths of his mind, and are not in their place till they have reached the depths of ours. The wisest man, we believe, may see in them a reflex of his own wisdom: but to him who is still learning, they become as seeds of knowledge; they take root in the mind, and ramify, as we meditate them, into a whole garden of thought. The sketch we mentioned is far too long for being extracted here: however, we give some scattered portions of it, which the reader will accept with fair allowance. As the wild suicidal Night-thoughts of *Werter* formed our first extract, this by way of counterpart may be the last. We must fancy Wilhelm in the "Pedagogic province," proceeding towards the "CHIEF, or the THREE,"

* "*Wanderjahre* denotes the period which a German artisan is, by law or usage, obliged to pass in travelling, to perfect himself in his craft, after the conclusion of his *Lehrjahre* (Apprenticeship), and before his Mastership can begin. In many guilds this custom is as old as their existence, and continues still to be indispensable: it is said to have originated in the frequent journeys of the German Emperors to Italy, and the consequent improvement observed in such workmen among their menials as had attended them thither. Most of the guilds are what is called *geschenkten,* that is, *presenting,* having presents to give to needy *wandering* brothers."

with intent to place his son under their charge, in that wonderful region, "where he was to see so many singularities."

"Wilhelm had already noticed that in the cut and colour of the young people's clothes, a variety prevailed, which gave the whole tiny population a peculiar aspect: he was about to question his attendant on this point, when a still stranger observation forced itself upon him; all the children, how employed soever, laid down their work, and turned, with singular yet diverse gestures, towards the party riding past them; or rather, as it was easy to infer, towards the Overseer, who was in it. The youngest laid their arms crosswise over their breasts and looked cheerfully up to the sky; those of middle size held their hands on their backs, and looked smiling on the ground; the eldest stood with a frank and spirited air; their arms stretched down, they turned their heads to the right, and formed themselves into a line; whereas the others kept separate, each where he chanced to be.

"The riders having stopped and dismounted here, as several children, in their various modes, were standing forth to be inspected by the Overseer, Wilhelm asked the meaning of these gestures; but Felix struck in and cried gaily: 'What posture am I to take then?' 'Without doubt,' said the Overseer, 'the first posture; the arms over the breast, the face earnest and cheerful towards the sky.' Felix obeyed, but soon cried: 'This is not much to my taste; I see nothing up there: does it last long? But yes!' exclaimed he joyfully, 'yonder are a pair of falcons flying from the west to the east; that is a good sign too?'—'As thou takest it, as thou behavest,' said the other: 'Now mingle among them as they mingle.' He gave a signal, and the children left their postures, and again betook them to work or sport as before."

Wilhelm a second time "asks the meaning of these gestures;" but the Overseer is not at liberty to throw much light on the matter; mentions only that they are symbolical, "nowise mere grimaces, but have a moral purport, which perhaps the Chief or the Three may further explain to him." The children themselves, it would seem, only know it in part; "secrecy having many advantages; for when you tell a man at once and straight forward the purpose of any object, he fancies there is nothing in it." By and by, however, having left Felix by the way, and parted with the Overseer, Wilhelm arrives at the abode of the Three "who preside over sacred things," and from whom further satisfaction is to be looked for.

"Wilhelm had now reached the gate of a wooded vale, surrounded with high walls: on a certain sign, the little door opened and a man of earnest, imposing look received our traveller. The latter found himself in a large beautifully umbrageous space, decked with the richest foliage, shaded with trees and bushes of all sorts; while stately walls and magnificent buildings were discerned only in glimpses through this thick natural boscage. A friendly reception from the Three, who by and by appeared, at last turned into a general conversation, the substance of which we now present in an abbreviated shape.

"'Since you intrust your son to us,' said they, 'it is fair that we admit you to a closer view of our procedure. Of what is external you have seen much that does not bear its meaning on its front. What part of this do you wish to have explained?'

"'Dignified yet singular gestures of salutation I have noticed; the import of which I would gladly learn: with you, doubtless, the exterior has a reference to the interior, and inversely: let me know what this reference is.'

"'Well-formed healthy children,' replied the Three, 'bring much into the world along with them; nature has given to each whatever he requires for time and duration; to unfold this is our duty; often it unfolds itself better of its own accord. One thing there is, however, which no child brings into the world with him; and yet it is on this one thing that all depends for making man in every point a man. If you can discover it yourself, speak it out.' Wilhelm thought a little while, then shook his head.

"The Three, after a suitable pause, exclaimed, 'Reverence!' Wilhelm seemed to hesitate. 'Reverence!' cried they, a second time. 'All want it, perhaps yourself.'

"'Three kinds of gestures you have seen; and we inculcate a threefold reverence, which when commingled and formed into one whole, attains its full force and effect. The first is Reverence for what is Above us. That posture, the arms crossed over the breast, the look turned joyfully towards heaven; that is what we have enjoined on young children; requiring from them thereby a testimony that there is a God above, who images and reveals himself in parents, teachers, superiors. Then comes the second; Reverence for what is Under us. Those hands folded over the back, and as it were tied together, that down-turned smiling look, announce that we are to regard the earth with attention and cheerfulness: from the bounty of the earth we are nourished: the earth affords unutterable joys; but disproportionate sorrows she also brings us. Should one of our children do himself external hurt, blamably or blamelessly; should others hurt him accidentally or purposely; should dead involuntary matter do him hurt; then let him well consider it; for such dangers will attend him all his days. But from this posture we delay not to free our pupil, the instant we become convinced that the instruction connected with it has produced sufficient influence on him. Then, on the contrary, we bid him gather courage, and, turning to his comrades, range himself along with them. Now, at last, he stands forth, frank and bold; not selfishly isolated; only in combination with his equals does he front the world. Further we have nothing to add.'

"'I see a glimpse of it!' said Wilhelm. 'Are not the mass of men so marred and stinted because they take pleasure only in the element of evil-wishing and evil-speaking? Whoever gives himself to this, soon comes to be indifferent towards God, contemptuous towards the world, spiteful towards his equals; and the true, genuine, indispensable sentiment of self-estimation corrupts into self-conceit and presumption. Allow me, however,' continued he, 'to state one difficulty. You say that reverence is not natural to man: now has not the reverence or fear of rude people for violent convulsions of nature, or other inexplicable mysteriously foreboding occurrences, been heretofore regarded as the germ out of which a higher feeling, a purer sentiment, was by degrees to be developed?'

"'Nature is indeed adequate to fear,' replied they, 'but to reverence not adequate. Men fear a known or unknown powerful being; the strong seeks to conquer it, the weak to avoid it: both endeavour to get quit of it, and feel themselves happy when for a short season they have put it aside, and their nature has in some degree restored itself to freedom and independence. The natural man repeats this operation millions of times in the course of his life; from fear he struggles to freedom; from freedom he is driven back to fear, and so makes no advancement. To fear is easy, but grievous; to reverence is difficult, but satisfactory. Man does not willingly submit himself to reverence, or rather he never so submits himself: it is a higher sense which must be communicated to his nature; which only in some favoured individuals unfolds itself spontaneously, who on this account too have of old been looked upon as Saints and Gods. Here lies the worth, here lies the business of all true Religions, whereof there are likewise only three, according to the objects towards which they direct our devotion.'

"The men paused; Wilhelm reflected for a time in silence; but feeling in himself no pretensions to unfold these strange words, he requested the Sages to proceed with their exposition. They immediately complied. 'No Religion that grounds itself on fear,' said they, 'is regarded among us. With the reverence to which a man should give dominion in his mind, he can, in paying honour, keep his own honour; he is not disunited with himself as in the former case. The Religion, which depends on Reverence for what is Above us, we denominate the Ethnic; it is the Religion of the Nations, and the first happy deliverance from a degrading fear; all Heathen religions, as we call them, are of this sort, whatsoever names they may bear. The Second Religion, which founds itself on Reverence for what is Around us, we denominate the Philosophical; for the Philosopher stations himself in the middle, and must draw down to him all that is higher, and up to him all that is lower, and only in this medium condition does he merit the title of Wise. Here, as he surveys with clear sight his relation to his equals, and therefore to the whole human race, his relation likewise to all other earthly circumstances and arrangements necessary or accidental, he alone, in a cosmic sense, lives in Truth. But now we have to speak of the Third Religion, grounded on Reverence for what is Under us; this we name the Christian; as in the Christian Religion such a temper is the most distinctly manifested; it is a last step to which mankind were fitted and destined to attain. But what a task was it not only to be patient with the Earth, and let it lie beneath us, we appealing to a higher birthplace; but also to recognise humility and poverty, mockery and despite, disgrace and wretchedness, suffering and death, to recognise these things as divine; nay, even on sin and crime to look not as hindrances, but to honour and love them as furtherances of what is holy. Of this, indeed, we find some traces in all ages; but the trace is not the goal; and this being now attained, the human species cannot retrograde; and we may say that the Christian Religion, having once appeared, cannot again vanish; having once assumed its divine shape, can be subject to no dissolution.'

"'To which of these Religions do you specially adhere?' inquired Wilhelm.

"'To all the three,' replied they, 'for in their union they produce what may properly be called the true Religion. Out of those three Reverences springs the highest Reverence, Reverence for One's self, and these again unfold themselves from this; so that man attains the highest elevation of which he is capable, that of being justified in reckoning himself the Best that God and Nature have produced; nay, of being able to continue on this lofty eminence, without being again by self-conceit and presumption drawn down from it into the vulgar level.'"

The Three undertake to admit him into the interior of their Sanctuary; whither, accordingly, he, "at the hand of the Eldest," proceeds on the morrow. Sorry are we that we cannot follow them into the "octagonal hall," so full of paintings, and the "gallery open on one side, and stretching round a spacious, gay, flowery garden." It is a beautiful figurative representation, by pictures and symbols of Art, of the First and the Second Religions, the Ethnic and the Philosophical; for the former of which the pictures have been composed from the Old Testament; for the latter from the New. We can only make room for some small portions.

"'I observe,' said Wilhelm, 'you have done the Israelites the honour to select their history as the groundwork of this delineation, or rather you have made it the leading object there.'

"'As you see,' replied the Eldest; 'for you will remark, that on the socles and friezes we have introduced another series of transactions and occurrences, not so much of a synchronistic as of a symphronistic kind; since, among all nations, we discover records of a similar import, and grounded on the same facts. Thus you perceive here, while, in the main field of the picture, Abraham receives a visit from his gods in the form of fair youths, Apollo among the herdsmen of Admetus is painted above on the frieze. From which we may learn, that the gods, when they appear to men, are commonly unrecognised of them.'

"The friends walked on. Wilhelm, for the most part, met with well-known objects; but they were here exhibited in a livelier, more expressive manner, than he had been used to see them. On some few matters, he requested explanation, and at last could not help returning to his former question: 'Why the Israelitish history had been chosen in preference to all others?'

"The Eldest answered: 'Among all Heathen religions, for such also is the Israelitish, this has the most distinguished advantages; of which I shall mention only a few. At the Ethnic judgment-seat, at the judgment-seat of the God of Nations, it is not asked whether this is best, the most excellent nation; but whether it lasts, whether it has continued. The Israelitish people never was good for much, as its own leaders, judges, rulers, prophets, have a thousand times reproachfully declared; it possesses few virtues, and most of the faults of other nations: but in cohesion, steadfastness, valour, and, when all this would not serve, in obstinate toughness, it has no match. It is the most perseverant nation in the world; it is, it was, and it will be, to glorify the name of Jehovah through all ages. We have set it up, therefore, as the pattern figure; as the main figure, to which the others only serve as a frame.'

"'It becomes not me to dispute with you,' said Wilhelm, 'since you have instruction to impart. Open to me, therefore, the other advantages of this people, or rather of its history, of its religion.'

"'One chief advantage,' said the other, 'is its excellent collection of Sacred Books. These stand so happily combined together, that even out of the most diverse elements, the feeling of a whole still rises before us. They are complete enough to satisfy; fragmentary enough to excite; barbarous enough to rouse; tender enough to appease; and for many other contradicting merits might not these Books, might not this one Book, be praised?'

* * * * *

"Thus wandering on, they had now reached the gloomy and perplexed periods of the History, the destruction of the City and the Temple, the murder, exile, slavery of whole masses of this stiff-necked people. Its subsequent fortunes were delineated in a cunning allegorical way; a real historical delineation of them would have lain without the limits of true Art.

"At this point, the gallery abruptly terminated in a closed door, and Wilhelm was surprised to see himself already at the end. 'In your historical series,' said he, 'I find a chasm. You have destroyed the Temple of Jerusalem, and dispersed the people; yet you have not introduced the divine Man who taught there shortly before; to whom, shortly before, they would give no ear.'

"'To have done this, as you require it, would have been an error. The life of that divine Man, whom you allude to, stands in no connection with the general history of the world in his time. It was a private life; his teaching was a teaching for individuals. What has publicly befallen vast masses of people, and the minor parts which compose them, belongs to the general History of the World, to the general Religion of the World; the Religion we have named the First. What inwardly befalls individuals belongs to the Second Religion, the Philosophical: such a Religion was it that Christ taught and practised, so long as he went about on earth. For this reason, the external here closes, and I now open to you the internal.'

"A door went back, and they entered a similar gallery; where Wilhelm soon recognised a corresponding series of Pictures from the New Testament. They seemed as if by another hand than the first: all was softer; forms, movements, accompaniments, light, and colouring."

Into this second gallery, with its strange doctrine about "Miracles and Parables," the characteristic of the Philosophical Religion, we cannot enter for the present, yet must give one hurried glance. Wilhelm expresses some surprise that these delineations terminate "with the Supper, with the scene where the Master and his Disciples part." He inquires for the remaining portion of the history.

"'In all sorts of instruction,' said the Eldest, 'in all sorts of communication, we are fond of separating whatever it is possible to separate; for by this means alone can the notion of importance and peculiar significance arise in the young mind. Actual experience of itself mingles and mixes all things together: here, accordingly, we have entirely disjoined that sublime Man's life from its termination. In life, he appears as a true Philosopher,—let not the expression stagger you,—as a Wise Man in the highest sense. He stands firm to this point: he goes on his way inflexibly, and while he exalts the lower to himself, while he makes the ignorant, the poor, the sick, partakers of his wisdom, of his riches, of his strength, he, on the other hand, in nowise conceals his divine origin; he dares to equal himself with God, nay, to declare that he himself is God. In this manner is he wont, from youth upwards, to astound his familiar friends; of these he gains a part to his own cause; irritates the rest against him; and shows to all men, who are aiming at a certain elevation in doctrine and life, what they have to look for from the world. And thus, for the noble portion of mankind, his walk and conversation are even more instructive and profitable than his death: for to those trials every one is called, to this trial but a few. Now, omitting all that results from this consideration, do but look at the touching scene of the Last Supper. Here the Wise Man, as it ever is, leaves those, that are his own, utterly orphaned behind him; aad while he is careful for the Good, he feeds along with them a traitor, by whom he and the Better are to be destroyed.'"

This seems to us to have "a deep, still meaning;" and the longer and closer we examine it, the more it pleases us. Wilhelm is not admitted into the shrine of the Third Religion, the Christian, or that of which Christ's sufferings and death were the symbols, as his walk and conversation had been the symbol of the Second, or Philosophical Religion. "That last Religion," it is said,—

"'That last Religion which arises from the Reverence of what is Beneath us; that veneration of the contradictory, the hated, the avoided, we give to each of our pupils, in small portions, by way of outfit, along with him into the world, merely that he may know where more is to be had, should such a want spring up within him. I invite you to return hither at the end of a year, to attend our general

Festival, and see how far your son is advanced: then shall you be admitted into the Sanctuary of Sorrow.'

"'Permit me one question,' said Wilhelm: 'as you have set up the life of this divine Man for a pattern and example, have you likewise selected his sufferings, his death, as a model of exalted patience?'

"'Undoubtedly we have,' replied the Eldest. 'Of this we make no secret; but we draw a veil over these sufferings, even because we reverence them so highly. We hold it a damnable audacity to bring forth that torturing Cross, and the Holy One who suffers on it, or to expose them to the light of the Sun, which hid its face when a reckless world forced such a sight on it; to take these mysterious secrets, in which the divine depth of Sorrow lies hid, and play with them, fondle them, trick them out, and rest not till the most reverend of all solemnities appears vulgar and paltry. Let so much for the present suffice—* * * The rest we must still owe you for a twelvemonth. The instruction, which in the interim we give the children, no stranger is allowed to witness: then, however, come to us, and you will hear what our best Speakers think it serviceable to make public on those matters.'"

Could we hope that, in its present disjointed state, this emblematic sketch would rise before the minds of our readers, in any measure as it stood before the mind of the writer; that, in considering it, they might seize only an outline of those many meanings which, at less or greater depth, lie hidden under it, we should anticipate their thanks for having, a first or a second time, brought it before them. As it is, believing that to open-minded, truth-seeking men, the deliberate words of an open-minded, truth-seeking man can in no case be wholly unintelligible, nor the words of such a man as Goethe indifferent, we have transcribed it for their perusal. If we induce them to turn to the original, and study this in its completeness, with so much else that environs it, and bears on it, they will thank us still more. To our own judgment, at least, there is a fine and pure significance in this whole delineation: such phrases even as "the Sanctuary of Sorrow," "the divine depth of Sorrow," have of themselves pathetic wisdom for us; as indeed a tone of devoutness, of calm, mild, priestlike dignity pervades the whole. In a time like ours, it is rare to see, in the writings of cultivated men, any opinion whatever, bearing any mark of sincerity, on such a subject as this: yet it is and continues the highest subject, and they that are highest are most fit for studying it, and helping others to study it.

Goethe's *Wanderjahre* was published in his seventy-second year; *Werter* in his twenty-fifth: thus in passing between these two works, and over *Meisters Lehrjahre*, which stands nearly midway, we have glanced over a space of almost fifty years, including within them, of course, whatever was most important in his public or private history. By means of these quotations, so diverse in their tone, we meant to make it visible that a great change had taken place in the moral disposition of the man; a change from inward imprisonment, doubt, and discontent, into freedom, belief, and clear activity: such a change as, in our opinion, must take place, more or less consciously, in every character that, especially in these times, attains to spiritual manhood; and in characters possessing any thoughtfulness and sensibility, will seldom take place without a too painful consciousness, without bitter conflicts, in which the character itself is too often maimed and impoverished, and which end too often not in victory, but in defeat, or fatal compromise with the enemy. Too often, we may well say; for though many gird on the harness, few bear it warrior-like; still fewer put it off with triumph. Among our own poets, Byron was almost the only man we saw faithfully and manfully struggling, to the end, in this cause; and he died while the victory was still doubtful, or at best, only beginning to be gained. We have already stated our opinion, that Goethe's success in this matter has been more complete than that of any other man in his age; nay, that, in the strictest sense, he may also be called the only one that has so succeeded. On this ground, were it on no other, we have ventured to say, that his spiritual history and procedure must deserve attention; that his opinions, his creations, his mode of thought, his whole picture of the world as it dwells within him, must to his contemporaries be an inquiry of no common interest; of an interest altogether peculiar, and not in this degree exampled in existing literature. These things can be but imperfectly stated here, and must be left, not in a state of demonstration, but, at the utmost, of loose fluctuating probability; nevertheless, if inquired into, they will be found to have a precise enough meaning, and, as we believe, a highly important one.

For the rest, what sort of mind it is that has passed through this change, that has gained this victory; how rich and high a mind; how learned by study in all that is wisest, by experience in all that is most complex, the brightest as well as the blackest, in man's existence; gifted with what insight, with what grace and power of utterance, we shall not for the present attempt discussing. All these the reader will learn, who studies his writings with such attention as they merit: and by no other means. Of Goethe's dramatic, lyrical, didactic poems, in their thousandfold expressiveness, for they are full of expressiveness, we can here say nothing. But in every department of Literature, of Art ancient and modern, in many provinces of Science, we shall often meet him; and hope to have other occasions of estimating what, in these respects, we and all men owe him.

Two circumstances, meanwhile we have remarked, which to us throw light on the nature of his original faculty for Poetry, and go far to convince us of the Mastery he has attained in that art; these we may here state briefly, for the judgment of such as already know his writings, or the help of such as are beginning to know them. The first is his singularly emblematic intellect; his perpetual never-failing tendency to transform into *shape*, into *life*, the opinion, the feeling that may dwell in him; which, in its widest sense, we reckon to be essentially the grand problem of the Poet. We do not mean mere metaphor and rhetorical trope: these are but the exterior concern, often but the scaffolding of the edifice, which is to be built up (within our thoughts) by means of them. In allusions, in similitudes, though no one known to us is happier, many are more copious, than Goethe. But we find this faculty of his in the very essence of his intellect; and trace it alike in the quiet, cunning epigram, the allegory, the quaint device, reminding us of some Quarles or Bunyan; and in the *Fausts*, the *Tassos*, the *Mignons*, which, in their pure and genuine personality, may almost remind us of the *Ariels* and *Hamlets* of Shakspeare. Every thing has form, every thing has visual existence; the poet's imagination *bodies forth* the forms of things unseen, his pen turns them to *shape*. This, as a natural endowment, exists in Goethe, we conceive, to a very high degree.

The other characteristic of his mind, which proves to us his acquired mastery in art, as this shows us the extent of his original capacity for it, is his wonderful variety, nay, universality; his entire freedom from Mannerism. We read Goethe for years before we come to see wherein the distinguishing peculiarity of his understanding, of his disposition, even of his way of writing, consists. It seems quite a simple style—that of his; remarkable chiefly for its calmness, its perspicuity, in short, its commonness: and yet it is the most uncommon of all styles: we feel as if every one might imitate it, and yet it is inimitable. As hard is it to discover in his writings,—though there also, as in every man's writings, the character of the writer must lie recorded,—what sort of spiritual construction he has, what are his temper, his affections, his individual specialities. For all lives freely within him; Philina and Clärchen, Mephistopheles and Mignon, are alike indifferent, or alike dear to him; he is of no sect or caste: he seems not this man or that man, but a man. We reckon this to be the characteristic of a Master in Art of any sort; and true especially of all great Poets. How true is it of Shakspeare and Homer! Who knows, or can figure what the Man Shakspeare was, by the first, by the twentieth perusal of his works? He is a Voice coming to us from the Land of Melody: his old, brick dwelling-place, in the mere earthly burgh of Stratford-on-Avon, offers us the most inexplicable enigma. And what is Homer in the *Ilias?* HE IS THE WITNESS; he has seen, and he reveals it; we hear and believe, but do not behold him. Now compare, with these two poets, any other two; not of equal genius, for there are none such, but of equal sincerity, who wrote as earnestly, and from the heart, like them. Take, for instance, Jean Paul and Lord Byron. The good Richter begins to show himself, in his broad, massive, kindly, quaint significance, before we have read many pages of even his slightest work; and to the last, he paints himself much better than his subject. Byron may almost be said to have painted nothing else than himself, be his subject what it might. Yet as a test for the culture of a Poet, in his poetical capacity, for his pretensions to mastery and completeness in his heart, we can but reckon this among the surest. Tried by this, there is no living writer that approaches within many degrees of Goethe.

Thus, it would seem, we consider Goethe to be a richly educated Poet, no less than a richly educated Man: a master both of Humanity, and of Poetry; one to whom Experience has given true wisdom, and the "Melodies Eternal" a perfect utterance for his wisdom. Of the particular form which this humanity, this wisdom has assumed; of his opinions, character, personality,—for these, with whatever difficulty, are and must be decipherable in his writings,—we had much to say: but this also we must decline. In the present state of matters, to speak adequately would be a task too hard for us, and one in which our readers could afford little help, nay, in which many of them might take little interest. Meanwhile, we have found a brief cursory sketch on this subject, already written in our language: some parts of it, by way of preparation, we shall here transcribe. It is written by a professed admirer of Goethe; nay, as might almost seem, by a grateful learner, whom he taught, whom he had helped to lead out of spiritual obstruction, into peace and light. Making due allowance for all this, there is little in the paper that we object to.

"In Goethe's mind," observes he, "the first aspect that strikes us is its calmness, then its beauty; a deeper inspection reveals to us its vastness and unmeasured strength. This man rules, and is not ruled. The stern and fiery energies of a most passionate soul lie silent in the centre of its being; a trembling sensibility has been enured to stand, without flinching or murmur, the sharpest trials. Nothing outward, nothing inward, shall agitate or control him. The brightest and most capricious fancy, the most piercing and inquisitive intellect, the wildest and deepest imagination; the highest thrills of joy, the bitterest pangs of sorrow: all these are his, he is not theirs. While he moves every heart from its steadfastness, his own is firm and still: the words that search into the inmost recesses of our nature, he pronounces with a tone of coldness and equanimity: in the deepest pathos he weeps not, or his tears are like water trickling from a rock of adamant. He is a king of himself and of this world; nor does he rule it like a vulgar great man, like Napoleon or Charles the Twelfth, by the mere brute exertion of his will, grounded on no principle, or on a false one: his faculties and feelings are not fettered or prostrated under the iron sway of Passion, but led and guided in kindly union under the mild sway of Reason; as the fierce primeval elements of Chaos were stilled at the coming of Light, and bound together, under its soft vesture, into a glorious and beneficent Creation.

"This is the true rest of man; the dim aim of every human soul, the full attainment of only a chosen few. It comes not unsought to any; but the wise are wise because they think no price too high for it. Goethe's inward home has been reared by slow and laborious efforts; but it stands on no hollow or deceitful basis: for his peace is not from blindness, but from clear vision; not from uncertain hope of alteration, but from sure insight into what cannot alter. His world seems once to have been desolate and baleful as that of the darkest skeptic: but he has covered it anew with beauty and solemnity, derived from deeper sources, over which Doubt can have no sway. He has acquired fearlessly, and fearlessly searched out and denied the False; but he has not forgotten, what is equally essential and infinitely harder, to search out and admit the True. His heart is still full of warmth, though his head is clear and cold; the world for him is still full of grandeur, though he clothes it with no false colours; his fellow-creatures are still objects of reverence and love, though their basenesses are plainer to no eye than to his. To reconcile these contradictions is the task of all good men, each for himself, in his own way and manner; a task which, in our age, is encompassed with difficulties peculiar to the time; and which Goethe seems to have accomplished with a success that few can rival. A mind so in unity with itself, even though it were a poor and small one, would arrest our attention, and win some kind regard from us; but when this mind ranks among the strongest and most complicated of the species, it becomes a sight full of interest, a study full of deep instruction.

"Such a mind as Goethe's is the fruit not only of a royal endowment by nature, but also of a culture proportionate to her bounty. In Goethe's original form of spirit, we discern the highest gifts of manhood, without any deficiency of the lower: he has an eye and a heart equally for the sublime, the common, and the ridiculous; the elements at once of a poet, a thinker, and a wit. Of his culture we have often spoken already; and it deserves again to be held up to praise and imitation. This, as he himself unostentatiously confesses, has been the soul of all his conduct, the great enterprise of his life; and few that understand him will be apt to deny that he has prospered. As a writer, his resources have been accumulated from nearly all the provinces of human intellect and activity; and he has trained himself to use these complicated instruments, with a light expertness which we might have admired in the professor of a solitary department. Freedom, and grace, and smiling earnestness are the characteristics of his works: the matter of them flows along in chaste abundance, in the softest combination; and their style is referred to by native critics as the highest specimen of the German tongue.

* * * * *

"But Goethe's culture as a writer is perhaps less remarkable than his culture as a man. He has learned not in head only, but also in heart; not from Art and Literature, but also by action and passion, in the rugged school of Experience. If asked what was the grand characteristic of his writings, we should not say knowledge, but wisdom. A mind that has seen, and suffered, and done, speaks to us of what it has tried and conquered. A gay delineation will give us notice of dark and toilsome experiences, of business done in the great deep of the spirit; a maxim, trivial to the careless eye, will rise with light and solution over long perplexed periods of our own history. It is thus that heart speaks to heart, that the life of one man becomes a possession to all. Here is a mind of the most subtile and tumultuous elements; but it is governed in peaceful diligence, and its impetuous and ethereal faculties work softly together for good and noble ends. Goethe may be called a Philosopher; for he loves and has practised as a man the wisdom which, as a poet, he inculcates. Composure and cheerful seriousness seem to breathe over all his character. There is no whining over human woes: it is understood that we must simply all strive to alleviate or remove them. There is no noisy battling for opinions; but a persevering effort to make Truth lovely, and recommend her, by a thousand avenues, to the hearts of all men. Of his personal manners we can easily believe the universal report, as often given in the way of censure as of praise, that he is a man of consummate breeding and the stateliest presence: for an air of polished tolerance, of courtly, we might almost say, majestic repose, and serene humanity, is visible throughout his works. In no line of them does he speak with asperity of any man: scarcely ever even of a thing. He knows the good, and loves it; he knows the bad and hateful, and rejects it; but in neither case with violence: his love is calm and active; his rejection is implied, rather than pronounced; meek and gentle, though we see that it is thorough, and never to be revoked. The noblest and the basest he not only seems to comprehend, but to personate and body forth in their most secret lineaments: hence actions and opinions appear to him as they are, with all the circumstances which extenuate or endear them to the hearts where they originated and are entertained. This also is the spirit of our Shakspeare, and perhaps of every great dramatic poet. Shakspeare is no sectarian; to all he deals with equity and mercy; because he knows all, and his heart is wide enough for all. In his mind the world is a whole; he figures it as Providence governs it; and to him it is not strange that the sun should be caused to shine on the evil and the good, and the rain to fall on the just and the unjust."

Considered as a transient, far-off view of Goethe in his personal character, all this, from the writer's peculiar point of vision, may have its true grounds, and wears at least the aspect of sincerity. We may also quote something of what follows on Goethe's character as a poet and thinker, and the contrast he exhibits in this respect with another celebrated, and now altogether European author.

"Goethe," observes this critic, "has been called the 'German Voltaire,' but it is a name which does him wrong and describes him ill. Except in the corresponding variety of their pursuits and knowledge, in which, perhaps, it does Voltaire wrong, the two cannot be compared. Goethe is all, or the best of all, that Voltaire was, and he is much that Voltaire did not dream of. To say nothing of his dig nified and truthful character as a man, he belongs, as a thinker and a writer, to a far higher class than this *enfant gâté du monde qu'il gâta*. He is not a questioner and a despiser, but a teacher and a reverencer; not a destroyer, but a builder up; not a wit only, but a wise man. Of him Montesquieu could not have said, with even epigrammatic truth: *Il a plus que personne l'esprit que tout le monde a.* Voltaire is the *cleverest* of all past and present men; but a great man is something more, and this he surely was not."

Whether this epigram, which we have seen in some Biographical Dictionary, really belongs to Montesquieu, we know not; but it does seem to us not wholly inapplicable to Voltaire, and at all events, highly expressive of an important distinction among men of talent generally. In fact, the popular man, and the man of true, at least of great originality, are seldom one and the same; we suspect that, till after a long struggle on the part of the latter, they are never so. Reasons are obvious enough. The popular man stands on our own level, or a hair's breadth higher; he shows us a truth which we can see without shifting our present intellectual position. This is a highly convenient arrangement. The original man, again, stands above us; he wishes to wrench us from our old fixtures, and elevate us to a higher and clearer level: but to quit our old fixtures, especially if we have sat in them with moderate comfort for some score or two of years, is no such easy business; accordingly we demur, we resist, we even give battle; we still suspect that he is above us, but try to persuade ourselves (Laziness and Vanity earnestly assenting) that he is below. For is it not the very essence of such a man that he be *new?* And who will warrant us that, at the same time, he shall only be an intensation and continuation of the *old*, which, in general, is what we long and look for? No one can warrant us. And, granting him to be a man of real genius, real depth, and that speaks not till after earnest meditation, what sort of a philosophy were his, could *we* estimate the length, breadth, and thickness of it at a single glance? And when did Criticism give two glances? Criticism, therefore, opens on such a man its greater and its lesser batteries, on every side: he has no security but to go on disregarding it; and "in the end," says Goethe, "Criticism itself comes to relish that method." But now let a speaker of the other class come forward; one of those men that "have more than any one, the opinion which all men have!" No sooner does he speak, than all and sundry of us feel as if we had been wishing to speak that very thing, as if we ourselves might have spoken it; and forthwith resounds from the united universe a celebration of that surprising feat. What clearness, brilliancy, justness, penetration! Who can doubt that this man is right, when so many thousand votes are ready to back him? Doubtless, he is right; doubtless, he is a clever man; and his praise will long be in all the Magazines.

Clever men are good, but they are not the best. "The instruction they can give us is like baked bread, savoury and satisfying for a single day;" but, unhappily, "flour cannot be sown, and seed-corn ought not to be ground." We proceed with our Critic in his contrast of Goethe with Voltaire.

"As poets," continues he, "the two live not in the same hemisphere, not in the same world. Of Voltaire's poetry, it were blindness to deny the polished, intellectual vigour, the logical symmetry, the flashes that from time to time give it the colour, if not the warmth, of fire: but it is in a far other sense than this that Goethe is a poet; in a sense of which the French literature has never afforded any example. We may venture to say of him, that his province is high and peculiar; higher than any poet but himself, for several generations, has so far succeeded in, perhaps even has steadfastly attempted. In reading Goethe's poetry, it perpetually strikes us that we are reading the poetry of our own day and generation. No demands are made on our credulity: the light, the science, the skepticism of our age, is not hid from us. He does not deal in antiquated mythologies, or ring changes on traditionary poetic forms; there are no supernal, no infernal influences, for *Faust* is an apparent, rather than a real exception; but there is the barren prose of the nineteenth century, the vulgar life which we are all leading, and it starts into strange beauty in his hands, and we pause in delighted wonder to behold the flowerage of poesy blooming in that parched and rugged soil. This is the end of his Mignons and Harpers, of his *Hermanns* and *Meisters*. Poetry, as he views it, exists not in time or place, but in the spirit of man; and Art with Nature is now to perform for the poet what Nature alone performed of old. The divinities and demons, the witches, spectres, and fairies, are vanished from the world, never again to be recalled: but the Imagination, which created these, still lives, and will for ever live, in man's soul; and can again pour its wizard light over the Universe, and summon forth enchantments as lovely or impressive, and which its sister faculties will not contradict. To say that Goethe has accomplished all this, would be to say that his genius is greater than was ever given to any man: for if it was a high and glorious mind, or rather series of minds, that peopled the first ages with their peculiar forms of poetry, it must be a series of minds much higher and more glorious that shall so people the present. The angels and demons, that can lay prostrate our hearts in the nineteenth century must be of another, and more cunning fashion, than those that subdued us in the ninth. To have attempted, to have begun this enterprise, may be accounted the greatest praise. That Goethe ever meditated it, in the form here set forth, we have no direct evidence: but, indeed, such is the end and aim of high poetry at all times and seasons; for the fiction of the poet is not falsehood, but the purest truth; and, if he would lead captive our whole being, not rest satisfied with a part of it, he must address us on interests that *are*, not that *were*, ours; and in a dialect which finds a response, and not a contradiction, within our bosoms."*

* German Romance, vol. iv. pp. 17—25.

Here, however, we must terminate our pilferings, or open robberies, and bring these straggling lucubrations to a close. In the extracts we have given, in the remarks made on them, and on the subject of them, we are aware that we have held the attitude of admirers and pleaders: neither is it unknown to us that the critic is, in virtue of his office, a judge, and not an advocate; sits there, not to do favour, but to dispense justice, which in most cases will involve blame as well as praise. But we are firm believers in the maxim that, for all right judgment of any man or thing, it is useful, nay, essential, to see his good qualities before pronouncing on his bad. This maxim is so clear to ourselves, that, in respect of poetry at least, we almost think we could make it clear to other men. In the first place, at all events, it is a much shallower and more ignoble occupation to detect faults than to discover beauties. The "critic fly," if it do but alight on any plinth or single cornice of a brave, stately building, shall be able to declare, with its half-inch vision, that here is a speck, and there an inequality; that, in fact, this and the other individual stone are nowise as they should be; for all this the "critic fly" will be sufficient: but to take in the fair relations of the Whole, to see the building as one object, to estimate its purpose, the adjustment of its parts, and their harmonious co-operation towards that purpose, will require the eye and the mind of a Vitruvius, or a Palladio. But further, the faults of a poem, or other piece of art, as we view them at first, will by no means continue unaltered when we view them after due and final investigation. Let us consider what we mean by a fault. By the word fault, we designate something that displeases us, that contradicts us. But here the question might arise. Who are *we?* This fault displeases, contradicts *us;* so far is clear; and had *we,* had *I,* and *my* pleasure and confirmation, been the chief end of the poet, then doubtless he has failed in that end, and his fault remains a fault irremediably, and without defence. But who shall say whether such really was his object, whether such ought to have been his object? And if it was not, and ought not to have been, what becomes of the fault? It must hang altogether undecided; we as yet know nothing of it; perhaps it may not be the poet's but our own fault; perhaps it may be no fault whatever. To see rightly into this matter, to determine with any infallibility, whether what we call a fault *is* in very deed a fault, we must previously have settled two points, neither of which may be so readily settled. First, we must have made plain to ourselves what the poet's aim really and truly was, how the task he had to do stood before his own eye, and how far, with such means as it afforded him, he has fulfilled it. Secondly, we must have decided whether and how far this aim, this task of his, accorded,—not with *us,* and our individual crotchets, and the crotchets of our little senate where we give or take the law,—but with human nature, and the nature of things at large; with the universal principles of poetic beauty, not as they stand written in our text-books, but in the hearts and imaginations of all men. Does the answer in either case come out unfavourable; was there an inconsistency between the means and the end; a discordance between the end and truth, there is a fault: was there not, there is no fault.

Thus it would appear that the detection of faults, provided they be faults of any depth and consequence, leads us of itself into that region where also the higher beauties of the piece, if it have any true beauties, essentially reside. In fact, according to our view, no man can pronounce dogmatically, with even a chance of being right, on the faults of a poem, till he has seen its very last and highest beauty; the last in becoming visible to any one, which few ever look after, which indeed in most pieces it were very vain to look after; the beauty of the poem as a Whole, in the strict sense; the clear view of it as an indivisible Unity; and whether it has grown up naturally from the general soil of Thought, and stands there like a thousand-years Oak, no leaf, no bough superfluous; or is nothing but a pasteboard Tree, cobbled together out of size and waste-paper and water-colours; altogether unconnected with the soil of Thought, except by mere juxtaposition, or at best united with it by some decayed *stump* and *dead boughs,* which the more cunning Decorationist (as in your Historic Novel) may have selected for the basis and support of his agglutinations. It is true, most readers judge of a poem by pieces, they praise and blame by pieces: it is a common practice, and for most poems and most readers may be perfectly sufficient; yet we would advise no man to follow this practice, who traces in himself even the slightest capability of following a better one; and if possible, we would advise him to practise only on worthy subjects; to read few poems that will not bear being studied as well as read.

That Goethe has his faults cannot be doubtful; for we believe it was ascertained long ago that there is no man free from them. Neither are we ourselves without some glimmering of certain actual limitations and inconsistencies by which he too, as he really lives, and writes, and is, may be hemmed in; which beset him too, as they do meaner men; which show us that he too is a son of Eve. But to exhibit these before our readers, in the present state of matters, we should reckon no easy labour, were it to be adequately, to be justly done; and done any how, no profitable one. Better is it we should first study him; better "to *see* the great man before attempting to *oversee* him." We are not ignorant that certain objections against Goethe already float vaguely in the English mind, and here and there, according to occasion, have even come to utterance: these, as the study of him proceeds, we shall hold ourselves ready, in due season, to discuss; but for the present we must beg the reader to believe, on our word, that we do not reckon them unanswerable, nay, that we reckon them in general the most answerable things in the world; and things which even a little increase of knowledge will not fail to answer without other help.

For furthering such increase of knowledge on this matter, may we beg the reader to accept two small pieces of advice, which we ourselves have found to be of use in studying Goethe. They seem applicable to the study of Foreign Literature generally; indeed to the study of all Literature that deserves the name.

The first is, nowise to suppose that Poetry is a superficial, cursory business, which may be seen through to the very bottom, so soon as one inclines to cast his eye on it. We reckon it the falsest of all maxims that a true Poem can be adequately *tasted;* can be judged of "as men judge of a dinner," by some internal *tongue*, that shall decide on the matter at once and irrevocably. Of the poetry which supplies spouting-clubs, and circulates in circulating libraries, we speak not here. That is quite another species; which has circulated, and will circulate, and ought to circulate, in all times; but for the study of which no man is required to give rules, the rules being already given by the thing itself. We speak of that Poetry which Masters write, which aims not "at furnishing a languid mind with fantastic shows and indolent emotions," but at incorporating the everlasting Reason of man in forms visible to his Sense, and suitable to it: and of this we say that to know it is no slight task; but rather that being the essence of all science, it requires the purest of all study for knowing it. "What!" cries the reader, "are we to *study* Poetry? To pore over it as we do over Fluxions?" Reader, it depends upon your object: if you want only *amusement*, choose your book, and you get along, without study, excellently well. "But is not Shakspeare plain, visible to the very bottom, without study?" cries he. Alas, no, gentle Reader; we cannot think so; we do not find that he is "visible to the very bottom," even to those that profess the study of him. It has been our lot to read some criticisms on Shakspeare, and to hear a great many; but for most part they amounted to no such "visibility." Volumes we have seen that were simply one huge Interjection printed over three hundred pages. Nine tenths of our critics have told us little more of Shakspeare, than what honest Franz Horn says our neighbours used to tell of him, "that he was a great spirit, and stept majestically along." Johnson's Preface, a sound and solid piece for its purpose, is a complete exception to this rule; and, so far as we remember, the only complete one. Students of poetry admire Shakspeare in their tenth year; but go on admiring him more and more, understanding him more and more, till their threescore-and-tenth. Grotius said, he read Terence otherwise than boys do. "Happy contractedness of youth," adds Goethe, "nay, of men in general; that at all moments of their existence they can look upon themselves as complete; and inquire neither after the True nor the False, nor the High nor the Deep; but simply after what is proportioned to themselves."

Our second advice we shall state in a few words. It is to remember that a Foreigner is no Englishman; that in judging a foreign work, it is not enough to ask whether it is suitable to our *modes*, but whether it is suitable to foreign *wants*; above all, whether it is suitable to *itself*. The fairness, the necessity of this can need no demonstration: yet how often do we find it, in practice, altogether neglected! We could fancy we saw some Bond-street Tailor criticising the costume of an ancient Greek; censuring the highly improper cut of collar and lapel; lamenting, indeed, that collar and lapel were nowhere to be seen. He pronounces the costume, easily and decisively, to be a barbarous one; to know whether it *is* a barbarous one, and how barbarous, the judgment of a Winkelmann might be required, and he would find it hard to give a judgment. For the questions set before the two were radically different. The Fraction asked himself: How will this look in Almacks, and before Lord Mahogany? The Winklemann asked himself: How will this look in the Universe, and before the Creator of Man?

Whether these remarks of ours may do any thing to forward a right appreciation of Goethe in this country, we know not; neither do we reckon this last result to be of any vital importance. Yet must we believe that, in recommending Goethe, we are doing our part to recommend a truer study of Poetry itself: and happy were we to fancy that any efforts of ours could promote such an object. Promoted, attained it will be, as we believe, by one means and another. A deeper feeling for Art is abroad over Europe; a purer, more earnest purpose in the study, in the practice of it. In this influence we too must participate: the time will come when our own ancient noble Literature will be studied and felt, as well as talked of; when Dilettantism will give place to Criticism in respect of it; and vague wonder end in clear knowledge, in sincere reverence, and, what were best of all, in hearty emulation.

BURNS.*

[EDINBURGH REVIEW, 1828.]

IN the modern arrangements of society, it is no uncommon thing that a man of genius must, like Butler, "ask for bread and receive a stone;" for, in spite of our grand maxim of supply and demand, it is by no means the highest excellence that men are most forward to recognise. The inventor of a spinning-jenny is pretty sure of his reward in his own day; but the writer of a true poem, like the apostle of a true religion, is nearly as sure of the contrary. We do not know whether it is not an aggravation of the injustice, that there is generally a posthumous retribution. Robert Burns, in the course of nature, might yet have been living; but his short life was spent in toil and penury; and he died, in the prime of his manhood, miserable and neglected; and yet already a brave mausoleum shines over his dust, and more than one splendid monument has been reared in other places to his fame: the street where he languished in poverty is called by his name; the highest personages in our literature have been proud to appear as his commentators and admirers, and here is the *sixth* narrative of his *Life*, that has been given to the world!

Mr. Lockhart thinks it necessary to apologize for this new attempt on such a subject: but his readers, we believe, will readily acquit him; or, at worst, will censure only the performance of his task, not the choice of it. The character of Burns, indeed, is a theme that cannot easily become either trite or exhausted; and will probably gain rather than lose in its dimensions by the distance to which it is removed by Time. No man, it has been said, is a hero to his valet: and this is probably true; but the fault is at least as likely to be the valet's as the hero's: For it is certain, that to the vulgar eye few things are wonderful that are not distant. It is difficult for men to believe that the man, the mere man whom they see, nay, perhaps, painfully feel, toiling at their side through the poor jostlings of existence, can be made of finer clay than themselves. Suppose that some dining acquaintance of Sir Thomas Lucy's, and neighbour of John a Combe's, had snatched an hour or two from the preservation of his game, and written us a Life of Shakspeare! What dissertations should we not have had,—not on *Hamlet* and *The Tempest*, but on the wool-trade, and deer-stealing, and the libel and vagrant laws! and how the Poacher became a Player; and how Sir Thomas and Mr. John had Christian bowels, and did not push him to extremities! In like manner, we believe, with respect to Burns, that till the companions of his pilgrimage, the honourable Excise Commissioners, and the Gentlemen of the Caledonian Hunt, and the Dumfries Aristocracy, and all the Squires and Earls, equally with the Ayr Writers, and the New and Old Light Clergy, whom he had to do with, shall have become invisible in the darkness of the Past, or visible only by light borrowed from *his* juxtaposition, it will be difficult to measure him by any true standard, or to estimate what he really was and did, in the eighteenth century, for his country and the world. It will be difficult, we say; but still a fair problem for literary historians; and repeated attempts will give us repeated approximations.

His former biographers have done something, no doubt, but by no means a great deal, to assist us. Dr. Currie and Mr. Walker, the principal of these writers, have both, we think, mistaken one essentially important thing:—Their own and the world's true relation to their author, and the style in which it became such men to think and to speak of such a man. Dr. Currie loved the poet truly; more perhaps than he avowed to his readers, or even to himself; yet he everywhere introduces him with a certain patronizing, apologetic air; as if the polite public might think it strange and half unwarrantable that he, a man of science, a scholar, and gentleman, should do such honour to a rustic. In all this, however, we readily admit that his fault was not want of love, but weakness of faith; and regret that the first and kindest of all our poet's biographers should not have seen farther, or believed more boldly what he saw. Mr. Walker offends more deeply in the same kind: and both err alike in presenting us with a detached catalogue of his several supposed attributes, virtues, and vices, instead of a delineation of the resulting character as a living unity. This, however, is not painting a portrait; but gauging the length and breadth of the several features, and jotting down their dimensions in arithmetical ciphers. Nay, it is not so much as this: for we are yet to learn by what arts or instruments the mind *could* be so measured and gauged.

Mr. Lockhart, we are happy to say, has avoided both these errors. He uniformly treats Burns as the high and remarkable man the public voice has now pronounced him to be: and in delineating him, he has avoided the method of separate generalities, and rather sought for characteristic incidents, habits, actions, sayings; in a word, for aspects which exhibit the whole man, as he looked and lived among his fellows. The book accordingly, with all its deficiencies, gives more insight, we think, into the true character of Burns, than any prior biography: though, being written on the very popular and condensed scheme of an article for *Constable's Miscellany*, it has less depth than we could have wished and expected from a writer of such power; and contains rather more, and more multifarious, quotations,

* The Life of Robert Burns. By J. G. Lockhart, LL. B. Edinburgh, 1828.

than belong of right to an original production. Indeed, Mr. Lockhart's own writing is generally so good, so clear, direct, and nervous, that we seldom wish to see it making place for another man's. However, the spirit of the work is throughout candid, tolerant, and anxiously conciliating; compliments and praises are liberally distributed, on all hands, to great and small; and, as Mr. Morris Birkbeck observes of the society in the backwoods of America, "the courtesies of polite life are never lost sight of for a moment." But there are better things than these in the volume; and we can safely testify, not only that it is easily and pleasantly read a first time, but may even be without difficulty read again.

Nevertheless, we are far from thinking that the problem of Burns's Biography has yet been adequately solved. We do not allude so much to deficiency of facts or documents,—though of these we are still every day receiving some fresh accession,—as to the limited and imperfect application of them to the great end of Biography. Our notions upon this subject may perhaps appear extravagant; but if an individual is really of consequence enough to have his life and character recorded for public remembrance, we have always been of opinion, that the public ought to be made acquainted with all the inward springs and relations of his character. How did the world and man's life, from his particular position, represent themselves to his mind? How did coexisting circumstances modify him from without; how did he modify these from within? With what endeavours and what efficacy rule over them; with what resistance and what suffering sink under them? In one word, what and how produced was the effect of society on him; what and how produced was his effect on society? He who should answer these questions, in regard to any individual, would, as we believe, furnish a model of perfection in biography. Few individuals, indeed, can deserve such a study; and many *lives* will be written, and, for the gratification of innocent curiosity, ought to be written, and read, and forgotten, which are not in this sense *biographies*. But Burns, if we mistake not, is one of these few individuals; and such a study, at least with such a result, he has not yet obtained. Our own contributions to it, we are aware, can be but scanty and feeble; but we offer them with good-will, and trust they may meet with acceptance from those for whom they are intended.

Burns first came upon the world as a prodigy; and was, in that character, entertained by it, in the usual fashion, with loud, vague, tumultuous wonder, speedily subsiding into censure and neglect; till his early and most mournful death again awakened an enthusiasm for him, which, especially as there was now nothing to be done, and much to be spoken, has prolonged itself even to our own time. It is true, the "nine days" have long since elapsed; and the very continuance of this clamour proves that Burns was no vulgar wonder. Accordingly, even in sober judgments, where, as years passed by, he has come to rest more and more exclusively on his own intrinsic merits, and may now be well nigh shorn of that casual radiance, he appears not only as a true British poet, but as one of the most considerable British men of the eighteenth century. Let it not be objected that he did little: He did much, if we consider where and how. If the work performed was small, we must remember that he had his very materials to discover; for the metal he worked in lay hid under the desert, where no eye but his had guessed its existence; and we may almost say, that with his own hand he had to construct the tools for fashioning it. For he found himself in deepest obscurity, without help, without instruction, without model; or with models only of the meanest sort. An educated man stands, as it were, in the midst of a boundless arsenal and magazine, filled with all the weapons and engines which man's skill has been able to devise from the earliest time; and he works, accordingly, with a strength borrowed from all past ages. How different is *his* state who stands on the outside of that storehouse, and feels that its gates must be stormed, or remain for ever shut against him? His means are the commonest and rudest; the mere work done is no measure of his strength. A dwarf behind his steam-engine may remove mountains; but no dwarf will hew them down with the pick-axe; and he must be a Titan that hurls them abroad with his arms.

It is in this last shape that Burns presents himself. Born in an age the most prosaic Britain had yet seen, and in a condition the most disadvantageous, where his mind, if it accomplished aught, must accomplish it under the pressure of continual bodily toil, nay, of penury and desponding apprehension of the worst evils, and with no furtherance but such knowledge as dwells in a poor man's hut, and the rhymes of a Ferguson or Ramsay for his standard of beauty, he sinks not under all these impediments: Through the fogs and darkness of that obscure region, his eagle eye discerns the true relations of the world and human life; he grows into intellectual strength, and trains himself into intellectual expertness. Impelled by the irrepressible movement of his inward spirit, he struggles forward into the general view, and with haughty modesty lays down before us, as the fruit of his labour, a gift, which Time has now pronounced imperishable. Add to all this, that his darksome, drudging childhood and youth was by far the kindliest era of his whole life; and that he died in his thirty-seventh year: and then ask if it be strange that his poems are imperfect, and of small extent, or that his genius attained no mastery in its art? Alas, his Sun shone as through a tropical tornado; and the pale Shadow of Death eclipsed it at noon! Shrouded in such baleful vapours, the genius of Burns was never seen in clear azure splendour, enlightening the world: But some beams from it did, by fits, pierce through; and it tinted those clouds with rainbow and orient colours into a glory and stern grandeur, which men silently gazed on with wonder and tears!

We are anxious not to exaggerate; for it is exposition rather than admiration that our readers require of us here; and yet to avoid some tendency to that side is no easy matter. We love Burns, and we pity him; and love and pity are prone to magnify. Criticism, it is sometimes thought, should be a cold business; we are not so sure of this; but, at all events, our concern with Burns is not exclusively that of critics. True and genial as his poetry must appear, it is not chiefly as a poet, but as a man, that he interests and affects us. He was often advised to write a tragedy: time and means were not lent him for this; but through life he enacted a tragedy, and one of the deepest. We question whether the world has since witnessed so utterly sad a scene; whether Napoleon himself, left to brawl with Sir Hudson Lowe, and perish on his rock, "amid the melancholy main," presented to the reflecting mind such a "spectacle of pity and fear," as did this intrinsically nobler, gentler, and perhaps greater soul, wasting itself away in a hopeless struggle with base entanglements, which coiled closer and closer round him, till only death opened him an outlet. Conquerors are a race with whom the world could well dispense; nor can the hard intellect, the unsympathizing loftiness, and high but selfish enthusiasm of such persons, inspire us in general with any affection; at best it may excite amazement; and their fall, like that of a pyramid, will be beheld with a certain sadness and awe. But a true Poet, a man in whose heart resides some effluence of Wisdom, some tone of the "Eternal Melodies," is the most precious gift that can be bestowed on a generation: we see in him a freer, purer, development of whatever is noblest in ourselves; his life is a rich lesson to us, and we mourn his death, as that of a benefactor who loved and taught us.

Such a gift had Nature in her bounty bestowed on us in Robert Burns; but with queen-like indifference she cast it from her hand, like a thing of no moment; and it was defaced and torn asunder, as an idle bauble, before we recognised it. To the ill-starred Burns was given the power of making man's life more venerable, but that of wisely guiding his own was not given. Destiny,—for so in our ignorance we must speak,—his faults, the faults of others, proved too hard for him; and that spirit, which might have soared, could it but have walked, soon sank to the dust, its glorious faculties trodden under foot in the blossom, and died, we may almost say, without ever having lived. And so kind and warm a soul; so full of inborn riches, of love to all living and lifeless things! How his heart flows out in sympathy over universal nature; and in her bleakest provinces discerns a beauty and a meaning! The "Daisy" falls not unheeded under his ploughshare; nor the ruined nest of that "wee, cowering, timorous beastie," cast forth, after all its provident pains, to "thole the sleety dribble, and cranreuch cauld." The "hoar visage" of Winter delights him: he dwells with a sad and oft-returning fondness in these scenes of solemn desolation; but the voice of the tempest becomes an anthem to his ears; he loves to walk in the sounding woods, for "it raises his thoughts to *Him that walketh on the wings of the wind*." A true Poet-soul, for it needs but to be struck, and the sound it yields will be music! But observe him chiefly as he mingles with his brother men. What warm, all-comprehending, fellow-feeling, what trustful, boundless love, what generous exaggeration of the object loved! His rustic friend, his nut-brown maiden, are no longer mean and homely, but a hero and a queen, whom he prizes as the paragons of Earth. The rough scenes of Scottish life, not seen by him in any Arcadian illusion, but in the rude contradiction, in the smoke and soil of a too harsh reality, are still lovely to him: Poverty is indeed his companion, but Love also, and Courage; the simple feelings, the worth, the nobleness, that dwell under the straw roof, are dear and venerable to his heart; and thus over the lowest provinces of man's existence he pours the glory of his own soul; and they rise, in shadow and sunshine, softened and brightened into a beauty which other eyes discern not in the highest. He has a just self-consciousness, which too often degenerates into pride; yet it is a noble pride, for defence, not for offence, no cold, suspicious feeling, but a frank and social one. The peasant Poet bears himself, we might say, like a King in exile: he is cast among the low, and feels himself equal to the highest; yet he claims no rank, that none may be disputed to him. The forward he can repel, the supercilious he can subdue; pretensions of wealth or ancestry are of no avail with him; there is a fire in that dark eye, under which the "insolence of condescension" cannot thrive. In his abasement, in his extreme need, he forgets not for a moment the majesty of Poetry and Manhood. And yet, far as he feels himself above common men, he wanders not apart from them, but mixes warmly in their interests; nay, throws himself into their arms; and, as it were, entreats them to love him. It is moving to see how, in his darkest despondency, this proud being still seeks relief from friendship; unbosoms himself, often to the unworthy; and, amid tears, strains to his glowing heart a heart that knows only the name of friendship. And yet he was "quick to learn;" a man of keen vision, before whom common disguises afforded no concealment. His understanding saw through the hollowness even of accomplished deceivers; but there was a generous credulity in his Heart. And so did our Peasant show himself among us; "a soul like an Æolian harp, in whose strings the vulgar wind, as it passed through them, changed itself into articulate melody." And this was he for whom the world found no fitter business than quarrelling with smugglers and vintners, computing excise dues upon tallow, and gauging alebarrels! In such toils was that mighty Spirit sorrowfully wasted: and a hundred years may pass on, before another such is given us to waste.

All that remains of Burns, the Writings he has left, seem to us, as we hinted above, no more than a poor mutilated fraction of what was in him; brief, broken glimpses of a genius that could never show itself complete; that wanted all things for completeness: culture, leisure, true effort, nay, even length of life. His poems are, with scarcely any exception, mere occasional effusions, poured forth with little premeditation, expressing, by such means as offered, the passion, opinion, or humour of the hour. Never in one instance was it permitted him to grapple with any subject with the full collection of his strength, to fuse and mould it in the concentrated fire of his genius. To try by the strict rules of Art such imperfect fragments, would be at once unprofitable and unfair. Nevertheless, there is something in these poems, marred and defective as they are, which forbids the most fastidious student of poetry to pass them by. Some sort of enduring quality they must have; for, after fifty years of the wildest vicissitudes in poetic taste, they still continue to be read; nay, are read more and more eagerly, more and more extensively; and this not only by literary virtuosos, and that class upon whom transitory causes operate most strongly, but by all classes, down to the most hard, unlettered, and truly natural class, who read little, and especially no poetry, except because they find pleasure in it. The grounds of so singular and wide a popularity, which extends, in a literal sense, from the palace to the hut, and over all regions where the English tongue is spoken, are well worth inquiring into. After every just deduction, it seems to imply some rare excellence in these works. What is that excellence?

To answer this question will not lead us far. The excellence of Burns is, indeed, among the rarest, whether in poetry or prose; but, at the same time, it is plain and easily recognised: his *Sincerity*, his indisputable air of Truth. Here are no fabulous woes or joys; no hollow fantastic sentimentalities; no wiredrawn refinings, either in thought or feeling: the passion that is traced before us has glowed in a living heart; the opinion he utters has risen in his own understanding, and been a light to his own steps. He does not write from hearsay, but from sight and experience; it is the scenes he has lived and laboured amidst, that he describes: those scenes, rude and humble as they are, have kindled beautiful emotions in his soul, noble thoughts, and definite resolves; and he speaks forth what is in him, not from any outward call of vanity or interest, but because his heart is too full to be silent. He speaks it, too, with such melody and modulation as he can; "in homely rustic jingle;" but it is his own, and genuine. This is the grand secret for finding readers and retaining them: let him who would move and convince others, be first moved and convinced himself. Horace's rule, *Si vis me flere*, is applicable in a wider sense than the literal one. To every poet, to every writer, we might say: Be true, if you would be believed. Let a man but speak forth with genuine earnestness the thought, the emotion, the actual condition, of his own heart; and other men, so strangely are we all knit together by the tie of sympathy, must and will give heed to him. In culture, in extent of view, we may stand above the speaker, or below him; but in either case, his words, if they are earnest and sincere, will find some response within us; for in spite of all casual varieties in outward rank, or inward, as face answers to face, so does the heart of man to man.

This may appear a very simple principle, and one which Burns had little merit in discovering. True, the discovery is easy enough: but the practical appliance is not easy; is indeed the fundamental difficulty which all poets have to strive with, and which scarcely one in the hundred ever fairly surmounts. A head too dull to discriminate the true from the false; a heart too dull to love the one at all risks, and to hate the other in spite of all temptations, are alike fatal to a writer. With either, or, as more commonly happens, with both, of these deficiencies, combine a love of distinction, a wish to be original, which is seldom wanting, and we have Affectation, the bane of literature, as Cant, its elder brother, is of morals. How often does the one and the other front us, in poetry, as in life! Great poets themselves are not always free of this vice; nay, it is precisely on a certain sort and degree of greatness that it is most commonly ingrafted. A strong effort after excellence will sometimes solace itself with a mere shadow of success, and he who has much to unfold, will sometimes unfold it imperfectly. Byron, for instance, was no common man: yet if we examine his poetry with this view, we shall find it far enough from faultless. Generally speaking, we should say that it is not true. He refreshes us, not with the divine fountain, but too often with vulgar strong waters, stimulating indeed to the taste, but soon ending in dislike or even nausea. Are his Harolds and Giaours, we would ask, real men, we mean, poetically consistent and conceivable men? Do not these characters, does not the character of their author, which more or less shines through them all, rather appear a thing put on for the occasion; no natural or possible mode of being, but something intended to look much grander than nature? Surely, all these stormful agonies, this volcanic heroism, superhuman contempt, and moody desperation, with so much scowling, and teeth-gnashing, and other sulphurous humours, is more like the brawling of a player in some paltry tragedy, which is to last three hours, than the bearing of a man in the business of life, which is to last three-score and ten years. To our minds, there is a taint of this sort, something which we should call theatrical, false, and affected, in every one of these otherwise powerful pieces. Perhaps *Don Juan*, especially the latter parts of it, is the only thing approaching to a *sincere* work, he ever wrote; the only work where he showed himself, in any measure, as he was; and seemed so intent on his subject, as, for moments, to forget himself. Yet Byron hated this vice; we believe, heartily detested it: nay, he had declared formal war against it in words. So difficult is it even for the strongest to make this primary attainment, which might seem the simplest of all: to *read its own consciousness without mistakes*, without errors involuntary or wilful! We recollect no poet of Burns's susceptibility who comes before us from the first, and abides with us to the last, with such a total want of affectation. He is an honest man, and an honest writer. In his successes and his failures, in his greatness and his littleness, he is ever clear, simple, true, and glitters with no lustre but his own. We reckon this to be a great virtue; to be, in fact, the root of most other virtues, literary as well as moral.

It is necessary, however, to mention, that it is to the poetry of Burns that we now allude; to those writings which he had time to meditate, and where no special reason existed to warp his critical feeling, or obstruct his endeavour to fulfil it. Certain of his Letters, and other fractions of prose composition, by no means deserve this praise. Here, doubtless, there is not the same natural truth of style; but on the contrary, something not only stiff, but strained and twisted; a certain high-flown, inflated tone; the stilting emphasis of which contrasts ill with the firmness and rugged simplicity of even his poorest verses. Thus no man, it would appear, is altogether unaffected. Does not Shakspeare himself sometimes premeditate the sheerest bombast! But even with regard to these Letters of Burns, it is but fair to state that he had two excuses. The first was his comparative deficiency in language. Burns, though for most part he writes with singular force, and even gracefulness, is not master of English prose, as he is of Scottish verse; not master of it, we mean, in proportion to the depth and vehemence of his matter. These Letters strike us as the effort of a man to express something which he has no organ fit for expressing. But a second and weightier excuse is to be found in the peculiarity of Burns's social rank. His correspondents are often men whose relation to him he has never accurately ascertained; whom therefore he is either forearming himself against, or else unconsciously flattering, by adopting the style he thinks will please them. At all events, we should remember that these faults, even in his Letters, are not the rule, but the exception. Whenever he writes, as one would ever wish to do, to trusted friends and on real interests, his style becomes simple, vigorous, expressive, sometimes even beautiful. His Letters to Mrs. Dunlop are uniformly excellent.

But we return to his poetry. In addition to its sincerity, it has another peculiar merit, which indeed is but a mode, or perhaps a means, of the foregoing. It displays itself in his choice of subjects, or rather in his indifference as to subjects, and the power he has of making all subjects interesting. The ordinary poet, like the ordinary man, is for ever seeking, in external circumstances, the help which can be found only in himself. In what is familiar and near at hand, he discerns no form or comeliness: home is not poetical but prosaic; it is in some past, distant, conventional world, that poetry resides for him; were he there and not here, were he thus and not so, it would be well with him. Hence our innumerable host of rose-coloured novels and iron-mailed epics, with their locality not on the Earth, but somewhere nearer to the Moon. Hence our Virgins of the Sun, and our Knights of the Cross, malicious Saracens in turbans, and copper-coloured Chiefs in wampum, and so many other truculent figures from the heroic times or the heroic climates, who on all hands swarm in our poetry. Peace be with them! But yet, as a great moralist proposed preaching to the men of this century, so would we fain preach to the poets, "a sermon on the duty of staying at home." Let them be sure that heroic ages and heroic climates can do little for them. That form of life has attraction for us, less because it is better or nobler than our own, than simply because it is different; and even this attraction must be of the most transient sort. For will not our own age, one day, be an ancient one; and have as quaint a costume as the rest; not contrasted with the rest, therefore, but ranked along with them, in respect of quaintness? Does Homer interest us now, because he wrote of what passed out of his native Greece, and two centuries before he was born; or because he wrote of what passed in God's world, and in the heart of man, which is the same after thirty centuries? Let our poets look to this: is their feeling really finer, truer, and their vision deeper than that of other men, they have nothing to fear, even from the humblest subject; is it not so,—they have nothing to hope, but an ephemeral favour, even from the highest.

The poet, we cannot but think, can never have far to seek for a subject: the elements of his art are in him, and around him on every hand; for him the Ideal world is not remote from the Actual, but under it and within it: nay, he is a poet, precisely because he can discern it there. Wherever there is a sky above him, and a world around him, the poet is in his place; for here too is man's existence, with its infinite longings and small acquirings; its ever-thwarted, ever-renewed endeavours; its unspeakable aspirations, its fears and hopes that wander through Eternity: and all the mystery of brightness and of gloom that it was ever made of, in any age or climate, since man first began to live. Is there not the fifth act of a Tragedy in every deathbed, though it were a peasant's and a bed of heath? And are wooings and weddings obsolete, that there can be Comedy no longer? Or are men suddenly grown wise, that Laughter must no longer shake his sides, but be cheated of his Farce? Man's life and nature is, as it was, and as it will ever be. But the poet must have an eye to read these things, and a heart to understand them; or they come and pass away before him in vain. He is a *vates*, a seer; a gift of vision has been given him. Has life no meanings for him, which another cannot equally decipher? then he is no poet, and Delphi itself will not make him one.

In this respect, Burns, though not perhaps absolutely a great poet, better manifests his capability, better proves the truth of his genius, than if he had, by his own strength, kept the whole Minerva Press going, to the end of his literary course. He shows himself at least a poet of Nature's own making; and Nature, after all, is still the grand agent in making poets. We often hear of this and the other external condition being requisite for the existence of a poet. Sometimes it is a certain sort of training; he must have studied certain things, studied for instance "the elder dramatists," and so learned a poetic language; as if poetry lay in the tongue, not in the heart. At other times we are told, he must be bred in a certain rank, and must be on a confidential footing with the higher classes; because, above all other things, he must see the world. As to seeing the world, we apprehend this will cause him little difficulty, if he have but an eye to see it with. Without eyes, indeed, the task might be hard. But happily every poet is born *in* the world, and sees it, with or against his will, every day and every hour he lives. The mysterious workmanship of man's heart, the true light and the inscrutable darkness of man's destiny, reveal themselves not only in capital cities, and crowded saloons, but in every hut and hamlet where men have their abode. Nay, do not the elements of all human virtues, and all human vices; the passions at once of a Borgia and of a Luther, lie written, in stronger or fainter lines, in the consciousness of every individual bosom, that has practised honest self-examination? Truly, this same world may be seen in Mossgiel and Tarbolton, if we look well, as clearly as it ever came to light in Crockford's, or the Tuileries itself.

But sometimes still harder requisitions are laid on the poor aspirant to poetry; for it is hinted that he should have *been born* two centuries ago; inasmuch as poetry, soon after that date, vanished from the earth, and became no longer attainable by men! Such cobweb speculations have, now and then, overhung the field of literature; but they obstruct not the growth of any plant there: the Shakspeare or the Burns, unconsciously, and merely as he walks onward, silently brushes them away. Is not every genius an impossibility till he appear? Why do we call him new and original, if *we* saw where his marble was lying, and what fabric he could rear from it? It is not the material but the workman that is wanting. It is not the dark *place* that hinders, but the dim *eye*. A Scottish peasant's life was the meanest and rudest of all lives, till Burns became a poet in it, and a poet of it; found it a *man's* life, and therefore significant to men. A thousand battle-fields remain unsung; but the *Wounded Hare* has not perished without its memorial; a balm of mercy yet breathes on us from its dumb agonies, because a poet was there. Our *Halloween* had passed and repassed, in rude awe and laughter, since the era of the Druids; but no Theocritus, till Burns, discerned in it the materials of a Scottish Idyl: neither was the *Holy Fair* any *Council of Trent*, or Roman *Jubilee*; but nevertheless, *Superstition*, and *Hypocrisy*, and *Fun* having been propitious to him, in this man's hand it became a poem, instinct with satire, and genuine comic life. Let but the true poet be given us, we repeat it, place him where and how you will, and true poetry will not be wanting.

Independently of the essential gift of poetic feeling, as we have now attempted to describe it, a certain rugged sterling worth pervades whatever Burns has written: a virtue, as of green fields and mountain breezes, dwells in his poetry; it is redolent of natural life, and hardy, natural men. There is a decisive strength in him; and yet a sweet native gracefulness: he is tender, and he is vehement, yet without constraint or too visible effort; he melts the heart, or inflames it, with a power which seems habitual and familiar to him. We see in him the gentleness, the trembling pity of a woman, with the deep earnestness, the force and passionate ardour of a hero. Tears lie in him, and consuming fire; as lightning lurks in the drops of the summer cloud. He has a resonance in his bosom for every note of human feeling: the high and the low, the sad, the ludicrous, the joyful, are welcome in their turns to his "lightly-moved and all-conceiving spirit." And observe with what a prompt and eager force he grasps his subject, be it what it may! How he fixes, as it were, the full image of the matter in his eye; full and clear in every lineament; and catches the real type and essence of it, amid a thousand accidents and superficial circumstances, no one of which misleads him! Is it of reason; some truth to be discovered? No sophistry, no vain surface-logic detains him; quick, resolute, unerring, he pierces through into the marrow of the question; and speaks his verdict with an emphasis that cannot be forgotten. Is it of description; some visual object to be represented? No poet of any age or nation is more graphic than Burns: the characteristic features disclose themselves to him at a glance; three lines from his hand, and we have a likeness. And, in that rough dialect, in that rude, often awkward, metre, so clear, and definite a likeness! It seems a draughtsman working with a burnt stick; and yet the burin of a Retzsch is not more expressive or exact.

This clearness of sight we may call the foundation of all talent; for in fact, unless we *see* our object, how shall we know how to place or prize it, in our understanding, our imagination, our affections? Yet it is not in itself perhaps a very high excellence; but capable of being united indifferently with the strongest, or with ordinary powers. Homer surpasses all men in this quality: but strangely enough, at no great distance below him are Richardson and Defoe. It belongs, in truth, to what is called a lively mind: and gives no sure indication of the higher endowments that may exist along with it. In all the three cases we have mentioned, it is combined with great garrulity; their descriptions are detailed, ample, and lovingly exact; Homer's fire bursts through, from time to time, as if by accident; but Defoe and Richardson have no fire. Burns, again, is not more distinguished by the clearness than by the impetuous force of his conceptions. Of the strength, the piercing emphasis with which he thought, his emphasis of expression may give an humble but the readiest proof. Who ever uttered sharper sayings than his; words more memorable, now by their burning vehemence, now by their cool vigour and laconic pith? A single phrase depicts a whole subject, a whole scene. Our Scottish forefathers in the battle-field struggled forward, he says, "*red-wat shod:*" giving, in this one word, a full vision of horror and carnage, perhaps too frightfully accurate for Art!

In fact, one of the leading features in the mind of Burns is this vigour of his strictly intellectual perceptions. A resolute force is ever visible in his judgments, as in his feelings and volitions. Professor Stewart says of him, with some surprise: "All the faculties of Burns's mind were, as far as I could judge, equally vigorous; and his predilection for poetry was rather the result of his own enthusiastic and impassioned temper, than of a genius exclusively adapted to that species of composition. From his conversation I should have pronounced him to be fitted to excel in whatever walk of ambition he had chosen to exert his abilities." But this, if we mistake not, is at all times the very essence of a truly poetical endowment. Poetry, except in such cases as that of Keats, where the whole consists in extreme sensibility, and a certain vague pervading tunefulness of nature, is no separate faculty, no organ which can be superadded to the rest, or disjoined from them; but rather the result of their general harmony and completion. The feelings, the gifts, that exist in the Poet, are those that exist, with more or less development, in every human soul: the imagination, which shudders at the Hell of Dante, is the same faculty, weaker in degree, which called that picture into being. How does the poet speak to all men, with power, but by being still more a man than they? Shakspeare, it has been well observed, in the planning and completing of his tragedies, has shown an Understanding, were it nothing more, which might have governed states, or indited a *Novum Organum.* What Burns's force of understanding may have been, we have less means of judging: for it dwelt among the humblest objects, never saw philosophy, and never rose, except for short intervals, into the region of great ideas. Nevertheless, sufficient indication remains for us in his works: we discern the brawny movements of a gigantic though untutored strength, and can understand how, in conversation, his quick, sure insight into men and things may, as much as aught else about him, have amazed the best thinkers of his time and country.

But, unless we mistake, the intellectual gift of Burns is fine as well as strong. The more delicate relations of things could not well have escaped his eye, for they were intimately present to his heart. The logic of the senate and the forum is indispensable, but not all-sufficient; nay, perhaps the highest Truth is that which will the most certainly elude it. For this logic works by words, and "the highest," it has been said, "cannot be expressed in words." We are not without tokens of an openness for this higher truth also, of a keen though uncultivated sense for it, having existed in Burns. Mr. Stewart, it will be remembered, "wonders," in the passage above quoted, that Burns had formed some distinct conception of the "doctrine of association." We rather think that far subtiler things than the doctrine of association had from of old been familiar to him. Here for instance:

"We know nothing," thus writes he, "or next to nothing, of the structure of our souls, so we cannot account for those seeming caprices in them, that one should be particularly pleased with this thing, or struck with that, which, on minds of a different cast, makes no extraordinary impression. I have some favourite flowers in spring, among which are the mountain-daisy, the hare-bell, the fox-glove, the wild-brier rose, the budding birch, and the hoary hawthorn, that I view and hang over with particular delight. I never hear the loud solitary whistle of the curlew in a summer noon, or the wild mixing cadence of a troop of gray plover in an autumnal morning, without feeling an elevation of soul like the enthusiasm of devotion or poetry. Tell me, my dear friend, to what can this be owing? Are we a piece of machinery, which, like the Æolian harp, passive, takes the impression of the passing accident; or do these workings argue something within us above the trodden clod? I own myself partial to such proofs of those awful and important realities: a God that made all things, man's immaterial and immortal nature, and a world of weal or wo beyond death and the grave."

Force and fineness of understanding are often spoken of as something different from general force and fineness of nature, as something partly independent of them. The necessities of language probably require this; but in truth these qualities are not distinct and independent: except in special cases, and from special causes, they ever go together. A man of strong understanding is generally a man of strong character; neither is delicacy in the one kind often divided from delicacy in the other. No one, at all events, is ignorant that in the poetry of Burns, keenness of insight keeps pace with keenness of feeling; that his *light* is not more pervading than his *warmth.* He is a man of the most impassioned temper; with passions not strong only, but noble, and of the sort in which great virtues and great poems take their rise. It is reverence, it is Love towards all Nature that inspires him, that opens his eyes to its beauty, and makes heart and voice eloquent in its praise. There is a true old saying, that "love furthers knowledge:" but above all, it is the living essence of that knowledge which makes poets; the first principle of its existence, increase, activity. Of Burns's fervid affection, his generous, all-embracing Love, we have spoken already, as of the grand distinction of his nature, seen equally in word and deed, in his Life and in his Writings. It were easy to multiply examples. Not man only, but all that environs man in the material and moral universe, is lovely in his sight: "the hoary hawthorn," the "troop of gray plover," the "solitary curlew," are all dear to him; all live in this Earth along with him, and to all he is knit as in mysterious brotherhood. How touching is it, for instance, that, amidst the gloom of personal misery, brooding over the wintry desolation without him and within him, he thinks of the "ourie cattle" and "silly sheep," and their sufferings in the pitiless storm!

I thought me on the ourie cattle,
Or silly sheep, wha bide this brattle
O' wintry war;
Or thro' the drift, deep-lairing, sprattle,
Beneath a scaur.

Ilk happing bird, wee helpless thing,
That in the merry month o' spring
Delighted me to hear thee sing,
What comes o' thee?
Where wilt thou cow'r thy chittering wing,
And close thy ee?

The tenant of the mean hut, with its "ragged roof and chinky wall," has a heart to pity even these! This is worth several homilies on Mercy: for it is the voice of Mercy herself. Burns, indeed, lives in sympathy; his soul rushes forth into all realms of being; nothing that has existence can be indifferent to him. The very Devil he cannot hate with right orthodoxy!

But fare you weel, auld Nickie-ben;
O wad ye tak a thought and men'!
Ye aiblins might,—I dinna ken,—
Still hae a stake;
I'm wae to think upo' yon den,
Even for your sake!

He did not know, probably, that Sterne had been beforehand with him. "'He is the father of curses and lies,' said Dr. Slop; 'and is cursed and damned already.'—'I am sorry for it,' quoth my uncle Toby!"—"A poet without Love, were a physical and metaphsyical impossibility."

Why should we speak of *Scots, wha hae wi' Wallace bled;* since all know it, from the king to the meanest of his subjects? This dithyrambic was composed on horseback; in riding in the middle of tempests, over the wildest Galloway moor, in company with a Mr. Syme, who, observing the poet's looks, forebore to speak, —judiciously enough,—for a man composing *Bruce's Address* might be unsafe to trifle with Doubtless this stern hymn was singing itself, as he formed it, through the soul of Burns; but to the external ear, it should be sung with the throat of the whirlwind. So long as there is warm blood in the heart of Scotchman or man, it will move in fierce thrills under this war-ode, the best, we believe, that was ever written by any pen.

Another wild stormful song, that dwells in our ear and mind with a strange tenacity, is *Macpherson's Farewell.* Perhaps there is something in the tradition itself that co-operates. For was not this grim Celt, this shaggy Northland Cacus, that "lived a life of sturt and strife, and died by treacherie," was not he too one of the Nimrods and Napoleons of the earth, in the arena of his own remote misty glens, for want of a clearer and wider one? Nay, was there not a touch of grace given him? A fibre of love and softness, of poetry itself, must have lived in his savage heart; for he composed that air the night before his execution; on the wings of that poor melody, his better soul would soar away above oblivion, pain, and all the ignominy and despair, which, like an avalanche, was hurling him to the abyss! Here also, as at Thebes, and in Pelops' line, was material Fate matched against man's Freewill; matched in bitterest though obscure duel; and the ethereal soul sunk not, even in its blindness, without a cry which has survived it. But who, except Burns, could have given words to such a soul; words that we never listen to without a strange half-barbarous, half-poetic fellow-feeling?

Sae rantingly, sae wantonly,
Sae dauntingly gaed he;
He play'd a spring, and danced it round,
Below the gallows tree.

Under a lighter and thinner disguise, the same principle of Love, which we have recognised as the great characteristic of Burns, and of all true poets, occasionally manifests itself in the shape of Humour. Everywhere, indeed, in his sunny moods, a full buoyant flood of mirth rolls through the mind of Burns; he rises to the high, and stoops to the low, and is brother and playmate to all Nature. We speak not of his bold and often irresistible faculty of caricature; for this is Drollery rather than Humour: but a much tenderer sportfulness dwells in him; and comes forth here and there, in evanescent and beautiful touches; as in his *Address to the Mouse*, or the *Farmer's Mare*, or in his *Elegy on Poor Mailie*, which last may be reckoned his happiest effort of this kind. In these pieces, there are traits of a Humour as fine as that of Sterne; yet altogether different, original, peculiar,—the Humour of Burns.

Of the tenderness, the playful pathos, and many other kindred qualities of Burns's poetry, much more might be said; but now, with these poor outlines of a sketch, we must prepare to quit this part of our subject. To speak of his individual writings, adequately, and with any detail, would lead us far beyond our limits. As already hinted, we can look on but few of these pieces as, in strict critical language, deserving the name of Poems; they are rhymed eloquence, rhymed pathos, rhymed sense; yet seldom essentially melodious, aerial, poetical. *Tam o' Shanter* itself, which enjoys so high a favour, does not appear to us, at all decisively, to come under this last category. It is not so much a poem, as a piece of sparkling rhetoric; the heart and body of the story still lies hard and dead. He has not gone back, much less carried us back, into that dark, earnest wondering age, when the tradition was believed, and when it took its rise; he does not attempt, by any new modelling of his supernatural ware, to strike anew that deep mysterious chord of human nature, which once responded to such things; and which lives in us too, and will for ever live, though silent, or vibrating with far other notes, and to far different issues. Our German readers will understand us, when we say, that he is not the Tieck but the Musäus of this tale. Externally it is all green and living; yet look closer, it is no firm growth, but only ivy on a rock. The piece does not properly cohere; the strange chasm which yawns in our incredulous imaginations between the Ayr public-house and the gate of Tophet, is nowhere bridged over, nay, the idea of such a bridge is laughed at; and thus the Tragedy of the adventure becomes a mere drunken phantasmagoria, painted on ale-vaporus, and the farce alone has any reality

We do not say that Burns should have made much more of this tradition; we rather think that, for strictly poetical purposes, not much *was* to be made of it. Neither are we blind to the deep, varied, genial power displayed in what he has actually accomplished; but we find far more "Shakspearian" qualities, as these of *Tam o' Shanter* have been fondly named, in many of his other pieces; nay, we incline to believe, that this latter might have been written, all but quite as well, by a man who, in place of genius, had only possessed talent.

Perhaps we may venture to say, that the most strictly poetical of all his "poems" is one, which does not appear in Currie's Edition; but has been often printed before and since, under the humble title of *The Jolly Beggars.* The subject truly is among the lowest in nature; but it only the more shows our poet's gift in raising it into the domain of Art. To our minds, this piece seems thoroughly compacted; melted together, refined; and poured forth in one flood of true *liquid* harmony. It is light, airy, and soft of movement; yet sharp and precise in its details; every face is a portrait: that *raucle carlin*, that *wee Apollo*, that *Son of Mars*, are Scottish, yet ideal; the scene is at once a dream, and the very Rag-castle of "Poosie-Nansie." Farther, it seems in a considerable degree complete, a real self-supporting Whole, which is the highest merit in a poem. The blanket of the night is drawn asunder for a moment; in full, ruddy, and flaming light, these rough tatterdemalions are seen in their boisterous revel; for the strong pulse of Life vindicates its right to gladness even here; and when the curtain closes, we prolong the action without effort; the next day as the last, our *Caird* and our *Balladmonger* are singing and soldiering; their "brats and callets" are hawking, begging, cheating; and some other night, in new combinations, they will wring from Fate another hour of wassail and good cheer. It would be strange, doubtless, to call this the best of Burns's writings; we mean to say only, that it seems to us the most perfect of its kind, as a piece of poetical composition, strictly so called. In the *Beggar's Opera*, in the *Beggar's Bush*, as other critics have already remarked, there is nothing which, in real poetic vigour, equals this *Cantata*: nothing, as we think, which comes within many degrees of it.

But by far the most finished, complete, and truly inspired pieces of Burns are, without dispute, to be found among his *Songs.* It is here that, although through a small aperture, his light shines with the least obstruction; in its highest beauty, and pure sunny clearness. The reason may be, that Song is a brief and simple species of composition: and requires nothing so much for its perfection as genuine poetic feeling, genuine music of heart. The song has its rules equally with the Tragedy; rules which in most cases are poorly fulfilled, in many cases are not so much as felt. We might write a long essay on the Songs of Burns; which we reckon by far the best that Britain has yet produced; for, indeed, since the era of Queen Elizabeth, we know not that, by any other hand, aught truly worth attention has been accomplished in this department. True, we have songs enough "by persons of quality;" we have tawdry, hollow, wine-bred, madrigals; many a rhymed "speech" in the flowing and watery vein of Ossorius the Portugal Bishop, rich in sonorous words, and, for moral, dashed perhaps with some tint of a sentimental sensuality; all which many persons cease not from endeavouring to sing: though for most part, we fear, the music is but from the throat outward, or at best from some region far enough short of the *Soul*; not in which, but in a certain inane Limbo of the Fancy, or even in some vaporous debatable land on the outside of the Nervous System, most of such madrigals and rhymed speeches seem to have originated. With the Songs of Burns we must not name these things. Independently of the clear, manly, heartfelt sentiment that ever pervades *his* poetry, his Songs are honest in another point of view: in form, as well as in spirit. They do not *affect* to be set to music, but they actually and in themselves are music; they have received their life, and fashioned themselves together, in the medium of Harmony, as Venus rose from the bosom of the sea. The story, the feeling, is not detailed, but suggested; not *said*, or spouted, in rhetorical completeness and coherence; but *sung*, in fitful gushes, in glowing hints, in fantastic breaks, in *warblings* not of the voice only, but of the whole mind. We consider this to be the essence of a song; and that no songs since the little careless catches, and, as it were, drops of song, which Shakspeare has here and there sprinkled over his plays, fulfil this condition in nearly the same degree as most of Burns's do. Such grace and truth of external movement, too, presupposes in general a corresponding force and truth of sentiment, and inward meaning. The Songs of Burns are not more perfect in the former quality than in the latter. With what tenderness he sings, yet with what vehemence and entireness! There is a piercing wail in his sorrow, the purest rapture in his joy: he burns with the sternest ire, or laughs with the loudest or slyest mirth; and yet he is sweet and soft, "sweet as the smile when fond lovers meet, and soft as their parting tear!" If we farther take into account the immense variety of his subjects; how, from the loud flowing revel in *Willie brew'd a peck o' Maut*, to the still, rapt enthusiasm of sadness for *Mary in Heaven*; from the glad kind greeting of *Auld Langsyne*, or the comic archness of *Duncan Gray*, to the fire-eyed fury of *Scots, wha hae wi' Wallace bled*, he has found a tone and words for every mood of man's heart,—it will seem a small praise if we rank him as the first of all our song-writers; for we know not where to find one worthy of being second to him.

It is on his Songs, as we believe, that Burns's chief influence as an author will ultimately be found to depend: nor, if our Fletcher's aphorism is true, shall we account this a small influence. "Let me make the songs of a people," said he, "and you shall make its laws." Surely, if ever any Poet might have equalled himself with Legislators, on this ground, it was Burns. His songs are already part of the mother tongue, not of Scotland only but of Britain, and of the millions that in all the ends of the earth speak a British language. In hut and hall, as the heart unfolds itself in the joy and wo of existence, the name, the voice of that joy and that wo, is the name and voice which Burns has given them. Strictly speaking, perhaps, no British man has so deeply affected the thoughts and feelings of so many men as this solitary and altogether private individual, with means apparently the humblest.

In another point of view, moreover, we incline to think that Burns's influence may have been considerable: we mean, as exerted specially on the Literature of his country, at least on the Literature of Scotland. Among the great changes which British, particularly Scottish literature, has undergone since that period, one of the greatest will be found to consist in its remarkable increase of nationality. Even the English writers, most popular in Burns's time, were little distinguished for their literary patriotism, in this its best sense. A certain attenuated cosmopolitanism had, in good measure, taken place of the old insular home-feeling; literature was, as it were, without any local environment; was not nourished by the affections which spring from a native soil. Our Grays and Glovers seemed to write almost as if *in vacuo;* the thing written bears no mark of place; it is not written so much for Englishmen, as for men; or rather, which is the inevitable result of this, for certain Generalizations which philosophy termed men. Goldsmith is an exception; not so Johnson; the scene of his *Rambler* is little more English than that of his *Rasselas*. But if such was, in some degree, the case with England, it was, in the highest degree, the case with Scotland. In fact, our Scottish literature had, at that period, a very singular aspect; unexampled, so far as we know, except perhaps at Geneva, where the same state of matters appears still to continue. For a long period after Scotland became British, we had no literature: at the date when Addison and Steele were writing their *Spectators*, our good Thomas Boston was writing, with the noblest intent, but alike in defiance of grammar and philosophy, his *Fourfold State of Man*. Then came the schisms in our National Church, and the fiercer schisms in our Body Politic: Theologic ink, and Jacobite blood, with gall enough in both cases, seemed to have blotted out the intellect of the country; however, it was only obscured, not obliterated. Lord Kames made nearly the first attempt, and a tolerably clumsy one, at writing English; and ere long, Hume, Robertson, Smith, and a whole host of followers, attracted hither the eyes of all Europe. And yet in this brilliant resuscitation of our "fervid genius," there was nothing truly Scottish, nothing indigenous; except, perhaps, the natural impetuosity of intellect, which we sometimes claim, and are sometimes upbraided with, as a characteristic of our nation. It is curious to remark that Scotland, so full of writers, had no Scottish culture, nor indeed any English; our culture was almost exclusively French. It was by studying Racine and Voltaire, Batteux and Boileau, that Kames had trained himself to be a critic and philosopher: it was the light of Montesquieu and Mably that guided Robertson in his political speculations; Quesnay's lamp that kindled the lamp of Adam Smith. Hume was too rich a man to borrow; and perhaps he reached on the French more than he was acted on by them: but neither had he aught to do with Scotland; Edinburgh, equally with La Flèche, was but the lodging and laboratory, in which he not so much morally *lived*, as metaphysically *investigated*. Never, perhaps, was there a class of writers, so clear and well-ordered, yet so totally destitute, to all appearance, of any patriotic affection, nay, of any human affection whatever. The French wits of the period were as unpatriotic: but their general deficiency in moral principle, not to say their avowed sensuality and unbelief in all virtue, strictly so called, render this accountable enough. We hope there is a patriotism founded on something better than prejudice; that our country may be dear to us, without injury to our philosophy; that in loving and justly prizing all other lands, we may prize justly, and yet love before all others, our own stern Motherland, and the venerable structure of social and moral Life, which Mind has through long ages been building up for us there. Surely there is nourishment for the better part of man's heart in all this: surely the roots, that have fixed themselves in the very core of man's being, may be so cultivated as to grow up not into briers, but into roses, in the field of his life! Our Scottish sages have no such propensities: the field of their life shows neither briers nor roses; but only a flat, continuous thrashing-floor for Logic, whereon all questions, from the "Doctrine of Rent," to the "Natural History of Religion, are thrashed and sifted with the same mechanical impartiality!

With Sir Walter Scott at the head of our literature, it cannot be denied that much of this evil is past, or rapidly passing away: our chief literary men, whatever other faults they may have, no longer live among us like a French Colony, or some knot of Propaganda Missionaries; but like natural-born subjects of the soil, partaking and sympathizing in all our attachments, humours, and habits. Our literature no longer grows in water, but in mould, and with the true racy virtues of the soil and climate. How much of this change may be due to Burns, or to any other individual, it might be difficult to estimate. Direct literary imitation of Burns was not to be looked for. But his example, in the fearless adoption of domestic subjects, could not but operate from afar; and certainly in no heart did the love of country ever burn with a warmer glow than in that of Burns: "a tide of Scottish prejudice," as he modestly calls this deep and generous feeling, "had been poured along his veins; and he felt that it would boil there till the flood-gates shut in eternal rest." It seemed to him, as if *he* could do so little for his country, and and yet would so gladly have done all. One small province stood, open for him; that of Scottish song, and how eagerly he entered on it; how devotedly he laboured there! In his most toilsome journeyings, this object never quits him; it is the little happy-valley of his careworn heart. In the gloom of his own affliction, he eagerly searches after some lonely brother of the muse, and rejoices to snatch one other name from the oblivion that was covering it! These were early feelings, and they abode with him to the end.

——a wish, (I mind its power,)
A wish, that to my latest hour
Will strongly heave my breast;
That I, for poor auld Scotland's sake,
Some useful plan or book could make,
Or sing a sang at least.
The rough bur Thistle spreading wide
Amang the bearded bear,
I turn'd my weeding-clips aside,
And spared the symbol dear.

But to leave the mere literary character of Burns, which has already detained us too long, we cannot but think that the Life he willed, and was fated to lead among his fellow-men, is both more interesting and instructive than any of his written works. These Poems are but like little rhymed fragments scattered here and there in the grand unrhymed Romance of his earthly existence; and it is only when intercalated in this at their proper places, that they attain their full measure of significance. And this too, alás, was but a fragment! The plan of a mighty edifice had been sketched; some columns, porticoes, firm masses of building, stand completed; the rest more or less clearly indicated; with many a far-stretching tendency, which only studious and friendly eyes can now trace towards the purposed termination. For the work is broken off in the middle, almost in the beginning; and rises among us, beautiful and sad, at once unfinished and a ruin! If charitable judgment was necessary in estimating his poems, and justice required that the aim and the manifest power to fulfil it must often be accepted for the fulfilment; much more is this the case in regard to his life, the sum and result of all his endeavours, where his difficulties came upon him not in detail only, but in mass; and so much has been left unaccomplished, nay, was mistaken, and altogether marred.

Properly speaking, there is but one era in the life of Burns, and that the earliest. We have not youth and manhood; but only youth: For, to the end, we discern no decisive change in the complexion of his character; in his thirty-seventh year, he is still, as it were, in youth. With all that resoluteness of judgment, that penetrating insight, and singular maturity of intellectual power, exhibited in his writings, he never attains to any clearness regarding himself; to the last he never ascertains his peculiar aim, even with such distinctness as is common among ordinary men; and therefore never can pursue it with that singleness of will, which insures success and some contentment to such men. To the last, he wavers between two purposes: glorying in his talent, like a true poet, he yet cannot consent to make this his chief and sole glory, and to follow it as the one thing needful, through poverty or riches, through good or evil report. Another far meaner ambition still cleaves to him; he must dream and struggle about a certain "Rock of Independence;" which, natural and even admirable as it might be, was still but a warring with the world, on the comparatively insignificant ground of his being more or less completely supplied with money, than others; of his standing at a higher, or at a lower altitude in general estimation, than others. For the world still appears to him, as to the young, in borrowed colours: he expects from it what it cannot give to any man; seeks for contentment, not within himself, in action and wise effort, but from without, in the kindness of circumstances, in love, friendship, honour, pecuniary ease. He would be happy, not actively and in himself, but passively, and from some ideal cornucopia of Enjoyments, not earned by his own labour, but showered on him by the beneficence of Destiny. Thus, like a young man, he cannot steady himself for any fixed or systematic pursuit, but swerves to and fro, between passionate hope, and remorseful disappointment: rushing onwards with a deep tempestuous force, he surmounts or breaks asunder many a barrier; travels, nay, advances far, but advancing only under uncertain guidance, is ever and anon turned from his path: and to the last, cannot reach the only true happiness of a man, that of clear, decided Activity in the sphere for which by nature and circumstances he has been fitted and appointed.

We do not say these things in dispraise of Burns: nay, perhaps, they but interest us the more in his favour. This blessing is not given soonest to the best; but rather, it is often the greatest minds that are latest in obtaining it; for where most is to be developed, most time may be required to develope it. A complex condition had been assigned him from without, as complex a condition from within: "no "pre-established harmony" existed between the clay soil of Mossgiel and the empyrean soul of Robert Burns; it was not wonderful, therefore, that the adjustment between them should have been long postponed, and his arm long cumbered, and his sight confused, in so vast and discordant an economy, as he had been appointed steward over. Byron was, at his death, but a year younger than Burns; and through life, as it might have appeared, far more simply situated; yet in him, too, we can trace no such adjustment, no such moral manhood; but at best, and only a little before his end, the beginning of what seemed such.

By much the most striking incident in Burns's Life is his journey to Edinburgh; but perhaps a still more important one is his residence at Irvine, so early as in his twenty-third year. Hitherto his life had been poor and toilworn; but otherwise not ungenial, and, with all its distresses, by no means unhappy. In his parentage, deducting outward circumstances, he had every reason to reckon himself fortunate: his father was a man of thoughtful, intense, earnest character, as the best of our peasants are; valuing knowledge, possessing some, and, what is far better and rarer, openminded for more; a man with a keen insight, and devout heart: reverent towards God, friendly therefore at once, and fearless towards all that God has made; in one word, though but a hard-handed peasant, a complete and fully unfolded *Man*. Such a father is seldom found in any rank in society; and was worth descending far in society to seek. Unfortunately, he was very poor; had he been even a little richer, almost ever so little, the whole might have issued far otherwise. Mighty events turn on a straw; the crossing of a brook decides the conquest of the world. Had this William Burns's small seven acres of nursery ground anywise prospered, the boy Robert had been sent to school; had struggled forward, as so many weaker men do, to some university; come forth not as a rustic wonder, but as a regular well-trained intellectual workman, and changed the whole course of British Literature,—for it lay in him to have done this! But the nursery did not prosper; poverty sank his whole family below the help of even our cheap school-system: Burns remained a hard-worked plough-boy, and British literature took its own course. Nevertheless, even in this rugged scene, there is much to nourish him. If he drudges, it is with his brother, and for his father and mother, whom he loves, and would fain shield from want. Wisdom is not banished from their poor hearth, nor the balm of natural feeling: the solemn words, *Let us worship God*, are heard there from a "priest-like father;" if threatenings of unjust men throw mother and children into tears, these are tears not of grief only, but of holiest affection; every heart in that humble group feels itself the closer knit to every other; in their hard warfare they are there together, a "little band of brethren." Neither are such tears, and the deep beauty that dwells in them, their only portion. Light visits the hearts as it does the eyes of all living: there is a force, too, in this youth, that enables him to trample on misfortune; nay, to bind it under his feet to make him sport. For a bold, warm, buoyant humour of character has been given him; and so the thick-coming shapes of evil are welcomed with a gay, friendly irony, and in their closest pressure he bates no jot of heart or hope. Vague yearnings of ambition fail not, as he grows up; dreamy fancies hang like cloud-cities around him; the curtain of Existence is slowly rising, in many-coloured splendour and gloom: and the auroral light of first love is gilding his horizon, and the music of song is on his path; and so he walks

> ——in glory and in joy,
> Behind his plough, upon the mountain side!

We know, from the best evidence, that up to this date, Burns was happy; nay, that he was the gayest, brightest, most fantastic, fascinating being to be found in the world; more so even than he ever afterwards appeared. But now, at this early age, he quits the paternal roof; goes forth into looser, louder, more exciting society; and becomes initiated in those dissipations, those vices, which a certain class of philosophers have asserted to be a natural preparative for entering on active life; a kind of mud-bath, in which the youth is, as it were, necessitated to steep, and, we suppose, cleanse himself, before the real toga of Manhood can be laid on him. We shall not dispute much with this class of philosophers; we hope they are mistaken: for Sin and Remorse so easily beset us at all stages of life, and are always such indifferent company, that it seems hard we should, at any stage, be forced and fated not only to meet, but to yield to them; and even serve for a term in their leprous armada. We hope it is not so. Clear we are, at all events, it cannot be the training one receives in this service, but only our determining to desert from it, that fits us for true manly Action. We become men, not after we have been dissipated, and disappointed in the chase of false pleasure; but after we have ascertained, in any way, what impassable barriers hem us in through this life; how mad it is to hope for contentment to our infinite soul from the *gifts* of this extremely finite world! that a man must be sufficient for himself; and that "for suffering and enduring there is no remedy but striving and doing." Manhood begins when we have in any way made truce with Necessity; begins, at all events, when we have surrendered to Necessity, as the most part only do; but begins joyfully and hopefully only when we have reconciled ourselves to Necessity; and thus, in reality, triumphed over it, and felt that in Necessity we are free. Surely, such lessons as this last, which, in one shape or other, is the grand lesson for every mortal man, are better learned from the lips of a devout mother, in the looks and actions of a devout father, while the heart is yet soft and pliant, than in collision with the sharp adamant of Fate, attracting us to shipwreck us, when the heart is grown hard, and may be broken before it will become contrite! Had Burns continued to learn this, as he was already learning it, in his father's cottage, he would have learned it fully, which he never did,—and been saved many a lasting aberration, many a bitter hour and year of remorseful sorrow.

It seems to us another circumstance of fatal import in Burns's history, that at this time too he became involved in the religious quarrels of his district; that he was enlisted and feasted, as the fighting man of the New-Light Priesthood, in their highly unprofitable warfare. At the tables of these free-minded clergy, he learned much more than was needful for him. Such liberal ridicule of fanaticism awakened in his mind scruples about Religion itself; and a whole world of Doubts, which it required quite another set of conjurors than these men to exorcise. We do not say that such an intellect as his could have escaped similar doubts, at some period of his history; or even that he could, at a later period, have come through them altogether victorious and unharmed: but it seems peculiarly unfortunate that this time, above all others, should have been fixed for the encounter. For now, with principles assailed by evil example from without, by "passions raging like demons" from within, he had little need of skeptical misgivings to whisper treason in the heat of the battle, or to cut off his retreat if he were already defeated. He loses his feeling of innocence; his mind is at variance with itself; the old divinity no longer presides there; but wild Desires and wild Repentance alternately oppress him. Ere long, too, he has committed himself before the world; his character for sobriety, dear to a Scottish peasant, as few corrupted worldlings can even conceive, is destroyed in the eyes of men; and his only refuge consists in trying to disbelieve his guiltiness, and is but a refuge of lies. The blackest desperation now gathers over him, broken only by the red lightnings of remorse. The whole fabric of his life is blasted asunder; for now not only his character, but his personal liberty, is to be lost; men and Fortune are leagued for his hurt; "hungry Ruin has him in the wind." He sees no escape but the saddest of all: exile from his loved country, to a country in every sense inhospitable and abhorrent to him. While the "gloomy night is gathering fast," in mental storm and solitude, as well as in physical, he sings his wild farewell to Scotland:

> Farewell, my friends, farewell my foes!
> My peace with these, my love with those:
> The bursting tears my heart declare;
> Adieu, my native banks of Ayr!

Light breaks suddenly in on him in floods; but still a false transitory light, and no real sunshine. He is invited to Edinburgh; hastens thither with anticipating heart; is welcomed as in triumph, and with universal blandishment and acclamation; whatever is wisest, whatever is greatest, or loveliest there, gathers round him, to gaze on his face, to show him honour, sympathy, affection. Burns's appearance among the sages and nobles of Edinburgh, must be regarded as one of the most singular phenomena in modern Literature; almost like the appearance of some Napoleon among the crowned sovereigns of modern Politics. For it is nowise as a "mockery king," set there by favour, transiently, and for a purpose, that he will let himself be treated; still less is he a mad Rienzi, whose sudden elevation turns his too weak head: but he stands there on his own basis; cool, unastonished, holding his equal rank from Nature herself; putting forth no claim which there is not strength *in* him, as well as about him, to vindicate. Mr. Lockhart has some forcible observations on this point:

"It needs no effort of imagination," says he, "to conceive what the sensations of an isolated set of scholars (almost all either clergymen or professors) must have been, in the presence of this big-boned, black-browed, brawny stranger, with his great flashing eyes, who, having forced his way among them from the plough-tail, at a single stride, manifested in the whole strain of his bearing and conversation, a most thorough conviction that in the society of the most eminent men of his nation, he was exactly where he was entitled to be; hardly deigned to flatter them by exhibiting even an occasional symptom of being flattered by their notice; by turns calmly measured himself against the most cultivated understandings of his time in discussion; overpowered the *bon mots* of the most celebrated convivialists by broad floods of merriment, impregnated with all the burning life of genius; astounded bosoms habitually enveloped in the thrice-piled folds of social reserve, by compelling them to tremble,—nay, to tremble visibly,—beneath the fearless touch of natural pathos; and all this without indicating the smallest willingness to be ranked among those professional ministers of excitement, who are content to be paid in money and smiles for doing what the spectators and auditors would be ashamed of doing in their own persons, even if they had the power of doing it; and last, and probably worst of all, who was known to be in the habit of enlivening societies which they would have scorned to approach, still more frequently than their own, with eloquence no less magnificent; with wit, in all likelihood still more daring; often enough as the superiors whom he fronted without alarm might have guessed from the beginning, and had, ere long, no occasion to guess, with wit pointed at themselves."—p. 131.

The farther we remove from this scene, the more singular will it seem to us: details of the exterior aspect of it are already full of interest. Most readers recollect Mr. Walker's personal interviews with Burns as among the best passages of his Narrative; a time will come when this reminiscence of Sir Walter Scott's, slight though it is, will also be precious.

"As for Burns," writes Sir Walter, "I may truly say *Virgilium vidi tantum*. I was a lad of fifteen in 1786—7, when he came first to Edinburgh, but had sense and feeling enough to be much interested in his poetry, and would have given the world to know him: but I had very little acquaintance with any literary people; and still less with the gentry of the west country, the two sets that he most frequented. Mr. Thomas Grierson was at that time a clerk of my father's. He knew Burns, and promised to ask him to his lodgings to dinner, but had no opportunity to keep his word; otherwise I might have seen more of this distinguished man. As it was, I saw him one day at the late venerable Professor Ferguson's, where there were several gentlemen of literary reputation, among whom I remember the celebrated Mr. Dugald Stewart. Of course, we youngsters sat silent, looked and listened. The only thing I remember, which was remarkable in Burns's manner, was the effect produced upon him by a print of Bunbury's, representing a soldier lying dead on the snow, his dog sitting in misery on one side,—on the other, his widow, with a child in her arms. These lines were written beneath:

> "Cold on Canadian hills, or Minden's plain,
> Perhaps that mother wept her soldier slain:
> Bent o'er her babe, her eye dissolved in dew,
> The big drops mingling with the milk he drew
> Gave the sad presage of his future years,
> The child of misery baptized in tears."

"Burns seemed much affected by the print, or rather by the ideas which it suggested to his mind. He actually shed tears. He asked whose the lines were, and it chanced that nobody but myself remembered that they occur in a half-forgotten poem of Langhorne's, called by the unpromising title of "The Justice of Peace." I whispered my information to a friend present, he mentioned it to Burns, who rewarded me with a look and a word, which, though of mere civility, I then received and still recollect with very great pleasure.

"His person was strong and robust; his manners rustic, not clownish; a sort of dignified plainness and simplicity, which received part of its effect perhaps from one's knowledge of his extraordinary talents. His features are represented in Mr. Nasmyth's picture: but to me it conveys the idea that they are diminished, as if seen in perspective. I think his countenance was more massive than it looks in any of the portraits. I should have taken the poet, had I not known what he was, for a very sagacious country farmer of the old Scotch school, *i. e.* none of your modern agriculturists who keep labourers for their drudgery, but the *douce gudeman* who held his own plough. There was a strong expression of sense and shrewdness in all his lineaments; the eye alone, I think, indicated the poetical character and temperament. It was large, and of a dark cast, which glowed (I say literally *glowed*) when he spoke with feeling or interest. I never saw such another eye in a human head, though I have seen the most distinguished men of my time. His conversation expressed perfect self-confidence, without the slightest presumption. Among the men who were the most learned of their time and country, he expressed himself with perfect firmness, but without the least intrusive forwardness; and when he differed in opinion, he did not hesitate to express it firmly, yet at the same time with modesty. I do not remember any part of his conversation distinctly enough to be quoted; nor did I ever see him again, except in the street, where he did not recognise me, as I could not expect he should. He was much caressed in Edinburgh: but (considering what literary emoluments have been since his day) the efforts made for his relief were extremely trifling.

"I remember, on this occasion I mention, I thought Burns's acquaintance with English poetry was rather limited; and also, that having twenty times the abilities of Allan Ramsay and of Ferguson, he talked of them with too much humility as his models: there was doubtless national predilection in his estimate.

"This is all I can tell you about Burns. I have only to add, that his dress corresponded with his manner. He was like a farmer dressed in his best to dine with the laird. I do not speak in *malam partem*, when I say, I never saw a man in company with his superiors in station or information more perfectly free from either the reality or the affectation of embarrassment. I was told, but did not observe it, that his address to females was extremely deferential, and always with a turn either to the pathetic or humorous, which engaged their attention particularly. I have heard the late Duchess of Gordon remark this.—I do not know any thing I can add to these recollections of forty years since."—pp. 112—115.

The conduct of Burns under this dazzling blaze of favour; the calm, unaffected, manly manner, in which he not only bore it, but estimated its value, has justly been regarded as the best proof that could be given of his real vigour and integrity of mind. A little natural vanity, some touches of hypocritical modesty, some glimmerings of affectation, at least some fear of being thought affected, we could have pardoned in almost any man; but no such indication is to be traced here. In his unexampled situation the young peasant is not a moment perplexed; so many strange lights do not confuse him, do not lead him astray. Nevertheless, we cannot but perceive that this winter did him great and lasting injury. A somewhat clearer knowledge of men's affairs, scarcely of their characters, it did afford him: but a sharper feeling of Fortune's unequal arrangements in their social destiny it also left with him. He had seen the gay and gorgeous arena, in which the powerful are born to play their parts; nay, had himself stood in the midst of it; and he felt more bitterly than ever, that here he was but a looker-on, and had no part or lot in that splendid game. From this time a jealous indignant fear of social degradation takes possession of him; and perverts, so far as aught could pervert, his private contentment, and his feelings towards his richer fellows. It was clear enough to Burns that he had talent enough to make a fortune, or a hundred fortunes, could he but have rightly willed this; it was clear also that he willed something far different, and therefore could not make one. Unhappy it was that he had not power to choose the one, and reject the other; but must halt for ever between two opinions, two objects; making hampered advancement towards either. But so is it with many men: we "long for the merchandise, yet would fain keep the price;" and so stand chaffering with Fate in vexatious altercation, till the Night come, and our fair is over!

The Edinburgh learned of that period were in general more noted for clearness of head than for warmth of heart: with the exception of the good old Blacklock, whose help was too ineffectual, scarcely one among them seems to have looked at Burns with any true sympathy, or indeed much otherwise than as at a highly curious *thing*. By the great, also, he is treated in the customary fashion; entertained at their tables, and dismissed: certain modica of pudding and praise are, from time to time, gladly exchanged for the fascination of his presence; which exchange once effected, the bargain is finished, and each party goes his several way. At the end of this strange season, Burns gloomily sums up his gains and losses, and meditates on the chaotic future. In money he is somewhat richer; in fame and the show of happiness, infinitely richer; but in the substance of it, as poor as ever. Nay poorer, for his heart is now maddened still more with the fever of mere worldly Ambition; and through long years the disease will rack him with unprofitable sufferings and weaken his strength for all true and nobler aims.

What Burns was next to do or avoid; how a man so circumstanced was now to guide himself towards his true advantage, might at this point of time have been a question for the wisest: and it was a question which he was left altogether to answer for himself: of his learned or rich patrons it had not struck any individual to turn a thought on this so trivial matter. Without claiming for Burns the praise of perfect sagacity, we must say, that his Excise and Farm scheme does not seem to us a very unreasonable one; and that we should be at a loss, even now, to suggest one decidedly better. Some of his admirers, indeed, are scandalized at his ever resolving to *gauge;* and would have had him apparently lie still at the pool, till the spirit of Patronage should stir the waters, and then heal with one plunge all his worldly sorrows! We fear such counsellors knew but little of Burns; and did not consider that happiness might in all cases be cheaply had by waiting for the fulfilment of golden dreams, were it not that in the interim the dreamer must die of hunger. It reflects credit on the manliness and sound sense of Burns, that he felt so early on what ground he was standing; and preferred self-help, on the humblest scale, to dependence and inaction, though with hope of far more splendid possibilities. But even these possibilities were not rejected in his scheme: he might expect, if it chanced that he *had* any friend, to rise, in no long period, into something even like opulence and leisure; while again, if it chanced that he had no friend, he could still live in security; and for the rest, he "did not intend to borrow honour from any profession." We think then that his plan was honest and well-calculated: all turned on the execution of it. Doubtless it failed; yet not, we believe, from any vice inherent in itself. Nay after all, it was no failure of external means, but of internal that overtook Burns. His was no bankruptcy of the purse, but of the soul; to his last day, he owed no man any thing.

Meanwhile he begins well: with two good and wise actions. His donation to his mother, munificent from a man whose income had lately been seven pounds a-year, was worthy of him, and not more than worthy. Generous also, and worthy of him, was his treatment of the woman whose life's welfare now depended on his pleasure. A friendly observer might have hoped serene days for him: his mind is on the true road to peace with itself: what clearness he still wants will be given as he proceeds; for the best teacher of duties, that still lie dim to us, is the Practice of those we see, and have at hand. Had the "patrons of genius," who could give him nothing, but taken nothing from him, at least nothing more!—the wounds of his heart would have healed, vulgar ambition would have died away. Toil and Frugality would have been welcome, since Virtue dwelt with them, and poetry would have shone through them as of old; and in her clear ethereal light, which was his own by birthright, he might have looked down on his earthly destiny, and all its obstructions, not with patience only, but with love.

But the patrons of genius would not have it so. Picturesque tourists,* all manner of fashionable danglers after literature, and, far worse, all manner of convivial Mecænases, hovered round him in his retreat; and his good as well as his weak qualities secured them influence over him. He was flattered by their notice; and his warm social nature made it impossible for him to shake them off, and hold on his way apart from them. These men, as we believe, were proximately the means of his ruin. Not that they meant him any ill; they only meant themselves a little good; if he suffered harm, let *him* look to it! But they wasted his precious time and his precious talent; they disturbed his composure, broke down his returning habits of temperance and assiduous contented exertion. Their pampering was baneful to him; their cruelty, which soon followed, was equally baneful. The old grudge against Fortune's inequality awoke with new bitterness in their neighbourhood, and Burns had no retreat but to the "Rock of Independence," which is but an air-castle, after all, that looks well at a distance, but will screen no one from real wind and wet. Flushed with irregular excitement, exasperated alternately by contempt of others, and contempt of himself, Burns was no longer regaining his peace of mind, but fast losing it for ever. There was a hollowness at the heart of his life, for his conscience did not now approve what he was doing.

Amid the vapours of unwise enjoyment, of bootless remorse, and angry discontent with Fate, his true loadstar, a life of Poetry, with Poverty, nay, with Famine if it must be so, was too often altogether hidden from his eyes. And yet he sailed a sea, where, without some such guide, there was no right steering. Meteors of French Politics rise before him, but these were not *his* stars. An accident this, which hastened, but did not originate, his worst distresses. In the mad contentions of that time, he comes in collision with certain official Superiors; is wounded by them; cruelly lacerated, we should say, could a dead mechanical implement, in any case, be called cruel: and shrinks, in indignant pain, into deeper self-seclusion, into gloomier moodiness than ever. His life has now lost its unity: it is a life of fragments; led with little aim, beyond the melancholy one of securing its own continuance,—in fits of wild false joy, when such offered, and of black despondency when they passed away. His character before the world begins to suffer: calumny is busy with him; for a miserable man makes more enemies than friends. Some faults he has fallen into, and a thousand misfortunes; but deep criminality is what he stands accused of, and they that are *not* without sin, cast the first stone at him! For is he not a well-wisher of the French Revolution, a Jacobin, and there-

* There is one little sketch by certain "English gentlemen" of this class, which though adopted in Currie's Narrative, and since then repeated in most others, we have all along felt an invincible disposition to regard as imaginary: "On a rock that projected into the stream they saw a man employed in angling, of a singular appearance. He had a cap made of fox-skin on his head, a loose great-coat fixed round him by a belt, from which depended an enormous Highland broad-sword. It was Burns." Now, we rather think, it was not Burns. For to say nothing of the fox-skin cap, loose and quite Hibernian watch-coat with the belt, what are we to make of this "enormous Highland broad-sword" depending from him? More especially, as there is no word of parish constables on the outlook to see whether, as Dennis phrases it, he had an eye to his own midriff, or that of the public! Burns, of all men, had the least tendency, to seek for distinction, either in his own eyes, or those of others, by such poor mummeries.

fore in that one act guilty of all? These accusations, political and moral, it has since appeared, were false enough: but the world hesitated little to credit them. Nay, his convivial Mecænases themselves were not the last to do it. There is reason to believe that, in his later years, the Dumfries Aristocracy had partly withdrawn themselves from Burns, as from a tainted person, no longer worthy of their acquaintance. That painful class, stationed, in all provincial cities, behind the outmost breastwork of Gentility, there to stand siege and do battle against the intrusion of Grocerdom, and Grazierdom, had actually seen dishonour in the society of Burns, and branded him with their veto; had, as we vulgarly say, *cut* him! We find one passage in this work of Mr. Lockhart's, which will not out of our thoughts:

"A gentleman of that country, whose name I have already more than once had occasion to refer to, has often told me that he was seldom more grieved, than when, riding into Dumfries one fine summer evening about this time to attend a country ball, he saw Burns walking alone, on the shady side of the principal street of the town, while the opposite side was gay with successive groups of gentlemen and ladies, all drawn together for the festivities of the night, not one of whom appeared willing to recognise him. The horseman dismounted, and joined Burns, who on his proposing to cross the street said: "Nay, nay, my young friend, that's all over now;" and quoted, after a pause, some verses of Lady Grizzel Baillie's pathetic ballad:

"His bonnet stood ance fu' fair on his brow,
His auld ane looked better than mony ane's new;
But now he lets't wear ony way it will hing,
And casts himsell dowie upon the corn-bing.

"O were we young, as we ance hae been,
We sud hae been galloping down on yon green,
And linking it ower the lily-white lea!
And werena my heart light I wad die."

It was little in Burns's character to let his feelings on certain subjects escape in this fashion. He immediately after reciting these verses, assumed the sprightliness of his most pleasing manner; and, taking his young friend home with him, entertained him very agreeably till the hour of the ball arrived."

Alas! when we think that Burns now sleeps "where bitter indignation can no longer lacerate his heart,"* and that most of these fair dames and frizzled gentlemen already lie at his side, where the breastwork of gentility is quite thrown down,—who would not sigh over the thin delusions and foolish toys that divide heart from heart, and make man unmerciful to his brother!

It was not now to be hoped that the genius of Burns would ever reach maturity, or accomplish ought worthy of itself. His spirit was jarred in its melody; not the soft breath of natural feeling, but the rude hand of Fate, was now sweeping over the strings. And yet what harmony was in him, what music even in his discords! How the wild tones had a charm for the simplest and the wisest; and all men felt and knew that here also was one of the Gifted! "If he entered an inn at midnight, after all the inmates were in bed, the news of his arrival circulated from the cellar to the garret; and ere ten minutes had elapsed, the landlord and all his guests were assembled!" Some brief, pure moments of poetic life were yet appointed him, in the composition of his Songs. We can understand how he grasped at this employment; and how, too, he spurned at all other reward for it but what the labour itself brought him. For the soul of Burns, though scathed and marred, was yet living in its full moral strength, though sharply conscious of its errors and abasement: and here, in his destitution and degradation, was one act of seeming nobleness and self-devotedness left even for him to perform. He felt, too, that with all the "thoughtless follies" that had "laid him low," the world was unjust and cruel to him; and he silently appealed to another and calmer time. Not as a hired soldier, but as a patriot, would he strive for the glory of his country; so he cast from him the poor sixpence a-day, and served zealously as a volunteer. Let us not grudge him this last luxury of his existence; let him not have appealed to us in vain! The money was not necessary to him; he struggled through without it; long since, these guineas would have been gone, and now the high-mindedness of refusing them will plead for him in all hearts for ever.

We are here arrived at the crisis of Burns's life; for matters had now taken such a shape with him as could not long continue. If improvement was not to be looked for, Nature could only for a limited time maintain this dark and maddening warfare against the world and itself. We are not medically informed whether any continuance of years was, at this period, probable for Burns; whether his death is to be looked on as in some sense an accidental event, or only as the natural consequence of the long series of events that had preceded. The latter seems to be the likelier opinion; and yet it is by no means a certain one. At all events, as we have said, *some* change could not be very distant. Three gates of deliverance, it seems to us, were open for Burns: clear poetical activity; madness; or death. The first, with longer life, was still possible, though not probable; for physical causes were beginning to be concerned in it: and yet Burns had an iron resolution; could he but have seen and felt, that not only his highest glory, but his first duty, and the true medicine for all his woes, lay here. The second was still less probable; for his mind was ever among the clearest and firmest. So the milder third gate was opened for him: and he passed, not softly, yet speedily, into that still country, where the hail-storms and fire-showers do not reach, and the heaviest-laden way-farer at length lays down his load!

Contemplating this sad end of Burns, and how he sank unaided by any real help, uncheered by any wise sympathy, generous minds have sometimes figured to themselves.

* *Ubi sæva indignatio cor ulterius lacerare nequit.*—SWIFT's Epitaph.

with a reproachful sorrow, that much might have been done for him; that by counsel, true affection, and friendly ministrations, he might have been saved to himself and the world. We question whether there is not more tenderness of heart than soundness of judgment in these suggestions. It seems dubious to us whether the richest, wisest, most benevolent individual, could have lent Burns any effectual help. Counsel, which seldom profits any one, he did not need; in his understanding, he knew the right from the wrong, as well perhaps as any man ever did; but the persuasion, which would have availed him, lies not so much in the head, as in the heart, where no argument or expostulation could have assisted much to implant it. As to money again, we do not really believe that this was his essential want; or well see how any private man could, even presupposing Burns's consent, have bestowed on him an independent fortune, with much prospect of decisive advantage. It is a mortifying truth, that two men in any rank of society could hardly be found virtuous enough to give money, and to take it, as a necessary gift, without injury to the moral entireness of one or both. But so stands the fact: Friendship, in the old heroic sense of that term, no longer exists; except in the cases of kindred or other legal affinity; it is in reality no longer expected, or recognised as a virtue among men. A close observer of manners has pronounced "Patronage," that is, pecuniary or other economic furtherance, to be "twice cursed;" cursing him that gives, and him that takes! And thus, in regard to outward matters also, it has become the rule, as in regard to inward it always was and must be the rule, that no one shall look for effectual help to another; but that each shall rest contented with what help he can afford himself. Such, we say, is the principle of modern Honour; naturally enough growing out of that sentiment of Pride, which we inculcate and encourage as the basis of our whole social morality. Many a poet has been poorer than Burns; but no one was ever prouder: we may question, whether, without great precautions, even a pension from Royalty would not have galled and encumbered, more than actually assisted him.

Still less, therefore, are we disposed to join with another class of Burns's admirers, who accuse the higher ranks among us of having ruined Burns by their selfish neglect of him. We have already stated our doubts whether direct pecuniary help, had it been offered, would have been accepted, or could have proved very effectual. We shall readily admit, however, that much was to be done for Burns; that many a poisoned arrow might have been warded from his bosom; many an entanglement in his path cut asunder by the hand of the powerful; and light and heat shed on him from high places, would have made his humble atmosphere more genial; and the softest heart then breathing might have lived and died with some fewer pangs. Nay, we shall grant further, and for Burns it is granting much, that with all his pride, he would have thanked, even with exaggerated gratitude, any one who had cordially befriended him: patronage, unless once cursed, needed not to have been twice so. At all events, the poor promotion he desired in his calling might have been granted: it was his own scheme, therefore, likelier than any other to be of service. All this it might have been a luxury, nay, it was a duty, for our nobility to have done. No part of all this, however, did any of them do; or apparently attempt, or wish to do; so much is granted against them. But what then is the amount of their blame? Simply that they were men of the world, and walked by the principles of such men; that they treated Burns, as other nobles and other commoners had done other poets; as the English did Shakspeare; as King Charles and his cavaliers did Butler, as King Philip and his Grandees did Cervantes. Do men gather grapes of thorns? or shall we cut down our thorns for yielding only a *fence*, and haws? How, indeed, could the "nobility and gentry of his native land" hold out any help to this "Scottish Bard, proud of his name and country?" Were the nobility and gentry so much as able rightly to help themselves? Had they not their game to preserve; their borough interests to strengthen; dinners, therefore, of various kinds to eat and give? Were their means more than adequate to all this business, or less than adequate? Less than adequate in general: few of them in reality were richer than Burns; many of them were poorer; for sometimes they had to wring their supplies, as with thumbscrews, from the hard hand; and, in their need of guineas, to forget their duty of mercy; which Burns was never reduced to do. Let us pity and forgive them. The game they preserved and shot, the dinners they ate and gave, the borough interests they strengthened, the *little* Babylons they severally builded by the glory of their might, are all melted, or melting back into the primeval Chaos, as man's merely selfish endeavours are fated to do: and here was an action extending, in virtue of its worldly influence, we may say, through all time; in virtue of its moral nature, beyond all time, being immortal as the Spirit of Goodness itself; this action was offered them to do, and light was not given them to do it. Let us pity and forgive them. But, better than pity, let us go and *do otherwise*. Human suffering did not end with the life of Burns; neither was the solemn mandate, "Love one another, bear one another's burdens," given to the rich only, but to all men. True, we shall find no Burns to relieve, to assuage by our aid or our pity: but celestial natures, groaning under the fardels of a weary life, we shall still find; and that wretchedness which Fate has rendered *voiceless* and *tuneless*, is not the least wretched, but the most.

Still we do not think that the blame of Burns's failure lies chiefly with the world. The world, it seems to us, treated him with more, rather than with less kindness, than it usually shows to such men. It has ever, we fear, shown but small favour to its Teachers; hunger and nakedness, perils and reviling, the prison, the cross, the poison-chalice, have, in most times and countries, been the market-place it has offered for Wisdom, the welcome with which it has greeted those who have come to enlighten and purify it. Homer and Socrates, and the Christian Apostles, belong to old days; but the world's Martyrology was not completed with these. Roger Bacon and Galileo languish in priestly dungeons, Tasso pines in the cell of a mad-house, Camoens dies begging on the streets of Lisbon. So neglected, so "persecuted they the Prophets," not in Judea only, but in all places where men have been. We reckon that every poet of Burns's order is, or should be, a prophet and teacher to his age; that he has no right therefore to expect great kindness from it, but rather is bound to do it great kindness; that Burns, in particular, experienced fully the usual proportion of the world's goodness; and that the blame of his failure, as we have said, lies not chiefly with the world.

Where then does it lie? We are forced to answer: With himself; it is his inward, not his outward misfortunes, that bring him to the dust. Seldom, indeed, is it otherwise; seldom is a life morally wrecked, but the grand cause lies in some internal mal-arrangement, some want less of good fortune than of good guidance. Nature fashions no creature without implanting in it the strength needful for its action and duration; least of all does she so neglect her masterpiece and darling, the poetic soul. Neither can we believe that it is in the power of *any* external circumstances utterly to ruin the mind of a man; nay, if proper wisdom be given him, even so much as to affect its essential health and beauty. The sternest sum-total of all worldly misfortunes is Death; nothing more *can* lie in the cup of human wo: yet many men, in all ages, have triumphed over Death, and led it captive; converting its physical victory into a moral victory for themselves, into a seal and immortal consecration for all that their past life had achieved. What has been done, may be done again; nay, it is but the degree and not the kind of such heroism that differs in different seasons; for without some portion of this spirit, not of boisterous daring, but of silent fearlessness, of Self-denial, in all its forms, no good man, in any scene or time, has ever attained to be good.

We have already stated the error of Burns; and mourned over it, rather than blamed it. It was the want of unity in his purposes, of consistency in his aims; the hapless attempt to mingle in friendly union the common spirit of the world with the spirit of poetry, which is of a far different and altogether irreconcilable nature. Burns was nothing wholly; and Burns could be nothing, no man formed as he was can be any thing, by halves. The heart, not of a mere hot-blooded, popular verse-monger, or poetical *Restaurateur*, but of a true Poet and Singer, worthy of the old religious heroic times, had been given him: and he fell in an age, not of heroism and religion, but of skepticism, selfishness, and triviality when true Nobleness was little understood, and its place supplied by a hollow, dissocial, altogether barren and unfruitful principle of Pride. The influences of that age, his open, kind, susceptible nature, to say nothing of his highly untoward situation, made it more than usually difficult for him to repel or resist; the better spirit that was within him ever sternly demanded its rights, its supremacy; he spent his life in endeavouring to reconcile these two; and lost it, as he must have lost it, without reconciling them here.

Burns was born poor; and born also to continue poor, for he would not endeavour to be otherwise: this it had been well could he have once for all admitted, and considered as finally settled. He was poor, truly; but hundreds even of his own class and order of minds have been poorer, yet have suffered nothing deadly from it: nay, his own Father had a far sorer battle with ungrateful destiny than his was; and he did not yield to it, but died courageously warring, and to all moral intents prevailing, against it. True, Burns had little means, had even little time for poetry, his only real pursuit and vocation; but so much the more precious was what little he had. In all these external respects his case was hard; but very far from the hardest. Poverty, incessant drudgery, and much worse evils, it has often been the lot of Poets and wise men to strive with, and their glory to conquer. Locke was banished as a traitor; and wrote his *Essay on the Human Understanding*, sheltering himself in a Dutch garret. Was Milton rich or at his ease, when he composed *Paradise Lost?* Not only low, but fallen from a height; not only poor but impoverished; in darkness and with dangers compassed round, he sang his immortal song, and found fit audience, though few. Did not Cervantes finish his work, a maimed soldier, and in prison? Nay, was not the *Araucana*, which Spain acknowledges as its Epic, written without even the aid of paper; on scraps of leather, as the stout fighter and voyager snatched any moment from that wild warfare?

And what then had these men, which Burns wanted? Two things; both which, it seems to us, are indispensable for such men. They had a true, religious principle of morals; and a single not a double aim in their activity. They were not self-seekers and self-worshippers: but seekers and worshippers of something far better than Self. Not personal enjoyment was their object; but a high, heroic idea of Religion, of Patriotism, of heavenly Wisdom in one or the other form, ever hovered before them; in which cause, they neither shrunk from suffering, nor called on the earth to witness it as something wonderful; but patiently endured, counting it blessedness enough so to spend and be spent. Thus the "golden-calf of Self-love," however curiously carved, was not their Deity; but the Invisible Goodness, which alone is man's reasonable service. This feeling was as a celestial fountain, whose streams refreshed into gladness and beauty all the provinces of their otherwise too desolate existence. In a word, they willed one thing, to which all other things were subordinated, and made subservient; and therefore they accomplished it. The wedge will rend rocks; but its edge must be sharp and single: if it be double, the wedge is bruised in pieces and will rend nothing.

Part of this superiority these men owed to their age; in which heroism and devotedness were still practised, or at least not yet disbelieved in: but much of it likewise they owed to themselves. With Burns again it was different. His morality, in most of its practical points, is that of a mere worldly man; enjoyment, in a finer or a coarser shape, is the only thing he longs and strives for. A noble instinct sometimes raises him above this; but an instinct only, and acting only for moments. He has no Religion; in the shallow age, where his days were cast, Religion was not discriminated from the New and Old Light *forms* of Religion; and was, with these, becoming obsolete in the minds of men. His heart, indeed, is alive with a trembling adoration, but there is no temple in his understanding. He lives in darkness and in the shadow of doubt. His religion, at best, is an anxious wish; like that of Rabelais, "a great Perhaps."

He loved Poetry warmly, and in his heart; could he but have loved it purely, and with his whole undivided heart, it had been well. For Poetry, as Burns could have followed it, is but another form of Wisdom, of Religion; is itself Wisdom and Religion. But this also was denied him. His poetry is a stray vagrant gleam, which will not be extinguished within him, yet rises not to be the true light of his path, but is often a wildfire that misleads him. It was not necessary for Burns to be rich, to be, or to seem, "independent;" but *it was* necessary for him to be at one with his own heart; to place what was highest in his nature, highest also in his life; "to seek within himself for that consistency and sequence, which external events would for ever refuse him." He was born a poet; poetry was the celestial element of his being, and should have been the soul of his whole endeavours. Lifted into that serene ether, whither he had wings given him to mount, he would have needed no other elevation: Poverty, neglect, and all evil, save the desecration of himself and his Art, were a small matter to him; the pride and the passions of the world lay far beneath his feet; and he looked down alike on noble and slave, on prince and beggar, and all that wore the stamp of man, with clear recognition, with brotherly affection, with sympathy, with pity. Nay, we question whether for his culture as a Poet, poverty, and much suffering for a season, were not absolutely advantageous. Great men, in looking back over their lives, have testified to that effect. "I would not for much," says Jean Paul, "that I had been born richer." And yet Paul's birth was poor enough; for, in another place, he adds: "The prisoner's allowance is bread and water; and I had often only the latter." But the gold that is refined in the hottest furnace comes out the purest; or, as he has himself expressed it, "the canary-bird sings sweeter the longer it has been trained in a darkened cage."

A man like Burns might have divided his hours between poetry and virtuous industry; industry which all true feeling sanctions, nay prescribes, and which has a beauty, for that cause, beyond the pomp of thrones: but to divide his hours between poetry and rich men's banquets, was an ill-starred and inauspicious attempt. How could he be at ease at such banquets? What had he to do there, mingling his music with the coarse roar of altogether earthly voices, and brightening the thick smoke of intoxication with fire lent him from heaven? Was it his aim to *enjoy* life? To-morrow he must go drudge as an Exciseman! We wonder not that Burns became moody, indignant, and at times an offender against certain rules of society; but rather that he did not grow utterly frantic, and run *a-muck* against them all. How could a man, so falsely placed, by his own or others' fault, ever know contentment or peaceable diligence for an hour? What he did, under such perverse guidance, and what he forbore to do, alike fill us with astonishment at the natural strength and worth of his character.

Doubtless there was a remedy for this perverseness: but not in others; only in himself; least of all in simple increase of wealth and worldly "respectability." We hope we have now heard enough about the efficacy of wealth for poetry, and to make poets happy. Nay, have we not seen another instance of it in these very days? Byron, a man of an endowment considerably less ethereal than that of Burns, is born in the rank not of a Scottish ploughman, but of an English peer: the highest worldly honours, the fairest worldly career, are his by inheritance: the richest harvest of fame he soon reaps, in another province, by his own hand. And what does all this avail him? Is he happy, is he good, is he true? Alas, he has a poet's soul, and strives towards the Infinite and the Eternal; and soon feels that all this is but mounting to the house-top to reach the stars! Like Burns, he is only a proud man; might like him have "purchased a pocket-copy of Milton to study the character of Satan;" for Satan also is Byron's grand exemplar, the hero of his poetry, and the model apparently of his conduct. As in Burns's case too, the celestial element will not mingle with the clay of earth; both poet and man of the world he must not be; vulgar Ambition will not live kindly with poetic Adoration; he *cannot* serve God and Mammon. Byron, like Burns, is not happy; nay, he is the most wretched of all men. His life is falsely arranged: the fire that is in him is not a strong, still, central fire, warming into beauty the products of a world; but it is the mad fire of a volcano; and now,—we look sadly into the ashes of a crater, which, erelong, will fill itself with snow!

Byron and Burns were sent forth as missionaries to their generation, to teach it a higher Doctrine, a purer Truth: they had a message to deliver, which, left them no rest till it was accomplished; in dim throes of pain, this divine behest lay smouldering within them; for they knew not what it meant, and felt it only in mysterious anticipation, and they had to die without articulately uttering it. They are in the camp of the Unconverted. Yet not as high messengers of rigorous though benignant truth, but as soft flattering singers, and in pleasant fellowship, will they live there; they are first adulated, then persecuted; they accomplish little for others; they find no peace for themselves, but only death and the peace of the grave. We confess, it is not without a certain mournful awe that we view the fate of these noble souls, so richly gifted, yet ruined to so little purpose with all their gifts. It seems to us there is a stern moral taught in this piece of history,—*twice* told us in our own time! Surely to men of like genius, if there be any such, it carries with it a lesson of deep impressive significance. Surely it would become such a man, furnished for the highest of all enterprises, that of being the Poet of his Age, to consider well what it is that he attempts, and in what spirit he attempts it. For the words of Milton are true in all times, and were never truer than in this: "He, who would write heroic poems, must make his whole life a heroic poem." If he cannot first so make his life, then let him hasten from this arena; for neither its lofty glories, nor its fearful perils, are for him. Let him dwindle into a modish ballad-monger; let him worship and be-sing the idols of the time, and the time will not fail to reward him,—if, indeed, he can endure to live in that capacity! Byron and Burns could not live as idol-priests, but the fire of their own hearts consumed them; and better it was for them that they could not. For it is not in the favour of the great, or of the small, but in a life of truth, and in the inexpugnable citadel of his own soul, that a Byron's or a Burns's strength must lie. Let the great stand aloof from him, or know how to reverence him. Beautiful is the union of wealth with favour and furtherance for literature; like the costliest flower-jar enclosing the loveliest amaranth. Yet let not the relation be mistaken. A true poet is not one whom they can hire by money or flattery to be a minister of their pleasures, their writer of occasional verses, their purveyor of table-wit; he cannot be their menial, he cannot even be their partisan. At the peril of both parties, let no such union be attempted! Will a Courser of the Sun work softly in the harness of a Dray-horse? His hoofs are of fire, and his path is through the heavens, bringing light to all lands; will he lumber on mud highways, dragging ale for earthly appetites, from door to door?

But we must stop short in these considerations, which would lead us to boundless lengths. We had something to say on the public moral character of Burns; but this also we must forbear. We are far from regarding him as guilty before the world, as guiltier than the average; nay, from doubting that he is less guilty than one of ten thousand. Tried at a tribunal far more rigid than that where the *Plebiscita* of common civic reputations are pronounced, he has seemed to us even there less worthy of blame than of pity and wonder. But the world is habitually unjust in its judgments of such men; unjust on many grounds, of which this one may be stated as the substance: It decides, like a court of law, by dead statutes; and not positively but negatively, less on what is done right, than on what is, or is not, done wrong. Not the few inches of reflection from the mathematical orbit, which are so easily measured, but the *ratio* of these to the whole diameter, constitutes the real aberration. This orbit may be a planet's, its diameter the breadth of the solar system; or it may be a city hippodrome; nay, the circle of a ginhorse, its diameter a score of feet or paces. But the inches of deflection only are measured; and it is assumed that the diameter of the ginhorse, and that of the planet, will yield the same ratio when compared with them. Here lies the root of many a blind, cruel condemnation of Burnses, Swifts, Rousseaus, which one never listens to with approval. Granted, the ship comes into harbour with shrouds and tackle damaged; and the pilot is therefore blameworthy; for he has not been all-wise and all-powerful; but to know *how* blameworthy, tell us first whether his voyage has been round the Globe, or only to Ramsgate and the Isle of Dogs.

With our readers in general, with men of right feeling anywhere, we are not required to plead for Burns. In pitying admiration, he lies enshrined in all our hearts, in a far nobler mausoleum than that one of marble; neither will his Works, even as they are, pass away from the memory of men. While the Shakspeares and Miltons roll on like mighty rivers through the country of Thought, bearing fleets of traffickers and assiduous pearl-fishers on their waves; this little Valclusa Fountain will also arrest our eye: For this also is of Nature's own and most cunning workmanship, bursts from the depths of the earth, with a full gushing current, into the light of day; and often will the traveller turn aside to drink of its clear waters, and muse among its rocks and pines!

THE LIFE OF HEYNE.*

[Foreign Review, 1828.]

The labours and merits of Heyne being better known, and more justly appreciated in England, than those of almost any other German, whether scholar, poet, or philosopher, we cannot but believe that some notice of his life may be acceptable to most readers. Accordingly, we here mean to give a short abstract of this volume, a miniature copy of the "biographical portrait," but must first say a few words on the portrait itself, and the limner by whom it has been drawn.

Professor Heeren is a man of learning, and known far out of his own Hanoverian circle,—indeed, more or less to all students of history,—by his researches on Ancient Commerce, a voluminous account of which from his hand enjoys considerable reputation. He is evidently a man of sense and natural talent, as well as learning; and his gifts seem to lie round him in quiet arrangement, and very much at his own command. Nevertheless, we cannot admire him as a writer; we do not even reckon that such endowments as he has are adequately represented in his books. His style both of diction and thought is thin, cold, formal, without force or character, and painfully reminds us of college lectures. He can work rapidly, but with no freedom, and, as it were, only in one attitude, and at one sort of labour. Not that we particularly blame Professor Heeren for this, but that we think he might have been something better: These "fellows in buckram," very numerous in certain walks of literature, are an unfortunate, rather than a guilty class of men; they have fallen, perhaps unwillingly, into the plan of writing by pattern, and can now do no other; for, in their minds, the beautiful comes at last to be simply synonymous with the neat. Every sentence bears a family-likeness to its precursor; most probably it has a set number of clauses; (three is a favourite number, as in Gibbon, for "the muses delight in odds;") has also a given rhythm, a known and foreseen music, simple but limited enough, like that of ill-bred fingers drumming on a table. And then it is strange how soon the outward rhythm carries the inward along with it; and the thought moves with the same stinted, hamstrung rub-a-dub as the words. In a state of perfection, this species of writing comes to resemble power-loom weaving: it is not the mind that is at work, but some scholastic machinery which the mind has of old constructed, and is from afar observing. Shot follows shot from the unwearied shuttle; and so the web is woven, ultimately and properly, indeed, by the wit of man, yet immediately, and in the meanwhile, by the mere aid of time and steam.

But our Professor's mode of speculation is little less intensely academic than his mode of writing. We fear he is something of what the Germans call a *Kleinstädter*;—mentally as well as bodily, a "dweller in a little town." He speaks at great length, and with undue fondness, of the "Georgia Augusta," which, after all, is but the University of Göttingen, an earthly, and no celestial institution: it is nearly in vain that he tries to contemplate Heyne as a European personage, or even as a German one; beyond the precincts of the Georgia Augusta, his view seems to grow feeble and soon die away into vague inanity; so we have not Heyne, the man and scholar, but Heyne, the Göttingen Professor. But neither is this habit of mind any strange or crying sin, or at all peculiar to Göttingen; as, indeed, most parishes of England can produce more than one example to show. And yet it is pitiful, when an establishment for universal science, which ought to be a watch-tower where a man might see all the kingdoms of the world, converts itself into a workshop, whence he sees nothing but his tool-box and bench, and the world, in broken glimpses, through one patched and highly discoloured pane!

Sometimes, indeed, our worthy friend rises into a region of the moral sublime, in which it is difficult for a foreigner to follow him. Thus he says, on one occasion, speaking of Heyne: "Immortal are his merits in regard to the catalogues"—of the Göttingen library. And, to cite no other instance, except the last and best one, we are informed, that, when Heyne died, "the guardian angels of the Georgia Augusta waited in that higher world to meet him with blessings." By day and night! There is no such guardian angel, that we know of, for the University of Göttingen; neither does it need one, being a good solid seminary of itself, with handsome stipends from Government. We had imagined, too, that if anybody welcomed people into heaven, it would be St. Peter, or at least some angel of old standing, and not a mere mushroom, as this of Göttingen must be, created since the year 1739.

But we are growing very ungrateful to the good Heeren, who meant no harm by these flourishes of rhetoric, and, indeed, does not often indulge in them. The grand questions with us here are, Did he know the truth in this matter? and was he disposed to tell it honestly? To both of which questions we can answer without reserve, that all appearances are in his favour. He was Heyne's pupil, colleague, son-in-law, and so knew him intimately for

* *Christian Gottlob Heyne, biographisch dargestellt von Arnold Hermann Ludwig Heeren.* (Christian Gottlob Heyne, biographically portrayed by Arnold Hermann Ludwig Heeren.) Göttingen.

thirty years: he has every feature also of a just, quiet, truth-loving man; so that we see little reason to doubt the authenticity, the innocence, of any statement in his volume. What more have we to do with him then, but to take thankfully what he has been pleased and able to give us, and, with all despatch, communicate it to our readers.

Heyne's Life is not without an intrinsic, as well as an external interest; for he had much to struggle with, and he struggled with it manfully; thus his history has a value independent of his fame. Some account of his early years we are happily enabled to give in his own words; we translate a considerable part of this passage, autobiography being a favourite sort of reading with us.

He was born at Chemnitz, in Upper Saxony, in September, 1729; the eldest of a poor weaver's family, poor almost to the verge of destitution.

"My good father, George Heyne," says he, "was a native of the principality of Glogau, in Silesia, from the little village of Gravenschutz. His youth had fallen in those times when the Evangelist party of that province were still exposed to the oppressions and persecutions of the Romish Church. His kindred, enjoying the blessing of contentment in an humble but independent station, felt, like others, the influence of this proselytizing bigotry, and lost their domestic peace by means of it. Some went over to the Romish faith. My father left his native village, and endeavoured, by the labour of his hands, to procure a livelihood in Saxony. 'What will it profit a man if he gain the whole world, and lose his own soul!' was the thought which the scenes of his youth had stamped the most deeply on his mind; but no lucky chance favoured his enterprises or endeavours to better his condition, ever so little. On the contrary, a series of perverse incidents kept him continually below the limits even of a moderate sufficiency. His old age was thus left a prey to poverty, and to her companions, timidity and depression of mind. Manufactures, at that time, were visibly declining in Saxony; and the misery among the working classes, in districts concerned in the linen trade, was unusually severe. Scarcely could the labour of the hands suffice to support the labourer himself, still less his family. The saddest aspect which the decay of civic society can exhibit has always appeared to me to be this, when honourable, honour-loving, conscientious diligence cannot, by the utmost efforts of toil, obtain the necessaries of life, or when the working man cannot even find work; but must stand with folded arms, lamenting his forced idleness, through which himself and his family are verging to starvation, or it may be, actually suffering the pains of hunger.

"It was in the extremest penury that I was born and brought up. The earliest companion of my childhood was Want; and my first impressions came from the tears of my mother, who had not bread for her children. How often have I seen her on Saturday-nights wringing her hands and weeping, when she had come back with what the hard toil, nay, often the sleepless nights, of her husband had produced, and could find none to buy it! Sometimes a fresh attempt was made through me or my sister; I had to return to the purchasers with the same piece of ware, to see whether we could not possibly get rid of it. In that quarter there is a class of so-called merchants, who, however, are in fact nothing more than forestallers, that buy up the linen made by the poorer people at the lowest price, and endeavour to sell it in other districts at the highest. Often have I seen one or other of these petty tyrants, with all the pride of a satrap, throw back the piece of goods offered him, or imperiously cut off some trifle from the price and wages required for it. Necessity constrained the poorer to sell the sweat of his brow at a *groschen* or two less, and again to make good the deficit by starving. It was the view of such things that awakened the first sparks of indignation in my young heart. The show of pomp and plenty among these purse-proud people, who fed themselves on the extorted crumbs of so many hundreds, far from dazzling me into respect or fear, filled me with rage against them. The first time I heard of tyrannicide at school, there rose vividly before me the project to become a Brutus on all those oppressors of the poor, who had so often cast my father and mother into straits: and here, for the first time, was an instance of a truth, which I have since had frequent occasion to observe, that if the unhappy man armed with feeling of his wrongs, and a certain strength of soul, does not risk the utmost and become an open criminal, it is merely the beneficent result of those circumstances in which Providence has placed him, thereby fettering his activity, and guarding him from such destructive attempts. That the oppressing part of mankind should be secured against the oppressed was, in the plan of inscrutable wisdom, a most important element of the present system of things.

"My good parents did what they could, and sent me to a child's school in the suburbs; I obtained the praise of learning very fast and being very fond of it. My schoolmaster had two sons, lately returned from Leipzig, a couple of depraved fellows, who took all pains to lead me astray; and, as I resisted, kept me for a long time, by threats and mistreatment of all sorts, extremely miserable. So early as my tenth year, to raise the money for my school wages, I had given lessons to a neighbour's child, a little girl, in reading and writing. As the common school-course could take me no farther, the point now was to get a private hour and proceed into Latin. But for that purpose a *guter groschen* weekly was required: this my parents had not to give. Many a day I carried this grief about with me: however, I had a godfather, who was in easy circumstances, a baker, and my mother's half-brother. One Saturday I was sent to this man to fetch a loaf. With wet eyes I entered his house, and chanced to find my godfather himself there. Being questioned why I was crying, I tried to answer, but a whole stream of tears broke loose, and scarcely could I make the cause of my sorrow intelligible. My magnanimous godfather offered to pay the weekly *groschen* out of his own pocket; and only this condition was imposed on me, that I should come to him every Sunday, and repeat what part of the Gospel I had learned by heart. This latter arrangement had one good effect for me,—it exercised my memory, and I learned to recite without bashfulness.

"Drunk with joy, I started off with my loaf; tossing it up time after time into the air, and barefoot as I was, I capered aloft after it. But hereupon my loaf fell into a puddle. This misfortune again brought me a little to reason; my mother heartily rejoiced at the good news; my father was less content. Thus passed a couple of years; and my schoolmaster intimated what I myself had long known, that I could now learn no more from him.

"This then was the time when I must leave school, and betake me to the handicraft of my father. Were not the artisan under oppressions of so many kinds, robbed of the fruits of his hard toil, and of so many advantages to which the useful citizen has a natural claim; I should still say,—Had I but continued in the station of my parents, what thousand-fold vexations would at this hour have been unknown to me! My father could not but be anxious to have a grown-up son for an assistant in his labour, and looked upon my repugnance to it with great dislike. I again longed to get into the grammar-school of the town; but for this all means were wanting. Where was a *gulden* of quarterly fees, where were books and a blue cloak to be come at; how wistfully my look often hung on the walls of the school when I learned it!

"A clergyman of the suburbs was my second godfather; his name was Sebastian Seydel; my schoolmaster, who likewise belonged to his congregation, had told him of me; I was sent for, and after a short examination, he promised me that I should go to the town-school; he himself would bear the charges. Who can express my happiness, as I then felt it! I was despatched to the first teacher, examined, and placed with approbation in the second class. Weakly from the first, pressed down with sorrow and want, without any cheerful enjoyment of childhood or youth, I was still of very small stature; my class-fellows judged by externals, and had a very slight opinion of me. Scarcely by various proofs of diligence, and by the praises I received, could I get so far that they tolerated my being put beside them.

"And certainly my diligence was not a little hampered! Of his promise, the clergyman, indeed, kept so much, that he paid my quarterly fees, provided me with a coarse cloak, and gave me some useless volumes that were lying on his shelves; but to furnish me with school-books he could not resolve. I thus found myself under the necessity of borrowing a class-fellow's books, and daily copying a part of them before the lesson. On the other hand, the honest man would have some hand himself in my instruction, and gave me from time to time some hours in Latin. In his youth he had learned to make Latin verses: scarcely was *Erasmus de Civilitate Morum* got over, when I too must take to verse-making; all this before I had read any authors, or could possibly possess any store of words. The man was withal passionate and rigorous; in every point repulsive; with a moderate income he was accused of avarice; he had the stiffness and self-will of an old bachelor, and at the same time the vanity of aiming to be a good Latinist, and, what was more, a Latin verse-maker, and consequently a literary clergyman. These qualities of his all contributed to overload my youth, and nip away in the bud every enjoyment of its pleasures."

In this plain but somewhat leaden style does Heyne proceed, detailing the crosses and losses of his school-years. We cannot pretend that the narrative delights us much; nay, that it is not rather bald and barren for such a narrative: but its fidelity may be relied on; and it paints the clear, broad, strong, and somewhat heavy nature of the writer, perhaps better than description could do. It is curious, for instance, to see with how little of a purely humane interest he looks back to his childhood: how Heyne the man has almost grown into a sort of teaching-machine, and sees in Heyne the boy little else than the incipient Gerund-grinder, and tells us little else but how this wheel after the other was developed in him, and he came at last to grind in complete perfection. We could have wished to get some view into the interior of that poor Chemnitz hovel, with its unresting loom and cheerless hearth, its squalor and devotion, its affection and repining; and the fire of natural genius struggling into flame amid such incumbrances, in an atmosphere so damp and close! But of all this we catch few farther glimpses; and hear only of Fabricius and Owen and Pasor, and school-examinations, and rectors that had been taught by Ernesti. Neither, in another respect, not of omission but of commission, can this piece of writing altogether content us. We must object a little to the spirit of it as too narrow, too intolerant. Sebastian Seydel must have been a very meager man; but is it right, that Heyne, of all others, should speak of him with asperity? Without question the unfortunate Seydel meant nobly, had not thrift stood in his way. Did he not pay down his *gulden* every quarter regularly, and give the boy a blue cloak, though a coarse one? Nay, he bestowed old books on him, and instruction, according to his gift, in the mystery of verse-making. And was not all this something? And if thrift and charity had a continual battle to fight, was not this better than a flat surrender on the part of the latter? The other pastors of Chemnitz are all quietly forgotten: why should Sebastian be remembered to his disadvantage for being only a little better than they?

Heyne continued to be much infested with tasks from Sebastian, and sorely held down by want, and discouragement of every sort. The school-course, moreover, he says, was bad, nothing but the old routine; vocables, translations, exercises; all without spirit or purpose. Nevertheless, he continued to make what we must call wonderful proficiency in these branches; especially as he had still to write every task before he could learn it. For he prepared "Greek versions," he says; "also Greek verses; and by and by could write down in Greek prose, and at last, in Greek as well as Latin verses, the discourses he heard in church!" Some ray of hope was beginning to spring up within his mind. A certain small degree of self-confidence had first been awakened in him, as he informs us, by a "pedantic adventure."

"There chanced to be a school-examination held, at which the superintendent, as chief school-inspector, was present. This man, Dr. Theodor Krüger, a theologian of some learning for his time, all at once interrupted the rector, who was teaching *ex cathedra*, and put the question: who among the scholars could tell him what might be made *per anagramma* from the word *Austria*. This whim had arisen from the circumstance that the first Silesian war was just begun; and some such anagram, reckoned very happy, had appeared in a newspaper.* No one of us knew so much as what an anagram was; even the rector looked quite perplexed. As none answered, the latter began to give us a description of anagrams in general. I set myself to work, and sprang forth with my discovery, *Vastari!* This was something different from the newspaper one: so much the greater was our superintendent's admiration, and the more as the successful aspirant was a little boy, on the lowest bench of the *secunda*. He growled out his applause to me, but at the same time set the whole school about my ears, as he stoutly upbraided them with being beaten by an *infimus*.

"Enough! this pedantic adventure gave the first impulse to the development of my powers. I began to take some credit to myself, and in spite of all the oppression and contempt in which I languished, to resolve on struggling forward. This first struggle was in truth ineffectual enough; was soon regarded as a piece of pride and conceitedness; it brought on me a thousand humiliations and disquietudes; at times it might degenerate on my part into defiance. Nevertheless, it kept me at the stretch of my diligence, ill-guided as it was, and withdrew me from the company of my class-fellows, among whom, as among children of low birth and bad nurture could not fail to be the case, the utmost coarseness and boorishness of every sort prevailed. The plan of these schools does not include any general inspection, but limits itself to mere intellectual instruction.

"Yet on all hands," continues he, "I found myself too sadly hampered. The perverse way in which the old parson treated me: at home the discontent and grudging of my parents, especially of my father, who could not get on with his work, and still thought, that had I kept by his way of life, he might now have had some help; the pressure of want, the feeling of being behind every other; all this would allow no cheerful thought, no sentiment of worth, to spring up within me. A timorous, bashful, awkward carriage shut me out still further from all exterior attractions. Where could I learn good manners, elegance, a right way of thought? where could I attain any culture for heart and spirit.

"Upwards, however, I still strove. A feeling of honour, a wish for something better, an effort to work myself out of this abasement, incessantly attended me; but without direction as it was, it led me rather to sullenness, misanthropy, and clownishness.

"At length a place opened for me, where some training in these points lay within my reach. One of our senators took his mother-in-law home to live with him; she had still two children with her, a son and a daughter, both about my own age. For the son private lessons were wanted; and happily I was chosen for the purpose.

"As these private hours brought me in a *gulden* monthly, I now began to defend myself a little against the grumbling of my parents. Hitherto I had been in the habit of doing work occasionally, that I might not be told how I was eating their bread for nothing; clothes, and oil for my lamp, I had earned by teaching in the house; these things I could now relinquish: and thus my condition was in some degree improved. On the other hand, I had now opportunity of seeing persons of better education. I gained the goodwill of the family; so that besides the lesson-hours I generally lived there. Such society afforded me some culture, extended my conceptions and opinions, and also polished a little the rudeness of my exterior."

In this senatorial house he must have been somewhat more at ease; for he now very privately fell in love with his pupil's sister, and made and burnt many Greek and Latin verses in her praise; and had sweet dreams of sometime rising "so high as to be worthy of her." Even as matters stood, he acquired her friendship and that of her mother. But the grand concern for the present was how to get to college at Leipzig. Old Sebastian had promised to stand good on this occasion; and unquestionably would have done so with the greatest pleasure, had it cost him nothing; but he promised and promised, without doing aught; above all, without putting his hand in his pocket; and elsewhere there was no hope or resource. At length, wearied perhaps with the boy's importunity, he determined to bestir himself; and so directed his assistant, who was just making a journey to Leipzig, to show Heyne the road; the two arrived in perfect safety: Heyne still longing after cash, for of his own he had only two *gulden*, about five shillings; but the assistant left him in a lodging house, and went his way, saying he had no farther orders!

The miseries of a poor scholar's life were now to be Heyne's portion in full measure. Ill-clothed, totally destitute of books, with five shillings in his purse, he found himself set down in the Leipzig university, to study all learning. Despondency at first overmastered the poor boy's heart, and he sunk into sickness, from which indeed he recovered; but only, as he says, "to fall into conditions of life where he became the prey of desperation." How he contrived to exist, much more to study, is scarcely apparent from this narrative. The unhappy old Sebastian did at length send him

* As yet Saxony was against Austria, not, as in the end, allied with her.

some pittance, and at rare intervals repeated the dole; yet ever with his own peculiar grace; not till after unspeakable solicitations; in quantities that were consumed by inextinguishable debt, and coupled with sour admonitions; nay, on one occasion addressed externally, "*A Mr. Heyne*, Etudiant negligeant." For half a year he would leave him without all help; then promise to come, and see what he was doing: come accordingly, and return without leaving him a penny; neither could the destitute youth ever obtain any public furtherance; no *freytisch* (free-table) or *stipendium* was to be procured. Many times he had no regular meal; "often not three-halfpence for a loaf at mid-day." He longed to be dead, for his spirit was often sunk in the gloom of darkness. "One good heart alone," says he, "I found, and that in the servant girl of the house where I lodged. She laid out money for my most pressing necessities, and risked almost all she had, seeing me in such frightful want. Could I but find thee in the world even now, thou good pious soul, that I might repay thee what thou then didst for me!"

Heyne declares it to be still a mystery to him how he stood all this. "What carried me forward," continues he, "was not ambition; my youthful dream of one day taking a place, or aiming to take one, among the learned. It is true, the bitter feeling of debasement, of deficiency in education and external polish; the consciousness of awkwardness in social life, incessantly accompanied me. But my chief strength lay in a certain defiance of fate. This gave me courage not to yield; everywhere to try to the uttermost whether I was doomed without remedy never to rise from this degradation."

Of order in his studies there could be little expectation. He did not even know what profession he was aiming after; old Sebastian was for theology; and Heyne, though himself averse to it, affected, and only affected to comply; besides he had no money to pay class fees: it was only to open lectures, or at most to ill-guarded class-rooms that he could gain admission. Of this ill-guarded sort was Winkler's; into which poor Heyne insinuated himself to hear philosophy. Alas! the first problem of all philosophy, the keeping of soul and body together, was wellnigh too hard for him. Winkler's students were of a riotous description, accustomed, among other improprieties, to *scharren*, scraping with the feet. One day they chose to receive Heyne in this fashion; and he could not venture back. "Nevertheless," adds he, simply enough, "the beadle came to me sometime afterwards, demanding the fee: I had my own shifts to take before I could raise it."

Ernesti was the only teacher from whom he derived any benefit: the man, indeed, whose influence seems to have shaped the whole subsequent course of his studies. By dint of excessive endeavours he gained admittance to Ernesti's lectures; and here first learned, says Heeren, "what interpretation of the classics meant." One Crist also, a strange, fantastic Sir Plume of a Professor, who built much on taste, elegance of manners, and the like, took some notice of him, and procured him a little employment as a private teacher. This might be more useful than his advice to imitate Scaliger, and read the ancients so as to begin with the most ancient, and proceed regularly to the latest. Small service it can do a bedrid man to convince him that waltzing is preferable to quadrilles! "Crist's Lectures," says he, "were a tissue of endless digressions, which, however, now and then contained excellent remarks."

But Heyne's best teacher was himself. No pressure of distresses, no want of books, advisers, or encouragement, not hunger itself could abate his resolute perseverance. What books he could come at he borrowed; and such was his excess of zeal in reading, that for a whole half year he allowed himself only two nights' sleep in the week, till at last a fever obliged him to be more moderate. His diligence was undirected, or ill-directed, but it never rested, never paused, and must at length prevail. Fortune had cast him into a cavern, and he was groping darkly round; but the prisoner was a giant, and would at length burst forth as a giant into the light of day. Heyne, without any clear aim, almost without any hope had set his heart on attaining knowledge; a force, as of instinct, drove him on, and no promise and no threat could turn him back. It was at the very depth of his destitution, when he had not "three *groschen* for a loaf to dine on," that he refused a tutorship, with handsome enough appointments, but which was to have removed him from the University. Crist had sent for him one Sunday, and made him the proposal: "There arose a violent struggle within me," says he, "which drove me to and fro for several days; to this hour it is incomprehensible to me where I found resolution to determine on renouncing the offer, and pursuing my object in Leipzig." A man with a half volition goes backwards and forwards, and makes no way on the smoothest road; a man with a whole volition advances on the roughest, and will reach his purpose if there be a little wisdom in it.

With his first two years' residence in Leipzig, Heyne's personal narrative terminates; not because the nodus of the history had been solved then, and his perplexities cleared up, but simply because he had not found time to relate further. A long series of straitened hopeless days were yet appointed him. By Ernesti's or Crist's recommendation, he occasionally got employment in giving private lessons; at one time, he worked as secretary and classical hodman to "Cruscius, the philosopher," who felt a little rusted in his Greek and Latin; everywhere he found the scantiest accommodation, and, shifting from side to side in dreary vicissitudes of want, had to spin out an existence, warmed by no ray of comfort, except the fire that burnt or smouldered unquenchably within his own bosom. However, he had now chosen a profession, that of law, at which, as at many other branches of learning, he was labouring with his old diligence. Of preferment in this province there was, for the present, little or no hope; but this was no new thing with Heyne. By degrees, too, his fine talents and endeavours, and his perverse situa tion, began to attract notice and sympathy; and here and there some well-wisher had his eye on him, and stood ready to do him a service. Two and twenty years of penury and joyless struggling had now passed over the man; how many more such might be added was still uncertain; yet, surely, the longest winter is followed by a spring.

Another trifling incident, little better than that old "pedantic adventure," again brought about important changes in Heyne's situation. Among his favourers in Leipzig had been the preacher of a French chapel, one Lacoste, who, at this time, was cut off by death. Heyne, it is said, in the real sorrow of his heart, composed a long Latin Epicedium on that occasion; the poem had nowise been intended for the press; but certain hearers of the deceased were so pleased with it, that they had it printed, and this in the finest style of typography and decoration. It was this latter circumstance, not the merit of the verses, which is said to have been considerable, that attracted the attention of Count Brühl, the well-known prime-minister and favourite of the Elector. Brühl's sons were studying in Leipzig; he was pleased to express himself contented with the poem, and to say, that he should like to have the author in his service. A prime minister's words are not as water spilt upon the ground, which cannot be gathered; but rather as heavenly manna, which is treasured up and eaten, not without a religious sentiment. Heyne was forthwith written to from all quarters, that his fortune was made: he had but to show himself in Dresden, said his friends, with one voice, and golden showers from the ministerial cornucopia would refresh him almost to saturation. For, was not the Count taken with him; and who in all Saxony, not excepting Serene Highness itself, could gainsay the Count? Over-persuaded, and against his will, Heyne at length determined on the journey; for which, as an indispensable preliminary, "fifty-one *thalers*" had to be borrowed; and so, following this hopeful quest, he actually arrived at Dresden in April, 1752. Count Brühl received him with the most captivating smiles; and even assured him in words, that he, Count Brühl, would take care of him. But a prime minister has so much to take care of! Heyne danced attendance all spring and summer, happier than our Johnson, inasmuch as he had not to "blow his fingers in a cold lobby," the weather being warm· and obtained not only promises, but useful experience of their value at courts.

He was to be made a secretary, with five hundred, with four hundred, or even with three hundred *thalers*, of income: only, in the meanwhile, his old stock of "fifty-one" had quite run out, and he had nothing to live upon. By great good luck, he procured some employment in his old craft, private teaching, which helped him through the winter; but as this ceased, he remained without resources. He tried working for the booksellers, and translated a French romance and a Greek one, Chariton's Loves of Chareas and Callirhoe; however, his emoluments would scarcely furnish him with salt, to to speak of victuals. He sold his few books. A licentiate in divinity, one Sonntag, took pity on his houselessness, and shared a garret with him; where, as there was no unoccupied bed, Heyne slept on the floor, with a few folios for his pillow. So fared he as to lodging: in regard to board, he gathered empty pease-cods, and had them boiled; this was not unfrequently his only meal.—O, ye poor naked wretches! what would Bishop Watson say to this?—At length, by dint of incredible solicitations, Heyne, in the autumn of 1753, obtained, not his secretaryship, but the post of under-clerk, (*copist*) in the Brühl Library, with one hundred *thalers* of salary; a sum barely sufficient to keep in life, which, indeed, was now a great point with him. In such sort was this young scholar "taken care of."

Nevertheless, it was under these external circumstances that he first entered on his proper career, and forcibly made a place for himself among the learned men of his day. In 1754, he prepared his edition of Tibullus, which was printed next year at Leipzig;* a work said to exhibit remarkable talent, inasmuch as "the rudiments of all those excellences, by which Heyne afterwards became distinguished as a commentator on the classics, are more or less apparent in it." The most illustrious Henry Count von Brühl, in spite of the dedication, paid no regard to this Tibullus; as indeed Germany at large paid little; but, in another country, it fell into the hands of Rhunken, where it was rightly estimated, and lay waiting, as in due season appeared, to be the pledge of better fortune for its author.

Meanwhile the day of difficulty for Heyne was yet far from past. The profits of his Tibullus served to cancel some debts; on the strength of his hundred *thalers*, the spindle of Clotho might still keep turning, though languidly; but, ere long, new troubles arose. His superior in the library was one Rost, a poetaster, atheist, and gold-maker, who corrupted his religious principles, and plagued him with caprices: Over the former evil Heyne at length triumphed, and became a rational Christian; but the latter was an abiding grievance; not, indeed, for ever, for it was removed by a greater. In 1756, the Seven Years' War broke out; Frederic advanced towards Dresden, animated with especial fury against Brühl; whose palaces accordingly were in a few months reduced to ashes, as his 70,000 splendid volumes were annihilated by fire and by water,† and all his domestics and dependents turned to the street without appeal.

Heyne had lately been engaged in studying Epictetus, and publishing, *ad fidem Codd. Muspt.*, an edition of his Enchiridion;‡ from which, quoth Heeren, his great soul had acquired much stoical nourishment. Such nourish-

---

* *Albii Tibulli quæ extant Carmina, novis Curis castigata. Illustrissimo Domino Henrico Comiti de Brühl Inscripta Lipsiæ*, 1755.

† One rich cargo, on its way to Hamburg, sank in the Elbe; another still more valuable portion had been, for safety, deposited in a vault, through which passed certain pipes of artificial waterworks; these the cannon broke, and, when the vault came to be opened, all was reduced to pulp and mould. The bomb-shells burnt the remainder.

‡ Lipsiæ, 1756. The *Codices*, or rather the *Codex*, was in Brühl's library.

ment never comes wrong in life; and, surely, at this time Heyne had need of it all. However, he struggled as he had been wont: translated pamphlets, sometimes wrote newspaper articles; eat, when he had wherewithal, and resolutely endured when he had not. By and by, Rabener, to whom he was a little known, offered him a tutorship in the family of a Herr von Schöuberg, which Heyne, not without reluctance, accepted. Tutorships were at all times his aversion; his rugged plebeian proud spirit made business of that sort grievous; but want stood over him, like an armed man, and was not to be reasoned with.

In this Schöuberg family, a novel and unexpected series of fortunes awaited him; but whether for weal or for wo might still be hard to determine. The name of Theresa Weiss has become a sort of classical word in biography; her union with Heyne forms, as it were, a green cypress-and-myrtle oasis in his otherwise hard and stony history. It was here that he first met with her; that they learned to love each other. She was the orphan of a "professor on the lute;" had long, amid poverty and afflictions, been trained, like the Stoics, to bear and forbear; was now in her twenty-seventh year, and the humble companion, as she had once been the school-mate, of the Frau von Schöuberg, whose young brother Heyne had come to teach. Their first interview may be described in his own words, which Hereen is here again happily enabled to introduce.

"It was on the 10th of October, (her future death-day!) that I first entered the Schöuberg house. Towards what mountains of mischances was I now proceeding! To what endless tissues of good and evil hap was the thread here taken up! Could I fancy that at this moment Providence was deciding the fortune of my life! I was ushered into a room, where sat several ladies engaged, with gay youthful sportiveness, in friendly confidential talk. Frau von Schöuberg, but lately married, yet at this time distant from her husband, was preparing for a journey to him at Prague, where his business detained him. On her brow still beamed the pure innocence of youth; in her eyes you saw a glad soft vernal sky; a smiling loving complaisance accompanied her discourse. This, too, seemed one of those souls, clear and uncontaminated as they come from the hands of their Maker. By reason of her brother, in her tender love of him, I must have been, to her, no unimportant guest.

"Beside her stood a young lady, dignified in aspect, of fair, slender shape, not regular in feature, yet soul in every glance. Her words, her looks, her every movement, impressed you with respect,—another sort of respect than what was paid to rank and birth. Good sense, good feeling disclosed itself in all she did. You forgot that more beauty, more softness, might have been demanded; you felt yourself under the influence of something noble, something stately and earnest, something decisive that lay in her look, in her gestures; not less attracted to her, than compelled to reverence her.

"More than esteem, the first sight of Theresa did not inspire me with. What I noticed most were the efforts she made to relieve my embarrassment, the fruit of my down-bent pride, and to keep me, a stranger, entering among familiar acquaintances, in easy conversation. Her good heart reminded her how much the unfortunate requires encouragement; especially when placed, as I was, among those to whose protection he must look up. Thus was my first kindness for her awakened by that good-heartedness, which made her, among thousands, a beneficent angel. She was one at this moment to myself; for I twice received letters from an unknown hand, containing money, which greatly alleviated my difficulties.

"In a few days, on the 14th of October, I commenced my task of instruction. Her I did not see again till the following spring, when she returned with her friend from Prague; and then only once or twice, as she soon accompanied Frau von Schöuberg to the country, to Ænsdorf, in Oberlausitz (Upper Lusatia.) They left us, after it had been settled that I was to follow them in a few days with my pupil. My young heart joyed in the prospect of rural pleasures, of which I had, from of old, cherished a thousand delightful dreams. I still remember the 6th of May, when we set out for Ænsdorf.

"The society of two cultivated females, who belonged to the noblest of their sex, and the endeavours to acquire their esteem, contributed to form my own character. Nature and religion were the objects of my daily contemplation; I began to act and live on principles, of which, till now, I had never thought: these, too, formed the subject of our constant discourse. Lovely nature and solitude exalted our feelings to a pitch of pious enthusiasm.

"Sooner than I, Theresa discovered that her friendship for me was growing into a passion. Her natural melancholy now seized her heart more keenly than ever: often our glad hours were changed into very gloomy and sad ones. Whenever our conversation chanced to turn on religion, (she was of the Roman Catholic faith,) I observed that her grief became more apparent. I noticed her redouble her devotions; and sometimes found her in solitude, weeping and praying with such a fulness of heart as I had never seen."

Theresa and her lover, or at least beloved, were soon separated, and for a long while kept much asunder; partly by domestic arrangements, still more by the tumults of war. Heyne attended his pupil to the Wittenberg University, and lived there a year; studying for his own behoof, chiefly in philosophy and German history, and with more profit, as he says, than of old. Theresa and he kept up a correspondence, which often passed into melancholy and enthusiasm. The Prussian cannon drove him out of Wittenberg: his pupil and he witnessed the bombardment of the place from the neighbourhood; and, having waited till their University became "a heap of rubbish," had to retire elsewhere for accommodation. The young man subsequently went to Erlangen, then to Göttingen. Heyne remained again without employment, alone in Dresden. Theresa was living in his neighbourhood, lovely and sad as ever; but a new bombardment drove her also to a distance. She left her little property with Heyne, who removed it to his lodging, and determined to abide the Prussian siege, having indeed no other resource. The sack of cities looks so well on paper, that we must find a little space here for Heyne's account of his experience in this business; though it is none of the brightest accounts; and indeed contrasts but poorly with Rabener's brisk sarcastic narrative of the same adventure; for he, too, was cannonaded out of Dresden at this time, and lost house and home, and books and manuscripts, and all but good humour.

"The Prussians advanced meanwhile, and on the 18th of July, (1760,) the bombardment of Dresden began. Several nights I passed, in company with others, in a tavern, and the days in my room; so that I could hear the balls from the battery, as they flew through the street, whizzing past my windows. An indifference to danger and to life took such possession of me, that on the last morning of the siege, I went early to bed, and, amid the frightfullest crashing of bombs and grenades, fell fast asleep of fatigue, and lay sound till midday. On awakening, I huddled on my clothes, and ran down stairs, but found the whole house deserted. I had returned to my room, considering what I was to do, whither, at all events, I was to take my chest, when with a tremendous crash, a bomb came down in the court of the house; did not, indeed, set fire to it, but, on all sides, shattered every thing to pieces. The thought, that where one bomb fell more would soon follow, gave me wings; I darted down stairs, found the house-door locked, ran to and fro; at last got entrance into one of the under-rooms, and sprung through the window into the street.

"Empty as the street where I lived had been, I found the principal thoroughfares crowded with fugitives. Amidst the whistling of balls, I ran along the Schlossgasse towards the Elbe-Bridge, and so forward to the Neustadt, out of which the Prussians had now been forced to retreat. Glad that I had leave to rest anywhere, I passed one part of the night on the floor of an empty house; the other, witnessing the frightful light of flying bombs, and a burning city.

"At break of day, a little postern was opened by the Austrian guard, to let the fugitives get out of the walls. The captain in his insolence called the people Lutheran dogs, and with this nick-name gave each of us a stroke as we passed through the gate.

"I was now at large; and the thought, whither bound? began for the first time to employ me. As I had run, indeed leapt from my house, in the night of terror, I had carried with me no particle of my property, and not a *groschen* of money. Only in hurrying along the street, I had chanced to see a tavern open (it was an Italian's) where I used to pass the nights. Here espying a fur-cloak, I had picked it up, and thrown it about me. With this I walked along, in one of the sultriest days, from the Neustadt, over the sand and the moor; and took the road for Ænsdorf, where Theresa with her friend was staying: the mother-in-law of the latter being also on a visit to them. In the fiercest heat of the sun, through tracts of country silent and deserted, I walked four leagues to Bischopfwerda, where I had to sleep in an inn among carriers. Towards midnight arrived a postilion with return horses; I asked him to let me ride one; and with him I proceeded, till my road turned off from the highway. All day, I heard the shots at poor Dresden re-echoing in the hills.

"Curiosity at first made my reception at Ænsdorf very warm. But as I came to appear in the light of an altogether destitute man, the family could see in me only a future burden: no invitations to continue with them followed. In a few days came a chance of conveyance, by a wagon for Neustadt, to a certain Frau von Fletscher a few miles on this side of it; I was favoured with some old linen for the road. The good Theresa suffered unspeakably under these proceedings: the noble lady, her friend, had not been allowed to act according to the dictates of her own heart.

"Not till now did I feel wholly how miserable I was! Spurning at destiny, and hardening my heart, I entered on this journey. With the Frau von Fletscher too my abode was brief; and by the first opportunity I returned to Dresden. There was still a possibility that my lodging might have been saved. With heavy heart I entered the city; hastened to the place where I had lived, and found—a heap of ashes."

Heyne took up his quarters in the vacant rooms of the Brühl Library. Some friends endeavoured to alleviate his distress; but war and rumors of war continued to harass him and drive him to and fro; and his Theresa, afterwards also a fugitive, was now as poor as himself. She heeded little the loss of her property; but inward sorrow and so many outward agitations preyed hard upon her; in the winter she fell violently sick at Dresden, was given up by her physicians; received extreme unction according to the rites of her church; and was for some hours believed to be dead. Nature however, again prevailed: a crisis had occurred in the mind as well as in the body; for with her first returning strength, Theresa declared her determination to renounce the Catholic, and publicly embrace the Protestant faith. Argument, representation of worldly disgrace and loss were unavailing; she could now, that all her friends were to be estranged, have little hope of being wedded to Heyne on earth; but she trusted that in another scene a like creed might unite them in a like destiny. He himself fell ill; and only escaped death by her nursing. Persisting the more in her purpose, she took priestly instruction, and on the 20th of May, in the Evangelical Schlosskirche, solemnly professed her new creed.

"Reverent admiration filled me," says he, "as I beheld the peace and steadfastness with which she executed her determination; and still more the courage with which she bore the consequences of it. She saw herself altogether cast out from her family: forsaken by her acquaintance, by every one; and by the fire deprived of all she had. Her courage exalted me to a higher duty, and admonished me to do mine. Imprudently I had, in former conversations, first awakened her religious scruples; the passion for me, which had so much increased her enthusiasm, increased her melancholy; even the secret thought of belonging more closely to me by sameness of belief had unconsciously influenced her. In a word, I formed the determination which could not but expose me to universal censure: helpless as I was, I united my destiny with hers. We were wedded at Ænsdorf, on the 4th of June, 1761."

This was a bold step, but a right one: Theresa had now no stay but him; it behoved them to struggle, and if better might not be, to sink together. Theresa, in this narrative, appears to us a noble, interesting being; noble not in sentiment only, but in action and suffering; a fair flower trodden down by misfortune, but yielding, like flowers, only the sweeter perfume for being crushed, and which it would have been a blessedness to raise up and cherish into free growth. Yet, in plain prose, we must question whether the two were happier than others in their union; both were quick of temper; she was all a heavenly light, he in good part a hard terrestrial mass, which perhaps she could never wholly illuminate; the balance of the love seems to have lain much on her side. Nevertheless Heyne was a steadfast, true, and kindly, if no ethereal man; he seems to have loved his wife honestly; and so amid light and shadow they made their pilgrimage together, if not better than other mortals, not worse, which was to have been feared.

Neither, for the present, did the pressure of distress weigh heavier on either than it had done before. He worked diligently, as he found scope, for his old Mæcenases, the Booksellers; the war-clouds grew lighter, or at least the young pair got better used to them; friends also were kind, often assisting and hospitably entertaining them. On occasion of such a visit to the family of a Herr von Löben, there occurred a little trait, which, for the sake of Theresa, must not be omitted. Heyne and she had spent some happy weeks with their infant, in this country-house, when the alarm of war drove the Von Löbens from their residence, which with the management of its concerns they left to Heyne. He says he gained some notion of "land-economy" truly; and Heeren states that he had a candle-manufactory to oversee.

But to our incident.

"Soon after the departure of the family, there came upon us an irruption of Cossacks, (disguised Prussians, as we subsequently learned.) After drinking to intoxication in the cellars, they set about plundering. Pursued by them, I ran up stairs, and no door being open but that of the room where my wife was with her infant, I rushed into it. She arose courageously, and placed herself, with the child on her arm, in the door against the robbers. This courage saved me, and the treasure which lay hidden in the chamber."

"O thou Lioness!" said Attila Schmelzle, on occasion of a similar rescue, "why hast thou never been in any deadly peril, that I might show thee the lion in thy husband?"

But better days were dawning. "On our return to Dresden," says Heyne, "I learned that inquiries had been made after me from Hanover; I knew not for what reason." The reason by and by came to light. Gessner, Professor of Eloquence in Göttingen, was dead: and a successor was wanted. These things, it would appear, cause difficulties in Hanover, which in many other places are little felt. But the Prime Minister Münchhausen had as good as founded the Georgia Augusta himself; and he was wont to watch over it with singular anxiety. The noted and notorious Klotz was already there, as assistant to Gessner, "but his beautiful latinity," says Heeren, "did not dazzle Münchhausen; so Klotz, with his pugnacity, was not thought of." The Minister applied to Ernesti for advice: Ernesti knew of no fit men in Germany, but recommended Rhunken of Leyden, or Saxe of Utrecht. Rhunken refused to leave his country, and added these words: "But why do you seek out of Germany, what Germany itself offers you? why not, for Gessner's successor, take Christian Gottlob Heyne, that true pupil of Ernesti, and man of fine talent, (excellenti virum ingenio,) who has shown how much he knows of Latin literature by his Tibullus; of Greek, by his Epictetus? In my opinion, and that of the greatest Hemsterhuis (Hemsterhusii τοῦ πάνυ,) Heyne is the only one that can replace your Gessner. Nor let any one tell me that Heyne's fame is not sufficiently illustrious and extended. Believe me, there is in this man such a richness of genius and learning, that ere long all Europe will ring with his praises."

This courageous and generous verdict of Rhunken's, in favour of a person as yet little known to the world, and to him known only by his writings, decided the matter. "Münchhausen," says our Heeren, "believed in the boldly prophesying man." Not without difficulty Heyne was unearthed; and after various excuses on account of competence on his part, —for he had lost all his books and papers in the siege of Dresden, and sadly forgotten his Latin and Greek in so many tumults,—and various prudential negotiations about dismission from the Saxon service, and salary, and privilege in the Hanoverian, he at length formally received his appointment; and some three months after, in June 1763, settled in Göttingen, with an official income of eight hundred *thalers*, which, it appears, was by several additions, in the course of time, increased to twelve hundred.

Here then had Heyne at last got to land. His long life was henceforth as quiet and fruitful in activity and comfort as the past period of it had been desolate and full of sorrows. He never left Göttingen, though frequently invited to do so, and sometimes with highly tempting offers;* but continued in his

* He was invited successively to be Professor at Cassel, and at Klosterbergen; to be Librarian at Dresden; and, most flattering of all, to be *Prokanzler* in the University of Copenhagen, and virtual Director of Education over all Denmark. He had a struggle on this last

place, busy in his vocation; growing in influence, in extent of connection at home and abroad; till Rhunken's prediction might almost be reckoned fulfilled to the letter; for Heyne in his own department was without any equal in Europe.

However, his history, from this point, even because it was so happy for himself, must lose most of its interest for the general reader. Heyne has now become a professor, and a regularly progressive man of learning; has a fixed household, his rents and comings in; it is easy to fancy how that man might flourish in calm sunshine of prosperity, whom in adversity we saw growing in spite of every storm. Of his proceedings in Göttingen, his reform of the Royal Society of Sciences, his editing of the *Gelehrte Anzeigen* (Gazette of Learning,) his exposition of the classics from Virgil to Pindar, his remodelling of the library, his passive quarrels with Voss, his armed neutrality with Michaelis; of all this we must say little. The best fruit of his endeavours lies before the world, in a long series of works, which, among us, as well as elsewhere, are known and justly appreciated. On looking over them, the first thing that strikes us is astonishment at Heyne's diligence; which, considering the quantity and quality of his writings, might have appeared singular even in one who had been without other duties. Yet Heyne's office involved him in the most laborious researches: he wrote letters by the hundred to all parts of the world, and on all conceivable subjects; he had three classes to teach daily; he appointed professors, for his recommendation was all-powerful; superintended schools; for a long time the inspection of the *Freytische* was laid on him, and he had cooks' bills to settle, and hungry students to satisfy with his purveyance. Besides all which, he accomplished, in the way of publication, as follows:

In addition to his *Tibullus* and *Epictetus*, the first of which went through three, the second through two editions, each time with large extensions and improvements:

His Virgil, (P. VIRGILIUS MARO *Varietate Lectionis et perpetuâ Annotatione illustratus,*) in various forms, from 1767 to 1803; no fewer than six editions.

His Pliny, (*Ex* C. PLINII SECUNDI *Historia Naturali excerpta, quas ad Artes spectant;*) two editions, 1790, 1811.

His Apollodorus, (APOLLODORI *Atheniensis Bibliothecæ Libri tres,* &c.;) two editions, 1787, 1803.

His Pindar, (PINDARI *Carmina, cum Lectionis Varietate, curavit* Ch. G. H.) three editions, 1774, 1797, 1798, the last with the Scholia, the Fragments, a Translation, and Hermann's Enq. *De Metris.*

His Conon and Parthenius, (CONONIS *Narrationes et* PARTHENII *Narrationes amatoriæ,*) 1798.

And lastly his Homer, (HOMERI ILIAS, *cum brevi Annotatione;*) 8 volumes, 1802; and a second, contracted edition, in 2 volumes, 1804.

occasion, but the Georgia Augusta again prevailed. Some increase of salary usually follows such refusals: it did not in this instance.

Next, almost a cartload of Translations; of which we shall mention only his version, (said to be with very important improvements,) of our *Universal History*, by Guthrie and Gray.

Then some ten or twelve thick volumes of Prolusions, Eulogies, Essays; treating of all subjects, from the French Directoral to the *Chest of Cyprolus.* Of these, six volumes are known in a separate shape, under the title of *Opuscula:* and contain some of Heyne's most valuable writings.

And lastly, to crown the whole with one most surprising item, seven thousand five hundred (Heeren says from seven to eight thousand) Reviews of Books, in the Göttingen *Gelehrte Anzeigen!* Shame on us degenerate Editors! Here of itself was work for a lifetime!

To expect that elegance of composition should prevail in these multifarious performances were unreasonable enough. Heyne wrote very indifferent German; and his Latin, by much the more common vehicle in his learned works, flowed from him with a copiousness which could not be Ciceronian. At the same time these volumes are not the folios of a Montfaucon, not mere classical ore and slag, but regularly melted metal, for most part exhibiting the essence, and only the essence of very great research, and enlightened by a philosophy, which, if it does not always wisely order its results, has looked far and deeply in collecting them.

To have performed so much evinces on the part of Heyne no little mastership in the great art of husbanding time. Heeren gives us sufficient details on this subject; explains Heyne's adjustment of his hours and various occupations; how he rose at five o'clock, and worked all the day, and all the year, with the regularity of a steeple-clock; nevertheless, how patiently he submitted to interruptions from strangers, or extraneous business; how, briefly, yet smoothly, he contrived to despatch such interruptions; how his letters were endorsed when they came to hand; and lay in a special drawer till they were answered: nay, we have a description of his whole "locality," his bureau and book-shelves and portfolios, his very bed and strong box are not forgotten. To the busy man, especially the busy man of letters, these details are far from uninteresting; if we judged by the result, many of Heyne's arrangements might seem worthy not of notice only, but of imitation.

His domestic circumstances continued on the whole highly favourable for such activity; though not now more than formerly were they exempted from the common lot; but still had several hard changes to encounter. In 1775, he lost his Theresa after long ill-health; an event which, stoic as he was, struck heavily and dolefully upon his heart. He forebore not to shed some natural tears, though from eyes little used to the melting mood. Nine days after her death, he thus writes to a friend with a solemn, mournful tenderness, which none of us will deny to be genuine:

"I have looked upon the grave that covers the remains of my Theresa: what a thousandfold pang, beyond the pitch of human feeling, pierced through my soul! How did my limbs tremble as I approached this holy spot! Here, then, reposes what is left of the dearest that heaven gave me; among the dust of her four children she sleeps. A sacred horror covered the place. I should have sunk altogether in my sorrow, had it not been for my two daughters that were standing on the outside of the church-yard; I saw their faces over the wall, directed to me with anxious fear. This called me to myself; I hastened in sadness from the spot where I could have continued for ever: where it cheered me to think that one day I should rest by her side; rest from all the carking care, from all the griefs which so often have embittered to me the enjoyment of life. Alas! among these griefs must I reckon even her love, the strongest, truest, that ever inspired the heart of woman, which may be the happiest of mortals, and yet was a fountain to me of a thousand distresses, inquietudes, and cares. To entire cheerfulness perhaps she never attained; but for what unspeakable sweetness, for what exalted, enrapturing joys is not Love indebted to Sorrow? Amidst gnawing anxieties, with the torture of anguish in my heart, I have been made even by the love which caused me this anguish, these anxieties, inexpressibly happy! When tears flowed over our cheeks, did not a nameless, seldom felt delight stream through my breast, oppressed equally by joy and by sorrow!"

But Heyne was not a man to brood over past griefs, or linger long where nothing was to be done, but mourn. In a short time, according to a good old plan of his, having reckoned up his grounds of sorrow, he fairly wrote down on paper, over against them, his "grounds of consolation;" concluding with these pious words, "So for all these sorrows too, these trials, do I thank thee, my God! And now, glorified friend, will I again turn me with undivided heart to my duty; thou thyself smilest approval on me!" Nay, it was not many months before a new marriage came on the anvil, in which matter, truly, Heyne conducted himself with the most philosophic indifference; leaving his friends, by whom the project had been started, to bring it to what issue they pleased. It was a scheme concerted by Zimmerman, (the author of *Solitude*, a man little known to Heyne,) and one Reich, a Leipzig bookseller, who had met at the Prymont Baths. Brandes, the Hanoverian Minister, successor of Münchhausen in the management of the University concerns, was there also with a daughter; upon her, the projectors cast their eye. Heyne, being consulted, seems to have comported himself like clay in the hands of the potter; father and fair one, in like manner, were of a compliant humour, and thus was the business achieved; and on the 9th of April, 1777, Heyne could take home a bride, won with less difficulty than most men have in choosing a pair of boots. Nevertheless, she proved an excellent wife to him; kept his house in the cheerfullest order; managed her step-children, and her own, like a true mother; and loved, and faithfully assisted her husband in whatever he undertook. Considered in his private relations, such a man might well reckon himself fortunate.

In addition to Heyne's claims as a scholar and teacher, Heeren would have us regard him as an unusually expert man of business and negotiator, for which line of life he himself seems indeed to have thought that his talent was more peculiarly fitted. In proof of this, we have long details of his procedure in managing the Library, the Royal Society, the University generally, and his incessant, and often rather complex correspondence with Münchhausen, Brandes, or other ministers, who presided over this department. Without detracting from Heyne's skill in such matters, what struck us more in this narrative of Heeren's was the singular contrast which the "Georgia Augusta," in its interior arrangement, as well as in its external relations to the Government, exhibits with our own universities. The prime minister of the country writes thrice weekly to the director of an institution for learning! He oversees all; knows the character, not only of every professor, but of every pupil that gives any promise. He is continually purchasing books, drawings, models; treating for this or the other help or advantage to the establishment. He has his eye over all Germany; and nowhere does a man of any decided talent show himself, but he strains every nerve to acquire him. And seldom or ever can he succeed; for the Hanoverian assiduity seems nothing singular; every state in Germany has its minister for education, as well as Hanover. They correspond, they inquire, they negotiate; everywhere there seems a canvassing, less for places, than for the best men to fill them. Heyne himself has his Seminarium, a private class of the nine most distinguished students in the university; these he trains with all diligence, and is in due time most probably enabled, by his connections, to place in stations fit for them. A hundred and thirty-five professors are said to have been sent from this Seminarium during his presidency. These things we state without commentary: we believe that the experience of all English, and Scotch, and Irish university-men will, of itself, furnish one. The state of education in Germany, and the structure of the establishments for conducting it, seems to us one of the most promising inquiries that could at this moment be entered on.

But to return to Heyne: We have said, that in his private circumstances, he might reckon himself fortunate. His public relations, on a more splendid scale, continued, to the last, to be of the same happy sort. By degrees, he had risen to be, both in name and office, the chief man of his establishment; his character stood high with the learned of all countries; and the best fruit of external reputation, increased respect in his own circle, was not denied to him. The burghers of Göttingen, so fond of their University, could not but be proud of Heyne; nay, as the time passed on, they found themselves laid under more than one specific obligation to him. He remodelled and reanimated their gymnasium (town-school), as he had before done that of Ilfeld; and what was still more important, in the rude times of the French war, by his skilful application, he succeeded in procuring from Napoleon, not only a protection for the University, but immunity from hostile invasion for the whole district it stands in. Nay, so happily were matters managed, or so happily did they turn of their own accord, that Göttingen rather gained than suffered by the war: Under Jerome of Westphalia, not only were all benefices punctually paid, but improvements even were effected; among other things, a new and very handsome extension, which had long been desired, was built for the library, at the charge of Government. To all these claims for public regard, add Heyne's now venerable age, and we can fancy how, among his townsmen and fellow-collegians, he must have been cherished, nay, almost worshipped. Already had the magistracy, by a special act, freed him from all public assessments; but, in 1809, on his eightieth birth-day, came a still more emphatic testimony; for the Ritter Franz, and all the public boards, and the faculties, *in corpore*, came to him in procession with good wishes; and students reverenced him; and young ladies sent him garlands, stitched together by their own fair fingers; in short, Göttingen was a place of jubilee; and good old Heyne, who nowise affected, yet could not dislike these things, was among the happiest of men.

In another respect, we must also reckon him fortunate; that he lived till he had completed all his undertakings; and then departed peacefully, and without sickness, from which, indeed, his whole life had been remarkably free. Three months before his death, in April, 1812, he saw the last volume of his works in print; and rejoiced, it is said, with an affecting thankfulness, that so much had been granted him. Length of life was not now to be hoped for; neither did Heyne look forward to the end with apprehension. His little German verses, and Latin translations, composed in sleepless nights, at this extreme period, are, to us, by far the most touching part of his poetry; so melancholy is the spirit of them, yet so mild; solemn, not without a shade of sadness, yet full of pious resignation. At length came the end; soft and gentle as his mother could have wished it for him. The 11th of July was a public day in the Royal Society; Heyne did his part in it; spoke at large, and with even more clearness and vivacity than usual.

"Next day," says Heeren, "was Sunday: I saw him in the evening, for the last time. He was resting in his chair, exhausted by the fatigue of yesterday. On Monday morning, he once more entered his class room, and held his Seminarium. In the afternoon he prepared his letters, domestic as well as foreign; among the latter, one on business; sealed them all but one, written in Latin, to Professor Thorlacius, in Copenhagen, which I found open, but finished, on his death. At supper, (none but his elder daughter was with him,) he talked cheerfully, and at his usual time retired to rest. In the night, the servant girl, that slept under his apartment, heard him walking up and down; a common practice with him when he could not sleep. However, he had again gone to bed. Soon after five, he arose, as usual; he joked with the girl when she asked him how he had been over-night. She left him, to make ready his coffee, as was her wont; and returning with it in a short quarter of an hour, she found him sunk down before his washing-stand, close by his work-table. His hands were wet; at the moment when he had been washing them, had death taken him into his arms. One breath more, and he ceased to live: when the hastening doctor opened a vein, no blood would flow."

Heyne was interred with all public solemnities: and, in epicedial language, it may be said without much exaggeration, that his country mourned for him. At Chemnitz, his birthplace, there assembled, under constituted authority, a grand meeting of the magistrates, to celebrate his memory; the old school-album, in which the little ragged boy had inscribed his name, was produced; grandiloquent speeches were delivered; and "in the afternoon, many hundreds went to see the poor cottage," where his father had weaved, and he starved and learned. How generous!

To estimate Heyne's intellectual character, to fix accurately his rank and merits as a critic and philologer, we cannot but consider as beyond our province, and at any rate superfluous here. By the general consent of the learned in all countries, he seems to be acknowledged as the first among recent scholars; his immense reading, his lynx-eyed skill in exposition and emendation are no longer here controverted; among ourselves his taste in these matters has been praised by Gibbon, and by Parr pronounced to be "exquisite." In his own country, Heyne is even regarded as the founder of a new epoch in classical study; as the first who with any decisiveness attempted to translate fairly beyond the letter of the classics; to read in the writings of the ancients, not the language alone, or even their detached opinions and records, but their spirit and character, their way of life and thought; how the world and nature painted themselves to the mind in those old ages; how, in one word, the Greeks and the Romans were men, even as we are. Such of our readers as have studied any one of Heyne's works, or even looked carefully into the *Lectures* of the Schlegels, the most ingenious and popular commentators of that school, will be at no loss to understand what we mean.

By his inquiries into antiquity, especially by his laboured investigation of its politics and its mythology, Heyne is believed to have carried the torch of philosophy towards, if not into, the mysteries of old time. What Winkelmann, his great contemporary did, or began to do, for ancient plastic art, the other, with equal success, began for ancient literature.* A high

* It is a curious fact that these two men, so singularly correspondent in their early sufferings, subsequent distinction, line of study, and rugged enthusiasm of character, were at one time, while both as yet were under the horizon, brought into partial contact. "An acquaintance of another sort," says Heeren, "the young Heyne was to make in the Brühl Library; with a person whose importance he could not then anticipate. One frequent visitor of this establishment was a certain almost wholly unknown man, whose visits could not be specially desirable for the librarians, such endless labour did he cost them. He seemed insatiable in reading; and

praise, surely; yet, as we must think, one not unfounded, and which, indeed, in all parts of Europe, is becoming more and more confirmed.

So much, in the province to which he devoted his activity, is Heyne allowed to have accomplished. Nevertheless, we must not assert that, in point of understanding and spiritual endowment, he can be called a complete, or even, in strict speech, a great man. Wonderful perspicuity, unwearied diligence, are not denied him; but to philosophic order, to classical adjustment, clearness, polish, whether in word or thought, he seldom attains; nay, many times, it must be avowed, he involves himself in tortures, long-winded verbosities, and stands before us little better than one of that old school which his admirers boast that he displaced. He appears, we might almost say, as if he had wings but could not well use them. Or, indeed, it might be that, writing constantly in a dead language, he came to write heavily; working for ever on subjects where learned armor-at-all-points cannot be dispensed with, he at last grew so habituated to his harness that he would not walk abroad without it; nay perhaps it had rusted together, and *could* not be unclasped! A sad fate for a thinker! Yet one which threatens many commentators, and overtakes many.

As a man encrusted and encased, he exhibits himself, moreover, to a certain degree, in his moral character. Here too, as in his intellect, there is an awkwardness, a cumbrous inertness; nay, there is a show of dulness, of hardness, which nowise intrinsically belongs to him. He passed, we are told, for less religious, less affectionate, less enthusiastic than he was. His heart, one would think, had no free course, or had found itself a secret one; outwardly he stands before us, cold and still, a very wall of rock; yet within lay a well, from which, as we have witnessed, the stroke of some Moses'-wand (the death of a Theresa) could draw streams of pure feeling. Callous as a man seems to us, he has a sense for all natural beauty; a merciful sympathy for his fellow-men: his own early distresses never left his memory: for similar distresses his pity and help were at all times in store. This form of character may also be the fruit partly of his employments, partly of his sufferings, and, perhaps, is not very singular among commentators.

For the rest, Heeren assures us, that in practice Heyne was truly a good man; altogether just; diligent in his own honest business, and ever ready to forward that of others; compassionate; though quick-tempered, placable; friendly, and satisfied with simple pleasures. He delighted in roses, and always kept a bouquet of them in water on his desk. His house was embowered among roses; and in his old days he used to wander through the bushes with a pair of scissors. Farther, says Heeren, in spite of his short sight, he was fond of the fields and skies, and could lie for hours reading on the grass. A kindly old man! With strangers, hundreds of whom visited him, he was uniformly courteous; though latterly, being a little hard of hearing, less fit to converse. In society he strove much to be polite; but had a habit (which ought to be general) of yawning, when people spoke to him and said nothing.

On the whole, the Germans have some reason to be proud of Heyne; who shall deny that they have here once more produced a scholar of the right old stock; a man to be ranked, for honesty of study and of life, with the Scaligers, the Bentleys, and old illustrious men, who, though covered with academic dust and harsh with polyglot vocables, were true men of endeavour, and fought like giants, with such weapons as they had, for the good cause? To ourselves, we confess, Heyne, highly interesting for what he did, is not less but more so for what he was. This is another of the proofs, which minds like his are from time to time sent hither to give, that the man is not the product of his circumstances, but that, in a far higher degree, the circumstances are the product of the man. While beneficed clerks and other sleek philosophers, reclining on their cushions of velvet, are demonstrating that to make a scholar and man of taste, there must be co-operation of the upper classes, society of gentlemen-commoners, and an income of four hundred a year;—arises the son of a Chemnitz weaver, and with the very wind of his stroke sweeps them from the scene. Let no man doubt the omnipotence of Nature, doubt the majesty of man's soul; let no lonely unfriended son of genius despair! Let him not despair; if he have the will, the right will, then the power also has not been denied him. It is but the artichoke that will not grow except in gardens; the acorn is cast carelessly abroad into the wilderness, yet it rises to be an oak; on the wild soil it nourishes itself, it defies the tempest, and lives for a thousand years.

---

called for so many books, that his reception there grew rather of the coolest. It was *Johann Winkelmann*. Meditating his journey for Italy, he was then laying in preparation for it. Thus did these two men become, if not confidential, yet acquainted; who at that time, both still in darkness and poverty, could little suppose, that in a few years, they were to be the teachers of cultivated Europe, and the ornaments of their nation."

GERMAN PLAYWRIGHTS.*

[FOREIGN REVIEW, 1829.]

In this stage of society, the playwright is as essential and acknowledged a character as the millwright, or cartwright, or any other wright whatever; neither can we see why, in general estimation, he should rank lower than these his brother artisans, except perhaps, for this one reason: that the former, working in timber and iron, for the wants of the body, produce a completely suitable machine, while the latter, working in thought and feeling, for the wants of the soul, produces a machine which is *in*completely suitable. In other respects, we confess, we cannot perceive that the balance lies against him: for no candid man, as it seems to us, will doubt but the talent, which constructed a *Virginius* or a *Bertram*, might have sufficed, had it been properly directed, to make not only wheelbarrows and wagons, but even mills of considerable complicacy. However, if the public is niggardly to the playwright in one point, it must be proportionably liberal in another; according to Adam Smith's observation, that trades which are reckoned less reputable have higher money-wages. Thus, one thing compensating the other, the playwright may still realize an existence; as, in fact, we find that he does: for playwrights were, are, and probably will always be; unless, indeed, in process of years, the whole dramatic concern be finally abandoned by mankind; or, as in the case of our Punch and Mathews, every player becoming his own playwright, this trade may merge in the other and older one.

The British nation has its own playwrights, several of them cunning men in their craft: yet here, it would seem, this sort of carpentry does not flourish; at least, not with that pre-eminent vigour which distinguishes most other branches of our national industry. In hardware and cotton goods, in all sorts of chemical, mechanical, or other material processes, England outstrips the world: nay, in many departments of literary manufacture also, as, for instance, in the fabrication of novels, she may safely boast herself peerless: but in this matter of the Drama, to whatever cause it be owing, one can claim no such superiority. In theatrical produce she yields considerably to France; and is, out of sight, inferior to Germany. Nay, do not we English hear daily, for the last twenty years, that the Drama is dead, or in a state of suspended animation; and are not medical men sitting on the case, and propounding their remedial appliances, weekly, monthly, quarterly, to no manner of purpose?—whilst in Germany the Drama is not only, to all appearance, alive, but in the very flush and hey-day of superabundant strength; indeed, as it were, still only sowing its first wild oats! For if the British Playwrights seem verging to ruin, and our Knowleses, Maturins, Shiels, and Shees stand few and comparatively forlorn, like firs on an Irish bog, the playwrights of Germany are a strong, triumphant body, so numerous that it has been calculated, in case of war, a regiment of foot might be raised, in which, from the colonel down to the drummer, every officer and private sentinel might show his drama or dramas.

To investigate the origin of so marked a superiority would lead us beyond our purpose. Doubtless the proximate cause must lie in a superior demand for the article of dramas; which superior demand again may arise either from the climate of Germany, as Montesquieu might believe; or perhaps more naturally and immediately from the political condition of that country; for man is not only a working but a talking animal, and where no Catholic Questions, and Parliamentary Reforms, and Select Vestries are given him to discuss in his leisure hours, he is glad to fall upon plays or players, or whatever comes to hand, whereby to fence himself a little against the inroads of Ennui. Of the fact, at least, that such a superior demand for dramas exists in Germany, we have only to open a newspaper to find proof. Is not every *Literaturblatt* and *Kunstblatt* stuffed to bursting, with theatricals? Nay, has not the "able Editor" established correspondents in every capital city of the civilized world, who report to him on this one matter and on no other? For, be our curiosity what it may, let us have profession of "intelligence from Munich," "intelligence from Vienna," intelligence from Berlin," is it intelligence of any thing but of greenroom controversies and negotiations, of tragedies and operas and farces acted and to be acted? Not of men, and their doings, by hearth and hall, in the firm earth; but of mere effigies and shells of men, and their doings in the world of pasteboard, do these unhappy correspondents write. Unhappy we call them; for, with all our tolerance of playwrights, we cannot but think that there are limits, and very strait ones, within which their activity should be restricted. Here, in England, our "theatrical reports" are

---

* *Die Ahnfrau.* (The Ancestress.) A Tragedy, in five Acts. By F. Grillparzer. Fourth Edition. Vienna, 1823.

König Ottokars Glück und Ende. (King Ottocar's Fortune and End.) A Tragedy, in five Acts. By F. Grillparzer. Vienna, 1825.

Sappho. A Tragedy, in five Acts. By F. Grillparzer. Third Edition. Vienna, 1822.

2. *Faust.* A Tragedy, in five Acts. By August Klingemann. Leipzig and Altenburg, 1815.

Ahasuer. A Tragedy, in five Acts. By August Klingemann. Brunswick, 1827.

3 *Müllner's Dramatische Werke. Erste rechtmässige, vollständige, und vom Verfasser verbesserte Gesammt-Ausgabe.* (Müllner's Dramatic Works. First legal collective Edition, complete and revised by the Author.) 7 vols. Brunswick, 1828.

nuisance enough; and many persons who love their life, and therefore "take care of their time, which is the stuff life is made of," regularly lose several columns of their weekly newspaper in that way: but our case is pure luxury, compared with that of the Germans, who, instead of a measurable and sufferable spicing of theatric matter, are obliged, metaphorically speaking, to breakfast and dine on it, have in fact nothing else to live on but that highly unnutritive victual. We ourselves are occasionally readers of German newspapers, and have often, in the spirit of Christian humanity, meditated presenting to the whole body of German editors a project, which, however, must certainly have ere now occurred to themselves, and for some reason been found inapplicable; it was, to address these correspondents of theirs, all and sundry, in plain language, and put the question: whether, on studiously surveying the Universe from their several stations, there was nothing in the Heavens above, on the earth beneath, or the waters under the earth, *nothing* visible but this one business, or rather shadow of business, that had an interest for the minds of men? If the correspondents still answered that nothing was visible, then of course they must be left to continue in this strange state: prayers, at the same time, being put up for them in all churches.

However, leaving every able Editor to fight his own battle, we address ourselves to the task in hand: meaning here to inquire a very little into the actual state of the dramatic trade in Germany, and exhibit some detached features of it to the consideration of our readers. For, seriously speaking, low as this province may be, it is a real, active, and ever-enduring province of the literary republic; nor can the pursuit of many men, even though it be a profitless and foolish pursuit, ever be without claim to some attention from us, either in the way of furtherance or of censure and correction. Our avowed object is to promote the sound study of foreign literature; which study, like all other earthly undertakings, has its negative as well as its positive side. We have already, as occasion served, borne testimony to the merits of various German poets, and must now say a word on certain German poetasters; hoping that it may be chiefly a regard to the former which has made us take even this slight notice of the latter: for the bad is in itself of no value, and only worth describing lest it be mistaken for the good. At the same time, let no reader tremble, as if we meant to overwhelm him, on this occasion, with a whole mountain of dramatic lumber, poured forth in torrents, like shot-rubbish, from the play-house-garrets, where it is mouldering and evaporating into nothing, silently and without harm to any one. Far be this from us! Nay, our own knowledge of this subject is in the highest degree limited; and, indeed, to exhaust it, or attempt discussing it with scientific precision, would be an impossible enterprise. What man is there that could assort the whole furniture of Milton's *Limbo of Vanity;* or where is the Hallam that would think it worth his while to write us the Constitutional History of a Rookery? Let the courteous reader take heart, then; for he is in hands that will not, nay, what is more, that cannot, do him much harm. One brief, shy glance into this huge bivouac of Playwrights, all sawing and planing with such tumult; and we leave it, probably for many years.

The German Parnassus, as one of its own denizens remarks, has a rather broad summit: yet only two Dramatists are reckoned, within the last half century, to have mounted thither; —Schiller and Goethe; if we are not, on the strength of his *Minna von Barnhelm* and *Emilie Galeotti*, to account Lessing of the number. On the slope of the Mountain may be found a few stragglers of the same brotherhood; among these, Tieck and Maler Müller, firmly enough stationed at considerable elevations; while, far below, appear various honest persons climbing vehemently, but against precipices of loose sand, to whom we wish all speed. But the reader will understand that the bivouac we speak of, and are about to enter, lies not on the declivity of the Hill at all; but on the level ground close to the foot of it; the essence of a Playwright being that he works not in Poetry, but in Prose, which more or less cunningly resembles it. And here, pausing for a moment, the reader observes that he is in a civilized country; for there, on the very boundary line of Parnassus, rises a gallows with the figure of a man hung in chains! It is the figure of August von Kotzebue, and has swung there for many years, as a warning to all too audacious Playwrights, who nevertheless, as we see, pay little heed to it. Ill-fated Kotzebue, once the darling of theatrical Europe! This was the prince of all Playwrights, and could manufacture Plays with a speed and felicity surpassing even Edinburgh novels. For his muse, like other doves, hatched twins in the month; and the world gazed on them with an admiration too deep for mere words. What is all past or present popularity to this? Were not these Plays translated into almost every language of articulate-speaking men; acted, at least, we may literally say, in every theatre from Kamtschatka to Cadiz? Nay, did they not melt the most obdurate hearts in all countries; and, like the music of Orpheus, draw tears down iron cheeks? We ourselves have known the flintiest men, who professed to have wept over them, for the first time in their lives. So was it twenty years ago; how stands it today? Kotzebue, lifted up on the hollow balloon of popular applause, thought wings had been given him that he might ascend to the Immortals: gay he rose, soaring, sailing, as with supreme dominion; but in the rarer azure deep, his windbag burst asunder, or the arrows of keen archers pierced it; and so at last we find him a compound-pendulum, vibrating in the character of scarecrow, to guard from forbidden fruit! O ye Playwrights, and literary quacks of every feather, weep over Kotzebue, and over yourselves! Know that the loudest roar of the million is not fame; that the windbag, are ye mad enough to mount it, *will* burst, or be shot through with arrows, and your bones too shall act as scarecrows.

But, quitting this idle allegorical vein, let us

at length proceed in plain English, and as beseems mere prose Reviewers, to the work laid out for us. Among the hundreds of German dramatists, as they are called, three individuals, already known to some British readers, and prominent from all the rest in Germany, may fitly enough stand here as representatives of the whole Playwright class; whose various craft and produce the procedure of these three may in some small degree serve to illustrate. Of Grillparzer, therefore, and Klingemann, and Mülner, in their order.

Franz Grillparzer seems to be an Austrian; which country is reckoned nowise fertile in poets; a circumstance that may perhaps have contributed a little to his own rather rapid celebrity. Our more special acquaintance with Grillparzer is of very recent date; though his name and samples of his ware have for some time been hung out, in many British and foreign Magazines, often with testimonials which might have beguiled less timeworn customers. Neither, after all, have we found there testimonials falser than other such are, but rather not so false; for, indeed, Grillparzer is a most inoffensive man, nay positively rather meritorious; nor is it without reluctance that we name him under this head of Playwrights, and not under that of Dramatists, which he aspires to. Had the law with regard to mediocre poets relaxed itself since Horace's time, all had been well with Grillparzer; for undoubtedly there *is* a small vein of tenderness and grace running through him, a seeming modesty also, and real love of his art, which gives promise of better things. But gods and men and columns are still equally rigid in that unhappy particular of mediocrity,—even pleasing mediocrity; and no scene or line is yet known to us of Grillparzer's which exhibits any thing more. *Non concessere,* therefore, is his sentence for the present; and the louder his well-meaning admirers extol him, the more emphatically should it be pronounced and repeated. Nevertheless Grillparzer's claim to the title of Playwright is perhaps more his misfortune than his crime. Living in a country where the Drama engrosses so much attention, he has been led into attempting it, without any decisive qualification for such an enterprise; and so his allotment of talent, which might have done good service in some prose department, or even in the sonnet, elegy, song, or other outlying province of Poetry, is driven, as it were, in spite of fate, to write Plays, which, though regularly divided into scenes and separate speeches, are essentially monological; and though swarming with characters, too often express only one character, and that no very extraordinary one, the character of Franz Grillparzer himself. What is an increase of misfortune, too, he has met with applause in this career, which therefore he is likely to follow farther and farther, let nature and his stars say to it what they will.

The characteristic of a Playwright is that he writes in Prose, which Prose he palms, probably, first on himself, and then on the simpler part of the public, for Poetry: and the manner, in which he effects this legerdemain, constitutes his specific distinction, fixes the species to which he belongs in the genus Playwright. But it is a universal feature of him that he attempts, by prosaic, and as it were mechanical means, to accomplish an end which, except by poetical genius, is absolutely not to be accomplished. For the most part, he has some knack, or trick of the trade, which by close inspection can be detected, and so the heart of his mystery be seen into. He may have one trick, or many; and the more cunningly he can disguise these, the more perfect is he as a craftsman; for were the public once to penetrate into this his slight of hand, it were all over with him,—Othello's occupation were gone. No conjuror, when we once understand his method of fire-eating, can any longer pass for a true thaumaturgist, or even entertain us in his proper character of quack, though he should eat Mount Vesuvius itself. But happily for Playwrights and others, the Public is a dim-eyed animal; gullible to almost all lengths,—nay, which often seems to prefer being gulled.

Of Grillparzer's peculiar knack, and recipe for play-making, there is not very much to be said. He seems to have tried various kinds of recipes, in his time; and, to his credit be it spoken, seems little contented with any of them. By much the worst Play of his, that we have seen, is the *Ahnfrau* (Ancestress); a deep tragedy of the Castle Spectre sort; the whole mechanism of which was discernible and condemnable at a single glance. It is nothing but the old Story of Fate; an invisible Nemesis visiting the sins of the fathers upon the children to the third and fourth generation; a method almost as common and sovereign in German Art, at this day, as the method of steam is in British mechanics; and of which we shall anon have more occasion to speak. In his Preface, Grillparzer endeavours to palliate or deny the fact of his being a *Schicksal-Dichter* (Fate-Tragedian); but to no purpose; for it is a fact grounded on the testimony of the seven senses: however, we are glad to observe that, with this one trial, he seems to have abandoned the Fate-line, and taken into better, at least into different ones. With regard to the *Ahnfrau* itself, we may remark that few things struck us so much as this little observation of Count Borotins, occurring, in the middle of the dismalest night-thoughts, so unexpectedly as follows:—

BERTHA.

* * * *

Und der Himmel, sternelos,
Starrt aus leeren Augenhöhlen
In das ungeheure Grab
Schwarz herab!

GRAF.

Wie sich doch die Stunden dehnen!
Was ist wohl die Glocke, Bertha?

BERTHA (*is just condoling with him, in these words*):—

* * * *

And the welkin, starless,
Glares from empty eye-holes,
Black down on that boundless grave!

COUNT.

How the hours do linger!
What o'clock is't, prithee, Bertha?

A more delicate turn, we venture to say, is rarely to be met with in tragic dialogue. As to the story of the *Ahnfrau*, it is, naturally enough, of the most heart-rending description. This Ancestress is a lady, or rather the ghost of a lady, for she has been defunct some centuries, who in life had committed what we call an "indiscretion;" which indiscretion the unpolite husband punished, one would have thought sufficiently, by running her through the body. However, the *Schicksal* of Grillparzer does not think it sufficient; but farther dooms the fair penitent to walk as goblin, till the last branch of her family be extinct. Accordingly she is heard, from time to time, slamming doors and the like, and now and then seen with dreadful goggle-eyes and other ghost appurtenances, to the terror not only of servant people, but of old Count Borotin, her now sole male descendant, whose afternoon nap she, on one occasion, cruelly disturbs. This Count Borotin is really a worthy, prosing old gentleman; only he had a son long ago drowned in a fish-pond (body not found); and has still a highly accomplished daughter, whom there is none offering to wed, except one Jaromir, a person of unknown extraction, and to all appearance, of the lightest purse; nay, as it turns out afterwards, actually the head of a Banditti establishment, which had long infested the neighbouring forests. However, a Captain of foot arrives, at this juncture, utterly to root out these Robbers; and now the strangest things come to light. For who should this Jaromir prove to be but poor old Borotin's drowned son, not drowned, but stolen and bred up by these Outlaws; the brother, therefore, of his intended; a most truculent fellow, who fighting for his life unwittingly kills his own father, and drives his bride to poison herself; in which wise, as was also Giles Scroggins' case, he "cannot get married." The reader sees all this is not to be accomplished without some jarring and tumult. In fact, there is a frightful uproar everywhere throughout that night; robbers dying, musquetry discharging, women shrieking, men swearing, and the Ahnfrau herself emerging at intervals, as the genius of the whole discord. But time and hours bring relief, as they always do. Jaromir, in the long run, likewise, succeeds in dying; whereupon the Borotin lineage having gone to the Devil, the Ancestress also retires thither,—at least makes the upper world rid of her presence,—and the piece ends in deep stillness. Of this poor Ancestress we shall only say farther: wherever she be, *requiescat! requiescat!*

As we mentioned above, the Fate method of manufacturing tragic emotion seems to have yielded Grillparzer himself little contentment; for after this *Ahnfrau*, we hear no more of it. His *König Ottokars Glück und Ende* (King Ottokar's Fortune and End) is a much more innocent piece, and proceeds in quite a different strain; aiming to subdue us not by old women's fables of Destiny, but by the accumulated splendour of thrones and principalities, the cruel or magnanimous pride of Austrian Emperors and Bohemian conquerors, the wit of chivalrous courtiers, and beautiful but shrewish queens; the whole set off by a proper intermixture of coronation ceremonies, Hungarian dresses, whiskered halberdiers, alarms of battle, and the pomp and circumstance of glorious war. There is even some attempt at delineating character in this play; certain of the *dramatis personæ* are evidently meant to differ from certain others, not in dress and name only, but in nature and mode of being; so much indeed they repeatedly assert, or hint, and do their best to make good,—unfortunately, however, with very indifferent success. In fact these *dramatis personæ* are rubrics and titles rather than persons; for most part, mere theatrical automata, with only a mechanical existence. The truth of the matter is, Grillparzer cannot communicate a poetic life to any character or object; and in this, were it in no other way, he evinces the intrinsically prosaic nature of his talent. These personages of his have, in some instances, a certain degree of metaphysical truth; that is to say, one portion of their structure, psychologically viewed, corresponds with the other;—so far all is well enough: but to unite these merely scientific and inanimate *qualities* into a living *man* is work not for a Playwright, but for a Dramatist. Nevertheless, *König Ottokar* is comparatively a harmless tragedy. It is full of action, striking enough, though without any discernible coherence; and with so much both of flirting, and fighting, with so many weddings, funerals, processions, encampments, it must be, we should think, if the tailor and decorationist do their duty, a very comfortable piece to see acted, especially on the Vienna boards, where it has a national interest, Rodolph of Hapsburg being a main personage in it.

The model of this *Ottokar* we imagine to have been Schiller's *Piccolomini;* a poem of similar materials and object; but differing from it as a living rose from a mass of dead rose-leaves, or even of broken Italian gum-flowers. It seems as though Grillparzer had hoped to subdue us by a sufficient multitude of wonderful scenes and circumstances, without inquiring, with any painful solicitude, whether the soul and meaning of them were presented to us or not. Herein truly, we believe, lies the peculiar knack or playwright-mystery of *Ottokar;* that its effect is calculated to depend chiefly on its quantity: on the mere number of astonishments, and joyful or deplorable adventures there brought to light; abundance in superficial contents compensating the absence of *callida junctura*. Which second method of tragic manufacture we hold to be better than the first, but still far from good. At the same time, it is a very common method, both in Tragedy and elsewhere; nay, we hear persons whose trade it is to write metre, or be otherwise "imaginative," professing it openly as the best they know. Do not these men go about collecting "features;" ferreting out strange incidents, murders, duels, ghost-apparitions, over the habitable globe; of which features and incidents, when they have gathered a sufficient stock, nothing more is needed than that they be ample enough, high-coloured enough, though huddled into any case (Novel, Tragedy, or Metrical Romance) that will hold it all? Nevertheless this is agglomeration, not creation; and avails little in Literature. Quantity, it is a certain fact, will *not* make up for defect of quality; nor are the gayest hues of any service, unless there be a likeness painted from them. Better were it for *König Ottokar* had the story been twice as short, and twice as expressive. For it is still true, as in Cervantes' time, *nunca lo bueno fué mucho.* What avails the dram of brandy while it swims chemically united with its barrel of wort? Let the distiller pass it and repass it through his limbecs; for it is the drops of pure alcohol that we want, not the gallons of water, which may be had in every ditch.

On the whole, however, we remember *König Ottokar* without animosity; and to prove that Grillparzer, if he could not make it poetical, might have made it less prosaic, and has in fact something better in him than is here manifested, we shall quote one passage, which strikes us as really rather sweet and natural. King Ottokar is in the last of his fields, no prospect before him but death or captivity: and soliloquizing on his past misdeeds:—

I have not borne me wisely in thy World,
Thou great, all-judging God! Like storm and tempest,
I traversed thy fair garden, wasting it:
'T is thine to waste, for thou alone canst heal.
Was evil not my aim, yet how did I,
Poor worm, presume to ape the Lord of Worlds,
And through the Bad seek out a way to the Good!

My fellow man, sent thither for his joy,
An end, a Self, within thy World a World,—
For thou hast fashion'd him a marvellous work,
With lofty brow, erect in look, strange sense,
And clothed him in the garment of thy Beauty,
And wondrously encircled him with wonders;
He hears, and sees, and feels, has pain and pleasure:
He takes him food, and cunning powers come forth,
And work and work, within their secret chambers,
And build him up his House: no royal Palace
Is comparable to the frame of Man!
And I have cast them from me by thousands,
For whims, as men throw rubbish from their door.

And none of all these slain but had a Mother
Who, as she bore him in sore travail,
Had clasped him fondly to her fostering breast;
A father who had bless'd him as his pride,
And nurturing, watch'd over him long years;
If he but hurt the skin upon his finger,
There would they run, with anxious look, to bind it,
And tend it, cheering him, until it heal'd;
And it was but a finger, the skin o' the finger!
And I have trod men down in heaps and squadrons,
For the stern iron open'd out a way
To their warm living hearts.—O God!
Wilt thou go into judgment with me, spare
My suffering people.

König Ottokar, 180–1.

Passages of this sort, scattered here and there over Grillparzer's Plays, and evincing at least an amiable tenderness of natural disposition, make us regret the more to condemn him. In fact, we have hopes that he is not born to be for ever a Playwright. A true though feeble vein of poetic talent he really seems to possess; and such purity of heart as may yet, with assiduous study, lead him into his proper field. For we do reckon him a conscientious man, and honest lover of Art: nay this incessant fluctuation in his dramatic schemes is itself a good omen. Besides this *Ahnfrau* and *Ottokar*, he has written two Dramas, *Sappho*, and *Der Goldene Vliess*, (The Golden Fleece,) on quite another principle; aiming apparently at some Classic model, or at least at some French reflect of such a model. *Sappho*, which we are sorry to learn is not his last piece, but his second, appears to us very considerably the most faultless production of his we are yet acquainted with. There is a degree of grace and simplicity in it, a softness, polish, and general good taste, little to be expected from the Author of the *Ahnfrau*: if he cannot bring out the full tragic meaning of Sappho's situation, he contrives, with laudable dexterity, to avoid the ridicule that lies within a single step of it; his Drama is weak and thin, but innocent, lovable;—nay, the last scene strikes us as even poetically meritorious. His *Goldene Vliess* we suspect to be of similar character, but have not yet found time and patience to study it. We repeat our hope of one day meeting Grillparzer in a more honourable calling than this of Playwright, or even fourth-rate Dramatist; which titles, as was said above, we have not given him without regret; and shall be truly glad to cancel for whatever better one he may yet chance to merit.

But if we felt a certain reluctance in classing Grillparzer among the Playwrights, no such feeling can have place with regard to the second name on our list, that of Doctor August Klingemann. Dr. Klingemann is one of the most indisputable Playwrights now extant: nay so superlative is his vigour in this department, we might even designate him *the* Playwright. His manner of proceeding is quite different from Grillparzer's; not a wavering overcharged method, or combination of methods, as the other's was; but a fixed principle of action, which he follows with unflinching courage; his own mind being, to all appearance, highly satisfied with it. If Grillparzer attempted to overpower us now by the method of Fate, now by that of pompous action, and grandiloquent or lachrymose sentiment, heaped on us in too rich abundance, Klingemann, without neglecting any of these resources, seems to place his chief dependence on a surer and readier stay: on his magazines of rosin, oil-paper, vizards, scarlet-drapery, and gunpowder. What thunder and lightning, magic-lantern transparencies, death's-heads, fire-showers, and plush cloaks can do,—is here done. Abundance of churchyard and chapel scenes, in most tempestuous weather; to say nothing of battle-fields, gleams of scoured arms here and there in the wood, and even occasional shots heard in the distance. Then there are such scowls and malignant side-glances, ashy paleness, stampings, and hysterics, as might, one would think, wring the toughest bosom into drops of pity. For not only are the looks and gestures of these people of the most heart-rending description, but their words and feelings also (for Klingemann is no half-artist) are of a piece with them; gorgeous inflations, the purest innocence, highest magnanimity; godlike sentiment of all sorts; everywhere the finest tragic humour. The moral too is genuine; there is the most anxious regard to virtue; indeed a distinct patronage both of Providence and the Devil. In this manner, does Dr. Klingemann compound his dramatic electuaries, no less cunningly than Dr. Kitchener did his "peptic persuaders;" and truly of the former we must say, that their operation is nowise unpleasant; nay, to our shame be it spoken, we have even read these Plays with a certain degree of satisfaction; and shall declare that if any man wish to amuse himself irrationally, here is the ware for his money.

Klingemann's latest dramatic undertaking is *Ahasuer;* a purely original invention, on which he seems to pique himself somewhat; confessing his opinion that now when the "birth-pains" are over, the character of *Ahasuer* may possibly do good service in many a future drama. We are not prophets, or sons of prophets; so shall leave this prediction resting on its own basis. Ahasuer, the reader will be interested to learn, is no other than the Wandering Jew or Shoemaker of Jerusalem, concerning whom there are two things to be remarked. The first is the strange name of this Shoemaker: why do Klingemann and all the Germans call the man *Ahasuer*, when his authentic Christian name is John; *Joannes a Temporibus Christi*, or, for brevity's sake, simply *Joannes a Temporibus?* This should be looked into. Our second remark is of the circumstance that no Historian or Narrator, neither Schiller, Strada, Thuanus, Monroe, nor Dugald Dalgetty, makes any mention of Ahasuer's having been present at the Battle of Lützen. Possibly they thought the fact too notorious to need mention. Here, at all events, he was; nay, as we infer, he must have been at Waterloo also; and probably at Trafalgar, though in which fleet is not so clear; for he takes a hand in all great battles and national emergencies, at least is witness of them, being bound to it by his destiny. Such is the peculiar occupation of the Wandering Jew, as brought to light in this Tragedy: his other specialities,—that he cannot lodge above three nights in one place; that he is of a melancholic temperament; above all, that he cannot die, not by hemp or steel, or Prussic-acid itself, but must travel on till the general consummation,—are familiar to all historical readers. Ahasuer's task at this Battle of Lützen seems to have been a very easy one; simply to see the Lion of the North brought down; not by a cannon-shot, as is generally believed, but, by the traitorous pistol-bullet of one Heinyn von Warth, a bigoted Catholic, who had pretended to desert from the Imperialists, that he might find some such opportunity. Unfortunately, Heinyn, directly after this feat, falls into a sleepless, half rabid state; comes home to Castle Warth, frightens his poor wife and worthy old noodle of a Father; then skulks about, for some time, now praying, oftener cursing and swearing; till at length the Swedes lay hold of him and kill him. Ahasuer, as usual, is in at the death: in the interim, however, he has saved Lady Heinyn from drowning, though as good as poisoned her with the look of his strange stony eyes; and now his business to all appearance being over, he signifies in strong language that he must begone; thereupon, he "steps solemnly into the wood; Wasaburg looks after him surprised; the rest kneel round the corpse; the *Requiem* faintly continues;" and what is still more surprising, "the curtain falls." Such is the simple action and stern catastrophe of this Tragedy; concerning which it were superfluous for us to speak farther in the way of criticism. We shall only add that there is a dreadful lithographic print in it, representing "Ludwig Derrient as Ahasuer;" in that very act of "stepping solemnly into the wood;" and uttering these final words: *Ich aber wandle weiter—weiter—weiter!*" We have heard of Herr Derrient as of the best actor in Germany; and can now bear testimony, if there be truth in this plate, that he is one of the ablest-bodied men. A most truculent, rawboned figure, "with bare legs and red leather shoes;" huge black beard; eyes turned inside out; and uttering these extraordinary words:—"But *I* go on—on—on!"

Now, however, we must give a glance at Klingemann's other chief performance in this line, the tragedy of *Faust*. Dr. Klingemann admits that the subject has been often treated; that Goethe's *Faust* in particular has "dramatic points," (*dramatische momente*:) but the business is to give it an entire dramatic superficies, to make it an *ächt dramatische*, a "genuinely" dramatic tragedy. Setting out with this laudable intention, Dr. Klingemann has produced a *Faust*, which differs from that of Goethe in more than one particular. The hero of this piece is not the old Faust, doctor in philosophy, driven desperate by the uncertainty of human knowledge: but plain John Faust, the printer, and even the inventor of gunpowder; driven desperate by his ambitious temper, and a total deficiency of cash. He has an excellent wife, an excellent blind father, both of whom would fain have him be peaceable, and work at his trade; but being an adept in the black art, he determines rather to relieve himself in that way. Accordingly he proceeds to make a contract with the Devil, on what we should consider pretty advantageous terms; the devil being bound to serve him in the most effectual manner, and Faust at liberty to commit *four* mortal sins before any hair of his head can be harmed. However, as will be seen, the devil proves Yorkshire; and Faust naturally enough finds himself quite jockeyed in the long run.

Another characteristic distinction of Klingemann is his manner of imbodying this same Evil Principle, when at last he resolves on introducing him to sight; for all these contracts and preliminary matters are very properly managed behind the scenes; only the main points of the transaction being indicated to the spectator by some thunder-clap, or the like. Here is no cold mocking Mephistopheles; but a swaggering, jovial, West-India-looking "Stranger," with a rubicund, indeed quite brick-coloured face, which Faust at first mistakes for the effect of hard drinking. However, it is a remarkable feature of this Stranger, that always on the introduction of any religious topic, or the mention of any sacred name, he strikes his glass down on the table, and generally breaks it.

For some time, after his grand bargain, Faust's affairs go on triumphantly, on the great scale, and he seems to feel pretty comfortable. But the Stranger shows him "his wife," Helena, the most enchanting creature in the world; and the most cruel hearted,—for notwithstanding the easy temper of her husband, she will not grant Faust the smallest encouragement, till he have killed Käthe, his own living helpmate, against whom he entertains no manner of grudge. Nevertheless, reflecting that he has a stock of four mortal sins to draw upon, and may well venture one for such a prize, he determines on killing Käthe. But here matters take a bad turn; for having poisoned poor Käthe, he discovers, most unexpectedly, that she is in the family way; and therefore that he has committed not one sin but two! Nay before the interment can take place, he is farther reduced, in a sort of accidental self-defence, to kill his father; thus accomplishing his third mortal sin; with which third, as we shall presently discover, his whole allotment is exhausted, a fourth, that he knew not of, being already on the score against him! From this point, it cannot but surprise us that bad grows worse: catchpoles are out in pursuit of him, "black masks" dance round him in a most suspicious manner, the brick-faced stranger seems to laugh at him, and Helena will nowhere make her appearance. That the sympathizing reader may see with his own eyes how poor Faust is beset at this juncture, we shall quote a scene or two. The first may, properly enough, be that of those "black masks."

SCENE SEVENTH. *A lighted Hall.*

(*In the distance is heard quick dancing-music. Masks pass from time to time over the Stage, but all dressed in black, and with vizards perfectly close. After a pause,* FAUST *plunges wildly in, with a full goblet in his hand.*)

FAUST (*rushing stormfully into the foreground.*)

Ha! Poison, 'stead of wine, that I intoxicate me!
Your wine makes sober,—burning fire bring us!
Off with your drink!—and blood is in it too!
(*Shuddering, he dashes the goblet from his hand.*)
My father's blood,—I've drunk my fill of *that!*
(*With increasing tumult.*)
Yet curses on him! curses, that he begot me!
Curse on my mother's bosom, that it bore me!
Curse on the gossip crone that stood by her,
And did not strangle me, at my first scream!
How could I help this being that was given me?
Accursed art thou, Nature, that hast mock'd me!
Accursed I, that let myself be mock'd!
And thou strong Being, that to make thee sport,
Enclosedst the fire-soul in this dungeon,
That so despairing it might strive for freedom—
Accur. . . (*He shrinks terror-struck.*)
No, not the *fourth* . . . . the blackest sin!
No! No!
(*In the excess of his outbreaking anguish, he hides his face in his hands.*)
O, I am altogether wretched!
(*Three black Masks come towards him.*)

FIRST MASK.

Hey! merry friend!

SECOND MASK.

Hey! Merry brother!

THIRD MASK (*reiterating with a cutting tone.*)

Merry!

FAUST (*breaking out in wild humour, and looking round among them.*)

Hey! Merry, then!

FIRST MASK.

Will any one catch flies?

SECOND MASK.

A long life yet; to midnight all the way!

THIRD MASK.

And after that, such pleasure without end!
(*The music suddenly ceases, and a clock strikes thrice.*)

FAUST (*astonished.*)

What is it?

FIRST MASK.

Wants a quarter, Sir, of twelve!

SECOND MASK.

Then we have time!

THIRD MASK.

Aye, time enough for jigging.

FIRST MASK.

And not till midnight comes the shot to pay!

FAUST (*shuddering.*)

What want ye?

FIRST MASK (*clasps his hand abruptly.*)

Hey! To dance a step with thee!

FAUST (*plucks his hand back.*)

Off!—Fire!!

FIRST MASK.

Tush! A spark or so of brimstone!

SECOND MASK.

Art dreaming, brother?

THIRD MASK.

Holla! Music, there!
(*The music begins again in the distance.*

FIRST MASK (*secretly laughing.*)

The spleen is biting him!

SECOND MASK.

Hark! at the gallows,
What jovial footing of it!

THIRD MASK.

Thither must I! (*Exit.*)

FIRST MASK.

Below, too! down in Purgatory! Hear ye?

SECOND MASK.

A stirring *there?* 'Tis time then! Hui, your servant!

FIRST MASK (*to* FAUST.)

Till midnight!
(*Exeunt both Masks hastily.*)

FAUST (*clasping his brow.*)

Ha! What begirds me here? (*Stepping vehemently forward.*)
Down with your masks! (*Violent knocking without.*)
What horrid uproar, next!
Is madness coming on me?—

VOICE (*violently, from without.*)

Open, in the king's name!
(*The music ceases. Thunderclap.*)

FAUST (*staggers back.*)

I have a heavy dream!—Sure, '*t is* not doomsday?

VOICE (*as before.*)

Here is the murderer! Open! open, then!

FAUST (*wipes his brow.*)

Has agony unmann'd me?—

SCENE EIGHTH.

BAILIFFS.

Where is he? where?

From these merely terrestrial constables, the jovial Stranger easily delivers Faust; but now comes the long-looked-for *tête-à-tête* with Helena.

SCENE TWELFTH.

(FAUST *leads* HELENA *on the stage. She also is close masked. The other Masks withdraw.*)

FAUST (*warm and glowing.*)

No longer strive, proud beauty!

HELENA.

Ha, wild stormer!

FAUST.

My bosom burns—!

HELENA.

The time is not yet come.—

—And so forth, through four pages of flame and ice, till at last,

FAUST (*insisting.*)

Off with the mask, then

HELENA (*still wilder.*)

Hey! the marriage-hour!

FAUST.

Off with the mask!!

HELENA.

'T is striking!!

FAUST.

One kiss!

HELENA.

Take it!!

(*The mask and head-dress fall from her: and she grins at him from a death's head: loud thunder: and the music ends, as with a shriek, in dissonances.*)

FAUST (*staggers back.*)

O Horror! wo!

HELENA.

The couch is ready, there!
Come, Bridegroom, to thy fire-nuptials!

(*She sinks, with a crashing thunder-peal, into the ground, out of which issue flames.*)

All this is bad enough; but mere child's-play to the "Thirteenth Scene," the last of this strange eventful history: with some parts of which we propose to send our readers weeping to their beds.

SCENE THIRTEENTH.

(*The* STRANGER *hurls* FAUST, *whose face is deadly pale, back to the stage, by the hair.*)

FAUST.

Ha, let me fly!—Come! Come!—

STRANGER (*with wild thundering tone.*)

'T is over now!

FAUST.

That horrid visage!—*throwing himself, in a tremor, on the* STTANGER'S *breast.*) Thou art my Friend!
Protect me!!

STRANGER (*laughing aloud.*)

Ha! ha! ha!

* * * * * * *

FAUST.

O, save me!!

STRANGER (*clutches him with irresistible force: whirls him round, so that* FAUST'S *face is towards the spectators, whilst his own is turned away: and thus he looks at him, and bawls with thundering voice:*)

'T is I!!—(A CLAP OF THUNDER. FAUST, *with gestures of deepest horror, rushes to the ground, uttering an inarticulate cry. The other, after a pause, continues, with cutting coolness:*)

Is that the mighty Hell-subduer,
That threatened *me?*—Ha, ME!! (*with highest contempt.*)
Worm of the dust!
I had reserved thy torment for—*myself!!*
Descend to other hands, be sport for slaves—
Thou art too small for me!!

FAUST (*rises erect, and seems to recover his strength.*)

Am I not Faust?

STRANGER.

Thou, no!

FAUST (*rising in his whole vehemence.*)

Accursed! Ha, I am! I am!
Down at my feet! I am thy master!

STRANGER.

No more!!

FAUST (*wildly.*)

More? Ha! My Bargain!!

STRANGER.

Is concluded!!

FAUST.

Three mortal sins.—

STRANGER.

The Fourth too is committed!

FAUST.

My wife, my child, and my old Father's blood—!

STRANGER (*holds up a Parchment to him.*)

And here *thy own!*—

FAUST.

That is my covenant!

STRANGER.

This *signature*—was thy most damning sin!

FAUST (*raging.*)

Ha, spirit of lies!! &c., &c.

* * * * * *

STRANGER (*in highest fury.*)

Down, thou accursed!

(*He drags him by the hair towards the back-ground; at this moment, amid violent thunder and lightning, the scene changes into a horrid wilderness; in the back-ground of which, a yawning Chasm: into this the Devil hurls Faust; on all sides Fire rains down, so that the whole interior of the Cavern seems burning: a black veil descends over both, so soon as Faust is got under.*)

FAUST (*huzzaing in wild defiance.*)

Ha, down! Down!

(*Thunder, lightning, and fire. Both sink. The Curtain falls.*)

On considering all which supernatural transactions, the bewildered reader has no theory for it, except that Faust must, in Dr. Cabanis's phrase, have laboured under "obstructions in the epigastric region," and all this of the Devil, and Helena, and so much murder and carousing, have been nothing but a waking dream, or other atrabilious phantasm; and regrets that the poor Printer had not rather applied to some Abernethy on the subject, or even, by one sufficient dose of Epsom-salt, on his own prescription, have put an end to the whole matter, and restored himself to the bosom of his afflicted family.

Such, then, for Dr. Klingemann's part, is his method of constructing Tragedies; to which method it may perhaps be objected that there is a want of originality in it; for do not our own British Playwrights follow precisely the same plan? We might answer that, if not his plan, at least, his infinitely superior execution of it, must distinguish Klingemann: but we rather think his claim to originality rests on a different ground, on the ground, namely, of his entire contentment with himself and with this his dramaturgy; and the cool heroism with which, on all occasions, he avows that contentment. Here is no poor, cowering, underfoot Playwright, begging the public for God's sake not to give him the whipping which he deserves; but a bold perpendicular Playwright, avowing himself as such; nay, mounted on the top of his joinery, and therefrom exercising a sharp critical superintendence over the German Drama generally. Klingemann, we understand, has lately executed a theatrical Tour, as Don Quixote did various Sallies; and thrown stones into most German Playhouses, and at various German Playwriters; of which we have seen only his assault on Tieck; a feat comparable perhaps to that "never-imagined adventure of the Windmills." Fortune, it is said, favours the brave; and the prayer of Burns's Kilmarnock weaver is not always unheard of Heaven. In conclusion, we congratulate Dr. Klingemann on his Manager-dignity in the Brunswick Theatre; a post he seems made for, almost as Bardolph was for the Eastcheap waitership.

But now, like his own Ahasuer, Doctor Klingemann must "go on—on—on;" for another and greater Doctor has been kept too long waiting, whose seven beautiful volumes of *Dramatische Werke* might well secure him a better fate. Dr. Müllner, of all these Playwrights, is the best known in England; some of his works have even, we believe, been translated into our language. In his own country, his fame, or at least notoriety, is also supreme over all; no Playwright of this age makes such a noise as Müllner; nay, many there are who affirm that he is something far better than a Playwright. Critics of the sixth and lower magnitudes, in every corner of Germany, have put the question a thousand times: Whether Müllner is not a Poet and Dramatist? To which question, as the higher authorities maintain an obstinate silence, or, if much pressed, reply only in groans, these sixth-magnitude men have been obliged to make answer themselves; and they have done it with an emphasis and vociferation calculated to dispel all remaining doubts in the minds of men. In Müllner's mind, at least, they have left little; a conviction the more excusable, as the play-going vulgar seem to be almost unanimous in sharing it; and thunders of applause, nightly through so many theatres, return him loud acclaim. Such renown is pleasant food for the hungry appetite of a man, and naturally he rolls it as a sweet morsel under his tongue: but, after all, it can profit him but little; nay, many times, what is sugar to the taste may be sugar-of-lead when it is swallowed. Better were it for Müllner, we think, had fainter thunders of applause, and from fewer theatres, greeted him. For what good is in it, even were there no evil? Though a thousand caps leap into the air at his name, his own stature is no hair's breadth higher; neither even can the final estimate of its height be thereby in the smallest degree enlarged. From gainsayers these greetings provoke only a stricter scrutiny; the matter comes to be accurately known at last; and he, who has been treated with foolish liberality at one period, must make up for it by the want of bare necessaries at another. No one will deny that Müllner is a person of some considerable talent: we understand he is, or was once, a Lawyer; and can believe that he may have acted, and talked, and written, very prettily in that capacity: but to set up for a Poet was quite a different enterprise, in which we reckon that he has altogether mistaken his road, and these mob-cheers have led him farther and farther astray.

Several years ago, on the faith of very earnest recommendation, it was our lot to read one of Dr. Müllner's Tragedies, the *Albanäserinn*; with which, such was its effect on us, we could willingly enough have terminated our acquaintance with Dr. Müllner. A palpable imitation of Schiller's *Braut von Messina*; without any philosophy or feeling that was not either perfectly commonplace or perfectly false, often both the one and the other; inflated, indeed, into a certain hollow bulk, but altogether without greatness; being built throughout on mere rant and clangour, and other elements of the most indubitable Prose: such a work could not but be satisfactory to us respecting Dr. Müllner's genius as a Poet; and time being precious, and the world wide enough, we had privately determined that we and Dr. Müllner were each henceforth to pursue his own course. Nevertheless, so considerable has been the progress of our worthy friend, since then, both at home and abroad, that his labours are again forced on our notice: for we reckon the existence of a true Poet in any country to be so important a fact, that even the slight probability of such is worthy of investigation. Accordingly, we have again perused the *Albanäserinn*, and along with it, faithfully examined the whole Dramatic works of Müllner, published in seven volumes, on beautiful paper, in small shape, and every way very fit for handling. The whole tragic works, we should rather say: for three or four of his comic performances sufficiently contented us; and some two volumes of farces, we confess, are still unread. We have also carefully gone through, and with much less difficulty, the Prefaces, Appendices, and other prose sheets, wherein the Author exhibits the "*fata libelli*;" defends himself from unjust criticisms, reports just ones, or himself makes such. The toils of this task we shall not magnify, well knowing that man's life is a fight throughout: only having now gathered what light is to be had on this matter, we proceed to speak forth our verdict thereon; fondly hoping that we shall then have done with it, for an indefinite period of time.

Dr. Müllner, then, we must take liberty to believe, in spite of all that has been said or sung on the subject, is no Dramatist; has never written a Tragedy, and in all human probability will never write one. Grounds for this harsh, negative opinion, did the "burden of proof" lie chiefly on our side, we might state in extreme abundance. There is one ground, however, which, if our observation be correct, would virtually include all the rest. Dr. Müllner's whole soul and character, to the deepest root we can trace of it, seems prosaic, not poetical; his Dramas, therefore, like whatever else he produces, must be manufactured, not created; nay, we think that his principle of manufacture is itself rather a poor and second-hand one. Vain were it for any reader to search in these seven volumes for an opinion any deeper or clearer, a sentiment any finer or higher, than may conveniently belong to the commonest practising advocate: except stilting heroics, which the man himself half knows to be false, and every other man easily waives aside, there is nothing here to disturb the quiescence of either heart or head. This man is a *Doctor Utriusque Juris*, most probably of good juristic talent; and nothing more whatever. His language, too, all accurately measured into feet, and good current German, so far as a foreigner may judge, bears similar testimony. Except the rhyme and metre, it exhibits no poetical symptom; without being verbose, it is essentially meager and watery; no idiomatic expressiveness, no melody, no virtue of any kind; the commonest vehicle for the commonest meaning. Not that our Doctor is destitute of metaphors and other rhetorical furtherances; but that these also are of the most trivial character: old threadbare material, scoured up into a state of shabby-gentility; mostly turning on "light" and "darkness;" "flashes through clouds," "fire of heart," "tempest of soul," and the like, which can profit no man or woman. In short, we must repeat it, Dr. Müllner has yet to show that there is any particle of poetic metal in him; that his genius is other than a sober clay-pit, from which good bricks may be made; but where, to look for gold or diamonds were sheer waste of labour.

When we think of our own Maturin and Sheridan Knowles, and the gala-day of popularity which they also once enjoyed with us, we can be at no loss for the genus under which Dr. Müllner is to be included in critical physiology. Nevertheless, in marking him as a distinct Playwright, we are bound to mention that in general intellectual talent he shows himself very considerably superior to his two German brethren. He has a much better taste than Klingemann; rejecting the aid of plush and gunpowder, we may say, altogether; is even at the pains to rhyme great part of his Tragedies; and on the whole, writes with a certain care and decorous composure, to which the Brunswick Manager seems totally indifferent. Moreover, he appears to surpass Grillparzer, as well as Klingemann, in a certain force both of judgment and passion; which indeed is no very mighty affair; Grillparzer being naturally but a treble pipe in these matters; and Klingemann blowing through such an enormous coach-horn, that the natural note goes for nothing, becomes a mere vibration in that all-subduing volume of sound. At the same time, it is singular enough that neither Grillparzer nor Klingemann should be nearly so tough reading as Müllner, which, however, we declare to be the fact. As to Klingemann, he is even an amusing artist; there is such a briskness and heart in him; so rich is he, nay, so exuberant in riches, so full of explosions, fire-flashes, execrations, and all manner of catastrophes: and then, good soul, he asks *no* attention from us, knows his trade better than to dream of asking any. Grillparzer again is a sadder and perhaps a wiser companion; long-winded a little, but peaceable and soft-hearted: his melancholy, even when he pules, is in the highest degree inoffensive, and we can often weep a tear or two *for* him, if not with him. But of all Tragedians, may the indulgent Heavens deliver us from any farther traffic with Dr. Müllner! This is the lukewarm, which we could wish to be either cold or hot. Müllner will not keep us awake, while we read him; yet neither will he, like Klingemann, let us fairly get asleep. Ever and anon, it is as if we came into some smooth quiescent country; and the soul flatters herself that here at last she may be allowed to fall back on her cushions, the eyes meanwhile, like two safe postillions, comfortably conducting her through that flat region, in which are nothing but flax-crops and milestones; and ever and anon some jolt or unexpected noise fatally disturbs her; and looking out, it is no waterfall or mountain chasm, but only the villanous highway, and squalls of October wind. To speak without figure, Dr. Müllner does seem to us a singularly oppressive writer; and perhaps, for this reason, that he hovers *too* near the verge of good writing; ever tempting us with some hope that here is a touch of poetry; and ever disappointing us with a touch of pure Prose. A stately sentiment comes tramping forth with a clank that sounds poetic and heroic: we start in breathless expectation, waiting to reverence the heavenly guest; and, alas, he proves to be but an old stager dressed in new buckram, a stager well known to us, nay, often a stager that has already been drummed out of most well-regulated communities. So it is ever with Dr. Müllner: no feeling can be traced much deeper in him than the tongue; or perhaps when we search more strictly, instead of an ideal of beauty, we shall find some vague aim after strength, or in defect of this, after mere size. And yet how cunningly he manages the counterfeit! A most plausible, fair-spoken, close-shaven man; a man whom you must not, for decency's-sake, throw out of the window; and yet you feel that being palpably a Turk in grain, his intents are wicked and not charitable!

But the grand question with regard to Müllner, as with regard to these other Playwrights, is: where lies his peculiar sleight of hand in this craft? Let us endeavour, then, to find out his secret,—his recipe for play-making; and communicate the same for behoof of the British nation. Müllner's recipe is no mysterious one; floats, indeed, on the very surface: might even be taught, one would suppose, on a few trials, to the humblest capacity. Our readers may perhaps recollect Zacharias Werner, and some short allusion, in our First Number, to a highly terrific piece of his, entitled *The Twenty-fourth of February.* A more detailed account of the matter may be found in Madame de Staël's *Allemagne;* in the Chapter which treats of that infatuated Zacharias generally. It is a story of a Swiss peasant and bankrupt, called Kurt Kuruh, if we mistake not; and of his wife, and a rich travelling stranger, lodged with them; which latter is, in the night of the Twenty-fourth of February, wilfully and feloniously murdered by the two former, and proves himself in the act of dying to be their own only son, who had returned home to make them all comfortable, could they only have had a little patience. But the foul deed is already accomplished, with a rusty knife or scythe; and nothing of course remains but for the whole batch to go to perdition. For it was written, as the Arabs say, "on the iron leaf;" these Kuruhs are doomed men; old Kuruh, the grandfather, had committed some sin or other; for which, like the sons of Atreus, his descendants are "prosecuted with the utmost rigour:" nay, so punctilious is Destiny, that this very Twenty-fourth of February, the day when that old sin was enacted, is still a fatal day with the family; and this very knife or scythe, the criminal tool on that former occasion, is ever the instrument of new crime and punishment; the Kuruhs, during all that half century, never having carried it to the smithy to make hob-nails; but kept it hanging on a peg, most injudiciously we think, almost as a sort of bait and bonus to Satan, a ready-made fulcrum for whatever machinery he might bring to bear against them. This is the tragic lesson taught in Werner's *Twenty-fourth of February;* and, as the whole *dramatis personæ* are either stuck through with old iron, or hanged in hemp, it is surely taught with some considerable emphasis.

Werner's Play was brought out at Weimar, in 1809; under the direction or permission, as he brags, of the great Goethe himself; and seems to have produced no faint impression on a discerning public. It is, in fact, a piece nowise destitute of substance and a certain coarse vigour; and if any one has so obstinate a heart that he must absolutely stand in a slaughter-house, or within wind of the gallows before tears will come, it may have a very comfortable effect on him. One symptom of merit it must be admitted to exhibit,—an adaptation to the general taste; for the small fibre of originality, which exists here, has already shot forth into a whole wood of imitations. We understand that the Fate-line is now quite an established branch of dramatic business in Germany: they have their Fate-dramatists, just as we have our gingham-weavers, and inkle-weavers. Of this Fate-manufacture we have already seen one sample in Grillparzer's *Ahnfrau;* but by far the most extensive Fate-manufacturer, the head and prince of all Fate-dramatists, is the Dr. Müllner, at present under consideration. Müllner deals in Fate and Fate only; it is the basis and staple of his whole tragedy-goods; cut off this one principle, you annihilate his raw material, and he can manufacture no more.

Müllner acknowledges his obligations to Werner; but, we think, not half warmly enough. Werner was in fact the making of him; great as he has now become, our Doctor is nothing but a mere misletoe growing from that poor oak, itself already half-dead; had there been no *Twenty-fourth of February,* there were then no *Twenty-ninth of February,* no *Schuld,* no *Albanüserinn,* most probably no *König Yngurd.* For the reader is to understand that Dr. Müllner, already a middle-aged, and as yet a perfectly undramatic man, began business with a direct copy of this *Twenty-fourth;* a thing proceeding by Destiny, and ending in murder, by a knife or scythe, as in the Kuruh case; with one improvement, indeed, that there was a grinding-stone introduced into the scene, and the spectator had the satisfaction of seeing the knife previously whetted. The Author too was honest enough publicly to admit his imitation; for he named this Play, the *Twenty-ninth of February;* and, in his Preface, gave thanks, though somewhat reluctantly, to Werner, as to his master and originator. For some inscrutable reason, this *Twenty-ninth* was not sent to the green-grocer, but became popular: there was even the weakest of parodies written on it, entitled *Eumenides Düster,* (Eumenides Gloomy,) which Müllner has reprinted; there was likewise "a wish expressed" that the termination might be made joyous, not grievous; with which wish also, the indefatigable wright has complied; and so, for the benefit of weak nerves, we have the *Wahn,* (Delusion,) which still ends in tears, but glad ones. In short, our Doctor has a peculiar merit with this *Twenty-ninth* of his; for who but he could have cut a second and a third face on the same cherry-stone, said cherry-stone having first to be borrowed, or indeed half-stolen?

At this point, however, Dr. Müllner apparently began to set up for himself; and ever henceforth he endeavours to persuade his own mind and ours that his debt to Werner terminates here. Nevertheless clear it is that fresh debt was every day contracting. For had not this one Wernerean idea taken complete hold of the Doctor's mind,—so that he was quite possessed with it; had, we might say, no other tragic idea whatever? That a man, on a certain day of the month, shall fall into crime; for which an invisible Fate shall silently pursue him; punishing the transgression, most probably on the same day of the month, annually (unless, as in the *Twenty-ninth,* it be leap-year, and Fate in this may be, to a certain extent, bilked; and never resting till the poor wight himself, and perhaps his last descendant, shall be swept away with the besom of destruction: such, more or less disguised, frequently without any disguise, is the tragic essence, the vital principle, natural or galvanic we are not deciding, of all Dr. Müllner's Dramas. Thus, in that everlasting

Twenty-ninth of February, we have the principle in its naked state: some old Woodcutter or Forester has fallen into deadly sin with his wife's sister, long ago, on that intercalary day; and so his whole progeny must, wittingly or unwittingly, proceed in incest and murder; the day of the catastrophe regularly occurring, every four years, on that same Twenty-ninth; till happily the whole are murdered, and there is an end. So likewise in the *Schuld*, (Guilt,) a much more ambitious performance, we have exactly the same doctrine of an anniversary; and the interest once more turns on that delicate business of murder and incest. In the *Albanäserinn*, (Fair Albanese,) again, which may have the credit, such as it is, of being Müllner's best Play, we find the Fate-theory a little coloured; as if the drug had begun to disgust, and the Doctor would hide it in a spoonful of syrup: it is a dying man's curse that operates on the criminal; which curse, being strengthened by a sin of very old standing in the family of the cursee, takes singular effect; the parties only weathering parricide, fratricide, and the old story of incest, by two self-banishments, and two very decisive self-murders. Nay, it seems as if our Doctor positively could not act at all without this Fate-panacea: in *König Yngurd*, we might almost think that he had made such an attempt, and found that it would not do. This König Yngurd, an imaginary Peasant-King of Norway, is meant, as we are kindly informed, to present us with some adumbration of Napoleon Bonaparte; and truly, for the two or three first Acts, he goes along with no small gallantry, in what drill-sergeants call a dashing or swashing style; a very virtuous kind of man, and as bold as Ruy Diaz or any other Christian: when suddenly in the middle of a battle, far on in the Play, he is seized with some caprice, or whimsical qualm; retires to a solitary place, among rocks, and there, in the most gratuitous manner, delivers himself over, *viva voce*, to the Devil; who indeed does not appear personally to take seisin of him, but yet, as afterwards comes to light, has with great readiness accepted the gift. For now Yngurd grows dreadfully sulky and wicked, does little henceforth but bully men and kill them; till at length, the measure of his iniquities being full, he himself is bullied and killed; and the Author, carried through by this his sovereign tragic elixir, contrary to expectation, terminates his piece with reasonable comfort.

This, then, is Dr. Müllner's dramatic mystery; this is the one patent hook by which he would hang his clay tragedies on the upper spiritual world; and so establish for himself a free communication, almost as if by block-and-tackle, between the visible Prose Earth and the invisible Poetic Heaven. The greater or less merit of this his invention, or rather improvement, for Werner is the real patentee, has given rise, we understand, to extensive argument. The small deer of criticism seem to be much divided in opinion on this point; and the higher orders, as we have stated, declining to throw any light whatever on it, the subject is still mooting with great animation. For our own share, we confess that we incline to rank it as a recipe for dramatic tears, a shade higher than the Page's split onion in the *Taming of the Shrew*. Craftily hid in the handkerchief, this onion was sufficient for the deception of Christopher Sly; in that way attaining its object; which, also, the Fate-invention seems to have done with the Christopher Slys of Germany, and these not one but many, and therefore somewhat harder to deceive. To this onion-superiority we think Dr. M. is fairly entitled; and with this it were, perhaps, good for him that he remained content.

Dr. Müllner's Fate-scheme has been attacked by certain of his traducers on the score of its hostility to the Christian religion. Languishing, indeed, should we reckon the condition of the Christian religion to be, could Dr. Müllner's play-joinery produce any perceptible effect on it. Nevertheless, we may remark, since the matter is in hand, that this business of Fate does seem to us nowise a Christian doctrine; not even a Mohammedan or Heathen one. The *Fate* of the Greeks, though a false, was a lofty hypothesis, and harmonized sufficiently with the whole sensual and material structure of their theology: a ground of deepest black, on which that gorgeous phantasmagoria was fitly enough painted. Besides, with them, the avenging Power dwelt, at least in its visible manifestations, among the high places of the earth; visiting only kingly houses, and world's criminals, from whom it might be supposed the world, but for such miraculous interferences, could have exacted no vengeance, or found no protection and purification. Never, that we recollect of, did the Erinnyes become mere sheriffs'-officers, and Fate a justice of the peace, haling poor drudges to the treadmill for robbery of henroosts, or scattering the earth with steel-traps to keep down poaching. And *what* has all this to do with the revealed Providence of these days; that power whose path is emphatically through the great deep; his doings and plans manifested, in completeness, not by the year, or by the century, on individuals or on nations, but stretching through eternity, and over the infinitude which he rules and sustains?

But there needs no recourse to theological arguments for judging this Fate-tenet of Dr. Müllner's. Its value, as a dramatic principle, may be estimated, it seems to us, by this one consideration: that in these days no person of either sex in the slightest degree believes it; that Dr. Müllner himself does not believe it. We are not contending that fiction should become fact, or that no dramatic incident is genuine, unless it could be sworn to before a jury; but simply that fiction should not be falsehood and delirium. How shall any one in the drama, or in poetry of any sort, present a consistent philosophy of life, which is the soul and ultimate essence of all poetry, if he and every mortal know that the whole moral basis of his ideal world is a lie? And is it other than a lie that man's life is, or was, or could be, grounded on this pettifogging principle of a Fate that pursues woodcutters and cowherds with miraculous visitations, on stated days of the month? Can we, with any profit, hold the mirror up to Nature in this wise? When our mirror is no mirror, but only as it were a nursery saucepan, and that long since grown rusty?

We might add, were it of any moment in this case, that we reckon Dr. Müllner's tragic knack altogether insufficient for a still more comprehensive reason; simply for the reason that it *is* a knack, a recipe, or secret of the craft, which, could it be never so excellent, must by repeated use degenerate into a mannerism, and therefore into a nuisance. But herein lies the difference between creation and manufacture; the latter has its manipulations, its secret processes, which can be learned by apprenticeship; the former has not. For in poetry we have heard of no secret possessing the smallest effectual virtue, except this one general secret: that the poet be a man of a purer, higher, richer nature than other men; which higher nature shall itself, after earnest inquiry, have taught him the proper form for imbodying its inspirations, as indeed the imperishable beauty of these will shine, with more or less distinctness, through any form whatever.

Had Dr. Müllner any visible pretension to this last great secret, it might be a duty to dwell longer and more gravely on his minor ones, however false and poor. As he has no such pretension, it appears to us that for the present we may take our leave. To give any further analysis of his individual dramas would be an easy task, but a stupid and thankless one. A Harrison's watch, though this too is but an earthly machine, may be taken asunder with some prospect of scientific advantage; but who would spend time in screwing and unscrewing the mechanism of ten pepper-mills? Neither shall we offer any extract, as a specimen of the diction and sentiment that reigns in these dramas. We have said already that it is fair, well-ordered stage-sentiment this of his; that the diction too is good, well-scanned, grammatical diction; no fault to be found with either, except that they pretend to be poetry, and are throughout the most unadulterated prose. To exhibit this fact in extracts would be a vain undertaking. Not the few sprigs of heath, but the thousand acres of it, characterize the wilderness. Let any one who covets a trim heath-nosegay, clutch at random into Müllner's seven volumes; for ourselves, we would not deal further in that article.

Besides his dramatic labours, Dr. Müllner is known to the public as a journalist. For some considerable time, he has edited a literary newspaper of his own originating, the *Mitternacht-Blatt* (Midnight Paper); stray leaves of which we occasionally look into. In this last capacity, we are happy to observe, he shows to much more advantage; indeed, the journalistic office seems quite natural to him; and would he take any advice from us, which he will not, here were the arena in which, and not in the Fate-drama, he would exclusively continue to fence, for his bread or glory. He is not without a vein of small wit; a certain degree of drollery there is, and grinning half-risible, half-impudent; he has a fair hand at the feebler sort of lampoon: the German Joe Millers also seem familiar to him, and his skill in the riddle is respectable; so that altogether, as we said, he makes a superior figure in this line, which indeed is but despicably managed in Germany, and his *Mitternacht-Blatt* is, by several degrees, the most readable paper of its kind we meet with in that country. Not that we, in the abstract, much admire Dr. Müllner's newspaper procedure; his style is merely the common-tavern-style, familiar enough in our own periodical literature; riotous, blustering, with some tincture of blackguardism; a half-dishonest style, and smells considerably of tobacco and spirituous liquor. Neither do we find that there is the smallest fraction of valuable knowledge or opinion communicated in the Midnight Paper; indeed, except it be the knowledge and opinion that Dr. Müllner *is* a great dramatist, and that all who presume to think otherwise are insufficient members of society, we cannot charge our memory with having gathered any knowledge from it whatever. It may be, too, that Dr. Müllner is not perfectly original in his journalistic manner: we have sometimes felt as if his light were, to a certain extent, a borrowed one; a rushlight kindled at the great pitch link of our own *Blackwood's Magazine*. But on this point we cannot take upon us to decide.

One of Müllner's regular journalistic articles is the *Kriegszeitung*, or War-intelligence, of all the paper-battles, feuds, defiances, and private assassinations, chiefly dramatic, which occur in the more distracted portion of the German Literary Republic. This *Kriegszeitung* Dr. Müllner evidently writes with great gusto, in a lively braggadocia manner, especially when touching on his own exploits; yet to us, it is far the most melancholy part of the *Mitternacht-Blatt*. Alas! this is not what we search for in a German newspaper; how "Herr Sapphir, or Herr Carbuncle, or so many other Herren Dousterswivel, are all busily molesting one another! We ourselves are pacific men; make a point "to shun discrepant circles rather than seek them:" and how sad is it to hear of so many illustrious-obscure persons living in foreign parts, and hear only, what was well known without hearing, that they also are instinct with the spirit of Satan! For what is the bone that these Journalists, in Berlin and elsewere, are worrying over; what is the ultimate purpose of all this barking and snarling? Sheer love of fight, you would say; simply to make one another's life a *little* bitterer, as if Fate had not been cross enough to the happiest of them. Were there any perceptible subject of dispute, *any* doctrine to advocate, even a false one, it would be something; but so far as we can discover, whether from Sapphire and Company, or the "Nabob of Weissenfels," (our own worthy Doctor,) there is none. And is this their appointed function? Are Editors scattered over the country, and supplied with victuals and fuel, purely to bite one another? Certainly not. But these Journalists, we think, are like the Academician's colony of spiders. This French virtuoso had found that cobwebs were worth something, could even be woven into silk stockings: whereupon, he exhibits a very handsome pair of cobweb hose to the Academy, is encouraged to proceed with the manufacture, and so collects some half-bushel of spiders, and puts them down in a spacious loft, with every convenience for making silk. But will the vicious creatures spin a thread? In place of it, they take to fighting with their whole vigour, in contempt of the poor Academician's utmost exertions to part them: and end not, till there is simply one spider left living, and not a shred of cobweb woven, or thenceforth to be expected! Could the weavers of paragraphs, like these of the cobweb, fairly exterminate and silence one another, it would perhaps be a little more supportable. But an Editor is made of sterner stuff. In general cases, indeed, when the brains are out, the man will die: but it is a well known fact in Journalistics, that a man may not only live, but support wife and children by his labours, in this line, years after the brain (if there ever was any) has been completely abstracted, or reduced, by time and hard usage, into a state of dry powder. What then is to be done? Is there no end to this brawling; and will the unprofitable noise endure for ever? By way of palliative, we have sometimes imagined that a Congress of all German Editors might be appointed, by proclamation, in some central spot, say the Nürnberg Market-place, if it would hold them all: here we would humbly suggest that the whole *Journalistik* might assemble on a given day, and under the eye of proper marshals, sufficiently and satisfactorily horsewhip one another simultaneously, each his neighbour, till the very toughest had enough both of whipping and of being whipped. In this way, it seems probable, little or no injustice would be done: and each Journalist, cleared of gall, for several months, might return home in a more composed frame of mind, and betake himself with new alacrity to the real duties of his office.

But, enough! enough! The humour of these men may be infectious; it is not good for us to be here. Wandering over the Elysian fields of German Literature, not watching the gloomy discords of its Tartarus, is what we wish to be employed in. Let the iron gate again close, and shut in the pallid kingdoms from view; we gladly revisit the upper air. Not in despite towards the German nation, which we love honestly, have we spoken thus of these its Playwrights and Journalists. Alas! when we look around us at home, we feel too well that the Germans might say to us,—Neighbour, sweep thy own floor! Neither is it with any hope of bettering the existence of these three individual Poetasters, still less with the smallest shadow of wish to make it more miserable, that we have spoken. After all, there must be Playwrights, as we have said: and these are among the best of the class. So long as it pleases them to manufacture in this line, and any body of German Thebans to pay them, in *groschen* or plaudits, for their ware, let both parties persist in so doing, and fair befall them! But the duty of Foreign Reviewers is of a two-fold sort. For not only are we stationed on the coast of the country, as watchers and spials, to report whatsoever remarkable thing becomes visible in the distance; but we stand there also as a sort of Tide-waiters and Preventive-servicemen, to contend, with our utmost vigour, that no improper article be landed. These offices, it would seem, as in the material world, so also in the literary and spiritual, usually fall to the lot of aged, invalided, impoverished, or otherwise decayed persons; but this is little to the matter. As true British subjects, with ready will, though it may be, with our last strength, we are here to discharge that double duty. Movements, we observe, are making along the beach, and signals out sea-wards, as if these Klingemanns and Müllners were to be landed on our soil: but through the strength of heaven this shall not be done, till the "most thinking people" know what it *is* that is landing. For the rest, if any one wishes to import that sort of produce, and finds it nourishing for his inward man, let him do so, and welcome. Only let him understand that it is not German Literature he is swallowing, but the froth and scum of German Literature; which scum, if he will only wait, we can further promise him that he may, ere long, enjoy in the new, and perhaps cheaper, form of *sediment*. And so let every one be active for himself.

Noch ist es Tag, da rühre sich der Mann,
Die Nacht tritt ein, wo niemand wirken kann.

VOLTAIRE.*

[Foreign Review, 1829.]

Could ambition always choose its own path, and were will in human undertakings synonymous with faculty, all truly ambitious men would be men of letters. Certainly, if we examine that love of power, which enters so largely into most practical calculations, nay, which our Utilitarian friends have recognised as the sole end and origin, both motive and reward, of all earthly enterprises, animating alike the philanthropist, the conqueror, the money-changer, and the missionary, we shall find that all other arenas of ambition, compared with this rich and boundless one of Literature, meaning thereby whatever respects the promulgation of Thought, are poor, limited, and ineffectual. For dull, unreflective, merely instinctive as the ordinary man may seem, he has nevertheless, as a quite indispensable appendage, a head that in some degree considers and computes; a lamp or rushlight of understanding has been given him, which, through whatever dim, besmoked, and strangely diffractive media it may shine, is the ultimate guiding light of his whole path: and here, as well as there, now as at all times in man's history, Opinion rules the world.

Curious it is, moreover, to consider, in this respect, how different appearance is from reality, and under what singular shape and circumstances the truly most important man of any given period might be found. Could some Asmodeus, by simply waiving his arm, open asunder the meaning of the Present, even so far as the Future will disclose it, how much more marvellous a sight should we have, than that mere bodily one through the roofs of Madrid! For we know not what we are, any more than what we shall be. It is a high, solemn, almost awful thought for every individual man, that his earthly influence, which has had a commencement, will never through all ages, were he the very meanest of us, have an end! What is done is done; has already blended itself with the boundless, ever-living, ever-working Universe, and will also work there, for good or for evil, openly or secretly, throughout all time. But the life of every man is as the well-spring of a stream, whose small beginnings are indeed plain to all, but whose ulterior course and destination, as it winds through the expanses of infinite years, only the Omniscient can discern. Will it mingle with neighbouring rivulets, as a tributary; or receive them as their sovereign? Is it to be a nameless brook, and will its tiny waters, among millions of other brooks and rills, increase the current of some world's-river? Or is it to be itself a Rhine or Danaw, whose goings forth are to the uttermost lands, its flood an everlasting boundary-line on the globe itself, the bulwark and highway of whole kingdoms and continents? We know not: only in either case, we know its path is to the great ocean: its waters, were they but a handful, are *here*, and cannot be annihilated or permanently held back.

As little can we prognosticate, with any certainty, the future influences from the present aspects of an individual. How many Demagogues, Crœsuses, Conquerors fill their own age with joy or terror, with a tumult that promises to be perennial; and in the next age die away into insignificance and oblivion! These are the forests of gourds, that overtop the infant cedars and aloe-trees, but, like the Prophet's gourd, wither on the third day. What was it to the Pharaohs of Egypt, in that old era, if Jethro the Midianitish priest and grazier accepted the Hebrew outlaw as his herdsman? Yet the Pharaohs, with all their chariots of war, are buried deep in the wrecks of time; and that Moses still lives, not among his own tribe only, but in the hearts and daily business of all civilized nations. Or figure Mahomet, in his youthful years, "travelling to the horse-fairs of Syria!" Nay, to take an infinitely higher instance, who has ever forgotten those lines of Tacitus; inserted as a small, transitory, altogether trifling circumstance in the history of such a potentate as Nero? To us it is the most earnest, sad, and sternly significant passage that we know to exist in writing: *Ergo abolendo rumori Nero subdidit reos, et quæsitissimis pœnis affecit, quos per flagitia invisos, vulgus* Christianos *appellabat. Auctor nominis ejus* Christus, *qui, Tiberio imperitante, per Procuratorem Pontium Pilatum supplicio affectus erat. Repressaque in præsens exitiabilis superstitio rursus erumpebat, non modo per Judæam originem ejus mali, sed per urbem etiam, quo cuncta undique atrocia aut pudenda confluunt, celebranturque.* "So, for the quieting of this rumour,* Nero judicially charged with the crime, and punished with most studied severities, that class, hated for their general wickedness, whom the vulgar call *Christians*. The originator of that name was one *Christ*, who, in the reign of Tiberius, suffered death by sentence of the procurator, Pontius Pilate. The baneful superstition, thereby repressed for the time, again broke out, not only over Judea, the native soil of that mischief, but in the City also, where from every side all

* *Mémoires sur Voltaire, et sur ses Ouvrages, par Longchamp et Wagnière, ses Secrétaires; suivis de divers E'crits inédits de la Marquise du Châtelet, du Président Henault, &c., tous relatifs à Voltaire.* (Memoirs concerning Voltaire and his Works, by Longchamp and Wagnière, his Secretaries; with various unpublished pieces by the Marquise du Châtelet, &c., all relating to Voltaire.) 2 Tomes. Paris, 1826.

* Of his having set fire to Rome.

atrocious and abominable things collect and flourish."* Tacitus was the wisest, most penetrating man of his generation; and to such depth, and no deeper, has he seen into this transaction, the most important that has occurred or can occur in the annals of mankind.

Nor is it only to those primitive ages, when religions took their rise, and a man of pure and high mind appeared not merely as a teacher and philosopher, but as a priest and prophet, that our observation applies. The same uncertainty, in estimating present things and men, holds more or less in all times; for in all times, even in those which seem most trivial, and open to research, human society rests on inscrutably deep foundations; which he is of all others the most mistaken, who fancies he has explored to the bottom. Neither is that sequence, which we love to speak of as "a chain of causes," properly to be figured as a "chain," or line, but rather as a tissue, or superficies of innumerable lines, extending in breadth as well as in length, and with a complexity, which will foil and utterly bewilder the most assiduous computation. In fact, the wisest of us must, for by far the most part, judge like the simplest; estimate importance by mere magnitude, and expect that what strongly affects our own generation, will strongly affect those that are to follow. In this way it is that conquerors and political revolutionists come to figure as so mighty in their influences; whereas truly there is no class of persons, creating such an uproar in the world, who in the long run produce so very slight an impression on its affairs. When Tamerlane had finished building his pyramid of seventy thousand human skulls, and was seen "standing at the gate Damascus, glittering in steel, with his battle-axe on his shoulder," till his fierce hosts filed out to new victories and new carnage, the pale onlooker might have fancied that Nature was in her death-throes; for havoc and despair had taken possession of the earth, the sun of manhood seemed setting in seas of blood. Yet, it might be, on that very gala-day of Tamerlane, a little boy was playing ninepins on the streets of Mentz, whose history was more important to men than that of twenty Tamerlanes. The Tartar Khan, with his shaggy demons of the wilderness, "passed away like a whirlwind" to be forgotten for ever; and that German artisan has wrought a benefit, which is yet immeasurably expanding itself, and will continue to expand itself through all countries and through all times. What are the conquests and expeditions of the whole corporation of captains, from Walter the Pennyless to Napoleon Bonaparte, compared with these "movable types" of Johannes Faust? Truly, it is a mortifying thing for your Conqueror to reflect, how perishable is the metal which he hammers with such violence: how the kind earth will soon shroud up his bloody footprints; and all that he achieved and skilfully piled together will be but like his own "canvas city" of a camp,—this evening loud with life, to-morrow all struck and vanished, "a few earth-pits and heaps of straw!" For here, as always, it continues true, that the deepest force is the stillest; that, as in the Fable, the mild shining of the sun shall silently accomplish what the fierce blustering of the tempest has in vain essayed. Above all, it is ever to be kept in mind, that not by material, but by moral power, are men and their actions governed. How noiseless is thought! No rolling of drums, no tramp of squadrons, or immeasurable tumult of baggage-wagons, attends its movements: in what obscure and sequestered places may the head be meditating, which is one day to be crowned with more than imperial authority; for Kings and Emperors will be among its ministering servants; it will rule not over, but *in* all heads, and with these its solitary combinations of ideas, as with magic formulas bend the world to its will! The time may come, when Napoleon himself will be better known for his laws than for his battles; and the victory of Waterloo prove less momentous than the opening of the first Mechanics' Institute.

We have been led into such rather trite reflections, by these volumes of *Memoirs on Voltaire;* a man in whose history the relative importance of intellectual and physical power is again curiously evinced. This also was a private person, by birth nowise an elevated one; yet so far as present knowledge will enable us to judge, it may be said, that to abstract Voltaire and his activity from the eighteenth century, were to produce a greater difference in the existing figure of things, than the want of any other individual, up to this day, could have occasioned. Nay, with the single exception of Luther, there is, perhaps, in these modern ages, no other man of a merely intellectual character, whose influence and reputation have become so entirely European as that of Voltaire. Indeed, like the great German Reformer's, his doctrines too, almost from the first, have affected not only the belief of the thinking world, silently propagating themselves from mind to mind; but in a high degree also, the conduct of the active and political world; entering as a distinct element into some of the most fearful civil convulsions which European history has on record.

Doubtless, to his own contemporaries, to such of them at least as had any insight into the actual state of men's minds, Voltaire already appeared as a note-worthy and decidedly historical personage: yet, perhaps, not the wildest of his admirers ventured to assign him such a magnitude as he now figures in, even with his adversaries and detractors. He has grown in apparent importance, as we receded from him, as the nature of his endeavours became more and more visible in their results. For, unlike many great men, but like all great agitators, Voltaire everywhere shows himself emphatically as the man of his century: uniting in his own person whatever spiritual accomplishments were most valued by that age; at the same time, with no depth to discern its ulterior tendencies, still less with any magnanimity to attempt withstanding these, his greatness and his littleness alike fitted him to produce an immediate effect; for he leads whither the multi-

* Tacit. Annal. xv. 44.

tude was of itself dimly minded to run, and keeps the van not less by skill in commanding, than by cunning in obeying. Besides, now that we look on the matter from some distance, the efforts of a thousand coadjutors and disciples, nay, a series of mighty political vicissitudes, in the production of which these efforts had but a subsidiary share, have all come, naturally in such a case, to appear as if exclusively his work; so that he rises before us as the paragon and epitome of a whole spiritual period, now almost passed away, yet remarkable in itself, and more than ever interesting to us, who seem to stand, as it were, on the confines of a new and better one.

Nay, had we forgotten that ours is the "Age of the Press," when he who runs may not only read, but furnish us with reading; and simply counted the books, and scattered leaves, thick as the autumnal in Vallombrosa, that have been written and printed concerning this man, we might almost fancy him the most important person, not of the eighteenth century, but of all the centuries from Noah's flood downwards. We have *Lives* of Voltaire by friend and by foe: Condorcet, Duvernet, Lepan, have each given us a whole; portions, documents, and all manner of authentic or spurious contributions have been supplied by innumerable hands; of which we mention only the labours of his various secretaries: Collini's, published some twenty years ago, and now these two massive octavos from Longchamp and Wagnière. To say nothing of the Baron de Grimm's Collections, unparalleled in more than one respect; or of the six-and-thirty volumes of scurrilous eavesdropping, long since printed under the title of *Mémoires de Bachaumont;* or of the daily and hourly attacks and defences that appeared separately in his lifetime, and all the judicial pieces, whether in the style of apotheosis or of excommunication, that have seen the light since then; a mass of fugitive writings, the very diamond edition of which might fill whole libraries. The peculiar talent of the French in all narrative, at least in all anecdotic, departments, rendering most of these works extremely readable, still further favoured their circulation, both at home and abroad: so that now, in most countries, Voltaire has been read of and talked of, till his name and life have grown familiar like those of a village acquaintance. In England, at least, where for almost a century the study of foreign literature has, we may say, confined itself to that of the French, with a slight intermixture from the elder Italians, Voltaire's writings and such writings as treated of him, were little likely to want readers. We suppose, there is no literary era, not even any domestic one, concerning which Englishmen in general have such information, at least have gathered so many anecdotes and opinions, as concerning this of Voltaire. Nor have native additions to the stock been wanting, and these of a due variety in purport and kind: maledictions, expostulations, and dreadful death-scenes, painted like Spanish *Sanbenitos*, by weak well-meaning persons of the hostile class; eulogies, generally of the gayer sort, by open or secret friends: all this has been long and extensively carried on among us. There is even an English *Life of Voltaire;** nay, we remember to have seen portions of his writings cited, *in terrorum*, and with criticisms, in some pamphlet, "by a country gentleman," either on the Education of the People, or else on the question of Preserving the Game.

With the "Age of the Press," and such manifestations of it on this subject, we are far from quarrelling. We have read great part of these thousand-and-first "Memoirs on Voltaire," by Longchamp and Wagnière, not without satisfaction; and can cheerfully look forward to still other "Memoirs" following in their train. Nothing can be more in the course of nature than the wish to satisfy one's self with knowledge of all sorts about any distinguished person, especially of our own era; the true study of his character, his spiritual individuality, and peculiar manner of existence, is full of instruction for all mankind: even that of his looks, sayings, habitudes, and indifferent actions, were not the records of them generally lies, is rather to be commended; nay, are not such lies themselves, when they keep within bounds, and the subject of them has been dead for some time, equal to snipe-shooting, or Colburn-Novels, at least little inferior in the great art of getting done with life, or, as it is technically called, killing time? For our own part, we say,—would that every Johnson in the world had his veridical Boswell, or leash of Boswells! We could then tolerate his Hawkins also, though not veridical. With regard to Voltaire, in particular, it seems to us not only innocent but profitable, that the whole truth regarding him should be well understood. Surely, the biography of such a man, who, to say no more of him, spent his best efforts, and as many still think, successfully, in assaulting the Christian religion, must be a matter of considerable import; what he did, and what he could not do; how he did it, or attempted it, that is, with what degree of strength, clearness, especially with what moral intents, what theories and feelings on man and man's life, are questions that will bear some discussing. To Voltaire, individually, for the last fifty-one years, the discussion has been indifferent enough; and to us it is a discussion not on one remarkable person only, and chiefly for the curious or studious, but involving considerations of highest moment to all men, and inquiries which the utmost compass of our philosophy will be unable to embrace.

Here, accordingly, we are about to offer some further observations on this *quæstio vexata;* not without hope that the reader may accept them in good part. Doubtless, when we look at the whole bearings of the matter, there seems little prospect of any unanimity respecting it, either now, or within a calculable period: it is probable that many will continue, for a long time, to speak of this "uni-

* "By Frank Hall Standish, Esq." (London, 1821): a work, which we can recommend only to such as feel themselves in extreme want of information on this subject, and, except in their own language, unable to acquire any. It is written very badly, though with sincerity, and not without considerable indications of talent; to all appearance, by a minor, many of whose statements and opinions (for he seems an inquiring, honest-hearted, rather decisive character) must have begun to astonish even himself, several years ago.

versal genius," this "apostle of Reason," and "father of sound Philosophy;" and many again of this "monster of impiety," this "sophist," and "atheist," and "ape-demon;" or, like the late Dr. Clarke of Cambridge, dismiss him more briefly with information that he is "a driveller:" neither is it essential that these two parties should, on the spur of the instant, reconcile themselves herein. Nevertheless, truth is better than error, were it only "on Hannibal's vinegar." It may be expected that men's opinions concerning Voltaire, which is of some moment, and concerning Voltairism, which is of almost boundless moment, will, if they cannot meet, gradually at every new comparison approach towards meeting; and what is still more desirable, towards meeting somewhere nearer the truth than they actually stand.

With honest wishes to promote such approximation, there is one condition, which, above all others, in this inquiry, we must beg the reader to impose on himself: the duty of fairness towards Voltaire, of Tolerance towards him, as towards all men. This, truly, is a duty, which we have the happiness to hear daily inculcated; yet which, it has been well said, no mortal is at bottom disposed to practise. Nevertheless, if we really desire to understand the truth on any subject, not merely, as is much more common, to confirm our already existing opinions, and gratify this and the other pitiful claim of vanity or malice in respect of it, tolerance may be regarded as the most indispensable of all prerequisites; the condition, indeed, by which alone any real progress in the question becomes possible. In respect of our fellow-men, and all real insight into their characters, this is especially true. No character, we may affirm, was ever rightly understood, till it had first been regarded with a certain feeling, not of tolerance only, but of sympathy. For here, more than in any other case, it is verified that the heart sees farther than the head. Let us be sure, our enemy is *not* that hateful being we are too apt to paint him. His vices and basenesses lie combined in far other order before his own mind, than before ours; and under colours which palliate them, nay, perhaps, exhibit them as virtues. Were he the wretch of our imagining, his life would be a burden to himself; for it is not by bread alone that the basest mortal lives; a certain approval of conscience is equally essential even to physical existence; is the fine all-pervading cement by which that wondrous union, a Self, is held together. Since the man, therefore, is not in Bedlam, and has not shot or hanged himself, let us take comfort, and conclude that he is one of two things: either a vicious *dog*, in man's guise, to be muzzled, and mourned over, and greatly marvelled at; or a real *man*, and, consequently, not without moral worth, which is to be enlightened, and so far approved of. But to judge rightly of his character, we must learn to look at it, not less with his eyes, than with our own; we must learn to pity him, to see him as a fellow-creature, in a word, to love him, or his real spiritual nature will ever be mistaken by us. In interpreting Voltaire, accordingly, it will be needful to bear some things carefully in mind, and to keep many other things as carefully in abeyance. Let us forget that *our* opinions were ever assailed by him, or ever defended; that *we* have to thank him, or upbraid him, for pain or for pleasure; let us forget that we are Deists, or Millenarians, Bishops, or Radical Reformers, and remember only that we are men. This is a European subject, or there never was one; and must, if we would in the least comprehend it, be looked at neither from the parish belfry, nor any Peterloo Platform; but, if possible, from some natural and infinitely higher point of vision.

It is a remarkable fact, that throughout the last fifty years of his life, Voltaire was seldom or never named, even by his detractors, without the epithet "great" being appended to him; so that, had the syllables suited such a junction, as they did in the happier case of *Charle-Magne*, we might almost have expected that, not *Voltaire*, but *Voltaire-ce-grand-homme* would be his designation with posterity. However, posterity is much more stinted in its allowances on that score; and a multitude of things remain to be adjusted, and questions of very dubious issue to be gone into, before such coronation titles can be conceded with any permanence. The million, even the wiser part of them, are apt to lose their discretion, when "tumultuously assembled;" for a small object, near at hand, may subtend a large angle; and often a Pennenden Heath has been mistaken for a Field of Runnymede; whereby the couplet on that immortal Dalhousie proves to be the emblem of many a man's real fortune with the public:

> And thou, Dalhousie, the great God of war,
> Lieutenant-Colonel to the Earl of Mar;

the latter end corresponding poorly with the beginning. To ascertain what was the true significance of Voltaire's history, both as respects himself and the world; what was his specific character and value as a man; what has been the character and value of his influence on society, of his appearance as an active agent in the culture of Europe; all this leads us into much deeper investigations; on the settlement of which, however, the whole business turns.

To our own view, we confess, on looking at Voltaire's life, the chief quality that shows itself is one for which *adroitness* seems the fitter name. Greatness implies several conditions, the existence of which, in his case, it might be difficult to demonstrate; but of his claim to this other praise there can be no disputing. Whatever be his aims, high or low, just or the contrary, he is at all times, and to the utmost degree, expert in pursuing them. It is to be observed, moreover, that his aims in general were not of a simple sort, and the attainment of them easy: few literary men have had a course so diversified with vicissitudes as Voltaire's. His life is not spent in a corner, like that of a studious recluse, but on the open theatre of the world; in an age full of commotion, when society is rending itself asunder, Superstition already armed for deadly battle against Unbelief; in which battle he himself plays a distinguished part. From his earliest years, we find him in perpetual conmunication with the higher personages of his time, often with the highest: it is in circles of authority, of reputation, at lowest, of fashion and rank, that he lives and works. Ninon de l'Enclos leaves the boy a legacy to buy books; he is still young, when he can say of his supper companions, "We are all Princes or Poets." In after life, he exhibits himself in company or correspondence with all manner of principalities and powers, from Queen Caroline of England to the Empress Catherine of Russia, from Pope Benedict to Frederic the Great. Meanwhile, shifting from side to side of Europe, hiding in the country, or living sumptuously in capital cities, he quits not his pen, with which, as with some enchanter's rod, more potent than any king's sceptre, he turns and winds the mighty machine of European Opinion; approves himself, as his schoolmaster had predicted, the *Coryphée du Déisme;* and, not content with this elevation, strives, and nowise ineffectually, to unite with it a poetical, historical, philosophic, and even scientific pre-eminence. Nay, we may add, a pecuniary one; for he speculates in the funds, diligently solicits pensions and promotions, trades to America, is long a regular victualling-contractor for armies; and thus, by one means and another, independently of literature, which would never yield much money, raises his income from 800 francs a-year to more than centuple that sum.* And now, having, besides all this commercial and economical business, written some thirty quartos, the most popular that were ever written, he returns after long exile to his native city, to be welcomed there almost as a religious idol; and closes a life, prosperous alike in the building of country-seats, and the composition of *Henriades* and *Philosophical Dictionaries,* by the most appropriate demise; by drowning, as it were, in an ocean of applause, so that as he lived for fame, he may be said to have died of it.

Such various, complete success, granted only to a small portion of men in any age of the world, presupposes, at least, with every allowance for good fortune, an almost unrivalled expertness of management. There must have been a great talent of some kind at work here: a cause proportionate to the effect. It is wonderful, truly, to observe with what perfect skill Voltaire steers his course through so many conflicting circumstances: how he weathers this Cape Horn, darts lightly through that Mahlstrom; always either sinks his enemy, or shuns him; here waters, and careens, and traffics with the rich savages; there lies land-locked till the hurricane is overblown; and so, in spite of all billows, and sea-monsters, and hostile fleets, finishes his long Manilla voyage, with streamers flying, and deck piled with ingots! To say nothing of his literary character, of which this same dexterous address will also be found to be a main feature, let us glance only at the general aspect of his conduct, as manifested both in his writings and actions. By turns, and ever at the right season, he is imperious and obsequious; now shoots abroad, from the mountain tops, Hyperion-like, his keen, innumerable shafts; anon, when danger is advancing, flies to obscure nooks; or, if taken in the fact, swears it was but in sport, and that he is the peaceablest of men. He bends to occasion; can, to a certain extent, blow hot or blow cold; and never attempts force, where cunning will serve his turn. The beagles of the Hierarchy and of the Monarchy, proverbially quick of scent, and sharp of tooth, are out in quest of him; but this is a lion-fox which cannot be captured. By wiles and a thousand doublings, he utterly distracts his pursuers; he can burrow in the earth, and all trace of him is gone.* With a strange system of anonymity and publicity, of denial and assertion, of Mystification in all senses, has Voltaire surrounded himself. He can raise no standing armies for his defence, yet he too is a "European power," and not undefended; an invisible, impregnable, though hitherto unrecognised bulwark, that of Public Opinion, defends him. With great art, he maintains this stronghold; though ever and anon sallying out from it, far beyond the permitted limits. But he has his coat of darkness, and his shoes of swiftness, like that other Killer of Giants. We find Voltaire a supple courtier, or a sharp satirist; he can talk blasphemy, and build churches, according to the signs of the times. Frederic the Great is not too high for his diplomacy, nor the poor Printer of his *Zadig* too low;† he manages the Cardinal Fleuri, and the Curé of St. Sulpice; and laughs in his sleeve at all the world. We should pronounce him to be one of the best politicians on record; as we have said, the *adroitest* of all literary men.

At the same time, Voltaire's worst enemies, it seems to us, will not deny that he had naturally a keen sense for rectitude, indeed, for all virtue: the utmost vivacity of temperament characterizes him; his quick susceptibility for every form of beauty is moral as well as intellectual. Nor was his practice without indubitable and highly creditable proofs of this. To the help-needing he was at all times a ready benefactor: many were the hungry adventurers who profited of his bounty, and then bit the hand that had fed them. If we enumerate his generous acts, from the case of the Abbé Desfontaines down to that of the widow Calas, and the Serfs of Saint Claude, we shall find that few private men have had so wide a circle of charity, and have watched over it so well. Should it be objected that love of reputation entered largely into these proceedings, Voltaire can afford a handsome deduction on that head: should the uncharitable even calculate that love of reputation was the sole motive, we can only remind them that love of *such* reputation is itself the effect of a social, humane disposition; and wish, as an immense

* See Tome ii. p. 328 of these *Mémoires.*

* Of one such "taking to cover," we have a curious and rather ridiculous account in this work, by Longchamp. It was with the Duchess du Maine that he sought shelter, and on a very slight occasion: nevertheless he had to lie perdue, for two months, at the Castle of Sceaux; and, with closed windows, and burning candles in daylight, compose *Zadig, Babouc, Memnon,* &c., for his amusement.

† See in Longchamp (pp. 154—163) how by natural legerdemain, a knave may be caught, and the *change rendu à des imprimeurs infidèles.*

improvement, that all men were animated with it. Voltaire was not without his experience of human baseness; but he still had a fellow-feeling for human sufferings; and delighted, were it only as an honest luxury, to relieve them. His attachments seem remarkably constant and lasting: even such sots as Thiriot, whom nothing but habit could have endeared to him, he continues, and after repeated injuries, to treat and regard as friends. To his equals we do not observe him envious, at least not palpably and despicably so; though this, we should add, might be in him, who was from the first so paramountly popular, no such hard attainment. Against Montesquieu, perhaps against him alone, he cannot help entertaining a small secret grudge; yet ever in public he does him the amplest justice: *l'Arlequin Grotius* of the fire-side becomes, on all grave occasions, the author of the *Esprit des Loix.* Neither to his enemies, and even betrayers, is Voltaire implacable or meanly vindictive: the instant of their submission is also the instant of his forgiveness; their hostility itself provokes only casual sallies from him; his heart is too kindly, indeed too light, to cherish any rancour, any continuation of revenge. If he has not the virtue to forgive, he is seldom without the prudence to forget: if, in his life-long contentions, he cannot treat his opponents with any magnanimity, he seldom, or perhaps never once, treats them quite basely; seldom or never with that absolute unfairness which the law of retaliation might so often have seemed to justify. We would say that, if not heroic, he is at all times a perfectly civilized man; which, considering that his war was with exasperated theologians, and a "war to the knife," on their part, may be looked upon as rather a surprising circumstance. He exhibits many minor virtues, a due appreciation of the highest; and fewer faults than, in his situation, might have been expected, and perhaps pardoned.

All this is well, and may fit out a highly expert and much esteemed man of business, in the widest sense of that term; but is still far from constituting a "great character." In fact, there is one deficiency in Voltaire's original structure, which, it appears to us, must be quite fatal to such claims for him: we mean his inborn levity of nature, his entire want of Earnestness. Voltaire was by birth a Mocker, and light *Pococurante*: which natural disposition his way of life confirmed into a predominant, indeed all-pervading habit. Far be it from us to say, that solemnity is an essential of greatness; that no great man can have other than a rigid vinegar aspect of countenance, never to be thawed or warmed by billows of mirth! There are things in this world to be laughed at, as well as things to be admired; and his is no complete mind, that cannot give to each sort its due. Nevertheless, contempt is a dangerous element to sport in; a deadly one, if we habitually live in it. How, indeed, to take the lowest view of this matter, shall a man accomplish great enterprises,—enduring all toil, resisting temptations, laying aside every weight,—unless he zealously love what he pursues? The faculty of love, of admiration, is to be regarded as the sign and the measure of high souls: unwisely directed, it leads to many evils; but without it, there cannot be any good. Ridicule, on the other hand, is indeed a faculty much prized by its possessors; yet, intrinsically, it is a small faculty; we may say, the smallest of all faculties that other men are at the pains to repay with any esteem. It is directly opposed to Thought, to Knowledge, properly so called; its nourishment and essence is Denial, which hovers only on the surface, while Knowledge dwells far below. Moreover, it is by nature selfish and morally trivial; it cherishes nothing but our Vanity, which may in general be left safely enough to shift for itself. Little "discourse of reason," in any sense, is implied in Ridicule: a scoffing man is in no lofty mood, for the time; shows more of the imp than of the angel. This too when his scoffing is what we call just, and has some foundation on truth: while again the laughter of fools, that vain sound, said in Scripture to resemble the "crackling of thorns under the pot,"—which they cannot heat, and only soil and begrime,—must be regarded, in these latter times, as a very serious addition to the sum of human wretchedness; and may not always, when considering the Increase of Crime in the Metropolis, escape the vigilance of Parliament.

We have, oftener than once, endeavoured to attach some meaning to that aphorism, vulgarly imputed to Shaftesbury, which, however, we can find nowhere in his works, that *ridicule is the test of truth.* But of all chimeras, that ever advanced themselves in the shape of philosophical doctrines, this is to us the most formless and purely inconceivable. Did or could the unassisted human faculties ever understand it, much more believe it? Surely, so far as the common mind can discern, laughter seems to depend not less on the laugher than on the laughee; and who gave laughers a patent to be always just, and always omniscient? If the philosophers of Nootka Sound were pleased to laugh at the manœuvres of Cook's seamen, did that render these manœuvres useless, and were the seamen to stand idle, or take to leather canoes, till the laughter abated? Let a discerning public judge.

But, leaving these questions for the present, we may observe at least that all great men have been careful to subordinate this talent or habit of ridicule; nay, in the ages which we consider the greatest, most of the arts that contribute to it have been thought disgraceful for freemen, and confined to the exercise of slaves. With Voltaire, however, there is no such subordination visible: by nature, or by practice, mockery has grown to be the irresistible bias of his disposition; so that for him, in all matters, the first question is not what is true, but what is false; not what is to be loved, and held fast, and earnestly laid to heart, but what is to be contemned, and derided, and sportfully cast out of doors. Here truly he earns abundant triumph as an image-breaker, but pockets little real wealth. Vanity, with its adjuncts, as we have said, finds rich solacement; but for aught better, there is not much. Reverence, the highest feeling that man's nature is capa ble of, the crown of his whole moral manhood, and precious, like fine gold, were it in the rudest forms, he seems not to understand, or have heard of, even by credible tradition. The glory of knowing and believing is all but a stranger to him; only with that of questioning and qualifying is he familiar. Accordingly, he sees but a little way into Nature: the mighty All, in its beauty, and infinite mysterious grandeur, humbling the small *Me* into nothingness, has never even for moments been revealed to him; only this and that other atom of it, and the differences and discrepancies of these two, has he looked into, and noted down. His theory of the world, his picture of man and man's life, is little; for a Poet and Philosopher, even pitiful. Examine it, in its highest developments, you find it an altogether vulgar picture; simply a reflex, from more or fewer mirrors of Self and the poor interests of Self. "The Divine Idea, that which lies at the bottom of Appearance," was never more invisible to any man. He reads History not with the eye of a devout Seer, or even of a Critic; but through a pair of mere anti-catholic spectacles. It is not a mighty drama, enacted on the theatre of Infinitude, with Suns for lamps, and Eternity as a back-ground; whose author is God, and whose purport and thousand-fold moral lead us up to the "dark with excess of light" of the Throne of God; but a poor wearisome debating-club dispute, spun through ten centuries, between the *Encyclopédie* and the *Sorbonne*. Wisdom or folly, nobleness or baseness, are merely superstitious or unbelieving: God's Universe is a larger Patrimony of St. Peter, from which it were well and pleasant to hunt the Pope.

In this way, Voltaire's nature, which was originally vehement rather than deep, came in its maturity, in spite of all his wonderful gifts, to be positively shallow. We find no heroism of character in him, from first to last; nay, there is not, that we know of, one great thought, in all his six-and-thirty quartos. The high worth implanted in him by Nature, and still often manifested in his conduct, does not shine there like a light, but like a coruscation. The enthusiasm, proper to such a mind, visits him; but it has no abiding virtue in his thought, no local habitation and no name. There is in him a rapidity, but at the same time a pettiness; a certain violence, and fitful abruptness, which takes from him all dignity. Of his *emportemens* and tragi-comical explosions, a thousand anecdotes are on record; neither is he, in these cases, a terrific volcano, but a mere bundle of rockets. He is nigh shooting poor Dorn, the Frankfort constable; actually fires a pistol, into the lobby, at him; and this, three days after that melancholy business of the "*Œuvre de Poésie du Roi mon Maitre*" had been finally adjusted. A bookseller, that, with the natural instinct of fallen mankind, overcharges him, receives from this Philosopher, by way of payment at sight, a slap on the face. Poor Longchamp, with considerable tact, and a praiseworthy air of second-table respectability, details various scenes of this kind: how Voltaire dashed away his combs, and maltreated his wig, and otherwise fiercely comported himself, the very first morning: how once, having a keenness of appetite, sharpened by walking, and a diet of weak tea, he became uncommonly anxious for supper; and Clairaut and Madame du Chatelet, sunk in algebraic calculations, twice promised to come down, but still kept the dishes cooling, and the Philosopher at last desperately battered open their locked door with his foot; exclaiming "*Vous êtes donc de concert pour me faire mourir?*"—And yet Voltaire had a true kindness of heart; all his domestics and dependents loved him, and continued with him. He has many elements of goodness, but floating loosely; nothing is combined in steadfast union. It is true, he presents in general a surface of smoothness, of cultured regularity; yet, under it, there is not the silent rock-bound strength of a World, but the wild tumults of a Chaos are ever bursting through. He is a man of power, but not of beneficent authority; we fear, but cannot reverence him; we feel him to be stronger, not higher.

Much of this spiritual short-coming and perversion might be due to natural defect: but much of it also is due to the age into which he was cast. It was an age of discord and division; the approach of a grand crisis in human affairs. Already we discern in it all the elements of the French Revolution; and wonder, so easily do we forget how entangled and hidden the meaning of the present generally is to us, that all men did not foresee the comings on of that fearful convulsion. On the one hand, a high all-attempting activity of Intellect: the most peremptory spirit of inquiry abroad on every subject; things human and things divine alike cited without misgivings before the same boastful tribunal of so-called Reason, which means here a merely argumentative Logic; the strong in mind excluded from his regular influence in the state, and deeply conscious of that injury. On the other hand, a privileged few, strong in the subjection of the many, yet in itself weak; a piebald, and for most part altogether decrepit battalion, of Clergy, of purblind Nobility, or rather of Courtiers, for as yet the Nobility is mostly on the other side: these cannot fight with Logic, and the day of Persecution is well-nigh done. The whole force of law, indeed, is still in their hands; but the far deeper force, which alone gives efficacy to law, is hourly passing away from them. Hope animates one side; fear the other; and the battle will be fierce and desperate. For there is wit without wisdom on the part of the self-styled Philosophers; feebleness with exasperation on the part of their opponents; pride enough on all hands, but little magnanimity; perhaps nowhere any pure love of truth, only everywhere the purest, most ardent love of self. In such a state of things, there lay abundant principles of discord: these two influences hung like fast-gathering electric clouds, as yet on opposite sides of the horizon, but with a malignity of aspect, which boded, whenever they might meet, a sky of fire and blackness, thunderbolts to waste the earth, and the sun and stars, though but for a season, to be blotted out from the heavens. For there is no conducting medium to unite softly these hostile elements;

there is no true virtue, no true wisdom, on the one side or on the other. Never perhaps, was there an epoch, in the history of the world, when universal corruption called so loudly for reform; and they who undertook that task were men intrinsically so worthless. Not by Gracchi, but by Catilines; not by Luthers, but by Aretines, was Europe to be renovated. The task has been a long and bloody one; and is still far from done.

In this condition of affairs, what side such a man as Voltaire was to take could not be doubtful. Whether he ought to have taken either side; whether he should not rather have stationed himself in the middle; the partisan of neither, perhaps hated by both; acknowledging, and forwarding, and striving to reconcile, what truth was in each; and preaching forth a far deeper truth, which, if his own century had neglected it, had persecuted it, future centuries would have recognised as priceless: all this was another question. Of no man, however gifted, can we require what he has not to give: but Voltaire called himself Philosopher, nay, *the* Philosopher. And such has often, indeed generally, been the fate of great men, and Lovers of Wisdom: their own age and country have treated them as of no account; in the great Corn-Exchange of the world, their pearls have seemed but spoiled barley, and been ignominiously rejected. Weak in adherents, strong only in their faith, in their indestructible consciousness of worth and well-doing, they have silently, or in words, appealed to coming ages, when their own ear would indeed be shut to the voice of love, and of hatred, but the Truth that had dwelt in them would speak with a voice audible to all. Bacon left his works to future generations, when some centuries should have elapsed. "Is it much for me," said Kepler, in his isolation, and extreme need, "that men should accept my discovery? If the Almighty waited six thousand years for one to see what He had made, I may surely wait two hundred, for one to understand what I have seen?" All this, and more, is implied in love of wisdom, in genuine seeking of truth; the noblest function that can be appointed for a man, but requiring also the noblest man to fulfil it.

With Voltaire, however, there is no symptom, perhaps there was no conception, of such nobleness; the high call for which, indeed, in the existing state of things, his intellect may have had as little the force to discern, as his heart had the force to obey. He follows a simpler course. Heedless of remoter issues, he adopts the cause of his own party; of that class with whom he lived, and was most anxious to stand well; he enlists in their ranks, not without hopes that he may one day rise to be their general. A resolution perfectly accordant with his prior habits, and temper of mind; and from which his whole subsequent procedure, and moral aspect as a man naturally enough evolves itself. Not that we would say, Voltaire was a mere prize-fighter; one of "Heaven's Swiss," contending for a cause which he only half, or not at all approved of. Far from it. Doubtless he loved truth, doubtless he partially felt himself to be advocating truth; nay, we know not that he has ever yet, in a single instance, been convicted of wilfully perverting his belief; of uttering, in all his controversies, one deliberate falsehood. Nor should this negative praise seem an altogether slight one, for greatly were it to be wished that even the best of his better-intentioned opponents had always deserved the like. Nevertheless, his love of truth is not that deep, infinite love, which beseems a Philosopher; which many ages have been fortunate enough to witness; nay, of which his own age had still some examples. It is a far inferior love, we should say, to that of poor Jean Jacques, half-sage, half-maniac as he was; it is more a prudent calculation than a passion. Voltaire loves Truth, but chiefly of the triumphant sort; we have no instance of his fighting for a quite discrowned and outcast Truth; it is chiefly when she walks abroad, in distress, it may be, but still with queen-like insignia, and knighthoods and renown are to be earned in her battles, that he defends her, that he charges gallantly against the Cades and Tylers. Nay, at all times, belief itself seems, with him, to be less the product of Meditation than of Argument. His first question with regard to any doctrine, perhaps his final test of its worth and genuineness, is: can others be convinced of this? Can I truck it, in the market, for power? "To such questioners," it has been said, "Truth, who buys not, and sells not, goes on her way, and makes no answer."

In fact, if we inquire into Voltaire's ruling motive, we shall find that it was at bottom but a vulgar one: ambition, the desire of ruling, by such means as he had, over other men. He acknowledges no higher divinity than Public Opinion; for whatever he asserts or performs, the number of votes is the measure of strength and value. Yet let us be just to him; let us admit that he, in some degree, estimates his votes, as well as counts them. If love of fame, which, especially for such a man, we can only call another modification of Vanity, is always his ruling passion, he has a certain taste in gratifying it. His vanity, which cannot be extinguished, is ever skilfully concealed; even his just claims are never boisterously insisted on; throughout his whole life he shows no single feature of the quack. Nevertheless, even in the height of his glory, he has a strange sensitiveness to the judgment of the world: could he have contrived a Dionysius' Ear, in the Rue Traversière, we should have found him watching at it, night and day. Let but any little evil-disposed Abbé, any Fréron, or Piron,

Pauvre Piron, qui ne fut jamais rien,
Pas même Académicien,

write a libel or epigram on him, what a fluster he is in! We grant he forbore much, in these cases; manfully consumed his own spleen, and sometimes long held his peace: but it was his part to have always done so. Why should such a man ruffle himself with the spite of exceeding small persons? Why not let these poor devils write; why should they not earn a dishonest penny, at his expense, if they had no readier way? But Voltaire cannot part with his "voices," his "most sweet voices;"

for they are his gods; take these, and what has he left? Accordingly, in literature and morals, in all his comings and goings, we find him striving, with a religious care, to sail strictly with the wind. In Art, the Parisian *Parterre* is his court of last appeal: he consults the *Café de Procope*, on his wisdom or his folly, as if it were a true Delphic Oracle. The following adventure belongs to his fifty-fourth year, when his fame might long have seemed abundantly established. We translate from the Sieur Longchamp's thin, half-roguish, mildly obsequious, most lackey-like Narrative:

"Judges could appreciate the merits of *Sémiramis*, which has continued on the stage, and always been seen there with pleasure. Every one knows how the two principal parts in this piece contributed to the celebrity of two great tragedians, Mademoiselle Dumèsnil, and M. le Kain. The enemies of M. de Voltaire renewed their attempts in the subsequent representations; but it only the better confirmed his triumph. Piron, to console himself for the defeat of his party, had recourse to his usual remedy; pelting the piece with some paltry epigrams, which did it no harm.

"Nevertheless, M. de Voltaire, who always loved to correct his works, and perfect them, became desirous to learn, more especially and at first hand, what good or ill the public were saying of his Tragedy; and it appeared to him that he could nowhere learn it better than in the *Café de Procope*, which was also called the *Antre* (cavern) *de Procope*, because it was very dark, even in full day, and ill-lighted in the evenings; and because you often saw there a set of lank, sallow poets, who had somewhat the air of apparitions. In this Café, which fronts the *Comédie Francaise*, had been held, for more than sixty years, the tribunal of those self-called *Aristarchs*, who fancied they could pass sentence without appeal, on plays, authors, and actors. M. de Voltaire wished to compeer there, but in disguise, and altogether *incognito*. It was on coming out from the playhouse that the judges usually proceeded thither, to open what they called their great sessions. On the second night of *Sémiramis*, he borrowed a clergyman's clothes; dressed himself in cassock and long clock: black stockings, girdle, bands, breviary itself; nothing was forgotten. He clapt on a large peruke, unpowdered, very ill combed, which covered more than the half of his cheeks, and left nothing to be seen but the end of a long nose. The peruke was surmounted by a large three-cornered hat, corners half bruised in. In this equipment, then, the author of *Sémiramis* proceeded on foot to the *Café de Procope*, where he squatted himself in a corner, and waiting for the end of the play, called for a *bavaroise*, a small roll of bread, and the gazette. It was not long till those familiars of the *Parterre* and tenants of the *Café* stept in. They instantly began discussing the new Tragedy. Its partisans and its adversaries pleaded their cause, with warmth; each giving his reasons. Impartial persons also spoke their sentiment; and repeated some fine verses of the piece. During all this time, M. de Voltaire, with spectacles on nose, head stooping over the gazette which he pretended to be reading, was listening to the debate: profiting by reasonable observations, suffering much to hear very absurd ones, and not answer them, which irritated him. Thus, during an hour and a half, had he the courage and patience to hear *Sémiramis* talked of and babbled of, without speaking a word. At last, all these pretended judges of the fame of authors having gone their ways, without converting one another, M. de Voltaire also went off; took a coach in the Rue Mazarine, and returned home about eleven o'clock. Though I knew of his disguise, I confess I was struck and almost frightened to see him accoutred so. I took him for a spectre, or shade of Ninus, that was appearing to me: or at least, for one of those ancient Irish debaters, arrived at the end of their career, after wearing themselves out in school-syllogisms. I helped him to doff all that apparatus, which I carried next morning to its true owner,—a doctor of the Sarbonne."

This stroke of art, which cannot in any wise pass for sublime, might have its uses and rational purpose in one case, and only in one: if *Sémiramis* was meant to be a popular show, that was to live or die by its first impression on the idle multitude; which accordingly we must infer to have been its real, at least its chief destination. In any other case, we cannot but consider this Haroun-Alraschid visit to the *Café de Procope* as questionable, and altogether inadequate. If *Sémiramis* was a Poem, a living Creation, won from the empyrean by the silent power, and long-continued Promethean toil of its author, what could the *Café de Procope* know of it, what could all Paris know of it, "on the second night?" Had it been a Milton's *Paradise Lost* they might have despised it till after the fiftieth year! True, the object of the Poet is, and must be, to "instruct by pleasing," yet not by pleasing this man and that man; only by pleasing *man*, by speaking to the pure nature of man, can any real "instruction," in this sense, be conveyed. Vain does it seem to search for a judgment of this kind, in the largest *Café*, in the largest Kingdom, "on the second night." The deep, clear consciousness of one mind comes infinitely nearer it, than the loud outcry of a million that have no such consciousness; whose "talk," or whose "babble," but distracts the listener; and to most genuine Poets has, from of old, been in a great measure indifferent. For the multitude of voices is no authority; a thousand voices may not, strictly examined, amount to one vote. Mankind in this world are divided into flocks, and follow their several bell-wethers. Now, it is well known, let the bell-wether rush through any gap, the rest rush after him, were it into bottomless quagmires. Nay, so conscientious are sheep in this particular, as a quaint naturalist and moralist has noted, "if you hold a stick upon the wether, so that he is forced to vault in his passage, the whole flock will do the like, when the stick is withdrawn; and the thousandth sheep shall be seen vaulting impetuously over air, as the first did over an otherwise impassable barrier!" A further peculiarity, which, in consulting Acts of Parliament, and other authentic records, not only as regards "Catholic Disabilities," but many other matters, you may find curiously verified in the human species also!—On the whole, we must consider this excursion to *Procope's* literary Cavern as illustrating Voltaire in rather pleasant style; but nowise much to his honour. Fame seems a far too high, if not the highest object with him; nay, sometimes even popularity is clutched at; we see no heavenly polar-star in this voyage of his; but only the guidance of a proverbially uncertain *wind.*

Voltaire reproachfully says of St. Louis, that "he ought to have been above his age;" but, in his own case, we can find few symptoms of such heroic superiority. The same perpetual appeal to his contemporaries, the same intense regard to reputation, as he viewed it, prescribes for him both his enterprises and his manner of conducting them. His aim is to please the more enlightened, at least the politer part of the world; and he offers them simply what they most wish for, be it in theatrical shows for their pastime, or in skeptical doctrines for their edification. For this latter purpose, Ridicule is the weapon he selects, and it suits him well. This was not the age of deep thoughts; no Duc de Richelieu, no Prince Conti, no Frederic the Great would have listened to such: only sportful contempt, and a thin conversational logic will avail. There may be wool-quilts, which the lath-sword of Harlequin will pierce, when the club of Hercules has rebounded from them in vain. As little was this an age for high virtues; no heroism, in any form, is required, or even acknowledged; but only, in all forms, a certain *bienséance.* To this rule, also, Voltaire readily conforms; indeed, he finds no small advantage in it. For a lax public morality not only allows him the indulgence of many a little private vice, and brings him in this and the other windfall of *menus plaisirs,* but opens him the readiest resource in many enterprises of danger. Of all men, Voltaire has the least disposition to increase the Army of Martyrs. No testimony will he seal with his blood; scarcely any will he so much as sign with ink. His obnoxious doctrines, as we have remarked, he publishes under a thousand concealments; with underplots and wheels within wheels; so that his whole track is in darkness, only his works see the light. No Proteus is so nimble, or assumes so many shapes; if, by rare chance, caught sleeping, he whisks through the smallest hole, and is out of sight, while the noose is getting ready. Let his judges take him to task, he will shuffle and evade; if directly questioned, he will even lie. In regard to this last point, the Marquis de Condorcet has set up a defence for him, which has, at least, the merit of being frank enough.

"The necessity of lying in order to disavow any work," says he, "is an extremity equally repugnant to conscience and nobleness of character: but the crime lies with those unjust men, who render such disavowal necessary to the safety of him whom they force to it. If you have made a crime of what is not one; if, by absurd or by arbitrary laws, you have infringed the natural right, which all men have, not only to form an opinion, but to render it public; then you deserve to lose the right which every man has of hearing the truth from the mouth of another; a right, which is the sole basis of that rigorous obligation, not to lie. If it is not permitted to deceive, the reason is, that to deceive any one, is to do him a wrong, or expose yourself to do him one; but a wrong supposes a right; and no one has the right of seeking to secure himself the means of committing an injustice."—*Vie de Voltaire,* p. 32.

It is strange, how scientific discoveries do maintain themselves: here, quite in other hands, and in an altogether different dialect, we have the old Catholic doctrine, if it ever was more than a Jesuitic one, "that faith need not be kept with heretics." Truth, it appears, is too precious an article for our enemies; is fit only for friends, for those who will pay us if we tell it them. It may be observed, however, that, granting Condorcet's premises, this doctrine also must be granted, as indeed is usual with that sharp-sighted writer. If the doing of right depends on the receiving of it; if our fellow-men, in this world, are not persons, but mere things, that for services bestowed will return services,—steam-engines that will manufacture calico, if we put in coals and water,—then, doubtless, the calico ceasing, our coals and water may also rationally cease; the questioner threatening to injure us for the truth, we may rationally tell him lies. But if, on the other hand, our fellow-man is no steam-engine, but a man; united with us, and with all men, and with the Maker of all men, in sacred, mysterious, indissoluble bonds, in an all-embracing Love, that encircles alike the seraph and the glow-worm; then will our duties to him rest on quite another basis than this very humble one of *quid pro quo;* and the Marquis de Condorcet's conclusion will be false; and might, in its practical extensions, be infinitely pernicious.

Such principles and habits, too lightly adopted by Voltaire, acted, as it seems to us, with hostile effect on his moral nature, not originally of the noblest sort, but which, under other influences, might have attained to far greater nobleness. As it is, we see in him simply a Man of the World, such as Paris and the eighteenth century produced and approved of: a polite, attractive, most cultivated, but essentially self-interested man; not without highly amiable qualities; indeed, with a general disposition which we could have accepted without disappointment in a mere Man of the World, but must find very defective, sometimes altogether out of place, in a Poet and Philosopher. Above this character of a Parisian "honourable man," he seldom or never rises; nay, sometimes we find him hovering on the very lowest boundaries of it, or, perhaps, even fairly below it. We shall nowise accuse him of excessive regard for money, of any wish to shine by the influence of mere wealth: let those commercial speculations, including even the victualing-contracts, pass for laudable prudence, for love of independence, and of the power to do good. But what are we to make of that hunting after pensions, and even a ter mere titles? There is an assiduity disp' ıyed here, which sometimes almost verges owards sneaking. Well might it provoke tae scorn of Alfieri; for there is nothing better than the spirit of "a French plebeian," apparent in it. Much, we know, very much should be allowed for difference of national manners, which in general mainly determine the meaning of such things: nevertheless, to our insular feelings, that famous *Trajan est-il-content?* especially when we consider who the Trajan was, will always remain an unfortunate saying. The more so, as Trajan himself turned his back on it, without answer; declining, indeed, through life, to listen to the voice of this charmer, or disturb his own "*âme paisible*," for one moment, though with the best philosopher in Nature. Nay, Pompadour herself was applied to; and even some considerable progress made, by that underground passage, had not an envious hand too soon and fatally intervened. D'Alembert says, there are two things that can reach the top of a pyramid, the eagle and the reptile. Apparently, Voltaire wished to combine both methods; and he had, with one of them, but indifferent success.

The truth is, we are trying Voltaire by too high a standard; comparing him with an ideal which he himself never strove after, perhaps never seriously aimed at. He is no great Man, but only a great *Persifleur;* a man for whom life, and all that pertains to it, has, at best, but a despicable meaning; who meets its difficulties not with earnest force, but with gay agility; and is found always at the top, less by power in swimming, than by lightness in floating. Take him in this character, forgetting that any other was ever ascribed to him, and we find that he enacted it almost to perfection. Never man better understood the whole secret of *Persiflage;* meaning, thereby, not only the external faculty of polite contempt, but that art of general inward contempt, by which a man of this sort endeavours to subject the circumstances of his Destiny to his Volition, and be, what is the instinctive effort of all men, though in the midst of material Necessity, morally Free. Voltaire's latent derision is as light, copious, and all-pervading as the derision which he utters. Nor is this so simple an attainment as we might fancy; a certain kind and degree of Stoicism, or approach to Stoicism, is necessary for the completed *Persifleur;* as for moral, or even practical completion, in any other way. The most indifferent-minded man is not by nature indifferent to his own pain and pleasure: this is an indifference, which he must by some method study to acquire, or acquire the show of; and which, it is fair to say, Voltaire manifests in a rather respectable degree. Without murmuring, he has reconciled himself to most things: the human lot, in this lower world, seems a strange business, yet, on the whole, with more of the farce in it, than of the tragedy; to him, it is nowise heart-rending, that this Planet of ours should be sent sailing through Space, like a miserable, aimless Ship-of-Fools, and he himself be a fool among the rest, and only a very little wiser than they. He does not, like Bolingbroke, "patronise Providence," though such sayings, as *Si Dieu n'existait pas il faudrait l'inventer*, seem now and then to indicate a tendency of that sort: but, at all events, he never openly levies war against Heaven; well knowing that the time spent in frantic malediction, directed *thither*, might be spent otherwise with more profit. There is, truly, no *Werterism* in him, either in its bad or its good sense. If he sees no unspeakable majesty in heaven and earth, neither does he see any unsufferable horror there. His view of the world is a cool, gently scornful, altogether prosaic one: his sublimest Apocalypse of Nature lies in the microscope and telescope; the Earth is a place for producing corn; the Starry Heavens are admirable as a nautical time-keeper. Yet, like a prudent man, he has adjusted himself to his condition, such as it is: he does not chant any *Miserere* over human life, calculating that no charitable dole, but only laughter, would be the reward of such an enterprise; does not hang or drown himself, clearly understanding that death of itself will soon save him that trouble. Affliction, it is true, has not for him any precious jewel in its head; on the contrary, it is an unmixed nuisance; yet, happily, not one to be howled over, so much as one to be speedily removed out of sight: if he does not learn from it Humility, and the sublime lesson of Resignation, neither does it teach him hardheartedness, and sickly discontent; but he bounds lightly over it, leaving both the jewel and the toad at a safe distance behind him.

Nor was Voltaire's history without perplexities enough to keep this principle in exercise; to try whether in life, as in literature, the *ridiculum* were really better than the *acer*. We must own, that on no occasion does it altogether fail him; never does he seem perfectly at a nonplus; no adventure is so hideous, that he cannot, in the long run, find some means to laugh at it, and forget it. Take, for instance, that last ill-omened visit of his to Frederic the Great. This was, probably, the most mortifying incident in Voltaire's whole life: an open experiment, in the sight of all Europe, to ascertain whether French Philosophy had virtue enough in it to found any friendly union, in such circumstances, even between its great master and his most illustrious disciple; and an experiment which answered in the negative, as was natural enough; for Vanity is of a devisive not of a uniting nature; and between the King of Letters and the King of Armies there existed no other tie. They should have kept up an interchange of flattery, from afar: gravitating towards one another like celestial luminaries, if they reckoned themselves such; yet always with a due centrifugal force; for if either shot madly from his sphere, nothing but collision, and concussion, and mutual recoil, could be the consequence. On the whole, we must pity Frederic, environed with that cluster of Philosophers: doubtless he meant rather well; yet the French at Rosbach, with guns in their hands, were but a small matter, compared with these French in Sans-Souci. Maupertuis sits sullen, monosyllabic; gloomy like the bear of his own arctic zone: Voltaire is the mad piper that will make him dance to tunes and amuse the people. In this roaly circle, with its parasites and bashaws, what heats and jealousies must there not have been; what secret heart-burnings, smooth-faced malice, plottings, counterplottings, and laurel-water pharmacy, in all its branches, before the ring of etiquette fairly burst asunder, and the establishment, so to speak, exploded! Yet over all these distressing matters Voltaire has thrown a soft veil of gayety: he remembers neither Doctor Akakia, nor Doctor Akakia's patron, with any animosity; but merely as actors in the grand farce of life along with him, a new scene of which has now commenced, quite displacing the other from the stage. The arrest at Frankfort, indeed, is a sour morsel; but this, too, he swallows, with an effort. Frederic, as we are given to understand, had these whims by kind; was, indeed, a wonderful scion from such a stock; for what could equal the avarice, malice, and rabid snappishness of old Frederic William, the father?

"He had a minister at the Hague, named Luicius," says the wit: "this Luicius was, of all royal ministers extant, the worst paid. The poor man, with a view to warm himself, had a few trees cut down, in the garden of Honslardik, then belonging to the House of Prussia; immediately thereafter he received despatches from the king, his master, keeping back a year of his salary. Luicius, in despair, cut his throat with the only razor he had (*avec le seul rasoir qu'il eût*:) an old lackey came to his assistance, and unfortunately saved his life. At an after period, I myself saw his Excellency at the Hague, and gave him an alms at the gate of that Palace called *La Vieille Cour*, which belongs to the King of Prussia, and where this unhappy Ambassador had lived twelve years."

With the *Roi-Philosophe* himself, Voltaire in a little while recommences correspondence; and to all appearance, proceeds quietly in his office of "buckwasher," that is, of verse-corrector to his Majesty, as if nothing whatever had happened.

Again, what human pen can describe the troubles this unfortunate Philosopher had with his women? A gadding feather-brained, capricious, old-coquettish, embittered, and embittering set of wantons from the earliest to the last! Widow Denis, for example, that disobedient niece, whom he rescued from furnished lodgings and spare diet, into pomp and plenty, how did she pester the last stage of his existence, for twenty-four years long! Blind to the peace and roses of Ferney; ever hankering and fretting after Parisian display; not without flirtation, though advanced in life; losing money at play, and purloining wherewith to make it good; scolding his servants, quarrelling with his secretaries, so that the too-indulgent uncle must turn off his beloved Collini, nay, almost be run through the body by him, for her sake! The good Wagnière, who succeeded this fiery Italian in the secretaryship, and loved Voltaire with a most creditable affection, cannot, though a simple, humble, and quite philanthropic man, speak of Madame Denis without visible overflowings of gall. He openly accuses her of hastening her uncle's death by her importunate stratagems to keep him in Paris, where was her heaven. Indeed it is clear that, his goods and chattels once made sure of, her chief care was that so fiery a patient might die soon enough; or, at best, according to her own confession, "how she was to get him buried." We have known superannuated grooms, nay effete saddle-horses, regarded with more real sympathy in their home, than was the best of uncles by the worst of nieces. Had not this surprising old man retained the sharpest judgment, and the gayest, easiest temper, his last days, and last years, must have been a continued scene of violence and tribulation.

Little better, worse in several respects, though at a time when he could better endure it, was the far-famed Marquise du Chatelet. Many a tempestuous day and wakeful night had he with that scientific and too-fascinating shrew. She speculated in mathematics and metaphysics; but was an adept also in far, very far different acquirements. Setting aside its whole criminality, which, indeed, perhaps went for little there, this literay amour wears but a mixed aspect; short sun-gleams, with long tropical tornadoes; touches of guitar-music, soon followed by Lisbon earthquakes. Marmontel, we remember, speaks of *knives* being used, at least brandished, and for quite other purposes than carving. Madame la Marquise was no saint, in any sense; but rather a Socrates' spouse, who would keep patience, and the whole philosophy of gayety, in constant practice. Like Queen Elizabeth, if she had the talents of a man, she had more than the caprices of a woman.

We shall take only one item, and that a small one, in this mountain of misery: her strange habits and methods of locomotion. She is perpetually travelling: a peaceful philosopher is lugged over the world, to Cirey, to Lunéville, to that *pied à terre* in Paris; resistance avails not; here, as in so many other cases, *il faut se ranger*. Sometimes, precisely on the eve of such departure, her domestics, exasperated by hunger and ill usage, will strike work, in a body; and a new set has to be collected at an hour's warning. Then Madame has been known to keep the postilion cracking and *sacre*-ing at the gate, from dawn till dewy eve, simply because she was playing cards, and the games went against her. But figure a lean and vivid-tempered philosopher starting from Paris at last; under cloud of night, for it is always at night; during hard frost; in a huge lumbering coach, or rather wagon, compared with which, indeed, the generality of modern wagons were a luxurious conveyance. With four starved, and perhaps spavined hacks, he slowly sets forth, "under a mountain of bandboxes:" at his side sits the wandering virago; in front of him, a serving-maid, with additional bandboxes "*et divers effets de sa maîtresse*." At the next stage, the postilions have to be beat up; they come out swearing. Cloaks and fur-pelisses avail little against the January-cold; "time and hours" are, once more, the only hope: but lo, at the tenth mile, this Tyburn-coach breaks down! One many-voiced discordant wail shrieks through the solitude, making night hideous,—

but in vain; the axle-tree has given way, the vehicle has overset, and marchionesses, chambermaids, bandboxes, and philosophers, are weltering in inextricable Chaos.

"The carriage was in the stage next Nangis, about half-way to that town, when the hind axle-tree broke, and it tumbled on the road, to M. de Voltaire's side: Madame du Chatelet, and her maid, fell above him, with all the bundles and bandboxes, for these were not tied to the front, but only piled up on both hands of the maid; and so observing the laws of equilibrium and gravitation of bodies, they rushed towards the corner where M. de Voltaire lay squeezed together. Under so many burdens, which half-suffocated him, he kept shouting bitterly (*poussait des cris aigus*); but it was impossible to change place; all had to remain as it was, till the two lackeys, one of whom was hurt by the fall, could come up, with the postilion, to disencumber the vehicle: they first drew out all the luggage, next the women, then M. de Voltaire. Nothing could be got out except by the top, that is, by the coach-door, which now opened upwards: one of the lackeys and a postilion clambering aloft, and fixing themselves on the body of the vehicle, drew them up, as from a well; seizing the first limb that came to hand, whether arm, or leg: and then passed them down to the two stationed below, who set them finally on the ground."—Vol. ii. p. 166.

What would Dr. Kitchener, with his *Traveller's Oracle*, have said to all this? For there is snow on the ground; and four peasants must be roused from a village half a league off, before that accursed vehicle can so much as be lifted from its beam ends! Vain is it for Longchamp, far in advance, sheltered in an hospitable though half-dismantled *chateau*, to pluck pigeons and be in haste to roast them: they will never, never be eaten to supper, scarcely to breakfast next morning!—Nor is it now only, but several times, that this unhappy axle-tree plays them foul; nay once, beggared by Madame's gambling, they have not cash to pay for mending it, and the smith, though they are in keenest flight, almost for their lives, will not trust them.

We imagine that these are trying things for any philosopher. Of the thousand other more private and perennial grievances; of certain discoveries and explanations, especially, which it still seems surprising that human philosophy could have tolerated, we make no mention; indeed, with regard to the latter, few earthly considerations could tempt a Reviewer of sensibility to mention them in this place.

The Marquise du Chatelet, and her husband, have been much wondered at in England: the calm magnanimity with which M. le Marquis conforms to the custom of the country, to the wishes of his helpmate, and leaves her, he himself meanwhile fighting, or at least drilling, for his King, to range over Space, in quest of loves and lovers; his friendly discretion, in this particular; no less so, his blithe benignant gullibility, the instant a *contretems de famille* renders his countenance needful,—have had all justice done them among us. His lady, too, is a wonder, offers no mean study to psychologists: she is a fair experiment to try how far that Delicacy, which we reckon innate in females, is only incidental and the product of fashion; how far a woman, not merely immodest, but without the slightest fig-leaf of common decency remaining, with the whole character, in short, of a *male* debauchee, may still have any moral worth as a woman. We ourselves have wondered a little over both these parties; and over the goal towards which so strange a "progress of society" might be tending. But still more wonderful, not without a shade of the sublime, has appeared to us the cheerful thraldom of this maltreated philosopher; and with what exhaustless patience, not being wedded, he endured all these forced-marches, whims, irascibilities, delinquencies, and thousand-fold unreasons; braving "the battle and the breeze," on that wild Bay of Biscay, for such a period. Fifteen long years, and was not mad, or a suicide at the end of them! But the like fate, it would seem, though worthy D'Israeli has omitted to enumerate it in his *Calamities of Authors*, is not unknown in literature. Pope also had his Mrs. Martha Blount; and, in the midst of that warfare with united Duncedom, his daily tale of Egyptian bricks to bake. Let us pity the lot of genius, in this sublunary sphere!

Every one knows the earthly termination of Madame la Marquise; and how, by a strange, almost satirical *Nemesis*, she was taken in her own nets, and her worst sin became her final punishment. To no purpose was the unparalleled credulity of M. le Marquis; to no purpose, the amplest toleration, and even helpful knavery of M. de Voltaire: "*les assiduités de M. de Saint-Lambert*," and the unimaginable consultations to which they gave rise at Cirey, were frightfully parodied in the end. The last scene was at Lunéville, in the peaceable court of King Stanislaus.

"Seeing that the aromatic-vinegar did no good, we tried to recover her from that sudden lethargy by rubbing her feet, and striking in the palms of her hands; but it was of no use: she had ceased to be. The maid was sent off to Madame de Boufflers' apartment, to inform the company that Madame du Chatelet was worse. Instantly they all rose from the supper-table: M. du Chatelet, M. de Voltaire, and the other guests rushed into the room. So soon as they understood the truth, there was a deep consternation; to tears, to cries, succeeded a mournful silence. The husband was led away, the other individuals went out successively, expressing the keenest sorrow. M. de Voltaire and M. de Saint-Lambert remained the last by the bedside, from which they could not be drawn away. At length, the former, absorbed in deep grief, left the room, and with difficulty reached the main door of the Castle, not knowing whither he went. Arrived there, he fell down at the foot of the outer stairs, and near the box of a sentry, where his head came on the pavement. His lackey, who was following, seeing him fall and struggle on the ground, ran forward and tried to lift him. At this moment, M. de Saint-Lambert, retiring by the same way, also arrived; and observing M. de Voltaire in that situation, hastened to assist the lackey. No sooner was M. de Voltaire on his feet, than opening his eyes, dimmed with tears, and recognising M. de Saint-Lambert, he said to him, with sobs and the most pathetic accent: 'Ah, my friend, it is you that have killed her!' Then, all on a sudden, as if he were starting from a deep sleep, he exclaimed in the tone of reproach and despair: *'Eh! mon Dieu! Monsieur, de quoi vous avisiez-vous de lui faire un enfant?'* They parted thereupon, without adding a single word; and retired to their several apartments, overwhelmed and almost annihilated by the excess of their sorrow."—Vol. ii. p. 250.

Among all threnetical discourses on record, this last, between men overwhelmed and almost annihilated by the excess of their sorrow, has probably an unexampled character. Some days afterwards, the first paroxysm of "reproach and despair" being somewhat assuaged, the sorrowing widower, not the glad legal one, composed this quatrain:

L'univers a perdu la sublime Emilie.
Elle aima les plaisirs, les arts, la vérité:
Les dieux, en lui donnant leur âme et leur génie,
N'avaient gardé pour eux que l'immortalité.

After which, reflecting, perhaps, that with this sublime Emilie, so meritoriously singular in loving pleasure, "his happiness had been chiefly on paper," he, like the bereaved Universe, consoled himself, and went on his way.

Woman, it has been sufficiently demonstrated, was given to man as a benefit, and for mutual support; a precious ornament and staff whereupon to lean in many trying situations: but to Voltaire she proved, so unlucky was he in this matter, little else than a broken reed, which only ran into his hand. We confess that looking over the manifold trials of this poor philosopher with the softer, or as he may have reckoned it, the harder sex,—from that Dutchwoman who published his juvenile letters, to the Niece Denis, who as good as killed him with racketing,—we see, in this one province, very great scope for almost all the cardinal virtues. And these internal convulsions add an incessant series of controversies and persecutions, political, religious, literary, from without; and we have a life quite rent asunder, horrent with asperities and chasms, where even a stout traveller might have faltered. Over all which Chamouni-needles and Staubbach-Falls, the great *Persifleur* skims along in this his little poetical air-ship, more softly than if he travelled the smoothest of merely prosaic roads.

Leaving out of view the worth or worthlessness of such a temper of mind, we are bound, in all seriousness, to say, both that it seems to have been Voltaire's highest conception of moral excellence, and that he has pursued and realized it with no small success. One great praise therefore he deserves,—that of unity with himself; that of *having* an aim, and steadfastly endeavouring after it, nay, as we have found, of attaining it; for his ideal Voltaire seems, to an unusual degree, manifested, made practically apparent, in the real one. There can be no doubt that this attainment of *Persifleur*, in the wide sense we here give it, was of all others the most admired and sought after in Voltaire's age and country; nay, in our own age and country, we have still innumerable admirers of it, and unwearied seekers after it, on every hand of us: nevertheless, we cannot but believe that its acme is past; that the best sense of our generation has already weighed its significance, and found it wanting. Voltaire himself, it seems to us, were he alive at this day, would find other tasks than that of mockery, especially of mockery in that style: it is not by Derision and Denial, but by far deeper, more earnest, diviner means that aught truly great has been effected for mankind; that the fabric of man's life has been reared, through long centuries, to its present height. If we admit that this chief of *Persifleurs* had a steady, conscious aim in life, the still higher praise of having had a right or noble aim cannot be conceded him without many limitations, and may, plausibly enough, be altogether denied.

At the same time, let it not be forgotten, that amid all these blighting influences, Voltaire maintains a certain indestructible humanity of nature; a soul never deaf to the cry of wretchedness; never utterly blind to the light of truth, beauty, goodness. It is even, in some measure, poetically interesting to observe this fine contradiction in him: the heart acting without directions from the head, or perhaps against its directions; the man virtuous, as it were, in spite of himself. For at all events, it will be granted that, as a private man, his existence was beneficial, not hurtful, to his fellow-men: the Calases, the Sirvens, and so many orphans and outcasts whom he cherished and protected, ought to cover a multitude of sins. It was his own sentiment, and, to all appearance, a sincere one:

J'ai fait un peu de bien; c'est mon meilleur ouvrage.

Perhaps there are few men, with such principles and such temptations as his were, that could have led such a life; few that could have done his work, and come through it with cleaner hands. If we call him the greatest of all *Persifleurs*, let us add that, morally speaking also, he is the best: if he excels all men in universality, sincerity, polished clearness of mockery, he perhaps combines with it as much worth of heart as, in any man, that habit can admit of.

It is now wellnigh time that we should quit this part of our subject: nevertheless, in seeking to form some picture of Voltaire's practical life, and the character, outward as well as inward, of his appearance in society, our readers will not grudge us a few glances at the last and most striking scene he enacted there. To our view, that final visit to Paris has a strange half-frivolous, half-fateful aspect; there is, as it were, a sort of dramatic justice in this catastrophe, that he, who had all his life hungered and thirsted after public favour, should at length die by excess of it; should find the door of his Heaven-on-earth unexpectedly thrown wide open, and enter there, only to be, as he himself said, "smothered under roses." Had Paris any suitable theogony or theology, as Rome and Athens had, this might almost be reckoned, as those ancients accounted of death by lightning, a sacred death, a death from the gods; from their many-headed god, POPULARITY. In the benignant quietude of Ferney, Voltaire had lived long, and, as his friends calculated, might still have lived long; but a series of trifling causes lured him to Paris, and in three months he is no more. At all hours of his history, he might have said with Alexander: "O Athenians, what toil do I undergo to please you;" and the last pleasure, his Athenians demand of him, is that he would die for them.

Considered with reference to the world at large, this journey is further remarkable. It is the most splendid triumph of that nature recorded in these ages; the loudest and showiest homage ever paid to what we moderns call Literature; to a man that had merely thought, and published his thoughts. Much false tumult, no doubt, there was in it; yet also a certain deeper significance. It is interesting to see how universal and eternal in man is love of wisdom; how the highest and the lowest, how supercilious princes, and rude peasants, and all men must alike show honour to Wisdom, or the appearance of Wisdom; nay, properly speaking, can show honour to nothing else. For it is not in the power of all Xerxes's hosts to bend one thought of our proud heart: these "may destroy the case of Anaxarchus; himself they cannot reach;" only to spiritual worth can the spirit do reverence; only in a soul deeper and better than ours can we see any heavenly mystery, and in humbling ourselves feel ourselves exalted. That the so ebullient enthusiasm of the French was in this case perfectly well directed, we cannot undertake to say; yet we rejoice to see and know that such a principle exists perennially in man's inmost bosom; that there is no heart so sunk and stupified, none so withered and pampered, but the felt presence of a nobler heart will inspire it and lead it captive.

Few royal progresses, few Roman triumphs, have equalled this long triumph of Voltaire. On his journey, at Bourg-en-Bresse, "he was recognised," says Wagnière, "while the horses were changing, and in a few moments the whole town crowded about the carriage; so that he was forced to lock himself for some time in a room of the inn." The Maitre-de-poste ordered his postilion to yoke better horses, and said to him with a broad oath: "*Va bon train, crève mes chevaux, je m' en f—; tu mènes M. de Voltaire.*" At Dijon, there were persons of distinction that wished even to dress themselves as waiters, that they might serve him at supper, and see him by this stratagem.

"At the barrier of Paris," continues Wagnière, "the officers asked if we had nothing with us contrary to the King's regulations: "On my word, gentlemen," (*Ma foi, Messieurs,*) replied M. de Voltaire, "I believe there is nothing contraband here except myself." I alighted from the carriage, that the inspector might more readily examine it. One of the guards said to his comrade: *C'est pardieu! M. de Voltaire.* He plucked at the coat of the person who was searching, and repeated the same words, looking fixedly at me. I could not help laughing; then all gazing with the greatest astonishment mingled with respect, begged M. de Voltaire to pass on whither he pleased."—Vol. i. p. 121.

Intelligence soon circulated over Paris; scarcely could the arrival of Kien-Long, or the Grand Lama of Thibet, have excited greater ferment. Poor Longchamp, demitted or rather dismissed from Voltaire's service, eight-and-twenty years before, and now, as a retired map-dealer (having resigned in favour of his son) living quietly "*dans un petit logement à part,*" a fine smooth, garrulous old man,—heard the news next morning in his remote *logement*, in the Estrapade; and instantly huddled on his clothes, though he had not been out for two days, to go and see what truth was in it.

"Several persons of my acquaintance, whom I met, told me that they had heard the same. I went purposely to the *Café Procope*, where this news formed the subject of conversation among several politicians, or men of letters, who talked of it with warmth. To assure myself still further, I walked thence towards the *Quai des Théatins*, where he had alighted the night before, and, as was said, taken up his lodging in a mansion near the church. Coming out from the Rue de la Seine, I saw afar off, a great number of people gathered on the Quai, not far from the Pont-Royal. Approaching nearer, I observed that this crowd was collected in front of the Marquis de Villette's Hotel, at the corner of the Rue de Beaune. I inquired what the matter was. The people answered me, that M. de Voltaire was in that house; and they were waiting to see him when he came out. They were not sure, however, whether he would come out that day; for it was natural to think that an old man of eighty-four might need a day or two of rest. From that moment, I no longer doubted the arrival of M. de Voltaire in Paris."—Vol. ii. p. 353.

By dint of address, Longchamp, in process of time, contrived to see his old master; had an interview of ten minutes; was for falling at his feet; and wept, with sad presentiments, at parting. Ten such minutes were a great matter; for Voltaire had his levees, and couchees, more crowded than those of any Emperor; princes and peers thronged his antechamber; and when he went abroad, his carriage was as the nucleus of a comet, whose train extended over whole districts of the city. He himself, says Wagnière, expressed dissatisfaction at much of this. Nevertheless, there were some plaudits, which, as he confessed, went to his heart. Condorcet mentions that once a person in the crowd inquiring who this great man was, a poor woman answered, "*C'est sauveur des Calas.*" Of a quite different sort was the tribute paid him by a quack, in the Place Louis XV., haranguing a mixed multitude on the art of juggling with cards; "*Here* gentlemen," said he, "is a trick I learned at Ferney, from that great man who makes so much noise among you, that famous M. de Voltaire, the master of us all!" In fact, mere gaping curiosity, and even ridicule was abroad as well as real enthusiasm. The clergy too were recoiling into ominous groups; already some Jesuitic drums eccelesiastic had beat to arms.

Figuring the lean, tottering, lonely old man in the midst of all this, how he looks into it, clear and alert, though no longer strong and calm, we feel drawn towards him by some tie of affection, of kindly sympathy. Longchamp says, he appeared "extremely worn, though still in the possession of all his senses, and with a very firm voice." The following little sketch, by a hostile journalist of the day, has fixed itself deeply with us:—

"M. de Voltaire appeared in full dress, on Tuesday, for the first time since his arrival in Paris. He had on a red coat lined with ermine; a large peruke, in the fashion of Louis XIV., black, unpowdered; and in which his withered figure was so buried that you saw only his two eyes shining like carbuncles. His head was surmounted by a square red cap in the form of a crown, which seemed only laid on. He had, in his hand, a small nibbed cane; and the public of Paris, not accustomed to see him in this accoutrement, laughed a good deal. This personage, singular in all, wishes doubtless to have nothing in common with ordinary men."—Vol. ii. p. 466.

This head—this wondrous microcosm in the *Grande peruque à la Louis XIV.*—was so soon to be distenanted of all its cunning gifts; these eyes, shining like carbuncles, were so soon to be closed in long night!—We must now give the coronation ceremony, of which the reader may have heard so much: borrowing from this same skeptical hand, which, however, is vouched for by Wagnière; as, indeed, La Harpe's more heroical narrative of that occurrence is well known, and hardly differs from the following, except in style:—

"On Monday, M. de Voltaire, resolving to enjoy the triumph which had been so long promised him, mounted his carriage, that azure-coloured vehicle, bespangled with gold stars, which a wag called the chariot of the empyrean; and so repaired to the Académie Française, which that day had a special meeting. Twenty-two members were present. None of the prelates, abbés, or other ecclesiastics, who belong to it, would attend, or take part in these singular deliberations. The sole exceptions were the Abbés de Boismont and Milot; the one a court rake-hell (*roué*), with nothing but the guise of his profession, the other a varlet (*cuistre*), having no favour to look for, either from the Court or the Church.

"The Académie went out to meet M. de Voltaire: he was led to the director's seat, which that office-bearer and the meeting invited him to accept. His portrait had been hung up above it. The company, without drawing lots, as is the custom, proceeded to work, and named him, by acclamation, Director for the April quarter. The old man, once set a going, was about to talk a great deal; but they told him, that they valued his health too much to hear him,—that they would reduce him to silence. M. d'Alembert accordingly occupied the session, by reading his *Eloge de Despreaux*, which had already been communicated on a public occasion, and where he had inserted various flattering things for the present visiter.

"M. de Voltaire then signified a wish to visit the Secretary of the Académie, whose apartments are above. With this gentleman he stayed some time; and at last set out for the Comédie Française. The court of the Louvre, vast as it is, was full of people waiting for him. So soon as his notable vehicle came in sight, the cry arose, *Le Voilà!* The Savoyards, the apple-women, all the rabble of the quarter, had assembled there: and the acclamations, *Vive Voltaire!* resounded as if they would never end. The Marquis de Villette, who had arrived before, came to hand him out of his carriage, where the Procureur Clos was seated beside him: both these gave him their arms, and could scarcely extricate him from the press. On his entering the playhouse, a crowd of more elegance, and seized with true enthusiasm for genius, surrounded him: the ladies, above all, threw themselves in his way, and stopped it, the better to look at him; some were seen squeezing forward to touch his clothes; some plucking hair from his fur. M. le Duc de Chartres, not caring to advance too near, showed, though at a distance, no less curiosity than others.

"The saint, or rather the god, of the evening, was to occupy the box belonging to the Gentlemen of the Bedchamber,* opposite that of the Counte d'Artois. Madame Denis and Madame de Villette were already there; and the pit was in convulsions of joy, awaiting the moment when the poet should appear. There was no end till he placed himself on the front seat, beside the ladies. Then rose a cry: *La Couronne!* and Brizard, the actor, came and put the garland on his head. "Ah, Heaven! will you kill me then?" (*Ah, Dieu! vous voulez donc me faire mourir!*) cried M. de Voltaire, weeping with joy, and resisting this honour. He took the crown in his hand, and presented it to *Belle-et-bonne*:† she withstood; and the Prince de Beauvau, seizing the laurel, replaced it on the head of our Sophocles, who could refuse no longer.

"The piece (*Irène*) was played, and with more applause than usual, though scarcely with enough to correspond to this triumph of its author. Meanwhile the players were in straits as to what they should do; and during their deliberations the tragedy ended; the curtain fell, and the tumult of the people was extreme, till it rose again, disclosing a show like that of the *Centénaire*. M. de Voltaire's bust, which had been placed shortly before in the *foyer* (green-room) of the Comédie Française, had been brought upon the stage, and elevated on a pedestal; the whole body of comedians stood round it in a semicircle, with palms and garlands in their hands: there was a crown already on the bust. The pealing of musical flourishes, of drums, of trumpets, had announced the ceremony; and Madame Vestris held in her hand a paper, which was soon understood to contain verses, lately composed by the Marquis de Saint-Marc. She recited them with an emphasis proportioned to the extravagance of the scene. They ran as follows:—

---

* He himself, as is perhaps too well known, was one.

† The Marquise de Villette, a foster-child of his.

Aux yeux de Paris enchanté,
Reçois en ce jour un hommage,
Que confirmera d'âge en âge
La sévère postérité!
Non tu n'as pas besoin d'atteindre au noir rivage
Pour jouir des honneurs de l'immortalité:
VOLTAIRE, *reçois la couronne*
Que l'on vient de te présenter;
Il est beau de la mériter,
*Quand c'est la France qui la donne!**

"This was encored: the actress recited it again, Next, each of them went forward and laid his garland round the bust. Mademoiselle Fanier, in a fanatical ecstasy, kissed it, and all the others imitated her.

"This long ceremony, accompanied with infinite *vivats*, being over, the curtain again dropped; and when it rose for *Nanine*, one of M. de Voltaire's comedies, his bust was seen on the right-hand side of the stage, where it remained during the whole play.

"M. le Comte d'Artois did not choose to show himself too openly; but being informed, according to his orders, as soon as M. de Voltaire appeared in the theatre, he had gone thither incognito; and it is thought that the old man, once when he went out for a moment, had the honour of a short interview with his Royal Highness.

"*Nanine* finished, comes a new hurly-burly,—a new trial for the modesty of our philosopher! He had got into his carriage, but the people would not let him go; they threw themselves on the horses, they kissed them: some young poets even cried to unyoke these animals, and draw the modern Apollo home with their own arms; unhappily, there were not enthusiasts enough to volunteer this service, and he at last got leave to depart, not without *vivats*, which he may have heard on the Pont-Royal, and even in his own house. . . .

"M. de Voltaire, on reaching home, wept anew; and modestly protested that if he had known the people were to play so many follies, he would not have gone."—Vol. ii.

On all these wonderful proceedings we shall leave our readers to their own reflections; remarking only, that this happened on the 30th of March, (1778,) and on the 30th of May, about the same hour, the object of such extraordinary adulation was in the article of death; the hearse already prepared to receive his remains, for which even a grave had to be stolen. "He expired," says Wagnière, "about a quarter past eleven at night, with the most perfect tranquillity, after having suffered the cruellest pains, in consequence of those fatal drugs, which his own imprudence, and especially that of the persons who should have looked to it, made him swallow. Ten minutes before his last breath, he took the hand of Morand, his valet-de-chambre, who was watching by him, pressed it and said *Adieu, mon cher Morand, je me meurs*, (Adieu, my dear Morand, I am gone.) These are the last words uttered by M. de Voltaire."†

We have still to consider this man in his specially intellectual capacity, which, as with every man of letters, is to be regarded as the clearest, and, to all practical intents, the most important aspect of him. Voltaire's intellectual endowment and acquirement, his talent or genius as a literary man, lies opened to us in a series of Writings, unexampled, as we believe, in two respects; their extent, and their diversity. Perhaps there is no writer, not a mere compiler, but writing from his own invention or elaboration, who has left so many volumes behind him; and if to the merely arithmetical, we add a critical estimate, the singularity is still greater; for these volumes are not written without an appearance of due care and preparation; perhaps there is not one altogether feeble and confused treatise, nay, one feeble and confused sentence, to be found in them. As to variety, again, they range nearly over all human subjects; from Theology down to Domestic Economy; from the Familiar Letter to the Political History; from the Pasquinade to the Epic Poem. Some strange gift, or union of gifts, must have been at work here; for the result is, at least, in the highest degree uncommon, and to be wondered at, if not to be admired.

If through all this many-coloured versatility, we try to decipher the essential, distinctive features of Voltaire's intellect, it seems to us that we find there a counterpart to our theory of his moral character; as, indeed, if that theory was accurate, we must do: for the thinking and the moral nature, distinguished by the necessities of speech, have no such distinction in themselves; but, rightly examined, exhibit in every case the strictest sympathy

*As Dryden said of Swift, so may we say: Our cousin Saint-Marc has no turn for poetry.

†On this sickness of Voltaire, and his death-bed deportment, many foolish books have been written; concerning which it is not necessary to say any thing. The conduct of the Parisian clergy, on that occasion, seems totally unworthy of their cloth; nor was their reward, so far as concerns these individuals, inappropriate: that of finding themselves once more bilked, once more *persifles* by that strange old man, in his last decrepitude, who, in his strength, had wrought them and others so many griefs. Surely the parting agonies of a fellow mortal, when the spirit of our brother, rapt in the whirlwinds and thick ghastly vapors of death, clutches blindly for help, and no help is there, are not the scenes where a wise faith would seek to exult, when it can no longer hope to alleviate! For the rest, to touch further on those their idle tales of dying horrors, remorse, and the like; to write of such, to believe them, or disbelieve them, or in any wise discuss them, were but a continuation of the same ineptitude. He, who, after the imperturbable exit of so many Cartouches and Thurtells, in every age of the world, can continue to regard the manner of a man's death as a test of his religious orthodoxy, may boast himself impregnable to merely terrestrial logic. Voltaire had enough of suffering, and of mean enough suffering, to encounter, without any addition from theological despair. His last interview with the clergy, who had been sent for by his friends, that the rites of burial might not be denied him, is thus described by Wagnière as it has been by all other credible reporters of it:—

"Two days before that mournful death, M. l'Abbé Mignot, his nephew, went to seek the Curé of Saint-Sulpice and the Abbé Guatier, and brought them into his uncle's sick-room; who, being informed that the Abbé Guatier was there, "Ah, well!" said he, "give him my compliments and my thanks." The Abbé spoke some words to him exhorting him to patience. The Curé of Saint-Sulpice then came forward, having announced himself, and asked of M. de Voltaire, elevating his voice, if he acknowledged the divinity of our Lord Jesus Christ? The sick man pushed one of his hands against the Curé's *calotte*, (coif,) shoving him back, and cried, turning abruptly to the other side, "Let me die in peace!" (*Laissez-moi mourir en paix!*) The Curé seemingly considered his person soiled, and his coif dishonoured, by the touch of a philosopher. He made the sick nurse give him a little brushing, and then went out with the Abbé Guatier."—Vol. i. p. 161.

and correspondence; are, indeed, but different phases of the same indissoluble unity,—a living mind. In life, Voltaire was found to be without good claim to the title of philosopher; and now, in literature, and for similar reasons, we find in him the same deficiencies. Here, too, it is not greatness, but the very extreme of expertness, that we recognise; not strength, so much as agility; not depth, but superficial extent. That truly surprising ability seems rather the unparalleled combination of many common talents, than the exercise of any finer or higher one: for here, too, the want of earnestness, of intense continuance, is fatal to him. He has the eye of a lynx; sees deeper, at the first glance, than any other man; but no second glance is given. Thus Truth, which, to the philospher, has from of old been said to live in a well, remains for the most part hidden from him; we may say for ever hidden, if we take the highest, and only philosophical species of Truth; for this does not reveal itself to any mortal, without quite another sort of meditation than Voltaire ever seems to have bestowed on it. In fact, his deductions are uniformly of a forensic, argumentative, immediately practical nature; often true, we will admit, so far as they go; but not the whole truth; and false, when taken for the whole. In regard to feeling, it is the same with him: he is, in general, humane, mildly affectionate, not without touches of nobleness; but light, fitful, discontinuous; "a smart freethinker, all things in an hour." He is no Poet and Philosopher, but a popular sweet Singer and Haranguer; in all senses, and in all styles, *Concionator*, which, for the most part, will turn out to be an altogether different character. It is true, in this last province he stands unrivalled; for such an audience, the most fit and perfectly persuasive of all preachers: but in many far higher provinces, he is neither perfect nor unrivalled; has been often surpassed; was surpassed even in his own age and nation. For a decisive, thoroughgoing, in any measure gigantic, force of thought, he is far inferior to Diderot; with all the liveliness, he has not the soft elegance; with more than the wit, he has but a small portion of the wisdom that belonged to Fontenelle: as in real sensibility, so in the delineation of it, in pathos, loftiness, and earnest eloquence, he cannot, making all fair abatements, and there are many, be compared with Rousseau.

Doubtless, an astonishing fertility, quickness, address; an openness also, and universal susceptibility of mind, must have belonged to him. As little can we deny that he manifests an assiduous perseverance, a capability of long-continued exertion, strange in so volatile a man; and consummate skill in husbanding and wisely directing his exertion. The very knowledge he had amassed, granting, which is but partly true, that it was superficial, remembered knowledge, might have distinguished him as a mere Dutch commentator. From Newton's *Principia* to the *Shaster* and *Vedam*, nothing has escaped him; he has glanced into all literatures and all sciences; nay, studied in them, for he can speak a rational word on all. It is known, for instance, that he understood Newton when no other man in France understood him; indeed, his countrymen may call Voltaire their discoverer of intellectual England,—a discovery, it is true, rather of the Curtis than of the Columbus sort, yet one which in his day still remained to be made. Nay, from all sides he brings new light into his country: now, for the first time, to the upturned wondering eyes of Frenchmen in general, does it become clear that Thought has actually a kind of existence in other kingdoms; that some glimmerings of civilization had dawned here and there on the human species, prior to the *Siècle de Louis Quatorze*. Of Voltaire's acquaintance with History, at least with what he called History, be it civil, religious, or literary; of his indescribable collection of facts, gathered from all sources,—from European Chronicles and State Papers, from eastern *Zends* and Jewish *Talmuds*, we need not remind any reader. It has been objected that his information was often borrowed at second-hand; that he had his plodders and pioneers, whom, as living dictionaries, he skilfully consulted in time of need. This also seems to be partly true, but deducts little from our estimate of him: for the skill *so* to borrow is even rarer than the power to lend. Voltaire's knowledge is not a mere show-room of curiosities, but truly a museum for purposes of teaching: every object is in its place, and there for its uses; nowhere do we find confusion, or vain display; everywhere intention, instructiveness, and the clearest order.

Perhaps it is this very power of Order, of rapid, perspicuous Arrangement, that lies at the root of Voltaire's best gifts; or rather, we should say, it is that keen, accurate intellectual vision, from which, to a mind of any intensity, Order naturally arises. This clear quick vision, and the methodic arrangement which springs from it, are looked upon as peculiarly French qualities; and Voltaire, at all times, manifests them in a more than French degree. Let him but cast his eye over any subject, in a moment he sees, though indeed only to a short depth, yet with instinctive decision, where the main bearings of it for that short depth lie; what is, or appears to be, its logical coherence; how causes connect themselves with effects; how the whole is to be seized, and in lucid sequence represented to his own or to other minds. In this respect, moreover, it is happy for him that, below the short depth alluded to, his view does not properly grow dim, but altogether terminates; thus there is nothing further to occasion him misgivings; has he not already sounded into that basis of bottomless Darkness on which all things firmly rest? What lies below is delusion, imagination, some form of Superstition or Folly; which he, nothing doubting, altogether casts away. Accordingly, he is the most intelligible of writers; everywhere transparent at a glance. There is no delineation or disquisition of his, that has not its whole purport written on its forehead; all is precise, all is rightly adjusted; that keen spirit of Order shows itself in the whole, and in every line of the whole.

If we say that this power of Arrangement, as applied both to the acquisition and to the communication of ideas, is Voltaire's most serviceable faculty in all his enterprises, we say nothing singular: for take the word in its largest acceptation, and it comprehends the whole office of Understanding, logically so called; is the means whereby man accomplishes whatever, in the way of outward force, has been made possible for him; conquers all practical obstacles, and rises to be the "king of this lower world." It is the organ of all that Knowledge which can properly be reckoned synonymous with Power; for hereby man strikes, with wise aim, into the infinite agencies of Nature, and multiplies his own small strength to unlimited degrees. It has been said also that man may rise to be the "god of this lower world;" but that is a far loftier height, not attainable by such powerful knowledge, but by quite another sort, for which Voltaire in particular shows hardly any aptitude.

In truth, readily as we have recognised his spirit of Method, with its many uses, we are far from ascribing to him any perceptible portion of that greatest praise in thinking, or in writing, the praise of philosophic, still less of poetic Method, which, especially the latter, must be the fruit of deep feeling as well as of clear vision,—of genius as well as of talent; and is much more likely to be found in the compositions of a Hooker, or a Shakspeare, than of a Voltaire. The Method discernible in Voltaire, and this on all subjects whatever, is a purely business Method. The order that arises from it is not Beauty, but, at best, Regularity. His objects do not lie round him in pictorial, not always in scientific grouping; but rather in commodious rows, where each may be seen and come at, like goods in a well-kept warehouse. We might say there is not the deep natural symmetry of a forest oak, but the simple artificial symmetry of a parlor chandelier. Compare, for example, the plan of the *Henriade* to that of our so barbarous *Hamlet*. The plan of the former is a geometrical diagram by Fermat; that of the latter a cartoon by Raphael. The *Henriade*, as we see it completed, is a polished, square-built Tuileries; *Hamlet* is a mysterious, star-paved Valhalla, and dwelling of the gods.

Nevertheless, Voltaire's style of Method is, as we have said, a business one; and for his purposes, more available than any other. It carries him swiftly through his work, and carries his reader swiftly through it; there is a prompt intelligence between the two; the whole meaning is communicated clearly, and comprehended without effort. From this also it may follow, that Voltaire will please the young more than he does the old; that the first perusal of him will please better than the second, if indeed any second be thought necessary. But what merit (and it is considerable) the pleasure and profit of this first perusal presupposes, must be honestly allowed him. Herein it seems to us lies the grand quality in all his performances. Those Histories of his, for instance, are felt, in spite of their sparkling rapidity, and knowing air of philosophic insight, to be among the shallowest of all histories; mere beadrolls of exterior occurrences, of battles, edifices, enactments, and other quite superficial phenomena; yet being clear beadrolls, well adapted for memory, and recited in a lively tone, we listen with satisfaction, and learn somewhat; learn much, if we began knowing nothing. Nay, sometimes the summary, in its skilful though crowded arrangement, and brilliant well-defined outlines, has almost a poetical as well as a didactic merit. *Charles the Twelfth* may still pass for a model in that often-attempted species of Biography: the clearest details are given in the fewest words; we have sketches of strange men and strange countries, of wars, adventures, negotiations, in a style which, for graphic brevity, rivals that of Sallust. It is a line-engraving, on a reduced scale, of that Swede and his mad life; without colours, yet not without the foreshortenings and perspective observances,—nay, not altogether without the deeper harmonies which belong to a true Picture. In respect of composition, whatever may be said of its accuracy or worth otherwise, we cannot but reckon it greatly the best of Voltaire's Histories.

In his other prose works, in his Novels, and innumerable Essays and fugitive pieces, the same clearness of order, the same rapid precision of view, again forms a distinguishing merit. His *Zadigs* and *Baboucs* and *Candides*, which, considered as products of imagination, perhaps rank higher with foreigners than any of his professedly poetical performances, are instinct with this sort of intellectual life: the sharpest glances, though from an oblique point of sight, into at least the surface of human life, into the old familiar world of business, which truly from his oblique station, looks oblique enough, and yields store of ridiculous combinations. The Wit, manifested chiefly in these and the like performances, but ever flowing, unless purposely restrained, in boundless abundance, from Voltaire's mind, has been often and duly celebrated. It lay deep-rooted in his nature; the inevitable produce of such an understanding with such a character, and was from the first likely, as it actually proved in the latter period of his life, to become the main dialect in which he spoke and even thought. Doing all justice to the inexhaustible readiness, the quick force, the polished acuteness, of Voltaire's Wit, we may remark, at the same time, that it was nowise the highest species of employment for such a mind as his; that, indeed, it ranks essentially among the lowest species even of Ridicule. It is at all times mere logical pleasantry; a gayety of the head, not of the heart; there is scarcely a twinkling of Humour in the whole of his numberless sallies. Wit of this sort cannot maintain a demure sedateness; a grave yet infinitely kind aspect, warming the inmost soul with true loving mirth; it has not even the force to laugh outright, but can only sniff and titter. It grounds itself, not on fond sportful sympathy, but on contempt, or at best, on indifference. It stands related to Humour as Prose does to Poetry; of which, in this department at least, Voltaire exhibits no symptom. The most determinedly ludicrous composition of his, the *Pucelle*, which cannot on other grounds be recommended to any reader, has no higher merit than that of an audacious caricature. True, he is not a buffoon; seldom or never violates the rules, we shall not say of propriety, yet of good breeding: to this negative praise he is entitled. But as for any high claim to positive praise, it cannot be made good. We look in vain, through his whole writings, for one lineament of a *Quixote* or a *Shandy;* even of a *Hudibras* or *Battle of the Books*. Indeed, it has been more than once observed that Humour is not a national gift with the French, in late times; that since Montaigne's day it seems to have well nigh vanished from among them.

Considered in his technical capacity of Poet, Voltaire need not, at present, detain us very long. Here too his excellence is chiefly intellectual, and shown in the way of business-like method. Every thing is well calculated for a given end; there is the utmost logical fitness of sentiment, of incident, of general contrivance. Nor is he without an enthusiasm that sometimes resembles inspiration; a clear fellow-feeling for the personages of his scene he always has; with a chameleon susceptibility he takes some hue of every object; if he cannot *be* that object, he at least plausibly enacts it. Thus we have a result everywhere consistent with itself; a contrivance, not without nice adjustments, and brilliant aspects, which pleases with that old pleasure of "difficulties overcome," and the visible correspondence of means to end. That the deeper portion of our soul sits silent, unmoved under all this; recognising no universal, everlasting Beauty, but only a modish Elegance, less the work of poetical creation than a process of the toilette, need occasion no surprise. It signifies only that Voltaire was a French Poet, and wrote as the French people of that day required and approved. We have long known that French poetry aimed at a different result than ours; that its splendour was what we should call a dead, artificial one; not the manifold soft summer glories of Nature, but a cold splendour, as of polished metal.

On the whole, in reading Voltaire's poetry, that adventure of the *Café de Procope* should ever be held in mind. He was not without an eye to have looked, had he seen others looking, into the deepest nature of poetry; nor has he failed here and there to cast a glance in that direction: but what preferment could such enterprises earn for him in the *Café de Procope?* What could it profit his all-precious "fame," to pursue them farther? In the end, he seems to have heartily reconciled himself to use and wont, and striven only to do better what he saw all others doing. Yet his private poetical creed, which could not be a catholic one, was, nevertheless, scarcely so bigoted as might have been looked for. That censure of Shakspeare, which elicited a re-censure in England, perhaps rather deserved a "recommendatory epistle," all things being considered. He calls Shakspeare "a genius full of force and fertility, of nature and sublimity," though unhappily "without the smallest spark of good taste, or the smallest acquaintance with the rules," which, in Voltaire's dialect, is not so false; Shakspeare having really almost no Parisian *bon goût* whatever, and walking through "*the* rules," so often as he sees good, with the most astonishing tranquillity. After a fair enough account of *Hamlet*, the best of those "*farces monstrueuses qu'on appelle tragedies*," where, however, there are "scenes so beautiful, and passages so grand and so terrible," Voltaire thus proceeds to resolve two great problems:

"The first, how so many wonders could accumulate in a single head? for it must be confessed that all the divine Shakspeare's plays are written in this taste: the second, how men's minds could have been elevated so as to look at these plays with transport; and how they are still followed after, in a century which has produced Addison's *Cato?*

"Our astonishment at the first wonder will cease, when we understand that Shakspeare took all his tragedies from histories or romances; and that in this case he only turned into verse the romance of *Claudius, Gertrude*, and *Hamlet*, written in full by Saxo Grammaticus, to whom be the praise.

"The second part of the problem, that is to say, the pleasure men take in these tragedies, presents a little more difficulty; but here is (*en voici*) the solution, according to the deep reflections of certain philosophers.

"The English chairmen, the sailors, hackney-coachmen, shop-porters, butchers, clerks even are passionately fond of shows: give them cock-fights, bull-baitings, fencing-matches, burials, duels, gibbets, witchcraft, apparitions, they run thither in crowds; nay, there is more than one patrician as curious as the populace. The citizens of London found in Shakspeare's tragedies, satisfaction enough for such a turn of mind. The courtiers were obliged to follow the torrent: how can you help admiring what the more sensible part of the town admires? There was nothing better for a hundred and fifty years; the admiration grew with age, and became an idolatry. Some touches of genius, some happy verses full of force and nature, which you remember in spite of yourself, atoned for the remainder, and soon the whole piece succeeded by the help of some beauties of detail."—*Œuvres*, t. xlvii. p. 300.

Here, truly, is a comfortable little theory, which throws light on more than one thing. However, it is couched in mild terms, comparatively speaking. Frederic the Great, for example, thus gives his verdict:

"To convince yourself of the wretched taste that up to this day prevails in Germany, you have only to visit the public theatres. You will there see, in action, the abominable plays of Shakspeare, translated into our language; and the whole audience fainting with rapture (*se pâmer d'aise*) in listening to those ridiculous farces, worthy of the savages of Canada. I call them such, because they sin against all the rules of the theatre. One may pardon those mad sallies in Shakspeare, for the birth of the arts is never the point of their maturity. But here, even now, we have a *Goetz de Berlichingen*, which has just made its appearance on the scene; a detestible imitation of those miserable English pieces; and the pit applauds, and demands with enthusiasm the repetition of these disgusting ineptitudes (*de ces dégoûtantes platitudes.*)—*De la Littérature Allemande.* Berlin, 1780.*

We have not cited these criticisms with a view to impugn them; but simply to ascertain where the critics themselves are standing. This passage of Frederic's has even a touch of pathos in it; may be regarded as the expiring cry of "*Goût*," in that country, who sees himself suddenly beleaguered by strange, appalling, Supernatural influences, which he mistakes for Lapland witchcraft, or Cagliostro jugglery; and so he drowns, grasping his opera-hat, in an ocean of "*Dégoûtantes platitudes.*" On the whole, it would appear that Voltaire's view of poetry was radically different from ours; that, in fact, of what we should strictly call poetry, he had almost no view whatever. A Tragedy, a Poem, with him is not to be "a manifestation of man's Reason in forms suitable to his Sense;" but rather a highly complex egg-dance, to be danced before the King, to a given tune, and without breaking a single egg. Nevertheless, let justice be shown to him, and to French poetry at large. This latter is a peculiar growth of our modern ages; has been labouriously cultivated, and is not without its own value. We have to remark also, as a curious fact, that it has been, at one time or other, transplanted into all countries, England, Germany, Spain; but though under the sunbeams of royal protection, it would strike root nowhere. Nay, now it seems falling into the sere and yellow leaf in its own natal soil: the axe has already been seen near its root; and perhaps, in no great lapse of years, this species of poetry may be to the French, what it is to all other nations, a pleasing reminiscence. Yet the elder French loved it with zeal; to them it must have had a true worth: indeed we can understand how, when Life itself consisted so much in Display, these representatives of Life may have been the only suitable ones. And now, when the nation feels itself called to a more grave and nobler destiny among nations, the want of a new literature also begins to be felt. As yet, in looking at their too purblind, scrambling controversies of *Romanticists* and *Classicists*, we cannot find that our ingenious neighbours have done much more than make a commencement in this enterprise: however, a commencement seems to be made; they are in what may be called the eclectic state; trying all things, German, English, Italian, Spanish, with a candour and real love of improvement, which give the best omens of a still higher success. From the peculiar gifts of the French, and their peculiar spiritual position, we may expect, had they once more attained to an original style, many important benefits, and important accessions to the Literature of the World. Meanwhile, in considering and duly estimating what that people has, in past times, accomplished, Voltaire must always be reckoned among their most meritorious Poets. Inferior in what we may call general poetic temperament to Racine; greatly inferior, in some points of it, to Corneille, he has an intellectual vivacity, a quickness both of sight and of invention, which belongs to neither of these two. We believe that, among foreign nations, his Tragedies, such works as *Zaire* and *Mahomet*, are considerably the most esteemed of this school.

However, it is nowise as a Poet, Historian, or Novelist, that Voltaire stands so prominent in Europe; but chiefly as a religious Polemic, as a vehement opponent of the Christian Faith. Viewed in this last character, he may give rise to many grave reflections, only a small portion of which can here be so much as glanced at. We may say, in general, that his style of controversy is of a piece with himself; not a higher, and scarcely a lower style than might have been expected from him. As in a moral point of view, Voltaire nowise wanted a love of truth, yet had withal a still deeper love of his own interest in truth; was, therefore, intrinsically no Philosopher, but a highly-accomplished Trivialist; so likewise, in an intellectual point of view, he manifests himself ingenious and adroit, rather than noble or comprehensive; fights for truth or victory, not by patient meditation, but by light sarcasm, whereby victory may indeed, for a time, be gained; but little Truth, what can be named Truth, especially in such matters as this, is to be looked for.

No one, we suppose, ever arrogated for Voltaire any praise of originality in this discussion; we suppose there is not a single idea, of any moment, relating to the Christian religion, in all his multifarious writings, that had not been set forth again and again before his enterprises commenced. The labours of a very mixed multitude, from Porphyry down to Shaftesbury, including Hobbeses, Tindals, Tolands, some of them skeptics of a much nobler class, had left little room for merit in this kind: nay, Bayle, his own countryman, had just finished a life spent in preaching skepticism precisely similar, and by methods precisely similar, when Voltaire appeared on the arena. Indeed, skepticism, as we have before observed, was at this period universal among the higher ranks in France, with whom Voltaire chiefly associated. It is only in the merit and demerit of grinding down this grain into food for the people, and inducing so many to eat of it, that Voltaire can claim any singularity. However, we quarrel not with him on this head: there may be cases where the want of originality is even a moral merit. But it is a much more serious ground of offence that he intermeddled in Religion without being himself, in any measure, Religious; that he entered the Temple and continued there, with a levity, which, in any Temple where men worship, can beseem no brother man; that, in a word, he ardently, and with long-continued effort, warred against Christianity, without understanding beyond the mere superficies of what Christianity was.

His polemical procedure in this matter, it appears to us, must now be admitted to have been, on the whole, a shallow one. Through all its manifold forms, and involutions, and repetitions, it turns, we believe exclusively, on

* We quote from the compilation: *Goethe in den Zeugnissen der Mitlebenden*, s. 124.

one point; what Theologians have called the "plenary Inspiration of the Scriptures." This is the single wall, against which, through long years, and with innumerable battering-rams and catapults and pop-guns, he unweariedly batters. Concede him this, and his ram swings freely, to and fro, through space; there is nothing further it can even aim at. That the Sacred Books could be aught else than a Bank-of-Faith Bill, for such and such quantities of Enjoyment, payable at sight in the other world, value received; which bill becomes waste paper, the stamp being questioned:—that the Christian Religion could have any deeper foundation than Books, could possibly be written in the purest nature of man, in mysterious, ineffaceable characters, to which Books, and all Revelations, and authentic traditions, were but a subsidiary matter, were but as the *light* whereby that divine *writing* was to be read;—nothing of this seems to have, even in the faintest manner, occurred to him. Yet herein, as we believe that the whole world has now begun to discover, lies the real essence of the question; by the negative or affirmative decision of which the Christian Religion, any thing that is worth calling by that name, must fall, or endure for ever. We believe, also, that the wiser minds of our age have already come to agreement on this question; or rather never were divided regarding it. Christianity, the "Worship of Sorrow," has been recognised as divine, on far other grounds than "Essays on Miracles," and by considerations infinitely deeper than would avail in any mere "trial by jury." He who argues against it or for it, in this manner, may be regarded as mistaking its nature: the Ithuriel, though to our eyes he wears a body, and the fashion of armour, cannot be wounded with material steel. Our fathers were wiser than we, when they said in deepest earnestness, what we often hear in shallow mockery, that Religion is "not of Sense, but of Faith;" not of Understanding, but of Reason. He who finds himself without this latter, who by all his studying has failed to unfold it in himself, may have studied to great or to small purpose, we say not which; but of the Christian Religion, as of many other things, he has and can have no knowledge.

The Christian Doctrine we often hear likened to the Greek Philosophy, and found, on all hands, some measurable way superior to it: but this also seems a mistake. The Christian Doctrine, that doctrine of Humility, in all senses, godlike, and the parent of all godlike virtues, is not superior, or inferior, or equal, to any doctrine of Socrates or Thales; being of a totally different nature; differing from these, as a perfect Ideal Poem does from a Correct Computation in Arithmetic. He who compares it with such standards may lament that, beyond the mere letter, the purport of this divine Humility has never been disclosed to him; that the loftiest feeling hitherto vouchsafed to mankind is as yet hidden from his eyes.

For the rest, the question how Christianity originated is doubtless a high question; resolvable enough, if we view only its surface, which was all that Voltaire saw of it; involved in sacred, silent, unfathomable depths, if we investigate its interior meanings; which meanings, indeed, it may be, every new age will develop to itself in a new manner, and with new degrees of light; for the whole truth may be called infinite, and to man's eye discernible only in parts: but the question itself is nowise the ultimate one in this matter.

We understand ourselves to be risking no new assertion, but simply reporting what is already the conviction of the greatest in our age, when we say,—that cheerfully recognising, gratefully appropriating whatever Voltaire has proved, or any other man has proved, or shall prove, the Christian Religion, once here, cannot again pass away; that, in one or the other form, it will endure through all time; that, as in Scripture, so also in the heart of man, is written, "the Gates of Hell shall not prevail against it." Were the memory of this Faith never so obscured, as, indeed, in all times, the coarse passions and perceptions of the world do all but obliterate it in the hearts of most; yet in every pure soul, in every Poet and Wise Man, it finds a new Missionary, a new Martyr, till the great volume of Universal History is finally closed, and man's destinies are fulfilled in this earth. "It is a height to which the human species were fated and enabled to attain; and from which, having once attained it, they can never retrograde."

These things, which it were far out of our place to attempt adequately elucidating here, must not be left out of sight, in appreciating Voltaire's polemical worth. We find no trace of these, or of any the like essential considerations having been present with him, in examining the Christian Religion; nor indeed was it consistent with his general habits that they should be so. Totally destitute of religious Reverence, even of common practical seriousness; by nature or habit, undevout both in heart and head; not only without any Belief, in other than a material sense, but without the possibility of acquiring any, he can be no safe or permanently useful guide in this investigation. We may consider him as having opened the way to future inquirers of a truer spirit; but for his own part, as having engaged in an enterprise, the real nature of which was well-nigh unknown to him; and engaged in it with the issue to be anticipated in such a case; producing chiefly confusion, dislocation, destruction, on all hands; so that the good he achieved is still, in these times, found mixed with an alarming proportion of evil, from which, indeed, men rationally doubt whether much of it will in any time be separable.

We should err widely, too, if in estimating what quantity, altogether overlooking what quality, of intellect Voltaire may have manifested on this occasion, we took the result produced as any measure of the force applied. His task was not one of Affirmation, but of Denial; not a task of erecting and rearing up, which is slow and laborious; but of destroying and overturning, which in most cases is rapid and far easier. The force necessary for him was nowise a great and noble one; but a small, in some respects a mean one, to be nimbly and seasonably put in use. The

Ephesian Temple, which it had employed many wise heads and strong arms, for a lifetime, to build, could be *un*-built by one madman, in a single hour.

Of such errors, deficiencies, and positive misdeeds, it appears to us, a just criticism must accuse Voltaire: at the same time, we can nowise join in the condemnatory clamour which so many worthy persons, not without the best intentions, to this day keep up against him. His whole character seems to be plain enough, common enough, had not extraneous influences so perverted our views regarding it: nor, morally speaking, is it a worse character, but considerably a better one, than belongs to the mass of men. Voltaire's aims in opposing the Christian Religion were unhappily of a mixed nature: yet, after all, very nearly such aims as we have often seen directed against it, and often seen directed in its favour: a little love of finding Truth, with a great love of making Proselytes; which last is in itself a natural, universal feeling; and if honest, is, even in the worst cases, a subject for pity, rather than for hatred. As a light, careless, courteous Man of the World, he offers no hateful aspect; on the contrary, a kindly, gay, rather amiable one: hundreds of men, with half his worth of disposition, die daily, and their little world laments them. It is time that he too should be judged of by his intrinsic, not by his accidental qualities; that justice should be done to him also; for injustice can profit no man and no cause.

In fact, Voltaire's chief merits belong to Nature and himself; his chief faults are of his time and country. In that famous era of the Pompadours and *Encyclopédies*, he forms the main figure; and was such, we have seen, more by resembling the multitude, than by differing from them. It was a strange age that of Louis XV.; in several points, a novel one in the history of mankind. In regard to its luxury and depravity, to the high culture of all merely practical and material faculties, and the entire torpor of all the purely contemplative and spiritual, this era considerably resembles that of the Roman Emperors. There, too, was external splendour and internal squalour; the highest completeness in all sensual arts, including among these not cookery and its adjuncts alone, but even "effect-painting" and "effect-writing;" only the art of virtuous living was a lost one. Instead of Love for Poetry, there was "Taste" for it; refinement in manners, with utmost coarseness in morals: in a word, the strange spectacle of a social system, embracing large, cultivated portions of the human species, and founded only on Atheism. With the Romans, things went what we should call their natural course: Liberty, public spirit, quietly declined into a *caput-mortuum;* Self-love, Materialism, Baseness even to the disbelief in all possibility of Virtue, stalked more and more imperiously abroad; till the body-politic, long since deprived of its vital circulating fluids, had now become a putrid carcass, and fell in pieces to be the prey of ravenous wolves. Then was there, under those Attilas and Alarics, a world's spectacle of destruction and despair, compared with which the often-commemorated "horrors of the French Revolution," and all Napoleon's wars, were but the gay jousting of a tournament to the sack of stormed cities. Our European community has escaped the like dire consummation; and by causes, which, as may be hoped, will always secure it from such. Nay, were there no other cause, it may be asserted, that in a commonwealth where the Christian religion exists, where it once has existed, public and private Virtue, the basis of all Strength, never can become extinct; but in every new age, and even from the deepest decline, there is a chance, and in the course of ages, a certainty of renovation.

That the Christian Religion, or any Religion, continued to exist; that some martyr heroism still lived in the heart of Europe to rise against mailed Tyranny when it rode triumphant,—was indeed no merit in the age of Louis XV., but a happy accident which it could not altogether get rid of. For that age too is to be regarded as an experiment, on the great scale, to decide the question, not yet, it would appear, settled to universal satisfaction: With what degree of vigour a political system, grounded on pure Self-interest, never so enlightened, but without a God, or any recognition of the godlike in man, can be expected to flourish; or whether, in such circumstances, a political system can be expected to flourish, or even to subsist at all? It is contended by many that our mere love of personal Pleasure, or Happiness as it is called, acting on every individual, with such clearness as he may easily have, will of itself lead him to respect the rights of others, and wisely employ his own: to fulfil, on a mere principle of economy, all the duties of a good patriot; so that, in what respects the State, or the merely social existence of mankind, Belief, beyond the testimony of the senses, and Virtue, beyond the very common Virtue of loving what is pleasant, and hating what is painful, are to be considered as supererogatory qualifications, as ornamental, not essential. Many there are, on the other hand, who pause over this doctrine; cannot discover, in such a universe of conflicting atoms, any principle by which the whole shall cohere: for, if every man's selfishness, infinitely expansive, is to be hemmed in only by the infinitely-expansive selfishness of every other man, it seems as if we should have a world of mutually-repulsive bodies with no centripetal force to bind them together; in which case, it is well known they would, by and by, diffuse themselves over space, and constitute a remarkable Chaos, but no habitable Solar or Stellar System.

If the age of Louis XV. was not made an *experimentum crucis* in regard to this question, one reason may be that such experiments are too expensive. Nature cannot afford, above once or twice in the thousand years, to destroy a whole world, for purposes of science; but must content herself with destroying one or two kingdoms. The age of Louis XV., so far as it went, seems a highly illustrative experiment. We are to remark, also, that its operation was clogged by a very considerable disturbing force; by a large remnant, namely, of the old faith in Religion, in the invisible, celestial nature of Virtue, which our French Purifiers, by their utmost efforts of lavation, had not been able to wash away. The men did their best, but no man can do more. Their worst enemy, we imagine, will not accuse them of any undue regard to things unseen and spiritual: far from practising this invisible sort of Virtue, they cannot even believe in its possibility. The high exploits and endurances of old ages were no longer virtues, but "passions;" these antique persons had a taste for being heroes, a certain fancy to die for the truth: the more fools they! With our *Philosophers*, the only virtue of any civilization was that they call "Honour," the sanctioning deity of which is that wonderful "Force of Public Opinion." Concerning which virtue of Honour, we must be permitted to say that she reveals herself too clearly, as the daughter and heiress of our old acquaintance Vanity, who indeed has been known enough, ever since the foundation of the world, at least since the date of that "Lucifer, son of the Morning;" but known chiefly in her proper character of strolling actress, or cast-clothes Abigail; and never till that new era had seen her issue set up as Queen and all-sufficient Dictatress of man's whole soul, prescribing with nicest precision what, in all practical and all moral emergencies, he was to do and to forbear. Again, with regard to this same Force of Public Opinion, it is a force well known to all of us, respected, valued as of indispensable utility, but nowise recognised as a final or divine force. We might ask what divine, what truly great thing had ever been effected by this force? Was it the Force of Public Opinion that drove Columbus to America; John Kepler, not to fare sumptuously among Rodolph's Astrologers and Fire-eaters, but to perish of want, discovering the true System of the Stars? Still more ineffectual do we find it as a basis of public or private Morals. Nay, taken by itself, it may be called a baseless basis; for without some ulterior sanction, common to all minds; without some belief in the necessary, eternal, or which is the same, in the supramundane, divine nature of Virtue, existing in each individual, what could the moral judgment of a thousand or a thousand thousand individuals avail us? Without some such celestial guidance, whencesoever derived, or howsoever named, it appears to us the Force of Public Opinion would, by and by, become an extremely unprofitable one. "Enlighten Self-interest!" cries the *Philosophe;* "Do but sufficiently enlighten it! We ourselves have seen enlightened Self-interests, ere now; and truly, for most part, their light was only as that of a horn-lantern, sufficient to guide the bearer himself out of various puddles: but to us and the world of comparatively small advantage. And figure the human species, like an endless host, seeking its way onwards through undiscovered Time, in black darkness, save that each had his horn-lantern, and the vanguard some few of glass!

However, we will not dwell on controversial niceties. What we had to remark was that this era, called of Philosophy, was in itself but a poor era; that any little morality it had was chiefly borrowed, and from those very ages which it accounted so barbarous. For this "Honour," this "Force of Public Opinion," is not asserted, on any side, to have much renovating, but only a sustaining or preventive power; it cannot create new Virtue, but at best may preserve what is already there. Nay, of the age of Louis XV., we may say that its very Power, its material strength, its knowledge, all that it had, was borrowed. It boasted itself to be an age of illumination; and truly illumination there was of its kind: only, except the illuminated windows, almost nothing to be *seen* thereby. None of those great Doctrines or Institutions that have "made man in all points a man;" none even of those Discoveries that have the most subjected external Nature to his purposes, were made in that age. What Plough, or Printing-press, what Chivalry, or Christianity; nay, what Steam-engine, or Quakerism, or Trial by Jury, did these Encyclopedists invent for mankind? They invented simply nothing; not one of man's virtues, not one of man's powers, is due to them: in all these respects, the age of Louis XV. is among the most barren of recorded ages. Indeed, the whole trade of our *Philosophes* was directly the opposite of invention: it was not to produce, that they stood there; but to criticise, to quarrel with, to rend in pieces, what had been already produced;—a quite inferior trade: sometimes a useful, but on the whole a mean trade; often the fruit, and always the parent, of meanness, in every mind that permanently follows it.

Considering the then position of affairs, it is not singular that the age of Louis XV. should have been what it was: an age without nobleness, without high virtues, or high manifestations of talent; an age of shallow clearness, of polish, self-conceit, skepticism, and all forms of *Persiflage*. As little does it seem surprising, or peculiarly blamable, that Voltaire, the leading man of that age, should have partaken largely of all its qualities. True, his giddy activity took serious effect, the light firebrands, which he so carelessly scattered abroad, kindled fearful conflagrations: but in these there has been good as well as evil; nor is it just that, even for the latter, he, a limited mortal, should be charged with more than mortal's responsibility. After all, that parched, blighted period, and the period of earthquakes and tornadoes which followed it, have now well-nigh cleared away: they belong to the Past, and for us and those that come after us, are not without their benefits, and calm historical meaning.

"The thinking heads of all nations," says a deep observer, "had in secret come to majority; and, in a mistaken feeling of their vocation, rose the more fiercely against antiquated constraint. The Man of Letters is, by instinct, opposed to a Priesthood of old standing: the literary class and the clerical must wage a war of extermination, when they are divided; for both strive after one place. Such division became more and more perceptible, the nearer we approached the period of European manhood, the epoch of triumphant Learning; and Knowledge and Faith came into more decided contradiction. In the prevailing Faith, as was thought, lay the reason of the universal degradation; and by a more and more searching Knowledge men hoped to remove it. On all hands, the Religious feeling suffered, under manifold attacks against its actual manner of existence, against the Forms in which hitherto it had imbodied itself. The result of that modern way of thought was named Philosophy; and in this all was included that opposed itself to the ancient way of thought, especially, therefore, all that opposed itself to Religion. The original personal hatred against the Catholic faith passed, by degrees, into hatred against the Bible; against the Christian Religion, and at last against Religion altogether. Nay, more, this hatred of Religion naturally extended itself over all objects of enthusiasm in general; proscribed Fancy and Feeling, Morality and love of Art, the Future and the Antique; placed man, with an effort, foremost in the series of natural productions; and changed the infinite, creative music of the Universe into the monotonous clatter of a boundless Mill, which, turned by the stream of Chance, and swimming thereon, was a Mill of itself, without Architect and Miller, properly, a genuine *perpetuum mobile*, a real, self-grinding Mill.

"One enthusiasm was generously left to poor mankind, and rendered indispensable as a touchstone of the highest culture, for all jobbers in the same: Enthusiasm for this magnanimous Philosophy, and above all, for these its priests and mystagogues. France was so happy as to be the birthplace and dwelling of this new Faith, which had thus, from patches of pure knowledge, been pasted together. Low as Poetry ranked in this new Church, there were some poets among them, who for effect's sake made use of the old ornaments and old lights; but, in so doing, ran a risk of kindling the new world-system by ancient fire. More cunning brethren, however, were at hand to help; and always in season poured cold water on the warming audience. The members of this Church were restlessly employed in clearing Nature, the Earth, the Souls of men, the Sciences, from all Poetry; obliterating every vestige of the Holy: disturbing, by sarcasms, the memory of all lofty occurrences, and lofty men; disrobing the world of all its variegated vesture. * * * * Pity that Nature continued so wondrous and incomprehensible, so poetical and infinite, all efforts to modernize her notwithstanding! However, if anywhere an old superstition, of a higher world and the like, came to light, instantly, on all hands, was a springing of rattles; that, if possible, the dangerous spark might be extinguished, by appliances of philosophy and wit: yet Tolerance was the watchword of the cultivated; and in France, above all, synonymous with Philosophy. Highly remarkable is this history of modern Unbelief; the key to all the vast phenomena of recent times. Not till last century, till the latter half of it, does the novelty begin; and in a little while, it expands to an immeasurable bulk and variety: a second Reformation, a more comprehensive, and more specific, was unavoidable: and naturally it first visited that land which was the most modernized, and had the longest lain in an asthenic state, from the want of freedom. * * *

"At the present epoch, however, we stand high enough to look back with a friendly smile on those bygone days; and even in those marvellous follies to discern curious crystallizations of historical matter. Thankfully will we stretch out our hands to those Men of Letters and *Philosophes:* for this delusion too required to be exhausted; and the scientific side of things to have full value given it. More beauteous and many-coloured stands Poesy, like a leafy India, when contrasted with the cold, dead Spitzbergen of that closet-logic That in the middle of the globe, an India, sc warm and lordly, might exist, must also a cold motionless sea, dead cliffs, mist instead of the starry sky, and a long night, make both Poles uninhabitable. The deep meaning of the laws of Mechanism lay heavy on those anchorites in the deserts of Understanding: the charm of the first glimpse into it overpowered them: the Old avenged itself on them; to the first feeling of self-consciousness, they sacrificed, with wondrous devotedness, what was holiest and fairest in the world! and were the first that, in practice, again recognised and preached forth the sacredness of Nature, the infinitude of Art, the independence of Knowledge, the worth of the Practical, and the all-presence of the Spirit of History; and so doing, put an end to a Spectre-dynasty, more potent, universal, and terrific than perhaps they themselves were aware of."*

How far our readers will accompany Novalis in such high-soaring speculation is not for us to say. Meanwhile, that the better part of them have already, in their own dialect, united with him, and with us, in candid tolerance, in clear acknowledgment, towards French Philosophy, towards this Voltaire and the spiritual period which bears his name, we do not hesitate to believe. Intolerance, animosity, can forward no cause; and least of all beseems the cause of moral and religious truth. A wise man has well reminded us, that "in any controversy, the instant we feel anger, we have already ceased striving for Truth, and begun striving for Ourselves." Let no man doubt that Voltaire and his disciples, like all men and all things that live and act in God's world, will one day be found to have "worked together for good." Nay that with all his evil, he has already accomplished good, must be admitted in the soberest calculation. How much do we include in this one little word: He gave the death-stab to modern Superstition. *That* horrid incubus, which dwelt in darkness, shunning the light, is passing away; with all its racks, and poison-chalices, and foul sleeping-draughts, is passing away without return. He who sees even a little way into the signs of the times, sees well that both the Smithfield fires and the Edinburgh thumbscrews (for these too must be held in remembrance) are things which have long, very long, lain behind us; divided from us by a wall of centuries, transparent indeed, but more impassable

* Novalis Schriften, i., s. 198.

than adamant. For, as we said, Superstition is in its death-lair; the last agonies may endure for decades, or for centuries; but it carries the iron in its heart, and will not vex the earth any more.

That, with Superstition, Religion is also passing away, seems to us a still more ungrounded fear. Religion cannot pass away. The burning of a little straw may hide the stars of the sky; but the stars are there, and will re-appear. On the whole, we must repeat the often-repeated saying, that it is unworthy a religious man to view an irreligious one either with alarm or aversion or with any other feeling than regret, and hope, and brotherly commiseration. If he seek Truth, is he not our brother, and to be pitied? If he do not seek truth, is he not still our brother, and to be pitied still more? Old Ludovicus Vives has a story of a clown that killed his ass because it had drunk up the moon, and he thought the world could ill spare that luminary. So he killed his ass, *ut lunam redderet*. The clown was well-intentioned, but unwise. Let us not imitate him; let us not slay a faithful servant who has carried us far. He has not drunk the moon; but only the *reflection* of the moon, in his own poor water-pail, where, too, it may be, he was drinking with purposes the most harmless.

NOVALIS.*

[Foreign Review, 1829.]

A number of years ago, Jean Paul's copy of *Novalis* led him to infer that the German reading world was of a quick disposition; inasmuch as with regard to books that required more than one perusal, it declined perusing them at all. Paul's *Novalis*, we suppose, was of the first Edition, uncut, dusty, and lent him from the Public Library with willingness, nay, with joy; but times, it would appear, must be considerably changed since then; indeed, were we to judge of German reading habits from these volumes of ours, we should draw quite an opposite conclusion of Paul's; for they are of the fourth Edition, perhaps therefore the ten-thousandth copy, and that of a Book demanding, whether deserving or not, to be oftener read than almost any other it has ever been our lot to examine.

Without at all entering into the merits of Novalis, we may observe that we should reckon it a happy sign of Literature, were so solid a fashion of study here and there established in all countries; for directly in the teeth of most "intellectual tea-circles," it may be asserted that no good Book, or good thing of any sort, shows its best face at first; nay, that the commonest quality in a true work of Art, if its excellence have any depth and compass, is that at first sight it occasions a certain disappointment; perhaps even, mingled with its undeniable beauty, a certain feeling of aversion. Not as if we meant, by this remark, to cast a stone at the old guild of literary Improvisators, or any of that diligent brotherhood whose trade it is to blow soap-bubbles for their fellow-creatures; which bubbles, of course, if they are not seen and admired this moment, will be altogether lost to men's eyes the next. Considering the use of these blowers, in civilized communities, we rather wish them strong lungs, and all manner of prosperity: but simply we would contend that such soap-bubble guild should not become the sole one in Literature; that being indisputably the strongest, it should content itself with this pre-eminence, and not tyrannically annihilate its less prosperous neighbours. For it should be recollected that Literature positively has other aims than this of amusement from hour to hour; nay, perhaps, that this, glorious as it may be, is not its highest or true aim. We do say, therefore, that the Improvisator corporation should be kept within limits; and readers, at least a certain small class of readers, should understand that some few departments of human inquiry have still their depths and difficulties; that the abstruse is not precisely synonymous with the absurd; nay, that light itself may be darkness, in a certain state of the eyesight; that, in short, cases may occur when a little patience and some attempt at thought would not be altogether superfluous in reading. Let the mob of gentlemen keep their own ground, and be happy and applauded there: if they overstep that ground, they indeed may flourish the better for it, but the reader will suffer damage. For in this way, a reader, accustomed to see through every thing in one second of time, comes to forget that his wisdom and critical penetration are finite and not infinite; and so commits more than one mistake in his conclusions. The Reviewer, too, who indeed is only a preparatory reader, as it were, a sort of sieve and drainer for the use of more luxurious readers, soon follows his example: these two react still further on the mob of gentlemen; and so among them all, with this action and reaction, matters grow worse and worse.

It rather seems to us as if, in this respect of faithfulness in reading, the Germans were somewhat ahead of us English; at least we have no such proof to show of it as that fourth Edition of *Novalis*. Our Coleridge's *Friend*, for example, and *Biographia Literaria*, are but a slight business compared with these *Schriften*; little more than the Alphabet, and that in

---

* *Novalis Schriften. Herausgegeben von Ludwig Tieck und Friedrich Schlegel.* (Novalis' Writings. Edited by Ludwig Tieck and Friedrich Schlegel.) Fourth Edition. 2 vols. Berlin, 1826.

gilt letters, of such Philosophy and Art as is here taught in the form of Grammar and Rhetorical Compend: yet Coleridge's works were triumphantly condemned by the whole reviewing world, as clearly unintelligible; and among readers they have still but an unseen circulation; like living brooks, hidden for the present under mountains of froth and theatrical snow-paper, and which only at a distant day, when these mountains shall have decomposed themselves into gas and earthly residuum, may roll forth in their true limpid shape, to gladden the general eye with what beauty and everlasting freshness does reside in them. It is admitted, too, on all hands, that Mr. Coleridge is a man of "genius," that is, a man having more intellectual insight than other men; and strangely enough, it is taken for granted, at the same time, that he has less intellectual insight than any other. For why else are his doctrines to be thrown out of doors, without examination, as false and worthless, simply because they are obscure? Or how is their so palpable falsehood to be accounted for to our minds, except on this extraordinary ground; that a man able to originate deep thoughts (such is the meaning of genius) is unable to *see* them when originated; that the creative intellect of a Philosopher is destitute of that mere faculty of logic which belongs to "all Attorneys, and men educated in Edinburgh?" The Cambridge carrier, when asked whether his horse could "draw inferences," readily replied, "Yes, any thing in reason;" but here, it seems, is a man of genius who has no similar gift.

We ourselves, we confess, are too young in the study of human nature to have met with any such anomaly. Never yet has it been our fortune to fall in with any man of genius, whose conclusions did not correspond better with his premises, and not worse, than those of other men; whose genius, when it once came to be understood, did not manifest itself in a deeper, fuller, truer view of all things human and divine, than the clearest of your so laudable "practical men" had claim to. Such, we say, has been our uniform experience; so uniform, that we now hardly ever expect to see it contradicted. True it is, the old Pythagorean argument of "the master said it," has long ceased to be available: in these days, no man, except the Pope of Rome, is altogether exempt from error of judgment; doubtless a man of genius may chance to adopt false opinions; nay, rather, like all other sons of Adam, except that same enviable Pope, *must* occasionally adopt such. Nevertheless, we reckon it a good maxim, that "no error is fully confuted till we have seen not only *that* it is an error, but *how* it became one;" till finding that it clashes with the principles of truth, established in our own mind, we find also in what way it had seemed to harmonize with the principles of truth established in that other mind, perhaps so unspeakably superior to ours. Treated by this method it still appears to us, according to the old saying, that the errors of the wise man are literally more instructive than the truths of a fool. For the wise man travels in lofty, far-seeing regions; the fool in low-lying, high-fenced lanes: retracing the footsteps of the former, to discover where he deviated, whole provinces of the Universe are laid open to us; in the path of the latter, granting even that he have not deviated at all, little is laid open to us but two wheel-ruts and two hedges.

On these grounds we reckon it more profitable, in almost any case, to have to do with men of depth, than with men of shallowness: and were it possible, we would read no book that was not written by one of the former class; all members of which we would love and venerate, how perverse soever they may seem to us at first; nay, though, after the fullest investigation, we still found many things to pardon in them. Such of our readers as at all participate in this predilection will not blame us for bringing them acquainted with Novalis, a man of the most indisputable talent, poetical and philosophical; whose opinions, extraordinary, nay, altogether wild and baseless as they often appear, are not without a strict coherence in his own mind, and will lead any other mind, that examines them faithfully, into endless considerations; opening the strangest inquiries, new truths, or new possibilities of truth, a whole unexpected world of thought, where, whether for belief or denial, the deepest questions await us.

In what is called reviewing such a book as this, we are aware that to the judicious craftsman two methods present themselves. The first and most convenient is for the Reviewer to perch himself resolutely, as it were, on the shoulder of his Author, and therefrom to show as if he commanded him, and looked down on him by natural superiority of stature. Whatsoever the great man says or does, the little man shall treat him with an air of knowingness and light condescending mockery; professing, with much covert sarcasm, that this and that other is beyond *his* comprehension, and cunningly asking his readers if they comprehend it! Herein it will help him mightily, if besides description, he can quote a few passages, which, in their detached state, and taken most probably in quite a wrong acceptation of the words, shall sound strange, and to certain hearers, even absurd; all which will be easy enough, if he have any handiness in the business, and address the right audience; truths, as this world goes, being true only for those that have *some* understanding of them; as, for instance, in the Yorkshire Wolds, and Thames Coal-ships, Christian men enough might be found, at this day, who, if you read them the Thirty-ninth of the *Principia*, would "grin intelligence from ear to ear." On the other hand, should our Reviewer meet with any passage, the wisdom of which, deep, plain, and palpable to the simplest, might cause misgivings in the reader, as if here were a man of half-unknown endowment, whom perhaps it were better to wonder at than laugh at, our Reviewer either quietly suppresses it, or citing it with an air of meritorious candour, calls upon his Author, in a tone of command and encouragement, to lay aside his transcendental crotchets, and write always thus, and *he* will admire him. Whereby the reader again feels comforted; proceeds swimmingly to the conclusion of the "Article," and shuts it with a victorious feeling, not only that he and the Reviewer understand this man, but also that, with some rays of fancy and the like, the man is little better than a living mass of darkness.

In this way does the small Reviewer triumph over great Authors: but it is the triumph of a fool. In this way, too, does he recommend himself to certain readers, but it is the recommendation of a parasite, and of no true servant. The servant would have spoken truth, in this case; truth, that it might have profited, however harsh: the parasite glosses his master with sweet speeches, that he may filch applause, and certain "guineas per sheet," from him; substituting for Ignorance, which was harmless, Error which is not so. And yet to the vulgar reader, naturally enough, that flattering unction is full of solacement. In fact, to a reader of this sort few things can be more alarming than to find that his own little Parish, where he lived so snug and absolute, is, after all, *not* the whole Universe; that beyond the hill which screened his house from the west wind, and grew his kitchen vegetables so sweetly, there are other hills and other hamlets, nay, mountains and towered cities; with all which, if he would continue to pass for a Geographer, he must forthwith make himself acquainted. Now this Reviewer, often his fellow Parishioner, is a safe man; leads him pleasantly to the hill top; shows him that indeed there are, or seem to be, other expanses, these, too, of boundless extent: but with only cloud mountains, and *fatamorgana* cities; the true character of that region being Vacuity, or at best a stony desert tenanted by Gryphons and Chimæras.

Surely, if printing is not, like courtier speech, "the art of *concealing* thought," all this must be blamable enough. Is it the Reviewer's real trade to be the pander of laziness, self-conceit, and all manner of contemptuous stupidity on the part of his reader; carefully ministering to these propensities; carefully fencing off whatever might invade that fool's-paradise with news of disturbance? Is he the priest of Literature and Philosophy, to interpret their mysteries to the common man; as a faithful preacher, teaching him to understand what is adapted for his understanding, to reverence what is adapted for higher understandings than his? Or merely the lackey of Dullness, striving for certain wages, of pudding or praise, by the month or quarter, to perpetuate the reign of presumption and triviality on earth? If the latter, will he not be counselled to pause for an instant, and reflect seriously, whether starvation were worse or were better than such a dog's-existence?

Our reader perceives that we are for adopting the second method with regard to Novalis; that we wish less to insult over this highly-gifted man, than to gain some insight into him; that we look upon his mode of being and thinking as very singular, but not, therefore, necessarily very contemptible; as a matter, in fact, worthy of examination, and difficult beyond most others to examine wisely and with profit. Let no small man expect that, in this case, a Samson is to be led forth, blinded and manacled, to make him sport. Nay, might it not, in a spiritual sense, be death, as surely it would be damage, to the small man himself? For is not this habit of sneering at all greatness, of forcibly bringing down all greatness to his own height, one chief cause which keeps that height so very inconsiderable? Come of it what may, we have no refreshing dew for the small man's vanity in this place, nay, rather, as charitable brethren, and fellow-sufferers from that same evil, we would gladly lay the sickle to that reed-grove of self-conceit, which has grown round him, and reap it altogether away, that so the true figure of the world, and his own true figure, might no longer be utterly hidden from him. Does this our brother, then, refuse to accompany us, without such allurements? He must even retain our best wishes, and abide by his own hearth.

Farther, to the honest few that still go along with us on this occasion, we are bound in justice to say that, far from looking down on Novalis, we cannot place either them or ourselves on a level with him. To explain so strange an individuality, to exhibit a mind of this depth and singularity before the minds of readers so foreign to him in every sense, would be a vain pretension in us. With the best will, and after repeated trials, we have gained but a feeble notion of Novalis for ourselves; his Volumes come before us with every disadvantage; they are the posthumous works of a man cut off in early life, while his opinions, far from being matured for the public eye were still lying crude and disjointed before his own: for most part written down in the shape of detached aphorisms, "none of them," as he says himself, "untrue or unimportant to his own mind," but naturally requiring to be remodelled, expanded, compressed, as the matter cleared up more and more into logical unity; at best but fragments of a great scheme which he did not live to realize. If his editors, Friedrich Schlegel and Ludwig Tieck, declined commenting on these Writings, we may well be excused for declining to do so. "It cannot be our purpose here," says Tieck, "to recommend the following Works, or to judge them; probable as it must be that any judgment delivered at this stage of the matter would be a premature and unripe one: for a spirit of such originality must first be comprehended, his will understood, and his loving intention felt and replied to; so that not till his ideas have taken root in other minds, and brought forth new ideas, shall we see rightly, from the historical sequence, what place he himself occupied, and what relation to his country he truly bore."

Meanwhile, Novalis is a figure of such importance in German Literature, that no student of it can pass him by without attention. If we must not attempt interpreting this Work for our readers, we are bound at least to point out its existence, and according to our best knowledge, direct such of them as take an interest in the matter how to investigate it farther for their own benefit. For this purpose, it may be well that we leave our Author to speak chiefly for himself; subjoining only such expositions as cannot be dispensed with for even verbal intelligibility, and as we can offer on our own surety with some degree of confidence. By way of basis to the whole inquiry, we prefix some particulars of his short life; a part of our task which Tieck's clear and graceful Narrative, given as "Preface to the Third Edition," renders easy for us.

Friedrich von Hardenberg, better known in Literature by the pseudonym "Novalis," was born on the 2d of May, 1772, at a country residence of his family in the Grafschaft of Mansfield, in Saxony. His father, who had been a soldier in youth, and still retained a liking for that profession, was at this time Director of the Saxon Salt-works; an office of some considerable trust and dignity. Tieck says, "he was a vigorous, unweariedly active man, of open, resolute character, a true German. His religious feelings made him a member of the Herrnhut Communion; yet his disposition continued gay, frank, rugged, and downright." The mother also was distinguished for her worth; "a pattern of noble piety and Christian mildness;" virtues which her subsequent life gave opportunity enough for exercising.

On young Friedrich, whom we may continue to call Novalis, the qualities of his parents must have exercised more than usual influence; for he was brought up in the most retired manner, with scarcely any associate but a sister one year older than himself, and the two brothers that were next to him in age. A decidedly religious temper seems to have diffused itself, under many benignant aspects, over the whole family: in Novalis especially it continued the ruling principle through life; manifested no less in his scientific speculation, than in his feelings and conduct. In childhood he is said to have been remarkable chiefly for the entire, enthusiastic affection with which he loved his mother; and for a certain still secluded disposition, such that he took no pleasure in boyish sports, and rather shunned the society of other children. Tieck mentions that, till his ninth year, he was reckoned nowise quick of apprehension; but, at this period, strangely enough, some violent biliary disease, which had almost cut him off, seemed to awaken his faculties into proper life, and he became the readiest, eagerest learner in all branches of his scholarship.

In his eighteenth year, after a few months of preparation in some *Gymnasium*, the only instruction he appears to have received in any public school, he repaired to Jena; and continued there for three years; after which he spent one season in the Leipzig University, and another, "to complete his studies," in that of Wittenberg. It seems to have been at Jena that he became acquainted with Friedrich Schlegel; where also, we suppose, he studied under Fichte. For both of these men he conceived a high admiration and affection; and both of them had, clearly enough, "a great and abiding effect on his whole life." Fichte, in particular, whose lofty eloquence, and clear calm enthusiasm are said to have made him irresistible as a teacher,* had quite gained Novalis to his doctrines; indeed the *Wissenschaftslehre*, which, as we are told of the latter, "he studied with unwearied zeal," appears to to have been the groundwork of all his future speculations in Philosophy. Besides these metaphysical inquiries, and the usual attainments in classical literature, Novalis seems "to have devoted himself with ardour to the Physical Sciences, and to Mathematics, the basis of them:" at an early period of his life, he had read much History "with extraordinary eagerness;" Poems had from of old been "the delight of his leisure;" particularly that species denominated *Mährchen*, (Traditionary Tale,) which continued a favourite with him to the last; as almost from infancy it had been a chosen amusement of his to read these compositions, and even to recite such, of his own invention. One remarkable piece of that sort he has himself left us, inserted in *Heinrich von Ofterdingen*, his chief literary performance.

But the time had now arrived, when study must become subordinate to action, and what is called a profession be fixed upon. At the breaking out of the French War, Novalis had been seized with a strong and altogether unexpected taste for a military life: however, the arguments and pressing entreaties of his friends ultimately prevailed over this whim; it seems to have been settled that he should follow his father's line of occupation; and so about the end of 1794, he removed to Arnstadt in Thuringia; "to train himself in practical affairs under the *Kreis-Amtmann* Just." In this *Kreis-Amtmann* (manager of a Circle) he found a wise and kind friend; applied himself honestly to business; and in all his serious calculations, may have looked forward to a life as smooth and commonplace as his past years had been. One incident, and that too of no unusual sort, appears in Tieck's opinion to have altered the whole form of his existence.

"It was not very long after his arrival at Arnstadt, when in a country mansion of the neighbourhood, he became acquainted with Sophie von K———. The first glance of this fair and wonderfully lovely form was decisive for his whole life; nay, we may say that the feeling, which now penetrated and inspired him, was the substance and essence of his whole life. Sometimes, in the look and figure of a child, there will stamp itself an expression, which, as it is too angelic and etherially beautiful, we are forced to call unearthly or celestial; and commonly at sight of such purified and almost transparent faces there comes on us a fear that they are too tender and delicately fashioned for this life: that it is Death, or Immortality, which looks forth so expressively on us from these glancing eyes; and too often a quick decay converts our mournful foreboding into certainty. Still more affecting are such figures, when their first period is happily passed over, and they come before us blooming on the eve of maidhood. All persons, that have known this wondrous loved one of our Friend, agree in testifying that no description can express in what grace and celestial harmony the fair being moved,

* Schelling, we have been informed, gives account of Fichte and his *Wissenschaftslehre*, to the following effect: "The Philosophy of Fichte was like lightning; it appeared only for a moment, but it kindled a fire which will burn for ever."

what beauty shone in her, what softness and majesty encircled her. Novalis became a poet every time he chanced to speak of it. She had concluded her thirteenth year when he first saw her: the spring and summer of 1795 were the blooming time of his life; every hour that he could spare from business he spent in Grüningen; and in the fall of that same year he obtained the wished-for promise from Sophie's parents."

Unhappily, however, these halcyon days were of too short continuance. Soon after this, Sophie fell dangerously sick "of a fever, attended with pains in the side;" and her lover had the worst consequences to fear. By and by, indeed, the fever left her; but not the pain, "which by its violence still spoiled for her many a fair hour," and gave rise to various apprehensions, though the Physician asserted that it was of no importance. Partly satisfied with this favourable prognostication, Novalis had gone to Weissenfels, to his parents, and was full of business; being now appointed Auditor in the department of which his father was Director; through winter the news from Grüningen were of a favourable sort; in spring he visited the family himself, and found his Sophie to all appearance well. But suddenly, in summer, his hopes and occupations were interrupted by tidings that, "she was in Jena, and had undergone a surgical operation." Her disease was an abscess in the liver: it had been her wish that he should not hear of her danger till the worst were over. The Jena surgeon gave hopes of a recovery though a slow one; but ere long the operation had to be repeated, and now it was feared that his patient's strength was too far exhausted. The young maiden bore all this with inflexible courage, and the cheerfulest resignation: her Mother and Sister, Novalis, with his Parents, and two of his Brothers, all deeply interested in the event, did their utmost to comfort her. In December, by her own wish, she returned home; but it was evident that she grew weaker and weaker. Novalis went and came between Grüningen and Weissenfels, where also he found a house of mourning; for Erasmus, one of these two Brothers, had long been sickly, and was now believed to be dying.

"The 17th of March," says Tieck, "was the fifteenth birthday of his Sophie; and on the 19th about noon she departed. No one durst tell Novalis these tidings: at last his Brother Carl undertook it. The poor youth shut himself up, and after three days and three nights of weeping, set out for Arnstadt, that there with his true friend he might be near the spot, which now hid the remains of what was dearest to him. On the 14th of April, his Brother Erasmus also left this world. Novalis wrote to inform his Brother Carl of the event, who had been obliged to make a journey into Lower Saxony: 'Be of good courage,' said he, 'Erasmus has prevailed; the flowers of our fair garland are dropping off Here, one by one, that they may be united Yonder, lovelier and for ever.'"

Among the papers published in these Volumes are three letters written about this time, which mournfully indicate the author's mood. "It has grown Evening around me," says he, "while I was looking into the red Morning. My grief is boundless as my love. For three years she has been my hourly thought. She alone bound me to life, to the country, to my occupations. With her I am parted from all; for now I scarcely have *myself* any more. But it has grown Evening; and I feel as if I had to travel early; and so I would fain be at rest, and see nothing but kind faces about me;—all in her spirit would I live, be soft and mild-hearted as she was." And again, some weeks later: "I live over the old, bygone life here, in still meditation. Yesterday I was twenty-five years old. I was in Grüningen, and stood beside her grave. It is a friendly spot; enclosed with a simple white railing; lies apart, and high. There is still room in it. The Village, with its blooming gardens, leans up around the hill; and at this point and that the eye loses itself in blue distances. I know you would have liked to stand by me, and stick the flowers, my birthday gifts, one by one into her hillock. This time two years, she made me a gay present, with a flag and national cockade on it. To-day her parents gave me the little things which she, still joyfully, had received on her last birthday. Friend,—it continues Evening, and will soon be Night. If you go away, think of me kindly, and visit, when you return, the still house, where your Friend rests for ever, with the ashes of his beloved. Fare you well!"—Nevertheless, a singular composure came over him: from the very depths of his griefs, arose a peace and pure joy, such as till then he had never known.

"In this season," observed Tieck, "Novalis lived only to his sorrow: it was natural for him to regard the visible and the invisible world as one; and to distinguish Life and Death, only by his longing for the latter. At the same time, too, Life became for him a glorified Life; and his whole being melted away as into a bright, conscious vision of a higher Existence. From the sacredness of Sorrow, from heartfelt love, and the pious wish for death, his temper, and all his conceptions are to be explained: and it seems possible that this time, with its deep griefs, planted in him the germ of death, if it was not, in any case, his appointed lot to be so soon snatched away from us.

"He remained many weeks in Thuringia; and came back comforted and truly purified, to his engagements: which he pursued more zealously than ever, though he now regarded himself as a stranger on the earth. In this period, some earlier, many later, especially in the Autumn of this year, occur most of those compositions, which, in the way of extract and selection, we have here given to the Public, under the title of *Fragments*: so likewise the *Hymns to the Night*."

Such is our Biographer's account of this matter, and of the weighty inference it has led him to. We have detailed it the more minutely, and almost in the very words of the text, the better to put our readers in a condition for judging on what grounds Tieck rests his opinion, that herein lies the key to the whole spiritual history of Novalis, that "the feeling which now penetrated and inspired him, may be said to have been the substance of his Life." It would ill become us to contradict one so well qualified to judge of all subjects, and who enjoyed such peculiar opportunities for forming a right judgment of this: meanwhile we may say that, to our own minds, after all consideration, the certainty of this hypothesis will nowise become clear. Or rather, perhaps, it is to the expression, to the too determinate and exclusive language in which the hypothesis is worded, that we should object; for so plain does the truth of the case seem to us, we cannot but believe that Tieck himself would consent to modify his statement. That the whole philosophical and moral existence of such a man as Novalis should have been shaped and determined by the death of a young girl, almost a child, specially distinguished, so far as is shown, by nothing save her beauty, which at any rate must have been very short-lived, will doubtless seem to every one a singular concatenation. We cannot but think that some result precisely similiar in moral effect might have been attained by many different means; nay, that by one means or another, it would not have failed to be attained. For spirits like Novalis, earthly fortune is in no instance so sweet and smooth, that it does not by and by teach the great doctrine of *Entsagen*, of "Renunciation," by which alone, as a wise man well known to Herr Tieck has observed, "can the real entrance on Life be properly said to begin." Experience, the grand School-master, seems to have taught Novalis this doctrine very early by the wreck of his first passionate wish; and herein lies the real influence of Sophie von K. on his character; an influence which, as we imagine, many other things might and would have equally exerted: for it is less the severity of the Teacher than the aptness of the Pupil that secures the lesson; nor do the purifying effects of frustrated Hope, and Affection that in this world will ever be homeless, depend on the worth or loveliness of its objects, but on that of the heart which cherished it, and can draw mild wisdom from so stern a disappointment. We do not say that Novalis continued the same as if this young maiden had not been; causes and effects connecting every man and thing with every other extend through all Time and all Space; but surely it appears unjust to represent him as so altogether pliant in the hands of Accident; a mere pipe for Fortune to play tunes on; and which sounded a mystic, deep, almost unearthly melody, simply because a young woman was beautiful and mortal.

We feel the more justified in these hard-hearted and so unromantic strictures on reading the very next paragraph of Tieck's Narrative. Directly on the back of this occurrence, Novalis goes to Freyberg; and there in 1798, it may be therefore somewhat more or somewhat less than a year after the death of his first love, forms an acquaintance, and engagement to marry, with a "Julie von Ch——!" Indeed, ever afterwards, to the end, his life appears to have been more than usually cheerful and happy. Tieck knows not what well to say of this betrothment, which in the eyes of most Novel-readers will have so shocking an appearance: he admits that "perhaps to any but his intimate friends it may seem singular;" asserts, notwithstanding, that "Sophie, as may be seen also in his writings, continued the centre of his thoughts; nay, as one departed, she stood in higher reverence with him than when visible and near;" and hurrying on, almost as over an unsafe subject, declares that Novalis felt nevertheless "as if loveliness of mind and person might in some measure replace his loss;" and so leaves us to our own reflections on the matter. We consider it as throwing light on the above criticism; and greatly restricting our acceptance of Tieck's theory. Yet perhaps, after all, it is only in a Minerva-Press Novel, or to the more tender Imagination, that such a proceeding would seem very blamable. Constancy, in its true sense, may be called the root of all excellence; especially excellent is constancy in active well-doing, in friendly helpfulness to those that love us, and to those that hate us: but constancy in passive suffering, again, in spite of the high value put upon it in Circulating Libraries, is a distinctly inferior virtue, rather an accident than a virtue, and, at all events, is of extreme rarity in this world. To Novalis, his Sophie might still be as a saintly presence, mournful and unspeakably mild, to be worshipped in the inmost shrine of his memory: but worship of this sort is not man's sole business; neither should we censure Novalis that he dries his tears, and once more looks abroad with hope on the earth, which is still, as it was before, the strangest complex of mystery and light, of joy as well as sorrow. "Life belongs to the living; and he that lives must be prepared for vicissitudes." The questionable circumstance with Novalis is his perhaps too great rapidity in that second courtship; a fault or misfortune the more to be regretted, as this marriage also was to remain a project, and only the anticipation of it to be enjoyed by him.

It was for the purpose of studying mineralogy, under the famous Werner, that Novalis had gone to Freyberg. For this science he had great fondness, as indeed for all the physical sciences: which, if we may judge from his writings, he seems to have prosecuted on a great and original principle, very different both from that of our idle theorizers and generalizers, and that of the still more melancholy class who merely "collect facts," and for the torpor or total extinction of the thinking faculty, strive to make up by the more assiduous use of the blowpipe and goniometer. The commencement of a work, entitled the *Disciples at Sais*, intended, as Tieck informs us, to be a "Physical Romance," was written in Freyberg, at this time: but it lay unfinished, unprosecuted; and now comes before us as a very mysterious fragment, disclosing scientific depths, which we have not light to see into, much less means to fathom and accurately measure. The various hypothetic views of "Nature," that is, of the visible Creation, which are here given out in the words of the several "Pupils," differ, almost all of them, more or less, from any that we have ever elsewhere met with. To this work we shall have occasion to refer more particularly in the sequel.

The acquaintance which Novalis formed, soon after this, with the elder Schlegel, (August

Wilhelm,) and still more that of Tieck, whom also he first met in Jena, seems to have operated a considerable diversion in his line of study. Tieck and the Schlegels, with some less active associates, among whom are now mentioned Wackenroder and Novalis, were at this time engaged in their far-famed campaign against Duncedom, or what called itself the "Old School" of Literature; which old and rather despicable "School" they had already, both by regular and guerrilla warfare, reduced to great straits; as ultimately, they are reckoned to have succeeded in utterly extirpating it, or at least driving it back to the very confines of its native Cimmeria. It seems to have been in connection with these men, that Novalis first came before the world as a writer: certain of his *Fragments*, under the title of *Blüthenstaub* (Pollen of Flowers;) his *Hymns to the Night*, and various poetical compositions, were sent forth in F. Schlegel's *Musen-Almanach*, and other periodicals under the same or kindred management. Novalis himself seems to profess that it was Tieck's influence which chiefly "reawakened Poetry in him." As to what reception these pieces met with, we have no information: however, Novalis seems to have been ardent and diligent in his new pursuit, as in his old ones; and no less happy than diligent.

"In the summer of 1800," says Tieck, "I saw him for the first time, while visiting my friend Wilhelm Schlegel; and our acquaintance soon became the most confidential friendship. They were bright days those, which we passed with Schlegel, Schelling, and some other friends. On my return homewards, I visited him in his house, and made acquaintance with his family. Here he read me the *Disciples at Sais*, and many of his *Fragments*. He escorted me as far as Halle; and we enjoyed in Giebichenstein, in the Reichardts' house, some other delightful hours. About this time, the first thought of his *Ofterdingen* had occurred. At an earlier period, certain of his *Spiritual Songs* had been composed; they were to form part of a Christian Hymn-book, which he meant to accompany with a collection of Sermons.' For the rest, he was very diligent in his professional labours; whatever he did was done with the heart; the smallest concern was not insignificant to him."

The professional labours here alluded to, seem to have left much leisure on his hands: room for frequent change of place, and even of residence. Not long afterwards, we find him "living for a long while in a solitary spot of the Güldne Aue in Thuringia, at the foot of the Kyffhaüser Mountain;" his chief society two military men, subsequently Generals; "in which solitude great part of his *Ofterdingen* was written." The first volume of this *Heinrich von Ofterdingen*, a sort of Art-Romance, intended, as he himself said, to be an "Apothesis of Poetry," was ere long published; under what circumstances, or with what result, we have, as before, no notice. Tieck had for some time been resident in Jena, and at intervals saw much of Novalis. On preparing to quit that abode, he went to pay him a farewell visit at Weissenfels; found him "somewhat paler," but full of gladness and hope; quite inspired with plans of his future happiness; his house was already fitted up; in a few months he was to be wedded: no less zealously did he speak of the speedy conclusion of *Ofterdingen*, and other books; his life seemed expanding in the richest activity and love." This was in 1800; four years ago Novalis had longed and looked for death, and it was not appointed him; now life is again rich, and far extending in his eyes, and its close is at hand. Tieck parted with him, and it proved to be for ever.

In the month of August, Novalis, preparing for his journey to Freyberg, on so joyful an occasion, was alarmed with an appearance of blood proceeding from the lungs. The Physician treated it as a slight matter; nevertheless, the marriage was postponed. He went to Dresden with his parents, for medical advice; abode there for some time in no improving state; on learning the accidental death of a young brother at home, he ruptured a blood-vessel; and the Doctor then declared his malady incurable. This, as usual in such maladies, was nowise the patient's own opinion; he wished to try a warmer climate, but was thought too weak for the journey. In January (1801) he returned home, visibly to all, but himself, in rapid decline. His bride had already been to see him, in Dresden. We may give the rest in Tieck's words:

"The nearer he approached his end, the more confidently did he expect a speedy recovery; for the cough diminished, and excepting languor, he had no feeling of sickness. With the hope and the longing for life, new talent and fresh strength seemed also to awaken in him; he thought, with renewed love, of all his projected labours; he determined on writing *Ofterdingen* over again from the very beginning; and shortly before his death, he said on one occasion, 'Never till now did I know what Poetry was; innumerable Songs and Poems, and of quite different stamp from any of my former ones, have arisen in me.' From the nineteenth of March, the death-day of his Sophie, he became visibly weaker: many of his friends visited him; and he felt great joy when, on the twenty-first, his true and oldest friend, Friedrich Schlegel, came to him from Jena. With him he conversed at great length; especially upon their several literary operations. During these days he was very lively; his nights too were quiet; and he enjoyed pretty sound sleep. On the twenty-fifth, about six in the morning, he made his brother hand him certain books, that he might look for something; then he ordered breakfast and talked cheerfully till eight; towards nine he bade his brother play a little to him on the harpsichord, and in the course of the music fell asleep. Friedrich Schlegel soon afterwards came into the room, and found him quietly sleeping: this sleep lasted till near twelve, when without the smallest motion he passed away, and unchanged in death, retained his common friendly looks as if he yet lived.

"So died," continues the affectionate Biographer, "before he had completed his twenty-ninth year, this our Friend; in whom his extensive acquirements, his philosophical talent, and his poetic genius, must alike obtain our love and admiration. As he had so far outrun his time, our country might have expected extraordinary things from such gifts, had this early death not overtaken him: as it is, the unfinished writings he left behind him have already had a wide influence; and many of his great thoughts will yet, in time coming, lend their inspiration, and noble minds and deep thinkers will be enlightened and enkindled by the sparks of his genius.

"Novalis was tall, slender, and of noble proportions. He wore his light-brown hair in long clustering locks, which at that time was less unusual than it would be now; his hazel eye was clear and glancing; and the colour of his face, especially of the fine brow, almost transparent. Hand and foot were somewhat too large, and without fine character. His look was at all times cheerful and kind. For those who distinguish a man only in so far as he puts himself forward, or by studious breeding, by fashionable bearing, endeavours to shine or to be singular, Novalis was lost in the crowd: to the more practised eye, again, he presented a figure which might be called beautiful. In outline and expression, his face strikingly resembled that of the Evangelist John, as we see him in the large noble painting by Albrecht Dürer, preserved at Nürnberg and München.

"In speaking, he was lively and loud, his gestures strong. I never saw him tired: though we had talked till far in the night, it was still only on purpose that he stopped, for the sake of rest, and even then he used to read before sleeping. Tedium he never felt, even in oppressive company, among mediocre men; for he was sure to find out one or other, who could give him some yet new piece of knowledge, such as he could turn to use, insignificant as it might seem. His kindliness, his frank bearing, made him a universal favourite: his skill in the art of social intercourse was so great, that smaller minds did not perceive how high he stood above them. Though in conversation he delighted the most to unfold the deeps of the soul, and spoke as inspired of the regions of invisible worlds, yet was he mirthful as a child; would jest in free artless gayety, and heartily give in to the jestings of his company. Without vanity, without learned haughtiness, far from every affectation and hypocrisy, he was a genuine, true man, the purest and loveliest imbodiment of a high immortal spirit."

So much for the outward figure and history of Novalis. Respecting his inward structure and significance, which our readers are here principally interested to understand, we have already acknowledged that we had no complete insight to boast of. The slightest perusal of his writings indicates to us a mind of wonderful depth and originality; but at the same time, of a nature or habit so abstruse, and altogether different from any thing we ourselves have notice or experience of, that to penetrate fairly into its essential character, much more to picture it forth in visual distinctness, would be an extremely difficult task. Nay, perhaps, if attempted by the means familiar to us, an impossible task; for Novalis belongs to that class of persons, who do not recognise the "syllogistic method," as the chief organ for investigating truth, or feel themselves bound at all times to stop short where its light fails them. Many of his opinions he would despair of proving in the most patient Court of Law; and would remain well content that they should be disbelieved there. He much loved, and had assiduously studied, Jacob Böhme and other mystical writers; and was, openly enough, in good part a Mystic himself. Not indeed what we English, in common speech, call a Mystic; which means only a man whom we do not understand, and, in self-defence, reckon or would fain reckon a Dunce. Novalis was a Mystic, or had an affinity with Mysticism, in the primary and true meaning of that word, exemplified in some shape among our own Puritan Divines, and which at this day carries no opprobrium with it in Germany, or except among certain more unimportant classes, in any other country. Nay, in this sense, great honours are recorded of Mysticism: Tasso, as may be seen in several of his prose writings, was professedly a Mystic; Dante is regarded as a chief man of that class.

Nevertheless, with all due tolerance or reverence for Novalis's Mysticism, the question still returns on us: How shall we understand it, and in any measure shadow it forth? How may that spiritual condition which by its own account is like pure Light, colourless, formless, infinite, be represented by mere Logic-Painters, mere Engravers we might say, who, except copper and burin, producing the most finite black-on-white, have no means of representing any thing? Novalis himself has a line or two, and no more, expressly on Mysticism; "What is Mysticism?" asks he. "What is it that should come to be treated mystically? Religion, Love, Nature, Polity.—All selected things (*alles Auserwählte*) have a reference to Mysticism. If all men were but one pair of lovers, the difference between Mysticism and Non-Mysticism were at an end." In which little sentence, unhappily, our reader obtains no clearness; feels rather as if he were looking into darkness visible. We must entreat him, nevertheless, to keep up his spirits in this business; and above all, to assist us with his friendliest, cheerfullest endeavour: perhaps some faint far-off view of that same mysterious Mysticism may at length rise upon us.

To ourselves, it somewhat illustrates the nature of Novalis's opinions, when we consider the then and present state of German metaphysical science generally; and the fact, stated above, that he gained his first notions on this subject from Fichte's *Wissenschaftslehre*. It is true, as Tieck remarks, "he sought to open for himself a new path in Philosophy; to unite Philosophy with Religion;" and so diverged in some degree from his first instructor; or, as it more probably seemed to himself, prosecuted Fichte's scientific inquiry into its highest practical results. At all events, his metaphysical creed, so far as we can gather it from these writings, appears everywhere in its essential lineaments, synonymous with what little we understand of Fichte's, and might indeed, safely enough for our present purpose, be classed under the head of Kantism, or German metaphysics generally.

Now, without entering into the intricacies of German Philosophy, we need here only advert to the character of Idealism, on which it is everywhere founded, and which universally pervades it. In all German systems, since the time of Kant, it is the fundamental principle to deny the existence of Matter; or rather we should say to believe it in a radically different sense from that in which the Scotch Philosopher strives to demonstrate it, and the English Unphilosopher believes it without demonstration. To any of our readers, who has dipped never so slightly into metaphysical reading, this Idealism will be no inconceivable thing. Indeed it is singular how widely diffused, and under what different aspects we meet with it among the most dissimilar classes of mankind. Our Bishop Berkeley seems to have adopted it from religious inducements: Father Boscovich was led to a very cognate result, in his *Theoria Philosophiæ Naturalis*, from merely mathematical considerations. Of the ancient Pyrrho or the modern Hume we do not speak: but in the opposite end of the Earth, as Sir W. Jones informs us, a similar theory, of immemorial age, prevails among the theologians of Hindostan. Nay, Professor Stuart has declared his opinion, that whoever at some time of his life has not entertained this theory, may reckon that he has yet shown no talent for metaphysical research. Neither is it any argument against the Idealist to say that, since he denies the absolute existence of Matter, he ought in conscience likewise to deny its relative existence; and plunge over precipices, and run himself through with swords, by way of recreation, since these, like all other material things, are only phantasms and spectra, and therefore of no consequence. If a man, corporeally taken, is but a phantasm and spectrum himself, all this will ultimately amount to much the same as it did before. Yet herein lies Dr. Reid's grand triumph over the Skeptics; which is as good as no triumph whatever. For as to the argument which he and his followers insist on, under all possible variety of figures, it amounts only to this very plain consideration, that "men naturally, and without reasoning, *believe* in the existence of Matter;" and seems, Philosophically speaking, not to have any value; nay, the introduction of it into Philosophy may be considered as an act of suicide on the part of that science, the life and business of which, that of "*interpreting* Appearances," is hereby at an end. Curious it is, moreover, to observe how these Common-sense Philosophers, men who brag chiefly of their irrefragable logic, and keep watch and ward, as if this were their special trade, against "Mysticism," and "Visionary Theories," are themselves obliged to base their whole system on Mysticism, and a Theory; on Faith, in short, and that of a very comprehensive kind; the Faith, namely, either that man's Senses are themselves Divine, or that they afford not only an honest, but a *literal* representation of the workings of some Divinity. So true is it that for these men also, all knowledge of the visible rests on belief of the invisible, and derives its first meaning and certainty therefrom!

The Idealist again boasts that his Philosophy is Transcendental, that is, "ascending *beyond* the senses;" which, he asserts, *all* Philosophy, properly so called, by its nature is and must be: and in this way he is led to various unexpected conclusions. To a Transcendentalist, Matter has an existence but only as a Phenomenon: were *we* not there, neither would it be there; it is a mere Relation, or rather the result of a Relation between our living Souls and the great First Cause; and depends for its apparent qualities on *our* bodily and mental organs; having itself *no* intrinsic qualities, being, in the common sense of that word, Nothing. The tree is green and hard, not of its own natural virtue, but simply because my eye and my hand are fashioned so as to discern such and such appearances under such and such conditions. Nay, as an Idealist might say, even on the most popular grounds, *must* it not be so? Bring a sentient Being, with eyes a little different, with fingers ten times harder than mine; and to him that Thing which I call Tree shall be yellow and soft, as truly as to me it is green and hard. Form his Nervous structure in all points the *reverse* of mine, and this same Tree shall not be combustible, or heat producing, but dissoluble and cold-producing, not high and convex, but deep and concave; shall simply have *all* properties exactly the reverse of those I attribute to it. There is, in fact, says Fichte, no Tree there; but only a Manifestation of Power from something which is *not I*. The same is true of material Nature at large, of the whole visible Universe, with all its movements, figures, accidents, and qualities; all are Impressions produced on *me* by something *different from me*. This, we suppose, may be the foundation of what Fichte means by his far-famed *Ich* and *Nicht-Ich* (I and Not-I); words which, taking lodging (to use the Hudibrastic phrase) in certain "heads that were to be let unfurnished," occasioned a hollow echo, as of Laughter, from the empty Apartments; though the words are in themselves quite harmless, and may represent the basis of a metaphysical Philosophy as fitly as any other words. But farther, and what is still stranger than such Idealism, according to these Kantean systems, the organs of the Mind too, what is called the Understanding, are of no less arbitrary, and, as it were, accidental character than those of the Body. Time and Space themselves are not external but internal entities: they have no outward existence, there is no Time and no Space *out* of the mind; they are mere *forms* of man's spiritual being, *laws* under which his thinking nature is constituted to act. This seems the hardest conclusion of all; but it is an important one with Kant; and is not given forth as a dogma; but carefully deduced in his *Critik der Reinen Vernunft* with great precision, and the strictest form of argument.

The reader would err widely who supposed that this Transcendental system of Metaphysics was a mere intellectual card-castle, or logical hocus-pocus, contrived from sheer idleness, and for sheer idleness, being without any bearing on the practical interests of men. On the contrary, however false, or however true, it is the most serious in its purport of all Philosophies propounded in these latter centuries; has been taught chiefly by men of the loftiest and most earnest character; and does bear, with a direct and highly comprehensive influence, on the most vital interests of men. To say nothing of the views it opens in regard to the course and management of what is called Natural Science, we cannot but perceive that its effects, for such as adopt it, on Morals and Religion, must in these days be of almost boundless importance. To take only that last and seemingly strangest doctrine, for example, concerning Time and Space, we shall find that to the Kantist it yields, almost immediately, a remarkable result of this sort. If Time and Space have no absolute existence out of our minds, it removes a stumbling-block from the very threshold of our Theology. For on this ground, when we say that the Deity is omnipresent and eternal, that with Him it is a universal Here and Now, we say nothing wonderful: nothing but that He also created Time and Space, that Time and Space are not laws of His being, but only of ours. Nay to the Transcendentalist, clearly enough, the whole question of the origin and existence of Nature must be greatly simplified: the old hostility of Matter is at an end, for Matter is itself annihilated, and the black Spectre, Atheism, "with all its sickly dews," melts into nothingness for ever. But farther, if it be, as Kant maintains, that the logical mechanism of the mind is arbitrary, so to speak, and might have been made different, it will follow that all inductive conclusions, all conclusions of the Understanding, have only a relative truth, are true only for *us*, and *if* some other thing be true. Thus far Hume and Kant go together, in this branch of the inquiry: but, here occurs the most total, diametrical divergence between them. We allude to the recognition, by these Transcendentalists, of a higher faculty in man than Understanding; of Reason, (*Vernunft*,) the pure, ultimate light of our nature; wherein, as they assert, lies the foundation of all Poetry, Virtue, Religion; things which are properly beyond the province of the Understanding, of which the Understanding *can* take no cognisance except a false one. The elder Jacobi, who indeed is no Kantist, says once, we remember—"It is the instinct of Understanding to *contradict* Reason." Admitting this last distinction and subordination, supposing it scientifically demonstrated, what numberless and weightiest consequences would follow from it alone! These we must leave the considerate reader to deduce for himself; observing only farther, that the *Teologia Mistica*, so much venerated by Tasso in his philosophical writings; the "Mysticism" alluded to above by Novalis; and generally all true Christian Faith and Devotion, appear, so far as we can see, more or less included in this doctrine of the Transcendentalists; under their several shapes, the essence of them all being what is here designated by the name Reason, and set forth as the true sovereign of man's mind.

How deep these and the like principles had impressed themselves on Novalis, we see more and more, the further we study his Writings. Naturally a deep, religious, contemplative spirit; purified also, as we have seen, by harsh Affliction, and familiar in the "Sanctuary of Sorrow," he comes before us as the most ideal of all Idealists. For him the material Creation is but an Appearance, a typical shadow in which the Deity manifests himself to Man. Not only has the unseen world a reality, but the only reality: the rest being not metaphorically, but literally and in scientific strictness, "a show;" in the words of the Poet, *Schall und Rauch umnebelnd Himmels Gluth*, "Sound and Smoke overclouding the Splendour of Heaven." The Invisible World is near us: or rather it is here, in us and about us; were the fleshly coil removed from our Soul, the glories of the Unseen were even now around us; as the Ancients fabled of the Spheral Music. Thus not in word only, but in truth and sober belief, he feels himself encompassed by the Godhead; feels in every thought, that "in Him he lives, moves, and has his being."

On his Philosophic and Poetic Procedure, all this has its natural influence. The aim of Novalis's whole Philosophy, we might say, is to preach and establish the Majesty of Reason, in that stricter sense; to conquer for it all provinces of human thought, and everywhere reduce its vassal, Understanding, into fealty, the right and only useful relation for it. Mighty tasks in this sort lay before himself; of which, in these Writings of his, we trace only scattered indications. In fact, all that he has left is in the shape of fragment; detached expositions and combinations, deep, brief glimpses: but such seems to be their general tendency. One character to be noted in many of these, often too obscure, speculations, is his peculiar manner of viewing Nature; his habit, as it were, of considering Nature rather in the concrete, not analytically and as a divisible Aggregate, but as a self-subsistent universally connected Whole. This also is perhaps partly the fruit of his Idealism. "He had formed the Plan," we are informed, "of a peculiar Encyclopedical Work, in which experiences and ideas from all the different Sciences were mutually to elucidate, confirm, and enforce each other." In this work he had even made some progress. Many of the "Thoughts," and short Aphoristic observations, here published, were intended for it; of such, apparently, it was, for the most part, to have consisted.

As a Poet, Novalis is no less Idealistic than as a Philosopher. His poems are breathings of a high devout soul, feeling always that here he has no home, but looking, as in clear vision, to a "city that hath foundations." He loves external Nature with a singular depth; nay, we might say, he reverences her, and holds unspeakable communings with her: for Nature is no longer dead, hostile Matter, but the veil and mysterious Garment of the Unseen; as it were, the Voice with which the Deity proclaims himself to man. These two qualities,—his pure religious temper, and heart-felt love of Nature,—bring him into true poetic relations both with the spiritual and the material World, and perhaps constitute his chief worth as a Poet; for which art he seems to have originally a genuine, but no exclusive or even very decided endowment.

His moral persuasions, as evinced in his Writings and Life, derive themselves naturally enough from the same source. It is the morality of a man, to whom the Earth and all its glories are in truth a vapour and a Dream, and the Beauty of Goodness the *only* real possession. Poetry, Virtue, Religion, which for other men have but, as it were, a traditionary and imagined existence, are for him the everlasting basis of the Universe; and all earthly acquirements, all with which ambition, Hope, Fear, can tempt us, to toil and sin, are in very deed but a picture of the brain, some reflex shadowed on the mirror of the Infinite, but in themselves air and nothingness. Thus, to live in that Light of Reason, to have, even while here, and encircled with this vision of Existence, our abode in that Eternal City, is the highest and sole duty of man. These things Novalis figures to himself under various images: sometimes he seems to represent the Primeval essence of Being as Love; at other times, he speaks in emblems, of which it would be still more difficult to give a just account; which, therefore, at present, we shall not further notice.

For now, with these far-off sketches of an exposition, the reader must hold himself ready to look into Novalis, for a little, with his own eyes. Whoever has honestly, and with attentive outlook, accompanied us along these wondrous outskirts of Idealism, may find himself as able to interpret Novalis as the majority of German readers would be; which, we think, is fair measure on our part. We shall not attempt any further commentary; fearing that it might be too difficult, and too unthankful a business. Our first extract is from the *Lehrlinge zu Sais*, (Pupil at Sais,) adverted to above. That "Physical Romance," which for the rest contains no story or indication of a story, but only poetized philosophical speeches, and the strangest shadowy allegorical allusions, and indeed is only carried the length of two Chapters, commences, without note of preparation, in this singular wise:

"I. The Pupil.—Men travel in manifold paths: whoso traces and compares these, will find strange Figures come to light; Figures which seem as if they belonged to that great Cipher-writing which one meets with everywhere, on wings of birds, shells of eggs, in clouds, in the snow, in crystals, in forms of rocks, in freezing waters, in the interior and exterior of mountains, of plants, animals, men, in the lights of the sky, in plates of glass and pitch when touched and struck on, in the filings round the magnet, and the singular conjunctures of Chance. In such Figures one anticipates the key to that wondrous Writing, the grammar of it; but this Anticipation will not fix itself into shape, and appears as if, after all, it would not become such a key for us. An *Alcahest* seems poured out over the senses of men. Only for a moment will their wishes, their thoughts thicken into form. Thus do their Anticipations arise; but after short whiles, all is again swimming vaguely before them, even as it did.

"From afar I heard say, that Unintelligibility was but the result of unintelligence; that this sought what itself had, and so could find nowhere else; also that we did not understand Speech, because Speech did not, would not, understand itself; that the genuine Sanscrit spoke for the sake of speaking, because speaking was its pleasure and its nature.

"Not long thereafter, said one: no explanation is required for Holy Writing. Whoso speaks truly is full of eternal life, and wonderfully related to genuine mysteries does his Writing appear to us, for it is a concord from the Symphony of the Universe.

"Surely this voice meant our Teacher; for it is he that can collect the indications which lie scattered on all sides. A singular light kindles in his looks, when at length the high Rune lies before us, and he watches in our eyes whether the star has yet risen upon us, which is to make the Figure visible and intelligible. Does he see us sad, that the darkness will not withdraw? he consoles us, and promises the faithful assiduous seer better fortune in time. Often has he told us how, when he was a child, the impulse to employ his senses, to busy, to fill them, left him no rest. He looked at the stars, and imitated their courses and positions in the sand. Into the ocean of air he gazed incessantly; and never wearied contemplating its clearness, its movements, its clouds, its lights. He gathered stones, flowers, insects, of all sorts, and spread them out in manifold wise, in rows, before him. To men and animals he paid heed; on the shore of the sea he sat, collected mussels. Over his own heart and his own thoughts he watched attentively. He knew not whither his longing was carrying him. As he grew up, he wandered far and wide; viewed other lands, other seas, new atmospheres, new rocks, unknown plants, animals, men; descended into caverns, saw how in courses and varying strata the edifice of the Earth was completed, and fashioned clay into strange figures of rocks. By and by, he came to find everywhere objects already known, but wonderfully mingled, united; and thus often extraordinary things came to shape in him. He soon became aware of combinations in all, of conjunctures, concurrences. Ere long, he no more saw any thing alone.—In great, variegated images, the perceptions of his senses crowded round him; he heard, saw, touched, and thought at once. He rejoiced to bring strangers together. Now the stars were men, now men were stars, the stones animals, the clouds plants; he sported with powers and appearances; he knew where and how this and that was to be found, to be brought into action; and so himself struck over the strings, for tones and touches of his own.

"What has passed with him since then he does not disclose to us. He tells us that we ourselves, led on by him and our own desire, will discover what has passed with him.

Many of us have withdrawn from him. They returned to their parents, and learned trades. Some have been sent out by him, we know not whither; he selected them. Of these, some had been but a short time there, others longer. One was still a child; scarcely was he come, when our Teacher was for passing him any more instruction. This Child had large dark eyes with azure ground, his skin shone like lilies, and his locks like light little clouds when it is growing evening. His voice pierced through all our hearts; willingly would we have given him our flowers, stones, pens, all we had. He smiled with an infinite earnestness; and we had a strange delight beside him. One day he will come again, said our Teacher, and then our lessons end.—Along with him he sent one, for whom we had often been sorry. Always sad he looked; he had been long years here; nothing would succeed with him; when we sought crystals or flowers, he seldom found. He saw dimly at a distance; to lay down variegated rows skilfully he had no power. He was so apt to break every thing. Yet none had such eagerness, such pleasure in hearing and listening. At last,—it was before that Child came into our circle,—he all at once grew cheerful and expert. One day he had gone out sad; he did not return, and the night came on. We were very anxious for him; suddenly as the morning dawned, we heard his voice in a neighbouring grove. He was singing a high, joyful song; we were all surprised; the Teacher looked to the East, such a look as I shall never see in him again. The singer soon came forth to us, and brought, with unspeakable blessedness on his face, a simple-looking little stone, of singular shape. The Teacher took it in his hand, and kissed him long; then looked at us with wet eyes, and laid this little stone on an empty space, which lay in the midst of other stones, just where, like radii, many rows of them met together.

"I shall in no time forget that moment. We felt as if we had had in our souls a clear passing glimpse into this wondrous World."

In these strange Oriental delineations, the judicious reader will suspect that more may be meant than meets the ear. But who this Teacher at Sais is, whether the personified Intellect of Mankind; and who this bright-faced golden-locked Child, (Reason, Religious Faith?) that was "to come again," to conclude these lessons; and that awkward unwearied Man, (Understanding?) that "was so apt to break every thing," we have no data for determining, and would not undertake to conjecture with any certainty. We subjoin a passage from the second chapter, or section, entitled "*Nature*," which, if possible, is of a still more surprising character than the first. After speaking at some length on the primeval views Man seems to have formed with regard to the external Universe, "the manifold objects of his Senses;" and how in those times his mind had a peculiar unity, and only by Practice divided itself into separate faculties, as by Practice it may yet further do, "our Pupil" proceeds to describe the conditions requisite in an inquirer into Nature, observing, in conclusion, with regard to this,—

"No one, of a surety, wanders further from the mark, than he who fancies to himself that he already understands this marvellous Kingdom, and can, in few words, fathom its constitution, and everywhere find the right path. To no one, who has broken off, and made himself an Island, will insight rise of itself, nor even without toilsome effort. Only to children, or child-like men, who know not what they do, can this happen. Long, unwearied intercourse, free and wise Contemplation, attention to faint tokens and indications; an inward poet-life, practised senses, a simple and devout spirit; these are the essential requisites of a true Friend of Nature; without these no one can attain his wish. Not wise does it seem to attempt comprehending and understanding a Human World without full perfected Humanity. No talent must sleep; and if all are not alike active, all must be alert, and not oppressed and enervated. As we see a future Painter in the boy who fills every wall with sketches and variedly adds colour to figure; so we see a future Philosopher in him who restlessly traces and questions all natural things, pays heed to all, brings together whatever is remarkable, and rejoices when he has become master and possessor of a new phenomenon, of a new power and piece of knowledge.

"Now to Some it appears not at all worth while to follow out the endless divisions of Nature; and moreover a dangerous undertaking, without fruit and issue. As we can never reach, say they, the absolutely smallest grain of material bodies, never find their simplest compartments, since all magnitude loses itself, forwards and backwards, in infinitude, so likewise is it with the species of bodies and powers; here too one comes on new species, new combinations, new appearances, even to infinitude. These seem only to stop, continue they, when our diligence tires; and so it is, spending precious time with idle contemplations and tedious enumerations; and this becomes at last a true delirium, a real vertigo over the horrid Deep. For Nature too remains, so far as we have yet come, ever a frightful Machine of Death: everywhere monstrous revolution, inexplicable vortices of movement; a kingdom of Devouring, of the maddest tyranny; a baleful Immense: the few light points disclose but a so much the more appalling Night, and terrors, of all sorts, must palsy every observer. Like a Saviour does Death stand by the hapless race of Mankind; for without Death, the maddest were the happiest. And precisely this striving to fathom that gigantic Mechanism is already a draught towards the Deep, a commencing giddiness; for every excitement is an increasing whirl, which soon gains full mastery over its victim, and hurls him forward with it into the fearful Night. Here, say those lamenters, lies the crafty snare for Man's understanding, which Nature everywhere seeks to annihilate as her greatest foe. Hail to that childlike ignorance and innocence of men, which kept them blind to the horrible perils, that everywhere, like grim thunder-clouds, lay round their peaceful dwelling, and each moment were ready to rush down on them. Only inward disunion among the powers of Nature has preserved men hitherto; nevertheless, that great epoch cannot fail to arrive, when the whole family of mankind, by a grand universal Resolve, will snatch themselves from this sorrowful condition, from this frightful imprisonment; and by a voluntary Abdication of their terrestrial abode, redeem their race from this anguish, and seek refuge in a happier world, with their ancient Father. Thus might they end worthily; and prevent a necessary, violent destruction; or a still more horrible degenerating into Beasts, by gradual dissolution of their thinking organs, through Insanity. Intercourse with the powers of Nature, with animals, plants, rocks, storms, and waves, must necessarily assimilate men to these objects; and this Assimilation, this Metamorphosis, and dissolution of the Divine and the Human, into ungovernable Forces, is even the Spirit of Nature, that frightfully voracious Power: and is not all that we see even now a prey from Heaven, a great Ruin of former Glories, the Remains of a terrific Repast?

"Be it so, cry a more courageous Class; let our species maintain a stubborn, well-planned war of destruction with this same Nature. By slow poisons must we endeavour to subdue her. The Inquirer into Nature is a noble hero, who rushes into the open abyss for the deliverance of his fellow Citizens. Artists have already played her many a trick; do but continue in this course; get hold of the secret threads, and bring them to act against each other. Profit by these discords, that so in the end you may lead her, like that fire-breathing Bull, according to your pleasure. To you she must become obedient. Patience and Faith beseem the children of men. Distant Brothers are united with us for one object; the wheel of the Stars must become the cistern-wheel of our life, and then, by our slaves, we can build us a new Fairyland. With heart-felt triumph let us look at her devastations, her tumults; she is selling herself to us, and every violence she will pay by a heavy penalty. In the inspiring feeling of our Freedom, let us live and die; here gushes forth the stream, which will one day overflow and subdue her; in it let us bathe, and refresh ourselves for new exploits. Hither the rage of the Monster does not reach; one drop of Freedom is sufficient to cripple her for ever, and for ever set limits to her havoc.

"They are right, say Several; here, or nowhere, lies the talisman. By the well of Freedom we sit and look; it is the grand magic Mirror, where the whole creation images itself, pure and clear; in it do the tender Spirits and Forms of all Natures bathe; all chambers we here behold unlocked. What need have we toilsomely to wander over the troublous World of visible things? The purer World lies even in us, in this Well. Here discloses itself the true meaning of the great, many-coloured, complected Scene; and if full of these sights we return into Nature, all is well known to us, with certainty we distinguish every shape. We need not to inquire long; a light Comparison, a few strokes in the sand, are enough to inform us. Thus, for us, is the whole a great Writing, to which we have the key; and nothing comes to us unexpected, for the course of the great Horologe is known to us beforehand. It is only we that enjoy Nature with full senses, because she does not frighten us from our senses; because no fever-dreams oppress us, and serene consciousness makes us calm and confiding.

"They are *not* right, says an earnest Man to these latter. Can they not recognise in Nature the true impress of their own Selves? It is even they that consume themselves in wild hostility to Thought. They know not that this so-called Nature of theirs is a Sport of the Mind, a waste Fantasy of their Dream. Of a surety, it is for them a horrible Monster, a strange grotesque Shadow of their own Passions. The waking man looks without fear at this offspring of his lawless Imagination; for he knows that they are but vain Spectres of his weakness. He feels himself lord of the world: his *Me* hovers victorious over the Abyss; and will through Eternities hover aloft above that endless Vicissitude. Harmony is what his spirit strives to promulgate, to extend. He will, even to infinitude, grow more and more harmonious with himself and with his Creation; and, at every step, behold the all-efficiency of a high moral order in the Universe, and what is purest of his *Me*, come forth into brighter and brighter clearness. The significance of the World is Reason; for her sake is the World here; and when it is grown to be the arena of a child-like, expanding Reason, it will one day become the divine Image of her Activity, the scene of a genuine Church. Till then let men honour Nature as the Emblem of his own Spirit; the Emblem ennobling itself, along with him, to unlimited degrees. Let him, therefore, who would arrive at knowledge of Nature, train his moral sense, let him act and conceive in accordance with the noble Essence of his Soul; and as if of herself, Nature will become open to him. Moral Action is that great and only Experiment, in which all riddles of the most manifold appearances explain themselves. Whoso understands it, and in rigid sequence of Thought can lay it open, is for ever Master of Nature."—*Bd.* ii. s. 43—57.

"The Pupil," it is added, "listens with alarm to these conflicting voices." If such was the case in half-supernatural Sais, it may well be much more so in mere sublunary London. Here again, however, in regard to these vaporous lucubrations, we can only imitate Jean Paul's Quintus Fixlein, who, it is said, in his elaborate *Catalogue of German Errors of the Press*, "states that important inferences are to be drawn from it, and advises the reader to draw them." Perhaps these wonderful paragraphs, which look, at this distance, so like chasms filled with mere sluggish mist, might prove valleys, with a clear stream, and soft pastures, were we near at hand. For one thing, either Novalis, with Tieck and Schlegel at his back, are men in a state of derangement; or there is more in Heaven and Earth than has been dreamt of in our Philosophy We may add that, in our view, this last Speaker, the "earnest Man," seems evidently to be Fichte; the first two Classes look like some skeptical or atheistic brood, unacquainted with Bacon's *Novum Organum*, or having, the First class at least, almost no faith in it. That theory of the human species ending by a universal simultaneous act of Suicide, will, to the more simple sort of readers, be new.

As further and more directly illustrating Novalis's scientific views, we may here subjoin two short sketches, taken from another department of this volume. To all who prosecute Philosophy, and take interest in its history and present aspects, they will not be without interest. The obscure parts of them are not perhaps unintelligible, but only obscure; which unluckily cannot, at all times, be helped in such cases:

"Common Logic is the Grammar of the higher Speech, that is, of Thought; it examines merely the *relations* of ideas to one another, the *Mechanics* of Thought, the pure Physiology of ideas. Now logical ideas stand related to one another, like words without thoughts. Logic occupies itself with the mere dead Body of the science of Thinking.—Metaphysics, again, is the *Dynamics* of Thought; treats of the primary *Powers* of Thought: occupies itself with the mere Soul of the Science of Thinking. Metaphysical ideas stand related to one another, like thoughts without words. Men often wondered at the stubborn Incompletibility of these two Sciences; each followed its own business by itself: there was a want everywhere, nothing would suit rightly with either. From the very First, attempts were made to unite them, as every thing about them indicated relationship; but every attempt failed; the one or the other Science still suffered in these attempts, and lost its essential character. We had to abide by metaphysical Logic, and Logical metaphysic, but neither of them was as it should be. With Physiology and Psychology, with Mechanics and Chemistry, it fared no better. In the latter half of this Century there arose, with us Germans, a more violent commotion than ever; the hostile masses towered themselves up against each other more fiercely than heretofore; the fermentation was extreme; there followed powerful explosions. And now some assert that a real Compenetration has somewhere or other taken place; that the germ of a union has arisen, which will grow by degrees, and assimilate all to one indivisible form: that this principle of Peace is pressing out irresistibly, on all sides, and that ere long there will be but one Science and one Spirit, as one Prophet and one God."—

"The rude, discursive Thinker is the Scholastic [Schoolman Logician]. The true Scholastic is a mystical Subtilist; out of logical Atoms he builds his Universe; he annihilates all living Nature, to put an Artifice of Thoughts [*Gedankenkunststück*, literally, Conjuror's-trick of Thoughts] in its room. His aim is an infinite Automaton. Opposite to him is the rude, intuitive Poet: this is a mystical Macrologist; he hates rules, and fixed form; a wild, violent life reigns instead of it in Nature; all is animate, no law; wilfulness and wonder everywhere. He is mere dynamical. Thus does he Philosophic Spirit arise at first, in altogether separate masses. In the *second* stage of culture these masses begin to come in contact, multifariously enough; and, as in the union of infinite Extremes, the Finite, the Limited arises, so here also arise 'Eclectic Philosophers' without number; the time of misunderstandings begins. The most limited is, in this stage, the most important, the purest Philosopher of the second stage. This class occupies itself wholly with the actual, present world, in the strictest sense. The Philosophers of the first class look down with contempt on those of the second; say, they are a little of every thing, and so nothing; hold their views as results of weakness, as Inconsequentism. On the contrary, the second class, in their turn, pity the first; lay the blame on their visionary enthusiasm, which they say is absurd, even to insanity. If, on the one hand, the Scholastics and Alchemists seem to be utterly at variance, and the Eclectics on the other hand quite at one, yet, strictly examined, it is altogether the reverse. The former, in essentials, are indirectly of one opinion; namely, as regards the non-dependence, and infinite character of Meditation, the both set out from the absolute: whilst the Eclectic and limited sort are essentially at variance; and agree only in what is deduced. The former are infinite but uniform, the latter bounded but multiform; the former have genius, the latter talent: those have Ideas, these have knacks, (*Handgriffe*;) those are heads without hands, these are hands without heads. The *third* stage is for the Artist, who can be at once implement and genius. He finds that that primitive Separation in the absolute Philosophical Activities [between the Scholastic, and the 'rude intuitive Poet'] is a deeper-lying Separation in his own Nature; which Separation indicates, by its existence as such, the possibility of being adjusted, of being joined: he finds that, heterogeneous as these Activities are, there is yet a faculty in him of passing from the one to the other, of changing his *polarity* at will. He discovers in them, therefore, necessary members of his spirit; he observes that both must be united in some common Principle. He infers that Eclecticism is nothing but the imperfect defective employment of this Principle. It becomes——"

But we need not struggle farther, wringing a significance out of these mysterious words: in delineating the genuine Transcendentalist, or "Philosopher of the third stage," properly speaking, *the* Philosopher, Novalis ascends into regions, whither few readers would follow him. It may be observed here, that British Philosophy, tracing it from Duns Scotus to Dugald Stewart, has now gone through the first and second of these "stages," the Scholastic and the Eclectic, and in considerable honour. With our amiable Professor Stewart, than whom no man, not Cicero himself, was ever more entirely Eclectic, that second or Eclectic class may be considered as having terminated; and now Philosophy is at a stand among us, or rather there is now no Philosophy visible in these Islands. It remains to be seen, whether we also are to have our "third stage;" and how that new and highest "class" will demean itself here. The French Philosophers seem busy studying Kant, and writing of him: but we rather imagine Novalis would pronounce them still only in the Eclectic stage. He says afterwards, that "all Eclectics are essentially and at bottom skeptics; the more comprehensive, the more skeptical."

These two passages have been extracted from a large series of *Fragments*, which, under the three divisions of Philosophical, Critical, Moral, occupy the greatest part of Volume second. They are fractions, as we hinted above, of that grand "encyclopedical work" which Novalis had planned. Friedrich Schlegel is said to be the selector of those published here. They come before us, without note or comment; worded for the most part in very unusual phraseology, and without repeated and most patient investigation, seldom yield any significance, or rather we should say, often yield a false one. A few of the clearest we have selected for insertion: whether the reader will think them "Pollen of Flowers," or a baser kind of dust, we shall not predict. We give them in a miscellaneous shape; overlooking those classifications which, even in the text, are not and could not be very rigidly adhered to.

"Philosophy can bake no bread; but she can procure for us God, Freedom, Immortality. Which then is more practical, Philosophy or Economy?—

"Philosophy is properly Home-sickness; the wish to be everywhere at home.—

"We are near awakening when we dream that we dream.—

"The true philosophical Act is annihilation of self, (*Selbsttödtung;*) this is the real beginning of all Philosophy; all requisites for being a Disciple of Philosophy point hither. This Act alone corresponds to all the conditions and characteristics of transcendental conduct.—

"To become properly acquainted with a truth, we must first have disbelieved it, and disputed against it.—

"Man is the higher Sense of our Planet; the star which connects it with the upper world; the eye which it turns towards Heaven.—

"Life is a disease of the spirit; a working incited by Passion. Rest is peculiar to the spirit.—

"Our Life is no Dream, but it may and will perhaps become one.—

"What is Nature? An encyclopedical, systematic Index, or Plan of our Spirit. Why will we content us with the mere Catalogue of our Treasures? Let us contemplate them ourselves, and in all ways elaborate and use them.—

"If our Bodily Life is a burning, our spiritual Life is a being-burnt, a Combustion (or, is precisely the inverse the case?); Death, therefore, perhaps a Change of Capacity.—

"Sleep is for the inhabitants of Planets only. In another time, Man will sleep and wake continually at once. The greater part of our Body, of our Humanity itself, yet sleeps a deep sleep.—

"There is but one Temple in the World; and that is the Body of Man. Nothing is holier than this high form. Bending before men is a reverence done to this Revelation in the Flesh.—We touch Heaven, when we lay our hand on a human body.—

"Man is a Sun; his Senses are the Planets.—

"Man has ever expressed some symbolical Philosophy of his Being in his Works and Conduct; he announces himself and his Gospel of Nature; he is the Messiah of Nature.—

"Plants are Children of the Earth; we are Children of the Æther. Our Lungs are properly our Root; we live, when we breathe; we begin our life with breathing.—

"Nature is an Eolian Harp, a musical instrument; whose tones again are keys to higher strings in us.—

"Every beloved object is the centre of a Paradise.—

"The first Man is the first Spiritseer; all appears to him as Spirit. What are children, but first men? The fresh gaze of the Child is richer in significance than the forecasting of the most indubitable Seer.—

"It depends only on the weakness of our organs and of our self-excitement (*Selbstberührung*) that we do not see ourselves in a Fairy-world. All Fabulous Tales, (*Mahrchen,*) are merely dreams of that home-world, which is everywhere and nowhere. The higher powers in us, which one day, as Genies, shall fulfil our will,* are, for the present, Muses, which refresh us on our toilsome course with sweet remembrances.—

"Man consists in Truth. If he exposes Truth, he exposes himself. If he betrays Truth, he betrays himself. We speak not here of Lies, but of acting against Conviction.

"A character is a completely fashioned will (*vollkommen gebildeter Wille.*)—

"There is, properly speaking, no Misfortune in the world. Happiness and Misfortune stand in continual balance. Every Misfortune is, as it were, the obstruction of a stream, which, after over-coming this obstruction, but bursts through with the greater force.—

"The ideal of Morality has no more dangerous rival than the ideal of highest Strength, of most powerful life; which also has been named (very falsely as it was there meant) the ideal of poetic greatness. It is the maximum of the savage; and has, in these times, gained, precisely among the greatest weaklings, very many proselytes. By this ideal, man becomes a Beast-Spirit, a Mixture; whose brutal wit has, for weaklings, a brutal power of attraction.—

"The spirit of Poesy is the morning light, which makes the statue of Memnon sound.—

"The division of Philosopher and Poet is only apparent, and to the disadvantage of both. It is a sign of disease, and of a sickly constitution.—

"The true Poet is all-knowing; he is an actual world in miniature.—

* Novalis's ideas, on what has been called the "perfectibility of man," ground themselves on his peculiar views of the constitution of material and spiritual Nature, and are of the most original and extraordinary character. With our utmost effort, we should despair of communicating other than a quite false notion of them. He asks, for instance, with scientific gravity: Whether any one, that recollects the first kind glance of her he loved, can doubt the possibility of *Magic?*

"Klopstock's works appear, for the most part, free Translations of an unknown Poet, by a very talented but unpoetical Philologist.—

"Goethe is an altogether practical poet. He is in his works what the English are in their wares: highly simple, neat, convenient, and durable. He has done in German Literature what Wedgewood did in English Manufacture. He has, like the English, a natural turn for Economy, and a noble Taste acquired by Understanding. Both these are very compatible, and have a near affinity in the chemical sense. * *—*Wilhelm Meister's Apprenticeship* may be called throughout prosaic and modern. The Romantic sinks to ruin, the Poesy of Nature, the Wonderful. The Book treats merely of common Worldly things: Nature and Mysticism are altogether forgotten. It is a poetized, civic, and household History; the Marvellous is expressly treated therein as imagination and enthusiasm. Artistic Atheism is the spirit of the Book. * * * It is properly a *Candide*, directed against Poetry; the Book is highly unpoetical in respect of spirit, poetical as the dress and body of it is. * * * The introduction of Shakspeare has almost a tragic effect. The hero retards the triumph of the Gospel of Economy; and economical Nature is finally the true and only remaining one.—

"When we speak of the aim and Art observable in Shakspeare's works, we must not forget that Art belongs to Nature; that it is, so to speak, self-viewing, self-imitating, self-fashioning Nature. The Art of a well-developed genius is far different from the Artfulness of the Understanding, of the merely reasoning mind. Shakspeare was no calculator, no learned thinker; he was a mighty many-gifted soul, whose feelings and works, like products of Nature, bear the stamp of the same spirit; and in which the last and deepest of observers will still find new harmonies with the infinite structure of the Universe; concurrences with later ideas, affinities with the higher powers and senses of man. They are emblematic, have many meanings, are simple, and inexhaustible, like products of Nature; and nothing more unsuitable could be said of them than that they are works of Art, in that narrow mechanical acceptation of the word."

The reader understands that we offer these specimens not as the best to be found in Novalis's *Fragments*, but simply as the most intelligible. Far stranger and deeper things there are, could we hope to make them in the smallest degree understood. But in examining and re-examining many of his *Fragments*, we find ourselves carried into more complex, more subtle regions of thought than any we are elsewhere acquainted with: here we cannot always find our own latitude and longitude, sometimes not even approximate to finding them; much less teach others such a secret.

What has been already quoted may afford some knowledge of Novalis, in the characters of Philosopher and Critic: there is one other aspect under which it would be still more curious to view and exhibit him, but still more difficult,—we mean that of his Religion. Novalis nowhere specially records his creed, in these Writings: he many times expresses, or implies, a zealous, heartfelt belief in the Christian system; yet with such adjuncts, and co existing persuasions, as to us might seem rather surprising. One or two more of these his Aphorisms, relative to this subject, we shall cite, as likely to be better than any description of ours. The whole essay at the end of volume first, entitled *Die Christenheit oder Europa* (Christianity or Europe), is also well worthy of study, in this as in many other points of view.

"Religion contains infinite sadness. If we are to love God, he must be in distress (*hülfbedürftig*, help-needing). In how far is this condition answered in Christianity?—

"Spinoza is a God-intoxicated-man (*Gott-trunkener Mensch.*)—

"Is the Devil, as Father of Lies, himself but a necessary illusion?—

"The Catholic Religion is to a certain extent applied Christianity. Fichte's Philosophy too is perhaps applied Christianity.—

"Can Miracles work Conviction? Or is not real Conviction, this highest function of our soul and personality, the only true God-announcing Miracle?

"The Christian Religion is especially remarkable, moreover, as it so decidedly lays claim to mere good will in Man, to his essential Temper, and values this independently of all Culture and Manifestation. It stands in opposition to Science and to Art, and *properly to Enjoyment.**

"Its origin is with the common people. It inspires the great majority of the *limited* in this Earth.

"It is the Light that begins to shine in the Darkness.

"It is the root of *all Democracy*, the highest Fact in the Rights of Man (*die höchste Thatsache der Popularität.*)

"Its unpoetical exterior, its resemblance to a modern family-picture, *seems only to be lent it.**—

"Martyrs are spiritual heroes. Christ was the greatest martyr of our species; through him has martyrdom become infinitely significant and holy.—

"The Bible begins nobly, with Paradise, the symbol of youth; and concludes with the Eternal Kingdom, the Holy City. Its two main divisions, also, are genuine grand-historical divisions (*ächt grosshistorisch.*) For in every grand-historical compartment, (*Glied*,) the grand history must lie, as it were, symbolically recreated, (*verjüngt*, made young again.) The beginning of the New Testament is the second higher Fall, (the Atonement of the Fall,) and the commencement of the new Period. The history of every individual man should be a Bible. Christ is the new Adam. A Bible is the highest problem of Authorship.—

"As yet there is no Religion. You must first make a Seminary (*Bildungs-schule*) of genuine Religion. Think ye that there is Religion? Religion has to be made and produced (*gemacht und hervorgebracht*) by the union of a number of persons."

Hitherto our readers have seen nothing of

* Italics also in the text.

Novalis in his character of Poet, properly so called; the *Pupils at Sais* being fully more of a scientific than poetic nature. As hinted above, we do not account his gifts in this latter province as of the first, or even of a high order; unless, indeed, it be true, as he himself maintains, that "the distinction of Poet and Philosopher is apparent only, and to the injury of both." In his professedly poetical compositions, there is an indubitable prolixity, a degree of languor, not weakness but sluggishness; the meaning is too much diluted; and diluted, we might say, not in a rich, lively, varying music, as we find in Tieck, for example; but rather in a low-voiced, not unmelodious monotony, the deep hum of which is broken only at rare intervals, though sometimes by tones of purest, and almost spiritual softness. We here allude chiefly to his unmetrical pieces, his prose fictions: indeed the metrical are few in number; for the most part on religious subjects; and in spite of a decided truthfulness both in feeling and word, seem to bespeak no great skill or practice in that form of composition. In his prose style he may be accounted happier; he aims in general at simplicity, and a certain familiar expressiveness; here and there, in his more elaborate passages, especially in his *Hymns to the Night*, he has reminded us of Herder.

These *Hymns to the Night*, it will be remembered, were written shortly after the death of his mistress: in that period of deep sorrow, or rather of holy deliverance from sorrow. Novalis himself regarded them as his most finished productions. They are of a strange veiled, almost enigmatical character; nevertheless, more deeply examined, they appear nowise without true poetic worth; there is a vastness, an immensity of idea; a still solemnity reigns in them, a solitude almost as of extinct worlds. Here and there, too, some lightbeam visits us in the void deep; and we cast a glance, clear and wondrous, into the secrets of that mysterious soul. A full commentary on the *Hymns to the Night* would be an exposition of Novalis's whole theological and moral creed; for it lies recorded there, though symbolically, and in lyric, not in didactic language. We have translated the third, as the shortest and simplest; imitating its light, half-measured style; above all, decyphering its vague deep-laid sense, as accurately as we could. By the word "Night," it will be seen, Novalis means much more than the common opposite of Day. "Light" seems, in these poems, to shadow forth our terrestrial life; Night the primeval and celestial life:

"Once when I was shedding bitter tears, when dissolved in pain my Hope had melted away, and I stood solitary by the grave that in its dark narrow space concealed the Form of my life; solitary as no other had been; chased by unutterable anguish; powerless; one thought and that of misery;—here now as I looked round for help; forward could not go, nor backward, but clung to a transient extinguished Life with unutterable longing;—lo, from the azure distance, down from the heights of my old Blessedness, came a chill Breath of Dusk, and suddenly the band of Birth, the fetter of Light was snapped asunder. Vanishes the Glory of Earth, and with it my Lamenting rushes together the infinite Sadness into a new unfathomable World: thou Night's-inspiration, Slumber of Heaven, camest over me; the scene rose gently aloft; over the scene hovered my enfranchised new-born spirit; to a cloud of dust that grave changed itself; through the cloud I beheld the transfigured features of my Beloved. In her eyes lay Eternity; I clasped her hands, and my tears became a glittering indissoluble chain. Centuries of Ages moved away into the distance, like thunder-clouds. On her neck I wept, for this new life, enrapturing tears.—It was my first only Dream; and ever since then do I feel this changeless everlasting faith in the Heaven of Night, and its Sun my Beloved."

What degree of critical satisfaction, what insight into the grand crisis of Novalis's spiritual history, which seems to be here shadowed forth, our readers may derive from this Third *Hymn to the Night*, we shall not pretend to conjecture. Meanwhile, it were giving them a false impression of the Poet, did we leave him here; exhibited only under his more mystic aspects: as if his Poetry were exclusively a thing of Allegory, dwelling amid Darkness and Vacuity, far from all paths of ordinary mortals and their thoughts. Novalis can write in the most common style, as well as in this most uncommon one; and there too not without originality. By far the greater part of his First volume is occupied with a Romance, *Heinrich von Ofterdingen*, written, so far as it goes, much in the every-day manner; we have adverted the less to it, because we nowise reckon it among his most remarkable compositions. Like many of the others, it has been left as a Fragment; nay, from the account Tieck gives of its ulterior plan, and how from the solid prose world of the first part, this "Apotheosis of Poetry" was to pass, in the Second, into a mythical, fairy, and quite fantastic world, critics have doubted, whether, strictly speaking, it *could* have been completed. From this work, we select two passages, as specimens of Novalis's manner in the more common style of composition; premising, which in this one instance we are entitled to do, that whatever excellence they may have will be universally appreciable. The first is the introduction to the whole Narrative, as it were, the text of the whole; the "Blue Flower" there spoken of being Poetry, the real object, passion and vocation of young Heinrich, which, through manifold adventures, exertions, and sufferings, he is to seek and find. His history commences thus:

"The old people were already asleep; the clock was beating its monotonous tick on the wall; the wind blustered over the rattling windows; by turns, the chamber was lighted by the sheen of the moon. The young man lay restless in his bed; and thought of the stranger and his stories. 'Not the treasures, is it,' said he to himself, 'that have awakened in me so unspeakable a desire; far from me is all covetousness; but the Blue Flower is what I long to behold. It lies incessantly in my heart, and I can think and fancy of nothing else. Never did I feel so before: it is as if, till now, I had been dreaming, or as if sleep had carried me into another world; for in the world I used to live in, who troubled himself about flowers? Such wild passion for a Flower was never heard of there. But whence could that stranger have come? None of us ever saw such a man; yet I know not how I alone was so caught with his discourse; the rest heard the very same, yet none seems to mind it. And then that I cannot even speak of my strange condition! I feel such rapturous contentment; and only then when I have not the Flower rightly before my eyes, does so deep heartfelt an eagerness come over me, these things no one will or can believe. I could fancy I were mad, if I did not see, did not think with such perfect clearness; since that day, all is far better known to me. I have heard tell of ancient times; how animals and trees and rocks used to speak with men. This is even my feeling; as if they were on the point of breaking out, and I could see in them, what they wished to say to me. There must be many a word which I know not: did I know more, I could better comprehend these matters. Once I liked dancing; now I had rather think to the music.'—The young man lost himself, by degrees, in sweet fancies, and fell asleep. He dreamed first of immeasurable distances, and wild unknown regions. He wandered over seas with incredible speed; strange animals he saw; he lived with many varieties of men, now in war, in wild tumult, now in peaceful huts. He was taken captive, and fell into the lowest wretchedness. All emotions rose to a height as yet unknown to him. He lived through an infinitely variegated life; died, and came back; loved to the highest passion, and then again was for ever parted from his loved one. At length towards morning, as the dawn broke up without, his spirit also grew stiller, the images grew clearer and more permanent. It seemed to him he was walking alone in a dark wood. Only here and there did day glimmer through the green net. Ere long he came to a rocky chasm, which mounted upwards. He had to climb over many crags, which some former stream had rolled down. The higher he came, the lighter grew the wood. At last he arrived at a little meadow, which lay on the declivity of the mountain. Beyond the meadow rose a high cliff, at the foot of which he observed an opening, that seemed to be the entrance of a passage hewn in the rock. The passage led him easily on, for some time, to a great subterranean expanse, out of which from afar a bright gleam was visible. On entering, he perceived a strong beam of light, which sprang as if from a fountain to the roof of the cave, and sprayed itself into innumerable sparks, which collected below in a great basin: the beam glanced like kindled gold: not the faintest noise was to be heard, a sacred silence encircled the glorious sight. He approached the basin, which waved and quivered with infinite hues. The walls of the cave were coated with this fluid, which was not hot but cool, and on the walls, threw out a faint bluish light. He dipt his hand in the basin, and wetted his lips. It was as if the breath of a spirit went through him; and he felt himself in his inmost heart strengthened and refreshed. An irresistible desire seized him to bathe; he undressed himself and stept into the basin. He felt as if a sunset cloud were floating round him; a heavenly emotion streamed over his soul; in deep pleasure innumerable thoughts strove to blend within him; new, unseen images arose, which also melted together, and became visible beings around him; and every wave of that lovely element pressed itself on him like a soft bosom. The flood seemed a Spirit of Beauty, which from moment to moment was taking form round the youth.

"Intoxicated with rapture, and yet conscious of every impression, he floated softly down that glittering stream, which flowed out from the basin into the rocks. A sort of sweet slumber fell upon him, in which he dreamed indescribable adventures, and out of which a new light awoke him. He found himself on a soft sward at the margin of a spring, which welled out into the air, and seemed to dissipate itself there. Dark-blue rocks, with many-coloured veins, rose at some distance; the daylight which encircled him was clearer and milder than the common; the sky was black-blue, and altogether pure. But what attracted him infinitely most was a high, light-blue Flower, which stood close by the spring, touching it with its broad glittering leaves. Round it stood innumerable flowers of all colours, and the sweetest perfume filled the air. He saw nothing but the Blue Flower; and gazed on it long with nameless tenderness. At last he was for approaching, when all at once it began to move and change; the leaves grew more resplendent, and clasped themselves round the waxing stem; the Flower bent itself towards him; and the petals showed like a blue spreading ruff, in which hovered a lovely face. His sweet astonishment at this transformation was increasing,—when suddenly his mother's voice awoke him, and he found himself in the house of his parents, which the morning sun was already gilding."

Our next and last extract is likewise of a dream. Young Heinrich with his mother travels a long journey to see his grandfather at Augsburg; converses, on the way, with merchants, miners, and red-cross warriors, (for it is in the time of the crusades;) and soon after his arrival, falls immeasurably in love with Matilda, the Poet Klingsohr's daughter, in whose face was that fairest one he had seen in his old vision of the Blue Flower. Matilda, it would appear, is to be taken from him by death (as Sophie was from Novalis:) meanwhile, dreading no such event, Heinrich abandons himself with full heart to his new emotions:

"He went to the window. The choir of the Stars stood in the deep heaven; and in the east, a white gleam announced the coming day.

"Full of rapture, Heinrich exclaimed: 'You, ye everlasting Stars, ye silent wanderers, I call you to witness my sacred oath. For Matilda will I live, and eternal faith shall unite my heart and hers. For me, too, the morn of an everlasting day is dawning. The night is by: to the rising Sun, I kindle myself, as a sacrifice that will never be extinguished.'

"Heinrich was heated; and not till late, towards morning, did he fall asleep. In strange dreams the thoughts of his soul imbodied themselves. A deep blue river gleamed from the plain. On its smooth surface floated a bark; Matilda was sitting there, and steering. She was adorned with garlands: was singing a simple Song, and looking over to him with fond sadness. His bosom was full of anxiety. He knew not why. The sky was clear, the stream calm. Her heavenly countenance was mirrored in the waves. All at once the bark began to whirl. He called earnestly to her. She smiled, and laid down her helm in the boat, which continued whirling. An unspeakable terror took hold of him. He dashed into the stream; but he could not get forward; the water carried him. She beckoned, she seemed as if she wished to say something to him; the bark was filling with water; yet she smiled with unspeakable affection, and looked cheerfully into the vortex. All at once it drew her in. A faint breath rippled over the stream, which flowed on as calm and glittering as before. His horrid agony robbed him of consciousness. His heart ceased beating. On returning to himself, he was again on dry land. It seemed as if he had floated far. It was a strange region. He knew not what had passed with him. His heart was gone. Unthinking he walked deeper into the country. He felt inexpressibly weary. A little well gushed from a hill; it sounded like perfect bells. With his hands he lifted some drops, and wetted his parched lips. Like a sick dream, lay the frightful event behind him. Farther and farther he walked; flowers and trees spoke to him. He felt so well, so at home in the scene. Then he heard that simple Song again. He ran after the sounds. Suddenly some one held him by the clothes. 'Dear Henry,' cried a well-known voice. He looked round, and Maltilda clasped him in her arms 'Why didst thou run from me, dear heart?' said she, breathing deep: 'I could scarcely overtake thee.' Heinrich wept. He pressed her to him. 'Where is the river?' cried he in tears.—'Seest thou not its blue waves above us?' He looked up, and the blue river was flowing softly over their heads. 'Where are we, dear Matilda!'—'With our Fathers.' —'Shall we stay together?'—'For ever,' answered she, pressing her lips to his, and so clasping him that she could not again quit hold. She put a wondrous, secret Word in his mouth, and it pierced through all his being. He was about to repeat it, when his Grandfather called, and he awoke. He would have given his life to remember that Word."

This image of Death, and of the River being the Sky in that other and eternal country, seems to us a fine and touching one; there is in it a trace of that simple sublimity, that soft still pathos, which are characteristics of Novalis, and doubtless the highest of his specially poetic gifts.

But on these, and what other gifts and deficiencies pertain to him, we can no farther insist: for now, after such multifarious quotations, and more or less stinted commentaries, we must consider our little enterprise in respect of Novalis to have reached its limits, to be, if not completed, concluded. Our reader has heard him largely; on a great variety of topics, selected and exhibited here in such manner as seemed the fittest for our object, and with a true wish on our part, that what little judgment was in the meanwhile to be formed of such a man, might be a fair and honest one Some of the passages we have translated will appear obscure; others, we hope, are not without symptoms of a wise and deep meaning; the rest may excite wonder, which wonder again it will depend on each reader for himself whether he turn to right account or to wrong account, whether he entertain as the parent of Knowledge, or as the daughter of Ignorance. For the great body of readers, we are aware, there can be little profit in Novalis, who rather employs our time than helps us to kill it; for such any farther study of him would be unadvisable. To others again, who prize Truth as the end of all reading, especially to that class who cultivate moral science as the development of purest and highest Truth, we can recommend the perusal and re-perusal of Novalis with almost perfect confidence. If they feel, with us, that the most profitable employment any book can give them, is to study honestly some earnest, deep-minded, truth-loving Man, to work their way into his manner of thought, till they see the world with his eyes, feel as he felt, and judge as he judged, neither believing nor denying, till they can in some measure so feel and judge,—then we may assert, that few books known to us are more worthy of their attention than this. They will find it, if we mistake not, an unfathomed mine of philosophical ideas, where the keenest intellect may have occupation enough; and in such occupation, without looking farther, reward enough. All this, if the reader proceed on candid principles; if not, it will be all otherwise. To no man, so much as to Novalis, is that famous motto applicable:

Leser, wie gefall' ich Dir?
Leser, wie gefüllst Du mir?

Reader, how likest thou me?
Reader, how like I thee?

For the rest, it were but a false proceeding did we attempt any formal character of Novalis in this place; did we pretend with such means as ours to reduce that extraordinary nature under common formularies; and in few words sum up the net total of his worth and worthlessness. We have repeatedly expressed our own imperfect knowledge of the matter, and our entire despair of bringing even an approximate picture of it before readers so foreign to him. The kind words, "amiable enthusiast," "poetic dreamer;" or the unkind ones, "German mystic," "crackbrained rhapsodist," are easily spoken and written; but would avail little in this instance. If we are not altogether mistaken, Novalis cannot be ranged under any of these noted categories; but, belongs to a higher and much less known one, the significance of which is perhaps also worth studying, at all events, will not till after long study become clear to us.

Meanwhile, let the reader accept some vague impressions of ours on this subject, since we have no fixed judgment to offer him. We might say that the chief excellence, we have remarked in Novalis, is his to us truly wonderful subtlety of intellect; his power of intense abstraction, of pursuing the deepest and most evanescent ideas, through their thousand complexities, as it were, with lynx vision, and to the very limits of human Thought. He was well skilled in mathematics, and, as we can easily believe, fond of that science; but his is a far finer species of endowment than any required in mathematics, where the mind, from the very beginning of *Euclid* to the end of *Laplace*, is assisted with visible symbols, with safe *implements* for thinking; nay, at least in what is called the higher mathematics, has often little more than a mechanical superintendence to exercise over these. This power of abstract meditation, when it is so sure and clear as we sometimes find it with Novalis, is a much higher and rarer one; its element is not mathematics, but that *Mathesis*, of which it has been said many a Great Calculist has not even a notion. In this power truly, so far as logical and not moral power is concerned, lies the summary of all Philosophic talent: which talent accordingly we imagine Novalis to have possessed in a very high degree; in a higher degree than almost any other modern writer we have met with.

His chief fault again figures itself to us as a certain undue softness, want of rapid energy; something which we might term *passiveness* extending both over his mind and his character. There is a tenderness in Novalis, a purity, a clearness, almost as of a woman; but he has not, at least not at all in that degree, the emphasis and resolute force of a man. Thus, in his poetical delineations, as we complained above, he is too diluted and diffuse; not verbose properly; not so much abounding in superfluous words, as in superfluous circumstances, which indeed is but a degree better. In his philosophical speculations, we feel as if, under a different form, the same fault were now and then manifested. Here again, he seems to us, in one sense, too languid, too passive. He *sits*, we might say, among the rich, fine, thousandfold combinations, which his mind almost of itself presents him; but, perhaps, he shows too little activity in the process, is too lax in separating the true from the doubtful, is not even at the trouble to express his truth with any laborious accuracy. With his stillness, with his deep love of Nature, his mild, lofty, spiritual tone of contemplation, he comes before us in a sort of Asiatic character, almost like our ideal of some antique Gymnosophist, and with the weakness as well as the strength of an Oriental. However, it should be remembered that his works both poetical and philosophical, as we now see them, appear under many disadvantages; altogether immature, and not as doctrines and delineations, but as the rude draught of such; in which, had they been completed, much was to have changed its shape, and this fault with many others might have disappeared. It may be, therefore, that this is only a superficial fault, or even only the appearance of a fault, and has its origin in these circumstances, and in our imperfect understanding of him. In personal and bodily habits, at least, Novalis appears to have been the opposite of inert; we hear expressly of his quickness and vehemence of movement.

In regard to the character of his genius, or rather perhaps of his literary significance, and the form under which he displayed his genius, Tieck thinks he may be likened to Dante. "For him," says he, "it had become the most natural disposition to regard the commonest and nearest as a wonder, and the strange, the supernatural as something common; men's everyday life itself lay round him like a wondrous fable, and those regions which the most dream of or doubt of as of a thing distant, incomprehensible, were for him a beloved home. Thus did he, uncorrupted by examples, find out for himself a new method of delineation; and in his multiplicity of meaning; in his view of Love, and his belief in Love, as at once his Instructor, his Wisdom, his Religion; in this too that a single grand incident of life, and one deep sorrow and bereavement grew to be the essence of his Poetry and Contemplation,—he alone among the moderns resembles the lofty Dante; and sings us, like him, an unfathomable, mystic song, far different from that of many imitators, who think to put on mysticism and put it off, like a piece of dress." Considering the tendency of his poetic endeavours, as well as the general spirit of his philosophy, this flattering comparison may turn out to be better founded than at first sight it seems to be. Nevertheless, were we required to illustrate Novalis in this way, which at all times must be a very loose one, we should incline rather to call him the German Pascal than the German Dante. Between Pascal and Novalis, a lover of such analogies might trace not a few points of resemblance. Both are of the purest, most affectionate moral nature; both of a high, fine, discursive intellect; both are mathematicians and naturalists, yet occupy themselves chiefly with Religion: nay, the best writings of both are left in the shape of "Thoughts," materials of a grand scheme, which each of them, with the views peculiar to his age, had planned, we may say, for the furtherance of Religion, and which neither of them lived to execute. Nor in all this would it fail to be carefully remarked, that Novalis was not the French but the *German* Pascal; and from the intellectual habits of the one and the other, many national contrasts and conclusions might be drawn; which we leave to those that have a taste for such parallels.

We have thus endeavoured to communicate some views, not of what is vulgarly called, but of what *is* German Mystic; to afford English readers a few glimpses into his actual household establishment, and show them by their own inspection how he lives and works. We have done it, moreover, not in the style of derision, which would have been so easy, but in that of serious inquiry, which seemed so much more profitable. For this we anticipate not censure, but thanks, from our readers. Mysticism, whatever it may be, should, like other actually existing things, be understood in well-informed minds. We have observed, indeed, that the old-established laugh on this subject has been getting rather hollow of late; and seems as if, ere long, it would in a great measure die away. It appears to us that, in England, there is a distinct spirit of tolerant and sober investigation abroad, in regard to this and other kindred matters; a persuasion, fast spreading wider and wider, that the plummet of French or Scotch Logic, excellent, nay, indispensable as it is for surveying all coasts and harbours, will absolutely not sound the deep-seas of human Inquiry; and that many a Voltaire and Hume, well-gifted and highly meritorious men, were far wrong in reckoning that when their six hundred fathoms were out, they had reached the bottom, which, as in the Atlantic, may lie unknown miles lower. Six hundred fathoms is the longest, and a most valuable nautical line: but many men sound with six and fewer fathoms, and arrive at precisely the same conclusion.

"The day will come," said Lichtenberg, in bitter irony, "when the belief in God will be like that in nursery Spectres;" or, as Jean Paul has it, "Of the World will be made a World-Machine, of the Æther a Gas, of God a Force, and of the Second World—a Coffin." We rather think, such a day will *not* come. At all events, while the battle is still waging, and that Coffin-and-Gas Philosophy has not yet secured itself with Tithes and penal Statutes, let there be free scope for Mysticism, or whatever else honestly opposes it. A fair field, and no favour, and the right *will* prosper! "Our present time," says Jean Paul elsewhere, "is indeed a criticising and critical time, hovering betwixt the wish and the inability to believe; a chaos of conflicting times; but even a chaotic world must have its centre, and revolution round that centre; there *is* no pure entire Confusion, but all such presupposes its opposite, before it can begin."

SIGNS OF THE TIMES.

[Edinburgh Review, 1829.]

It is no very good symptom either of nations or individuals, that they deal much in vaticination. Happy men are full of the present, for its bounty suffices them; and wise men also, for its duties engage them. Our grand business undoubtedly is, not to *see* what lies dimly at a distance, but to *do* what lies clearly at hand.

> Know'st thou *Yesterday*, its aim and reason?
> Work'st thou well *To-day*, for worthy things?
> Then calmly wait the *Morrow's* hidden season,
> And fear not thou, what hap soe'er it brings!

But man's "large discourse of reason" *will* look "before and after;" and, impatient of "the ignorant present time," will indulge in anticipation far more than profits him. Seldom can the unhappy be persuaded that the evil of the day is sufficient for it; and the ambitious will not be content with present splendour, but paints yet more glorious triumphs, on the cloud-curtain of the future.

The case, however, is still worse with nations. For here the prophets are not one, but many; and each incites and confirms the other; so that the fatidical fury spreads wider and wider, till at last even Saul must join in it. For there is still a real magic in the action and reaction of minds on one another. The casual deliration of a few becomes, by this mysterious reverberation, the frenzy of many; men lose the use, not only of their understandings, but of their bodily senses; while the most obdurate, unbelieving hearts melt, like the rest, in the furnace where all are cast as victims and as fuel. It is grievous to think, that this noble omnipotence of Sympathy has been so rarely the Aaron's-rod of Truth and Virtue, and so often the Enchanter's-rod of Wickedness and Folly! No solitary miscreant, scarcely any solitary maniac, would venture on such actions and imaginations, as large communities of sane men have, in such circumstances, entertained as sound wisdom. Witness long scenes of the French Revolution! a whole people drunk with blood and arrogance, and then with terror and cruelty, and with desperation, and blood again! Levity is no protection against such visitations, nor the utmost earnestness of character. The New England Puritan burns witches, wrestles for months with the horrors of Satan's invisible world, and all ghastly phantasms, the daily and hourly precursors of the Last Day; then suddenly bethinks him that he is frantic, weeps bitterly, prays contritely, and the history of that gloomy season lies behind him like a frightful dream.

And Old England has had her share of such frenzies and panics; though happily, like other old maladies, they have grown milder of late: and since the days of Titus Oates, have mostly passed without loss of men's lives, or indeed without much other loss than that of reason, for the time, in the sufferers. In this mitigated form, however, the distemper is of pretty regular recurrence; and may be reckoned on at intervals, like other natural visitations; so that reasonable men deal with it, as the Londoners do with their fogs,—go cautiously out into the groping crowd, and patiently carry lanterns at noon; knowing, by a well-grounded faith, that the sun is still in existence, and will one day reappear. How often have we heard, for the last fifty years, that the country was wrecked, and fast sinking; whereas, up to this date, the country is entire and afloat! The "State in Danger" is a condition of things, which we have witnessed a hundred times; and as for the church, it has seldom been out of "danger" since we can remember it.

All men are aware, that the present is a crisis of this sort; and why it has become so. The repeal of the Test Acts, and then of the Catholic disabilities, has struck many of their admirers with an indescribable astonishment. Those things seemed fixed and immovable; deep as the foundations of the world; and lo! in a moment they have vanished, and their place knows them no more! Our worthy friends mistook the slumbering Leviathan for an island; often as they had been assured, that intolerance was, and could be nothing but a Monster; and so, mooring under the lee, they had anchored comfortably in his scaly rind, thinking to take good cheer; as for some space they did. But now their Leviathan has suddenly dived under; and they can no longer be fastened in the stream of time; but must drift forward on it, even like the rest of the world; no very appalling fate, we think, could they but understand it: which, however, they will not yet, for a season. Their little island is gone, and sunk deep amid confused eddies; and what is left worth caring for in the universe? What is it to them, that the great continents of the earth are still standing; and the polestar and all our loadstars, in the heavens, still shining and eternal? Their cherished little haven is gone, and they will not be comforted! And therefore, day after day, in all manner of periodical or perennial publications, the most lugubrious predictions are sent forth. The king has virtually abdicated; the church is a widow, without jointure; public principle is gone; private honesty is going; society, in short, is fast falling in pieces; and a time of unmixed evil is come on us. At such a period, it was to be expected that the rage of prophecy should be more than usually excited. Accordingly, the Millenarians have come forth on the right hand, and the Millites on the left. The Fifth-monarchy men prophesy from the Bible, and the Utilitarians from Bentham. The one announces that the last of the seals is to be opened, positively, in the year 1860; and the other assures us, that "the greatest happiness principle" is to make a heaven of earth, in a still shorter time. We know these symptoms too well, to think it necessary or safe to interfere with them. Time and the hours will bring relief to all parties. The grand encourager of Delphic or other noises is—the Echo. Left to themselves, they will soon dissipate, and die away in space.

Meanwhile, we too admit that the present is an important time; as all present time necessarily is. The poorest day that passes over us is the conflux of two Eternities! and is made up of currents that issue from the remotest Past, and flow onwards into the remotest Future. We were wise indeed, could we discern truly the signs of our own time; and by knowledge of its wants and advantages, wisely adjust our own position in it. Let us then, instead of gazing idly into the obscure distance, look calmly around us for a little, on the perplexed scene where we stand. Perhaps, on a more serious inspection, something of its perplexity will disappear, some of its distinctive characters, and deeper tendencies, more clearly reveal themselves; whereby our own relations to it, our own true aims and endeavours in it, may also become clearer.

Were we required to characterize this age of ours by any single epithet, we should be tempted to call it, not an Heroical, Devotional, Philosophical, or Moral Age, but, above all others, the Mechanical Age. It is the Age of Machinery, in every outward and inward sense of that word; the age which, with its whole undivided might, forwards, teaches, and practises the great art of adopting means to ends. Nothing is now done directly, or by hand; all is by rule and calculated contrivance. For the simplest operation, some helps and accompaniments, some cunning, abbreviating process is in readiness. Our old modes of exertion are all discredited, and thrown aside. On every hand, the living artisan is driven from his workshop, to make room for a speedier, inanimate one. The shuttle drops from the fingers of the weaver, and falls into iron fingers that ply it faster. The sailor furls his sail, and lays down his oar, and bids a strong, unwearied servant, on vapourous wings, bear him through the waters. Men have crossed oceans by steam; the Birmingham Fire-king has visited the fabulous East; and the genius of the Cape, were there any Camoens now to sing it, has again been alarmed, and with far stranger thunders than Gama's. There is no end to machinery. Even the horse is stripped of his harness, and finds a fleet fire-horse yoked in his stead. Nay, we have an artist that hatches chickens by steam; the very brood-hen is to be superseded! For all earthly, and for some unearthly purposes, we have machines and mechanic furtherances; for mincing our cabbages; for casting us into magnetic sleep. We remove mountains, and make seas our smooth highway; nothing can resist us. We war with rude nature; and, by our resistless engines, come off always victorious, and loaded with spoils.

What wonderful accessions have thus been made, and are still making, to the physical power of mankind; how much better fed, clothed, lodged, and, in all outward respects, accommodated, men now are, or might be, by a given quantity of labour, is a grateful reflection which forces itself on every one. What changes, too, this addition of power is introducing into the social system; how wealth has more and more increased, and at the same time gathered itself more and more into masses, strangely altering the old relations, and increasing the distance between the rich and the poor, will be a question for Political Economists, and a much more complex and important one than any they have yet engaged with. But leaving these matters for the present, let us observe how the mechanical genius of our time has diffused itself into quite other provinces. Not the external and physical alone is now managed by machinery, but the internal and spiritual also. Here, too, nothing follows its spontaneous course, nothing is left to be accomplished by old, natural methods. Every thing has its cunningly devised implements, its pre-established apparatus; it is not done by hand, but by machinery. Thus we have machines for Education: Lancastrian machines; Hamiltonian machines; Monitors, maps, and emblems. Instruction, that mysterious communing of Wisdom with Ignorance, is no longer an indefinable tentative process, requiring a study of individual aptitudes, and a perpetual variation of means and methods, to attain the same end; but a secure, universal, straight-forward business, to be conducted in the gross, by proper mechanism, with such intellect as comes to hand. Then, we have Religious machines, of all imaginable varieties; the Bible Society, professing a far higher and heavenly structure, is found, on inquiry, to be altogether an earthly contrivance, supported by collection of moneys, by fomenting of vanities, by puffing, intrigue, and chicane; and yet, in effect, a very excellent machine for converting the heathen. It is the same in all other departments. Has any man, or any society of men, a truth to speak, a piece of spiritual work to do, they can nowise proceed at once, and with the mere natural organs, but must first call a public meeting, appoint committees, issue prospectuses, eat a public dinner; in a word, construct or borrow machinery, wherewith to speak it and do it. Without machinery they were hopeless, helpless; a colony of Hindoo weavers squatting in the heart of Lancashire. Then every machine must have its moving power, in some of the great currents of society: Every little sect among us, Unitarians, Utilitarians, Anabaptists, Phrenologists, must each have its periodical, its monthly or quarterly magazine,—hanging out, like its windmill, into the *popularis aura*, to grind meal for the society.

With individuals, in like manner, natural strength avails little. No individual now hopes to accomplish the poorest enterprise single-handed, and without mechanical aids; he must make interest with some existing corporation, and till his field with their oxen. In these days, more emphatically than ever, "to live, signifies to unite with a party, or to make one." Philosophy, Science, Art, Literature, all depend on machinery. No Newton, by silent meditation, now discovers the system of the world from the falling of an apple; but some quite other than Newton stands in his Museum, his Scientific Institution, and behind whole batteries of retorts, digesters, and galvanic piles imperatively "interrogates Nature,"—who, however, shows no haste to answer. In defect of Raphaels, and Angelos, and Mozarts, we have Royal Academies of Painting, Sculpture, Music; whereby the languishing spirit of art may be strengthened by the more generous diet of a Public Kitchen. Literature, too, has its Paternoster-row mechanism, its Trade dinners, its Editorial conclaves, and huge subterranean puffing bellows; so that books are not only printed, but, in a great measure, written and sold, by machinery. National culture, spiritual benefit of all sorts, is under the same management. No Queen Christina, in these times, needs to send for her Descartes; no King Frederic for his Voltaire, and painfully nourish him with pensions and flattery: but any sovereign of taste, who wishes to enlighten his people, has only to impose a new tax, and with the proceeds establish Philosophic Institutes. Hence the Royal and Imperial Societies, the Bibliothèques, Glyptothèques, Technothèques, which front us in all capital cities, like so many well-finished hives, to which it is expected the stray agencies of Wisdom will swarm of their own accord, and hive and make honey. In like manner, among ourselves, when it is thought that religion is declining, we have only to vote half a million's worth of bricks and mortar, and build new churches. In Ireland, it seems they have gone still farther; having actually established a "Penny-a-week Purgatory Society!" Thus does the Genius of Mechanism stand by to help us in all difficulties and emergencies; and, with his iron back, bears all our burdens.

These things, which we state lightly enough here, are yet of deep import, and indicate a mighty change in our whole manner of existence. For the same habit regulates not our modes of action alone, but our modes of thought and feeling. Men are grown mechanical in head and in heart, as well as in hand. They have lost faith in individual endeavour, and in natural force, of any kind. Not for internal perfection, but for external combinations and arrangements, for institutions, constitutions,—for Mechanism of one sort or other, do they hope and struggle. Their whole efforts, attachments, opinions, turn on mechanism, and are of a mechanical character.

We may trace this tendency, we think, very distinctly, in all the great manifestations of our time; in its intellectual aspect, the studies it most favours, and its manner of conducting them; in its practical aspects, its politics, arts, religion, morals; in the whole sources, and throughout the whole currents, of its spiritual, no less than its material activity.

Consider, for example, the state of Science generally, in Europe, at this period. It is admitted, on all sides, that the Metaphysical and Moral Sciences are falling into decay, while the Physical are engrossing, every day, more respect and attention. In most of the European nations, there is now no such thing as a Science of Mind; only more or less advancement in the general science, or the special sciences, of matter. The French were the first to desert this school of Metaphysics; and though they have lately affected to revive it, it has yet no signs of vitality. The land of Malebranche, Pascal, Descartes, and Fenelon, has now only its Cousins and Villemains; while, in the department of Physics, it reckons far other names. Among ourselves, the Philosophy of Mind, after a rickety infancy, which never reached the vigour of manhood, fell suddenly into decay, languished, and finally died out, with its last amiable cultivator, Professor Stewart. In no nation but Germany has any decisive effort been made in psychological science; not to speak of any decisive result. The science of the age, in short, is physical, chemical, physiological, and, in all shapes, mechanical. Our favourite Mathematics, the highly prized exponent of all these other sciences, has also become more and more mechanical. Excellence, in what is called its higher departments, depends less on natural genius, than on acquired expertness in wielding its machinery. Without undervaluing the wonderful results which a Lagrange, or Laplace, educes by means of it, we may remark, that its calculus, differential and integral, is little else than a more cunningly-constructed arithmetical mill, where the factors being put in, are, as it were, ground into the true product, under cover, and without other effort, on our part, than steady turning of the handle. We have more Mathematics certainly than ever; but less Mathesis. Archimedes and Plato could not have read the *Mécanique Céleste;* but neither would the whole French Institute see aught in that saying, "God geometrizes!" but a sentimental rodomontade.

From Locke's time downwards, our whole Metaphysics have been physical; not a spiritual Philosophy, but a material one. The singular estimation in which his Essay was so long held as a scientific work, (for the character of the man entitled all he said to veneration,) will one day be thought a curious indication of the spirit of these times. His whole doctrine is mechanical, in its aim and origin, in its method and its results. It is a mere discussion concerning the origin of our consciousness, or ideas, or whatever else they are called; a genetic history of what we see *in* the mind. But the grand secrets of Necessity and Free-will, of the mind's vital or non-vital dependence on matter, of our mysterious relations to Time and Space, to God, to the universe, are not, in the faintest degree, touched on in these inquiries; and seem not to have the smallest connection with them.

The last class of our Scotch Metaphysicians had a dim notion that much of this was wrong; but they knew not how to right it. The school of Reid had also from the first taken a mechanical course, not seeing any other. The singular conclusions at which Hume, setting out from their admitted premises, was arriving, brought this school into being; they let loose Instinct, as an undiscriminating ban-dog, to guard them against these conclusions;—they tugged lustily at the logical chain by which Hume was so coldly towing them and the world into bottomless abysses of Atheism and Fatalism. But the chain somehow snapped between them; and the issue has been that nobody now cares about either,—any more than about Hartley's, Darwin's, or Priestley's contemporaneous doings in England. Hartley's vibrations and vibratiuncles one would think were material and mechanical enough; but our continental neighbours have gone still farther. One of their philosophers has lately discovered, that "as the liver secretes bile, so does the brain secrete thought;" which astonishing discovery Dr. Cabanis, more lately still, in his *Rapports du Physique et du Morale de l' Homme,* has pushed into its minutest developments. The metaphysical philosophy of this last inquirer is certainly no shadowy or unsubstantial one. He fairly lays open our moral structure with his dissecting-knives and real metal probes; and exhibits it to the inspection of mankind, by Leuwenhoek microscopes and inflation with the anatomical blowpipe. Thought, he is inclined to hold, is still secreted by the brain; but then Poetry and Religion (and it is really worth knowing) are "a product of the smaller intestines!" We have the greatest admiration for this learned doctor: with what scientific stoicism he walks through the land of wonders, unwondering; like a wise man through some huge, gaudy, imposing Vauxhall, whose fire-works, cascades, and symphonies, the vulgar may enjoy and believe in,—but where he finds nothing real but the saltpetre, pasteboard, and catgut. His book may be regarded as the ultimatum of mechanical metaphysics in our time; a remarkable realization of what in Martinus Scriblerus was still only an idea, that "as the jack had a meat-roasting quality, so had the body a thinking quality"—upon the strength of which the Nurembergers were to build a wood and leather man, "who should reason as well as most country parsons." Vaucanson did indeed make a wooden duck, that seemed to eat and digest; but that bold scheme of the Nurembergers remained for a more modern virtuoso.

This condition of the two great departments of knowledge—the outward, cultivated exclusively on mechanical principles; the inward finally abandoned, because, cultivated on such principles, it is found to yield no result—sufficiently indicates the intellectual bias of our time, its all-pervading disposition towards that line of inquiry. In fact, an inward persuasion has long been diffusing itself, and now and then even comes to utterance, that, except the external, there are no true sciences; that to the inward world (if there be any) our only conceivable road is through the outward; that, in short, what cannot be investigated and understood mechanically, cannot be investigated and understood at all. We advert the more particularly to these intellectual propensities, as to prominent symptoms of our age; because Opinion is at all times doubly related to Action, first as cause, then as effect; and the speculative tendency of any age will therefore give us, on the whole, the best indications of its practical tendency.

Nowhere, for example, is the deep, almost exclusive faith, we have in Mechanism, more visible than in the Politics of this time. Civil government does, by its nature, include much that is mechanical, and must be treated accordingly. We term it, indeed, in ordinary language, the Machine of Society, and talk of it as the grand working wheel from which all private machines must derive, or to which they must adapt, their movements. Considered merely as a metaphor, all this is well enough; but here, as in so many other cases, the "foam hardens itself into a shell," and the shadow we have wantonly evoked stands terribly before us, and will not depart at our bidding. Government includes much also that is not mechanical, and cannot be treated mechanically; of which latter truth, as appears to us, the political speculations and exertions of our time are taking less and less cognisance.

Nay, in the very outset, we might note the mighty interest taken in *mere political arrangements,* as itself the sign of a mechanical age. The whole discontent of Europe takes this di rection. The deep, strong cry of all civilized nations—a cry which every one now sees, must and will be answered—is, Give us a reform of Government! A good structure of legislation,—a proper check upon the executive,—a wise arrangement of the judiciary, is *all* that is wanting for human happiness. The Philosopher of this age is not a Socrates, a Plato, a Hooker, or Taylor, who inculcates on men the necessity and infinite worth of moral goodness, the great truth that our happiness depends on the mind which is within us, and not on the circumstances which are without us; but a Smith, a De Lolme, a Bentham, who chiefly inculcates the reverse of this,—that our happiness depends entirely on external circumstances; nay, that the strength and dignity of the mind within us is itself the creature and consequence of these. Were the laws, the government, in good order, all were well with us; the rest would care for itself! Dissentients from this opinion, expressed or implied, are now rarely to be met with; widely and angrily as men differ in its application, the principle is admitted by all.

Equally mechanical, and of equal simplicity, are the methods proposed by both parties for completing or securing this all-sufficient perfection of arrangement. It is no longer the moral, religious, spiritual condition of the people that is our concern, but their physical, practical, economical condition, as regulated by public laws. Thus is the Body-politic more than ever worshipped and tended: but the Soul-politic less than ever. Love of country, in any high or generous sense, in any other than an almost animal sense, or mere habit, has little importance attached to it in such reforms, or in the opposition shown them. Men are to be guided only by their self-interests. Good government is a good balancing of these; and, except a keen eye and appetite for self-interest, requires no virtue in any quarter. To both parties it is emphatically a machine: to the discontented, a "taxing machine;" to the contented, a "machine for securing property." Its duties and its faults are not those of a father, but of an active parish constable.

Thus it is by the mere condition of the machine; by preserving it untouched, or else by re-constructing it, and oiling it anew, that man's salvation as a social being is to be insured and indefinitely promoted. Contrive the fabric of law aright, and without farther effort on your part, that divine spirit of freedom, which all hearts venerate and long for, will of herself come to inhabit it; and under her healing wings every noxious influence will wither, every good and salutary one more and more expand. Nay, so devoted are we to this principle, and at the same time so curiously mechanical, that a new trade, specially grounded in it, has arisen among us, under the name of "Codification," or code-making in the abstract; whereby any people, for a reasonable consideration, may be accommodated with a patent code,—more easily than curious individuals with patent breeches, for the people does *not* need to be measured first.

To us who live in the midst of all this, and see continually the faith, hope, and practice of every one founded on Mechanism of one kind or other, it is apt to seem quite natural, and as if it could never have been otherwise. Nevertheless, if we recollect or reflect a little, we shall find both that it has been, and might again be, otherwise. The domain of Mechanism,—meaning thereby political, ecclesiastical, or other outward establishments,—was once considered as embracing, and we are persuaded can at any time embrace but a limited portion of man's interests, and by no means the highest portion.

To speak a little pedantically, there is a science of *Dynamics* in man's fortunes and nature, as well as of *Mechanics*. There is a science which treats of, and practically addresses, the primary, unmodified forces and energies of man, the mysterious springs of Love, and Fear, and Wonder, of Enthusiasm, Poetry, Religion, all which have a truly vital and *infinite* character; as well as a science which practically addresses the finite, modified developments of these, when they take the shape of immediate "motives," as hope of reward, or as fear of punishment.

Now it is certain, that in former times the wise men, the enlightened lovers of their kind, who appeared generally as Moralists, Poets, or Priests, did, without neglecting the Mechanical province, deal chiefly with the Dynamical; applying themselves chiefly to regulate, increase, and purify the inward primary powers of man; and fancying that herein lay the main difficulty, and the best service they could undertake. But a wide difference is manifest in our age. For the wise men, who now appear as Political Philosophers, deal exclusively with the Mechanical province; and occupying themselves in counting up and estimating men's motives, strive by curious checking and balancing, and other adjustments of Profit and Loss, to guide them to their true advantage: while, unfortunately, those same "motives" are so innumerable, and so variable in every individual, that no really useful conclusion can ever be drawn from their enumeration. But though Mechanism, wisely contrived, has done much for man, in a social and moral point of view, we cannot be persuaded that it has ever been the chief source of his worth or happiness. Consider the great elements of human enjoyment, the attainments and possessions that exalt man's life to its present height, and see what part of these he owes to institutions, to Mechanism of any kind; and what to the instinctive, unbounded force, which Nature herself lent him, and still continues to him. Shall we say, for example, that Science and Art are indebted principally to the founders of Schools and universities? Did not Science originate rather, and gain advancement, in the obscure closets of the Roger Bacons, Keplers, Newtons; in the workshops of the Fausts and the Watts; wherever, and in what guise soever Nature, from the first times downwards, had sent a gifted spirit upon the earth? Again, were Homer and Shakspeare members of any beneficial guild, or made Poets by means of it? Were Painting and Sculpture created by forethought, brought into the world by institutions for that end? No; Science and Art have, from first to last, been the free gift of Nature; an unsolicited, unexpected gift: often even a fatal one. These things rose up, as it were by spontaneous growth, in the free soil and sunshine of Nature. They were not planted or grafted, nor even greatly multiplied or improved by the culture or manuring of institutions. Generally speaking, they have derived only partial help from these: often have suffered damage. They made constitutions for themselves. They originated in the Dynamical nature of man, and not in his Mechanical nature.

Or, to take an infinitely higher instance, that of the Christian Religion, which, under every theory of it, in the believing or the unbelieving mind, must be ever regarded as the crowning glory, or rather the life and soul, of our whole modern culture: How did Christianity arise and spread abroad among men? Was it by institutions, and establishments, and well-arranged systems of mechanism? Not so; on the contrary, in all past and existing institutions for those ends, its divine spirit has invariably been found to languish and decay. It arose in the mystic deeps of man's soul; and was spread abroad by the "preaching of the word," by simple, altogether natural and individual efforts; and flew, like hallowed fire, from heart to heart, till all were purified and illuminated by it; and its heavenly light shone, as it still shines, and as sun or star will ever shine, through the whole dark destinies of man. Here again was no Mechanism; man's highest attainment was accomplished, Dynamically, not Mechanically. Nay, we will venture to say, that no high attainment, not even any far-extending movement among men, was ever accomplished otherwise. Strange as it may seem, if we read History with any degree of thoughtfulness, we shall find, that the checks and balances of Profit and Loss have never been the grand agents with man; that they have never been roused into deep, thorough, all-pervading efforts by any computable prospect of Profit and Loss, for any visible, finite object; but always for some invisible and infinite one. The Crusades took their rise in Religion; their visible object was, commercially speaking, worth nothing. It was the boundless, Invisible world that was laid bare in the imaginations of those men; and in its burning light, the visible shrunk as a scroll. Not mechanical, nor produced by mechanical means, was this vast movement. No dining at Freemasons' Tavern, with the other long train of modern machinery; no cunning reconciliation of "vested interests," was required here: only the passionate voice of one man, the rapt soul looking through the eyes of one man; and rugged, steel-clad Europe trembled beneath his words, and followed him whither he listed. In later ages, it was still the same. The Reformation had an invisible, mystic, and ideal aim; the result was indeed to be embodied in external things; but its spirit, its worth, was internal, invisible, infinite. Our English Revolution, too, originated in Religion. Men did battle, in those days, not for Purse sake, but for Conscience sake. Nay, in our own days, it is no way different. The French Revolution itself had something higher in it than cheap bread and a Habeas-corpus act. Here, too, was an Idea; a Dynamic, not a Mechanic force. It was a struggle, though a blind and at last an insane one, for the infinite, divine nature of Right, of Freedom, of Country.

Thus does man, in every age, vindicate, consciously or unconsciously, his celestial birthright. Thus does nature hold on her wondrous, unquestionable course; and all our systems and theories are but so many froth-eddies or sand-banks, which from time to time she casts up and washes away. When we can drain the Ocean into our mill-ponds, and bottle up the Force of Gravity, to be sold by retail, in our gas-jars; then may we hope to comprehend the infinitudes of man's soul under formulas of Profit and Loss; and rule over this too, as over a patent engine, by checks, and valves, and balances.

Nay, even with regard to Government itself, can it be necessary to remind any one that Freedom, without which indeed all spiritual life is impossible, depends on infinitely more complex influences than either the extension or the curtailment of the "democratic interest?" Who is there that, "taking the high *priori* road," shall point out what these influences are; what deep, subtle, inextricably entangled influences they have been, and may be? For man is not the creature and product of Mechanism; but, in a far truer sense, its creator and producer: it is the noble people that makes the noble Government; rather than conversely. On the whole, Institutions are much; but they are not all. The freest and highest spirits of the world have often been found under strange outward circumstances: Saint Paul and his brother Apostles were politically slaves; Epictetus was personally one. Again, forget the influences of Chivalry and Religion, and ask, —what countries produced Columbus and Las Casas? Or, descending from virtue and heroism, to mere energy and spiritual talent: Cortes, Pizarro, Alba, Ximenes? The Spaniards of the sixteenth century were indisputably the noblest nation of Europe; yet they had the Inquisition, and Philip II. They have the same government at this day; and are the lowest nation. The Dutch, too, have retained their old constitution; but no Siege of Leyden, no William the Silent, not even an Egmont or De Witt, any longer appears among them. With ourselves, also, where much has changed, effect has nowise followed cause, as it should have done: two centuries ago, the Commons' Speaker addressed Queen Elizabeth on bended knees, happy that the virago's foot did not even smite him; yet the people were then governed, not by a Castlereagh, but by a Burghley; they had their Shakspeare and Philip Sidney, where we have our Sheridan Knowles and Beau Brummel.

These and the like facts are so familiar, the truths which they preach so obvious, and have in all past times been so universally believed and acted on, that we should almost feel ashamed for repeating them; were it not that, on every hand, the memory of them seems to have passed away, or at best died into a faint tradition, of no value as a practical principle. To judge by the loud clamour of our Constitution builders, Statists, Economists, directors, creators, reformers of Public Societies; in a word, all manner of Mechanists, from the Cartwright up to the Code-maker; and by the nearly total silence of all Preachers and Teachers who should give a voice to Poetry, Religion, and Morality, we might fancy either that man's Dynamical nature was, to all spiritual intents, extinct, or else so perfected, that nothing more was to be made of it by the old means; and henceforth only in his Mechanical contrivances did any hope exist for him.

To define the limits of these two departments of man's activity, which work into one another, and by means of one another, so intricately and inseparably, were by its nature an impossible attempt. Their relative importance, even to the wisest mind, will vary in different times, according to the special wants and dispositions of these times. Meanwhile, it seems clear enough that only in the right co-ordination of the two, and the vigorous forwarding of *both*, does our true line of action lie. Undue cultivation of the inward or Dynamical province leads to idle, visionary, impracticable courses, and, especially in rude eras, to Superstition and Fanaticism, with their long train of baleful and well-known evils. Undue cultivation of the outward, again, though less immediately prejudicial, and even for the time productive of many palpable benefits, must, in the long run, by destroying Moral Force, which is the parent of all other Force, prove not less certainly, and perhaps still more hopelessly, pernicious. This, we take it, is the grand characteristic of our age. By our skill in Mechanism, it has come to pass that, in the management of external things, we excel all other ages; while in whatever respects the pure moral nature, in true dignity of soul and character, we are perhaps inferior to most civilized ages.

In fact, if we look deeper, we shall find that this faith in Mechanism has now struck its roots deep into men's most intimate, primary sources of conviction; and is thence sending up, over his whole life and activity, innumerable stems,—fruit-bearing and poison-bearing. The truth is, men have lost their belief in the Invisible, and believe, and hope, and work only in the Visible; or, to speak it in other words, This is not a Religious age. Only the material, the immediately practical, not the divine and spiritual, is important to us. The infinite, absolute character of Virtue has passed into a finite, conditional one; it is no longer a worship of the Beautiful and Good; but a calculation of the Profitable. Worship, indeed, in any sense, is not recognised among us, or is mechanically explained into Fear of pain, or Hope of pleasure. Our true Deity is Mechanism. It has subdued external Nature for us, and, we think, it will do all other things. We are Giants in physical power: in a deeper than a metaphorical sense, we are Titans, that strive, by heaping mountain on mountain, to conquer Heaven also.

The strong mechanical character, so visible in the spiritual pursuits and methods of this age, may be traced much farther into the condition and prevailing disposition of our spiritual nature itself. Consider, for example, the general fashion of Intellect in this era. Intellect, the power man has of knowing and believing, is now nearly synonymous with Logic, or the mere power of arranging and communicating. Its implement is not Meditation, but Argument. "Cause and effect" is almost the only category under which we look at, and work with, all Nature. Our first question with regard to any object is not, What is it?, but, How is it? We are no longer instinctively driven to apprehend, and lay to heart, what is Good and Lovely, but rather to inquire, as onlookers, how it is produced, whence it comes, whither it goes. Our favourite Philosophers have no love and no hatred; they stand among us not to do, nor to create any thing, but as a sort of Logic-mills to grind out the true causes and effects of all that is done and created. To the eye of a Smith, a Hume, or a Constant, all is well that works quietly. An Order of Ignatius Loyola, a Presbyterianism of John Knox, a Wickliffe, or a Henry the Eighth, are simply so many mechanical phenomena, caused or causing.

The *Euphuist* of our day differs much from his pleasant predecessors. An intellectual dapperling of these times boasts chiefly of his irresistible perspicacity, his "dwelling in the daylight of truth," and so forth; which, on examination, turns out to be a dwelling in the *rush*-light of "closet-logic," and a deep unconsciousness that there is any other light to dwell in; or any other objects to survey with it. Wonder indeed, is, on all hands, dying out: it is the sign of uncultivation to wonder. Speak to any small man of a high, majestic Reformation, of a high, majestic Luther to lead it, and forthwith he sets about "accounting" for it! how the "circumstances of the time" called for such a character, and found him, we suppose, standing girt and road-ready, to do its errand; how the "circumstances of the time" created, fashioned, floated him quietly along into the result; how, in short, this small man, had he been there, could have performed the like himself! For it is the "force of circumstances" that does every thing; the force of one man can do nothing. Now all this is grounded on little more than a metaphor. We figure Society as a "Machine," and that mind is opposed to mind, as body is to body; whereby two, or at most ten, little minds must be stronger than one great mind. Notable absurdity! For the plain truth, very plain, we think, is, that minds are opposed to minds in quite a different way; and *one* man that has a higher Wisdom, a hitherto unknown spiritual Truth in him, is stronger, not than ten men that have it not, or than ten thousand, but than *all* men, that have it not; and stands among them with a quite ethereal, angelic power, as with a sword out of Heaven's own armory, sky-tempered, which no buckler, and no tower of brass, will finally withstand.

But to us, in these times, such considerations rarely occur. We enjoy, we see nothing by direct vision; but only by reflection, and in anatomical dismemberment. Like Sir Hudibras, for every Why, we must have a Wherefore. We have our little *theory* on all human and divine things. Poetry, the workings of genius itself, which in all times, with one or another meaning, has been called Inspiration, and held to be mysterious and inscrutable, is no longer without its scientific exposition. The building of the lofty rhyme is like any other masonry or bricklaying: we have theories of its rise, height, decline, and fall,—which latter, it would seem, is now near, among all people. Of our "Theories of Taste," as they are called, wherein the deep, infinite, unspeakable Love of Wisdom and Beauty, which dwells in all men, is "explained," made mechanically visible, from "Association," and the like, why should we say any thing? Hume has written us a "Natural History of Religion;" in which one Natural History, all the rest are included. Strangely, too, does the general feeling coincide with Hume's in this wonderful problem; for whether his "Natural History" be the right one or not, that Religion must have a Natural History, all of us, cleric and laic, seem to be agreed. He indeed regards it as a Disease, we again as Health; so far there is a difference; but in our first principle we are at one.

To what extent theological Unbelief, we mean intellectual dissent from the Church, in its view of Holy Writ, prevails at this day, would be a highly important, were it not, under any circumstances, an almost impossible inquiry. But the Unbelief, which is of a still more fundamental character, every man may see prevailing, with scarcely any but the faintest contradiction, all around him; even in the Pulpit itself. Religion in most countries, more or less in every country, is no longer what it was, and should be,—a thousand-voiced psalm from the heart of Man to his invisible Father, the fountain of all Goodness, Beauty, Truth, and revealed in every revelation of these; but for the most part, a wise, prudential feeling grounded on a mere calculation; a matter, as all others now are, of Expediency and Utility: whereby some smaller quantum of earthly enjoyment may be exchanged for a far larger quantum of celestial enjoyment. Thus Religion, too, is Profit; a working for wages; not Reverence, but vulgar Hope or Fear. Many, we know, very many, we hope, are still religious in a far different sense; were it not so, our case were too desperate: But to witness that such is the temper of the times, we take any calm observant man, who agrees or disagrees in our feeling on the matter, and ask him whether our *view* of it is not in general well-founded.

Literature, too, if we consider it, gives similar testimony. At no former era has Literature, the printed communication of Thought, been of such importance as it is now. We often hear that the Church is in danger; and truly so it is,—in a danger it seems not to know of: For, with its tithes in the most perfect safety, its functions are becoming more and more superseded. The true Church of England, at this moment, lies in the Editors of its Newspapers. These preach to the people daily, weekly; admonishing kings themselves; advising peace or war, with an authority which only the first Reformers and a long-past class of Popes were possessed of; inflicting moral censure; imparting moral encouragement, consolation, edification; in all ways, diligently "administering the Discipline of the Church." It may be said, too, that in private disposition, the new Preachers somewhat resemble the Mendicant Friars of old times: outwardly full of holy zeal; inwardly not without stratagem, and hunger for terrestrial things. But omitting this class, and the boundless host of watery personages who pipe, as they are able, on so many scrannel straws, let us look at the higher regions of Literature, where, if anywhere, the pure melodies of Poesy and Wisdom should be heard. Of natural talent there is no deficiency: one or two richly-endowed individuals even give us a superiority in this respect. But what is the song they sing? Is it a tone of the Memnon Statue, breathing music as the *light* first touches it? a "liquid wisdom," disclosing to our sense the deep, infinite harmonies of Nature and man's soul? Alas, no! It is not a matin or vesper hymn to the Spirit of all Beauty, but a fierce clashing of cymbals, and shouting of multitudes, as children pass through the fire to Molech! Poetry itself has no eye for the Invisible. Beauty is no longer the god it worships, but some brute image of Strength; which we may well call an idol, for true Strength is one and the same with Beauty, and its worship also is a hymn. The meek, silent Light can mould, create, and purify all Nature; but the loud Whirlwind, the sign and product of Disunion, of Weakness, passes on, and is forgotten. How widely this veneration for the physically Strongest has spread itself through Literature, any one may judge, who reads either criticism or poem. We praise a work, not as "true," but as "strong;" our highest praise is that it has "affected" us, has "terrified" us. All this, it has been well observed, is the "maximum of the Barbarous," the symptom, not of vigorous refinement, but of luxurious corruption. It speaks much, too, for men's indestructible love of truth, that nothing of this kind will abide with them; that even the talent of a Byron cannot permanently seduce us into idol-worship; but that he, too, with all his wild syren charming, already begins to be disregarded and forgotten.

Again, with respect to our Moral condition: here also, he who runs may read that the same physical, mechanical influences are everywhere busy. For the "superior morality," of which we hear so much, we too, would desire to be thankful: at the same time, it were but blindness to deny that this "superior morality" is properly rather an "inferior criminality," produced not by greater love of Virtue, but by greater perfection of Police; and of that far subtler and stronger Police, called Public Opinion. This last watches over us with its Argus eyes more keenly than ever; but the "inward eye" seems heavy with sleep. Of any belief in invisible, divine things, we find as few traces in our Morality as elsewhere. It is by tangible, material considerations that we are guided, not by inward and spiritual. Self-denial, the parent of all virtue, in any true sense of that word, has perhaps seldom been rarer: so rare is it, that the most, even in their abstract speculations, regard its existence as a chimera. Virtue is Pleasure, is Profit; no celestial, but an earthly thing. Virtuous men, Philanthropists, Martyrs, are happy accidents; their "taste" lies the right way! In all senses, we worship and follow after Power; which may be called a physical pursuit. No man now loves Truth, as Truth must be loved, with an infinite love; but only with a finite love, and as it were *par amours*. Nay, properly speaking, he does not *believe* and know it, but only "*thinks*" it, and that "there is every probability!" He preaches it aloud, and rushes courageously forth with it,—if there is a multitude huzzaing at his back! yet ever keeps looking over his shoulder, and the instant the huzzaing languishes, he too stops short. In fact, what morality we have takes the shape of Ambition, of Honour; beyond money and money's worth, our only rational blessedness is popularity. It were but a fool's trick to die for conscience. Only for "character," by duel, or in case of extremity, by suicide, is the wise man bound to die. By arguing on the "force of circumstances," we have argued away all force from ourselves; and stand leashed together, uniform in dress and movement, like the rowers of some boundless galley. This and that may be right and true; *but* we must not do it. Wonderful "Force of Public Opinion!" We must act and walk in all points as it prescribes; follow the traffic it bids us, realize the sum of money, the degree of "influence" it expects of us, *or* we shall be lightly esteemed; certain mouthfuls of articulate wind will be blown at us, and this, what mortal courage can front? Thus, while civil Liberty is more and more secured to us, our moral Liberty is all but lost. Practically considered, our creed is Fatalism: and, free in hand and foot, we are shackled in heart and soul, with far straiter than Feudal chains. Truly may we say with the Philosopher, "the deep meaning of the laws of Mechanism lies heavy on us;" and in the closet, in the market-place, in the temple, by the social hearth, encumbers the whole movements of our mind, and over our noblest faculties is spreading a night-mare sleep.

These dark features, we are aware, belong more or less to other ages, as well as to ours. This faith in Mechanism, in the all-importance of physical things, is in every age the common refuge of Weakness and blind Discontent; of all who believe, as many will ever do, that man's true good lies without him, not within. We are aware also, that, as applied to ourselves in all their aggravation, they form but half a picture; that in the whole picture there are bright lights as well as gloomy shadows. If we here dwell chiefly on the latter, let us not be blamed: it is in general more profitable to reckon up our defects, than to boast of our attainments.

Neither, with all these evils more or less clearly before us, have we at any time despaired of the fortunes of society. Despair, or even despondency, in that respect, appears to us, in all cases, a groundless feeling. We have a faith in the imperishable dignity of man; in the high vocation to which, throughout this his earthly history, he has been appointed. However it may be with individual nations, whatever melancholic speculators may assert, it seems a well-ascertained fact that, in all times, reckoning even from those of the Heracleids and Pelasgi, the happiness and greatness of mankind at large have been continually progressive. Doubtless this age also is advancing. Its very unrest, its ceaseless activity, its discontent, contains matter of promise. Knowledge, education, are opening the eyes of the humblest,—are increasing the number of thinking minds without limit. This is as it should be; for, not in turning back, not in resisting, but only in resolutely struggling forward, does our life consist. Nay, after all, our spiritual maladies are but of Opinion; we are but fettered by chains of our own forging, and which ourselves also can rend asunder. This deep, paralyzed subjection to physical objects comes not from Nature, but from our own unwise mode of *viewing* Nature. Neither can we understand that man wants, at this hour, any faculty of heart, soul, or body, that ever belonged to him. "He, who has been born, has been a First Man;" has had lying before his young eyes, and as yet unhardened into scientific shapes, a world as plastic, infinite, divine, as lay before the eyes of Adam himself. If Mechanism, like some glass bell, encircles and imprisons us, if the soul looks forth on a fair heavenly country which it cannot reach, and pines, and in its scanty atmosphere is ready to perish,—yet the bell is but of glass; "one bold stroke to break the bell in pieces, and thou art delivered!" Not the invisible world is wanting, for it dwells in man's soul, and this last is still here. Are the solemn temples in which the Divinity was once visibly revealed among us, crumbling away? We can repair them, we can rebuild them. The wisdom, the heroic worth of our forefathers, which we have lost, we can recover. That admiration of old nobleness, which now so often shows itself as a faint *dilettantism*, will one day become a generous emulation, and man may again be all that he has been, and more than he has been. Nor are these the mere daydreams of fancy; they are clear possibilities; nay, in this time, they are even assuming the character of hopes. Indications we do see, in other countries and in our own, signs infinitely cheering to us, that Mechanism is not always to be our hard taskmaster, but one day to be our pliant, all-ministering servant; that a new and brighter spiritual era is slowly evolving itself for all men. But on these things our present course forbids us to enter.

Meanwhile, that great outward changes are in progress can be doubtful to no one. The time is sick and out of joint. Many things have reached their height; and it is a wise adage that tells us, "the darkest hour is nearest the dawn." Whenever we can gather any indication of the public thought, whether from printed books, as in France or Germany, or from Carbonari rebellions and other political tumults, as in Spain, Portugal, Italy, and Greece, the voice it utters is the same. The thinking minds of all nations call for change.

There is a deep-lying struggle in the whole fabric of society; a boundless, grinding collision of the New with the Old. The French Revolution, as is now visible enough, was not the parent of this mighty movement, but its offspring. Those two hostile influences, which always exist in human things, and on the constant intercommunion of which depends their health and safety, had lain in separate masses, accumulating through generations, and France was the scene of their fiercest explosion; but the final issue was not unfolded in that country: nay, it is not yet anywhere unfolded. Political freedom is hitherto the object of these efforts; but they will not and cannot stop there. It is towards a higher freedom than mere freedom from oppression by his fellow-mortal that man dimly aims. Of this higher, heavenly freedom, which is "man's reasonable service," all his noble institutions, his faithful endeavours, and loftiest attainments, are but the body, and more and more approximated emblem.

On the whole, as this wondrous planet, Earth, is journeying with its fellows through infinite space, so are the wondrous destinies embarked on it journeying through infinite time, under a higher guidance than ours. For the present, as our astronomy informs us, its path lies towards *Hercules*, the constellation of *Physical Power:* But that is not our most pressing concern. Go where it will, the deep HEAVEN will be around it. Therein let us have hope and sure faith. To reform a world, to reform a nation, no wise man will undertake; and all but foolish men know that the only solid, though a far slower reformation, is what each begins and perfects on *himself.*

JEAN PAUL FRIEDRICH RICHTER AGAIN.*

[FOREIGN REVIEW, 1830.]

IT is some six years since the name "Jean Paul Friedrich Richter" was first printed with English types; and some six-and-forty since it has stood emblazoned and illuminated on all true literary Indicators among the Germans; a fact, which, if we consider the history of many a Kotzebue and Chateaubriand, within that period, may confirm the old doctrine, that the best celebrity does not always spread the fastest; but rather, quite contrariwise, that as blown bladders are far more easily carried than metallic masses, though gold ones, of equal bulk, so the Playwright, Poetaster, Philosophe, will often pass triumphantly beyond seas, while the Poet and Philosopher abide quietly at home. Such is the order of nature: a Spurzheim flies from Vienna to Paris and London, within the year; a Kant, slowly advancing, may, perhaps, reach us from Königsberg within the century: Newton, merely to cross the narrow Channel, required fifty years; Shakspeare, again, three times as many. It is true there are examples of an opposite sort; now and then, by some rare chance, a Goethe, a Cervantes, will occur in literature, and Kings may laugh over *Don Quixote* while it is yet unfinished, and scenes from *Werter* be painted on Chinese tea-cups, while the author is still a stripling. These, however, are not the rule, but the exceptions; nay, rightly interpreted, the exceptions which confirm it. In general, that sudden tumultuous popularity comes more from partial delirium on both sides, than from clear insight; and is of evil omen to all concerned with it. How many loud Bacchus-festivals of this sort have we seen prove to be Pseudo-Bacchanalia, and end in directly the inverse of Orgies! Drawn by his team of lions, the jolly god advances as a real god, with all his thyrsi, cymbals, Phallophori, and Mænadic women: the air, the earth is giddy with their clangor, their Evohes; but, alas! in a little while, the lion-team shows long ears, and becomes too clearly an ass-team in lion-skins; the Mænads wheel round in amazement; and then the jolly god, dragged from his chariot, is trodden into the kennels as a drunk mortal.

That no such apotheosis was appointed for Richter in his own country, or is now to be anticipated in any other, we cannot but regard as a natural, and nowise unfortunate circumstance. What divinity lies in him requires a calmer worship, and from quite another class of worshippers. Neither, in spite of that forty years' abeyance, shall we accuse England of any uncommon blindness towards him: nay, taking all things into account, we should rather consider his actual footing among us, as evincing not only an increased rapidity in literary intercourse, but an intrinsic improvement in the manner and objects of it. Our feeling of foreign excellence, we hope, must be becoming truer: our Insular taste must be opening more and more into a European one. For Richter is by no means a man whose merits, like his singularities, force themselves on the general eye; indeed, without great patience, and some considerable catholicism of disposition, no reader is likely to prosper much with him. He has a fine, high, altogether unusual talent; and a manner of expressing it perhaps still more unusual. He is a Humorist heartily and throughout; not only in low provinces of thought, where this is more common, but in the loftiest provinces, where it is well nigh unexampled; and thus, in wild sport, "playing bowls with the sun and moon," he fashions the strangest ideal world, which at first glance looks no better than a chaos. The Germans themselves find much to bear with in him;

---

* *Wahrheit aus Jean Paul's Leben.* (Biography of Jean Pau..) *1stes, 2tes, 3tes Bändchen.* Breslau, 1826, '27, '28.

and for readers of any other nation, he is involved in almost boundless complexity; a mighty maze, indeed, but in which the plan, or traces of a plan, are nowhere visible. Far from appreciating and appropriating the spirit of his writings, foreigners find it in the highest difficult to seize their grammatical meaning. Probably there is not, in any modern language, so intricate a writer; abounding, without measure, in obscure allusions, in the most twisted phraseology; perplexed into endless entanglements and dislocations, parenthesis within parenthesis; not forgetting elisions, sudden whirls, quibs, conceits, and all manner of inexplicable crotchets: the whole moving on in the gayest manner, yet nowise in what seem military lines, but rather in huge party-coloured mob-masses. How foreigners must find themselves bested in this case, our readers may best judge from the fact, that a work with the following title was undertaken some twenty years ago, for the benefit of Richter's own countrymen: "*K. Reinhold's Lexicon for Jean Paul's works, or explanation of all the foreign words and unusual modes of speech which occur in his writings; with short notices of the historical persons and facts therein alluded to; and plain German versions of the more difficult passages in the context: —a necessary assistance for all who would read those works with profit!*" So much for the dress or vehicle of Richter's thoughts; now let it only be remembered farther, that the thoughts themselves are often of the most abstruse description; so that not till after laborious meditation, can much, either of truth or of falsehood, be discerned in them; and we have a man, from whom readers with weak nerves, and a taste in any degree sickly, will not fail to recoil, perhaps with a sentiment approaching to horror. And yet, as we said, notwithstanding all these drawbacks, Richter already meets with a certain recognition in England; he has his readers and admirers; various translations from his works have been published among us; criticisms, also, not without clear discernment, and nowise wanting in applause; and to all this, so far as we can see, even the un-German part of the public has listened with some curiosity and hopeful anticipation. From which symptoms we should infer two things, both very comfortable to us in our present capacity: First, that the old strait-laced, microscopic sect of *Belles-lettres-men*, whose divinity was "Elegance," a creed of French growth, and more admirable for men-milliners than for critics and philosophers, must be rapidly declining in these Islands; and, secondly, which is a much more personal consideration, that, in still farther investigating and exhibiting this wonderful Jean Paul, we have attempted what will be, for many of our readers, no unwelcome service.

Our inquiry naturally divides itself into two departments, the Biographical and the Critical; concerning both of which, in their order, we have some observations to make; and what, in regard to the latter department at least, we reckon more profitable, some rather curious documents to present.

It does not appear that Richter's life, externally considered, differed much in general character from other literary lives, which, for most part, are so barren of incident: the earlier portion of it was straitened enough, but not otherwise distinguished; the latter and busiest portion of it was, in like manner, altogether private; spent chiefly in provincial towns, and apart from high scenes or persons; its principal occurrences the new books he wrote, its whole course a spiritual and silent one. He became an author in his nineteenth year; and with a conscientious assiduity, adhered to that employment; not seeking, indeed carefully avoiding, any interruption or disturbance therein, were it only for a day or an hour. Nevertheless, in looking over those sixty volumes of his, we feel as if Richter's history must have another, much deeper interest and worth, than outward incidents could impart to it. For the spirit which shines more or less completely through his writings, is one of perennial excellence; rare in all times and situations, and perhaps nowhere and in no time more rare than in literary Europe, at this era. We see in this man a high, self-subsistent, original, and, in many respects, even great character. He shows himself a man of wonderful gifts, and with, perhaps, a still happier combination and adjustment of these: in whom Philosophy and Poetry are not only reconciled, but blended together into a purer essence, into Religion; who, with the softest, most universal sympathy for outward things, is inwardly calm, impregnable; holds on his way through all temptations and afflictions, so quietly, yet so inflexibly; the true literary man, among a thousand false ones, the Apollo among neatherds; in one word, a man understanding the nineteenth century, and living in the midst of it; yet whose life is, in some measure, an heroic and devout one. No character of this kind, we are aware, is to be formed without manifold and victorious struggling with the world; and the narrative of such struggling, what little of it can be narrated and interpreted, will belong to the highest species of history. The acted life of such a man, it has been said, "is itself a Bible;" it is a "Gospel of Freedom," preached abroad to all men; whereby, among mean unbelieving souls, we may know that nobleness has not yet become impossible; and, languishing amid boundless triviality and despicability, still understand that man's nature is indefeasibly divine, and so hold fast what is the most important of all faith, the faith in ourselves.

But if the acted life of a *pius Vates* is so high a matter, the written life, which, if properly written, would be a translation and interpretation thereof, must also have great value. It has been said that no Poet is equal to his Poem, which saying is partially true; but, in a deeper sense, it may also be asserted, and with still greater truth, that no Poem is equal to its Poet. Now, it is Biography that first gives us both Poet and Poem; by the significance of the one, elucidating and completing that of the other. That ideal outline of himself, which a man unconsciously shadows forth in his writings, and which, rightly deciphered, will be truer than any other representation of him, it is the task of the Biographer to fill up into an actual coherent figure, and bring home to our experience, or at least clear, undoubting admiration, thereby to instruct and edify us in many ways. Conducted on such principles, the Biography of great men, especially of great Poets, that is, of men in the highest degree noble minded and wise, might become one of the most dignified and valuable species of composition. As matters stand, indeed, there are few Biographies that accomplish any thing of this kind; the most are mere Indexes of a Biography, which each reader is to write out for himself, as he peruses them; not the living body, but the dry bones of a body, which should have been alive. To expect any such Promethean virtue in a common Life-writer were unreasonable enough. How shall that unhappy Biographic brotherhood, instead of writing like Index-makers and Government-clerks, suddenly become enkindled with some sparks of intellect, or even of genial fire; and not only collecting dates and facts, but making use of them, look beyond the surface and economical form of a man's life, into its substance and spirit? The truth is, Biographies are in a similar case with Sermons and Songs: they have their scientific rules, their ideal of perfection and of imperfection, as all things have; but hitherto their rules are only, as it were, unseen Laws of Nature, not critical Acts of Parliament, and threaten us with no immediate penalty: besides, unlike Tragedies and Epics, such works may be something without being all: their simplicity of form, moreover, is apt to seem easiness of execution; and thus, for one artist in those departments, we have a thousand bunglers.

With regard to Richter, in particular, to say that his biographic treatment has been worse than usual, were saying much; yet worse than we expected it has certainly been. Various "Lives of Jean Paul," anxiously endeavouring to profit by the public excitement, while it lasted, and communicating, in a given space, almost a minimum of information, have been read by us, within the last four years, with no great disappointment. We strove to take thankfully what little they had to give; and looked forward, in hope, to that promised "Autobiography," wherein all deficiencies were to be supplied. Several years before his death, it would seem, Richter had determined on writing some account of his own life; and with his customary honesty, had set about a thorough preparation for this task. After revolving many plans, some of them singular enough, he at last determined on the form of composition; and with a half-sportful allusion to Goethe's *Dichtung und Wahrheit aus meinem Leben*, had prefixed to his work the title *Wahrheit aus meinem Leben* (Truth from my Life); having relinquished, as impracticable, the strange idea of writing, parallel to it, a *Dichtung* (Fiction) also, under cover of "Nicolaus Margraf,"—a certain Apothecary, existing only as hero of one of his last Novels! In this work, which weightier avocations had indeed retarded or suspended, considerable progress was said to have been made; and on Richter's decease, Herr Otto, a man of talents, who had been his intimate friend for half a life-time, undertook the editing and completing of it; not without sufficient proclamation and assertion, which in the meanwhile was credible enough, that to him only could the post of Richter's biographer belong.

Three little Volumes of that *Wahrheit aus Jean Paul's Leben*, published in the course of as many years, are at length before us. The First volume, which came out in 1826, occasioned some surprise, if not disappointment yet still left room for hope. It was the commencement of a real Autobiography, and written with much heartiness and even dignity of manner, though taken up under a quite unexpected point of view, in that spirit of genial humour, of gay earnestness, which, with all its strange fantastic accompaniments, often sat on Jean Paul so gracefully, and to which, at any rate, no reader of his works could be a stranger. By virtue of an autocratic ukase, Paul had appointed himself "Professor of his own History," and delivered to the Universe three beautiful "Lectures" on that subject; boasting, justly enough, that, in his special department, he was better informed than any other man whatever. He was not without his oratorical secrets and professorial habits: thus, as Mr. Wortley, in writing his parliamentary speech to be read within his hat, had marked, in various passages, "Here cough," so Paul with greater brevity, had an arbitrary hieroglyph introduced here and there, among his papers, and purporting, as he tells us, *Meine Herren, niemand scharre, niemand gähne!*—"Gentlemen, no scraping, no yawning!"—a hieroglyph, we must say, which many public speakers might stand more in need of than he.

Unfortunately, in the Second volume, no other Lectures came to light, but only a string of disconnected, indeed quite heterogeneous Notes, intended to have been fashioned into such; the full free stream of oratory dissipated itself into unsatisfactory drops. With the Third volume, which is by much the longest, Herr Otto appears more decidedly in his own person, though still rather with the scissors than with the pen; and, behind a multitude of circumvallations and outposts, endeavours to advance his history a little; the Lectures having left it still almost at the very commencement. His peculiar plan, and the too manifest purpose to continue speaking in Jean Paul's manner, greatly obstruct his progress; which, indeed, is so inconsiderable, that at the end of this third volume, that is, after some seven hundred small octavo pages, we find the hero, as yet, scarcely beyond his twentieth year, and the history proper still only, as it were, beginning. We cannot but regret that Herr Otto, whose talent and good purpose, to say nothing of his relation to Richter, demand regard from us, had not adopted some straightforward method, and spoken out in plain prose, which seems a more natural dialect for him, what he had to say on this matter. Instead of a multifarious combination, tending so slowly, if at all, towards unity, he might, without omitting those "Lectures," or any "Note" that had value, have given us a direct Narrative, which, if it had wanted the line of Beauty, might have had the still more indispensable line of Regularity, and been, at all events, far shorter. Till Herr Otto's work is completed, we cannot speak positively; but, in the meanwhile, we must say that it wears an unprosperous aspect, and leaves room to fear that, after all, Richter's Biography may still long continue a problem. As for ourselves, in this state of matters, what help, towards characterizing Jean Paul's practical Life, we can afford, is but a few slight facts gleaned from Herr Otto's and other meaner works; and which, even in our own eyes, are extremely insufficient.

Richter was born at Wonsiedel in Baireuth, in the year 1763; and as his birth-day fell on the 21st of March, it was sometimes wittily said that he and the Spring were born together. He himself mentions this, and with a laudable intention: "this epigrammatic fact," says he, "that I the Professor and the Spring came into the world together, I have indeed brought out a hundred times in conversation, before now; but I fire it off here purposely, like a cannon-salute, for the hundred and first time, that so by printing I may ever henceforth be unable to offer it again as *bonmot-bonbon*, when, through the Printer's Devil, it has already been presented to all the world." Destiny, he seems to think, made another witticism on him; the word *Richter* being appellative as well as proper, in the German tongue, where it signifies *Judge*. His Christian name, Jean Paul, which long passed for some freak of his own, and a pseudonym, he seems to have derived honestly enough, from his maternal grandfather, Johann Paul Kuhn, a substantial cloth-maker, in Hof; only translating the German *Johann* into the French *Jean*. The Richters, for at least two generations, had been schoolmasters, or very subaltern churchmen, distinguished for their poverty and their piety; the grandfather, it appears, is still remembered in his little circle, as a man of quite remarkable innocence and holiness; "in Neustadt," says his descendant, "they will show you a bench behind the organ, where he knelt on Sundays, and a cave he had made for himself in what is called the Little Culm, where he was wont to pray." Holding, and laboriously discharging, three school or church offices, his yearly income scarcely amounted to fifteen pounds: "and at this Hunger-fountain, common enough for Baireuth school-people, the man stood thirty-five years long, and cheerfully drew." Preferment had been slow in visiting him: but at length, "it came to pass," says Paul, "just in my birth-year, that, on the 6th of August, probably through special connections with the *Higher Powers*, he did obtain one of the most important places; in comparison with which, truly, Rectorate, and Town, and cave in the Culmberg, were well worth exchanging; a place, namely, in the Neustadt Churchyard.*—His good wife had been promoted thither twenty years before him. My parents had taken me, an infant, along with them to his death-bed. He was in the act of departing, when a clergyman (as my father has often told me) said to them: Now, let the old Jacob lay his hand on the child, and bless him. I was held into the bed of death, and he laid his hand on my head.—Thou good old grandfather! Often have I thought of thy hand, blessing as it grew cold,—when Fate led me out of dark hours into clearer,—and already I can believe in thy blessing, in this material world, whose life, foundation, and essence is Spirit!"

The father, who at this time occupied the humble post of *Tertius*, (under schoolmaster) and Organist at Wonsiedel, was shortly afterwards appointed clergyman in the hamlet of Jodiz; and thence, in the course of years, transferred to Schwarzenbach on the Saale. He too was of a truly devout disposition, though combining with it more energy of character, and, apparently, more general talent; being noted in his neighbourhood as a bold, zealous preacher; and still partially known to the world, we believe, for some meritorious compositions in Church-music. In poverty he cannot be said to have altogether equalled his predecessor, who through life ate nothing but bread and beer; yet poor enough he was; no less cheerful than poor. The thriving burgher's daughter, whom he took to wife, had, as we guess, brought no money with her, but only habits little advantageous for a schoolmaster, or parson; at all events, the worthy man, frugal as his household was, had continual difficulties, and even died in debt. Paul, who in those days was called Fritz, narrates gaily, how his mother used to despatch him to Hof, her native town, with a provender bag strapped over his shoulders, under pretext of purchasing at a cheaper rate there; but in reality to get his groceries and dainties furnished gratis by his grandmother. He was wont to kiss his grandfather's hand behind the loom, and speak with him; while the good old lady, parsimonious to all the world, but lavish to her own, privily filled his bag with the good things of this life, and even gave him almonds for himself, which, however, he kept for a friend. One other little trait, quite new in ecclesiastical annals, we must here communicate. Paul, in summing up the joys of existence at Jodiz, mentions this among the number:

"In Autumn evenings (and though the weather were bad) the Father used to go in his night-gown, with Paul and Adam, into a potatoe-field lying over the Saale. The one younker carried a mattock, the other a hand-basket. Arrived on the ground, the Father set to digging new potatoes, so many as were wanted for supper; Paul gathered them from the bed into the basket, whilst Adam, clambering in the hazel thickets, looked out for the best nuts. After a time, Adam had to come down from his boughs into the bed, and Paul in his turn ascended. And thus, with potatoes and nuts, they returned contentedly home; and the pleasure of having run abroad, some mile in space, some hour in time, and then of celebrating the harvest-home, by candle light, when they came

* *Gottesacker* (God's-field,) not *Kirchhof*, the more common term, and exactly corresponding to ours, is the word Richter uses here,—and almost always elsewhere, which in his writings he has often occasion to do.

back,—let every one paint to himself as brilliantly as the receiver thereof."

To such persons as argue that the respectability of the cloth depends on its price at the clothier's, it must appear surprising that a Protestant clergyman, who not only was in no case to keep fox-hounds, but even saw it convenient to dig his own potatoes, should not have fallen under universal odium, and felt his usefulness very considerably diminished. Nothing of this kind, however, becomes visible in the history of the Jodiz Parson: we find him a man powerful in his vocation; loved and venerated by his flock; nay, associating at will, and ever as an honoured guest, with the gentry of Voigtland, not indeed in the character of gentleman, yet in that of priest, which he reckoned far higher. Like an old Lutheran, says his son, he believed in the great, as he did in ghosts; but without any shade of fear. The truth is, the man had a cheerful, pure, religious heart; was diligent in business, and fervent in spirit: and, in all the relations of his life, found this well-nigh sufficient for him.

To our Professor, as to Poets in general, the recollections of childhood had always something of an ideal, almost celestial character. Often, in his fictions, he describes such scenes, with a fond minuteness; nor is poverty any deadly, or even unwelcome ingredient in them. On the whole, it is not by money, or money's worth, that man lives and has his being. "Is not God's Universe *within* our head, whether there be a torn scull-cap or a king's diadem *without?*" Let no one imagine that Paul's young years were unhappy; still less that he looks back on them in a lachrymose, sentimental manner, with the smallest symptom either of boasting or whining. Poverty of a far sterner sort than this would have been a light matter to him; for a kind mother, Nature herself, had already provided against it; and, like the mother of Achilles, rendered him invulnerable to outward things. There was a bold, deep, joyful spirit looking through those young eyes; and to such a spirit the world *has* nothing poor, but all is rich, and full of loveliness and wonder. That our readers may glance with us into this foreign Parsonage, we shall translate some paragraphs from Paul's second Lecture, and thereby furnish, at the same time, a specimen of his professorial style and temper.

"To represent the Jodiz life of our Hans Paul,—for by this name we shall for a time distinguish him, yet ever changing it with others,—our best course, I believe, will be to conduct him through a whole Idyl-year; dividing the normal year into four seasons, as so many quarterly Idyls; four Idyls exhaust his happiness.

"For the rest, let no one marvel at finding an Idyl-kingdom and pastoral-world in a little hamlet and parsonage. In the smallest bed you can raise a tulip-tree, which shall extend its flowery boughs over all the garden; and the life-breath of joy can be inhaled as well through a window, as in the open wood and sky. Nay, is not Man's Spirit (with all its infinite celestial-spaces) walled in within a six-feet Body, with integuments, and Malpighian mucuses, and capillary tubes; and has only five strait world-windows, of Senses, to open for the boundless, round-eyed, round-sunned All;—and yet it discerns and reproduces an All!

"Scarcely do I know with which of the four quarterly Idyls to begin; for each is a little heavenly forecourt to the next: however, the climax of joys, if we start with Winter and January, will perhaps be most apparent. In the cold, our Father had commonly, like an Alpine herdsman, come down from the upper altitude of his study; and, to the joy of the children, was dwelling on the plain of the general family-room. In the morning, he sat by a window, committing his Sunday's sermon to memory; and the three sons, Fritz, (who I myself am,) and Adam, and Gottlieb, carried, by turns, the full coffee-cup to him, and still more gladly carried back the empty one, because the carrier was then entitled to pick the unmelted remains of the sugar-candy (taken against cough) from the bottom thereof. Out of doors, truly, the sky covered all things with silence; the brook with ice, the village with snow: but in our room, there was life: under the stove a pigeon-establishment; on the windows, finch cages; on the floor the invincible bull brach, our *Bonne*, the night-guardian of the court-yard; and a poodle, and the pretty *Scharmantel*, (Poll,) a present from the Lady von Plotho;—and close by, the kitchen, with two maids; and farther off, against the other end of the house, our stable, with all sorts of bovine, swinish, and feathered cattle, and their noises: the threshers, with their flails, also at work within the court-yard, I might reckon as another item. In this way, with nothing but society on all hands, the whole male portion of the house hold easily spent their fore-noon in tasks of memory, not far from the female portion, as busily employed in cooking.

"Holidays occur in every occupation; thus I too had my airing holidays,—analogous to watering holidays,—so that I could travel out in the snow of the court-yard, and to the barn with its threshing. Nay, was there a delicate embassy to be transacted in the village,—for example, to the schoolmaster, to the tailor,—I was sure to be despatched thither in the middle of my lessons: and thus I still got forth into the open air and the cold, and measured myself with the new snow. At noon, before our own dinner, we children might also, in the kitchen, have the hungry satisfaction to see the threshers fall to and consume their victuals.

"The afternoon, again, was still more important, and richer in joys. Winter shortened and sweetened our lessons. In the long dusk, our Father walked to and fro; and the children, according to ability, trotted under his night-gown, holding by his hands. At sound of the Vesper bell, we placed ourselves in a circle, and in concert devotionally chanted the hymn, *Die finstre Nacht bricht stark herein*, (The gloomy Night is gathering round.) Only in villages, not in towns, where properly there is more night than day labour, have the evening chimes a meaning and beauty, and are the swan-song of the day: the evening-bell is as it were the muffle of the over loud heart, and like a *rance des vaches* of the plains, calls men from their running and toiling, into the land of silence and dreams. After a pleasant watching about the kitchen door, for the moonrise of candle-light, we saw our wide room at once illuminated and barricaded; to wit, the window shutters were closed and bolted; and behind these window bastions and breast-works, the child felt himself snugly nestled, and well secured against Knecht Ruprecht,* who on the outside could not get in, but only in vain keep growling and humming.

"About this period too it was that we children might undress, and in long train-shirts skip up and down. Idyllic joys of various sorts alternated: our Father either had his quarto Bible, interleaved with blank folio sheets, before him, and was marking, at each verse, the book wherein he had read any thing concerning it;—or more commonly he had his ruled music-paper; and, undisturbed by this racketting of children, was composing whole concerts of church-music, with all their divisions; constructing his internal melody without any help of external tones, (as Reichard too advises,) or rather, in spite of all external mistones. In both cases, in the last with the more pleasure, I looked on as he wrote; and rejoiced specially, when, by pauses of various instruments, whole pages were at once filled up. The children all sat sporting *on* that long writing and eating table, or even *under* it. ***

"Then, at length, how did the winter evening, once a week, mount in worth, when the old errand-woman, coated in snow, with her fruit, flesh, and general ware basket, entered the kitchen from Hof; and we all, in this case, had the distant town in miniature before our eyes, nay, before our noses, for there were pastry cakes in it!"

Thus in dull winter imprisonment, among all manner of bovine, swinish, and feathered cattle, with their noises, may Idyllic joys be found, if there is an eye to see them, and a heart to taste them. Truly happiness is cheap, did we apply to the right merchant for it. Paul warns us elsewhere not to believe, for these Idyls, that there were no sour days, no chidings, and the like, at Jodiz: yet, on the whole, he had good reason to rejoice in his parents. They loved him well; his Father, he says, would "shed tears" over any mark of quickness or talent in little Fritz: they were virtuous also, and devout, which, after all, is better than being rich. "Ever and anon," says he, "I was hearing some narrative from my Father, how he and other clergymen had taken parts of their dress and given them to the poor; he related these things with joy, not as an admonition, but merely as a necessary occurrence: O God! I thank Thee for my Father!"

Richter's education was not of a more sumptuous sort than his board and lodging. Some disagreement with the Schoolmaster at Jodiz had induced the Parson to take his sons from school, and determine to teach them himself. This determination he executed faithfully indeed, yet in the most limited style; his method being no Pestalozzian one, but simply the old scheme of task-work and force-work, operating on a Latin grammar and a Latin vocabulary: and the two boys sat all day, and all year, at home, without other preceptorial nourishment than getting by heart long lists of words. Fritz learned honestly nevertheless, and in spite of his brother Adam's bad example. For the rest, he was totally destitute of books, except such of his Father's theological ones as he could come at by stealth: these, for want of better, he eagerly devoured; understanding, as he says, nothing whatever of their contents. With no less impetuosity, and no less profit, he perused the antiquated sets of Newspapers, which a kind patroness, the Lady von Plotho, already mentioned, was in the habit of furnishing to his Father, not in separate sheets, but in sheaves monthly. This was the extent of his reading. Jodiz too was the most sequestered of all hamlets; had neither natural nor artificial beauty; no memorable thing could be seen there, in a lifetime. Nevertheless, under an immeasurable Sky, and in a quite wondrous World it did stand; and glimpses into the infinite spaces of the Universe, and even into the infinite spaces of Man's Soul, could be had there as well as elsewhere. Fritz had his own thoughts, in spite of schoolmasters: a little heavenly seed of Knowledge, nay of Wisdom, had been laid in him, and with no gardener, but Nature herself, it was silently growing. To some of our readers, the following circumstance may seem unparalleled, if not unintelligible; to others nowise so:

"In the future Literary History of our hero, it will become doubtful whether he was not born more for Philosophy than for Poetry. In earliest times, the word *Weltweisheit*, (Philosophy, *World-wisdom*,)—yet also another word, *Morgenland*, (East, *Morning-land*,)—was to me an open Heaven's-gate, through which I looked in, over long, long gardens of joy.—Never shall I forget that inward occurrence, till now narrated to no mortal, wherein I witnessed the birth of my Self-consciousness, of which I can still give the place and time. One forenoon, I was standing, a very young child, in the outer door, and looking leftward at the stack of fuel wood, —when, all at once the internal vision,—I am a Me, (*ich bin ein Ich*,) came like a flash from heaven before me, and in gleaming light ever afterwards continued: then had my Me, for the first time, seen itself, and for ever. Deceptions of memory are scarcely conceivable here; for, in regard to an event occurring altogether in the veiled Holy-of-Holies of man, and whose novelty alone has given permanence to such everyday recollections accompanying it, no posterior description from another party would have mingled itself with accompanying circumstances at all."

It was in his thirteenth year that the family removed to that better church-living at Schwarzenbach; with which change, so far as school education was concerned, prospects considerably brightened for him. The public Teacher there was no deep scholar or thinker, yet a lively, genial man, and warmly interested in his pupils; among whom he soon learned to distinguish Fritz, as a boy of altogether superior gifts. What was of still more importance, Fritz now got access to books; entered into a

* The *Rawhead* (with bloody bones) of Germany.

course of highly miscellaneous, self-selected reading; and what with Romances, what with Belles-Lettres works, and Hutchesonian Philosophy, and controversial Divinity, saw an astonishing scene opening round him on all hands. His Latin and Greek were now better taught; he even began learning Hebrew. Two clergymen of the neighbourhood took pleasure in his company, young as he was; and were of great service now and afterwards: it was under their auspices that he commenced composition, and also speculating on Theology, wherein he "inclined strongly to the heterodox side."

In the "family room," however, things were not nearly so flourishing. The Professor's three Lectures terminate before this date; but we gather from his Notes that surly clouds hung over Schwarzenbach, that "his evil days began there." The Father was engaged in more complex duties than formerly, went often from home, was encumbered with debt, and lost his former cheerfulness of humour. For his sons he saw no outlet except the hereditary craft of School-keeping; and let the matter rest there, taking little farther charge of them. In some three years, the poor man, worn down with manifold anxieties, departed this life; leaving his pecuniary affairs, which he had long calculated on rectifying by the better income of Schwarzenbach, sadly deranged.

Meanwhile, Friedrich had been sent to the Hof *Gymnasium*, (Town-school,) where, notwithstanding this event, he continued some time, two years in all, apparently the most profitable period of his whole tuition; indeed, the only period when, properly speaking, he had any tutor but himself. The good old cloth-making grandfather and grandmother took charge of him, under their roof; and he had a body of teachers, all notable in their way. Herr Otto represents him as a fine, trustful, kindly, yet resolute youth, who went through his persecutions, preferments, studies, friendships, and other school-destinies in a highly creditable manner; and demonstrates this, at great length, by various details of facts, far too minute for insertion here. As a trait of Paul's intellectual habitudes, it may be mentioned that, at this time, he scarcely made any progress in History or Geography, much as he profited in all other branches; nor was the dull teacher entirely to blame, but also the indisposed pupil: indeed, it was not till long afterwards, that he overcame or suppressed his contempt for those studies, and with an effort of his own acquired some skill in them.* The like we have heard of other Poets and Philosophers, especially when their teachers chanced to be prosaists and unphilosophical. Richter boasts that he was never punished at school; yet between him and the Historico-geographical *Conrector* (Second Master) no good understanding could subsist. On one tragi-comical occasion, of another sort, they came into still more decided collision. The zealous Conrector, a most solid, painstaking man, desirous to render his Gymnasium as like a University as possible, had imagined that a series of "Disputations," some foreshadow of those held at College, might be a useful, as certainly enough it would be an ornamental thing. By ill luck, the worthy President had selected some church-article for the theme of such a Disputation: one boy was to defend, and it fell to Paul's lot to impugn the dogma, a task which, as hinted above, he was very specially qualified to undertake. Now, honest Paul knew nothing of the limits of this game; never dreamt but he might argue with his whole strength, to whatever results it might lead. In a very few rounds, accordingly, his antagonist was borne out of the ring, as good as lifeless; and the Conrector himself, seeing the danger, had, as it were, to descend from his presiding chair, and clap the gauntlets on his own more experienced hands. But Paul, nothing daunted, gave him also a Rowland for an Oliver; nay, as it became more and more manifest to all eyes, was fast reducing him also to the frightfullest extremity. The Conrector's tongue threatened cleaving to the roof of his mouth; for his brain was at a stand, or whirling in eddies, only his gall was in active play. Nothing remained for him but to close the debate abruptly by a "Silence, Sirrah!"—and leave the room, with a face (like that of the much more famous Subrector Hans von Füchslein)* "of a mingled colour, like red bole, green chalk, tinsel-yellow, and *vomissement de la reine*."

With his studies in the Leipzig University, whither he proceeded in 1781, begins a far more important era for Paul; properly, the era of his manhood, and first entire dependence on himself. In regard to literary or scientific culture, it is not clear that he derived much furtherance from Leipzig; much more, at least, than the mere neighbourhood of libraries and fellow-learners might anywhere else have afforded him. Certain professorial courses he did attend, and with diligence; but too much in the character of critic, as well as of pupil: he was in the habit of "measuring minds" with men so much older and more honourable than he; and ere long, his respect for many of them had not a little abated. What his original plan of studies was, or whether he had any fixed plan, we do not learn; at Hof, without election or rejection on his own part, he had been trained with some view to Theology; but this and every other professional view soon faded away in Leipzig, owing to a variety of causes; and Richter, now still more decidedly a self-teacher, broke loose from all corporate guilds whatsoever, and in intellectual culture, as in other respects, endeavoured to seek out a basis of his own. He read multitudes of books, and wrote down whole volumes of excerpts, and private speculations; labouring in all directions with insatiable eagerness; but

* "All History," thus he writes in his thirty-second year, "in so far as it is an affair of memory, can only be reckoned a sapless, heartless, thistle for pedantic chaffinches;—but, on the other hand, like Nature, it has highest value, in as far as we, by means of it, as by means of Nature, can divine and read the Infinite Spirit, who, with Nature and History, as with letters, legibly writes to us. He who finds a God in the physical world, will also find one in the moral, which is History. Nature orces on our heart a Creator; History, a Providence."

* See *Quintus Fixlein*, c. 7.

from the University he derived little guidance, and soon came to expect little. Ernesti, the only truly eminent man of the place, had died shortly after Paul's arrival there.

Nay, it was necessity as well as choice that detached him from professions: he had not the means to enter any. Quite another and far more pressing set of cares lay around him: not how he could live easily in future years, but how he could live at all in the present, was the grand question with him. Whatever it might be in regard to intellectual matters, certainly in regard to moral matters, Leipzig was his true seminary, where, with many stripes, Experience taught him the wisest lessons. It was here that he first saw Poverty, not in the shape of Parsimony, but in the far sterner one of actual Want; and, unseen and single-handed, wrestling with Fortune for life and death, first proved what a rugged, deep-rooted, indomitable strength, under such genial softness, dwelt in him; and from a buoyant cloud-capt Youth, perfected himself into a clear, free, benignant and lofty-minded Man.

Meanwhile the steps toward such a consummation were painful enough. His old Schoolmaster at Schwarzenbach, himself a Leipziger, had been wont to assure him that he might live for nothing in Leipzig, so easily were "free-tables," "*stipendia*," private teaching, and the like, to be procured there, by youths of merit. That Richter was of this latter species, the Rector of the Hof Gymnasium bore honourable witness; inviting the Leipzig dignitaries, in his *Testimonium*, to try the candidate themselves; and even introducing him in person (for the two had travelled together) to various influential men: but all these things availed him nothing. The Professors he found beleaguered by a crowd of needy sycophants, diligent in season, and out of season, whose whole tactics were too loathsome to him; on all hands, he heard the sad saying: *Lipsia vult expectari*, Leipzig preferments must be waited for. Now, waiting was of all things the most inconvenient for poor Richter. In his pocket he had little; friends, except one fellow-student, he had none; and at home the finance department had fallen into a state of total perplexity, fast verging towards final ruin. The worthy old Cloth-Manufacturer was now dead; his wife soon followed him: and the Widow Richter, her favourite daughter, who had removed to Hof, though against the advice of all her friends, that she might be near her, now stood alone there, with a young family, and in the most forlorn situation. She was appointed chief heir, indeed; but former benefactions had left far less to inherit than had been expected; nay, the other relatives contested the whole arrangement, and she had to waste her remaining substance in lawsuits, scarcely realizing from it, in the shape of borrowed pittances and by forced sales, enough to supply her with daily bread. Nor was it poverty alone that she had to suffer, but contumely no less; the Hof public openly finding her guilty of Unthrift, and, instead of assistance, repeating to her dispraise, over their coffee, the old proverb, "Hard got, soon gone;" for which all evils she had no remedy but loud complainings to Heaven and Earth. The good woman, with the most honest dispositions, seems, in fact, to have had but a small share of wisdom: far too small for her present trying situation. Herr Otto says that Richter's portraiture of Lenette, in the *Blumen-Frucht und Dornen-Stücke*, (Flower, Fruit, and Thorn Pieces,) contains many features of his mother: Lenette is of "an upright, but common and limited nature;" assiduous, even to excess, in sweeping and scouring: true-hearted, religious in her way, yet full of discontents, suspicion, and headstrong whims: a spouse for ever plagued and plaguing; as the brave Sebastian Siebenkäs, that true Diogenes of impoverished Poors'-Advocates, often felt, to his cost, beside her. Widow Richter's family, as well as her fortune, was under bad government, and sinking into lower and lower degradation: Adam, the brother, mentioned above, as Paul's yokefellow in Latin and potatoe-digging, had now fallen away even from the humble pretension of being a Schoolmaster, or, indeed, of being any thing; for, after various acts of vagrancy, he had enlisted in a marching regiment; with which, or in other devious courses, he marched on, and only the grand billet-master, Death, found him fixed quarters. The Richter establishment had parted from its old moorings, and was now, with wind and tide, fast drifting towards fatal whirlpools.

In this state of matters, the scarcity of Leipzig could nowise be supplied from the fulness of Hof: but rather the two households stood like concave mirrors reflecting one another's keen hunger into a still keener for both. What outlook was there for the poor Philosopher of nineteen? Even his meagre "bread and milk" could not be had for nothing; it became a serious consideration for him that the shoemaker, who was to sole his boots, "did not trust." Far from affording him any sufficient moneys, his straitened mother would willingly have made him borrow for her own wants; and was incessantly persuading him to get places for his brothers. Richter felt, too, that except himself, desolate, helpless as he was, those brothers, that old mother, had no stay on earth. There are men with whom it is as with Schiller's Friedland: "Night must it be ere Friedland's star will beam." On this forsaken youth Fortune seemed to have let loose her bandogs, and hungry Ruin had him in the wind; without was no help, no counsel: but there lay a giant force within; and so from the depths of that sorrow and abasement, his better soul rose purified and invincible, like Hercules from his long Labours. A high, cheerful Stoicism grew up in the man. Poverty, Pain, and all Evil, he learned to regard, not as what they seemed, but as what they were; he learned to despise them, nay, in kind mockery to sport with them, as with bright-spotted wild beasts which he had tamed and harnessed. "What is Poverty," said he, "who is the man that whines under it? The pain is but as that of piercing the ears of a maiden, and you hang jewels in the wound." Dark thoughts he had, but they settled into no abiding gloom: "sometimes," says Otto, "he would wave his finger across his brow, as if driving back some hostile series of ideas;" and farther complaint he did not utter.* During this sad period, he wrote out for himself a little manual of practical philosophy, naming it *Andachtsbuch*, (Book of Devotion,) which contains such maxims as these:

"Every unpleasant feeling is a sign that I have become untrue to my resolutions.—Epictetus was not unhappy.—

"Not chance, but I am to blame for my sufferings.

"It were an impossible miracle if none befel thee: look for their coming, therefore; each day make thyself sure of many.

"Say not, were my sorrows other than these, I should bear them better.

"Think of the host of Worlds, and of the plagues on this World-mote.—Death puts an end to the whole.—

"For virtue's sake I am here: but if a man, for his task, forgets and sacrifices all, why shouldst not thou?—

"Expect injuries, for men are weak, and thou thyself doest such too often.

"Mollify thy heart by painting out the sufferings of thy enemy; think of him as of one spiritually sick, who deserves sympathy.—

"Most men judge so badly; why wouldst thou be praised by a child?—No one would respect thee in a beggar's coat: what is a respect that is paid to woollen cloth, not to thee?"

These are wise maxims for so young a man; but what was wiser still, he did not rest satisfied with mere maxims, which, how true soever, are only a dead letter, till Action first gives them life and worth. Besides devout prayer to the gods, he set his own shoulder to the wheel. "Evil," says he, "is like a nightmare; the instant you begin to strive with it, to bestir yourself, it has already ended." Without farther parleying, there as he stood, Richter grappled with his Fate, and resolutely determined on self-help. His means, it is true, were of the most unpromising sort, yet the only means he had: the writing of Books! He forthwith commenced writing them. The *Grönländische Prozesse*, (Greenland Lawsuits,) a collection of satirical sketches, full of wild, gay wit, and keen insight, was composed in that base environment of his, with unpaid milkscores and unsoled boots; and even still survives, though the Author, besides all other disadvantages, was then only in his nineteenth year. But the heaviest part of the business yet remained; that of finding a purchaser and publisher. Richter tried all Leipzig with his manuscript, in vain; to a man, with that total contempt of Grammar which Jedediah Cleishbotham also complains of, they "declined the *article*." Paul had to stand by, as so many have done, and see his sunbeams weighed on hay-scales, and the hay-balance give no symptoms of moving. But Paul's heart moved as little as the balance; Leipzig being now exhausted, the World was all before him where to try; he had nothing for it, but to search till he found, or till he died searching. One Voss of Berlin at length bestirred himself; accepted, printed the Book, and even gave him sixteen *Louis d'or* for it. What a Potosi was here! Paul determined to be an author henceforth, and nothing but an author; now that his soul might even be kept in his body by that trade. His mother, hearing that he had written a book, thought that perhaps he could even write a sermon, and was for his coming down to preach in the High Church of Hof. "What is a sermon," said Paul, "which every miserable student can spout forth? Or, think you, there is a parson in Hof that, not to speak of writing my Book, can, in the smallest degree, understand it?"

But unfortunately his Potosi was like other mines; the metalliferous vein did not last; what miners call a *shift* or *trouble* occurred in it, and now there was nothing but hard rock to hew on. The *Grönländische Prozesse*, though printed, did not sell; the public was in quest of pap and treacle, not of fierce curry like this. The Reviewing world mostly passed it by without notice; one poor dog in Leipzig even lifted up his leg over it. "For any thing we know," saith he, "much, if not all of what the Author here, in bitter tone, sets forth on book-making, theologians, women, and so on, may be true; but throughout the whole work, the determination to be witty acts on him so strongly, that we cannot doubt but his book will excite in all rational readers so much disgust, that they will see themselves constrained to close it again without delay." And herewith the ill-starred quadruped passes on, as if nothing special had happened. "Singular!" adds Herr Otto, "this review, which, at the time pretended to some ephemeral attention, and likely enough obtained it, would have fallen into everlasting oblivion, had not its connection with that very work, which every rational reader was to close again, or rather never to open, raised it up for a moment!" One moment, say we, is enough: let it drop again into that murky pool, and sink there to endless depths; for all flesh, and reviewer-flesh too, is fallible and pardonable.

Richter's next Book was soon ready; but, in this position of affairs, no man would buy it. The *Selection from the Papers of the Devil*, such was its wonderful title, lay by him, on quite another principle than the Horatian one, for seven long years. It was in vain that he exhibited, and corresponded, and left no stone unturned; ransacking the world for a publisher; there was none anywhere to be met with. The unwearied Richter tried other plans. He presented Magazine Editors with essays, some one in ten of which might be accepted; he made joint stock with certain provincial literati of the Hof district, who had cash, and published for themselves; he sometimes borrowed, but was in hot haste to repay it; he lived as the young ravens; he was often in danger of starving. "The prisoner's allowance," says he, "is bread and water, but I had only the latter."

"Nowhere," observes Richter on another

*In bodily pain, he was wont to show the like endurance and indifference. At one period of his life, he had violent headaches, which forced him, for the sake of a slight alleviation, to keep his head perfectly erect; you might see him talking with a calm face, and all his old gaiety, and only known by this posture that he was suffering.

occasion, "can you collect the stress-memorials and siege-medals of Poverty more pleasantly and philosophically than at College: the Academic Burschen exhibit to us how many Humorists and Diogeneses Germany has in it.* Travelling through this parched Sahara, with nothing round him but stern sandy solitude, and no landmark on Earth, but only loadstars in the Heaven, Richter does not anywhere appear to have faltered in his progress; for a moment to have lost heart, or even to have lost good humour. 'The man who fears not death,' says the Greek Poet, 'will start at no shadows.' Paul had looked Desperation full in the face, and found that for him she was not desperate. Sorely pressed on from without, his inward energy, his strength both of thought and resolve did but increase, and establish itself on a surer and surer foundation; he stood like a rock amid the beating of continual tempests; nay, a rock crowned with foliage; and in its clefts, nourishing flowers of sweetest perfume. For there was a passionate fire in him, as well as a stoical calmness; tenderest Love was there, and devout Reverence; and a deep genial Humour lay, like warm sunshine, softening the whole, blending the whole into light sportful harmony. In these its hard trials, whatever was noblest in his nature came out in still surer clearness. It was here that he learned to distinguish what is perennial and imperishable in man, from what is transient and earthly; and to prize the latter, were it king's crowns and conqueror's triumphal chariots, but as the wrappage of the jewel; we might say, but as the finer or coarser Paper on which the Heroic Poem of Life is to be written. A lofty indestructible faith in the dignity of man took possession of him, and a disbelief in all other dignities; and the vulgar world, and what it could give him, or withhold from him, was, in his eyes, but a small matter. Nay, had he not found a voice for these things; which, though no man would listen to it, he felt to be a true one, and that if true no tone of it could be altogether lost. Preaching forth the Wisdom, which in the dark deep wells of Adversity he had drawn up, he felt himself strong, courageous, even gay. He had "an internal world wherewith to fence himself against the frosts and heats of the external." Studying, writing, in this mood, though grim Scarcity looked in on him through the windows, he ever looked out again on that fiend with a quiet, half-satirical eye. Surely, we should find it hard to wish any generous nature such fortune: yet is one such man, nursed into manhood, amid these stern, truth-telling influences, worth a thousand popular ballad-mongers, and sleek literary gentlemen, kept in perpetual boyhood by influences that always lie.

"In my Historical Lectures," says Paul, "the business of Hungering will in truth more and more make its appearance,—with the hero it rises to a great height,—about as often as Feasting in *Thummel's Travels*, and Tea-drinking in Richardson's *Clarissa;* nevertheless, I cannot help saying to Poverty: Welcome! so thou come not at quite too late a time! Wealth bears heavier on talent than Poverty; under gold-mountains and thrones, who knows how many a spiritual giant may lie crushed down and buried! When among the flames of youth, and above all of hotter powers as well, the oil of Riches is also poured in,—little will remain of the phœnix but his ashes; and only a Goethe has force to keep, even, at the sun of good fortune, his phœnix-wings unsinged. The poor Historical Professor, in this place, would not, for much money, have had much money in his youth. Fate manages Poets, as men do singing birds; you overhang the cage of the singer and make it dark, till at length he has caught the tunes you play to him, and can sing them rightly."

There have been many Johnsons, Heynes, and other meaner natures, in every country, that have passed through as hard a probation as Richter's was, and borne permanent traces of its good and its evil influences; some, with their modesty and quiet endurance, combining a sickly dispiritment, others a hardened dullness or even deadness of heart: nay, there are some whom Misery itself cannot teach, but only exasperate; who, far from parting with the mirror of their Vanity, when it is trodden in pieces, rather collect the hundred fragments of it, and with more fondness and more bitterness than ever, behold not one but a hundred images of Self therein; to these men Pain is a pure evil, and as school-dunces their hard Pedagogue will only whip them to the end. But, in modern days, and even among the better instances, there is scarcely one that we remember who has drawn, from Poverty and suffering, such unmixed advantage as Jean Paul; acquiring under it not only Herculean strength, but the softest tenderness of soul; a view of man and man's life not less cheerful, even sportful, than it is deep and calm. To Fear he is a stranger; not only the rage of men, "the ruins of nature would strike him fearless;" yet he has a heart vibrating to all the finest thrills of Mercy, a deep loving sympathy with all created things. There is, we must say, something Old-Grecian in this form of mind; yet Old-Grecian under the new conditions of our own time; not an Ethnic, but a Christian greatness. Richter might have stood beside Socrates, as a faithful, though rather tumultuous disciple: or better still, he might have bandied repartees with Diogenes, who, if he could nowhere find Men, must at least have admitted that this too was a Spartan Boy. Diogenes and he, much as they differed, mostly to the disadvantage of the former, would have

* By certain speculators on German affairs, much has been written and talked about what is, after all, a very slender item in German affairs, the *Burschenleben*, or manners of the young men at Universities. We must regret that in discussing this matter, since it was thought worth discussing, the true significance and soul of it should not have been, by some faint indication, pointed out to us. Apart from its duelling punctilios, and beer-songs, and tobacco-smoking, and other fopperies of the system, which are to the German student merely what coach-driving and horse-dealing, and other kindred fopperies, are to the English, Burschenism is not without its meaning more than Oxfordism or Cambridgeism. The Bursch strives to say in the strongest language he can: "See! I am an unmonied scholar, and a free *man;*" the Oxonian and Cantab again endeavour to say: "See! I am a monied scholar, and a spirited *gentleman.*" We rather think the Bursch's assertion, were it rightly worded, would be the more profitable of the two.

found much in common: above all, that resolute self-dependence, and quite settled indifference to the "force of public opinion." Of this latter quality, as well as of various other qualities in Richter, we have a curious proof in the Episode, which Herr Otto here for the first time details with accuracy, and at large, "concerning the Costume controversies." There is something great as well as ridiculous in this whole story of the Costume, which we must not pass unnoticed. It was in the second year of his residence at Leipzig, and when, as we have seen, his necessities were pressing enough, that Richter, finding himself unpatronised by the World, thought it might be reasonable if he paid a little attention, as far as convenient, to the wishes, rational orders, and even whims of his only other Patron, namely, of Himself. Now the long visits of the hair-dresser, with his powders, puffs, and pomatums, were decidedly irksome to him, and even too expensive; besides, his love of Swift and Sterne made him love the English and their modes; which things being considered, Paul made free to cut off his cue altogether, and with certain other alterations in his dress, to walk abroad in what was called the English fashion. We rather conjecture that, in some points, it was after all but Pseudo-English; at least, we can find no tradition of any such mode having then or ever been prevalent here in its other details. For besides the docked cue, he had shirts *à la Hamlet;* wore his breast open, without neckcloth: in such guise did he appear openly. Astonishment took hold of the minds of men. German students have more license than most people in selecting fantastic garbs; but the bare neck and want of cue seemed graces beyond the reach of true art. We can figure the massive, portly cynic, with what humour twinkling in his eye he came forth among the elegant gentlemen; feeling, like that juggler-divinity Ram-Dass, well-known to Baptist Missionaries, that "he had fire enough in his stomach to burn away all the sins of the world." It was a species of pride, even of foppery, we will admit; but a tough, strong-limbed species, like that which in ragged gown "trampled on the pride of Plato."

Nowise in so respectable a light, however, did a certain *Magister*, or pedagogue dignitary of Richter's neighbourhood, regard the matter. Poor Richter, poor in purse, rich otherwise, had, at this time, hired himself a small mean garden-house, that he might have a little fresh air, through summer, in his studies: the Magister, who had hired a large sumptuous one in the same garden, naturally met him in his walks, bare-necked, cue-less; and perhaps not liking the cast of his countenance, strangely twisted into Sardonic wrinkles, with all its broad honest benignity,—took it in deep dudgeon that such an unauthorized character should venture to enjoy nature beside him. But what was to be done? Supercilious looks, even frowning, would accomplish nothing; the Sardonic visage was not to be frowned into the smallest terror. The Magister wrote to the landlord, demanding that this nuisance should be abated. Richter, with a praiseworthy love of peace, wrote to the Magister, promising to do what he could: he would not approach his (the Magister's) house so near as last night, would walk only in the evenings and mornings, and thereby for most part keep out of sight the apparel "which convenience, health, and poverty had prescribed for him." These were fair conditions of a boundary-treaty; but the Magister interpreted them in too literal a sense, and soon found reason to complain that they had been infringed. He again took pen and ink, and in peremptory language represented that Paul had actually come past a certain Statue, which, without doubt, stood within the debatable land; threatening him, therefore, with Herr Körner, the landlord's vengeance, and withal openly testifying his own contempt and just rage against him. Paul answered, also in writing, that he had nowise infringed his promise, this Statue or any other Statue having nothing to do with it; but that now he did altogether revoke said promise, and would henceforth walk whensoever and wheresoever seemed good to him, seeing he too paid for the privilege. "To me," observed he, "Herr Körner is not dreadful (*fürchterlich;*)" and for the Magister himself he put down these remarkable words: "You despise my mean name; *nevertheless take note of it; for you will not have done the latter long, till the former will not be in your power to do*: I speak ambiguously, that I may not speak arrogantly." Be it noted, at the same time, that with a noble spirit of accommodation, Richter proposed yet new terms of treaty; which being accepted, he, pursuant thereto, with bag and baggage forthwith evacuated the garden, and returned to his "town-room at the Three Roses, in Peterstrasse;" glorious in retreat, and "leaving his Paradise," as Herr Otto with some conceit remarks, "no less guiltlessly than voluntarily, for a certain bareness of breast and neck; whereas our First Parents were only allowed to retain theirs, so long as they felt themselves innocent in total nudity." What the Magister thought of the "mean name," some years afterwards, we do not learn.

But if such tragical things went on in Leipzig, how much more when he went down to Hof in the holidays, where, at any rate, the Richters stood in slight esteem! It will surprise our readers to learn that Paul, with the mildest tempered pertinacity, resisted all expostulations of friends, and persecutions of foes, in this great cause; and went about *à la Hamlet*, for the space of no less than seven years! He himself seemed partly sensible that it was affectation; but the man would have his humour out. "On the whole," says he, "*I hold the constant regard we pay, in all our actions, to the judgment of others, as the poison of our peace, our reason, and our virtue.* At this slave-chain I have long filed, and I scarcely ever hope to break it entirely asunder. I wish to accustom myself to the censure of others, and *appear* a fool, that I may learn to endure fools." So speaks the young Diogenes, embracing his frozen pillar by way of "exercitation;" as if the world did not give us frozen pillars enough in this kind without our wilfully stepping aside to seek them! Better is that other maxim: "He who differs from the world in important matters should the more carefully conform to it in indifferent ones." Nay, by degrees Richter himself saw into this, and having now proved satisfactorily enough that he could take his own way when he so pleased, —leaving, as is fair, the "most sweet voices" to take theirs also,—he addressed to his friends (chiefly the Voigtland Literati above alluded to) the following circular:

"ADVERTISEMENT.

"The undersigned begs to give notice, that whereas cropt hair has as many enemies as red hair, and said enemies of the hair are enemies likewise of the person it grows on; whereas farther, such a fashion is in no respect Christian, since otherwise Christian persons would have it; and whereas, especially, the Undersigned has suffered no less from his hair than Absalom did from his, though on contrary grounds; and whereas it has been notified that the public purposed to send him into his grave, since the hair grew there without scissors: he hereby gives notice that he will not push matters to such extremity. Be it known, therefore, to the nobility, gentry, and a discerning public in general, that the Undersigned proposes, on Sunday next, to appear in various important streets (of Hof) with a short false cue; and with this cue as with a magnet, and cord-of-love, and magic-rod, to possess himself forcibly of the affections of all and sundry, be they who they may."

And thus ended "gloriously," as Herr Otto thinks, the long "clothes-martyrdom;" from the course of which, besides its intrinsic comicality, we may learn two things: first, that Paul nowise wanted a due indifference to the popular wind, but, on fit or unfit occasion, could stand on his own basis stoutly enough, wrapping his cloak as himself listed; and secondly, that he had such a buoyant, elastic humour of spirit, that besides counter-pressure against Poverty, and Famine itself, there was still a clear overplus left to play fantastic tricks withal, at which the angels could not indeed weep, but might well shake their heads and smile. We return to our history.

Several years before the date of this "Advertisement," namely, in 1784, Paul, who had now determined on writing, with or without readers, to the end of the chapter, finding no furtherance in Leipzig, but only hunger and hardship, bethought him that he might as well write in Hof beside his mother, as there. His publishers, when he had any, were in other cities; and the two households, like two dying embers, might perhaps show some feeble point of red-heat between them, if cunningly laid together. He quitted Leipzig, after a three years' residence there; and fairly commenced housekeeping on his own score. Probably there is not in the whole history of Literature any record of a literary establishment like this at Hof; so ruggedly independent, so simple, not to say altogether unfurnished. Lawsuits had now done their work, and the Widow Richter, with her family, was living in a "house containing one apartment." Paul had no books, except "twelve manuscript volumes of excerpts," and the considerable library which he carried in his head; with which small resources, the public, especially as he had still no cue, could not well see what was to become of him. Two great furtherances, however, he had, of which the public took no sufficient note: a real Head on his shoulders, not as is more common, a mere hat-wearing, empty *effigies* of a head; and the strangest, stoutest, indeed, a quite noble Heart within him. Here, then, he could, as is the duty of man, "prize his existence, more than his manner of existence," which latter was, indeed, easily enough dis-esteemed. Come of it what might, he determined, on his own strength, to try issues to the uttermost with Fortune; nay, while fighting like a very Ajax against her, to keep laughing in her face till she too burst into laughter, and ceased frowning at him. He would nowise slacken in his Authorship, therefore, but continued stubbornly toiling, as at his right work, let the weather be sunny or snowy. For the rest, Poverty was written on the posts of his door, and within on every equipment of his existence; he that ran might read in large characters: "Good Christian people, you perceive that I have little money; what inference do you draw from it?" So hung the struggle, and as yet were no signs of victory for Paul. It was not till 1788 that he could find a publisher for his *Teufels Papieren;* and even then few readers. But no disheartenment availed with him: authorship was once for all felt to be his true vocation; and by it he was minded to continue at all hazards. For a short while, he had been tutor in some family, and had again a much more tempting offer of the like sort, but he refused it, purposing henceforth to "bring up no children but his own,—his books," let Famine say to it what she pleased.

"With his mother," says Otto, "and at times also with several of his brothers, but always with one, he lived in a mean house, which had only a single apartment; and this went on even when,—after the appearance of the *Mümien,*—his star began to rise, ascending higher and higher, and never again declining. * * *

"As Paul, in the characters of Walt and Vult,* (it is his direct statement in these Notes,) meant to depict himself; so it may be remarked, that in the delineation of Lenette, his mother stood before his mind, at the period when this down-pressed and humiliated woman began to gather heart, and raise herself up again;† seeing she could no longer doubt the truth of his predictions, that Authorship must, and would prosper with him. She now the more busily, in one and the same room where

* *Gottwalt* and *Quoddeusvult,* two Brothers (see Paul's *Flegeljahre*) of the most opposite temperaments: the former a still, soft-hearted tearful enthusiast, the other a madcap humourist, honest at bottom, but bursting out on all hands with the strangest explosions, speculative and practical.

† "Quite up indeed, she could never more rise; and in silent humility, avoiding any loud expression of satisfaction, she lived to enjoy with timorous gladness, the delight of seeing her son's worth publicly recognised, and his acquaintance sought by the most influential men, and herself, too, honoured, on this account, as she had never before been."

Paul was writing and studying, managed the household operations; cooking, washing, scouring, handling the broom, and these being finished, spinning cotton. Of the painful income earned by this latter employment, she kept a written account. One such revenue-book, under the title, *Was ich ersponnen*, (Earned by spinning,) which extends from March, 1793, to September, 1794, is still in existence. The produce of March, the first year, stands entered there as 2 florins, 51 kreutzers, 3 pfennings, [somewhere about four shillings!]; that of April, &c.; 'at last that of September, 1794, as 2 fl. 1 kr.; and on the last page of the little book, stands marked, that Samuel (the youngest son) had, on the 9th of this same September, got new boots, which cost 3 thalers,—almost a whole quarter's revenue!'"

Considering these things, how mournful would it have seemed to Paul that Bishop Dogbolt could not get translated, because of Politics; and the too high-souled Viscount Plumcake, thwarted in courtship, was seized with a perceptible dyspepsia!

We have dwelt the longer on this portion of Paul's history, because we reckon it interesting in itself; and that if the spectacle of a great man struggling with adversity be a fit one for the gods to look down on, much more must it be so for mean fellow-mortals to look up to. For us in Literary England, above all, such conduct as Richter's has a peculiar interest, in these times; the interest of entire novelty. Of all literary phenomena, that of a literary man daring to believe that he is *poor*, may be regarded as the rarest. Can a man without capital actually open his lips and speak to mankind? Had he no landed property, then: no connection with the higher classes; did he not even keep a gig? By these documents it would appear so. This was not a nobleman, nor gentleman, nor gigman;* but simply a man!

On the whole, what a wondrous spirit of gentility does animate our British Literature at this era! We have no Men of Letters now, but only Literary Gentlemen. Samuel Johnson was the last that ventured to appear in that former character, and support himself, on his own legs, without any crutches, purchased or stolen: rough old Samuel, the last of all the Romans! Time was, when in English Literature, as in English Life, the comedy of "Every Man in his Humour" was daily enacted among us; but how the poor French word, French in every sense, "*Qu'en dira-t-on?*" spellbinds us all, and we have nothing for it but to drill and cane each other into one uniform, regimental "nation of gentlemen." "Let him who would write heroic poems," said Milton, "make his life a heroic poem." Let him who would write heroic poems, say we, put money in his purse; or if he have no gold money, let him put in copper-money, or pebbles, and chink with it as with true metal, in the ears of mankind, that they may listen to him. Herein does the secret of good writing now consist, as that of good living has always done. When we first visited Grub-street, and with bared head did reverence to the genius of the place, with a "*Salve, magna parens!*" we were astonished to learn, on inquiry, that the Authors did not dwell there now, but had all removed, years ago, to a sort of "High Life below Stairs," far in the West. For why, what remedy was there; did not the wants of the age require it? How can men write without High Life; and how, except below Stairs, as Shoulder-knot, or as talking Katerfelto, or by secondhand communication with these two, can the great body of men acquire any knowledge thereof? Nay, has not the Atlantis, or true Blissful Island of Poesy, been, in all times, understood to lie Westward, though never rightly discovered till now? Our great fault with writers used to be, not that they were intrinsically more or less completed Dolts, with no eye or ear for the "open secret," of the world, or for any thing, save the "open display" of the world,—for its gilt ceilings, marketable pleasures, war-chariots, and all manner, to the highest manner, of Lord Mayor shows, and Guildhall dinners, and their own small part and lot therein; but the head and front of their offence lay in this, that they had not "frequented the society of the upper classes." And now, with our improved age, and this so universal extension of "High Life below Stairs," what a change has been introduced, what benign consequences will follow! One consequence has already been a degree of Dapperism and Dilettantism and ricketty Debility unexampled in the history of Literature, and enough of itself to "make us the envy of surrounding nations;" for hereby the Literary man, once so dangerous to the quiescence of society, has now become perfectly innoxious, so that a look will quail him, and he can be tied hand and foot by a spinster's thread. Hope there is, that henceforth neither Church nor State will be put in jeopardy by literature. The old Literary man, as we have said, stood on his own legs; had a whole heart within him, and might be provoked into many things. But the new Literary man, on the other hand, cannot stand at all, save in stays; he must first gird up his weak sides with the whalebone of a certain fashionable, knowing, half-squirarchal air,—be it inherited, bought, or, as is more likely, borrowed or stolen, whalebone; and herewith he stands a little without collapsing. If the man now twang his jew's-harp to please the children, what is to be feared from him; what more is to be required of him?

Seriously speaking, we must hold it a remarkable thing that every Englishman should be a "gentleman;" that in so democratic a country, our common title of honour, which all men assert for themselves, should be one which professedly depends on station, on accidents rather than on qualities; or at best, as Coleridge interprets it, "on a certain indifference to money matters," which certain indiffer-

* In Thurtell's trial (says the *Quarterly Review*) occurred the following colloquy: "Q. What sort of person was Mr. Weare? *A.* He was always a respectable person. Q. What do you mean by respectable? *A.* He kept a gig."—Since then we have seen a "*Defensio Gigmanica*, or Apology for the Gigmen of Great Britain," composed not without eloquence, and which we hope one day to prevail on our friend, a man of some whims, to give to the public.

ence again must be wise or mad, you would think, exactly as one possesses much money, or possesses little! We suppose it must be the commercial genius of the nation, counteracting and suppressing its political genius; for the Americans are said to be still more notable in this respect than we. Now, what a hollow, windy vacuity of internal character this indicates; how, in place of a rightly ordered heart, we strive only to exhibit a full purse; and all pushing, rushing, elbowing on towards a false aim, the courtier's kibes are more and more galled by the toe of the peasant; and on every side, instead of Faith, Hope, and Charity, we have Neediness, Greediness, and Vain-glory; all this is palpable enough. Fools that we are! Why should we wear our knees to horn and sorrowfully beat our breasts, praying day and night to Mammon, who, if he would even hear us, has almost nothing to give? For granting that the deaf brute-god were to relent for our sacrificings; to change our gilt brass into solid gold, and instead of hungry actors of rich gentility, make us all in very deed Rothschild-Howards to-morrow, what good were it? Are we not already denizens of this wondrous England, with its high Shakspeares and Hampdens; nay, of this wondrous Universe, with its Galaxies and Eternities, and unspeakable Splendours, that we should so worry and scramble, and tear one another in pieces, for some acres, (nay, still oftener, for the *show* of some acres,) more or less, of clay property, the largest of which properties, the Sutherland itself, is invisible even from the Moon? Fools that we are! To dig, and bore like ground-worms in those acres of ours, even if we have acres; and far from beholding and enjoying the heavenly Lights, not to know of them except by unheeded and unbelieved report! Shall certain pounds sterling that we have in the Bank of England, or the ghosts of certain pounds that we would fain seem to have, hide from us the treasures we are all born to in this the "City of God?"

> My inheritance how wide and fair!
> TIME is my estate, to TIME I'm heir.

But leaving the money-changers, and honour-hunters, and gigmen of every degree, to their own wise ways, which they will not alter, we must again remark as a singular circumstance, that the same spirit should, to such an extent, have taken possession of Literature also. This is the eye of the world, enlightening all, and instead of the shows of things unfolding to us things themselves: has the eye too gone blind; has the Poet and Thinker adopted the philosophy of the Grocer and Valet in Livery? Nay, let us hear Lord Byron himself on the subject. Some years ago, there appeared in the Magazines, and to the admiration of most editorial gentlemen, certain extracts from Letters of Lord Byron's, which carried this philosophy to rather a high pitch. His Lordship, we recollect, mentioned, that, "all rules for Poetry were not worth a d—n," (saving and excepting, doubtless, the ancient Rule-of-Thumb, which must still have place here;) after which aphorism his Lordship proceeded to state that the great ruin of all British Poets sprang from a simple source; their exclusion from High Life in London, excepting only some shape of that High Life below Stairs, which, however, was nowise adequate: "he himself and Thomas Moore were perfectly familiar in such upper life: he by birth, Moore by happy accident, and so they could both write Poetry; the others were not familiar, and so could not write it."—Surely it is fast growing time that all this should be drummed out of our Planet, and forbidden to return.

Richter, for his part, was quite excluded from the West-end of Hof: for Hof too has its West-end; "every mortal longs for his parade-place; would still wish, at banquets, to be master of some seat or other, wherein to overtop this or that plucked goose of the neighbourhood." So poor Richter could only be admitted to the West-end of the Universe, where truly he had a very superior establishment. The legal, clerical, and other conscript fathers of Hof might, had they so inclined, have lent him a few books, told or believed some fewer lies of him, and thus positively and negatively shown the young adventurer many a little service; but they inclined to none of these things, and happily he was enabled to do without them. Gay, gentle, frolicsome as a lamb, yet strong, forbearant, and royally courageous as a lion, he worked along, amid the scouring of kettles, the hissing of frying-pans, the hum of his mother's wheel;—and it is not without a proud feeling that our reader (for he too is a man) hears of victory being at last gained, and of Works, which the most reflective nation in Europe regards as classical, being written under such accompaniments.

However, it is at this lowest point of the Narrative that Herr Otto for the present stops short; leaving us only the assurance that better days are coming: so that concerning the whole ascendant and dominant portion of Richter's history, we are left to our own resources; and from these we have only gathered some scanty indications, which may be summed up with a very disproportionate brevity. It appears that the *Unsichtbare Loge*, (Invisible Lodge,) sent forth from the Hof spinning establishment in 1793, was the first of his works that obtained any decisive favour. A long trial of faith; for the man had now been besieging the literary citadel upwards of ten years, and still no breach visible! With the appearance of *Hesperus*, another wondrous Novel, which proceeded from the same "single apartment," in 1796, the siege may be said to have terminated by storm; and Jean Paul, whom the most knew not what in the world to think of, whom here and there a man of weak judgment had not even scrupled to declare half-mad, made it universally indubitable, that though encircled with dusky vapours, and shining out only in strange many-hued irregular bursts of flame, he was and would be one of the celestial Luminaries of his day and generation. The keen intellectual energy displayed in *Hesperus*, still more the nobleness of mind, the sympathy with Nature, the warm, impetuous, yet pure and lofty delineations of Friendship and Love; in a less degree perhaps, the wild boisterous Humour that everywhere prevails in it, secured

Richter not only admirers, but personal well-wishers in all quarters of his country. Gleim, for example, though then eighty years of age, and among the last survivors of a quite different school, could not contain himself with rapture. "What a divine genius (*Gottgenius*)," thus wrote he some time afterwards, "is our Friedrich Richter! I am reading his *Blumenstücke* for the second time: here is more than Shakspeare, said I, at fifty passages I have marked. What a divine genius! I wonder over the human head, out of which these streams, these books, these Rhinefalls, these Blandusian fountains pour forth over human nature to make human nature humane; and if to-day I object to the plan, object to phrases, to words, I am contented with all to-morrow." The kind, lively old man, it appears, had sent him a gay letter, signed "Septimus Fixlein," with a present of money in it; to which Richter, with great heartiness and some curiosity to penetrate the secret, made answer in this very *Blumenstücke;* and so ere long a joyful acquaintance and friendship was formed; Paul had visited Halberstadt, with warmest welcomes, and sat for his picture there, (an oil painting by Pfenninger,) which is still to be seen in Gleim's *Ehrentempel*, (Temple of Honour.) About this epoch too, the Reviewing world, after a long conscientious silence, again opened its thick lips, and in quite another dialect, screeching out a rusty *Nunc Domine dimittas*, with considerable force of pipe, instead of its last monosyllabic and very unhandsome *grunt*. For the credit of our own guild, we could have wished that the Reviewing world had struck up its *Dimittas* a little sooner.

In 1797, the Widow Richter was taken away from the strange variable climate of this world, we shall hope, into a sunnier one; her kettles hung unscoured on the wall; and the spool, so often filled with her cotton-thread and wetted with her tears, revolved no more. Poor old weather-beaten, heavy-laden soul! And yet a "light-beam from on high" was in her also; and the "twelve shillings for Samuel's new boots" were more bounteous and more blessed than many a King's ransom. Nay, she saw, before departing, that she, even she, had "borne a mighty man;" and her early sunshine, long drowned in deluges, again looked out at evening with farewell sweet.

The Hof household being thus broken up, Richter for some years led a wandering life. In the course of this same 1797, we find him once more in Leipzig; and truly under far other circumstances than of old. For instead of silk-stockinged, shovel-hatted, but too imperious Magisters, that would not let him occupy his own hired dog-hutch in peace, "he here," says Heinrich Doering,* "became acquainted with the three Princesses, adorned with every charm of person and of mind, the daughters of the Dutchess of Hildburghausen! The Duke, who also did justice to his extraordinary merits, conferred on him, some years afterwards, the title of *Legationsrath*, (Councillor of Legation.") To Princes and Princesses, indeed, Jean Paul seems, ever henceforth, to have had what we should reckon a surprising access. For example:—"the social circles where the Duchess Amelia (of Weimar) was wont to assemble the most talented men, first, in Ettersburg, afterwards in Tiefurt;"—then the "Duke of Meinungen at Coburg, who had with pressing kindness invited him;"—the Prince Primate Dalberg, who did much more than invite him; —late in life, "the gifted Duchess Dorothea, in Lobichau, of which visit he has himself commemorated the festive days," &c. &c.;—all which small matters, it appears to us, should be taken into consideration by that class of British philosophers, troublesome in many an intellectual tea-circle, who deduce the "German bad taste" from our own old everlasting "want of intercourse;" whereby, if it so seemed good to them, their tea, till some less self-evident proposition were started, might be "consumed with a certain stately silence."

But next year (1798) there came on Paul a far grander piece of good fortune than any of these, namely, a good wife; which, as Solomon has long ago recorded, is a "good thing." He had gone from Leipzig to Berlin, still busily writing; "and during a longer residence in this latter city," says Doering, "Caroline Mayer, daughter of the Royal Prussian Privy Councillor and Professor of Medicine, Dr. John Andrew Mayer," (these are all his titles,) "gave him her hand; nay even," continues the microscopic Doering, "as is said in a public paper, bestowed on him (*aufdrückte*) the bride-kiss of her own accord." What is still more astonishing, she is recorded to have been a "chosen one of her sex," one that "like a gentle, guardian, care-dispelling genius, went by his side through all his pilgrimage."

Shortly after this great event, Paul removed with his new wife to Weimar, where he seems to have resided some years, in high favour with whatever was most illustrious in that city. His first impression on Schiller is characteristic enough. "Of Hesperus," thus writes Schiller, "I have yet made no mention to you. I found him pretty much what I expected; foreign like a man fallen from the Moon; full of good will, and heartily inclined to see things about him, but without the organ for seeing them. However, I have only spoken to him once, and so can say little of him."* In answer to which, Goethe also expresses his love for Richter, but "doubts whether in literary practice he will ever fall in with them two, much as his theoretical creed inclined that way." Hesperus proved to have more "organ" than Schiller gave him credit for; nevertheless Goethe's doubt had not been unfounded. It was to Herder that Paul chiefly attached himself here; esteeming the others as high-gifted, friendly men, but only Herder as a teacher and spiritual father; of which latter relation, and the warm love and gratitude accompanying it on Paul's side, his writings give frequent proof. "If Herder was not a Poet, says he once, "he was something more,—a Poem!" With Wieland too he stood on the friendliest footing, often walking out to visit him at

* *Leben Jean Paul's.* Gotha, 1826.

* *Briefwechsel zwischen Schiller und Goethe* (Correspondence between Schiller and Goethe.) B. ii. 77.

Osmanstädt, whither the old man had now retired. Perhaps these years spent at Weimar, in close intercourse with so many distinguished persons, were, in regard to outward matters, among the most instructive of Richter's life: in regard to inward matters, he had already served, and with credit, a hard apprenticeship elsewhere. We must not forget to mention that *Titan*, one of his chief romances, (published at Berlin in 1800,) was written during his abode at Weimar; so likewise the *Flegeljahre*, (Wild Oats;) and the eulogy of *Charlotte Corday*, which last, though originally but a Magazine Essay, deserves notice for its bold eloquence, and the antique republican spirit manifested in it. With respect to *Titan*, which, together with its *Comic Appendix*, forms six very extraordinary volumes, Richter was accustomed, on all occasions, to declare it his master-piece, and even the best he could ever hope to do; though there are not wanting readers who continue to regard *Hesperus* with preference. For ourselves, we have read *Titan* with a certain disappointment, after hearing so much of it; yet on the whole, must incline to the Author's opinion. One day we hope to afford the British public some sketch of both these works, concerning which, it has been said, "there is solid metal enough in them to fit out whole circulating libraries, were it beaten into the usual filigree; and much which, attenuate it as we might, no Quarterly Subscriber could well carry with him." Richter's other Novels published prior to this period are the *Invisible Lodge;* the *Siebenkäs*, (or Flower, Fruit, and Thorn pieces;) the *Life of Quintus Fixlein;* the *Jubelsenior*, (Parson in Jubilee:) *Jean Paul's Letters and future History;* the *Dejeuner in Kuhschnappel;* the *Biographical Recreations under the Cranium of a Giantess*, scarcely belong to this species. The Novels published afterwards, which we may as well catalogue here, are the *Leben Fibels*, (Life of Fibel;) *Katzenbergers Badereise*, (Katzenberger's Journey to the Bath;) *Schmelzle's Reise nach Flatz*, (Schmelzle's Journey to Flätz;) the *Comet*, named also *Nicolaus Margraf*.

It seems to have been about the year 1802, that Paul had a pension bestowed on him by the *Fürst Primas* (Prince Primate) von Dalberg, a prelate famed for his munificence, whom we have mentioned above. What the amount was we do not find specified, but only that it "secured him the means of a comfortable life," and was "subsequently," we suppose after the Prince Primate's decease, "paid him by the King of Bavaria." On the strength of which fixed revenue, Paul now established for himself a fixed household: selecting for this purpose, after various intermediate wanderings, the city of Baireuth, "with its kind picturesque environment," where, with only brief occasional excursions, he continued to live and write. We have heard that he was a man universally loved, as well as honoured there: a friendly, true, and high-minded man; copious in speech, which was full of grave genuine humour; contented with simple people and simple pleasures; and himself of the simplest habits and wishes. He had three children; and a guardian angel, doubtless not without her flaws, yet a reasonable angel notwithstanding. For a man with such obdured Stoicism, like triple steel, round his breast; and of such gentle, deep-lying, ever-living springs of Love within it,—all this may well have made a happy life. Besides Paul was of exemplary, unwearied diligence in his vocation; and so had, at all times, "perennial, fire-proof Joys, namely, Employments." In addition to the latter part of the novels named above, which, with the others, as all of them are more or less genuine poetical productions, we feel reluctant to designate even transiently by so despicable an English word,—his philosophical and critical performances, especially the *Vorschule der Aesthetik*, (Introduction to Æsthetics,) and the *Levana*, (Doctrine of Education,) belong wholly to Baireuth, not to enumerate a multitude of miscellaneous writings, (on moral, literary, scientific subjects, but always in a humourous, fantastic, poetic dress,) which of themselves would have made the fortune of no mean man. His heart and conscience, as well as his head and hand, were in the work; from which no temptation could withdraw him. "I hold my duty," says he in these Biographical Notes, "not to lie in enjoying or acquiring, but in writing,—whatever time it may cost, whatever money may be forborne,—nay whatever pleasure; for example that of seeing Switzerland, which nothing but the sacrifice of time forbids."—"I deny myself my evening meal (*Vesperessen*) in my eagerness to work, but the interruptions by my children I cannot deny myself." And again: "A Poet, who presumes to give poetic delight, should contemn and willingly forbear all enjoyments, the sacrifice of which affects not his creative powers; that so he may perhaps delight a century and a whole people." In Richter's advanced years, it was happy for him that he could say: "When I look at what has been made out of me, I must thank God that I paid no heed to external matters, neither to time or toil, nor profit, nor loss; the thing is there, and the instruments that did it I have forgotten and none else knows them. In this wise, has the unimportant series of moments been changed into something higher that remains."—"I have described so much," says he elsewhere, "and I die without ever having seen Switzerland, and the Ocean, and so many other sights. But the ocean of eternity I shall in no case fail to see."

A heavy stroke fell on him in the year 1821, when his only son, a young man of great promise, died at the University. Paul lost not his composure; but was deeply, incurably wounded. "Epistolary lamentations on my misfortune," says he, "I read unmoved, for the bitterest is to be heard within myself, and I must shut the ears of my soul to it; but a single new trait of Max's fair nature opens the whole lacerated heart asunder again, and it can only drive its blood into the eyes." New personal sufferings awaited him: a decay of health, and what to so indefatigable a reader and writer was still worse, a decay of eye-sight, increasing at last into almost total blindness. This too he bore with his old steadfastness, cheerfully seeking what help was to be had; and when no more of help remained, still cheerfully labouring at his vocation, though in sickness and in blindness.* Dark without, he was inwardly full of light; busied on his favourite theme, the *Immortality of the Soul;* when (on the 14th November, 1825) Death came, and Paul's work was all accomplished, and that great question settled for him on far higher and indisputable evidence. The unfinished Volume (which under the title of *Selina* we now have) was carried on his bier to the grave: for his funeral was public, and in Baireuth, and elsewhere, all possible honour was done to his memory.

In regard to Paul's character as a man, we have little to say beyond what the facts of this Narrative have already said more plainly than in words. We learn from all quarters, in one or the other dialect, that the pure high morality which adorns his writings, stamped itself also on his life and actions. "He was a tender husband and father," says Doering, "and goodness itself towards his friends and all that was near him." The significance of such a spirit as Richter's, practically manifested in such a life, is deep and manifold, and at this era will merit careful study. For the present, however, we must leave it, in this degree, to the reader's own consideration; another and still more immediately needful department of our task still remains for us.

Richter's intellectual and Literary character is, perhaps, in a singular degree the counterpart and image of his practical and moral character: his Works seem to us a more than usually faithful transcript of his mind; written with great warmth direct from the heart, and, like himself, wild, strong, original, sincere. Viewed under any aspect, whether as Thinker, Moralist, Satirist, Poet, he is a phenomenon; a vast, many-sided, tumultuous, yet noble nature; for faults, as for merits, "Jean Paul the Unique." In all departments, we find in him a subduing force; but a lawless, untutored, as it were, half savage force. Thus, for example, few understandings known to us are of a more irresistible character than Richter's; but its strength is a natural, unarmed, Orson-like strength: he does not cunningly undermine his subject, and lay it open, by syllogistic implements, or any rule of art; but he crushes it to pieces in his arms, he treads it asunder, not without gay triumph, under his feet; and so in almost monstrous fashion, yet with piercing clearness, lays bare the inmost heart and core of it to all eyes. In passion again, there is the same wild vehemence: it is a voice of softest pity, of endless, boundless wailing, a voice as of Rachel weeping for her children;—or the fierce bellowing of lions amid savage forests. Thus, too, he not only loves Nature, but he revels in her; plunges into her infinite bosom, and fills his whole heart to intoxication with her charms. He tells us that he was wont to study, to write, almost to live, in the open air; and no skyey aspect was so dismal that it altogether wanted beauty for him. We know of no Poet with so deep and passionate and universal a feeling towards Nature: "from the solemn phases of the starry heaven to the simple floweret of the meadow, his eye and his heart are open for her charms and her mystic meanings." But what most of all shadows forth the inborn, essential temper of Paul's mind, is the sportfulness, the wild heartfelt Humour, which, in his highest as in his lowest moods, ever exhibits itself as a quite inseparable ingredient. His Humour, with all its wildness, is of the gravest and kindliest, a genuine Humour; "consistent with utmost earnestness, or rather, inconsistent with the want of it." But on the whole, it is impossible for him to write in other than a humorous manner, be his subject what it may. His Philosophical Treatises, nay, as we have seen, his Autobiography itself, every thing that comes from him, is encased in some quaint fantastic framing; and roguish eyes (yet with a strange sympathy in the matter, for his Humour, as we said, is heartfelt and true) look out on us through many a grave delineation. In his Novels, above all, this is ever an indispensable quality, and, indeed, announces itself in the very entrance of the business, often even on the title-page. Think, for instance, of that *Selection from the Papers of the Devil; Hesperus,* OR *the Dog-post-days; Siebenkas's Wedded-life, Death* AND *Nuptials!*

"The first aspect of these peculiarities," says one of Richter's English critics, "cannot prepossess us in his favour; we are too forcibly reminded of theatrical clap-traps and literary quackery: nor on opening one of the works themselves is the case much mended. Piercing gleams of thought do not escape us; singular truths, conveyed in a form as singular; grotesque, and often truly ludicrous delineations; pathetic, magnificent, far-sounding passages; effusions full of wit, knowledge, and imagination, but difficult to bring under any rubric whatever; all the elements, in short, of a glorious intellect, but dashed together in such wild arrangement, that their order seems the very ideal of confusion. The style and structure of the book appear alike incomprehensible. The narrative is every now and then suspended, to make way for some 'Extra-leaf,' some wild digression upon any subject but the one in hand; the language groans with indescribable metaphors, and allusions to all things human and divine; flowing onward, not like a river, but like an inundation; circling in complex eddies, chafing and gurgling, now this way, now that, till the proper current sinks out of view, amid the boundless uproar. We close the work with a mingled feeling of astonishment, oppression, and perplexity; and Richter stands before us in brilliant cloudy vagueness, a giant mass of intellect, but withou form, beauty, or intelligible purpose.

"To readers who believe that intrinsic is inseparable from superficial excellence, and that nothing can be good or beautiful which is not to be seen through in a moment, Richter can occasion little difficulty. They admit him to be a man of vast natural endowments, but he

* He begins a letter applying for spectacles (August, 1824) in these terms:—"Since last winter, my eyes (the left had, already without cataract, been long half-blind, and like Reviewers and *Litterateurs*, read nothing but title pages) have been seized by a daily increasing Night-Ultra and Enemy-to-Light, who, did I not withstand him, would shortly drive me into the Orcus of Amaurosia. Then, *Addio, opera omnia!*"—*Doering*, 32.

is utterly uncultivated, and without command of them; full of monstrous affectation, the very high-priest of Bad Taste; knows not the art of writing, scarcely that there is such an art; an insane visionary, floating for ever among baseless dreams that hide the firm earth from his view: an intellectual Polyphemus, in short, a *monstrum horrendum, informe, ingens*, (carefully adding) *cui lumen ademptum*; and they close their verdict reflectively with his own praiseworthy maxim: 'Providence has given to the English the empire of the sea, to the French that of the land, to the Germans that of—the air.'

"In this way the matter is adjusted; briefly, comfortably, and wrong. The casket was difficult to open: did we know, by its very shape, that there was nothing in it, that so we should cast it into the sea? Affectation is often singularity, but, singularity is not always affectation. If the nature and condition of a man be really and truly, not conceitedly and untruly, singular, so also will his manner be, so also ought it to be. Affectation is the product of Falsehood, a heavy sin, and the parent of numerous heavy sins; let it be severely punished, but not too lightly imputed. Scarcely any mortal is absolutely free from it, neither most probably is Richter; but it is in minds of another substance than his that it grows to be the ruling product. Moreover, he is actually not a visionary; but, with all his visions, will be found to see the firm Earth, in its whole figures and relations, much more clearly than thousands of such critics, who too probably can see nothing else. Far from being untrained or uncultivated, it will surprise these persons to discover that few men have studied the art of writing, and many other arts besides, more carefully than he; that his *Vorschule der Aesthetik* abounds with deep and sound maxims of criticism; in the course of which, many complex works, his own among others, are rigidly and justly tried, and even the graces and minutest qualities of style are by no means overlooked or unwisely handled.

"Withal, there is something in Richter that incites us to a second, to a third perusal. His works are hard to understand, but they always *have* a meaning, often a true and deep one. In our closer, more comprehensive glance, their truth steps forth with new distinctness, their error dissipates and recedes, passes into veniality, often even into beauty; and at last the thick haze which encircled the form of the writer melts away, and he stands revealed to us in his own steadfast features, a colossal spirit, a lofty and original thinker, a genuine poet, a high-minded, true, and most amiable man.

"I have called him a colossal spirit, for this impression continues with us: to the last we figure him as something gigantic: for all the elements of his structure are vast, and combined together in living and life-giving, rather than in beautiful or symmetrical order. His intellect is keen, impetuous, far-grasping, fit to rend in peaces the stubbornest materials, and extort from them their most hidden and refractory truth. In his Humour he sports with the highest and the lowest, he can play at bowls with the Sun and Moon. His Imagination opens for us the Land of Dreams; we sail with him through the boundless Abyss; and the secrets of Space, and Time, and Life, and Annihilation, hover round us in dim, cloudy forms; and darkness, and immensity, and dread encompass and overshadow us. Nay, in handling the smallest matter, he works it with the tools of a giant. A common truth is wrenched from its old combinations, and presented us in new, impassable, abysmal contrast with its opposite error. A trifle, some slender character, some jest, or quip, or spiritual toy, is shaped into most quaint, yet often truly living form; but shaped somehow as with the hammer of Vulcan, with three strokes that might have helped to forge an Ægis. The treasures of his mind are of a similar description with the mind itself; his knowledge is gathered from all the kingdoms of Art, and Science, and Nature, and lies round him in huge unwieldy heaps. His very language is Titanian; deep, strong, tumultuous; shining wiih a thousand hues, fused from a thousand elements, and winding in labyrinthic mazes.

"Among Richter's gifts," continues this critic, "the first that strikes us as truly great is his Imagination; for he loves to dwell in the loftiest and most solemn provinces of thought; his works abound with mysterious allegories, visions, and typical adumbrations; his Dreams, in particular, have a gloomy vastness, broken here and there by wild far-darting splendour; and shadowy forms of meaning rise dimly from the bosom of the void Infinite. Yet, if I mistake not, Humour is his ruling quality, the quality which lives most deeply in his inward nature, and most strongly influences his manner of being. In this rare gift, for none is rarer than true Humour, he stands unrivalled in his own country, and among late writers, in every other. To describe Humour is difficult at all times, and would perhaps be more than usually difficult in Richter's case. Like all his other qualities, it is vast, rude, irregular; often perhaps overstrained and extravagant; yet, fundamentally, it is genuine Humour, the Humour of Cervantes and Sterne; the product not of Contempt, but of Love, not of superficial distortion of natural forms, but of deep though playful sympathy with all forms of Nature. * * *

"So long as Humour will avail him, his management even of higher and stronger characters may still be pronounced successful; but wherever Humour ceases to be applicable, his success is more or less imperfect. In the treatment of heroes proper he is seldom completely happy. They shoot into rugged exaggeration in his hands: their sensibility becomes too copious and tearful, their magnanimity too fierce, abrupt, and thorough-going. In some few instances, they verge towards absolute failure: compared with their less ambitious brethren, they are almost of a vulgar cast; with all their brilliancy and vigour, too like that positive, determinate, volcanic class of personages whom we meet with so frequently in Novels; they call themselves Men, and do their utmost to prove the assertion, but they cannot make us believe it; for after all their vapouring and storming, we see well enough that they are but Engines, with no more life than the Freethinkers' model in *Martinus Scriblerus,* the Nuremberg Man, who operated by a combination of pipes and levers, and though he could breath and digest perfectly, and even reason as well as most country parsons, was made of wood and leather. In the general conduct of such histories and delineations, Richter seldom appears to advantage: the incidents are often startling and extravagant; the whole structure of the story has a rugged, broken, huge, artificial aspect, and will not assume the air of truth. Yet its chasms are strangely filled up with the costliest materials; a world, a universe of wit, and knowledge, and fancy, and imagination has sent its fairest products to adorn the edifice; the rude and rent Cyclopean walls are resplendent with jewels and beaten gold; rich stately foliage screens it, the balmiest odours encircle it; we stand astonished if not captivated, delighted if not charmed, by the artist and his art."

With these views, so far as they go, we see little reason to disagree. There is doubtless a deeper meaning in the matter, but perhaps this is not the season for evolving it. To depict, with true scientific accuracy, the essential purport and character of Richter's genius and literary endeavour; how it originated, whither it tends, how it stands related to the general tendencies of the world in this age; above all, what is its worth and want of worth to ourselves,—may one day be a necessary problem; but, as matters actually stand, would be a difficult, and not very profitable one. The English public has not yet seen Richter; and must know him before it can judge him. For us, in the present circumstances, we hold it a more promising plan to exhibit some specimens of his workmanship itself, than to attempt describing it anew or better. The general outline of his intellectual aspect, as sketched in few words by the writer already quoted, may stand here by way of preface to these Extracts: as was the case above, whatever it may want, it contains nothing that we dissent from.

"To characterize Jean Paul's works," says he, "would be difficult after the fullest inspection: to describe them to English readers would be next to impossible. Whether poetical, philosophical, didactic, fantastic, they seem all to be emblems, more or less complete, of the singular mind where they originated. As a whole, the first perusal of them, more particularly to a foreigner, is almost infallibly offensive; and neither their meaning nor their no-meaning is to be discerned without long and sedulous study. They are a tropical wilderness, full of endless tortuosities; but with the fairest flowers and the coolest fountains; now overarching us with high umbrageous gloom, now opening in long gorgeous vistas. We wander through them, enjoying their wild grandeur; and, by degrees, our half-contemptuous wonder at the Author passes into reverence and love. His face was long hid from us; but we see him at length, in the firm shape of spiritual manhood; a vast and most singular nature, but vindicating his singular nature by the force, the beauty, and benignity which pervade it. In fine, we joyfully accept him for what he is and was meant to be. The graces, the polish, the sprightly elegancies, which belong to men of lighter make, we cannot look for or demand from him. His movement is essentially slow and cumbrous, for he advances not with one faculty, but with a whole mind; with intellect, and pathos, and wit, and humour, and imagination, moving onward like a mighty host, motley, ponderous, irregular, irresistible. He is not airy, sparkling, and precise; but deep, billowy, and vast. The melody of his nature is not expressed in common note-marks, or written down by the critical gamut: for it is wild and manifold; its voice is like the voice of cataracts, and the sounding of primeval forests. To feeble ears it is discord, but to ears that understand it, deep majestic music."*

As our first specimen, which also may serve for proof that Richter, in adopting his own extraordinary style, did it with clear knowledge of what excellence in style, and the various kinds and degrees of excellence therein properly signified, we select, from his *Vorschule der Aesthetik* (above mentioned and recommended) the following miniature sketches: the reader, acquainted with the persons, will find these sentences, as we believe, strikingly descriptive and exact.

"Visit Herder's creations, where Greek life-freshness, and Hindoo life-weariness are wonderfully blended: you walk, as it were, amid moonshine, into which the red dawn is already falling; but one hidden sun is the painter of both."

"Similar, but more compacted into periods, is Friedrich Heinrich Jacobi's vigorous, German-hearted prose; musical in every sense, for even his images are often derived from tones. The rare union between cutting force of intellectual utterance, and infinitude of sentiment, gives us the tense metallic chord with its soft tones."

"In Goethe's prose, on the other hand, his fixedness of form gives us the Memnon's-tone. A plastic rounding, a pictorial determinateness, which even betrays the manual artist, make his works a fixed still gallery of figures and bronze statues."

"Luther's prose is a half-battle; few deeds are equal to his words."

"Klopstock's prose frequently evinces a sharpness of diction bordering on poverty of matter; a quality peculiar to Grammarians, who most of all know *distinctly*, but least of all know *much*. From want of matter, one is apt to think too much of language. New views of the world, like these other poets, Klopstock scarcely gave. Hence the naked winter-boughs, in his prose; the multitude of circumscribed propositions; the brevity; the return of the same small sharp-cut figures, for instance, of the Resurrection, as of a Harvest-field."

"The perfection of pomp-prose we find in Schiller: what the utmost splendour of reflection in images, in fulness and antithesis can give, he gives. Nay, often he plays on the po-

*German Romance, iii. 6, 18.

etic strings with so rich and jewel-loaded a hand, that the sparkling mass disturbs, if not the playing, yet our hearing of it."—*Vorschule*, s. 545.

That Richter's own playing and painting differed widely from all of these, the reader has already heard, and may now convince himself. Take, for example, the following of a fair-weather scene, selected from a thousand such that may be found in his writings; nowise as the best, but simply as the briefest. It is in the May season, the last evening of Spring:

"Such a May as the present, (of 1794,) Nature has not in the memory of man—begun; for this is but the fifteenth of it. People of reflection have long been vexed once every year, that our German singers should indite May-songs, since several other months deserve such a poetical Night-music better; and I myself have often gone so far as to adopt the idiom of our market-women, and instead of May butter to say June butter, as also June, March, April songs. But thou, kind May of this year, thou deservest to thyself all the songs which were ever made on thy rude namesakes!—By Heaven! when I now issue from the wavering chequered acacia-grove of the Castle, in which I am writing this Chapter, and come forth into the broad living light, and look up to the warming Heaven, and over its Earth budding out beneath it,—the Spring rises before me like a vast full cloud, with a splendour of blue and green. I see the Sun standing amid roses in the western sky, into which he has *thrown his ray-brush wherewith he has to-day been painting the Earth*;—and when I look round a little in our picture exhibition,—his enamelling is still hot on the mountains; on the moist chalk of the moist earth, the flowers, full of sap-colours, are laid out to dry, and the forget-me-not with miniature colours; under the varnish of the streams the skyey Painter has pencilled his own eye; and the clouds like a decoration-painter, he has touched off with wild outlines, and single tints; and so he stands at the border of the Earth, and looks back on his stately Spring, whose robe-folds are valleys, whose breast-bouquet is gardens, and whose blush is a vernal evening, and who, when she rises, will be—Summer!"—*Fixlein*, z. 11.

Or the following, in which moreover are two happy living figures, a bridegroom and a a bride on their marriage-day:

"He led her from the crowded dancing-room into the cool evening. Why does the evening, does the night, put warmer love in our hearts? Is it the nightly pressure of helplessness; or is it the exalting separation from the turmoils of life, that veiling of the world, in which for the soul nothing then remains but souls:—is it, therefore, that the letters in which the loved name stands written in our spirit, appear, like phosphorus writing, by night, *on fire*, while by day in their *cloudy* traces they but smoke?

"He walked with his bride into the Castle-garden: she hastened quickly through the Castle, and past its servant's-hall, where the fair flowers of her young life had been crushed broad and dry, under a long dreary pressure; and her soul expanded, and breathed in the free open garden, on whose flowery soil Destiny had cast forth the first seeds of the blossoms which to-day were gladdening her existence. Still Eden! Green, flower-chequered *chiaroscuro!*—The moon is sleeping under ground, like a dead one, but beyond the garden, the sun's red evening-clouds have fallen down like roseleaves; and the evening-star, the brideman of the sun, hovers like a glancing butterfly above the rosy red, and, modest as a bride, deprives no single starlet of its light.

"The wandering pair arrived at the old gardener's-hut; now standing locked and dumb, with dark windows in the light garden, like a fragment of the Past surviving in the Present. Bared twigs of trees were folding, with clammy half-formed leaves, over the thick intertwisted tangles of the bushes. The Spring was standing, like a conqueror, with Winter at his feet. In the blue pond now bloodless, a dusky evening-sky lay hollowed out; and the gushing waters were moistening the flower-beds. The silver sparks of stars were rising on the altar of the East, and falling down extinguished in the red-sea of the West."

"The wind whirred, like a night-bird, louder through the trees; and gave tones to the acacia-grove, and the tones called to the pair who had first become happy within it: 'Enter, new mortal pair, and think of what is past, and of my withering and your own; and be holy as Eternity, and weep, not for joy only, but for gratitude also!' * * *

"They reached the blazing, rustling marriage-house, but their softened hearts sought stillness; and a foreign touch, as in the blossoming vine, would have disturbed the flower-nuptials of their souls. They turned rather, and winded up into the churchyard, to preserve their mood. Majestic on the groves and mountains stood the Night before man's heart, and made it also great. Over the white steeple-obelisk the sky rested bluer and darker; and behind it wavered the withered summit of the Maypole with faded flag. The son noticed his father's grave, on which the wind was opening and shutting, with harsh noise, the small lid on the metal cross, to let the year of his death be read on the brass plate within. An overpowering grief seized his heart with violent streams of tears, and drove him to the sunk hillock; and he led his bride to the grave, and said: 'Here sleeps he, my good father: in his thirty-second year he was carried hither to his long rest. O thou good dear father, couldst thou but see the happiness of thy son, like my mother! But thy eyes are empty, and thy breast is full of ashes, and thou seest us not.'—He was silent. The bride wept aloud; she saw the mouldering coffins of her parents open, and the two dead arise, and look round for their daughter, who had stayed so long behind them, forsaken on the earth. She fell on his neck and faltered: 'O beloved, I have neither father nor mother, do not forsake me!'

"O thou who hast still a father and a mother, thank God for it on the day when thy soul is full of glad tears, and needs a bosom wherein to shed them. . . .

"And with this embracing at a father's grave, let this day of joy be holily concluded."—*Fixlein*, z. 9.

In such passages, slight as they are, we fancy an experienced eye will trace some features of originality, as well as of uncommonness: an open sense for Nature, a soft heart, a warm rich fancy, and here and there some under-current of Humour are distinctly enough discernible. Of this latter quality, which, as has been often said, forms Richter's grand characteristic, we would fain give our readers some correct notion; but see not well how it is to be done. Being genuine poetic humour, not drollery or vulgar caricature, it is like a fine essence, like a soul; we discover it only in whole works and delineations; as the soul is only to be seen in the living body, not in detached limbs and fragments. Richter's Humour takes a great variety of forms, some of them sufficiently grotesque and piebald; ranging from the light kindly-comic vein of Sterne in his *Trim* and *Uncle Toby*, over all intermediate degrees, to the rugged grim farce-tragedy often manifested in Hogarth's pictures; nay, to still darker and wilder moods than this. Of the former sort are his characters of Fixlein, Schmelzle, Fibel; of the latter his Vult, Giannozzo, Leibgebber, Schoppe, which last two are indeed one and the same. Of these, of the spirit that reigns in them, we should despair of giving other than the most inadequate and even incorrect idea, by any extracts or expositions that could possibly be furnished here. Not without reluctance we have accordingly renounced that enterprise; and must content ourselves with some "Extra-leaf," or other separable passage, which, if it afford no emblem of Richter's Humour, may be, in these circumstances, our best approximation to such. Of the "Extra-leaves," in *Hesperus* itself, a considerable volume might be formed, and truly one of the strangest. Most of them, however, are national; could not be apprehended without a commentary; and even then, much to their disadvantage, for Humour must be seen, not through a glass, but face to face. The following is nowise one of the best; but it turns on what we believe is a quite European subject, at all events is certainly an English one.

"*Extra-leaf on Daughter-full Houses.*

"The Minister's house was an open bookshop, the books in which (the daughters) you might read there, but could not take home with you. Though five other daughters were already standing in five private libraries, as wives, and one under the ground at Majenthal was sleeping off the child's-play of life, yet still in this daughter-warehouse there remained three gratis copies to be disposed of to good friends. The Minister was always prepared, in drawings from the office-lottery, to give his daughters as premiums to winners, and holders of the lucky ticket. Whom God gives an office, he also gives, if not sense for it, at least a wife. In a daughter-full house, there must, as in the Church of St. Peter's, be *confessionals* for all nations, for all characters, for all faults; that the daughters may sit as confessoresses therein, and absolve from all, bachelorship only excepted. As a Natural-Philosopher, I have many times admired the wise methods of Nature for distributing daughters and plants: is it not a fine arrangement, said I to the Natural-Historian Goeze, that Nature should have bestowed specially on young women, who for their growth require a rich mineralogical soil, some sort of hooking apparatus, whereby to stick themselves on miserable marriage-cattle, that may carry them to fat places? Thus Linnæus,* as you know, observes that such seeds as can flourish only in fat earth are furnished with barbs, and so fasten themselves the better on grazing quadrupeds, which transport them to stalls and dunghills. Strangely does Nature, by the wind,—which father and mother must raise,—scatter daughters and fir-seeds into the arable spots of the forest. Who does not remark the final cause here, and how Nature has equipped many a daughter with such and such charms, simply that some Peer, some mitred Abbot, Cardinal-deacon, appanaged Prince, or mere country Baron, may lay hold of said charmer, and in the character of Father or Brideman, hand over her ready-made to some gawk of the like sort, as a wife acquired by purchase? And do we find in bilberries a slighter attention on the part of Nature? Does not the same Linnæus notice, in the same treatise, that they, too, are cased in a nutritive juice to incite the Fox to eat them; after which, the villain,—digest them he cannot,—in such sort as he may, becomes their sower?—

"O, my heart is more in earnest than you think; the parents anger me who are soul-brokers; the daughters sadden me, who are made slave-Negresses.—Ah, is it wonderful that these, who in their West-Indian market-place, must dance, laugh, speak, sing, till some lord of a plantation take them home with him,—that these, I say, should be as slavishly treated, as they are sold and bought? Ye poor lambs!—And yet ye, too, are as bad as your sale-mothers and sale-fathers: what is one to do with his enthusiasm for your sex, when one travels through German towns, where every heaviest pursed, every longest-tilled individual, were he second cousin to the Devil himself, can point with his finger to thirty houses, and say: 'I know not, shall it be from the pearl-coloured, or the nut-brown, or the steel-green house, that I wed; open to customers are they all!'—How, my girls, is your heart so little worth that you cut it, like old clothes, after any fashion, to fit any breast; and does it wax or shrink, then, like a Chinese ball, to fit itself into the ball-mould and marriage ring-case of any male heart whatever?—'Well, it must; unless we would sit at home, and grow Old Maids,' answer they; whom I will not answer, but turn scornfully away from them to address that same Old Maid in these words:

"'Forsaken, but patient one! misknown and mistreated! Think not of the times when thou hadst hope of a better than the present are, and

---

*His *Amœn. Acad.*—The Treatise on the Habitable Globe.

repent the noble pride of thy heart never! It is not always our duty to marry, but it is always our duty to abide by right, not to purchase happiness by loss of honour, not to avoid unweddedness by untruthfulness. Lonely, unadmired heroine! in thy last hour, when all Life and the bygone possessions and scaffoldings of Life shall crumble in pieces, ready to fall down; in that hour thou wilt look back on thy untenanted life: no children, no husband, no wet eyes will be there; but in the empty dusk, one high, pure, angelic, smiling, beaming Figure, godlike and mounting to the Godlike, will hover, and beckon thee to mount with her,—mount thou with her, the Figure is thy Virtue.' "

We have spoken above, and warmly, of Jean Paul's Imagination, of his high devout feeling, which it were now a still more grateful part of our task to exhibit. But in this also our readers must content themselves with some imperfect glimpses. What religious opinions and aspirations he specially entertained, how that noblest portion of man's interests represented itself in such a mind, were long to describe, did we even know it with certainty. He hints somewhere that "the soul, which by nature looks Heavenward, is without a Temple in this age;" in which the careful reader will decipher much.

"But there will come another era," says Paul, "when it shall be light, and man will awaken from his lofty dreams, and find—his dreams still there, and that nothing is gone save his sleep.

"The stones and rocks, which two veiled Figures, (Necessity and Vice,) like Deucalion and Pyrrha, are casting behind them, at Goodness, will themselves become men.

"And on the Western Gate (*Abendthor*, evening-gate) of this century stands written: Here is the way to Virtue and Wisdom; as on the Western-Gate at Cherson stands the proud Inscription: Here is the way to Byzance.

"Infinite Providence, Thou wilt cause the day to dawn.

"But as yet, struggles the twelfth-hour of the Night: the nocturnal birds of prey are on the wing, spectres uproar, the dead walk, the living dream."—*Hesperus. Preface.*

Connected with this, there is one other piece, which also for its singular poetic qualities, we shall translate here. The reader has heard much of Richter's Dreams, with what strange prophetic power he rules over that chaos of spiritual Nature, bodying forth a whole world of Darkness, broken by pallid gleams, or wild sparkles of light, and peopled with huge, shadowy, bewildered shapes, full of grandeur and meaning. No Poet known to us, not Milton himself, shows such a vastness of Imagination; such a rapt, deep, old Hebrew spirit, as Richter in these scenes. He mentions in his Biographical Notes the impression which these lines of the *Tempest* had on him, as recited by one of his companions:

> "We are such stuff
> As dreams are made of, and our little Life
> Is rounded with a sleep."

"The passage of Shakspeare," says he, "*rounded with a sleep*, (*mit Schlaf umgeben*,) in Plattner's mouth, created whole books in me."—The following dream is perhaps his grandest, as, undoubtedly, it is among his most celebrated. We shall give it entire, long as it is, and therewith finish our quotations. What value he himself put on it, may be gathered from the following Note: "If ever my heart," says he, "were to grow so wretched and so dead, that all feelings in it which announce the being of a God were extinct there, I would terrify myself with this sketch of mine; it would heal me, and give me my feelings back." We translate it from *Siebenkäs*, where it forms the first chapter, or *Blumenstück*, (Flower-piece.)

"The purpose of this fiction is the excuse of its boldness. Men deny the Divine Existence with as little feeling as the most assert it. Even in our true systems we go on collecting mere words, playmarks, and medals, as the misers do coins; and not till late do we transform the words into feelings, the coins into enjoyments. A man may, for twenty years, believe the Immortality of the Soul;—in the one-and-twentieth, in some great moment, he for the first time discovers with amazement the rich meaning of this belief, and the warmth of this Naptha-well.

"Of such sort, too, was my terror at the poisonous stifling vapour which floats out round the heart of him who for the first time enters the school of Atheism. I could with less pain deny Immortality, than Deity; there I should lose but a world covered with mists, here I should lose the present world, namely, the Sun thereof: the whole Spiritual Universe is dashed asunder by the hand of Atheism, into numberless quicksilver-points of *Me's*, which glitter, run, waver, fly together or asunder, without unity or continuance. No one in Creation is so alone, as the denier of God; he mourns, with an orphaned heart that has lost its great Father, by the corpse of Nature, which no World-spirit moves and holds together, and which grows in its grave; and he mourns by that Corpse till he himself crumble off from it. The whole world lies before him, like the Egyptian Sphinx of stone, half-buried in the sand; and the All is the cold iron mask of a formless Eternity.* * *

"I merely remark farther, that with the belief of Atheism, the belief of Immortality is quite compatible; for the same Necessity, which in this Life threw my light dew-drop of a *Me* into a flower-bell and under a Sun, can repeat that process in a second life;—nay, more easily imbody me—the second time than the first.

"If we hear, in childhood, that the dead, about midnight, when our *sleep reaches near the soul*, and darkens even our dreams, awake out of theirs, and in the church mimic the worship of the living, we shudder at Death by reason of the dead, and in the night-solitude turn away our eyes from the long silent windows of the church, and fear to search in their gleaming, whether it proceed from the moon.

"Childhood, and rather its terrors than its raptures, take wings and radiance again in dreams, and sport like fire-flies in the little night of the soul. Crush not these flickering sparks!—Leave us even our dark painful dreams as higher half-shadows of reality! And wherewith will you replace to us *those* dreams, which bear us away from under the tumult of the waterfall into the still heights of childhood, where the stream of life yet ran silent in its little plain, and flowed towards its abysses, a mirror of the Heaven?—

"I was lying once, on a summer-evening, in the sunshine; and I fell asleep. Methought I awoke in the churchyard. The down-rolling wheels of the steeple-clock, which was striking eleven, had awoke me. In the emptied night-heaven I looked for the Sun; for I thought an eclipse was veiling him with the Moon. All the Graves were open, and the iron doors of the charnel-house were swinging to and fro by invisible hands. On the walls, flitted shadows, which proceeded from no one, and other shadows stretched upwards in the pale air. In the open coffins none now lay sleeping, but the children. Over the whole heaven hung, in large folds, a gray sultry mist, which a giant shadow like vapour was drawing down, nearer, closer, and hotter. Above me I heard the distant fall of avalanches; under me the first step of a boundless earthquake. The Church wavered up and down with two interminable Dissonances, which struggled with each other in it; endeavouring in vain to mingle in unison. At times, a gray glimmer hovered along the windows, and under it the lead and iron fell down molten. The net of the mist, and the tottering Earth brought me into that hideous Temple; at the door of which, in two poison-bushes, two glittering Basilisks lay brooding. I passed through unknown Shadows, on whom ancient centuries were impressed.—All the Shadows were standing round the empty Altar; and in all, not the heart, but the breast quivered and pulsed. One dead man only, who had just been buried there, still lay on his coffin without quivering breast; and on his smiling countenance, stood a happy dream. But at the entrance of one Living, he awoke, and smiled no longer; he lifted his heavy eyelids, but within was no eye; and in his beating breast there lay, instead of heart, a wound. He held up his hands, and folded them to pray; but the arms lengthened out, and dissolved; and the hands, still folded together, fell away. Above, on the Church-dome stood the dial-plate of *Eternity* whereon no number appeared, and which was its own index: but a black finger pointed thereon, and the Dead sought to see the time by it.

"Now sank from aloft a noble, high Form, with a look of uneffaceable sorrow, down to the Altar, and all the Dead cried out, 'Christ! is there no God?' He answered 'There is none!' The whole Shadow of each then shuddered, not the breast alone; and one after the other, all, in this shuddering, shook into pieces.

"Christ continued: 'I went through the Worlds, I mounted into the Suns, and flew with the Galaxies through the wastes of Heaven; but there is no God! I descended as far as Being casts its shadow, and looked down into the Abyss and cried, Father, where art thou? But I heard only the everlasting storm which no one guides, and the gleaming Rainbow of Creation hung without a Sun that made it, over the Abyss, and trickled down. And when I looked up to the immeasurable world for the Divine *Eye*, it glared on me with an empty, black, bottomless *Eye-socket*; and Eternity lay upon Chaos, eating it and ruminating it. Cry on, ye Dissonances; cry away the Shadows, for He is not!'

"The pale-grown Shadows flitted away, as white vapour which frost has formed with the warm breath disappears; and all was void. O, then came, fearful for the heart, the dead Children who had been awakened in the Churchyard, into the temple, and cast themselves before the high Form on the Altar, and said, 'Jesus, have we no Father?' And he answered, with streaming tears, 'We are all orphans, I and you; we are without Father!'

"Then shrieked the Dissonances still louder, —the quivering walls of the Temple parted asunder; and the Temple and the Children sank down, and the whole Earth and the Sun sank after it, and the whole Universe sank with its immensity before us; and above, on the summit of immeasurable Nature, stood Christ, and gazed down into the Universe chequered with its thousand Suns, as into the Mine bored out of the Eternal Night, in which the Suns run like mine-lamps, and the Galaxies like silver veins.

"And as he saw the grinding press of Worlds, the torch-dance of celestial wildfires, and the coral-banks of beating hearts; and as he saw how world after world shook off its glimmering souls upon the Sea of Death, as a water-bubble scatters swimming lights on the waves, then majestic as the Highest of the Finite, he raised his eyes towards the Nothingness, and towards the void Immensity, and said: 'Dead, dumb Nothingness! Cold, everlasting Necessity! Frantic Chance! Know ye what this is that lies beneath you? When will ye crush the Universe in pieces, and me? Chance, knowest thou what thou doest, when with thy hurricanes thou walkest through that snow-powder of Stars, and extinguishest Sun after Sun, and that sparkling dew of heavenly light goes out, as thou passest over it? How is each so solitary in this wide grave of the All! I am alone with myself! O Father, O Father! where is thy infinite bosom that I might rest on it? Ah, if each soul is its own father and creator, why can it not be its own destroyer too?

"'Is this beside me yet a Man? Unhappy one! Your little life is the sigh of Nature, or only its echo; a convex-mirror throws its rays into that dust-cloud of dead men's ashes, down on the Earth, and thus you, cloud-formed wavering phantoms, arise.—Look down into the Abyss, over which clouds of ashes are moving; mists full of Worlds reek up from the Sea of Death; the *Future* is a mounting mist, and the *Present* is a falling one.—Knowest thou thy Earth again?'

"Here Christ looked down, and his eye filled with tears, and he said: 'Ah, I was once there; I was still happy then; I had still my Infinite Father, and looked up cheerfully from the mountains, into the immeasurable Heaven, and pressed my mangled breast on his healing form, and said even in the bitterness of death: Father, take thy son from this bleeding hull, and lift him to thy heart!—Ah, ye too happy inhabitants of Earth, ye still believe in *Him*. Perhaps even now your Sun is going down, and ye kneel amid blossoms, and brightness, and tears, and lift trustful hands, and cry with joy-streaming eyes, to the opened Heaven: "Me too thou knowest, Omnipotent, and all my wounds; and at death thou receivest me, and closest them all!" Unhappy creatures, at death they will not be closed! Ah, when the sorrow-laden lays himself, with galled back, into the Earth, to sleep till a fairer Morning full of Truth, full of Virtue and Joy, he awakens in a stormy Chaos, in the everlasting Midnight, —and there comes no Morning, and no soft healing hand, and no Infinite Father!—Mortal, beside me! if thou still livest, pray to *Him;* else hast thou lost him for ever!'

"And as I fell down, and looked into the sparkling Universe, I saw the upborne Rings of the Giant-Serpent, the Serpent of Eternity, which had coiled itself round the All of Worlds, —and the Rings sank down, and encircled the All doubly;—and then it wound itself, innumerable ways, round Nature, and swept the Worlds from their places, and crashing, squeezed the Temple of Immensity together, into the Church of a Burying-ground,—and all grew strait, dark, fearful,—and an immeasurably extended Hammer was to strike the last hour of Time, and shiver the Universe asunder, . . . WHEN I AWOKE.

"My soul wept for joy that I could still pray to God; and the joy, and the weeping, and the faith on him were my prayer. And as I arose, the Sun was glowing deep behind the full purpled corn-ears, and casting meekly the gleam of its twilight-red on the little Moon, which was rising in the East without an Aurora; and between the sky and the earth, a gay transient air-people was stretching out its short wings and living, as I did, before the Infinite Father; and from all Nature around me flowed peaceful tones as from distant evening-bells."

Without commenting on this singular piece, we must here for the present close our lucubrations on Jean Paul. To delineate, with any correctness, the specific features of such a genius, and of its operations and results in the great variety of provinces where it dwelt and worked, were a long task; for which, perhaps, some groundwork may have been laid here, and which, as occasion serves, it will be pleasant for us to resume.

Probably enough, our readers, in considering these strange matters, will too often bethink them of that "Episode concerning Paul's Costume;" and conclude that, as in living, so in writing, he was a Mannerist, and man of continual Affectations. We will not quarrel with them on this point; we must not venture among the intricacies it would lead us into. At the same time, we hope, many will agree with us in honouring Richter, such as he was; and "in spite of his hundred real, and his ten thousand seeming faults," discern under this wondrous guise the spirit of a true Poet and Philosopher. A Poet, and among the highest of his time, we must reckon him, though he wrote no verses; a Philosopher, though he promulgated no systems: for on the whole, that "Divine Idea of the World" stood in clear ethereal light before his mind; he recognised the Invisible, even under the mean forms of these days, and with a high, strong, not uninspired heart, strove to represent it in the Visible, and published tidings of it to his fellow men. This one virtue, the foundation of all other virtues, and which a long study more and more clearly reveals to us in Jean Paul, will cover far greater sins than his were. It raises him into quite another sphere than that of the thousand elegant sweet-singers, and cause-and-effect *philosophers*, in his own country, or in this; the million Novel-manufacturers, Sketchers, practical Discoursers, and so forth, not once reckoned in. Such a man we can safely recommend to universal study; and for those who, in the actual state of matters, may the most blame him, repeat the old maxim: "What is extraordinary try to look at with your own eyes."

ON HISTORY.

[FRASER'S MAGAZINE, 1830.]

CLIO was figured by the ancients as the eldest daughter of Memory, and chief of the Muses; which dignity, whether we regard the essential qualities of her art, or its practice and acceptance among men, we shall still find to have been fitly bestowed. History, as it lies at the root of all science, is also the first distinct product of man's spiritual nature; his earliest expression of what can be called Thought. It is a looking both before and after; as, indeed, the coming Time already waits, unseen, yet definitely shaped, predetermined, and inevitable, in the Time come: and only by the combination of both is the meaning of either completed. The Sibylline Books, though old, are not the oldest. Some nations have prophecy, some have not: but, of all mankind, there is no tribe so rude that it has not attempted History, though several have not arithmetic enough to count Five. History has been written with quipo-threads, with feather-pictures, with wampum-belts; still oftener with earth-mounds and monumental stone-heaps, whether as pyramid or cairn; for the

Celt and the Copt, the Red man as well as the White, lives between two eternities, and, warring against Oblivion, he would fain unite himself in clear, conscious relation, as in dim unconscious relation he is already united, with the whole Future and the whole Past.

A talent for History may be said to be born with us, as our chief inheritance. In a certain sense all men are historians. Is not every memory written quite full with Annals, wherein joy and mourning, conquest and loss, manifoldly alternate; and, with or without philosophy, the whole fortunes of one little inward kingdom, and all its politics, foreign and domestic, stand ineffaceably recorded? Our very speech is curiously historical. Most men, you may observe, speak only to narrate; not in imparting what they have thought, which indeed were often a very small matter, but in exhibiting what they have undergone or seen, which is a quite unlimited one, do talkers dilate. Cut us off from Narrative, how would the stream of conversation, even among the wisest, languish into detached handfuls, and among the foolish utterly evaporate! Thus, as we do nothing but enact History, we say little but recite it; nay, rather, in that widest sense, our whole spiritual life is built thereon. For, strictly considered, what is all Knowledge too but recorded Experience, and a product of History; of which, therefore, Reasoning and Belief, no less than Action and Passion, are essential materials?

Under a limited, and the only practicable shape, History proper, that part of History which treats of remarkable action, has, in all modern as well as ancient times, ranked among the highest arts, and perhaps never stood higher than in these times of ours. For whereas, of old, the charm of History lay chiefly in gratifying our common appetite for the wonderful, for the unknown; and her office was but as that of a Minstrel and Story-teller, she has now farther become a Schoolmistress, and professes to instruct in gratifying. Whether, with the stateliness of that venerable character, she may not have taken up something of its austerity and frigidity; whether, in the logical terseness of a Hume or Robertson, the graceful ease and gay pictorial heartiness of a Herodotus or Froissart may not be wanting, is not the question for us here. Enough that all learners, all inquiring minds of every order, are gathered round her footstool, and reverently pondering her lessons, as the true basis of Wisdom. Poetry, Divinity, Politics, Physics, have each their adherents and adversaries; each little guild supporting a defensive and offensive war for its own special domain; while the domain of History is as a Free Emporium, where all these belligerents peaceably meet and furnish themselves; and Sentimentalist and Utilitarian, Skeptic and Theologian, with one voice advise us: Examine History, for it is "Philosophy teaching by Experience."

Far be it from us to disparage such teaching, the very attempt at which must be precious. Neither shall we too rigidly inquire, how much it has hitherto profited? Whether most of what little practical wisdom men have, has come from study of professed History, or from other less boasted sources, whereby, as matters now stand, a Marlborough may become great in the world's business, with no History save what he derives from Shakspeare's Plays? Nay, whether in that same teaching by Experience, historical Philosophy has yet properly deciphered the first element of all science in this kind? What is the aim and significance of that wondrous changeful life it investigates and paints? Whence the course of man's destinies in this Earth originated, and whither they are tending? Or, indeed, if they have any course and tendency, are really guided forward by an unseen mysterious Wisdom, or only circle in blind mazes without recognisable guidance? Which questions, altogether fundamental, one might think, in any Philosophy of History, have, since the era when Monkish Annalists were wont to answer them by the long-ago extinguished light of their Missal and Breviary, been by most philosophical Historians only glanced at dubiously, and from afar; by many, not so much as glanced at. The truth is, two difficulties, never wholly surmountable, lie in the way. Before philosophy can teach by Experience, the Philosophy has to be in readiness, the Experience must be gathered and intelligibly recorded. Now, overlooking the former consideration, and with regard only to the latter, let any one who has examined the current of human affairs—and how intricate, perplexed, unfathomable, even when seen into with our own eyes, are their thousand-fold, blending movements—say whether the true representing of it is easy or impossible. Social Life is the aggregate of all the individual men's Lives who constitute society; History is the essence of innumerable Biographies. But if one Biography, nay, our own Biography, study and recapitulate it as we may, remains in so many points unintelligible to us, how much more must these million, the very facts of which, to say nothing of the purport of them, we know not, and cannot know!

Neither will it adequately avail us to assert that the general inward condition of Life is the same in all ages; and that only the remarkable deviations from the common endowment, and common lot, and the more important variations which the outward figure of Life has from time to time undergone, deserve memory and record. The inward condition of life, it may rather be affirmed, the conscious or half-conscious aim of mankind, so far as men are not mere digesting machines, is the same in no two ages; neither are the more important outward variations easy to fix on, or always well capable of representation. Which was the greater innovator, which was the more important personage in man's history, he who first led armies over the Alps, and gained the victories of Cannæ and Thrasymene; or the nameless boor who first hammered out for himself an iron spade? When the oak tree is felled, the whole forest echoes with it; but a hundred acorns are planted silently by some unnoticed breeze. Battles and war-tumults, which for the time din every ear, and with joy or terror intoxicate every heart, pass away like tavern-brawls; and, except some few Marathons and Morgartens, are remembered by accident, not by desert. Laws themselves, political Constitutions, are not our Life, but only the house wherein our life is led: nay, they are but the bare walls of the house; all whose essential furniture, the inventions and traditions, and daily habits that regulate and support our existence, are the work not of Dracos and Hampdens, but of Phœnician mariners, of Italian masons and Saxon metallurgists, of philosophers, alchemists, prophets, and all the long forgotten train of artists and artisans; who from the first have been jointly teaching us how to think and how to act, how to rule over spiritual and over physical Nature. Well may we say that of our History the more important part is lost without recovery, and,—as thanksgivings were once wont to be offered for unrecognised mercies,—look with reverence into the dark untenanted places of the past, where, in formless oblivion, our chief benefactors, with all their sedulous endeavours, but not with the fruit of these, lie entombed.

So imperfect is that same Experience, by which Philosophy is to teach. Nay, even with regard to those occurrences that do stand recorded, that, at their origin, have seemed worthy of record, and the summary of which constitutes what we now call History, is not our understanding of them altogether incomplete; it is even possible to represent them as they were? The old story of Sir Walter Raleigh's looking from his prison window, on some street tumult, which afterwards three witnesses reported in three different ways, himself differing from them all, is still a true lesson for us. Consider how it is that historical documents and records originate; even honest records, where the reporters were unbiassed by personal regard; a case which, where nothing more were wanted, must ever be among the rarest. The real leading features of an historical transaction, those movements that essentially characterize it, and alone deserve to be recorded, are nowise the foremost to be noted. At first, among the various witnesses, who are also parties interested, there is only vague wonder, and fear or hope, and the noise of Rumour's thousand tongues; till, after a season, the conflict of testimonies has subsided into some general issue; and then it is settled, by a majority of votes, that such and such a "Crossing of the Rubicon," an "Impeachment of Stafford," a "Convocation of the Notables," are epochs in the world's history, cardinal points on which grand world-revolutions have hinged. Suppose, however, that the majority of votes was all wrong; that the real cardinal points lay far deeper, and had been passed over unnoticed, because no Seer, but only mere Onlookers, chanced to be there! Our clock strikes when there is a change from hour to hour; but no hammer in the Horologe of Time peals through the universe, when there is a change from Era to Era. Men understand not what is among their hands: as calmness is the characteristic of strength, so the weightiest causes may be the most silent. It is, in no case, the real historical Transaction, but only some more or less plausible scheme and theory of the Transaction, or the harmonized result of many such schemes, each varying from the other, and all varying from Truth, that we can ever hope to behold.

Nay, were our faculty of insight into passing things never so complete, there is still a fatal discrepancy between our manner of observing these, and their manner of occurring. The most gifted man can observe, still more can record, only the *series* of his own impressions: his observation, therefore, to say nothing of its other imperfections, must be *successive*, while the things done were often *simultaneous*; the things done were not a series, but a group. It is not in acted, as it is in written History: actual events are nowise so simply related to each other as parent and offspring are; every single event is the offspring not of one, but of all other events prior or contemporaneous, and will in its turn combine with all others to give birth to new: it is an ever-living, ever-working Chaos of Being, wherein shape after shape bodies itself forth from innumerable elements. And this Chaos, boundless as the habitation and duration of man, unfathomable as the soul and destiny of man, is what the historian will depict, and scientifically gauge, we may say, by threading it with single lines of a few ells in length! For as all Action is, by its nature, to be figured as extended in breadth, and in depth, as well as in length; that is to say, is based on Passion and Mystery, if we investigate its origin; and spreads abroad on all hands, modifying and modified; as well as advances towards completion, so,—all Narrative is, by its nature, of only one dimension; only travels forward towards one, or towards successive points: Narrative is *linear*, Action is *solid*. Alas, for our "chains," or chainlets, of "causes and effects," which we so assiduously track through certain handbreadths of years and square miles, when the whole is a broad, deep, Immensity, and each atom is "chained" and complected with all! Truly, if History is Philosophy teaching by Experience, the writer fitted to compose history is hitherto an unknown man. The Experience itself would require All-knowledge to record it, were the All-wisdom needful for such Philosophy as would interpret it, to be had for asking. Better were it that mere earthly Historians should lower such pretensions, more suitable for Omniscience than for human science; and aiming only at some picture of the things acted, which picture itself will at best be a poor approximation, leave the inscrutable purport of them an acknowledged secret; or, at most, in reverent Faith, far different from that teaching of Philosophy, pause over the mysterious vestiges of Him, whose path is in the great deep of Time, whom History indeed reveals, but only all History, and in Eternity will clearly reveal.

Such considerations truly were of small profit, did they, instead of teaching us vigilance and reverent humility in our inquiries into History, abate our esteem for them, or discourage us from unweariedly prosecuting them. Let us search more and more into the Past; let all men explore it as the true fountain of knowledge; by whose light alone, consciously or unconsciously employed, can the Present and the Future be interpreted or guessed at. For though the whole meaning lies far beyond our ken; yet in that complex Manuscript, covered over with formless, inextricably entangled, unknown characters,—nay, which is a *Palympsest*, and had once prophetic writing, still dimly legible there,—some letters, some words, may be deciphered; and if no complete Philosophy, here and there an intelligible precept, available in practice, be gathered; well understanding, in the mean while, that it is only a little portion we have deciphered, that much still remains to be interpreted; that history is a real prophetic Manuscript, and can be fully interpreted by no man.

But the Artist in History may be distinguished from the Artisan in History; for here, as in all other provinces, there are Artists and Artisans; men who labour mechanically in a department, without eye for the Whole, not feeling that there is a Whole; and men who inform and ennoble the humblest department with an Idea of the Whole, and habitually know that only in the Whole is the Partial to be truly discerned. The proceedings, and the duties of these two, in regard to History, must be altogether different. Not, indeed, that each has not a real worth, in his several degree. The simple Husbandman can till his field, and by knowledge he has gained of its soil, sow it with the fit grain, though the deep rocks and central fires are unknown to him: his little crop hangs under and over the firmament of stars, and sails through whole untracked celestial spaces, between Aries and Libra; nevertheless, it ripens for him in due season, and he gathers it safe into his barn. As a husbandman he is blameless in disregarding those higher wonders; but as a Thinker, and faithful inquirer into nature, he were wrong. So, likewise, is it with the Historian, who examines some special aspect of history, and from this or that combination of circumstances, political, moral, economical, and the issues it has led to, infers that such and such properties belong to human society, and that the like circumstance will produce the like issues; which inference, if other trials confirm it, must be held true and practically valuable. He is wrong only, and an artisan, when he fancies that these properties, discovered or discoverable, exhaust the matter, and sees not at every step that it is inexhaustible.

However, that class of cause-and-effect speculators, with whom no wonder would remain wonderful, but all things in Heaven and Earth must be "computed and accounted for;" and even the Unknown, the Infinite, in man's life, had, under the words Enthusiasm, Superstition, Spirit of the Age, and so forth, obtained, as it were, an algebraical symbol, and given value,—have now well-nigh played their part in European culture; and may be considered, as in most countries, even in England itself, where they linger the latest, verging towards extinction. He who reads the inscrutable Book of Nature, as if it were a Merchant's Ledger, is justly suspected of having never seen that Book, but only some school Synopsis thereof; from which, if taken for the real Book, more error than insight is to be derived.

Doubtless, also, it is with a growing feeling of the infinite nature of history, that in these times, the old principle, Division of Labour, has been so widely applied to it. The political Historian, once almost the sole cultivator of History, has now found various associates, who strive to elucidate other phases of human Life; of which, as hinted above, the political conditions it is passed under, are but one; and though the primary, perhaps not the most important, of the many outward arrangements. Of this historian himself, moreover, in his own special department, new and higher things are now beginning to be expected. From of old, it was too often to be reproachfully observed of him, that he dwelt with disproportionate fondness in Senate-houses, in Battle-fields, nay, even in King's Antechambers; forgetting, that far away from such scenes, the mighty tide of Thought, and Action, was still rolling on its wondrous course, in gloom and brightness: and in its thousand remote valleys, a whole world of Existence, with or without an earthly sun of Happiness to warm it, with or without a heavenly sun of Holiness to purify and sanctify it, was blossoming and fading, whether the "famous victory" were won or lost. The time seems coming when much of this must be amended; and he who sees no world but that of courts and camps; and writes only how soldiers were drilled and shot, and how this ministerial conjurer out-conjured that other, and then guided, or at least held, something which he called the rudder of government, but which was rather the spigot of Taxation, wherewith, in place of steering, he could tap, and the more cunningly the nearer the lees,—will pass for a more or less instructive Gazetteer, but will no longer be called an Historian.

However, the Political Historian, were his work performed with all conceivable perfection, can accomplish but a part, and still leaves room for numerous fellow-labourers. Foremost among these comes the Ecclesiastical Historian; endeavouring with catholic or sectarian view, to trace the progress of the Church, of that portion of the social establishment, which respects our religious condition, as the other portion does our civil, or rather, in the long run, our economical condition. Rightly conducted, this department were undoubtedly the more important of the two; inasmuch as it concerns us more to understand how man's moral well-being had been and might be promoted, than to understand in the like sort his physical well-being; which latter is ultimately the aim of all political arrangements. For the physically happiest is simply the safest, the strongest; and in all conditions of Government, Power (whether of wealth as in these days, or of arms and adherents as in old days) is the only outward emblem and purchase-money of Good. True Good, however, unless we reckon Pleasure synonymous with it, is said to be rarely, or rather never, offered for sale in the market where that even passes current. So that, for man's true advantage, not the outward condition of his life, but the inward and spiritual, is of prime influence; not the form of government he lives under, and the power he can accumulate there, but the Church he is a member of, and the degree of moral Elevation he can acquire by means of its instruction. Church History, then, did it speak wisely, would have momentous secrets to teach us: nay, in its highest degree, it were a sort of continued Holy Writ; our sacred books being, indeed, only a History of the primeval Church, as it first arose in man's soul, and symbolically imbodied itself in his external life. How far our actual Church Historians fall below such unattainable standards, nay, below quite attainable approximations thereto, we need not point out. Of the Ecclesiastical Historian we have to complain, as we did of his Political fellow-craftsman, that his inquiries turn rather on the outward mechanism, the mere hulls and superficial accidents of the object, than on the object itself; as if the church lay in Bishop's Chapter-houses, and Ecumenic Council Halls, and Cardinals' Conclaves, and not far more in the hearts of Believing Men, in whose walk and conversation, as influenced thereby, its chief manifestations were to be looked for, and its progress or decline ascertained. The history of the Church is a History of the Invisible as well as of the Visible Church; which latter, if disjoined from the former, is but a vacant edifice; gilded, it may be, and overhung with old votive gifts, yet useless, nay, pestilentially unclean; to write whose history is less important than to forward its downfall.

Of a less ambitious character are the Histories that relate to special separate provinces of human Action; to Sciences, Practical Arts, Institutions, and the like; matters which do not imply an epitome of man's whole interest and form of life; but wherein, though each is still connected with all, the spirit of each, at least its material results, may be in some degree evolved without so strict reference to that of the others. Highest in dignity and difficulty, under this head, would be our histories of Philosophy, of man's opinions and theories respecting the nature of his Being, and relations to the Universe, Visible and Invisible; which History, indeed, were it fitly treated, or fit for right treatment, would be a province of Church History; the logical or dogmatical province of it; for Philosophy, in its true sense, is or should be the soul, of which Religion, Worship, is the body; in the healthy state of things the Philosopher and Priest were one and the same. But Philosophy itself is far enough from wearing this character; neither have its Historians been men, generally speaking, that could in the smallest degree approximate it thereto. Scarcely since the rude era of the Magi and Druids has that same healthy identification of Priest and Philosopher had place in any country: but rather the worship of divine things, and the scientific investigation of divine things, have been in quite different hands, their relations not friendly but hostile. Neither have the Brückers and Bühles, to say nothing of the many unhappy Enfields who have treated of that latter department, been more than barren reporters, often unintelligent and unintelligible reporters, of the doctrine uttered, without force to discover how the doctrine originated, or what reference it bore to its time and country, to the spiritual position of mankind there and then. Nay, such a task did not perhaps lie before them, as a thing to be attempted.

Art, also, and Literature are intimately blended with Religion; as it were, outworks and abutments, by which that highest pinnacle in our inward world gradually connects itself with the general level, and becomes accessible therefrom. He who should write a proper History of Poetry, would depict for us the successive Revelations which man had obtained of the Spirit of Nature; under what aspects he had caught and endeavoured to body forth some glimpse of that unspeakable Beauty, which in its highest clearness is Religion, is the inspiration of a Prophet, yet in one or the other degree must inspire every true Singer, were his theme never so humble. We should see by what steps men had ascended to the Temple; how near they had approached; by what ill hap they had, for long periods, turned away from it, and grovelled on the plain with no music in the air, or blindly struggled towards other heights. That among all our Eichhorns and Wartons there is no such Historian, must be too clear to every one. Nevertheless let us not despair of far nearer approaches to that excellence. Above all, let us keep the Ideal of it ever in our eye; for thereby alone have we even a chance to reach it.

Our histories of Laws and Constitutions, wherein many a Montesquieu and Hallam has laboured with acceptance, are of a much simpler nature, yet deep enough, if thoroughly investigated; and useful, when authentic, even with little depth. Then we have Histories of Medicine, of Mathematics, of Astronomy, Commerce, Chivalry, Monkery; and Goguets and Beckmanns have come forward with what might be the most bountiful contribution of all, a History of Inventions. Of all which sorts, and many more not here enumerated, not yet devised and put in practice, the merit and the proper scheme may require no exposition.

In this manner, though, as above remarked, all Action is extended three ways, and the general sum of human Action is a whole Universe, with all limits of it unknown, does History strive by running path after path, through the Impassable, in manifold directions and intersections, to secure for us some oversight of the Whole; in which endeavour, if each Historian look well around him from his path, tracking it out with the *eye*, not, as is more common, with the *nose*, he may at last prove not altogether unsuccessful. Praying only that increased division of labour do not here, as elsewhere, aggravate our already strong Mechanical tendencies, so that in the manual dexterity for parts we lose all command over the whole; and the hope of any Philosophy of History be farther off than ever; let us all wish her great, and greater success.

LUTHER'S PSALM.

[FRASER'S MAGAZINE, 1831.]

AMONG Luther's Spiritual Songs, of which various collections have appeared of late years,* the one entitled *Eine feste Burg ist unser Gott* is universally regarded as the best; and indeed still retains its place and devotional use in the Psalmodies of Protestant Germany. Of the Tune, which also is by Luther, we have no copy, and only a second-hand knowledge: to the original Words, probably never before printed in England, we subjoin the following translation; which, if it possesses the only merit it can pretend to, that of literal adherence to the sense, will not prove unacceptable to our readers. Luther's music is heard daily in our churches, several of our finest Psalm-tunes being of his composition. Luther's sentiments, also, are, or should be, present in many an English heart; the more interesting to us is any the smallest articulate expression of these.

The great Reformer's love of music, of poetry, it has often been remarked, is one of the most significant features in his character. But, indeed, if every great man, Napoleon himself, is intrinsically a poet, an idealist, with more or less completeness of utterance, which of all our great men, in these modern ages, had such an endowment in that kind as Luther? He it was, emphatically, who stood based on the Spiritual World of man, and only by the footing and miraculous power he had obtained there, could work such changes in the Material World. As a participant and dispenser of divine influences, he shows himself among human affairs a true connecting medium and visible Messenger between Heaven and Earth; a man, therefore, not only permitted to enter the sphere of Poetry, but to dwell in the purest centre thereof: perhaps the most inspired of all Teachers since the first apostles of his faith; and thus not a poet only but a Prophet and God-ordained Priest, which is the highest form of that dignity, and of all dignity.

Unhappily, or happily, Luther's poetic feeling did not so much learn to express itself in fit Words that take captive every ear, as in fit Actions, wherein truly, under still more impressive manifestation, the spirit of spheral Melody resides, and still audibly addresses us. In his written Poems we find little, save that Strength of one "whose words," it has been said, "were half-battles;" little of that still Harmony and blending softness of union which is the last perfection of Strength; less of it than even his conduct often manifested. With words he had not learned to make pure music; it was by deeds of Love, or heroic Valour, that he spoke freely; in tones, only through his Flute, amid tears, could the sigh of that strong soul find utterance.

* For example: Luther's *geistliche Lieder nebst dessen Gedanken über die musica*, (Berlin, 1817): *Die Lieder* Luther's *gesammelt von Kosegarten und Rambach, &c.*

Nevertheless, though in imperfect articulation, the same voice, if we will listen well, is to be heard also in his writings, in his Poems. The following, for example, jars upon our ears; yet is there something in it like the sound of Alpine avalanches, or the first murmur of Earthquakes; in the very vastness of which dissonance a higher unison is revealed to us. Luther wrote this Song in a time of blackest threatenings, which, however, could in no wise become a time of Despair. In those tones, rugged, broken as they are, do we not recognise the accent of that summoned man, (summoned not by Charles the Fifth, but by God Almighty also,) who answered his friend's warning not to enter Worms in this wise: "Were there as many devils in Worms as there are roof-tiles, I would on;"—of him who, alone in that assemblage, before all emperors, and principalities, and powers, spoke forth these final and for ever memorable words: "It is neither safe nor prudent to do aught against conscience. Here stand I, I cannot otherwise. God assist me. Amen!"* It is evident enough that to this man all Popes' conclaves, and imperial Diets, and hosts and nations were but weak; weak as the forest, with all its strong *Trees*, may be to the smallest spark of electric *Fire*.

EINE FESTE BURG IST UNSER GOTT.

Ein' feste Burg ist unser Gott,
Ein' gute Wehr und Waffen;
Er hilft uns frey aus aller Noth,
Die uns jetzt hat betroffen.
Der alte böse Fiend,
Mit Ernst ers jetzt meint;
Gross Macht und viel List
Sein grausam' Rüstzeuch ist,
Auf Erd'n ist nicht seins Gleichen.

Mit unsrer Macht ist nichts gethan,
Wir sind gar bald verloren:
Es streit't für uns der rechte Mann,
Den Gott selbst hat erkoren.
Fragst du wer er ist?
Er heisst Jesus Christ,
Der Herre Zebaoth,
Und ist kein ander Gott,
Das Feld muss er behalten.

Und wenn die Welt voll Teufel wär,
Und wollt'n uns gar verschlingen,
So fürchten wir uns nicht so sehr,
Es soll uns doch gelingen.
Der Fürste dieser welt,
Wie sauer er sich stellt,
Thut er uns doch nichts;
Das macht er ist gerichtt,
Ein Wörtlein kann ihn fällen.

* "Till such time, as either by proofs from Holy Scripture, or by fair reason and argument, I have been confuted and convicted, I cannot and will not recant, *weil weder sicher noch gerathen ist, etwas wider Gewissen zu thun. Hier stehe ich, ich kann nicht anders. Gott helfe mir. Amen!*"

Das Wort sie sollen lassen stahn
Und Keimen Dank dazu haben
Er ist bey uns wohl auf dem Plan
Mit seinen Geist und Gaben.
Nehmen sie uns den Leib,
Gut', Ehr', Kind und Weib,
Lass fahren dahin.
Sie haben's kein Gewinn,
Das Reich Gottes muss uns bleiben.

A safe stronghold our God is still,
A trusty shield and weapon;
He'll help us clear from all the ill
That hath us now o'ertaken.
The ancient Prince of Hell,
Hath risen with purpose fell;
Strong mail of Craft and Power
He weareth in this hour,
On Earth is not his fellow.

With force of arms we nothing can,
Full soon were we down-ridden;
But for us fights the proper Man,
Whom God himself hath bidden.
Ask ye, Who is this same?
Christ Jesus is his name,
The Lord Zebaoth's Son,
He and no other one
Shall conquer in the battle.

And were this world all Devils o'er
And watching to devour us,
We lay it not to heart so sore,
Not they can overpower us.
And let the Prince of Ill
Look grim as e'er he will,
He harms us not a whit,
For why? His doom is writ,
A word shall quickly slay him.

God's Word, for all their craft and force,
One moment will not linger,
But spite of Hell, shall have its course,
'T is written by his finger.
And though they take our life,
Goods, honour, children, wife,
Yet is their profit small;
These things shall vanish all,
The City of God remaineth.

SCHILLER.*

[FRASER'S MAGAZINE, 1831.]

To the student of German Literature, or of Literature in general, these volumes, purporting to lay open the private intercourse of two men eminent beyond all others of their time in that department, will doubtless be a welcome appearance. Neither Schiller nor Goethe has ever, that we have hitherto seen, written worthlessly on any subject, and the writings here offered us are confidential Letters, relating moreover to a highly important period in the spiritual history, not of the parties themselves, but of their country likewise; full of topics, high and low, on which far meaner talents than theirs might prove interesting. We have heard and known so much of both these venerated persons; of their friendship, and true co-operation in so many noble endeavours, the fruit of which has long been plain to every one: and now are we to look into the secret constitution and conditions of all this; to trace the public result, which is Ideal, down to its roots in the Common; how Poets may live and work poetically among the Prose things of this world, and *Fausts* and *Tells* be written on rag-paper, and with goose-quills, like mere Minerva Novels, and songs by a Person of Quality! Virtuosos have glass bee-hives, which they curiously peep into; but here truly were a far stranger sort of honey-making. Nay, apart from virtuosoship, or any technical object, what a hold have such things on our universal curiosity as men! If the sympathy we feel with one another is infinite, or nearly so,—in proof of which, do but consider the boundless ocean of Gossip (imperfect, undistilled Biography) which is emitted and imbibed by the human species daily;—if every secret-history, every closed-door's conversation, how trivial soever, has an interest for us, then might the conversation of a Schiller with a Goethe, so rarely do Schillers meet with Goethes among us, tempt Honesty itself into eaves-dropping.

Unhappily the conversation flits away for ever with the hour that witnessed it; and the Letter and Answer, frank, lively, genial as they may be, are only a poor emblem and epitome of it. The living dramatic movement is gone; nothing but the cold historical net-product remains for us. It is true, in every confidential Letter, the writer will, in some measure, more or less directly depict himself: but nowhere is Painting, by pen or pencil, so inadequate as in delineating spiritual Nature. The Pyramid can be measured in geometric feet, and the draughtsman represents it, with all its environment, on canvas, accurately to the eye, nay Mont-Blanc is embossed in coloured stucco; and we have his very type, and miniature fac-simile, in our museums. But for great Men, let him who would know such, pray that he may see them daily face to face: for, in the dim distance, and by the eye of the imagination, our vision, do what we may, will be too imperfect. How pale, thin, ineffectual do the great figures we would fain summon from History rise before us! Scarcely as palpable men does our utmost effort body them forth; oftenest only like Ossian's ghosts, in hazy twilight, with "stars dim twinkling through their forms." Our Socrates, our Luther, after all that we have talked and argued

* *Briefwechsel zwischen Schiller und Goethe, in den jahren* 1794 *bis* 1805. (Correspondence between Schiller and Goethe in the years 1794—1805.) 1st—3d Volumes (1794—1797.) Stuttgart and Tübingen, 1828, 1829.

of them, are to most of us quite invisible; the Sage of Athens, the Monk of Eisleben: not Persons but Titles. Yet such men, far more than any Alps or Coliseums, are the true world-wonders, which it concerns us to behold clearly, and imprint for ever on our remembrance. Great men are the Fire-pillars in this dark pilgrimage of mankind; they stand as heavenly Signs, ever-living witnesses of what has been, prophetic tokens of what may still be, the revealed, imbodied Possibilities of human nature; which greatness he who has never seen, or rationally conceived of, and with his whole heart passionately loved and reverenced, is himself for ever doomed to be little. How many weighty reasons, how many innocent allurements attract our curiosity to such men! We would know them, see them visibly, even as we know and see our like: no hint, no notice that concerns them is superfluous or too small for us. Were Gulliver's conjurer but here, to recall and sensibly bring back the brave Past, that we might look into it, and scrutinize it at will! But, alas, in Nature there is no such conjuring: the great spirits that have gone before us can survive only as disembodied Voices; their form and distinctive aspect, outward and even in many respects inward, all whereby they were known as living, breathing men, has passed into another sphere; from which only History, in scanty memorials, can evoke some faint resemblance of it. The more precious, in spite of all imperfections, is such History, are such memorials, that still in some degree preserve what had otherwise been lost without recovery.

For the rest, as to the maxim, often enough inculcated on us, that close inspection will abate our admiration, that only the obscure can be sublime, let us put small faith in it. Here, as in other provinces, it is not knowledge, but a little knowledge, that puffeth up, and for wonder at the thing known substitutes mere wonder at the knower thereof: to a sciolist, the starry heavens revolving in dead mechanism, may be less than a Jacob's vision; but to the Newton they are more; for the same God still dwells enthroned there, and holy Influences, like Angels, still ascend and descend; and this clearer vision of a little but renders the remaining mystery the deeper and more divine. So likewise is it with true spiritual greatness. On the whole, that theory of "no man being a hero to his valet," carries us but a little way into the real nature of the case. With a superficial meaning which is plain enough, it essentially holds good only of such heroes as are false, or else of such valets as are too genuine, as are shoulder-knotted and brass-lackered in soul as well as in body: of other sorts it does not hold. Milton was still a hero to the good Elwood. But we dwell not on that mean doctrine, which, true or false, may be left to itself, the more safely, as in practice it is of little or no immediate import. For were it never so true, yet, unless we preferred huge bug-bears to small realities, our practical course were still the same: to inquire, to investigate by all methods, till we saw clearly.

What worth in this biographical point of view, the "Correspondence of Schiller and Goethe" may have, we shall not attempt determining here; the rather as only a portion of the work, and to judge by the space of time included in it, only a small portion, is yet before us. Nay, perhaps its full worth will not become apparent till a future age, when the persons and concerns it treats of shall have assumed their proper relative magnitude and stand disencumbered, and for ever separated from contemporary trivialities, which, for the present, with their hollow, transient bulk, so mar our estimate. Two centuries ago, Leicester and Essex might be the wonders of England; their Kenilworth festivities and Cadiz Expeditions seemed the great occurrences of that day; but what should we now give, were these all forgotten and some "Correspondence between Shakspeare and Ben Jonson" suddenly brought to light!

One valuable quality these letters of Schiller and Goethe everywhere exhibit, that of truth: whatever we do learn from them, whether in the shape of fact or of opinion, may be relied on as genuine. There is a tone of entire sincerity in that style: a constant natural courtesy nowhere obstructs the right freedom of word or thought; indeed, no ends but honourable ones, and generally of a mutual interest, are before either party; thus neither needs to veil, still less to mask himself from the other; the two self-portraits, so far as they are filled up, may be looked upon as real likenesses. Perhaps, to most readers, some larger intermixture of what we should call domestic interest, of ordinary human concerns, and the hopes, fears, and other feelings these excite, would have improved the work; which as it is, not indeed without pleasant exceptions, turns mostly on compositions, and publications, and philosophies, and other such high matters. This, we believe, is a rare fault in modern Correspondences; where generally the opposite fault is complained of, and except mere temporalities, good and evil hap of the corresponding parties, their state of purse, heart, and nervous system, and the moods and humours these give rise to,—little stands recorded for us. It may be too that native readers will feel such a want less than foreigners do, whose curiosity in this instance is equally minute, and to whom so many details, familiar enough in the country itself, must be unknown. At all events, it is to be remembered that Schiller and Goethe are, in strict speech, Literary Men; for whom their social life is only as the dwelling-place and outward tabernacle of their spiritual life; which latter is the one thing needful; the other, except in subserviency to this, meriting no attention, or the least possible. Besides, as cultivated men, perhaps even by natural temper, they are not in the habit of yielding to violent emotions of any kind, still less of unfolding and depicting such, by letter, even to closest intimates; a turn of mind which, if it diminished the warmth of their epistolary intercourse, must have increased their private happiness, and so, by their friends, can hardly be regretted. He who wears his heart on his sleeve, will often have to lament aloud that daws peck at it: he who does not, will spare himself such lamenting. Of Rousseau's Confessions, whatever value we assign that sort of ware, there is no vestige in this Correspondence.

Meanwhile, many cheerful, honest little domestic touches are given here and there; which we can accept gladly, with no worse censure than wishing that there had been more. But this Correspondence has another and more proper aspect, under which, if rightly considered, it possesses a far higher interest than most domestic delineations could have imparted. It shows us two high, creative, truly poetic minds, unweariedly cultivating themselves, unweariedly advancing from one measure of strength and clearness to another; whereby to such as travel, we say not on the same road, for this few can do, but in the same direction, as all should do, the richest psychological and practical lesson is laid out; from which men of every intellectual degree may learn something, and he that is of the highest degree will probably learn the most. What value lies in this lesson, moreover, may be expected to increase in an increasing ratio as the Correspondence proceeds, and a larger space, with broader differences of advancement, comes into view; especially as respects Schiller, the younger and more susceptive of the two; for whom, in particular, these eleven years may be said to comprise the most important era of his culture; indeed, the whole history of his progress therein, from the time when he first found the right path, and properly became progressive.

But to enter farther on the merits and special qualities of these Letters, which, on all hands, will be regarded as a publication of real value, both intrinsic and extrinsic, is not our task now. Of the frank, kind, mutually-respectful relation that manifests itself between the two Correspondents; of their several epistolary styles, and the worth of each, and whatever else characterizes this work as a series of biographical documents, or of philosophical views, we may at some future period have occasion to speak; certain detached speculations and indications will of themselves come before us in the course of our present undertaking. Meanwhile to British readers, the chief object is not the Letters, but the writers of them. Of Goethe the public already know something: of Schiller, less is known, and our wish is to bring him into closer approximation with our readers.

Indeed, had we considered only his importance in German, or we may now say, in European Literature, Schiller might well have demanded an earlier notice in our Journal. As a man of true poetical and philosophical genius, who proved this high endowment both in his conduct, and by a long series of Writings which manifest it to all; nay, even as a man so eminently admired by his nation, while he lived, and whose fame, there and abroad, during the twenty-five years since his decease, has been constantly expanding and confirming itself, he appears with such claims as can belong only to a small number of men. If we have seemed negligent of Schiller, want of affection was nowise the cause. Our admiration for him is of old standing, and has not abated, as it ripened into calm, loving estimation. But to English expositors of Foreign Literature, at this epoch, there will be many more pressing duties than that of expounding Schiller. To a considerable extent, Schiller may be said to expound himself. His greatness is of a simple kind; his manner of displaying it is, for most part, apprehensible to every one.—Besides, of all German Writers, ranking in any such class as his, Klopstock scarcely excepted, he has the least nationality: his character indeed is German, if German mean true, earnest, nobly-humane; but his mode of thought, and mode of utterance, all but the mere vocables of it, are European. Accordingly, it is to be observed, no German Writer has had such acceptance with foreigners; has been so instantaneously admitted into favour, at least any favour which proved permanent. Among the French, for example, Schiller is almost naturalized; translated, commented upon, by men of whom Constant is one; even brought upon the stage, and by a large class of critics vehemently extolled there. Indeed, to the Romanticist class, in all countries, Schiller is naturally the pattern man and great master; as it were a sort of ambassador and mediator, were mediation possible, between the Old School and the New; pointing to his own Works, as to a glittering bridge, that will lead pleasantly from the Versailles gardening and artificial hydraulics of the one, into the true Ginnistan and wonderland of the other. With ourselves too, who are troubled with no controversies on Romanticism and Classicism,—the Bowles controversy on Pope having long since evaporated without result, and all critical guild-brethren now working diligently with one accord, in the calmer sphere of Vapidism, or even Nullism,—Schiller is no less universally esteemed by persons of any feeling for poetry. To readers of German, and these are increasing everywhere a hundred fold, he is one of the earliest studies; and the dullest cannot study him without some perception of his beauties. For the un-German, again, we have Translations in abundance and superabundance; through which, under whatever distortion, however shorn of his beams, some image of this poetical sun must force itself; and in susceptive hearts, awaken love, and a desire for more immediate insight. So that now, we suppose, anywhere in England, a man who denied that Schiller was a Poet would himself be, from every side, declared a Prosaist, and thereby summarily enough put to silence.

All which being so, the weightiest part of our duty, that of preliminary pleading for Schiller, of asserting rank and excellence for him while a stranger, and to judges suspicious of counterfeits, is taken off our hands. The knowledge of his works is silently and rapidly proceeding; in the only way by which true knowledge can be attained, by loving study of them, in many an inquiring, candid mind. Moreover, as remarked above, Schiller's works, generally speaking, require little commentary: for a man of such excellence, for a true Poet we should say that his worth lies singularly open;

nay, in great part of his writings, beyond such open universally recognisable worth, there is no other to be sought.

Yet doubtless if he is a Poet, a genuine interpreter of the Invisible, Criticism will have a deeper duty to discharge for him. Every Poet, be his outward lot what it may, finds himself born in the midst of Prose; he has to struggle from the littleness and obstruction of an Actual world, into the freedom and infinitude of an Ideal; and the history of such struggle, which is the history of his life, cannot be other than instructive. His is a high, laborious, unrequited, or only self-requited endeavour, which, however, by the law of his being, he is compelled to undertake, and must prevail in, or be permanently wretched; nay the more wretched, the nobler his gifts are. For it is the deep, inborn claim of his whole spiritual nature, and will not and must not go unanswered. His youthful unrest, that "unrest of genius," often so wayward in its character, is the dim anticipation of this; the mysterious, all-powerful mandate, as from Heaven, to prepare himself, to purify himself, for the vocation wherewith he is called. And yet how few can fulfil this mandate, how few ever earnestly give heed to it! Of the thousand jingling dilettanti, whose jingle dies with the hour which it harmlessly or hurtfully amused, we say nothing here: to these, as to the mass of men, such calls for spiritual perfection speak only in whispers, drowned without difficulty in the din and dissipation of the world. But even for the Byron, for the Burns, whose ear is quick for celestial messages, in whom "speaks the prophesying spirit," in awful prophetic voice, how hard is it to "take no counsel with flesh and blood," and instead of living and writing for the Day that passes over them, live and write for the Eternity that rests and abides over them; instead of living commodiously in the Half, the Reputable, the Plausible, "to live resolutely in the Whole, the Good, the True!"* Such Halfness, such halting between two opinions, such painful, altogether fruitless negotiating between Truth and Falsehood, has been the besetting sin, and chief misery, of mankind in all ages. Nay, in our age, it has christened itself Moderation, a prudent taking of the middle course; and passes current among us as a virtue. How virtuous it is, the withered condition of many a once ingenious nature that has lived by this method—the broken or breaking heart of many a noble nature that could not live by it—speak aloud, did we but listen.

And now, when from among so many shipwrecks and misventures one goodly vessel comes to land, we joyfully survey its rich cargo, and hasten to question the crew on the fortunes of their voyage. Among the crowd of uncultivated and miscultivated writers, the high, pure Schiller stands before us with a like distinction. We ask, how was this man successful?—From what peculiar point of view did he attempt penetrating the secret of spiritual Nature?—From what region of Prose rise into Poetry?—Under what outward accidents—with what inward faculties—by what methods —with what result?

* *Im Ganzen, Guten, Wahren resolut zu leben.*—Goethe.

For any thorough or final answer to such questions, it is evident enough, neither our own means, nor the present situation of our readers, in regard to this matter, are in any measure adequate. Nevertheless, the imperfect beginning must be made, before the perfect result can appear. Some slight far-off glance over the character of the man, as he looked and lived, in Action and in Poetry, will not, perhaps, be unacceptable from us: for such as know little of Schiller, it may be an opening of the way to better knowledge; for such as are already familiar with him, it may be, a stating in words of what they themselves have often thought; and welcome, therefore, as the confirming testimony of a second witness.

Of Schiller's personal history there are accounts in various accessible publications; so that, we suppose, no formal Narrative of his Life, which may now be considered generally known, is necessary here. Such as are curious on the subject, and still uninformed, may find some satisfaction in the *Life of Schiller*, (London, 1824;) in the *Vie de Schiller*, (prefixed to the French Translation of his Dramatic Works;) in the *Account of Schiller*, (prefixed to the English Translation of his Thirty-Years' War, Edinburgh, 1828;) and, doubtless, in many other Essays, known to us only by title. Nay, in the survey we propose to make of his character, practical as well as speculative, the main facts of his outward history will of themselves come to light.

Schiller's Life is emphatically a literary one; that of a man existing only for Contemplation; guided forward by the pursuit of ideal things, and seeking and finding his true welfare therein. A singular simplicity characterizes it,—a remoteness from whatever is called business; an aversion to the tumults of business, an indifference to its prizes, grows with him from year to year. He holds no office; scarcely for a little while a University Professorship; he covets no promotion; has no stock of money; and shows no discontent with these arrangements. Nay, when permanent sickness, continual pain of body, is added to them, he still seems happy: these last fifteen years of his life are, spiritually considered, the clearest and most productive of all. We might say, there is something priest-like in that Life of his: under quite another colour and environment, yet with aims differing in form rather than in essence, it has a priest-like stillness, a priest-like purity; nay, if for the Catholic Faith, we substitute the Ideal of Art, and for Convent Rules, Moral, Æsthetic Laws, it has even something of a monastic character. By the three monastic vows he was not bound; yet vows of as high and difficult a kind, both to do and to forbear, he had taken on him; and his happiness and whole business lay in observing them. Thus immured, not in cloisters of stone and mortar, yet in cloisters of the mind, which separate him as impassably from the vulgar, he works and meditates only on what we may call Divine things; his familiar talk, his very recreations, the whole actings and fancyings of his daily existence, tend thither.

As in the life of a Holy Man, too, so in that of Schiller, there is but one great epoch: that of taking on him these Literary Vows; of finally extricating himself from the distractions of the world, and consecrating his whole future days to Wisdom. What lies before this epoch, and what lies after it, have two altogether different characters. The former is worldly, and occupied with worldly vicissitudes; the latter is spiritual, of calm tenor, marked to himself only by his growth in inward clearness, to the world only by the peaceable fruits of this. It is to the first of these periods that we shall here chiefly direct ourselves.

In his parentage, and the circumstances of his earlier years, we may reckon him fortunate. His parents, indeed, are not rich, nor even otherwise independent: yet neither are they meanly poor; and warm affection, a true honest character, ripened in both into religion, not without an openness for knowledge, and even considerable intellectual culture, makes amends for every defect. The Boy, too, is himself of a character in which, to the observant, lies the richest promise. A modest, still nature, apt for all instruction in heart or head; flashes of liveliness, of impetuosity, from time to time breaking through. That little anecdote of the Thunder-storm is so graceful in its littleness, that one cannot but hope it may be authentic.

"Once, it is said, during a tremendous thunder-storm, his father missed him in the young group within doors; none of the sisters could tell what was become of Fritz, and the old man grew at length so anxious that he was forced to go out in quest of him. Fritz was scarcely passed the age of infancy, and knew not the dangers of a scene so awful. His father found him at last, in a solitary place of the neighbourhood, perched on the branch of a tree, gazing at the tempestuous face of the sky, and watching the flashes as in succession they spread their lurid gloom over it. To the reprimands of his parent, the whimpering truant pleaded in extenuation, 'that the Lightning was so beautiful, and he wished to see where it was coming from!'"

In his village-school he reads the Classics with diligence, without relish; at home, with far deeper feelings, the Bible; and already his young heart is caught with that mystic grandeur of the Hebrew Prophets. His devout nature, moulded by the pious habits of his parents, inclines him to be a clergyman: a clergyman, indeed, he proved; only the Church he ministered in was the Catholic, a far more Catholic than that false Romish one. But already in his ninth year, not without rapturous amazement, and a lasting remembrance, he had seen the "splendours of the Ludwigsburg Theatre;" and so, unconsciously, cast a glimpse into that world, where, by accident or natural preference, his own genius was one day to work out its noblest triumphs.

Before the end of his boyhood, however, begins a far harsher era for Schiller; wherein, under quite other nurture, other faculties were to be developed in him. He must enter on a scene of oppression, distortion, isolation; under which, for the present, the fairest years of his existence are painfully crushed down. But this too has its wholesome influences on him; for there is in genius that alchymy which converts all metals into gold; which from suffering educes strength, from error clearer wisdom, from all things good.

"The Duke of Wurtemberg had lately founded a free seminary for certain branches of professional education: it was first set up at Solitude, one of his country residences; and had now been transferred to Stuttgard, where, under an improved form, and with the name of *Karls-schule*, we believe it still exists. The Duke proposed to give the sons of his military officers a preferable claim to the benefits of this institution; and having formed a good opinion both of Schiller and his father, he invited the former to profit by this opportunity. The offer occasioned great embarrassment: the young man and his parents were alike determined in favour of the Church, a project with which this new one was inconsistent. Their embarrassment was but increased, when the Duke, on learning the nature of their scruples, desired them to think well before they decided. It was out of fear, and with reluctance that his proposal was accepted. Schiller enrolled himself in 1773; and turned, with a heavy heart, from freedom and cherished hopes, to Greek, and seclusion, and Law.

"His anticipations proved to be but too just: the six years which he spent in this Establishment were the most harassing and comfortless of his life. The Stuttgard system of education seems to have been formed on the principle, not of cherishing and correcting nature, but of rooting it out, and supplying its place by something better. The process of teaching and living was conducted with the stiff formality of military drilling; every thing went on by statute and ordinance; there was no scope for the exercise of free-will, no allowance for the varieties of original structure. A scholar might possess what instincts or capacities he pleased; the 'regulations of the school' took no account of this; he must fit himself into the common mould, which, like the old Giant's bed, stood there, appointed by superior authority, to be filled alike by the great and the little. The same strict and narrow course of reading and composition was marked out for each beforehand, and it was by stealth if he read or wrote any thing beside. Their domestic economy was regulated in the same spirit as their preceptorial: it consisted of the same sedulous exclusion of all that could border on pleasure, or give any exercise to choice. The pupils were kept apart from the conversation or sight of any person but their teachers; none ever got beyond the precincts of despotism to snatch even a fearful joy; their very amusements proceeded by the word of command.

"How grievous all this must have been it is easy to conceive. To Schiller it was more grievous than to any other. Of an ardent and impetuous, yet delicate nature, whilst his discontentment devoured him internally, he was too modest to give it the relief of utterance by deeds or words. Locked up within himself, he suffered deeply, but without complaining Some of his Letters written during this period have been preserved: they exhibit the ineffectual struggles of a fervid and busy mind, veiling its many chagrins under a certain dreamy patience, which only shows them more painfully. He pored over his lexicons, and grammars, and insipid tasks, with an artificial composure; but his spirit pined within him like a captive's, when he looked forth into the cheerful world, or recollected the affection of parents, the hopes and frolicsome enjoyments of past years."

Youth is to all the glad season of life; but often only by what it hopes, not by what it attains, or what it escapes. In these sufferings of Schiller's, many a one may say, there is nothing unexampled: could not the history of every Eton Scholar, of every poor Midshipman, with his rudely-broken domestic ties, his privations, persecutions, and cheerless solitude of heart, equal or outdo them? In respect of these, its palpable hardships, perhaps it might; and be still very miserable. But the hardship which presses heaviest on Schiller lies deeper than all these; out of which the natural fire of almost any young heart will sooner or later rise victorious. His worst oppression is an oppression of the moral sense; a fettering not of the Desires only, but of the pure reasonable Will: for besides all outward sufferings, his mind is driven from its true aim, dimly yet invincibly felt to be the true one; and turned, by sheer violence, into one which it feels to be false. Not in Law, with its profits and dignities; not in Medicine, which he willingly, yet still hopelessly exchanged for Law; not in the routine of any marketable occupation, how gainful or honoured soever, can his soul find content and a home: only in some far purer and higher region of Activity; for which he has yet no name; which he once fancied to be the Church, which at length he discovers to be Poetry. Nor is this any transient, boyish wilfulness, but a deep-seated, earnest, ineradicable longing, the dim purpose of his whole inner man. Nevertheless as a transient, boyish wilfulness his teachers must regard it, and deal with it; and not till after the fiercest contest, and a clear victory, will its true nature be recognised. Herein lay the sharpest sting of Schiller's ill fortune; his whole mind is wrenched asunder; he has no rallying point in his misery; he is suffering and toiling for a wrong object. "A singular miscalculation of Nature," he says long afterwards, "had combined my poetical tendencies with the place of my birth. Any disposition to Poetry did violence to the laws of the Institution where I was educated, and contradicted the plan of its founder. For eight years, my enthusiasm struggled with military discipline; but the passion for Poetry is vehement and fiery as a first love. What discipline was meant to extinguish, it blew into a flame. To escape from arrangements that tortured me, my heart sought refuge in the world of ideas, when as yet I was unacquainted with the world of realities, from which iron bars excluded me."

Doubtless Schiller's own prudence had already taught him that in order to live poetically, it was first requisite to live; that he should and must, as himself expresses it, "forsake the balmy climate of Pindus for the Greenland of a barren and dreary science of terms." But the dull work of this Greenland once accomplished, he might rationally hope that his task was done; that the "leisure gained by superior diligence" would be his own, for Poetry, or whatever else he pleased. Truly, it was "intolerable and degrading to be hemmed in still farther by the caprices of severe and formal pedagogues." No wonder that Schiller "brooded gloomily" over his situation. But what was to be done? "Many plans he formed for deliverance; sometimes he would escape in secret to catch a glimpse of the free and busy world, to him forbidden: sometimes he laid schemes for utterly abandoning a place which he abhorred, and trusting to fortune for the rest." But he is young, inexperienced, unprovided; without help, or counsel: there is nothing to be done, but endure.

"Under such corroding and continual vexations," says his Biographer, "an ordinary spirit would have sunk at length; would have gradually given up its loftier aspirations, and sought refuge in vicious indulgence, or at best have sullenly harnessed itself into the yoke, and plodded through existence; weary, discontented, and broken, ever casting back a hankering look on the dreams of his youth, and ever without power to realize them. But Schiller was no ordinary character, and did not act like one. Beneath a cold and simple exterior, dignified with no artificial attractions, and marred in its native amiableness by the incessant obstruction, the isolation and painful destitutions under which he lived, there was concealed a burning energy of soul, which no obstruction could extinguish. The hard circumstances of his fortune had prevented the natural development of his mind; his faculties had been cramped and misdirected; but they had gathered strength by opposition and the habit of self-dependence which it encouraged. His thoughts, unguided by a teacher, had sounded into the depths of his own nature and the mysteries of his own fate; his feelings and passions, unshared by any other heart, had been driven back upon his own; where, like the volcanic fire that smoulders and fuses in secret, they accumulated till their force grew irresistible.

"Hitherto Schiller had passed for an unprofitable, discontented, and a disobedient Boy: but the time was now come when the gyves of school-discipline could no longer cripple and distort the giant might of his nature: he stood forth as a Man, and wrenched asunder his fetters with a force that was felt at the extremities of Europe. The publication of the *Robbers* forms an era not only in Schiller's history, but in the literature of the World; and there seems no doubt that, but for so mean a cause as the perverted discipline of the Stuttgard school, we had never seen this tragedy. Schiller commenced it in his nineteenth year; and the circumstances under which it was composed are to be traced in all its parts.

"Translations of the work soon appeared in almost all the languages of Europe,* and

* Our English translation, one of the washiest, was executed (we have been told) in Edinburgh by a "Lord of Session," otherwise not unknown in Literature: who

were read in almost all of them with a deep interest, compounded of admiration and aversion, according to the relative proportions of sensibility and judgment in the various minds which contemplated the subject. In Germany, the enthusiasm which the *Robbers* excited was extreme. The young author had burst upon the world like a meteor; and surprise, for a time, suspended the power of cool and rational criticism. In the ferment produced by the universal discussion of this single topic, the poet was magnified above his natural dimensions, great as they were: and though the general sentence was loudly in his favour, yet he found detractors as well as praisers, and both equally beyond the limits of moderation.

"But the tragedy of the *Robbers* produced for its Author some consequences of a kind much more sensible than these. We have called it the signal of Schiller's deliverance from school tyranny and military constraint; but its operation in this respect was not immediate. At first it seemed to involve him more deeply than before. He had finished the original sketch of it in 1778; but for fear of offence, he kept it secret till his medical studies were completed. These, in the mean time, he had pursued with sufficient assiduity to merit the usual honours. In 1780, he had, in consequence, obtained the post of Surgeon to the regiment *Augé*, in the Wurtemberg army. This advancement enabled him to complete his project,—to print the *Robbers* at his own expense; not being able to find any bookseller that would undertake it. The nature of the work, and the universal interest it awakened, drew attention to the private circumstances of the Author, whom the *Robbers*, as well as other pieces of his writing that had found their way into the periodical publications of the time, sufficiently showed to be no common man. Many grave persons were offended at the vehement sentiments expressed in the *Robbers;* and the unquestioned ability with which these extravagances were expressed but made the matter worse. To Schiller's superiors, above all, such things were inconceivable; he might perhaps be a very great genius, but was certainly a dangerous servant for His Highness, the Grand Duke of Wurtemberg. Officious people mingled themselves in the affair: nay, the graziers of the Alps were brought to bear upon it. The Grisons' magistrates, it appeared, had seen the book, and were mortally huffed at their people's being there spoken of, according to a Swabian adage, as *common highwaymen.** They complained in the *Hamburg Correspondent;* and a sort of jackall, at Ludwigsburg, one Walter, whose name deserves to be thus kept in mind, volunteered to plead their cause before the Grand Duke.

"Informed of all these circumstances, the Grand Duke expressed disapprobation of Schiller's poetical labours in the most unequivocal terms. Schiller was at length summoned before him; and it then turned out, that his Highness was not only dissatisfied with the moral or political errors of the work, but scandalized moreover at its want of literary merit. In this latter respect, he was kind enough to proffer his own services. But Schiller seems to have received the proposal with no sufficient gratitude; and the interview passed without advantage to either party. It terminated in the Duke's commanding Schiller to abide by medical subjects: or at least, to beware of writing any more poetry, without submitting it to *his* inspection.

* * * * * *

"Various new mortifications awaited Schiller. It was in vain that he discharged the humble duties of his station with the most strict fidelity, and even, it is said, with superior skill: he was a suspected person, and his most innocent actions were misconstrued, his slightest faults were visited with the full measure of official severity. * * * His free spirit shrunk at the prospect of wasting its strength in strife against the pitiful constraints, the minute and endless persecutions of men, who knew him not, yet had his fortune in their hands: the idea of dungeons and jailers haunted and tortured his mind; and the means of escaping them, the renunciation of poetry, the source of all his joy, if likewise of many woes, the radiant guiding-star of his turbid and obscure existence, seemed a sentence of death to all that was dignified, and delightful, and worth retaining, in his character. * * * With the natural feeling of a young author, he had ventured to go in secret, and witness the first representation of his Tragedy, at Manheim. His incognito did not conceal him; he was put under arrest, during a week, for this offence: and as the punishment did not deter him from again transgressing in a similar manner, he learned that it was in contemplation to try more rigorous measures with him. Dark hints were given to him of some exemplary as well as imminent severity: and Dalberg's aid, the sole hope of averting it by quiet means, was distant and dubious. Schiller saw himself reduced to extremities. Beleaguered with present distresses, and the most horrible forebodings, on every side; roused to the highest pitch of indignation, yet forced to keep silence, and wear the face of patience, he could endure this maddening constraint no longer. He resolved to be free, at whatever risk; to abandon advantages which he could not buy at such a price; to quit his step-dame home, and go forth, though friendless and alone, to seek his fortune in the great market of life. Some foreign Duke or Prince was arriving at Stuttgard; and all the people were in movement, witnessing the spectable of his entrance: Schiller seized this opportunity of retiring from the city, careless whither he went, so he got be

went to work under deepest concealment, lest evil might befal him. The confidential Devil, now an Angel, who mysteriously carried him the proof-sheets, is our informant.

*The obnoxious passage has been carefully expunged from subsequent editions. It was in the third Scene of the second Act. Spiegelberg, discoursing with Razmann, observes, "An honest man you may form of windle-straws; but to make a rascal you must have grist: besides there is a national genius in it—a certain rascal-climate, so to speak." In the first Edition there was added, "*Go to the Grisons, for instance; that is what I call the Thief's Athens.*" The patriot who stood forth, on this occasion, for the honour of the Grisons, to deny this weighty charge, and denounce the crime of making it, was (not Dogberry or Verges, but) "one of the noble family of Salis."

yond the reach of turnkeys, and Grand Dukes, and commanding officers. It was in the month of October, 1782, his twenty-third year."—*Life of Schiller*, Part I.

Such were the circumstances under which Schiller rose to manhood. We see them permanently influence his character; but there is also a strength in himself which on the whole triumphs over them. The kindly and the unkindly alike lead him towards the goal. In childhood, the most unheeded, but by far the most important era of existence,—as it were, the still Creation-days of the whole future man,—he had breathed the only wholesome atmosphere, a soft atmosphere of affection and joy: the invisible seeds which are one day to ripen into clear Devoutness, and all humane Virtue, are happily sown in him. Not till he has gathered force for resistance, does the time of contradiction, of being "purified by suffering," arrive. For this contradiction, too, we have to thank those Stuttgard Schoolmasters and their purblind Duke. Had the system they followed been a milder, more reasonable one, we should not indeed have altogether lost our Poet, for the Poetry lay in his inmost soul, and could not remain unuttered; but we might well have found him under a far inferior character; not dependent on himself and truth, but dependent on the world and its gifts; not standing on a native, everlasting basis, but on an accidental, transient one.

In Schiller himself, as manifested in these emergencies, we already trace the chief features which distinguish him through life. A tenderness, a sensitive delicacy, aggravated under that harsh treatment, issues in a certain shyness and reserve: which, as conjoined moreover with habits of internal and not of external activity, might in time have worked itself, had his natural temper been less warm and affectionate, into timorous self-seclusion, dissociality, and even positive misanthropy. Nay, generally viewed, there is much in Schiller at this epoch that to a careless observer might have passed for weakness; as indeed, for such observers, weakness, and fineness of nature are easily confounded. One element of strength, however, and the root of all strength, he throughout evinces: he wills one thing, and knows what he wills. His mind has a purpose, and still better, a right purpose. He already loves true spiritual Beauty, with his whole heart and his whole soul; and for the attainment, for the pursuit of this, is prepared to make all sacrifices. As a dim instinct, under vague forms, this aim first appears; gains force with his force, clearness in the opposition it must conquer; and at length declares itself, with a peremptory emphasis which will admit of no contradiction.

As a mere piece of literary history, these passages of Schiller's life are not without interest; this is a "persecution for conscience-sake," such as has oftener befallen heresy in Religion, than heresy in Literature; a blind struggle to extinguish, by physical violence, the inward, celestial light of a human soul; and here in regard to Literature, as in regard to Religion, it always is an ineffectual struggle. Doubtless, as religious Inquisitors have often done, these secular Inquisitors meant honestly in persecuting; and since the matter went well in spite of them, their interference with it may be forgiven and forgotten. We have dwelt the longer on these proceedings of theirs, because they bring us to the grand crisis of Schiller's history, and for the first time show us his will decisively asserting itself, decisively pronouncing the law whereby his whole future life is to be governed. He himself says, he "went empty away; empty in purse and hope." Yet the mind that dwelt in him was still there with its gifts; and the task of his existence now lay undivided before him. He is henceforth a Literary Man; and need appear in no other character. "All my connections," he could ere long say, "are now dissolved. The public is now all to me; my study, my sovereign, my confidant. To the public alone I from this time belong; before this and no other tribunal will I place myself; this alone do I reverence and fear. Something majestic hovers before me, as I determine now to wear no other fetters, but the sentence of the world, to appeal to no other throne but the soul of man."*

In his subsequent life, with all varieties of outward fortune, we find a noble inward unity. That love of Literature, and that resolution to abide by it at all hazards, do not forsake him. He wanders through the world, looks at it under many phases; mingles in the joys of social life; is a husband, father; experiences all the common destinies of man; but the same "radiant guiding-star" which, often obscured, had led him safe through the perplexities of his youth, now shines on him with unwavering light. In all relations and conditions, Schiller is blameless, amiable; he is even little tempted to err. That high purpose after spiritual perfection, which with him was a love of Poetry, and an unwearied, active love, is itself, when pure and supreme, the necessary parent of good conduct, as of noble feeling. With all men it should be pure and supreme; for in one or the other shape it is the true end of man's life. Neither in any man is it ever wholly obliterated; with the most, however, it remains a passive sentiment, an idle wish. And even with the small residue of men in whom it attains some measure of activity, who would be Poets in act or word, how seldom is it the sincere and highest purpose, how seldom unmixed with vulgar ambition, and low, mere earthly aims, which distort or utterly pervert its manifestations! With Schiller, again, it, was the one thing needful; the first duty, for which all other duties worked together, under which all other duties quietly prospered, as under their rightful sovereign. Worldly preferment, fame itself, he did not covet: yet of fame he reaps the most plenteous harvest; and of worldly goods what little he wanted is in the end made sure to him. His mild, honest character everywhere gains him friends: that upright, peaceful, simple life is honourable in the eyes of all; and they who know him the best love him the most.

Perhaps, among all the circumstances of

* Preface to the *Thalia*.

Schiller's literary life there was none so important for him as his connection with Goethe. To use our old figure, we might say, that if Schiller was a Priest, then was Goethe the Bishop from whom he first acquired clear spiritual light, by whose hands he was ordained to the priesthood. Their friendship has been much celebrated, and deserved to be so; it is a pure relation; unhappily too rare in Literature; where if a Swift and Pope can even found an imperious Duumvirate, on little more than mutually-tolerated pride, and part the spoils, for some time, without quarrelling, it is thought a credit. Seldom do men combine so steadily and warmly for such purposes,—which when weighed in the economical balance are but gossamer. It appears also that preliminary difficulties stood in the way; prepossessions of some strength had to be conquered on both sides. For a number of years, the two, by accident or choice, never met, and their first interview scarcely promised any permanent approximation. "On the whole," says Schiller, "this personal meeting has not at all diminished the idea, great as it was, which I had previously formed of Goethe; but I doubt whether we shall ever come into close communication with each other. Much that still interests me has already had its epoch with him. His whole nature is, from its very origin, otherwise constructed than mine: his world is not my world; our modes of conceiving things appear to be essentially different. From such a combination no secure substantial intimacy can result."

Nevertheless, in spite of far graver prejudices on the part of Goethe,—to say nothing of the poor jealousies which in another man so circumstanced would openly or secretly have been at work,—a secure substantial intimacy did result—manifesting itself by continual good offices, and interrupted only by death. If we regard the relative situation of the parties, and their conduct in this matter, we must recognise in both of them no little social virtue; at all events, a deep disinterested love of worth. In the case of Goethe, more especially, who, as the elder and every way greater of the two, has little to expect in comparison with what he gives, this friendly union, had we space to explain its nature and progress, would give new proof that, as poor Jung Stilling also experienced, "the man's heart, which few know, is as true and noble as his genius, which all know." By Goethe, and this even before the date of their friendship, Schiller's outward interests had been essentially promoted: he was introduced under that sanction, into the service of Weimar, to an academic office, to a pension: his whole way was made smooth for him. In spiritual matters, this help, or rather let us say co-operation, for it came not in the shape of help, but of reciprocal service, was of still more lasting consequence. By the side of his friend, Schiller rises into the highest regions of Art he ever reached; and in all worthy things is sure of sympathy, of one wise judgment amid a crowd of unwise ones, of one helpful hand amid many hostile. Thus outwardly and inwardly assisted and confirmed, he henceforth goes on his way with new steadfastness, turning neither to the right hand, nor to the left; and while days are given him, devotes them wholly to his best duty. It is rare that one man can do so much for another, can permanently benefit another; so mournfully, in giving and receiving, as in most charitable affections and finer movements of our nature, are we all held in by that paltry vanity, which, under reputable names, usurps, on both sides, a sovereignty it has no claim to. Nay, many times, when our friend would honestly help us, and strives to do it, yet will he never bring himself to understand what we really need, and so to forward us on our own path; but insists more simply on us taking his path, and leaves us as incorrigible because we will not and cannot. Thus "men are solitary among each other;" no one will help his neighbour; each has even to assume a defensive attitude lest his neighbour hinder him!

Of Schiller's zealous, entire devotedness to Literature we have already spoken as of his crowning virtue, and the great source of his welfare. With what ardour he pursued this object his whole life, from the earliest stage of it, had given proof: but the clearest proof, clearer even than that youthful self-exile, was reserved for his later years, when a lingering, incurable disease had laid on him its new and ever-galling burden. At no period of Schiller's history does the native nobleness of his character appear so decidedly, as now in this season of silent, unwitnessed heroism, when the dark enemy dwelt within himself, unconquerable, yet ever, in all other struggles, to be kept at bay. We have medical evidence that during the last fifteen years of his life, not a moment could have been free of pain. Yet he utters no complaint. In this "Correspondence with Goethe" we see him cheerful, laborious; scarcely speaking of his maladies, and then only historically, in the style of a third party, as it were, calculating what force and length of days might still remain at his disposal. Nay, his highest poetical performances, we may say all that are truly poetical, belong to this era. If we recollect how many poor valetudinarians, Rousseaus, Cowpers, and the like, men otherwise of fine endowment, dwindle under the influence of nervous disease, into pining wretchedness, some into madness itself; and then that Schiller, under the like influence, wrote some of his deepest speculations, and all his genuine dramas, from *Wallenstein* to *Wilhelm Tell*, we shall the better estimate his merit.

It has been said that only in Religion, or something equivalent to Religion, can human nature support itself under such trials. But Schiller too had his Religion! was a Worshipper, nay, as we have often said, a Priest; and so in his earthly sufferings wanted not a heavenly stay. Without some such stay his life might well have been intolerable; stript of the Ideal, what remained for him in the Real was but a poor matter. Do we talk of his "happiness?" Alas, what is the loftiest flight of genius, the finest frenzy that ever for moments united Heaven with Earth, to the perennial never-failing joys of a digestive-apparatus thoroughly eupeptic? Has not the turtle-eating man an eternal sunshine of the breast? Does not his

Soul,—which, as in some Sclavonic dialects, means his Stomach,—sit for ever at his ease, enwrapped in warm condiments, amid spicy odours; enjoying the past, the present and the future; and only awakening from its soft trance to the sober certainty of a still higher bliss each meal-time—three or even four visions of Heaven in the space of one solar day! While for the sick man of genius, "whose world is of the mind, ideal, internal; when the mildew of lingering disease has struck that world, and begun to blacken and consume its beauty, what remains but despondency, and bitterness, and desolate sorrow felt and anticipated to the end?"

"Wo to him," continues this Jeremiah, "if his will likewise falter, if his resolution fail, and his spirit bend its neck to the yoke of this new enemy! Idleness and a disturbed imagination will gain the mastery of him, and let loose their thousand fiends to harass him, to torment him into madness. Alas! the bondage of Algiers is freedom compared with this of the sick man of genius, whose heart has fainted, and sunk beneath its load. His clay dwelling is changed into a gloomy prison; every nerve has become an avenue of disgust or anguish, and the soul sits within in her melancholy loneliness, a prey to the spectres of despair, or stupified with excess of suffering; doomed, as it were, to a life-in-death, to a consciousness of agonized existence, without the consciousness of power which should accompany it. Happily death, or entire fatuity, at length puts an end to such scenes of ignoble misery, which, however, ignoble as they are, we ought to view with pity rather than contempt."—*Life of Schiller*, p. 167.

Yet on the whole, we say, it is a shame for the man of genius to complain. Has he not a "light from Heaven" within him, to which the splendour of all earthly thrones and principalities is but darkness? And the head that wears such a crown grudges to lie uneasy? If that same "light from Heaven," shining through the falsest media, supported Syrian Simon through all weather on his sixty-feet pillar, or the still more wonderful Eremite, who walled himself, for life, up to the chin, in stone and mortar; how much more should it do, when shining direct and pure from all intermixture? Let the modern Priest of wisdom either suffer his small persecutions and inflictions, though sickness be of the number, in patience, or admit that ancient fanatics and bedlamites were truer worshippers than he.

A foolish controversy on this subject of happiness now and then occupies some intellectual dinner-party; speculative gentlemen we have seen, more than once, almost forget their wine in arguing whether Happiness was the chief end of man. The most cry out, with Pope: "Happiness, our being's end and aim;" and ask whether it is even conceivable that we should follow any other. How comes it, then, cry the Opposition, that the gross are happier than the refined; that even though we know them to be happier, we would not change places with them? Is it not written, "increase of knowledge is increase of sorrow?" And yet also written, in characters still more ineffaceable, "Pursue knowledge, attain clear vision, as the beginning of all good?" Were your doctrine right, for what should we struggle with our whole might, for what pray to Heaven, if not that the "malady of thought" might be utterly stifled within us, and a power of digestion and secretion, to which that of the tiger were trifling, be imparted instead thereof? Whereupon the others deny that thought is a malady; that increase of knowledge is increase of sorrow; that Aldermen have a sunnier life than Aristotle's, though the Stagyrite himself died exclaiming, *Fœdè mundum intravi, anxius vixi, perturbatus morior, &c.*; and thus the argument circulates, and the bottles stand still.

So far as that Happiness question concerns the symposia of speculative gentlemen,—the rather as it really is a good enduring hacklog whereon to chop logic, for those so minded,—we with great willingness leave it resting on its own bottom. But there are earnest natures for whom Truth is no plaything, but the staff of life; men whom the "solid reality of things" will not carry forward; who when the "inward voice" is silent in them, are powerless, nor will the loud huzzaing of millions supply the want of it. To these men, seeking anxiously for guidance; feeling that did they once clearly see the right, they would follow it cheerfully to weal or to wo, comparatively careless which; to these men the question, what is the proper aim of man, has a deep and awful interest.

For the sake of such, it may be remarked that the origin of this argument, like that of every other argument under the sun, lies in the confusion of language. If Happiness mean Welfare, there is no doubt but all men should and must pursue their Welfare, that is to say, pursue what is worthy of their pursuit. But if, on the other hand, Happiness mean, as for most men it does, "agreeable sensations," Enjoyment refined or not, then must we observe that there *is* a doubt; or rather that there is a certainty the other way. Strictly considered, this truth, that man has in him something higher than a Love of Pleasure, take Pleasure in what sense you will, has been the text of all true Teachers and Preachers, since the beginning of the world; and in one or another dialect, we may hope, will continue to be preached and taught till the world end. Neither is our own day without its asserters thereof: what, for example, does the astonished reader make of this little sentence from Schiller's *Æsthetic Letters?* It is on that old question the "improvement of the species;" which, however, is handled here in a very new manner.

"The first acquisitions, then, which men gathered in the Kingdom of Spirit were *Anxiety* and *Fear;* both, it is true, products of Reason, not of Sense; but of a Reason that mistook its object, and mistook its mode of application. Fruits of this same tree are all your Happiness-Systems, (*Glückseligkeitssysteme,*) whether they have for object the passing Day, or the whole of life, or what renders them no whit more venerable, the whole of Eternity. A boundless duration of Being and Well-being (*Daseyns und Wohlseyns*) simply for Being and Well-being's sake, is an Ideal belonging to Appetite alone, and which only the struggle of mere Animalism, (*Thierheit,*) longing to be infinite, gives rise to. Thus without gaining any thing for his Manhood, he, by this first effort of Reason, loses the happy limitation of the Animal; and has now only the unenviable superiority of missing the Present in an effort directed to the Distance, and whereby still, in the whole boundless Distance, nothing but the Present is sought for."—*Briefe über die Aesthetische Erziehung des Menschen*, B. 24.

The *Æsthetic Letters*, in which this and many far deeper matters come into view, will one day deserve a long chapter to themselves. Meanwhile we cannot but remark, as a curious symptom of this time, that the pursuit of merely sensuous good, of personal Pleasure in one shape or other, should be the universally admitted formula of man's whole duty. Once, Epicurus had his Zeno; and if the herd of mankind have at all times been the slaves of Desire, Drudging anxiously for their mess of pottage, or filling themselves with swine's husks,—earnest natures were not wanting, who, at least in theory, asserted for their kind a higher vocation than this; declaring, as they could, that man's soul was no dead Balance for "motives" to sway hither and thither, but a living, divine Soul, indefeasibly Free, whose birthright it was to be the servant of Virtue, Goodness, God, and in such service to be blessed without fee or reward. Now-a-days, however, matters are, on all hands, managed far more prudently. The choice of Hercules could not occasion much difficulty in these times to any young man of talent. On the one hand—by a path which is steep, indeed, yet smoothed by much travelling, and kept in constant repair by many a moral Macadam—smokes (in patent calefactors) a Dinner of innumerable courses; on the other, by a downward path, through avenues of very mixed character, frowns in the distance a grim Gallows, probably "improved drop." Thus is Utility the only God of these days; and our honest Benthamites are but a small Provincial Synod of that boundless Communion. Without gift of prophecy we may predict, that the straggling bush-fire which is kept up here and there against that body of well-intentioned men, must one day become a universal battle; and the grand question, Mind *versus* Matter, be again under new forms judged of and decided. —But we wander too far from our task; to which, therefore, nothing doubtful of a prosperous issue in due time to that Utilitarian struggle, we hasten to return.

In forming for ourselves some picture of Schiller as a man, of what may be called his moral character, perhaps the very perfection of his manner of existence tends to diminish our estimate of its merits. What he aimed at he has attained in a singular degree. His life, at least from the period of manhood, is still unruffled,—of clear even course. The completeness of the victory hides from us the magnitude of the struggle. On the whole, however, we may admit, that his character was not so much a great character as a holy one. We have often named him a Priest; and this title, with the quiet loftiness,—the pure, secluded, only internal, yet still heavenly worth that should belong to it, perhaps best describes him. One high enthusiasm takes possession of his whole nature. Herein lies his strength, as well as the task he has to do; for this he lived, and we may say also he died for it. In his life we see not that the social affections played any deep part. As a son, husband, father, friend, he is ever kindly, honest, amiable; but rarely, if at all, do outward things stimulate him into what can be called passion. Of the wild loves and lamentations, and all the fierce ardour that distinguish, for instance, his Scottish contemporary, Burns, there is scarcely any trace here. In fact, it was towards the Ideal, not towards the Actual, that Schiller's faith and hope was directed. His highest happiness lay not in outward honour, pleasure, social recreation, perhaps not even in friendly affection, such as the world could show it; but in the realm of Poetry, a city of the mind, where, for him, all that was true and noble had foundation. His habits, accordingly, though far from dissocial, were solitary; his chief business and chief pleasure lay in silent meditation.

"His intolerance of interruptions," we are told at an early period of his life, "first put him on the plan of studying by night; an alluring, but pernicious practice, which began at Dresden, and was never afterwards given up. His recreations breathed a similar spirit: he loved to be much alone, and strongly moved. The banks of the Elbe were the favourite resort of his mornings: here, wandering in solitude, amid groves and lawns, and green and beautiful places, he abandoned his mind to delicious musings; or meditated on the cares and studies which had lately been employing, and were again soon to employ him. At times he might be seen floating on the river, in a gondola, feasting himself with the loveliness of earth and sky. He delighted most to be there when tempests were abroad; his unquiet spirit found a solace in the expression of its own unrest on the face of Nature; danger lent a charm to his situation; he felt in harmony with the scene, when the rack was sweeping stormfully across the heavens, and the forests were sounding in the breeze, and the river was rolling its chafed waters into wild eddying heaps."

"During summer," it is mentioned at a subsequent date, "his place of study was in a garden which he at length purchased, in the suburbs of Jena, not far from the Weselhoft's house, where, at that time, was the office of the *Allgemeine Litteraturzeitung*. Reckoning from the market-place of Jena, it lies on the southwest border of the town, between the Engelgatter and the Neuthor, in a hollow defile, through which a part of the Leutrabach flows round the city. On the top of the acclivity, from which there is a beautiful prospect into the valley of the Saal, and the fir-mountains of the neighbouring forest, Schiller built himself a small house with a single chamber. It was his favourite abode during hours of composition; a great part of the works he then wrote were written here. In winter he likewise dwelt apart from the tumult of men,—in Griesbach's house, on the outside of the city trench. On sitting down to his desk at night, he was wont to keep some strong coffee, or wine-chocolate, but more frequently a flask of old Rhenish, or Champagne, standing by him, that he might from time to time repair the exhaustion of nature. Often the neighbours used to hear him earnestly declaiming in the silence of the night; and whoever had an opportunity of watching him on such occasions—a thing very easy to be done, from the heights lying opposite his little garden-house, on the other side of the dale—might see him now speaking aloud, and walking swiftly to and fro in his chamber, then suddenly throwing himself down into his chair, and writing; and drinking the while, sometimes more than once, from the glass standing near him. In winter he was to be found at his desk till four, or even five o'clock, in the morning; in summer till towards three. He then went to bed, from which he seldom rose till nine or ten."

And again:

"At Weimar his present way of life was like his former one at Jena: his business was to study and compose; his recreations were in the circle of his family, where he could abandon himself to affections grave or trifling, and in frank cheerful intercourse with a few friends. Of the latter he had lately formed a social club, the meetings of which afforded him a regular and innocent amusement. He still loved solitary walks: in the Park at Weimar he might frequently be seen, wandering among the groves and remote avenues, with a note-book in his hand; now loitering slowly along, now standing still, now moving rapidly on; if any one appeared in sight, he would dart into another alley, that his dream might not be broken. One of his favourite resorts, we are told, was the thickly overshadowed, rocky path, which leads to the *Römische Haus*, a pleasure-house of the Duke's, built under the direction of Goethe. There he would often sit in the gloom of the crags overgrown with cypresses and boxwood; shady thickets before him; not far from the murmur of a little brook, which there gushes in a smooth slaty channel, and where some verses of Goethe are cut upon a brown plate of stone, and fixed in the rock."—*Life of Schiller.*

Such retirement, alike from the tumults and the pleasures of busy men, though it seems to diminish the merit of virtuous conduct in Schiller, is itself, as hinted above, the best proof of his virtue. No man is born without ambitious worldly desires; and for no man, especially for no man like Schiller, can the victory over them be too complete. His duty lay in that mode of life; and he had both discovered his duty, and addressed himself with his whole might to perform it. Nor was it in estrangement from men's interests that this seclusion originated: but rather in deeper concern for those. From many indications, we can perceive that to Schiller the task of the Poet appeared of far weightier import to mankind, in these times, than that of any other man whatever. It seemed to him that he was "casting his bread upon the waters, and would find it after many days;" that when the noise of all conquerors, and demagogues, and political reformers had quite died away, some tone of heavenly wisdom that had dwelt even in him might still linger among men, and be acknowledged as heavenly and priceless, whether as his or not; whereby, though dead, he would yet speak, and his spirit would live throughout all generations, when the syllables that once formed his name had passed into forgetfulness for ever. We are told, "he was in the highest degree philanthropic and humane: and often said that he had no deeper wish than to know all men happy." What was still more, he strove, in his public and private capacity, to do his utmost for that end. Honest, merciful, disinterested, he is at all times found: and for the great duty laid on him no man was ever more unweariedly ardent. It was "his evening song and his morning prayer." He lived for it; and he died for it; "sacrificing," in the words of Goethe, "his Life itself to this delineating of Life."

In collision with his fellow-men, for with him as with others this also was a part of his relation to society, we find him no less noble than in friendly union with them. He mingles in none of the controversies of the time; or only like a god in the battles of men. In his conduct towards inferiors, even ill-intentioned and mean inferiors, there is everywhere a true, dignified, patrician spirit. Ever witnessing, and inwardly lamenting, the baseness of vulgar Literature in his day, he makes no clamorous attacks on it; alludes to it only from afar: as in Milton's writings, so in his, few of his contemporaries are named, or hinted at; it was not with men, but with things that he had a warfare. The *Review of Bürger*, so often descanted on, was doubtless highly afflicting to that down-broken, unhappy poet; but no hostility to Bürger, only love and veneration for the Art he professed, is to be discerned in it. With Bürger, or with any other mortal, he had no quarrel: the favour of the public, which he himself enjoyed in the highest measure, he esteemed at no high value. "The Artist," said he in a noble passage, already known to English readers, "the Artist, it is true, is the son of his time; but pity for him if he is its pupil, or even its favourite! Let some beneficent divinity snatch him, when a suckling, from the breast of his mother, and nurse him with the milk of a better time; that he may ripen to his full stature beneath a distant Grecian sky. And having grown to manhood, let him return, a foreign shape, into his century; not, however, to delight it by his presence, but, dreadful like the son of Agamemnon, to purify it!" On the whole, Schiller has no trace of vanity; scarcely of pride, even in its best sense, for the modest self-consciousness, which characterizes genius, is with him rather implied than openly expressed. He has no hatred; no anger, save against Falsehood and Baseness, where it may be called a holy anger. Presumptuous triviality stood bared in his keen glance; but his look is the noble scowl that curls the lip of an Apollo, when, pierced with sun-arrows, the serpent expires before him. In a word, we can say of Schiller, what can be said only of few in any country or time: He was a high ministering servant at Truth's altar; and bore him worthily of the office he held. Let this, and that it was even in our age, be for ever remembered to his praise.

Schiller's intellectual character has, as indeed is always the case, an accurate conformity with his moral one. Here too he is simple in his excellence; lofty rather than expansive or varied; pure, divinely ardent rather than great. A noble sensibility, the truest sympathy with Nature, in all forms, animates him; yet scarcely any creative gift altogether commensurate with this. If to his mind's eye all forms of Nature have a meaning and beauty, it is only under a few forms, chiefly of the severe or pathetic kind, that he can body forth this meaning, can represent as a Poet what as a Thinker he discerns and loves. We might say, his music is true spheral music; yet only with few tones, in simple modulation; no full choral harmony is to be heard in it. That Schiller, at least in his later years, attained a genuine poetic style, and dwelt, more or less, in the perennial regions of his Art, no one will deny: yet still his poetry shows rather like a partial than a universal gift; the laboured product of certain faculties rather than the spontaneous product of his whole nature. At the summit of the pyre, there is indeed white flame; but the materials are not all in flame, perhaps not all ignited. Nay, often it seems to us, as if poetry were, on the whole, not his essential gift; as if his genius were reflective in a still higher degree than creative; philosophical and oratorical rather than poetic. To the last, there is a stiffness in him, a certain infusibility. His genius is not an Æolian-harp for the common wind to play with, and make wild, free melody; but a scientific harmonica, that being artfully touched will yield rich notes, though in limited measure. It may be, indeed, or rather it is highly probable, that of the gifts which lay in him only a small portion was unfolded: for we are to recollect that nothing came to him without a strenuous effort; and that he was called away at middle age. At all events, here as we find him we should say, that of all his endowments the most perfect is understanding. Accurate, thorough insight, is a quality we miss in none of his productions, whatever else may be wanting. He has an intellectual vision, clear, wide, piercing, methodical,—a truly philosophic eye. Yet in regard to this also it is to be remarked, that the same simplicity, the same want of universality again displays itself. He looks aloft rather than around. It is in high, far-seeing philosophic views that he delights; in speculations on Art,—on the dignity and destiny of Man, rather than on the common doings and interests of Men. Nevertheless these latter, mean as they seem, are boundless in significance; for every the poorest aspect of Nature, especially of living Nature, is a type and manifestation of the invisible spirit that works in Nature. There is properly no object trivial or insignificant: but every finite thing, could we look well, is as a window, through which solemn vistas are opened into Infinitude itself. But neither as a Poet nor as a Thinker, neither in delineation nor in exposition and discussion, does Schiller more than glance at such objects. For the most part, the Common is to him still the Common, or is idealized, rather as it were by mechanical art than by inspiration: not by deeper poetic or philosophic inspection, disclosing new beauty in its everyday features, but rather by deducting these, by casting them aside, and dwelling on what brighter features may remain in it. Herein Schiller, as, indeed, himself was modestly aware, differs essentially from most great poets; and from none more than from his great contemporary, Goethe. Such intellectual pre-eminence as this, valuable though it be, is the easiest and the least valuable; a pre-eminence that, indeed, captivates the general eye, but may, after all, have little intrinsic grandeur. Less in rising into lofty abstractions lies the difficulty, than in seeing well and lovingly the complexities of what is at hand. He is wise who can instruct us and assist us in the business of daily virtuous living; he who trains us to see old truth under Academic formularies may be wise or not as it chances; but we love to see Wisdom in unpretending forms, to recognise her royal features under week-day vesture.—There may be more true spiritual force in a Proverb than in a philosophical System. A King in the midst of his body-guards, with all his trumpets, war-horses, and gilt standard-bearers, will look great though he be little; but only some Roman Carus can give audience to satrap-ambassadors, while seated on the ground, with a woollen cap, and supping on boiled pease, like a common soldier.

In all Schiller's earlier writings, nay, more or less, in the whole of his writings, this aristocratic fastidiousness, this comparatively barren elevation, appears as a leading characteristic. In speculation he is either altogether abstract and systematic, or he dwells on old, conventionally-noble themes; never looking abroad, over the many-coloured stream of life, to elucidate and ennoble it; or only looking on it, so to speak, from a college window. The philosophy even of his Histories, for example, founds itself mainly on the perfectibility of man, the effect of constitutions, of religions, and other such high, purely scientific objects. In his Poetry we have a similar manifestation. The interest turns on prescribed, old-established matters, common love-mania, passionate greatness, enthusiasm for liberty, and the like. This, even in *Don Carlos*, a work of what may be called his transition-period, the turning-point between his earlier and his later period, where still we find Posa, the favourite hero, "towering aloft, far-shining, clear and cold, as a sea-beacon." In after years, Schiller himself saw well that the greatest lay not here. With unwearied effort he strove to lower and to widen his sphere, and not without success, as many of his Poems testify; for example, the *Lied der Glocke*, (Song of the Bell,) every way a noble composition; and, in a still higher degree, the tragedy of *Wilhelm Tell*, the last, and, so far as spirit and style are concerned, the best of all his dramas.

Closely connected with this imperfection, both as cause and as consequence, is Schiller's singular want of Humour. Humour is properly the exponent of low things; that which first renders them poetical to the mind. The man of Humour sees common life, even mean life, under the new light of sportfulness and love; whatever has existence has a charm for him. Humour has justly been regarded as the finest perfection of poetic genius. He who wants it, be his other gifts what they may, has only half a mind; an eye for what is above him, not for what is about him or below him. Now, among all writers of any real poetic genius, we cannot recollect one who, in this respect, exhibits such total deficiency as Schiller. In his whole writings there is scarcely any vestige of it, scarcely any attempt that way. His nature was without Humour; and he had too true a feeling to adopt any counterfeit in its stead. Thus no drollery or caricature, still less any barren mockery, which, in the hundred cases, are all that we find passing current as Humour, discover themselves in Schiller. His works are full of laboured earnestness; he is the gravest of all writers. Some of his critical discussions, especially in the *Aesthetische Briefe*, where he designates the ultimate height of man's culture by the title *Spieltrieb*, (literally, Sport-impulse,) prove that he knew what Humour was, and how essential; as indeed, to his intellect, all forms of excellence, even the most alien to his own, were painted with a wonderful fidelity. Nevertheless, he himself attains not that height which he saw so clearly; to the last the *Spieltrieb* could be little more than a theory with him. With the single exception of *Wallenstein's Lager*, where, too, the Humour, if it be such, is not deep, his other attempts at mirth, fortunately very few, are of the heaviest. A rigid intensity, a serious enthusiastic ardour, majesty rather than grace, still more than lightness or sportfulness, characterizes him. Wit he had, such wit as keen intellectual insight can give; yet even of this no large endowment. Perhaps he was too honest, too sincere, for the exercise of wit; too intent on the deeper relations of things to note their more transient collisions. Besides, he dealt in Affirmation, and not in Negation; in which last, it has been said, the material of wit chiefly lies.

These observations are to point out for us the special department and limits of Schiller's excellence; nowise to call in question its reality. Of his noble sense for Truth, both in speculation and in action; of his deep, genial insight into nature; and the living harmony in which he renders back what is highest and grandest in Nature, no reader of his works need be reminded. In whatever belongs to the pathetic, the heroic, the tragically elevating, Schiller is at home; a master; nay, perhaps the greatest of all late poets. To the assiduous student, moreover, much else that lay in Schiller, but was never worked into shape, will become partially visible: deep inexhaustible mines of thought and feeling; a whole world of gifts, the finest produce of which was but beginning to be realized. To his high-minded, unwearied efforts what was impossible, had length of years been granted him! There is a tone in some of his later pieces, which here and there breathes of the very highest region of Art. Nor are the natural or accidental defects we have noticed in his genius, even as it stands, such as to exclude him from the rank of great Poets. Poets whom the whole world reckons great, have, more than once, exhibited the like. Milton, for example, shares most of them with him: like Schiller he dwells, with full power, only in the high and earnest; in all other provinces exhibiting a certain inaptitude, an elephantine unpliancy: he too has little Humour; his coarse invective has in it contemptuous emphasis enough, yet scarcely any graceful sport. Indeed, on the positive side, also, these two worthies are not without a resemblance. Under far other circumstances, with less massiveness, and vehement strength of soul, there is in Schiller the same intensity; the same concentration, and towards similar objects, towards whatever is Sublime in Nature and in Art, which sublimities they both, each in his several way, worship with undivided heart. There is not in Schiller's nature the same rich complexity of rhythm, as in Milton's, with its depth of linked sweetness; yet in Schiller too there is something of the same pure, swelling force, some tone which, like Milton's, is deep, majestic, solemn.

It was as a Dramatic Author that Schiller distinguished himself to the world: yet often we feel as if chance rather than a natural tendency had led him into this province; as if his talent were essentially, in a certain style, lyrical, perhaps even epic, rather than dramatic. He dwelt within himself, and could not without effort, and then only within a certain range, body forth other forms of being. Nay, much of what is called his poetry seems to us, as hinted above, oratorical rather than poetical; his first bias might have led him to be a speaker, rather than a singer. Nevertheless, a pure fire dwelt deep in his soul; and only in Poetry, of one or the other sort, could this find utterance. The rest of his nature, at the same time, has a certain prosaic rigour; so that not without strenuous and complex endeavours, long persisted in, could its poetic quality evolve itself. Quite pure, and as the all-sovereign element, it perhaps never did evolve itself; and among such complex endeavours, a small accident might influence large portions in its course.

Of Schiller's honest, undivided zeal in this great problem of self-cultivation, we have often spoken. What progress he had made, and in spite of what difficulties, appears, if we contrast his earlier compositions with those of his later years. A few specimens of both sorts we shall here present. By this means, too, such of our readers as are unacquainted with Schiller, may gain some clearer notion of his poetic individuality than any description of ours could give. We shall take the *Robbers*, as his first performance, what he himself calls "a monster produced by the unnatural union of Genius with Thraldom;" the fierce fuliginous fire that burns in that singular piece will still be discernible in separated passages. The following Scene, even in the yeasty vehicle of our common English version, has not wanted its admirers; it is the Second of the Third Act.

Country on the Danube.

THE ROBBERS.

(*Camped on a Height, under Trees: the Horses are grazing on the Hill further down.*)

MOOR. I can no farther (*throws himself on the ground.*) My limbs ache as if ground to pieces. My tongue parched as a potsherd. (*Schweitzer glides away unperceived.*) I would ask you to fetch me a handful of water from the stream; but ye all are wearied to death.

SCHWARZ. And the wine too is all down there, in our jacks.

MOOR. See, how lovely the Harvest looks!—The Trees almost breaking under their load. The vine full of hope.

GRIMM. It is a plentiful year.

MOOR. Think'st thou?—And so *one* toil in the world will be repaid. *One?*—Yet over night there may come a hailstorm, and shatter it all to ruin.

SCHWARZ. Possible enough, it might all be ruined two hours before reaping.

MOOR. Ay, so say I. It will all be ruined. Why should man prosper in what he has from the Ant; when he fails in what makes him like the Gods?—or is this the true aim of his Destiny?

SCHWARZ. I know it not.

MOOR. Thou hast said well; and done still better, if thou never tri'dst to know it!—Brother,—I have looked at men, at their insect-anxieties, and giant projects—their godlike schemes and mouselike occupations—their wondrous race-running after Happiness;—he trusting to the gallop of his horse,—he to the nose of his ass,—a third to his own legs; this whirling lottery of life, in which so many a creature stakes his innocence, and—his Heaven! all trying for a prize, and—blanks are the whole drawing,—there was not a prize in the batch. It is a drama, Brother, to bring tears into thy eyes, if it tickle thy midriff to laughter.

SCHWARZ. How gloriously the sun is setting yonder!

MOOR (*lost in the view.*) So dies a Hero!—To be worshipped!

GRIMM. It seems to move thee.

MOOR. When I was a lad—it was my darling thought to live so, to die so—(*with suppressed pain.*) It was a lad's thought!

GRIMM. I hope so, truly.

MOOR (*draws his hat down on his face.*) There was a time—Leave me alone, comrades.

SCHWARZ. Moor! Moor! What, Devil?—How his colour goes!

GRIMM. Ha! What ails him! Is he ill?

MOOR. There was a time when I could not sleep, if my evening prayer had been forgotten—

GRIMM. Art thou going crazed? Will Moor let such milksop fancies tutor him?

MOOR (*lays his head on Grimm's breast.*) Brother! Brother!

GRIMM. Come! don't be a child,—I beg—

MOOR. Were I a child!—Oh, were I one!

GRIMM. Pooh! Pooh!

SCHWARZ. Cheer up. Look at the brave landscape,—the fine evening.

MOOR. Yes, Friends, this world is all so lovely.

SCHWARZ. There now—that's right.

MOOR. This Earth is so glorious.

GRIMM. Right,—Right—that is it.

MOOR (*sinking back.*) And I so hideous in this lovely world, and I a monster in this glorious Earth.

GRIMM. Out on it!

MOOR. My innocence! My innocence!—See, all things are gone forth to bask in the peaceful beam of the Spring,—why must I alone inhale the torments of Hell out of the joys of Heaven?—That all should be so happy, all so married together by the spirit of peace!—The whole world *one* family, its Father above—that Father not *mine!*—I alone the castaway,—I alone struck out from the company of the just;—for me no child to lisp my name,—never for me the languishing look of one whom I love; never, never, the embracing of a bosom friend (*dashing wildly back.*) Encircled with murderers,—serpents hissing round me,—rushing down to the gulph of perdition on the eddying torrent of wickedness,—amid the flowers of the glad world, a howling Abaddon!

SCHWARZ (*to the rest.*) How *is* this? I never saw him so.

MOOR (*with piercing sorrow.*) Oh, that I might return into my mother's womb,—that I might be born a beggar!—No! I durst not pray, O Heaven, to be as one of these day-labourers—Oh! I would toil till the blood ran down my temples to buy myself the pleasure of one noontide sleep,—the blessedness of a single tear.

GRIMM (*to the rest.*) Patience, a moment. The fit is passing.

MOOR. There *was* a time too when I could weep—O ye days of peace, thou castle of my father, ye green lovely valleys! O all ye Elysian scenes of my childhood! will ye never come again, never with your balmy sighing cool my burning bosom? Mourn with me, Nature! They will never come again, never cool my burning bosom with their balmy sighing. They are gone! gone! and will not return!

Or take that still wilder monologue of Moor's on the old subject of suicide; in the midnight Forest, among the sleeping Robbers:

(*He lays aside the lute, and walks up and down in deep thought.*)

Who shall warrant me?——'Tis all so dark,—perplexed labyrinths,—no outlet, no loadstar—were it but *over* with this last draught of breath—*Over*, like a sorry farce. But whence this fierce *Hunger* after *Happiness?* whence this ideal of a *never-reached* perfection? this *continuation* of uncompleted plans?—if the pitiful pressure of this pitiful thing (*holding out a pistol*) makes the wise man equal with the fool, the coward with the brave, the nobleminded with the caitiff?—There is so divine a harmony in all irrational Nature, why should there be this dissonance in rational? No! no! there is somewhat beyond, for I have yet never known happiness.

Think ye, I will tremble? spirits of my murdered ones! I will not tremble. (*Trembling violently.*)—Your feeble dying moan,—your black-choked faces,—your frightfully gaping wounds are but links of an unbreakable chain of Destiny; and depend at last on my childish sports, on the whims of my nurses and pedagogues, on the temperament of my father, on the blood of my mother—(*shaken with horror.*) Why has my Perillus made of me a Brazen Bull to roast mankind in my glowing belly?

(*Gazing on the Pistol.*) Time and Eternity—linked together by a single moment!—Dread key, that shuttest behind me the prison of life, and before me openest the dwelling of eternal Night—say—O say—*whither,—whither* wilt thou lead me? Foreign, never circumnavigated Land!—See, manhood waxes faint under *this* image; the effort of the finite gives up, and Fancy, the capricious ape of Sense, juggles our credulity with strange shadows.—No! No! It becomes not a man to waver. Be what thou wilt, *nameless Yonder*—so this me keep but true. Be what thou wilt, so I take *myself* along with me—!—Outward things are but the colouring of the man—I am my Heaven and my Hell.

What if thou shouldst send me *companionless* to some burnt and blasted circle of the Universe; which thou hast banished from thy sight; where the lone darkness and the motionless desert were my prospects—for ever?—I would people the silent wilderness with my fantasies; I should have Eternity for leisure to unravel the perplexed image of the boundless wo.—Or wilt Thou lead me through still other births! still other scenes of pain, from stage to stage—Onwards to Annihilation? The life-threads that are to be woven for me Yonder, cannot I tear them asunder, as I do these?—Thou canst make me Nothing;—this freedom canst Thou not take from me. (*He loads the Pistol. Suddenly he Stops.*) And shall I for terror of a miserable life—die?—Shall I give wretchedness the victory over me?—No, I will endure it. (*He throws the Pistol away.*) Let misery blunt itself on my pride! I will go through with it.—Act IV. Scene VI.

And now with these ferocities, and Sybilline frenzies, compare the placid strength of the following delineation, also of a stern character, from the *Maid of Orleans;* where Talbot, the gray veteran, dark, unbelieving, indomitable, passes down, as he thinks, to the land of utter Nothingness, contemptuous even of the Fate that destroys him, and—

"In death reposes on the soil of France,
Like hero on his unsurrender'd shield."

It is the sixth Scene of the third Act; in the heat of a Battle:

(*The scene changes to an open Space encircled with Trees. During the music, Soldiers are seen hastily retreating across the Background.*)

Talbot, *leaning on* Fastolf, *and accompanied by Soldiers. Soon after,* Lionel.

TALBOT.

Here, set me down beneath this tree, and you
Betake yourselves again to battle: quick!
I need no help to die.

FASTOLF.

O day of wo! (*Lionel enters.*)
Look what a sight awaits you, Lionel!
Our leader wounded, dying!

LIONEL.

God forbid!
O noble Talbot, this is not a time to die.
Yield not to Death; force faltering Nature
By your strength of soul, that life depart not!

TALBOT.

In vain! the day of Destiny is come
That levels with the dust our power in France.
In vain, in the fierce clash of desp'rate battle,
Have I risk'd our utmost to withstand it:
The bolt has smote and crush'd me, and I lie
To rise no more for ever. Rheims is lost;
Make haste to rescue Paris.

LIONEL.

Paris is the Dauphin's:
A post arrived even now with th' evil news
It had surrender'd.

TALBOT (*tears away his bandages.*)

Then flow out, ye life-streams;
This Sun is growing loathsome to me.

LIONEL.

Fastolf,
Convey him to the rear: this post can hold
Few instants more; you coward knaves, fall back,
Resistless comes the Witch, and havoc round her.

TALBOT.

Madness, thou conquerest, and I must yield:
Against Stupidity the Gods themselves are powerless.
High Reason, radiant Daughter of the head of God,
Wise Foundress of the system of the Universe,
Conductress of the Stars, who art thou, then,
If tied to th' tail o' th' wild horse, Superstition,
Thou must plunge, eyes open, vainly shrieking,
Sheer down with that drunk Beast to the Abyss?
Cursed who sets his life upon the great
And dignified; and with forecasting spirit
Lays out wise plans! The Fool-King's is this World.

LIONEL.

Oh! Death is near! Think of your God, and pray!

TALBOT.

Were we, as brave men, worsted by the brave,
'T had been but Fortune's common fickleness:
But that a paltry farce should tread us down!—
Did toil and peril, all our earnest life,
Deserve no graver issue?

LIONEL (*grasps his hand.*)

Talbot, farewell!
The meed of bitter tears I'll duly pay you,
When the fight is done, should I outlive it
But now Fate calls me to the field, where yet
She wav'ring sits, and shakes her doubtful urn.
Farewell! we meet beyond the unseen shore.
Brief parting for long friendship! God be with you! [*Exit.*

TALBOT.

Soon it is over, and to the earth I render,
To th' everlasting Sun, the transient atoms
Which for pain and pleasure join'd to form me;
And of the mighty Talbot, whose renown
Once fill'd the world, remains nought but a handful
Of flitting dust. Thus man comes to his end;
And all our conquest in the fight of Life
Is knowledge that 't is Nothing, and contempt
For hollow shows which once we chas'd and worship'd.

SCENE VII.

Enter Charles, Burgundy, Dunois, Du Chatel, *and Soldiers.*

BURGUNDY.

The trench is stormed.

DUNOIS.

Bravo! The fight is ours.

CHARLES (*observing* TALBOT.)

Ha! who is this that to the light of day
Is bidding his constrained and sad farewell?
His bearing speaks no common man; go, haste,
Assist him, if assistance yet avail.
(*Soldiers from the Dauphin's suite step forward.*)

FASTOLF.

Back! Keep away! Approach not the Departing,
Him whom in life ye never wished too near.

BURGUNDY.

What do I see? Great Talbot in his blood!
(*He goes towards him.* TALBOT *gazes fixedly at him and dies.*)

FASTOLF.

Off, Burgundy! With the aspect of a Traitor
Disturb not the last moment of a Hero.

The "Power-words and Thunder-words," as the Germans call them, so frequent in the *Robbers*,* are altogether wanting here; that volcanic fury has assuaged itself; instead of smoke and red lava, we have sunshine and a verdant world. For still more striking examples of this benignant change, we might refer to many scenes, (too long for our present purposes) in *Wallenstein*, and indeed in all the Dramas which followed this, and most of all in *Wilhelm Tell*, which is the latest of them. The careful, and in general truly poetic structure of these works, considered as complete Poems, would exhibit it infinitely better; but for this object, larger limits than ours at present, and studious Readers as well as a Reviewer, were essential.

In his smaller Poems, the like progress is visible. Schiller's works should all be dated, as we study them; but indeed the most, by internal evidence, date themselves.—Besides the *Lied der Glocke*, already mentioned, there are many lyrical pieces of high merit; particularly a whole series of *Ballads*, nearly every one of which is true and poetical. The *Ritter Toggenberg*, the *Dragon-fight*, the *Diver*, are all well known; the *Cranes of Ibycus* has in it, under this simple form, something Old-Grecian, an emphasis, a prophetic gloom, which might seem borrowed even from the spirit of Æschylus. But on these, or any farther on the other poetical works of Schiller, we must not dilate at present. One little piece, which lies by us translated, we may give as a specimen of his style in this lyrical province, and therewith terminate this part of our subject. It is entitled *Alpenlied*, (Song of the Alps,) and seems to require no commentary. Perhaps something of the clear, melodious, yet still somewhat metallic tone of the original may penetrate even through our version:

SONG OF THE ALPS.

By the edge of the chasm is a slippery Track,
The torrent beneath, and the mist hanging o'er thee:
The cliffs of the mountain, huge, rugged, and black,
Are frowning like Giants before thee;
And, wouldst thou not waken the sleeping Lawine,
Walk silent and soft through the deadly ravine.

That Bridge with its dizzying, perilous span
Aloft o'er the gulph and its flood suspended,
Think'st thou it was built by the art of man,
By his hand that grim old arch was bended?
Far down in the jaws of the gloomy abyss
The water is boiling and hissing—for ever will hiss.

That Gate through the rocks is as darksome and drear,
As if to the region of Shadows it carried:
Yet enter! A sweet laughing landscape is here,
Where the Spring with the Autumn is married.
From the world with its sorrows and warfare and wail,
O could I but hide in this bright little vale!

Four Rivers rush down from on high,
Their spring will be hidden for ever;
Their course is to all the four points of the sky,
To each point of the sky is a river;
And fast as they start from their old Mother's feet,
They dash forth, and no more will they meet.

Two Pinnacles rise to the depths of the Blue;
Aloft on their white summits glancing,
Bedeck'd in their garments of golden dew,
The Clouds of the Sky are dancing;
There threading alone their lightsome maze,
Uplifted apart from all mortals' gaze.

And high on her ever-enduring throne
The Queen of the mountain reposes;
Her head serene, and azure, and lone
A diamond crown encloses;
The Sun with his darts shoots round it keen and hot,
He gilds it always, he warms it not.

Of Schiller's Philosophic talent, still more of the results he had arrived at in philosophy, there were much to be said and thought, which we must not enter upon here. As hinted above, his primary endowment seems to us fully as much philosophical as poetical; his intellect, at all events, is peculiarly of that character; strong, penetrating, yet systematic and scholastic, rather than intuitive; and manifesting this tendency both in the objects it treats, and in its mode of treating them. The transcendental Philosophy, which arose in Schiller's busiest era, could not remain without influence on him; he had carefully studied Kant's System, and appears to have not only admitted but zealously appropriated its fundamental doctrines; remoulding them, however, into his own peculiar forms, so that they seem no longer borrowed, but permanently acquired, not less Schiller's than Kant's. Some, perhaps, little aware of his natural wants and tendencies, are of opinion that these speculations did not profit him: Schiller himself, on the other hand, appears to have been well contented with his Philosophy; in which, as harmonized with his Poetry, the assurance and safe anchorage for his moral nature might lie.

"From the opponents of the New Philosophy," says he, "I expect not that tolerance, which is shown to every other system, no better seen into than this: for Kant's Philosophy itself, in its leading points, practises no tolerance; and bears much too rigorous a character, to leave any room for accommodation. But in my eyes this does it honour; proving how little it can endure to have truth tampered with. Such a Philosophy will not be discussed with a mere shake of the head. In the open, clear, accessible field of Inquiry it builds up its system; seeks no shade, makes no reservation; but even as it treats its neighbours, so it requires to be treated; and may

* Thus, to take one often cited instance, Moor's simple question, "Whether there is any powder left?" receives this emphatic answer, "Powder enough to blow the Earth into the Moon!"

be forgiven for lightly esteeming every thing but Proofs. Nor am I terrified to think that the law of Change, from which no human and no divine work finds grace, will operate on this Philosophy, as on every other, and one day its Form will be destroyed: but its Foundations will not have this destiny to fear; for ever since mankind has existed, and any Reason among mankind, these same first principles have been admitted, and on the whole acted upon."—*Correspondence with Goethe*, I. 58.

Schiller's philosophical performances relate chiefly to matters of Art; not, indeed, without significant glances into still more important regions of speculation: nay, Art, as he viewed it, has its basis on the most important interests of man, and of itself involves the harmonious adjustment of these. We have already undertaken to present our readers, on a future occasion, with some abstract of the *Æsthetic Letters*, one of the deepest, most compact pieces of reasoning we are anywhere acquainted with: by that opportunity, the general character of Schiller, as a Philosopher, will best fall to be discussed. Meanwhile, the two following brief passages, as some indication of his views on the highest of all philosophical questions, may stand here without commentary. He is speaking of *Wilhelm Meister*, and in the first extract, of the *Fair Saint's Confessions*, which occupy the Fifth Book of that work:

"The transition from Religion in general to the Christian Religion, by the experience of sin, is excellently conceived. * * * I find virtually in the Christian System the rudiments of the Highest and Noblest; and the different phases of this System, in practical life, are so offensive and mean, precisely because they are bungled representations of that same Highest. If you study the specific character of Christianity, what distinguishes it from all monotheistic Religion, it lies in nothing else than in that *making dead of the Law*, the removal of that Kantean Imperative, instead of which Christianity requires a free Inclination. It is thus, in its pure form, a representing of Moral Beauty, or the Incarnation of the Holy; and in this sense, the only *æsthetic* Religion: hence, too, I explain to myself why it so prospers with female natures, and only in women is now to be met with under a tolerable figure." —*Correspondence*, I. 195.

"But in seriousness," he says elsewhere, "whence may it proceed that you have had a man educated, and in all points equipt, without ever coming upon certain wants which only Philosophy can meet? I am convinced, it is entirely attributable to the *æsthetic direction* you have taken through the whole Romance. Within the æsthetic temper there arises no want of those grounds of comfort, which are to be drawn from speculation: such a temper has self-subsistence, has infinitude, within itself; only when the Sensual and the Moral in man strive hostilely together, need help be sought of pure Reason. A healthy poetic nature wants, as you yourself say, no Moral Law, no Rights of Man, no Political Metaphysics. You might have added as well, it wants no Deity, no Immortality, to stay and uphold itself withal. Those three points round which, in the long run, all speculation turns, may in truth afford such a nature matter for poetic play, but can never become serious concerns and necessities for it."—II. 131.

This last seems a singular opinion; and may prove, if it be correct, that Schiller himself was no "healthy poetic nature;" for undoubtedly with him those three points were "serious concerns and necessities;" as many portions of his works, and various entire treatises, will testify. Nevertheless, it plays an important part in his theories of Poetry; and often, under milder forms, returns on us there.

But, without entering farther on those complex topics, we must here for the present take leave of Schiller. Of his merits we have all along spoken rather on the negative side; and we rejoice in feeling authorized to do so. That any German writer, especially one so dear to us, should already stand so high with British readers that, in admiring him, the critic may also, without prejudice to right feeling on the subject, coolly judge of him, cannot be other than a gratifying circumstance. Perhaps there is no other true Poet of that nation with whom the like course would be suitable.

Connected with this there is one farther observation we must make before concluding. Among young students of German Literature, the question often arises, and is warmly mooted: whether Schiller or Goethe is the greater Poet? Of this question we must be allowed to say that it seems rather a slender one, and for two reasons. First, because Schiller and Goethe are of totally dissimilar endowments and endeavours, in regard to all matters intellectual, and cannot well be compared together as Poets. Secondly, because if the question mean to ask, which Poet is on the whole the rarer and more excellent, as probably it does, it must be considered as long ago abundantly answered. To the clear-sighted and modest Schiller, above all, such a question would have appeared surprising. No one knew better than himself, that as Goethe was a born Poet, so he was in great part a made Poet; that as the one spirit was intuitive, all-embracing, instinct with melody, so the other was scholastic, divisive, only partially and as it were artificially melodious. Besides, Goethe has lived to perfect his natural gift, which the less happy Schiller was not permitted to do. The former, accordingly, is the national Poet; the latter is not, and never could have been. We once heard a German remark that readers till their twenty-fifth year usually preferred Schiller; after their twenty-fifth year, Goethe. This probably was no unfair illustration of the question. Schiller can seem higher than Goethe only because he is narrower. Thus to unpractised eyes, a Peak of Teneriffe, nay, a Strasburg Minster, when we stand on it, may seem higher than a Chimborazo; because the former rise abruptly, without abutment or environment; the latter rises gradually, carrying half a world aloft with it; and only the deeper azure of the heavens, the widened horizon, the "eternal sunshine," disclose to the geographer that the "Region of Change" lies far below him.

However, let us not divide these two Friends, who in life were so benignantly united. Without asserting for Schiller any claim that even enemies can dispute, enough will remain for him. We may say that, as a Poët and Thinker, he attained to a perennial Truth, and ranks among the noblest productions of his century and nation. Goethe may continue *the* German Poet, but neither through long generations can Schiller be forgotten. "His works, too, the memory of what he did and was, will arise afar off like a towering landmark in the solitude of the Past, when distance shall have dwarfed into invisibility many lesser people that once encompassed him, and hid him from the near beholder."

THE NIBELUNGEN LIED.*

[WESTMINSTER REVIEW, 1831.]

IN the year 1757, the Swiss Professor Bodmer printed an ancient poetical manuscript, under the title of *Chriemhilden Rache und die Klage*, (Chriemhilde's Revenge, and the Lament;) which may be considered as the first of a series, or stream of publications, and speculations still rolling on, with increased current, to the present day. Not, indeed, that all these had their source or determining cause in so insignificant a circumstance; their source, or rather thousand sources, lay far elsewhere. As has often been remarked, a certain antiquarian tendency in Literature, a fonder, more earnest looking back into the Past, began about that time to manifest itself in all nations, (witness our own *Percy's Reliques*:) this was among the first distinct symptoms of it in Germany: where, as with ourselves, its manifold effects are still visible enough.

Some fifteen years after Bodmer's publication, which, for the rest, is not celebrated as an editorial feat, one C. H. Müller undertook a *Collection of German Poems from the Twelfth, Thirteenth, and Fourteenth Centuries*; wherein, among other articles, he reprinted Bodmer's *Chriemhilde* and *Klage*, with a highly remarkable addition prefixed to the former, essential indeed to the right understanding of it; and the whole now stood before the world as one Poem, under the name of the *Nibelungen Lied*, or Lay of the Nibelungen. It has since been ascertained that the *Klage* is a foreign inferior appendage; at best, related only as epilogue to the main work: meanwhile out of this *Nibelungen*, such as it was, there soon proceeded new inquiries, and kindred enterprises. For much as the Poem, in the shape it here bore, was defaced and marred, it failed not to attract observation: to all open-minded lovers of poetry, especially where a strong patriotic feeling existed, this singular, antique *Nibelungen* was an interesting appearance. Johannes Müller, in his famous *Swiss History*, spoke of it in warm terms: subsequently, August Wilhelm Schlegel, through the medium of *Das Deutsche Museum*, succeeded in awakening something like a universal popular feeling on the subject; and, as a natural consequence, a whole host of Editors and Critics, of deep and of shallow endeavour, whose labours we yet see in progress. The *Nibelungen* has now been investigated, translated, collated, commented upon, with more or less result, to almost boundless lengths: besides the Work named at the head of this Paper, and which stands there simply as one of the latest, we have Versions into the modern tongue by Von der Hagen, by Hinsberg, Lachmann, Büsching, Zeune, the last in Prose, and said to be worthless; Criticisms, Introductions, Keys, and so forth, by innumerable others, of whom we mention only Docen and the Brothers Grimm.

By which means, not only has the Poem itself been elucidated with all manner of researches, but its whole environment has come forth in new light; the scene and personages it relates to, the other fictions and traditions connected with it, have attained a new importance and coherence. Manuscripts, that for ages had lain dormant, have issued from their archives into public view; books that had circulated only in mean guise for the amusement of the people, have become important, not to one or two *virtuosos*, but to the general body of the learned: and now a whole System of antique Teutonic Fiction and Mythology unfolds itself, shedding here and there a real though feeble and uncertain glimmer over what was once the total darkness of the old Time. No fewer than Fourteen ancient Traditionary Poems, all strangely intertwisted, and growing out of and into one another, have come to light among the Germans; who now, in looking back, find that they too, as well as the Greeks, have their Heroic Age, and round the old Valhalla, as their Northern Pantheon, a world of demi-gods and wonders.

Such a phenomenon, unexpected till of late, cannot but interest a deep-thinking, enthusiastic people. For the *Nibelungen* especially, which lies as the centre and distinct keystone of the whole too chaotic System,—let us say rather, blooms as a firm sunny island in the middle of these cloud-covered, ever-shifting, sand-whirlpools,—they cannot sufficiently testify their love and veneration. Learned professors lecture on the *Nibelungen*, in public schools, with a praiseworthy view to initiate the German youth in love of their fatherland; from many zealous and nowise ignorant critics we hear talk of a "great Northern Epos," of a "German Iliad;" the more saturnine are shamed into silence, or hollow mouth-homage; thus from all quarters comes a sound of joyful

---

* *Das Nibelungen Lied, übersetzt von Karl Simrock.* (The *Nibelungen Lied*, translated by Karl Simrock.) 2 vols. 12mo. Berlin, 1827.

acclamation: the *Nibelungen* is welcomed as a precious national possession, recovered after six centuries of neglect, and takes undisputed place among the sacred books of German literature.

Of these curious transactions, some rumour has not failed to reach us in England, where our minds, from their own antiquarian disposition, were willing enough to receive it. Abstracts and extracts of the *Nibelungen* have been printed in our language; there have been disquisitions on it in our Reviews; hitherto, however, such as nowise to exhaust the subject. On the contrary, where so much was to be told at once, the speaker might be somewhat puzzled where to begin: it was a much readier method to begin with the end, or with any part of the middle, than like Hamilton's Ram (whose example is too little followed in literary narrative) to begin with the beginning. Thus has our stock of intelligence come rushing out on us quite promiscuously and pell-mell; whereby the whole matter could not but acquire a tortuous, confused, altogether inexplicable, and even dreary aspect; and the class of "well-informed persons" now find themselves in that uncomfortable position, where they are obliged to profess admiration, and at the same time feel that, except by name, they know not what the thing admired is. Such a position towards the venerable *Nibelungen*, which is no less bright and graceful than historically significant, cannot be the right one. Moreover, as appears to us, it might be somewhat mended by very simple means. Let any one that had honestly read the *Nibelungen*, which in these days is no surprising achievement, only tell us what he found there, and nothing that he did not find: we should then know something, and, what were still better, be ready for knowing more. To search out the secret roots of such a production, ramified through successive layers of centuries, and drawing nourishment from each, may be work, and too hard work, for the deepest philosopher and critic; but to look with natural eyes on what part of it stands visibly above ground, and record his own experiences thereof, is what any reasonable mortal, if he will take heed, can do.

Some such slight service we here intend proffering to our readers: let them glance with us a little into that mighty maze of Northern Archæology; where, it may be, some pleasant prospects will open. If the *Nibelungen* is what we have called it, a firm sunny island amid the weltering chaos of antique tradition, it must be worth visiting on general grounds; nay, if the primeval rudiments of it have the antiquity assigned them, it belongs especially to us English *Teutones* as well as to the German.

Far be it from us, meanwhile, to venture rashly or farther than is needful, into that same traditionary chaos, fondly named the "Cycle of Northern Fiction," with its Fourteen Sectors, (or separate Poems,) which are rather Fourteen shoreless Limbos, where we hear of pieces containing "a hundred thousand verses," and "seventy thousand verses," as of a quite natural affair! How travel through that inane country; by what art discover the little grain of Substance that casts such multiplied immeasurable Shadows? The primeval Mythus, were it at first philosophical truth, or were it historical incident, floats too vaguely on the breath of men: each successive Singer and Redactor furnishes it with new personages, new scenery, to please a new audience; each has the privilege of inventing, and the far wider privilege of borrowing and new-modelling from *all* that have preceded him. Thus though Tradition may have but one root, it grows like a Banian, into a whole overarching labyrinth of trees. Or rather might we say, it is a Hall of Mirrors, where in pale light each mirror reflects, convexly or concavely, not only some real Object, but the Shadows of this in other mirrors; which again do the like for it: till in such reflection and re-reflection the whole immensity is filled with dimmer and dimmer shapes; and no firm scene lies round us, but a dislocated, distorted chaos, fading away on all hands, in the distance, into utter night. Only to some brave Von der Hagen, furnished with indefatigable ardour, and a deep, almost a religious love, is it given to find sure footing there, and see his way. All those *Dukes of Aquitania*, therefore, and *Etzel's Court-holdings*, and *Dietriche* and *Sigenots*, we shall leave standing where they are. Such as desire farther information, will find an intelligible account of the whole Series or Cycle, in Messrs. Weber and Jamieson's *Illustrations of Northern Antiquities;* and all possible furtherance, in the numerous German works above alluded to; among which Von der Hagen's writings, though not the readiest, are probably the safest guides. But for us, our business here is with the *Nibelungen*, the inhabited poetic country round which all these wildernesses lie; only as environments of which, as routes to which, are they of moment to us. Perhaps our shortest and smoothest route will be through the *Heldenbuch*, (Hero-book;) which is greatly the most important of these subsidiary Fictions, not without interest of its own, and closely related to the *Nibelungen*. This *Heldenbuch*, therefore, we must now address ourselves to traverse with all despatch. At the present stage of the business, too, we shall forbear any historical inquiry and argument concerning the date and local habitation of those Traditions; reserving what little is to be said on that matter till the Traditions themselves have become better known to us. Let the reader, on trust, for the present, transport himself into the twelfth or thirteenth century; and therefrom looking back into the sixth or fifth, see what presents itself.

Of the *Heldenbuch*, tried on its own merits, and except as illustrating that other far worthier Poem, or at most as an old national, and still in some measure popular book, we should have felt strongly inclined to say, as the curate in *Don Quixote* so often did, *Al corral con ello*, Out of window with it! Doubtless there are touches of beauty in the work, and even a sort of heartiness and antique quaintness in its wildest follies; but on the whole that George-and-Dragon species of composition has long ceased to find favour with any one; and except for its groundwork, more or less discernible, of old

Northern Fiction, this *Heldenbuch* has little to distinguish it from these. Nevertheless, what is worth remark, it seems to have been a far higher favourite than the *Nibelungen*, with ancient readers: it was printed soon after the invention of printing: some think in 1472, for there is no place or date on the first edition; at all events, in 1491, in 1509, and repeatedly since; whereas the *Nibelungen*, though written earlier, and in worth immeasurably superior, had to remain in manuscript three centuries longer. From which, for the thousandth time, inferences might be drawn as to the infallibility of popular taste, and its value as a criterion for poetry. However, it is probably in virtue of this neglect, that the *Nibelungen* boasts of its actual purity; that it now comes before us, clear and graceful as it issued from the old singer's head and heart; not over-loaded with Ass-eared Giants, Fiery Dragons, Dwarfs, and Hairy Women, as the *Heldenbuch* is, many of which, as charity would hope, may be the produce of a later age than that famed *Swabian Era*, to which these poems, as we now see them, are commonly referred. Indeed, one Casper von Roen is understood to have passed the whole *Heldenbuch* through his limbec, in the fifteenth century; but like other rectifiers, instead of purifying it, to have only drugged it with still fiercer ingredients to suit the sick appetite of the time.

Of this drugged and adulterated *Hero-Book* (the only one we yet have, though there is talk of a better) we shall quote the long Title-page of Lessing's Copy, the edition of 1560; from which, with a few intercalated observations, the reader's curiosity may probably obtain what little satisfaction it wants.

Das Heldenbuch Welchs aufs neue corrigirt und gebessert ist, mit shönen Figuren geziert. Gedruckt zu Frankfurt am Mayn, durch Weygand Han und Sygmund Feyerabend, &c. That is to say:

"The *Hero-Book*, which is of new corrected and improved, adorned with beautiful Figures. Printed at Frankfurt on the Mayn, through Weygand Han, and Sygmund Feyerabend.

"*Part First* saith of Kaiser Ottnit and the little King Elberich, how they with great peril, over sea, in Heathendom, won from a king his daughter, (and how he in lawful marriage took her to wife.")

From which announcement the reader already guesses the contents: how this little King Elberich was a Dwarf, or Elf, some half-span long, yet full of cunning practices, and the most helpful activity; nay, stranger still, had been Kaiser Ottnit of *Lampartei*, or Lombardy's father,—having had his own ulterior views in that indiscretion. How they sailed with Messina ships, into Paynim land; fought with that unspeakable Turk, King Machabol, in and about his fortress and metropolis of Montebur, which was all stuck round with Christian heads; slew from seventy to a hundred thousand of the Infidels at one heat; saw the lady on the battlements; and at length, chiefly by Dwarf Elberich's help, carried her off in triumph: wedded her in Messina; and without difficulty, rooting out the Mohammedan prejudice, converted her to the creed of Mother Church. The fair runaway seems to have been of a gentle, tractable disposition, very different from old Machabol; concerning whom it is chiefly to be noted that Dwarf Elberich, rendering himself invisible on their first interview, plucks out a handful of hair from his chin; thereby increasing to a tenfold pitch the royal choler; and, what is still more remarkable, furnishing the poet Wieland, six centuries afterwards, with the critical incident in his *Oberon*. As for the young lady herself, we cannot but admit that she was well worth sailing to Heathendom for; and shall here, as our sole specimen of that old German doggerel, give the description of her, as she first appeared on the battlements during the fight; subjoining a version as verbal and literal as the plainest prose can make it. Considered as a detached passage, it is perhaps the finest we have met with in the *Heldenbuch*.

Ihr herz brann also schone,
Recht als ein rot rubein,
Gleich dem vollen mone
Gaben ihr äuglein schein
Sich hett die maget reine
Mit rosen wohl bekleid
Und auch mit Berlin Kleine,
Niemand da tröst die meid.

Sie war schön an dem leibe,
Und zu den Seiten schmal
Recht als ein Kertze Scheibe
Wohlgeschaffen überall:
Ihr beyden händ gemeine
Dars ihr gentz nichts gebrach;
Ihr näglein schön und reine,
Das man sich darin besach.

Ihr har war schön umbfangen
Mit elder seiden fein;
Das liess sie nieder hangen,
Das hübsche Magedlein.
Sie trug ein kron mit steinen
Sie war von gold so rot;
Elberich dem viel kleinen
War zu der Magte not.

Da vornen in den Kronen
Lag ein Karfunkelstein,
Der in dem Pallast schone
Recht als ein Kertz erschein;
Auf jrem haupt das hare
War lauter und auch fein
Es leuchtet also klare
Recht als der Sonnen schein.

Die Magt die stand alleine,
Gar trawrig war jr mut;
Ihr farb und die war reine,
Lieblich we Milch und Blut:
Her durch jr zöpffe reinen
Schien jr hals als der Schnee
Elberich dem viel Kleinen
That der Maget Jammer weh.

Her heart burnt (with anxiety) as beautiful
Just as a red ruby,
Like the full moon
Her eyes (eyelings, pretty eyes) gave sheen.
Herself had the maiden pure
Well adorned with roses,
And also with pearls small:
No one there comforted the maid.

She was fair of body,
And in the waist slender;
Right as a (golden) candlestick
Well-fashioned everywhere:
Her two hands proper,
So that she wanted nought;
Her little nails fair and pure,
That you could see yourself therein.

Her hair was beautifully girt
With noble silk (band) fine;

She let it flow down,
The lovely maidling.
She wore a crown with jewels,
It was of gold so red:
For Elberich the very small
The maid had need (to console her.)

There in front of the crown
Lay a carbuncle-stone,
Which in the palace fair
Even as a taper seemed;
On her head the hair
Was glossy and also fine,
It shone as bright
Even as the sun's sheen.

The maid she stood alone,
Right sad was her mind;
Her colour it was pure,
Lovely as milk and blood:
Out through her pure locks
Shone her neck like the snow.
Elberich the very small
Was touched with the maiden's sorrow.

Happy man was Kaiser Ottnit, blessed with such a wife, after all his travail;—had not the Turk Machabol cunningly sent him, in revenge, a box of young Dragons, or Dragon-eggs, by the hands of a caitiff Infidel, contriver of mischief; by whom in due course of time they were hatched and nursed to the infinite wo of all Lampartie, and ultimately to the death of Kaiser Ottnit himself, whom they swallowed and attempted to digest, once without effect, but the next time too fatally, crown and all!

"*Part Second* announceth (*meldet*) of Herr Hugdietrich and his son Wolfdietrich; how they for justice's sake, oft by their doughty acts succoured distressed persons, with other bold heroes that stood by them in extremity."

Concerning which Hugdietrich, Emperor of Greece, and his son Wolfdietrich, one day the renowned Dietrich of Bern, we can here say little more than that the former trained himself to sempstress work; and for many weeks, plied his needle, before he could get wedded and produce Wolfdietrich; who coming into the world in this clandestine manner, was let down into the castle-ditch, and like Romulus and Remus nursed by a Wolf, whence his name. However, after never-imagined adventures, with enchanters and enchantresses, pagans, and giants, in all quarters of the globe, he finally, with utmost effort, slaughtered those Lombardy Dragons; then married Kaiser Ottnit's widow, whom he had rather flirted with before; and so lived universally respected in his new empire, performing yet other notable achievements. One strange property he had, sometimes useful to him, sometimes hurtful: that his breath, when he became angry, grew flame, red hot, and would take the temper out of swords. We find him again in the *Nibelungen*, among King Etzel's (Attila's) followers: a staid, cautious, yet still invincible man; on which occasion, though with great reluctance, he is forced to interfere, and does so with effect. Dietrich is the favourite hero of all those Southern Fictions, and well acknowledged in the Northern also, where the chief man, however, as we shall find, is not he, but Siegfried.

"*Part Third* showeth of the Rose-garden at Worms, which was planted by Chrimhilte, King Gibrich's daughter; whereby afterwards most part of those Heroes and Giants came to destruction and were slain."

In this Third Part the Southern or Lombard Heroes come into contact and collision with another as notable, Northern class; and for us much more important. Chriemhild, whose ulterior history makes such a figure in the *Nibelungen*, had, it would seem, near the ancient City of Worms, a Rose-garden, some seven English miles in circuit; fenced only by a silk thread; wherein, however, she maintained Twelve stout fighting men; several of whom, as Hagen, Volker, her three Brothers, above all the gallant Siegfried her betrothed, we shall meet with again: these, so unspeakable was their prowess, sufficed to defend the silk-thread Garden against all mortals. Our good antiquary, Von der Hagen, imagines that this Rose-garden business (in the primeval Tradition) glances obliquely at the Ecliptic with its Twelve Signs, at Jupiter's fight with the Titans, and we know not what confused skirmishing in the Utgard, or Asgard, or Midgard of the Scandinavians. Be this as it may, Chriemhild, we are here told, being very beautiful, and very wilful, boasts in the pride of her heart, that no heroes on earth are to be compared with hers; and hearing accidentally that Dietrich of Bern has a high character in this line, forthwith challenges him to visit Worms, and with eleven picked men, to do battle there against those other Twelve champions of Christendom that watch her Rose-garden. Dietrich, in a towering passion at the style of the message, which was "surly and stout," instantly pitches upon his eleven seconds, who also are to be principals; and with a retinue of other sixty thousand, by quick stages, in which obstacles enough are overcome, reaches Worms, and declares himself ready. Among these eleven Lombard heroes of his, are likewise several whom we meet with again in the *Nibelungen*; besides Dietrich himself, we have the old Duke Hildebrand, Wolfhart, Ortwin. Notable among them, in another way, is Monk Ilsan, a truculent, gray-bearded fellow, equal to any Friar Tuck in *Robin Hood*.

The conditions of fight are soon agreed on: there are to be twelve successive duels, each challenger being expected to find his match; and the prize of victory is a Rose-garland from Chriemhild, and *ein Helssen und ein Küssen*, that is to say virtually, one kiss from her fair lips, to each. But here, as it ever should do, Pride gets a fall; for Chriemhild's bully-hectors, are in divers ways all successively felled to the ground by the Berners; some of whom, as old Hildebrand, will not even take her Kiss when it is due: even Siegfried himself, most reluctantly engaged with by Dietrich, and for a while victorious, is at last forced to seek shelter in her lap. Nay, Monk Ilsan, after the regular fight is over, and his part in it well performed, calls out, in succession, fifty-two other idle Champions of the Garden, part of them Giants, and routs the whole fraternity: thereby earning, besides his own regular allowance, fifty-two spare Garlands, and fifty-two several kisses; in the course of which latter, Chriemhild's cheek, a just punishment as seemed, was scratched to the drawing of blood by his rough beard. It only remains to be added that King Gibrich, Chriemhild's Father, is now fain to do homage for his kingdom to Dietrich; who returns triumphant to his own country; where also, Monk Ilsan, according to promise, distributes these fifty-two Garlands among his fellow Friars, crushing a garland on the bare crown of each, till "the red blood ran over their ears." Under which hard but not undeserved treatment, they all agreed to pray for remission of Ilsan's sins: indeed, such as continued refractory he tied together by the beards, and hung pair-wise over poles; whereby the stoutest soon gave in.

> So endeth here this ditty
> Of strife from woman's pride:
> God on our griefe take pity,
> And Mary still by us abide.

"In *Part Fourth* is announced (*gemelt*) of the little King Laurin, the Dwarf, how he encompassed his Rose-garden with so great manhood and art-magic, till at last he was vanquished by the heroes, and forced to become their Juggler, with, &c. &c."

Of which Fourth and happily last part we shall here say nothing; inasmuch as, except that certain of our old heroes again figure there, it has no coherence or connection with the rest of the *Heldenbuch;* and is simply a new tale, which by way of episode Heinrich von Ofterdingen, as we learn from his own words, had subsequently appended thereto. He says:

> Heinrich von Ofterdingen
> This story hath been singing,
> To the joy of Princes bold,
> They gave him silver and gold,
> Moreover pennies and garments rich!
> Here endeth this Book the which
> Doth sing our noble Heroes' story:
> God help us all to heavenly glory.

Such is some outline of the famous *Heldenbuch;* on which it is not our business here to add any criticism. The fact that it has so long been popular betokens a certain worth in it; the kind and degree of which is also in some measure apparent. In poetry "the rude man," it has been said, "requires only to see something going on; the man of more refinement wishes to feel; the truly refined man must be made to reflect." For the first of these classes our *Hero-Book,* as has been apparent enough, provides in abundance; for the other two scantily, indeed; for the second not not at all. Nevertheless our estimate of this work, which as a series of Antique Traditions may have considerable meaning, is apt rather to be too low. Let us remember that this is not the original *Heldenbuch* which we now see; but only a version of it into the Knight-errant dialect of the thirteenth, indeed partly of the fourteenth and fifteenth centuries, with all the fantastic monstrosities, now so trivial, pertaining to that style; under which disguises the really antique earnest groundwork, interesting as old Thought, if not as old Poetry, is all but quite obscured from us. But Antiquarian diligence is now busy with the *Heldenbuch* also, from which what light is in it will doubtless be elicited, and here and there a deformity removed. Though the Ethiop cannot change his skin, there is no need that even he should go abroad unwashed.*

Casper von Roen, or whoever was the ultimate redactor of the *Heldenbuch,* whom Lessing designates as "a highly ill-informed man," would have done better had he quite omitted that little King Laurin, "and his little Rose-garden," which properly is no Rose-garden at all; and instead thereof introduced the *Gehörnte Siegfried,* (Behorned Siegfried,) whose history lies at the heart of the whole Northern Traditions; and, under a rude prose dress, is to this day a real child's-book and people's-book among the Germans. Of this Siegfried we have already seen somewhat in the Rose-garden at Worms; and shall ere long see much more elsewhere; for he is the chief hero of the *Nibelungen:* indeed nowhere can we dip into those old Fictions, whether in Scandinavia or the Rhine-land, but under one figure or another, whether as Dragon-killer and Prince-royal, or as Blacksmith and Horse-subduer, as Sigurd, Sivrit, Siegfried, we are sure to light on him. As his early adventures belong to the strange sort, and will afterwards concern us not a little, we shall here endeavour to piece together some consistent outline of them; so far indeed as that may be possible, for his biographers, agreeing in the main points, differ widely in the details.

First, then, let no one from the title *Gehörnte,* (Horned, Behorned,) fancy that our brave Siegfried, who was the loveliest as well as the bravest of men, was actually cornuted, and had horns on his brow, though like Michael Angelo's Moses; or even that his skin, to which the epithet *Behorned* refers, was hard like a crocodile's, and not softer than the softest shamoy: for the truth is, his Hornedness means only an Invulnerability, like that of Achilles, which he came by in the following manner. All men agree that Siegfried was a king's son; he was born, as we here have good reason to know, "at Santen in Netherland," of Siegemund and the fair Siegelinde: yet by some family misfortune or discord, of which the accounts are very various, he came into singular straits during boyhood; having passed that happy period of life, not under the canopies of costly state, but by the sooty stithy, in one Mimer a Blacksmith's shop. Here, however, he was nowise in his proper element; ever quarrelling with his fellow apprentices; nay, as some say, breaking the hardest anvils into shivers by his too stout hammering. So that Mimer, otherwise a first-rate Smith, could by no means do with him there. He sends him, accordingly, to the neighbouring forest, to fetch charcoal; well aware that a monstrous Dragon, one Regin, the Smith's own Brother, would meet him and devour him.

* Our inconsiderable knowledge of the *Heldenbuch* is derived from various secondary sources; chiefly from Lessing's *Werke* [B. XIII.], where the reader will find an epitome of the whole Poem, with Extracts by Herr Fülleborn, from which the above are taken. A still more accessible and larger Abstract, with long specimens translated into verse, stands in the *Illustrations of Northern Antiquities,* [p. 45—167.] Von der Hagen has since been employed specially on the *Heldenbuch;* with what result we have not yet learned.

But far otherwise it proved: Siegfried by main force slew this Dragon, or rather Dragonized Smith's-Brother; made broth of him; and, warned by some significant phenomena, bathed therein; or, as others assert, bathed directly in the monster's blood without cookery; and hereby attained that Invulnerability, complete in all respects, save that between his shoulders where a limetree leaf chanced to settle and stick during the process, there was one little spot, a fatal spot as afterwards turned out, left in its natural state.

Siegfried, now seeing through the craft of the Smith, returned home and slew him; then set forth in search of adventures, the bare catalogue of which were long to recite. We mention only two, as subsequently of moment both for him and for us. He is by some said to have courted and then jilted the fair and proud Queen Brunhild of Isenland; nay, to have thrown down the seven gates of her Castle; and then ridden off with her wild horse Gana, having mounted him in the meadow, and instantly broken him. Some cross passages between him and Queen Brunhild, who understood no jesting, there must clearly have been, so angry is her recognition of him in the *Nibelungen;* nay, she bears a lasting grudge against him there, as he, and indeed, she also, one day too sorely felt.

His other grand adventure is with the two sons of the deceased King Nibelung, in Nibelungen-land: these two youths, to whom their father had bequeathed a Hoard or Treasure, beyond all price or computation, Siegfried, "riding by alone," found on the side of a mountain, in a state of great perplexity. They had brought out the treasure from the cave where it usually lay; but how to part it was the difficulty; for not to speak of gold, there were as many jewels alone "as twelve wagons in four days and nights each going three journeys could carry away;" nay, "however much you took from it there was no diminution;" besides, in real property, a Sword, Balmung, of great potency; a Divining-rod "which gave power over every one;" and a *Tarnkappe*, (or Cloak of Darkness,) which not only rendered the wearer invisible, but also gave him twelve men's strength. So that the two Princes Royal, without counsel save from their Twelve stupid Giants, knew not how to fall upon any amicable arrangement; and, seeing Siegfried ride by so opportunely, requested him to be arbiter; offering also the Sword Balmung for his trouble. Siegfried, who readily undertook the impossible problem, did his best to accomplish it; but, of course, without effect; nay the two Nibelungen Princes, being of choleric temper, grew impatient, and provoked him; whereupon, with the Sword Balmung he slew them both, and their Twelve Giants (perhaps originally Signs of the Zodiac) to boot. Thus did the famous *Nibelungen Hort*, (Hoard,) and indeed the whole Nibelungen-land come into his possession; wearing the Sword Balmung, and having slain the two Princes and their champions, what was there farther to oppose him? Vainly did the Dwarf Alberich, our old friend Elberich of the *Heldenbuch*, who had now become special keeper of this Hoard, attempt some resistance with a Dwarf Army; he was driven back into the cave: plundered of his *Tarnkappe;* and obliged with all his myrmidons to swear fealty to the conqueror, whom indeed thenceforth he and they punctually obeyed.

Whereby Siegfried might now farther style himself King of the Nibelungen; master of the infinite Nibelungen Hoard (collected doubtless by art-magic in the beginning of Time, in the deep bowels of the Universe) with the *Wünschelruthe*, (Wishing or Divining-rod,) pertaining thereto; owner of the *Tarnkappe*, which he ever after kept by him, to put on at will; and though last not least, Bearer and Wielder of the Sword Balmung,* by the keen edge of which all this gain had come to him. To which last acquisitions, adding his previously acquired Invulnerability, and his natural dignities as Prince of Netherland, he might well show himself before the foremost at Worms or elsewhere; and attempt any the highest adventure that fortune could cut out for him. However, his subsequent history belongs all to the *Nibelungen Song;* at which fair garden of poesy we are now, through all these shaggy wildernesses and enchanted woods, finally arrived.

Apart from its antiquarian value, and not only as by far the finest monument of old German art, but intrinsically, and as a mere detached composition, this *Nibelungen* has an excellence that cannot but surprise us. With little preparation, any reader of poetry, even in these days, might find it interesting. It is not without a certain Unity of interest and purport, an internal coherence and completeness; it is a Whole, and some spirit of Music informs it: these are the highest characteristics of a true Poem. Considering farther what intellectual environment we now find it in, it is doubly to be prized and wondered at; for it differs from those *Hero-Books*, as molten or

* By this Sword Balmung also hangs a tale. Doubtless it was one of those invaluable weapons sometimes fabricated by the old Northern Smiths, compared with which our modern Foxes, and Ferraras, and Toledos are mere leaden tools. Von der Hagen seems to think it simply the Sword Mimung under another name; in which case Siegfried's old master, Mimer, had been the maker of it, and called it after himself, as if it had been his son. In Scandinavian chronicles, veridical or not, we have the following account of that transaction. Mimer (or as some have it, surely without ground, one Veliant, once an apprentice of his) was challenged by another Craftsman, named Amilias, who boasted that he had made a suit of armour which no stroke could dint,—to equal that feat, or own himself the second Smith then extant. This last the stout Mimer would in no case do, but proceeded to forge the Sword Mimung; with which, when it was finished, he, "in presence of the King," cut asunder "a thread of wool floating on water." This would have seemed a fair fire-edge to most Smiths: not so to Mimer: he sawed the blade in pieces, welded it in "a red hot fire for three days," tempered it with "milk and oatmeal," and by much other cunning, brought out a sword that severed "a ball of wool floating on water." But neither would this suffice him; he returned to his smithy; and by means known only to himself, produced in the course of seven weeks a third and final edition of Mimung, which split asunder a whole floating pack of wool. The comparative trial now took place forthwith. Amilias, cased in his impenetrable coat of mail, sat down on a bench, in presence of assembled thousands, and bade Mimer strike him. Mimer fetched of course his best blow, on which Amilias observed that there was a strange feeling of cold iron in his inwards. "Shake thyself," said Mimer; the luckless wight did so, and fell in two halves, being cleft sheer through from collar to haunch, never more to swing hammer in this world.—See *Illustrations of Northern Antiquities*, p. 31.

carved metal does from rude agglomerated ore; almost as some Shakspeare from his fellow Dramatists, whose *Tamburlaines* and *Island Princesses*, themselves not destitute of merit, first show us clearly in what pure loftiness and loneliness the *Hamlets* and *Tempests* reign.

The unknown Singer of the *Nibelungen*, though no Shakspeare, must have had a deep, poetic soul; wherein things discontinuous and inanimate shaped themselves together into life, and the Universe with its wondrous purport stood significantly imaged; overarching, as with heavenly firmaments and eternal harmonies, the little scene where men strut and fret their hour. His Poem, unlike so many old and new pretenders to that name, has a basis and organic structure, a beginning, middle, and end; there is one great principle and idea set forth in it, round which all its multifarious parts combine in living union. Remarkable it is, moreover, how along with this essence and primary condition of all poetic virtue, the minor external virtues of what we call Taste, and so forth, are, as it were, presupposed; and the living soul of Poetry being there, its body of incidents, its garment of language, come of their own accord. So, too, in the case of Shakspeare: his feeling of propriety, as compared with that of the Marlowes and Fletchers, his quick sure sense of what is fit and unfit, either in act or word, might astonish us, had he no other superiority. But true Inspiration, as it may well do, includes that same Taste, or rather a far higher and heartfelt Taste, of which that other "elegant" species is but an ineffectual, irrational apery: let us see the herald Mercury actually descend from his Heaven, and the bright wings, and the graceful movement of these, will not be wanting.

With an instinctive art, far different from acquired artifice, this Poet of the *Nibelungen*, working in the same province with his contemporaries of the *Heldenbuch*, on the same material of tradition, has, in a wonderful degree, possessed himself of what these could only strive after; and with his "clear feeling of fictitious truth," avoided as false the errors and monstrous perplexities in which they vainly struggled. He is of another species than they; in language, in purity and depth of feeling, in fineness of invention, stands quite apart from them.

The language of the *Heldenbuch*, as we saw above, was a feeble half-articulate child's-speech, the metre nothing better than a miserable doggerel; whereas here in the old Frankish (*Oberdutsch*) dialect of the *Nibelungen*, we have a clear decisive utterance, and in a real system of verse, not without essential regularity, great liveliness, and now and then even harmony of rhythm. Doubtless we must often call it a diffuse diluted utterance; at the same time it is genuine, with a certain antique garrulous heartiness, and has a rhythm in the thoughts as well as the words. The simplicity is never silly, even in that perpetual recurrence of epithets, sometimes of rhymes, as where two words for instance *lib* (body, life, *leib*) and *wip* (woman, wife, *weip*) are indissolubly wedded together, and the one never shows itself without the other following,—there is something which reminds us not so much of poverty, as of trustfulness and child-like innocence. Indeed a strange charm lies in those old tones, where, in gay dancing melodies, the sternest tidings are sung to us; and deep floods of Sadness and Strife play lightly in little curling billows, like seas in summer. It is as a meek smile, in whose still, thoughtful depths a whole infinitude of patience, and love, and heroic strength lie revealed. But in other cases, too, we have seen this outward sport and inward earnestness offer grateful contrast, and cunning excitement; for example, in Tasso; of whom, though otherwise different enough, this old Northern Singer has more than once reminded us. There, too, as here, we have a dark solemn meaning in light guise; deeds of high temper, harsh self-denial, daring, and death, stand embodied in that soft, quick-flowing, joyfully-modulated verse. Nay, farther, as if the implement, much more than we might fancy, had influenced the work done, these two Poems, could we trust our individual feeling, have in one respect the same poetical result for us: in the *Nibelungen* as in the *Gerusalemme*, the persons and their story are indeed brought vividly before us, yet not near and palpably present; it is rather as if we looked on that scene through an inverted telescope, whereby the whole was carried far away into the distance, the life-large figures comprised into brilliant miniatures, so clear, so real, yet tiny, elf-like, and beautified as well as lessened, their colours being now closer and brighter, the shadows and trivial features no longer visible. This, as we partly apprehend, comes of *Singing* Epic Poems; most part of which only pretend to be sung. Tasso's rich melody still lives among the Italian people; the *Nibelungen* also is what it professes to be, a *Song*.

No less striking than the verse and language is the quality of the invention manifested here. Of the Fable, or narrative material of the *Nibelungen*, we should say that it had high, almost the highest merit; so daintily, yet firmly, is it put together; with such felicitous selection of the beautiful, the essential, and no less felicitous rejection of whatever was unbeautiful or even extraneous. The reader is no longer afflicted with that chaotic brood of Fire-drakes, Giants, and malicious turbaned Turks, so fatally rife in the *Heldenbuch*: all this is swept away, or only hovers in faint shadows afar off; and a free field is opened for legitimate perennial interests. Yet neither is the *Nibelungen* without its wonders; for it is poetry and not prose; here too, a supernatural world encompasses the natural; and, though at rare intervals and in a calm manner, reveals itself there. It is truly wonderful with what skill our simple, untaught Poet deals with the marvellous; admitting it without reluctance or criticism, yet precisely in the degree and shape that will best avail him. Here, if in no other respect, we should say that he has a decided superiority to Homer himself. The whole story of the *Nibelungen* is fateful, mysterious, guided on by unseen influences; yet the actual marvels are few, and done in the far distance: those Dwarfs, and Cloaks of Darkness, and charmed Treasure-caves, are heard of rather than beheld, the tidings of them seem to issue from unknown space. Vain were it to inquire where that Nibelungen land specially is: its very name is *Nebel-land* or *Nifl-land*, the land of Darkness, of Invisibility. The "Nibelungen Heroes," that muster in thousands and tens of thousands, though they march to the Rhine or Danube, and we see their strong limbs and shining armour, we could almost fancy to be children of the air. Far beyond the firm horizon, that wonder-bearing region swims on the infinite waters; unseen by bodily eye, or at most discerned as a faint streak, hanging in the blue depths, uncertain whether island or cloud. And thus the *Nibelungen Song*, though based on the bottomless foundation of Spirit, and not unvisited of skyey messengers, is a real, rounded, habitable Earth, where we find firm footing, and the wondrous and the common live amicably together. Perhaps it would be difficult to find any Poet of ancient or modern times, who in this trying problem has steered his way with greater delicacy and success.

To any of our readers, who may have personally studied the *Nibelungen*, these high praises of ours will not seem exaggerated: the rest, who are the vast majority, must endeavour to accept them with some degree of faith, at least, of curiosity; to vindicate, and judicially substantiate them would far exceed our present opportunities. Nay, in any case, the criticisms, the alleged Characteristics of a Poem are so many Theorems, which are indeed enunciated, truly or falsely, but the Demonstration of which must be sought for in the reader's own study and experience. Nearly all that can be attempted here, is some hasty epitome of the mere Narrative; no substantial image of the work, but a feeble outline and shadow. To which task, as the personages and their environment have already been in some degree illustrated, we can now proceed without obstacle.

The *Nibelungen* has been called the Northern Epos; yet it has, in great part, a Dramatic character: those thirty-nine *Aventiuren* (Adventures) which it consists of, might be so many scenes in a Tragedy. The catastrophe is dimly prophesied from the beginning; and, at every fresh step, rises more and more clearly into view. A shadow of coming Fate, as it were, a low inarticulate voice of Doom falls from the first, out of that charmed Nibelungen-land: the discord of two women, is as a little spark of evil passion, that ere long enlarges itself into a crime; foul murder is done; and now the Sin rolls on like a devouring fire, till the guilty and the innocent are alike encircled with it, and a whole land is ashes, and a whole race is swept away.

Uns ist in alten mæren Wunders vil geseit,
Von helden lobebæren Von grozer chuonheit,
Von vrouden und hoch-geziten Von weinen und von chlagen,
Von chuner rechen striten Muget ir nu wunder hören sagen.

We find in ancient story, Wonders many told,
Of heroes in great glory, With spirit free and bold,
Of joyances, and high-tides, Of weeping and of wo,
Of noble Recken striving, Mote ye now wonders know.

This is the brief artless Proem; and the promise contained in it proceeds directly towards fulfilment. In the very second stanza we learn:—

Es wühs in Burgonden Ein vil edel magedin,
Das in allen landen Niht schoners mohte sin,
Chriemhilt was si gehein Si wart ein schöne wip,
Darumbe müsen degene Vil verliesen den lip.

A right noble maiden Did grow in Burgundy,
That in all lands of earth Nought fairer mote there be;
Chriemhild of Worms she hight, She was a fairest *wife*:
For the which must warriors A many lose their life.*

Chriemhild, this world's-wonder, a king's daughter and king's sister, and no less coy and proud than fair, dreams one night that "she had petted a falcon, strong, beautiful, and wild; which two eagles snatched away from her: this she was forced to see; greater sorrow felt she never in the world." Her mother, Ute, to whom she relates the vision, soon redes it for her; the falcon is a noble husband, whom, God keep him, she must suddenly lose. Chriemhild declares warmly for the single state; as indeed, living there at the Court of Worms, with her brothers, Gunther, Gernot, Geiselher, "three kings noble and rich," in such pomp and renown, the pride of Burgunden-land and Earth, she might readily enough have changed for the worse. However, dame Ute bids her not be too emphatical; for "if ever she have heart-felt joy in life, it will be from man's love, and she shall be a fair wife, (*wip*), when God sends her a right worthy Ritter's *lip*." Chriemhild is more in earnest than maidens usually are when they talk thus; it appears, she guarded against love "for many a lief-long day;" nevertheless, she too must yield to destiny. "Honourably she was to become a most noble Ritter's wife." "This," adds the old Singer, "was that same falcon she dreamed of: how sorely she since revenged him on her nearest kindred! For that one death died full many a mother's son."

It may be observed that the Poet, here, and all times, shows a marked partiality for Chriemhild; ever striving, unlike his fellow singers, to magnify her worth, her faithfulness, and loveliness; and softening, as much as may be, whatever makes against her. No less a favourite with him is Siegfried, the prompt, gay, peaceably fearless hero; to whom, in the Second *Aventiure*, we are here suddenly introduced, at Santen (Xanten) the Court of Netherland; whither, to his glad parents, after achievements (to us partially known) "of which one might sing and tell for ever," that noble prince has returned. Much as he has done and conquered, he is but just arrived at man's

* This is the first of a thousand instances, in which the two inseparables, *Wip* and *Lip*, or in modern tongue, *Weib* and *Leib*, as mentioned above, appear together. From these two opening stanzas of the *Nibelungen Lied*, in its purest form, the reader may obtain some idea of the versification; it runs on in more or less regular Alexandrines, with a cæsural pause in each, where the capital letter occurs; indeed, the lines seem originally to have been divided into two at that point, for sometimes, as in Stanza First, the middle words (*mæren*, *lobebæren*; *geziten*, *striten*) also rhyme; but this is rather a rare case. The word *Rechen* or *Recken*, used in the First Stanza, is the constant designation for bold fighters, and has the same root with *rich*, (thus in old French, *hommes riches*; in Spanish, *ricos hombres*,) which last is here also synonymous with *powerful*, and is applied to kings, and even to the Almighty, *Got dem richen*.

years: it is on occasion of this joyful event, that a high-tide (*hochgezit*) is now held there, with infinite joustings, minstrelsy, largesses, and other chivalrous doings, all which is sung with utmost heartiness. The old King Siegemund offers to resign his crown to him; but Siegfried has other game a-field: the unparalleled beauty of Chriemhild has reached his ear and his fancy; and now he will to Worms, and woo her, at least "see how it stands with her." Fruitless is it for Siegemund and the mother Siegelinde to represent the perils of that enterprise, the pride of those Burgundian Gunthers and Gernots, the fierce temper of their uncle Hagen; Siegfried is as obstinate as young men are in these cases, and can hear no counsel. Nay, he will not accept the much more liberal proposition, to take an army with him, and conquer the country, if it must be so; he will ride forth, like himself, with twelve champions only, and so defy the future. Whereupon, the old people finding that there is no other course, proceed to make him clothes;*—at least, the good queen with "her fair women sitting night and day," and sewing, does so, the father furnishing noblest battle and riding gear;—and so dismiss him with many blessings and lamentations. "For him wept sore the king and his *wife*, but he comforted both their bodies (*lip*); he said, 'ye must not weep, for my body ever shall ye be without care.'"

Sad was it to the Recken, Stood weeping many a maid,
I ween, their heart had them The tidings true foresaid
That of their friends so many Death thereby should find;
Cause had they of lamenting Such boding in their mind.

Nevertheless, on the seventh morning, that adventurous company "ride up the sand," (on the Rhine beach to Worms,) in high temper, in dress and trappings, aspect and bearing, more than kingly.

Siegfried's reception at King Gunther's court, and his brave sayings and doings there for some time, we must omit. One fine trait of his chivalrous delicacy it is that, for a whole year, he never hints at his errand; never once sees or speaks of Chriemhild, whom, nevertheless, he is longing day and night to meet. She, on her side, has often through her lattices noticed the gallant stranger victorious in all tiltings and knightly exercises; whereby it would seem, in spite of her rigorous predeterminations, some kindness for him is already gliding in. Meanwhile, mighty wars and threats of invasion arise, and Siegfried does the state good service. Returning victorious, both as general and soldier, from Hessen, (Hessia,) where, by help of his own courage and the sword Balmung, he has captured a Danish King, and utterly discomfited a Saxon one; he can now show himself before Chriemhild without other blushes than those of timid love. Nay, the maiden has herself inquired pointedly of the messengers, touching his exploits; and "her fair face grew rose-red when she heard them." A gay High-tide, by way of triumph, is appointed; several kings, and two-and-thirty princes, and knights enough with "gold-red saddles," come to joust; and better than whole infinities of kings and princes with their saddles, the fair Chriemhild herself, under guidance of her mother, chiefly too in honour of the victor, is to grace that sport. "Ute the full rich" fails not to set her needle-women to work, and "clothes of price are taken from their presses," for the love of her child, "wherewith to deck many women and maids." And now, "on the Whitsun-morning," all is ready, and glorious as heart could desire it: brave Ritters "five thousand or more," all glancing in the lists; but grander still, Chriemhild herself is advancing beside her mother, with a hundred body-guards, all sword-in-hand and many a noble maid "wearing rich raiment," in her train!

"Now issued forth the lovely one, (*minnechliche*,) as the red morning doth from troubled clouds; much care fled away from him, who bore her in his heart, and long had done; he saw the lovely one stand in her beauty.

"There glanced from her garments full many precious stones, her rose-red colour shone full lovely; try what he might, each man must confess that in this world he had not seen aught so fair.

"Like as the light moon stands before the stars, and its sheen so clear goes over the clouds, even so stood she now before many fair women; whereat cheered was the mind of the hero.

"The rich chamberlains you saw go before her, the high spirited Recken would not forbear, but pressed on where they saw the lovely maiden. Siegfried the lord was both glad and sad.

"He thought in his mind, how could this be that I should woo thee? That was a foolish dream; yet must I for ever be a stranger, I were rather (*sanfter*, softer) dead. He became from these thoughts, in quick changes, pale and red.

"Thus stood so lovely the child of Siegelinde, as if he were limned on parchment by a master's art; for all granted that hero so beautiful they had never seen."

In this passage, which we have rendered, from the Fifth *Aventiure*, into the closest prose, it is to be remarked, among other singularities, that there are two similes: in which figure of speech our old Singer deals very sparingly. The first, that comparison of Chriemhild to the moon among stars with its sheen going over the clouds, has now for many centuries had little novelty or merit; but the second, that of Siegfried to a Figure in some illuminated Manuscript, is graceful in itself; and unspeakably so to antiquaries, seldom honoured, in their Black-letter stubbing and grubbing, with such a poetic windfall.

A prince and a princess of this quality are clearly made for one another. Nay, on the motion of young Herr Gernot, fair Chriemhild is bid specially to salute Siegfried, she who had never before saluted man: which unparalleled grace the lovely one, in all courtliness, openly does him. "Be welcome," said she, "Herr Siegfried, a noble Ritter good;" from which salute, for this seems to have been all, "much raised was his mind." He bowed

* This is a never-failing preparative for all expeditions, and always specified and insisted on with a simple, loving, almost female impressiveness.

with graceful reverence, as his manner was with women; she took him by the hand, and with fond stolen glances, they looked at each other. Whether in that ceremonial joining of hands there might not be some soft, slight pressure, of far deeper import, is what our Singer will not take upon him to say; however, he thinks the affirmative more probable. Henceforth, in that bright May weather, the two were seen constantly together: nothing but felicity around and before them.—In these days, truly, it must have been that the famous Prize-fight with Dietrich of Bern and his eleven Lombardy champions, took place, little to the profit of the two Lovers, were it not rather that the whole of that Rose-garden transaction, as given in the *Heldenbuch*, might be falsified and even imaginary; for no mention or hint of it occurs here. War or battle is not heard of; Siegfried, the peerless, walks wooingly by the side of Chriemhild the peerless: matters, it is evident, are in the best possible course.

But now comes a new side-wind, which, however, in the long run also forwards the voyage. Tidings, namely, reached over the Rhine, not so surprising we might hope, "that there was many a fair maiden;" whereupon Gunther the King "thought with himself to win one of them." It was an honest purpose in King Gunther, only his choice was not the discreetest. For no fair maiden will content him but Queen Brunhild, a lady who rules in *Isenland*, far over sea, famed indeed for her beauty, yet no less for her caprices. Fables we have met with of this Brunhild being properly a *Valkyr*, or Scandinavian Houri, such as were wont to lead old northern warriors from their last battle field, into Valhalla; and that her castle of *Isenstein* stood amidst a lake of fire; but this, as we said, is fable and groundless calumny, of which there is not so much as notice taken here. Brunhild, it is plain enough, was a flesh-and-blood maiden, glorious in look and faculty, only with some preternatural talents given her, and the strangest, wayward habits. It appears, for example, that any suitor proposing for her has this brief condition to proceed upon: he must try the adorable in the three several games of hurling the Spear (at one another), Leaping, and throwing the Stone; if victorious, he gains her hand; if vanquished, he loses his own head; which latter issue, such is the fair Amazon's strength, frequent fatal experiment has shown to be the only probable one.

Siegfried, who knows something of Burnhild and her ways, votes clearly against the whole enterprise; however, Gunther has once for all got the whim in him, and must see it out. The prudent Hagen von Toneg, uncle to love-sick Gunther, and ever true to him, then advises that Siegfried be requested to take part in the adventure; to which request Siegfried readily accedes on one condition; that should they prove fortunate he himself is to have Chriemhild to wife, when they return. This readily settled, he now takes charge of the business, and throws a little light on it for the others. They must lead no army thither, only two, Hagen and Dankwart, besides the king and himself, shall go. The grand subject of *waete** (clothes) is next hinted at, and in general terms elucidated; whereupon a solemn consultation with Chriemhild ensues; and a great cutting out, on her part, of white silk from Araby, of green silk from Zazemang, of strange fish-skins covered with morocco silk; a great sewing thereof for seven weeks, on the part of her maids; lastly a fitting-on of the three suits by each hero, for each had three; and heartiest thanks in return, seeing all fitted perfectly, and was of grace and price unutterable. What is still more to the point, Siegfried takes his Cloak of Darkness with him, fancying he may need it there. The good old Singer, who has hitherto alluded only in the faintest way to Siegfried's prior adventures and miraculous possessions, introduces this of the *Tarnkappe* with great frankness and simplicity. "Of wild dwarfs, (*getwargen*,)" says he, "I have heard tell, they are in hollow mountains, and for defence wear somewhat called *Tarnkappe*, of wondrous sort:" the qualities of which garment, that it renders invisible, and gives twelve men's strength, are already known to us.

The voyage to Isenstein, Siegfried steering the ship thither, is happily accomplished in twenty days. Gunther admires to a high degree the fine masonry of the place; as indeed he well might, there being some eighty-six towers, three immense palaces, and one immense hall, the whole built of "marble green as grass;" farther he sees many fair women looking from the windows down on the bark, and thinks the loveliest is she in the snow-white dress; which, Siegfried informs him, is a worthy choice; the snow-white maiden being no other than Brunhild. It is also to be kept in mind that Siegfried, for reasons known best to himself, had previously stipulated that, though a free king, they should all treat him as vassal of Gunther; for whom accordingly he holds the stirrup, as they mount on the beach; thereby giving rise to a misconception, which in the end led to saddest consequences.

Queen Brunhild, who had called back her maidens from the windows, being a strict disciplinarian, and retired into the interior of her green marble Isenstein, to dress still better, now inquires of some attendant, Who these strangers of such lordly aspect are, and what brings them. The attendant professes himself at a loss to say; one of them looks like Siegfried, the other is evidently by his port a noble king. His notice of Von Troneg Hagen is peculiarly vivid.

The third of those companions, He is of aspect stern,
And yet with lovely body, Rich queen, as ye might discern;
From those *his rapid glances*, For the eyes nought rest in him,
Meseems this foreign Recke Is of temper fierce and grim.

This is one of those little graphic touches, scattered all over our Poem, which do more for picturing out an object, especially a man, than whole pages of enumeration and mensuration. Never after do we hear of this stout, in-

* Hence our English *weeds*, and Scotch *wad* (pledge); and, say the etymologists, *wadding*, and even *wedding*.

domitable Hagen, in all the wild deeds and sufferings he passes through, but those *swinden blicken* of his come before us, with the restless, deep, dauntless spirit that looks through them.

Brunhild's reception of Siegfried is not without tartness; which, however, he, with polished courtesy, and the nimblest address, ever at his command, softens down, or hurries over: he is here, without will of his own, and so forth, only as attendant on his master, the renowned King Gunther, who comes to sue for her hand, as the summit and keystone of all earthly blessings. Brunhild, who had determined on fighting Siegfried himself, if he so willed it, makes small account of this King Gunther, or his prowess; and instantly clears the ground, and equips her for battle. The royal wooer must have looked a little blank when he saw a shield brought in for his fair one's handling, "three spans thick with gold and iron," which four chamberlains could hardly bear, and a spear or javelin she meant to shoot or hurl, which was a burden for three. Hagen, in angry apprehension for his king and nephew, exclaims that they shall all lose their life, (*lip*,) and that she is the *tiuvels wip*, or Devil's wife. Nevertheless Siegfried is already there in his Cloak of Darkness, twelve men strong, and privily whispers in the ear of royalty to be of comfort; takes the shield to himself, Gunther only affecting to hold it, and so fronts the edge of battle. Brunhild performs prodigies of spear-hurling, of leaping, and stone-pitching; but Gunther, or rather Siegfried, "who does the work, he only acting the gestures," nay, who even snatches him up into the air and leaps carrying him,—gains a decided victory, and the lovely Amazon must own with surprise and shame, that she is fairly won. Siegfried presently appears without *Tarnkappe*, and asks with a grave face, When the games then are to begin?

So far well; yet somewhat still remains to be done. Brunhild will not sail for Worms, to be wedded, till she have assembled a fit train of warriors: wherein the Burgundians, being here without retinue, see symptoms or possibilities of mischief. The deft Siegfried, ablest of men, again knows a resource. In his *Tarnkappe* he steps on board the bark, which, seen from the shore, appears to drift off of its own accord; and therein, stoutly steering towards *Nibelungen-land*, he reaches that mysterious country and the mountain where his Hoard lies, before the second morning; finds Dwarf Alberich and all his giant sentinels at their post, and faithful almost to the death; these soon rouse him thirty thousand Nibelungen Recken, from whom he has only to choose one thousand of the best; equip them splendidly enough; and therewith return to Gunther, simply as if they were that sovereign's own body-guard, that had been delayed a little by stress of weather.

The final arrival at Worms; the bridal feasts, for there are two, Siegfried also receiving his reward; and the joyance and splendour of man and maid, at this lordliest of hightides; and the joustings, greater than those at Aspramont or Montauban—every reader can fancy for himself. Remarkable only is the evil eye with which queen Brunhild still continues to regard the noble Siegfried. She cannot understand how Gunther, the Landlord of the Rhine,* should have bestowed his sister on a vassal: the assurance that Siegfried also is a prince and heir-apparent, the prince namely of Netherland, and little inferior to Burgundian majesty itself, yields no complete satisfaction; and Brunhild hints plainly that, unless the truth be told her, unpleasant consequences may follow. Thus is there ever a ravelled thread in the web of life! But for this little cloud of spleen, these bridal feasts had been all bright and balmy as the month of June. Unluckily, too, the cloud is an electric one; spreads itself in time into a general earthquake; nay, that very night becomes a thunder-storm, or tornado, unparalleled we may hope in the annals of connubial happiness.

The Singer of the *Nibelungen*, unlike the Author of *Roderick Random*, cares little for intermeddling with "the chaste mysteries of hymen." Could we, in the corrupt, ambiguous, modern tongue, hope to exhibit any shadow of the old, simple, true-hearted, merely historical spirit, with which, in perfect purity of soul, he describes things unattempted yet in prose or rhyme,—we could a tale unfold! Suffice it to say, King Gunther, Landlord of the Rhine, falling sheer down from the third heaven of hope, finds his spouse the most athletic and intractable of women; and himself, at the close of the adventure, nowise encircled in her arms, but tied hard and fast, hand and foot, in her girdle, and hung thereby, at considerable elevation, on a nail in the wall. Let any reader of sensibility figure the emotions of the royal breast, there as he vibrates suspended on his peg, and his inexorable bride sleeping sound in her bed below! Towards morning he capitulates; engaging to observe the prescribed line of conduct with utmost strictness, so he may but avoid becoming a laughing-stock to all men.

No wonder the dread king looked rather grave next morning, and received the congratulations of mankind in a cold manner. He confesses to Siegfried, who partly suspects how it may be, that he has brought the "evil devil" home to his house in the shape of wife, whereby he is wretched enough. However, there are remedies for all things but death. The ever-serviceable Siegfried undertakes even here to make the crooked straight. What may not an honest friend with Tarnkappe and twelve men's strength perform? Proud Brunhild, next night, after a fierce contest, owns herself again vanquished; Gunther is there to reap the fruits of another's victory; the noble Siegfried withdraws, taking nothing with him but the luxury of doing good, and the proud queen's Ring and Girdle gained from her in that struggle; which small trophies he, with the last infirmity of a noble mind, presents to his own fond wife, little dreaming that they would one day cost him and her, and all of

* *Der Wirt vom Rine:* singular enough the word *Wirth*, often applied to royalty in that old dialect, is now also the title of innkeepers. To such base uses may we come.

them, so dear. Such readers as take any interest in poor Gunther will be gratified to learn, that from this hour Brunhild's preternatural faculties quite left her, being all dependent on her maidhood; so that any more spear-hurling, or other the like extraordinary work, is not to be apprehended from her.

If we add that Siegfried formally made over to his dear Chriemhild the Nibelungen Hoard, by way of *Morgengabe*, (or, as we may say, Jointure;) and the high-tide, though not the honeymoon being past, returned to Netherland with his spouse, to be welcomed there with infinite rejoicings,—we have gone through as it were the First Act of this Tragedy, and may here pause to look round us for a moment. The main characters are now introduced on the scene, the relations that bind them together are dimly sketched out: there is the prompt, cheerfully heroic, invulnerable, and invincible Siegfried, now happiest of men; the high Chriemhild, fitly-mated, and if a moon, revolving gloriously round her sun, or *Friedel* (joy and darling); not without pride and female aspirings, yet not prouder than one so gifted and placed is pardonable for being. On the other hand, we have King Gunther, or rather let us say king's-mantle Gunther, for never except in that one enterprise of courting Brunhild, in which too, without help, he would have cut so poor a figure, does the worthy sovereign show will of his own, or character other than that of good potter's clay; farther, the suspicious, forecasting, yet stout and reckless Hagen, him with the *rapid glances*, and these turned not too kindly on Siegfried, whose prowess he has used yet dreads, whose Nibelungen Hoard he perhaps already covets; lastly, the rigorous and vigorous Brunhild, of whom also more is to be feared than hoped. Considering the fierce nature of these now mingled ingredients, and how, except perhaps in the case of Gunther there is no menstruum of placid stupidity to soften them, except in Siegfried, no element of heroic truth to master them and bind them together,—unquiet fermentation may readily be apprehended.

Meanwhile, for a season all is peace and sunshine. Siegfried reigns in Netherland, of which his father has surrendered him the crown; Chriemhild brings him a son, whom in honour of the uncle he christens Gunther, which courtesy the uncle and Brunhild repay in kind. The Nibelungen Hoard is still open and inexhaustible; Dwarf Alberich and all the Recken there still loyal; outward relations friendly, internal supremely prosperous: these are halcyon days. But, alas, they cannot last. Queen Brunhild, retaining with true female tenacity her first notion, right or wrong, reflects one day that Siegfried, who is and shall be nothing but her husband's vassal, has for a long while paid him no service; and, determined on a remedy, manages that Siegfried and his queen shall be invited to a high-tide at Worms, where opportunity may chance for enforcing that claim. Thither accordingly, after ten years' absence, we find these illustrious guests returning; Siegfried escorted by a thousand Nibelungen Ritters, and farther by his father Siegemund, who leads a train of Netherlanders. Here for eleven days, amid infinite joustings, there is a true heaven on earth: but the apple of Discord is already lying in the knightly ring, and two Women, the proudest and keenest-tempered of the world, simultaneously stoop to lift it. *Aventiure* Fourteenth is entitled "How the two queens rated one another." Never was courtlier Billingsgate uttered, or which came more directly home to the business and bosoms of women. The subject is that old story of Precedence, which indeed, from the time of Cain and Abel downwards, has wrought such effusion of blood and bile both among men and women; lying at the bottom of all armaments and battle-fields, whether Blenheims and Waterloos, or any plate-displays, and tongue-and eye skirmishes, in the circle of domestic Tea: nay, the very animals have it; and horses, were they but the miserablest Shelties and Welsh ponies, will not graze together till it has been ascertained, by clear fight, who is master of whom, and a proper drawing-room etiquette established.

Brunhild and Chriemhild take to arguing about the merits of their husbands: the latter fondly expatiating on the pre-eminence of her *Friedel*, how he walks "like the moon among stars" before all other men, is reminded by her sister that one man at least must be excepted, the mighty king Gunther of Worms, to whom, by his own confession long ago at Isenstein, he is vassal and servant. Chriemhild will sooner admit that clay is above sunbeams, than any such proposition; which therefore she, in all politeness, requests of her sister never more to touch upon while she lives. The result may be foreseen: rejoinder follows reply, statement grows assertion; flint-sparks have fallen on the dry flax, which from smoke bursts into conflagration. The two queens part in hottest, though still clear-flaming anger. Not, however, to let their anger burn out, only to feed it with more solid fuel. Chriemhild dresses her forty maids in finer than royal apparel; orders out all her husband's Recken; and so attended, walks foremost to the Minster, where mass is to be said; thus practically asserting that she is not only a true queen, but the worthier of the two. Brunhild, quite outdone in splendour, and enraged beyond all patience, overtakes her at the door of the Minster, with peremptory order to stop: "before king's wife shall vassal's never go."

Then said the fair Chriemhilde, Right angry was her mood:
"Couldest thou but hold thy peace, It were surely for thy good,
Thyself hast all polluted With shame thy fair bodye;
How can a Concubine By right a King's wife be?"

"Whom hast thou Concubined?" The King's wife quickly spake;
"That do I thee," said Chriemhilde; "For thy pride and vaunting's sake;
Who first had thy fair body Was Siegfried my beloved Man;
My brother was it not That thy maidhood from thee wan."

In proof of which outrageous saying, she produces that Ring and Girdle; the innocent conquest of which, as we well know, had a far other origin. Brunhild bursts into tears; "sadder day she never saw." Nay, perhaps a new light now rose on her over much that had been dark in her late history; "she rued full sore that ever she was born."

Here, then, is the black injury, which only blood will wash away. The evil fiend has begun his work; and the issue of it lies beyond man's control. Siegfried may protest his innocence of that calumny, and chastise his indiscreet spouse for uttering it even in the heat of anger: the female heart is wounded beyond healing; the old springs of bitterness against this hero unite into a fell flood of hate; while he sees the sunlight, she cannot know a joyful hour. Vengeance is soon offered her: Hagen, who lives only for his prince, undertakes this bad service; by treacherous professions of attachment, and anxiety to guard Siegfried's life, he gains from Chriemhild the secret of his vulnerability; Siegfried is carried out to hunt; and in the hour of frankest gayety is stabbed through the fatal spot; and, felling the murderer to the ground, dies upbraiding his false kindred, yet, with a touching simplicity, recommending his child and wife to their protection. "Let her feel that she is your sister; was there ever virtue in princes, be true to her: for me my Father and my men shall long wait." "The flowers all round were wetted with blood, then he struggled with death; not long did he this, the weapon cut him too keen; so he could speak nought more. the Recke bold and noble."

At this point, we might say, ends the Third Act of our Tragedy; the whole story henceforth takes a darker character; it is as if a tone of sorrow and fateful boding became more and more audible in its free, light music. Evil has produced new evil in fatal augmentation: injury is abolished; but in its stead there is guilt and despair. Chriemhild, an hour ago so rich, is now robbed of all: her grief is boundless as her love has been. No glad thought can ever more dwell in her; darkness, utter night, has come over her, as she looked into the red of morning. The spoiler too walks abroad unpunished; the bleeding corpse witnesses against Hagen, nay he himself cares not to hide the deed. But who is there to avenge the friendless? Siegfried's father has returned in haste to his own land; Chriemhild is now alone on the earth, her husband's grave is all that remains to her; there only can she sit, as if waiting at the threshold of her own dark home; and in prayers and tears, pour out the sorrow and love that have no end. Still farther injuries are heaped on her: by advice of the crafty Hagen, Gunther, who had not planned the murder, yet permitted and witnessed it, now comes with whining professions of repentance and good-will; persuades her to send for the Nibelungen Hoard to Worms: where no sooner is it arrived, than Hagen and the rest forcibly take it from her; and her last trust in affection or truth from mortal is rudely cut away. Bent to the earth, she weeps only for her lost Siegfried, knows no comfort, but will weep for ever.

One lurid gleam of hope, after long years of darkness, breaks in on her, in the prospect of revenge. King Etzel sends from his far country to solicit her hand: the embassy she hears at first, as a woman of ice might do; the good Rudiger, Etzel's spokesman, pleads in vain that his king is the richest of all earthly kings; that he is so lonely "since Frau Helke died;" that though a Heathen he has Christians about him, and may one day be converted: till, at length, when he hints distantly at the power of Etzel to avenge her injuries, she on a sudden becomes all attention. Hagen, foreseeing such possibilities, protests against the match; but is overruled: Chriemhild departs with Rudiger for the land of the Huns; taking cold leave of her relations; only two of whom, her brothers Gernot and Geiselher, innocent of that murder, does she admit near her as convoy to the Donau.

The Nibelungen Hoard has hitherto been fatal to all its possessors; to the two sons of Nibelung; to Siegfried its conqueror: neither does the Burgundian Royal House fare better with it. Already, discords threatening to arise, Hagen sees prudent to sink it in the Rhine; first taking oath of Gunther and his brothers, that none of them shall reveal the hiding-place, while any of the rest is alive. But the curse that clave to it could not be sunk there. The Nibelungen-land is now theirs: they themselves are henceforth called Nibelungen; and this history of their fate is the Nibelungen Song, or *Nibelungen Noth*, (Nibelungen's Need, extreme need, or final wreck and abolition.)

The Fifth Act of our strange eventful history now draws on. Chriemhild has a kind husband, of hospitable disposition, who troubles himself little about her secret feelings and intents. With his permission, she sends two minstrels, inviting the Burgundian Court to a high-tide, at Etzel's: she has charged the messengers to say that she is happy, and to bring all Gunther's champions with them. Her eye was on Hagen, but she could not single him from the rest. After seven days' deliberation, Gunther answers that he will come. Hagen has loudly dissuaded the journey, but again been overruled. "It is his fate," says a commentator, "like Cassandra's, ever to foresee the evil, and ever to be disregarded. He himself shut his ear against the inward voice; and now his warnings are uttered to the deaf." He argues long, but in vain: nay, young Gernot hints at last that this aversion originates in personal fear:

> Then spake Von Troneg Hagen: "Nowise is it through fear;
> So you command it, Heroes, Then up, gird on your gear;
> I ride with you the foremost Into King Etzel's land."
> Since then full many a helm Was shivered by his hand.

Frau Ute's dreams and omens are now unavailing with him; "whoso heedeth dreams," said Hagen, "of the right story wotteth not:" he has computed the worst issue, and defied it.

Many a little touch of pathos, and even solemn beauty lies carelessly scattered in these rhymes, had we space to exhibit such here. As specimen of a strange, winding, diffuse, yet innocently graceful style of narrative, we had translated some considerable portion of this Twenty-fifth *Aventiure*, "How the Nibelungen marched (fared) to the Huns," into verses as literal as might be; which now, alas, look mournfully different from the original; almost like Scriblerus's shield when the barbarian housemaid had scoured it. Nevertheless, to do for the reader what we can, let somewhat of that modernized ware, such as it is, be set before him. The brave Nibelungen are on the eve of departure; and about ferrying over the Rhine; and here it may be noted that Worms,* with our old Singer, lies not in its true position, but at some distance from the river; a proof at least that he was never there, and probably sang and lived in some very distant region:

The boats were floating ready, And many men there were;
What clothes of price they had They took and stow'd them there,
Was never a rest from toiling Until the even tide,
Then they took the flood right gaily, Would longer not abide.

Brave tents and hutches You saw raised on the grass,
Other side the Rhine-stream That camp it pitched was:
The king to stay a while Was besought of his fair wife;
That night she saw him with her, And never more in life.

Trumpets and flutes spoke out, At dawning of the day,
That time was come for parting, So they rose to march away:
Who loved-one had in arms Did kiss that same, I ween;
And fond farewells were bidden By cause of Etzel's Queen.

Frau Ute's noble sons They had a serving man,
A brave one and a true: Or ever the march began,
He speaketh to King Gunther, What for his ear was fit,
He said: "Wo for this journey, I grieve because of it."

He Rumold hight, the Sewer, Was known as hero true;
He spake: "Whom shall his people And land be trusted to?
Wo on't, will nought persuade ye, Brave Recken, from this road!
Frau Chriemhild's flattering message No good doth seem to bode."

"The land to thee be trusted, And my fair boy also,
And serve thou well the women, I tell thee ere I go,
Whomso thou findest weeping Her heart give comfort to:
No harm to one of us King Etzel's wife will do."

The steeds were standing ready, For the Kings and for their men;
With kisses tenderest, Took leave full many then,
Who, in gallant cheer and hope, To march were nought afraid!
Them since that day bewaileth Many a noble wife and maid.

But when the rapid Recken Took horse and prickt away,
The women shent in sorrow You saw behind them stay;
Of parting all too long Their hearts to them did tell;
When grief so great is coming, The mind forebodes not well.

Nathless the brisk Burgonden All on their way did go,
Then rose the country over A mickle dole and wo;
On both sides of the hills, Woman and man did weep:
Let their folk do how they list, These gay their course did keep.

The Nibelungen Recken*, Did march with them as well,
In a thousand glittering hauberks, Who at home had ta'en farewell
Of many a fair woman Should see them never more:
The wound of her brave Siegfried Did grieve Chriemhilde sore.

Then 'gan they shape their journey Towards the River Maine,
All on through East-Franconia, King Gunther and his train:
Hagen he was their leader, Of old did know the way,
Dankwart did keep, as marshal, their ranks in good array.

As they, from East-Franconia, The Salfield rode along,
Might you have seen them prancing, A bright and lordly throng,
The Princes and their vassals, All heroes of great fame:
The twelfth morn brave king Gunther Unto the Donau came.

There rode Von Troneg Hagen, The foremost of that host,
He was to the Nibelungen The guide they loved the most:
The Ritter keen dismounted, Set foot on the sandy ground,
His steed to a tree he tied, Look'd wistful all around.

"Much scaith," Von Troneg said, "May lightly chance to thee,
King Gunther, by this tide, As thou with eyes mayst see:
The river is overflowing, Full strong runs here its stream,
For crossing of this Donau Some counsel might well beseem."

"What counsel hast thou, brave Hagen," King Gunther then did say,
Of thy own wit and cunning? Dishearten me not I pray:
Thyself the ford will find us, If knightly skill it can,
That safe to yonder shore We may pass both horse and man."

* This City of Worms, had we a right imagination, ought to be as venerable to us Moderns, as any Thebes or Troy was to the Ancients. Whether founded by the Gods or not, it is of quite unknown antiquity, and has witnessed the most wonderful things. Within authentic times, the Romans were here, and if tradition may be credited, Attila also; it was the seat of the Austrasian kings; the frequent residence of Charlemagne himself; innumerable Festivals, Hightides, Tournaments, and Imperial Diets were held in it, of which latter, one at least, that where Luther appeared in 1521, will be for ever remembered by all mankind. Nor is Worms more famous in history than, as indeed we may see here, it is in romance; whereof many monuments and vestiges remain to *this day*. "A pleasant meadow there," says Von der Hagen, "is still called Chriemhild's *Rosengarten*. The name *Worms* itself is derived (by Legendary Etymology) from the Dragon, or *Worm*, which Siegfried slew, the figure of which once formed the City Arms; in past times, there was also to be seen here an ancient strong *Riesen-Haus*, (Giant's house,) and many a memorial of Siegfried: his Lance, 60 feet long, (almost 80 English feet,) in the Cathedral; his Statue, of gigantic size on the *Neue Thurm* (New Tower) on the Rhine;" &c. &c. "And lastly the Siegfried's Chapel, in primeval Pre-Gothic architecture, not long since pulled down. In the time of the *Meistersängers*, too, the Stadtrath was bound to give every Master, who sang the Lay of Siegfried (*Meisterlied von Siegfrieden*, the purport of which is now unknown) without mistake, a certain gratuity."—*Glossary* to the *Nibelungen*, § *Worms*.

One is sorry to learn that this famed Imperial City is no longer Imperial, but much fallen in every way from its palmy state; the 30,000 inhabitants (to be found there in Gustavus Adolphus's time) having now declined into some 6,800,—"who maintain themselves by wine-growing, Rhine-boats, tobacco-manufacture, and making sugar-of-lead." So hard has war, which respects nothing, pressed on Worms, ill-placed for safety, on the hostile border: Louvois, or Louis XIV., in 1689, had it utterly devastated; whereby in the interior, "spaces that were once covered with buildings are now gardens."—See *Conv. Lexicon*, § *Worms*.

* These are the Nibelungen proper who had come to Worms with Siegfried, on the famed bridal journey from Isenstein, long ago. Observe, at the same time, that ever since the *Nibelungen Hoard* was transferred to Rhineland, the whole subjects of King Gunther are often called Nibelungen, and their subsequent history is this *Nibelungen Song*.

"To me I trow," spake Hagen, "Life hath not grown so cheap,
To go with will and drown me In riding these waters deep;
But first, of men some few By this hand of mine shall die,
In great King Etzel's country, As best good will have I.

"But bide ye here by the River, Ye Ritters brisk and sound,
Myself will seek some boatman, If boatman, here be found,
To row us at his ferry, Across to Gelfrat's land:"
The Troneger grasped his buckler, Fared forth along the strand.

He was full bravely harness'd, Himself the knightly bore,
With buckler and with helmet, Which bright enough he wore:
And, bound above his hauberk, A weapon broad was seen,
That cut with both its edges, Was never sword so keen.

Then hither he and thither Search'd for the Ferryman,
He heard a splashing of waters, To watch the same he 'gan;
It was the white Mer-women, That in a Fountain clear,
To cool their fair bodyes, Were merrily bathing here.

From these Mer-women, who "skimmed aloof like white cygnets, at sight of him," Hagen snatches up "their wondrous raiment;" on condition of returning which, they rede him his fortune; how this expedition is to speed. At first favourably:

She said: "To Etzel's country, Of a truth ye well may hie,
For here I pledge my hand, Now kill me if I lie;
That heroes seeking honour Did never arrive thereat
So richly as ye shall do, Believe thou surely that."

But no sooner is the wondrous raiment restored them, than they change their tale; for in spite of that matchless honour, it appears, every one of the adventurous Recken is to perish.

Outspake the wild Mer-woman: "I tell thee it will arrive,
Of all your gallant host No man shall be left alive,
Except king Gunther's chaplain, As we full well do know;
He only, home returning, To the Rhine-land back shall go."

Then spake Von Troneg Hagen, His wroth did fiercely swell:
"Such tidings to my master I were right wroth to tell,
That in king Etzel's country We all must lose our life:
Yet show me over the water, Thou wise all-knowing *wife*."

Thereupon, seeing him bent on ruin, she gives directions how to find the ferry, but withal counsels him to deal warily: the ferry-house stands on the other side of the river; the boatman, too, is not only the hottest-tempered of men, but rich and indolent; nevertheless, if nothing else will serve, let Hagen call himself Amelrich, and that name will bring him. All happens as predicted: the boatman, heedless of all shouting and offers of gold clasps, bestirs himself lustily at the name of Amelrich; but the more indignant is he, on taking in his fare, to find it a counterfeit. He orders Hagen, if he loves his life, to leap out.

"Now say not that," spake Hagen; "Right hard am I bested,
Take from me for good friendship This clasp of gold so red;
And row our thousand heroes And steeds across this river:"
Then spake the wrathful boatman, "That will I surely never."

Then one of his oars he lifted, Right broad it was and long,
He struck it down on Hagen, Did the hero mickle wrong,
That in the boat he staggered, and alighted on his knee;
Other such wrathful boatman Did never the Troneger see.

His proud unbidden guest He would now provoke still more,
He struck his head so stoutly That it broke in twain the oar,
With strokes on head of Hagen; He was a sturdy wight:
Nathless had Gelfrat's boatman Small profit of that fight.

With fiercely raging spirit, the Troneger turn'd him round,
Clutch'd quick enough his scabbard, And a weapon there he found;
He smote his head from off him, And cast it on the sand,
Thus had that wrathful boatman His death from Hagen's hand.

Even as Von Troneg Hagen The wrathful boatmen slew,
The boat whirl'd round to the river, He had work enough to do;
Or ever he turn'd it shorewards, To weary he began,
But kept full stoutly rowing, The bold king Gunther's man.

He wheel'd it back brave Hagen, With many a lusty stroke,
The strong oar, with such rowing, In his hand asunder broke;
He fain would reach the Recken, All waiting on the shore,
No tackle now he had; Hei,* how deftly he spliced the oar.

With throng from off his buckler! It was a slender band;
Right over against a forest He drove the boat to land;
Where Gunther's Recken waited, In crowds along the beach;
Full many a goodly hero Moved down his boat to reach.

Hagen ferries them over himself "into the unknown land," like a right yare steersman; yet ever brooding fiercely on that prediction of the wild Mer-woman, which had outdone even his own dark forebodings. Seeing the Chaplain, who alone of them all was to return, standing in the boat beside his *chappelsoume*, (pyxes and other sacred furniture,) he determines to belie at least this part of the prophecy, and on a sudden hurls the chaplain overboard. Nay, as the poor priest swims after the boat, he pushes him down, regardless of all remonstrance, resolved that he shall die. Nevertheless it proved not so: the chaplain made for the other side; when his strength failed, "then God's hand helped him," and at length he reached the shore. Thus does the stern truth stand revealed to Hagen by the very

* These apparently insignificant circumstances, down even to mending the oar from his shield, are preserved with a singular fidelity, in the most distorted editions of the tale: see, for example, the Danish ballad, *Lady Grimhild's Wrack* (translated in the *Northern Antiquities*, p. 275, by Mr. Jamieson.) This "*Hei!*" is a brisk interjection, whereby the worthy old Singer now and then introduces his own person, when any thing very eminent is going forward.

means he took for eluding it: "he thought with himself these Recken must all lose their lives." From this time, a grim reckless spirit takes possession of him; a courage, an audacity, waxing more and more into the fixed strength of desperation. The passage once finished, he dashes the boat in pieces, and casts it in the stream, greatly as the others wonder at him.

"Why do ye this, good brother?" Said the Ritter Dankwart then,
"How shall we cross this river, When the road we come again?
Returning home from Hunland, Here must we lingering stay?"
Not then did Hagen tell him That return no more could they.

In this shipment "into the unknown land" there lies, for the more penetrating sort of commentators, some hidden meaning and allusion. The destruction of the unreturning Ship, as of the Ship Argo, of Æneas's Ships, and the like, is a constant feature of such traditions: it is thought, this ferrying of the Nibelungen has a reference to old Scandinavian Mythuses; nay, to the oldest, most universal emblems shaped out by man's Imagination; Hagen the ferryman being, in some sort, a type of Death, who ferries over his thousands and tens of thousands into a Land still more unknown.*

But leaving these considerations, let us remark the deep fearful interest, which, in gathering strength, rises to a really tragical height in the close of this Poem. Strangely has the old Singer, in these his loose melodies, modulated the wild narrative into a poetic whole, with what we might call true art, were it not rather an instinct of genius still more unerring. A fateful gloom now hangs over the fortunes of the Nibelungen, which deepens and deepens as they march onwards to the judgment-bar, till all are engulphed in utter night.

Hagen himself rises in tragic greatness; so helpful, so prompt and strong is he, and true to the death, though without hope. If sin can ever be pardoned, then that one act of his is pardonable; by loyal faith, by free daring, and heroic constancy, he has made amends for it. Well does he know what is coming; yet he goes forth to meet it, offers to Ruin his sullen welcome. Warnings thicken on him, which he treats lightly, as things now superfluous. Spite of our love for Siegfried, we must pity and almost respect the lost Hagen, now in his extreme need, and fronting it so nobly. "Mixed was his hair with a gray colour, his limbs strong, and threatening his look." Nay, his sterner qualities are beautifully tempered by another feeling, of which till now we understood not that he was capable,—the feeling of friendship. There is a certain Volker of Alsace here introduced, not for the first time, yet first in decided energy, who is more to Hagen than a brother. This Volker, a courtier and noble, is also a *Spielmann*, (minstrel,) a *Fidelere gut*, (fiddler good;) and surely the prince of all *Fideleres*; in truth a very phœnix, melodious as the soft nightingale, yet strong as the royal eagle: for also in the brunt of battle he can play tunes; and with a *Steel Fiddlebow*, beats strange music from the cleft helmets of his enemies. There is, in this continual allusion to Volker's *Schwertfidelbogen*, (Sword-fiddlebow,) as rude as it sounds to us, a barbaric greatness and depth; the light minstrel of kingly and queenly halls is gay also in the storm of Fate, its dire rushing pipes and whistles, to him: is he not the image of every brave man fighting with Necessity, be that duel when and where it may; smiting the fiend with giant strokes, yet every stroke *musical?*—This Volker and Hagen are united inseparably, and defy death together. "Whatever Volker said pleased Hagen; whatever Hagen did pleased Volker."

But into these last Ten *Aventiures*, almost like the image of a Doomsday, we must hardly glance at present. Seldom, perhaps, in the poetry of that or any other age, has a grander scene of pity and terror been exhibited than here, could we look into it clearly. At every new step new shapes of fear arise. Dietrich of Bern meets the Nibelungen on their way, with ominous warnings: but warnings, as we said, are now superfluous, when the evil itself is apparent and inevitable. Chriemhild, wasted and exasperated here into a frightful Medea, openly threatens Hagen, but is openly defied by him; he and Volker retire to a seat before her palace, and sit there, while she advances in angry tears, with a crowd of armed Huns to destroy them. But Hagen has Siegfried's Balmung lying naked on his knee, the Minstrel also has drawn his keen Fiddlebow, and the Huns dare not provoke the battle. Chriemhild would fain single out Hagen for vengeance; but Hagen, like other men, stands not alone: and sin is an infection which will not rest with one victim. Partakers or not of his crime, the others also must share his punishment. Singularly touching, in the meanwhile, is king Etzel's ignorance of what every one else understands too well; and how, in peaceful hospitable spirit, he exerts himself to testify his joy over these royal guests of his, who are bidden hither for far other ends. That night the wayworn Nibelungen are sumptuously lodged; yet Hagen and Volker see good to keep watch: Volker plays them to sleep: "under the door of the house he sat on the stone: bolder fiddler was there never any; when the tones flowed so sweetly they all gave him thanks. Then sounded his strings till all the house rang; his strength and the art were great, sweeter and sweeter he began to play, till flitted forth from him into sleep full many a care-worn soul." It was their last lullaby; they were to sleep no more. Armed men appear, but suddenly vanish, in the night; assassins sent by Chriemhild, expecting no sentinel: it is plain that the last hour draws nigh.

In the morning the Nibelungen are for the Minster to hear mass; they are putting on gay raiment; but Hagen tells them a different tale: "Ye must take other garments, Recken;" "instead of silk shirts, hauberks; for rich mantles your good shields;" "and, beloved masters, moreover squires and men, ye shall

* See Von der Hagen's *Nibelungen ihre Bedeutung*, &c.

full earnestly go to the church, and plain to God the powerful (*Got dem richen*) of your sorrow and utmost need; and know of a surety that death for us is nigh." In Etzel's Hall, where the Nibelungen appear at the royal feast in complete armour, the Strife, incited by Chriemhild, begins: the first answer to her provocation is from Hagen, who hews off the head of her own and Etzel's son, making it bound into the mother's bosom:" "then began among the Recken a murder grim and great." Dietrich, with a voice of preternatural power, commands pause; retires with Etzel and Chriemhild; and now the bloody work has free course. We have heard of battles, and massacres, and deadly struggles in siege and storm; but seldom has even the poet's imagination pictured any thing so fierce and terrible as this. Host after host, as they enter that huge vaulted Hall, perish in the conflict with the doomed Nibelungen; and even after the terrific uproar, ensues a still more terrific silence. All night, and through morning it lasts. They throw the dead from the windows; blood runs like water; the Hall is set fire to, they quench it with blood, their own burning thirst they slake with blood. It is a tumult like the Crack of Doom, a thousand voiced, wild stunning hubbub: and, frightful like a Trump of Doom, the *Sword-fiddlebow* of Volker, who guards the door, makes music to that death-dance. Nor are traits of heroism wanting, and thrilling tones of pity and love; as in that act of Rudiger, Etzel's and Chriemhild's champion, who, bound by oath, "lays his soul in God's hand," and enters that Golgotha to die fighting against his friends; yet first changes shields with Hagen, whose own, also given him by Rudiger in a far other hour, had been shattered in the fight. "When he so lovingly bade give him the shield, there were eyes enough red with hot tears; it was the last gift which Rudiger of Bechelaren gave to any Recke. As grim as Hagen was, and as hard of mind, he wept at this gift which the hero good, so near his last times, had given him; full many a noble Ritter began to weep."

At last Volker is slain; they are all slain, save only Hagen and Gunther, faint and wounded, yet still unconquered among the bodies of the dead. Dietrich the wary, though strong and invincible, whose Recken too, except old Hildebrand, he now finds are all killed, though he had charged them strictly not to mix in the quarrel, at last arms himself to finish it. He subdues the two wearied Nibelungen, binds them, delivers them to Chriemhild; "and Herr Dietrich went away with weeping eyes, worthily from the heroes." These never saw each other more. Chriemhild demands of Hagen, Where the Nibelungen Hoard is? But he answers her that he has sworn never to disclose it, while any of her brothers live. "I bring it to an end," said the infuriated woman; orders her brother's head to be struck off, and holds it up to Hagen. "Thou hast it now according to thy will," said Hagen; "of the Hoard knoweth none but God and I; from thee, she-devil, (*Valendinne,*) shall it for ever be hid." She kills him with his own sword, once her husband's; and is herself struck dead by Hildebrand, indignant at the wo she has wrought; King Etzel, there present, not opposing the deed. Whereupon the curtain drops over that wild scene, "the full highly honoured were lying dead; the people, all had sorrow and lamentation, in grief had the king's feast ended, as all love is wont to do;

Ine chan iu nicht bescheiden Waz sider da geschach,
Wan ritter unde wrovven Weinen man do sach
Dar-zuo die edeln chnechte Ir lieben vriunde tot:
Da hat das mære ein ende; Diz ist der Nibelunge not.

I cannot say you now What hath befallen since,
The women all were weeping, And the Ritters and the prince,
Also the noble squires, Their dear friends lying dead:
Here hath the story ending; This is the *Nibelungen's Need.*

We have now finished our slight analysis of this Poem; and hope that readers, who are curious in this matter, and ask themselves, What is the *Nibelungen?* may have here found some outlines of an answer, some help towards farther researches of their own. To such readers another question will suggest itself: Whence this singular production comes to us, When and How it originated? On which point also, what little light our investigation has yielded may be summarily given.

The worthy Von der Hagen, who may well understand the *Nibelungen* better than any other man, having rendered it into the modern tongue, and twice edited it in the original, not without collating some eleven manuscripts, and travelling several thousands of miles to make the last edition perfect,—writes a Book some years ago, rather boldly denominated *The Nibelungen, its meaning for the present and for ever;* wherein, not content with any measurable antiquity of centuries, he would fain claim an antiquity beyond all bounds of dated time. Working his way with feeble mine-lamps of etymology and the like, he traces back the rudiments of his beloved *Nibelungen,* "to which the flower of his whole life has been consecrated," into the thick darkness of the Scandinavian *Niflheim und Muspelheim,* and the Hindoo Cosmogony; connecting it farther (as already in part we have incidentally pointed out) with the Ship Argo, with Jupiter's goatskin Ægis, the fire-creed of Zerdusht, and even with the heavenly Constellations. His reasoning is somewhat abstruse; yet an honest zeal, very considerable learning and intellectual force bring him tolerably through. So much he renders plausible or probable: that in the *Nibelungen,* under more or less defacement, lie fragments, scattered like mysterious Runes, yet still in part decipherable, of the earliest Thoughts of men; that the fiction of the Nibelungen was at first a religious or philosophical Mythus; and only in later ages, incorporating itself more or less completely with vague traditions of real events, took the form of a story, or mere Narrative of earthly transactions; in which last form, moreover, our actual *Nibelungen Lied* is nowise the original Narrative, but the second, or even third redaction of one much earlier.

At what particular era the primeval fiction

of the *Nibelungen* passed from its Mythological into its Historical shape; and the obscure spiritual elements of it wedded themselves to the obscure remembrances of the Northern Immigrations; and the Twelve Signs of the Zodiac became Twelve Champions of Attila's Wife,—there is no fixing with the smallest certainty. It is known from history that Eginhart, the secretary of Charlemagne, compiled, by order of that monarch, a collection of the ancient German Songs; among which, it is fondly believed by antiquaries, this *Nibelungen*, (not indeed our actual *Nibelungen Lied*, yet an older one of similar purport,) and the main traditions of the *Heldenbuch* connected therewith, may have had honourable place. Unluckily Eginhart's Collection has quite perished; and only his Life of the Great Charles, in which this circumstance stands noted, survives to provoke curiosity. One thing is certain, Fulco, Archbishop of Rheims, in the year 885, is introduced as "citing certain German books," to enforce some argument of his by instance of "King Ermerich's crime towards his relations;" which King Ermerich and his crime are at this day part and parcel of the "Cycle of German Fiction," and presupposed in the *Nibelungen*.* Later notices, of a more decisive sort, occur in abundance. Saxo Grammaticus, who flourished in the twelfth century, relates that about the year 1130, a Saxon minstrel being sent to Seeland, with a treacherous invitation from one royal Dane to another; and not daring to violate his oath, yet compassionating the victim, sang to him by way of indirect warning "the Song of Chriemhild's Treachery to her Brothers;" that is to say, the latter portion of the Story which we still read at greater length in the existing *Nibelungen Lied*. To which direct evidence, that these traditions were universally known in the twelfth century, nay, had been in some shape committed to writing, as "German Books," in the ninth or rather in the eighth,—we have still to add the probability of their being "ancient songs," even at that earliest date; all which may perhaps carry us back into the seventh or even sixth century; yet not farther, inasmuch as certain of the poetic personages that figure in them belong historically to the fifth.

Other and more open proof of antiquity lies in the fact, that these Traditions are so universally diffused. There are Danish and Icelandic versions of them, externally more or less altered and distorted, yet substantially real copies, professing indeed to be borrowed from the German; in particular we have the *Niflinga* and the *Wilkina Saga*, composed in the thirteenth century, which still in many ways illustrate the German original. Innumerable other songs and sagas point more remotely in the same direction. Nay, as Von der Hagen informs us, certain rhymed tales, founded on these old adventures, have been recovered from popular recitation, in the Faroe Islands, within these few years.

If we ask now, what lineaments of Fact still exist in these Traditions; what are the Historical events and persons which our primeval Mythuses have here united with, and so strangely metamorphosed? the answer is unsatisfactory enough. The great Northern Immigrations, unspeakably momentous and glorious as they were for the Germans, have well nigh faded away utterly from all vernacular records. Some traces, nevertheless, some names, and dim shadows of occurrences in that grand movement, still linger here: which, in such circumstances, we gather with avidity. There can be no doubt, for example, but this "Etzel, king of Hunland," is the Attila of history; several of whose real achievements and relations are faintly, yet still recognisably pictured forth in these Poems. Thus his first queen is named Halke, and in the Scandinavian versions, Herka; which last (Erca) is also the name that Priscus gives her, in the well-known Account of his embassy to Attila. Moreover, it is on his second marriage, which had in fact so mysterious and tragical a character, that the whole catastrophe of the *Nibelungen* turns. It is true, the "Scourge of God" plays but a tame part here; however, his great acts, though all past, are still visible in their fruits: besides, it is on the Northern or German personages that the tradition chiefly dwells.

Taking farther into account the general "Cycle" or System of Northern Tradition, whereof this *Nibelungen* is the centre and keystone, there is, as indeed we saw in the *Heldenbuch*, a certain Kaiser Ottnit and a Dietrich of Bern; to whom also it seems unreasonable to deny historical existence. This *Bern*, (Verona,) as well as the *Rabenschlacht*, (Battle of Ravenna,) is continually figuring in these Fictions; though whether under Ottnit we are to understand Odoacer the vanquished, and under Dietrich of Bern, Theodoricus Veronensis, the victor both at Verona and Ravenna, is by no means so indubitable. Chronological difficulties stand much in the way. For our Dietrich of Bern, as we saw in the *Nibelungen*, is represented as one of Etzel's Champions: now Attila died about the year 450; and this Ostrogoth Theodoric did not fight his great Battle at Verona till 489; that of Ravenna, which was followed by a three years' siege, beginning next year. So that before Dietrich could become Dietrich *of Bern*, Etzel had been gone almost half a century from the scene. Startled by this anachronism, some commentators have fished out another Theodoric, eighty years prior to him of Verona, and who actually served in Attila's hosts, with a retinue of Goths and Germans; with which New Theodoric, however, the old Ottnit, or Odoacer, of the *Heldenbuch*, must, in his turn, part company; whereby the case is in no whit mended. Certain it seems, in the mean time, that *Dietrich*, which signifies *Rich in People*, is the same name which in Greek becomes Theodoricus; for, at first, (as in Procopius,) this very *Theodoricus* is always written Θευδεριχ, which almost exactly corresponds with the German sound. But such are the inconsistencies involved in both hypotheses, that we are forced to conclude one of two things: either that the singers of those old lays were little versed in the niceties of History, and unambitious of passing for authorities therein,

* Von der Hagen's *Nibelungen*, Einleitung, § vii.

which seems a remarkably easy conclusion; or else, with Lessing, that they meant some quite other series of persons and transactions, some Kaiser Otto, and his two Anti-Kaisers, (in the twelfth century:) which, from what has come to light since Lessing's day, seems now an untenable position.

However, as concerns the *Nibelungen*, the most remarkable coincidence, if genuine, remains yet to be mentioned. "Thwortz," a Hungarian Chronicler, (or perhaps chronicle,) of we know not what authority, relates, "that Attila left his kingdom to his two sons Chaba and Aladar, the former by a Grecian mother, the latter by Kremheilch, (Chriemhild,) a German; that Theodoric, one of his followers, sowed dissension between them; and along with the Teutonic hosts took part with his half-countryman, the younger son; whereupon rose a great slaughter, which lasted for fifteen days, and terminated in the defeat of Chaba, (the Greek,) and his flight into Asia."* Could we but put faith in this Thwortz, we might fancy that some vague rumour of that Kremheilch tragedy, swoln by the way, had reached the German ear and imagination; where, gathering round older Ideas and Mythuses, as Matter round its Spirit, the first rude form of *Chriemhilde's Revenge and the Wreck of the Nibelungen* bodied itself forth in Song.

Thus any historical light, emitted by these old Fictions, is little better than darkness visible; sufficient at most to indicate that great Northern Immigrations, and wars and rumours of wars, have been; but nowise how and what they have been. Scarcely clearer is the special history of the Fictions themselves: where they were first put together, who have been their successive redactors and new-modellers. Von der Hagen, as we said, supposes that there may have been three several series of such. Two, at all events, are clearly indicated. In their present shape, we have internal evidence that none of these Poems can be older than the twelfth century; indeed great part of the *Hero-Book* can be proved to be considerably later. With this last it is understood that Wolfram von Eschenbach and Heinrich von Ofterdingen, two singers, otherwise noted in that era, were largely concerned; but neither is there any demonstration of this vague belief: while again, in regard to the Author of our actual *Nibelungen* not so much as a plausible conjecture can be formed.

Some vote for a certain Conrad von Würzburg; others for the above-named Eschenbach and Ofterdingen; others again for Klingsohr of Ungerland, a minstrel who once passed for a magician. Against all and each of which hypotheses there are objections; and for none of them the smallest conclusive evidence. Who this gifted Singer may have been, only in so far as his Work itself proves that there was but One, and the style points to the latter half of the twelfth century,—remains altogether dark: the unwearied Von der Hagen himself, after fullest investigation, gives for verdict, "we know it not." Considering the high worth of the *Nibelungen*, and how many feeble ballad-mongers of that *Swabian Era* have transmitted us their names, so total an oblivion, in this infinitely more important case, may seem surprising. But those *Minnelieder* (Love-songs) and Provençal Madrigals were the Court Poetry of that time, and gained honour in high places; while the old National Traditions were common property and plebeian, and to sing them an unrewarded labour.

Whoever he may be, let him have our gratitude, our love. Looking back with a farewell glance, over that wondrous old Tale, with its many-coloured texture "of joyances and high-tides, of weeping and of wo," so skilfully yet artlessly knit up into a whole, we cannot but repeat that a true epic spirit lives in it; that in many ways, it has meaning and charms for us. Not only as the oldest Tradition of Modern Europe, does it possess a high antiquarian interest; but farther, and even in the shape we now see it under, unless the "Epics of the Son of Fingal" had some sort of authenticity, it is our oldest Poem also; the earliest product of these New Ages, which on its own merits, both in form and essence, can be named Poetical. Considering its chivalrous, romantic tone, it may rank as a piece of literary composition, perhaps considerably higher than the Spanish *Cid;* taking in its historical significance, and deep ramifications into the remote Time, it ranks indubitably and greatly higher.

It has been called a Northern *Iliad;* but except in the fact that both poems have a narrative character, and both sing "the destructive rage" of men, the two have scarcely any similarity. The Singer of the *Nibelungen* is a far different person from Homer; far inferior both in culture and in genius. Nothing of the glowing imagery, of the fierce bursting energy, of the mingled fire and gloom, that dwell in the old Greek, makes its appearance here. The German Singer is comparatively a simple nature; has never penetrated deep into life; never "questioned Fate," or struggled with fearful mysteries; of all which we find traces in Homer, still more in Shakspeare; but with meek believing submission, has taken the Universe as he found it represented to him; and rejoices with a fine childlike gladness in the mere outward shows of things. He has little power of delineating character; perhaps he had no decisive vision thereof. His persons are superficially distinguished, and not altogether without generic difference; but the portraiture is imperfectly brought out; there lay no true living original within him. He has little Fancy; we find scarcely one or two similitudes in his whole Poem; and these one or two, which, moreover, are repeated, betoken no special faculty that way. He speaks of the "moon among stars;" says often, of sparks struck from steel armour in battle, and so forth, that they were *wie es wehte der wind*, "as if the wind were blowing them." We have mentioned Tasso along with him; yet neither in this case is there any close resemblance; the light playful grace, still more, the Italian pomp and sunny luxuriance of Tasso are wanting in the other. His are humble, wood-notes wild; and no nightingale's, but yet a sweet

* Weber, (*Illustrations of Northern Antiquities*, p. 39,) who cites Görres (*Zeitung für Einsiedler*) as his authority.

sky-hidden lark's. In all the rhetorical gifts, to say nothing of rhetorical attainments, we should pronounce him even poor.

Nevertheless, a noble soul he must have been, and furnished with far more essential requisites for Poetry, than these are: namely, with the heart and feeling of a Poet. He has a clear eye for the Beautiful and True; all unites itself gracefully and compactly in his imagination: it is strange with what careless felicity he winds his way in that complex narrative, and be the subject what it will, comes through it unsullied, and with a smile. His great strength is an unconscious instinctive strength; wherein truly lies its highest merit. The whole spirit of Chivalry, of Love, and heroic Valour, must have lived in him, and inspired him. Everywhere he shows a noble Sensibility; the sad accents of parting friends, the lamentings of women, the high daring of men, all that is worthy and lovely prolongs itself in melodious echoes through his heart. A true old Singer, and taught of Nature herself! Neither let us call him an inglorious Milton, since now he is no longer a mute one. What good were it that the four or five Letters composing his Name could be printed, and pronounced, with absolute certainty? All that was mortal in him is gone utterly; of his life, and its environment, as of the bodily tabernacle he dwelt in, the very ashes remain not: like a fair heavenly Apparition, which indeed he was, he has melted into air, and only the Voice he uttered, in virtue of its inspired gift, yet lives and will live.

To the Germans this *Nibelungen Song* is naturally an object of no common love; neither if they sometimes overvalue it, and vague antiquarian wonder is more common than just criticism, should the fault be too heavily visited. After long ages of concealment, they have found it in the remote wilderness, still standing like the trunk of some almost antediluvian oak; nay with boughs on it still green, after all the wind and weather of twelve hundred years. To many a patriotic feeling, which lingers fondly in solitary places of the Past, it may well be a rallying-point, and "Lovers' *Trysting-Tree.*"

For us also it has its worth. A creation from the old ages, still bright and balmy, if we visit it; and opening into the first History of Europe, of Mankind. Thus all is not oblivion; but on the edge of the abyss, that separates the Old world from the New, there hangs a fair rainbow-land; which also in (three) curious repetitions, as it were, in a secondary, and even a ternary reflex, sheds some feeble twilight far into the deeps of the primeval Time.

GERMAN LITERATURE OF THE FOURTEENTH AND FIFTEENTH CENTURIES.*

[FOREIGN QUARTERLY REVIEW, 1831.]

It is not with Herr Soltau's work, and its merits or demerits, that we here purpose to concern ourselves. The old Low-German Apologue was already familiar under many shapes; its versions into Latin, English, and all modern tongues: if it now comes before our German friends under a new shape, and they can read it not only in Gottsched's prosaic Prose, and Goethe's poetic Hexameters, but also "in the metre of the original," namely, in Doggerel; and this, as would appear, not without comfort, for it is "the second edition;"—doubtless the Germans themselves will look to it, will direct Herr Soltau aright in his praiseworthy labours, and, with all suitable speed, forward him from his second edition into a third. To us strangers the fact is chiefly interesting, as another little memento of the indestructible vitality there is in worth, however rude; and to stranger Reviewers, as it brings that wondrous old Fiction, with so much else that holds of it, once more specifically into view.

The Apologue of *Reynard the Fox* ranks undoubtedly among the most remarkable Books, not only as a German, but, in all senses, as a European one; and yet for us perhaps its extrinsic, historical character, is even more noteworthy than its intrinsic. In Literary History it forms, so to speak, the culminating point, or highest manifestation of a Tendency which had ruled the two prior centuries: ever downwards from the last of the Hohenstauffen Emperors, and the end of their Swabian Era, to the borders of the Reformation, rudiments and fibres of this singular Fable are seen, among innumerable kindred things, fashioning themselves together; and now, after three other centuries of actual existence, it still stands visible and entire, venerable in itself, and the enduring memorial of much that has proved more perishable. Thus, naturally enough, it figures as the representative of a whole group that historically cluster round it; in studying its significance, we study that of a whole intellectual period.

As this section of German Literature closely connects itself with the corresponding section of European Literature, and indeed offers an expressive, characteristic epitome thereof, some insight into it, were such easily procurable,

* *Reinecke der Fuchs, übersetzt von D. W. Soltau.* (Reynard the Fox, translated by D. W. Soltau.) 2d edition, 8vo. Lüneburg, 1830.

might not be without profit. No Literary Historian that we know of, least of all any in England, having looked much in this direction, either as concerned Germany or other countries, whereby a long space of time, once busy enough, and full of life, now lies barren and void in men's memories,—we shall here endeavour to present, in such clearness as first attempts may admit, the result of some slight researches of our own in regard to it.

The *Troubadour Period* in general Literature, to which the *Swabian Era* in German answers, has, especially within the last generation, attracted inquiry enough; the French have their Raynouards, we our Webers, the Germans their Haugs, Gräters, Langs, and numerous other Collectors and Translators of *Minnelieder;* among whom Ludwig Tieck, the foremost in far other provinces, has not disdained to take the lead. We shall suppose that this Literary Period is partially known to all readers. Let each recall whatever he has learned or figured regarding it; represent to himself that brave young heyday of Chivalry and Minstrelsy, when a stern Barbarossa, a stern Lion-heart, sang *sirventes*, and with the hand that could wield the sword and sceptre twanged the melodious strings; when knights-errant tilted, and ladies' eyes rained bright influences; and suddenly, as at some sunrise, the whole Earth had grown vocal and musical. Then truly was the time of singing come; for princes and prelates, emperors and squires, the wise and the simple, men, women, and children, all sang and rhymed, or delighted in hearing it done. It was a universal noise of Song; as if the Spring of Manhood had arrived, and warblings from every spray, not indeed without infinite twitterings also, which, except their gladness, had no music, were bidding it welcome. This was the *Swabian Era;* justly reckoned not only superior to all preceding eras, but properly the First Era of German Literature. Poetry had at length found a home in the life of men; and every pure soul was inspired by it; and in words, or still better, in actions, strove to give it utterance.

"Believers," says Tieck, "sang of Faith; Lovers of Love; Knights described knightly actions and battles; and loving, believing knights were their chief audience. The Spring, Beauty, Gayety, were objects that could never tire; great duels and deeds of arms carried away every hearer; the more surely the stronger they were painted; and as the pillars and dome of the Church encircled the flock, so did Religion, as the Highest, encircle Poetry and Reality; and every heart, in equal love humbled itself before her."*

Let the reader, we say, fancy all this, and moreover that, as earthly things do, it is all passing away. And now, from this extreme verge of the *Swabian Era*, let us look forward into the inane of the next two centuries, and see whether there also some shadows and dim forms, significant in their kind, may not begin to grow visible. Already, as above indicated, *Reinecke de Fos* rises clear in the distance, as the goal of our survey: let us now, restricting ourselves to the German aspects of the matter, examine what may lie between.

Conrad the Fourth, who died in 1254, was the last of the Swabian Emperors: and Conradin his son, grasping too early at a Southern Crown, perished on the scaffold at Naples in 1268; with which stripling, more fortunate in song than in war, and whose death, or murder, with fourteen years of other cruelty, the *Sicilian Vespers* so frightfully avenged, the imperial line of the Hohenstauffen came to an end. Their House, as we have seen, gives name to a Literary Era; and truly, if dates alone were regarded, we might reckon it much more than a name. For with this change of dynasty, a great change in German Literature begins to indicate itself; the fall of the Hohenstauffen is close followed by the decay of Poetry; as if that fair flowerage and umbrage, which blossomed far and wide round the Swabian Family, had in very deed depended on it for growth and life; and now, the stem being felled, the leaves also were languishing, and soon to wither and drop away. Conradin, as his father and his grandfather had been, was a singer; some lines of his, though he died in his sixteenth year, have even come down to us; but henceforth no crowned poet, except, long afterwards, some few with cheap laurel crowns, is to be met with: the Gay Science was visibly declining. In such times as now came, the court and the great could no longer patronize it; the polity of the Empire was, by one convulsion after another, all but utterly dismembered; ambitious nobles, a sovereign without power; contention, violence, distress, everywhere prevailing. Richard of Cornwall, who could not so much as keep hold of his sceptre, not to speak of swaying it wisely; or even the brave Rudolf of Hapsburg, who manfully accomplished both these duties, had other work to do than sweet singing. Gay *Wars of the Wartburg* were now changed to stern *Battles of the Marchfield;* in his leisure hours, a good Emperor, instead of twanging harps, must hammer from his helmet the dints it had got in his working and fighting hours.* Amid such rude tumults the Minne-Song could not but change its scene and tone; if, indeed, it continued at all, which, however, it scarcely did; for now, no longer united in courtly choir, it seemed to lose both its sweetness and its force, gradually became mute, or in remote obscure corners lived on, feeble and inaudible, till after several centuries, when, under a new title, and with far inferior claims, it again solicits some notice from us.

Doubtless, in this posture of affairs political, the progress of Literature could be little forwarded from without; in some directions, as in that of Court-Poetry, we may admit that it was

* *Minnelieder aus dem Schwäbischen Zeitalter.* (*Vorrede*, x.)

* It was on this famous plain of the Marchfield that Ottocar, King of Bohemia, conquered Bela of Hungary, in 1260; and was himself, in 1278, conquered and slain by Rudolf of Hapsburg, at that time much left to his own resources; whose talent for mending helmets, however, is perhaps but a poetical tradition. Curious, moreover: it was here again, after more than five centuries, that the House of Hapsburg received its worst overthrow, and from a new and greater Rudolf, namely, from Napoleon, at Wagram, which lies in the middle of this same Marchfield.

obstructed or altogether stopped. But why not only Court-Poetry, but Poetry of all sorts should have declined, and as it were gone out, is quite another question; to which, indeed, as men must have their theory on every thing, answer has often been attempted, but only with partial success. To most of the German Literary Historians this so ungenial condition of the Court and Government appears enough: by the warlike, altogether practical character of Rudolf, by the imbecile ambition of his successors, by the general prevalence of feuds and lawless disorder, the death of Poetry seems fully accounted for. In which conclusion of theirs, allowing all force to the grounds it rests on, we cannot but perceive that there lurks some fallacy; the fallacy, namely, so common in these times, of deducing the inward and spiritual exclusively from the outward and material; of tacitly, perhaps unconsciously, denying all independent force, or even life, to the former, and looking out for the secret of its vicissitudes solely in some circumstance belonging to the latter. Now it cannot be too often repeated, where it continues still unknown or forgotten, that man has a soul as certainly as he has a body; nay, much more certainly; that properly it is the course of his unseen, spiritual life, which informs and rules his external visible life, rather than receives rule from it; in which spiritual life, indeed, and not in any outward action or condition arising from it, the true secret of his history lies, and is to be sought after, and indefinitely approached. Poetry, above all, we should have known long ago, is one of those mysterious things whose origin and developments never can be what we call explained; often it seems to us like the wind, blowing where it lists, coming and departing with little or no regard to any the most cunning theory that has yet been devised of it. Least of all does it seem to depend on court patronage, the form of government, or any modification of politics or economics, catholic as these influences have now become in our philosophy: it lives in a snow-clad, sulphureous Iceland, and not in a sunny, wine-growing France; flourishes under an arbitrary Elizabeth, and dies out under a constitutional George; Philip II. has his Cervantes, and in prison; Washington and Jackson have only their Coopers and Browns. Why did poetry appear so brightly after the Battles of Thermopylæ and Salamis, and quite turn away her face and wings from those of Lexington and Bunker's Hill? We answer, the Greeks were a poetical people, the Americans are not; that is to say, it appeared because it did appear! On the whole, we could desire that one of two things should happen: Either that our theories and genetic histories of Poetry should henceforth cease, and mankind rest satisfied, once for all, with Dr. Cabanis's theory, which seems to be the simplest, that "Poetry is a product of the smaller intestines," and must be cultivated medically by the exhibition of castor-oil: Or else that, in future speculations of this kind, we should endeavour to start with some recognition of the fact, once well known, and still in words admitted, that Poetry is Inspiration; has in it a certain spirituality and divinity which no dissecting-knife will discover; arises in the most secret and most sacred region of man's soul, as it were in our Holy of Holies; and as for external things, depends only on such as can operate in that region; among which it will be found that Acts of Parliament, and the state of the Smithfield markets, nowise play the chief parts.

With regard to this change in German Literature, especially, it is to be remarked, that the phenomenon was not a German, but a European one; whereby we easily infer, so much at least, that the roots of it must have lain deeper than in any change from Hohenstauffen Emperors to Hapsburg ones. For now the Troubadours and Trouveres, as well as the Minnesingers, were sinking into silence; the world seemed to have rhymed itself out; those chivalrous roundelays, heroic tales, mythologies, and quaint love-sicknesses, had grown unprofitable to the ear. In fact, Chivalry itself was in the wane; and with it that gay melody, like its other pomp. More earnest business, not sportfully, but with harsh endeavour, was now to be done. The graceful minuet-dance of Fancy must give place to the toilsome thorny pilgrimage of Understanding. Life and its appurtenances and possessions, which had been so admired and besung, now disclosed, the more they came to be investigated, the more contradictions. The Church no longer rose with its pillars "like a venerable dome over the united flock;" but, more accurately seen into, was a straight prison, full of unclean creeping things; against which thraldom all better spirits could not but murmur and struggle. Everywhere greatness and littleness seemed so inexplicably blended: Nature, like the Sphinx, her emblem, with her fair woman's face and neck, showed also the claws of a Lioness. Now too her Riddle had been propounded; and thousands of subtle, disputatious School-men were striving earnestly to read it, that they might live, morally live, that the monster might not devour them. These, like strong swimmers, in boundless bottomless, vortices of Logic, swam manfully, but could not get to land.

On a better course, yet with the like aim, Physical Science was also unfolding itself. A Roger Bacon, an Albert the Great, are cheering appearances in this era: not blind to the greatness of Nature, yet no longer with poetic reverence of her, but venturing fearlessly into her recesses, and extorting from her many a secret; the first victories of that long series which is to make man more and more her King. Thus everywhere we have the image of contest, of effort. The spirit of man, which once, in peaceful, loving communion with the Universe, had uttered forth its gladness in Song, now feels hampered and hemmed in, and struggles vehemently to make itself room. Power is the one thing needful, and that Knowledge which is Power: thus also Intellect becomes the grand faculty, in which all the others are well nigh absorbed.

Poetry, which has been defined as "the harmonious unison of Man with Nature," could not flourish in this temper of the times. The number of poets, or rather versifiers, henceforth greatly diminishes; their style also, and topics, are different and less poetical. Men wish to be practically instructed rather than poetically amused: Poetry itself must assume a preceptorial character, and teach wholesome saws and moral maxims, or it will not be listened to. Singing for the Song's sake is now nowhere practised; but in its stead there is everywhere the jar and bustle of argument, investigation, contentious activity. Such throughout the fourteenth century is the general aspect of mind over Europe. In Italy alone is there a splendid exception: the mystic song of Dante, with its sterne, indignant moral, is followed by the light love-rhymes of Petrarch, the Troubadour of Italy, when this class was extinct elsewhere: the master minds of that country, peculiar in its social and moral condition, still more in its relations to classical Antiquity, pursue a course of their own. But only the master minds; for Italy too has its Dialecticians, and projectors, and reformers; nay, after Petrarch, these take the lead; and there, as elsewhere, in their discords and loud assiduous toil, the voice of Poetry dies away.

To search out the causes of this great revolution, which lie not in Politics nor Statistics, would lead us far beyond our depth. Meanwhile let us remark that the change is nowise to be considered as a relapse, or fall from a higher state of spiritual culture to a lower; but rather, so far as we have objects to compare it with, as a quite natural progress and higher development of culture. In the history of the universal mind, there is a certain analogy to that of the individual. Our first self-consciousness is the first revelation to us of a whole universe, wondrous and altogether good: it is a feeling of joy and new-found strength, of mysterious infinite hope and capability; and in all men, either by word or act, expresses itself poetically. The world without us and within us, beshone by the young light of Love, and all instinct with a divinity, is beautiful and great: it seems for us a boundless happiness that we are privileged to live. This is the season of generous deeds and feelings; which also, on the lips of the gifted, form themselves into musical utterance, and give spoken poetry as well as acted. Nothing is calculated and measured, but all is loved, believed, appropriated. All action is spontaneous; high sentiment, a sure, imperishable good: and thus the youth stands, like the First Man, in his fair Garden, giving Names to the bright Appearances of this Universe which he has inherited, and rejoicing in it as glorious and divine. Ere long, however, comes a harsher time. Under the first beauty of man's life appears an infinite, earnest rigour; high sentiment will not avail, unless it can continue to be translated into noble action; which problem, in the destiny appointed for man born to toil, is difficult, interminable, capable of only approximate solution. What flowed softly in melodious coherence when seen and sung from a distance, proves rugged and unmanageable when practically handled. The fervid, lyrical gladness of past years gives place to a collected thoughtfulness and energy; nay often—so painful, so unexpected are the contradictions everywhere met with—to gloom, sadness, and anger; and not till after long struggles and hard-contested victories is the youth changed into a man.

Without pushing the comparison too far, we may say that in the culture of the European mind, or in Literature, which is the symbol and product of this, a certain similarity of progress is manifested. That tuneful Chivalry, that high cheerful devotion to the God-like in heaven, and to Women, its emblems on earth; those Crusades and vernal Love-songs were the heroic doings of the world's youth; to which also a corresponding manhood succeeded. Poetic recognition is followed by scientific examination: the reign of Fancy, with its gay images, and graceful, capricious sports, has ended; and now Understanding, which, when reunited to Poetry, will one day become Reason and a nobler Poetry, has to do its part. Meantime, while there is no such union, but a more and more widening controversy, prosaic discord and the unmusical sounds of labour and effort are alone audible.

The era of the Troubadours, who in Germany are the Minnesingers, gave place in that country, as in all others, to a period which we might name the Didactic; for Literature now ceased to be a festal melody, and addressing itself rather to the intellect than to the heart, became as it were a school lesson. Instead of that cheerful, warbling Song of Love and Devotion, wherein nothing was taught, but all was believed and worshipped, we have henceforth only wise Apologues, Fables, Satires, Exhortations, and all manner of edifying Moralities. Poetry, indeed, continued still to be the form of composition for all that can be named Literature, except Chroniclers, and others of that genus, valuable not as doers of the work, but as witnesses of the work done; these Teachers all wrote in verse: nevertheless, in general there are few elements of Poetry in their performances: the internal structure has nothing poetical, it is a mere business-like prose: in the rhyme alone, at most in the occasional graces of expression, could we discover that it reckoned itself poetical. In fact we may say that Poetry, in the old sense, had now altogether gone out of sight: instead of her heavenly vesture and Ariel-harp, she had put on earthly weeds, and walked abroad with ferula and horn-book. It was long before this new guise would sit well on her; only in late centuries that she could fashion it into beauty, and learn to move with it, and mount with it gracefully as of old.

Looking now more specially to our historical task, if we inquire how far into the subsequent time this Didactic Period extended, no precise answer can well be given. On this side there seem no positive limits to it; with many superficial modifications, the same fundamental element pervades all spiritual efforts of mankind through the following centuries. We may say that it is felt even in the Poetry of our own time; nay, must be felt through all time; inasmuch as Inquiry once awakened cannot fall asleep, or exhaust itself; thus Literature must continue to have a didactic character; and the Poet of these days is he who, not indeed by mechanical but by poetical methods, can instruct us, can more and more evolve for us the mystery of our Life. However, after a certain space, this Didactic Spirit in Literature cannot, as an historical partition and landmark, be available here. At the era of the Reformation, it reaches its acme; and, in singular shapes, steps forth on the high places of Public Business, and amid storms and thunder, not without brightness and true fire from Heaven, conclusively renovates the world. This is, as it were, the apotheosis of the Didactic Spirit, where it first attains a really poetical concentration, and stimulates mankind into heroism of word and of action also. Of the latter, indeed, still more than of the former; for not till a much more recent time, almost till our own time, has Inquiry in some measure again reconciled itself to Belief; and Poetry, though in detached tones, arisen on us, as a true musical Wisdom. Thus is the deed, in certain circumstances, readier and greater than the word: Action strikes fiery light from the rocks it has to hew through; Poetry reposes in the skyey splendour which that rough passage has led to. But after Luther's day, this Didactic Tendency again sinks to a lower level; mingles with manifold other tendencies; among which, admitting that it still forms the main stream, it is no longer so pre-eminent, positive, and universal, as properly to characterize the whole. For minor Periods and subdivisions in Literary History, other more superficial characteristics must, from time to time, be fixed on.

Neither, examining the other limit of this Period, can we say specially where it begins; for, as usual in these things, it begins not at once, but by degrees; Kings' reigns and changes in the form of Government have their day and date; not so changes in the spiritual condition of a people. The Minnesinger Period and the Didactic may be said to commingle, as it were, to overlap each other, for above a century: some writers partially belonging to the latter class occur even prior to the times of Friedrich II.; and a certain echo of the Minne-Song had continued down to Manesse's day, under Ludwig the Bavarian.

Thus from the Minnesingers to the Church Reformers, we have a wide space of between two and three centuries; in which, of course, it is impossible for us to do more than point out one or two of the leading appearances; a minute survey and exposition being foreign from our object.

Among the Minnesingers themselves, as already hinted, there are not wanting some with an occasionally didactic character; Gottfried of Strasburg, known also as a translator of *Sir Tristrem*, and two other Singers, Reinmar von Zweter, and Walter von der Vogelweide, are noted in this respect; the last two especially, for their oblique glances at the Pope and his Monks, the unsound condition of which body could not escape even a Love-minstrel's eye.*

But perhaps the special step of transition may be still better marked in the works of a rhymer named the *Stricker*, whose province was the epic, or narrative; into which he seems to have introduced this new character in unusual measure. As the *Stricker* still retains some shadow of a place in Literary History, the following notice of him may be borrowed here. Of his personal history, it may be premised, nothing whatever is known; not even why he bears this title; unless it be, as some have fancied, that *Stricker*, which now signifies *Knitter*, in those days meant *Schriber*, (Writer:)

"In truth," says Bouterwek, "this painstaking man was more a writer than a Poet, yet not altogether without talent in that latter way. Voluminous enough, at least, is his redaction of an older epic work on the *War of Charlemagne with the Saracens in Spain*, the old German original of which is perhaps nothing more than a translation from the Latin or French. Of a Poet in the Stricker's day, when the romantic Epos had attained such polish among the Germans, one might have expected that this ancient Fiction, since he was pleased to remodel it, would have served as the material to a new poetic creation; or at least, that he would have breathed into it some new and more poetic spirit. But such a development of these Charlemagne Fables was reserved for the *Italian* Poets. The Stricker has not only left the matter of the old Tale almost unaltered, but has even brought out its unpoetical lineaments in stronger light. The fanatical piety with which it is overloaded probably appeared to him its chief merit. To convert these castaway Heathens, or failing this, to annihilate them, Charlemagne takes the field. Next to him, the hero Roland plays a main part there. Consultations are held, ambassadors negotiate; war breaks out with all its terrors: the Heathen fought stoutly: at length comes the well known defeat of the Franks at Ronceval, or Roncevaux; where, however, the Saracens also lose so many men, that their King Marsilies dies of grief. The Narrative is divided into chapters, each chapter again into sections,

---

* Reinmar Von Zweter, for example, says once:

Har und bart nach Klostersitten gesnitten
Des vind ich gennog,
Ich vinde aber der nit vil dies rehte tragen;
Halb visch halb man ist visch noch man,
Gar visch ist visch, gar man ist man,
Als ich erkennen Kan:
Von hofmunchen und von Klosterrittern
Kan ich niht gesagen:
Hofmunchen, Klosterrittern, diesen beiden
Wolt ich reht ze rehte wol bescheiden,
Ob sie sich wolten lassen vinden,
Da sie ze rehte solten wesen;
In Kloster munche solten genesen,
So suln des hofs sich ritter unterwinden.

Hair and beard cut in the cloister fashion
Of this find I enough,
But of those that wear it well I find not many;
Half-fish half-man is neither fish nor man,
Whole fish is fish, whole man is man,
As I discover can:
Of court-monks and of cloister-knights
Can I not speak:
Court-monks, cloister-knights, these both
Would I rightly put to rights,
Whether they would let themselves be found
Where they by right should be;
In their cloister monks should flourish,
And knights obey at court.

See also in *Flögel*, (*Geschichte der Romischen Litteratur*, b. iii. s. 11,) immediately following this Extract, a formidable dinner-course of *Lies*,—boiled lies, roasted lies, lies with saffron, forced-meat lies, and other varieties, arranged by this same artist;—farther, (in page 9,) a rather gallant onslaught from Walter von der Vogelweide, on the *Babest* (Pope *Papst*) himself. All this was before the middle of the thirteenth century.

an epitome of which is always given at the outset. Miracles occur in the story, but for most part only such as tend to evince how God himself inspirited the Christians against the Heathen. Of any thing like free, bold flights of imagination there is little to be met with: the higher features of the genuine romantic epos are altogether wanting. In return, it has a certain didactic temper, which, indeed, announces itself even in the Introduction. The latter, it should be added, prepossesses us in the Poet's favour; testifying with what warm interest the noble and great in man's life affected him."*

The *Wälsche Gast* (Italian Guest) of Zirkler or Tirkeler, who professes, truly or not, to be from Friuli, and, as a benevolent stranger, or *Guest*, tells the Germans hard truths somewhat in the spirit of Juvenal; even the famous *Meister Freidank*, (Master Freethought,) with his wise Book of rhymed Maxims, entitled *Die Bescheidenheit*, (Modesty;) still more the sagacious *Tyro, King of Scots*, quite omitted in history, but who teaches *Friedebrand, his Son*, with some discrimination, how to choose a good priest;—all these, with others of still thinner substance, rise before us only as faint shadows, and must not linger in our field of vision. Greatly the most important figure in the earlier part of this era is Hugo von Trimberg, to whom we must now turn; author of various poetico-preceptorial works, one of which, named the *Renner*, (Runner,) has long been known not only to antiquarians, but, in some small degree, even to the general reader. Of Hugo's Biography he has himself incidentally communicated somewhat. His surname he derives from Trimberg, his birth-place, a village on the Saale, not far from Würzburg, in Franconia. By profession he appears to have been a Schoolmaster: in the conclusion of his *Renner*, he announces that "he kept school for forty years at Thürstadt, near Bamberg;" farther, that his Book was finished in 1300, which date he confirms by other local circumstances.

Der dies Buch gedichtet hat,
Der pflag der schlen zu Thürstat.
Vierzig jar vor Babenberg,
Und heiss Hugo von Trymberg.
Es ward follenbracht das ist wahr,
Da tausent und dreyhundert jar
Nach Christus Geburt vergangen waren,
Drithalbs jar gleich vor den jaren
Da die Juden in Franken wurden erschlagen.
Bey der zeit und in den tagen,
Da bischoff Leopolt bischoff was
Zu Babenberg.

Some have supposed that the Schoolmaster dignity, claimed here, refers not to actual wielding of the birch, but to a Mastership and practice of instructing in the art of Poetry, which about this time began to have its scholars and even guild-brethren, as the feeble remnants of Minne-Song gradually took the new shape, in which we afterwards see it, of *Meistergesang*, (Master-song:) but for this hypothesis, so plain are Hugo's own words, there seems little foundation. It is uncertain whether he was a clerical personage, certain enough that he was not a monk: at all events, he must have been a man of reading and knowledge; industrious in study, and superior in literary acquirement to most in that time. By a collateral account, we find that he had gathered a library of two hundred Books; among which were a whole dozen by himself, five in Latin, seven in German, hoping that by means of these, and the furtherance they would yield in the pedagogic craft, he might live at ease in his old days; in which hope, however, he had been disappointed: seeing, as himself rather feelingly complains, "no one now cares to study knowledge, (*Kunst*,) which, nevertheless, deserves honour and favour." What these twelve Books of Hugo's own writing were, can, for most part, only be conjectured. Of one, entitled the *Sammler*, (Collector,) he himself makes mention in the *Renner:* he had begun it about thirty years before this latter: but having by ill accident lost great part of his manuscript, abandoned it in anger. Of another work Flögel has discovered the following notice in Johann Wolf:

"About this time (1599) did that virtuous and learned nobleman, Conrad von Liebenstein, present to me a manuscript of Hugo von Trimberg, who flourished about the year 1300. It sets forth the short-comings of all ranks, and especially complains of the clergy. It is entitled *Reu ins Land*, (Repentance to the Land;) and now lies with the Lord of Zillhart."*

The other ten appear to have vanished even to the last vestige.

Such is the whole sum-total of information which the assiduity of commentators has collected touching worthy Hugo's life and fortunes. Pleasant it were to see him face to face; gladly would we penetrate through that long vista of five hundred years, and peep into his book-presses, his frugal fireside, his noisy mansion with its disobedient urchins, now that it has all grown so silent; but the distance is too far, the intervening medium intercepts our light; only in uncertain, fluctuating dusk, will Hugo and his environment appear to us. Nevertheless Hugo, as he had in Nature, has in History, an immortal part; as to his inward man, we can still see that he was no mere bookworm, or simple Parson Adams; but of most observant eye; shrewd, inquiring, considerate, who from his Thürstadt school-chair, as from his *sedes exploratorio*, had looked abroad into the world's business; and formed his own theory about many things. A cheerful, gentle heart had been given him; a quiet, sly humour; light to see beyond the garments and outer hulls of Life into Life itself: the long-necked purse, the threadbare gabardine, the languidly-simmering pot of his pedagogic household establishment were a small matter to him: he was a man to look on these things with a meek smile; to nestle down quietly, as the

*Bouterwek, ix. 245. Other versified Narratives by this worthy *Stricker* still exist, but for the most part only in manuscript. Of these the History of *Wilhelm von Blumethal*, a Round-table adventurer, appears to be the principal. The Poem on Charlemagne stands printed in Schilter's *Thesaurus*; its exact date is matter only of conjecture.

*Flögel, (iii. 15,) who quotes for it, *Wolfii Lexicon, Memorab*. t. ii. p. 1061.

lark, in the lowest furrow; nay, to mount therefrom singing, and soar above all mere earthly heights. How many potentates, and principalities, and proud belligerents have evaporated into utter oblivion, while the poor Thürstadt Schoolmaster still holds together!

This *Renner*, which seems to be his final work, probably comprises the essence of all those lost Volumes: and indeed a synopsis of Hugo's whole Philosophy of Life, such as his two hundred books and long decades of quiet observation and reflection had taught him. Why it has been named the *Renner*, whether by Hugo himself, or by some witty editor and Transcriber, there are two guesses forthcoming, and no certain reason. One guess is that this Book was to *run* after the lost Tomes, and make good to mankind the deficiency occasioned by want of them; which happy thought, hidebound though it be, might have seemed sprightly enough to Hugo and that age. The second guess is that our author, in the same style of easy wit, meant to say this book must *hasten* and run out into the world, and do him a good turn quickly, while it was yet time, he being so very old. But leaving this, we may remark, with certainty enough, that what we have left of Hugo was first printed under this title of *Renner*, at Frankfort on the Mayn, in 1549; and quite incorrectly, being modernized to all lengths, and often without understanding of the sense; the Edition moreover is now rare, and Lessing's project of a new one did not take effect; so that, except in Manuscripts, of which there are many, and in printed Extracts, which also are numerous, the *Renner* is to most readers a sealed book.

In regard to its literary merit opinions seem to be nearly unanimous. The highest merit, that of poetical unity, or even the lower merit of logical unity, is not ascribed to it by the warmest panegyrist. Apparently this work had been a kind of store-chest, wherein the good Hugo had, from time to time, deposited the fruits of his meditation as they chanced to ripen for him; here a little, and there a little, in all varieties of kind; till the chest being filled, or the fruits nearly exhausted, it was sent forth and published to the world, by the easy process of turning up the bottom.

"No theme," says Bouterwek, "leads with certainty to the other; satirical descriptions, proverbs, fables, jests, and other narratives all huddled together at random, to teach us in a poetical way a series of moral lessons. A strained and frosty Allegory opens the work: then follows the chapter of *Meyden*, (Maids;) of Wicked Masters; of Pages; of Priests, Monks, and Friars, with great minuteness: then of a young Minx with an Old Man; then of Bad Landlords, and of Robbers. Next come divers Virtues and Vices, all painted out, and judged of. Towards the end, there follows a sort of Moral Natural History; Considerations on the dispositions of various Animals; a little Botany and Physiology; then again all manner of didactic Narratives; and finally a Meditation on the Last Day."

Whereby it would appear clearly, as hinted, that Hugo's *Runner* pursues no straight course; and only through the most labyrinthic mazes, here wandering in deep thickets, or even sinking in moist bogs, there panting over mountain-tops by narrow sheep tracks; but for most part jigging lightly on sunny greens, accomplishes his wonderful journey.

Nevertheless, as we ourselves can testify, there is a certain charm in the worthy man; his work, such as it is, seems to flow direct from the heart, in natural, spontaneous abundance; is at once cheerful and earnest; his own simple, honest, mildly-decided character is everywhere visible. Besides, Hugo, as we said, is a person of understanding; has looked over many provinces of Life, not without insight; in his quiet, sly way, can speak forth a shrewd word on occasion. There is a genuine though slender vein of Humour in him; nor in his satire does he ever lose temper, but rebukes sportfully; not indeed laughing aloud, scarcely even sardonically smiling, yet with a certain subdued roguery, and patriarchal knowingness. His fancy too, if not brilliant, is copious almost beyond measure; no end to his crotchets, suppositions, minute specifications. Withal he is original; his maxims, even when professedly borrowed, have passed through the test of his own experience; all carries in it some stamp of his personality. Thus the *Renner*, though in its whole extent perhaps too boundless and planless for ordinary nerves, makes, in the fragmentary state, no unpleasant reading: that old doggerel is not without significance; often in its straggling, broken, entangled strokes some vivid antique picture is strangely brought out for us.

As a specimen of Hugo's general manner, we select a small portion of his Chapter on *The Maidens;* that passage where he treats of the highest enterprise a maiden can engage in, the choosing of a husband. It will be seen at once that Hugo is no Minnesinger, glozing his fair audience with madrigals and hypocritical gallantry; but a quiet Natural Historian, reporting such facts as he finds, in perfect good nature, it is true, yet not without an under-current of satirical humour. His quaint style of thought, his garrulous minuteness of detail, are partly apparent here. The first few lines we may give in the original also; not as they stand in the Frankfort edition, but as professing to derive themselves from a genuine ancient source:

Kortzyn mut und lange haar
han die meyde sunderbar
dy zu yren jaren kommen synt
dy wal machen yn daz hertze blynt
dy auchgn wyren yn den weg
von den auchgn get eyn steg
tzu dem hertzen nit gar lang
uff deme stege ist vyl mannig gedang
*wen sy woln memen oder nit.**

Short of sense and long of hair,
Strange enough the maidens are;
Once they to their teens have got,
Such a choosing, this or that:
Eyes they have that ever spy,
From the Eyes a Path doth lie
To the Heart, and is not long,
Hereon travel thoughts a throng,
Whomso they will have or not.

* Horn, *Geschichte, und Kritik der deutschen Poesie*, s. 44.

"Wo's me," continues Hugo, "how often this same is repeated; till they grow all confused how to choose, from so many, whom they have brought in without number. First they bethink them so: This one is short, that one is long; he is courtly and old, the other young and ill-favoured: this is lean, that is bald, here is one fat, there one thin; this is noble, that is weak; he never yet broke a spear: one is white, another black; that other is named Master Hack, (*hartz;*) this is pale, that again is red; he seldom eateth cheerful bread;" and so on, through endless other varieties, in new streams of soft-murmuring doggerel, whereon, as on the Path it would represent, do travel thoughts a throng, whomso these fair irresolutes will have or not.

Thus, for Hugo, the age of Minstrelsy is gone: not soft Love-ditties, and Hymns of Lady-worship, but a skeptical criticism, importunate animadversion, not without a shade of mockery, will he indite. The age of Chivalry is gone also. To a Schoolmaster, with empty larder, the pomp of tournaments could never have been specially interesting; but now such passages of arms, how free and gallant soever, appear to him no other than the probable product of delirium. "God might well laugh, could it be," says he, "to see his mannikins live so wondrously on this Earth: two of them will take to fighting, and nowise let it alone; nothing serves but with two long spears they must ride and stick at one another greatly to their hurt; when one is by the other skewered through the bowels or through the weasand, he hath small profit thereby. But who forced them to such straits?" The answer is too plain: some modification of Insanity. Nay, so contemptuous is Hugo of all chivalrous things, that he openly grudges any time spent in reading of them. In Don Quixote's Library he would have made short work:

How Master Dietrich fought with Ecken,
And how of old the Stalwart Recken
Were all by women's craft betrayed:
Such things you oft hear sung and said,
And wept at, like a case of sorrow;—
Of our own sins we'll think to-morrow.

This last is one of Hugo's darker strokes; for commonly, though moral perfection is ever the one thing needful with him, he preaches in a quite cheerful tone; nay, ever and anon, enlivens us with some timely joke. Considerable part, and apparently much the best part, of his work is occupied with satirical Fables, and *Schwänke* (jests, comic tales;) of which latter classes we have seen some possessing true humour, and the simplicity which is their next merit. These, however, we must wholly omit; and indeed, without farther parleying, here part company with Hugo. We leave him, not without esteem, and a touch of affection due to one so true-hearted, and, under that old humble guise, so gifted with intellectual talent. Safely enough may be conceded him the dignity of chief moral Poet of his time; nay, perhaps, for his solid character, and modest manly ways, a much higher dignity. Though his Book can no longer be considered, what the Frankfort Editor describes it in his interminable title-page, as a universal *vademecum* for mankind, it is still so adorned with many fine sayings, and in itself of so curious a texture, that it seems well worth preserving. A proper Edition of the *Renner* will one day doubtless make its appearance among the Germans. Hugo is further remarkable as the precursor and prototype of Sebastian Brandt, whose *Narrenschiff* (Ship of Fools) has, with perhaps less merit, had infinitely better fortune than the *Renner.*

Some half century later in date, and no less didactic in character than Hugo's *Renner*, another work, still rising visible above the level of those times, demands some notice from us. This is the *Edelstein* (Gem) of Bonerius, or Boner, which at one time, to judge by the number of Manuscripts, whereof fourteen are still in existence, must have enjoyed great popularity; and indeed, after long years of oblivion, it has, by recent critics and redactors, been again brought into some circulation. Boner's *Gem* is a collection of a Hundred Fables done into German rhyme; and derives its proud designation not more perhaps from the supposed excellence of the work, than from a witty allusion to the title of Fable First, which, in the chief Manuscript, chances to be that well-known one of the Cock scraping for Barleycorns, and finding instead there a precious stone (*Edelstein*) or Gem: *Von einem Hanen und dem Edelen steine;* whereupon the author, or some kind friend, remarks in a sort of Prologue:

Dies Büchlein mag der Edelstein
Wol heiszen wand es in treit (in sich trägt)
Bischaft (Beispiel) manger kluogheit.

"This Bookling may well be called the Gem, sith it includes examples of many a prudence:"—which name, accordingly, as we see, it bears even to this day.

Boner and his Fables have given rise to much discussion among the Germans: scattered at short distances throughout the last hundred years, there is a series of Selections, Editions, Translations, Critical Disquisitions, some of them in the shape of Academic Program; among the labourers in which enterprise we find such men as Gellert and Lessing. A *Bonerii Gemma*, or Latin version of the work, was published by Oberlin, in 1782; Eschenburg sent forth an Edition in modern German, in 1810; Benecke a reprint of the antique original, in 1816. So that now a faithful duty has been done to Boner; and what with Bibliographical Inquiries, what with vocabularies and learned collations of Texts, he that runs may read whatever stands written in the *Gem.*

Of these diligent lucubrations, with which we strangers are only in a remote degree concerned, it will be sufficient here to report in few words the main results,—not indeed very difficult to report. First then, with regard to Boner himself, we have to say that nothing whatever has been discovered: who, when, or what that worthy moralist was, remains, and may always remain, entirely uncertain. It is merely conjectured, from the dialect, and other more minute indications, that his place of abode was the north-west quarter of Switzerland; with still higher probability that he lived about the middle of the fourteenth century; from his learning and devout pacific temper, some have inferred that he was a monk or priest; however, in one Manuscript of his *Gem*, he is designated, apparently by some ignorant Transcriber, a knight, *ein Ritter gotz alsus*: from all which, as above said, our only conclusion is, that nothing can be concluded.

Johann Scherz, about the year 1710, in what he called *Philosophiæ moralis Germanorum medii ævi Specimen*, sent forth certain of these Fables, with expositions, but apparently without naming the Author; to which *Specimen* Gellert in his *Dissertatio de poesi apologorum* had again, some forty years afterwards, invited attention. Nevertheless, so total was the obscurity which Boner had fallen into, that Bodmer, already known as the resuscitator of the *Nibelungen Lied*, in printing the *Edelstein* from an old Manuscript, in 1752, mistook its probable date by about a century, and gave his work the title of *Fables from the Minnesinger Period*,* without naming the Fabulist, or guessing whether there were one or many. In this condition stood the matter, when several years afterwards, Lessing, pursuing another inquiry, came across the track of this Boner; was allured into it; proceeded to clear it; and moving briskly forward with a sure eye, and sharp critical axe, hewed away innumerable entanglements; and so opened out a free avenue and vista, where strangely, in remote depth of antiquarian woods, the whole ancient Fable-manufactory, with Boner and many others working in it, becomes visible, in all the light which probably will ever be admitted to it. He who has perplexed himself with *Romulus and Rimicius*, and Nevelet's *Anonymus*, and *Avianus*, and still more, with the false guidance of their many commentators, will find help and deliverance in this light, thorough-going Inquiry of Lessing's.†

Now, therefore, it became apparent: first, that those supposed *Fables from the Minnesinger Period*, of Bodmer, were in truth written by one Boner, in quite another Period; secondly, that Boner was not properly the author of them, but the borrower and free versifier from certain Latin originals; farther, that the real title was *Edelstein*; and strangest of all, that the work had been printed three centuries before Bodmer's time, namely, at Bamberg, in 1461; of which Edition, indeed, a tattered copy, typographically curious, lay, and probably lies, in the Wolfenbüttel Library, where Lessing then waited and wrote. The other discoveries, touching Boner's personality, and locality, are but conjectures, due also to Lessing, and have been stated already.

As to the *Gem* itself, about which there has been such scrambling, we may say, now when it is cleaned and laid out before us, that though but a small seed-pearl, it has a genuine value. To us Boner is interesting by his antiquity, as the speaking witness of many long-past things; to his contemporaries again he must have been still more interesting as the reporter of so many new things. These Fables of his, then for the first time rendered out of inaccessible Latin* into German metre, contain no little edifying matter, had we not known it before: our old friends, the Fox with the musical Raven; the Man and Boy taking their Ass to market, and so inadequate to please the public in their method of transporting him: the Bishop that gave his Nephew a Cure of Souls, but durst not trust him with a Basket of Pears; all these and many more figure here. But apart from the material of his Fables, Boner's style and manner has an abiding merit. He is not so much a Translator as a free Imitator: he tells the story in his own way; appends his own moral, and except that in the latter department he is apt to be a little prolix, acquits himself to high satisfaction. His narrative, in those old limping rhymes, is cunningly enough brought out: artless, lively, graphic, with a spicing of innocent humour, a certain childlike archness, which is the chief merit of a Fable. Such is the German Æsop; a character whom, in the North-west district of Switzerland, at that time of day, we should hardly have looked for.

Could we hope that to many of our readers the old rough dialect of Boner would be intelligible, it were easy to vindicate these praises. As matters stand, we can only venture on one translated specimen, which in this shape claims much allowance; the Fable, also, is nowise the best, or perhaps the worst, but simply one of the shortest. For the rest, we have rendered the old doggerel into new, with all possible fidelity:

THE FROG AND THE STEER.

Of him that striveth after more honour than he should.

A Frog with Frogling by his side
Came hopping through the plain, one tide:
There he an Ox at grass did spy,
Much anger'd was the Frog thereby;
He said: "Lord God, what was my sin
Thou madest me so small and thin?
Likewise I have no handsome feature,
And all dishonoured is my nature,

*Koch also, with a strange deviation from his usual accuracy, dates Boner, in one place, 1220; and in another, "towards the latter half of the fourteenth century." See his *Compendium*, p. 28, and p. 200, vol. i.

† *Sammtliche Schriften*, B. 8.

*The two originals to whom Lessing has traced all his Fables are *Avianus* and Nevelet's *Anonymus*; concerning which personages the following brief notice by Jörden (*Lexicon*, i. 161) may be inserted here: "Flavius Avianus (who must not be confounded with another Latin Poet, *Avienus*) lived, as is believed, under the two Antonines in the second century: he has left us forty-two Fables in elegiac measure, the best Editions of which are that by Kannegiesser, (Amsterdam, 1731,) that by," &c., &c. With respect to the *Anonymus* again: "under this designation is understood the half-barbarous Latin Poet, whose sixty Fables, in elegiac measure, stand in the collection, which Nevelet, under the title *Mythologia Æsopica*, published at Frankfort in 1610, and which directly follow those of Avianus in that work. They are nothing else than versified translations of the Fables written in prose by *Romulus*, a noted Fabulist, whose era cannot be fixed, nor even his name made out to complete satisfaction."—The reader who wants deeper insight into these matters may consult Lessing, as cited above.

To other creatures far and near,
For instance, this same grazing Steer."
The Frog would fain with Bullock cope,
"Gan brisk outblow himself in hope.
Then spake his Frogling: "Father o' me,
It boots not, let thy blowing be;
Thy nature hath forbid this battle,
Thou canst not vie with the black-cattle."
Nathless let be the Frog would not,
Such prideful notion had he got;
Again to blow right sore 'gan he,
And said: "Like Ox could I but be
In size, within this world there were
No Frog so glad, to thee I swear."
The Son spake: "Father, me is wo
Thou should'st torment thy body so,
I fear thou art to lose thy life,
Come follow me and leave this strife;
Good father, take advice of me
And let thy boastful blowing be."
Frog said: "Thou need'st not beck and nod,
I will not do 't, so help me God;
Big as this Ox is, I must turn,
Mine honour now it doth concern."
He blew himself, and burst in twain,
Such of that blowing was his gain.

The like hath oft been seen of such
Who grasp at honour overmuch;
They must with none at all be doing,
But sink full soon and come to ruin.
He that, with wind of Pride accursed,
Much puffs himself, will surely burst;
He men miswishes and misjudges,
Inferiors scorns, superiors grudges,
Of all his equals is a hater,
Much grieved he is at any better;
Wherefore it were a sentence wise
Were his whole body set with eyes,
Who envy hath, to see so well
What lucky hap each man befel,
That so he filled were with fury,
And burst asunder in a hurry;
And so full soon betid him this
Which to the Frog betided is.

Readers to whom such stinted twanging of the true Poetic Lyre, such cheerful fingering, though only of one and its lowest string, has any melody, may find enough of it in Benecke's *Boner*, a reproduction, as above stated, of the original *Edelstein;* which Edition we are authorized to recommend as furnished with all helps for such a study: less adventurous readers may still, from Eschenburg's half-modernized Edition, derive some contentment and insight.

Hugo von Trimberg and Boner, who stand out here as our chief Literary representatives of the Fourteenth Century, could play no such part in their own day, when the great men, who shone in the world's eye, were Theologians and Jurists, Politicians at the Imperial Diet; at best, Professors in the new Universities; of whom all memory has long since perished. So different is universal from temporary importance, and worth belonging to our manhood from that merely of our station or calling. Nevertheless, as every writer, of any true gifts, is "citizen both of his time and of his country," and the more completely the greater his gifts; so in the works of these two secluded individuals, the characteristic tendencies and spirit of their age may best be discerned.

Accordingly, in studying their commentators, one fact, that cannot but strike us, is the great prevalence and currency which this species of Literature, cultivated by them, had obtained in that era. Of Fable Literature, especially, this was the summer tide and highest efflorescence. The Latin originals which Boner partly drew from, descending, with manifold transformations and additions, out of classical times, were in the hands of the learned; in the living memories of the people, were numerous fragments of primeval Oriental Fable, derived perhaps through Palestine; from which two sources, curiously intermingled, a whole stream of Fables evolved itself; whereat the morally athirst, such was the genius of that time, were not slow to drink. Boner, as we have seen, worked in a field then zealously cultivated: nay was not Æsop himself, what we have for Æsop, a contemporary of his; the Greek Monk Planudes and the Swiss Monk Boner might be chanting their Psalter at one and the same hour!

Fable, indeed, may be regarded as the earliest and simplest product of Didactic Poetry, the first attempt of Instruction clothing itself in Fancy: hence the antiquity of Fables, their universal diffusion in the childhood of nations, so that they have become a common property of all: hence also their acceptance and diligent culture among the Germans, among the Europeans, in this the first stage of an era when the whole bent of Literature was Didactic. But the Fourteenth Century was the age of Fable in a still wider sense: it was the age when whatever Poetry there remained took the shape of Apologue and moral Fiction: the higher spirit of Imagination had died away, or withdrawn itself into Religion; the lower and feebler not only took continual counsel of Understanding, but was content to walk in its leading-strings. Now was the time when human life and its relations were looked at with an earnest practical eye; and the moral perplexities that occur there, when man, hemmed in between the Would and the Should, or the Must, painfully hesitates, or altogether sinks in that collision, were not only set forth in the way of precept, but imbodied, for still clearer instruction, in Examples and edifying Fictions. The Monks themselves, such of them as had any talent, meditated and taught in this fashion: witness that strange *Gesta Romanorum*, still extant, and once familiar over all Europe;—a Collection of Moral Tales, expressly devised for the use of Preachers, though only the Shakspeares, and in subsequent times, turned it to right purpose.* These and the like old *Gests*, with most of which the *Romans* had so little to do, were the staple Literature of that period: cultivated with great assiduity, and so far as mere invention, or compilation, of incident goes, with no little merit; for already almost all the grand destinies, and fundamental, ever-recurring entanglements of human life, are laid hold of and depicted here; so that, from the first, our modern Novelists and Dramatists could find nothing new under the sun, but everywhere, in contrivance of their Story, saw themselves forestalled. The boundless abundance of Narratives then current, the singular derivations and transmigrations

*See an account of this curious Book in Douce's learned and ingenious *Illustrations of Shakspeare.*

of these, surprise antiquarian commentators: but, indeed, it was in this same century that Boccaccio, refining the gold from that so copious dross, produced his *Decamerone*, which still indicates the same fact in more pleasant fashion, to all readers. That in these universal tendencies of the time the Germans participated and co-operated, Boner's Fables, and Hugo's many Narrations, serious and comic, may, like two specimens from a great multitude, point out to us. The Madrigal had passed into the Apologue; the Heroic Poem, with its supernatural machinery and sentiment, into the Fiction of practical Life: in which latter species a prophetic eye might have discerned the coming *Tom Joneses* and *Wilhelm Meisters;* and with still more astonishment, the *Minerva Presses* of all nations, and this their huge transit-trade in Rags, all lifted from the dunghill, printed on, and returned thither, to the comfort of parties interested.

The Drama, as is well known, had an equally Didactic origin; namely, in those *Mysteries* contrived by the clergy for bringing home religious truth, with new force, to the universal comprehension. That this cunning device had already found its way into Germany, we have proof in a document too curious to be omitted here:

"In the year 1322, there was a play shown at Eisenach, which had a tragical enough effect. Markgraf Friedrich of Misnia, Landgraf also of Thuringia, having brought his tedious warfares to a conclusion, and the country beginning now to revive under peace, his subjects were busy repaying themselves for the past distresses by all manner of diversions; to which end, apparently by the Sovereign's order, a dramatic representation of the *Ten Virgins* was schemed, and at Eisenach, in his presence, duly executed. This happened fifteen days after Easter, by indulgence of the Preaching Friars. In the *Chronicon Sampetrinum*, stands recorded that the play was enacted in the Bear-garden, (*in horto ferarum*,) by the Clergy and their Scholars. But now, when it came to pass that the Wise Virgins would give the Foolish no oil, and these latter were shut out from the Bridegroom, they began to weep bitterly, and called on the Saints to intercede for them; who, however, even with Mary at their head, could effect nothing from God; but the Foolish Virgins were all sentenced to damnation. Which things the Landgraf seeing and hearing, he fell into a doubt, and was very angry; and said, 'What then is the Christian Faith, if God will not take pity on us, for intercession of Mary and all the Saints?' In this anger he continued five days; and the learned men could hardly enlighten him to understand the Gospel. Thereupon he was struck with apoplexy, and became speechless and powerless; in which sad state he continued, bedrid, two years and seven months, and so died, being then fifty-five."*

Surely a serious warning, would they but take it, to Dramatic Critics, not to venture beyond their depth! Had this fiery old Landgraf given up the reins of his imagination into his author's hands, he might have been pleased he knew not why; whereas the meshes of Theology, in which he kicks and struggles, here strangle the life out of him; and the Ten Virgins at Eisenach are more fatal to warlike men, than Æschylus' Furies at Athens were to weak women.

Neither were the unlearned People without their Literature, their Narrative Poetry; though how, in an age without printing and bookstalls, it was circulated among them; whether by strolling *Fiedelers*, (Minstrels,) who might recite as well as fiddle, or by other methods, we have not learned. However, its existence and abundance in this era is sufficiently evinced by the multitude of *Volksbücher* (People's-Books) which issued from the Press, next century, almost as soon as there was a Press. Several of these, which still languidly survive among the people, or at least the children, of all countries, were of German composition; of most, so strangely had they been sifted and winnowed to and fro, it was impossible to fix the origin. But borrowed or domestic, they nowhere wanted admirers in Germany: the *Patient Helena*, the *Fair Magelone*, *Blue-Beard*, *Fortunatus;* these, and afterwards the *Seven Wise Masters*, with other more directly Æsopic ware, to which the introduction of the old Indian Stock, or *Book of Wisdom*, translated from John of Capua's Latin,* one day formed a rich accession, were in all memories, and on all tongues.

Beautiful traits of Imagination and a pure genuine feeling, though under the rudest forms, shine forth in some of these old Tales: for instance, in *Magelone* and *Fortunatus;* which two, indeed, with others of a different stamp, Ludwig Tieck has, with singular talent, ventured, not unsuccessfully, to reproduce in our own time and dialect. A second class distinguish themselves by a homely, honest-hearted Wisdom, full of character and quaint devices; of which class the *Seven Wise Masters*, extracted chiefly from that *Gesta Romanorum* above mentioned, and containing "proverb-philosophy, anecdotes, fables, and jests, the seeds of which, on the fertile German soil, spread luxuriantly through several generations," is perhaps the best example. Lastly, in a third class, we find in full play that spirit of broad drollery, of rough, saturnine Humour, which the Germans claim as a special characteristic; among these, we must not omit to mention the *Schiltbürger*, correspondent to our own *Wise Men of Gotham;* still less, the far-famed *Tyll Eulenspiegel*, (Tyll Owlglass,) whose rogueries and waggeries belong, in the fullest sense, to this era.

This last is a true German work; for both the man Tyll Eulenspiegel, and the Book which is his history, were produced there. Nevertheless, Tyll's fame has gone abroad into all lands: this, the narrative of his exploits, has been published in innumerable editions, even with all manner of learned glosses, and translated into Latin, English, French, Dutch, Polish; nay, in several lan-

* Flögel, (*Geschichte der Romischen Literatur*, iv. 287,) who founds on that old *Chronicon Sampetrinum Erfurtense*, contained in Menke's Collection.

* In 1483, by command of a certain Eberhard, Duke of Würtemberg. What relation this old *Book of Wisdom* bears to our actual *Pilpay*, we have not learned.

guages, as in his own, an *Eulenspiegelerei*, an *Espièglerie*, or dog's trick, so named after him, still, by consent of lexicographers, keeps his memory alive. We may say, that to few mortals has it been granted to earn such a place in Universal History as Tyll: for now after five centuries, when Wallace's birth-place is unknown even to the Scots; and the admirable Crichton still more rapidly is grown a shadow; and Edward Longshanks sleeps unregarded save by a few Antiquarian English,—Tyll's native village is pointed out with pride to the traveller, and his tombstone, with a sculptured pun on his name, an Owl, namely, and a Glass, still stands, or pretends to stand, "at Möllen, near Lubeck," where, since 1350, his once nimble bones have been at rest. Tyll, in the calling he had chosen, naturally led a wandering life, as place after place became too hot for him; by which means he saw into many things with his own eyes: having been not only over all Westphalia and Saxony, but even in Poland, and as far as Rome. That in his old days, like other great men, he became an Autobiographer, and in trustful winter evening, not on paper, but on air, and to the laughter-lovers of Möllen, composed this work himself, is purely an hypothesis; certain only that it came forth originally in the dialect of this region, namely, the *Platt-Deutsch*; and was therefrom translated, probably about a century afterwards, into its present High German, as Lessing conjectures, by one Thomas Mürner, who on other grounds is not unknown to antiquarians. For the rest, write it who might, the Book is here, "abounding," as a wise Critic remarks, "in inventive humour, in rough merriment and broad drollery, not without a keen rugged shrewdness of insight; which properties must have made it irresistibly captivating to the popular sense; and, with all its fantastic extravagancies and roguish crotchets, in many points instructive."

From Tyll's so captivating achievements, we shall here select one to insert some account of; the rather as the tale is soon told, and by means of it, we catch a little trait of manners, and, through Tyll's spectacles, may peep into the interior of a Household, even of a Parsonage, in those old days.

"It chanced after so many adventures, that Eulenspiegel came to a Parson, who promoted him to be his Sacristan, or as we now say, Sexton. Of this Parson it is recorded that he kept a Concubine, who had but one eye; she also had a spite at Tyll, and was wont to speak evil of him to his master, and report his rogueries. Now while Eulenspiegel held this Sextoncy, the Easter-season came, and there was to be a play set forth of the Resurrection of Our Lord. And as the people were not learned, and could not read, the Parson took his Concubine and stationed her in the holy Sepulchre by way of Angel. Which thing Eulenspiegel seeing, he took to him three of the simplest persons that could be found there, to enact the Three Marys; and the Parson himself, with a flag in his hand, represented Christ. Thereupon spake Eulenspiegel to the simple persons: 'When the Angel asks you, whom ye seek, ye must answer, The Parson's one-eyed Concubine.' Now it came to pass that the time arrived when they were to act, and the Angel asked them: 'Whom seek ye here?' and they answered, as Eulenspiegel had taught and bidden them, and said: 'We seek the Parson's one-eyed Concubine.' Whereby did the Parson observe that he was made a mock of. And when the Parson's Concubine heard the same, she started out of the Grave, and aimed a box at Eulenspiegel's face, but missed him, and hit one of the simple persons, who were representing the Three Marys. This latter then returned her a slap on the mouth, whereupon she caught him by the hair. But his wife seeing this, came running thither, and fell upon the Parson's Harlot. Which thing the Parson discerning, he threw down his flag, and sprang forward to his Harlot's assistance. Thus gave they one another hearty thwacking and basting, and there was great uproar in the Church. But when Eulenspiegel perceived that they all had one another by the ears in the Church, he went his ways, and came no more back."*

These and the like pleasant narratives were the People's Comedy in those days. Neither was their Tragedy wanting; as indeed both spring up spontaneously in all regions of human Life; however, their chief work of this latter class, the wild, deep, and now world-renowned, *Legend of Faust*, belongs to a somewhat later date.†

Thus, though the Poetry which spoke in rhyme was feeble enough, the spirit of Poetry could nowise be regarded as extinct; while Fancy, Imagination, and all the intellectual faculties necessary for that art, were in active exercise. Neither had the Enthusiasm of

* Flögel, iv. 290. For more of Eulenspiegel, see Görres's *Ueber die Volksbücher*.

† To the fifteenth century, say some who fix it on Johann Faust, the Goldsmith and partial Inventor of Printing: to the sixteenth century, say others, referring it to Johann Faust, Doctor in Philosophy; which individual did actually, as the Tradition also bears, study first at Wittenberg (where he might be one of Luther's pupils,) then at Ingolstadt, where also he taught, and had a *Famulus* named Wagner, son of a clergyman at Wasserberg. Melancthon, Tritheim, and other credible witnesses, some of whom had seen the man, vouch sufficiently for these facts. The rest of the Doctor's history is much more obscure. He seems to have been of a vehement, unquiet temper; skilled in Natural Philosophy, and perhaps in the occult science of Conjuring, by aid of which two gifts, a much shallower man, wandering in Need and Pride over the world in those days, might, without any Mephistopheles, have worked wonders enough. Nevertheless, that he rode off through the air on a wine-cask, from Auerbach's Keller at Leipzig, in 1523, seems questionable; though an old carving, in that venerable Tavern, still mutely asserts it to the toper of this day. About 1560, his term of Thaumaturgy being over, he disappeared: whether, under feigned name, by the rope of some hangman; or "frightfully torn in pieces by the Devil, near the village of Rimlich, between Twelve and One in the morning," let each reader judge for himself. The latter was clearly George Rudolf Weidman's opinion, whose *Veritable History of the abominable Sins of Dr. Johann Faust* came out at Hamburg in 1599; and is no less circumstantially announced in the old "People's-Book, *That everywhere-infamous Arch-Black-Artist and Conjurer, Dr. Faust's Compact with the Devil, Wonderful-Walk and Conversation, and terrible End*, printed, seemingly without date, at Köln (Cologne) and Nurnberg; read by every one; written by we know not whom." See again, for farther insight, Görres's *Ueber die deutschen Volksbücher*. Another Work, (Liepzig, 1824,) expressly "On Faust and the Wandering Jew," which latter, in those times, wandered much in Germany, is also referred to.—*Conv. Lexicon*, ♮ *Faust*.

heart, on which it still more intimately depends, died out; but only taken another form. In lower degrees it expressed itself as an ardent zeal for Knowledge, and Improvement; for spiritual excellence such as the time held out and prescribed. This was no languid, low-minded age, but of earnest busy effort; in all provinces of culture, resolutely struggling forward. Classical Literature, after long hindrances, had now found its way into Germany also: old Rome was open, with all its wealth, to the intelligent eye; scholars of Chrysoloras were fast unfolding the treasures of Greece. School Philosophy, which had never obtained firm footing among the Germans, was in all countries drawing to a close; but the subtile, piercing vision, which it had fostered and called into activity, was henceforth to employ itself with new profit on more substantial interests. In such manifold praiseworthy endeavours the most ardent mind had ample arena.

A higher, purer enthusiasm, again, which no longer found its place in chivalrous Minstrelsy, might still retire to meditate and worship in religious Cloisters, where, amid all the corruption of monkish manners, there were not wanting men who aimed at, and accomplished, the highest problem of manhood, a life of spiritual Truth. Among the Germans, especially, that deep-feeling, deep-thinking, devout temper, now degenerating into abstruse theosophy, now purifying itself into holy eloquence, and clear apostolic light, was awake in this era; a temper which had long dwelt, and still dwells there; which ere long was to render that people worthy the honour of giving Europe a new Reformation, a new Religion. As an example of monkish diligence and zeal, if of nothing more, we here mention the German Bible of Mathias von Behaim, which, in his Hermitage at Halle, he rendered from the Vulgate, in 1343; the Manuscript of which is still to be seen in Leipzig. Much more conspicuous stand two other German Priests of this Period; to whom, as connected with Literature also, a few words must now be devoted.

Johann Tauler is a name which fails in no Literary History of Germany: he was a man famous in his own day as the most eloquent of preachers; is still noted by critics for his intellectual deserts; by pious persons, especially of the class called Mystics, is still studied as a practical instructor; and by all true inquirers prized as a person of high talent and moral worth. Tauler was a Dominican Monk; seems to have lived and preached at Strasburg; where, as his grave-stone still testifies, he died in 1361. His devotional works have been often edited: one of his modern admirers has written his biography; wherein perhaps this is the strangest fact, if it be one, that once in the pulpit "he grew suddenly dumb, and did nothing but weep; in which despondent state he continued for two whole years." Then, however, he again lifted up his voice, with new energy and new potency. We learn farther, that he "renounced the dialect of Philosophy, and spoke direct to the heart in language of the heart." His Sermons, composed in Latin and delivered in German, in which language, after repeated renovations and changes of dialect, they are still read, have, with his other writings, been characterized, by a native critic worthy of confidence, in these terms:

"They contain a treasure of meditations, hints, indications full of heartfelt piety, which still speak to the inmost longings and noblest wants of man's Mind. His style is abrupt, compressed, significant in its conciseness; the nameless depth of feelings struggles with the phraseology. He was the first that wrested from our German speech the fit expression for ideas of moral Reason and Emotion, and has left us riches in that kind, such as the zeal for purity and fulness of language in our own days cannot leave unheeded."—Tauler, it is added, "was a man who, imbued with genuine Devotedness, as it springs from the depths of a soul strengthened in self-contemplation, and, free and all-powerful, rules over Life and Effort,—attempted to train and win the people for a duty which had hitherto been considered as that of the learned class alone: to raise the Lay-world into moral study of Religion for themselves, that so, enfranchised from the bonds of unreflecting custom, they might regulate Creed and Conduct by strength self-acquired. He taught men to look within; by spiritual contemplation to feel the secret of their higher Destiny; to seek in their own souls what from without is never, or too scantily afforded; self-believing, to create what, by the dead letter of foreign Tradition, can never be brought forth."*

Known to all Europe, as Tauler is to Germany, and of a class with him, as a man of antique Christian walk, of warm, devoutly-feeling, poetic spirit, and insight and experience in the deepest regions of man's heart and life, follows, in the next generation, Thomas Hamerken, or Hammerlein, (*Malleolus;*) usually named *Thomas à Kempis*, that is, *Thomas of Kempen*, a village near Cologne, where he was born in 1388. Others contend that Kampen in Overyssel was his birthplace; however, in either case, at that era, more especially, considering what he did, we can here regard him as a *Deutscher*, a German. For his spiritual and intellectual character we may refer to his works, written in the Latin tongue, and still known; above all, to his far-famed work *De Imitatione Christi*, which has been praised by such men as Luther, Leibnitz, Haller; and, what is more, has been read, and continues to be read, with moral profit, in all Christian languages and communions, having passed through upwards of a thousand editions, which number is yet daily increasing. A new English *Thomas à Kempis* was published only the other year. But the venerable man deserves a word from us, not only as a high, spotless Priest, and father of the Church, at a time when such were rare, but as a zealous promotor of learning, which, in his own country, he accomplished much to forward. Hammerlein, the son of poor parents, had been educated at the famous school of Deventer; he himself instituted a

* Wachler, *Vorlesungen über die Geschichte der deutschen National-literatur* (Lectures onthe History of German National Literature,) b. i. s. 131.

similar one at Zwoll, which long continued the grand classical seminary of the North. Among his own pupils we find enumerated Moritz von Spiegelberg, Rudolf von Lange, Rudolf Agricola, Antonius Liber, Ludwig Dringenberg, Alexander Hegius; of whom Agricola, with other two, by advice of their teacher, visited Italy to study Greek; the whole six, united through manhood and life, as they had been in youth and at school, are regarded as the founders of true classical literature among the Germans. Their scholastico-monastic establishments at Derventer, with Zwoll and its other numerous offspring, which rapidly extended themselves over the Northwest of Europe from Artois to Silesia, and operated powerfully both in a moral and intellectual view, are among the characteristic redeeming features of that time; but the details of them fall not within our present limits.*

If now, quitting the Cloister and Library, we look abroad over active Life, and the general state of culture and spiritual endeavour as manifested there, we have on all hands the cheering prospect of a society in full progress. The Practical Spirit, which had pressed forward into Poetry itself, could not but be busy and successful in those provinces where its home specially lies. Among the Germans, it is true, so far as political condition was concerned, the aspect of affairs had not changed for the better. The Imperial Constitution was weakened and loosened into the mere semblance of a Government; the head of which had still the title, but no longer the reality of sovereign power; so that Germany, ever since the times of Rudolf, had, as it were, ceased to be one great nation, and become a disunited, often conflicting aggregate of small nations. Nay, we may almost say, of petty districts, or even of households: for now, when every pitiful Baron claimed to be an independent potentate, and exercised his divine right of peace and war, too often in plundering the industrious Burgher, public Law could no longer vindicate the weak against the strong; except the venerable unwritten code of *Faustrécht*, (Club-Law,) there was no other valid. On every steep rock, or difficult fastness, these dread sovereigns perched themselves; studding the country with innumerable *Raubschlösser*, (Robber-Towers,) which now in the eye of the picturesque tourist look interesting enough, but in those days were interesting on far other grounds. Herein dwelt a race of persons, proud, ignorant, hungry; who, boasting of an endless pedigree, talked familiarly of living on the produce of their "Saddles," (*vom Sattel zu leben*,) that is to say, by the profession of highwaymen, for which, unluckily, as mentioned, there was then no effectual gallows. Some, indeed, might plunder as the eagle, others as the vulture and crow; but, in general, from men cultivating that walk of life, no profit in any other was to be looked for. Vain was it, however, for the Kaiser to publish edict on edict against them; nay, if he destroyed their Robber-Towers, new ones were built; was the old wolf hunted down, the cub had escaped, who re-appeared when his teeth were grown. Not till industry and social cultivation had everywhere spread, and risen supreme, could that brood, in detail, be extirpated or tamed.

Neither was this miserable defect of police the only misery in such a state of things. For the Saddle-eating Baron, even in pacific circumstances, naturally looked down on the fruit-producing Burgher; who, again, feeling himself a wiser, wealthier, better, and, in time, a stronger man, ill brooked this procedure, and retaliated, or, by quite declining such communications, avoided it. Thus, throughout long centuries, and after that old code of Club-Law had been well-nigh abolished, the effort of the nation was still divided into two courses; the Noble and the Citizen would not work together, freely imparting and receiving their several gifts; but the culture of the polite arts, and that of the useful arts, had to proceed with mutual disadvantage, each on its separate footing. Indeed that supercilious and too marked distinction of ranks, which so ridiculously characterized the Germans, has only in very recent times disappeared.

Nevertheless here, as it ever does, the strength of the country lay in the middle classes; which were sound and active, and, in spite of all these hindrances, daily advancing. The Free towns, which, in Germany as elsewhere, the sovereign favoured, held within their walls a race of men as brave as they of the Robber-Tower, but exercising their bravery on fitter objects; who, by degrees, too, ventured into the field against even the greatest of these kinglets, and in many a stout fight taught them a juristic doctrine, which no head, with all its helmets, was too thick for taking in. The Four Forest Cantons had already testified in this way; their Tells and Stauffachers preaching, with apostolic blows and knocks, like so many Luthers; whereby, from their remote Alpine glens, all lands and all times have heard them, and believed them. By dint of such logic it began to be understood everywhere, that a Man, whether clothed in purple cloaks or in tanned sheep-skins, wielding the sceptre or the ox-goad, is neither Deity nor Beast, but simply a Man, and must comport himself accordingly.

But commerce of itself was pouring new strength into every peaceable community; the Hanse League, now in full vigour, secured the fruits of industry over all the North. The havens of the Netherlands, thronged with ships from every sea, transmitted or collected their wide-borne freight over Germany; where, far inland, flourished market-cities, with their cunning workmen, their spacious warehouses, and merchants who in opulence vied with the richest. Except perhaps in the close vicinity of Robber-Towers, and even there not always nor altogether, Diligence, good Order, peaceful abundance were everywhere conspicuous in Germany. Petrarch has celebrated, in warm terms, the beauties of the Rhine, as he witnessed them; the rich, embellished, cultivated aspect of land and people: Æneas Sylvius, afterwards Pope Pius the Second, expresses himself, in the next century, with still greater emphasis; he says, and he could judge, having seen both, "that the King of Scotland did not

* See Eichhorn's *Geschichte der Literatur*, b. ii. s. 134.

live so handsomely as a moderate Citizen of Nürnberg:" indeed Conrad Celtes, another contemporary witness, informs us, touching these same citizens, that their wives went abroad loaded with the richest jewels, that "most of their household utensils were of silver and gold." For, as Æneas Sylvius adds, "their mercantile activity is astonishing; the greater part of the German nation consists of merchants." Thus, too, in Augsburg, the Fugger family, which sprang, like that of the Medici, from smallest beginnings, were fast rising into that height of commercial greatness, such that Charles V., in viewing the Royal Treasury at Paris, could say, "I have a weaver in Augsburg able to buy it all with his own gold."* With less satisfaction, the same haughty Monarch had to see his own Nephew wedded to the fair Philippine Welser, daughter of another merchant in that city, and for wisdom and beauty the paragon of her time.†

In this state of economical prosperity, Literature and Art, such kinds of them at least as had a practical application, could not want encouragement. It is mentioned as one of the furtherances to Classical Learning among the Germans, that these Free Towns, as well as numerous petty Courts of Princes, exercising a sovereign power, required individuals of some culture to conduct their Diplomacy; one man able at least to write a handsome Latin style was an indispensable requisite. For a long while even this small accomplishment was not to be acquired in Germany; where, such had been the troublous condition of the Governments, there were yet, in the beginning of the fourteenth century, no Universities: however, a better temper and better fortune began at length to prevail among the German Sovereigns; the demands of the time insisted on fulfilment. The University of Prague was founded in 1348, that of Vienna in 1364;* and now, as if to make up for the delay, princes and communities on all hands made haste to establish similar Institutions; so that before the end of the century we find three others, Heidelberg, Cologne, Erfurt; in the course of the next no fewer than eight more, of which Leipzig (in 1404) is the most remarkable. Neither did this honourable zeal grow cool in the sixteenth century, or even down to our own, when Germany, boasting of some forty great Schools and twenty-two Universities, four of which date within the last thirty years, may fairly reckon itself the best school-provided country in Europe; as, indeed, those who in any measure know it are aware that it is also indisputably the best educated.

Still more decisive are the proofs of national activity, of progressive culture among the Germans, if we glance at what concerns the practical Arts. Apart from Universities and learned show, there has dwelt, in those same Nürnbergs and Augsburgs, a solid, quietly-perseverant spirit, full of old Teutonic character and old Teutonic sense; whereby, ever and anon, from under the bonnet of some rugged German artisan or staid Burgher, this and the other World's Invention has been starting forth, where such was least of all looked for. Indeed with regard to practical Knowledge in General, if we consider the present history and daily life of mankind, it must be owned that while each nation has contributed a share,—the largest share, at least of such shares as can be appropriated and fixed on any special contributor, belongs to Germany. Copernic, Hevel, Kepler, Otto Guericke, are of other times; but in this era also the spirit of Inquiry, of Invention, was especially busy. Gunpowder, (of the thirteenth century,) though Milton gives the credit of it to Satan, has helped mightily to lessen the horrors of war: thus much at least must be admitted in its favour, that it secures the dominion of

* Charles had his reasons for such a speech. This same Auton Fugger, to whom he alluded here, had often stood by him in straits, showing a munificence and even generosity worthy of the proudest princes. During the celebrated Diet of Augsburg, in 1530, the Emperor lodged for a whole year in Auton's house; and Auton was a man to warm his Emperor "at a fire of cinnamon wood," and to burn therein "the bonds for large sums owing him by his majesty." For all which, Auton and his kindred had countships and princeships in abundance; also the right to coin money, but no solid bullion to exercise such right on; which, however, they repeatedly did on bullion of their own. This Auton left six millions of gold-crowns in cash: "besides precious articles, jewels, properties in all countries of Europe, and both the Indies." The Fuggers had ships on every sea, wagons on every highway; they worked the Carinthian Mines; even Albrecht Dürer's Pictures must pass through their warehouses to the Italian market. However, this family had other merits than their mountains of metal, their kindness to needy sovereigns, and even their all-embracing spirit of commercial enterprise. They were famed for acts of general beneficence, and did much charity where no imperial thanks were to be looked for. To found Hospitals and Schools, on the most liberal scale, was a common thing with them. In the sixteenth century, three benevolent brothers of the House purchased a suburb of Augsburg; rebuilt it with small commodious houses, to be let to indigent industrious burghers for a trifling rent: this is the well-known *Fuggerei*, which, still existing, with its own walls and gate, maintains their name in daily currency there. —The founder of this remarkable family did actually drive the shuttle in the village of Göggingen, near Augsburg, about the middle of the Fourteenth century; "but in 1619," says the *Spiegel der Ehren*, (Mirror of Honour,) "the noble stem had so branched out that there were forty-seven Counts and Countesses belonging to it, and of young descendants as many as there are days in the year." Four stout boughs of the same noble stem, in the rank of Princes, still subsist and flourish. "Thus in the generous Fuggers," says that above-named *Mirror*, "was fulfilled our Saviour's promise: 'Give, and it shall be given you.'"—*Conv. Lexicon*, ☧ *Fugger-Geschlecht*.

† The Welsers were of patrician descent, and had for many centuries followed commerce at Augsburg, where, next only to the Fuggers, they played a high part. It was they, for example that, at their own charges, first colonized Venezuela; that equipped the first German ship to India, "the Journal of which still exists;" they united with the Fuggers to lend Charles V. twelve *Tonnen Gold*, 1,200,000 Florins. The fair Philippine, by her pure charms and honest wiles, worked out a reconciliation with Kaiser Ferdinand the First, her Father-in law; lived thirty happy years with her husband; and had medals struck by him, *Divæ Philippinæ*, in honour of her, when (at Innspruck in 1580) he became a widower. —*Conv. Lexicon*, ☧ *Welser*.

* There seems to be some controversy about the precedence here: Bouterwek gives Vienna, with a date 1333, as the earliest; Koch again puts Heidelberg, 1346, in front; the dates in the Text profess to be taken from Meiner's *Geschichte der Enstehung und Entwickelung der Hohen Schulen unsers Erdtheils*, (History of the Origin and Development of High Schools in Europe,) Göttingen, 1802. The last established University is that of München, (Munich,) in 1826. Prussia alone has 21,000 Public Schoolmasters, specially trained to their profession, sometimes even sent to travel for improvement at the cost of Government. What says "the most enlightened nation in the world" to this?—Eats its pudding, and says little or nothing.

civilized over savage man: nay, hereby, in personal contests, not brute Strength, but Courage and Ingenuity, can avail; for the Dwarf and the Giant are alike strong with pistols between them. Neither can Valour now find its best arena in War, in Battle, which is henceforth a matter of calculation and strategy, and the soldier a chess-pawn to shoot and be shot at: whereby that noble quality may at length come to reserve itself for other more legitimate occasions, of which, in this our Life-Battle with Destiny, there are enough. And thus Gunpowder, if it spread the havoc of War, mitigates it in a still higher degree; like some Inoculation,—to which may an extirpating Vaccination one day succeed! It ought to be stated, however, that the claim of Schwartz to the original invention is dubious; to the sole invention altogether unfounded: the recipe stands under disguise in the writings of Roger Bacon; the article itself was previously known in the East.

Far more indisputable are the advantages of Printing: and if the story of Brother Schwartz's mortar giving fire and driving his pestle through the ceiling, in the city of Mentz, as the painful Monk and Alchymist was accidentally pounding the ingredients of our first Gunpowder, is but a fable,—that of our first Book being printed there is much better ascertained. Johann Gutenberg was a native of Mentz; and there, in company with Faust and Schöffer, appears to have completed his invention, between the years 1440 and 1449: the famous "Forty-two line Bible" was printed there in 1455.* Of this noble art, which is like an infinitely intensated organ of Speech, whereby the Voice of a small transitory man may reach not only through all earthly Space, but through all earthly Time, it were needless to repeat the often-repeated praises; or speculate on the practical effects, the most momentous of which are, perhaps, but now becoming visible. On this subject of the Press, and its German origin, a far humbler remark may be in place here; namely, that Rag-paper, the material on which Printing works and lives, was also invented in Germany some hundred and fifty years before. "The oldest specimens of this article yet known to exist," says Eichhorn, "are some Documents, of the year 1318, in the Archives of the Hospital at Kaufbeuern. Breitkopf (*Vom Ursprung der Spielkarten*, On the Origin of Cards) has demonstrated our claim to the invention; and that France and England borrowed it from Germany, and Spain from Italy."†

On the invention of Printing there followed naturally a multiplication of Books, and a new activity, which has ever since proceeded at an accelerating rate, in the business of Literature; but for the present, no change in its character or objects. Those Universities, and other Establishments and Improvements, were so many tools which the spirit of the time had devised, not for working out new paths, which was their ulterior issue, but, in the mean while, for proceeding more commodiously on the old path. In the Prague University, it is true, whither Wickliffe's writings had found their way, a teacher of more earnest tone had risen, in the person of John Huss, Rector there; whose Books, *Of the Six Errors* and *Of the Church*, still more his energetic, zealously polemical Discourses to the people, were yet unexampled on the Continent. The shameful murder of this man, who lived and died as beseemed a Martyr; and the stern vengeance which his countrymen took for it, unhappily not on the Constance Cardinals, but on less offensive Bohemian Catholics, kept up during twenty years, on the Eastern Border of Germany, an agitating tumult, not only of opinion, but of action: however, the fierce, indomitable Zisca being called away, and the pusillanimous Emperor offering terms, which, indeed, he did not keep, this uproar subsided, and the national activity proceeded in its former course.

In German Literature, during those years, nothing presents itself as worthy of notice here. Chronicles were written; Class-books for the studious, edifying Homilies, in varied guise, for the busy, were compiled: a few Books of Travels made their appearance, among which Translations from our too fabulous countryman, Mandeville, are perhaps the most remarkable. For the rest, Life continued to be looked at less with poetic admiration, than in a spirit of observation and comparison: not without many a protest against clerical and secular error; such, however, seldom rising into the style of grave hate and hostility, but playfully expressing themselves in satire. The old effort towards the Useful; in Literature, the old prevalence of the Didactic, especially of the Æsopic, is everywhere manifest. Of this Æsopic spirit, what phases it successively assumed, and its significance in these, there were much to be said. However, in place of multiplying smaller instances and aspects, let us now take up the highest; and with the best of all Apologues, *Reynard the Fox*, terminates our survey of that Fable-loving time.

The story of *Reinecke Fuchs*, or, to give it the original Low-German name, *Reineke de Fos*, is, more than any other, a truly European performance: for some centuries, a universal household possession and secular Bible, read everywhere, in the palace and the hut; it still interests us, moreover, by its intrinsic worth, being on the whole the most poetical and meritorious production of our Western World in that kind; or perhaps of the whole World, though in such matters, the West has generally yielded to, and learned from, the East.

Touching the origin of this Book, as often happens in like cases, there is a controversy, perplexed not only by inevitable ignorance, but also by anger and false patriotism. Into this vexed sea we have happily no call to venture; and shall merely glance for a moment, from the firm land, where all that can specially concern us in the matter stands secured and safe. The oldest printed Edition of our actual

* As to the Dutch claim, it rests only on vague local traditions, which were never heard of publicly till their Lorenz Coster had been dead almost a hundred and fifty years; so that, out of Holland, it finds few partisans.

† B. ii. s. 91.—"The first German Paper-mill we have sure account of," says Koch, "worked at Nürnberg in 1390."—Vol. i. p. 35.

Reynard is that of Lübeck, in 1498; of which there is a copy, understood to be the only one, still extant in the Wolfenbüttel Library. This oldest Edition is in the Low-German or Saxon tongue, and appears to have been produced by Hinrek van Alkmer, who in the Preface calls himself "Schoolmaster and Tutor of that noble virtuous Prince and Lord, the Duke of Lorraine;" and says farther, that by order of this same worthy sovereign, he "sought out and rendered the present Book from the Walloon and French tongue into German, to the praise and honour of God, and wholesome edification of whoso readeth therein." Which candid and business-like statement would doubtless have continued to yield entire satisfaction; had it not been that, in modern days, and while this first Lübeck Edition was still lying in its dusty recess unknown to Bibliomaniacs, another account, dated some hundred years later, and supported by a little subsequent hearsay, had been raked up: how the real Author was Nicholas Baumann, Professor at Rostock; how he had been Secretary to the Duke of Juliers, but was driven from his service by wicked cabals; and so in revenge composed this satirical adumbration of the Juliers Court; putting on the title-page, to avoid consequences, the feigned tale of its being rendered from the French and Walloon tongue, and the feigned name of Hinrek van Alkmer, who, for the rest, was never Schoolmaster and Tutor at Lorraine, or anywhere else, but a mere man of straw, created for the nonce, out of so many Letters of the Alphabet. Hereupon excessive debate, and a learned sharp-shooting, with victory-shouts on both sides; into which we nowise enter. Some touch of human sympathy does draw us towards Hinrek, whom, if he was once a real man, with bones and sinews, stomach and provender-scrip, it is mournful to see evaporated away into mere vowels and consonants: however, beyond a kind wish, we can give him no help. In Literary History, except on this one occasion, as seems indisputable enough, he is nowhere mentioned or hinted at.

Leaving Hinrek and Nicolaus, then, to fight out their quarrel as they may, we remark that the clearest issue of it would throw little light on the origin of *Reinecke*. The victor could at most claim to be the first German redactor of this Fable, and the happiest; whose work had superseded and obliterated all preceding ones whatsoever; but nowise to be the inventor thereof, who must be sought for in a much remoter period. There are even two printed versions of the Tale, prior in date to this of Lübeck: a Dutch one, at Delft in 1484; and one by Caxton in English, in 1481, which seems to be the earliest of all.* These two differ essentially from Hinrek's; still more so does the French *Roman du nouveau Renard*, composed "by Jacquemars Gielée at Lisle, about the year 1290," which yet exists in manuscript: however, they sufficiently verify that statement, by some supposed to be feigned, of the German redactor's having "sought and rendered" his work from the Walloon and French; in which latter tongue, as we shall soon see, some shadow of it had been known and popular, long centuries before that time. For besides Gielée's work, we have a *Renard Couronné* of still earlier, a *Renard Contrefait* of somewhat later date: and Chroniclers inform us that, at the noted Festival given by Philip the Fair, in the beginning of the fourteenth century, among the dramatic entertainments, was a whole Life of Reynard; wherein it must not surprise us that he "ended by becoming Pope, and still, under the Tiara, continued to eat poultry." Nay, curious inquirers have discovered on the French and German borders, some vestige of the Story even in Carlovingian times, which, indeed, again makes it a German original: they will have it that a certain Reinhard, or Reinecke, Duke of Lorraine, who, in the ninth century, by his craft and exhaustless stratagems worked strange mischief in that region, many times overreaching King Zwentibald himself, and at last, in his stronghold of Durfos, proving impregnable to him,—had in satirical songs of that period been celebrated as a *fox*, as *Reinhard the Fox*, and so given rise afar off to this Apologue, at least to the title of it. The name *Isegrim*, as applied to the Wolf, these same speculators deduce from an Austrian Count Isengrin, who, in those old days, had revolted against Kaiser Arnulph, and otherwise exhibited too wolfish a disposition. Certain it is, at least, that both designations were in universal use during the twelfth century; they occur, for example, in one of the two *sirventes* which our Cœur-de-Lion has left us: "ye have promised me fidelity," says he, "but ye have kept it as the Wolf did to the Fox," as *Isangrin* did to *Reinhart*.* Nay, perhaps the ancient circulation of some such Song, or Tale, among the French, is best of all evinced by the fact that this same *Reinhart*, or *Renard*, is still the only word in their language for *Fox;* and thus, strangely enough, the Proper may have become an Appellative; and sly Duke Reinhart, at an era when the French tongue was first evolving itself from the rubbish of Latin and German, have insinuated his name into Natural as well as Political History.

From all which, so much at least would appear: That the Fable of *Reynard the Fox*, which in the German version we behold completed, nowise derived its completeness from the individual there named Hinrek van Alkmer, or from any other individual, or people: but rather, that being in old times universally current, it was taken up by poets and satirists of all countries; from each received some acces-

* Caxton's Edition, a copy of which is in the British Museum, bears title: *Hystorye of Reynart the Foxe:* and begins thus:—"It was aboute the tyme of Pentecoste or Whytsontyde that the wodes comynly be lusty and gladsome, and the trees clad with levys and blossoms, and the grounds with herbes and flowers sweete smellyng;"—where, as in many other passages, the fact that Caxton and Alkmer had the same original before them is manifest enough. Our venerable Printer says in conclusion: "I have not added ne mynnsshed but have followed as nyghe as I can my copye whych was in dutche; and by me Willm Caxton translated in to this rude and symple englyssh in thabbey of Westminster, and fynnyshed the vi daye of Juyn the yere of our lord 1481, the 21 yere of the regne of Kynge Edward the iiijth."

* Flögel, (iii. 31,) who quotes the *Histoire Litteraire des Troubadours*, t. i. p. 63.

sion or improvement; and properly has no single author. We must observe, however, that as yet it had attained no fixation or consistency; no version was decidedly preferred to every other. Caxton's and the Dutch appear, at best, but as the skeleton of what afterwards became a body; of the old Walloon version, said to have been discovered lately, we are taught to entertain a similar opinion:* in the existing French versions, which are all older, either in Gielée's, or in the others, there is even less analogy. Loosely conjoined, therefore, and only in the state of dry bones, was it that Hinrek, or Nicolaus, or some Lower-Saxon whoever he might be, found the story; and blowing on it with the breath of genius, raised it up into a consistent Fable. Many additions and some exclusions he must have made; was probably enough assisted by personal experience of a Court, whether that of Juliers or some other; perhaps also he admitted personal allusions, and doubtless many an oblique glance at existing things: and thus was produced the Low-German *Reineke de Fos*, which version, shortly after its appearance, had extinguished all the rest, and come to be, what it still is, the sole veritable representative of *Reynard*, inasmuch as all subsequent translations and editions have derived themselves from it.

The farther history of *Reinecke* is easily traced. In this new guise, it spread abroad over all the world, with a scarcely exampled rapidity; fixing itself also as a firm possession in most countries, where, indeed, in this character, we still find it. It was printed and rendered, innumerable times: in the original dialect alone, the last Editor has reckoned up more than twenty Editions; on one of which, for example, we find such a name as that of Heinrich Voss. It was first translated into High-German in 1545; into Latin in 1567, by Hartmann Schopper, whose smooth style and rough fortune keep him in memory with Scholars:† a new version into short German verse appeared next century; in our own times, Goethe has not disdained to re-produce it, by means of his own, in a third shape: Of Soltau's version, into literal doggerel, we have already testified. Long generations before, it had been manufactured into Prose, for the use of the people, and was sold on stalls; where still, with the needful changes in spelling, and printed on grayest paper, it tempts the speculative eye.

Thus has our old Fable, rising like some River in the remote distance, from obscure rivulets, gathered strength out of every valley, out of every country, as it rolled on. It is European in two senses; for as all Europe contributed to it, so all Europe has enjoyed it. Among the Germans, *Reinecke Fuchs* was long a House-book and universal Best-companion: it has been lectured on in Universities, quoted in Imperial Council-halls; it lay on the toilette of Princesses, and was thumbed to pieces on the bench of the Artisan; we hear of grave men ranking it only next to the Bible. Neither, as we said, was its popularity confined to home; Translations ere long appeared in French, Italian, Danish, Swedish, Dutch, English:* nor was that same stall-honour, which has been reckoned the truest literary celebrity, refused it here; perhaps many a reader of these pages may, like the writer of them, recollect the hours, when, hidden from unfeeling gaze of pedagogue, he swallowed *The most pleasant and delightful History of Renard the Fox*, like stolen waters, with a timorous joy.

So much for the outward fortunes of this remarkable Book. It comes before us with a character such as can belong only to a very few; that of being a true world's-Book, which through centuries was everywhere at home, the spirit of which diffused itself into all languages and all minds. These quaint Æsopic figures have painted themselves in innumerable heads; that rough, deep-lying humour has been the laughter of many generations. So that, at worst, we must regard this *Reinecke* as an ancient Idol, once worshipped, and still interesting for that circumstance, were the sculpture never so rude. We can love it, moreover, as being indigenous, wholly of our own creation: it sprang up from European sense and character, and was a faithful type and organ of these.

But independently of all extrinsic considerations, this Fable of *Reinecke* may challenge a judgment on its own merits. Cunningly constructed, and not without a true poetic life, we must admit it to be: great power of conception and invention, great pictorial fidelity, a warm, sunny tone of colouring, are manifest enough. It is full of broad, rustic mirth; inexhaustible in comic devices; a World-Saturnalia, where Wolves tonsured into Monks, and

---

* See Scheller; (*Reineke de Fos, To Brunswyk*, 1825;) *Vorrede*.

† While engaged in this Translation, at Freiburg in Baden, he was impressed as a soldier, and carried, apparently in fetters, to Vienna, having given his work to another to finish. At Vienna he stood not long in the ranks; having fallen violently sick, and being thrown out into the streets to recover there. He says, "he was without bed, and had to seek quarters on the muddy pavement, in a Barrel." Here too, in the night, some excessively straitened individual stole from him his cloak and sabre. However, men were not all hyenas; one Josias Hufnagel, unknown to him, but to whom by his writings he was known, took him under roof, procured medical assistance, equipped him anew; so that "in the harvest season, being half-cured, he could return or rather re-crawl to Frankfort on the Mayn." There too "a Magister Johann Cuipius, Christian Egenolph's son-in-law, kindly received him," and encouraged him to finish his Translation; as accordingly he did, dedicating it to the Emperor, with doleful complaints, fruitless or not is unknown. For now poor Hartmann, no longer an Autobiographer, quite vanishes, and we can understand only that he laid his wearied back one day in a most still bed, where the blanket of the Night softly enwrapped him and all his woes.——His Book is entitled *Opus poeticum de admirabili Fallaciâ et Astutiâ Vulpeculæ Reinekes*, &c. &c.; and in the Dedication and Preface contains all these details.

* Besides Caxton's original, of which little is known among us but the name, we have two versions; one in 1667, "with excellent Morals and Expositions," which was reprinted in 1681, and followed in 1684 by a continuation, called the *Shifts of Reynardine the Son of Reynard*, of English growth; another in 1708, slightly altered from the former, explaining what appears doubtful or allegorical; "it being originally written," says the brave editor elsewhere, "by an eminent Statesman of the German Empire, to show some Men their Follies, and correct the Vices of the Times he lived in." Not only *Reynardine* but a second Appendix, *Cawood the Rook*, appears here; also there are "curious Devices, or Pictures."—Of editions "printed for the Flying-Stationers," we say nothing.

nigh starved by short commons, Foxes pilgriming to Rome for absolution, Cocks pleading at the judgment-bar, make strange mummery. Nor is this wild Parody of Human Life without its meaning and moral: it is an Air-pageant from Fancy's Dream-grotto, yet Wisdom lurks in it; as we gaze, the vision becomes poetic and prophetic. A true Irony must have dwelt in the Poet's heart and head; here, under grotesque shadows, he gives us the saddest picture of Reality; yet for us without sadness; his figures mask themselves in uncouth, bestial vizards, and enact, gamboling: their Tragedy dissolves into sardonic grins. He has a deep, heartfelt Humour, sporting with the world and its evils in kind mockery: this is the poetic *soul*, round which the outward *material* has fashioned itself into living coherence. And so, in that rude old Apologue, we have still a mirror, though now tarnished and time-worn, of true magic reality; and can discern there, in cunning reflex, some image both of our destiny and of our duty: for now, as then, "Prudence is the only virtue sure of its reward," and cunning triumphs where Honesty is worsted; and now, as then, it is the wise man's part to know this, and cheerfully look for it, and cheerfully defy it:

> *Ut vulpis adulatio*
> Here through his own world moveth,
> *Sic hominis et ratio*
> Most like to Reynard's proveth.*

If *Reinecke* is nowise a perfect Comic Epos, it has various features of such, and, above all, a genuine Epic spirit, which is the rarest feature.

Of the Fable, and its incidents and structure, it is perhaps superfluous to offer any sketch; to most readers the whole may be already familiar. How Noble, King of the Beasts, holding a solemn Court, one Whitsuntide, is deafened on all hands with complaints against Reinecke; Hinze the Cat, Lampe the Hare, Isegrim the Wolf, with innumerable others, having suffered from his villany, Isegrim especially, in a point which most keenly touches honour; nay, Chanticleer the Cock, (*Henning de Hane*,) amid bitterest wail, appearing even with the *corpus delicti*, the body of one of his children, whom that arch-knave has feloniously murdered with intent to eat. How his indignant Majesty thereupon despatches Bruin the Bear to cite the delinquent in the King's name; how Bruin, inveigled into a Honey-Expedition, returns without his errand, without his ears, almost without his life; Hinze the Cat, in a subsequent expedition, faring no better. How at last Reinecke, that he may not have to stand actual siege in his fortress of Malapertus, does appear for trial, and is about to be hanged, but on the gallows-ladder makes a speech unrivalled in forensic eloquence, and saves his life; nay, having incidentally hinted at some Treasures, the hiding-place of which is well known to him, rises into high favour; is permitted to depart on that pious pilgrimage to Rome he has so much at heart, and furnished even with shoes, cut from the living hides of Isegrim and Isegrim's much-injured spouse, his worst enemies. How, the Treasures not making their appearance, but only new misdeeds, he is again haled to judgment; again glozes the general ear with sweetest speeches; at length, being challenged to it, fights Isegrim in knightly tourney, and by the cunningest, though the most unchivalrous method, not to be farther specified in polite writing, carries off a complete victory; and having thus, by wager of battle, manifested his innocence, is overloaded with royal favour; created Chancellor, and Pilot to weather the Storm; and so, in universal honour and authority, reaps the fair fruit of his gifts and labours.

> Whereby shall each to wisdom turn,
> Evil eschew, and virtue learn,
> Therefore was this same story wrote,
> That is its aim, and other not.
> This Book for little price is sold,
> But image clear of world doth hold;
> Whoso into the world would look,
> My counsel is,—he buy this book.
> So endeth Reynard's Fox's story:
> God help us all to heavenly glory!

It has been objected that the animals in *Reinecke* are not Animals, but Men disguised; to which objection, except in so far as grounded on the necessary indubitable fact that this is an Apologue or emblematic Fable, and no Chapter of Natural History, we cannot in any considerable degree accede. Nay, that very contrast between Object and Effort, where the Passions of men develope themselves on the Interests of animals, and the whole is huddled together in chaotic mockery, is a main charm of the picture. For the rest, we should rather say, these bestial characters were moderately well sustained: the vehement, futile vociferation of Chanticleer; the hysterical promptitude, and earnest profession and protestation of poor Lampe the Hare; the thick-headed ferocity of Isegrim; the sluggish, gluttonous opacity of Bruin; above all, the craft, the tact, and inexhaustible knavish adroitness of Reinecke himself, are in strict accuracy of costume. Often also their situations and occupations are bestial enough. What quantities of bacon and other provant do Isegrim and Reinecke forage; Reinecke contributing the scheme,—for the two were then in partnership,—and Isegrim paying the shot in broken bones! What more characteristic than the fate of Bruin, when, ill-counselled, he introduces his stupid head into Rustefill's half-split log, has the wedges whisked away, and stands clutched there, as in a vice, and uselessly roaring, disappointed of honey, sure only of a beating without parallel! Not to forget the Mare, whom, addressing her by the title of Good-wife, with all politeness, Isegrim, sore-pinched with hunger, asks whether she will sell her foal: she answers, that the price is written on her hinder hoof; which document the intending purchaser, being "an Erfurt graduate," declares his full ability to read; but finds there no writing, or print, save only the print of six horsenails on his own mauled visage. And abundance of the like; sufficient

* *Ut vulpis adulatio*
Nu in de werlde blikket:
Sic hominis et ratio
Gelyk dem Fos sik shikket.—Motto to *Reinecke.*

to excuse our old Epos on this head, or altogether justify it. Another objection, that, namely, which points to the great, and excessive coarseness of the work, here and there, it cannot so readily turn aside; being indeed rude, old-fashioned, and homespun, apt even to draggle in the mire: neither are its occasional dulness and tediousness to be denied; but only to be set against its frequent terseness and strength, and pardoned as the product of poor humanity, from whose hands nothing, not even a *Reineke de Fos*, comes perfect.

He who would read, and still understand this old Apologue, must apply to Goethe, whose version, for poetical use, we have found infinitely the best; like some copy of an ancient, bedimmed, half-obliterated woodcut, but new-done on steel, on India-paper, and with all manner of graceful, yet appropriate appendages. Nevertheless, the old Low-German original has also a certain charm, and, simply as the original, would claim some notice. It is reckoned greatly the best performance that was ever brought out in that dialect; interesting, moreover, in a philological point of view, especially to us English; being properly the language of our old Saxon Fatherland; and still curiously like our own, though the two, for some twelve centuries, have had no brotherly communication. One short specimen, with the most verbal translation, we shall here insert, and then have done with *Reinecke:*

"De Greving was Reinken broder's söne,
The Badger was Reinke's brother's son,
De sprak do, un was sêr köne.
He spake there, and was (sore) very (keen) bold.
He forantworde in dem Hove den Fos,
He (for-answered) defended in the Court the fox,
De dog was sêr falsh un lôs.
That (though) yet was very false and loose.
He sprak to deme Wulve also fôrd:
He spake to the Wolf so forth:
Here Isegrim, it is ein ôldspräken wôrd,
Master Isegrim, it is an old-spoken word,
Des fyendes mund shaffe, selden frôm!
The (fiends) enemy's mouth (shapeth) bringeth seldom advantage!
So do ji ôk by Reinken, mimen ôm.
So do ye (eke) too by Reinke, mine (eme) uncle.
Were he so wol alse ji hyre to Hove,
Were he as well as ye here at Court,
Un stunde he also in des Koninge's love,
And stood he so in the King's favour,
Here Isegrim, alse ji dôt,
Master Isegrim, as ye do,
It sholde ju nigt dünken gôd,
It should you not (think) seem good,
Dat ji en hyr alsus forspräken
That ye him here so forspake
Un de ôlden stükke hyr fôrräken.
And the old tricks here forth-raked.
Men dat kwerde, dat ji Reinken hävven gedân,
But the ill that ye Reinke have done,
Dat late ji al agter stan.
That let ye all (after stand) stand by.
It is nog etliken heren wol kund,
It is yet to some gentlemen well known,
Wo ji mid Reinken maken den ferbund,
How ye with Rienke made (bond) alliance,
Un wolden wären twe like gesellen;
And would be two (like) equal partners;
Dat mok ik dirren heren fortällen.
That mote I these gentlemen forth-tell.
Wente Reinke, myn ôm, in wintersnôd,
Since Reinke, mine uncle, in winter's-need,
Umme Isegrim's willen, fylna was dôd.
For Isegrim's (will) sake, full-nigh was dead.
Wente it geshang dat ein kwam gefaren,
For it chanced that one came (faring) driving,
De hadde grotte fishe up ener karen:
Who had many fishes upon a car:
Isegrim hadde geren der fishe gehaled,
Isegrim had fain the fishes (have haled) have got,
Men he hadde nigt, darmid se wörden betaled.
But he had not wherewith they should be (betold) paid.
He bragte minen ôm in de grote nôd,
He brought mine uncle into great (need) straits,
Um sinen willen ging he liggen for dôd,
For his sake went he to (lig) lie for dead,
Regt in den wäg, un stund äventur.
Right in the way, and stood (adventure) chance.
Market, worden em ôk de fishe sûr?
Mark, were him eke the fishes (sour) dear-bought?
Do jenne mid der kare gefaren kwam
When (yonder) he with the car driving came
Un minen ôm darsülvest fornem,
And mine uncle (there-self) even there perceived,
Hastigen tôg he syn swërd un snel,
Hastily (took) drew he his sword and (snell) quick,
Un wolde mineme ome torrüken en fel.
And would my uncle (tatter in fell) tear in pieces.
Men he rögede sik nigt klên nog grôt:
But he stirred himself not (little nor great) more or less;
Do mênde he dat he were dôd;
Then (meaned) thought he that he was dead;
He läde ön up de kar, und dayte on to fillen,
He laid him upon the car, and thought him to skin,
Dat wagede he all dorg Isegrim's willen!
That risked he all through Isegrim's will!
Do he fordan begunde to faren,
When he forth-on began to fare,
Wärp Reinke etlike fishe fan der karen,
Cast Reinke some fishes from the car.
Isegrim fan ferne agteona kwam
Isegrim from afar after came
Un derre fishe al to sik nam.
And these fishes all to himself took.
Reinke sprang wedder fan der karen;
Reinke sprang again from the car;
Em lüstede to nigt länger to faren,
Him listed not longer to fare.
He hadde ôk gêrne der fishe begërd,
He (had) would have also fain of the fishes required,
Men Isegrim hadde se alle fortêrd.
But Isegrim had them all consumed.
He hadde getan dat he wolde barsten,
He had eaten so that he would burst,
Un moste darumme gên torn arsten.
And must thereby go to the doctor.
Do Isegrim der graden nigt en mogte,
As Isegrim the fish-bones not liked,
Der sülven he em ein weinig brogte.
Of these same he him a little brought.

Whereby it would appear, if we are to believe Grimbart the Badger, that Reinecke was not only the cheater in this case, but also the cheatee; however, he makes matters straight again in that other noted fish expedition, where Isegrim minded not to steal but to catch fish, and having no fishing-tackle, by Reinecke's advice, inserts his tail into the lake, in winter-season; but before the promised string of trouts, all hooked to one another, and to him, will bite, is frozen in, and left there to his own bitter meditations.

We here take leave of Reineke de Fos, and of the whole Æsopic genus, of which it is almost the last, and by far the most remarkable example. The Age of Apologue, like that of Chivalry and Love-singing, is gone; for no thing in this Earth has continuance. If we ask, where are now our People's Books? the answer might give room for reflections. Hinrek van Alkmer has passed away, and Dr. Birkbeck has risen in his room. What good and evil lie in that little sentence!—But doubtless the day is coming when what is wanting here will be supplied; when as the Logical, so likewise the Poetical susceptibility and faculty of the people,—their Fancy, Humour, Imagination, wherein lie the main elements of spiritual life,—will no longer be left uncultivated, barren, or bearing only spontaneous thistles, but in new and finer harmony, with an improved Understanding, will flourish in new vigour; and in our inward world there will again be a sunny Firmament and verdant Earth, as well as a Pantry and culinary Fire; and men will learn not only to recapitulate and compute, but to worship, to love; in tears or in laughter, hold mystical as well as logical communion with the high and the low of this wondrous Universe; and read, as they should live, with their whole being. Of which glorious consummation there is at all times, seeing these endowments are indestructible, nay, essentially supreme, in man, the firmest ulterior certainty, but, for the present, only faint prospects and far-off indications. Time brings Roses!

TAYLOR'S HISTORIC SURVEY OF GERMAN POETRY.*

[Edinburgh Review, 1831.]

German Literature has now for upwards of half a century been making some way in England; yet by no means at a constant rate, rather in capricious flux and reflux,—deluge alternating with desiccation: never would it assume such moderate, reasonable currency, as promised to be useful and lasting. The history of its progress here would illustrate the progress of more important things; would again exemplify what obstacles a new spiritual object, with its mixture of truth and of falsehood, has to encounter from unwise enemies, still more from unwise friends; how dross is mistaken for metal, and common ashes are solemnly labelled as fell poison; how long, in such cases, blind Passion must vociferate before she can awaken Judgment; in short, with what tumult, vicissitude, and protracted difficulty, a foreign doctrine adjusts and locates itself among the homeborn. Perfect ignorance is quiet, perfect knowledge is quiet; not so the transition from the former to the latter. In a vague, all-exaggerating twilight of wonder, the new has to fight its battle with the old; Hope has to settle accounts with Fear: thus the scales strangely waver; public opinion, which is as yet baseless, fluctuates without limit; periods of foolish admiration and foolish execration must elapse, before that of true inquiry and zeal according to knowledge can begin.

Thirty years ago, for example, a person of influence and understanding thought good to emit such a proclamation as the following: "Those ladies, who take the lead in society, are loudly called upon to act as guardians of the public taste as well as of the public virtue. They are called upon, therefore, to oppose, with the whole weight of their influence, the irruption of those swarms of Publications now daily issuing from the banks of the Danube, which, like their ravaging predecessors of the darker ages, though with far other and more fatal arms, are overrunning civilized society. Those readers, whose purer taste has been formed on the correct models of the old classic school, see with indignation and astonishment the Huns and Vandals once more overpowering the Greeks and Romans. They behold our minds, with a retrograde but rapid motion, hurried back to the reign of Chaos and old Night, by distorted and unprincipled Compositions, which, in spite of strong flashes of genius, unite the taste of the Goths with the morals of Bagshot."—"The newspapers announce that Schiller's *Tragedy of the Robbers*, which inflamed the young nobility of Germany to enlist themselves into a band of highwaymen, to rob in the forests of Bohemia, is now acting in England by persons of quality!"*

Whether our fair Amazons, at sound of this alarm-trumpet, drew up in array of war to discomfit those invading Compositions, and snuff out the lights of that questionable private theatre, we have not learned; and see only that, if so, their campaign was fruitless and needless. Like the old Northern Immigrators, those new Paper Goths marched on resistless whither they were bound; some to honour, some to dishonour, the most to oblivion and the impalpable inane; and no weapon or artillery, not even the glances of bright eyes, but only the omnipotence of Time, could tame and assort them. Thus, Kotzebue's truculent armaments, once so threatening, all turned out to be mere Fantasms and Night apparitions; and so rushed onwards, like some Spectre Hunt, with loud howls indeed, yet

* Historic Survey of German Poetry, interspersed with various Translations. By W. Taylor, of Norwich. 3 vols. 8vo, London, 1830.

* *Strictures on the Modern System of Female Education.* By Hannah More. The Eighth Edition, p. 41.

hurrying nothing into chaos but themselves. While again, Schiller's *Tragedy of the Robbers*, which did not inflame either the young or the old nobility of Germany to rob in the forests of Bohemia, or indeed to do any thing, except perhaps yawn a little less, proved equally innocuous in England, and might still be acted without offence, could living individuals, idle enough for that end, be met with here. Nay, this same Schiller, not indeed by *Robbers*, yet by *Wallensteins*, by *Maids of Orleans*, and *Wilhelm Tells*, has actually conquered for himself a fixed dominion among us, which is yearly widening; round which other German kings, of less intrinsic prowess, and of greater, are likewise erecting thrones. And yet, as we perceive, civilized society still stands in its place; and the public taste, as well as the public virtue, live on, though languidly, as before. For, in fine, it has become manifest that the old Cimmerian forest is now quite felled and tilled; that the true Children of Night, whom we have to dread, dwell not on the banks of the Danube, but nearer hand.

Could we take our progress in knowledge of German Literature since that diatribe was written, as any measure of our progress in the science of Criticism, above all in the grand science of national Tolerance, there were some reason for satisfaction. With regard to Germany itself, whether we yet stand on the right footing, and know at last how we are to live in profitable neighbourhood and intercourse with that country; or whether the present is but one of those capricious tides, which also will have its reflux, may seem doubtful: meanwhile, clearly enough, a rapidly growing favour for German Literature comes to light; which favour too is the more hopeful, as it now grounds itself on better knowledge, on direct study and judgment. Our knowledge is better, if only because more general. Within the last ten years, independent readers of German have multiplied perhaps a hundred fold; so that now this acquirement is almost expected as a natural item in liberal education. Hence, in a great number of minds, some immediate personal insight into the deeper significance of German Intellect and Art;—everywhere, at least a feeling that it has some such significance. With independent readers, moreover, the writer ceases to be independent, which of itself is a considerable step. Our British Translators, for instance, have long been unparalleled in modern literature, and, like their country, "the envy of surrounding nations:" but now there are symptoms that, even in the remote German province, they must no longer range quite at will; that the butchering of a *Faust* will henceforth be accounted literary homicide, and practitioners of that quality must operate on the dead subject only. While there are Klingemanns and Claurens in such abundance, let no merely ambitious, or merely hungry Interpreter, fasten on Goethes and Schillers. Remark, too, with satisfaction, how the old established British Critic now feels that it has become unsafe to speak delirium on this subject; wherefore he prudently restricts himself to one of two courses: either to acquire some understanding of it, or, which is the still surer course, altogether to hold his peace. Hence freedom from much babble that was wont to be oppressive: probably no watchhorn with such a note as that of Mrs. More's can again be sounded, by male or female Dogberry, in these Islands. Again, there is no one of our younger, more vigorous Periodicals, but has its German craftsman, gleaning what he can: we have seen Jean Paul quoted in English Newspapers. Nor, among the signs of improvement, at least of extended curiosity, let us omit our British Foreign Reviews, a sort of merchantmen that regularly visit the Continental, especially the German ports, and bring back such ware as luck yields them, with the hope of better. Last, not least among our evidences of Philo-Germanism, here is a whole *Historic Survey of German Poetry*, in three sufficient octavos; and this not merely in the eulogistic and recommendatory vein, but proceeding in the way of criticism, and indifferent, impartial narrative: a man of known character, of talent, experience, penetration, judges that the English public is prepared for such a service, and likely to reward it.

These are appearances, which, as advocates for the friendly approximation of all men and all peoples, and the readiest possible interchange of whatever each produces of advantage to the others, we must witness gladly. Free Literary intercourse with other nations, what is it but an extended Freedom of the Press; a liberty to read (in spite of Ignorance, of Prejudice, which is the worst of Censors) what our foreign teachers also have printed for us?—ultimately, therefore, a liberty to speak and to hear, were it with men of all countries and of all times; to use, in utmost compass, those precious natural organs, by which not Knowledge only but mutual Affection is chiefly generated among mankind! It is a natural wish in man to know his fellow-passengers in this Strange Ship, or Planet, on this strange Life-voyage: neither need his curiosity restrict itself to the cabin where he himself chances to lodge; but may extend to all accessible departments of the vessel. In all he will find mysterious beings, of Wants and Endeavours like his own; in all he will find Men; with these let him comfort and manifoldly instruct himself. As to German Literature, in particular, which professes to be not only new, but original, and rich in curious information for us; which claims, moreover, nothing that we have not granted to the French, Italian, Spanish, and in a less degree to far meaner literatures, we are gratified to see that such claims can no longer be resisted. In the present fallow state of our English Literature, when no Poet cultivates his own poetic field, but all are harnessed into Editorial teams, and ploughing in concert, for Useful Knowledge, or Bibliopolic Profit, we regard this renewal of our intercourse with poetic Germany, after twenty years of languor or suspension, as among the most remarkable and even promising features of our recent intellectual history. In the absence of better tendencies, let this, which is no idle, but, in some points of view, a deep and earnest one, be encouraged. For ourselves, in the midst of so many louder and more exciting interests, we feel it a kind of duty to cast some glances now and then on this little stiller interest; since the matter is once for all to be inquired into, sound notions on it should be furthered, unsound ones cannot be too speedily corrected. It is on such grounds that we have taken up this *Historic Survey*.

Mr. Taylor is so considerable a person, that no Book deliberately published by him, on any subject, can be without weight. On German Poetry, such is the actual state of public information and curiosity, his guidance will be sure to lead or mislead a numerous class of inquirers. We are therefore called on to examine him with more than usual strictness and minuteness. The Press, in these times, has become so active; Literature—what is still called Literature—has so dilated in volume, and diminished in density, that the very Reviewer feels at a nonplus, and has ceased to review. Why thoughtfully examine what was written without thought; or note faults and merits, where there is neither fault nor merit? From a Nonentity, imbodied, with innocent deception, into foolscap and printer's ink, and named Book; from the common wind of Talk, even when it is conserved by such mechanism, for days, in the shape of Froth,—how shall the hapless Reviewer filter aught in that once so profitable colander of his? He has ceased, as we said, to attempt the impossible,—cannot review, but only discourse; he dismisses his too unproductive Author, generally with civil words, not to quarrel needlessly with a fellow-creature; and must try, as he best may, to grind from his own poor garner. Authors long looked with an evil, envious eye on the Reviewer, strove often to blow out his light, which only burnt the clearer for such blasts; but now, cunningly altering their tactics, they have extinguished it by want of oil. Unless for some unforeseen change of affairs, or some new-contrived machinery, of which there is yet no trace, the trade of Reviewer is well nigh done.

The happier are we that Mr. Taylor's Book is of the old stamp, and has substance in it for our uses. If no honour, there will be no disgrace, in having carefully examined it; which service, indeed, is due to our readers, not without curiosity in this matter, as well as to the Author. In so far as he seems a safe guide, and brings true tidings from the promised land, let us proclaim that fact, and recommend him to all pilgrims: if, on the other hand, his tidings are false, let us hasten to make this also known; that the German Canaan suffer not, in the eyes of the fainthearted, by spurious samples of its produce and reports of bloodthirsty sons of Anak dwelling there, which this harbinger and spy brings out of it. In either case, we may hope, our Author, who loves the Germans in his way, and would have his countrymen brought into closer acquaintance with them, will feel that, in purpose at least, we are co-operating with him.

First, then, be it admitted without hesitation, that Mr. Taylor, in respect of general talent and acquirement, takes his place above all our expositors of German things; that his book is greatly the most important we yet have on this subject. Here are upwards of fourteen hundred solid pages of commentary, narrative, and translation, submitted to the English reader; numerous statements and personages, hitherto unheard of, or vaguely heard of, stand here in fixed shape; there is, if no map of intellectual Germany, some first attempt at such. Farther, we are to state that our author is a zealous, earnest man; no hollow dilettante hunting after shadows, and prating he knows not what; but a substantial, distinct, remarkably decisive man; has his own opinion on many subjects, and can express it adequately. We should say, precision of idea was a striking quality of his: no vague transcendentalism, or mysticism of any kind; nothing but what is measurable and tangible, and has a meaning which he that runs may read, is to be apprehended here. He is a man of much classical and other reading; of much singular reflection; stands on his own basis, quiescent yet immovable: a certain rugged vigour of natural power, interesting even in its distortions, is everywhere manifest. Lastly, we venture to assign him the rare merit of honesty: he speaks out in plain English what is in him; seems heartily convinced of his own doctrines, and preaches them because they are his own; not for the sake of sale, but of truth; at worst, for the sake of making proselytes.

On the strength of which properties, we reckon that this *Historic Survey* may, under certain conditions, be useful and acceptable to two classes. First, to incipient students of German Literature in the original; who in any History of their subject, even in a bare catalogue, will find help; though for that class, unfortunately, Mr. Taylor's help is much diminished in value by several circumstances; by this one, were there no other, that he nowhere cites any authority: the path he has opened may be the true or the false one; for farther researches and lateral surveys there is no direction or indication. But, secondly, we reckon that this Book may be welcome to many of the much larger miscellaneous class, who read less for any specific object than for the sake of reading; to whom any book, that will, either in the way of contradiction or of confirmation, by new wisdom, or new perversion of wisdom, stir up the stagnant inner man, is a windfall; the rather if it bring some historic tidings also, fit for remembering, and repeating; above all, if, as in this case, the style, with many singularities, have some striking merits, and so the book be a light exercise, even an entertainment.

To such praise and utility the work is justly entitled; but this is not all it pretends to; and more cannot without many limitations be conceded it. Unluckily the *Historic Survey* is not what it should be, but only what it would be. Our Author hastens to correct in his Preface any false hopes his Titlepage may have excited: "A complete History of German Poetry," it seems, "is hardly within reach of his local command of library: so comprehensive an undertaking would require another residence in a country from which he has now been separated more than forty years;" and which various considerations render it unadvisable to revisit. Nevertheless, "having long been in the practice of importing the productions of its fine literature," and of working in that material, as critic, biographer, and translator, for more than one "periodic publication of this country," he has now composed "introductory and connective sections," filled up deficiencies, retrenched superfluities; and so, collecting and remodelling those "successive contributions," cements them together into the "new and entire work" here offered to the public. "With fragments," he concludes, "long since hewn, as it were, and sculptured, I attempt to construct an English Temple of Fame to the memory of those German Poets."

There is no doubt but a Complete History of German Poetry exceeds any local or universal command of books which a British man can at this day enjoy; and, farther, presents obstacles of an infinitely more serious character than this. A History of German, or of any national Poetry, would form, taken in its complete sense, one of the most arduous enterprises any writer could engage in. Poetry, were it the rudest, so it be sincere, is the attempt which man makes to render his existence harmonious, the utmost he can do for that end: it springs therefore from his whole feelings, opinions, activity, and takes its character from these. It may be called the music of his whole manner of being; and, historically considered, is the test how far Music, or Freedom, existed therein; how far the feeling of Love, of Beauty, and Dignity, could be elicited from that peculiar situation of his, and from the views he there had of Life and Nature, of the Universe, internal and external. Hence, in any measure to understand the Poetry, to estimate its worth, and historical meaning, we ask as a quite fundamental inquiry: What that situation was? Thus the History of a nation's Poetry is the essence of its History, political, economic, scientific, religious. With all these the complete Historian of a national Poetry will be familiar; the national physiognomy, in its finest traits, and through its successive stages of growth, will be clear to him: he will discern the grand spiritual Tendency of each period, what was the highest Aim and Enthusiasm of mankind in each, and how one epoch naturally evolved itself from the other. He has to record this highest Aim of a nation, in its successive directions and developments; for by this the Poetry of the nation modulates itself, this *is* the Poetry of the nation.

Such were the primary essence of a true History of Poetry; the living principle round which all detached facts and phenomena, all separate characters of Poems and Poets, would fashion themselves into a coherent whole, if they are by any means to cohere. To accomplish such a work for any Literature would require not only all outward aids, but an excellent inward faculty: all telescopes and observatories were of no avail, without the seeing eye and the understanding heart.

Doubtless, as matters stand, such models remain in great part ideal; the stinted result of actual practice must not be too rigidly tried by them. In our language, we have yet no example of such a performance. Neither elsewhere, except perhaps in the well-meant, but altogether ineffectual, attempt of Denina, among the Italians, and in some detached, though far more successful, sketches by German writers, is there any that we know of. To expect an English History of German Literature in this style were especially unreasonable; where not only the man to write it, but the people to read and enjoy it, are wanting. Some *Historic Survey*, wherein such an ideal standard, if not attained, if not approached, might be faithfully kept in view, and endeavoured after, would suffice us. Neither need such a Survey, even as a British Surveyor might execute it, be deficient in striking objects, and views of a general interest. There is the spectacle of a great people, closely related to us in blood, language, character, advancing through fifteen centuries of culture; with the eras and changes that have distinguished the like career in other nations. Nay, perhaps, the intellectual history of the Germans is not without peculiar attraction, on two grounds: first, that they are a separate unmixed people; that in them one of the two grand stem-tribes, from which all modern European countries derive their population and speech, is seen growing up distinct, and in several particulars following its own course; secondly, that by accident and by desert, the Germans have more than once been found playing the highest part in European culture; at more than one era the grand Tendencies of Europe have first imbodied themselves into action in Germany, the main battle between the New and the Old has been fought and gained there. We mention only the Swiss Revolt, and Luther's Reformation. The Germans have not indeed so many classical works to exhibit as some other nations; a Shakspeare, a Dante, has not yet been recognised among them; nevertheless, they too have had their Teachers and inspired Singers; and in regard to popular Mythology, traditionary possessions and spirit, what we may call the *inarticulate* Poetry of a nation, and what is the element of its spoken or written Poetry, they will be found superior to any other modern people.

The Historic Surveyor of German Poetry will observe a remarkable nation struggling out of Paganism; fragments of that stern Superstition, saved from the general wreck, and still, amid the new order of things, carrying back our view, in faint reflexes, into the dim primeval time. By slow degrees the chaos of the Northern Immigrations settles into a new and fairer world; arts advance; little by little, a fund of Knowledge, of Power over Nature, is accumulated for man; feeble glimmerings, even of a higher knowledge, of a poetic, break forth; till at length in the *Swabian Era*, as it is named, a blaze of true though simple Poetry bursts over Germany, more splendid, we might say, than the Troubadour Period of any other nation; for that famous *Nibelungen Song*, produced, at least ultimately fashioned in those times, and still so significant in these, is altogether without parallel elsewhere.

To this period, the essence of which was

young Wonder, and an enthusiasm for which Chivalry was still the fit exponent, there succeeds, as was natural, a period of Inquiry, a Didactic period; wherein, among the Germans, as elsewhere, many a Hugo von Trimberg delivers wise saws, and moral apothegms, to the general edification: later, a Town-clerk of Strasburg sees his *Ship of fools* translated into all living languages, twice into Latin, and read by Kings; the Apologue of *Reynard the Fox* gathering itself together, from sources remote and near, assumes its Low-German vesture; and becomes the darling of high and low, nay still lives with us, in rude genial vigour, as one of the most remarkable indigenous productions of the Middle Ages. Nor is acted poetry of this kind wanting; the Spirit of Inquiry translates itself into Deeds which are poetical, as well as into words: already at the opening of the fourteenth century, Germany witnesses the first assertion of political right, the first vindication of Man against Nobleman; in the early history of the German Swiss. And again, two centuries later, the first assertion of intellectual right, the first vindication of Man against Clergyman; in the history of Luther's Reformation. Meanwhile the Press has begun its incalculable task; the indigenous Fiction of the Germans, what we have called their inarticulate Poetry, issues in innumerable *Volks-Bücher*, (People's-Books,) the progeny and kindred of which still live in all European countries: the People have their Tragedy and their Comedy; *Tyll Eulenspiegel* shakes every diaphragm with laughter; the rudest heart quails with awe at the wild mythus of *Faust*.

With Luther, however, the Didactic Tendency has reached its poetic acme; and now we must see it assume a prosaic character, and Poetry for a long while decline. The Spirit of Inquiry, of Criticism, is pushed beyond the limits, or two exclusively cultivated: what had done so much, is capable of doing all; Understanding is alone listened to, while Fancy and Imagination languish inactive, or are forcibly stifled; and all poetic culture gradually dies away. As if with the high resolute genius, and noble achievements, of its Luthers and Huttens, the genius of the country had exhausted itself, we behold generation after generation of mere Prosaists succeed these high Psalmists. Science indeed advances, practical manipulation in all kinds improves; Germany has its Copernics, Hevels, Guerickes, Keplers; later, a Leibnitz opens the path of true Logic, and teaches the mysteries of Figure and Number: but the finer Education of mankind seems at a stand. Instead of Poetic recognition and worship, we have stolid Theologic controversy, or still shallower Freethinking; pedantry, servility, mode-hunting, every species of Idolatry and Affectation holds sway. The World has lost its beauty, Life its infinite majesty, as if the Author of it were no longer divine: instead of admiration and creation of the True, there is at best criticism and denial of the False; to Luther there has succeeded Thomasius. In this era, so unpoetical for all Europe, Germany torn in pieces by a Thirty Year's War, and its consequences, is pre-eminently prosaic; its few Singers are feeble echoes of foreign models little better than themselves. No Shakspeare, no Milton appears there; such, indeed, would have appeared earlier, if at all, in the current of German history; but instead, they have only at best Opitzes, Flemmings, Logans, as we had our Queen Anne Wits; or, in their Lohensteines, Gryphs, Hoffmannswaldaus, though in inverse order, an unintentional parody of our Drydens and Lees.

Nevertheless from every moral death there is a new birth; in this wondrous course of his, man may indeed linger but cannot retrograde or stand still. In the middle of last century, from among the Parisian Erotics, rickety Sentimentalism, Court aperies, and hollow Dulness, striving in all hopeless courses, we behold the giant spirit of Germany awaken as from long slumber; shake away these worthless fetters, and by its Lessings and Klopstocks, announce, in true German dialect, that the Germans also are men. Singular enough in its circumstances was this rescuscitation; the work as of a "spirit on the waters,"—a movement agitating the great popular mass; for it was favoured by no court or king: all sovereignties, even the pettiest, had abandoned their native Literature, their native language, as if to irreclaimable barbarism. The greatest King produced in Germany since Barbarossa's time, Frederick the Second, looked coldly on the native endeavour, and saw no hope but in aid from France. However, the native endeavour prospered without aid: Lessing's announcement did not die away with him, but took clearer utterance, and more inspired modulation from his followers; in whose works it now speaks, not to Germany alone, but to the whole world. The results of this last Period of German Literature are of deep significance, the depth of which is perhaps but now becoming visible. Here, too, it may be, as in other cases, the Want of the Age has first taken voice and shape in Germany; that change from Negation to Affirmation, from Destruction to Reconstruction, for which all thinkers in every country are now prepared, is perhaps already in action there. In the nobler Literature of the Germans, say some, lie the rudiments of a new spiritual era, which it is for this, and for succeeding generations to work out and realize. The ancient creative Inspiration, it would seem, is still possible in these ages; at a time when Skepticism, Frivolity, Sensuality, had withered Life into a sand desert, and our gayest prospect was but the *false mirage*, and even our Byrons could utter but a death-song or despairing howl, the Moses'-wand has again smote from that Horeb refreshing streams, towards which the better spirits of all nations are hastening, if not to drink, yet wistfully and hopefully to examine. If the older Literary History of Germany has the common attractions, which in a greater or a less degree belong to the successive epochs of other such Histories; its newer Literature, and the historical delineation of this, has an interest such as belongs to no other.

It is somewhat in this way, as appears to

us, that the growth of German Poetry must be construed and represented by the historian: these are the general phenomena and vicissitudes, which, if elucidated by proper individual instances, by specimens fitly chosen, presented in natural sequence, and worked by philosophy into union, would make a valuable book; on any and all of which the observations and researches of so able an inquirer as Mr. Taylor would have been welcome. Sorry are we to declare that of all this, which constitutes the essence of any thing calling itself *Historic Survey*, there is scarcely a vestige in the book before us. The question, What is the German mind; what is the culture of the German mind; what course has Germany followed in that matter; what are its national characteristics as manifested therein? appears not to have presented itself to the author's thought. No theorem of Germany and its intellectual progress, not even a false one, has he been at pains to construct for himself. We believe, it is impossible for the most assiduous reader to gather from these three Volumes any portraiture of the national mind of Germany,—not to say in its successive phases and the historical sequence of these, but in any one phase or condition. The work is made up of critical, biographical, bibliographical dissertations, and notices concerning this and the other individual poet; interspersed with large masses of translation: and except that all these are strung together in the order of time, has no historical feature whatever. Many literary lives as we read, the nature of literary life in Germany,—what sort of moral, economical, intellectual element it is that a German writer lives in and works in,—will nowhere manifest itself. Indeed, far from depicting Germany, scarcely on more than one or two occasions does our author even look at it, or so much as remind us that it were capable of being depicted. On these rare occasions, too, we were treated with such philosophic insight as the following: "The Germans are not an imitative, but they are a listening people: they can do nothing without directions, and any thing with them. As soon as Gottsched's rules for writing German correctly had made their appearance, everybody began to write German." Or we have theoretic hints, resting on no basis, about some new tribunal of taste which at one time had formed itself "in the mess-rooms of the Prussian officers!"

In a word, the "connecting sections," or indeed by what alchymy such a congeries could be connected into an *Historic Survey*, have not become plain to us. Considerable part of it consists of quite detached little Notices, mostly of altogether insignificant men; heaped together as separate fragments; fit, had they been unexceptionable in other respects, for a Biographical Dictionary, but nowise for an *Historic Survey*. Then we have dense masses of Translation, sometimes good, but seldom of the characteristic pieces; an entire *Iphigenia*, an entire *Nathan the Wise:* nay worse, a *Sequel to Nathan*, which when we have conscientiously struggled to pursue, the Author turns round, without any apparent smile and tells us that it is by a nameless writer, and worth nothing. Not only Mr. Taylor's own Translations, which are generally good, but contributions from a whole body of labourers in that department, are given: for example, near sixty pages, very ill rendered by a Miss Plumtre, of a *Life of Kotzebue*, concerning whom, or whose life, death, or burial, there is now no curiosity extant among men. If in that "English Temple of Fame," with its hewn and sculptured stones, those Biographical-Dictionary fragments and fractions are so much dry *rubble-work* of whinstone, is not this quite despicable *Autobiography of Kotzebue* a rood or two of mere *turf*, which, as ready-cut, our architect, to make up measure, has packed in among his marble ashlar, whereby the whole wall will the sooner bulge? But indeed, generally speaking, symmetry is not one of his architectural rules. Thus, in volume First, we have a long story translated from a German Magazine, about certain antique Hyperborean *Baresarks*, amusing enough, but with no more reference to Germany than to England; while, in return, the *Nibelungen Lied* is despatched in something less than one line, and comes no more to light. Tyll Eulenspiegel, who was not an "anonymous Satire, entitled the *Mirror of Owls*," but a real flesh-and-blood hero of that name, whose tombstone is standing to this day near Lubeck, has some four lines for his share; *Reineke de Vos* about as many, which also are inaccurate. Again, if Wieland have his half-volume, and poor Ernest Schulze, poor Zacharias Werner, and numerous other poor men, each his chapter; Luther also has his two sentences, and is in these weighed against—Dr. Isaac Watts. Ulrich Hutten does not occur here; Hans Sachs and his Master-singers escape notice, or even do worse; the poetry of the Reformation is not alluded to. The name of Jean Paul Friedrich Richter appears not to be known to Mr. Taylor; or if want of Rhyme was to be the test of a Prosaist, how comes Salomon Gesner here? Stranger still, Ludwig Tieck is not once mentioned; neither is Novalis; neither is Maler Müller. But why dwell on these omissions and commissions? is not all included in this one well-nigh incredible fact, that one of the largest articles in the Book, a tenth part of the whole *Historic Survey of German Poetry*, treats of that delectable genius, August von Kotzebue?

The truth is, this *Historic Survey* has not any thing historical in it; but is a mere aggregate of Dissertations, Translations, Notices, and Notes, bound together indeed by the circumstance that they are all about German Poetry, "about it and about it;" also by the sequence of time, and still more strongly by the Bookbinder's packthread; but by no other sufficient tie whatever. The authentic title, were not some mercantile varnish allowable in such cases, might be: "General Jail-delivery of all Publications and Manuscripts, original or translated, composed or borrowed, on the subject of German Poetry; by," &c.

To such Jail-delivery, at least when it is from the prison of Mr. Taylor's Desk at Norwich, and relates to a subject in the actual predicament of German Poetry among us, we have no fundamental objection: and for the name, now that it is explained, there is nothing in a name; a rose by any other name would smell as sweet. However, even in this lower and lowest point of view, the *Historic Survey* is liable to grave objections: its worth is of no unmixed character. We mentioned that Mr. Taylor did not often cite authorities: for which doubtless he may have his reasons. If it be not from French Prefaces, and the *Biographie Universelle*, and other the like sources, we confess ourselves altogether at a loss to divine whence any reasonable individual gathered such notices as these. Books indeed are scarce; but the most untoward situation may command Wachler's *Vorlesungen*, Horn's *Poesie und Beredsamkeit*, Meister's *Characteristiken*, Koch's *Compendium*, or some of the thousand and one compilations of that sort, numerous and accurate in German, more than in any other literature: at all events, Jörden's *Lexicon Deutscher und Prosaisten*, and the world-renowned Leipsic *Conversations-Lexicon*. No one of these appears to have been in Mr. Taylor's possession;—Bouterwek alone, and him he seems to have consulted perfunctorily. A certain proportion of errors in such a work is pardonable and unavoidable: scarcely so the proportion observed here. The *Historic Survey* abounds with errors, perhaps beyond any book it has ever been our lot to review. Of these, many, indeed, are harmless enough: as, for instance, where we learn that Görres was born in 1804, (not in 1776;) though in that case he must have published his *Shah-Nameh* at the age of three years; or where it is said that Werner's epitaph "begs Mary Magdalene to pray for his soul," which it does not do, if indeed any one cared what it did. Some are of a quite mysterious nature; either impregnated with a wit which continues obstinately latent, or indicating that, in spite of Railways and Newspapers, some portions of this Island are still impermeable. For example, "It (*Goetz von Berlichingen*) was admirably translated into English, in 1799, at Edinburgh, by *William* Scott, Advocate; no doubt, the same person who, under the poetical but assumed name of *Walter*, has since become the most extensively popular of the British writers."—Others again are the fruit of a more culpable ignorance; as when we hear that Goethe's *Dichtung und Wahrheit* is literally meant to be a fictitious narrative, and no genuine Biography; that his *Stella* ends quietly in Bigamy, (to Mr. Taylor's satisfaction,) which, however the French Translation may run, in the original it certainly does not. Mr. Taylor likewise complains that his copy of *Faust* is incomplete: so, we grieve to state, is ours. Still worse is it when speaking of distinguished men, who probably have been at pains to veil their sentiments on certain subjects, our author takes it upon him to lift such veil, and with perfect composure pronounces this to be a Deist, that a Pantheist, that other an Atheist, often without any due foundation. It is quite erroneous, for example, to describe Schiller by any such unhappy term as that of Deist: it is very particularly erroneous to say that Goethe anywhere "avows himself an Atheist," that he "is a Pantheist;"—indeed, that he is, was, or is like to be any *ist* to which Mr. Taylor would attach just meaning.

But on the whole, what struck us most in these errors, is their surprising number. In the way of our calling, we at first took pencil, with intent to mark such transgressions; but soon found it too appalling a task, and so laid aside our black-lead and our art (*cæstus artemque.*) Happily, however, a little natural invention, assisted by some tincture of arithmetic, came to our aid. Six pages, studied for that end, we did mark; finding therein thirteen errors: the pages are 167—173 of Volume Third, and still in our copy, have their marginal stigmas, which can be vindicated before a jury of Authors. Now if 6 give 13, who sees not that 1455, the entire number of pages, will give 3152, and a fraction? Or, allowing for translations, which are freer from errors, and for philosophical Discussions, wherein the errors are of another sort; nay, granting with a perhaps unwarranted liberality, that these six pages may yield too high an average, which we know not that they do,—may not, in round numbers, Fifteen Hundred be given as the approximate amount, not of Errors, indeed, yet of Mistakes and Misstatements, in these three octavos?

Of errors in doctrine, false critical judgments, and all sorts of philosophical hallucination, the number, more difficult to ascertain, is also unfortunately great. Considered, indeed, as in any measure a picture of what is remarkable in German Poetry, this *Historic Survey* is one great Error. We have to object to Mr. Taylor on all grounds; that his views are often partial and inadequate, sometimes quite false and imaginary; that the highest productions of German Literature, those works in which properly its characteristic and chief worth lie, are still as a sealed book to him; or, what is worse, an open book that he will not read, but pronounces to be filled with blank paper. From a man of such intellectual vigour, who has studied his subject so long, we should not have expected such a failure.

Perhaps the main principle of it may be stated, if not accounted for, in this one circumstance, that the *Historic Survey*, like its Author, stands separated from Germany by "more than forty years." During this time Germany has been making unexampled progress; while our author has either advanced in the other direction, or continued quite stationary. Forty years, it is true, make no difference in a classical Poem; yet much in the readers of that Poem, and its position towards these. Forty years are but a small period in some Histories, but in the history of German Literature, the most rapidly extending, incessantly fluctuating object even in the spiritual world, they make a great period. In Germany, within these forty years, how much has been united, how much has fallen asunder! Kant has superseded Wolfe; Fichte, Kant; Schelling, Fichte; and now, it seems, Hegel is bent on superseding Schelling. Baumgarten has given place to Schlegel; the *Deutsche Bibliothek* to the Berlin *Hermes*: Lessing still towers in the distance like an Earthborn Atlas; but in the poetical Heaven, Wieland and Klopstock burn fainter, as new and more radiant luminaries have arisen. Within the last forty years, German Literature has become national, idiomatic, distinct from all others; by its productions during that period, it is either something or nothing.

Nevertheless it is still at the distance of forty years, sometimes we think it must be fifty, that Mr. Taylor stands. "The fine Literature of Germany," no doubt, he has "imported;" yet only with the eyes of 1780 does he read it. Thus Sulzer's *Universal Theory* continues still to be his roadbook to the temple of German taste; almost as if the German critic should undertake to measure *Waverley* and *Manfred* by the scale of Blair's *Lectures*. Sulzer was an estimable man, who did good service in his day; but about forty years ago sunk into a repose, from which it would now be impossible to rouse him. The superannuation of Sulzer appears not once to be suspected by our Author; as indeed little of all the great work that has been done or undone, in Literary Germany within that period, has become clear to him. The far-famed *Xenien* of Schiller's *Musenalmanach* are once mentioned, in some half-dozen lines, wherein also there are more than half-a-dozen inaccuracies, and one rather egregious error. Of the results that followed from these *Xenien;* of Tieck, Wackenroder, the two Schlegels, and Novalis, whose critical Union, and its works, filled all Germany with tumult, discussion, and at length with new conviction, no whisper transpires here. The *New School*, with all that it taught, untaught, and mistaught, is not so much as alluded to. Schiller and Goethe, with all the poetic world they created, remain invisible, or dimly seen: Kant is a sort of Political Reformer. It must be stated with all distinctness, that of the newer and higher German Literature, no reader will obtain the smallest understanding from these Volumes.

Indeed, quite apart from his inacquaintance with actual Germany, there is that in the structure or habit of Mr. Taylor's mind, which singularly unfits him for judging of such matters well. We must complain that he reads German Poetry, from first to last, with English eyes; will not accommodate himself to the spirit of the Literature he is investigating, and do his utmost, by loving endeavour, to win its secret from it; but plunges in headlong, and silently assuming that all this was written for him and for his objects, makes short work with it, and innumerable false conclusions. It is sad to see an honest traveller confidently gauging all foreign objects with a measure that will not mete them; trying German Sacred Oaks by their fitness for British shipbuilding; walking from Dan to Beersheba, and finding so little that he did not bring with him. This, we are too well aware, is the commonest of all errors, both with vulgar readers, and with vulgar critics; but from Mr. Taylor we had expected something better; nay, let us confess, he himself now and then seems to attempt something better, but too imperfectly succeeds in it.

The truth is, Mr. Taylor, though a man of talent, as we have often admitted, and as the world well knows, though a downright, independent, and to all appearance most praiseworthy man, is one of the most peculiar critics to be found in our times. As we construe him from these volumes, the basis of his nature seems to be polemical; his whole view of the world, of its Poetry, and whatever else it holds, has a militant character. According to this philosophy, the whole duty of man, it would almost appear, is to lay aside the opinion of his grandfather. Doubtless, it is natural, it is indispensable, for a man to lay aside the opinion of his grandfather, when it will no longer hold together on him; but we had imagined that the great and infinitely harder duty was—To turn the opinion that does hold together, to some account. However, it is not in receiving the New, and creating good with it, but solely in pulling to pieces the Old, that Mr. Taylor will have us employed. Often, in the course of these pages, might the British reader sorrowfully exclaim: "Alas! is this the year of grace 1831, and are we still *here?* Armed with the hatchet and tinder-box; still no symptom of the sower's-sheet and plough?" These latter, for our Author, are implements of the dark ages; the ground is full of thistles and jungle; cut down and spare not. A singular aversion to Priests, something like a natural horror and hydrophobia, gives him no rest night nor day: the gist of all his speculations is to drive down more or less effectual palisades against that class of persons; nothing that he does but they interfere with or threaten; the first question he asks of every passer-by, be it German Poet, Philosopher, Farce-writer, is, "Arian or Trinitarian? Wilt thou help me or not?" Long as he has now laboured, and though calling himself Philosopher, Mr. Taylor has not yet succeeded in sweeping this arena clear; but still painfully struggles in the questions of Naturalism and Supernaturalism, Liberalism and Servilism.

Agitated by this zeal, with its fitful hope and fear, it is that he goes through Germany; scenting out Infidelity with the nose of an ancient Heresy-hunter, though for opposite purposes; and, like a recruiting sergeant, beating aloud for recruits; nay, where in any corner he can spy a tall man, clutching at him, to crimp him or impress him. Goethe's and Schiller's creed we saw specified above; those of Lessing and Herder are scarcely less edifying; but take rather this sagacious exposition of Kant's Philosophy:

"The Alexandrian writings do not differ so widely as is commonly apprehended from those of the Königsberg School, for they abound with passages, which, while they seem to flatter the popular credulity, resolve into allegory the stories of the gods, and into an illustrative personification the soul of the world; thus insinuating to the more alert and penetrating, the speculative rejection of opinions with which they are encouraged and commanded in action to comply. With analogous spirit, Professor Kant studiously introduces a distinction between Practical and Theoretical Reason; and while he teaches that rational conduct will indulge the hypothesis of a God, a revelation, and a future state, (this, we presume is meant by calling them *inferences of Practical Reason,*) he pretends that Theoretical Reason can adduce no one satisfactory argument in their behalf: so that his morality amounts to a defence of the old adage, 'Think with the wise, and act with the vulgar;' a plan of behaviour which secures to the vulgar an ultimate victory over the wise. * * Philosophy is to be withdrawn within a narrower circle of the initiated; and these must be induced to conspire in favouring a vulgar superstition. This can best be accomplished by enveloping with enigmatic jargon the topics of discussion; by employing a cloudy phraseology, which may intercept from below the war-whoop of impiety, and from above the evulgation of infidelity; by contriving a kind of 'cipher of illuminism,' in which public discussions of the most critical nature can be carried on from the press, without alarming the prejudices of the people, or exciting the precautions of the magistrate. Such a cipher, in the hands of an adept, is the dialect of Kant. Add to this, the notorious Gallicanism of his opinions, which must endear him to the patriotism of the philosophers of the Lyceum; and it will appear probable that the reception of his forms of syllogising should extend from Germany to France; should completely and exclusively establish itself on the Continent; entomb with the Reasonings the Reason of the modern world; and form the tasteless fretwork which seems about to convert the halls of liberal Philosophy into churches of mystical Supernaturalism."

These are, indeed, fearful symptoms, and enough to quicken the diligence of any recruiting officer that has the good cause at heart. Reasonably may such officer, beleagured with "witchcraft and demonology, trinitarianism, intolerance," and a considerable list of *et-ceteras*, and, still seeing no hearty followers of his flag, but a mere Falstaff regiment, smite upon his thigh, and, in moments of despondency, lament that Christianity had ever entered, or, as we here have it, "intruded" into Europe at all; that, at least, some small slip of heathendom, "Scandinavia, for instance," had not been "left to its natural course, unmisguided by ecclesiastical missionaries and monastic institutions. Many superstitions, which have fatigued the credulity, clouded the intellect, and impaired the security of man, and which, alas! but too naturally followed in the train of the sacred books, would there, perhaps, never have struck root; and in one corner of the world, the inquiries of reason might have found an earlier asylum, and asserted a less circumscribed range." Nevertheless, there is still hope, preponderating hope. "The general tendency of the German school," it would appear, could we but believe such tidings, "is to teach French opinions in English forms." Philosophy can now look down with some approving glances on Socinianism. Nay, the literature of Germany, "very liberal and tolerant," is gradually overflowing even into the Slavonian nations, "and will found, in new languages and climates, those latest inferences of a corrupt but instructed refinement, which are likely to rebuild the morality of the Ancients on the ruins of Christian Puritanism."

Such retrospections and prospections bring to mind an absurd rumour which, confounding our author with his namesake, the celebrated translator of Plato and Aristotle, represented him as being engaged in the repair and re-establishment of the Pagan religion. For such rumour, we are happy to state, there is not, and was not, the slightest foundation. Wieland may, indeed, at one time, have put some whims into his disciple's head; but Mr. Taylor is too solid a man to embark in speculations of that nature. Prophetic day-dreams are not practical projects; at all events, as we here see, it is not the old Pagan gods that we are to bring back, but only the ancient Pagan morality, a refined and reformed Paganism;—as some middle-aged householder, if distressed by tax-gatherers and duns, might resolve on becoming thirteen again, and a bird-nesting schoolboy. Let no timid Layman apprehend any overflow of Priests from Mr. Taylor, or even of Gods. Is not this commentary on the hitherto so inexplicable conversion of Friedrich Leopold, Count Stolberg, enough to quiet every alarmist?

"On the Continent of Europe, the gentleman, and Frederic Leopold was emphatically so, is seldom brought up with much solicitude for any positive doctrine: among the Catholics, the moralist insists on the duty of conforming to the religion of one's ancestors; among the Protestants, on the duty of conforming to the religion of the magistrate; but Frederic Leopold seems to have invented a new point of honour, and a most rational one, the duty of conforming to the religion of one's father-in-law.

"A young man is the happier, while single, for being unencumbered with any religious restraints; but when the time comes for submitting to matrimony, he will find the precedent of Frederic Leopold well entitled to consideration. A predisposition to conform to the religion of the father-in-law facilitates advantageous matrimonial connections; it produces in a family the desirable harmony of religious profession; it secures the sincere education of the daughters in the faith of their mother; and it leaves the young men at liberty to apostatize in their turn, to exert their right of private judgment, and to choose a worship for themselves. Religion, if a blemish in the male, is surely a grace in the female sex: courage of mind may tend to acknowledge nothing above itself; but timidity is ever disposed to look upwards for protection, for consolation, and for happiness."

With regard to this latter point, whether Religion is "a blemish in the male, and surely a grace in the female sex," it is possible judgments may remain suspended. Courage of mind, indeed, will prompt the squirrel to set itself in posture against an armed horseman; yet whether for men and women, who seem to stand, not only under the Galaxy and Stellar system, and under Immensity and Eternity, but even under any bare bodkin or drop of prussic acid, "such courage of mind as may tend to acknowledge nothing above itself," were ornamental or the contrary; whether, lastly, religion is grounded on Fear, or on something infinitely higher and inconsistent with Fear,—may be questions. But they are of a kind we are not at present called to meddle with.

Mr. Taylor promulgates many other strange articles of faith, for he is a positive man, and has a certain quiet wilfulness; these, however, cannot henceforth much surprise us. He still calls the Middle Ages, during which nearly all the inventions and social institutions, whereby we yet live as civilized men, were originated or perfected, "a Millennium of Darkness;" on the faith chiefly of certain long-past Pedants, who reckoned every thing barren, because Chrysolaras had not yet come, and no Greek Roots grew there. Again, turning in the other direction, he criticizes Luther's Reformation, and repeats that old, and indeed quite foolish, story of the Augustine Monk's having a merely commercial grudge against the Dominican; computes the quantity of blood shed for Protestantism; and, forgetting that men shed blood, in all ages, for any cause, and for no cause, for Sansculottism, for Bonapartism, thinks that, on the whole, the Reformation was an error and failure. Pity that Providence (as King Alphonso wished in the Astronomical case) had not created its man three centuries sooner, and taken a little counsel from him! On the other hand, "Voltaire's Reformation" was successful; and here, for once, Providence was right. Will Mr. Taylor mention what it was that Voltaire *reformed?* Many things he *de*formed, deservedly and undeservedly, but the thing that he *formed* or *re*-formed is still unknown to the world.

It is perhaps unnecessary to add, that Mr. Taylor's whole Philosophy is sensual; that is, he recognises nothing that cannot be weighed, measured, and, with one or the other organ, eaten and digested. Logic is his only lamp of life; where this fails, the region of Creation terminates. For him there is no Invisible, Incomprehensible; whosoever, under any name, believes in an invisible, he treats, with leniency and the loftiest tolerance, as a mystic and lunatic; and if the unhappy crackbrain has any handicraft, literary or other, allows him to go at large, and work at it. Withal he is a great-hearted, strong-minded, and, in many points, interesting man. There is a majestic composure in the attitude he has assumed; massive, immovable, uncomplaining, he sits in a world of Delirium; and for his Future looks with sure faith,—only in the direction of the Past. We take him to be a man of sociable turn, not without kindness; at all events of the most perfect courtesy. He despises the entire Universe, yet speaks respectfully of Translators from the German, and always says that they "English beautifully." A certain mild Dogmatism sits well on him; peaceable, incontrovertible, uttering the palpably absurd, as if it were a mere truism. On the other hand, there are touches of a grave, scientific obscenity, which are questionable. This word Obscenity we use with reference to our readers, and might also add Profanity, but not with reference to Mr. Taylor; he, as we said, is scientific merely; and where there is no *cœnum* and no *fanum*, there can be no obscenity and no profanity.

To a German we might have compressed all this long description into a single word: Mr. Taylor is simply what they call a *Philister;* every fibre of him is Philistine. With us such men usually take into Politics, and become Code-makers and Utilitarians: it was only in Germany that they ever meddled much with Literature; and there worthy Nicolai has long since terminated his Jesuit-hunt; no Adelung now writes books, *Ueber die Nützlichkeit der Empfindung,* (On the Utility of Feeling.) Singular enough, now, when that old species had been quite extinct for almost half a century in their own land, appears a native-born English Philistine, made in all points as they were. With wondering welcome we hail the Strongboned; almost as we might a resuscitated Mammoth. Let no David choose smooth stones from the brook to sling at him: is he not our own Goliath, whose limbs were made in England, whose thews and sinews any soil might be proud of? Is he not, as we said, a man that can stand on his own legs without collapsing when left by himself? in these days one of the greatest rarities, almost prodigies.

We cheerfully acquitted Mr. Taylor of Religion; but must expect less gratitude when we farther deny him any feeling for true Poetry, as indeed the feelings for Religion and for Poetry of this sort are one and the same. Of Poetry, Mr. Taylor knows well what will make a grand, especially a large, *picture* in the imagination: he has even a creative gift of this kind himself, as his style will often testify; but much more he does not know. How indeed should he? Nicolai, too, "judged of Poetry as he did of Brunswick Mum, simply by *tasting* it." Mr. Taylor assumes, as a fact known to all thinking creatures, that Poetry is neither more nor less than "a stimulant." Perhaps above five hundred times in the *Historic Survey* we see this doctrine expressly acted on. Whether the piece to be judged of is a Poetical Whole, and has what the critics have named a genial life, and what that life is, he inquires not; but, at best, whether it is a logical Whole, and for most part, simply, whether it is stimulant. The praise is, that it has fine situations, striking scenes, agonizing scenes, harrows his feelings, and the like. Schiller's *Robbers* he finds to be stimulant; his *Maid of Orleans* is not stimulant, but "among the weakest of his tragedies, and composed apparently in ill health." The author of *Pizarro* is supremely stimulant; he of *Torquato Tasso* is "too quotidian to be stimulant." We had understood that alcohol was stimulant in all its shapes; opium also, tobacco, and indeed the whole class of narcotics; but heretofore found Poetry in none of the Pharmacopœias. Nevertheless, it is edifying to observe with what fearless consistency Mr. Taylor, who is no half-man, carries through this theory of stimulation. It lies privily in the heart of many a reader and reviewer; nay, Schiller, at one time, said that "Molière's old woman seemed to have become sole Editress of all Reviews;"

but seldom, in the history of Literature, has she had the honesty to unveil, and ride triumphant as in these volumes. Mr. Taylor discovers that the only Poet to be classed with Homer is Tasso; that Shakspeare's Tragedies are cousins-german to those of Otway; that poor, moaning, monotonous Macpherson is an epic poet. Lastly, he runs a laboured parallel between Schiller, Goethe, and Kotzebue; one is more this, the other more that; one strives hither, the other thither, through the whole string of critical predicables; almost as if we should compare scientifically Milton's *Paradise Lost*, the *Prophecies of Isaiah*, and Mat Lewis's *Tales of Terror*.

Such is Mr. Taylor; a strong-hearted oak, but in an unkindly soil, and beat upon from infancy by Trinitarian and Tory Southwesters: such is the result which native vigour, wind-storms, and thirsty mould have made out among them; grim boughs dishevelled in multangular complexity, and of the stiffness of brass; a tree crooked every way, unwedgeable and gnarled. What bandages or cordages of ours, or of man's, could straighten it, now that it has grown there for half a century? We simply point out that there is excellent tough *knee-timber* in it, and of straight timber little or none.

In fact, taking Mr. Taylor as he is and must be, and keeping a perpetual account and protest with him on these peculiarities of his, we find that on various parts of his subject he has profitable things to say. The Göttingen group of Poets, "Bürger and his set," such as they were, are pleasantly delineated. The like may be said of the somewhat earlier Swiss brotherhood, whereof Bodmer and Breitinger are the central figures; though worthy, wonderful Lavater, the wandering Physiognomist and Evangelist, and Protestant Pope, should not have been first forgotten, and then crammed into an insignificant paragraph. Lessing, again, is but poorly managed; his main performance, as was natural, reckoned to be the writing of *Nathan the Wise;* we have no original portrait here, but a pantagraphical reduced copy of some foreign sketches or scratches, quite unworthy of such a man, in such an historical position, standing on the confines of Light and Darkness, like Day on the misty mountain tops. Of Herder also there is much omitted; the *Geschichte der Menscheit* scarcely alluded to; yet some features are given, accurately and even beautifully. A slow-rolling grandiloquence is in Mr. Taylor's best passages, of which this is one: if no poetic light, he has occasionally a glow of true rhetorical heat. Wieland is lovingly painted, yet on the whole faithfully, as he looked some fifty years ago, if not as he now looks: this is the longest article in the *Historic Survey*, and much too long; those Paganizing *Dialogues* in particular had never much worth, and at present have scarcely any.

Perhaps the best of all these Essays is that on Klopstock. The sphere of Klopstock's genius does not transcend Mr. Taylor's scale of poetic altitudes; though it perhaps reaches the highest grade there; the "stimulant" theory recedes into the back-ground; indeed there is a rhetorical amplitude and brilliancy in the *Messias* which elicits in our critic an instinct truer than his philosophy is. He has honestly studied the *Messias*, and presents a clear outline of it; neither has the still purer spirit of Klopstock's *Odes* escaped him. We have English Biographies of Klopstock, and a miserable Version of his great Work; but perhaps there is no writing in our language that offers so correct an emblem of him as this analysis. Of the *Odes* we shall here present one, in Mr. Taylor's translation, which, though in prose, the reader will not fail to approve of. It is perhaps, the finest passage in his whole *Historic Survey*.

"THE TWO MUSES.

"I saw—tell me, was I beholding what now happens, or was I beholding futurity?—I saw with the Muse of Britain the Muse of Germany engaged in competitory race—flying warm to the goal of coronation.

"Two goals, where the prospect terminates, bordered the career: Oaks of the forest shaded the one; near to the other waved Palms in the evening shadow.

"Accustomed to contest, stepped she from Albion proudly into the arena; as she stepped, when, with the Grecian Muse and with her from the Capitol, she entered the lists.

"She beheld the young trembling rival, who trembled yet with dignity; glowing roses worthy of victory streamed flaming over her cheek, and her golden hair flew abroad.

"Already she retained with pain in her tumultuous bosom the contracted breath; already she hung bending forward towards the goal; already the herald was lifting the trumpet, and her eyes swam with intoxicating joy.

"Proud of her courageous rival, prouder of herself, the lofty Britoness measured, but with noble glance, thee, Tuiskone: 'Yes, by the bards, I grew up with thee in the grove of oaks:

"'But a tale had reached me that thou wast no more. Pardon, O Muse, if thou beest immortal, pardon that I but now learn it. Yonder at the goal alone will I learn it.

"'There it stands. But dost thou see the still further one, and its crowns also? This represt courage, this proud silence, this look which sinks fiery upon the ground, I know:

"'Yet weigh once again, ere the herald sound a note dangerous to thee. Am I not she who have measured myself with her from Thermopylæ, and with the stately one of the Seven Hills?"

"She spake: the earnest decisive moment drew nearer with the herald. 'I love thee,' answered quick with looks of flame, Teutona, 'Britoness, I love thee to enthusiasm;

"'But not warmer than immortality and those Palms: Touch, if so wills thy genius, touch them before me; yet will I, when thou seizest it, seize also the crown.

"'And, Oh how I tremble! O ye Immortals, perhaps I may reach first the high goal: then, oh then, may thy breath attain my loose-streaming hair!'

"The herald shrilled. They flew with eagle-speed. The wide career smoked up clouds of dust. I looked. Beyond the Oak billowed yet thicker the dust, and I lost them."

"This beautiful allegory," adds Mr. Taylor, "requires no illustration; but it constitutes one of the reasons for suspecting that the younger may eventually be the victorious Muse." We hope not, but that the generous race may yet last through long centuries. Tuiskone has shot through a mighty space, since this Poet saw her: what if she were now slackening her speed, and the Britoness quickening hers?

If the Essay on Klopstock is the best, that on Kotzebue is undoubtedly the worst, in this book, or perhaps in any book written by man of ability in our day. It is one of those acts which, in the spirit of philanthropy, we could wish Mr. Taylor to conceal in profoundest secrecy; were it not that hereby the "stimulant" theory, a heresy which still lurks here and there even in our better criticism, is in some sort brought to a crisis, and may the sooner depart from this world, or at least from the high places of it, into others more suitable. Kotzebue, whom all nations, and kindreds, and tongues, and peoples, his own people the foremost, after playing with him for some foolish hour, have swept out of doors as a lifeless bundle of dyed rags, is here scientifically examined, measured, pulse-felt, and pronounced to be living, and a divinity. He has such prolific "invention," abounds so in "fine situations," in passionate scenes, is so soul-harrowing, so stimulant. The *Proceedings at Bow Street* are stimulant enough; neither is prolific invention, interesting situations, or soul-harrowing passion wanting among the Authors that compose there; least of all if we follow them to Newgate, and the gallows: but when did the *Morning Herald* think of inserting its *Police Reports* among our Anthologies? Mr. Taylor is at the pains to analyze very many of Kotzebue's productions, and translates copiously from two or three: how the Siberian Governor took on when his daughter was about to run away with one Benjowsky, who however, was enabled to surrender his prize, there on the beach, with sails hoisted, by "looking at his wife's picture;" how the people "lift young Burgundy from the Tun," not indeed to drink him, for he is not wine but a Duke; how a certain stout-hearted West Indian, that has made a fortune, proposes marriage to his two sisters, but finding the ladies reluctant, solicits their serving-woman, whose reputation is not only cracked, but visibly quite rent asunder, accepts her nevertheless, with her thriving cherub, and is the happiest of men;—with more of the like sort. On the strength of which we are assured that, "according to my judgment, Kotzebue is the greatest dramatic genius that Europe has evolved since Shakspeare." Such is the table which Mr. Taylor has spread for pilgrims in the Prose Wilderness of Life: thus does he sit like a kind host, ready to carve; and though the viands and beverage are but, as it were, stewed garlic, Yarmouth herrings, and *blue-ruin*, praise them as "stimulant," and courteously presses the universe to fall to.

What a purveyor with this palate shall say to Nectar and Ambrosia, may be curious as a question in Natural History, but hardly otherwise. The most of what Mr. Taylor has written on Schiller, on Goethe, and the new Literature of Germany, a reader that loves him, as we honestly do, will consider as unwritten, or written in a state of somnambulism. He who has just quitted Kotzebue's Bear-garden, and Fives-court, and pronounces it to be all stimulant and very good, what is there for him to do in the Hall of the Gods? He looks transiently in; asks with mild authority, "Arian or Trinitarian? Quotidian or Stimulant?" and receiving no answer but a hollow echo, which almost sounds like laughter, passes on, muttering that they are dumb idols, or mere Nürnberg waxwork.

It remains to notice Mr. Taylor's Translations. Apart from the choice of subjects, which in probably more than half the cases is unhappy, there is much to be said in favour of these. Compared with the average of British Translations, they may be pronounced of almost ideal excellence; compared with the best translations extant, for example, the German *Shakspeare*, *Homer*, *Calderon*, they may still be called better than indifferent. One great merit Mr. Taylor has: rigorous adherence to his original; he endeavours at least to copy with all possible fidelity the turn of phrase, the tone, the very metre, whatever stands written for him. With the German language he has now had a long familiarity, and, what is no less essential, and perhaps still rarer among our translators, has a decided understanding of English. All this of Mr. Taylor's own Translations: in the borrowed pieces, whereof there are several, we seldom, except indeed in those by Shelley and Coleridge, find much worth; sometimes a distinct worthlessness. Mr. Taylor has made no conscience of clearing those unfortunate performances even from their gross blunders. Thus, in that "excellent version by Miss Plumptre," we find this statement: Professor Müller could not utter a period without introducing the words *with under*, "whether they had business there or not;" which statement, were it only on the ground that Professor Müller was not sent to Bedlam, there to utter periods, we venture to deny. Doubtless his besetting sin was *mitunder*, which indeed means *at the same time*, or the like, (etymologically, *with among*,) but nowise *with under*. One other instance we shall give, from a much more important subject. Mr. Taylor admits that he does not make much of *Faust:* however, he inserts Shelley's version of the *Mayday Night;* and another scene, evidently rendered by quite a different artist. In this latter, Margaret is in the Cathedral during High-Mass, but her whole thoughts are turned inwards on a secret shame and sorrow: an Evil Spirit is whispering in her ear, the Choir chant fragments of the *Dies iræ;* she is like to choke and sink. In the original, this passage is in verse; and, we presume, in the translation also,—founding on the capital letters. The concluding lines are these:

"MARGARET.

I feel imprison'd. The thick pillars gird me.
The vaults low'r o'er me. Air, air, I faint.

EVIL SPIRIT.

Where wilt thou lie concealed? for sin and shame
Remain not hidden—wo is coming *down*.

THE CHOIR.

Quid sum miser tum dicturus?
Quem patronum rogaturus?
Cum vix justus sit securus.

EVIL SPIRIT.

From thee the glorified *avert their view*,
The pure *forbear* to offer thee a hand.

THE CHOIR.

Quid sum miser tum dicturus?

MARGARET.

Neighbour, your ——"

—Your what?—Angels and ministers of grace defend us!—"*Your Drambottle.*" Will Mr. Taylor have us understand, then, that "the noble German nation," more especially the fairer half thereof, (for the "Neighbour" is *Nachbarin*, Neighbouress,) goes to church with a decanter of brandy in its pocket? Or would he not rather, even forcibly, interpret *Fläschchen* by *vinaigrette*, by *volatile-salts*?—The world has no notice that this passage is a borrowed one, but will, notwithstanding, as the more charitable theory, hope and believe so.

We have now done with Mr. Taylor; and would fain, after all that has come and gone, part with him in good nature and good will. He has spoken freely, we have answered freely. Far as we differ from him in regard to German Literature, and to the much more important subjects here connected with it; deeply as we feel convinced that his convictions are wrong and dangerous, are but half true, and, if taken for the whole truth, wholly false and fatal, we have nowise blinded ourselves to his vigorous talent, to his varied learning, his sincerity, his manful independence and self-support. Neither is it for speaking out plainly that we blame him. A man's honest, earnest opinion is the most precious of all he possesses: let him communicate this, if he is to communicate any thing. There is, doubtless, a time to speak, and a time to keep silence; yet Fontenelle's celebrated aphorism, *I might have my hand full of truth, and would open only my little finger*, may be practised also to excess, and the little finger itself kept closed. That reserve, and knowing silence, long so universal among us, is less the fruit of active benevolence, of philosophic tolerance, than of indifference and weak conviction. Honest Skepticism, honest Atheism, is better than that withered, lifeless Dilettantism and amateur Eclecticism, which merely toys with all opinions; or than that wicked Machiavelism, which, in thought denying every thing, except that Power is Power, in words, for its own wise purposes, loudly believes every thing: of both which miserable habitudes the day, even in England, is wellnigh over. That Mr. Taylor belongs not, and at no time belonged, to either of these classes, we account a true praise. Of his *Historic Survey* we have endeavoured to point out the faults and the merits: should he reach a second edition, which we hope, perhaps he may profit by some of our hints, and render the work less unworthy of himself and of his subject. In its present state and shape, this English Temple of Fame can content no one. A huge, anomalous, heterogeneous mass, no section of it like another, oriel-window alternating with rabbit-hole, wrought capital on pillar of dried mud; heaped together out of marble, loose earth, rude boulder-stone; hastily roofed in with shingles,—such is the Temple of Fame; uninhabitable either for priest or statue, and which nothing but a continued suspension of the laws of gravity can keep from rushing ere long into a chaos of stone and dust. For the English worshipper, who in the meanwhile has no other temple, we search out the least dangerous apartments; for the future builder, the materials that will be valuable.

And now, in washing our hands of this all-too sordid but not unnecessary task, one word on a more momentous object. Does not the existence of such a Book, do not many other indications, traceable in France, in Germany, as well as here, betoken that a new era in the spiritual intercourse of Europe is approaching; that instead of isolated, mutually repulsive National Literatures, a World-Literature may one day be looked for? The better minds of all countries begin to understand each other; and, which follows naturally, to love each other and help each other; by whom ultimately all countries in all their proceedings are governed.

Late in man's history, yet clearly at length, it becomes manifest to the dullest, that mind is stronger than matter, that mind is the creator and shaper of matter; that not brute Force, but only Persuasion and Faith is the king of this world. The true Poet, who is but the inspired Thinker, is still an Orpheus whose Lyre tames the savage beasts, and evokes the dead rocks to fashion themselves into palaces and stately inhabited cities. It has been said, and may be repeated, that Literature is fast becoming all in all to us; our Church, our Senate, our whole Social Constitution. The true Pope of Christendom is not that feeble old man in Rome; nor is its Autocrat the Napoleon, the Nicolas, with his half million even of obedient bayonets; such Autocrat is himself but a more cunningly-devised bayonet and military engine in the hands of a mightier than he. The true Autocrat and Pope is that man, the real or seeming Wisest of the past age; crowned after death; who finds his Hierarchy of gifted Authors, his Clergy of assiduous Journalists; whose Decretals, written not on parchment, but on the living souls of men, it were an inversion of the Laws of Nature to *dis*obey. In these times of ours, all Intellect has fused itself into Literature: Literature, Printed Thought, is the molten sea and wonder-bearing Chaos, into which mind after mind casts forth its opinion, its feeling, to be molten into the general mass, and to work there; Interest after Interest is engulfed in it, or embarked on it: higher, higher it rises round all the Edifices of Existence; they must all be molten into it, and anew bodied forth from it, or stand unconsumed among its fiery surges. Wo to him whose Edifice is not built of true Asbest, and on the everlasting Rock; but on the false sand, and of the drift-wood of Accident, and the paper and parchment of antiquated Habit! For the power, or powers, exist not on our Earth, that can say to that sea, roll back, or bid its proud waves be still.

What form so omnipotent an element will assume; how long it will welter to and fro as a wild Democracy, a wild Anarchy; what Constitution and Organization it will fashion for itself, and for what depends on it, in the depths of Time, is a subject for prophetic conjecture, wherein brightest hope is not unmingled with fearful apprehension and awe at the boundless unknown. The more cheering is this one thing which we do see and know—That its tendency is to a universal European Commonweal; that the wisest in all nations will communicate and co-operate; whereby Europe will again have its true Sacred College, and Council of Amphictyous; wars will become rarer, less inhuman, and, in the course of centuries, such delirious ferocity in nations, as in individuals it already is, may be proscribed, and become obsolete for ever.

TRAGEDY OF THE NIGHT-MOTH.

[FRASER'S MAGAZINE, 1831.]

Magna Ausus.

'T is placid midnight, stars are keeping
Their meek and silent course in heaven;
Save pale recluse, all things are sleeping,
His mind to study still is given.

But see! a wandering Night-moth enters,
Allured by taper gleaming bright;
A while keeps hovering round, then ventures
On Goethe's mystic page to light.

With awe she views the candle blazing;
A universe of fire it seems
To moth-*savante* with rapture gazing,
Or fount whence Life and Motion streams.

What passions in her small heart whirling,
Hopes boundless, adoration, dread;
At length her tiny pinions twirling,
She darts and—puff!—the moth is dead!

The sullen flame, for her scarce sparkling,
Gives but one hiss, one fitful glare;
Now bright and busy, now all darkling,
She snaps and fades to empty air.

Her bright gray form that spread so slimly,
Some fan she seemed of pigmy Queen;
Her silky cloak that lay so trimly,
Her wee, wee eyes that looked so keen,

Last moment here, now gone for ever,
To nought are passed with fiery pain;
And ages circling round shall never
Give to this creature shape again?

Poor moth! near weeping I lament thee,
Thy glossy form, thy instant wo;
'T was zeal for "things too high" that sent thee
From cheery earth to shades below.

Short speck of boundless space was needed
For home, for kingdom, world to thee!
Where passed unheeding as unheeded,
Thy slender life from sorrow free.

But syren hopes from out thy dwelling,
Enticed thee, bade thee Earth explore,—
Thy frame, so late with rapture swelling,
Is swept from Earth for evermore!

Poor moth! thy fate my own resembles:
Me too a restless asking mind
Hath sent on far and weary rambles,
To seek the good I ne'er shall find.

Like thee, with common lot contented,
With humble joys and vulgar fate,
I might have lived and ne'er lamented,
Moth of a larger size, a longer date!

But Nature's majesty unveiling,
What seemed her wildest, grandest charms,
Eternal Truth and Beauty hailing,
Like thee, I rushed into her arms.

What gained we, little moth? Thy ashes,
Thy one brief parting pang may show:
And withering thoughts for soul that dashes
From deep to deep, are but a death more slow.

CHARACTERISTICS.*

[EDINBURGH REVIEW, 1831.]

THE healthy know not of their health, but only the sick: this is the Physician's Aphorism; and applicable in a far wider sense than he gives it. We may say, it holds no less in moral, intellectual, political, poetical, than in merely corporeal therapeutics; that wherever, or in what shape soever, powers of the sort which can be named *vital* are at work, herein lies the test of their working right, or working wrong.

In the Body, for example, as all doctors are agreed, the first condition of complete health is, that each organ perform its function unconsciously, unheeded; let but any organ announce its separate existence, were it even boastfully, and for pleasure, not for pain, then already has one of those unfortunate "false centres of sensibility" established itself, already is derangement there. The perfection of bodily well-being is, that the collective bodily activities seem one; and be manifested, moreover, not in themselves, but in the action they accomplish. If a Dr. Kitchener boast that his system is in high order, Dietetic Philosophy may indeed take credit; but the true Peptician was that Countryman who answered that, "for his part, he had no system." In fact, unity, agreement, is always silent, or soft-voiced; it is only discord that loudly proclaims itself. So long as the several elements of Life, all fitly adjusted, can pour forth their movement like harmonious tuned strings, it is a melody and unison; Life, from its mysterious fountains, flows out as in celestial music and diapason,—which also, like that other music of the spheres, even because it is perennial and complete, without interruption and without imperfection, might be fabled to escape the ear. Thus, too, in some languages, is the state of health well denoted by a term expressing unity; when we feel ourselves as we wish to be, we say that we are *whole.*

Few mortals, it is to be feared, are permanently blessed with that felicity of "having no system:" nevertheless, most of us, looking back on young years, may remember seasons of a light, aërial translucency and elasticity, and perfect freedom; the body had not yet become the prison-house of the soul, but was its vehicle and implement, like a creature of the thought, and altogether pliant to its bidding. We knew not that we had limbs, we only lifted, hurled, and leapt; through eye and ear, and all avenues of sense, came clear unimpeded tidings from without, and from within issued clear victorious force; we stood as in the centre of Nature, giving and receiving, in harmony with it all; unlike Virgil's Husbandmen, "too happy *because* we did not know our blessedness." In those days, health and sickness were foreign traditions that did not concern us; our whole being was as yet One, the whole man like an incorporated Will. Such, were Rest or ever-successful Labour the human lot, might our life continue to be: a pure, perpetual, unregarded music; a beam of perfect white light, rendering all things visible, but itself unseen, even because it was of that perfect whiteness, and no irregular obstruction had yet broken it into colours. The beginning of Inquiry is Disease: all Science, if we consider well, as it must have originated in the feeling of something being wrong, so it is and continues to be but Division, Dismemberment, and partial healing of the wrong. Thus, as was of old written, the Tree of Knowledge springs from a root of evil, and bears fruits of good and evil. Had Adam remained in Paradise, there had been no Anatomy and no Metaphysics.

But, alas, as the Philosopher declares, "Life itself is a disease; a working incited by suffering;" action from passion! The memory of that first state of Freedom and paradisiac Unconsciousness has faded away into an ideal poetic dream. We stand here too conscious of many things: with Knowledge, the symptom of Derangement, we must even do our best to restore a little Order. Life is, in few instances, and at rare intervals, the diapason of a heavenly melody; oftenest the fierce jar of disruptions and convulsions, which, do what we will, there is no disregarding. Nevertheless, such is still the wish of Nature on our behalf; in all vital action, her manifest purpose and effort is, that we should be unconscious of it, and, like the peptic Countryman, never know that we "have a system." For indeed vital action everywhere is emphatically a means, not an end; Life is not given us for the mere sake of Living, but always with an ulterior external Aim: neither is it on the process, on the means, but rather on the result, that Nature, in any of her doings, is wont to intrust us with insight and volition. Boundless as is the domain of man, it is but a small fractional proportion of it that he rules with Consciousness and by Forethought: what he can contrive, nay, what he can altogether know and comprehend, is essentially the mechanical, small; the great is ever, in one sense or other, the vital; it is essentially the mysterious, and only the surface of it can be understood. But Nature, it might seem, strives, like a kind mother, to hide from us even this, that she is a mystery: she will have us rest on her beautiful and awful bosom as if it were our secure home; on he bottomless, boundless Deep,

* 1. An Essay on the Origin and Prospects of Man. By Thomas Hope. 3 vols. 8vo. London, 1831.

2. *Philosophische Vorlesungen, insbesondere über Philosophie der sprache und des Wortes. Geschrieben und vorgetragen zu Dresden im December*, 1828, *und in den ersten Tagen des Januars* 1829. (Philosophical Lectures, especially on the Philosophy of Language and the Gift of Speech. Written and delivered at Dresden in December, 1828, and the early days of January, 1829.) By Friedrich von Schlegel. 8vo. Vienna, 1830.

whereon all human things fearfully and wonderfully swim, she will have us walk and build, as if the film which supported us there (which any scratch of a bare bodkin will rend asunder, any sputter of a pistol-shot instantaneously burn up) were no film, but a solid rock-foundation. For ever in the neighbourhood of an inevitable Death, man can forget that he is born to die; of his Life, which, strictly meditated, contains in it an Immensity and an Eternity, he can conceive lightly, as of a simple implement wherewith to do day-labour and earn wages. So cunningly does Nature, the mother of all highest art, which only apes her from afar, "body forth the Finite from the Infinite;" and guide man safe on his wondrous path, not more by endowing him with vision, than, at the right place, with blindness! Under all her works, chiefly under her noblest work, Life, lies a basis of Darkness, which she benignantly conceals; in Life, too, the roots and inward circulations which stretch down fearfully to the regions of Death and Night, shall not hint of their existence, and only the fair stem with its leaves and flowers, shone on by the fair sun, disclose itself, and joyfully grow.

However, without venturing into the abstruse, or too eagerly asking Why and How, in things where our answer must needs prove, in great part, an echo of the question, let us be content to remark farther, in the merely historical way, how that Aphorism of the bodily Physician holds good in quite other departments. Of the Soul, with her activities, we shall find it no less true than of the Body: nay, cry the Spiritualists, is not that very division of the unity, Man, into a dualism of Soul and Body, itself the symptom of disease; as, perhaps, your frightful theory of Materialism, of his being but a Body, and therefore, at least, once more a unity, may be the paroxysm which was critical, and the beginning of cure! But omitting this, we observe, with confidence enough, that the truly strong mind, view it as Intellect, as Morality, or under any other aspect, is nowise the mind acquainted with its strength; that here as before the sign of health is Unconsciousness. In our inward, as in our outward world, what is mechanical lies open to us: not what is dynamical and has vitality. Of our Thinking, we might say, it is but the mere upper surface that we shape into articulate Thoughts;—underneath the region of argument and conscious discourse lies the region of meditation; here, in its quiet mysterious depths, dwells what vital force is in us; here, if aught is to be created, and not merely manufactured and communicated, must the work go on. Manufacture is intelligible, but trivial; Creation is great, and cannot be understood. Thus if the Debator and Demonstrator, whom we may rank as the lowest of true thinkers, knows what he has done, and how he did it, the Artist, whom we rank as the highest, knows not; must speak of Inspiration, and, in one or the other dialect, call his work the gift of a divinity.

But on the whole, "genius is ever a secret to itself;" of this old truth we have, on all sides, daily evidence. The Shakspeare takes no airs for writing *Hamlet* and the *Tempest*, understands not that it is any thing surprising: Milton, again, is more conscious of his faculty, which accordingly is an inferior one. On the other hand, what cackling and strutting must we not often hear and see, when, in some shape of academical prolusion, maiden speech, review article, this or the other well-fledged goose has produced its goose-egg, of quite measurable value, were it the pink of its whole kind; and wonders why all mortals do not wonder!

Foolish enough, too, was the College Tutor's surprise at Walter Shandy; how, though unread in Aristotle, he could nevertheless argue; and not knowing the name of any dialectic tool, handled them all to perfection. Is it the skilfullest Anatomist that cuts the best figure at Sadler's Wells? or does the Boxer hit better for knowing that he has a flexor longus and a flexor brevis? But, indeed, as in the higher case of the Poet, so here in that of the Speaker and Inquirer, the true force is an unconscious one. The healthy Understanding, we should say, is not the Logical, argumentative, but the Intuitive; for the end of Understanding is not to prove, and find reasons, but to know and believe. Of Logic, and its limits, and uses and abuses, there were much to be said and examined; one fact, however, which chiefly concerns us here, has long been familiar; that the man of logic and the man of insight; the Reasoner and the Discoverer, or even Knower, are quite separable,—indeed, for most part, quite separate characters. In practical matters, for example, has it not become almost proverbial that the man of logic cannot prosper? This is he whom business people call Systematic and Theorizer and Wordmonger; his *vital* intellectual force lies dormant or extinct, his whole force is mechanical, conscious: of such a one it is foreseen that, when once confronted with the infinite complexities of the real world, his little compact theorem of the world will be found wanting; that unless he can throw it overboard, and become a new creature, he will necessarily founder. Nay, in mere Speculation itself, the most ineffectual of all characters, generally speaking, is your dialectic man-at-arms; were he armed cap-a-pie in syllogistic mail of proof, and perfect master of logic-fence, how little does it avail him! Consider the old Schoolmen, and their pilgrimage towards Truth: the faithfullest endeavour, incessant unwearied motion, often great natural vigour; only no progress: nothing but antic feats of one limb poised against the other; there they balanced, somersetted, and made postures; at best gyrated swiftly, with some pleasure, like Spinning Dervishes, and ended where they began. So it is, so will it always be, with all System-makers and builders of logical card-castles; of which class a certain remnant must, in every age, as they do in our own, survive and build. Logic is good, but it is not the best. The Irrefragable Doctor, with his chains of induction, his corollaries, dilemmas, and other cunning logical diagrams and apparatus, will cast you a beautiful horoscope, and speak reasonable things; nevertheless your stolen jewel, which you wanted him to find you, is not forthcoming. Often by some winged word, winged as the thunderbolt is, of a Luther, a Napoleon, a Goethe, shall we see the difficulty split asunder, and its secret laid bare; while the Irrefragable, with all his logical tools, hews at it, and hovers round it, and finds it on all hands too hard for him.

Again in the difference between Oratory and Rhetoric, as indeed everywhere in that superiority of what is called the Natural over the Artificial, we find a similar illustration. The Orator persuades and carries all with him, he knows not how; the Rhetorician can prove that he ought to have persuaded and carried all with him; the one is in a state of healthy unconsciousness, as if he "had no system;" the other, in virtue of regimen and dietetic punctuality, feels at best that "his system is in high order." So stands it, in short, with all forms of Intellect, whether as directed to the finding of Truth, or to the fit imparting thereof; to Poetry, to Eloquence, to depth of Insight, which is the basis of both these; always the characteristic of right performance is a certain spontaneity, an unconsciousness; "the healthy know not of their health, but only the sick." So that the old precept of the critic, as crabbed as it looked to his ambitious disciple, might contain in it a most fundamental truth, applicable to us all, and in much else than Literature: "Whenever you have written any sentence that looks particularly excellent, be sure to blot it out." In like manner, under milder phraseology, and with a meaning purposely much wider, a living Thinker has taught us: "Of the Wrong we are always conscious, of the Right never."

But if such is the law with regard to Speculation and the Intellectual power of man, much more is it with regard to Conduct, and the power, manifested chiefly therein, which we name Moral. "Let not thy left hand know what thy right hand doeth:" whisper not to thy own heart, How worthy is this action; for then it is already becoming worthless. The good man is he who *works* continually in well-doing; to whom well-doing is as his natural existence, awakening no astonishment, requiring no commentary; but there, like a thing of course, and as if it could not but be so. Self-contemplation, on the other hand, is infallibly the symptom of disease, be it or be it not the sign of cure: an unhealthy Virtue is one that consumes itself to leanness in repenting and anxiety; or, still worse, that inflates itself into dropsical boastfulness and vain glory: either way, it is a self-seeking; an unprofitable looking behind us to measure the way we have made: whereas the sole concern is to walk continually forward, and make more way. If in any sphere of Man's Life, then in the moral sphere, as the inmost and most vital of all, it is good that there be wholeness; that there be unconsciousness, which is the evidence of this. Let the free, reasonable Will, which dwells in us, as in our Holy of Holies, be indeed free, and obeyed like a Divinity, as is its right and its effort: the perfect obedience will be the silent one. Such perhaps were the sense of that maxim, enunciating, as is usual, but the half of a truth: "To say that we have a clear conscience is to utter a solecism; had we never sinned, we should have had no conscience." Were defeat unknown, neither would victory be celebrated by songs of triumph.

This, true enough, is an ideal, impossible state of being; yet ever the goal towards which our actual state of being strives; which it is the more perfect the nearer it can approach. Nor, in our actual world, where Labour must often prove ineffectual, and thus in all senses Light alternate with Darkness, and the nature of an ideal Morality be much modified, is the case, thus far, materially different. It is a fact, which escapes no one, that, generally speaking, whoso is acquainted with his worth has but a little stock to cultivate acquaintance with. Above all, the public acknowledgment of such acquaintance, indicating that it has reached quite an intimate footing, bodes ill. Already, to the popular judgment, he who talks much about Virtue in the abstract, begins to be suspicious; it is shrewdly guessed that where there is great preaching, there will be little almsgiving. Or again, on a wider scale, we can remark that ages of Heroism are not ages of Moral Philosophy; Virtue, when it can be philosophized of, has become aware of itself, is sickly, and beginning to decline. A spontaneous habitual all-pervading spirit of Chivalrous Valour shrinks together, and perks itself up into shrivelled Points of Honour; humane Courtesy and Nobleness of mind dwindles into punctilious Politeness, "avoiding meats;" "paying tithe of mint and anise, neglecting the weightier matters of the law." Goodness, which was a rule to itself, must appeal to Precept, and seek strength from Sanctions; the Freewill no longer reigns unquestioned and by divine right, but like a mere earthly sovereign, by expediency, by Rewards and Punishments: or rather, let us say, the Freewill, so far as may be, has abdicated and withdrawn into the dark, and a spectral nightmare of a Necessity usurps its throne; for now that mysterious Self-impulse of the whole man, heaven-inspired, and in all senses partaking of the Infinite, being captiously questioned in a finite dialect, and answering, as it needs must, by silence,—is conceived as non-extant, and only the outward Mechanism of it remains acknowledged: of Volition, except as the synonym of Desire, we hear nothing; of "Motives," without any Mover, more than enough.

So, too, when the generous Affections have become well-nigh paralytic, we have the reign of Sentimentality. The greatness, the profitableness, at any rate the extremely ornamental nature of high feeling, and the luxury of doing good; charity, love, self-forgetfulness, devotedness, and all manner of godlike magnanimity are everywhere insisted on, and pressingly inculcated in speech and writing, in prose and verse; Socinian Preachers proclaim "Benevolence" to all the four winds, and have TRUTH engraved on their watchseals: unhappily with little or no effect. Were the Limbs in right Walking order, why so much demonstrating of Motion? The barrenest of all mortals is the Sentimentalist. Granting even that he were sincere, and did not wilfully deceive us, or without first deceiving himself, what good is in him? Does he not lie there as a perpetual lesson of despair, and type of bedrid valetudinarian impotence? His is emphatically a Virtue that has become, through every fibre, conscious of itself; it is all sick, and feels as if it were made of glass and durst not touch or be touched: in the shape of work, it can do nothing; at the utmost, by incessant nursing and caudling, keep itself alive. As the last stage of all, when Virtue, properly so called, has ceased to be practised, and become extinct, and a mere remembrance, we have the era of Sophists, descanting of its existence, proving it, denying it, mechanically "accounting" for it;—as dissectors and demonstrators cannot operate till once the body be dead.

Thus is true Moral genius, like true intellectual, which indeed is but a lower phasis thereof, "ever a secret to itself." The healthy moral nature loves Goodness, and without wonder wholly lives in it; the unhealthy makes love to it, and would fain get to live in it; or, finding such courtship fruitless, turns round, and not without contempt, abandons it. These curious relations of the Voluntary and Conscious to the Involuntary and Unconscious, and the small proportion which, in all departments of our life, the former bears to the latter,—might lead us into deep questions of Psychology and Physiology: such, however, belong not to our present object. Enough, if the fact itself become apparent, that Nature so meant it with us; that in this wise we are made. We may now say, that view man's individual Existence under what aspect we will, under the highest Spiritual, as under the merely Animal aspect, everywhere the grand vital energy, while in its sound state, is an unseen, unconscious one; or, in the words of our old Aphorism, "the healthy know not of their health, but only the sick."

To understand man, however, we must look beyond the individual man and his actions or interests, and view him in combination with his fellows. It is in Society that man first feels what he is; first becomes what he can be. In Society an altogether new set of spiritual activities are evolved in him, and the old immeasurably quickened and strengthened. Society is the genial element wherein his nature first lives and grows; the solitary man were but a small portion of himself, and must continue for ever folded in, stunted, and only half alive. "Already," says a deep Thinker, with more meaning than will disclose itself at once, "my opinion, my conviction, gains *infinitely* in strength and sureness, the moment a second mind has adopted it." Such, even in its simplest form, is association; so wondrous the communion of soul with soul as directed to the mere act of Knowing! In other higher acts, the wonder is still more manifest; as in that portion of our being which we name the Moral: for properly, indeed, all communion is of a moral sort, whereof such intellectual communion, (in the act of knowing,) is itself an example. But with regard to Morals strictly so called, it is in Society, we might almost say, that Morality begins; here at least it takes an altogether new form, and on every side, as in living growth, expands itself. The Duties of Man to himself, to what is Highest in himself, make but the First Table of the Law: to the First Table is now superadded a Second, with the duties of Man to his Neighbour; whereby also the significance of the first now assumes its true importance. Man has joined himself with man; soul acts and reacts on soul; a mystic miraculous unfathomable Union establishes itself; Life, in all its elements, has become intensated, consecrated. The lightning-spark of Thought, generated, or say rather heaven-kindled, in the solitary mind, awakens its express likeness in another mind, in a thousand other minds, and all blaze up together in combined fire; reverberated from mind to mind, fed also with fresh fuel in each, it acquires incalculable new Light as Thought, incalculable new Heat as converted into Action. By and by, a common store of Thought can accumulate, and be transmitted as an everlasting possession: Literature, whether as preserved in the memory of Bards, in Runes and Hieroglyphs engraved on stone, or in Books of written or printed paper, comes into existence, and begins to play its wondrous part. Politics are formed; the weak submitting to the strong; with a willing loyalty, giving obedience that he may receive guidance: or say rather, in honour of our nature, the ignorant submitting to the wise; for so it is in all even the rudest communities, man never yields himself wholly to brute Force, but always to moral Greatness; thus the universal title of respect, from the Oriental *Scheik*, from the *Sachem* of the red Indians, down to our English *Sir*, implies only that he whom we mean to honour is our *senior*. Last, as the crown and all-supporting keystone of the fabric, Religion arises. The devout meditation of the isolated man, which flitted through his soul, like a transient tone of Love and Awe from unknown lands, acquires certainty, continuance, when it is shared in by his brother-men. "Where two or three are gathered together" in the name of the Highest, then first does the Highest, as it is written, "appear among them to bless them;" then first does an Altar and act of united Worship open a way from Earth to Heaven; whereon, were it but a simple Jacob's-ladder, the heavenly Messengers will travel, with glad tidings, and unspeakable gifts for men. Such is Society, the vital articulation of many individuals into a new collective individual: greatly the most important of man's attainments on this earth; that in which, and by virtue of which, all his other attainments and attempts find their arena, and have their value. Considered well, Society is the standing wonder of our existence; a true region of the Supernatural; as it were, a second all-embracing Life, wherein our first individual Life becomes doubly and trebly alive, and whatever of infinitude was in us bodies itself forth, and becomes visible and active.

To figure society as endowed with Life is scarcely a metaphor; but rather the statement of a fact by such imperfect methods as language affords. Look at it closely, that mystic Union, Nature's highest work with man, wherein man's volition plays an indispensable yet so subordinate a part, and the small Mechanical grows so mysteriously and indissolubly out of the infinite

Dynamical, like body out of Spirit,—is truly enough vital, what we can call vital, and bears the distinguishing character of life. In the same style also, we can say that Society has its periods of sickness and vigour, of youth, manhood, decrepitude, dissolution, and new-birth; in one or other of which stages, we may, in all times and all places where men inhabit, discern it; and do ourselves in this time and place, whether as co-operating or as contending, as healthy members or as diseased ones, to our joy and sorrow, form part of it. The question, what is the actual condition of Society? has in these days unhappily become important enough. No one of us is unconcerned in that question; but for the majority of thinking men a true answer to it, such is the state of matters, appears almost as the one thing needful. Meanwhile as the true answer, that is to say, the complete and fundamental answer and settlement, often as it has been demanded, is nowhere forthcoming, and indeed by its nature is impossible, any honest approximation towards such is not without value. The feeblest light, or even so much as a more precise recognition of the darkness, which is the first step to attainment of light, will be welcome.

This once understood, let it not seem idle if we remark that here too our old Aphorism holds; that again in the Body Politic, as in the animal body, the sign of right performance is Unconsciousness. Such, indeed, is virtually the meaning of that phrase "artificial state of society," as contrasted with the natural state, and indicating something so inferior to it. For, in all vital things, men distinguish an Artificial and a Natural; founding on some dim perception or sentiment of the very truth we here insist on; the Artificial is the conscious, mechanical; the Natural is the unconscious, dynamical. Thus as we have an artificial Poetry, and prize only the natural; so likewise we have an artificial Morality, an artificial Wisdom, an artificial Society. The artificial Society is precisely one that knows its own structure, its own internal functions; not in watching, not in knowing which, but in working outwardly to the fulfilment of its aim, does the well-being of a Society consist. Every Society, every Polity, has a spiritual principle; is the imbodiment, tentative, and more or less complete, of an Idea: all its tendencies of endeavour, specialities of custom, its laws, politics, and whole procedure, (as the glance of some Montesquieu across innumerable superficial entanglements can partly decipher,) are prescribed by an Idea, and flow naturally from it, as movements from the living source of motion. This idea, be it of devotion to a Man or class of Men, to a Creed, to an institution, or even, as in more ancient times, to a piece of land, is ever a true Loyalty; has in it something of a religious, paramount, quite infinite character; it is properly the Soul of the State, its Life: mysterious as other forms of Life, and like these working secretly, and in a depth beyond that of consciousness.

Accordingly, it is not in the vigorous ages of a Roman Republic that Treatises of the Commonwealth are written: while the Decii are rushing with devoted bodies on the enemies of Rome, what need of preaching Patriotism? The virtue of Patriotism has already sunk from its pristine, all-transcendant condition, before it has received a name. So long as the Commonwealth continues rightly athletic, it cares not to dabble in anatomy. Why teach Obedience to the sovereign; why so much as admire it, or separately recognise it, while a divine idea of Obedience perennially inspires all men? Loyalty, like Patriotism, of which it is a form, was not praised until it had begun to decline; the *Preux Chevaliers* first became rightly admirable, when "dying for their king" had ceased to be a habit with chevaliers. For if the mystic significance of the State, let this be what it may, dwells vitally in every heart, encircles every life as with a second higher life, how should it stand self-questioning? It must rush outward, and express itself by works. Besides, if perfect, it is there as by necessity, and does not excite inquiry: it is also by nature, infinite, has no limits; therefore can be circumscribed by no conditions and definitions; cannot be reasoned of; except *musically*, or in the language of Poetry, cannot yet so much as be spoken of.

In those days, Society was what we name healthy, sound at heart. Not, indeed, without suffering enough; not without perplexities, difficulty on every side: for such is the appointment of man; his highest and sole blessedness is, that he toil, and know what to toil at: not in ease, but in united victorious labour, which is at once evil and the victory over evil, does his Freedom lie. Nay, often, looking no deeper than such superficial perplexities of the early Time, historians have taught us that it was all one mass of contradiction and disease; and in the antique Republic, or feudal Monarchy, have seen only the confused chaotic quarry, not the robust labourer, or the stately edifice he was building of it. If society, in such ages, had its difficulty, it had also its strength; if sorrowful masses of rubbish so encumbered it, the tough sinews to hurl them aside, with indomitable heart, were not wanting. Society went along without complaint; did not stop to scrutinize itself, to say, How well I perform, or, Alas, how ill! Men did not yet feel themselves to be "the envy of surrounding nations;" and were enviable on that very account. Society was what we can call *whole*, in both senses of the word. The individual man was in himself a whole, or complete union; and could combine with his fellows as the living member of a greater whole. For all men, through their life, were animated by one great Idea; thus all efforts pointed one way, everywhere there was *wholeness*. Opinion and Action had not yet become disunited; but the former could still produce the latter, or attempt to produce it, as the stamp does its impression while the wax is not hardened. Thought, and the Voice of thought, were also a unison; thus, instead of Speculation we had Poetry; Literature, in its rude utterance, was as yet a heroic Song, perhaps too a devotional Anthem. Religion was everywhere; Philosophy lay hid under it, peacefully included in it. Herein, as in the life-centre of all, lay the true health and oneness. Only at a later era must Religion split itself into Philosophies; and thereby the vital union of thought being lost, disunion and mutual collision in all provinces of Speech and of Action more and more prevail. For if the Poet, or Priest, or by whatever title the inspired thinker may be named, is the sign of vigour and wellbeing; so likewise is the Logician, or uninspired thinker, the sign of disease, probably of decrepitude and decay. Thus, not to mention other instances, one of them much nearer hand,—so soon as Prophecy among the Hebrews had ceased, then did the reign of Argumentation begin; and the ancient Theocracy, in its Sadduceeisms and Phariseeisms, and vain jangling of sects and doctors, give token that the *soul* of it had fled, and that the *body* itself by natural dissolution, "with the old forces still at work, but working in reverse order," was on the road to final disappearance.

We might pursue this question into innumerable other ramifications; and everywhere, under new shapes, find the same truth, which we here so imperfectly enunciate, disclosed: that throughout the whole world of man, in all manifestations and performances of his nature, outward and inward, personal and social, the Perfect, the Great is a mystery to itself, knows not itself; whatsoever does know itself is already little, and more or less imperfect. Or otherwise, we may say, Unconsciousness belongs to pure unmixed Life; Consciousness to a diseased mixture and conflict of Life and Death: Unconsciousness is the sign of Creation; Consciousness at best, that of Manufacture. So deep, in this existence of ours, is the significance of Mystery. Well might the Ancients make silence a god; for it is the element of all godhood, infinitude, or transcendental greatness; at once the source and the ocean wherein all such begins and ends. In the same sense, too, have Poets sung "Hymns to the Night;" as if "Night" were nobler than day; as if Day were but a small motley-coloured veil spread transiently over the infinite bosom of Night, and did but deform and hide from us its purely transparent, eternal deeps. So likewise have they spoken and sung as if Silence were the grand epitome and complete sum-total of all Harmony; and Death, what mortals call Death, properly the beginning of Life. Under such figures, since except in figures there is no speaking of the Invisible, have men endeavoured to express a great Truth;—a Truth, in our times, as nearly as is perhaps possible, forgotten by the most; which nevertheless continues for ever true, for ever all-important, and will one day, under new figures, be again brought home to the bosoms of all.

But, indeed, in a far lower sense, the rudest mind has still some intimation of the greatness there is in Mystery. If Silence was made a god of by the Ancients, he still continues a government clerk among us Moderns. To all Quacks, moreover, of what sort soever, the effect of Mystery is well known: here and there some Cagliostro, even in latter days, turns it to notable account: the Blockhead also, who is ambitious, and has no talent, finds sometimes in "the talent of silence," a kind of succedaneum. Or again, looking on the opposite side of the matter, do we not see, in the common understanding of mankind, a certain distrust, a certain contempt of what is altogether self-conscious and mechanical? As nothing that is wholly seen through has other than a trivial character; so any thing professing to be great, and yet wholly to see through itself, is already known to be false, and a failure. The evil repute your "theoretical men" stand in, the acknowledged inefficiency of "Paper Constitutions," and all that class of objects, are instances of this. Experience often repeated, and perhaps a certain instinct of something far deeper that lies under such experiences, has taught men so much. They know, beforehand, that the loud is generally the insignificant, the empty. Whatsoever can proclaim itself from the house-tops may be fit for the hawker, and for those multitudes that must needs buy of him; but for any deeper use, might as well continue unproclaimed. Observe, too, how the converse of the proposition holds; how the insignificant, the empty, is usually the loud; and, after the manner of a drum, is loud even because of its emptiness. The uses of some Patent Dinner Calefactor can be bruited abroad over the whole world in the course of the first winter; those of the Printing Press are not so well seen into for the first three centuries: the passing of the Select Vestries Bill raises more noise and hopeful expectancy among mankind, than did the promulgation of the Christian Religion. Again, and again, we say, the great, the creative, and enduring, is ever a secret to itself; only the small, the barren, and transient, is otherwise.

If we now, with a practical medical view, examine, by this same test of Unconsciousness, the Condition of our own Era, and of man's Life therein, the diagnosis we arrive at is nowise of a flattering sort. The state of Society in our days is of all possible states the least an unconscious one: this is especially the Era when all manner of Inquiries into what was once the unfelt, involuntary sphere of man's existence, find their place, and as it were occupy the whole domain of thought. What, for example, is all this that we hear, for the last generation or two, about the Improvement of the Age, the Spirit of the Age, Destruction of Prejudice, Progress of the Species, and the March of Intellect, but an unhealthy state of self-sentience, self-survey: the precursor and prognostic of still worse health? That Intellect do march, if possible at double-quick time, is very desirable; nevertheless why should she turn round at every stride, and cry: See you what a stride I have taken! Such a marching of Intellect is distinctly of the spavined kind; what the Jockeys call "all action and no go." Or at best, if we examine well, it is the marching of that gouty Patient, whom his Doctors had clapt on a metal floor artificially heated to the searing point, so that he was obliged to march, and marched with a vengeance—nowhither. Intellect did not awaken for the first time yesterday; but has been under way from Noah's Flood downwards: greatly her best progress, moreover, was in the old times, when she said nothing about it. In those same dark "ages," Intellect (metaphorically as well as literally) could invent *glass*, which now she has enough ado to grind into *spectacles.* Intellect built not only Churches, but a Church, *the* Church, based on this firm Earth, yet reaching up, and leading up, as high as Heaven; and now it is all she can do to keep its doors bolted, that there be no tearing of the Surplices, no robbery of the Alms-box. She built a Senate-house likewise, glorious in its kind; and now it costs her a wellnigh mortal effort to sweep it clear of vermin, and get the roof made rain-tight.

But the truth is, with Intellect, as with most other things, we are now passing from that first or boastful stage of Self-sentience into the second or painful one: out of these often asseverated declarations that "our system is in high order," we come now, by natural sequence, to the melancholy conviction that it is altogether the reverse. Thus, for instance, in the matter of Government, the period of the "Invaluable Constitution" must be followed by a Reform Bill; to laudatory De Lolmes succeed objurgatory Benthams. At any rate, what Treatises on the Social Contract, on the Elective Franchise, the Rights of Man, the Rights of Property, Codifications, Institutions, Constitutions, have we not, for long years, groaned under! Or again, with a wider survey, consider those Essays on Man, Thoughts on Man, Inquiries concerning Man; not to mention Evidences of the Christian Faith, Theories of Poetry, Consideration on the Origin of Evil, which during the last century have accumulated on us to a frightful extent. Never since the beginning of Time was there, that we hear or read of, so intensely self-conscious a Society. Our whole relations to the Universe and to our fellow man have become an Inquiry, a Doubt: nothing will go on of its own accord, and do its functions quietly; but all things must be probed into, the whole working of man's world be anatomically studied. Alas, anatomically studied, that it may be medically aided! Till at length, indeed, we have come to such a pass, that except in this same Medicine, with its artifices and appliances, few can so much as imagine any strength or hope to remain for us. The whole Life of Society must now be carried on by drugs: doctor after doctor appears with his nostrum, of Co-operative Societies, Universal Suffrage, Cottage-and-Cow systems, Repression of Population, Vote by Ballot. To such height has the dyspepsia of Society reached; as indeed the constant grinding internal pain, or from time to time the mad spasmodic throes, of all Society do otherwise too mournfully indicate.

Far be it from us to attribute, as some unwise persons do, the disease itself to this unhappy sensation that there is a disease! The Encyclopedists did not produce the troubles of France; but the troubles of France produced the Encyclopedists, and much else. The Self-consciousness is the symptom merely; nay, it is also the attempt towards cure. We record the fact, without special censure; not wondering that Society should feel itself, and in all ways complain of aches and twinges, for it has suffered enough. Napoleon was but a Job's comforter, when he told his wounded Staff-officer, twice unhorsed by cannon balls, and with half his limbs blown to pieces: *Vous vous écoutez trop!*

On the outward, or as it were Physical diseases of Society, it were beside our purpose to insist here. These are diseases which he who runs may read; and sorrow over, with or without hope. Wealth has accumulated itself into masses; and Poverty, also in accumulation enough, lies impassably separated from it; opposed, uncommunicating, like forces in positive and negative poles. The gods of this lower world sit aloft on glittering thrones, less happy than Epicurus' gods, but as indolent, as impotent; while the boundless living chaos of Ignorance and Hunger welters terrific, in its dark fury, under their feet. How much among us might be likened to a whited sepulchre; outwardly all Pomp and Strength; but inwardly full of horror and despair and dead men's bones! Iron highways, with their wains fire-winged, are uniting all ends of the firm Land; quays and moles, with their innumerable stately fleets, tame the Ocean into our pliant bearer of burdens; Labour's thousand arms, of sinew and of metal, all-conquering, everywhere, from the tops of the mountain down to the depths of the mine and the caverns of the sea, ply unweariedly for the service of man: Yet man remains unserved. He has subdued this Planet, his habitation and inheritance, yet reaps no profit from the victory. Sad to look upon, in the highest stage of civilization, nine-tenths of mankind must struggle in the lowest battle of savage or even animal man, the battle against Famine. Countries are rich, prosperous in all manner of increase, beyond example: but the Men of those countries are poor, needier than ever of all sustenance outward and inward; of Belief, of Knowledge, of Money, of Food. The rule, *Sic vos non vobis,* never altogether to be got rid of in men's Industry, now presses with such incubus weight, that Industry must shake it off, or utterly be strangled under it; and, alas, can as yet but gasp and rave, and aimlessly struggle, like one in the final deliration. Thus Change, or the inevitable approach of Change, is manifest everywhere. In one Country we have seen lava-torrents of fever-frenzy envelope all things; Government succeed Government, like the phantasms of a dying brain: in another Country, we can even now see, in maddest alternation, the Peasant governed by such guidance as this: To labour earnestly one month in raising wheat, and the next month labour earnestly in burning it. So that Society, were it not by nature immortal, and its death ever a new-birth, might appear, as it does in the eyes of some, to be sick to dissolution, and even now writhing in its last agony. Sick enough we must admit it to be, with disease enough, a whole nosology of diseases; wherein he perhaps is happiest that is not called to prescribe as physician;—wherein, however, one small piece of policy, that of summoning the Wisest in the Commonwealth, by the sole method yet known or thought of, to come together and with their whole soul consult for it, might, but for late tedious experiences, have seemed unquestionable enough.

But leaving this, let us rather look within, into the Spiritual condition of Society, and see what aspects and prospects offer themselves there. For, after all, it is there properly that the secret and origin of the whole is to be sought: the Physical derangements of Society are but the image and impress of its Spiritual; while the heart continues sound, all other sickness is superficial, and temporary. False Action is the fruit of false Speculation; let the spirit of Society be free and strong, that is to say, let true Principles inspire the members of Society, then neither can disorders accumulate in its Practice; each disorder will be promptly, faithfully inquired into, and remedied as it arises. But alas, with us the Spiritual condition of Society is no less sickly than the Physical. Examine man's internal world, in any of its social relations and performances, here too all seems diseased self-consciousness, collision, and mutually-destructive struggle. Nothing acts from within outwards in undivided healthy force; every thing lies impotent, lamed, its force turned inwards, and painfully "listens to itself."

To begin with our highest Spiritual function, with Religion, we might ask, whither has Religion now fled? Of Churches and their establishments we here say nothing; nor of the unhappy domains of Unbelief, and how innumerable men, blinded in their minds, must "live without God in the world;" but, taking the fairest side of the matter, we ask, What is the nature of that same Religion, which still lingers in the hearts of the few who are called, and call themselves, specially the Religious? Is it a healthy Religion, vital, unconscious of itself; that shines forth spontaneously in doing of the Work, or even in preaching of the Word? Unhappily, no. Instead of heroic martyr Conduct, and inspired and soul-inspiring Eloquence, whereby Religion itself were brought home to our living bosoms, to live and reign there, we have "Discourses on the Evidences," endeavouring, with smallest result, to make it probable that such a thing as Religion exists. The most enthusiastic Evangelicals do not preach a Gospel, but keep describing how it should and might be preached; to awaken the sacred fire of Faith, as by a sacred contagion, is not their endeavour; but, at most, to describe how Faith shows and acts, and scientifically distinguish true Faith from false. Religion, like all else, is conscious of itself, listens to itself; it becomes less and less creative, vital; more and more mechanical. Considered as a whole, the Christian Religion, of late ages has been continually dissipating itself into Metaphysics; and threatens now to disappear, as some rivers do, in deserts of barren sand.

Of Literature, and its deep-seated, wide-spread maladies, why speak? Literature is but a branch of Religion, and always participates in its character. However, in our time, it is the only branch that still shows any greenness; and, as some think, must one day become the main stem. Now, apart from the subterranean and tartarean regions of Literature;—leaving out of view the frightful, scandalous statistics of Puffing, the mystery of Slander, Falsehood, Hatred, and other convulsion-work of rabid Imbecility, and all that has rendered Literature on that side a perfect "Babylon the mother of Abominations," in very deed, making the world "drunk" with the wine of her iniquity;—forgetting all this, let us look only to the regions of the upper air; to such Literature as can be said to have some attempt towards truth in it, some tone of music, and if it be not poetical, to hold of the poetical. Among other characteristics, is not this manifest enough: that it knows itself? Spontaneous devotedness to the object, being wholly possessed by the object, what we can call Inspiration, has well-nigh ceased to appear in Literature. Which melodious Singer forgets that he is singing melodiously? We have not the love of greatness, but the love of the love of greatness. Hence infinite Affectations, Distractions; in every case inevitable Error. Consider, for one example, this peculiarity of Modern Literature, the sin that has been named View-hunting. In our elder writers, there are no paintings of scenery for its own sake; no euphuistic gallantries with Nature, but a constant heart-love for her, a constant dwelling in communion with her. View-hunting, with so much else that is of kin to it, first came decisively into action through the *Sorrows of Werter;* which wonderful Performance, indeed, may in many senses be regarded as the progenitor of all that has since become popular in Literature; whereof, in so far as concerns spirit and tendency, it still offers the most instructive image; for nowhere, except in its own country, above all in the mind of its illustrious Author, has it yet fallen wholly obsolete. Scarcely ever, till that late epoch, did any worshipper of Nature become entirely aware that he was worshipping, much to his own credit, and think of saying to himself: Come let us make a description! Intolerable enough: when every puny whipster draws out his pencil, and insists on painting you a scene; so that the instant you discern such a thing as "wavy outline," "mirror of the lake," "stern headland," or the like, in any Book, you must timorously hasten on; and scarcely the Author of Waverley himself can tempt you not to skip.

Nay, is not the diseased self-conscious state of Literature disclosed in this one fact, which lies so near us here, the prevalence of Reviewing! Sterne's wish for a reader "that would give up the reins of his imagination into his author's hands and be pleased he knew not why, and cared not wherefore," might lead him a long journey now. Indeed, for our best class of readers, the chief pleasure, a very stinted one, is this same knowing of the Why; which many a Kames and Bossu has been, ineffectually enough, endeavouring to teach us: till at last these also have laid down their trade; and now your Reviewer is a mere *taster,* who tastes, and says, by the evidence of such palate, such tongue, as he has got—It is good; it is bad. Was it thus that the French carried out certain inferior creatures on their Algerine Expedition, to taste the wells for them, and try whether they were poisoned? Far be it from us to disparage our own craft, whereby we have our living! Only we must note these things: that Reviewing spreads with strange vigour; that such a man as Byron reckons the Reviewer and the Poet equal; that at the last Leipsic Fair, there was advertised a Review of Reviews. By and by it will be found that "all Literature has become one boundless self-devouring Review; and as in London routs, we have to *do* nothing, but only to *see* others do nothing."—Thus does Literature also, like a sick thing, superabundantly "listen to itself."

No less is this unhealthy symptom manifest, if we cast a glance on our Philosophy, on the character of our speculative Thinking. Nay, already, as above hinted, the mere existence and necessity of a Philosophy is an evil. Man is sent hither not to question, but to work: "the end of man," it was long ago written, "is an Action, not a Thought." In the perfect state, all Thought were but the Picture and inspiring Symbol of Action; Philosophy, except as Poetry and Religion, had no being. And yet how, in this imperfect state, can it be avoided, can it be dispensed with? Man stands as in the centre of Nature; his fraction of Time encircled by Eternity, his handbreadth of Space encircled by Infinitude: how shall he forbear asking himself, What am I; and Whence; and Whither? How too, except in slight partial hints, in kind asseverations and assurances, such as a mother quiets her fretfully inquisitive child with, shall he get answer to such inquiries?

The disease of Metaphysics, accordingly, is a perennial one. In all ages, those questions of Death and Immortality, Origin of Evil, Freedom and Necessity, must, under new forms, anew make their appearance; ever, from time to time, must the attempt to shape for ourselves some Theorem of the Universe be repeated. And ever unsuccessfully: for what Theorem of the Infinite can the Finite render complete? We, the whole species of Mankind, and our whole existence and history, are but a floating speck in the illimitable ocean of the All; yet *in* that ocean; indissoluble portion thereof; partaking of its infinite tendencies; borne this way and that by its deep-swelling tides, and grand ocean currents;—of which what faintest chance is there that we should ever exhaust the significance, ascertain the goings and comings? A region of Doubt, therefore, hovers for ever in the background; in Action alone can we have certainty. Nay, properly, Doubt is the indispensable, inexhaustible material whereon Action works, which Action has to fashion into Certainty and Reality; only on a canvas of Darkness, such is man's way of being, could the many-coloured picture of our Life paint itself and shine.

Thus if our oldest system of Metaphysics is as old as the *Book of Genesis*, our latest is that of Mr. Thomas Hope, published only within the current year. It is a chronic malady that of Metaphysics, as we said, and perpetually recurs on us. At the utmost, there is a better and a worse in it; a stage of convalescence, and a stage of relapse with new sickness: these for ever succeed each other, as is the nature of all Life-movements here below. The first, or convalescent stage, we might also name of that Dogmatical or Constructive Metaphysics; when the mind constructively endeavours to scheme out, and assert for itself an actual Theorem of the Universe, and therewith for a time rests satisfied. The second or sick stage might be called that of Skeptical or Inquisitory Metaphysics; when the mind having widened its sphere of vision, the existing Theorem of the Universe no longer answers the phenomena, no longer yields contentment; but must be torn in pieces, and certainty anew sought for in the endless realms of Denial. All Theologies and sacred Cosmogonies belong, in some measure, to the first class: in all Pyrrhonism from Pyrrho down to Hume and the innumerable disciples of Hume, we have instances enough of the second. In the former, so far as it affords satisfaction, a temporary anodyne to Doubt, an arena for wholesome action, there may be much good; indeed in this case, it holds rather of Poetry than of Metaphysics, might be called Inspiration rather than Speculation. The latter is Metaphysics proper; a pure, unmixed, though from time to time a necessary evil.

For truly, if we look into it, there is no more fruitless endeavour than this same, which the Metaphysician proper toils in: to educe Conviction out of Negation. How, by merely testing and rejecting what is not, shall we ever attain knowledge of what is? Metaphysical Speculation, as it begins in No or Nothingness, so it must needs end in Nothingness; circulates and must circulate in endless vortices; creating, swallowing—itself. Our being is made up of Light and Darkness, the Light resting on the Darkness, and balancing it; everywhere there is Dualism, Equipoise; a perpetual Contradiction dwells in us: "where shall I place myself to escape from my own shadow?" Consider it well, Metaphysics is the attempt of the mind to rise above the mind; to environ, and shut in, or as we say, *comprehend* the mind. Hopeless struggle, for the wisest, as for the foolishest! What strength of sinew, or athletic skill, will enable the stoutest athlete to fold his own body in his arms, and, by lifting, lift up *himself?* The Irish Saint swam the Channel "carrying his head in his teeth:" but the feat has never been imitated.

That this is the age of Metaphysics, in the proper, or skeptical Inquisitory sense; that there was a necessity for its being such an age, we regard as our indubitable misfortune. From many causes, the arena of free Activity has long been narrowing, that of skeptical Inquiry becoming more and more universal, more and more perplexing. The Thought conducts not to the Deed; but in boundless chaos, self-devouring, engenders monstrosities, fantasms, fire-breathing chimeras. Profitable Speculation were this: What is to be done; and How is it to be done? But with us not so much as the What can be got sight of. For some generations, all Philosophy has been a painful, captious, hostile question towards every thing in the Heaven above, in the Earth beneath: Why art thou there? Till at length it has come to pass that the worth and authenticity of all things seems dubitable or deniable: our best effort must be unproductively spent, not in working, but in ascertaining our mere Whereabout, and so much as whether we are to work at all. Doubt, which, as was said, ever hangs in the back-ground of our world, has now become our middle-ground and foreground; whereon, for the time, no fair Life-picture can be painted, but only the dark air-canvas itself flow round us, bewildering and benighting.

Nevertheless, doubt as we will, man is actually Here; not to ask questions, but to do work: in this time, as in all times, it must be the heaviest evil for him, if his faculty of Action lie dormant, and only that of skeptical Inquiry exert itself. Accordingly, whoever looks abroad upon the world, comparing the Past with the Present, may find that the practical condition of man, in these days, is one of the saddest; burdened with miseries which are in a considerable degree peculiar. In no time was man's life what he calls a happy one; in no time can it be so. A perpetual dream there has been of Paradises, and some luxurious Lubberland, where the brooks should run wine, and the trees bend with ready-baked viands; but it was a dream merely, an impossible dream. Suffering, Contradiction, Error, have their quite perennial, and even indispensable, abode in this Earth. Is not Labour the inheritance of man? And what Labour for the present is joyous, and not grievous? Labour, Effort, is the very interruption of that Ease, which man foolishly enough fancies to be his Happiness: and yet without Labour there were no Ease, no Rest, so much as conceivable. Thus Evil, what we call Evil, must ever exist while man exists: Evil, in the widest sense we can give it, is precisely the dark, disordered material out of which man's Free-will has to create an edifice of order, and Good. Ever must Pain urge us to Labour; and only in free Effort can any blessedness be imagined for us.

But if man has, in all ages, had enough to encounter, there has, in most civilized ages, been an inward force vouchsafed him, whereby the pressure of things outward might be withstood. Obstruction abounded; but Faith also was not wanting. It is by Faith that man removes mountains: while he had Faith, his limbs might be wearied with toiling, his back galled with bearing; but the heart within him was peaceable and resolved. In the thickest gloom there burnt a lamp to guide him. If he struggled and suffered, he felt, that it even should be so; knew for what he was suffering and struggling. Faith gave him an inward Willingness; a world of Strength wherewith to front a world of Difficulty. The true wretchedness lies here: that the Difficulty remain and the Strength be lost; that Pain cannot relieve itself in free Effort; that we have the Labour, and want the Willingness. Faith strengthens us, enlightens us, for all endeavours and endurances; with Faith we can do all, and dare all, and life itself has a thousand times been joyfully given away. But the sum of man's misery is even this, that he feel himself crushed under the Juggernaut wheels and know that Juggernaut is no divinity, but a dead mechanical idol.

Now this is specially the misery which has fallen on man in our Era. Belief, Faith has wellnigh vanished from the world. The youth on awakening in this wondrous Universe, no longer finds a competent theory of its wonders. Time was when, if he asked himself: What is man; what are the duties of man? the answer stood ready written for him. But now the ancient "ground-plan of the All" belies itself when brought into contact with reality; Mother Church has, to the most, become a superannuated Stepmother, whose lessons go disregarded; or are spurned at, and scornfully gainsayed. For young Valour and thirst of Action no ideal Chivalry invites to heroism, prescribes what is heroic: the old ideal of Manhood has grown obsolete, and the new is still invisible to us, and we grope after it in darkness, one clutching this phantom, another that; Werterism, Byronism, even Brummelism, each has its day. For contemplation and love of Wisdom no Cloister now opens its religious shades; the Thinker must, in all senses, wander homeless, too often aimless, looking up to a Heaven which is dead for him, round to an Earth which is deaf. Action, in those old days, was easy, was voluntary, for the divine worth of human things lay acknowledged; Speculation was wholesome, for it ranged itself as the handmaid of Action; what could not so range itself died out by its natural death, by neglect. Loyalty still hallowed obedience, and made rule noble; there was still something to be loyal to; the Godlike stood embodied under many a symbol in men's interests and business; the Finite shadowed forth the Infinite; Eternity looked through Time. The Life of man was encompassed and overcanopied by a glory of Heaven, even as his dwelling-place by the azure vault.

How changed in these new days! Truly may it be said, the Divinity has withdrawn from the Earth; or veils himself in that wide-wasting Whirlwind of a departing Era, wherein the fewest can discern his goings. Not Godhead, but an iron, ignoble circle of Necessity embraces all things; binds the youth of these times into a sluggish thrall, or else exasperates him into a rebel. Heroic Action is paralyzed; for what worth now remains unquestionable with him? At the fervid period when his whole nature cries aloud for Action, there is nothing sacred under whose banner he can act; the course and kind and conditions of free Action are all but undiscoverable. Doubt storms in on him through every avenue: inquiries of the deepest, painfullest sort must be engaged with; and the invincible energy of young years waste itself in skeptical, suicidal cavillings; in passionate "questionings of Destiny," whereto no answer will be returned.

For men, in whom the old perennial principle of Hunger (be it Hunger of the poor Day-drudge who stills it with eighteenpence a day, or of the ambitious Place-hunter who can nowise still it with so little) suffices to fill up existence, the case is bad; but not the worst. These men have an aim, such as it is; and can steer towards it, with chagrin enough truly; yet, as their hands are kept full, without desperation. Unhappier are they to whom a higher instinct has been given; who struggle to be persons, not machines; to whom the Universe is not a warehouse, or at best fancy-bazaar, but a mystic temple and hall of doom. For such men there lie properly two courses open. The lower, yet still an estimable class, take up with worn-out Symbols of the Godlike; keep trimming and trucking between these and Hypocrisy, purblindly enough, miserably enough. A numerous intermediate class end in Denial; and form a theory that there is no theory; that nothing is certain in the world, except this fact of Pleasure being pleasant; so they try to realize what trifling modicum of Pleasure they can come at, and to live contented therewith, winking hard. Of these we speak not here; but only of the second nobler class, who also have dared to say No, and cannot yet say Yea; but feel that in the No they dwell as in a Golgotha, where life enters not, where peace is not appointed them. Hard, for most part, is the fate of such men; the harder the nobler they are. In dim forecastings, wrestles within them the "Divine Idea of the World," yet will nowhere visibly reveal itself. They have to realize a Worship for themselves, or live unworshipping. The Godlike has vanished from the world; and they, by the strong cry of their soul's agony, like true wonder-workers, must again evoke its presence. This miracle is their appointed task; which they must accomplish, or die wretchedly: this miracle has been accomplished by such: but not in our land; our land yet knows not of it. Behold a Byron, in melodious tones, "cursing his day:" he mistakes earthborn passionate Desire for heaven-inspired Freewill; without heavenly loadstar, rushes madly into the dance of meteoric lights that hover on the mad Mahlstrom; and goes down among its eddies. Hear a Shelley filling the earth with inarticulate wail; like the infinite, inarticulate grief and weeping of forsaken infants. A noble Friedrich Schlegel, stupified in that fearful loneliness, as of a silenced battle-field, flies back to Catholicism; as a child might to its slain mother's bosom, and cling there. In lower regions, how many a poor Hazlitt must wander on God's verdant earth, like the Unblest on burning deserts; passionately dig wells, and draw up only the dry quicksand; believe that he is seeking Truth, yet only wrestle among endless Sophisms, doing desperate battle as with spectre-hosts; and die and make no sign!

To the better order of such minds any mad joy of Denial has long since ceased: the problem is not now to deny, but to ascertain and perform. Once in destroying the False, there was a certain inspiration; but now the genius of Destruction has done its work, there is now nothing more to destroy. The doom of the Old has long been pronounced, and irrevocable; the Old has passed away: but, alas, the New appears not in its stead; the Time is still in pangs of travail with the New. Man has walked by the light of conflagrations, and amid the sound of falling cities; and now there is darkness, and long watching till it be morning. The voice even of the faithful can but exclaim: "As yet struggles the twelfth hour of the Night: birds of darkness are on the wing, spectres uproar, the dead walk, the living dream.—Thou, Eternal Providence, wilt cause the day to dawn!"*

Such being the condition, temporal and spiritual, of the world at our Epoch, can we wonder that the world "listens to itself," and struggles and writhes, everywhere externally and internally, like a thing in pain? Nay, is not even this unhealthy action of the world's Organization, if the symptom of universal disease, yet also the symptom and sole means of restoration and cure? The effort of Nature, exerting her medicative force to cast out foreign impediments, and once more become One, become whole? In Practice, still more in Opinion, which is the precursor and prototype of Practice, there must needs be collision, convulsion; much has to be ground away. Thought must needs be Doubt and Inquiry, before it can again be Affirmation and Sacred Precept. Innumerable "Philosophies of Man," contending in boundless hubbub, must annihilate each other, before an inspired Poesy and Faith for Man can fashion itself together.

From this stunning hubbub, a true Babylonish confusion of tongues, we have here selected two voices; less as objects of praise or condemnation, than as signs how far the confusion has reached, what prospect there is of its abating. Friedrich Schlegel's *Lectures*, delivered at Dresden, and Mr. Hope's *Essay*, published in London, are the latest utterances of European Speculation: far asunder in external place, they stand at a still wider distance in inward purport; are, indeed, so opposite and yet so cognate that they may, in many senses, represent the two Extremes of our whole modern system of Thought; and be said to include between them all the Metaphysical Philosophies, so often alluded to here, which, of late times, from France, Germany, England, have agitated and almost overwhelmed us. Both in regard to matter and to form, the relation of these two Works is significant enough.

Speaking first of their cognate qualities, let us remark, not without emotion, one quite extraneous point of agreement; the fact that the Writers of both have departed from this world; they have now finished their search, and had all doubts resolved: while we listen to the voice, the tongue that uttered it has gone silent for ever. But the fundamental, all-pervading similarity lies in this circumstance, well worthy of being noted, that both these Philosophies are of the Dogmatic, or Constructive sort: each in its way is a kind of Genesis; an endeavour to bring the Phenomena of man's Universe once more under some theoretic Scheme; in both there is a decided principle of unity; they strive after a result which shall be positive; their aim is not to question, but to establish. This, especially if we consider with what comprehensive concentrated force it is here exhibited, forms a new feature in such works.

Under all other aspects, there is the most irreconcilable opposition; a staring contrariety, such as might provoke contrasts were there

* Jean Paul's *Hesperus*. *Vorrede*.

far fewer points of comparison. If Schlegel's Work is the apotheosis of Spiritualism; Hope's again is the apotheosis of Materialism: in the one, all matter is evaporated into a Phenomenon, and terrestrial Life itself, with its whole doings and showings, held out as a Disturbance (*Zerrüttung*) produced by the *Zeitgeist*, (Spirit of Time;) in the other, Matter is distilled and sublimated into some semblance of Divinity: the one regards Space and Time as mere forms of man's mind, and without external existence or reality; the other supposes Space and Time to be "incessantly created," and rayed in upon us like a sort of "gravitation." Such is their difference in respect of purport; no less striking is it in respect of manner, talent, success, and all outward characteristics. Thus, if in Schlegel we have to admire the power of Words, in Hope we stand astonished, it might almost be said, at the want of an articulate Language. To Schlegel his Philosophic Speech is obedient, dexterous, exact, like a promptly-ministering genius; his names are so clear, so precise and vivid, that they almost (sometimes altogether) become things for him: with Hope there is no Philosophical Speech; but a painful, confused stammering, and struggling after such; or the tongue, as in dotish forgetfulness, maunders low, longwinded, and speaks not the word intended, but another; so that here the scarcely intelligible, in these endless convolutions, becomes the wholly unreadable; and often we could ask, as that mad pupil did of his tutor in Philosophy, "But whether is Virtue a fluid, then, or a gas?" If the fact, that Schlegel, in the city of Dresden, could find audience for such high discourse, may excite our envy; this other fact, that a person of strong powers, skilled in English Thought and master of its Dialect, could write the *Origin and Prospects of Man*, may painfully remind us of the reproach, "that England has now no language for Meditation; that England, the most Calculative, is the least Meditative, of all civilized countries."

It is not our purpose to offer any criticism of Schlegel's Book; in such limits as were possible here, we should despair of communicating even the faintest image of its significance. To the mass of readers, indeed, both among the Germans themselves, and still more elsewhere, it nowise addresses itself, and may lie for ever sealed. We point it out as a remarkable document of the Time and of the Man; can recommend it, moreover, to all earnest Thinkers, as a work deserving their best regard: a work full of deep meditation, wherein the infinite mystery of Life, if not represented, is decisively recognised. Of Schlegel himself, and his character, and spiritual history, we can profess no thorough or final understanding; yet enough to make us view him with admiration and pity, nowise with harsh contemptuous censure; and must say, with clearest persuasion, that the outcry of his being "a renegade," and so forth, is but like other such outcries, a judgment where there was neither jury, nor evidence, nor judge. The candid reader, in this Book itself, to say nothing of all the rest, will find traces of a high, far-seeing, earnest spirit, to whom "Austrian Pensions," and the Kaiser's crown, and Austria altogether, were but a light matter to the finding and vitally appropriating of Truth. Let us respect the sacred mystery of a Person; rush not irreverently into man's Holy of Holies! Were the lost little one, as we said already, found "sucking its dead mother, on the field of carnage," could it be other than a spectacle for tears? A solemn mournful feeling comes over us when we see this last Work of Friedrich Schlegel, the unwearied seeker, end abruptly in the middle; and, as if he *had not* yet found, as if emblematically of much, end with an "Aber—," with a "But—!" This was the last word that came from the Pen of Friedrich Schlegel: about eleven at night he wrote it down, and there paused sick; at one in the morning, Time for him had merged itself in Eternity; he was, as we say, no more.

Still less can we attempt any criticism of Mr. Hope's new Book of Genesis. Indeed, under any circumstances, criticism of it were now impossible. Such an utterance could only be responded to in peals of laughter; and laughter sounds hollow and hideous through the vaults of the dead. Of this monstrous Anomaly, where all sciences are heaped and huddled together, and the principles of all are, with a childlike innocence, plied hither and thither, or wholly abolished in case of need; where the First Cause is figured as a huge Circle, with nothing to do but radiate "gravitation" towards its centre; and so construct a Universe, wherein all, from the lowest cucumber with its coolness, up to the highest seraph with his love, were but, "gravitation," direct or reflex, "in more or less central globes," —what can we say, except, with sorrow and shame, that it could have originated nowhere save in England? It is a general agglomerate of all facts, notions, whims, and observations, as they lie in the brain of an English gentleman; as an English gentleman, of unusual thinking power, is led to fashion them, in his schools and in his world: all these thrown into the crucible, and if not fused, yet soldered or conglutinated with boundless patience; and now tumbled out here, heterogeneous, amorphous, unspeakable, a world's wonder. Most melancholy must we name the whole business; full of long-continued thought, earnestness, loftiness of mind; not without glances into the Deepest, a constant fearless endeavour after truth; and with all this nothing accomplished, but the perhaps absurdest Book written in our century by a thinking man. A shameful Abortion; which, however, need not now be smothered or mangled, for it is already dead; only, in our love and sorrowing reverence for the writer of *Anastasius*, and the heroic seeker of Light, though not bringer thereof, let it be buried and forgotten.

For ourselves, the loud discord which jars in these two Works, in innumerable works of the like import, and generally in all the Thought and Action of this period, does not any longer utterly confuse us. Unhappy who, in such a time, felt not, at all conjunctures, ineradicably in his heart the knowledge that a God made this Universe, and a Demon not! And shall

Evil always prosper, then? Out of all Evil comes Good; and no Good that is possible but shall one day be real. Deep and sad as is our feeling that we stand yet in the bodeful Night; equally deep, indestructible is our assurance that the Morning also will not fail. Nay, already, as we look round, streaks of a day-spring are in the east: it is dawning; when the time shall be fulfilled, it will be day. The progress of man towards higher and nobler Developments of whatever is highest and noblest in him, lies not only prophesied to Faith, but now written to the eye of Observation, so that he who runs may read.

One great step of progress, for example, we should say, in actual circumstances, was this same; the clear ascertainment that we are in progress. About the grand Course of Providence, and his final Purposes with us, we can know nothing, or almost nothing: man begins in darkness, ends in darkness; mystery is everywhere around us and in us, under our feet, among our hands. Nevertheless so much has become evident to every one, that this wondrous Mankind is advancing somewhither; that at least all human things are, have been, and for ever will be, in Movement and Change; —as, indeed, for beings that exist in Time, by virtue of Time, and are made of Time, might have been long since understood. In some provinces, it is true, as in Experimental Science, this discovery is an old one; but in most others it belongs wholly to these latter days. How often, in former ages, by eternal Creeds, eternal Forms of Government, and the like, has it been attempted, fiercely enough, and with destructive violence, to chain the Future under the Past; and say to the Providence, whose ways with man are mysterious, and through the great Deep: Hitherto shalt thou come, but no farther! A wholly insane attempt; and for man himself, could it prosper, the frightfullest of all enchantments, a very Life-in-Death. Man's task here below, the destiny of every individual man, is to be in turns Apprentice and Workman; or say rather, Scholar, Teacher, Discoverer: by nature he has a strength for learning, for imitating; but also a strength for acting, for knowing on his own account. Are we not in a World seen to be Infinite; the relations lying closest together modified by those latest-discovered, and lying farthest asunder? Could you ever spell-bind man into a Scholar merely, so that he had nothing to discover, to correct; could you ever establish a Theory of the Universe that were entire, unimprovable, and which needed only to be got by heart; man then were spiritually defunct, the species We now name Man had ceased to exist. But the gods, kinder to us than we are to ourselves, have forbidden such suicidal acts. As Phlogiston is displaced by Oxygen, and the Epicycles of Ptolemy by the Ellipses of Kepler; so does Paganism give place to Catholicism, Tyranny to Monarchy, and Feudalism to Representative Government, —where also the process does not stop. Perfection of Practice, like completeness of Opinion, is always approaching, never arrived; Truth, in the words of Schiller, *immer wird, nie ist*; never *is*, always *is a-being*.

Sad, truly, were our condition did we kno but this, that Change is universal and inev table. Launched into a dark shoreless sea o Pyrrhonism, what would remain for us but sail aimless, hopeless; or make madly merr while the devouring Death had not yet engulfe us? As, indeed, we have seen many, and sti see many do. Nevertheless so stands it no The venerator of the Past (and to what pu heart is the Past, in that "moonlight of m mory," other than sad and holy?) sorrows n over its departure, as one utterly bereave The true Past departs not, nothing that wa worthy in the Past departs; no Truth or Goo ness realized by man ever dies, or can die but is all still here, and recognised or nc lives and works through endless changes. all things, to speak in the German dialect, ar discerned by us, and exist for us, in an elemer of Time, and therefore of Mortality and Mut bility; yet Time itself reposes on Eternity the truly Great and Transcendental has i basis and substance in Eternity; stands r vealed to us as Eternity in a vesture of Tim Thus in all Poetry, Worship, Art, Society, a one form passes into another, nothing is lost it is but the superficial, as it were the *bod* only, that grows obsolete and dies; under th mortal body lies a *soul* that is immortal; th anew incarnates itself in fairer revelation; an the Present is the living sum-total of the whol Past.

In Change, therefore, there is nothing te rible, nothing supernatural: on the contrar it lies in the very essence of our lot, and li in this world. To-day is not yesterday: w ourselves change; how can our Works an Thoughts, if they are always to be the fittes continue always the same? Change, indee is painful; yet ever needful: and if Memor have its force and worth, so also has Hop Nay, if we look well to it, what is all Derang ment, and necessity of great Change, in itse such an evil, but the product simply of *in creased resources* which the old *methods* can n longer administer; of new wealth which th old coffers will no longer contain? What i it, for example, that in our own day burst asunder the bonds of ancient Political Sys tems, and perplexes all Europe with the fea of Change, but even this: the increase o social resources, which the old social method will no longer sufficiently administer? Th new omnipotence of the Steam-engine is hew ing asunder quite other mountains than th physical. Have not our economical distresse those barnyard Conflagrations themselves, th frightfullest madness of our mad epoch, thei rise also in what is a real increase: increas of Men; of human Force; properly, in such Planet as ours, the most precious of all in creases? It is true again, the ancient method of administration will no longer suffice. Mus the indomitable millions, full of old Saxo energy and fire, lie cooped up in this Wester Nook, choking one another, as in a Blackhol of Calcutta, while a whole fertile untenante Earth, desolate for want of the ploughshare cries: Come and till me, come and reap me If the ancient Captains can no longer yiel guidance, new must be sought after: for th difficulty lies not in nature, but in artifice: the European Calcutta-Blackhole has no walls but air ones, and paper ones.—So, too, Skepticism itself, with its innumerable mischiefs, what is it but the sour fruit of a most blessed increase, that of Knowledge; a fruit, too, that will not always continue *sour?*

In fact, much as we have said and mourned about the unproductive prevalence of Metaphysics, it was not without some insight into the use that lies in them. Metaphysical Speculation, if a necessary evil, is the forerunner of much good. The fever of Skepticism must needs burn itself out, and burn out thereby the Impurities that caused it; then again will there be clearness, health. The principle of Life, which now struggles painfully, in the outer, thin, and barren domain of the Conscious or Mechanical, may then withdraw into its inner Sanctuaries, its abysses of mystery and miracle; withdraw deeper than ever into that domain of the Unconscious, by nature infinite and inexhaustible; and creatively work there. From that mystic region, and from that alone, all wonders, all Poesies, and Religions, and Social Systems have proceeded: the like wonders, and greater and higher, lie slumbering there; and, brooded on by the spirit of the waters, will evolve themselves, and rise like exhalations from the Deep.

Of our modern Metaphysics, accordingly, may not this already be said, that if they have produced no Affirmation, they have destroyed much Negation? It is a disease expelling a disease: the fire of Doubt, as above hinted, consuming away the Doubtful; that so the Certain come to light, and again lie visible on the surface. English or French Metaphysics, in reference to this last stage of the speculative process, are not what we allude to here; but only the Metaphysics of the Germans. In France or England, since the days of Diderot and Hume, though all thought has been of a skeptico-metaphysical texture, so far as there were any Thought, we have seen no Metaphysics; but only more or less ineffectual questionings whether such could be. In the Pyrrhonism of Hume and the Materialism of Diderot, Logic had, as it were, overshot itself, overset itself. Now, though the athlete, to use our old figure, cannot, by much lifting, lift up his own body, he may shift it out of a laming posture, and get to stand in a free one. Such a service have German Metaphysics done for man's mind. The second sickness of Speculation has abolished both itself and the first. Friedrich Schlegel complains much of the fruitlessness, the tumult and transiency of German as of all Metaphysics; and with reason: yet in that wide-spreading, deep-whirling vortex of Kantism, so soon metamorphosed into Fichteism, Schellingism, and then as Hegelism, and Cousinism, perhaps finally evaporated, is not this issue visible enough, that Pyrrhonism and Materialism, themselves necessary phenomena in European culture, have disappeared; and a Faith in Religion has again become possible and inevitable for the scientific mind; and the word *Free*-thinker no longer means the Denier or Caviller, but the Believer, or the Ready to believe? Nay, in the higher Literature of Germany, there already lies, for him that can read it, the beginning of a new revelation of the Godlike; as yet unrecognised by the mass of the world; but waiting there for recognition, and sure to find it when the fit hour comes. This age also is not wholly without its Prophets.

Again, under another aspect, if Utilitarianism, or Radicalism, or the Mechanical Philosophy, or by whatever name it is called, has still its long task to do; nevertheless we can now see through it and beyond it: in the better heads, even among us English, it has become obsolete; as in other countries it has been, in such heads, for some forty or even fifty years. What sound mind among the French, for example, now fancies that men can be governed by "Constitutions;" by the never so cunning mechanizing of Self-interests, and all conceivable adjustments of checking and balancing: in a word, by the best possible solution of this quite insoluble and impossible problem, *Given a world of Knaves, to produce an Honesty from their united action?* Were not experiments enough of this kind tried before all Europe, and found wanting, when, in that doomsday of France, the infinite gulf of human Passion shivered asunder the thin rinds of Habit; and burst forth all-devouring, as in seas of Nether Fire? Which cunningly-devised "Constitution," constitutional, republican, democratic, sans-culottic, could bind that raging chasm together? Were they not all burnt up, like Paper as they were, in its molten eddies; and still the fire-sea raged fiercer than before? It is not by Mechanism, but by Religion; not by Self-interest, but by Loyalty, that men are governed or governable.

Remarkable it is, truly, how everywhere the eternal fact begins again to be recognised, that there is a Godlike in human affairs; that God not only made us and beholds us, but is in us and around us; that the Age of Miracles, as it ever was, now is. Such recognition we discern on all hands, and in all countries: in each country after its own fashion. In France, among the younger nobler minds, strangely enough; where, in their loud contention with the Actual and Conscious, the Ideal or Unconscious is, for the time, without exponent; where Religion means not the parent of Polity, as of all that is highest, but Polity itself; and this and the other earnest man has not been wanting, who could whisper audibly: "Go to, I will make a religion." In England still more strangely; as in all things, worthy England will have its way: by the shrieking of hysterical women casting out of devils, and other "gifts of the Holy Ghost." Well might Jean Paul say, in this his twelfth hour of the Night, "the living dream;" well might he say, "the dead walk." Meanwhile let us rejoice rather that so much has been seen into, were it through never so diffracting media, and never so madly distorted; that in all dialects, though but half-articulately, this high Gospel begins to be preached: "Man is still Man." The genius of Mechanism, as was once before predicted, will not always sit like a choking incubus on our soul; but at length, when by a new magic Word the old spell is broken, become our slave, and as familiar-spirit do all our bidding. "We are near awakening when we dream that we dream."

He that has an eye and a heart can even now say: Why should I falter? Light has come into the world; to such as love Light, so as Light must be loved, with a boundless all-doing, all-enduring love. For the rest, let that vain struggle to read the mystery of the Infinite cease to harass us. It is a mystery which, through all ages, we shall only read here a line of, there another line of. Do we not already know that the name of the Infinite is Good, is God? Here on Earth we are as Soldiers, fighting in a foreign land; that understand not the plan of the campaign, and have no need to understand it; seeing well what is at our hand to be done. Let us do it like Soldiers, with submission, with courage, with a heroic joy. "Whatsoever thy hand findeth to do, do it with all thy might." Behind us, behind each one of us, lie Six Thousand years of human effort, human conquest: before us is the boundless Time, with its as yet uncreated and unconquered Continents and Eldorados, which we, even we, have to conquer, to create: and from the bosom of Eternity shine for us celestial guiding stars.

"My inheritance how wide and fair!
Time is my fair seed-field, of Time I 'm heir."

GOETHE'S PORTRAIT.*

[Fraser's Magazine, 1832.]

Reader! thou here beholdest the Eidolon of Johann Wolfgang von Goethe. So looks and lives, now in his eighty-third year, afar in the bright little friendly circle of Weimar, "the clearest, most universal man of his time." Strange enough is the cunning that resides in the ten fingers, especially what they bring to pass by pencil and pen! Him who never saw England, England now sees: from Fraser's "Gallery" he looks forth here, wondering, doubtless, how *he* came into such *Lichtstrasse* ("light-street," or galaxy;) yet with kind recognition of all neighbours, even as the moon looks kindly on lesser lights, and, were they but fish-oil cressets, or terrestrial Vauxhall stars, (of clipped tin,) forbids not their shining. Nay, the very soul of the man thou canst likewise behold. Do but look well in those forty volumes of "musical wisdom," which, under the title of *Goethe's Werke*, Cotta of Tübingen, or Black and Young of Covent Garden—once offer them a trifle of drink-money—will cheerfully hand thee: greater sight, or more profitable, thou wilt not meet with in this generation. The German language, it is presumable, thou knowest; if not, shouldst thou undertake the study thereof for that sole end, it were well worth thy while.

Croquis (a man otherwise of rather satirical turn) surprises us, on this occasion, with a fit of enthusiasm. He declares often, that here is the finest of all living heads; speaks much of blended passion and repose; serene depths of eyes; the brow, the temples, royally arched, a very palace of thought;—and so forth.

The writer of these Notices is not without decision of character, and can believe what he knows. He answers Brother Croquis, that it is no wonder the head should be royal and a palace; for a most royal work was appointed to be done therein. Reader! within that head the whole world lies mirrored, in such clear, ethereal harmony, as it has done in none since Shakspeare left us: even *this* Rag-fair of a world, wherein thou painfully strugglest, and (as is like) stumblest—all lies transfigured here, and revealed authentically to be still holy, still divine. What alchymy was that: to find a mad universe full of skepticism, discord, desperation; and *transmute* it into a wise universe of belief, and melody, and reverence! Was not *there* an *opus magnum*, if one ever was? This, then, is he who, heroically doing and enduring, has accomplished it.

In this distracted time of ours, wherein men have lost their old loadstars, and wandered after night-fires and foolish will-o'-wisps; and all things, in that "shaking of the nations," have been tumbled into chaos, the high made low and the low high, and ever and anon some duke of this, and king of that, is gurgled aloft, to float there for moments; and fancies himself the governor and head-director of it all, and *is* but the topmost froth-bell, to burst again and mingle with the wild fermenting mass,—in this so despicable time, we say, there were nevertheless—be the bounteous heavens ever thanked for it!—*two great men* sent among us. The one, in the island of St. Helena now sleeps "dark and lone, amid the ocean's everlasting lullaby;" the other still rejoices in the blessed sunlight, on the banks of the Ilme.

Great was the part allotted each, great the talent given him for the same; yet, mark the contrast! Bonaparte walked through the war-convulsed world like an all-devouring earthquake, heaving, thundering, hurling kingdom over kingdom; Goethe was as the mild-shining, inaudible light, which, notwithstanding, can again make that chaos into a creation. Thus, too, we see Napoleon, with his Austerlitzes, Waterloos, and Borodinos, is quite gone—all departed, sunk to silence like a tavern-brawl. While this other!—*he* still shines with his direct radiance; his inspired words are to abide

* By Stieler of Munich; the copy in Fraser's Magazine proved a total failure and involuntary caricature,—resembling, as was said at the time, a wretched old-clothesman carrying behind his back a hat which he seemed to have stolen.

in living hearts, as the life and inspiration of thinkers, born and still unborn. Some fifty years hence, his thinking will be found translated, and ground down, even to the capacity of the diurnal press; acts of parliament will be passed in virtue of him:—this man, if we well consider of it, is appointed to be ruler of the world.

Reader! to thee thyself, even now, he has one counsel to give, the secret of his whole poetic alchymy: GEDENKE ZU LEBEN. Yes, "think of living!" Thy life, wert thou the "pitifullest of all the sons of earth," is no idle dream, but a solemn reality. It is thy own; it is all thou hast to front eternity with. Work, then, even as he has done, and does—"LIKE A STAR UNHASTING, YET UNRESTING."—*Sic va leas.*

BIOGRAPHY.*

[FRAZER'S MAGAZINE, 1832.]

MAN'S sociality of nature evinces itself, in spite of all that can be said, with abundant evidence by this one fact, were there no other: the unspeakable delight he takes in Biography. It is written, "The proper study of mankind is man;" to which study, let us candidly admit, he, by true or by false methods, applies himself, nothing loath. "Man is perennially interesting to man; nay, if we look strictly to it, there is nothing else interesting." How inexpressibly comfortable to know our fellow-creature; to see into him, understand his goings forth, decipher the whole heart of his mystery: nay, not only to see into him, but even to see out of him, to view the world altogether as he views it; so that we can theoretically construe him, and could almost practically personate him; and do now thoroughly discern both what manner of man he is, and what manner of thing he has got to work on and live on!

A scientific interest and a poetic one alike inspire us in this matter. A scientific: because every mortal has a Problem of Existence set before him, which, were it only, what for the most it is, the Problem of keeping soul and body together, must be to a certain extent *original*, unlike every other; and yet, at the same time, so *like* every other; like our own, therefore; instructive, moreover, since we also are indentured to *live*. A poetic interest still more: for precisely this same struggle of human Free-will against material Necessity, which every man's Life, by the mere circumstance that the man continues alive, will more or less victoriously exhibit,—is that which above all else, or rather inclusive of all else, calls the Sympathy of mortal hearts into action; and whether as acted, or as represented and written of, not only is Poetry, but is the sole Poetry possible. Borne onwards by which two all-embracing interests, may the earnest Lover of Biography expand himself on all sides, and indefinitely enrich himself. Looking with the eyes of every new neighbour, he can discern a new world different for each: feeling with the heart of every neighbour, he lives with every neighbour's life, even as with his own. Of these millions of living men each individual is a mirror to us: a mirror both scientific and poetic; or, if you will, both natural and magical;—from which one would so gladly draw aside the gauze veil; and, peering therein, discern the image of his own natural face, and the supernatural secrets that prophetically lie under the same!

Observe, accordingly, to what extent, in the actual course of things, this business of Biography is practised and relished. Define to thyself, judicious Reader, the real significance of these phenomena, named Gossip, Egotism, Personal Narrative, (miraculous or not,) Scandal, Raillery, Slander, and such like; the sum-total of which (with some fractional addition of a better ingredient, generally too small to be noticeable) constitutes that other grand phenomenon still called "Conversation." Do they not mean wholly: *Biography* and *Autobiography?* Not only in the common Speech of men; but in all Art, too, which is or should be the concentrated and conserved essence of what men can speak and show, Biography is almost the one thing needful.

Even in the highest works of Art our interest, as the critics complain, is too apt to be strongly or even mainly of a Biographic sort. In the Art, we can nowise forget the Artist: while looking on the *Transfiguration*, while studying the *Iliad*, we ever strive to figure to ourselves what spirit dwelt in Raphael; what a head was that of Homer, wherein, woven of Elysian light and Tartarian gloom, that old world fashioned itself together, of which these written Greek characters are but a feeble though perennial copy. The Painter and the Singer are present to us; we partially and for the time become the very Painter and the very Singer, while we enjoy the Picture and the Song. Perhaps, too, let the critic say what he will, this is the highest enjoyment, the clearest recognition, we can have of these. Art indeed is Art; yet Man also is Man. Had the *Transfiguration* been painted without human hand, had it grown merely on the canvas, say by atmospheric influences, as lichen-pictures do on rocks,—it were a grand Picture doubtless; yet nothing like so grand as *the* Picture, which, on opening our eyes, we everywhere in Heaven and in Earth see painted; and every-

* The Life of Samuel Johnson, LL.D.: including a Tour to the Hebrides: By James Boswell, Esq. A new Edition, with numerous Additions and Notes. By John Wilson Croker, LL.D., F. R. S. 5 vols. London, 1831.

where pass over with indifference,—because the Painter was not a Man. Think of this; much lies in it. The Vatican is great; yet poor to Chimborazo or the Peake of Teneriffe: its dome is but a foolish Big-endian or Little-endian chip of an egg-shell, compared with that star-fretted Dome where Arcturus and Orion glance for ever; which latter, notwithstanding, who looks at, save perhaps some necessitous star-gazer bent to make Almanacs, some thick-quilted watchman, to see what weather it will prove? The Biographic interest is wanting: no Michael Angelo was He who built that "Temple of Immensity;" therefore do we, pitiful Littlenesses as we are, turn rather to wonder and to worship in the little toybox of a Temple built by our like.

Still more decisively, still more exclusively does the Biographic interest manifest itself, as we descend into lower regions of spiritual communication; through the whole range of what is called Literature. Of History, for example, the most honoured, if not honourable species of composition, is not the whole purport biographic? "History," it has been said, "is the essence of innumerable Biographies." Such, at least, it should be: whether it is, might admit of question. But, in any case, what hope have we in turning over those old interminable Chronicles, with their garrulities and insipidities; or still worse, in patiently examining those modern Narrations, of the Philosophic kind, where "Philosophy, teaching by Experience," must sit like owl on housetop, *seeing* nothing, *understanding* nothing, uttering only, with solemnity enough, her perpetual most wearisome *hoo-hoo*:—what hope have we, except for the most part fallacious one of gaining some acquaintance with our fellow-creatures, though dead and vanished, yet dear to us; how they got along in those old days, suffering and doing; to what extent, and under what circumstances, they resisted the Devil and triumphed over him, or struck their colours to him, and were trodden under foot by him; how, in short, the perennial Battle went, which men name Life, which we also in these new days, with indifferent fortune, have to fight, and must bequeath to our sons and grandsons to go on fighting,—till the Enemy one day be quite vanquished and abolished, or else the great Night sink and part the combatants; and thus, either by some Millennium or some new Noah's Deluge, the Volume of Universal History wind itself up! Other hope, in studying such Books, we have none: and that it is a deceitful hope, who that has tried knows not? A feast of widest Biographic insight is spread for us; we enter full of hungry anticipation: alas! like so many other feasts, which Life invites us to, a mere Ossian's "feast of *shells*,"—the food and liquor being all emptied out and clean gone, and only the vacant dishes and deceitful emblems thereof left! Your modern Historical Restaurateurs are indeed little better than high-priests of Famine; that keep choicest china dinner-sets, only no dinner to serve therein. Yet such is our Biographic appetite, we run trying from shop to shop, with ever new hope; and, unless we could eat the wind, with ever new disappointment.

Again, consider the whole class of Fictitious Narratives; from the highest category of epic or dramatic Poetry, in Shakspeare and Homer, down to the lowest of froth Prose in the Fashionable Novel. What are all these but so many mimic Biographies? Attempts, here by an inspired Speaker, there by an uninspired Babbler, to deliver himself, more or less ineffectually, of the grand secret wherewith all hearts labour oppressed: The significance of Man's Life;—which deliverance, even as traced in the unfurnished head, and printed at the Minerva Press, finds readers. For, observe, though there is *a* greatest Fool, as a superlative in every kind; and *the* most Foolish man in the Earth is now indubitably living and breathing, and did this morning or lately eat breakfast, and is even now digesting the same; and looks out on the world, with his dim horn-eyes, and inwardly forms some unspeakable theory thereof: yet where shall the authentically Existing be personally met with! Can one of us, otherwise than by guess, know that we have got sight of him, have orally communed with him? To take even the narrower sphere of this our English metropolis, can any one confidently say to himself, that he has conversed with the identical, individual, Stupidest man now extant in London? No one. Deep as we dive in the Profound, there is ever a new depth opens: where the ultimate bottom may lie, through what new scenes of being we must pass before reaching it, (except that we know it does lie somewhere, and might by human faculty and opportunity be reached,) is altogether a mystery to us. Strange, tantalizing pursuit! We have the fullest assurance, not only that there is a Stupidest of London men actually resident, with bed and board of some kind, in London; but that several persons have been or perhaps are now speaking face to face with him: while for us, chase it as we may, such scientific blessedness will too probably be for ever denied!—But the thing we meant to enforce was this comfortable fact, that no known Head was so wooden, but there might be other heads to which it were a genius and Friar Bacon's Oracle. Of no given Book, not even of a Fashionable Novel, can you predicate with certainty that its vacuity is absolute; that there are not other vacuities which shall partially replenish themselves therefrom, and esteem it a *plenum*. How knowest thou, may the distressed Novelwright exclaim, that I, here where I sit, am the Foolishest of existing mortals; that this my Long-ear of a Fictitious Biography shall not find one and the other, into whose still longer ears it may be the means, under Providence, of instilling somewhat? We answer, None knows, none can certainly know: therefore, write on, worthy Brother, even as thou canst, as it has been given thee.

Here, however, in regard to "Fictitious Biographies," and much other matter of like sort, which the greener mind in these days inditeth, we may as well insert some singular sentences on the importance and significance of

Reality, as they stand written for us in Professor Gottfried Sauerteig's *Æsthetische Springwürzel*: a Work, perhaps, as yet new to most English readers. The Professor and Doctor is not a man whom we can praise without reservation; neither shall we say that his *Springwürzel* (a sort of magical pick-locks, as he affectedly names them) are adequate to "*start*" every *bolt* that locks up an æsthetic mystery; nevertheless, in his crabbed, one-sided way, he sometimes hits masses of the truth. We endeavour to translate faithfully, and trust the reader will find it worth serious perusal:

"The significance, even for poetic purposes," says Sauerteig, "that lies in Reality, is too apt to escape us; is perhaps only now beginning to be discerned. When we named *Rousseau's Confessions* an elegiaco-didactic Poem, we meant more than an empty figure of speech; we meant an historical scientific fact.

"Fiction, while the feigner of it knows that he is feigning, partakes, more than we suspect, of the nature of *lying*; and has ever an, in some degree, unsatisfactory character. All Mythologies were once Philosophies; were *believed*: the Epic Poems of old time, so long as they continued *epic*, and had any complete impressiveness, were Histories, and understood to be narratives of *facts*. In so far as Homer employed his gods as mere ornamental fringes, and had not himself, or at least did not expect his hearers to have, a belief that they were real agents in those antique doings; so far did he fail to be *genuine*; so far was he a partially *hollow* and false singer; and sang to please only a portion of man's mind, not the whole thereof.

"Imagination is, after all, but a poor matter when it must part company with Understanding, and even front it hostilely in flat contradiction. Our mind is divided in twain: there is contest; wherein that which is weaker must needs come to the worse. Now of all feelings, states, principles, call it what you will, in man's mind, is not Belief the clearest, strongest; against which all others contend in vain? Belief is, indeed, the beginning and first condition of all spiritual Force whatsoever: only in so far as Imagination, were it but momentarily, is *believed*, can there be any use or meaning in it, any enjoyment of it. And what is momentary Belief? The enjoyment of a moment. Whereas a perennial Belief were enjoyment perennially, and with the whole united soul.

"It is thus that I judge of the Supernatural in an Epic Poem; and would say, the instant it had ceased to be authentically supernatural, and become what you call 'Machinery;' sweep it out of sight (*schaff'es mir vom Halse*)! Of a truth, that same 'Machinery,' about which the critics make such hubbub, was well named *Machinery*; for it is in very deed mechanical, nowise inspired or poetical. Neither for us is there the smallest æsthetic enjoyment in it; save only in this way: that we believe it *to have been believed*,—by the Singer or his Hearers; into whose case we now laboriously struggle to transport ourselves; and so, with stinted enough result, catch some reflex of the Reality, which for them was wholly real, and visible face to face. Whenever it has come so far that your 'Machinery' is avowedly mechanical and unbelieved,—what is it else, if we dare tell ourselves the truth, but a miserable, meaningless Deception kept up by old use and wont alone? If the gods of an *Iliad* are to us no longer authentic Shapes of Terror, heart-stirring, heart-appalling, but only vague-glittering Shadows,—what must the dead Pagan gods of an *Epigoniad* be, the dead-living Pagan-Christian gods of a *Lusiad*, the concrete-abstract, evangelical-metaphysical gods of a *Paradise Lost*? Superannuated lumber! Cast raiment, at best; in which some poor mime, strutting and swaggering, may or may not set forth new noble Human Feelings, (again a Reality,) and so secure, or not secure, our pardon of such hoydenish masking,—for which, in any case, he has a pardon to *ask*.

"True enough, none but the earliest Epic Poems can claim this distinction of entire credibility, of Reality: after an *Iliad*, a *Shaster*, a *Koran*, and other the like primitive performances, the rest seem, by this rule of mine, to be altogether excluded from the list. Accordingly, what *are* all the rest from Virgil's *Æneid* downwards, in comparison?—Frosty, artificial, heterogeneous things; more of gumflowers than of roses; at best, of the two mixed incoherently together: to some of which, indeed, it were hard to deny the title of Poems; yet to no one of which can that title belong in any sense even resembling the old high one it, in those old days, conveyed,—when the epithet 'divine' or 'sacred,' as applied to the uttered Word of man, was not a vain metaphor, a vain sound, but a real name with meaning. Thus, too, the farther we recede from those early days, when Poetry, as true Poetry is always, was still sacred or divine, and inspired, (what ours, in great part, only pretends to be,)—the more impossible becomes it to produce any, we say not true Poetry, but tolerable semblance of such; the hollower, in particular, grow all manner of Epics; till at length, as in this generation, the very name of Epic sets men a-yawning, the announcement of a new Epic is received as a public calamity.

"But what if the *impossible* being once for all quite discarded, the *probable* be well adhered to; how stands it with fiction *then*? Why, then, I would say, the evil is much mended, but nowise completely cured. We have then, in place of the wholly dead modern Epic, the partially living modern Novel; to which latter it is much easier to lend that above-mentioned, so essential 'momentary credence,' than to the former: indeed infinitely easier: for the former being flatly incredible, no mortal *can* for a moment credit it, for a moment enjoy it. Thus, here and there, a *Tom Jones*, a *Meister*, a *Crusoe*, will yield no little solacement to the minds of men: though still immeasurably less than a *Reality* would, were the significance thereof as impressively unfolded, were the genius that could so unfold it once given us by the kind Heavens. Neither say thou that proper Realities are wanting; for Man's Life, now as of old, is the genuine work of God; wherever there is a Man, a God also is revealed, and all that is Godlike: a whole epitome of the Infinite, with its meanings, lies enfolded in the Life of every

Man. Only, alas, that the Seer to discern this same Godlike, and with fit utterance *un*fold it for us, is wanting, and may long be wanting!

"Nay, a question arises on us here, wherein the whole German reading-world will eagerly join: Whether man *can* any longer be so interested by the spoken Word, as he often was in those primeval days, when, rapt away by its inscrutable power, he pronounced it, in such dialect as he had, to be *transcendental*, (to *transcend* all measure,) to be sacred, prophetic, and the inspiration of a god? For myself, I, (*ich meines Ortes*,) by faith or by insight, do heartily understand that the answer to such question will be, Yea! For never, that I could in searching find out, has Man been, by Time which devours so much, deprivated of any faculty whatsoever that he in any era was possessed of. To my seeming, the babe born yesterday has all the organs of Body, Soul, and Spirit, and in exactly the same combination and entireness, that the oldest Pelasgic Greek, or Mesopotamian Patriarch, or Father Adam himself could boast of. Ten fingers, one heart with venous and arterial blood therein, still belong to man that is born of woman: when did he lose any of his spiritual Endowments either: above all, his highest spiritual Endowment, that of revealing Poetic Beauty, and of adequately receiving the same? Not the material, not the susceptibility is wanting; only the poet, or long series of Poets, to work on these. True, alas too true, the Poet *is* still utterly wanting, or all but utterly: nevertheless have we not centuries enough before us to produce him in? Him and much else!—I, for the present, will but predict that chiefly by working more and more on Reality, and evolving more and more wisely *its* inexhaustible meanings; and, in brief, speaking forth in fit utterance whatsoever our whole soul *believes*, and ceasing to speak forth what thing soever our whole soul does not believe,—will this high emprise be accomplished, or approximated to."

These notable, and not unfounded, though partial and *deep*-seeing rather than *wide*-seeing observations on the great import of Reality, considered even as a poetic material, we have inserted the more willingly, because a transient feeling to the same purpose may often have suggested itself to many readers; and, on the whole, it is good that every reader and every writer understand, with all intensity of conviction, what quite infinite worth lies in *Truth*; how all-pervading, omnipotent, in man's mind, is the thing we name *Belief*. For the rest, Herr Sauerteig, though one-sided, on this matter of Reality, seems heartily persuaded, and is not perhaps so ignorant as he looks. It cannot be unknown to him, for example, what noise is made about "Invention;" what a supreme rank this faculty is reckoned to hold in the poetic endowment. Great truly is Invention; nevertheless, that is but a poor exercise of it with which Belief is not concerned. "An Irishman with whisky in his head," as poor Byron said, will invent you, in this kind, till there is enough and to spare. Nay, perhaps, if we consider well, the highest exercise of Invention has, in very deed, nothing to do with Fiction; but is an invention of new Truth, what we can call a Revelation; which last does undoubtedly transcend all other poetic efforts, nor can Herr Sauerteig be too loud in its praises. But, on the other hand, whether such effort is still possible for man, Herr Sauerteig and the bulk of the world are probably at issue,—and will probably continue so till that same "Revelation" or new "Invention of Reality," of the sort he desiderates, shall itself make its appearance.

Meanwhile, quitting these airy regions, let any one bethink him how impressive the smallest historical *fact* may become, as contrasted with the grandest *fictitious event*; what an incalculable force lies for us in this consideration: The Thing which I here hold imaged in my mind did actually occur; was, in very truth, an element in the system of the All, whereof I too form part; had therefore, and has, through all time, an authentic being; is not a dream, but a reality! We ourselves can remember reading in *Lord Clarendon*, with feelings perhaps somehow accidentally opened to it,—certainly with a depth of impression strange to us then and now,—that insignificant looking passage, where Charles, after the battle of Worcester, glides down, with Squire Careless, from the Royal Oak, at night-fall, being hungry: how, "making a shift to get over hedges and ditches, after walking at least eight or nine miles, which were the more grievous to the King by the weight of his boots, (for he could not put *them* off, when he cut off his hair, for want of shoes,) before morning they came to *a poor cottage, the owner whereof being a Roman Catholic was known to Careless*." How this poor drudge, being knocked up from his snoring, "carried them into a little barn full of hay, which was a better lodging than he had for himself;" and by and by, not without difficulty, brought his Majesty "a piece of bread and a great pot of butter-milk," saying candidly that "he himself lived by his daily labour, and that what he had brought him was the fare he and his wife had:" on which nourishing diet his Majesty, "staying upon the haymow," feeds thankfully for two days; and then departs, under new guidance, having first changed clothes down to the very shirt and "old pair of shoes," with his landlord; and so as worthy Bunyan has it, "goes on his way, and sees him no more."* Singular enough if we will think of it! This then was a genuine flesh-and-blood Rustic of the year 1651: he did actually swallow bread and butter-milk (not having ale and bacon,) and do field labour; with these hob-nailed "shoes" has sprawled through mud-roads in winter, and, jocund or not, driven his team a-field in summer; he made bargains; had chafferings and higglings, now a sore heart, now a glad one; was born; was a son, was a father;—toiled in many ways, being forced to it, till the strength was all worn out of him: and then—lay down "to rest his galled back," and sleep there till the long-distant morning!—How comes it, that he alone of all the British rustics who tilled and lived along with him, on whom the blessed sun on that same "fifth

* History of the Rebellion, iii. 625.

day of September" was shining, should have chanced to rise on us; that this poor pair of clouted Shoes, out of a million million hides that have been tanned, and cut, and worn, should still subsist, and hang visibly together? We see him but for a moment; for one moment, the blanket of the Night is rent asunder, so that we behold and see, and then closes over him—for ever.

So too, in some *Boswell's Life of Johnson*, how indelible, and magically bright, does many a little *Reality* dwell in our remembrance! There is no need that the personages on the scene be a King and Clown; that the scene be the Forest of the Royal Oak, "on the borders of Staffordshire:" need only that the scene lie on this old firm Earth of ours, where we also have so surprisingly arrived; that the personages be *men*, and *seen* with the eyes of a man. Foolish enough, how some slight, perhaps mean and even ugly incident—if *real*, and well presented—will fix itself in a susceptive memory, and lie ennobled there; silvered over with the pale cast of thought, with the pathos which belongs only to the Dead. For the Past is all holy to us; the Dead are all holy, even they that were base and wicked while alive. Their baseness and wickedness was not *They*, was but the heavy unmanageable Environment that lay round them, with which they fought unprevailing: *they* (the ethereal God-given Force that dwelt in them, and was their *Self*) have now shuffled off that heavy Environment, and are free and pure: their life-long Battle, go how it might, is all ended, with many wounds or with fewer; they have been recalled from it, and the once harsh-jarring battle-field has become a silent awe-inspiring Golgotha, and *Gottesacker*—Field of God!—Boswell relates this in itself smallest and poorest of occurrences: "As we walked along the Strand to-night, arm in arm, a woman of the town accosted us in the usual enticing manner. 'No, no, my girl,' said Johnson; 'it won't do.' He, however, did not treat her with harshness, and we talked of the wretched life of such women." Strange power of *Reality!* Not even this poorest of occurrences, but now, after seventy years are come and gone, has a meaning for us. Do but consider that it is *true;* that it did in very deed occur! That unhappy Outcast, with all her sins and woes, her lawless desires, too complex mischances, her wailings and her riotings, has departed utterly: alas! her siren finery has got all besmutched; ground, generations since, into dust and smoke, of her degraded body, and whole miserable earthly existence, all is away: *she* is no longer here, but far from us, in the bosom of Eternity,—whence we too came, whither we too are bound! Johnson said, "No, no, my girl; it won't do;" and then "we talked;"—and herewith the wretched one, seen but for the twinkling of an eye, passes on into the utter Darkness. No high Calista, that ever issued from Story-teller's brain, will impress us more deeply than this meanest of the mean; and for a good reason: That *she* issued from the Maker of Men.

It is well worth the Artist's while to examine for himself what it is that gives such pitiful incidents their memorableness; his aim likewise is, above all things, to be *memorable.* Half the effect, we already perceive, depends on the object, on its being *real*, on its being really *seen.* The other half will depend on the observer; and the question now is: How are real objects to be *so* seen; on what quality of observing, or of style in describing, does this so intense pictorial power depend? Often a slight circumstance contributes curiously to the result: some little, and perhaps to appearance accidental, feature is presented; a light-gleam, which instantaneously *excites* the mind, and urges it to complete the picture, and evolve the meaning thereof for itself. By critics, such light-gleams and their almost magical influence have frequently been noted: but the power to produce such, to select such features as will produce them, is generally treated as a knack, or trick of the trade, a secret for being "graphic;" whereas these magical feats are, in truth, rather inspirations; and the gift of performing them, which acts unconsciously, without forethought, and as if by nature alone, is properly a *genius* for description.

One grand, invaluable secret there is, however, which includes all the rest, and, what is comfortable, lies clearly in every man's power: *To have an open, loving heart, and what follows from the possession of such!* Truly has it been said, emphatically in these days ought it to be repeated: A loving heart is the beginning of all Knowledge. This it is that opens the whole mind, quickens every faculty of the intellect to do its fit work, that of *knowing;* and therefrom, by sure consequence, of *vividly uttering forth.* Other secret for being "graphic" is there none, worth having: but this is an all-sufficient one. See, for example, what a small Boswell can do! Hereby, indeed, is the whole man made a living mirror, wherein the wonders of this ever-wonderful Universe are, in their true light, (which is ever a magical, miraculous one,) represented, and reflected back on us. It has been said, "the heart sees farther than the head:" but, indeed, without the seeing heart there is no true seeing for the head so much as possible; all is mere *oversight*, hallucination, and vain superficial phantasmagoria, which can permanently profit no one.

Here, too, may we not pause for an instant, and make a practical reflection? Considering the multitude of mortals that handle the Pen in these days, and can mostly spell, and write without daring violations of grammar, the question naturally arises: How is it, then, that no Work proceeds from them, bearing any stamp of authenticity and permanence; of worth for more than one day? Ship-loads of Fashionable Novels, Sentimental Rhymes, Tragedies, Farces, Diaries of Travel, Tales by flood and field, are swallowed monthly into the bottomless Pool; still does the Press toil: innumerable Paper-makers, Compositors, Printers' Devils, Bookbinders, and Hawkers grown hoarse with loud proclaiming, rest not from their labour; and still, in torrents, rushes on the great array of Publications, unpausing, to their final home; and still Oblivion, like the Grave, cries: Give! Give! How is it that of all these countless multitudes, no one can attain to the smallest mark of excellence, or produce ought that shall endure longer than "snow-flake on the river," or the foam of penny-beer? We answer: Because they *are* foam; because there is no *Reality* in them. These Three Thousand men, women, and children, that make up the army of British Authors, do not, if we will well consider it, *see* any thing whatever; consequently *have* nothing that they can record and utter, only more or fewer things that they can plausibly pretend to record. The Universe, of Man and Nature, is still quite shut up from them; the "open secret" still utterly a secret; because no sympathy with Man or Nature, no love and free simplicity of heart has yet unfolded the same. Nothing but a pitiful Image of their own pitiful Self, with its vanities, and grudgings, and ravenous hunger of all kinds, hangs for ever painted in the retina of these unfortunate persons: so that the starry ALL, with whatsoever it embraces, does but appear as some expanded magic-lantern shadow of that same Image,—and naturally looks pitiful enough.

It is vain for these persons to allege that they are naturally without gift, naturally stupid and sightless, and so *can* attain to no knowledge of any thing; therefore, in writing of any thing, must needs write falsehoods of it, there being in it no truth for them. Not so, good Friends. The stupidest of you has a certain faculty; were it but that of articulate speech, (say, in the Scottish, the Irish, the Cockney dialect, or even in "Governess-English,") and of physically discerning what lies under your nose. The stupidest of you would perhaps grudge to be compared in faculty with James Boswell; yet see what he has produced! You do not use your faculty honestly; your heart is shut up; full of greediness, malice, discontent; so your intellectual sense cannot be open. It is vain also to urge that James Boswell had opportunities; saw great men and great things, such as you can never hope to look on. What make ye of Parson White in Selborne? He had not only no great men to look on, but not even men; merely sparrows and cock-chafers: yet has he left us a *Biography* of these; which, under its title *Natural History of Selborne*, still remains valuable to us; which has copied a little sentence or two *faithfully* from the inspired volume of Nature, and so is itself not without inspiration. Go ye and do likewise. Sweep away utterly all frothiness and falsehood from your heart; struggle unweariedly to acquire, what is possible for every God-created Man, a free, open, humble soul: *speak not at all, in any wise, till you have somewhat to speak;* care not for the *reward* of your speaking, but simply and with undivided mind for the *truth* of your speaking: then be placed in what section of Space and of Time soever, do but open your eyes, and they shall actually *see*, and bring you real *knowledge*, wondrous, worthy of *belief;* and instead of one Boswell and one White, the world will rejoice in a thousand,—stationed on their thousand several watch-towers, to instruct us by indubitable documents, of whatsoever in our so stupendous world comes to light and *is!* O, had the Editor of this Magazine but a magic rod to turn all that not inconsiderable Intellect, which now deluges us with artificial fictitious soap-lather, and mere Lying, into the faithful study of Reality,—what knowledge of great, everlasting Nature, and of Man's ways and doings therein, would not every year bring us in! Can we but change one single soap-latherer and mountebank Juggler, into a true Thinker and Doer, that even *tries* honestly to think and do—great will be our reward.

But to return; or rather from this point to begin our journey! If now, what with Herr Sauerteig's *Springwürzel*, what with so much lucubration of our own, it have become apparent how deep, immeasurable is the "worth that lies in *Reality*," and farther, how exclusive the interest which man takes in the Histories of Man,—may it not seem lamentable, that so few genuinely good *Biographies* have yet been accumulated in Literature; that in the whole world, one cannot find, going strictly to work, above some dozen, or baker's dozen, and those chiefly of very ancient date? Lamentable; yet, after what we have just seen, accountable. Another question might be asked: How comes it that in England we have simply one good Biography, this *Boswell's Johnson;* and of good, indifferent, or even bad attempts at Biography, fewer than any civilized people? Consider the French and Germans, with their Moreris, Bayles, Jördenses, Jöchers, their innumerable *Mémoires*, and *Schilderungen*, and *Biographies Universelles;* not to speak of Rousseaus, Goethes, Schubarts, Jung-Stillings: and then contrast with these our poor Birches, and Kippises and Pecks,—the whole breed of whom, moreover, is now extinct!

With this question, as the answer might lead us far, and come out unflattering to patriotic sentiment, we shall not intermeddle; but turn rather, with greater pleasure, to the fact, that one excellent Biography *is* actually English;—and even now lies, in Five new Volumes, at our hand, soliciting a new consideration from us; such as, age after age (the Perennial showing ever new phases as *our* position alters,) it may long be profitable to bestow on it;—to which task we here, in this age, gladly address ourselves.

First, however, Let the foolish April-fool day pass by; and our Reader, during these twenty-nine days of uncertain weather that will follow, keep pondering, according to convenience, the purport of BIOGRAPHY in general: then, with the blessed dew of May-day, and in unlimited convenience of space, shall all that we have written on *Johnson*, and *Boswell's Johnson*, and *Croker's Boswell's Johnson*, be faithfully laid before him.

BOSWELL'S LIFE OF JOHNSON.*

[Fraser's Magazine, 1832.]

Æsop's Fly, sitting on the axle of the chariot, has been much laughed at for exclaiming: What a dust I do raise! Yet which of us, in his way, has not sometimes been guilty of the like? Nay, so foolish are men, they often, standing at ease and as spectators on the highway, will volunteer to exclaim of the Fly (not being tempted to it, as *he* was) exactly to the same purport: What a dust *thou* dost raise! Smallest of mortals, when mounted aloft by circumstances, come to seem great; smallest of phenomena connected with them are treated as important, and must be sedulously scanned, and commented upon with loud emphasis.

That Mr. Croker should undertake to edit *Boswell's Life of Johnson*, was a praiseworthy but no miraculous procedure: neither could the accomplishment of such undertaking be, in an epoch like ours, anywise regarded as an event in Universal History; the right or the wrong accomplishment thereof was, in very truth, one of the most insignificant of things. However, it sat in a great environment, on the axle of a high, fast-rolling, parliamentary chariot; and all the world has exclaimed over it, and the author of it: What a dust thou dost raise! List to the Reviews, and "Organs of Public Opinion," from the *National Omnibus* upwards; criticisms, vituperative and laudatory, stream from their thousand throats of brass and leather; here chanting *Io pæans;* there grating harsh thunder, or vehement shrewmouse squeaklets; till the general ear is filled, and nigh deafened. Boswell's Book had a noiseless birth, compared wtth this Edition of Boswell's Book. On the other hand, consider with what degree of tumult *Paradise Lost* and the *Iliad* were ushered in!

To swell such clamor, or prolong it beyond the time, seems nowise our vocation here. At most, perhaps we are bound to inform simple readers, with all possible brevity, what manner of performance and Edition this is; especially, whether, in our poor judgment, it is worth laying out three pounds sterling upon, yea or not. The whole business belongs distinctly to the lower ranks of the trivial class.

Let us admit, then, with great readiness, that as Johnson once said, and the Editor repeats, "all works which describe manners, require notes in sixty or seventy years, or less;" that, accordingly, a new Edition of Boswell was desirable; and that Mr. Croker has given one. For this task he had various qualifications: his own voluntary resolution to do it; his high place in society unlocking all manner of archives to him; not less, perhaps, a certain anecdotico-biographic turn of mind, natural or acquired; we mean, a love for the *minuter* events of History, and talent for investigating these. Let us admit, too, that he has been very diligent; seems to have made inquiries perseveringly far and near; as well as drawn freely from his own ample stores; and so tells us to appearance quite accurately, much that he has not found lying on the highways, but has had to seek and dig for. Numerous persons, chiefly of quality, rise to view in these Notes; when and also where they came into this world, received office or promotion, died, and were buried (only what they *did*, except digest, remaining often too mysterious,)—is faithfully enough set down. Whereby all that their various and doubtless widely-scattered Tombstones could have taught us, is here presented, at once, in a bound Book. Thus is an indubitable conquest, though a small one, gained over our great enemy, the all-destroyer Time; and as such shall have welcome.

Nay, let us say that the spirit of Diligence, exhibited in this department, seems to attend the Editor honestly throughout: he keeps everywhere a watchful outlook on his Text; reconciling the distant with the present, or at least indicating and regretting their irreconcilability; elucidating, smoothing down; in all ways, exercising, according to ability, a strict editorial superintendence. Any little Latin or even Greek phrase is rendered into English, in general with perfect accuracy; citations are verified, or else corrected. On all hands, moreover, there is a certain spirit of Decency maintained and insisted on: if not good morals, yet good manners, are rigidly inculcated; if not Religion, and a devout Christian heart, yet Orthodoxy, and a cleanly, Shovel-hatted look,—which, as compared with flat Nothing, is something very considerable. Grant too, as no contemptible triumph of this latter spirit, that though the Editor is known as a decided Politician and Party-man, he has carefully subdued all temptations to transgress in that way: except by quite involuntary indications, and rather as it were the pervading temper of the whole, you could not discover on which side of the Political Warfare he is enlisted and fights. This, as we said, is a great triumph of the Decency-principle: for this, and for these other graces and performances, let the Editor have all praise.

Herewith, however, must the praise unfortunately terminate. Diligence, Fidelity, Decency, are good and indispensable; yet, without Faculty, without Light, they will not do the work. Along with that Tombstone information, perhaps even without much of it, we could have liked to gain some answer, in one way or other, to this wide question: What and how was *English Life* in Johnson's time; wherein has ours grown to differ therefrom? In other words: What things have we to forget, what to fancy and remember, before we, from such distance, can put ourselves in Johnson's *place;* and so, in the full sense of

* The Life of Samuel Johnson, LL.D.: including a Tour to the Hebrides. By James Boswell, Esq.—A new Edition, with numerous Additions and Notes. By John Wilson Croker, LL.D., F. R. S. 5 vols. London, 1831.

the term, *understand* him, his sayings and his doings? This was indeed specially the problem which a Commentator and Editor had to solve: a complete solution of it should have lain in him, his whole mind should have been filled and prepared with perfect insight into it; then, whether in the way of express Dissertation, of incidental Exposition and Indication, opportunities enough would have occurred of bringing out the same: what was dark in the figure of the Past had thereby been enlightened; Boswell had, not in show and word only, but in very fact, been made *new* again, readable to us who are divided from him, even as he was to those close at hand. Of all which very little has been attempted here; accomplished, we should say, next to nothing, or altogether nothing.

Excuse, no doubt, is in readiness for such omission; and, indeed, for innumerable other failings;—as where, for example, the Editor will punctually explain what is already sunclear; and then anon, not without frankness, declare frequently enough that "the Editor does not understand," that "the Editor cannot guess,"—while, for most part, the Reader cannot help both guessing and seeing. Thus, if Johnson say, in one sentence, that "English names should not be used in Latin verses;" and then, in the next sentence, speak blamingly of "Carteret being used as a dactyl," will the generality of mortals detect any puzzle there? Or again, where poor Boswell writes: "I always remember a remark made to me by a Turkish lady, educated in France: '*Ma foi, monsieur, notre bonheur depend de la façon que notre sang circule;*' "—though the Turkish lady here speaks English-French, where is the call for a Note like this: "Mr. Boswell no doubt fancied these words had some meaning, or he would hardly have quoted them; but what that meaning is the Editor cannot guess?" The Editor is clearly no witch at a riddle.—For these and all kindred deficiencies, the excuse, as we said, is at hand; but the fact of their existence is not the less certain and regretable.

Indeed, it, from a very early stage of the business, becomes afflictively apparent, how much the Editor, so well furnished with all external appliances and means, is from within unfurnished with means for forming to himself any just notion of Johnson, or of Johnson's Life; and therefore of speaking on that subject with much hope of edifying. Too lightly is it from the first taken for granted that *Hunger*, the great basis of our life, is also its apex and ultimate perfection; that as "Neediness and Greediness and Vain-glory" are the chief qualities of most men, so no man, not even a Johnson, acts or can think of acting on any other principle. Whatsoever, therefore, cannot be referred to the two former categories, (Need and Greed,) is without scruple ranged under the latter. It is here properly that our Editor becomes burdensome; and, to the weaker sort, even a nuisance. "What good is it," will such cry, "when we had still some faint shadow of belief that man was better than a selfish Digesting-machine; what good is it to poke in, at every turn, and explain how this and that which we thought noble in old Samuel, was vulgar, base; that for him too there was no reality but in the Stomach; and except Pudding, and the finer species of pudding which is named Praise, life had no pabulum? Why, for instance, when we know that Johnson *loved* his good Wife, and says expressly that their marriage was "a love-match on both sides,"—should two closed lips open to tell us only this: "Is it not possible that the obvious advantage of having a woman of experience to superintend an establishment of this kind (the Edial School) may have contributed to a match so disproportionate in point of age— Ed.?" Or again, when in the Text, the honest cynic speaks freely of his former poverty, and it is known that he once lived on fourpence halfpenny a-day,—need a Commentator advance, and comment thus: "When we find Dr. Johnson tell unpleasant truths to, or of, other men, let us recollect that he does not appear to have spared himself, on occasions in which he might be forgiven for doing so?" "Why in short," continues the exasperated Reader, "should Notes of this species stand affronting me, when there might have been no Note at all?"—Gentle Reader, we answer, Be not wroth. What other could an honest Commentator do, than give thee the best he had? Such was the picture and theorem he had fashioned for himself of the world and of man's doings therein: take it, and draw wise inferences from it. If there did exist a Leader of Public Opinion, and Champion of Orthodoxy in the Church of Jesus of Nazareth, who reckoned that man's glory consisted in not being poor; and that a Sage, and Prophet of his time, must needs blush because the world had paid him at that easy rate of fourpence halfpenny *per diem*,—was not the fact of such existence worth knowing, worth considering?

Of a much milder hue, yet to us practically of an all-defacing, and for the present enterprise quite ruinous character,—is another grand fundamental failing; the last we shall feel ourselves obliged to take the pain of specifying here. It is that our Editor has fatally, and almost surprisingly, mistaken the limits of an Editor's function; and so, instead of working on the margin with his Pen, to elucidate as best might be, strikes boldly into the body of the page with his Scissors, and there clips at discretion! Four Books Mr. C. had by him, wherefrom to gather light for the fifth, which was Boswell's. What does he do but now, in the placidest manner,—slit the whole five into slips, and sew these together into a *sextum quid*, exactly at his own convenience; giving Boswell the credit of the whole! By what art-magic, our readers ask, has he united them? By the simplest of all: by Brackets. Never before was the full virtue of the Bracket made manifest. You begin a sentence under Boswell's guidance, thinking to be carried happily through it by the same: but no; in the middle, perhaps after your semicolon, and some consequent "for,"—starts up one of these Bracket-ligatures, and stitches you in from half a page, to twenty or thirty pages of a Hawkins, Tyers, Murphy, Piozzi; so that often one must make the old sad reflection, "where we are we know, whither we are going no man knoweth!" It is truly said also, "There is much between the cup and the lip;" but here the case is still sadder: for not till after consideration can you ascertain, now when the cup is *at* the lip, what liquor is it you are imbibing; whether Boswell's French wine which you began with, or some Piozzi's ginger-beer, or Hawkins's entire, or perhaps some other great Brewer's penny-swipes or even alegar, which has been surreptitiously substituted instead thereof. A situation almost original; not to be tried a second time! But, in fine, what ideas Mr. Croker entertains of a literary *whole* and the thing called *Book*, and how the very Printer's Devils did not rise in mutiny against such a conglomeration as this, and refuse to print it,—may remain a problem.

But now happily our say is said. All faults, the Moralists tell us, are properly *shortcomings;* crimes themselves are nothing other than a *not doing enough;* a *fighting*, but with defective vigour. How much more a mere insufficiency, and this after good efforts, in handicraft practice! Mr. Croker says: "The worst that can happen is that all the present Editor has contributed may, if the reader so pleases, be rejected as *surplusage*." It is our pleasant duty to take with hearty welcome what he has given; and render thanks even for what he meant to give. Next and finally, it is our painful duty to declare, aloud if that be necessary, that his gift, as weighed against the hard money which the Booksellers demand for giving it you, is (in our judgment) very greatly the lighter. No portion, accordingly, of our small floating capital has been embarked in the business, or shall ever be; indeed, were we in the market for such a thing, there is simply *no* Edition of *Boswell* to which this last would seem preferable. And now enough, and more than enough!

We have next a word to say of James Boswell. Boswell has already been much commented upon; but rather in the way of censure and vituperation, than of true recognition. He was a man that brought himself much before the world; confessed that he eagerly coveted fame, or if that were not possible, notoriety; of which latter as he gained far more than seemed his due, the public were incited, not only by their natural love of scandal, but by a special ground of envy, to say whatever ill of him could be said. Out of the fifteen millions that then lived, and had bed and board, in the British Islands, this man has provided us a greater *pleasure* than any other individual, at whose cost we now enjoy ourselves; perhaps has done us a greater *service* than can be specially attributed to more than two or three: yet, ungrateful that we are, no written or spoken eulogy of James Boswell anywhere exists; his recompense in solid pudding (so far as copyright went) was not excessive; and as for the empty praise, it has altogether been denied him. Men are unwiser than children; they do not know the hand that feeds.

Boswell was a person whose mean or bad qualities lay open to the general eye; visible, palpable to the dullest. His good qualities again, belonged not to the Time he lived in; were far from common then, indeed, in such a degree, were almost unexampled; not recognisable therefore by every one; nay, apt even (so strange had they grown) to be confounded with the very vices they lay contiguous to, and had sprung out of. That he was a wine-bibber and gross liver; gluttonously fond of whatever would yield him a little solacement, were it only of a stomachic character, is undeniable enough. That he was vain, heedless, a babbler; had much of the sycophant, alternating with the braggadocio, curiously spiced too with an all-pervading dash of the coxcomb; that he gloried much when the Tailor, by a court-suit, had made a new man of him; that he appeared at the Shakspeare Jubilee with a riband, imprinted "CORSICA BOSWELL," round his hat; and in short, if you will, lived no day of his life without doing and saying more than one pretentious ineptitude: all this unhappily is evident as the sun at noon. The very look of Boswell seems to have signified so much. In that cocked nose, cocked partly in triumph over his weaker fellow-creatures, partly to snuff up the smell of coming pleasure, and scent it from afar; in those bag-cheeks, hanging like half-filled wine-skins, still able to contain more; in that coarsely protruded shelf mouth, that fat dewlapped chin; in all this, who sees not sensuality, pretension, boisterous imbecility enough; much that could not have been ornamental in the temper of a great man's overfed great man, (what the Scotch name *flunky*,) though it had been more natural there. The under part of Boswell's face is of a low, almost brutish character.

Unfortunately, on the other hand, what great and genuine good lay in him was nowise so self-evident. That Boswell was a hunter after spiritual Notabilities, that he loved such, and longed, and even crept and crawled to be near them; that he first (in old Touchwood Auchinleck's phraseology) "took on with Paoli," and then being off with "the Corsican landlouper," took on with a schoolmaster, "ane that keeped a schule, and ca'd it an academe;" that he did all this, and could not help doing it, we account a very singular merit. The man, once for all, had an "open sense," an open loving heart, which so few have: where Excellence existed, he was compelled to acknowledge it; was drawn towards it, and (let the old sulphur-brand of a Laird say what he liked) *could not but* walk with it,—if not as superior, if not as equal, then as inferior and lackey, better so than not at all. If we reflect now that this love of Excellence had not only *such* an evil *nature* to triumph over; but also what an *education* and social position withstood it and weighed it down, its innate strength, victorious over all these things, may astonish us. Consider what an inward impulse there must have been, how many mountains of impediment hurled aside, before the Scottish Laird could, as humble servant, embrace the knees (the bosom was not permitted him) of the English Dominie! "Your Scottish Laird," says an English naturalist of these days, "may be defined as the hungriest and vainest of all bipeds yet known." Boswell too was a Tory; of quite peculiarly feudal, genealogical, pragmatical temper, had been nurtured in an atmosphere of Heraldry; at the feet of a very Gamaliel in that kind; within bare walls, adorned only with pedigrees, amid serving-men in threadbare livery; all things teaching him, from birth upwards, to remember, that a Laird was a Laird. Perhaps there was a special vanity in his very blood: old Auchinleck had, if not the gay, tail-spreading, peacock vanity of his son, no little of the slow-stalking, contentious, hissing vanity of the gander; a still more fatal species. Scottish Advocates will yet tell you how the ancient man, having chanced to be the first sheriff appointed (after the abolition of "hereditary jurisdiction") by royal authority, was wont, in dull pompous tone, to preface many a deliverance from the bench, with these words: "I, the first king's Sheriff in Scotland."

And now behold the worthy Bozzy, so prepossessed and held back by nature and by art, fly nevertheless like iron to its magnet, whither his better genius called! You may surround the iron and the magnet with what enclosures and encumbrances you please,—with wood, with rubbish, with brass: it matters not, the two feel each other, they struggle restlessly towards each other, they *will* be together. The iron may be a Scottish squirelet, full of gulosity and "gigmanity;"* the magnet an English plebeian, and moving rag-and-dust mountain, coarse, proud, irascible, imperious: nevertheless, behold how they embrace, and inseparably cleave to one another! It is one of the strangest phenomena of the past century, that at a time when the old reverent feeling of Discipleship (such as brought men from far countries, with rich gifts, and prostrate soul, to the feet of the Prophets) had passed utterly away from men's practical experience, and was no longer surmised to exist, (as it does,) perennial, indestructible, in man's inmost heart, —James Boswell should have been the individual, of all others, predestined to recall it, in such singular guise, to the wondering, and, for a long while, laughing, and unrecognising world. It has been commonly said, The man's vulgar vanity was all that attached him to Johnson; he delighted to be seen near him, to be thought connected with him. Now let it be at once granted that no consideration springing out of vulgar vanity could well be absent from the mind of James Boswell, in this his intercourse with Johnson, or in any considerable transaction of his life. At the same time ask yourself: Whether such vanity, and nothing else, actuated him therein; whether this was the true essence and moving principle of the phenomenon, or not rather its outward vesture, and the accidental environment (and defacement) in which it came to light? The man was, by nature and habit, vain; a sycophant-coxcomb, be it granted: but had there been nothing more than vanity in him, was Samuel Johnson the man of men to whom he must attach himself? At the date when Johnson was a poor rusty-coated "scholar," dwelling in Temple-lane, and indeed throughout their whole intercourse afterwards, were there not chancellors and prime ministers enough; graceful gentlemen, the glass of fashion: honour-giving noblemen; dinner giving rich men; renowned fire-eaters, swordsmen, gownsmen; Quacks and Realities of all hues,—any one of whom bulked much larger in the world's eye than Johnson ever did? To any one of whom, by half that submissiveness and assiduity, our Bozzy might have recommended himself; and sat there, the envy of surrounding lickspittles; pocketing now solid emolument, swallowing now well-cooked viands and wines of rich vintage; in each case, also, shone on by some glittering reflex of Renown or Notoriety, so as to be the observed of innumerable observers. To no one of whom, however, though otherwise a most diligent solicitor and purveyor, did he so attach himself: such vulgar courtierships were his paid drudgery, or leisure-amusement; the worship of Johnson was his grand, ideal, voluntary business. Does not the frothy-hearted yet enthusiastic man, doffing his Advocate's-wig, regularly take post, and hurry up to London, for the sake of his Sage chiefly; as to a Feast of Tabernacles, the Sabbath of his whole year? The plate-licker and wine-bibber dives into Bolt Court, to sip muddy coffee with a cynical old man, and a sour-tempered blind old woman (feeling the cups, whether they are full, with her finger;) and patiently endured contradictions without end; too happy so he may but be allowed to listen and live. Nay, it does not appear that vulgar vanity could ever have been much flattered by Boswell's relation to Johnson. Mr. Croker says, Johnson was, to the last, little regarded by the great world; from which, for a vulgar vanity, all honour, as from its fountain, descends. Bozzy, even among Johnson's friends and special admirers, seems rather to have been laughed at than envied: his officious, whisking, consequential ways, the daily reproofs and rebuffs he underwent, could gain from the world no golden, but only leaden, opinions. His devout Discipleship seemed nothing more than a mean Spanielship, in the general eye. His mighty "constellation," or sun, round whom he, as satellite, observantly gyrated, was, for the mass of men, but a huge ill-snuffed tallow-light, and he a weak night-moth, circling foolishly, dangerously about it, not knowing what he wanted. If he enjoyed Highland dinners and toasts, as henchman to a new sort of chieftain, Henry Erskine, in the domestic "Outer-House," could hand him a shilling "for the sight of his Bear." Doubtless the man was laughed at, and often heard himself laughed at for his Johnsonism. To be envied, is the grand and sole aim of vulgar vanity; to be filled with good things is that of sensuality: for Johnson perhaps no man living *envied* poor Bozzy; and of good things (except himself paid for them) there was no vestige in that acquaintanceship. Had nothing other or better than vanity and sensuality been there, Johnson and Boswell had never come together, or had soon and finally separated again.

In fact, the so copious terrestrial Dross that

* Q "What do you mean by 'respectable'?"—*A.* He always kept a gig."—(*Thurtell's Trial.*)—"Thus," it has been said, "does society naturally divide itself into four classes: Noblemen, Gentlemen, Gigmen, and Men."

welters chaotically, as the outer sphere of this man's character, does but render for us more remarkable, more touching, the celestial spark of goodness, of light, and Reverence for Wisdom, which dwelt in the interior, and could struggle through such encumbrances, and in some degree illuminate and beautify them. There is much lying yet undeveloped in the love of Boswell for Johnson. A cheering proof, in a time which else utterly wanted and still wants such, that living Wisdom is quite *infinitely* precious to man, is the symbol of the Godlike to him, which even weak eyes may discern; that Loyalty, Discipleship, all that was ever meant by *Hero-worship*, lives perennially in the human bosom, and waits, even in these dead days, only for occasions to unfold it, and inspire all men with it, and again make the world alive! James Boswell we can regard as a practical witness (or real *martyr*) to this high, everlasting truth. A wonderful martyr, if you will; and in a time which made such martyrdom doubly wonderful: yet the time and its martyr perhaps suited each other. For a decrepit, death-sick Era, when CANT had first decisively opened her poison-breathing lips to proclaim that God-worship and Mammon-worship were one and the same, that Life was a *Lie*, and the Earth Beelzebub's, which the *Supreme Quack* should inherit; and so all things were fallen into the yellow leaf, and fast hastening to noisome corruption: for such an Era, perhaps no better Prophet than a parti-coloured Zany-Prophet, concealing (from himself and others) his prophetic significance in such unexpected vestures,—was deserved, or would have been in place. A precious medicine lay hidden in floods of coarsest, most composite treacle: the world swallowed the treacle, for it suited the world's palate; and now, after half a century, may the medicine also begin to show itself! James Boswell belonged, in his corruptible part, to the lowest classes of mankind; a foolish, inflated creature, swimming in an element of self-conceit: but in his corruptible there dwelt an incorruptible, all the more impressive and indubitable for the strange lodging it had taken.

Consider, too, with what force, diligence, and vivacity, he has rendered back, all this which, in Johnson's neighbourhood, his "open sense" had so eagerly and freely taken in. That loose-flowing, careless-looking Work of his is as a picture by one of Nature's own Artists; the best possible resemblance of a Reality; like the very image thereof in a clear mirror. Which indeed it was: let but the mirror be *clear*, this is the great point; the picture must and will be genuine. How the babbling Bozzy, inspired only by love, and the recognition and vision which love can lend, epitomizes nightly the words of Wisdom, the deeds and aspects of Wisdom, and so, by little and little, unconsciously works together for us a whole *Johnsoniad;* a more free, perfect, sunlit, and spirit-speaking likeness, than for many centuries had been drawn by man of man! Scarcely since the days of Homer has the feat been equalled: indeed, in many senses, this also is a kind of Heroic Poem. The fit *Odyssey* of our unheroic age was to be written, not sung; of a Thinker, not of a Fighter; and (for want of a Homer) by the first open soul that might offer,—looked such even through the organs of a Boswell. We do the man's intellectual endowment great wrong, if we measure it by its mere logical outcome; though here, too, there is not wanting a light ingenuity, a figurativeness, and fanciful sport, with glimpses of insight far deeper than the common. But Boswell's grand intellectual talent was (as such ever is) an *unconscious* one, of far higher reach and significance than Logic; and showed itself in the whole, not in parts. Here again we have that old saying verified, "The heart sees farther than the head."

Thus does poor Bozzy stand out to us as an ill-assorted, glaring mixture of the highest and the lowest. What, indeed, is man's life generally but a kind of beast-godhood; the god in us triumphing more and more over the beast; striving more and more to subdue it under his feet? Did not the Ancients, in their wise, perennially significant way, figure Nature itself, their sacred All, or PAN, as a portentous commingling of these two discords; as musical, humane, oracular in its upper part, yet ending below in the cloven hairy feet of a goat? The union of melodious, celestial Freewill and Reason, with foul Irrationality and Lust; in which, nevertheless, dwelt a mysterious unspeakable Fear and half-mad *panic* Awe; as for mortals there well might! And is not man a microcosm, or epitomized mirror of that same Universe; or, rather, is not that Universe even Himself, the reflex of his own fearful and wonderful being, "the waste fantasy of his own dream?" No wonder that man, that each man, and James Boswell like the others, should resemble it! The peculiarity in his case was the unusual defect of amalgamation and subordination: the highest lay side by side with the lowest; not morally combined with it and spiritually transfiguring it; but tumbling in half-mechanical juxtaposition with it, and from time to time, as the mad alternation chanced, irradiating it, or eclipsed by it.

The world, as we said, has been but unjust to him; discerning only the outer terrestrial and often sordid mass; without eye, as it generally is, for his inner divine secret; and thus figuring him nowise as a god Pan, but simply of the bestial species, like the cattle on a thousand hills. Nay, sometimes a strange enough hypothesis has been started of him; as if it were in virtue even of these same bad qualities that he did his good work; as if it were the very fact of his being among the worst men in this world that had enabled him to write one of the best books therein! Falser hypothesis, we may venture to say, never rose in human soul. *Bad* is by its nature negative, and can do *nothing;* whatsoever enables us to *do* any thing is by its very nature *good.* Alas, that there should be teachers in Israel, or even learners, to whom this world-ancient fact is still problematical, or even deniable! Boswell wrote a good Book because he had a heart and an eye to discern Wisdom, and an utterance to render it forth; because of his free insight, his lively talent, above all, of his Love and childlike Open-mindedness. His sneaking sycophancies, his greediness and forwardness, whatever was bestial and earthy in him, are so many blemishes in his Book, which still disturb us in its clearness: wholly hindrances, not helps. Towards Johnson, however, his feeling was not Sycophancy, which is the lowest, but Reverence, which is the highest of human feelings. None but a *reverent* man (which so unspeakably few are) could have found his way from Boswell's environment to Johnson's: if such worship for real God-made superiors showed itself also as worship for apparent Tailor-made superiors, even as hollow, interested mouth-worship for such,—the case, in this composite human nature of ours, was not miraculous, the more was the pity! But for ourselves, let every one of us cling to this last article of Faith, and know it as the beginning of all knowledge worth the name: That neither James Boswell's good Book, nor any other good thing, in any time or in any place, was, is, or can be performed by any man in virtue of his *badness*, but always and solely in spite thereof.

As for the Book itself, questionless the universal favour entertained for it is well merited. In worth as a Book we have rated it beyond any other product of the eighteenth century: all Johnson's own Writings, laborious and in their kind genuine above most, stand on a quite inferior level to it; already, indeed, they are becoming obsolete for this generation; and for some future generation, may be valuable chiefly as Prolegomena and expository Scholia to this *Johnsoniad* of Boswell. Which of us but remembers, as one of the sunny spots in his existence, the day when he opened these airy volumes, fascinating him by a true natural-magic! It was as if the curtains of the Past were drawn aside, and we looked mysteriously into a kindred country, where dwelt our Fathers; inexpressibly dear to us, but which had seemed for ever hidden from our eyes. For the dead Night had engulfed it; all was gone, vanished as if it had not been. Nevertheless, wondrously given back to us, there once more it lay; all bright, lucid, blooming; a little island of Creation amid the circumambient Void. There it still lies; like a thing stationary, imperishable, over which changeful Time were now accumulating itself in vain, and could not, any longer, harm it, or hide it.

If we examine by what charm it is that men are still held to this *Life of Johnson*, now when so much else has been forgotten, the main part of the answer will perhaps be found in that speculation "on the import of *Reality*," communicated to the world, last Month, in this Magazine. The *Johnsoniad* of Boswell turns on objects that in very deed existed; it is all *true*. So far other in melodiousness of tone, it vies with the *Odyssey* or surpasses it, in this one point: to us these read pages, as those chanted hexameters were to the first Greek heroes, are in the fullest, deepest sense, wholly *credible*. All the wit and wisdom, lying embalmed in Boswell's Book, plenteous as these are, could not have saved it. Far more scientific *instruction* (mere excitement and enlightenment of the *thinking power*) can be found in twenty other works of that time, which make but a quite secondary impression on us. The other works of that time, however, fall under one of two classes: Either they are professedly Didactic; and, in that way, mere Abstractions, Philosophic Diagrams, incapable of interesting us much otherwise than as *Euclid's Elements* may do: Or else, with all their vivacity, and pictorial richness of colour, *they are Fictions and not Realities*. Deep, truly, as Herr Sauerteig urges, is the force of this consideration: The thing here stated is a fact; these figures, that local habitation, are not shadow but substance. In virtue of such advantages, see how a very Boswell may become Poetical!

Critics insist much on the Poet that he should communicate an "Infinitude" to his delineation; that by intensity of conception, by that gift of "transcendental Thought," which is fitly named *genius*, and inspiration, he should *inform* the Finite with a certain Infinitude of significance; or as they sometimes say, ennoble the Actual into Idealness. They are right in their precept; they mean rightly. But in cases like this of the *Johnsoniad*, (such is the dark grandeur of that "Time-element," wherein man's soul here below lives imprisoned,) the Poet's task is, as it were, done to his hand: Time itself, which is the outer veil of Eternity, invests, of its own accord, with an authentic, felt "infinitude," whatsoever it has once embraced in its mysterious folds. Consider all that lies in that one word, *Past!* What a pathetic, sacred, in every sense *poetic*, meaning is implied in it; a meaning growing ever the clearer, the farther we recede in Time, —the *more* of that same Past we have to look through!—On which ground indeed must Sauerteig have built, and not without plausibility, in that strange thesis of his: "that History after all is the true Poetry; that Reality if rightly interpreted is grander than Fiction; nay, that even in the right interpretation of Reality and History does genuine Poetry consist."

Thus for *Boswell's Life of Johnson* has Time done, is Time still doing, what no ornament of Art or Artifice could have done for it. Rough Samuel and sleek wheedling James *were*, and *are not*. Their Life and whole personal Environment has melted into air. The Mitre Tavern still stands in Fleet Street: but where now is its scot-and-lot paying, beef-and-ale loving, cocked-hatted, potbellied Landlord; its rosy-faced, assiduous Landlady, with all her shining brass-pans, waxed tables, well-filled larder-shelves; her cooks, and bootjacks, and errand-boys, and watery-mouthed hangers-on? Gone! Gone! The becking waiter, that with wreathed smiles, wont to spread for Samuel and Bozzy their "supper of the gods," has long since pocketed his last sixpence; and vanished, sixpences and all, like a ghost at cock-crowing. The Bottles they drank out of are all broken, the Chairs they sat on all rotted and burnt; the very Knives and Forks they ate with have rusted to the heart, and become brown oxide of iron, and mingled with the indiscriminate clay. All, all, has vanished; in very deed and truth, like that baseless fabric of Prospero's air-vision. Of the Mitre Tavern nothing but the bare walls remain there: of London, of England, of the World, nothing but the bare walls remain; and these also decaying, (were they of adamant,) only slower. The mysterious River of Existence rushes on: a new Billow thereof has arrived, and lashes wildly as ever round the old embankments; but the former Billow with *its* loud, mad eddyings, where is it?—Where!—Now this Book of Boswell's, this is precisely a Revocation of the Edict of Destiny; so that Time shall not utterly, not so soon by several centuries, have dominion over us. A little row of Naphtha-lamps, with its line of Naphtha-light, burns clear and holy through the dead Night of the Past: they who are gone are still here; though hidden they are revealed, though dead they yet speak. There it shines, that little miraculously lamp-lit Pathway; shedding its feebler and feebler twilight into the boundless dark Oblivion, for all that our Johnson *touched* has become illuminated for us: on which miraculous little Pathway we can still travel, and see wonders.

It is not speaking with exaggeration, but with strict measured sobriety, to say that this Book of Boswell's will give us more real insight into the *History of England* during those days than twenty other Books, falsely entitled "Histories," which take to themselves that special aim. What good is it to me though innumerable Smolletts and Belshams keep dinning in my ears that a man named George the Third was born and bred up, and a man named George the Second died; that Walpole, and the Pelhams, and Chatham, and Rockingham, and Shelburne, and North, with their Coalition or their Separation Ministries, all ousted one another; and vehemently scrambled for "the thing they called the Rudder of Government, but which was in reality the Spigot of Taxation?" That debates were held, and infinite jarring and jargoning took place; and road-bills and enclosure-bills, and game-bills and India-bills, and Laws which no man can number, which happily few men needed to trouble their heads with beyond the passing moment, were enacted, and printed by the King's Stationer? That he who sat in Chancery, and rayed out speculation from the Woolsack, was now a man that squinted, now a man that did not squint? To the hungry and thirsty mind all this avails next to nothing. These men and these things, we indeed know, did swim, by strength or by specific levity, (as apples or as horse-dung,) on the top of the current: but is it by painfully noting the courses, eddyings, and bobbings hither and thither of such drift-articles, that you will unfold to me the nature of the current itself; of that mighty-rolling, loud-roaring, Life-current, bottomless as the foundations of the Universe, mysterious as its Author? The thing I want to see is not Redbook Lists, and Court Calendars, and Parliamentary Registers, but the Life of Man in England: what men did, thought, suffered, enjoyed; the form, especially the spirit, of their terrestrial existence, its outward environment, its inward principle; *how* and *what* it was; whence it proceeded, whither it was tending.

Mournful, in truth, is it to behold what the business called "History," in these so enlightened and illuminated times, still continues to be. Can you gather from it, read till your eyes go out, any dimmest shadow of an answer to that great question: How men lived and had their being; were it but economically, as what wages they got, and what they bought with these? Unhappily you cannot. History will throw no light on any such matter. At the point where living memory fails, it is all darkness; Mr. Senior and Mr. Sadler must still debate this simplest of all elements in the condition of the past: Whether men were better off, in their mere larders and pantries, or were worse off than now! History, as it stands all bound up in gilt volumes, is but a shade more instructive than the wooden volumes of a Backgammon-board. How my Prime Minister was appointed is of less moment to me than How my House Servant was hired. In these days, ten ordinary Histories of Kings and Courtiers were well exchanged against the tenth part of one good History of Booksellers.

For example, I would fain know the History of Scotland; who can tell it me? "Robertson," cry innumerable voices; "Robertson against the world." I open Robertson; and find there, through long ages too confused for narrative, and fit only to be presented in the way of epitome and distilled essence, a cunning answer and hypothesis, not to this question: By whom, and by what means, when and how, was this fair broad Scotland, with its Arts and Manufactures, Temples, Schools, Institutions, Poetry, Spirit, National Character, created and made arable, verdant, peculiar, great, here as I can see some fair section of it lying, kind and strong, (like some Bacchus-tamed Lion,) from the Castle-hill of Edinburgh?—but to this other question: How did the King keep himself alive in these old days; and restrain so many Butcher-Barons and ravenous Henchmen from utterly extirpating one another, so that killing went on in some sort of moderation? In the one little Letter of Æneas Sylvius, from old Scotland, there is more of History than in all this.—At length, however, we come to a luminous age, interesting enough; to the age of the Reformation. All Scotland is awakened to a second higher life: the Spirit of the highest stirs in every bosom, agitates every bosom; Scotland is convulsed, fermenting, struggling to body itself forth anew. To the herdsman among his cattle in remote woods; to the craftsman, in his rude, heath-thatched workshop, among his rude guild-brethren; to the great and to the little, a new light has arisen: in town and hamlet groups are gathered, with eloquent looks, and governed or ungovernable tongues; the great and the little go forth together to do battle for the Lord against the mighty. We ask, with breathless eagerness: How was it; how went it on? Let us understand it, let us see it, and know it!—In reply, is handed us a really graceful, and most dainty little Scandalous Chronicle (as for some Journal of Fashion) of two persons: Mary Stuart, a Beauty, but over lightheaded; and Henry Darnley, a Booby, who had fine legs. How these first courted, billed and cooed, according to nature; then pouted, fretted, grew utterly enraged, and blew one another up with gunpowder: this, and not the History of Scotland, is what we goodnaturedly read. Nay, by other hands, something like a horseload of other Books have been written to prove that it was the Beauty who blew up the Booby, and that it was not she. Who or what it was, the thing once for all *being* so effectually done, concerns us little. To know Scotland, at that great epoch, were a valuable increase of knowledge: to know poor Darnley and see him with burning candle, from centre to skin, were no increase of knowledge at all.—Thus is History written.

Hence, indeed, comes it that History, which should be "the essence of innumerable Biographies," will tell us, question it as we like, less than one genuine Biography may do, pleasantly and of its own accord! The time is approaching when History will be attempted on quite other principles; when the Court, the Senate, and Battle-field, receding more and more into the background, the Temple, the Workshop, and Social Hearth, will advance more and more into the foreground; and History will not content itself with shaping some answer to that question: How are men *taxed* and *kept quiet* then? but will seek to answer this other infinitely wider and higher question: How and what *were men* then? Not our Government only, or the "*House* wherein our life was led," but the *Life* itself we led there, will be inquired into. Of which latter it may be found that Government, in any modern sense of the word, is after all but a secondary condition: in the mere sense of *Taxation* and *Keeping quiet*, a small, almost a pitiful one.—Meanwhile let us welcome such Boswells, each in his degree, as bring us any genuine contribution, were it never so inadequate, so inconsiderable.

An exception was early taken against this *Life of Johnson*, and all similar enterprises, which we here recommend; and has been transmitted from critic to critic, and repeated in their several dialects, uninterruptedly, ever since: That such jottings down of careless conversation are an infringement of social privacy; a crime against our highest Freedom, the Freedom of man's intercourse with man. To this accusation, which we have read and heard oftener than enough, might it not be well for once to offer the flattest contradiction, and plea of *Not at all guilty?* Not that conversation is noted down, but that conversation should not deserve noting down, is the evil. Doubtless, if conversation be falsely recorded, then is it simply a Lie; and worthy of being swept, with all despatch, to the Father of Lies. But if, on the other hand, conversation can be authentically recorded, and any one is ready for the task, let him by all means proceed with it; let conversation be kept in remembrance to the latest date possible. Nay, should the consciousness that a man may be among us "taking notes" tend, in any measure, to restrict those floods of idle insincere *speech* with which the *thought* of mankind is well nigh drowned,—were it other than the most indubitable benefit? He who speaks honestly cares not, needs not care, though his words be preserved to remotest time: for him who speaks *dis*honestly, the fittest of all punishments seems to be this same, which the nature of the case provides. The dishonest speaker, not he only who purposely utters falsehoods, but he who does not purposely, and with sincere heart, utter Truth, and Truth alone; who babbles he knows not what, and has clapped no bridle on his tongue, but lets it run racket, ejecting chatter and futility,—is among the most indubitable malefactors omitted, or inserted, in the Criminal Calendar. To him that will well consider it, idle speaking is precisely the beginning of all Hollowness, Halfness, *Infidelity*, (want of Faithfulness;) the genial atmosphere in which rank weeds of every kind attain the mastery over noble fruits in man's life, and utterly choke them out: one of the most crying maladies of these days, and to be testified against, and in all ways to the uttermost withstood. Wise, of a wisdom far beyond our shallow depth, was that old precept: *Watch thy tongue;* out of it are the issues of Life! "Man is properly an *incarnated word*:" the *word* that he speaks is the *man* himself. Were eyes put into our head, that we might *see;* or only that we might fancy, and plausibly pretend, we had *seen?* Was the tongue suspended there, that it might tell truly what we had seen, and make man the soul's brother of man; or only that it might utter vain sounds, jargon, soul-confusing, and so *divide* man, as by enchanted walls of Darkness, from union with man? Thou who wearest that cunning, Heaven-made organ, a Tongue, think well of this. Speak not, I passionately entreat thee, till thy thought have silently matured itself, till thou have other than mad and mad-making noises to emit: *hold thy tongue* (thou hast it a-holding) till *some* meaning lie behind, to set it wagging. Consider the significance of SILENCE: it is boundless, never by meditating to be exhausted; unspeakably profitable to thee! Cease that chaotic hubbub, wherein thy own soul runs to waste, to confused suicidal dislocation and stupor: out of Silence comes thy strength. "Speech is silvern, Silence is golden; Speech is human, Silence is divine." Fool! thinkest thou that because no Boswell is there with ass-skin and black-lead to note thy jargon, it therefore dies and is harmless? Nothing dies, nothing can die. No idlest word thou speakest but is a seed cast into Time, and grows through all Eternity! The Recording Angel, consider it well, is no fable, but the truest of truths: the paper tablets thou canst burn; of the "iron leaf" there is no burning.—Truly, if we can permit God Almighty to note down our conversation, thinking it good enough for Him,—any poor Boswell need not scruple to work his will of it.

Leaving now this our English *Odyssey*, with its Singer and Scholiast, let us come to the *Ulysses;* that great Samuel Johnson himself, the far-experienced, "much-enduring man," whose labours and pilgrimage are here sung. A full-length image of his Existence has been preserved for us: and he, perhaps of all living Englishmen, was the one who best deserved that honour. For if it is true and now almost proverbial, that "the Life of the lowest mortal, if faithfully recorded, would be interesting to the highest;" how much more when the mortal in question was already distinguished in fortune and natural quality, so that his thinkings and doings were not significant of himself only, but of large masses of mankind! "There is not a man whom I meet on the streets," says one, "but I could like, were it otherwise convenient, to know his Biography:" nevertheless, could an enlightened curiosity be so far gratified, it must be owned the Biography of most ought to be, in an extreme degree, *summary.* In this world, there is so wonderfully little self-subsistence among men; next to no originality, (though never absolutely *none:*) one Life is too servilely the copy of another; and so in whole thousands of them you find little that is properly new; nothing but the old song sung by a new voice, with better or worse execution, here and there an ornamental quaver, and false notes enough: but the fundamental tune is ever the same; and for the *words,* these, all that they meant stands written generally on the Churchyard stone: *Natus sum: esuriebam, quærebam; nunc repletus requiesco.* Mankind sail their Life-voyage in huge fleets, following some single whale-fishing or herring-fishing Commodore: the log-book of each differs not, in essential purport, from that of any other; nay the most have no legible log-book (reflection, observation not being among their talents;) keep no reckoning, only *keep in sight* of the flagship,—and fish. Read the Commodore's Papers, (know *his* Life;) and even your lover of that street Biography will have learned the most of what he sought after.

Or, the servile *imitancy,* and yet also a nobler relationship and mysterious union to one another which lies in such imitancy, of Mankind might be illustrated under the different figure (itself nowise *original*) of a Flock of Sheep. Sheep go in flocks for three reasons: First, because they are of a gregarious temper, and *love* to be together: Secondly, because of their cowardice; they are afraid to be left alone: Thirdly, because the common run of them are dull of sight, to a proverb, and can have no choice in roads; sheep can in fact *see* nothing; in a celestial Luminary, and a scoured pewter Tankard, would discern only that both dazzled them, and were of unspeakable glory. How like their fellow creatures of the human species! Men, too, as was from the first maintained here, are gregarious: then surely faint-hearted enough, trembling to be left by themselves: above all, dull-sighted, down to the verge of utter blindness. Thus are we seen ever running in torrents, and mobs, if we run at all; and after what foolish scoured Tankards, mistaking them for Suns! Foolish Turnip-lanterns likewise, to all appearance supernatural, keep whole nations quaking, their hair on end. Neither know we, except by blind habit, where the good pastures lie: solely when the sweet grass is between our teeth, we know it, and chew it; also when grass is bitter and scant, we know it,—and bleat and butt: these last two facts we know of a truth, and in very deed.—Thus do Men and Sheep play their parts on this Nether Earth; wandering restlessly in large masses, they know not whither; for most part, each following his neighbour, and his own nose.

Nevertheless, not always; look better, you shall find certain that do, in some small degree, *know whither.* Sheep have their Bell-wether; some ram of the folds, endued with more valour, with clearer vision than other sheep; he leads them through the wolds, by height and hollow, to the woods and water-courses, for covert or for pleasant provender; courageously marching, and if need be, leaping, and with hoof and horn doing battle, in the van: him they courageously, and with assured heart, follow. Touching it is, as every herdsman will inform you, with what chivalrous devotedness these woolly Hosts adhere to their Wether; and rush after him, through good report and through bad report, were it into safe shelters and green thymy nooks, or into asphaltic lakes and the jaws of devouring lions. Ever also must we recall that fact which we owe Jean Paul's quick eye: "If you hold a stick before the Wether, so that he, by necessity, leaps in passing you, and then withdraw your stick, the Flock will nevertheless all leap as he did; and the thousandth sheep shall be found impetuously vaulting over air, as the first did over an otherwise impassable barrier." Reader, wouldst thou understand Society, ponder well those ovine proceedings: thou wilt find them all curiously significant.

Now if sheep always, how much more must men always, have their Chief, their Guide! Man, too, is by nature quite thoroughly *gregarious:* nay, ever he struggles to be something more, to be *social;* not even when Society has become impossible, does that deep-seated tendency and effort forsake him. Man, as if by miraculous magic, imparts his Thoughts, his Mood of mind to man; an unspeakable communion binds all past, present, and future men into one indissoluble whole, almost into one living individual. Of which high, mysterious Truth, this disposition to *imitate,* to lead and be led, this impossibility *not* to imitate, is the most constant, and one of the simplest manifestations. To "imitate!" which of us all can measure the significance that lies in that one word? By virtue of which the infant Man, born at Woolsthorpe, grows up not to be a hairy Savage, and chewer of Acorns, but an Isaac Newton, and Discoverer of Solar Systems!—Thus both in a celestial and terrestrial sense, are we a *Flock,* such as there is no other: nay, looking away from the base and ludicrous to the sublime and sacred side of the matter, (since in every matter there are two sides,) have not we also a SHEPHERD, "if we will but hear his voice?" Of those stupid multitudes there is no one but has an immortal Soul within him; a reflex, and living image of God's whole Universe: strangely, from its dim environment, the light of the Highest looks through him; for which reason, indeed, it is that we claim a brotherhood with him, and so love to know his History, and come into clearer and clearer union with all that he feels, and says, and does.

However, the chief thing to be noted was this: Amid those dull millions, who, as a dull flock, roll hither and thither, whithersoever they are led, and seem all sightless and slavish, accomplishing, attempting little save what the animal instinct (in its somewhat higher kind) might teach, (to keep themselves and their young ones alive,)—are scattered here and there superior natures, whose eye is not destitute of free vision, nor their heart of free volition. These latter, therefore, examine and determine, not what others do, but what it is right to do; towards which, and which only, will they, with such force as is given them, resolutely endeavour: for if the Machine, living or inanimate, is merely *fed*, or desires to be fed, and so *works*; the Person can *will*, and so *do*. These are properly our Men, our Great Men; the guides of the dull host,—which follows them as by an irrevocable decree. They are the chosen of the world: they had this rare faculty not only of "supposing" and "inclining to think," but of *knowing* and *believing*; the nature of their being was, that they lived not by Hearsay but by clear Vision; while others hovered and swam along, in the grand Vanity-fair of the World, blinded by the mere "Shows of things," these saw into the Things themselves, and could walk as men having an eternal load-star, and with their feet on sure paths. Thus was there a *Reality* in their existence; something of a perennial character; in virtue of which indeed it is that the memory of them is perennial. Whoso belongs only to his own age, and reverences only *its* gilt Popinjays or soot-smeared Mumbojumbos, must needs die with it: though he have been crowned seven times in the Capitol, or seventy and seven times, and Rumour have blown his praises to all the four winds, deafening every ear therewith,—it avails not; there was nothing universal, nothing eternal in him; he must fade away, even as the Popinjay-gildings and Scarecrow-apparel, which he could not see through. The great man does, in good truth, belong to his own age; nay, more so than any other man; being properly the synopsis and epitome of such age with its interests and influences: but belongs likewise to all ages, otherwise he is not great. What was transitory in him passes away; and an immortal part remains, the significance of which is in strict speech inexhaustible,—as that of every *real* object is. Aloft, conspicuous, on his enduring basis, he stands there, serene, unaltering; silently addresses to every new generation a new lesson and monition. Well is his Life worth writing, worth interpreting; and ever, in the new dialect of new times, of re-writing and re-interpreting.

Of such chosen men was Samuel Johnson: not ranking among the highest, or even the high, yet distinctly admitted into that sacred band; whose existence was no idle Dream, but a Reality which he transacted *awake;* nowise a Clothes-horse and Patent Digester, but a genuine Man. By nature he was gifted for the noblest of earthly tasks, that of Priesthood, and Guidance of mankind; by destiny, moreover, he was appointed to this task, and did actually, according to strength, fulfil the same: so that always the question, *How; in what spirit; under what shape?* remains for us to be asked and answered concerning him. For as the highest Gospel was a Biography, so is the Life of every good man still an indubitable Gospel, and preaches to the eye and heart and whole man, that Devils even must believe and tremble, these gladdest tidings: "Man is heaven-born; not the thrall of Circumstances, of Necessity, but the victorious subduer thereof: behold how he can become the 'Announcer of himself and of his Freedom;' and is ever what the Thinker has named him, 'the Messias of Nature!'"—Yes, Reader, all this that thou hast so often heard about "force of circumstances," "the creature of the time," "balancing of motives," and who knows what melancholy stuff to the like purport, wherein thou, as in a nightmare Dream, sittest paralyzed, and hast no force left,—was in very truth, if Johnson and waking men are to be credited, little other than a hag-ridden vision of death-sleep: some *half*-fact, more fatal at times than a whole falsehood. Shake it off; awake; up and be doing, even as it is given thee!

The Contradiction which yawns wide enough in every Life, which it is the meaning and task of Life to reconcile, was in Johnson's wider than in most. Seldom, for any man, has the contrast between the ethereal heavenward side of things, and the dark sordid earthward, been more glaring: whether we look at Nature's work with him or Fortune's, from first to last, heterogeneity, as of sunbeams and miry clay, is on all hands manifest. Whereby indeed, only this was declared, That *much Life* had been given him; many things to triumph over, a great work to *do*. Happily also he did it; better than the most.

Nature had given him a high, keen-visioned, almost poetic soul; yet withal imprisoned it in an inert, unsightly body: he that could never rest had not limbs that would move with him, but only roll and waddle: the inward eye, all-penetrating, all embracing, must look through bodily windows that were dim, half-blinded; he so loved men, and "never once *saw* the human face divine!" Not less did he prize the love of men; he was eminently social; the approbation of his fellows was dear to him, "valuable," as he owned, "if from the meanest of human beings:" yet the first impression he produced on every man was to be one of aversion, almost of disgust. By Nature it was farther ordered that the imperious Johnson should be born poor: the ruler-soul, strong in its native royalty, generous, uncontrollable, like the lion of the woods, was to be housed, then, in such a dwelling-place: of Disfigurement, Disease, and lastly of a Poverty which itself made him the servant of servants. Thus was the born King likewise a born Slave: the divine spirit of Music must awake imprisoned amid dull-croaking universal Discords; the Ariel finds himself encased in the coarse hulls of a Caliban. So is it more or less, we know, (and thou, O Reader, knowest and feelest even now,) with all men: yet with the fewest men in any such degree as with Johnson.

Fortune, moreover, which had so managed his first appearance in the world, lets not her hand lie idle, or turn the other way, but works unweariedly in the same spirit, while he is journeying through the world. What such a mind, stamped of Nature's noblest metal, though in so ungainly a die, was specially and best of all fitted for, might still be a question. To none of the world's few Incorporated Guilds could he have adjusted himself without difficulty, without distortion; in none been a Guild-Brother well at ease. Perhaps, if we look to the strictly practical nature of his faculty, to the strength, decision, method that manifests itself in him, we may say that his calling was rather towards Active than Speculative life; that as Statesman, (in the higher, now obsolete sense,) Lawgiver, Ruler: in short, as Doer of the Work, he had shone even more than as Speaker of the Word. His honesty of heart, his courageous temper, the value he set on things outward and material, might have made him a King among Kings. Had the golden age of those new French Prophets, when it shall be: *A chacun selon sa capacité; à chaque capacité selon ses œuvres*, but arrived! Indeed even in our brazen and Birmingham-lacker age, he himself regretted that he had not become a Lawyer, and risen to be Chancellor, which he might well have done. However, it was otherwise appointed. To no man does Fortune throw open all the kingdoms of this world, and say: It is thine; choose where thou wilt dwell! To the most she opens hardly the smallest cranny or doghutch, and says, not without asperity: There, that is thine whilst thou canst keep it: nestle thyself there, and bless Heaven! Alas, men must fit themselves into many things: some forty years ago, for instance, the noblest and ablest man in all the British lands might be seen not swaying the royal sceptre, or the pontiff's censer, on the pinnacle of the World, but gauging ale-tubs in the little burgh of Dumfries! Johnson came a little nearer the mark than Burns: but with him too, "Strength was mournfully denied its arena;" he too had to fight Fortune at strange odds, all his life long.

Johnson's disposition for *royalty*, (had the Fates so ordered it,) is well seen in early boyhood. "His favourites," says Boswell, "used to receive very liberal assistance from him; and such was the submission and deference with which he was treated, that three of the boys, of whom Mr. Hector was sometimes one, used to come in the morning as his humble attendants, and carry him to school. One in the middle stooped, while he sat upon his back, and one on each side supported him; and thus was he borne triumphant." The purfly, sand-blind lubber and blubber, with his open mouth and his face of bruised honeycomb: yet already dominant, imperial, and irresistible! Not in the "King's chair" (of human arms) as we see, do his three satellites carry him along: rather on the *Tyrant's-saddle*, the back of his fellow-creature, must he ride prosperous!—The child is father of the man. He who had seen fifty years into coming Time, would have felt that little spectacle of mischievous schoolboys to be a great one. For us, who look back on it, and what followed it, now from afar, there arise questions enough: How looked these urchins? What jackets and galligaskins had they; felt headgear, or of dogskin leather? What was old Lichfield doing then; what thinking?—and so on, through the whole series of Corporal Trim's "auxiliary verbs." A picture of it all fashions itself together;—only unhappily we have no brush, and no fingers.

Boyhood is now past; the ferula of Pedagogue waves harmless, in the distance: Samuel has struggled up to uncouth bulk and youthhood, wrestling with Disease and Poverty, all the way; which two continue still his companions. At College we see little of him: yet thus much, that things went not well. A rugged wild-man of the desert, awakened to the feeling of himself; proud as the proudest, poor as the poorest: stoically shut up, silently enduring the incurable: what a world of blackest gloom, with sun-gleams, and pale, tearful moon-gleams, and flickerings of a celestial and an infernal splendour, was this that now opened for him! But the weather is wintry; and the toes of the man are looking through his shoes. His muddy features grow of a purple and sea-green colour; a flood of black indignation mantling beneath. A truculent, raw-boned figure! Meat he has probably little; hope he has less; his feet, as we said, have come into brotherhood with the cold mire.

"Shall I be particular," inquires Sir John Hawkins, "and relate a circumstance of his distress, that cannot be imputed to him as an effect of his own extravagance or irregularity, and consequently reflects no disgrace on his memory? He had scarce any change of raiment, and, in a short time after Corbet left him, but one pair of shoes, and those so old that his feet were seen through them: a gentleman of his college, the father of an eminent clergyman now living, directed a servitor one morning to place a new pair at the door of Johnson's chamber; who seeing them upon his first going out, so far forgot himself and the spirit which must have actuated his unknown benefactor, that, with all the indignation of an insulted man, he threw them away."

How exceedingly surprising!—The Rev. Dr. Hall remarks: "As far as we can judge from a cursory view of the weekly account in the buttery books, Johnson appears to have lived as well as other commoners and scholars." Alas! such "cursory view of the buttery books," now from the safe distance of a century, in the safe chair of a College Mastership, is one thing; the continual view of the empty (or locked) buttery itself was quite a different thing. But hear our Knight, how he farther discourses. "Johnson," quoth Sir John, "could not at this early period of his life divest himself of an idea that poverty was disgraceful; and was very severe in his censures of that economy in both our Universities, which exacted at meals the attendance of poor scholars, under the several denominations of Servitors in the one and Sizers in the other: he thought that the Scholar's, like the Christian life, levelled all distinctions of rank and worldly pre-eminence; but in this he was *mistaken:* civil polity," &c., &c.—Too true! it is man's lot to err.

However, Destiny, in all ways, means to prove the mistaken Samuel, and see what stuff is in him. He must leave these butteries of Oxford, Want like an armed man compelling him; retreat into his father's mean home; and there abandon himself for a season to inaction, disappointment, shame, and nervous melancholy nigh run mad; he is probably the wretchedest man in wide England. In all ways, he too must "become perfect through *suffering.*"—High thoughts have visited him; his College Exercises have been praised beyond the walls of College; Pope himself has seen that *Translation*, and approved of it: Samuel had whispered to himself: I too am "one and somewhat." False thoughts; that leave only misery behind! The fever-fire of Ambition is too painfully extinguished (but not cured) in the frost-bath of Poverty. Johnson has knocked at the gate, as one having a right; but there was no opening: the world lies all encircled as with brass; nowhere can he find or force the smallest entrance. An ushership at Market Bosworth, and "a disagreement between him and Sir Wolstan Dixie, the Patron of the school," yields him bread of affliction and water of affliction; but so bitter, that unassisted human nature cannot swallow them. Young Samson will grind no more in the Philistine mill of Bosworth; quits hold of Sir Wolstan and the "domestic chaplaincy, so far at least as to say grace at table," and also to be "treated with what he represented as intolerable harshness;" and so, after "some months of such complicated misery," feeling doubtless that there are worse things in the world than quick death by Famine, "relinquishes a situation, which all his life afterwards he recollected with the strongest aversion, and even horror." Men like Johnson are properly called the Forlorn Hope of the World: judge whether his hope was forlorn or not, by this letter to a dull oily Printer, who called himself *Sylvanus Urban:*

"Sir,—As you appear no less sensible than your readers, of the defect of your poetical article, you will not be displeased if (in order to the improvement of it) I communicate to you the sentiments of a person who will undertake, on reasonable terms, sometimes to fill a column.

"His opinion is, that the public would," &c., &c.

"If such a correspondence will be agreeable to you, be pleased to inform me in two posts, what the conditions are on which you shall expect it. Your late offer (for a Prize Poem) gives me no reason to distrust your generosity. If you engage in any literary projects besides this paper, I have other designs to impart."

Reader, the generous person, to whom this Letter goes addressed, is "Mr. Edmund Cave, at St. John's Gate, London;" the addresser of it is Samuel Johnson, in Birmingham, Warwickshire.

Nevertheless, Life rallies in the man; re-asserts its right to be *lived*, even to be enjoyed. "Better a small bush," say the Scotch, "than no shelter:" Johnson learns to be contented with humble human things; and is there not already an actually realized human Existence, all stirring and living on every hand of him? Go thou and do likewise! In Birmingham itself, with his own purchased goose-quill, he can earn "five pounds;" nay, finally, the choicest terrestrial good: a Friend, who will be Wife to him! Johnson's marriage with the good Widow Porter has been treated with ridicule by many mortals, who apparently had no understanding thereof. That the purblind, seamy-faced Wildman, stalking lonely, wo-stricken, like some Irish Gallow-glass with peeled club, whose speech no man knew, whose look all men both laughed at and shuddered at, should find any brave female heart, to acknowledge, at first sight and hearing of him, "This is the most sensible man I ever met with;" and then, with generous courage, to take him to itself, and say, Be thou mine; be thou warmed here, and thawed into life!—in all this, in the kind Widow's love and pity for him, in Johnson's love and gratitude, there is actually no matter for ridicule. Their wedded life, as is the common lot, was made up of drizzle and dry weather; but innocence and worth dwelt in it; and when death had ended it, a certain sacredness: Johnson's deathless affection for his Tetty was always venerable and noble. However, be this as it might, Johnson is now minded to wed; and will live by the trade of Pedagogy, for by this also may life be kept in. Let the world therefore take notice: "*At Edial near Lichfield, in Staffordshire, young gentlemen are boarded, and taught the Latin and Greek languages, by* Samuel Johnson." Had this Edial enterprise prospered, how different might the issue have been! Johnson had lived a life of unnoticed nobleness, or swoln into some amorphous Dr. Parr, of no avail to us; Bozzy would have dwindled into official insignificance, or risen by some other elevation; old Auchinleck had never been afflicted with "ane that kept a schule," or obliged to violate hospitality by a "Cromwell do? God, sir, he gart kings ken that there was a *lith* in their neck!" But the Edial enterprise did not prosper; Destiny had other work appointed for Samuel Johnson; and young gentlemen got board where they could elsewhere find it. This man was to become a Teacher of grown gentlemen, in the most surprising way; a man of Letters, and Ruler of the British Nation for some time,—not of their bodies merely, but of their minds; not *over* them, but *in* them.

The career of Literature could not, in Johnson's day, any more than now, be said to lie along the shores of a Pactolus: whatever else might be gathered there, gold-dust was nowise the chief produce. The world, from the times of Socrates, St. Paul, and far earlier, has always had its Teachers; and always treated them in a peculiar way. A shrewd Town-clerk, (not of Ephesus,) once, in founding a Burgh-Seminary, when the question came, How the Schoolmasters should be maintained? delivered this brief counsel: "D—n them, keep them *poor!*" Considerable wisdom may lie in this aphorism. At all events, we see, the world has acted on it long, and indeed improved on it,—putting many a Schoolmaster of its great Burgh-Seminary to a death, which even *cost* it something. The world, it is true, had for some time been too busy to go out of its way, and *put* any Author to death; however, the old sentence pronounced against them was found to be pretty sufficient. The first Writers (being Monks) were sworn to a vow of Poverty; the modern Authors had no need to swear to it. This was the epoch when an Otway could still die of hunger: not to speak of your innumerable Scrogginses, whom "the Muse found stretched beneath a rug," with "rusty grate unconscious of a fire," stocking-nightcap, sanded floor, and all the other escutcheons of the craft, time out of mind the heirlooms of Authorship. Scroggins, however, seems to have been but an idler; not at all so diligent as worthy Mr. Boyce, whom we might have seen *sitting up* in bed with his wearing apparel of Blanket about him, and a hole slit in the same, that his hand might be at liberty to work in its vocation. The worst was, that too frequently a blackguard recklessness of temper ensued, incapable of turning to account what good the gods even here had provided: your Boyces acted on some stoico-epicurean principle of *carpe diem*, as men do in bombarded towns, and seasons of raging pestilence;—and so had lost not only their life, and presence of mind, but their status as persons of respectability. The trade of Author was about one of its lowest ebbs, when Johnson embarked on it.

Accordingly we find no mention of Illuminations in the city of London, when this same Ruler of the British nation arrived in it: no cannon-salvoes are fired; no flourish of drums and trumpets greets his appearance on the scene. He enters quite quietly, with some copper half-pence in his pocket; creeps into lodgings in Exeter Street, Strand; and has a Coronation Pontiff also, of not less peculiar equipment, whom, with all submissiveness, he must wait upon, in his Vatican of St. John's Gate. This is the dull oily Printer alluded to above.

"Cave's temper," says our Knight Hawkins, "was phlegmatic: though he assumed, as the publisher of the Magazine, the name of Sylvanus Urban, he had few of those qualities that constitute urbanity. Judge of his want of them by this question, which he once put to an author: "Mr.——, I hear you have just published a pamphlet, and am told there is a very good paragraph in it upon the subject of music: did you write that yourself?" His discernment was also slow; and as he had already at his command some writers of prose and verse, who, in the language of Booksellers, are called good hands, he was the backwarder in making advances, or courting an intimacy with Johnson. Upon the first approach of a stranger, his practice was to continue sitting; a posture in which he was ever to be found, and for a few minutes to continue silent: if at any time he was inclined to begin the discourse, it was generally by putting a leaf of the Magazine, then in the press, into the hand of his visitor, and asking his opinion of it. * * *

"He was so incompetent a judge of Johnson's abilities, that meaning at one time to dazzle him with the splendour of some of those luminaries in Literature, who favoured him with their correspondence, he told him that if he would, in the evening, be at a certain alehouse in the neighbourhood of Clerkenwell, he might have a chance of seeing Mr. Browne and another or two of those illustrious contributors: Johnson accepted the invitation; and being introduced by Cave, dressed in a loose horseman's coat, and such a great bushy wig as he constantly wore, to the sight of Mr. Browne, whom he found sitting at the upper end of a long table, in a cloud of tobacco-smoke, had his curiosity gratified."—*Hawkins*, 46—50.

In fact, if we look seriously into the condition of Authorship at that period, we shall find that Johnson had undertaken one of the ruggedest of all possible enterprises; that here, as elsewhere, Fortune had given him unspeakable Contradictions to reconcile. For a man of Johnson's stamp, the Problem was twofold: *First*, not only as the humble but indispensable condition of all else, to keep himself, if so might be, *alive*; but *secondly*, to keep himself alive by speaking forth the *Truth* that was in him, and speaking it *truly*, that is, in the clearest and fittest utterance the Heavens had enabled him to give it, let the earth say to this what she liked. Of which twofold Problem if it be hard to solve either member separately, how incalculably more so to solve it, when both are conjoined, and work with endless complication into one another! He that finds himself already *kept alive* can sometimes unhappily not always speak a little truth; he that finds himself able and willing, to all lengths, to *speak lies*, may, by watching how the wind sits, scrape together a livelihood, sometimes of great splendour: he, again, who finds himself provided with *neither* endowment, has but a ticklish game to play, and shall have praises if he win it. Let us look a little at both faces of the matter; and see what front they then offered our Adventurer, what front he offered them.

At the time of Johnson's appearance on the field, Literature, in many senses, was in a transitional state; chiefly in this sense, as respects the pecuniary subsistence of its cultivators. It was in the very act of passing from the protection of Patrons into that of the Public; no longer to supply its necessities by laudatory Dedications to the Great, but by judicious Bargains with the Booksellers. This happy change has been much sung and celebrated; many a "lord of the lion heart and eagle-eye" looking back with scorn enough on the bygone system of Dependency: so that now it were perhaps well to consider, for a moment, what good might also be in it, what gratitude we owe it. That a good was in it, admits not of doubt. Whatsoever has existed has had its value: without some truth and worth lying in it, the thing could not have hung together, and been the organ and sustenance, and method of action, for men that reasoned and were alive. Translate a Falsehood which is wholly false into Practice, the result comes out *zero*; there is no fruit or issue to be derived from it. That in an age, when a Nobleman was still noble, still, with his wealth the protector of worthy and humane things, and still venerated as such, a poor man of Genius, his brother in nobleness, should, with unfeigned reverence, address him and say: "I have found Wisdom here, and would fain proclaim it abroad; wilt thou, of thy abundance, afford me the means?" —in all this there was no baseness; it was wholly an honest proposal, which a free man might make, and a free man listen to. So might a Tasso, with a *Gerusalemme* in his hand or in his head, speak to a Duke of Ferrara; so might a Shakspeare to his Southampton; and Continental Artists generally to their rich Protectors,—in some countries, down almost to these days. It was only when the reverence became *feigned*, that baseness entered into the transaction on both sides; and, indeed, flourished there with rapid luxuriance, till that became disgraceful for a Dryden, which a Shakspeare could once practise without offence.

Neither, it is very true, was the new way of Bookseller Mæcenasship worthless; which opened itself at this juncture, for the most important of all transport-trades, now when the old way had become too miry and impassable. Remark, moreover, how this second sort of Mæcenasship, after carrying us through nearly a century of Literary Time, appears now to have wellnigh discharged *its* functions also; and to be working pretty rapidly towards some *third* method, the exact conditions of which are yet nowise visible. Thus all things have their end; and we should part with them all, not in anger but in peace. The Bookseller System, during its peculiar century, the whole of the eighteenth, did carry us handsomely along; and many good Works it has left us, and many good Men it maintained: if it is now expiring, by PUFFERY, as the Patronage System did by FLATTERY, (for *Lying* is ever the forerunner of Death, nay is itself Death,) let us not forget its benefits; how it nursed Literature through boyhood and school-years, as Patronage had wrapped it in soft swaddling-bands;—till now we see it about to put on the *toga virilis*, could it but *find* any such!

There is tolerable travelling on the beaten road run how it may; only on the new road, not yet levelled and paved, and on the old road, all broken into ruts and quagmires, is the travelling bad or impracticable. The difficulty lies always in the *transition* from one method to another. In which state it was that Johnson now found Literature; and out of which, let us also say, he manfully carried it. What remarkable mortal *first paid copyright* in England we have not ascertained; perhaps for almost a century before, some scarce visible or ponderable pittance of wages had occasionally been yielded by the Seller of Books to the Writer of them: the original Covenant, stipulating to produce *Paradise Lost* on the one hand, and *Five Pounds Sterling* on the other, still lies, (we have been told,) in black-on-white for inspection and purchase by the curious, at a Bookshop in Chancery Lane. Thus had the matter gone on, in a mixed, confused way, for some threescore years;—as ever, in such things, the old system *overlaps* the new, by some generation or two, and only dies quite out when the new has got a complete organization, and weather-worthy surface of its own. Among the first authors, the very first of any significance, who lived by the day's wages of his craft, and composedly faced the world on that basis, was Samuel Johnson.

At the time of Johnson's appearance, there were still two ways, on which an Author might attempt proceeding; there were the Mæcenases proper in the West End of London; and the Mæcenases virtual of St. John's Gate and Paternoster Row. To a considerate man it might seem uncertain which methods were preferable: neither had very high attractions; the Patron's aid was now wellnigh *necessarily* polluted by sycophancy, before it could come to hand; the Bookseller's was deformed with greedy stupidity, not to say entire wooden-headedness and disgust, (so that an Osborne even required to be knocked down, by an author of spirit,) and could barely keep the thread of life together. The one was the wages of suffering and poverty; the other, unless you gave strict heed to it, the wages of sin. In time, Johnson had opportunity of looking into both methods, and ascertaining what they were; but found, at first trial, that the former would in no wise do for him. Listen, once again, to that far-famed Blast of Doom, proclaiming into the ear of Lord Chesterfield, and, through him, of the listening world, that Patronage should be no more!

"Seven years, my Lord, have now passed, since I waited in your outward rooms, or was repulsed from your door; during which time I have been pushing on my work* through difficulties, of which it is useless to complain, and have brought it at last to the verge of publication, without one act of assistance,† one word of encouragement, or one smile of favour.

"The shepherd in Virgil grew at last acquainted with Love, and found him a native of the rocks.

"Is not a patron, my Lord, one who looks with unconcern on a man struggling for life in the water, and when he has reached ground, encumbers him with help? The notice which you have been pleased to take of my labours, had it been early, had been kind: but it has been delayed till I am indifferent and cannot enjoy it; till I am solitary and cannot impart it; till I am known and do not want it. I hope, it is no very cynical asperity, not to confess obligations, where no benefit has been received, or to be unwilling that the public should consider me as owing that to a patron which Providence has enabled me to do for myself.

---

* The *English Dictionary*.

† Were time and printer's space of no value, it were easy to wash away certain foolish soot-stains dropped here as "Notes;" especially two: the one on this word (and on Boswell's Note to it;) the other on the paragraph which follows. Let "ED." look a second time; he will find that Johnson's sacred regard for *Truth* is the only thing to be "noted," in the former case; also, in the latter, that this of "Love's being a native of the rocks" actually *has* a "meaning."

"Having carried on my Work thus far with so little obligation to any favourer of learning; I shall not be disappointed though I should conclude it, if less be possible, with less: for I have long been awakened from that dream of hope, in which I once boasted myself with so much exultation.

"My Lord, your Lordship's most humble, most obedient servant,

"SAM. JOHNSON."

And thus must the rebellious "Sam. Johnson" turn him to the Bookselling guild, and the wondrous chaos of "Author by trade;" and, though ushered into it only by that dull oily Printer, "with loose horseman's coat, and such a great bushy wig as he constantly wore," and only as subaltern to some commanding-officer, "Browne, sitting amid tobacco-smoke at the head of a long table in the alehouse at Clerkenwell,"—gird himself together for the warfare; having no alternative!

Little less contradictory was that other branch of the two-fold Problem now set before Johnson: the speaking forth of *Truth.* Nay, taken by itself, it had in those days become so complex as to puzzle strongest heads, with nothing else imposed on them for solution; and even to turn high heads of that sort into mere hollow *vizards*, speaking neither truth nor falsehood, nor any thing but what the Prompter and Player (ὑποκριτής) put into them. Alas! for poor Johnson, Contradiction abounded; in spirituals and in temporals, within and without. Born with the strongest unconquerable love of just Insight, he must begin to live and learn in a scene where Prejudice flourishes with rank luxuriance. England was all confused enough, sightless and yet restless, take it where you would; but figure the best intellect in England nursed up to manhood in the idol-cavern of a poor Tradesman's house, in the cathedral city of Lichfield! What is Truth? said jesting Pilate; What is Truth? might earnest Johnson much more emphatically say. Truth, no longer, like the Phœnix, in rainbow plumage, "poured, from her glittering beak, such tones of sweetest melody as took captive every ear:" the Phœnix (waxing old) had wellnigh ceased her singing, and empty wearisome Cuckoos, and doleful monotonous Owls, innumerable Jays also, and twittering Sparrows on the housetop, pretended they were repeating her.

It was wholly a divided age, that of Johnson; Unity existed nowhere, in its Heaven, or in its Earth. Society, through every fibre, was rent asunder: all things, it was then becoming visible, but could not then be understood, were moving onwards, with an impulse received ages before, yet now first with a decisive rapidity, towards that great chaotic gulf, where, whether in the shape of French Revolutions, Reform Bills, or what shape soever, bloody or bloodless, the descent and engulfment assume, we now see them weltering and boiling. Already Cant, as once before hinted, had begun to play its wonderful part (for the hour was come): two ghastly Apparitions, unreal *simulacra* both, HYPOCRISY and ATHEISM, are already, in silence, parting the world. Opinion and Action, which should live together as wedded pair, "one flesh," more properly as Soul and Body, have commenced their open quarrel, and are suing for a separate maintenance,—as if they could exist separately. To the earnest mind, in any position, firm footing and a life of Truth was becoming daily more difficult: in Johnson's position, it was more difficult than in almost any other.

If, as for a devout nature was inevitable and indispensable, he looked up to Religion, as to the pole-star of his voyage, already there was no *fixed* pole-star any longer visible; but two stars, a whole constellation of stars, each proclaiming itself as the true. There was the red portentous comet-star of Infidelity; the dimmer and dimmer-burning fixed-star (uncertain now whether not an atmospheric *meteor*) of Orthodoxy: which of these to choose? The keener intellects of Europe had, almost without exception, ranged themselves under the former: for some half-century, it had been the general effort of European Speculation to proclaim that Destruction of Falsehood was the only Truth; daily had Denial waxed stronger and stronger, Belief sunk more and more into decay. From our Bolingbrokes and Tolands, the skeptical fever had passed into France, into Scotland; and already it smouldered, far and wide, secretly eating out the heart of England. Bayle had played his part; Voltaire, on a wider theatre, was playing his,—Johnson's senior by some fifteen years: Hume and Johnson were children of the same year. To this keener order of intellects did Johnson's indisputably belong: was he to join them? Was he to oppose them? A complicated question: for, alas! the Church itself is no longer, even to him, wholly of true adamant, but of adamant and baked mud conjoined: the zealously Devout must find his Church tottering; and pause amazed to see, instead of inspired Priest, many a swine-feeding Trulliber ministering at her altar. It is not the least curious of the incoherences which Johnson had to reconcile, that, though by nature contemptuous and incredulous, he was, at that time of day, to find his safety and glory in defending, with his whole might, the traditions of the elders.

Not less perplexingly intricate, and on both sides hollow or questionable, was the aspect of Politics. Whigs struggling blindly forward, Tories holding blindly back; each with some forecast of a half truth; neither with any forecast of the whole! Admire here this other Contradiction in the life of Johnson: that, though the most ungovernable, and in practice the most independent of men, he must be a Jacobite, and worshipper of the Divine Right. In politics also there are Irreconcilables enough for him. As, indeed, how could it be otherwise? For when religion is torn asunder, and the very heart of man's existence set against itself, then, in all subordinate departments there must needs be hollowness, incoherence. The English Nation had rebelled against a Tyrant; and, by the hands of religious tyrannicides, exacted stern vengeance of him: Democracy had risen iron-sinewed, and "like an infant Hercules, strangled serpents in its cradle." But as yet none knew the meaning or extent of the phenomenon.

Europe was not ripe for it; not to be ripened for it, but by the culture and various experience of another century and half. And now, when the King-killers were all swept away, and a milder *second* picture was painted over the canvas of the *first*, and betitled "Glorious Revolution," who doubted but the catastrophe was over, the whole business finished, and Democracy gone to its long sleep? Yet was it like a business finished and not finished; a lingering uneasiness dwelt in all minds: the deep-lying, resistless Tendency, which had still to be *obeyed*, could no longer be *recognised;* thus was there half-ness, insincerity, uncertainty in men's ways; instead of heroic Puritans and heroic Cavaliers, came now a dawdling set of argumentative Whigs, and a dawdling set of deaf-eared Tories; each half-foolish, each half-false. The Whigs were false and without basis; inasmuch as their whole object was Resistance, Criticism, Demolition,—they knew not why, or towards what issue. In Whiggism, ever since a Charles and his Jeffries had ceased to meddle with it, and to have any Russel or Sidney to meddle with, there could be no divineness of character; not till, in these latter days, it took the figure of a thorough-going, all-defying, Radicalism, was there any solid footing for it to stand on. Of the like uncertain, half-hollow nature had Toryism become, in Johnson's time; preaching forth indeed an everlasting truth, the duty of Loyalty; yet now (ever since the final expulsion of the Stuarts), having no *Person* but only an *Office* to be loyal to, no living *Soul* to worship, but only a dead velvet-cushioned *Chair*. Its attitude, therefore, was stiff-necked refusal to move; as that of Whiggism was clamorous command to move,—let rhyme and reason, on both hands, say to it what they might. The consequence was: Immeasurable floods of contentious jargon, tending nowhither; false conviction; false resistance to conviction; decay (ultimately to become decease) of whatsoever was once understood by the words, *Principle*, or *Honesty* of heart; the louder and louder triumph of *Half*-ness and Plausibility over *Whole*-ness and Truth;—at last, this all-overshadowing efflorescence of QUACKERY, which we now see, with all its deadening and killing fruits, in all its innumerable branches, down to the lowest. How, between these jarring extremes, wherein the rotten lay so inextricably intermingled with the sound, and as yet no eye could see through the ulterior meaning of the matter, was a faithful and true man to adjust himself?

That Johnson, in spite of all drawbacks, adopted the Conservative side; stationed himself as the unyielding opponent of Innovation, resolute to hold fast the form of sound words, could not but increase, in no small measure, the difficulties he had to strive with. We mean, the *moral* difficulties; for in *economical* respects, it might be pretty equally balanced; the Tory servant of the Public had perhaps about the same chance of promotion as the Whig: and all the promotion Johnson aimed at was the privilege *to live*. But, for what, though unavowed, was no less indispensable, for his peace of conscience, and the clear ascertainment and feeling of his Duty as an inhabitant of God's world, the case was hereby rendered much more complex. To resist Innovation is easy enough on one condition: that you resist Inquiry. This is, and was, the common expedient of your common Conservatives; but it would not do for Johnson: he was a zealous recommender and practiser of Inquiry; once for all, could not and would not believe, much less speak and act, a Falsehood; the *form* of sound words, which he held fast, must have a *meaning* in it. Here lay the difficulty: to behold a portentous mixture of True and False, and feel that he must dwell and fight there; yet to love and defend only the True. How worship, when you cannot and will not be an idolater; yet cannot help discerning that the Symbol of your Divinity has half become idolatrous? This was the question, which Johnson, the man both of clear eye and devout believing heart, must answer,—at peril of his life. The Whig or Skeptic, on the other hand, had a much simpler part to play. To him only the idolatrous side of things, nowise the divine one, lay visible: not *worship*, therefore, nay in the strict sense not heart-honesty, only at most lip, and hand-honesty, is required of him. What spiritual force is his, he can conscientiously employ in the work of cavilling, of pulling down what is False. For the rest, that there is or can be any Truth of a higher than sensual nature, has not occurred to him. The utmost, therefore, that he as man has to aim at, is RESPECTABILITY, the suffrages of his fellow-men. Such suffrages he may weigh as well as count; or count only: according as he is a Burke, or a Wilkes. But beyond these there lies nothing divine for him; these attained, all is attained. Thus is his whole world distinct and rounded in; a clear goal is set before him; a firm path, rougher or smoother; at worst a firm region wherein to seek a path: let him gird up his loins, and travel on without misgivings! For the honest Conservative, again, nothing is distinct, nothing rounded in: RESPECTABILITY can nowise be his highest Godhead; not one aim, but two conflicting aims to be continually reconciled by him, has he to strive after. A difficult position, as we said; which accordingly the most did, even in those days, but half defend,—by the surrender, namely, of their own too cumbersome *honesty* or even *understanding;* after which the completest defence was worth little. Into this difficult position Johnson, nevertheless, threw himself: found it indeed full of difficulties; yet held it out manfully, as an honest-hearted, open-sighted man, while the life was in him.

Such was that same "twofold Problem" set before Samuel Johnson. Consider all these moral difficulties; and add to them the fearful aggravation, which lay in that other circumstance, that he needed a continual appeal to the Public, must continually produce a certain impression and conviction on the Public; that if he did not, he ceased to have "provision for the day that was passing over him," he could not any longer live! How a vulgar character, once launched into this wild element; driven onwards by Fear and Famine: without other aim than to clutch what Provender (of Enjoyment in any kind) he could get, always if possible keeping *quite* clear of the Gallows and Pillory, (that is to say, minding heedfully both "person" and "character,")—would have floated hither and thither in it; and contrived to eat some three repasts daily, and wear some three suits yearly, and then to depart, and disappear, having consumed his last ration: all this might be worth knowing, but were in itself a trivial knowledge. How a noble man, resolute for the Truth, to whom Shams and Lies were once for all an abomination,—was to act in it: *here* lay the mystery. By what methods, by what gifts of eye and hand, does a heroic Samuel Johnson, now when cast forth into that waste Chaos of Authorship, maddest of things, a mingled Phlegethon and Fleet-ditch, with its floating lumber, and sea-krakens, and mud-spectres,—shape himself a voyage; of the *transient* driftwood, and the *enduring* iron, built him a seaworthy Life-boat, and sail therein, undrowned, unpolluted, through the roaring "mother of dead dogs," onwards to an eternal Landmark, and City that hath foundations? This high question is even the one answered in Boswell's Book; which Book we, therefore not so falsely, have named a *Heroic Poem;* for in it there lies the whole argument of such. Glory to our brave Samuel! He accomplished this wonderful Problem; and now through long generations, we point to him, and say: Here also was a Man; let the world once more have assurance of a Man!

Had there been in Johnson, now when afloat on that confusion worse confounded of grandeur and squalor, no light but an earthly outward one, he too must have made shipwreck. With his diseased body, and vehement voracious heart, how easy for him to become a *carpe-diem* Philosopher, like the rest, and live and die as miserably as any Boyce of that Brotherhood! But happily there was a higher light for him; shining as a lamp to his path; which, in all paths, would teach him to act and walk not as a fool, but as wise in those evil days also, "redeeming the time." Under dimmer or clearer manifestations, a Truth had been revealed to him: I also am a Man; even in this unutterable element of Authorship, I may live as beseems a Man! That Wrong is not only different from Right, but that it is in strict scientific terms, *infinitely* different; even as the gaining of the whole world set against the losing of one's own soul, or (as Johnson had it) a Heaven set against a Hell; that in all situations (out of the Pit of Tophet), wherein a living Man has stood or can stand, there is actually a Prize of quite *infinite* value placed within his reach, namely a *Duty* for him to do: this highest Gospel, which forms the basis and worth of all other Gospels whatsoever, had been revealed to Samuel Johnson; and the man had believed it, and laid it faithfully to heart. Such knowledge of the *transcendental*, immeasurable character of Duty, we call the basis of all Gospels, the essence of all Religion: he who with his whole soul knows not this, as yet knows nothing, as yet *is* properly nothing.

This, happily for him, Johnson was one of those that knew: under a certain authentic Symbol, it stood for ever present to his eyes: a Symbol, indeed, waxing old as doth a garment; yet which had guided forward, as their Banner and celestial Pillar of Fire, innumerable saints and witnesses, the fathers of our modern world; and for him also had still a sacred significance. It does not appear that, at any time, Johnson was what we call irreligious: but in his sorrows and isolation, when hope died away, and only a long vista of suffering and toil lay before him to the end, then first did Religion shine forth in its meek, everlasting clearness; even as the stars do in black night, which in the daytime and dusk were hidden by inferior lights. How a true man, in the midst of errors and uncertainties, shall work out for himself a sure Life-truth; and adjusting the transient to the eternal, amid the fragments of ruined Temples build up, with toil and pain, a little Altar for himself, and worship there; how Samuel Johnson, in the era of Voltaire, can purify and fortify his soul, and hold real communion with the Highest, "in the Church of St. Clement Danes:" this too stands all unfolded in his Biography, and is among the most touching and memorable things there; a thing to be looked at with pity, admiration, awe. Johnson's Religion was as the light of life to him; without it, his heart was all sick, dark, and had no guidance left.

He is now enlisted, or impressed, into that unspeakable shoe-black seraph Army of Authors; but can feel hereby that he fights under a celestial flag, and will quit him like a man. The first grand requisite, an assured heart, he therefore has: what his outward equipments and accoutrements are, is the next question; an important, though inferior one. His intellectual stock, intrinsically viewed, is perhaps inconsiderable: the furnishings of an English School and English University; good knowledge of the Latin tongue, a more uncertain one of Greek: this is a rather slender stock of Education wherewith to front the world. But then it is to be remembered that his world was England; that such was the culture England commonly supplied and expected. Besides, Johnson has been a voracious reader, though a desultory one, and oftenest in strange scholastic, too obsolete Libraries; he has also rubbed shoulders with the press of actual Life, for some thirty years now: views or hallucinations of innumerable things are weltering to and fro in him. Above all, be his weapons what they may, he has an arm that can wield them. Nature has given him her choicest gift: an open eye and heart. He will look on the world, wheresoever he can catch a glimpse of it, with eager curiosity: to the last, we find this a striking characteristic of him: for all human interests he has a sense; the meanest handicraftsman could interest him, even in extreme age, by speaking of his craft: the ways of men are all interesting to him; any human thing, that he did not know, he wished to know. Reflection, moreover, Meditation, was what he practised incessantly, with or without his will: for the mind of the man was earnest, deep as well as humane. Thus would the world, such fragments of it as he could survey, form itself, or continually tend to form itself, into a coherent Whole; on any and on all phases of which, his vote and voice must be well worth listening to. As a Speaker of the Word, he will speak real words; no idle jargon, no hollow triviality will issue from him. His aim too is clear, attainable, that of *working for his wages;* let him *do* this honestly, and all else will follow of its own accord.

With such omens, into such a warfare, did Johnson go forth. A rugged, hungry Kerne, or Gallowglass, as we called him: yet indomitable; in whom lay the true spirit of a Soldier. With giant's force he toils, since such is his appointment, were it but at hewing of wood and drawing of water for old sedentary, bushy-wigged Cave; distinguishes himself by mere quantity, if there is to be no other distinction. He can write all things; frosty Latin verses, if these are the saleable commodity; Book-prefaces, Political Philippics, Review Articles, Parliamentary Debates: all things he does rapidly; still more surprising, all things he does thoroughly and well. How he sits there, in his rough-hewn, amorphous bulk, in that upper room at St. John's Gate, and trundles off sheet after sheet of those Senate-of-Lilliput Debates, to the clamorous Printer's Devils waiting for them, with insatiable throat, down stairs; himself perhaps *impransus* all the while! Admire also the greatness of Literature; how a grain of mustard-seed cast into its Nile-waters, shall settle in the teeming mould, and be found, one day, as a Tree, in whose branches all the fowls of heaven may lodge. Was it not so with these Lilliput Debates? In that small project and act, began the stupendous Fourth Estate; whose wide world-embracing influences what eye can take in; in whose boughs are there not already fowls of strange feather lodged? Such things, and far stranger, were done in that wondrous old Portal, even in latter times. And then figure Samuel dining "behind the screen," from a trencher covertly handed in to him, at a preconcerted nod from the "great bushy wig;" Samuel, too ragged to show face, yet "made a happy man of" by hearing his praise spoken. If to Johnson himself, then much more to us, may that St. John's Gate be a place we can "never pass without veneration."*

Poverty, Distress, and as yet Obscurity, are his companions: so poor is he that his Wife must leave him, and seek shelter among other relations; Johnson's household has accommodation for one inmate only. To all his ever-varying, ever-recurring troubles, moreover, must be added this continual one of ill health, and its concomitant depressiveness: a galling load, which would have crushed most common mortals into desperation, is his appointed ballast and life-burden; he "could not remember the day he had passed free from pain." Nevertheless, Life, as we said before, is always Life: a healthy soul, imprison it as you will, in squalid garrets, shabby coat, bodily sickness, or whatever else, will assert its heaven-granted indefeasible Freedom, its right to conquer difficulties, to do work, even to feel gladness. Johnson does not whine over his existence, but manfully makes the most and best of it. "He said, a man might live in a garret at eighteen-pence a week; few people would inquire where he lodged; and if they did, it was easy to say, 'Sir, I am to be found at such a place.' By spending threepence in a coffee-house, he might be for some hours every day in very good company; he might dine for sixpence, breakfast on bread and milk for a penny, and do without supper. On *clean-shirt-day* he went abroad, and paid visits." Think by whom, and of whom this was uttered, and ask then, Whether there is more pathos in it than in a whole circulating-library of *Giaours* and *Harolds*, or less pathos? On another occasion, "when Dr. Johnson, one day, read his own Satire, in which the life of a scholar is painted with the various obstructions thrown in his way to fortune and to fame, he burst into a passion of tears: Mr. Thrale's family and Mr. Scott only were present, who, in a jocose way, clapped him on the back, and said, 'What's all this, my dear sir? Why you, and I, and *Hercules*, you know, were all troubled with *melancholy.*' He was a very large man, and made out the triumvirate with Johnson and Hercules comically enough." These were sweet tears; the sweet victorious remembrance lay in them of toils indeed frightful, yet never flinched from, and now triumphed over. "One day it shall delight you to re-

* All Johnson's places of resort and abode are venerable, and now indeed to the many as well as to the few; for his name has become great; and, as we must often with a kind of sad admiration recognise, there is, even to the rudest man, no greatness so venerable as intellectual, as spiritual greatness; nay properly there is no other venerable at all. For example, what soul-subduing magic, for the very clown or craftsman of our England, lies in the word "Scholar!" "He is a Scholar:" he is a man *wiser* than we; of a wisdom to us *boundless*, infinite: who shall speak his worth! Such things, we say, fill us with a certain pathetic admiration of defaced and obstructed yet glorious man; archangel though in ruins,—or rather, though in *rubbish*, of encumbrances and mud-incrustations, which also are not to be perpetual.

Nevertheless, in this mad-whirling all-forgetting London, the haunts of the mighty that were, can seldom without a strange difficulty be discovered. Will any man, for instance, tell us which *bricks* it was in Lincoln's Inn Buildings, that Ben Jonson's hand and trowel laid? No man, it is to be feared,—and also grumbled at. With Samuel Johnson may it prove otherwise! A Gentleman of the British Museum is said to have made drawings of all *his* residences: the blessing of Old Mortality be upon him! We ourselves, not without labour and risk, lately discovered Gough Square, between Fleet Street and Holborn (adjoining both to Bolt Court and Johnson's Court;) and, on the second day of search, the very House there, wherein the *English Dictionary* was composed. It is the first or corner house on the right hand, as you enter through the arched way from the North-west. The actual occupant, an elderly, well-washed, decent-looking man, invited us to enter; and courteously undertook to be *cicerone;* though in his memory lay nothing but the foolishest jumble and hallucination. It is a stout old-fashioned, oak-balustraded house: "I have spent many a pound and penny on it since then," said the worthy Landlord: "here, you see, this Bedroom was the Doctor's study; that was the garden" (a plot of delved ground somewhat larger than a bed-quilt) "where he walked for exercise; these three garret Bedrooms" (where his three Copyists sat and wrote) "were the place he kept his—*Pupils* in!" *Tempus edax rerum!* Yet *ferax* also: for our friend now added, with a wistful look, which strove to seem merely historical: "I let it all in Lodgings, to respectable gentlemen; by the quarter, or the month; it's all one to me."—"To me also," whispered the Ghost of Samuel, as we went pensively our ways.

member labour done !"—Neither, though Johnson is obscure and poor, need the highest enjoyment of existence, that of heart freely communing with heart, be denied him. Savage and he wander homeless through the streets; without bed, yet not without friendly converse; such another conversation not, it is like, producible in the proudest drawing-room of London. Nor, under the void Night, upon the hard pavement, are their own woes the only topic: nowise; they "will stand by their country," the two "Back-woods-men" of the Brick Desart!

Of all outward evils Obscurity is perhaps in itself the least. To Johnson, as to a healthy-minded man, the fantastic article, sold or given under the title of *Fame*, had little or no value but its intrinsic one. He prized it as the means of getting him employment and good wages; scarcely as any thing more. His light and guidance came from a loftier source; of which, in honest aversion to all hypocrisy or pretentious talk, he spoke not to men; nay, perhaps, being of a *healthy* mind, had never spoken to himself. We reckon it a striking fact in Johnson's history, this carelessness of his to Fame. Most authors speak of their "Fame" as if it were a quite priceless matter; the grand ultimatum, and heavenly Constantine's-Banner they had to follow, and conquer under.—Thy "Fame!" Unhappy mortal, where will it and thou both be in some fifty years? Shakspeare himself has lasted but two hundred; Homer (partly by accident) three thousand: and does not already an ETERNITY encircle every *Me* and every *Thee?* Cease, then, to sit feverishly hatching on that "Fame" of thine; and flapping, and shrieking with fierce hisses, like brood-goose on her last egg, if man shall or dare approach it! Quarrel not with me, hate me not, my Brother: make what thou canst of thy egg, and welcome: God knows, I will not steal it; I believe it to be *addle*.—Johnson, for his part, was no man to be killed "by a review;" concerning which matter, it was said by a benevolent person: "If any author *can* be reviewed to death, let it be, with all convenient despatch, *done*." Johnson thankfully receives any word spoken in his favour; is nowise disobliged by a lampoon, but will look at it, if pointed out to him, and show how it might have been done better: the lampoon itself is indeed *nothing*, a soap-bubble that, next moment, will become a drop of sour suds; but in the meanwhile, if it do any thing, it keeps him more in the world's eye, and the next *bargain* will be all the richer: "Sir, if they should cease to talk of me, I must starve." Sound heart and understanding head! these fail no man, not even a man of Letters.

Obscurity, however, was, in Johnson's case, whether a light or heavy evil, likely to be no lasting one. He is animated by the spirit of a true *workman*, resolute to do his work well; and he *does* his work well; all his work, that of writing, that of living. A man of this stamp is unhappily not so common in the literary or in any other department of the world, that he can continue always unnoticed. By slow degrees, Johnson emerges; looming, at first, huge and dim in the eye of an observant few; at last disclosed, in his real proportions, to the eye of the whole world, and encircled with a "light-nimbus" of glory, so that whoso is not blind must and shall behold him. By slow degrees, we said; for this also is notable; slow but sure: as his fame waxes not by exaggerated clamour of what he *seems* to be, but by better and better insight of what he *is*, so it will last and stand wearing, being genuine. Thus indeed is it always, or nearly always, with true fame. The heavenly Luminary rises amid vapours: star-gazers enough must scan it, with critical telescopes; it makes no blazing, the world can either look at it, or forbear looking at it; not till after a time and times, does its celestial, eternal nature become indubitable. Pleasant, on the other hand, is the blazing of a Tarbarrel; the crowd dance merrily round it, with loud huzzaing, universal three-times-three, and, like Homer's peasants, "bless the useful light:" but unhappily it so soon ends in darkness, foul choking smoke, and is kicked into the gutters, a nameless imbroglio of charred staves, pitch-cinders, and *vomissement du Diable!*

But indeed, from the old, Johnson has enjoyed all or nearly all that Fame can yield any man: the respect, the obedience of those that are about him and inferior to him; of those whose opinion alone can have any forcible impression on him. A little circle gathers round the Wise man; which gradually enlarges as the report thereof spreads, and more can come to see, and to believe; for Wisdom is precious, and of irresistible attraction to all. "An inspired-idiot," Goldsmith, hangs strangely about him; though, as Hawkins says, "he loved not Johnson, but rather envied him for his parts'; and once entreated a friend to desist from praising him, 'for in doing so,' said he, 'you harrow up my very soul!'" Yet on the whole, there is no evil in the "gooseberry-fool;" but rather much good; of a finer, if of a weaker, sort than Johnson's; and all the more genuine that he himself could never become *conscious* of it,—though unhappily never cease *attempting* to become so: the Author of the genuine *Vicar of Wakefield*, nill he, will he, must needs fly towards such a mass of genuine Manhood; and Dr. Minor keep gyrating round Dr. Major, alternately attracted and repelled. Then there is the chivalrous Topham Beauclerk, with his sharp wit, and gallant, courtly ways: there is Bennet Langton, an orthodox gentleman, and worthy; though Johnson once laughed, louder almost than mortal, at his last will and testament; and "could not stop his merriment, but continued it all the way till he got without the Temple-gate; then burst into such a fit of laughter that he appeared to be almost in a convulsion; and, in order to support himself, laid hold of one of the posts at the side of the foot-pavement, and sent forth peals so loud that, in the silence of the night, his voice seemed to resound from Temple-bar to Fleet-ditch!" Lastly comes his solid-thinking, solid-feeding Thrale, the well-beloved man; with *Thralia*, a bright papilionaceous creature, whom the elephant loved to play with, and wave to and fro upon his trunk. Not to speak of a reverent Bozzy, for what need is there farther?—Or of the spiritual Luminaries, with tongue or pen, who made that age remarkable; or of Highland Lairds drinking, in fierce usquebaugh, "Your health, Toctor Shonson!"—still less of many such as that poor "Mr. F. Lewis," older in date, of whose birth, death, and whole terrestrial *res gestæ*, this only, and strange enough this actually, survives: "Sir, he lived in London, and hung loose upon society!" *stat* PARVI *nominis umbra.*—

In his fifty-third year, he is beneficed, by the royal bounty, with a Pension of three hundred pounds. Loud clamour is always more or less insane: but probably the insanest of all loud clamours in the eighteenth century, was this that was raised about Johnson's Pension. Men seem to be led by the noses; but in reality, it is by the ears,—as some ancient slaves were, who had their ears bored; or as some modern quadrupeds may be, whose ears are long. Very falsely was it said, "Names do not change Things;" Names do change Things; nay for most part they are the only substance, which mankind can discern in Things. The whole sum that Johnson, during the remaining twenty-two years of his life, drew from the public funds of England, would have supported some Supreme Priest for about half as many weeks; it amounts very nearly to the revenue of our poorest Church-Overseer for one twelvemonth. Of secular Administrators of Provinces, and Horse-subduers, and Game-destroyers, we shall not so much as speak: but who were the Primates of England, and the Primates of all England, during Johnson's days? No man has remembered. Again, is the Primate of all England something, or is he nothing? If something, then what but the man who, in the supreme degree, teaches and spiritually edifies, and leads towards Heaven by guiding wisely through the Earth, the living souls that inhabit England? We touch here upon deep matters; which but remotely concern us, and might lead us into still deeper: clear, in the meanwhile, it is that the true Spiritual Edifier and Soul's-Father of all England was, and till very lately continued to be, the man named Samuel Johnson,—whom this scot-and-lot-paying world cackled reproachfully to see remunerated like a Supervisor of Excise!

If Destiny had beaten hard on poor Samuel, and did never cease to visit him too roughly, yet the last section of his Life might be pronounced victorious, and on the whole happy. He was not Idle; but now no longer goaded on by want; the light which had shone irradiating the dark haunts of Poverty, now illuminates the circles of Wealth, of a certain culture and elegant intelligence; he who had once been admitted to speak with Edmund Cave and Tobacco Browne, now admits a Reynolds and a Burke to speak with him. Loving friends are there; Listeners, even Answerers: the fruit of his long labours lies round him in fair legible Writings, of Philosophy, Eloquence, Morality, Philology; some excellent, all worthy and genuine Works; for which, too, a deep, earnest murmur of thanks reaches him from all ends of his Fatherland. Nay, there are works of Goodness, of undying Mercy, which even he has possessed the power to do: "What I gave I have; what I spent I had!" Early friends had long sunk into the grave; yet in his soul they ever lived, fresh and clear, with soft pious breathings towards them, not without a still hope of one day meeting them again in purer union. Such was Johnson's Life: the victorious Battle of a free, true Man. Finally he died the death of the free and true: a dark cloud of Death, solemn, and not untinged with haloes of immortal Hope "took him away," and our eyes could no longer behold him; but can still behold the trace and impress of his courageous, honest spirit, deep-legible in the World's Business, wheresoever he walked and was.

To estimate the quantity of Work that Johnson performed, how much poorer the World were had it wanted him, can, as in all such cases, never be accurately done; cannot, till after some longer space, be approximately done. All work is as seed sown; it grows and spreads, and sows itself anew, and so, in endless palingenesia, lives and works. To Johnson's Writings, good and solid, and still profitable as they are, we have already rated his Life and Conversation as superior. By the one and by the other, who shall compute what effects have been produced, and are still, and into deep Time, producing?

So much, however, we can already see: It is now some three quarters of a century that Johnson has been the Prophet of the English; the man by whose light the English people, in public and in private, more than by any other man's, have guided their existence. Higher light than that immediately *practical* one; higher virtue than an honest PRUDENCE, he could not then communicate; nor perhaps could they have received: such light, such virtue, however, he did communicate. How to thread this labyrinthic Time, the fallen and falling Ruin of Times; to silence vain Scruples, hold firm to the last the fragments of old Belief, and with earnest eye still discern some glimpses of a true path, and go forward thereon, "in a world where there is much to be done, and little to be known:" this is what Samuel Johnson, by act and word, taught his nation, what his nation received and learned of him, more than of any other. We can view him as the preserver and transmitter of whatsoever was genuine in the spirit of Toryism; which genuine spirit, it is now becoming manifest, must again imbody itself in all new forms of Society, be what they may, that are to exist, and have continuance—elsewhere than on Paper. The *last* in many things, Johnson was the last genuine Tory; the last of Englishmen who, with strong voice, and wholly-believing heart, preached the Doctrine of Standing still; who, without selfishness or slavishness, reverenced the existing Powers, and could assert the privileges of rank, though himself poor, neglected, and plebeian; who had heart-devoutness with heart-hatred of cant, was orthodox-religious with his eyes open; and in all things and everywhere spoke out in plain English, from a soul wherein jesuitism could find no harbour, and with the front and tone not of a diplomatist but of a man.

This last of the Tories was Johnson: not Burke, as is often said; Burke was essentially a Whig, and only, on reaching the verge of the chasm towards which Whiggism from the first was inevitably leading, recoiled; and, like a man vehement rather than earnest, a resplendent far-sighted Rhetorician rather than a deep sure Thinker, recoiled with no measure, convulsively, and damaging what he drove back with him.

In a world which exists by the balance of Antagonisms, the respective merit of the Conservator and the Innovator must ever remain debateable. Great, in the meanwhile, and undoubted, for both sides, is the merit of him who, in a day of Change, walks wisely, honestly. Johnson's aim was in itself an impossible one; this of stemming the eternal Flood of Time; of clutching all things, and anchoring them down, and saying, Move not!—how could it, or should it, ever have success? The strongest man can but retard the current partially and for a short hour. Yet even in such shortest retardation, may not an estimable value lie? If England has escaped the blood-bath of a French Revolution; and may yet, in virtue of this delay and of the experience it has given, work out her deliverance calmly into a new Era, let Samuel Johnson, beyond all contemporary or succeeding men, have the praise for it. We said above that he was appointed to be Ruler of the British nation for a season: whoso will look beyond the surface, into the heart of the world's movements, may find that all Pitt Administrations, and Continental Subsidies, and Waterloo victories, rested on the possibility of making England, yet a little while, *Toryish*, Loyal to the Old; and this again on the anterior reality, that the Wise had found such Loyalty still practicable, and recommendable. England had its Hume, as France had its Voltaires and Diderots; but the Johnson was peculiar to us.

If we ask now by what endowment it mainly was that Johnson realized such a Life for himself and others; what quality of character the main phenomena of his Life may be most naturally deduced from, and his other qualities most naturally subordinated to, in our conception of him, perhaps the answer were: The quality of Courage, of Valour; that Johnson was a Brave Man. The Courage that can go forth, once and away, to Chalk-Farm, and have itself shot, and snuffed out, with decency, is nowise wholly what we mean here. Such Courage we indeed esteem an exceeding small matter; capable of coexisting with a life full of falsehood, feebleness, poltroonery, and despicability. Nay oftener it is Cowardice rather that produces the result: for consider, Is the Chalk-Farm Pistoleer inspired with any reasonable Belief and Determination; or is he hounded on by haggard, indefinable Fear,—how he will be *cut* at public places, and "plucked geese of the neighbourhood" will wag their tongues at him a plucked goose? If he go then, and be shot without shrieking, or audible uproar, it is well for him: nevertheless there is nothing amazing in it. Courage to manage all this has not perhaps been denied to any man, or to any woman. Thus, do not recruiting sergeants drum through the streets of manufacturing towns, and collect ragged losels enough; every one of whom, if once dressed in red, and trained a little, will receive fire cheerfully for the small sum of one shilling *per diem*, and have the soul blown out of him at last, with perfect propriety. The Courage that dares only *die*, is on the whole no sublime affair; necessary indeed, yet universal: pitiful when it begins to parade itself. On this Globe of ours, there are some thirty-six persons that manifest it, seldom with the smallest failure, during every second of time. Nay look at Newgate: do not the offscourings of Creation, when condemned to the gallows, as if they were not men but vermin, walk thither with decency, and even to the scowls and hootings of the whole Universe give their stern good-night in silence? What is to be undergone only once, we may undergo; what must be, comes almost of its own accord. Considered as Duelist, what a poor figure does the fiercest Irish Whiskerando make, compared with any English Game-cock, such as you may buy for fifteen-pence!

The Courage we desire and prize is not the Courage to die decently, but to live manfully. This, when by God's grace it has been given, lies deep in the soul; like genial heat, fosters all other virtues and gifts; without it they could not live. In spite of our innumerable Waterloos and Peterloos, and such campaigning as there has been, this Courage we allude to, and call the only true one, is perhaps rarer in these last ages, than it has been in any other since the Saxon Invasion under Hengist. Altogether extinct it can never be among men; otherwise the species Man were no longer for this world: here and there, in all times, under various guises, men are sent hither not only to demonstrate but exhibit it, and testify, as from heart to heart, that it is still possible, still practicable.

Johnson, in the eighteenth century, and as Man of Letters, was one of such; and, in good truth, "the bravest of the brave." What mortal could have more to war with? Yet, as we saw, he yielded not, faltered not; he fought, and even, such was his blessedness, prevailed. Whoso will understand what it is to have a man's heart, may find that, since the time of John Milton, no braver heart had beat in any English bosom than Samuel Johnson now bore. Observe too that he never called himself brave, never felt himself to be so; the more completely *was* so. No Giant Despair, no Golgotha-Death-dance or Sorcerer's-Sabbath of "Literary Life in London," appals this pilgrim; he works resolutely for deliverance; in still defiance, steps stoutly along. The thing that is given him to do he can make himself do; what is to be endured he can endure in silence.

How the great soul of old Samuel, consuming daily his own bitter unalleviable allotment of misery and toil, shows beside the poor flimsy little soul of young Boswell; one day flaunting in the ring of vanity, tarrying by the wine-cup, and crying, Aha, the wine is red; the next day deploring his downpressed, night-shaded, quite poor estate; and thinking it unkind that the whole movement of the Universe should go on, while *his* digestive-apparatus had stopped! We reckon Johnson's "talent of silence" to be among his great and too rare gifts. Where there is nothing farther to be done, there shall nothing farther be said: like his own poor blind Welshwoman, he accomplished somewhat, and also "endured fifty years of wretchedness with unshaken fortitude." How grim was Life to him; a sick Prison-house and Doubting-castle! "His great business," he would profess, "was to escape from himself." Yet towards all this he has taken his position and resolution; can dismiss it all "with frigid indifference, having little to hope or to fear." Friends are stupid and pusillanimous and parsimonious; "wearied of his stay, yet offended at his departure:" it is the manner of the world. "By popular delusion," remarks he with a gigantic calmness, "illiterate writers will rise into renown:" it is portion of the History of English Literature; a perennial thing, this same popular delusion; and will—alter the character of the Language.

Closely connected with this quality of Valour, partly as springing from it, partly as protected by it, are the more recognisable qualities of Truthfulness in word and thought, and Honesty in action. There is a reciprocity of influence here: for as the realizing of Truthfulness and Honesty is the Life-light and great aim of Valour, so without Valour they cannot, in anywise, be realized. Now, in spite of all practical shortcomings, no one that sees into the significance of Johnson, will say that his prime object was not Truth. In conversation, doubtless, you may observe him, on occasion, fighting as if for victory;—and must pardon these ebulliences of a careless hour, which were not without temptation and provocation. Remark likewise two things; that such prize-arguings were ever on merely superficial debatable questions; and then that they were argued generally by the fair laws of battle, and logic-fence, by one cunning in that same. If their purpose was excusable, their effect was harmless, perhaps beneficial: that of taming noisy mediocrity, and showing it another side of a debatable matter; to see *both* sides of which was, for the first time, to see the Truth of it. In his Writings themselves, are errors enough, crabbed prepossessions enough, yet these also of a quite extraneous and accidental nature; nowhere a wilful shutting of the eyes to the Truth. Nay, is there not everywhere a heartfelt discernment, singular, almost admirable, if we consider through what confused conflicting lights and hallucinations it had to be attained, of the highest everlasting Truth, and beginning of all Truths: this, namely, that man is ever, and even in the age of Wilkes and Whitfield, a Revelation of God to man; and lives, moves, and has his being in Truth only; is either true, or, in strict speech, *is* not at all?

Quite spotless, on the other hand, is Johnson's love of Truth, if we look at it as expressed in Practice, as what we have named Honesty of action. "Clear your mind of Cant;" *clear* it, throw Cant utterly away: such was his emphatic, repeated precept; and did not he himself faithfully conform to it? The Life of this man has been, as it were, turned inside out, and examined with microscopes by friend and foe; yet was there no Lie found in him. His Doings and Writings are not *shows* but *performances*: you may weigh them in the balance, and they will stand weight. Not a line, not a sentence is dishonestly done, is other than it pretends to be. Alas! and he wrote not out of inward inspiration, but to earn his wages: and with that grand perennial tide of "popular delusion" flowing by; in whose waters he nevertheless refused to fish, to whose rich oyster-beds the dive was too muddy for him. Observe, again, with what innate hatred of Cant, he takes for himself, and offers to others the lowest possible view of his business, which he followed with such nobleness. Motive for writing he had none, as he often said, but money; and yet he wrote *so*. Into the region of Poetic Art he indeed never rose; there was no *ideal* without him avowing itself in his work: the nobler was that unavowed *ideal* which lay within him, and commanded, saying, Work out thy Artisanship in the spirit of an Artist! They who talk loudest about the dignity of Art, and fancy that they too are Artistic guild-brethren, and of the Celestials,—let them consider well what manner of man this was, who felt himself to be only a hired day-labourer. A labourer that was worthy of his hire; that has laboured not as an eye-servant, but as one found faithful! Neither was Johnson in those days perhaps wholly a unique. Time was when, for money, you might have ware: and needed not, in all departments, in that of the Epic Poem, in that of the Blacking Bottle, to rest content with the mere *persuasion* that you had ware. It was a happier time. But as yet the seventh Apocalyptic Bladder (of PUFFERY) had not been rent open,—to whirl and grind, as in a West-Indian Tornado, all earthly trades and things into wreck, and dust, and consummation,—and regeneration. Be it quickly, since it must be!—

That Mercy can dwell only with Valour, is an old sentiment or proposition; which, in Johnson, again receives confirmation. Few men on record have had a more merciful, tenderly affectionate nature than old Samuel. He was called the Bear; and did indeed too often look, and roar, like one; being forced to it in his own defence: yet within that shaggy exterior of his, there beat a heart warm as a mother's, soft as a little child's. Nay generally, his very roaring was but the anger of affection: the rage of a Bear, if you will; but of a Bear bereaved of her whelps. Touch his Religion, glance at the Church of England, or the Divine Right; and he was upon you! These things were his Symbols of all that was good, and precious for men; his very Ark of the Covenant: whoso laid hand on them tore asunder his heart of hearts. Not out of hatred to the opponent, but of love to the thing opposed, did Johnson grow cruel, fiercely contradictory: this is an important distinction; never to be forgotten in our censure of his conversational outrages. But observe also with what humanity, what openness of love, he can attach himself to all things: to a blind old woman, to a Doctor Levett, to a Cat "Hodge." "His thoughts in the latter part of his life were frequently employed on his deceased friends; he often muttered these or such-like sentences: "Poor man! and then he died." How he patiently converts his poor home into a Lazaretto; endures, for long years, the contradiction of the miserable and unreasonable; with him unconnected, save that they had no other to yield them refuge! Generous old man! Worldly possession he has little; yet of this he gives freely; from his own hard-earned shilling, the half-pence for the poor, that "waited his coming out," are not withheld: the poor "waited the coming out" of one not quite so poor! A Sterne can write sentimentalities on Dead Asses: Johnson has a rough voice; but he finds the wretched Daughter of Vice fallen down in the streets; carries her home, on his own shoulders, and like a good Samaritan, gives help to the help-needing, worthy or unworthy. Ought not Charity, even in that sense, to cover a multitude of Sins? No Penny-a-week Committee-Lady, no manager of Soup-Kitchens, dancer at Charity Balls, was this rugged, stern-visaged man: but where, in all England, could there have been found another soul so full of Pity, a hand so heavenlike bounteous as his? The widow's mite, we know, was greater than all the other gifts.

Perhaps it is this divine feeling of Affection, throughout manifested, that principally attracts us towards Johnson. A true brother of men is he; and filial lover of the Earth; who, with little bright spots of Attachment, "where lives and works some loved one," has beautified "this rough solitary Earth into a peopled garden." Litchfield, with its mostly dull and limited inhabitants, is to the last one of the sunny islets for him: *Salve magna parens!* Or read those Letters on his Mother's death: what a genuine solemn grief and pity lies recorded there; a looking back into the Past, unspeakably mournful, unspeakably tender. And yet calm, sublime; for he must now act, not look: his venerated Mother has been taken from him; but he must now write a *Rasselas* to defray her interment! Again in this little incident, recorded in his Book of Devotion, are not the tones of sacred Sorrow and Greatness deeper than in many a blank-verse Tragedy; as, indeed, "the fifth act of a Tragedy" (though unrhymed) does "lie in every death-bed, were it a peasant's, and of straw:"

"Sunday, October 18, 1767. Yesterday, at about ten in the morning, I took my leave for ever of my dear old friend, Catherine Chambers, who came to live with my mother about 1724, and has been but little parted from us since. She buried my father, my brother, and my mother. She is now fifty-eight years old.

"I desired all to withdraw; then told her that we were to part for ever; that as Christians, we should part with prayer; and that I would, if she was willing, say a short prayer beside her. She expressed great desire to hear me; and held up her poor hands as she lay in bed, with great fervour, while I prayed kneeling by her. * * *

"I then kissed her. She told me that to part was the greatest pain she had ever felt, and that she hoped we should meet again in a better place. I expressed with swelled eyes, and great emotion of tenderness, the same hopes. We kissed and parted; I humbly hope, to meet again, and to part no more."

Tears trickling down the granite rock: a soft swell of Pity springs within! Still more tragical is this other scene: "Johnson mentioned that he could not in general accuse himself of having been an undutiful son. "Once indeed," said he, "I was disobedient: I refused to attend my father to Uttoxeter market. Pride was the source of that refusal, and the remembrance of it was painful. A few years ago I desired to atone for this fault."—But by what method?—What method was now possible? Hear it; the words are again given as his own, though here evidently by a less capable reporter:

"Madam, I beg your pardon for the abruptness of my departure in the morning, but I was compelled to do it by conscience. Fifty years ago, Madam, on this day, I committed a breach of filial piety. My father had been in the habit of attending Uttoxeter market, and opening a stall there for the sale of his Books. Confined by indisposition, he desired me, that day, to go and attend the stall in his place. My pride prevented me; I gave my father a refusal.—And now to-day I have been at Uttoxeter; I went into the market, at the time of business, uncovered my head, and stood with it bare, for an hour, on the spot where my father's stall used to stand. In contrition I stood, and I hope the penance was expiatory."

Who does not figure to himself this spectacle, amid the "rainy weather, and the sneers," or wonder, "of the by-standers?" The memory of old Michael Johnson, rising from the far distance; sad-beckoning in the "moonlight of memory:" how he had toiled faithfully hither and thither; patiently among the lowest of the low; been buffetted and beaten down, yet ever risen again, ever tried it anew—And oh! when the wearied old man, as Bookseller, or Hawker, or Tinker, or whatsoever it was that Fate had reduced him to, begged help of *thee* for one day,—how savage, diabolic, was that mean Vanity, which answered, No! He sleeps now; after life's fitful fever, he sleeps: but thou, O Merciless, how now wilt thou still the sting of that remembrance?—The picture of Samuel Johnson standing bareheaded in the market there, is one of the grandest and saddest we can paint. "Repentance! Repentance!" he proclaims, as with passionate sobs:—but only to the ear of Heaven, if Heaven will give him audience: the earthly ear, and heart, that should have heard it, are now closed, unresponsive for ever.

That this so keen-loving, soft-trembling Affectionateness, the inmost essence of his being, must have looked forth, in one form or another, through Johnson's whole character, practical and intellectual, modifying both, is not to be doubted. Yet through what singular distortions and superstitions, moping melancholies, blind habits, whims about "entering with the right foot," and "touching every post as he walked along;" and all the other mad chaotic lumber of a brain that, with sun-clear intellect, hovered for ever on the verge of insanity,—must that same inmost essence have looked forth; unrecognisable to all but the most observant! Accordingly it was not recognised; Johnson passed not for a fine nature, but for a dull, almost brutal one. Might not, for example, the first-fruit of such a Lovingness, coupled with his quick Insight, have been expected to be a peculiarly courteous demeanour as man among men? In Johnson's "Politeness," which he often, to the wonder of some, asserted to be great, there was indeed somewhat that needed explanation. Nevertheless, if he insisted always on handing lady-visitors to their carriage; though with the certainty of collecting a mob of gazers in Fleet Street,—as might well be, the beau having on, by way of court dress, "his rusty brown morning suit, a pair of old shoes for slippers, a little shrivelled wig sticking on the top of his head, and the sleeves of his shirt and the knees of his breeches hanging loose:"—in all this we can see the spirit of true Politeness, only shining through a strange medium. Thus again, in his apartments, at one time, there were unfortunately no chairs. "A gentleman who frequently visited him whilst writing his *Idlers*, constantly found him at his desk, sitting on one with three legs; and on rising from it, he remarked that Johnson never forgot its defect; but would either hold it in his hand, or place it with great composure against some support; taking no notice of its imperfection to his visitor,"—who meanwhile, we suppose, sat upon folios, or in the sartorial fashion. "It was remarkable in Johnson," continues Miss Reynolds, ("Renny dear,") "that no external circumstances ever prompted him to make any apology, or to seem even sensible of their existence. Whether this was the effect of philosophic pride, or of some partial notion of his respecting high breeding, is doubtful." That it *was*, for one thing, the effect of genuine Politeness, is nowise doubtful. Not of the Pharisaical Brummellian Politeness, which would suffer crucifixion rather than ask twice for soup: but the noble universal Politeness of a man, that knows the dignity of men, and feels his own; such as may be seen in the patriarchial bearing of an Indian Sachem; such as Johnson himself exhibited, when a sudden chance brought him into dialogue with his King. To us, with our view of the man, it nowise appears "strange" that he should have boasted himself cunning in the laws of Politeness; nor "stranger still," habitually attentive to practise them.

More legibly is this influence of the Loving heart to be traced in his intellectual character. What, indeed, is the beginning of intellect, the first inducement to the exercise thereof, but attraction towards somewhat, *affection* for it? Thus too, who ever saw, or will see, any true talent, not to speak of genius, the foundation of which is not goodness, love? From Johnson's strength of Affection, we deduce many of his intellectual peculiarities; especially that threatening array of perversions, known under the name of "Johnson's Prejudices." Looking well into the root from which these sprung, we have long ceased to view them with hostility, can pardon and reverently pity them. Consider with what force early-imbibed opinions must have clung to a soul of this Affection. Those evil-famed Prejudices of his, that Jacobitism, Church-of-Englandism, hatred of the Scotch, belief in Witches, and such like, what were they but the ordinary beliefs of well-doing, well-meaning provincial Englishmen in that day? First gathered by his Father's hearth; round the kind "country fires" of native Staffordshire; they grew with his growth and strengthened with his strength: they were hallowed by fondest sacred recollections: to part with them was parting with his heart's blood. If the man who has no strength of Affection, strength of Belief, have no strength of Prejudice, let him thank Heaven for it, but to himself take small thanks.

Melancholy it was, indeed, that the noble Johnson could not work himself loose from these adhesions; that he could only purify them, and wear them with some nobleness. Yet let us understand how they grew out from the very centre of his being: nay, moreover, how they came to cohere in him with what formed the business and worth of his Life, the sum of his whole Spiritual Endeavour. For it is on the same ground that he became throughout an Edifier and Repairer, not, as the others of his make were, a Puller-down; that in an age of universal Skepticism, England was still to produce its Believer. Mark too his candour even here; while a Dr. Adams, with placid surprise, asks, "Have we not evidence enough of the soul's immortality?" Johnson answers, "I wish for more." But the truth is, in Prejudice, as in all things, Johnson was the product of England; one of those *good* yeomen whose limbs were made in England: alas, the last of *such* Invincibles, their day being now done! His culture is wholly English; that not of a Thinker but of a "Scholar:" his interests are wholly English; he sees and knows nothing but England; he is the John Bull of Spiritual Europe: let him live, love him, as he was and could not but be! Pitiable it is, no doubt, that a Samuel Johnson must confute Hume's irreligious Philosophy by some "story from a Clergyman of the Bishopric of Durham;" should see nothing in the great Frederick but "Voltaire's lackey;" in Voltaire himself but a man *acerrimi ingenii, paucarum literarum;* in Rousseau but one worthy to be hanged; and in the universal, long-prepared, inevitable Tendency of European Thought but a greensick milkmaid's crotchet of (for variety's sake) "milking the Bull." Our good, dear John! Observe too what it is that he sees in the city of Paris: no feeblest glimpse of those D'Alemberts and Diderots, or of the strange questionable work they did; solely some Benedictine Priests, to talk kitchen-latin with them about *Editiones Principes*. "*Monsheer Nongtongpaw!*"—Our dear, foolish John; yet is there a lion's heart within him!—Pitiable all these things were, we say; yet nowise inexcusable; nay, as basis or as foil to much else that was in Johnson, almost venerable. Ought we not, indeed, to honour England, and English Institutions and Way of Life, that they could still equip such a man; could furnish him in heart and head to be a Samuel Johnson, and yet to love them, and unyieldingly fight for them? What truth and living vigour must such Institutions once have had, when, in the middle of the Eighteenth century, there was still enough left in them for this!

It is worthy of note that, in our little British Isle, the two grand Antagonisms of Europe should have stood imbodied, under their very highest concentration, in two men produced simultaneously among ourselves. Samuel Johnson and David Hume, as was observed, were children of the same year: through life they were spectators of the same Life-movement; often inhabitants of the same city. Greater contrast, in all things, between two great men, could not be. Hume, well-born, competently provided for, whole in body and mind, of his own determination forces a way into Literature: Johnson, poor, moonstruck, diseased, forlorn, is forced into it "with the bayonet of necessity at his back." And what a part did they severally play there! As Johnson became the father of all succeeding Tories; so was Hume the father of all succeeding Whigs, for his own Jacobitism was but an accident, as worthy to be named Prejudice as any of Johnson's. Again, if Johnson's culture was exclusively English; Hume's, in Scotland, became European;—for which reason too we find his influence spread deeply over all quarters of Europe, traceable deeply in all speculation, French, German, as well as domestic; while Johnson's name, out of England, is hardly anywhere to be met with. In spiritual stature they are almost equal; both great, among the greatest: yet how unlike in likeness! Hume has the widest methodizing, comprehensive eye; Johnson the keenest for perspicacity and minute detail: so had, perhaps chiefly, their education ordered it. Neither of the two rose into Poetry; yet both to some approximation thereof: Hume to something of an Epic clearness and method, as in his delineation of the Commonwealth Wars; Johnson to many a deep Lyric tone of plaintiveness, and impetuous graceful power, scattered over his fugitive compositions. Both, rather to the general surprise, had a certain rugged Humour shining through their earnestness: the indication, indeed, that they *were* earnest men, and had *subdued* their wild world into a kind of temporary home, and safe dwelling. Both were, by principle and habit, Stoics: yet Johnson with the greater merit, for he alone had very much to triumph over; farther, he alone ennobled his Stoicism into Devotion. To Johnson Life was as a Prison, to be endured with heroic faith: to Hume it was little more than a foolish Bartholomew-Fair Show-booth, with the foolish crowdings and elbowings of which it was not worth while to quarrel; the whole would break up, and be at liberty, so *soon*. Both realized the highest task of Manhood, that of living like men; each died not unfitly, in his way: Hume as one, with factitious, half-false gayety, taking leave of what was itself wholly but a Lie: Johnson as one, with awe-struck, yet resolute and piously expectant heart, taking leave of a Reality, to enter a Reality still higher. Johnson had the harder problem of it, from first to last: whether, with some hesitation, we can admit that he was intrinsically the better-gifted, —may remain undecided.

These two men now rest; the one in Westminster Abbey here; the other in the Calton Hill Churchyard of Edinburgh. Through Life they did not meet: as contrasts, "like in unlike," love each other; so might they two have loved, and communed kindly,—had not the terrestrial dross and darkness, that was in them, withstood! One day their spirits, what truth was in each, will be found working, living in harmony and free union, even here below. They were the two half-men of their time: whoso should combine the intrepid Candour, and decisive scientific Clearness of Hume, with the Reverence, the Love, and devout Humility of Johnson, were the whole man of a new time. Till such whole man arrive for us, and the distracted time admit of such, might the heavens but bless poor England with half-men worthy to tie the shoe-latchets of these, resembling these even from afar! Be both attentively regarded, let the true Effort of both prosper;—and for the present, both take our affectionate farewell!

DEATH OF GOETHE.

[NEW MONTHLY MAGAZINE, 1832.]

IN the obituary of these days stands one article of quite peculiar import; the time, the place, and particulars of which will have to be often repeated, and re-written, and continue in remembrance many centuries: this, namely, that Johann Wolfgang von Goethe died at Weimar, on the 22d March, 1832. It was about eleven in the morning; "he expired," says the record, "without any apparent suffering, having a few minutes previously, called for paper for the purpose of writing, and expressed his delight at the arrival of spring." A beautiful death; like that of a soldier found faithful at his post, and in the cold hand his arms still grasped! The Poet's last words are a greeting of the new-awakened earth; his last movement is to work at his appointed task. Beautiful: what we might call a Classic, sacred death; if it were not rather an Elijah-translation,—in a chariot, not of fire and terror, but of hope and soft vernal sunbeams! It was at Frankfort on the Mayn, on the 28th of August, 1749, that this man entered the world—and now, gently welcoming the birth-day of his eighty-second spring, he closes his eyes, and takes farewell.

So then, our greatest has departed. That melody of life, with its cunning tones, which took captive ear and heart, has gone silent; the heavenly force that dwelt here victorious over so much, is here no longer; thus far, not farther, by speech and by act, shall the wise man utter himself forth. The End! What solemn meaning lies in that sound, as it peals mournfully through the soul, when a living friend has passed away! All now is closed, irrevocable; the changeful life-picture, growing daily into new coherence, under new touches and hues, has suddenly become completed and unchangeable; there, as it lay, it is dipped, from this moment, in the æther of the Heavens, and shines transfigured, to endure even so—for ever, Time and Time's Empire; stern, wide devouring, yet not without their grandeur! The week-day man, who was one of us, has put on the garment of Eternity, and become radiant and triumphant; the present is all at once the past; Hope is suddenly cut away, and only the backward vistas of Memory remain, shone on by a light that proceeds not from this earthly sun.

The death of Goethe, even for the many hearts that personally loved him, is not a thing to be lamented over; is to be viewed, in his own spirit, as a thing full of greatness and sacredness. "For all men it is appointed once to die." To this man the full measure of a man's life had been granted, and a course and task such as to only a few in the whole generations of the world; what else could we hope or require but that now he should be called hence and have leave to depart, "having finished the work that was given him to do?" If his course, as we may say of him more justly than of any other, was like the Sun's, so also was his going down. For indeed, as the material Sun is the eye and revealer of all things, so is Poetry, so is the World-Poet in a spiritual sense. Goethe's life, too, if we examine it, is well represented in that emblem of a solar Day. Beautifully rose our summer sun, gorgeous in the red fervid East, scattering the spectres and sickly damps (of both of which there were enough to scatter)—strong, benignant in his noon-day clearness, walking triumphant through the upper realms; and now, mark also how he sets! *So Stirbt ein Held: anbetungsvoll!* "So dies a hero; sight to be worshipped."

And yet, when the inanimate, material sun has sunk and disappeared, it will happen that we stand to gaze into the still glowing West; and here rise great, pale, motionless clouds, like coulisses or curtains, to close the flame-theatre within; and then, in that death-pause of the Day, an unspeakable feeling will come over us; it is as if the poor sounds of Time, those hammerings of tired Labour on his anvils, those voices of simple men, had become awful and supernatural; as if in listening, we could hear them "mingle with the ever-pealing tones of old Eternity." In such moments the secrets of Life lie opener to us; mysterious things flit over the soul; Life itself seems holier, wonderful, and fearful. How much more when our sunset was of a living sun; and *its* bright countenance and shining return to us, not on the morrow, but "no more again, at all, for ever!" In such a scene, silence, as over the mysterious great, is for him that has some feeling thereof, the fittest mood. Nevertheless by silence, the distant is not brought into communion: the feeling of each is without response from the bosom of his brother. There are now, what some years ago there were not, English hearts that know something of what those three words, "Death of Goethe," mean; to such men, among their many thoughts on the event, which are not to be translated into speech, may these few, through that imperfect medium, prove acceptable.

"Death," says the Philosopher, "is a commingling of Eternity with Time; in the death of a good man, Eternity is seen looking through Time." With such a sublimity here offered to eye and heart, it is not unnatural to look with new earnestness before and behind, and ask, what space in those years and æons of computed Time, this man with his activity may influence; what relation to the world of change and mortality, which the earthly name Life, he who is even now called to the Immortals has borne and may bear.

Goethe, it is commonly said, made a new era in Literature; a Poetic era began with him, the end or ulterior tendencies of which are yet nowise generally visible. This common saying is a true one, and true with a far deeper meaning than, to the most, it conveys Were the Poet but a sweet sound and singer, solacing the ear of the idle with pleasant songs, and the new Poet one who could sing his idle, pleasant song, to a new air, we should account him a small matter, and his performance small. But this man, it is not unknown to many, was a Poet in such a sense as the late generations have witnessed no other; as it is, in this generation, a kind of distinction to believe in the existence of, in the possibility of. The true Poet is ever, as of old, the Seer; whose eye has been gifted to discern the godlike mystery of God's universe, and decipher some new lines of its celestial writing; we can still call him a *Vates* and Seer; for he *sees* into this greatest of secrets "the open secret;" hidden things become clear; how the future (both resting on Eternity) is but another phasis of the present; thereby are his words in very truth prophetic; what he has spoken shall be done.

It begins now to be everywhere surmised that the real Force, which in this world all things must obey, is Insight, Spiritual Vision, and Determination. The Thought is parent of the Deed, nay, is living soul of it, and last and continual, as well as first mover of it; is the foundation, and beginning, and essence, therefore, of man's whole existence here below. In this sense, it has been said, the WORD of man (the uttered thoughts of man) is still a magic formula, whereby he rules the world. Do not the winds and waters, and all tumultuous powers, inanimate and animate, obey him? A poor, quite mechanical, Magician speaks—and fire-winged ships cross the ocean at his bidding. Or mark, above all, that "raging of the nations," wholly in contention, desperation, and dark chaotic fury; how the meek voice of a Hebrew Martyr and Redeemer stills it into order, and a savage Earth becomes kind and beautiful, and the "habitation of horrid cruelty" a temple of peace. The true sovereign of the world, who moulds the world like soft wax, according to his pleasure, is he who lovingly *sees* into the world; the "inspired Thinker," whom in these days we name Poet. The true sovereign is the Wise Man.

However, as the Moon, which can heave up the Atlantic, sends not in her obedient billows at once, but gradually; and, for example, the Tide, which swells to-day on our shores, and washes every creek, rose in the bosom of the great ocean (astronomers assure us) eight and forty hours ago; and indeed all world-movements, by nature deep, are by nature calm, and flow and swell onwards with a certain majestic slowness—so, too, with the impulse of a Great Man, and the effect he has to manifest on other men. To such an one we may grant some generation or two before the celestial impulse he impressed on the world will universally proclaim itself, and become (like the working of the moon) if still not intelligible, yet palpable, to all men; some generation or two more, wherein it has to grow, and expand, and envelop all things, before it can reach its acme; and thereafter mingling with other movements and new impulses, at length cease to require a specific observation or designation. Longer or shorter such period may be, according to the nature of the impulse itself, and of the elements it works in; according, above all, as the impulse was intrinsically great and deep-reaching, or only wide-spread, superficial, and transient. Thus, if David Hume is at this hour pontiff of the world, and rules most hearts, and guides most tongues, (the hearts and tongues, even in those that in vain rebel against him,) there are, nevertheless, symptoms that his task draws towards completion; and now in the distance his successor becomes visible. On the other hand, we have seen a Napoleon, like some gunpowder force (with which sort he, indeed, was appointed chiefly to work) explode his whole virtue suddenly, and thunder himself out and silent, in a space of five-and-twenty years. While again, for a man of true greatness, working with spiritual implements, two centuries is no uncommon period; nay, on this Earth of ours, there have been men whose impulse had not completed its development till after fifteen hundred years, and might, perhaps, be seen still individually subsistent after two thousand.

But, as was once written, "though our clock strikes when there is a change from hour to hour, no hammer in the horologe of time peals through the universe to proclaim that there is a change from era to era." The true beginning is oftenest unnoticed, and unnoticeable. Thus do men go wrong in their reckoning; and grope hither and thither, not knowing where they are, in what course their history runs. Within this last century, for instance, with its wild doings and destroyings, what hope, grounded in miscalculation, ending in disappointment! How many world-famous victories were gained and lost, dynasties founded and subverted, revolutions accomplished, constitutions sworn to; and ever the "new era" was come, was coming, yet still it came not, but the time continued sick! Alas, all these were but spasmodic convulsions of the death-sick time; the crisis of cure and regeneration to the time was not there indicated. The real new era was when a Wise Man came into the world, with clearness of vision and greatness of soul to accomplish this old high enterprise, amid these new difficulties, yet again: A Life of Wisdom. Such a man became, by Heaven's pre-appointment, in very deed, the Redeemer of the time. Did he not bear the curse of the time? He was filled full with its skepticism, bitterness, hollowness, and thousandfold contradictions, till his heart was like to break; but he subdued all this, rose victorious over this, and manifoldly by word and act showed others that come after, how to do the like. Honour to him who first, "through the impassable, paves a road!" Such indeed is the task of every great man; nay, of every good man in one or the other sphere, since goodness is greatness, and the good man, high or humble, is ever a martyr, and a "spiritual hero that ventures forward into the gulf for our deliverance." The gulf into which this man ventured, which he tamed and rendered habitable, was the greatest and most perilous of all, wherein truly all others lie included: *The whole distracted Existence of man in an age of unbelief.* Whoso lives, whoso with earnest mind studies to live wisely in that mad element, may yet know, perhaps, too well, what an enterprise was here; and for the chosen of our time, who could prevail in that same, have the higher reverence, and a gratitude such as belong to no other.

How far he prevailed in it, and by what means, with what endurances and achievements, will in due season be estimated; those volumes called *Goethe's Works,* will receive no further addition or alteration; and the record of his whole spiritual Endeavour lies written there,—were the man or men but ready who could read it rightly! A glorious record; wherein he that would understand himself and his environment, and struggles for escape out of darkness into light, as for the one thing needful, will long thankfully study. For the whole chaotic time, what it has suffered, attained, and striven after, stands imaged there; interpreted, ennobled into poetic clearness. From the passionate longings and wailings of "Werter" spoken as from the heart of all Europe; onwards through the wild unearthly melody of "Faust" (like the spirit song of falling worlds;) to that serenely smiling wisdom of "Meisters Lehrjahre," and the "German Hafiz,"—what an interval; and all enfolded in an ethereal music, as from unknown spheres, harmoniously uniting all! A long interval; and wide as well as long; for this was a universal man. History, Science, Art, human Activity under every aspect; the laws of light in his "Farbenlehre;" the laws of wild Italian life in his "Benvenuto Cellini;"—nothing escaped him, nothing that he did not look into, that he did not see into. Consider too the genuineness of whatsoever he did; his hearty, idiomatic way; simplicity with loftiness, and nobleness, and aerial grace.—Pure works of art, completed with an antique Grecian polish as "Torquato Tasso," as "Iphigenie," Proverbs; "Xenien;" Patriarchal Sayings, which, since the Hebrew Scriptures were closed, we know not where to match; in whose homely depths lie often the materials for volumes.

To measure and estimate all this, as we said, the time is not come; a century hence will be the fitter time. He who investigates it best will find its meaning greatest, and be the readiest to acknowledge that it transcends him.—Let the reader have *seen*, before he attempts to *oversee*. A poor reader, in the meanwhile were he, who discerned not here the authentic rudiments of that same New Era, whereof we have so often had false warning. Wondrously, the wrecks and pulverized rubbish of ancient things, institutions, religions, forgotten noblenesses, made alive again by the breath of Genius, lie here in new coherence and incipient union, the spirit of Art working creative through the mass: that *chaos*, into which the eighteenth century with its wild war of hypocrites and skeptics had reduced the Past, begins here to be once more a *world*.—This, the highest that can be said of written books, is to be said of these; there is in them a new time, the prophecy and beginning of a new time. The corner stone of a new social edifice for mankind is laid there; firmly, as before, on the natural rock, far extending traces of a ground-plan we can also see, which future centuries may go on to enlarge, amend, and work into reality. These sayings seem strange to some; nevertheless they are not empty exaggerations, but expressions, in their way, of a belief, which is not now of yesterday; perhaps when Goethe has been read and meditated for another generation, they will not seem so strange.

Precious is the new light of knowledge which our teacher conquers for us; yet small to the new light of Love which also we derive from him; the most important element of any man's performance is the life he has accomplished. Under the intellectual union of man and man, which works by precept, lies a holier union of affection, working by example: the influences of which latter, mystic, deep-reaching, all-embracing, can still less be computed. For Love is ever the beginning of Knowledge, as fire is of light; works also more in the manner of *fire*. That Goethe was a great teacher of men, means already that he was a good man; that he himself learned; in the school of experience had striven and proved victorious. To how many hearers languishing, nigh dead, in the airless dungeon of Unbelief (a true vacuum and nonentity) has the assurance that there was such a man, that such a man was still possible, come like tidings of great joy! He who would learn to reconcile Reverence with clearness, to deny and defy what is false, yet believe and worship what is true; amid raging factions, bent on what is either altogether empty or has substance in it only for a day, which stormfully convulse and tear hither and thither a distracted, expiring system of society, to adjust himself aright: and, working for the world, and in the world, keep himself unspotted from the world,—let him look here. This man, we may say, became morally great, by being in his own age what in some other ages many might have been—a genuine man. His grand excellency was this, that he was genuine. As his primary faculty, the foundation of all others, was Intellect, depth and force of Vision, so his primary virtue was Justice, was the courage to be just. A giant's strength we admired in him; yet, strength ennobled into softest mildness; even like that "silent rock-bound strength of a world," on whose bosom, that rests on the adamant, grow flowers. The greatest of hearts was also the bravest: fearless, unwearied, peacefully invincible. A completed man; the trembling sensibility, the wild enthusiasm of a Mignon, can assort with the scornful world-mockery of a Mephistophiles; and each side of many-sided life receives its due from him.

Goethe reckoned Schiller happy that he died young, in the full vigour of his days: that he could "figure him as a youth for ever." To himself a different, higher destiny was appointed. Through all the changes of man's life, onwards to its extreme verge, he was to go; and through them all nobly. In youth, flatterings of fortune, uninterrupted outward prosperity cannot corrupt him; a wise observer must remark, "only a Goethe, at the sum of earthly happiness, can keep his Phœnix-wings unsinged."—Through manhood, in the most complex relation, as poet, courtier, politician, man of business, man of speculation; in the middle of revolutions and counter-revolutions, outward and spiritual; with the world loudly for him, with the world loudly or silently against him; in all seasons and situations, he holds equally on his way. Old age itself, which is called dark and feeble, he was to render lovely: who that looked upon him there, venerable in himself, and in the world's reverence, ever the clearer, the purer, but could have prayed that he too were such an old man? And did not the kind Heavens continue kind, and grant to a career so glorious the worthiest end?

Such was Goethe's life; such has his departure been—he sleeps now beside his Schiller and his Carl August: so had the Prince willed it, that between these two should be his own final rest. In life they were united, in death they are not divided. The unwearied Workman now rests from his labours; the fruit of these is left growing, and to grow. His earthly years have been numbered and ended: but of his activity (for it stood rooted in the Eternal) there is no end. All that we mean by the higher Literature of Germany, which is the higher Literature of Europe, already gathers round this man, as its creator; of which grand object, dawning mysterious on a world that hoped not for it, who is there that can assume the significance and far-reaching influences? The Literature of Europe will pass away; Europe itself, the Earth itself will pass away; this little life-boat of an Earth, with its noisy crew of Mankind, and all their troubled History, will one day have vanished, faded like a cloud-speck from the azure of the All! What then is man? What then is man? He endures but for an hour, and is crushed before the moth. Yet in the being and in the working of a faithful man is there already (as all faith, from the beginning, gives assurance) a something that pertains not to this wild death-element of TIME; that triumphs over Time, and *is*, and will be, when Time shall be no more.

And now we turn back into the world, withdrawing from this new made grave. The man whom we love lies there: but glorious, worthy: and his spirit yet lives in us with an authentic life. Could each here vow to do his little task, even as the Departed did his great one; in the manner of a true man, not for a Day, but for Eternity! To live, as he counselled and commanded, not commodiously in the Reputable, the Plausible, the Half, but resolutely in the Whole, the Good, the True:

"Im Ganzen, Guten, Wahren resolut zu leben!

GOETHE'S WORKS.*

[FOREIGN QUARTERLY REVIEW, 1832.]

IT is now four years since we specially invited attention to this Book; first in an essay on the graceful little fantasy-piece of *Helena*, then in a more general one on the merits and workings of Goethe himself: since which time two important things have happened in reference to it; for the publication, advancing with successful regularity, reached its fortieth and last volume in 1830; and now, still more emphatically to conclude both this "completed final edition," and all other editions, endeavours and attainments of one in whose hands lay so much, come tidings that the venerable man has been recalled from our earth, and of his long labours and high faithful stewardship we have had what was appointed us.

The greatest epoch in a man's life is not always his death; yet for bystanders, such as contemporaries, it is always the most noticeable. All other epochs are transition-points from one visible condition to another visible; the days of their occurrence are like any other days, from which only the clearer-sighted will distinguish them; bridges they are, over which the smooth highway runs continuous, as if no Rubicon were there. But the day in a mortal's destinies which is like no other, is his death-day: here too is a transition, what we may call a bridge, as at other epochs; but now from the keystone onwards half the arch rests on invisibility; this is a transition out of visible Time into invisible Eternity.

Since death, as the palpable revelation (not to be overlooked by the dullest) of the mystery of wonder, and depth, and fear, which everywhere from beginning to ending through its whole course and movement lies under life, is in any case so great, we find it not unnatural that hereby a new look of greatness, a new interest should be impressed on whatsoever has preceded it and led to it; that even towards some man, whose history did not then first become significant, the world should turn, at his departure, with a quite peculiar earnestness, and now seriously ask itself a question, perhaps never seriously asked before: What the purport and character of his presence here was: now when he has gone hence, and is not present here, and will remain absent for evermore. It is the conclusion that crowns the work; much more the irreversible conclusion wherein all is concluded: thus is there no life so mean but a death will make it memorable.

At all lykewakes, accordingly, the doings and endurances of the Departed are the theme: rude souls, rude tongues grow eloquently busy with him; a whole septuagint of beldames are striving to render, in such dialect as they have, the small bible, or apochrypha, of his existence, for the general perusal. The least famous of mankind will for once become public, and have his name printed, and read not without interest: in the Newspaper obituaries; on some frail memorial, under which he has crept to sleep. Foolish lovesick girls know that there is one method to impress the obdurate, false Lovelace, and wring his bosom; the method of drowning: foolish ruined dandies, whom the tailor will no longer trust, and the world turning on its heel is about forgetting, can recall it to attention by report of pistol; and so, in a worthless death, if in a worthless life no more, re-attain the top-gallant of renown,—for one day. Death is ever a sublimity, and supernatural wonder, were there no other left: the last act of a most strange drama, which is not dramatic but has now become real: wherein, miraculously, Furies, god-missioned, have in actual person risen from the abyss, and do verily dance there in that terror of all terrors, and wave their dusky-glaring torches, and shake their serpent-hair! Out of which heart-thrilling, so authentically tragic fifth act there goes, as we said, a new meaning over all the other four: making them likewise tragic and authentic, and memorable in some measure, were they formerly the sorriest pickle-herring farce.

But above all, when a Great Man dies, then has the time come for putting us in mind that he was alive: biographies and biographic sketches, criticisms, characters, anecdotes

* *Goethes Werke. Vollständige Ausgabe letzer Hand,* (Goethe's Works. Completed, final edition,) 40 voll. Stuttgard and Tübingen. 1827-30.

reminiscences, issue forth as from opened springing fountains; the world, with a passion whetted by impossibility, will yet a while retain, yet a while speak with, though only to the unanswering echoes, what it has lost without remedy: thus is the last event of life often the loudest; and real spiritual *Apparitions*, (who have been named Men,) as false imaginary ones are fabled to do, vanish in thunder.

For ourselves, as regards the great beauty, if not seeking to be foremost in this natural movement, neither do we shun to mingle in it. The life and ways of such men as he, are, in all seasons, a matter profitable to contemplate, to speak of; if in this death season, long with a sad reverence looked forward to, there has little increase of light, little change of feeling arisen for the writer, a readier attention, nay a certain expectance, from some readers is call sufficient. Innumerable meditations and disquisitions on this subject must yet pass through the minds of men; on all sides must it be taken up, by various observers, by successive generations, and ever a new light may evolve itself: why should not this observer, on this side, set down what he partially has seen into, and the necessary process thereby be forwarded, at any rate, continued?

A continental Humourist, of deep-piercing, resolute, though strangely perverse faculty, whose works are as yet but sparingly if at all cited in English literature, has written a chapter, somewhat in the nondescript manner of metaphysico-rhetorical, homiletic-exegetic rhapsody, on the *Greatness of great men;* which topic we agree with him in reckoning one of the most pregnant. The time, indeed, is come when much that was once found visibly subsistent Without must anew be sought for Within; many a human feeling, indestructible, and to man's well-being indispensable, which once manifested itself in expressive forms to the Sense, now lies hidden in the *formless* depths of the Spirit, or at best struggles out obscurely in forms become superannuated, altogether inexpressive, and unrecognisable; from which paralysed, imprisoned state, often the best effort of the thinker is required, and moreover were well applied, to deliver it. For if the Present is to be the "living sum-total of the whole Past," nothing that ever lived in the Past must be let wholly die; whatsoever was done, whatsoever was said or written aforetime, was done and written for our edification. In such state of imprisonment, paralysis and unrecognisable defacement, as compared with its condition in the old ages, lies this our feeling towards great men; wherein, and in the much that else belongs to it, some of the deepest human interests will be found involved. A few words from Herr Professor Teufelsdreck, if they help to set this preliminary matter in a clearer light, may be worth translating here. Let us first remark with him, however, "how wonderful in all cases, great or little, is the importance of man to man:"

"Deny it as he will," says Teufelsdreck, "man reverently loves man, and daily by action evidences his belief in the divineness of man. What a more than regal mystery encircles the poorest of living souls for us! The highest is not independent of him; his suffrage has value: could the highest monarch convince himself that the humblest beggar with sincere mind despised him, no serried ranks of halberdiers and body-guards could shut out some little twinge of pain; some emanation from the low had pierced into the bosom of the high. Of a truth, men are mystically united; a mystic bond of brotherhood makes all men one.

"Thus too has that fierce hunting after Popularity, which you often wonder at, and laugh at, a basis on something true: nay, under the other aspect, what is that wonderful spirit of Interference, were it but manifested as the paltriest scandal and tea-table backbiting, other than, inversely or directly, a heartfelt indestructible sympathy of man with man? Hatred itself is but an inverse love. The philosopher's wife complained to the philosopher that certain two-legged animals without feathers spake evil of him, spitefully criticised his goings out and comings in; wherein she too failed not of her share: 'Light of my life,' answered the philosopher, 'it is their love of us, unknown to themselves, and taking a foolish shape; thank them for it, and do thou love them more wisely. Were we mere steam-engines working here under this rooftree, they would scorn to speak of us once in a twelve-month.' The last stage of human perversion, it has been said, is when sympathy corrupts itself into envy; and the indestructible interest we take in men's doings has become a joy over their faults and misfortunes: this is the last and lowest stage; lower than this we cannot go: the absolute petrifaction of indifference is not attainable on this side total death.

"And now," continues the Professor, "rising from these lowest tea-table regions of human communion into the higher and highest, is there not still in the world's demeanour towards Great Men, enough to make the old practice of *Hero-worship* intelligible, nay, significant? Simpleton! I tell thee Hero-worship still continues; it is the only creed which never and nowhere grows or can grow obsolete. For always and everywhere this remains a true saying: *Il y a dans le cœur humain un fibre religieux.* Man always *worships* something; always he sees the Infinite shadowed forth in something finite; and indeed can and must so see it in *any* finite thing, once tempt him well to *fix* his eyes thereon. Yes, in practice, be it in theory or not, we are all Supernaturalists; and have an infinite happiness or an infinite wo not only waiting us hereafter, but looking out on us through any pitifullest present good or evil;—as, for example, on a high poetic Byron through his lameness; as on all young souls through their first lovesuit; as on older souls, still more foolishly, through many a lawsuit, paper-battle, political horse-race or ass-race. Atheism, it has been said, is impossible; and truly, if we will consider it, no Atheist denies a Divinity, but only some NAME (*Nomen, Numen*) of a Divinity: the God is still present there, working in that benighted heart, were it only as a god of darkness. Thousands of stern Sansculottes, to seek no other instance, go chanting martyr hymns to their guillotine; these spurn at the name of a God; yet worship one (as hapless 'Proselytes without the Gate') under the new pseudonym of Freedom. What indeed is all this that is called political fanaticism, revolutionary madness, force of hatred, force of love, and so forth; but merely under new designations, that same wondrous, wonder-working reflex from the Infinite, which in all times has given the Finite its empyrean or tartarean hue, thereby its blessedness or cursedness, its marketable worth or unworth?

"Remark, however, as illustrative of several things, and more to the purpose here, that man does in strict speech always remain the clearest symbol of the Divinity to man. Friend Novalis, the devoutest heart I knew, and of purest depth, has not scrupled to call man what the Divine Man is called in Scripture, a 'Revelation in the Flesh.' 'There is but one temple in the world,' says he, 'and that is the body of man. Bending before men is a reverence done to this revelation in the flesh. We touch heaven when we lay our hand on a human body.' In which notable words, a reader that meditates them, may find such meaning and scientific accuracy as will surprise him.

"The age of superstition, it appears to be sufficiently known, are behind us. To no man, were he never so heroic, are shrines any more built, and vows offered as to one having supernatural power. The sphere of the TRANSCENDENTAL cannot now, by that avenue of heroic worth, of eloquent wisdom, or by any other avenue, be so easily reached. The worth that in these days could *transcend* all estimate or survey, and lead men willingly captive into *infinite* admiration, into worship, is still waited for (with little hope) from the unseen Time. All that can be said to offer itself in that kind, at present, is some slight household devotion, (*Haus-Andacht*,) whereby this or the other enthusiast, privately in all quietness, can love his hero or sage without measure, and idealize, and, so in a sense, idolize him;—which practice, as man is by necessity an idol-worshipper, (no offence in him *so* long as *idol* means accurately *vision*, clear *symbol*,) and all wicked idolatry is but a *more* idolatrous worship, may be excusable, in certain cases, praiseworthy. Be this as it will, let the curious eye gratify itself in observing how the old antediluvian feeling still, though now struggling out so imperfectly, and forced into unexpected shapes, asserts its existence in the newest man: and the Chaldeans or old Persians, with their Zerdusht, differ only in vesture and dialect from the French, with their Voltaire *étouffé sous des roses*."*

This, doubtless, is a wonderful phraseology, but referable, as the Professor urges, to that capacious reservoir and convenience, "the nature of the time:" "A time," says he, "when as in some Destruction of a Roman Empire, wrecks of old things are everywhere confusedly jumbled with rudiments of new; so that, till once the mixture and amalgamation be complete, and even have long continued complete, and universally apparent, no grammatical *langue d'oc* or *langue d'oui* can establish itself, but only some barbarous mixed *lingua rustica*, more like a jargon than a language, must prevail; and thus the deepest matters be either barbarously spoken of, or wholly omitted and lost sight of, which were still worse." But to let the homily proceed:

"Consider, at any rate," continues he elsewhere, "under how many categories, down to the most impertinent, the world inquires concerning Great Men, and never wearies striving to represent to itself their whole structure, aspect, procedure, outward and inward! Blame not the world for such minutest curiosity about its great ones: this comes of the world's old-established necessity to worship: and, indeed, whom but its great ones, that "like celestial fire-pillars go before it on the march," ought it to worship? Blame not even that mistaken worship of sham great ones, that are not celestial fire-pillars, but terrestrial glass-lanterns with wick and tallow, under no guidance but a stupid fatuous one; of which worship the litanies, and gossip-homilies are, in some quarters of the globe, so inexpressibly uninteresting. Blame it not; pity it rather, with a certain loving respect.

"Man is never, let me assure thee, altogether a clothes-horse; under the clothes there is always a body and a soul. The Count von Bügeleisen, so idolized by our fashionable classes, is not, as the English Swift asserts, created wholly by the Tailor: but partially, also, by the supernatural Powers. His beautifully cut apparel, and graceful expensive tackle and environment of all kinds, are but the symbols of a beauty and gracefulness supposed to be inherent in the Count himself; under which predicament come also our reverence for his counthood, and in good part that other notable phenomenon of his being worshipped, because he *is* worshipped, of one idolater, sheep-like, running after him, because many have already run. Nay, on what other principle but this latter hast thou, O reader, (if thou be not one of a thousand,) read, for example, thy *Homer*, and found some real joy therein? All these things, I say, the apparel, the counthood, the existing popularity, and whatever else can combine them, are symbols;—bank notes, which, whether there be gold behind them, or only bankruptcy and empty drawers, pass current for gold. But how, now, could they so pass, if gold itself were not prized, and believed and known to be somewhere extant? Produce the actual gold visibly, and mark how, in these distrustful days, your most accredited bank-paper stagnates in the market! No holy Alliance, though plush, and gilding, and genealogical parchment, to the utmost that the time yields, be hung round it, can gain for itself a dominion in the heart of any man; some thirty or forty millions of men's hearts being, on the other hand, subdued into loyal reverence by a Corsican Lieutenant of Artillery. Such is the difference between God-creation and Tailor-creation. Great is the tailor, but not the greatest. So, too, in matters spiritual, what avails it that a man be Doctor of the Sorbonne, Doctor of Laws, of Both Laws, and can cover half a square foot in pica-type with the list of his fellowships, arranged as equilateral triangle,

* *Die Kleider: ihr Werden und Wirken* Von D. TEUFELSDRECK. Weissnichtwo. Stillschweign'sche Buchhandlung, 1830.

at the vertex an '&c.' over and above, and with the parchment of his diplomas could thatch the whole street he lives in: What avails it? The man is but an owl; of prepossessing gravity indeed; much respected by simple neighbours; but to whose sorrowful hootings no creature hastens, eager to listen. While, again, let but some riding gauger arrive under cloud of night at a Scottish inn, and word be whispered that it is Robert Burns; in few instants all beds and truckle-beds, from garret to cellar, are left vacant, and gentle and simple, with open eyes and erect ears, are gathered together."

Whereby, at least, from amid this questionable *lingua*, "more like a jargon than a language," so much may have become apparent: What unspeakable importance the world attaches, has ever attached, (expressing the same by all possible methods,) and will ever attach, to its great men. Deep and venerable, whether looked at in the Teufelsdreck manner or otherwise, is this love of men for great men, this their exclusive admiration of great men; a quality of vast significance, if we consider it well; for, as in its origin it reaches up into the highest and even holiest provinces of man's nature, so, in his practical history it will be found to play the most surprising part. Does not, for one example, the fact of such a temper indestructibly existing in all men, point out man as an essentially governable and teachable creature, and for ever refute that calumny of his being by nature insubordinate, prone to rebellion? Men seldom, or rather never for a length of time and deliberately, rebel against any thing that does not deserve rebelling against. Ready, ever zealous is the obedience and devotedness they show to the great, to the really high; prostrating their whole possession and self, body, heart, soul, and spirit, under the feet of whatsoever is authentically above them. Nay, in most times, it is rather a slavish devotedness to those who only seem and pretend to be above them that constitutes their fault.

But why seek special instances? Is not Love, from of old, known to be the beginning of all things? And what is admiration of the great but love of the truly loveable? The first product of love is *imitation*, that all-important peculiar gift of man, whereby Mankind is not only held socially together in the present time, but connected in like union with the past and the future; so that the attainment of the innumerable Departed can be conveyed down to the Living, and transmitted with increase to the Unborn. Now great men, in particular spiritually great men, for all men have a spirit to guide, though all have not kingdoms to govern and battles to fight, are the men universally imitated and learned of, the glass in which whole generations survey and shape themselves.

Thus is the Great Man of an age, beyond comparison, the most important phenomenon therein; all other phenomena, were they Waterloo Victories, Constitutions of the year One, glorious revolutions, new births of the golden age, in what sort you will, are small and trivial. Alas, all these pass away, and are left extinct behind, like the tar-barrels they were celebrated with, and the new-born golden age proves always to be still-born: neither is there, was there, or will there, be any other golden age possible, save only in this: in new increase of worth and wisdom;—that is to say, therefore, in the new arrival among us of wise and worthy men. Such arrivals are the great occurrences, though unnoticed ones; all else that can occur, in what kind soever, is but the *road*, up hill or down hill, rougher or smoother: nowise the *power* that will nerve us for travelling forward thereon. So little comparatively can forethought or the cunningest mechanical pre-contrivance do for a nation, for a world! Ever must we wait on the bounty of Time, and see what leader shall be born for us, and whither he will lead. Thus too, in defect of great men, noted men become important: the Noted Man of an age is the emblem and living summary of the Ideal which that age has fashioned for itself: show me the noted man of an age, you show me the age that produced him. Such figures walk in the van, for great good, or for great evil; if not leading, then driven and still farther misleading. The apotheosis of Beau Brummel has marred many a pretty youth; landed him not at any *goal* where oak garlands, earned by faithful labour and valour, carry men to the immortal gods; but, by a fatal inversion, at the King's Bench *gaol*, where he that has never sowed shall not any longer reap, still less any longer burn his barn, but scrape himself with potsherds among the ashes thereof, and consider with all deliberation "what he wanted, and what he wants."

To enlighten this principle of reverence for the great, to teach us reverence, and whom we are to revere and admire, should ever be a chief aim of Education, (indeed it is herein that instruction properly both begins and ends;) and in these late ages, perhaps more than ever, so indispensable is now our need of clear reverence, so inexpressibly poor our supply. "Clear reverence!" it was once responded to a seeker of light: "all want it, perhaps thou thyself." What wretched idols, of Leeds cloth, stuffed out with bran of one kind or other, do men either worship, or being tired of worshipping, (so expensively without fruit,) rend in pieces and kick out of doors, amid loud shouting and crowing, what they call "tremendous cheers," as if the feat were miraculous! In private life, as in public, delusion in this sort does its work; the blind leading the blind, both fall into the ditch.

"For alas!" cries Teufelsdreck on this occasion, "though in susceptive hearts it is felt that a great man is unspeakably great, the specific marks of him are mournfully mistaken: thus must innumerable pilgrims journey, in toil and hope, to shrines where there is no healing. On the fairer half of the creation, above all, such error presses hard. Women are born worshippers; in their good little hearts lies the most craving relish for greatness: it is even said, each chooses her husband on the hypothesis of his being a great man—in his way. The good creatures, yet the foolish! For their choices, no insight, or next to none, being vouchsafed them, are unutterable. Yet how touching, also to see, for example, Parisian ladies of quality, all rustling in silks and laces, visit the condemned-cell of a fierce Cartouche, and in silver accents, and with the looks of angels, beg locks of hair from him; as from the greatest, were it only in the profession of highwayman! Still more fatal is that other mistake, the commonest of all, whereby the devotional youth, seeking for a great man to worship, finds such within his own worthy person, and proceeds with all zeal to worship *there*. Unhappy enough! to realize, in an age of such gas-light illumination, this basest superstition of the ages of Egyptian darkness.

"Remark, however, and not without emotion, that of all rituals, and divine services, and ordinances ever instituted for the worship of any god, this of Self-worship is the ritual most faithfully observed. Trouble enough has the Hindoo devotee, with his washings, and cookings, and perplexed formularies, tying him up at every function of his existence: but is it greater trouble than that of his German self-worshipping brother; is it trouble even by the devoutest Fakir, so honestly undertaken and fulfilled? I answer, No; for the German's heart is in it. The German worshipper, for whom does he work, and scheme, and struggle, and fight, at his rising up and lying down, in all times and places, but for his god only? Can he escape from that divine presence of Self; can his heart waver, or his hand wax faint in that sacred service? The Hebrew Jonah, prophet as he was, rather than take a message to Nineveh, took ship to Tarshish, hoping to hide there from his Sender; but in what ship-hull or whale's belly, shall the madder German Jonah cherish hope of hiding from—Himself! Consider too the temples he builds, and the services of (shoulder-knotted) priests he ordains and maintains; the smoking sacrifices, thrice a day or oftener, with perhaps a psalmist or two, of broken-winded laureats and literators, if such are to be had. Nor are his votive gifts wanting, of rings, and jewels, and gold embroideries, such as our Lady of Loretto might grow yellower to look upon. A toilsome, perpetual worship, heroically gone through; and then with what issue? Alas, with the worst. The old Egyptian leek-worshipper had, it is to be hoped, seasons of light and faith: his leek-god seems to smile on him; he is humbled, and in humility exalted, before the majesty of something, were it only that of germinative Physical Nature, seen through a germinating, not unnourishing potherb. The Self-worshipper, again, has no seasons of light, which are not of blue sulphur-light; hungry, envious pride, not humility in any sort, is the ashy fruit of his worship; his self-god growls on him with the perpetual wolf-cry, Give! Give! and your devout Byron, as the Frau Hunt, with a wise simplicity (*geistreich naiv*,) once said, 'must sit sulking like a great schoolboy, in pet because they have given him a plain bun and not a spiced one.'—His bun was a life-rent of God's universe, with the tasks it offered, and the tools to do them with; *à priori*, one might have fancied it could be put up with for once."

After which wondrous glimpses into the Teufelsdreck Homily on the *Greatness of Great Men*, it may now be high time to proceed with the matter more in hand; and remark that our much calumniated age, so fruitful in noted men, is also not without its great. In noted men, undoubtedly enough, we surpass all ages since the creation of the world; and from two plain causes: First, that there has been a French Revolution, and that there is now pretty rapidly proceeding a European Revolution; whereby every thing, as in the Term-day of a great city, when all mortals are removing, has been, so to speak, set out into the street; and many a foolish vessel of dishonour, unnoticed, and worth no notice in its own dark corner, has become universally recognisable when once mounted on the summit of some furniture-wagon, and tottering there—(as committee-president, or other head-director,) with what is put under it, slowly onwards to its new lodging and arrangement, itself, alas, hardly to get thither without *breakage*. Secondly, that the Printing Press, with stitched and loose leaves, has now come into full action; and makes, as it were, a sort of universal day-light for removal and revolution, and every thing else, to proceed in, far more commodiously, yet also far more conspicuously. A complaint has accordingly been heard that famous men abound, that we are quite overrun with famous men: however, the remedy lies in the disease itself; crowded succession already means quick oblivion. For wagon after wagon rolls off, and either arrives or is overset; and so, in either case the vessel of dishonour, which, at worst, we saw only in crossing some street, will afflict us no more.

Of great men, among so many millions of noted men, it is computed that in our time there have been two; one in the practical, another in the speculative province: Napoleon Bonaparte and Johann Wolfgang von Goethe. In which dual number, inconsiderable as it is, our time may, perhaps, specially pride itself, and take precedence of many others; in particular, reckon itself the flower-time of the whole last century and half. Every age will, no doubt, have its superior man or men: but one *so* superior as to take rank among the high of all ages; this is what we call a great man; this rarely makes his appearance, such bounty of nature and accident must combine to produce and unfold him. Of Napoleon and his works all ends of the world have heard; for *such* a host marched not in silence through the frighted deep: few heads there are in this Planet which have not formed to themselves some featured or featureless image of him; his history has been written about, on the great scale and on the small, some millions of times, and still remains to be written: one of our highest literary problems. For such a "light-nimbus" of glory and renown encircled the man; the environment he walked in was itself so stupendous that the eye grew dazzled and mistook his proportions; or quite turned away from him in pain and temporary blindness. Thus even among the clear-sighted there is no unanimity about Napoleon; and only here and there does his own greatness begin to be interpreted, and accurately separated from the mere greatness of his fame and fortune.

Goethe, again, though of longer continuance in the world, and intrinsically of much more unquestionable greatness, and even importance there, could not be so noted by the world: for if the explosion of powder-mines and artillery-parks naturally attracts every eye and ear; the approach of a new-created star (dawning on us in new-created radiance, from the eternal Deeps!) though *this*, and not the artillery-parks, is to shape our destiny and *rule* the lower earth, is notable at first only to certain star-gazers and weather-prophets. Among ourselves, especially, Goethe had little recognition: indeed, it was only of late that his existence, as a man and not as a mere sound, became authentically known to us; and some shadow of his high endowments and endeavours, and of the high meaning that might lie therein, arose in the general mind of England, even of intelligent England. Five years ago, to rank him with Napoleon, like him as rising unattainable beyond his class, like him and more than he of quite peculiar moment to all Europe, would have seemed a wonderful procedure; candour even, and enlightened liberality, to grant him place beside this and the other home-born ready-writer, blessed with that special privilege of "English cultivation," and able thereby to write novels, heart captivating, heart-rending, or of enchaining interest.

Since which time, however, let us say, the progress of clearer apprehension has been rapid and satisfactory: innumerable unmusical voices have already fallen silent on this matter; for in fowls of every feather, even in the pertest choughs and thievish magpies, there dwells a singular reverence of the eagle; no Dullness is so courageous, but if you once show it any gleam of a heavenly Resplendence, it will, at lowest, shut its eyes and say nothing. So fares it here with the "old established British critic;" who, indeed in these days of ours, begins to be strangely situated; so many new things rising on his horizon, black indefinable shapes, magical or not; the old brickfield (where he kneaded insufficient marketable bricks) all stirring under his feet; preternatural, mad-making tones in the earth and air:—with all which what shall an old-established British critic and brickmaker do, but, at wisest, put his hands in his pockets, and, with the face and heart of a British mastiff, though amid dismal enough forebodings, see what it will turn to?

In the younger, more hopeful minds, again, in most minds that can be considered as in a state of growth, German literature is taking its due place: in such, and in generations of other such that are to follow them, some thankful appreciation of the greatest in German literature cannot fail; at all events this feeling that he *is* great and the greatest, whereby appreciation, and, what alone is of much value, appropriation, first becomes rightly possible. To forward such on their way towards appropriating what excellence this man realized and created for them, somewhat has already been done, yet not much; much still waits to be done. The field, indeed, is large: there are forty volumes of the most significant Writing that has been produced for the last two centuries; there is the whole long Life and heroic Character of him who produced them; all this to expatiate over and inquire into; in both which departments the deepest thinker, and most far-sighted, may find scope enough.

Nevertheless, in these days of the ten-pound franchise, when all the world (perceiving now like the Irish innkeeper, that "death and destruction are just coming in") will have itself represented in parliament; and the wits of so many are gone in this direction to gather wool, and must needs return more or less shorn; it were foolish to invite either young or old into great depths of thought on such a remote matter; the tendency of which is neither for the Reform Bill nor against it, but quietly *through* it and beyond it; nowise to prescribe this or that mode of *electing* members, but only to produce a few members *worth* electing. Not for many years (who knows how many!) in these harassed, hand-to-mouth circumstances, can the world's bleared eyes open themselves to study the true import of such topics; of this topic the highest of such. As things actually stand, some quite cursory glances, and considerations close on the surface, to remind a few (unelected, unelective) parties interested, that it lies over for study, are all that can be attempted here: could we, by any method, in any measure, disclose for such the wondrous wonder-working *element* it hovers in, the *light* it is to be studied and inquired after in, what is needfullest at present were accomplished.

One class of considerations, near enough the surface, we avoid; all that partakes of an elegiac character. True enough, nothing can be *done*, or suffered, but there is something to be *said*, wisely or unwisely. The departure of our Greatest contemporary Man could not be other than a great event; fitted to awaken, in all who with understanding beheld it, feeling sad, but high and sacred, of mortality and immortality, of mourning and of triumph; far lookings into the Past and into the Future; so many changes, fearful and wonderful, of fleeting Time; glimpses too of the Eternity these rest on, which knows no change. At the present date and distance, however, all this pertains not to us; has been uttered elsewhere, or may be left for utterance there. Let us consider the Exequies as past; that the high Rogus, with its sweet scented wood, amid the wail of music eloquent to speechless hearts, has flamed aloft, heaven-kissing, in sight of all the Greeks; and that now the ashes of the Hero are gathered into their urn, and the host has marched onwards to new victories and new toils; ever to be mindful of the dead, not to mourn for him any more. The host of the Greeks, in this case, was all thinking Europe: whether their funeral games were appropriate and worthy we stop not to inquire; the time, in regard to such things, is empty or ill provided, and this was what the time could conveniently do. All canonization and solemn cremation are gone by; and as yet nothing suitable, nothing that does not border upon parody, has appeared in their room. A Bentham bequeaths his remains to be lectured over in a school of anatomy; and perhaps, even in this way, finds, as chief of the Utilitarians, a really nobler funeral than any other, which the prosaic age, rich only in crapes and hollow scutcheons, (of timber as of words,) could have afforded him.

The matter in hand being *Goethe's Works*, and the greatest work of every man, or rather the summary and net amount of all his works, being the Life he has led, we ask, as the first question:—How it went with Goethe in that matter; what was the practical basis, of want and fulfilment, of joy and sorrow, from which his spiritual productions grew forth; the characters of which they must more or less legibly bear? In which sense, those Volumes entitled by him *Dichtung und Wahrheit*, wherein his personal history, what he has thought fit to make known of it, stands delineated, will long be valuable. A noble commentary, instructive in many ways, lies opened there, and yearly increasing in worth and interest; which all readers, now when the true quality of it is ascertained, will rejoice that circumstances induced and allowed him to write: for surely if old Cellini's counsel have any propriety, it is doubly proper in this case; the autobiographic practice he recommends (of which the last century in particular has seen so many worthy and worthless examples) was never so much in place as here. "All men, of what rank soever," thus counsels the brave Benvenuto, "who have accomplished aught virtuous or virtuous-like, should, provided they be conscious of really good purposes, write down their own life; nevertheless, not put hand to so worthy an enterprise till after they have reached the age of forty." All which ukase-regulations Goethe had abundantly fulfilled—the last as abundantly as any, for he had now reached the age of sixty-two.

"This year, 1811," says he, "distinguishes itself for me by persevering outward activity. The *Life of Philip Hackert* went to press; the papers committed to me all carefully elaborated as the case required. By this task I was once more attracted to the South: the occurrences which, at that period, had befallen me there, in Hackert's company or neighbourhood, became alive in the imagination; I had cause to ask, Why this which I was doing for another should not be attempted for myself? I turned, accordingly, before completion of that volume, to my own earliest personal history; and, in truth, found here that I had delayed too long. The work should have been undertaken while my mother yet lived; thereby had I got nigher those scenes of childhood, and been, by her great strength of memory, transported into the midst of them. Now, however, must these vanished apparitions be recalled by my own help; and, first, with labour, many an incitement to recollection, like a necessary magic-apparatus be devised. To represent the development of a child who had grown to be remarkable, how this exhibited itself under given circumstances, and yet how in general it could content the student of human nature and his views: such was the thing I had to do.

"In this sense, unpretendingly enough, to a work treated, with anxious fidelity, I gave the name *Wahrheit und Dichtung*, (Truth and Fiction;) deeply convinced that man, in immediate Presence, still more in Remembrance, fashions and models the external world according to his own peculiarities.

"The business, as, with historical studying, and otherwise recalling of places and persons, I had much time to spend on it, busied me wheresoever I went or stood, at home and abroad, to such a degree that my actual condition became like a secondary matter; though again, on all hands, when summoned outwards by occasion, I with full force and undivided sense proved myself present."—*Werke* xxxii. 62.

These Volumes, with what other supplementary matter has been added to them, (the rather as Goethe's was a life of manifold relation, of the widest connection with important or elevated persons, not to be carelessly laid before the world, and he had the rare good fortune of arranging all things that regarded even his posthumous concernment with the existing generation, according to his own deliberate judgment,) are perhaps likely to be, for a long time, our only authentic reference. By the last will of the deceased, it would seem, all his papers and effects are to lie exactly as they are, till after another twenty years.

Looking now into these magically-recalled scenes of childhood and manhood, the student of human nature will, under all manner of shapes, from first to last, note one thing: The singularly complex Possibility offered from without, yet along with it the deep never-failing Force from within, whereby all this is conquered and realized. It was as if accident and primary endowment had conspired to produce a character on the great scale; a will is cast abroad into the widest, wildest element, and gifted also in an extreme degree, to prevail over this, to fashion this to its own form: in which subordinating and self-fashioning of its circumstances, a character properly consists. In external situations, it is true, in occurrences such as could be recited in the Newspapers, Goethe's existence is not more complex than other men's; outwardly rather a pacific smooth existence: but in his inward specialities and depth of faculty and temper, in his position spiritual and temporal towards the world as it was and the world as he could have wished it, the observant eye may discern complexity, perplexity enough; an extent of data greater, perhaps, than had lain in any life-problem for some centuries. And now, as mentioned, the force for solving this was, in like manner, granted him in extraordinary measure; so that we must say, his possibilities were faithfully and with wonderful success turned into acquisitions; and this man fought the good fight, not only victorious, as all true men are, but victorious without damage, and with an ever-increasing strength for new victory, as only great and happy men are. Not wounds and loss (beyond fast-healing, skin-deep wounds) has the unconquerable to suffer; only ever-enduring toil; weariness—from which, after rest, he will rise stronger than before.

Good fortune, what the world calls good for

tune, awaits him from beginning to end; but also a far deeper felicity than this. Such worldly gifts of good fortune are what we called possibilities: happy he that can rule over them; but *doubly* unhappy he that cannot. Only in virtue of good guidance does that same good fortune prove good. Wealth, health, fiery light with Proteus manysidedness of mind, peace, honour, length of days: with all this you may make no Goethe, but only some Voltaire; with the most that was fortuitous in all this, make only some short-lived, unhappy, unprofitable Byron.

At no period of the World's History can a gifted man be born when he will not find enough to do; in no circumstances come into life but there will be contradictions for him to reconcile, difficulties which it will task his whole strength to surmount, if his whole strength suffice. Everywhere the human soul stands between a hemisphere of light and another of darkness; on the confines of two everlastingly hostile empires, Necessity and Freewill. A pious adage says, "the back is made for the burden:" we might with no less truth invert it, and say, the burden was made for the back. Nay, so perverse is the nature of man, it has in all times been found that an external allotment superior to the common was more dangerous than one inferior; thus for a hundred that can bear adversity, there is hardly one that can bear prosperity.

Of riches, in particular, as of the grossest species of prosperity, the perils are recorded by all moralists; and ever, as of old, must the sad observation from time to time occur: "Easier for a camel to pass through the eye of a needle!" Riches in a cultured community are the strangest of things: a power all-moving, yet which any the most powerless and skilless can *put* in motion; they are the *readiest* of possibilities; the readiest to become a great blessing or a great curse. "Beneath gold thrones and mountains," says Jean Paul, "who knows how many giant spirits lie entombed!" The first fruit of riches, especially for the man born rich, is to teach him faith in them, and all but hide from him that there is any other faith: thus is he trained up in the miserable eye-service of what is called Honour, Respectability; instead of a man we have but a *gigman*,—one who "always kept a gig," two-wheeled or four-wheeled. Consider too what this same gigmanhood issues in; consider that first and most stupendous of gigmen, Phaeton, the son of Sol, who drove the brightest of all conceivable gigs, yet with the sorrowfullest result. Alas, Phaeton was his father's heir; born to attain the highest fortune without earning it: he had *built* no sun-chariot, (could not build the simplest wheelbarrow,) but could and would insist on *driving* one; and so broke his own stiff neck, sent gig and horses spinning through infinite space, and set the universe on fire!—Or, to speak in more modest figures, Poverty, we may say, surrounds a man with ready-made barriers, which, if they mournfully gall and hamper, do at least prescribe for him and force on him a sort of course and goal; a safe and beaten though a circuitous course; great part of his guidance is secure against fatal error, is withdrawn from his control. The rich, again, has his whole life to guide, without goal or barrier, save of his own choosing; and, tempted as we have seen, is too likely to guide it ill; often, instead of walking straight forward, as he might, does but, like Jeshurun, wax fat and kick; in which process, it is clear, not the adamantine circle of Necessity whereon the World is built, but only his own limb-bones must go to pieces!—Truly, in plain prose, if we bethink us what a road many a Byron and Mirabeau, especially in these latter generations, have gone, it is proof of an uncommon inward wealth in Goethe; that the outward wealth, whether of money or other happiness which Fortune offered him, did in no case exceed the power of Nature to appropriate and wholesomely assimilate; that all outward blessedness grew to inward strength, and produced only blessed effects for him. Those "gold mountains" of Jean Paul, to the giant that *can* rise above them, are excellent, both fortified and speculatory, heights; and do in fact become a *throne*, where happily they have not been a *tomb*.

Goethe's childhood is throughout of riant, joyful character: kind plenty, in every sense, security, affection, manifold excitement, instruction, encircles him: wholly an element of sun and azure, wherein the young spirit, awakening and attaining, can on all hands richly unfold itself. A beautiful boy, of earnest, lucid, serenely deep nature, with the peaceful completeness yet infinite incessant expansiveness of a boy, has, in the fittest environment, begun to *be*: beautiful he looks and moves; rapid, gracefully prompt, like the son of Maia; wise, noble, like Latona's son: nay (as all men may *now* see) he is, in very truth, a miniature incipient world-poet; of all heavenly figures the beautifullest we know of that can visit this lower earth. Lovely enough shine for us those young years in old Teutonic Frankfort; mirrored in the far remembrance of the Self-historian, real yet ideal, they are among our most genuine poetic Idyls. No smallest matter is too small for us, when we think *who* it was that did it or suffered it. The little long-clothed urchin, mercurial enough with all his stillness, can throw a whole cargo of new-marketed crockery, piece by piece, from the balcony into the street, (once the feat is suggested to him;) and comically shatters cheap delf-ware with the same right hand, which tragically wrote and hurled forth the demonic scorn of Mephistophiles, or as "right hand" of Faust, "smote the universe to ruins." Neither smile more than enough (if thou be wise) that the gray-haired, all-experienced man remembers how the boy walked on the Mayn bridge, and "liked to look at the bright weather-cock" on the barrier there. That foolish piece of gilt wood, there glittering sun-lit, with its reflex wavering in the Mayn waters, is awakening quite another glitter in the young gifted soul: is not this foolish sun-lit splendour also, now when there is an *eye* to behold it, one of Nature's doings? The eye of the young seer is here, through the paltriest chink, looking into the infinite Splendours of Nature—where, one day, himself is to enter and dwell.

Goethe's mother appears to have been the more gifted of the parents; a woman of altogether genial character, great spiritual faculty and worth; whom the son, at an after time, put old family friends in mind of. It is gratifying for us that she lived to witness his maturity in works and honours; to know that the little infant she had nursed was grown to be a mighty man, the first man of his nation and time. In the father, as prosperous citizen of Frankfort, skilled in many things, improved by travel, by studies both practical and ornamental; decorated with some diplomatic title, but passing, among his books, paintings, collections and household possessions, social or intellectual, spiritual or material, a quite undiplomatic independent life, we become acquainted with a German (not country) but city *gentleman* of the last century; a character scarcely ever familiar in our Islands; now perhaps almost obsolete among the Germans too. A positive, methodical man, sound-headed, honest-hearted, sharp-tempered; with an uncommon share of volition, among other things, so that scarcely any obstacle would turn him back, but whatsoever he could not mount over he would struggle round, and in any case *be* at the end of his journey: many or all of whose good qualities passed also over by inheritance; and, in fairer combination, on nobler objects, to the whole world's profit, were seen a second time in action.

Family incidents; house-buildings, or re-buildings; arrivals, departures; in any case, new-year's-days and birth-days, are not wanting: nor city-incidents; many coloured tumult of Frankfort fairs; Kaisers' coronations, expected and witnessed; or that glorious ceremonial of the yearly *Pfeiffergericht*, wherein the grandfather himself plays so imperial a part. World incidents too roll forth their billows into the remotest creek, and alter the current there. The Earthquake of Lisbon hurls the little Frankfort boy into wondrous depths of another sort; enunciating dark theological problems, which no theology of his will solve. Direction, instruction, in like manner, awaits him in the Great Frederic's Seven Years' War; especially in that long billetting of King's Lieutenant Comte de Thorane, with his serjeants and adjutants, with his painters and picture-easels, his quick precision and decision, his "dry gallantry" and stately Spanish bearing;—though collisions with the "house-father," whose German house-stairs (though he silently endures the inevitable) were not new-built to be made a French highway of; who besides loves not the French, but the great invincible Fritz they are striving to beat down. Think, for example, of that singular congratulation on the victory at Bergen:

"So then, at last, after a restless Passion-week, Passion-Friday, 1759, arrived. A deep stillness announced the approaching storm. We children were forbidden to leave the house; our father had no rest, and went out. The battle began; I mounted to the top story, where the field, indeed, was still out of my sight, but the thunder of the cannon and the volleys of the small arms could be fully discerned. After some hours, we saw the first tokens of the battle, in a row of wagons, whereon wounded men, in all sorts of sorrowful dismemberment and gesture, were driven softly past us to the Liebfrauen-Kloster, which had been changed into a hospital. The compassion of the citizens forthwith awoke. Beer, wine, bread, money were given to such as had still power of receiving. But when, ere long, wounded and captive Germans also were noticed in that train, the pity had no limits; it seemed as if each were bent to strip himself of whatever movable thing he had, to aid his countrymen therewith in their extremity.

"The prisoners, meanwhile, were the symptom of a battle unprosperous for the Allies. My father, in his partiality, quite certain that these would gain, had the passionate rashness to go out to meet the expected visitors; not reflecting that the beaten side would in that case have to run over him. He went first into his garden, at the Friedberg Gate, where he found all quiet and solitary; then ventured forth to the Bornheim Heath, where soon, however, various scattered outrunners and baggage-men came in sight, who took the satisfaction, as they passed, of shooting at the boundary-stones, and sent our eager wanderer the reverberated lead singing about his ears. He reckoned it wiser, therefore, to come back; and learned on some inquiry, what the sound of the firing might already have taught him, that for the French all went well, and no retreat was thought of. Arriving home full of black humour, he quite, at sight of his wounded and prisoner countrymen, lost all composure. From him also many a gift went out for the passing wagons, but only Germans were to taste of it; which arrangement, as Fate had so huddled friends and foes together, could not always be adhered to.

"Our mother, and we children, who had from the first built upon the Count's word, and so passed a tolerably quiet day, were greatly rejoiced, and our mother doubly comforted, as she that morning, on questioning the oracle of her jewel box by the scratch of a needle, had obtained a most consolatory answer not only for the present but for the future. We wished our father a similar belief and disposition: we flattered him what we could, we entreated him to take some food, which he had forborne all day; he refused our caresses and every enjoyment, and retired to his room. Our joy, in the meanwhile, was not disturbed; the business was over: the King's Lieutenant, who to-day, contrary to custom, had been on horseback, at length returned; his presence at home was more needful than ever. We sprang out to meet him, kissed his hands, testified our joy. It seemed to please him greatly. 'Well!' said he, with more softness than usual, 'I am glad too for your sake, dear children.' He ordered us sweetmeats, sweet wine, every thing the best, and went to his chamber, where already a mass of importuners, solicitors, petitioners, were crowded.

"We held now a dainty collation; deplored our good father, who could not participate therein, and pressed our mother to bring him down; she, however, knew better, and how uncheering such gifts would be to him. Meanwhile she had put some supper in order, and would fain have sent him up a little to his room; but such irregularity was a thing he never suffered, not in extremest cases; so the sweet gifts being once put aside, she set about entreating him to come down in his usual way. He yielded at last, unwillingly, and little did we know what mischief we were making ready. The stairs ran free through the whole house, past the door of every anti-chamber. Our father, in descending, had to pass the Count's apartments. His anti-chamber was so full of people that he had at length resolved to come out, and despatch several at once; and this happened, alas, just at the instant our father was passing down. The Count stept cheerfully out, saluted him, and said: 'You will congratulate us and yourself that this dangerous affair has gone off so happily.'—'Not at all!' replied my father, with grim emphasis: 'I wish they had chased you to the Devil, had I myself gone too.' The Count held in for a moment, then burst forth with fury: 'You shall repent this! You shall not'———"

Father Goethe, however, has "in the meanwhile quietly descended," and sat down to sup, much cheerfuller than formerly; he little caring, "we little knowing, in what questionable way he had rolled the stone from his heart," and how official friends must interfere and secret negotiations enough go on, to keep him out of military prison, and worse things that might have befallen there. On all which may we be permitted once again to make the simple reflection: What a plagued and plaguing world, with its battles and bombardments, wars and rumours of war, (which sow or reap no ear of corn for any man,) this is! The boy, who here watches the musket-volleys and cannon-thunders of the great Fritz, shall, as man, witness the siege of Mentz; fly with Brunswick Dukes before Doumouriez and his Sansculottes, through a country champed into one red world of mud, "like Pharaoh," (for the carriage too breaks down,) "through the Red Sea;" and finally become involved in the universal fire-consummation of Napoleon, and by skill defend himself from hurt therein!—

The father, with occasional subsidiary private tutors, is his son's schoolmaster; a somewhat pedantic pedagogue, with ambition enough and faithful good will, but more of rigour than of insight; who, however, works on a subject that he *cannot* spoil. Languages, to the number of six or seven, with whatsoever pertains to them; histories, syllabuses, knowledges-made-easy; not to speak of dancing, drawing, music, or, in due time, riding and fencing: all is taken in with boundless appetite and aptitude; all is but fuel, injudiciously piled, and of wet quality, yet under which works an unquenchable Greek-fire that will feed itself therewith, that will one day make it *all* clear and glowing. The paternal grandmother, recollected as a "pale, thin, ever white and clean dressed figure," provides the children many a satisfaction; and at length, on some festive night the crowning one of a puppet-show: whereupon ensues a long course of theatrical speculatings and practisings, somewhat as delineated, for another party, in the first book of *Meister's Apprenticeship;* in which work, indeed, especially in the earlier portion of it, some shadow of the author's personal experience and culture is more than once traceable. Thus Meister's desperate burnt-offering of his young "Poems on various Occasions," was the image of a reality which took place in Leipsic, made desperately enough, "on the kitchen hearth, the thick smoke from which, flowing through the whole house, filled our good landlady with alarm."

Old "Imperial Freetown" Frankfort is not without its notabilities, tragic or comic; in any case, impressive and didactic. The young heart is filled with boding to look into the *Juden-gasse,* (Jew-gate,) where squalid painful Hebrews are banished to scour old clothes, and in hate, and greed, and Old-Hebrew obstinacy and implacability, work out a wonderful prophetic existence, as "a people terrible from the beginning;" manages, however, to get admittance to their synagogue, and see a wedding and a circumcision. On its spike, aloft on one of the steeples, grins, for the last two hundred years, the bleached skull of a malefactor and traitor; properly, indeed, not so much a traitor, as a Radical whose Reform Bill could not be carried through. The future book-writer also, on one occasion, sees the execution of a book; how the huge printed reams rustle in the flames, are stirred up with oven-forks, and fly half-charred aloft, the sport of winds; from which half-charred leaves, diligently picked up, he pieces himself a copy together, as did many others, and with double earnestness reads it.

As little is the old Freetown deficient in notable men; all accessible to a grandson of the Schultheiss,* who besides is a youth like no other. Of which originals, curious enough, and long since "vanished from the sale-catalogues," take only these two specimens:

"Von Reineck, of an old-noble house; able, downright, but stiff-necked; a lean black-brown man, whom I never saw smile. The misfortune befel him that his only daughter was carried off by a friend of the family. He prosecuted his son-in-law with the most vehement suit; and as the courts, in their formality, would neither fast enough, nor with force enough obey his vengeance, he fell out with them; and there arose quarrel on quarrel, process on process. He withdrew himself wholly into his house and the adjoining garden, lived in a spacious but melancholy under-room, where for many years no brush of a painter, perhaps scarcely the besom of a maid, had got admittance. Me he would willingly endure; had specially recommended me to his younger son. His oldest friends, who knew how to humour him, his men of business and agents, he often had at table: and on such occasions failed not to invite me. His board was well furnished, his buffet still better. His guests, however, had one torment, a large stove smoking out of many cracks. One of the most intimate ven-

---

* *Schultheiss* is the title of the chief magistrate in some free-towns and republics, for instance, in Berne. It seems to derive itself from *Schuld-heissen,* and may mean the teller of duty, him by whom what *should* be is *hight.*

tured once to take notice of it, and ask the host whether he could stand such an inconvenience the whole winter. He answered, like a second Timon, and Heautontimorumenos: 'Would to God this were the worst mischief of those that plague me!' Not till late would he be persuaded to admit daughter and grandson to his sight: the son-in-law was never more to show face before him.

"On this brave and unfortunate man my presence had a kind effect; for as he gladly spoke with me, in particular instructed me on political and state concerns, he seemed himself to feel assuaged and cheered. Accordingly, the few old friends who still kept about him, would often make use of me when they wished to soothe his indignant humour, and persuade him to any recreation. In fact he now more than once went out with us, and viewed the neighbourhood again, on which, for so many years, he had not turned an eye." * * *

"Hofrath Huisgen, not a native of Frankfort; of the Reformed religion, and thus incapable of public office, of advocacy among the rest, which latter, however, as a man much trusted for juristic talent, he, under another's signature, contrived quite calmly to practise, as well in Frankfort as in the Imperial Courts, —might be about sixty when I happened to have writing lessons along with his son, and so came into the house. His figure was large; tall without being bony, broad without corpulency. His face, deformed not only by smallpox, but wanting one of the eyes, you could not look on, for the first time, without apprehension. On his bald head he wore always a perfectly white bell-shaped cap, (*Glockenmütze,*) tied at top with a ribbon. His night-gowns, of calamanco or damask, were always as if new washed. He inhabited a most cheerful suite of rooms on the ground floor in the *Allee*, and the neatness of every thing about him corresponded to it. The high order of his books, papers, maps, made a pleasant impression. His son, Heinrich Sebastian, who afterwards became known by various writings on Art, promised little in his youth. Good-natured but heavy, not rude yet artless, and without wish to instruct himself, he sought rather to avoid his father, as from his mother he could get whatever he wanted. I, on the other hand, came more and more into intimacy with the master the more I knew of him. As he meddled with none but important law-cases, he had time enough to amuse and occupy himself with other things. I had not long been about him, and listened to his doctrine, till I came to observe that in respect of God and the World he stood on the opposition side. One of his pet books was, *Agrippa de Vanitate Scientiarum;* this he particularly recommended me to read, and did therewith set my young brain, for a while, into considerable tumult. I, in the joy of youth, was inclined to a sort of optimism, and with God or the Gods had now tolerably adjusted myself again; for, by a series of years, I had got to experience that there is many a balance against evil, that misfortunes are things one recovers from, that in dangers one finds deliverance and does not always break his neck. On what men did and tried, moreover, I looked with tolerance, and found much praiseworthy which my old gentleman would nowise be content with. Nay, once, as he had been depicting me the world not a little on the crabbed side, I noticed in him that he meant still to finish with a trump-card. He shut, as in such cases his wont was, the blind left eye close; looked with the other broad out; and said, in a snuffing voice: '*Auch in Gott entdeck' ich Fehler.*'"

Of a gentler character is the reminiscence of the maternal grandfather, old Schultheiss Textor; with his gift of prophetic dreaming, "which endowment none of his descendants inherited;" with his kind, mild ways; there as he glides about in his garden, at evening, "in black velvet cap," trimming "the finer sort of fruit-trees," with aid of those antique embroidered gloves or gauntlets, yearly handed him at the *Pfeiffergericht:* a soft, spirit-looking figure; the farthest out-post of the Past, which behind him melts into dim vapour. In Frau von Klestenberg, a religious associate of the mother's, we become acquainted with the *Schöne Seele* (Fair Saint) of *Meister;* she, at an after period, studied to convert her *Philo*, but only very partially succeeded. Let us notice also, as a token for good, how the young universal spirit takes pleasure in the workshops of handicraftsmen, and loves to understand their methods of labouring and of living:

"My father had early accustomed me to manage little matters for him. In particular, it was often my commission to stir up the craftsman he employed; who were too apt to loiter with him; as he wanted to have all accurately done, and finally for prompt payment to have the price moderated. I came in this way, into almost all manner of work-shops; and as it lay in my nature to shape myself into the circumstances of others, to feel every species of human existence, and with satisfaction participate therein, I spent many pleasant hours in such places; grew to understand the procedure of each, and what of joy and of sorrow, advantage or drawback, the indispensable conditions of this or that way of life brought with them.* * * The household economy of the various crafts, which took its figure and colour from the occupation of each, was also silently an object of attention; and so unfolded, so confirmed itself in me the feeling of the equality, if not of all men, yet of all men's situations; existence by itself appearing as the head condition, all the rest as indifferent and accidental."

And so, amid manifold instructive influences, has the boy grown out of boyhood; when now a new figure enters on the scene, bringing far higher revelations:

"As at last the wine was failing, one of them called the maid; but instead of her there came a maiden of uncommon, and, to see her in this environment, of incredible beauty. 'What is it?' said she, after kindly giving us good-evening: 'the maid is ill and gone to bed: can I serve you?'—'Our wine is done,' said one; 'couldst thou get us a couple of bottles over the way, it were very good of thee.'—'Do it, Gretchen,' said another, 'it is but a cat's leap.' —'Surely!' said she; took a couple of empty bottles from the table, and hastened out. Her figure, when she turned away from you, was almost prettier than before: the little cap sat so neat on the little head, which a slim neck so gracefully united with back and shoulders. Every thing about her seemed select; and you could follow the whole form more calmly, as attention was not now attracted and arrested by the true still eyes and the lovely mouth alone."

It is at the very threshold of youth that this episode of Gretchen (Margarete, Mar-*g'ret'-kin*) occurs; the young critic of slim necks and true still eyes shall now know something of natural magic, and the importance of one mortal to another; the wild-flowing bottomless sea of human Passion, glorious in Auroral light, (which, alas, may become infernal lightning,) unveils itself a little to him. A graceful little episode we reckon it; and Gretchen better than most first loves: wholly an innocent, wise, dainty maiden; pure and poor,—who vanishes from us here; but, we trust, in some quiet nook of the Rhineland, became wife and mother, and was the joy and sorrow of some brave man's heart,—according as it is appointed. To the boy himself it ended painfully and almost fatally, had not sickness come to his deliverance; and here too he may experience how "a shadow chases us in all manner of sunshine," and in this *What-d'ye-call-it* of Existence the tragic element is not wanting. The name of Gretchen, not her story, which had nothing in it of that guilt and terror, has been made world-famous in the play of *Faust.*—

Leipsic University has the honour of matriculating him. The name of his "propitious mother" she may boast of, but not of the reality: alas, in these days, the University of the Universe is the only propitious mother of such; all other propitious mothers are but unpropitious superannuated dry-nurses fallen bedrid, from whom the famished nurseling has to *steal* even bread and water, if he will not die; whom for most part he soon takes leave of, giving perhaps, (as in Gibbon's case,) for farewell thanks, some rough tweak of the nose; and rushes desperate into the wide world an orphan. The time is advancing, slower or faster, when the bedrid dry-nurse will decease, and be succeeded by a walking and stirring wet one. Goethe's employments and culture at Leipsic lay in quite other groves than the academic: he listened to the Ciceronian Ernesti with eagerness, but the life-giving word flowed not from his mouth; to the sacerdotal, eclectic-sentimental Gellert, (the divinity of all tea-table moral philosophers of both sexes;) witnessed "the pure soul, the genuine will of the noble man," heard "his admonitions, warnings, and entreaties, uttered in a somewhat hollow and melancholy tone," —and then the Frenchman say to it all, *Laissez le faire, il nous forme des dupes.* "In logic it seemed to me very strange that I must now take up those spiritual operations which from of old I had executed with the utmost convenience, and tatter them asunder, insulate, and as if destroy them, that their right employment might become plain to me. Of the Thing of the World, of God, I fancied I knew almost about as much as the Doctor himself; and he seemed to me, in more than one place, to hobble dreadfully (*gewaltig zu hapern*)."

However, he studies to some profit with the Painter Oeser; hears, one day, at the door, with horror, that there is no lesson, for news of Winkelmann's assassination have come. With the ancient Gottsched, too, he has an interview: alas, it is a young Zeus come to dethrone old Saturn, whose time in the literary heaven is nigh run; for on Olympus itself, one Demiurgus passeth away and another cometh. Gottsched had introduced the reign of *water*, in all shapes liquid and solid, and long gloriously presided over the same; but now there is enough of it, and the "rayless majesty" (had he been prophetic) here beheld the rayed one, before whom he was to melt away:

"We announced ourselves. The servant led us into a large room, and said his master would come immediately. Whether we misinterpreted a motion he made I cannot say; at any rate, we fancied he had beckoned us to advance into an adjoining chamber. We did advance, and to a singular scene; for, at the same moment, Gottsched, the huge broad gigantic man, entered from the opposite door, in green damask nightgown, lined with red taffeta; but his enormous head was bald and without covering. This, however, was the very want to be now supplied: for the servant came springing in at a side-door, with a full-bottomed wig on his hand, (the locks fell down to his elbows,) and held it out, with terrified gesture, to his master. Gottsched, without uttering the smallest complaint, lifted the head-gear with his left hand from the servant's arm; and very deftly swinging it up to its place on the head, at the same time, with his right hand, gave the poor man a box on the ear, which, as is seen in comedies, dashed him spinning out of the apartment, whereupon the respectable-looking Patriarch quite gravely desired us to be seated, and with proper dignity went through a tolerably long discourse."

In which discourse, however, it is likely, little edification for the young inquirer could lie. Already by multifarious discoursings and readings he has convinced himself, to his despair, of the watery condition of the Gottschedic world, and how "the *Noachide* (Noaheid) of Bodmer is a true symbol of the deluge that has swelled up round the German Parnassus," and in literature as in philosophy there is neither landmark nor loadstar. Here, too, he resumes his inquiries about religion, falls into "black scruples" about most things, and in "the bald and feeble deliverances" propounded him, has sorry comfort. Outward things, moreover, go not as they should: the copious philosophic harlequinades of that wag Beyrish, "with the long nose," unsettle rather than settle; as do, in many ways, other wise and foolish mortals of both sexes: matters grow worse and worse. He falls sick, becomes wretched enough; yet unfolds withal "an audacious humour which feels itself superior to the moment; not only fears no danger, but even wilfully courts it." And thus, somewhat in a wrecked state, he quits his propitious mother, and returns home.

Nevertheless let there be no reflections: he must now in earnest get forward with his Law, and on to Strasburg to complete himself therein; so has the paternal judgment arranged it. A lawyer, the thing in these latter days called Lawyer, of a man in whom ever bounteous Nature has sent us a Poet for the World! O blind mortals, blind over what lies closest to us, what we have the truest wish to see! In this young colt that caprioles there in young lustihood, and snuffs the wind with an "audacious humour," rather dangerous looking, no Sleswick Dobbin, to rise to dromedary stature, and draw three tons avoirdupois, (of street-mud or whatever else,) has been vouchsafed; but a winged miraculous Pegasus to carry us to the heavens!—Whereon too (if we consider it) many a heroic Bellerophon shall, in times coming, mount and destroy Chimæras, and deliver afflicted nations on the lower earth.

Meanwhile, be this as it may, the youth is gone to Strasburg to prepare for the *examen rigorosum;* though, as it turned out, for quite a different than the Law one. Confusion enough is in his head and heart; poetic objects too have taken root there, and will not rest till they have worked themselves into form. "These," says he, "were Götz von Berlichingen and Faust. The written Life of the former had seized my inmost soul. The figure of a rude well-meaning self-helper, in wild anarchic time, excited my deepest sympathy. The impressive puppet-show Fable of the other sounded and hummed through me many-toned enough."—"Let us withdraw, however," subjoins he, "into the free air, to the high broad platform of the Minster; as if the time were still here, when we young ones often rendezvoused thither to salute, with full rummers, the sinking sun." They had good telescopes with them; "and one friend after another searched out the spot in the distance which had become the dearest to him; neither was I without a little eye-mark of the like, which, though it rose not conspicuous in the landscape, drew me to it beyond all else with a kindly magic." This alludes, we perceive, to that Alsatian Vicar of Wakefield, and his daughter the fair Frederike; concerning which matter a word may not be useless here. Exception has been taken by certain tender souls, of the all-for-love sort, against Goethe's conduct in this matter. He flirted with this blooming blue-eyed Alsatian, she with him, innocently enough, thoughtlessly enough, till they both came to love each other; and then, when the marrying point began to grow visible in the distance, he stopt short, and would no farther. Adieu, he cried, and waved his lily hand. "The good Frederike was weeping; I too was sick enough at heart." Whereupon arises the question: Is Goethe a bad man; or is he not a bad man? Alas, worthy souls! if this world were all a wedding dance, and *thou shalt* never come into collision with *thou wilt,* what a new improved time we had of it! It is man's miserable lot, in the meanwhile to eat and labour as well as wed; alas, how often, like Corporal Trim, does he spend the whole night; one moment dividing the world into two halves with his fair Beguine; next moment remembering that he has only a knapsack and fifteen florins to divide with any one! Besides, you do not consider that our dear Frederike, whom we too could weep for if it served, had a sound German heart within her stays; had furthermore abundance of *work* to do, and not even leisure to die of love; above all, that at this period, in the country parts of Alsatia, there were no circulating library novels.

With regard to the false one's cruelty of temper, who, if we remember, saw a ghost in broad noon that day he rode away from her, let us, on the other hand, hear Jung Stilling, for he also had experience thereof at this very date. Poor Jung, a sort of German Dominie Sampson, awkward, honest, irascible, "in old-fashioned clothes and bag-wig," who had been several things, charcoal-burner, and, in repeated alternation, tailor and school-master, was now come to Strasburg to study medicine; with purse long-necked, yet with head that had brains in it, and heart full of trust in God. A pious soul, who if he did afterwards write books on the Nature of Departed Spirits, also restored to sight (by his skill in eye-operations) above *two thousand poor blind persons,* without fee or reward, even supporting many of them in the hospital at his own expense.

"There dined," says he, "at this table about twenty people, whom the two comrades saw one after the other enter. One especially, with large eyes, magnificent brow, and fine stature, walked (*muthig*) gallantly in. He drew Herr Troost's and Stilling's eyes on him; Herr Troost said, 'That must be a superior man.' Stilling assented, yet thought they would both have much vexation from him, as he looked like one of your wild fellows. This did Stilling infer from the frank style which the student had assumed; but here he was far mistaken. They found, meanwhile, that this distinguished individual was named Herr Goethe.

"Herr Troost whispered to Stilling, 'Here it were best one sat seven days silent.' Stilling felt this truth; they sat silent, therefore, and no one particularly minded them, except that Goethe now and then hurled over (*herüberwälzte*) a look: he sat opposite Stilling, and had the government of the table without aiming at it.

"Herr Troost was neat, and dressed in the fashion; Stilling likewise tolerably so. He had a dark brown coat with fustian under garments: only that a scratch-wig also remained to him, which, among his bag-wigs, he would wear out. This he had put on one day, and came therewith to dinner. Nobody took notice of it except Herr Waldberg of Vienna. That gentleman looked at him, and as he had already heard that Stilling was greatly taken up about religion, he began, and asked him, Whether he thought, Adam in Paradise had worn a scratch-wig? All laughed heartily, except Salzman, Goethe, and Troost; these did not laugh. In Stilling wrath rose and burnt, and he answered: 'Be ashamed of this jest; such a trivial thing is not worth laughing at!' But Goethe struck in and added: 'Try a man first whether he deserves mockery. It is devil-like to fall upon an honest-hearted person who has injured nobody, and make sport of him!' From that time Herr Goethe took up Stilling, visited him, liked him, made friendship and brothership with him, and strove by all opportunities to do him kindness. Pity that so few are acquainted with this noble man in respect of his heart!"*

Here, indeed, may be the place to mention, that this noble man, in respect of his heart, and goodness and badness, is not altogether easy to get acquainted with; that innumerable persons, of the man-milliner, parish-clerk, and circulating-library sort, will find him a hard nut to crack. Hear in what questionable manner, so early as the year 1773, he expresses himself towards Herr Sulzer, whose beautiful hypothesis, that "Nature meant, by the constant influx of satisfactions streaming in upon us, to fashion our minds, on the whole, to softness and sensibility," he will not leave a leg to stand on. "*On the whole*," says he, "she does no such thing; she rather, God be thanked, hardens her genuine children against the pains and evils she incessantly prepares for them; so that we name him the happiest man who is the strongest to make front against evil, to put it aside from him, and in defiance of it go the road of his own will." "Man's art in all situations is to fortify himself against Nature, to avoid her thousand-fold ills, and only to enjoy his measure of the good; till at length he manages to include the whole circulation of his true and factitious wants in a palace, and fix as far as possible all scattered beauty and felicity within his glass walls, where accordingly he grows ever the weaker, takes to 'joys of the soul,' and his powers, roused to their natural exertion by no contradiction, melt away into" (*horresco referens*)—"Virtue, Benevolence, Sensibility!" In Goethe's Writings, too, we all know the moral lesson is seldom so easily educed as one would wish. Alas, how seldom is he so direct in tendency as his own plain-spoken moralist at Plundersweilern:

"Dear Christian People, one and all,
When will you cease your sinning?
Else can your comfort be but small,
Good hap scarce have beginning;
For Vice is hurtful unto man,
In Virtue lies the surest plan,"

or, to give it in the original words, the emphasis of which no foreign idiom can imitate:

"*Die Tugend ist das hochste Gut,*
Das Laster Weh dem Menschen thut!"

In which emphatic couplet, does there not, as the critics say in other cases, lie the essence of whole volumes, such as we have read?—

Goethe's far most important relation in Strasburg was the accidental temporary one with Herder; which issued, indeed, in a more permanent, though at no time an altogether intimate one. Herder, with much to give, had always something to require; living with him seems never to have been wholly a sinecure. Goethe and he moreover were fundamentally different, not to say discordant; neither could the humour of the latter be peculiarly sweetened by his actual business in Strasburg, that of undergoing a surgical operation on "the lachrymatory duct," and, above all, an unsuccessful one:

"He was attending the prince of Holstein-Eutin, who laboured under mental distresses, on a course of travel; and had arrived with him at Strasburg. Our society, so soon as his presence there was known, felt a strong wish to get near him; which happiness, quite unexpectedly and by chance, befel me first. I had gone to the Inn *zum Geist*, visiting I forget what stranger of rank. Just at the bottom of the stairs I came upon a man, like myself about to ascend, whom by his look I could take to be a clergyman. His powdered hair was fastened up into a round lock; the black coat also distinguished him; still more a long black silk mantle, the end of which he had gathered together and stuck into his pocket. This in some measure surprising, yet on the whole gallant and pleasing figure, of whom I had already heard speak, left me no doubt but it was the famed Traveller; and my address soon convinced him that he was known to me. He asked my name, which could be of no significance to him; however my openness seemed to give pleasure, for he replied to it in friendly style, and as we stepped up stairs forthwith showed himself ready for a lively communication. Our visit also was to the same party; and before separation I begged permission to wait upon himself, which he kindly enough accorded me. I delayed not to make repeated use of this preferment; and was the longer the more attracted towards him. He had something softish in his manner, which was fit and dignified, without strictly being bred. A round face; a fine brow; a somewhat short blunt nose; a somewhat projected, yet highly characteristic, pleasant, amiable mouth. Under black eye-brows, a pair of coal-black eyes, which failed not of their effect, though one of them was wont to be red and inflamed."

With this gifted man, by five years his senior, whose writings had already given him a name, and announced the much that lay in him, the open-hearted disciple could manifoldly communicate, learning and enduring. Ere long, under that "softish manner," there disclosed itself a "counter-pulse" of causticity, of ungentle, almost noisy banter; the blunt nose was too often curled in an aduncosuspensive manner. Whatsoever of self-complacency, of acquired attachment and insight, of self-sufficiency well or ill grounded, lay in the youth, was exposed, we can fancy, to the severest trial. In Herder too, as in an expressive microcosm, he might see imaged the whole wild world of German literature, of European Thought; its old workings and misworkings, its best recent tendencies and efforts; what its past and actual wasteness, perplexity, confusion worse confounded, was. In all which, moreover, the bantered, yet imperturbably inquiring brave young man had quite other than a theoretic interest, being himself minded to dwell there. It is easy to conceive that Herder's presence, stirring up in that fashion so many new and old matters, would mightily aggravate the former "fermentation;"

* *Stilling's Wanderschaft.* Berlin and Leipsic, 1778.

and thereby, it is true, unintentionally or not, forward the same towards clearness.

In fact, with the hastiest glance over the then position of the world spiritual, we shall find that as Disorder is never wanting, (and for the young spiritual hero, who is there only to destroy Disorder and make it order, can least of all be wanting,) so, at the present juncture, it specially abounded. Why dwell on this often delineated Epoch? Over all Europe the reign of Earnestness had now wholly dwindled into that of Dilettantism. The voice of a certain modern "closet logic," which called itself, and could not but call itself, Philosophy, had gone forth, saying, Let there be darkness, and there was darkness. No divinity any longer dwelt in the world; and as men cannot do without a divinity, a sort of terrestrial upholstery one had been got together, and named TASTE, with medallic virtuosi and picture cognoscenti, and enlightened letter and belles-lettres men enough for priests. To which worship, with its stunted formularies and hungry results, must the earnest mind, like the hollow and shallow one, adjust itself, as best might be. To a new man, no doubt the Earth is always new, never wholly without interest. Knowledge, were it only that of dead languages, or of dead actions, the foreign tradition of what others had acquired and done, was still to be searched after; fame might be enjoyed if procurable; above all, the culinary and brewing arts remained in pristine completeness, their results could be relished with pristine vigour. Life lumbered along, better or worse, in pitiful discontent, not yet in decisive desperation, as through a dim day of languor, sultry and sunless. Already too on the horizon might be seen clouds, might be heard murmurs, which by and by proved themselves of an electric character, and were to cool and clear that same sultriness in wondrous deluges.

To a man standing in the midst of German literature, and looking out thither for his highest good, the view was troubled perhaps with various peculiar perplexities. For two centuries, German literature had lain in the sere leaf. The Luther, "whose words were half battles," and such half battles as could shake and overset half Europe with their cannonading, had long since gone to sleep; and all other words were but the miserable bickering of (theological) camp-suttlers in quarrel over the stripping of the slain. Ulrich Hutten slept silent, in the little island of the Zurich Lake; the weary and heavy-laden had wiped the sweat from his brow, and laid him down to rest there: the valiant fire-tempered heart, with all its woes and loves and loving indignations, mouldered, cold, forgotten; with such a pulse no new heart rose to beat. The tamer Opitzes and Flemmings of a succeeding era had, in like manner, long fallen obsolete. One unhappy generation after another of pedants, "rhizophagous," living on roots, Greek or Hebrew; of farce-writers, gallant verse-writers, journalists, and other jugglars of nondescript sort wandered in nomadic wise, whither provender was to be had; among whom, if a passionate Gunther go with some emphasis to ruin; if an illuminated Thomasius, earlier than the general herd, deny witchcraft, we are to esteem it a felicity. This too, however, has passed; and now, in manifold enigmatical signs a new Time announces itself. Well-born Hagedorns, munificent Gleims have again rendered the character of Author honourable; the polish of correct, assiduous Rabeners and Ramlers have smoothed away the old impurities; a pious Klopstock, to the general enthusiasm, rises anew into something of seraphic music, though by methods wherein he can have no follower; the brave spirit of a Lessing pierces, in many a life-giving ray, through the dark inertness: Germany has risen to a level with Europe, is henceforth participant of all European influences; nay it is now appointed, though not yet ascertained, that Germany is to be the leader of spiritual Europe. A deep movement agitates the universal mind of Germany, though as yet no one sees towards what issue; only that heavings and eddyings, confused, conflicting tendencies, work unquietly everywhere; the movement is begun and will not stop, but the course of it is yet far from ascertained. Even to the young man now looking on with such anxious intensity had this very task been allotted: To find it a course and set it flowing thereon.

Whoever will represent this confused revolutionary condition of all things, has but to fancy how it would act on the most susceptive and comprehensive of living minds; what a Chaos he had taken in, and was dimly struggling to body forth into a Creation. Add to which his so confused, contradictory, personal condition; appointed by a positive father to be practitioner of Law, by a still more positive mother (old Nature herself) to be practitioner of Wisdom, and Captain of spiritual Europe; we have confusion enough for him, doubts economic and doubts theologic, doubts moral and æsthetical, a whole world of confusion and doubt.

Nevertheless to the young Strasburg student the gods had given their most precious gift, which is worth all others, without which all others are worth nothing—a seeing eye and a faithful loving heart:

> "*Er hatt' ein Auge treu und klug,*
> *Und war auch liebevoll genug,*
> *Zu schauen manches klar und rein,*
> *Und wieder alles gut zu machen sein;*
> *Hatt' auch eine Zunge die sich ergross,*
> *Und leicht und fein in Worte floss;*
> *Dess thaten die Musen sich erfreun,*
> *Wollten ihn zum Meistersänger weihn.*"*

A mind of all-piercing vision, of sunny strength, not made to ray out darker darkness, but to bring warm sunlight, all purifying, all uniting. A clear, invincible mind, and "consecrated to be Master-singer" in quite another guild than that Nürnberg one.

His first literary productions fall in his twenty-third year; *Werter*, the most celebrated of these, in his twenty-fifth. Of which won-

* *Hans Sachsens Poetische Sendung*, (*Goethe's Werke*, XIII.;) a beautiful piece, (a very *Hans Sachs beatified*, both in character and style,) which we wish there was any possibility of translating.

derful Book, and its now recognised character as poetic (and prophetic) utterance of the World's Despair, it is needless to repeat what has elsewhere been written. This and *Götz von Berlichingen*, which also, as a poetic looking back into the past, was a word for the world, have produced incalculable effects;—which now, indeed, however some departing echo of them may linger in the wrecks of our own Moss-trooper and Satanic Schools, do at length all happily lie behind us. Some trifling incidents at Wetzlar, and the suicide of an unhappy acquaintance were the means of "crystallizing" that wondrous, perilous stuff, which the young heart oppressively held dissolved in it, into this world-famous, and as it proved world-medicative *Werter*. He had gone to Wetzlar with an eye still to Law; which now, however, was abandoned, never to be resumed. Thus did he too, "like Saul the son of Kish, go out to seek his father's asses, and instead thereof find a kingdom."

With the completion of these two Works (a completion in every sense, for they were not only emitted, but speedily also *de*mitted, and seen over, and left behind,) commences what we can specially call his Life, his activity as Man. The outward particulars of it, from this point where his own Narrative ends, have been briefly summed up in these terms:

"In 1776, the Heir-apparent of Weimar was passing through Frankfort, on which occasion, by the intervention of some friends, he waited upon Goethe. The visit must have been mutually agreeable; for a short time afterwards the young author was invited to court; apparently to contribute his assistance in various literary institutions and arrangements then proceeding or contemplated; and in pursuance of this honourable call, he accordingly settled at Weimar, with the title of *Legationsrath*, and the actual dignity of a place in the in the *Collegium*, (Council.) The connection begun under such favourable auspices, and ever afterwards continued under the like or better, has been productive of important consequences, not only to Weimar but to all Germany. The noble purpose undertaken by the Duchess Amelia was zealously forwarded by the young Duke on his accession; under whose influence, supported and directed by his new Councillor, this inconsiderable state has gained for itself a fairer distinction than any of its larger, richer, or more warlike neighbours. By degrees whatever was brightest in the genius of Germany had been gathered to this little court; a classical theatre was under the superintendence of Goethe and Schiller; here Wieland taught and sung; in the pulpit was Herder; and possessing such a four, the small town of Weimar, some five-and-twenty years ago, might challenge the proudest capital of the world to match it in intellectual wealth. Occupied so profitably to his country, and honourably to himself, Goethe continued rising in favour with his Prince; by degrees a political was added to his literary trust; in 1779 he became Privy Councillor; President in 1782; and at length after his return from Italy, where he had spent two years in varied studies and observation, he was appointed Minister; a post which he only a few years ago resigned, on his final retirement from public affairs."

Notable enough that little Weimar should, in this particular, have brought back, as it were, an old Italian Commonwealth into the nineteenth century! For the Petrarcas and Bocaccios, though reverenced as Poets, were not supposed to have lost their wits as men; but could be employed in the highest services of the state, not only as fit, but as the fittest, to discharge these. Very different with us, where Diplomatists and Governors can be picked up from the highways, or chosen in the manner of blindman's buff, (the first figure you clutch, say rather that clutches *you*, will make a governor;) and, even in extraordinary times, it is thought much if a Milton can become Latin Clerk under some Bulstrode Whitelock, and be called "one Mr. Milton." As if the poet, with his poetry, were no other than a pleasant mountebank, with faculty of a certain ground-and-lofty tumbling which would amuse; for which you must throw him a few coins, a little flattery, otherwise he would not amuse you with it. As if there were any talent whatsoever; above all, as if there were any talent of Poetry, (by the consent of all ages the highest talent, and sometimes pricelessly high,) the first foundation of which were not even these two things, (properly but one thing:) intellectual Perspicacity, with force and honesty of Will. Which two, do they not, in their simplest, quite naked form, constitute the very equipment a Man of Business needs; the very implements whereby *all* business, from that of the delver and ditcher to that of the legislator and imperator, is accomplished; as in their noblest concentration they are still the moving faculty of the Artist and Prophet!

To Goethe himself, this connection with Weimar opened the happiest course of life, which probably the age he lived in could have yielded him. Moderation yet abundance; elegance without luxury or sumptuosity: Art enough to give a heavenly firmament to his existence; Business enough to give it a solid earth. In his multifarious duties, he comes in contact with all manner of men; gains experience and tolerance of all men's ways. A faculty like his, which could master the highest spiritual problems, and conquer Evil Spirits in their own domain, was not likely to be foiled by such when they put on the simpler shape of material clay. The greatest of Poets is also the skilfullest of Managers: the little terrestrial Weimar trust committed to him prospers; and one sees with a sort of smile, in which may lie a deep seriousness, how the Jena Museums, University arrangements, Weimar Art-exhibitions and Palace-buildings, are guided smoothly on, by a hand which could have worthily swayed imperial sceptres. The world, could it intrust its imperial sceptres to such hands, were blessed: nay to this man, without the world's consent, given or asked, a still higher function *had* been committed. But on the whole, we name his external life happy, among the happiest, in this, that a noble princely Courtesy could dwell in it based on the worship, by speech and practice, of Truth only, (for his victory, as we said above, was so complete, as almost to hide that there had been a struggle,) and the worldly could praise him as the most agreeable of men, and the spiritual as the highest and clearest; but happy, above all, in this, that it forwarded him, as no other could have done, in his inward life, the good or evil hap of which was alone of permanent importance.

The inward life of Goethe, onwards from this epoch, lies nobly recorded in the long series of his Writings. Of these, meanwhile, the great bulk of our English world has nowise yet got to such understanding and mastery, that we could, with much hope of profit, go into a critical examination of their merits and characteristics. Such a task can stand over till the day for it arrive; be it in this generation, or the next, or after the next. What has been elsewhere already set forth suffices the present want, or needs only to be repeated and enforced; the expositor of German things must say, with judicious Zanga in the play: "First recover that, then shalt thou know more." A glance over the grand outlines of the matter, and more especially under the aspect suitable to these days, can alone be in place here.

In *Goethe's Works*, Chronologically arranged, we see this above all things: A mind working itself into clearer and clearer freedom; gaining a more and more perfect dominion of its world. The pestilential fever of Skepticism runs through its stages: but happily it ends and disappears at the last stage, not in death, not in chronic malady (the commonest) way, but in clearer, henceforth invulnerable health. *Werter* we called the voice of the world's despair: passionate, uncontrollable is this voice; not yet melodious and supreme,—as nevertheless we at length hear it in the wild apocalyptic *Faust*: like a death-song of departing worlds; no voice of joyful "morning stars singing together" over a Creation; but of red nigh-extinguished midnight stars, in spheral swan-melody, proclaiming: It is ended!

What follows, in the next period, we might, for want of a fitter term, call Pagan or Ethnic in character; meaning thereby an anthropomorphic character, akin to that of old Greece and Rome. *Wilhelm Meister* is of that stamp: warm, hearty, sunny human Endeavour; a free recognition of Life in its depth, variety, and majesty; as yet no Divinity recognised there. The famed *Venetian Epigrams* are of the like Old-Ethnic tone: musical, joyfully strong; true, yet not the whole truth, and sometimes in their blunt realism, jarring on the sense. As in this, oftener cited, perhaps, by a certain class of wise men, than the due proportion demanded:

"Why so bustleth the People and crieth? Would find itself victual,
Children too would beget, feed on the best may be had:
Mark in thy notebooks, Traveller, this, and at home go do likewise;
Farther reacheth no man, make he what stretching he will."

Doubt reduced into Denial, now lies prostrate under foot: the fire has done its work, an old world is in ashes; but the smoke and the flame are blown away, and a sun again shines clear over the ruin, to raise therefrom a new nobler verdure and flowerage. Till at length, in the third, or final period, melodious Reverence becomes triumphant; a deep all-pervading Faith, with mild voice, grave as gay, speaks forth to us in a *Meisters Wanderjahre*, in a *West-Ostlicher Divan*; in many a little *Zahme Xenie*, and true-hearted little rhyme, "which," it has been said, "for pregnancy and genial significance, except in the Hebrew Scriptures, you will nowhere match." As here, striking in almost at a venture:

"Like as a Star,
That maketh not haste,
That taketh not rest,
Be each one fulfilling
His god-given Hest."*

* *Wie das Gestirn,*
Ohne Hast,
Aber ohne Rast,
Drehe sich jeder
Um die eigne Last.

So stands it in the original: hereby, however, hangs a tale:

"A fact," says one of our fellow labourers in this German vineyard, "has but now come to our knowledge, which we take pleasure and pride in stating. Fifteen Englishmen, entertaining that high consideration for the Good Goethe, which the labours and high deserts of a long life usefully employed so richly merit from all mankind, have presented him with a highly wrought Seal, as a token of their veneration. We must pass over the description of the gift, for it would be too elaborate;" suffice it to say, that amid tasteful carving and emblematic embossing enough, stood these words engraven on a gold belt, on the four sides respectively: *To the German Master: From Friends in England: 28th August:* 1831; finally, that the impression was a star encircled with a serpent-of-eternity, and this motto: *Ohne Hast Aber Ohne Rast.*

"The following is the letter which accompanied it:

"'*To the Poet Goethe, on the* 28*th of August*, 1831.

"'Sir,—Among the friends whom this interesting Anniversary calls round you, may we "English friends," in thought and symbolically, since personally it is impossible, present ourselves to offer you our affectionate congratulations. We hope you will do us the honour to accept this little Birth-Day Gift, which, as a true testimony of our feelings, may not be without value.

"'We said to ourselves: As it is always the highest duty and pleasure to show reverence to whom reverence is due, and our chief, perhaps our only benefactor is he who by act and word instructs us in wisdom,—so we, undersigned, feeling towards the Poet Goethe as the spiritually taught towards their spiritual teacher, are desirous to express that sentiment openly and in common; for which end we have determined to solicit his acceptance of a small English gift, proceeding from us all equally, on his approaching birth-day; that so, while the venerable man still dwells among us, some memorial of the gratitude we owe him, and think the whole world owes him, may not be wanting.

"'And thus our little tribute, perhaps among the purest that men could offer to man, now stands in visible shape, and begs to be received. May it be welcome, and speak permanently of a most close relation, though wide seas flow between the parties!

"'We pray that many years may be added to a life so glorious, that all happiness may be yours, and strength given to complete your high task, even as it has hitherto proceeded, like a star, without haste, yet without rest.

"'We remain, Sir, your friends and Servants,
FIFTEEN ENGLISHMEN.'

"The wonderful old man, to whom distant and unknown friends had paid such homage, could not but be moved at sentiments expressed in such terms. We hear that he values the token highly, and has condescended to return the following lines for answer;—

"'DEN FUNFZEHN ENGLISCHEN FREUNDEN.

Worte die der Dichter spricht,
Treu, in heimischen Bezirken,
Wirken gleich, doch weiss er nicht
Ob sie in die Ferne wirken.

Or this small Couplet, which the reader, if he will, may substitute for whole horse-loads of *Essays on the Origin of Evil;* a spiritual manufacture, which in these enlightened times ought ere now to have gone out of fashion:

"'What shall I teach thee, the foremost thing?'
Couldst teach me off my own Shadow to spring!"

Or the pathetic picturesqueness of this:

"A rampart-breach is every Day,
Which many mortals are storming:
Fall in the gap who may,
Of the slain no heap is forming."

Eine Bresche ist jeder Tag.
Die viele Menschen erstürmen;
Wer da auch fallen mag,
Die Todten sich niemals thürmen.

In such spirit, and with an eye that takes in all provinces of human Thought, Feeling, and Activity, does the Poet stand forth as the true prophet of his time: victorious over its contradiction, possessor of its wealth; embodying the nobleness of the past into a new whole, into a new vital nobleness for the present and the future. Antique nobleness in all kinds, yet worn with new clearness; the spirit of it is preserved and again revealed in shape, when the former shape and vesture had become old, (as vestures do,) and was dead and cast forth; and we mourned as if the spirit too were gone. This, we are aware, is a high saying; applicable to no other man living, or that has lived for some two centuries; ranks Goethe, not only as the highest man of his time, but as a man of universal Time, important for all generations—one of the landmarks in the History of Men.

Thus from our point of view does Goethe rise on us as the Uniter, and victorious Reconciler, of the distracted clashing elements of the most distracted and divided age, that the world has witnessed since the Introduction of the Christian Religion; to which old chaotic Era, of world-confusion and world-*re*fusion, of blackest darkness, succeeded by a dawn of light and nobler "dayspring from on high," this wondrous Era of ours is, indeed, often likened. To the faithful heart let no era be a desperate one! It is ever the nature of Darkness to be followed by a new nobler Light; nay, to produce such. The woes and contradictions of an Atheistic time; of a world sunk in wickedness and baseness and unbelief, wherein also physical wretchedness, the disorganization and broken-heartedness of whole classes struggling in ignorance and pain will not fail: all this, the view of all this, falls like a Sphinx-question on every new-born earnest heart, a life-and-death entanglement for every earnest heart to deliver itself from, and the world from. Of Wisdom cometh Strength: only when there is "no vision" do the people perish. But, by natural vicissitudes, the age of *Persiflage* goes out, and that of earnest unconquerable Endeavour must come in: for the ashes of the old fire will not warm men anew; the new generation is too desolate to indulge in mockery,—unless, perhaps, in bitter suicidal mockery of itself! Thus after Voltaires enough have laughed and sniffed at what is false, appear some Turgots to ask what is true. Wo to the land where, in these seasons, no prophet arises; but only censors, satirists, and embittered desperadoes to make the evil worse; at best but to accelerate a consummation, which, in accelerating, they have aggravated! Old Europe had its Tacitus and Juvenal; but these availed not. New Europe too has had its Mirabeaus, and Byrons, and Napoleons, and innumerable red-flaming meteors, shaking pestilence from their hair; and earthquakes and deluges, and Chaos come again; but the clear Star, day's harbinger, (*Phosphorus*, the bringer of *light*,) had not yet been recognised.

That in Goethe there lay Force to educe reconcilement out of such contradiction as man is now born into, marks him as the Strong One of his time; the true *Earl*, though now with quite other weapons than those old steel *Jarls* were used to! Such reconcilement of contradictions, indeed, is the task of every man: the weakest reconciles somewhat; reduces old chaotic elements into new higher order; ever, according to faculty and endeavour, brings good out of evil. Consider now what faculty and endeavour must belong to the highest of such tasks, which virtually includes all others whatsoever! The thing that was given this man to reconcile (to begin reconciling, and teach us how to reconcile) was the inward spiritual chaos; the centre of all other confusions, outward and inward: he was to close the Abyss out of which such manifold destruction, moral, intellectual, social, was proceeding.

The greatness of his Endowment, manifested in such a work, has long been plain to all men. That it belongs to the highest class of human endowments, entitling the wearer thereof, who so nobly used it to the appellation in its strictest sense, of Great Man,—is also becoming plain. A giant strength of Character is to be traced here; mild and kindly and calm, even as strength ever is. In the midst of so much spasmodic Byronism, bellowing till its windpipe is cracked, how very different looks *this* symptom of strength: "He appeared to aim at pushing away from him every thing that did hang upon his individual will." "In his own imperturbable firmness of character, he had grown into the habit of *never contradicting any one.* On the contrary, he listened with a friendly air to every one's opinion, and would himself elucidate and strengthen it by instances and reasons of his own. All who did not know him fancied that he thought as they did; for he was possessed of a preponderating intellect, and could transport himself into the mental state of any man and imitate his manner of conceiving."* Beloved brethren, who wish to be strong! Had not the man, who could take this smooth method of it, more strength in him than any teeth-grinding, glass-eyed "lone Caloyer" you have yet fallen in with? Consider

---

Britten! habt sie aufgefasst:
"*Thätigen Sinn, das Thun gezügelt;*
Stetig Streben ohne Hast;"
Und so wollt Ihrs denn besiegelt!
'*Weimar, d. 28ten August,* 1831.' GOETHE.'"
(*Fraser's Magazine,* XXII. 447.)

And thus, as it chanced, was the poet's *last* birth-day celebrated by an outward ceremony of a peculiar kind; wherein, too, it is to be hoped, might lie some inward meaning and sincerity.

* *Wilhelm Meister,* book vi.

your ways; consider first, Whether you cannot do with being *weak!* If the answer still prove negative, consider, secondly, what strength actually is, and where you are to try for it. A certain strong man, of former time, fought stoutly at Lepanto; worked stoutly as Algerine slave; stoutly delivered himself from such working, with stout cheerfulness endured famine and nakedness and the world's ingratitude; and sitting in jail, with the one arm left him, wrote our joyfullest, and all but our deepest, modern book, and named it *Don Quixote:* this was a genuine strong man. A strong man, of recent time, fights little for any good cause anywhere; works weakly as an English lord; weakly delivers himself from such working; with weak despondency endures the cackling of plucked geese at St. James's, and, sitting in sunny Italy, in his coach-and-four, at a distance of two thousand miles from them, writes, over many reams of paper, the following sentence, with variations: *Saw ever the world one greater or unhappier?* this was a sham strong man. Choose ye.—

Of Goethe's spiritual Endowment, looked at on the Intellectual side, we have, (as indeed lies in the nature of things, for moral and intellectual are fundamentally one and the same,) to pronounce a similar opinion; that it is great among the very greatest. As the first gift of all, may be discerned here, utmost Clearness; all-piercing faculty of Vision; whereto, as we ever find it, all other gifts are superadded; nay, properly they are but other forms of the same gift. A nobler power of insight than this of Goethe, you in vain look for, since Shakspeare passed away. In fact, there is much every way, here in particular, that these two minds have in common. Shakspeare too does not look *at* a thing, but into it, through it; so that he constructively comprehends it, can take it asunder, and put it together again; the thing melts, as it were, into light under his eye, and anew *creates* itself before him. That is to say, he is a Thinker in the highest of all senses: he is a Poet. For Goethe, as for Shakspeare, the world lies all translucent, all *fusible*, (we might call it,) encircled with Wonder; the Natural in reality the Supernatural, for to the seer's eyes both become one. What are the *Hamlets* and *Tempests*, the *Fausts* and *Mignons*, but glimpses accorded us into this translucent, wonder-encircled world: revelations of the mystery of all mysteries, Man's Life as it actually is?

Under other secondary aspects, the poetical faculty of the two will still be found cognate. Goethe is full of *figurativeness;* this grand light-giving Intellect, as all such are, is an imaginative one,—and in a quite other sense than most of our unhappy Imaginatives will imagine. Gall the Craniologist declared him to be a born *Volksredner*, (popular orator,) both by the figure of his brow, and what was still more decisive, because "he could not speak but a figure came." Gall saw what was high as his own nose reached,

"High as the nose doth reach, all clear!
What higher lies, they ask: Is it here?"

A far different figurativeness was this of Goethe than popular oratory has work for. In figures of the popular oratory kind, Goethe, throughout his Writings at least, is nowise the most copious man known to us, though on a stricter scrutiny we may find him the richest. Of your ready-made, coloured-paper metaphors, such as can be sewed or plastered on the surface, by way of giving an ornamental finish to the rag-web already woven, we speak not; there is not one such to be discovered in all his Works. But even in the use of genuine metaphors, that are not haberdashery ornament, but the genuine new vesture of new thoughts, he yields to lower men, (for example, to Jean Paul;) that is to say, in fact, he is more master of the *common* language, and can oftener make *it* serve him. Goethe's figurativeness lies in the very centre of his being; manifests itself as the constructing of the inward elements of a thought, as the *vital* imbodyment of it: such figures as those of Goethe you will look for through all modern literature, and except here and there in Shakspeare, nowhere find a trace of. Again, it is the same faculty in higher exercise, that enables the poet to construct a Character. Here too Shakspeare and Goethe, unlike innumerable others, are *vital;* their construction begins at the *heart* and flows outward as the life-streams do: fashioning the *surface*, as it were, spontaneously. Those Macbeths and Falstaffs, accordingly, these Fausts and Philinas, have a verisimilitude and life that separates them from all other fictions of late ages. All others, in comparison, have more or less the nature of hollow vizards, constructed from without inwards, painted *like*, and deceptively put in motion. Many years ago on finishing our first perusal of *Wilhelm Meister*, with a very mixed sentiment in other respects, we could not but feel that here lay more insight into the elements of human nature, and a more poetically perfect combining of these than in all the other fictitious literature of our generation.

Neither, as an additional similarity, (for the great is ever like itself,) let the majestic Calmness of both be omitted; their perfect tolerance for all men and all things. This too proceeds from the same source, perfect clearness of vision: he who comprehends an object cannot hate it, has already begun to love it. In respect of style, no less than of character, this calmness and graceful smooth-flowing softness is again characteristic of both: though in Goethe the quality is more complete, having been matured by far more assiduous study. Goethe's style is perhaps to be reckoned the most excellent that our modern world, in any language, can exhibit. "Even to a foreigner," says one, "it is full of character and secondary meanings; polished, yet vernacular and cordial, it sounds like the dialect of wise, antique-minded, true-hearted men: in poetry, brief, sharp, simple, and expressive: in prose, perhaps, still more pleasing; for it is at once concise and full, rich, clear, unpretending, and melodious; and the sense, not presented in alternating flashes, piece after piece revealed and withdrawn, rises before us as in continuous dawning, and stands at last simultaneously complete, and bathed in the mellowest and ruddiest sunshine. It brings to mind what the prose of Hooker, Bacon, Milton, Browne, would have been, had they written under the good, without the bad influences of that French precision, which has polished and attenuated, trimmed and impoverished all modern languages; made our meaning clear, and too often shallow as well as clear." *

Finally, as Shakspeare is to be considered as the greater nature of the two, on the other hand we must admit him to have been the less cultivated, and much the more careless. What Shakspeare *could* have done we nowhere discover. A careless mortal, open to the Universe and its influences, not caring strenuously to open himself; who, Prometheus-like, will scale Heaven, (if it so must be,) and is satisfied if he therewith pay the rent of his London Playhouse; who, had the Warwickshire Justice let him hunt deer unmolested, might, for many years more, have lived quiet on the green earth without such aerial journeys: an unparalleled mortal. In the great Goethe, again, we see a man through life at his utmost strain; a man that, as he says himself, "struggled toughly;" laid hold of all things, under all aspects, scientific or poetic: engaged passionately with the deepest interests of man's existence, in the most complex age of man's history. What Shakspeare's thoughts on "God, Nature, Art," would have been, especially had he lived to number fourscore years, were curious to know: Goethe's, delivered in many-toned melody, as the apocalypse of our era, are here, for us to know.

Such was the noble talent intrusted to this man; such the noble employment he made thereof. We can call him, once more, "a clear and universal man;" we can say that, in his universality, as thinker, as singer, as worker, he lived a life of antique nobleness under these new conditions; and, in so living, is alone in all Europe; the foremost, whom others are to learn from and follow. In which great act, or rather great sum total of many acts, who shall compute what treasure of new strengthening, of faith become hope and vision, lies secured for all! The question, Can man still live in devoutness, yet without blindness or contraction; in unconquerable steadfastness for the right, yet without tumultuous exasperation against the wrong; as an antique worthy, yet with the expansion and increased endowment of a modern? is no longer a question, but has become a certainty, and ocularly-visible fact.

We have looked at Goethe, as we engaged to do, "on *this* side," and with the eyes of "this generation;" that is to say, chiefly as a world-changer, and benignant spiritual revolutionist: for in our present so astonishing condition of "progress of the species," such is the category under which we must try all things, wisdom itself. And, indeed, under this aspect too, Goethe's Life and Works are doubtless of incalculable value, and worthy our most earnest study; for his Spiritual History is, as it were, the ideal emblem of all true men's in these days; the goal of Manhood, which he attained, we too in our degree have to aim at; let us mark well the road he fashioned for himself, and in the dim weltering chaos rejoice to find a paved way.

Here, moreover, another word of explanation is perhaps worth adding. We mean in regard to the controversy agitated (as about many things pertaining to Goethe) about his Political Creed and practice, whether he was Ministerial or in Opposition? Let the political admirer of Goethe be at ease: Goethe was both, and also neither! The "rotten white-washed (*gebrechliche übertünchte*) condition of society" was plainer to few eyes than to his, sadder to few hearts than to his. Listen to the Epigrammatist at Venice:

"To this stithy I liken the land, the hammer its ruler,
And the people that plate, beaten between them that writhes:
Wo to the plate, when nothing but wilful bruises on bruises
Hit at random; and made, cometh no Kettle to view!"

But, alas, what is to be done?

"No Apostle-of-Liberty much to my heart ever found I:
License, each for himself, this was at bottom their want.
Liberator of many! first dare to be Servant of many:
What a business is that, wouldst thou know it, go try!"

Let the following also be recommended to all inordinate worshippers of Septennials, Triennials, Elective Franchise, and the Shameful parts of the Constitution; and let each be a little tolerant of his neighbour's "festoon," and rejoice that he has himself found out *Freedom*,—a thing much wanted:

"Walls I can see tumbled down, walls I see also a-building;
Here sit prisoners, there likewise do prisoners sit:
Is the world then itself a huge prison? Free only the madman,
His chains knitting still up into some graceful festoon?"

So that for the Poet what remains but to leave Conservative and Destructive pulling one another's locks and ears off, as they will and can, (the ulterior issue being long since indubitable enough;) and, for his own part, strive day and night to forward the small suffering remnant of *Productives*, of those who, in true manful endeavour, were it under despotism or under sansculottism, create some what,—with whom, alone, in the end, does the hope of the world lie. Go thou and do likewise! Art thou *called* to politics, work therein, as this man would have done, like a real and not an imaginary workman. Understand well, meanwhile, that to no man is his political constitution "a life, but only a house wherein his life is led:" and hast thou a nobler task than such *house*-pargeting and smoke-doctoring, and pulling down of ancient rotten rat-inhabited walls, leave such to the proper craftsman; honour the higher Artist, and good-humouredly say with him:

"All this is neither my coat nor my cake,
Why fill my hand with other men's charges?
The fishes swim at ease in the lake,
And take no thought of the barges."

Goethe's political practice, or rather no-practice, except that of self-defence, is a part of his conduct quite inseparably coherent with the

* *German Romance*, iv.

rest; a thing we could recommend to universal study, that the spirit of it might be understood by all men, and by all men imitated.

Nevertheless it is nowise alone on this revolutionary or "progress-of-the-species" side that Goethe has significance; his Life and Work is no painted show but a solid reality, and may be looked at with profit on all sides, from all imaginable points of view. Perennial, as a possession for ever, Goethe's History and Writings abide there; a thousand-voiced "Melody of Wisdom," which he that has ears may hear. What the experience of the most complexly-situated, deep-searching, every way *far-experienced* man has yielded him of insight, lies written for all men here. He who was of compass to know and feel more than any other man, this is the record of his knowledge and feeling. "The deepest heart, the highest head to scan" was not beyond his faculty; thus, then, did he scan and interpret: let many generations listen, according to their want; let the generation which has no need of listening, and nothing new to learn there, esteem itself a happy one.

To us, meanwhile, to all that wander in darkness and seek light, as the one thing needful, be this possession reckoned among our choicest blessings and distinctions. *Colite talem virum;* learn of him, imitate, emulate him! So did *he* catch the Music of the Universe, and unfold it into clearness, and in authentic celestial tones bring it home to the hearts of men, from amid that soul-confusing Babylonish hubbub of this our new Tower-of-Babel era! For now, too, as in that old time, had men said to themselves: Come, let us build a tower which shall reach to heaven; and by our steam-engines, and logic-engines, and skilful mechanism and manipulation, vanquish not only Physical Nature, but the divine Spirit of Nature, and scale the empyrean itself. Wherefore they must needs again be stricken with confusion of tongues (or of printing-presses,) and *dispersed*,—to other work; wherein also let us hope, their hammers and trowels shall better avail them.—

Of Goethe, with a feeling such as can be due to no other man, we now take farewell: *vixit, vivit.*

CORN-LAW RHYMES.*

[Edinburgh Review, 1832.]

Smelfungus Redivivus, throwing down his critical assaying-balance, some years ago, and taking leave of the Belles-Lettres function, expressed himself in this abrupt way: "The end having come, it is fit that we end. Poetry having ceased to be read, or published, or written, how can it continue to be reviewed? With your Lake Schools, and Border-Thief Schools, and Cockney and Satanic Schools, there has been enough to do; and now, all these Schools having burnt or smouldered themselves out, and left nothing but a wide-spread wreck of ashes, dust, and cinders,—or perhaps dying embers, kicked to and fro under the feet of innumerable women and children in the Magazines, and at best blown here and there into transient sputters, with vapour enough, so as to form what you might name a boundless Green-sick, or New-Sentimental, or Sleep-Awake School,—what remains but to adjust ourselves to circumstances? Urge me not," continues the able Editor, suddenly changing his figure, "with considerations that Poetry, as the inward voice of Life, must be perennial, only dead in one form to become alive in another; that this still abundant deluge of Metre, seeing there must needs be fractions of Poetry floating scattered in it, ought still to be net-fished, at all events, surveyed and taken note of: the survey of English Metre, at this epoch, perhaps transcends the human faculties; to hire out the reading of it, by estimate, at a remunerative rate per page, would, in few Quarters, reduce the cash-box of any extant Review to the verge of insolvency."

What our distinguished contemporary has said remains said. Far be it from us to censure or counsel any able Editor; to draw aside the Editorial veil, and, officiously prying into his interior mysteries, impugn the laws he walks by! For Editors, as for others, there are times of perplexity, wherein the cunning of the wisest will scantily suffice his own wants, say nothing of his neighbour's.

To us, on our side, meanwhile, it remains clear that Poetry, or were it but Metre, should nowise be altogether neglected. Surely it is the Reviewer's trade to sit watching, not only the tillage, crop-rotation, marketings, and good or evil husbandry of the Economic Earth, but also the weather-symptoms of the Literary Heaven, on which those former so much depend: if any promising or threatening meteoric phenomenon make its appearance, and he proclaim not tidings thereof, it is at his peril. Farther, be it considered how, in this singular poetic epoch, a small matter constitutes a novelty. If the whole welkin hang overcast in drizzly dinginess, the feeblest light-gleam, or speck of blue, cannot pass unheeded.

The Works of this Corn-Law Rhymer we might liken rather to some little fraction of a rainbow: hues of joy and harmony, painted

* 1. Corn-Law Rhymes. Third Edition. 8vo. London, 1831.
2. Love; a Poem. By the Author of Corn-Law Rhymes. Third Edition. 8vo. London, 1831.
3. The Village Patriarch; a Poem. By the Author of Corn-Law Rhymes. 12mo. London, 1831.

out of troublous tears. No round full bow, indeed; gloriously spanning the heavens; shone on by the full sun; and, with seven-striped, gold-crimson border (as is in some sort the office of Poetry) dividing Black from Brilliant: not such; alas, still far from it! Yet, in very truth, a little prismatic blush, glowing genuine among the wet clouds; which proceeds, if you will, from a sun cloud-hidden, yet indicates that a sun does shine, and above those vapours, a whole azure vault and celestial firmament stretch serene.

Strange as it may seem, it is nevertheless true, that here we have once more got sight of a Book calling itself Poetry, yet which actually is a kind of Book, and no empty paste-board Case, and simulacrum or "ghost-defunct" of a Book, such as is too often palmed on the world, and handed over Booksellers' counters, with a demand of real money for it, as if it too were a reality. The speaker here is of that singular class, who have something to say; whereby, though delivering himself in verse, and in these days, he does not deliver himself wholly in jargon, but articulately, and with a certain degree of meaning, that has been *believed*, and therefore is again believable.

To some the wonder and interest will be heightened by another circumstance: that the speaker in question is not school-learned, or even furnished with pecuniary capital; is, indeed, a quite unmoneyed, russet-coated speaker; nothing or little other than a Sheffield worker in brass and iron, who describes himself as "one of the lower, little removed above the lowest class." Be of what class he may, the man is provided, as we can perceive, with a rational god-created soul; which too has fashioned itself into some clearness, some self-subsistence, and can actually see and know with its own organs; and in rugged substantial English, nay, with tones of poetic melody, utter forth what it has seen.

It used to be said that lions do not paint, that poor men do not write; but the case is altering now. Here is a voice coming from the deep Cyclopean forges, where Labour, in real soot and sweat, beats with his thousand hammers "the red son of the furnace;" doing personal battle with Necessity, and her dark brute Powers, to make them reasonable and serviceable; an intelligible voice from the hitherto Mute and Irrational, to tell us at first hand how it is with him, what in very deed is the theorem of the world and of himself, which he, in those dim depths of his, in that wearied head of his, has put together. To which voice, in several respects significant enough, let good ear be given.

Here too, be it premised, that nowise under the category of "Uneducated Poets," or in any fashion of dilettante patronage, can our Sheffield friend be produced. His position is unsuitable for that: so is ours. Genius, which the French lady declared to be of no sex, is much more certainly of no rank; neither when "the spark of Nature's fire" has been imparted, should Education take high airs in her artificial light,—which is too often but phosphorescence and putrescence. In fact, it now begins to be suspected here and there, that this same aristocratic recognition, which looks down with an obliging smile from its throne, of bound Volumes and gold Ingots, and admits that it is wonderfully well for one of the uneducated classes, may be getting out of place. There are unhappy times in the world's history, when he that is the least educated will chiefly have to say that he is the least perverted; and with the multitude of false eye-glasses, convex, concave, green, even yellow, has not lost the natural use of his eyes. For a generation that reads Cobbett's Prose, and Burns's Poetry, it need be no miracle that here also is a man who can handle both pen and hammer like a man.

Nevertheless, this serene-highness attitude and temper is so frequent, perhaps it were good to turn the tables for a moment, and see what look it has under that reverse aspect. How were it if we surmised, that for a man gifted with natural vigour, with a man's character to be developed in him, more especially if in the way of Literature, as Thinker and Writer, it is actually, in these strange days, no special misfortune to be trained up among the Uneducated classes, and not among the Educated; but rather of two misfortunes the smaller?

For all men doubtless obstructions abound; spiritual growth must be hampered and stunted, and has to struggle through with difficulty, if it do not wholly stop. We may grant too that, for a mediocre character, the continual training and tutoring, from language-masters, dancing-masters, posture-masters of all sorts, hired and volunteer, which a high rank in any time and country assures, there will be produced a certain superiority, or at worst, air of superiority, over the corresponding mediocre character of low rank: thus we perceive the vulgar Do-nothing, as contrasted with the vulgar Drudge, is in general a much prettier man; with a wider, perhaps clearer, outlook into the distance; in innumerable superficial matters, however it may be when we we go deeper, he has a manifest advantage. But with the man of uncommon character, again, in whom a germ of irrepressible Force has been implanted, and *will* unfold itself into some sort of freedom,—altogether the reverse may hold. For such germs, too, there is undoubtedly enough, a proper soil where they will grow best, and an improper one where they will grow worst. True also, where there is a will, there is a way; where a genius has been given, a possibility, a certainty of its growing is also given. Yet often it seems as if the injudicious gardening and manuring were worse than none at all; and killed what the inclemencies of blind chance would have spared. We find accordingly that few Frederics or Napoleons, indeed none since the great Alexander, who unfortunately drank himself to death too soon for proving what lay in him, were nursed up with an eye to their vocation: mostly with an eye quite the other way, in the midst of isolation and pain, destitution and contradiction. Nay, in our own times, have we not seen two men of genius, a Byron and a Burns; they both, by mandate of Nature, struggle and must struggle towards clear Manhood, stormfully enough, for the space of six-and-thirty years; yet only the gifted Ploughman can partially prevail therein: the gifted Peer must toil and strive, and shoot out in wild efforts, yet die at last in Boyhood, with the promise of his Manhood still but announcing itself in the distance. Truly, as was once written, "it is only the artichoke that will not grow except in gardens; the acorn is cast carelessly abroad into the wilderness, yet on the wild soil it nourishes itself, and rises to be an oak." All woodmen, moreover, will tell you that fat manure is the ruin of your oak; likewise that the thinner and wilder your soil, the tougher, more iron-textured is your timber,—though, unhappily, also, the smaller. So too with the spirits of men: they become pure from their errors, by suffering for them; he who has battled, were it only with poverty and hard toil, will be found stronger, more expert, than he who could stay at home from the battle, concealed among the Provision-wagons, or even not unwatchfully "abiding by the stuff." In which sense, an observer, not without experience of our time, has said: "Had I a man of clearly developed character, (clear, sincere within its limits,) of insight, courage, and real applicable force of head and of heart, to search for; and not a man of luxuriously distorted character, with haughtiness for courage, and for insight and applicable force, speculation and plausible show of force,—it were rather among the lower than the higher classes that I should look for him."

A hard saying, indeed, seems this same: that he whose other wants were all beforehand supplied; to whose capabilities no problem was presented except even this, How to cultivate them to best advantage, should attain less real culture than he whose first grand problem and obligation was nowise spiritual culture, but hard labour for his daily bread! Sad enough must the perversion be where preparations of such magnitude issue in abortion; and a so sumptuous Art with all its appliances can accomplish nothing, not so much as necessitous Nature would of herself have supplied! Nevertheless, so pregnant is Life with evil as with good; to such height in an age rich, plethorically overgrown with means, can means be accumulated in the wrong place, and immeasurably aggravate wrong tendencies, instead of righting them, this sad and strange result may actually turn out to have been realized.

But what, after all, is meant by *uneducated*, in a time when Books have come into the world; come to the household furniture in every habitation of the civilized world? In the poorest cottage are Books: is one Book, wherein for several thousands of years the spirit of man has found light, and nourishment, and an interpreting response to whatever is Deepest in him; wherein still, to this day, for the eye that will look well, the Mystery of Existence reflects itself, if not resolved, yet revealed, and prophetically emblemed; if not to the satisfying of the outward sense, yet to the opening of the inward sense, which is the far grander result. "In Books lie the creative Phœnix-ashes of the whole Past." All that men have devised, discovered, done, felt, or imagined, lies recorded in Books; wherein whoso has learned the mystery of spelling printed letters, may find it, and appropriate it.

Nay, what indeed is all this? As if it were by universities and libraries and lecture-rooms, that man's Education, what we can call Education, were accomplished: solely, or mainly, by instilling the dead letter and record of other men's Force, that the living Force of a new man were to be awakened, enkindled, and purified into victorious clearness! Foolish Pedant, that sittest there compassionately descanting on the Learning of Shakspeare! Shakspeare had penetrated into innumerable things; far into Nature with her divine Splendours and infernal Terrors, her Ariel Melodies, and mystic mandragora Moans; far into man's workings with Nature, into man's Art and Artifice; Shakspeare knew (*kenned*, which in those day's still partially meant *can-ned*) innumerable things; what men are, and what the world is, and how and what men aim at there, from the Dame Quickly of modern Eastcheap to the Cæsar of ancient Rome, over many countries, over many centuries: of all this he had the clearest understanding and constructive comprehension; all this was his Learning and Insight: what now is thine? Insight into none of those things; perhaps, strictly considered, into no thing whatever: solely into thy own sheepskin diplomas, fat academic honours, into vocables and alphabetic letters, and but a little way into these!—The grand result of schooling is a mind with just vision to discern, with free force to do: the grand schoolmaster is Practice.

And now, when *kenning* and *can-ning* have become two altogether different words; and this, the first principle of human culture, the foundation-stone of all but false imaginary culture, that men must, before every other thing, be trained to *do* somewhat, has been, for some generations, laid quietly on the shelf, with such result as we see,—consider what advantage those same uneducated Working classes have over the educated Unworking classes, in one particular; herein, namely, that they must *work*. To work! What incalculable sources of cultivation lie in that process, in that attempt; how it lays hold of the whole man, not of a small theoretical calculating fraction of him, but of the whole practical, doing and daring and enduring man; thereby to awaken dormant faculties, root out old errors, at every step! He that has done nothing has known nothing. Vain is it to sit scheming and plausibly discoursing: up and be doing! If thy knowledge be real, put it forth from thee: grapple with real Nature; try thy theories there, and see how they hold out. *Do* one thing, for the first time in thy life do a thing: a new light will rise to thee on the doing of all things whatsoever. Truly, a boundless significance lies in work: whereby the humblest craftsman comes to attain much, which is of indispensable use, but which he who is of no craft, were he never so high, runs the risk of missing. Once turn to Practice, Error and Truth will no longer consort together: the result of

Error involves you in the square-root of a negative quantity; try to *extract* it, or any earthly substance or sustenance from it, if you will! The honourable Member can discover that "there is a reaction," and believe it, and wearisomely reason on it, in spite of all men, while he so pleases, for still his wine and his oil will not fail him: but the sooty Brazier, who discovered that brass was green-cheese, has to act on his discovery; finds, therefore, that, singular as it may seem, brass cannot be masticated for dinner, green-cheese will not beat into fireproof dishes: that such discovery, therefore, has no legs to stand on, and must even be let fall. Now, take this principle of difference through the entire lives of two men, and calculate what it will amount to! Necessity, moreover, which we here see as the mother of Accuracy, is well known as the mother of Invention. He who wants every thing, must know many things, do many things, to procure even a few: different enough with him, whose indispensable knowledge is this only, that a finger will pull the bell.

So that, for all men who live, we may conclude, this Life of Man is a school, wherein the naturally foolish will continue foolish though you bray him in a mortar, but the naturally wise will gather wisdom under every disadvantage. What, meanwhile, must be the condition of an Era, when the highest advantages there become perverted into drawbacks; when, if you take two men of genius, and put the one between the handles of a plough, and mount the other between the painted coronets of a coach-and-four, and bid them both move along, the former shall arrive a Burns, the latter a Byron: two men of talent, and put the one into a Printer's chapel, full of lampblack, tyrannous usage, hard toil, and the other into Oxford universities, with lexicons and libraries, and hired expositors and sumptuous endowments, the former shall come out a Dr. Franklin, the latter a Dr. Parr!—

However, we are not here to write an Essay on Education, or sing *misereres* over a "world in its dotage;" but simply to say that our Corn-Law Rhymer, educated or uneducated as Nature and Art have made him, asks not the smallest patronage or compassion for his rhymes, professes not the smallest contrition for them. Nowise in such attitude does he present himself; not supplicatory, deprecatory, but sturdy, defiant, almost menacing. Wherefore, indeed, should he supplicate or deprecate? It is out of the abundance of the heart that he has spoken; praise or blame cannot make it truer or falser than it already is. By the grace of God this man is sufficient for himself; by his skill in metallurgy, can beat out a toilsome but a manful living, go how it may; has arrived too at that singular audacity of believing what he knows, and acting on it, or writing on it, or thinking on it, without leave asked of any one: there shall he stand, and work, with head and with hand, for himself and the world; blown about by no wind of doctrine; frightened at no Reviewer's shadow; having, in his time, looked substances enough in the face, and remained unfrightened.

What is left, therefore, but to take what he brings, and as he brings it? Let us be thankful, were it only for the day of small things. Something it is that we have lived to welcome once more a sweet Singer wearing the likeness of a Man. In humble guise, it is true, and of stature more or less marred in its development; yet not without a genial robustness, strength and valour, built on honesty and love; on the whole, a genuine man, with somewhat of the eye and speech and bearing that beseems a man. To whom all other genuine men, how different soever in subordinate particulars, can gladly hold out the right hand of fellowship.

The great excellence of our Rhymer, be it understood then, we take to consist even in this, often hinted at already, that he *is genuine.* Here is an earnest, truth-speaking man; no theorizer, sentimentalizer, but a practical man of work and endeavour, man of sufferance and endurance. The thing that he speaks is not a hearsay, but a thing which he has himself known, and by experience become assured of. He has used his eyes for seeing; uses his tongue for declaring what he has seen. His voice, therefore, among the many noises of our Planet, will deserve its place better than the most; will be well worth some attention. Whom else should we attend to but such? The man who speaks with some half shadow of a Belief, and supposes, and inclines to think; and considers not with undivided soul, what is true, but only what is plausible, and will find audience and recompense; do we not meet him at every street-turning, on all highways and byways; is he not stale, unprofitable, ineffectual, wholly grown a weariness of the flesh? So rare is his opposite in any rank of Literature, or of Life, so very rare, that even in the lowest he is precious. The authentic insight and experience of any human soul, were it but insight and experience in hewing of wood and drawing of water, is real knowledge, a real possession and acquirement, how small soever: *palabra*, again, were it a supreme pontiff's, is wind merely, and nothing, or less than nothing. To a considerable degree, this man, we say, has worked himself loose from cant, and conjectural halfness, idle pretences and hallucinations, into a condition of Sincerity. Wherein, perhaps, as above argued, his hard social environment, and fortune to be "a workman born," which brought so many other retardations with it, may have forwarded and accelerated him.

That a man, Workman, or Idleman, encompassed, as in these days, with persons in a state of willing or unwilling Insincerity, and necessitated, as man is to learn whatever he does traditionally learn by *imitating* these, should nevertheless shake off Insincerity, and struggle out from that dim pestiferous marsh-atmosphere, into a clearer and purer height,—betokens in him a certain originality; in which rare gift Force of all kinds is presupposed. To our Rhymer, accordingly, as hinted more than once, vision and determination have not been denied: a rugged, homegrown understanding is in him; whereby, in his own way, he has mastered this and that, and looked into various things, in general honesty and to purpose, sometimes deeply, piercingly, and with a Seer's eye. Strong thoughts are not wanting, beautiful thoughts; strong and beautiful expressions of thought. As traceable for instance in this new illustration of an old argument, the mischief of Commercial Restrictions:

"These, O ye quacks, these are your remedies:
Alms for the Rich, a bread-tax for the Poor!
Soul-purchased harvests on the indigent moor!
Thus the winged victor of a hundred fights,
The warrior Ship, bows low her banner'd head,
When through her planks the seaborn reptile bites
Its deadly way;—and sinks in ocean's bed,
Vanquish'd by worms. What then? The worms were fed.—
Will not God smite thee black, thou whited wall?
Thy law is lifeless, and thy law a lie,
Or Nature is a dream unnatural:
Look on the clouds, the streams, the earth, the sky;
Lo all is interchange and harmony!
Where is the gorgeous pomp which, yester morn,
Curtained yon Orb, with amber, fold on fold?
Behold it in the blue of Rivelin, borne
To feed the all-feeding sea! the molten gold
Is flowing pale in Loxley's waters cold,
To kindle into beauty tree and flower,
And wake to verdant life hill, vale, and plain.
Cloud trades with river, and exchange is power:
But should the clouds, the streams, the winds disdain
Harmonious intercourse, nor dew nor rain
Would forest-crown the mountains: airless day
Would blast on Kinderscout the heathy glow;
No purply green would meeken into gray
O'er Don at eve; no sound of river's flow
Disturb the Sepulchre of all below."

Nature and the doings of men have not passed by this man unheeded, like the endless cloud-rack in dull weather; or lightly heeded, like a theatric phantasmagoria; but earnestly inquired into, like a thing of reality; reverently loved and worshipped, as a thing with divine significance in its reality, glimpses of which divineness he has caught and laid to heart. For his vision, as was said, partakes of the genuinely Poetical: he is not a Rhymer and Speaker only, but, in some genuine sense, something of a Poet.

Farther we must admit him, what indeed is already herein admitted, to be, if clear-sighted, also brave-hearted. A troublous element is his; a Life of painfulness, toil, insecurity, scarcity, yet he fronts it like a man; yields not to it, tames into some subjection, some order; its wild fearful dinning and tumult, as of a devouring Chaos, becomes a sort of wild war-music for him; wherein too are passages of beauty, of melodious melting softness, of lightness and briskness, even of joy. The stout heart is also a warm and kind one; Affection dwells with Danger, all the holier and the lovelier for such stern environment. A working man is this; yet, as we said, a man: in his sort, a courageous, much loving, faithfully enduring and endeavouring man.

What such a one, so gifted and so placed, shall say to a Time like ours; how he will fashion himself into peace, or war, or armed neutrality, with the world and his fellow men, and work out his course in joy and grief, in victory and defeat, is a question worth asking: which in these three little Volumes partly receives answer. He has turned, as all thinkers up to a very high and rare order in these days must do, into Politics; is a Reformer, at least a stern Complainer, Radical to the heart: his poetic melody takes an elegiaco-tragical character: much of him is converted into Hostility, and grim, hardly-suppressed Indignation, such as Right long denied, Hope long deferred, may awaken in the kindliest heart. Not yet as a rebel against any thing does he stand; but as a free man, and the spokesman of free men, not far from rebelling against much; with sorrowful, appealing dew, yet also with incipient lightning, in his eyes; whom it were not desirable to provoke into rebellion. He says in Vulcanic dialect, his feelings have been *hammered* till they are *cold-short;* so they will no longer bend; "they snap, and fly off,"—in the face of the hammerer. Not unnatural, though lamentable! Nevertheless, under all disguises of the Radical, the Poet is still recognisable: a certain music breathes through all dissonances, as the prophecy and ground-tone of returning harmony; the man, as we said, is of a poetical nature.

To his Political Philosophy there is perhaps no great importance attachable. He feels, as all men that live must do, the disorganization, and hard-grinding, unequal pressure of the Social Affairs; but sees into it only a very little farther than far inferior men do. The frightful condition of a Time, when public and private Principle, as the word was once understood, having gone out of sight, and Self-interest being left to plot, and struggle, and scramble, as it could and would, Difficulties had accumulated till they were no longer to be borne, and the spirit that should have fronted and conquered them seemed to have forsaken the world;—when the Rich, as the utmost they could resolve on, had ceased to govern, and the Poor, in their fast-accumulating numbers, and ever-widening complexities, had ceased to be able to do without governing; and now the plan of "Competition" and "*Laissez-faire*" was, on every side, approaching its consummation; and each bound up in the circle of his own wants and perils, stood grimly distrustful of his neighbour, and the distracted Commonweal was a Common-wo, and to all men it became apparent that the end was drawing nigh:—all this black aspect of Ruin and Decay, visible enough, experimentally known to our Sheffield friend, he calls by the name of "Corn-Law," and expects to be in good part delivered from, were the accursed Bread-tax repealed.

In this system of political Doctrine, even as here so emphatically set forth, there is not much of novelty. Radicals we have many; loud enough on this and other grievances; the removal of which is to be the one thing needful. The deep, wide flood of Bitterness, and Hope becoming hopeless, lies acrid, corrosive in every bosom; and flows fiercely enough through any orifice Accident may open: through Law Reform, Legislative Reform, Poor Laws, want of Poor Laws, Tithes, Game Laws, or, as we see here, Corn Laws. Whereby indeed only this becomes clear, that a deep, wide flood of evil does exist and corrode; from which, in all ways, blindly and seeingly, men seek deliverance, and cannot rest till they find it; least of all till they know what part and proportion of it is to *be* found. But with us foolish sons of Adam this is ever the way; some evil that lies nearest us, be it a chronic sickness, or but a smoky chimney, is ever the acme and sum-total of all evil: the black hydra that shuts us out from a Promised Land: and so, in poor Mr. Shandy' s fashion, must we "shift from trouble to trouble, and from side to side; button up one cause of vexation, and unbutton another."

Thus for our keen-hearted singer, and sufferer, has "the Bread-tax," in itself a considerable but no immeasurable smoke-pillar, swoln out to be a world embracing Darkness, that darkens and suffocates the whole Earth, and has blotted out the heavenly stars. Into the merit of the Corn Laws, which has often been discussed, in fit season, by competent hands, we do not enter here; least of all in the way of argument, in the way of blame, towards one who, if he read such merit with some emphasis "on the scantier trenchers of his children," may well be pardoned. That the "Bread-tax," with various other taxes, may ere long be altered and abrogated, and the Corn Trade become as free as the poorest "bread-taxed drudge" could wish "it, or the richest satrap bread-tax-fed" could fear it, seems no extravagant hypothesis: would that the mad Time could, by such simple hellebore-dose, be healed! Alas, for the diseases of a "world lying in wickedness," in heart-sickness and atrophy, quite another alcahest is needed;—a long, painful course of medicine and regimen, surgery and physic, not yet specified or indicated in the Royal-College Books!

But if there is little novelty in our friend's Political Philosophy, there is some in his political Feeling and Poetry. The peculiarity of this Radical is, that with all his stormful destructiveness, he combines a decided loyalty and faith. If he despise and trample under foot on the one hand, he exalts and reverences on the other: the "landed pauper in his coach-and-four" rolls all the more glaringly, contrasted with the "Rockinghams and Savilles" of the past, with the "Lansdowns and Fitzwilliams," many a "Wentworth's lord," still "a blessing" to the present. This man, indeed, has in him the root of all reverence,—a principle of Religion. He believes in a Godhead, not with the lips only, but apparently with the heart; who, as has been written, and often felt, "reveals Himself in Parents, in all true Teachers, and Rulers,"—as in false Teachers and Rulers quite Another may be revealed! Our Rhymer, it would seem, is no Methodist: far enough from it. He makes "the Ranter," in his hot-headed way, exclaim over

> "The hundred Popes of England's Jesuitry;"

and adds, by way of note, in his own person, some still stronger sayings: How "this baneful corporation," "dismal as its Reign of Terror is, and long armed its Holy Inquisition, must condescend to learn and teach what is useful, or go where all nuisances go." As little perhaps is he a Churchman; the "Cadi-Dervish" being nowise to his mind. Scarcely, however, if at all, does he show aversion to the Church as Church; or, among his many griefs, touch upon Tithes as one. But, in any case, the black colours of Life, even as here painted, and brooded over, do not hide from him that a God is the Author and sustainer thereof; that God's world, if made a House of Imprisonment, can also be a House of Prayer; wherein for the weary and heavy-laden, Pity and Hope are not altogether cut away.

It is chiefly in virtue of this inward temper of heart, with the clear disposition and adjustment which for all else results therefrom, that our Radical attains to be Poetical; that the harsh groanings, contentions, upbraidings, of one who unhappily has felt constrained to adopt such mode of utterance, become ennobled into something of music. If a land of bondage, this is still his Father's land, and the bondage endures not for ever. As worshipper and believer, the captive can look with seeing eye: the aspect of the Infinite Universe still fills him with an infinite feeling; his chains, were it but for moments, fall away; he soars free aloft, and the sunny regions of Poesy and Freedom gleam golden afar on the widened horizon. Gleamings we say, prophetic dawnings, from those far regions, spring up for him; nay, beams of actual radiance. In his ruggedness, and dim contractedness, (rather of place than of organ,) he is not without touches of a feeling and vision, which, even in the strictest sense, is to be named poetical.

One deeply poetical idea, above all others, seems to have taken hold of him: the idea of Time. As was natural to a poetic soul, with few objects of Art in its environment, and driven inward, rather than invited outward, for occupation. This deep mystery of ever-flowing Time; "bringing forth," and as the Ancients wisely fabled, "devouring" what it has brought forth; rushing on, *in* us, yet above us, all uncontrollable by us; and under it, dimly visible athwart it, the bottomless Eternal;—this is, indeed, what we may call the Primary idea of Poetry: the first that introduces itself into the poetic mind. As here:

> "The bee shall seek to settle on his hand,
> But from the vacant bench haste to the moor,
> Mourning the last of England's high-soul'd Poor,
> And bid the mountains weep for Enoch Wray.
> And for themselves,—albeit of things that last
> Unalter'd most: for they shall pass away
> Like Enoch, though their iron roots seem fast,
> Bound to the eternal future as the past:
> The Patriarch died, and they shall be no more!
> Yes, and the sailless worlds, which navigate
> The unutterable Deep that hath no shore,
> Will lose their starry splendour soon or late,
> Like tapers, quench'd by him whose will is fate!
> Yes, and the Angel of Eternity
> Who numbers worlds and writes their names in light,
> One day, O Earth, will look in vain for thee,
> And start and stop in his unerring flight,
> And with his wings of sorrow and affright,
> Veil his impassion'd brow and heavenly tears!"

And not the first idea only, but the greatest, properly the parent of all others. For if it can rise in the remotest ages, in the rudest states of culture, wherever an "inspired thinker" happens to exist, it connects itself still with all great things; with the highest results of new Philosophy, as of primeval Theology: and for the Poet, in particular, is as the life-element wherein alone his conceptions can take poetic form, and the whole world become miraculous and magical.

> "We *are such stuff*
> As Dreams are made of: and our little life
> Is rounded with a Sleep!"

Figure that, believe that, O Reader; then say whether the *Arabian Tales* seem wonderful! —"Rounded with a sleep, (*mit Schlaf umgeben*)!" says Jean Paul: "these three words created whole volumes in me."

To turn now on our worthy Rhymer, who has brought us so much, and stingily insist on his errors and shortcomings, were no honest procedure. We had the whole poetical encyclopædia to draw upon, and say commodiously, Such and such an item is *not* here; of which encyclopædia the highest genius can fill but a portion. With much merit, far from common in his time, he is not without something of the faults of his time. We praised him for originality; yet is there a certain remainder of imitation in him; a tang of the Circulating Libraries, as in Sancho's wine, with its key and thong, there was a tang of iron and leather. To be reminded of Crabbe, with his truthful severity of style, in such a place, we cannot object; but what if there were a slight bravura dash of the fair tuneful Hemans? Still more, what have we to do with Byron, and his fierce vociferous mouthings, whether "passionate," or not passionate and only theatrical? King Cambyses' vein is, after all, but a worthless one; no vein for a wise man. Strength, if that be the thing aimed at, does not manifest itself in spasms, but in stout bearing of burdens. Our Author says, "It is too bad to exalt into a hero the coxcomb who would have gone into hysterics if a tailor had laughed at him." Walk not in his footsteps, then, we say, whether as hero or as singer; repent a little, for example, over somewhat in that fuliginous, blue-flaming, pitch-and-sulphur "Dream of Enoch Wray," and write the next otherwise.

We mean no imitation in a bad palpable sense; only that there is a tone of such occasionally audible; which ought to be removed; —of which, in any case, we make not much. Imitation is a leaning on something foreign; incompleteness of individual development, defect of free utterance. From the same source, spring most of our Author's faults; in particular, his worst, which after all is intrinsically a defect of manner. He has little or no Humour. Without Humour of character he cannot well be; but it has not yet got to utterance. Thus, where he has mean things to deal with, he knows not how to deal with them; oftenest deals with them more or less meanly. In his vituperative prose Notes, he seems embarrassed; and but ill hides his embarrassment, under an air of predetermined sarcasm, of knowing briskness, almost of vulgar pertness. He says, he cannot help it; he is poor, hard-worked, and "soot is soot." True, indeed; yet there is no connection between Poverty and Discourtesy; which latter originates in Dullness alone. Courtesy is the due of Man to Man; not of suit of clothes to suit of clothes. He who could master so many things, and make even Corn-Laws rhyme, we require of him this further thing,—a bearing worthy of himself, and of the order he belongs to,—the highest and most ancient of all orders, that of Manhood. A pert snappishness is no manner for a brave man; and then the manner so soon influences the matter; a far worse result. Let him speak wise things, and speak them wisely; which latter may be done in many dialects, grave and gay, only in the snappish seldom or never.

The truth is, as might have been expected, there is still much lying in him to be developed; the hope of which development it were rather sad to abandon. Why, for example, should not his view of the world, his knowledge of what is and has been in the world, indefinitely extend itself? Were he merely the "uneducated Poet," we should say, he had read largely; as he is not such, we say, Read still more, much more largely. Books enough there are in England, and of quite another weight and worth than that circulating-library sort; may be procured too, may be read, even by a hard-worked man; for what man (either in God's service or the Devil's, as himself chooses it) is not hard-worked? But here again, where there is a will there is a way. True, our friend is no longer in his teens; yet still, as would seem, in the vigour of his years: we hope too that his mind is not finally shut in, but of the improvable and enlargeable sort. If Alfieri (also kept busy enough, with horse-breaking and what not) learned Greek after he was fifty, why is the Corn-Law Rhymer too old to learn?

However, be in the future what there may, our Rhymer has already done what was much more difficult, and better than reading printed books;—looked into the great prophetic-manuscript Book of Existence, and read little passages there. Here, for example, is a sentence tolerably spelled:

> "Where toils the Mill by ancient woods embraced,
> Hark, how the cold steel screams in hissing fire!
> Blind Enoch sees the Grinder's wheel no more,
> Couch'd beneath rocks and forests, that admire
> Their beauty in the waters, ere they roar
> Dashed in white foam the swift circumference o'er.
> There draws the Grinder his laborious breath:
> There coughing at his deadly trade he bends:
> Born to die young, he fears nor man nor death;
> Scorning the future, what he earns he spends;
> Debauch and riot are his bosom friends."
> "Behold his failings! Hath he virtues too?
> He is no Pauper, blackguard though he be:
> Full well he knows what minds combined can do,
> Full well maintains his birthright: he is free,
> And, frown for frown, outstares monopoly.
> Yet Abraham and Elliot both in vain
> Bid Science on his cheek prolong the bloom;
> He *will* not live! He seems in haste to gain
> The undisturbed asylum of the tomb,
> And, old at two-and-thirty, meets his doom!"

Or this "of Jem, the rogue avowed,

> "Whose trade is Poaching! Honest Jem works not,
> Begs not, but thrives by plundering beggars here.
> Wise as a lord, and quite as good a shot,
> He, like his betters, lives in hate and fear
> And feeds on partridge because bread is dear.
> Sire of six sons apprenticed to the jail,
> He prowls in arms, the Tory of the night;
> With them he shares his battles and his ale,

With him they feel the majesty of might,
No Despot better knows that Power is Right.
Mark his unpaidish sneer, his lordly frown;
Hark how he calls the beadle and flunky liars;
See how magnificently he breaks down
His neighbour's fence, if so his will requires,
And how his struttle emulates the squire's!"
"Jem rises with the Moon; but when she sinks,
Homeward with sack-like pockets, and quick heels,
Hungry as boroughmongering gowl, he slinks.
He reads not, writes not, thinks not; scarcely feels;
Steals all he gets; serves Hell with all he steals!"

It is rustic, rude existence; barren moors, with the smoke of Forges rising over the waste expanse. Alas, no Arcadia; but the actual dwelling-place of actual toil-grimed sons of Tubal-cain: yet are there blossoms and the wild natural fragrance of gorse and broom; yet has the Craftsman pauses in his toil; the Craftsman too has an inheritance in Earth; and even in Heaven.

"Light! All is not corrupt, for thou art pure,
Unchanged and changeless. Though frail man is vile,
Thou look'st on him; serene, sublime, secure,
Yet, like thy Father, with a pitying smile.
Even on this wintry day, as marble cold,
Angels might quit their home to visit thee,
And match their plumage with thy mantle roll'd
Beneath God's Throne, o'er billows of a sea
Whose isles are Worlds, whose bounds Infinity.
Why then is Enoch absent from my side?
I miss the rustle of his silver hair;
A guide no more, I seem to want a guide,
While Enoch journeys to the house of prayer;
Ah, ne'er came Sabbath-day but he was there!
Lo, how, like him, erect and strong, though gray,
Yon village tower time-touch'd to God appeals!
And hark! the chimes of morning die away:
Hark! to the heart the solemn sweetness steals,
Like the heart's voice, unfelt by none who feels
That God is Love, that Man is living Dust;
Unfelt by none whom ties of brotherhood
Link to his kind; by none who puts his trust
In naught of Earth that hath survived the flood,
Save those mute charities, by which the good
Strengthen poor worms, and serve their Maker best.
"Hail Sabbath! Day of mercy, peace, and rest!
Thou o'er loud cities throw'st a noiseless spell,
The hammer there, the wheel, the saw molest
Pale Thought no more: o'er Trade's contentious hell
Meek Quiet spreads her wings invisible.
And when thou com'st, less silent are the fields,
Through whose sweet paths the toil-freed townsman steals,
To him the very air a banquet yields.
Envious he watches the poised hawk that wheels
His flight on chainless winds. Each cloud reveals
A paradise of beauty to his eye.
His little Boys are with him, seeking flowers,
Or chasing the too venturous gilded fly.
So by the daisy's side he spends the hours,
Renewing friendship with the budding bowers:
And while might, beauty, good without alloy
Are mirror'd in his children's happy eyes,—
In His great Temple offering thankful joy
To Him, the infinitely Great and Wise,
With soul attuned to Nature's harmonies,
Serene and cheerful as a sporting child,—
His *heart* refuses to believe that man
Could turn into a hell the blooming wild,
The blissful country where his childhood ran
A race with infant rivers, ere began—"

—"King-humbling" bread-tax, "blind Misrule" and enough else.

And so our Corn-Law Rhymer plays his part. In this wise, does he indite and act his Drama of Life, which for him is all too Domestic-Tragical. It is said, "the good actor soon makes us forget the bad theatre, were it but a barn; while, again, nothing renders so apparent the badness of the bad actor as a theatre of peculiar excellence." How much more in a theatre and drama such as these of Life itself! One other item, however, we must note in that ill-decorated Sheffield theatre: the back-scene and bottom-decoration of it all; which is no other than a Workhouse. Alas, the Workhouse is the bourne whither all these actors and workers are bound; whence none that has once passed it returns! A bodeful sound, like the rustle of approaching world-devouring tornadoes, quivers through their whole existence; and the voice of it is, Pauperism! The thanksgiving they offer up to Heaven is, that they are not yet Paupers; the earnest cry of their prayer is, that "God would shield them from the bitterness of Parish Pay."

Mournful enough, that a white European Man must pray wistfully for what the horse he drives is sure of,—That the strain of his whole faculties may not fail to earn him food and lodging. Mournful that a gallant manly spirit, with an eye to discern the world, a heart to reverence it, a hand cunning and willing to labour in it, must be haunted with such a fear. The grim end of it all, Beggary! A soul loathing, what true souls ever loathe, Dependence, help from the unworthy to help; yet sucked into the world-whirlpool,—able to do no other: the highest in man's heart struggling vainly against the lowest in man's destiny! In good truth, if many a sickly and sulky Byron, or Byronlet, glooming over the woes of existence, and how unworthy God's Universe is to have so distinguished a resident, could transport himself into the patched coat and sooty apron of a Sheffield Blacksmith, made with as strange faculties and feelings as he, made by God Almighty all one as he was,—it would throw a light on much for him.

Meanwhile, is it not frightful as well as mournful to consider how the wide-spread evil is spreading wider and wider? Most persons, who have had eyes to look with, may have verified, in their own circle, the statement of this Sheffield Eye-witness, and "from their own knowledge and observation fearlessly declare that the little master-manufacturer," that the working man generally, "is in a much worse condition than he was in twenty-five years ago." Unhappily, the fact is too plain; the reason and scientific necessity of it is too plain. In this state of things, every new man is a new misfortune; every new market a new complexity; the chapter of chances grows ever more incalculable; the hungry gamesters (whose stake is their life) are ever increasing in numbers; the world-movement rolls on: by what method shall the weak and help-needing, who has none to help him, withstand it? Alas, how many brave hearts, ground to pieces in that unequal battle, have already sunk; in every sinking heart, a Tragedy, less famous than that of the Sons of Atreus; wherein, however, if no "kingly house," yet a manly house went to the dust, and a whole manly "lineage was swept away." Must it grow worse and worse till the last brave heart is broken in England; and this same "brave Peasantry" has become a kennel of wild-howling ravenous Paupers? God be thanked! There is some feeble shadow of hopes that the change may have begun while it was yet time. You may lift the pressure from the free man's shoulders, and bid him go forth rejoicing; but lift the slave's burden, he will only wallow the more composedly in his sloth: a nation of degraded men cannot be raised up, except by what we rightly name a miracle.

Under which point of view also, these little Volumes, indicating such a character in such a place, are not without significance. One faint symptom perhaps that clearness will return, that there is a possibility of its return. It is as if from that Gehenna of Manufacturing Radicalism, from amid its loud roaring and cursing, whereby nothing became feasible, nothing knowable, except this only, that misery and malady existed there, we heard now some manful tone of reason and determination, wherein alone can there be profit, or promise of deliverance. In this Corn-Law Rhymer we seem to trace something of the antique spirit; a spirit which had long become invisible among our working as among other classes; which here, perhaps almost for the first time, reveals itself in an altogether modern political vesture. "The Pariahs of the Isle of Woe," as he passionately names them, are no longer Pariahs if they have become Men. Here is one man of their tribe; in several respects a true man; who has abjured Hypocrisy and Servility, yet not therewith trodden Religion and Loyalty under foot; not without justness of insight, devoutness, peaceable heroism of resolve; who, in all circumstances, even in these strange ones, will be found quitting himself like a man. One such that has found a voice: who knows how many mute but not inactive brethren he may have in his own and in all other ranks? Seven thousand that have not bowed the knee to Baal! These are the men, wheresoever found, who are to stand forth in England's evil day, on whom the hope of England rests. For it has been often said, and must often be said again, that all Reform except a moral one will prove unavailing. Political Reform, pressingly enough wanted, can indeed root out the weeds (gross deep-fixed lazy dock-weeds, poisonous obscene hemlocks, ineffectual spurry in abundance;) but it leaves the ground *empty*,—ready either for noble fruits, or for new worse tares! And how else is a Moral Reform to be looked for but in this way, that more and more Good Men are, by a bountiful Providence, sent hither to disseminate Goodness; literally to *sow* it, as in seeds shaken abroad by the living tree? For such, in all ages and places, is the nature of a Good Man; he is ever a mystic creative centre of Goodness; his influence, if we consider it, is not to be measured; for his works do not die, but being of Eternity, are eternal; and in new transformation, and ever wider diffusion, endure, living and life-giving. Thou who exclaimest over the horrors and baseness of the Time, and how Diogenes would now need *two* lanterns in daylight, think of this; over the Time thou hast no power: to redeem a World sunk in dishonesty has not been given thee; solely over one man therein thou hast a quite absolute uncontrollable power; him redeem, him make honest; it will be something, it will be much, and thy life and labour not in vain.

We have given no epitomized abstract of these little Books, such as is the Reviewer's wont: we would gladly persuade many a reader, high and low, who takes interest not in rhyme only, but in reason, and the condition of his fellow-man, to purchase and peruse them for himself. It is proof of an innate love of worth, and how willingly the Public, did not thousand-voiced Puffery so confuse it, would have to do with substances, and not with deceptive shadows, that these Volumes carry "Third Edition" marked on them,—on all of them but the newest, whose fate with the reading world we yet know not; which, however, seems to deserve not worse but better than either of its forerunners.

Nay, it appears to us as if in this humble chant of the *Village Patriarch* might be traced rudiments of a truly great idea; great though all undeveloped. The Rhapsody of "Enoch Wray" is, in its nature, and unconscious tendency, Epic; a whole world lies shadowed in it. What we might call an inarticulate, half-audible Epic! The main figure is a blind aged man; himself a ruin, and encircled with the ruin of a whole Era. Sad and great does that image of a universal Dissolution hover visible as a poetic background. Good old Enoch! He could do so much, was so wise, so valiant. No Ilion had he destroyed; yet somewhat he had built up: where the Mill stands noisy by its cataract, making corn into bread for men, it was Enoch that reared it, and made the rude rocks send it water; where the mountain Torrent now boils in vain, and is mere passing music to the traveller, it was Enoch's cunning that spanned it with that strong Arch, grim, time-defying. Where Enoch's hand or mind has been, Disorder has become Order; Chaos has receded some little handbreadth; must give up some new handbreath of his realm. Enoch too has seen his followers fall round him, (by stress of hardship, and the arrows of the gods,) has performed funeral games for them, and raised sandstone memorials, and carved his *Abiit ad Plures* thereon, with his own hand. The living chronicle and epitome of a whole century; when he departs, a whole century will become dead, historical.

Rudiments of an Epic, we say; and of the true Epic of our Time,—were the genius but arrived that could sing it! Not "Arms and the Man;" "Tools and the Man," that were now our Epic. What indeed are Tools, from the Hammer and Plummet of Enoch Wray to this Pen we now write with, but Arms, wherewith to do battle against UNREASON without or within, and smite in pieces not miserable fellow-men, but the Arch Enemy that makes us all miserable; henceforth the only legitimate battle!

Which Epic, as we granted, is here altogether imperfectly sung; scarcely a few notes thereof brought freely out: nevertheless with indication, with prediction that it will be sung

Such is the purport and merit of the *Village Patriarch;* it struggles towards a noble utterance, which however it can nowise find. Old Enoch is from the first speechless, heard of rather than heard or seen; at best, mute, motionless like a stone-pillar of his own carving. Indeed, to find fit utterance for such meaning as lies struggling here is a problem, to which the highest poetic minds may long be content to accomplish only approximate solutions. Meanwhile, our honest Rhymer, with no guide but the instinct of a clear natural talent, has created and adjusted somewhat, not without vitality of union: has avoided somewhat, the road to which lay open enough. His *Village Patriach,* for example, though of an elegiac strain, is not wholly lachrymose, not without touches of rugged gayety;—is like Life itself, with tears and toil, with laughter and rude play, such as metallurgic Yorkshire sees it:—in which sense, that wondrous Courtship of the sharp-tempered, oft-widowed Alice Green may pass, questionable, yet with a certain air of soot-stained genuineness. And so has, not a Picture, indeed, yet a sort of genial Study or Cartoon come together for him: and may endure there, after some flary oil-daubings, which we have seen framed with gilding, and hung up in proud galleries, have become rags and rubbish.

To one class of readers especially, such Books as these ought to be interesting;—to the highest, that is to say, the richest class. Among our Aristocracy, there are men, we trust there are many men, who feel that they also are workmen, born to toil, ever in their great Taskmaster's eye, faithfully with heart and head for those that with heart and hand do, under the same great Taskmaster, toil for them;—who have even this noblest and hardest work set before them—To deliver out of that Egyptian bondage to Wretchedness, and Ignorance, and Sin, the hardhanded millions, of whom this hardhanded, earnest witness, and writer, is here representative. To such men his writing will be as a Document, which they will lovingly interpret: what is dark and exasperated and acrid, in their humble Brother, they for themselves will enlighten and sweeten; taking thankfully what is the real purport of his message, and laying it earnestly to heart. Might an instructive relation and interchange between High and Low, at length ground itself, and more and more perfect itself, to the unspeakable profit of all parties; for if all parties are to love and help one another, the first step towards this is, that all thoroughly understand one another. To such rich men an authentic message from the hearts of poor men, from the heart of one poor man, will be welcome.

To another class of our Aristocracy, again, who unhappily feel rather that they are *not* workmen; and profess not so much to bear any burden, as to be themselves, with utmost attainable *steadiness,* and if possible, *gracefulness,* borne,—such a phenomenon as this of the Sheffield Corn-Law Rhymer, with a Manchester Detrosier, and much else, pointing the same way, will be quite unwelcome; indeed, to the clearer-sighted, astonishing and alarming. It indicates that they find themselves, as Napoleon was wont to say, "in a new position;"—a position wonderful enough; of extreme singularity; to which, in the whole course of History, there is perhaps but one case in some measure parallel. The case alluded to stands recorded in the *Book of Numbers:* the case of Balaam the son of Beor. Truly, if we consider it, there are few passages more notable and pregnant in their way, than this of Balaam. The Midianitish Soothsayer (Truth-speaker, or as we should now say, Counsel-giver and Senator) is journeying forth, as he has from of old quite prosperously done, in the way of his vocation; not so much to "curse the people of the Lord," as to earn for himself a comfortable penny by such means as are possible and expedient; something, it is hoped, midway between cursing and blessing; which shall not, except in case of necessity, be either a curse or a blessing, or any thing so much as a Nothing that will look like a Something and bring wages in. For the man is not dishonest; far from it; still less is he honest; but above all things, he is, has been, and will be, respectable. Did calumny ever dare to fasten itself on the fair fame of Balaam? In his whole walk and conversation, has he not shown consistency enough; ever doing and speaking the thing that was decent; with proper spirit, maintaining his status; so that friend and opponent must often compliment him, and defy the spiteful world to say, Herein art thou a Knave? And now as he jogs along, in official comfort, with brave official retinue, his heart filled with good things, his head with schemes for the suppression of Vice, and the Cause of civil and religious Liberty all over the world;—consider what a spasm, and life-clutching, ice-taloned pang, must have shot through the brain and pericardium of Balaam, when his Ass not only on the sudden stood stock-still, defying spur and cudgel, but—*began to talk,* and that in a reasonable manner! Did not his face, elongating, collapse, and tremor occupy his joints? For the thin crust of Respectability has cracked asunder; and a bottomless preternatural Inane yawns under him instead. Farewell, a long farewell to all my greatness! the spirit-stirring Vote, ear-piercing Hear; the big Speech that makes ambition virtue; soft Palm-greasing first of raptures, and Cheers that emulate sphere-music: Balaam's occupation's gone!—

As for our stout Corn-Law Rhymer, what can we say by way of valediction but this,—Well done; come again, doing better? Advices enough there were; but all lie included under one,—To keep his eyes open, and do honestly whatsoever his hand shall find to do. We have praised him for sincerity; let him become more and more sincere; casting out all remnants of Hearsay, Imitation, ephemeral Speculation; resolutely "*clearing* his mind of Cant." We advised a wider course of reading: would he forgive us if we now suggested the question, Whether Rhyme is the only dialect he can write in; whether Rhyme is, after all, the natural or fittest dialect for him? In good Prose, which differs inconceivably from bad Prose, what may not be written, what may not be read; from a Waverley Novel, to an Arabic Koran, to an English Bible! Rhyme has plain advantages; which, however, are often purchased too dear. If the inward thought *can* speak itself and not sing itself, let it, especially in these quite unmusical days, do the former. In any case, if the inward Thought do not sing itself, that singing of the outward Phrase is a timber-toned, false matter we could well dispense with. Will our Rhymer consider himself, then; and decide for what is actually best. Rhyme, up to this hour, never seems altogether obedient to him; and disobedient Rhyme,—who would ride on it that had once learned walking?

He takes amiss that some friends have admonished him to quit Politics; we will not repeat that admonition. Let him, on this as on all other matters, take solemn counsel with his own Socrates'-Demon; such as dwells in every mortal: such as he is a happy mortal who can hear the voice of, follow the behests of, like an unalterable law. At the same time, we could truly wish to see such a mind as his engaged rather in considering what, in his own sphere, could be *done*, than what, in his own or other spheres, ought to be *destroyed*; rather in producing or preserving the True, than in mangling and slashing asunder the False. Let him be at ease: the False is already dead, or lives only with a mock life. The death-sentence of the False was of old, from the first beginning of it, written in Heaven; and is now proclaimed in the Earth, and read aloud at all market-crosses; nor are innumerable volunteer tipstaves and headsmen wanting to execute the same: for which needful service men inferior to him may suffice. Why should the heart of the Corn-Law Rhymer be troubled? Spite of "Bread-tax," he and his brave children, who will emulate their sire, have yet bread: the Workhouse, as we rejoice to fancy, has receded into the safe distance; and is now quite shut out from his poetic pleasure-ground. Why should he afflict himself with devices of "Boroughmongering gowls," or the rage of the Heathen imagining a vain thing? This matter, which he calls Corn-Law, will not have completed itself, adjusted itself into clearness, for the space of a century or two: nay, after twenty centuries, what will there, or can there be for the son of Adam, but Work, Work, two hands quite *full* of Work! Meanwhile, is not the Corn-Law Rhymer already a king, though a belligerent one; king of his own mind and faculty, and what man in the long run is king of more? Not one in the thousand, even among sceptered kings, of so much. Be diligent in business, then; fervent in spirit. Above all things, lay aside anger, uncharitableness, hatred, noisy tumult; avoid them, as worse than Pestilence, worse than "Bread-tax" itself:

> For it well beseemeth kings, all mortals it beseemeth well,
> To possess their souls in patience, and await what can betide.

NOVELLE.

TRANSLATED FROM GOETHE.

[Fraser's Magazine, 1832.]

The spacious courts of the Prince's Castle were still veiled in thick mists of an autumnal morning; through which veil, meanwhile, as it melted into clearness, you could more or less discern the whole Hunter-company, on horseback and on foot, all busily astir. The hasty occupations of the nearest were distinguishable: there was lengthening, shortening of stirrup-leathers; there was handling of rifles and shot-pouches, there was putting of game-bags to rights; while the hounds, impatient in their leashes, threatened to drag their keepers off with them. Here and there, too, a horse showed spirit more than enough; driven on by its fiery nature, or excited by the spur of its rider, who even now in the half-dusk could not repress a certain self-complacent wish to exhibit himself. All waited, however, on the Prince, who, taking leave of his young consort, was now delaying too long.

United a short while ago, they already felt the happiness of consentaneous dispositions; both were of active vivid character; each willingly participated in the tastes and endeavours of the other. The Prince's father had already, in his time, discerned and improved the season when it became evident that all members of the commonwealth should pass their days in equal industry; should all, in equal working and producing, each in his kind, first earn and then enjoy.

How well this had prospered was visible in these very days, when the head-market was a holding, which you might well enough have named a fair. The Prince yester-even had led his Princess on horseback through the tumult of the heaped-up wares; and pointed out to her how on this spot the Mountain region met the Plain country in profitable barter: he could here, with the objects before him, awaken her attention to the various industry of his Land.

If the Prince at this time occupied himself and his servants almost exclusively with these pressing concerns, and in particular worked incessantly with his Finance-minister, yet would the Hunt-master too have his right; on whose pleading, the temptation could not be resisted to undertake, in this choice autumn weather, a Hunt that had already been postponed; and so for the household itself, and for the many stranger visitants, prepare a peculiar and singular festivity.

The Princess stayed behind with reluctance: but it was proposed to push far into the Mountains, and stir up the peaceable inhabitants of the forests there with an unexpected invasion.

At parting, her lord failed not to propose a ride for her, with Friedrich, the Prince-Uncle, as escort: "I will leave thee," said he, "our Honorio too, as Equerry and Page, who will manage all." In pursuance of which words, he, in descending, gave to a handsome young man the needful injunctions; and soon thereafter disappeared with guests and train.

The Princess, who had waved her handkerchief to her husband while still down in the court, now retired to the back apartments, which commanded a free prospect towards the Mountains; and so much the lovelier, as the Castle itself stood on a sort of elevation, and thus, behind as well as before, afforded manifold magnificent views. She found the fine telescope still in the position where they had left it yester-even, when amusing themselves over bush and hill and forest-summit, with the lofty ruins of the primeval Stammburg, or Family Tower; which in the clearness of evening stood out noteworthy, as at that hour, with its great light-and-shade masses, the best aspect of so venerable a memorial of old time was to be had. This morning too, with the approximating glasses, might be beautifully seen the autumnal tinge of the trees, many in kind and number, which had struggled up through the masonry unhindered and undisturbed during long years. The fair dame, however, directed the tube somewhat lower, to a waste stony flat, over which the Hunting-train was to pass: she waited the moment with patience, and was not disappointed; for with the clearness and magnifying power of the instrument her glancing eyes plainly distinguished the Prince and the Head-Equerry; nay, she forbore not again to wave her handkerchief, as some momentary pause and looking-back was fancied perhaps, rather than observed.

Prince-Uncle, Friedrich by name, now with announcement, entered, attended by his Painter, who carried a large portfolio under his arm. "Dear Cousin," said the hale old gentleman, "we here present you with the Views of the Stammburg, taken on various sides to show how the mighty Pile, warred on and warring, has from old times fronted the year and its weather; how here and there its wall had to yield, here and there rush down into waste ruins. However, we have now done much to make the wild mass accessible; for more there wants not to set every traveller, every visitor, into astonishment, into admiration."

As the Prince now exhibited the separate leaves, he continued: "Here where, advancing up the hollow-way, through the outer ring-walls, you reach the Fortress proper, rises against us a rock, the firmest of the whole mountain; on this there stands a tower built, yet when Nature leaves off, and Art and Handicraft begin, no one can distinguish. Farther you perceive sidewards walls abutting on it, and donjons terrace-wise stretching down. But I speak wrong, for to the eye it is but a wood that encircles that old summit; these hundred and fifty years no axe has sounded there, and the massiest stems have on all sides sprung up; wherever you press inwards to the walls, the smooth maple, the rough oak, the taper pine, with trunk and roots oppose you; round these we have to wind, and pick our footsteps with skill. Do but look how artfully our Master has brought the character of it on paper; how the roots and stems, the species of each distinguishable, twist themselves among the masonry, and the huge boughs come looping through the holes. It is a wilderness like no other; an accidentally unique locality, where ancient traces of long-vanished power of Man, and the ever-living, ever-working power of Nature show themselves in the most earnest conflict."

Exhibiting another leaf, he went on: "What say you now to the Castle-court, which, become inaccessible by the falling in of the old gate-tower, had for immemorial time been trodden by no foot? We sought to get at it by a side; have pierced through walls, blasted vaults asunder, and so provided a convenient but secret way. Inside it needed no clearance; here stretches a flat rock-summit, smoothed by nature: but yet strong trees have in spots found luck and opportunity for rooting themselves there; they have softly but decidedly grown up, and now stretch out their boughs into the galleries where the knights once walked to and fro; nay, through the doors and windows into the vaulted halls; out of which we would not drive them: they have even got the mastery, and may keep it. Sweeping away deep strata of leaves, we have found the notablest place all smoothed, the like of which were perhaps not to be met with in the world.

"After all this, however, it is still to be remarked, and on the spot itself well worth examining, how on the steps that lead up to the main tower, a maple has struck root and fashioned itself to a stout tree, so that you can hardly with difficulty press by it, to mount the battlements and gaze over the unbounded prospect. Yet here too, you linger pleased in the shade; for that tree is it which high over the whole wondrously lifts itself into the air.

"Let us thank the brave Artist, then, who so deservingly in various pictures teaches us the whole, even as if we saw it: he has spent the fairest hours of the day and of the season therein, and for weeks long kept moving about these scenes. Here in this corner has there for him, and the warder we gave him, been a little pleasant dwelling fitted up. You could not think, my Best, what a lovely outlook into the country, into court and walls, he has got there. But now when all is once in outline, so pure, so characteristic, he may finish it down here at his ease. With these pictures we will decorate our garden-hall; and no one shall recreate his eyes over our regular parterres, our groves and shady walks, without wishing himself up there, to follow, in actual sight of the old and of the new, of the stubborn, inflexible, indestructible, and of the fresh, pliant, irresistible, what reflections and comparisons would rise for him."

Honorio entered, with notice that the horses were brought out; then said the Princess, turning to the Uncle: "Let us ride up; and you will show me in reality what you have here set before me in image. Ever since I came among you, I have heard of this undertaking; and should now like of all things to see with my own eyes what in the narrative seemed impossible, and in the depicting remains improbable.—"Not yet, my Love," answered the Prince: "what you here saw is what it can become and is becoming; for the present much in the enterprise stands still amid impediments; Art must first be complete, if Nature is not to shame it."—"Then let us ride at least upwards, were it only to the foot: I have the greatest wish to-day to look about me far in the world."—"Altogether as you will it," replied the Prince.—"Let us ride through the Town, however," continued the Lady, "over the great market-place, where stands the innumerable crowd of booths, looking like a little city, like a camp. It is as if the wants and occupations of all the families in the land were turned outwards, assembled in this centre, and brought into the light of day: for the attentive observer can descry whatsoever it is that man performs and needs; you fancy, for the moment, there is no money necessary, that all business could here be managed by barter, and so at bottom it is. Since the Prince, last night, set me on these reflections, it is pleasant to consider how here, where Mountain and Plain meet together, both so clearly speak out what they require, and wish. For as the Highlander can fashion the timber of his woods into a hundred shapes, and mould his iron for all manner of uses, so these others from below come to meet him with most manifold wares, in which often you can hardly discover the material or recognise the aim."

"I am aware," answered the Prince, "that my Nephew turns his utmost care to these things; for specially, on the present occasion, this main point comes to be considered, that one receive more than one give out: which to manage is, in the long run, the sum of all Political Economy, as of the smallest private housekeeping. Pardon me, however, my Best: I never like to ride through markets; at every step you are hindered and kept back; and then flames up in my imagination the monstrous misery which, as it were, burnt itself into my eyes, when I witnessed one such world of wares go off in fire. I had scarcely got to ——"

"Let us not lose the bright hours," interrupted the Princess, for the worthy man had already more than once afflicted her with the minute description of that mischance: how he being on a long journey, resting in the best inn, on the market-place which was just then swarming with a fair, had gone to bed exceedingly fatigued; and in the night-time been, by shrieks, and flames rolling up against his lodging, hideously awakened.

The Princess hastened to mount her favourite horse: and led, not through the backgate upwards, but through the foregate downwards, her reluctant-willing attendant; for who but would gladly have ridden by her side, who but would gladly have followed after her. And so Honorio too had without regret stayed back from the otherwise so wished-for Hunt, to be exclusively at her service.

As was to be anticipated, they could only ride through the market step by step: but the fair Lovely one enlivened every stoppage by some sprightly remark, "I repeat my lesson of yester-night," said she, "since Necessity is trying our patience." And in truth, the whole mass of men so crowded about the riders, that their progress was slow. The people gazed with joy at the young dame; and, on so many smiling countenances, might be read the pleasure they felt to see that the first woman in the land was also the fairest and gracefullest.

Promiscuously mingled stood, Mountaineers, who had built their still dwellings amid rocks, firs, and spruces; Lowlanders from hills, meadows, and leas; craftsmen of the little towns; and what else had all assembled there. After a quiet glance, the Princess remarked to her attendant, how all these, whencesoever they came, had taken more stuff than necessary for their clothes, more cloth and linen, more ribands for trimming. It is as if the women could not be bushy enough, the men not puffy enough, to please themselves.

"We will leave them that," answered the uncle: "spend his superfluity on what he will, a man is happy in it; happiest when he therewith decks and dizens himself." The fair dame nodded assent.

So had they by degrees got upon a clear space, which led out to the suburbs, when, at the end of many small booths and stands, a larger edifice of boards showed itself, which was scarcely glanced at till an ear-lacerating bellow sounded forth from it. The feeding-hour of the wild beasts there exhibited seemed to have come: the Lion let his forest and desert-voice be heard in all vigour; the horses shuddered, and all must remark how, in the peaceful ways and workings of the cultivated world, the King of the wilderness so fearfully announced himself. Coming nearer the booth, you could not overlook the variegated colossal pictures representing with violent colours and strong emblems those foreign beasts; to a sight of which the peaceful burgher was to be irresistibly enticed. The grim monstrous tiger was pouncing on a blackamoor, on the point of tearing him in shreds; a lion stood earnest and majestic, as if he saw no prey worthy of him; other wondrous party-coloured creatures, beside these mighty ones, deserved less attention.

"As we come back," said the Princess, "we will alight and take a nearer view of these gentry."—"It is strange," observed the Prince, "that man always seeks excitement by Terror. Inside, there, the Tiger lies quite quiet in his cage; and here must he ferociously dart upon a black, that the people may fancy the like is to be seen within; of murder and sudden death,

48 2 I 2

of burning and destruction, there is not enough; but ballad-singers must at every corner keep repeating it. Good man will have himself frightened a little; to feel the better, in secret, how beautiful and laudable it is to draw breath in freedom."

Whatever of apprehensiveness from such bugbear images might have remained, was soon all and wholly effaced, as, issuing through the gate, our party entered on the cheerfullest of scenes. The road led first up the River, as yet but a small current, and bearing only light boats, but which by and by, as renowned world-stream, would carry forth its name and waters, and enliven distant lands. They proceeded next through well cultivated fruit-gardens and pleasure-grounds, softly ascending; and by degrees you could look about you in the now-disclosed much-peopled region, till first a thicket, then a little wood admitted our riders, and the gracefullest localities refreshed and limited their view. A meadow vale leading upwards, shortly before mown for the second time, velvet-like to look upon, watered by a brook rushing out lively, copious at once from the uplands above, received them as with welcome; and so they approached a higher, freer station, which, on issuing from the wood, after a stiff ascent, they gained; and could now descry, over new clumps of trees, the old Castle, the goal of their pilgrimage, rising in the distance, as pinnacle of the rock and forest. Backwards, again, (for never did one mount hither without turning round,) they caught, through accidental openings of the high trees, the Prince's Castle, on the left, lightened by the morning sun; the well-built higher quarter of the Town softened under light smoke-clouds; and so on, rightwards, the under Town, the River in several bendings, with its meadows and mills; on the farther side, an extensive fertile region.

Having satisfied themselves with the prospect, or rather as usually happens when we look round from so high a station, become doubly eager for a wider, less limited view, they rode on, over a broad stony flat, where the mighty Ruin stood fronting them, as a green-crowned summit, a few old trees far down about its foot: they rode along; and so arrived there, just at the steepest, most inaccessible side. Great rocks jutting out from of old, insensible of every change, firm, well-founded, stood clenched together there; and so it towered upwards: what had fallen at intervals lay in huge plates and fragments confusedly heaped, and seemed to forbid the boldest any attempt. But the steep, the precipitous is inviting to youth: to undertake it, to storm and conquer it, is for young limbs an enjoyment. The Princess testified desire for an attempt; Honorio was at her hand; the Prince-Uncle, if easier to satisfy, took it cheerfully, and would show that he too had strength: the horses were to wait below among the trees; our climbers make for a certain point, where a huge projecting rock affords a standing-room, and a prospect, which indeed is already passing over into the bird's-eye kind, yet folds itself together there picturesquely enough.

The sun, almost at its meridian, lent the clearest light; the Prince's Castle, with its compartments, main buildings, wings, domes, and towers, lay clear and stately; the upper Town in its whole extent; into the lower also you could conveniently look, nay, by the telescope distinguish the booths in the market-place. So furthersome an instrument Honorio would never leave behind: they looked at the River upwards and downwards, on this side the mountainous, terrace-like, interrupted expanse, on that the upswelling, fruitful land, alternating in level and low hill; places innumerable; for it was long customary to dispute how many of them were here to be seen.

Over the great expanse lay a cheerful stillness, as is common at noon; when, as the Ancients were wont to say, Pan is asleep, and all Nature holds her breath not to awaken him.

"It is not the first time," said the Princess, "that I, on some such high far-seeing spot, have reflected how Nature all clear looks so pure and peaceful, and gives you the impression as if there were nothing contradictory in the world; and yet when you return back into the habitation of man, be it lofty or low, wide or narrow, there is ever somewhat to contend with, to battle with, to smooth and put to rights."

Honorio, who, meanwhile, was looking through the glass at the Town, exclaimed: "See! see! There is fire in the market!" They looked, and could observe some smoke, the flames were smothered in the daylight. "The fire spreads!" cried he, still looking through the glass; the mischief indeed now became noticeable to the good eyes of the Princess; from time to time you observed a red burst of flame; the smoke mounted aloft; and Prince-Uncle said: "Let us return: that is not good; I always feared I should see that misery a second time." They descended, got back to their horses. "Ride," said the Princess to the Uncle, "fast, but not without a groom; leave me Honorio, we will follow without delay. The Uncle felt the reasonableness, nay necessity of this; and started off down the waste stony slope, at the quickest pace the ground allowed.

As the Princess mounted, Honorio said: "Please your Excellency to ride slow! In the Town as in the Castle, the fire-apparatus is in perfect order; the people, in this unexpected accident, will not lose their presence of mind. Here, moreover, we have bad ground, little stones and short grass; quick riding is unsafe; in any case, before we arrive, the fire will be got under." The Princess did not think so; she observed the smoke spreading, she fancied that she saw a flame flash up, that she heard an explosion; and now in her imagination all the terrific things awoke, which the worthy Uncle's repeated narrative of his experiences in that market-conflagration had too deeply implanted there.

Frightful doubtless had that business been, alarming and impressive enough to leave behind it, painfully through life long, a boding and image of its recurrence, when, in the night-season, on the great booth-covered market-space, a sudden fire had seized booth after booth, before the sleepers in these light huts could be shaken out of deep dreams: the Prince himself, as a wearied stranger arriving only for rest, started from his sleep, sprang to the window, saw all fearfully illuminated; flame after flame, from the right, from the left, darting through each other, rolls quivering towards him. The houses of the market-place, reddened in the shine, seemed already glowing, threatened every moment to kindle, and burst forth in fire: below, the element raged without let; planks cracked, laths cracked, the canvas flew abroad, and its dusky fire-peaked tatters whirled themselves round and aloft, as if bad spirits, in their own element, with perpetual change of shape, were, in capricious dance, devouring one another; and there and yonder would dart up out from their penal fire. And then with wild howls each saved what was at hand: servants and masters laboured to drag forth bales already seized by the flames, to snatch away yet somewhat from the burning shelves, and pack it into the chests, which too they must at last leave a prey to the hastening flame. How many a one could have prayed but for a moment's pause to the loud-advancing fire; as he looked round for the possibility of some device, and was with all his possession already seized: on the one side, burnt and glowed already, what on the other still stood in dark night. Obstinate characters, will-strong men grimly fronted the grim foe, and saved much, with loss of their eyebrows and hair. Alas, all this waste confusion now rose anew before the fair spirit of the Princess; the gay morning prospect was all overclouded, and her eyes darkened; wood and meadow had put on a look of strangeness, of danger.

Entering the peaceful vale, heeding little its refreshing coolness, they were but a few steps down from the copious fountain of the brook which flowed by them, when the Princess descried, quite down in the thickets, something singular, whieh she soon recognised for the tiger: springing on, as she a short while ago had seen him painted, he came towards her; and this image, added to the frightful ones she was already busy with, made the strangest impression. "Fly! your Grace," cried Honorio, "fly!" She turned her horse towards the steep hill they had just descended. The young man, rushing on towards the monster, drew his pistol and fired when he thought himself near enough; but, alas, without effect; the tiger sprang to a side, the horse faltered, the provoked wild beast followed his course, upwards straight after the Princess. She galloped, what her horse could, up the steep stony space; scarcely apprehending that so delicate a creature, unused to such exertion, could not hold out. It overdid itself, driven on by the necessitated Princess; it stumbled on the loose gravel of the steep, and again stumbled; and at last fell, after violent efforts, powerless to the ground. The fair dame, resolute and dextrous, failed not instantly to get upon her feet; the horse too rose, but the tiger was approaching; though not with vehement speed; the uneven ground, the sharp stones seemed to damp his impetuosity; and only Honorio flying after him, riding with checked speed along with him, appeared to stimulate and provoke his force anew. Both runners, at the same instant, reached the spot where the Princess was standing by her horse: the Knight bent himself, fired, and with this second pistol hit the monster through the head, so that it rushed down; and now, stretched out in full length, first clearly disclosed the might and terror whereof only the bodily hull was left lying. Honorio had sprung from his horse; was already kneeling on the beast, quenching its last movements, and held his drawn hanger in his right hand. The youth was beautiful; he had come dashing on as in sports of the lance and the ring the Princess had often seen him do. Even so in the riding-course would his bullet, as he darted by, hit the Turk's-head on the pole, right under the turban in the brow; even so would he, lightly prancing up, prick his naked sabre into the fallen mass, and lift it from the ground. In all such arts he was dextrous and felicitous; both now stood him in good stead.

"Give him the rest," said the Princess: "I fear he will hurt you with his claws."—"Pardon!" answered the youth: "he is already dead enough; and I would not hurt the skin, which next winter shall shine upon your sledge."—"Sport not," said the Princess: "whatsoever of pious feeling dwells in the depth of the heart unfolds itself in such a moment."—"I too," cried Honorio, "was never more pious than even now; and therefore do I think of what is joyfullest; I look at the tiger's fell only as it can attend you to do you pleasure."—"It would for ever remind me," said she, "of this fearful moment."—"Yet is it," replied the youth with glowing cheeks, "a more harmless spoil than when the weapons of slain enemies are carried for show before the victor."—"I shall bethink me, at sight of it, of your boldness and cleverness; and need not add that you may reckon on my thanks and the Prince's favour for your life long. But rise; the beast is clean dead, let us consider what is next: before all things rise!"—"As I am once on my knees," replied the youth, "once in a posture which in other circumstances would have been forbid, let me beg at this moment to receive assurance of the favour, of the grace which you vouchsafe me. I have already asked so often of your high consort for leave and promotion to go on my travels. He who has the happiness to sit at your table, whom you honour with the privilege to entertain your company, should have seen the world. Travellers stream in on us from all parts; and when a town, an important spot in any quarter of the world comes in course, the question is sure to be asked of us, were we ever there? Nobody allows one sense, till one has seen all that: it is as if you had to instruct yourself only for the sake of others."

"Rise!" repeated the Princess: "I were loth to wish or request aught that went against the will of my Husband; however, if I mistake not, the cause why he has retained you hitherto will soon be at an end. His intention was to see you ripened into a complete, self-guided nobleman, to do yourself and him credit in foreign parts, as hitherto at court; and I should think this deed of yours was as good a recommendatory passport as a young man could wish for to take abroad with him."

That, instead of a youthful joy, a certain mournfulness came over his face, the Princess had not time to observe, nor had he to indulge his emotion; for, in hot haste, up the steep, came a woman, with a boy at her hand, straight to the group so well known to us; and scarcely had Honorio, bethinking him, arisen, when they howling and shrieking cast themselves on the carcass; by which action, as well as by their cleanly decent, yet party-coloured and unusual dress, might be gathered that it was the mistress of this slain creature, and the black-eyed, black-locked boy, holding a flute in his hand, her son; weeping like his mother, less violent but deeply moved, kneeling beside her.

Now came strong outbreakings of passion from this woman; interrupted, indeed, and pulse-wise; a stream of words, leaping like a stream in gushes from rock to rock. A natural language, short and discontinuous, made itself impressive and pathetic: in vain should we attempt translating it into our dialects; the approximate purport of it we must not omit. "They have murdered thee, poor beast! murdered without need! Thou wert tame, and wouldst fain have laid down at rest and waited our coming; for thy foot-balls were sore, thy claws had no force left. The hot sun to ripen them was wanting. Thou wert the beautifullest of thy kind: who ever saw a kingly tiger so gloriously stretched out in sleep, as thou here liest, dead, never to rise more. When thou awokest in the early dawn of morning, and openedst thy throat, stretching out thy red tongue, thou wert as if smiling on us; and even when bellowing, thou tookest thy food from the hands of a woman, from the fingers of a child. How long have we gone with thee on thy journeys; how long has thy company been useful and fruitful to us! To us, to us of a very truth, meat came from the eater, and sweetness out of the strong. So will it be no more. Wo! wo!"

She had not done lamenting, when over the smoother part of the Castle Mountain, came riders rushing down; soon recognised as the Prince's Hunting-train, himself the foremost. Following their sport, in the backward hills, they had observed the fire-vapours; and fast through dale and ravine, as in fierce chase, taken the shortest path towards this mournful sign. Galloping along the stony vacancy, they stopped and stared at sight of the unexpected group, which in that empty expanse stood out so markworthy. After the first recognition there was silence; some pause of breathing-time; and then what the view itself did not impart, was with brief words explained. So stood the Prince, contemplating the strange unheard-of incident; a circle round him of riders, and followers that had run on foot. What to do was still undetermined; the Prince intent on ordering, executing, when a man pressed forward into the circle; large of stature, party-coloured, wondrously-apparelled, like wife and child. And now the family in union testified their sorrow and astonishment. The man, however, soon restrained himself, bowed in reverent distance before the Prince, and said: "It is not the time for lamenting; alas, my lord and mighty hunter, the lion too is loose, hither towards the mountains is he gone: but spare him, have mercy that he perish not like this good beast."

"The Lion!" said the Prince: "Hast thou the trace of him?"—"Yes, Lord! A peasant down there, who had heedlessly taken shelter on a tree, directed me farther up this way, to the left; but I saw the crowd of men and horses here; anxious for tidings of assistance, I hastened hither."—"So then," commanded the Prince, "draw to the left, Huntsmen; you will load your pieces, go softly to work, if you drive him into the deep woods, it is no matter: but in the end, good man, we shall be obliged to kill your animal; why were you improvident enough to let him loose?"—"The fire broke out," replied he, "we kept quiet and attentive; it spread fast, but at a distance from us, we had water enough for our defence; but a heap of powder blew up, and threw the brands on to us, and over our heads; we were too hasty, and are now ruined people."

The Prince was still busy directing; but for a moment all seemed to pause, as a man was observed hastily springing down from the heights of the old Castle; whom the troop soon recognised for the watchman that had been stationed there to keep the Painter's apartments, while he lodged there and took charge of the workmen. He came running, out of breath, yet in few words soon made known that the Lion had laid himself down, within the high ring-wall, in the sunshine, at the foot of a large beech, and was behaving quite quietly. With an air of vexation, however, the man concluded: "Why did I take my rifle to town yester-night, to have it cleaned; he had never risen again, the skin had been mine, and I might all my life have had the credit of the thing."

The Prince, whom his military experiences here also stood in stead, for he had before now been in situations where from various sides inevitable evil seemed to threaten, said hereupon: "What surety do you give me that if we spare your lion, he will not work destruction among us, among my people?"

"This woman and this child," answered the father hastily, "engage to tame him, to keep him peaceable, till I bring up the cage, and then we can carry him back unharmed and without harming any one."

The boy put his flute to his lips; an instrument of the kind once named soft, or sweet flutes; short-beaked like pipes: he, who understood the art, could bring out of it the gracefullest tones. Meanwhile the Prince had inquired of the watchman how the lion came up. "By the hollow-way," answered he, "which is walled in on both sides, and was formerly the only entrance, and is to be the only one still: two footpaths, which led in elsewhere, we have so blocked up and destroyed that no human being, except by that first narrow passage, can reach the Magic Castle which Prince Friedrich's talent and taste is making of it."

After a little thought, during which the Prince looked round at the boy, who still continued as if softly preluding, he turned to Honorio, and said: "Thou hast done much to-day, complete thy task. Secure that narrow path; keep your rifles in readiness, but do not shoot till the creature can no otherwise be driven back: in any case, kindle a fire, which will frighten him if he make downwards. The man and woman take charge of the rest." Honorio rapidly bestirred himself to execute these orders.

The child continued his tune, which was no tune; a series of notes without law, and perhaps even on that account so heart-touching: the by-standers seemed as if enchanted by the movement of a song-like melody, when the father with dignified enthusiasm began to speak in this sort:

"God has given the Prince wisdom, and also knowledge to discern that all God's works are wise, each after its kind. Behold the rock, how he stands fast and stirs not, defies the weather and the sunshine; primeval trees adorn his head, and so crowned he looks abroad; neither if a mass rush away, will this continue what it was, but falls broken into many pieces and covers the side of the descent. But there too they will not tarry, capriciously they leap far down, the brook receives them, to the river he bears them. Not resisting, not contradictory, angular; no, smooth and rounded they travel now quicker on their way, arrive, from river to river, finally at the ocean, whither march the giants in hosts, and in the depths whereof dwarfs are busy.

"But who shall exalt the glory of the Lord, whom the stars praise from Eternity to Eternity! Why look ye far into the distance? Consider here the bee: late at the end of harvest she still busily gathers, builds her a house, tight of corner, straight of wall, herself the architect and mason. Behold the ant: she knows her way, and loses it not; she piles her a dwelling of grass-halms, earth-crumbs, and needles of the fir; she piles it aloft and arches it in; but she has laboured in vain, for the horse stamps, and scrapes it all in pieces: lo! he has trodden down her beams, and scattered her planks; impatiently he snorts and cannot rest; for the Lord has made the horse comrade of the wind and companion of the storm, to carry man whither he wills, and woman whither she desires. But in the Wood of Palms arose he, the Lion, with earnest step traversed the wildernesses; there rules he over all creatures, his might who shall withstand? Yet man can tame him; and the fiercest of living things has reverence for the image of God, in which too the angels are made, who serve the Lord and his servants. For in the den of Lions Daniel was not afraid: he remained fast and faithful, and the wild bellowing interrupted not his song of praise."

This speech, delivered with expression of a natural enthusiasm, the child accompanied here and there with graceful tones; but now, the father having ended, he, with clear melodious voice and skilful passaging, struck up his warble, whereupon the father took the flute, and gave note in unison, while the child sang:

From the Dens, I, in a deeper,
Prophet's song of praise can hear;
Angel-host he hath for keeper,
Needs the good man there to fear?

Lion, Lioness, agazing,
Mildly pressing round him came;
Yea, that humble, holy praising,
It hath made them tame.

The father continued accompanying this strophe with his flute; the mother here and there touched in as second voice.

Impressive, however, in a quite peculiar degree, it was, when the child now began to shuffle the lines of the strophe into other arrangement; and thereby if not bring out a new sense, yet heighten the feeling by leading it into self-excitement:

Angel-host around doth hover,
Us in heavenly tones to cheer:
In the dens our head doth cover:
Needs the poor child there to fear?

For that humble holy praising
Will permit no evil nigh:
Angels hover, keeping, gazing,
Who so safe as I?

Hereupon with emphasis and elevation began all three:

For th' Eternal rules above us,
Lands and oceans rules his will;
Lions even as lambs shall love us,
And the proudest waves be still.

Whetted sword to scabbard cleaving,
Faith and Hope victorious see:
Strong, who, loving and believing,
Prays, O Lord, to thee.

All were silent, hearing, hearkening; and only when the tones ceased could you remark and distinguish the impression they had made. All was as if appeased; each affected in his way. The Prince, as if he now first saw the misery that a little ago had threatened him, looked down on his spouse, who leaning on him forebore not to draw out the little embroidered handkerchief, and therewith covered her eyes. It was blessedness for her to feel her young bosom relieved from the pressure with which the preceding minutes had loaded it. A perfect silence reigned over the crowd; they seemed to have forgotten the dangers: the conflagration below; and above, the rising up of a dubiously-reposing Lion.

By a sign to bring the horses, the Prince first restored the group to motion; he turned to the woman, and said: "You think then that, once find the lion, you could, by your singing, by the singing of this child, with help of these flute-tones, appease him, and carry him back to his prison, unhurt and hurting no one?" They answered Yes, assuring and affirming; the Castellan was given them as guide. And now the Prince started off in all speed with a few; the Princess followed slower with the rest of the train: mother and son, on their side, under conduct of the warder, who had got himself a musket, mounted up the steeper part of the height.

Before the entrance of the hollow-way which opened their access to the Castle, they found the hunters busy heaping up dry brushwood, to have, in any case, a large fire ready for kindling. "There is no need," said the woman: "it will all go well and peaceably, without that."

Farther on, sitting on a wall, his double-barrel resting in his lap, Honorio appeared; at his post, as if ready for every occurrence. However, he seemed hardly to notice our party; he sat as if sunk in deep thoughts, he looked round like one whose mind was not there. The woman addressed him with a prayer not to let the fire be lit; he appeared not to heed her words; she spoke on with vivacity, and cried: "Handsome young man, thou hast killed my tiger, I do not curse thee; spare my lion, good young man, I will bless thee."

Honorio was looking straight out before him, to where the sun on his course began to sink. "Thou lookest to the west," cried the woman; "thou dost well, there is much to do there; hasten, delay not, thou wilt conquer. But first conquer thyself." At this he appeared to give a smile; the woman stept on; could not, however, but look back once more at him: a ruddy sun was overshining his face; she thought she had never seen a handsomer youth.

"If your child," said the warder now, "with his fluting and singing, can, as you are persuaded, entice and pacify the lion, we shall soon get mastery of him after, for the creature has lain down quite close to the perforated vaults through which, as the main passage was blocked up with ruins, we had to bore ourselves an entrance into the Castle-Court. If the child entice him into this latter, I can close the opening with little difficulty; then the boy, if he like, can glide out by one of the little spiral stairs he will find in the corner. We must conceal ourselves; but I shall so take my place that a rifle-ball can, at any moment, help the poor child in case of extremity."

"All these precautions are unnecessary; God and skill, piety and a blessing, must do the work."—"May be," replied the warder, "however, I know my duties. First, I must lead you, by a difficult path to the top of the wall, right opposite the vaults and opening I have mentioned: the child may then go down, as into the arena of the show, and lead away the animal, if it will follow him." This was done: warder and mother looked down in concealment as the child, descending the screw-stairs, showed himself in the open space of the Court, and disappeared opposite them in the gloomy opening; but forthwith gave his flute voice, which by and by grew weaker, and at last sank dumb. The pause was bodeful enough; the old Hunter, familiar with danger, felt heart-sick at the singular conjuncture; the mother, however, with cheerful face, bending over to listen, showed not the smallest discomposure.

At last the flute was again heard; the child stept forth from the cavern with glittering satisfied eyes, the lion after him, but slowly, and as it seemed, with difficulty. He showed here and there desire to lie down; yet the boy led him in a half-circle through the few disleaved, many-tinted trees, till at length, in the last rays of the sun which poured in through a hole in the ruins, he set him down, as if transfigured in the bright red light; and again commenced his pacifying song, the repetition of which we also cannot forbear:

From the Dens, I, in a deeper,
  Prophet's song of praise can hear;
Angel-host he hath for keeper,
  Needs the good man there to fear?

Lion, Lioness, agazing,
  Mildly pressing round him came;
Yea, that humble, holy praising,
  It hath made them tame.

Meanwhile the lion had laid itself down quite close to the child, and lifted its heavy right fore-paw into his bosom; the boy as he sung gracefully stroked it; but was not long in observing that a sharp thorn had stuck itself between the balls. He carefully pulled it out; with a smile, took the party-coloured silk handkerchief from his neck, and bound up the frightful paw of the monster; so that his mother for joy bent herself back with outstretched arms, and perhaps, according to custom, would have shouted and clapped applause, had not a hard hand gripe of the warder reminded her that the danger was not yet over.

Triumphantly the child sang on, having with a few tones preluded:

For th' Eternal rules above us,
  Lands and oceans rules his will;
Lions even as lambs shall love us,
  And the proudest waves be still.

Whetted sword to scabbard cleaving,
  Faith and Hope victorious see:
Strong, who, loving and believing,
  Prays, O Lord, to thee.

Were it possible to fancy that in the countenance of so grim a creature, the tyrant of the woods, the despot of the animal kingdom, an expression of friendliness, of thankful contentment could be traced, then here was such traceable; and truly the child in his illustrated look had the air as of a mighty triumphant victor; the other figure, indeed, not of that one vanquished, for his strength lay concealed in him; but yet of one tamed, of one given up to his own peaceful will. The child fluted and sang on, changing the lines according to his way, and adding new:

And so to good children bringeth
  Blessed Angel help in need;
Fetters o'er the cruel flingeth,
  Worthy art with wings doth speed.

So have tamed, and firmly iron'd
  To a poor child's feeble knee,
Him the forest's lordly tyrant,
  Song and Piety.

THE TALE.

BY GOETHE.

[FRASER'S MAGAZINE, 1832.]

THAT Goethe, many years ago, wrote a piece named *Das Mährchen*, (The Tale;) which the admiring critics of Germany contrived to criticise by a stroke of the pen; declaring that it was indeed *The* Tale, and worthy to be called the Tale of Tales, (*das Mährchen aller Mährchen,*) —may appear certain to most English readers, for they have repeatedly seen as much in print. To some English readers it may appear certain, furthermore, that they personally know this Tale of Tales; and can even pronounce it to deserve no such epithet, and the admiring critics of Germany to be little other than blockheads.

English readers! the first certainty is altogether indubitable; the second certainty is not worth a rush.

That same *Mährchen aller Mährchen* you may see with your own eyes, at this hour, in the Fifteenth Volume of *Goethe's Werke;* and seeing is believing. On the other hand, that English "Tale of Tales," put forth some years ago as the Translation thereof, by an individual connected with the Periodical Press of London, (his Periodical vehicle, if we remember, broke down soon after, and was rebuilt, and still runs, under the name of *Court Journal,*)—was a Translation, miserable enough, of a quite different thing; a thing, not a *Mährchen* (Fabulous Tale) at all, but an *Erzählung* or common fictitious Narrative; having no manner of relation to the real piece, (beyond standing in the same volume;) not so much as Milton's *Tetrachordon* of Divorce has to his *Allegro* and *Penseroso!* In this way do individuals connected with the Periodical Press of London play their part, and commodiously befool thee, O Public of English readers, and can serve thee with a mass of roasted grass, and name it stewed venison; and will continue to do so, till thou—open thy eyes, and from a blind monster become a seeing one.

This mistake we did not publicly note at the time of its occurrence; for two good reasons: first, that while mistakes are increasing, like Population, at the rate of Twelve Hundred a day, the benefit of seizing *one,* and throttling it, would be perfectly inconsiderable: second, that we were not then in existence. The highly composite, astonishing Entity, which here as "O. Y." addresses mankind for a season, still slumbered (his elements scattered over Infinitude, and working under other shapes) in the womb of Nothing! Meditate on us a little, O Reader: if thou wilt consider who and what we are; what Powers, of Cash, Esurience, Intelligence, Stupidity, and Mystery created us, and what work we do and will do, there shall be no end to thy amazement.

This mistake, however, we do now note; induced thereto by occasion. By the fact, namely, that a genuine English Translation of that *Mährchen* has been handed in to us for judgment; and now (such judgment having proved merciful) comes out from us in the way of publication. Of the Translation we cannot say much; by the colour of the paper, it may be some seven years old, and have lain perhaps in smoky repositories: it is not a good Translation; yet also not wholly bad; faithful to the original, (as we can vouch, after strict trial;) conveys the real meaning, though with an effort: here and there our pen has striven to help it, but could not do much. The poor Translator, who signs himself "D. T.," and affects to carry matters with a high hand, though, as we have ground to surmise, he is probably in straits for the necessaries of life, —has, at a more recent date, appended numerous Notes; wherein he will convince himself that more meaning lies in his Mährchen "than in all the Literature of our century:" some of these we have retained, now and then with an explanatory or exculpatory word of our own; the most we have cut away, as superfluous and even absurd. Superfluous and even absurd, we say: D. T. can take this of us as he likes; we know him, and what is in him, and what is not in him; believe that he will prove reasonable; can do either way. At all events, let one of the notablest Performances produced for the last thousand years, be now, through his organs, (since no other, in this elapsed half-century, have offered themselves,) set before an undiscerning public.

We too will premise our conviction that this *Mährchen* presents a phantasmagoric Adumbration, pregnant with deepest significance; though nowise that D. T. has so accurately evolved the same. Listen notwithstanding to a remark or two, extracted from his immeasurable Proem:

"Dull men of this country," says he, "who pretend to admire Goethe, smiled on me when I first asked the meaning of this Tale. 'Meaning!' answered they: 'it is a wild arabesque, without meaning or purpose at all, except to dash together, copiously enough, confused hues of Imagination, and see what will come of them.' Such is still the persuasion of several heads; which nevertheless would perhaps grudge to be considered wigblocks."—Not impossible: the first Sin in our Universe was Lucifer's, that of Self-conceit. But hear again; what is more to the point:

"The difficulties of interpretation are exceedingly enhanced by one circumstance, not unusual in other such writings of Goethe's; namely, that this is no Allegory; which, as in the *Pilgrim's Progress,* you have only once for all to find the key of, and so go on unlocking: it is a Phantasmagory, rather; wherein things the most heterogeneous are, with homogeneity of figure, emblemed forth: which would require not one key to unlock it, but, at different stages of the business, a dozen successive keys." Here you have epochs of time shadowed forth, there Qualities of the Human

Soul; now it is Institutions, Historical Events, now Doctrines, Philosophic Truths: thus are all manner of 'entities and quiddities and ghosts of defunct bodies' set flying; you have the whole Four Elements chaotico-creatively jumbled together, and spirits enough imbodying themselves, and roguishly peering through, in the confused wild-working mass!" * * *

"So much, however, I will stake my whole money capital and literary character upon: that here is a wonderful EMBLEM OF UNIVERSAL HISTORY set forth; more especially a wonderful Emblem of this our wonderful and woful 'Age of Transition;' what men have been and done, what they are to be and do, is, in this Tale of Tales, poetico-prophetically typified, in such a style of grandeur and celestial brilliancy and life, as the Western Imagination has not elsewhere reached; as only the Oriental Imagination, and in the primeval ages, was wont to attempt."—Here surely is good wine, with a big bush! Study the Tale of Tales, O reader: even in the bald version of D. T., there will be meaning found. He continues in this triumphant style:

"Can any mortal head (not a wigblock) doubt that the Giant of this Poem means SUPERSTITION? That the Ferryman has something to do with the PRIESTHOOD; his Hut with the CHURCH?

"Again, might it not be presumed that the River were TIME; and that it flowed (as Time does) between two worlds? Call the world, or country on this side, where the fair Lily dwells, the world of SUPERNATURALISM; the country on that side, NATURALISM, the working week-day world where we all dwell and toil: whosoever or whatsoever introduces itself, and appears in the firm earth of human business, or as we well say, *comes into* Existence, must proceed *from* Lily's supernatural country; whatsoever of a material sort deceases and disappears might be expected to go *thither*. Let the reader consider this, and note what comes of it.

"To get a free solid communication established over this same wondrous River of Time, so that the Natural and Supernatural may stand in friendliest neighbourhood and union, forms the grand action of this Phantasmagoric Poem: is not such also, let me ask thee, the grand action and summary of Universal History; the one problem of Human Culture; the thing which Mankind (once the three daily meals of victual were moderately secured) has ever striven after, and must ever strive after?—Alas! we observe very soon, matters stand on a most distressful footing, in this of Natural and Supernatural: there are three conveyances across, and all bad, all incidental, temporary, uncertain: the worst of the three, one would think, and the worst conceivable, were the Giant's Shadow, at sunrise and sunset; the best that Snake-bridge at noon, yet still only a bad best. Consider again our trustless, rotten, revolutionary 'age of transition,' and see whether this too does not fit it!

"If you ask next, Who these other strange characters are, the Snake, the Will-o'-Wisps, the Man with the Lamp? I will answer, in general and afar off, that *Light* must signify human Insight, Cultivation, in one sort or other. As for the Snake, I know not well what name to call it by; nay perhaps, in our scanty vocabularies, there is no *name* for it, though that does not hinder its being a thing, genuine enough. Meditation; Intellectual Research; Understanding; in the most general acceptation, Thought: all these come near designating it; none actually designates it. Were I bound, under legal penalties, to give the creature a name, I should say THOUGHT rather than another.

"But what if our Snake, and so much else that works here beside it, were neither a *quality*, nor a *reality*, nor a *state*, nor an *action*, in any kind; none of these things purely and alone, but something intermediate and partaking of them all! In which case, to *name* it, in vulgar speech, were a still more frantic attempt: it is unnameable in speech; and remains only the allegorical Figure known in this Tale by the name of Snake, and more or less *resembling* and shadowing forth somewhat that speech has named, or might name. It is this heterogeneity of nature, pitching your solidest Predicables heels over head, throwing you half a dozen Categories into the melting-pot at once,—that so unspeakably bewilders a Commentator, and for moments is nigh reducing him to *delirium saltans*.

"The Will-o'-wisps, that laugh and jig, and compliment the ladies, and eat gold and shake it from them, I for my own share take the liberty of viewing as some shadow of ELEGANT CULTURE, or modern Fine Literature; which by and by became so skeptical-destructive; and did, as French Philosophy, eat Gold (or Wisdom) enough, and shake it out again. In which sense, their coming (into Existence) by the old Ferryman's (by the Priesthood's) assistance, and almost oversetting his boat, and then laughing at him, and trying to skip off from him, yet being obliged to stop till they had satisfied him: all this, to the discerning eye, has its significance.

"As to the Man with the Lamp, in him and his gold-*giving*, jewel-forming, and otherwise so miraculous Light, which 'casts no shadow,' and 'cannot illuminate what is wholly otherwise in darkness,'—I see what you might name the celestial REASON of Man, (Reason as contrasted with Understanding, and superordinated to it,) the purest essence of his seeing Faculty; which manifests itself as the Spirit of Poetry, of Prophecy, or whatever else of highest in the intellectual sort man's mind can do. We behold this respectable, venerable Lamp-bearer everywhere present in time of need; directing, accomplishing, working, wonder-working, finally victorious;—as, in strict reality, it is ever (if we will study it) the Poetic Vision that lies at the bottom of all other Knowledge or Action; and is the source and creative fountain of whatsoever mortal *ken* or *can*, and mystically and miraculously guides them forward whither they are to go. Be the Man with the Lamp, then, named REASON; mankind's noblest inspired Insight and Light; whereof all the other lights are but effluences, and more or less discoloured emanations.

"His Wife, poor old woman, we shall call

Practical Endeavour; which as married to Reason, to spiritual Vision and Belief, first makes up man's being here below. Unhappily the ancient couple, we find, are but in a decayed condition: the better emblems are they of Reason and Endeavour in this our "transitionary age!" The Man presents himself in the garb of a peasant, the Woman has grown old, garrulous, querulous; both live nevertheless in their 'ancient cottage,' better or worse, the roof-tree of which still holds together over them. And then those mischievous Will-o'-wisps, who pay the old lady such court, and eat all the old gold (all that was wise and beautiful and desirable) off her walls; and show the old stones, quite ugly and bare, as they had not been for ages! Besides, they have killed poor Mops, the plaything, and joy and fondling of the house;—as has not that same Elegant Culture, or French Philosophy done, wheresoever it has arrived? Mark, notwithstanding, how the Man with the Lamp puts it all right again, reconciles every thing, and makes the finest business out of what seemed the worst.

"With regard to the Four Kings, and the Temple which lies fashioned under ground, please to consider all this as the Future lying prepared and certain under the Present: you observe, not only inspired Reason (or the Man with the Lamp) but scientific Thought (or the Snake) can discern it lying there: nevertheless much work must be done, innumerable difficulties fronted and conquered, before it can rise out of the depths, (of the Future,) and realize itself as the actual worshipping-place of man, and 'the most frequented Temple in the whole Earth.'

"As for the fair Lily and her ambulatory necessitous Prince, these are objects that I shall admit myself incapable of naming; yet nowise admit myself incapable of attaching meaning to. Consider them as the two disjointed Halves of this singular Dualistic Being of ours; a Being, I must say, the most utterly Dualistic; fashioned, from the very heart of it, out of Positive and Negative, (what we happily call Light and Darkness, necessity and Freewill, Good and Evil, and the like;) everywhere out of *two* mortally opposed things, which yet must be united in vital love, if there is to be any *Life;*—a being, I repeat, Dualistic beyond expressing; which will split in two, strike it in *any* direction, on *any* of its six sides; and does of itself split in two, (into Contradiction,) every hour of the day,—were not *Life* perpetually there, perpetually knitting it together again! But as to that cutting up, and parcelling, and labelling of the indivisible Human Soul into what are called "Faculties," it is a thing I have from of old eschewed, and even hated. A thing which you *must* sometimes do, (or you cannot *speak;*) yet which is never done without Error hovering near you; for most part, without her pouncing on you, and quite blindfolding you.

"Let not us, therefore, in looking at Lily and her Prince be tempted to that practice: why should we try to *name* them at all? Enough if we do feel that man's whole Being is riven asunder every way (in this 'transitionary age,') and yawning in hostile, irreconcilable contradiction with itself: what good were it to know farther in what *direction* the rift (as our Poet here pleased to represent it) had taken effect? Fancy, however, that these two Halves of Man's Soul and Being are separated, in pain and enchanted obstruction, from one another. The better, fairer Half sits in the Supernatural country, deadening and killing; alas, not permitted to come across into the Natural visible country, and there make all blessed and alive! The rugged stronger Half, in such separation, is quite lamed and paralytic; wretched, forlorn, in a state of death-life, must he wander to and fro over the River of Time; all that is dear and essential to him, imprisoned there; which if he look at he grows still weaker, which if he touch, he dies. Poor Prince! And let the judicious reader, who had read the Era he lives in, or even spelt the alphabet thereof, say whether, with the paralytic-lamed Activity of man (hampered and hamstrung 'in a transitionary age' of Skepticism, Methodism; atheistic Sarcasm, hysteric Orgasm; brazen-faced Delusion, Puffery, Hypocrisy, Stupidity, and the whole Bill and nothing but the Bill,) it is not even so? Must not poor man's Activity (like this poor Prince) wander from Natural to Supernatural, and back again, disconsolate enough; unable to *do* any thing, except merely wring its hands, and, whimpering and blubbering, lamentably inquire: *What* shall I do?

"But Courage! Courage! The Temple is built, (though under-ground;) the Bridge shall arch itself, the divided Two shall clasp each other as flames do, rushing into one; and all that ends well shall be well! Mark only how, in this imitable Poem, worthy an Olympic crown, or prize of the Literary Society, it is represented as proceeding!"

So far D. T.; a commentator who at least does not want confidence in himself; whom we shall only caution not to be too confident; to remember always that, as he once says, "Phantasmagory is not Allegory;" that much exists, under our very noses, which has no "name," and can get none; that the "River of Time" and so forth may be one thing, or more than one, or none; that, in short, there is risk of the too valiant D. T.'s bamboozling himself in this matter; being led from puddle to pool; and so left standing at last, like a foolish mystified nose-of-wax, wondering where the devil he is.

To the simpler sort of readers we shall also extend an advice; or be it rather, proffer a petition. It is to fancy themselves, for the time being, delivered altogether from D. T.'s company; and to read this *Mährchen*, as if it were there only for its own sake, and those tag-rag Notes of his were so much blank paper. Let the simpler sort of readers say now how they like it! If unhappily on looking back, some spasm of "the malady of thought," begin afflicting them, let such Notes be then inquired of, but not till then, and then also with distrust. Pin thy faith to no man's sleeve; hast thou not two eyes of thy own?

The Commentator himself cannot, it is to be hoped, imagine that he has exhausted the matter. To decipher and represent the *genesis* of this extraordinary Production, and what was the Author's state of mind in producing it; to *see*, with dim, common eyes, what the great Goethe, with inspired poetic eyes, then saw; and paint to oneself the thick-coming shapes and many-coloured splendours of his "Prospero's Grotto," at that hour: this were what we could call complete criticism and commentary; what D. T. is far from having done, and ought to fall on his face, and confess that he can never do.

We shall conclude with remarking two things. First, that D. T. does not appear to have set eye on any of those German Commentaries on this Tale of Tales; or even to have heard, credently, that such exist: an omission, in a professed Translator, which he himself may answer for. Secondly, that with all his boundless preluding, he has forgot to insert the Author's own prelude; the passage, namely, by which this *Mährchen* is especially ushered in, and the key-note of it struck by the Composer himself, and the tone of the whole prescribed! This latter altogether glaring omission we now charitably supply; and then let D. T., and his illustrious Original, and the Readers of this Magazine take it among them. Turn to the latter part of the *Deutschen Ausgewanderten* (page 208, Volume XV. of the last Edition of *Goethe's Werke;*) it is written there as we render it:

"'The Imagination,' said Karl, 'is a fine faculty; yet I like not when she works on what has actually happened: the airy forms she creates are welcome as things of their own kind; but uniting with Truth she produces oftenest nothing but monsters; and seems to me, in such cases, to fly into direct variance with Reason and Common sense. She ought, you might say, to hang upon no object, to force no object on us; she must, if she is to produce Works of Art, play like a sort of music upon us; move us within ourselves, and this in such a way that we forget there is any thing without us producing the movement.'

"'Proceed no farther,' said the old man, 'with your conditionings! To enjoy a product of Imagination this also is a condition, that we enjoy it unconditionally; for Imagination herself cannot condition and bargain; she must wait what shall be given her. She forms no plans, prescribes for herself no path; but is borne and guided by her own pinions; and hovering hither and thither, marks out the strangest courses; which in their direction are ever altering. Let me but, on my evening walk, call up again to life within me, some wondrous figures I was wont to play with in earlier years. This night I promise you a Tale, which shall remind you of Nothing and of All.'"

And now for it! O. Y.

THE TALE.

In his little Hut, by the great River, which a heavy rain had swoln to overflowing, lay the ancient Ferryman, asleep, wearied by the toil of the day. In the middle of the night,* loud voices awoke him; he heard that it was travellers wishing to be carried over.

Stepping out, he saw two large Will-o'-wisps, hovering to and fro on his boat, which lay moored; they said, they were in violent haste, and should have been already on the other side. The old Ferryman made no loitering; pushed off, and steered with his usual skill obliquely through the stream: while the two strangers whiffled and hissed together, in an unknown very rapid tongue, and every now and then broke out in loud laughter, hopping about, at one time on the gunwale and the seats, at another on the bottom of the boat.

"The boat is heeling!" cried the old man "if you don't be quiet, it will overset; be seated, gentlemen of the wisp!"

At this advice they burst into a fit of laughter, mocked the old man, and were more unquiet than ever. He bore their mischief with patience, and soon reached the farther shore.

"Here is for your labour!" cried the travellers, and as they shook themselves, a heap of glittering gold-pieces jingled down into the wet boat. "For Heaven's sake, what are you about?" cried the old man; "you will ruin me for ever! Had a single piece of gold got into the water, the stream which cannot suffer gold, would have risen in horrid waves, and swallowed both my skiff and me; and who knows how it might have fared with you in that case: here, take back your gold."

"We can take nothing back, which we have once shaken from us," said the Lights.

"Then you give me the trouble," said the old man, stooping down, and gathering the pieces into his cap, "of raking them together, and carrying them ashore, and burying them."

The Lights had leaped from the boat, but the old man cried: "Stay; where is my fare?"

"If you take no gold, you may work for nothing," cried the Will-o'-wisps.—"You must know that I am only to be paid with fruits of the earth."—"Fruits of the earth? we despise them and have never tasted them."—"And yet I cannot let you go, till you have promised that you will deliver me three Cabbages, three Artichokes, and three large Onions."

The Lights were making off with jests; but they felt themselves, in some inexplicable manner, fastened to the ground: it was the unpleasantest feeling they had ever had. They engaged to pay him his demand as soon as possible: he let them go, and pushed away. He was gone a good distance, when they called to him: "Old Man! Holla, old man! the main point is forgotten!"* He was off, however, and did not hear them. He had fallen quietly down that side of the River, where, in a rocky spot, which the water never reached, he meant to bury the pernicious gold. Here, between two high crags, he found a monstrous chasm; shook

* In the middle of the night truly! In the middle of the Dark Ages, when what with Mohammedan Conquests, what with Christian Crusadings, Destructions of Constantinople, Discoveries of America, the TIME-RIVER was indeed swoln to overflowing; and the *Ignes Fatui* (of Elegant Culture, of Literature,) must needs feel in haste to get over into Existence, being much wanted; and apply to the Priesthood, (respectable old Ferryman, roused out of sleep thereby!) who willingly introduced them, mischievous, ungrateful imps as they were.—D. T.

* What could this be? To ask whither their next road lay? It was useless to ask there: the respectable old Priesthood "did not hear them."—D. T.

the metal into it, and steered back to his cottage.

Now, in this chasm, lay the fair green Snake, who was roused from her sleep by the gold coming chinking down.* No sooner did she fix her eye on the glittering coins, than she ate them all up, with the greatest relish, on the spot; and carefully picked out such pieces as were scattered in the chinks of the rock.

Scarcely had she swallowed them, when, with extreme delight, she began to feel the metal melting in her inwards, and spreading all over her body; and soon, to her lively joy, she observed that she was grown transparent and luminous. Long ago she had been told that this was possible; but now being doubtful whether such a light could last, her curiosity and the desire to be secure against the future, drove her from her cell, that she might see who it was that had shaken in this precious metal. She found no one. The more delightful was it to admire her own appearance, and her graceful brightness, as she crawled along through roots and bushes, and spread out her light among the grass. Every leaf seemed of emerald, every flower was dyed with new glory. It was in vain that she crossed the solitary thickets; but her hopes rose high, when, on reaching the open country, she perceived from afar a brilliancy resembling her own. "Shall I find my like at last, then?" cried she, and hastened to the spot. The toil of crawling through bog and reeds gave her little thought; for though she liked best to live in dry grassy spots of the mountains, among the clefts of rocks, and for most part fed on spicy herbs, and slaked her thirst with mild dew and fresh spring water, yet for the sake of this dear gold, and in the hope of this glorious light, she would have undertaken any thing you could propose to her.

At last, with much fatigue, she reached a wet rushy spot in the swamp, where our two Will-o'-wisps were frisking to and fro. She shoved herself along to them; saluted them, was happy to meet such pleasant gentlemen related to her family. The Lights glided towards her, skipped up over her, and laughed in their fashion. "Lady Cousin," said they, "you are of the horizontal line, yet what of that? It is true we are related only by the look; for observe you," here both the Flames, compressing their whole breadth, made themselves as high and peaked as possible, "how prettily this taper length beseems us gentlemen of the vertical line! Take it not amiss of us, good Lady; what family can boast of such a thing? Since there ever was a Jack-o'-lanthorn in the world, no one of them has either sat or lain."

The Snake felt exceedingly uncomfortable in the company of these relations; for let her hold her head as high as possible, she found that she must bend it to the earth again, would she stir from the spot;† and if in the dark thicket she had been extremely satisfied with her appearance, her splendour in the presence of these cousins seemed to lesson every moment, nay she was afraid that at last it would go out entirely.

In this embarrassment she hastily asked: if the gentlemen could not inform her, whence the glittering gold came, that had fallen a short while ago into the cleft of the rock; her own opinion was, that it had been a golden shower, and had trickled down direct from the sky. The Will-o'-wisps laughed, and shook themselves, and a multitude of gold-pieces came clinking down about them. The snake pushed nimbly forward to eat the coin. "Much good may it do you, Mistress," said the dapper gentlemen: "we can help you to a little more." They shook themselves again several times with great quickness, so that the Snake could scarcely gulp the precious victuals fast enough. Her splendour visibly began increasing; she was really shining beautifully, while the Lights had in the mean time grown rather lean and short of stature, without however in the smallest losing their good-humour.

"I am obliged to you for ever," said the Snake, having got her wind again after the repast; "ask of me what you will; all that I can I will do."

"Very good!" cried the Lights. "Then tell us where the fair Lily dwells? Lead us to the fair Lily's palace and garden; and do not lose a moment, we are dying of impatience to fall down at her feet."

"This service," said the Snake with a deep sigh, "I cannot now do for you. The fair Lily dwells, alas, on the other side of the water."—"Other side of the water? And we have come across it, this stormy night! How cruel is the River to divide us! Would it not be possible to call the old man back?"

"It would be useless," said the Snake; "for if you found him ready on the bank, he would not take you in; he can carry any one to this side, none to yonder."

"Here is a pretty kettle of fish!" cried the Lights: "are there no other means of getting through the water?"—"There are other means, but not at this moment. I myself could take you over, gentlemen, but not till noon."—"That is an hour we do not like to travel in."—"Then you may go across in the evening, on the great Giant's shadow."—"How is that?"—"The great Giant lives not far from this; with his body he has no power; his hands cannot lift a straw, his shoulders could not bear a fagot of twigs; but with his shadow he has power over much, nay all.* At sunrise and sunset therefore he is strongest; so at evening you merely put yourself upon the back of his shadow, the Giant walks softly to the bank, and the shadow carries you across the water. But if you please, about the hour of noon, to be in waiting at that corner of the wood, where the bushes overhang the bank, I myself will take you over and present you to the fair Lily: or on the other hand, if you dislike the noontide, you have just to go at nightfall to that bend of the rocks, and pay a visit to

* THOUGHT, Understanding, roused from her long sleep by the first produce of modern Belles Lettres; which she eagerly devours.—D. T.

† True enough: Thought cannot fly and dance, as your wildfire of Belles Lettres may; she proceeds in the systole-diastole, up-and-down method; and must ever "bend her head to the earth again," (in the way of Baconian Experiment,) or she will not stir from the spot.—D. T.

* Is not SUPERSTITION strongest when the sun is low? with body, powerless; with shadow, omnipotent?—D. T.

the Giant; he will certainly receive you like a gentleman."

With a slight bow, the flames went off; and the Snake at bottom was not discontented to get rid of them; partly that she might enjoy the brightness of her own light, partly satisfy a curiosity with which, for a long time, she had been agitated in a singular way.

In the chasm, where she often crawled hither and thither, she had made a strange discovery. For although in creeping up and down this abyss, she had never had a ray of light, she could well enough discriminate the objects in it, by her sense of touch. Generally she met with nothing but irregular productions of nature; at one time she would wind between the teeth of large crystals, at another she would feel the barbs and hairs of native silver, and now and then carry out with her to the light some straggling jewels.* But to her no small wonder, in a rock which was closed on every side, she had come on certain objects which betrayed the shaping hand of man: smooth walls on which she could not climb, sharp regular corners, well-formed pillars; and what seemed strangest of all, human figures which she had entwined more than once, and which appeared to her to be of brass, or of the finest polished marble. All these experiences she now wished to combine by the sense of sight, thereby to confirm what as yet she only guessed. She believed she could illuminate the whole of that subterranean vault by her own light; and hoped to get acquainted with these curious things at once. She hastened back; and soon found, by the usual way, the cleft by which she used to penetrate the Sanctuary.

On reaching the place, she gazed around with eager curiosity; and though her shining could not enlighten every object in the rotunda, yet those nearest her were plain enough. With astonishment and reverence she looked up into a glancing niche, where the image of an august King stood formed of pure Gold. In size the figure was beyond the stature of man, but by its shape it seemed the likeness of a little rather than a tall person. His handsome body was encircled with an unadorned mantle; and a garland of oak bound his hair together.

No sooner had the Snake beheld this reverend figure, than the King began to speak, and asked: "Whence comest thou?"—"From the chasms where the gold dwells," said the Snake. "What is grander than gold?" inquired the King.—"Light," replied the Snake. "What is more refreshing than light?" said he.—"Speech," answered she.

During this conversation she had squinted to a side, and in the nearest niche perceived another glorious image. It was a Silver King in a sitting posture; his shape was long and rather languid; he was covered with a decorated robe; crown, girdle, and sceptre were adorned with precious stones: the cheerfulness of pride was in his countenance; he seemed about to speak, when a vein which ran dimly-coloured over the marble wall, on a sudden became bright, and diffused a cheerful light throughout the whole Temple. By this brilliancy the Snake perceived a third King, made of Brass, and sitting mighty in shape, leaning on his club, adorned with a laurel garland, and more like a rock than a man. She was looking for the fourth, which was standing at the greatest distance from her; but the wall opened, while the glittering vein started and split, as lightning does, and disappeared.

A Man of middle stature, entering through the cleft, attracted the attention of the Snake. He was dressed like a peasant, and carried in his hand a little Lamp, on whose still flame you liked to look, and which in a strange manner, without casting any shadow, enlightened the whole dome.*

"Why comest thou, since we have light?" said the golden King.—"You know that I may not enlighten what is dark."†—"Will my Kingdom end?" said the silver King.—"Late or never," said the old Man.

With a stronger voice the brazen King began to ask: "When shall I arise?"—"Soon," replied the Man.—"With whom shall I combine?" said the King.—"With thy elder brothers," said the Man.—"What will the youngest do?" inquired the King.—"He will sit down," replied the Man.

"I am not tired," cried the fourth King, with a rough faltering voice.‡

While this speech was going on, the Snake had glided softly round the temple, viewing every thing; she was now looking at the fourth King close by him. He stood leaning on a pillar; his considerable form was heavy rather than beautiful. But what metal it was made of could not be determined. Closely inspected, it seemed a mixture of the three metals which its brothers had been formed of. But in the founding, these materials did not seem to have combined together fully; gold and silver veins ran irregularly through a brazen mass, and gave the figure an unpleasant aspect.

Meanwhile the gold King was asking of the Man, "How many secrets knowest thou?"—"Three," replied the Man.—"Which is the most important?" said the silver King.—"The open one," replied the other.§—"Wilt thou open it to us also?" said the brass King.—"When I know the fourth," replied the Man.—"What care I?" grumbled the composite King, in an under tone.

"I know the fourth," said the Snake; approached the old Man, and hissed somewhat in his ear. "The time is at hand!" cried the old Man, with a strong voice. The temple re-

* Primitive employments, and attainments, of Thought, in this dark den whither it is sent to dwell. For many long ages, it discerns "nothing but irregular productions of Nature;" having indeed to pick material bed and board out of Nature and her irregular productions.—D. T.

* Poetic Light, celestial Reason!—D. T.

Let the reader, in one word, attend well to these four Kings: much annotation from D. T. is here necessarily swept out.—O. Y.

† What is wholly dark. Understanding precedes Reason: modern Science is come: modern Poesy is still but coming,—in Goethe, (and whom else?)—D. T.

‡ Consider these Kings as Eras of the World's History; co, not as Eras, but as Principles which jointly or severally rule Eras. Alas, poor we, in this chaotic soft-soldered "transitionary age," are so unfortunate as to live under the Fourth King.—D. T.

§ Reader, hast thou any glimpse of the "open secret?" I fear, not.—D. T.—Writer, art thou a goose? I fear, yes.—O. Y.

echoed, the metal statues sounded; and that instant the old Man sank away to the westward, and the Snake to the eastward; and both of them passed through the clefts of the rock, with the greatest speed.

All the passages, through which the old Man travelled, filled themselves immediately behind him with gold; for his Lamp had the strange property of changing stone into gold, wood into silver, dead animals into precious stones, and of annihilating all metals. But to display this power, it must shine alone. If another light were beside it, the Lamp only cast from it a pure clear brightness, and all living things were refreshed by it.*

The old Man entered his cottage, which was built on the slope of the hill. He found his Wife in extreme distress. She was sitting at the fire weeping, and refusing to be consoled. "How unhappy am I!" cried she: "Did I not entreat thee not to go away to-night?"—"What is the matter, then?" inquired the husband, quite composed.

"Scarcely wert thou gone," said she, sobbing, "when there came two noisy Travellers to the door: unthinkingly I let them in; they seemed to be a couple of genteel, very honourable people; they were dressed in flames, you would have taken them for Will-o'-wisps. But no sooner were they in the house, than they began, like impudent varlets, to compliment me,† and grew so forward that I feel ashamed to think of it."

"No doubt," said the husband with a smile, "the gentlemen were jesting: considering thy age, they might have held by general politeness."

"Age! what age?" cried the Wife: "wilt thou always be talking of my age? How old am I then?—General politeness! But I know what I know. Look round there what a face the walls have; look at the old stones, which I have not seen these hundred years; every film of gold have they licked away, thou couldst not think how fast; and still they kept assuring me that it tasted far beyond common gold. Once they had swept the walls, the fellows seemed to be in high spirits, and truly in that little while they had grown much broader and brighter. They now began to be impertinent again, they patted me, and called me their queen, they shook themselves, and a shower of gold pieces sprang from them! See how they are shining there under the bench! But ah! what misery! Poor Mops ate a coin or two; and look, he is lying in the chimney, dead. Poor Pug! O well-a-day! I did not see it till they were gone; else I had never promised to pay the Ferryman the debt they owe him."—"What do they owe him?" said the Man.—"Three Cabbages," replied the Wife, "three Artichokes and three Onions: I engaged to go when it was day, and take them to the River."

"Thou mayest do them that civility," said the old Man; "they may chance to be of use to us again."

"Whether they will be of use to us I know not; but they promised and vowed that they would."

Meantime the fire on the hearth had burnt low; the old Man covered up the embers with a heap of ashes, and put the glittering gold pieces aside; so that his little Lamp now gleamed alone, in the fairest brightness. The walls again coated themselves with gold, and Mops changed into the prettiest onyx that could be imagined. The alternation of the brown and black in this precious stone made it the most curious piece of workmanship.

"Take thy basket," said the Man, "and put the onyx into it; then take the three Cabbages, the three Artichokes, and the three Onions; place them round little Mops, and carry them to the River. At noon the Snake will take thee over; visit the fair Lily, give her the onyx, she will make it alive by her touch, as by her touch she kills whatever is alive already. She will have a true companion in the little dog. Tell her not to mourn; her deliverance is near; the greatest misfortune she may look upon as the greatest happiness; for the time is at hand."

The old Woman filled her basket, and set out as soon as it was day. The rising sun shone clear from the other side of the River, which was glittering in the distance: the old Woman walked with slow steps, for the basket pressed upon her head, and it was not the onyx that so burdened her. Whatever lifeless thing she might be carrying, she did not feel the weight of it; on the other hand, in those cases the basket rose aloft, and hovered along above her head. But to carry any fresh herbage, or any little living animal, she found exceedingly laborious.* She had travelled on for some time, in a sullen humour, when she halted suddenly in fright, for she had almost trod upon the Giant's shadow, which was stretching towards her across the plain. And now, lifting up her eyes, she saw the monster of a Giant himself, who had been bathing in the River, and was just come out,† and she knew not how she should avoid him. The moment he perceived her, he began saluting her in sport, and the hands of his shadow soon caught hold of the basket; with dexterous ease they picked away from it a Cabbage, an Artichoke, and an Onion, and brought them to the Giant's mouth, who then went his way up the River, and let the Woman go in peace.

She considered whether it would not be better to return, and supply from her garden the pieces she had lost; and amid these doubts, she still kept walking on, so that in a little while she was at the bank of the River. She sat long waiting for the Ferryman, whom she perceived at last, steering over with a very

* In Illuminated Ages, the Age of Miracles is said to cease; but it is only we that cease to see it, for we are still "refreshed by it."—D. T.

† Poor old Practical Endeavour! Listen to many an *Encyclopédie*-Diderot, humanized *Philosophe*, didactic singer, march-of-intellect men, and other "impudent varlets" (that would never put their own finger to the work;) and hear what "compliments" they uttered.—D. T.

* Why so? Is it because with "lifeless things" (with inanimate *machinery*) all goes like clock-work, which it is, and "the basket hovers aloft;" while with living things, (were it but the culture of forest-trees) poor Endeavour has more difficulty?—D. T.—Or, is it chiefly because a Tale must be a Tale?—O. Y.

† Very proper in the huge Loggerhead *Superstition*, to bathe himself in the element of TIME, and get refreshment thereby.—D. T.

singular traveller. A young, noble-looking, handsome man, whom she could not gaze upon enough, stepped out of the boat.

"What is it you bring?" cried the old man. "The greens which those two Will-o'-wisps owe you," said the Woman, pointing to her ware. As the Ferryman found only two of each sort he grew angry, and declared he would have none of them. The Woman earnestly entreated him to take them; told him that she could not now go home, and that her burden for the way which still remained was very heavy. He stood by his refusal, and assured her that it did not rest with him. "What belongs to me," said he "I must leave lying nine hours in a heap, touching none of it, till I have given the River its third." After much higgling, the old man at last replied: "There is still another way. If you like to pledge yourself to the River, and declare yourself its debtor, I will take the six pieces; but there is some risk in it."—"If I keep my word, I shall run no risk?"—"Not the smallest. Put your hand into the stream," continued he, "and promise that within four-and-twenty hours you will pay the debt."

The old Woman did so; but what was her affright, when, on drawing out her hand, she found it black as coal! She loudly scolded the old Ferryman; declared that her hands had always been the fairest part of her; that in spite of her hard work, she had all along contrived to keep these noble members white and dainty. She looked at the hand with indignation, and exclaimed in a despairing tone: "Worse and worse! Look, it is vanishing entirely; it is grown far smaller than the other."*

"For the present it but seems so," said the old man; if you do not keep your word, however, it may prove so in earnest. The hand will gradually diminish, and at length disappear altogether, though you have the use of it as formerly. Every thing as usual you will be able to perform with it, only nobody will see it."—"I had rather that I could not use it, and no one could observe the want," cried she; "but what of that, I will keep my word, and rid myself of this black skin, and all anxieties about it." Thereupon she hastily took up her basket, which mounted of itself over her head, and hovered free above her in the air, as she hurried after the Youth, who was walking softly and thoughtfully down the bank. His noble form and strange dress had made a deep impression on her.

His breast was covered with a glittering coat of mail; in whose wavings might be traced every motion of his fair body. From his shoulders hung a purple cloak; around his uncovered head flowed abundant brown hair in beautiful locks: his graceful face, and his well-formed feet were exposed to the scorching of the sun. With bare soles he walked composedly over the hot sand; and a deep inward sorrow seemed to blunt him against all external things.

* A dangerous thing to pledge yourself to the Time-River;—as many a National Debt, and the like, blackening, bewitching the "beautiful hand" of Endeavour, can witness.—D. T.—Heavens!—O. Y.

The garrulous old Woman tried to lead him into conversation; but with his short answers he gave her small encouragement or information; so that in the end, notwithstanding the beauty of his eyes, she grew tired of speaking with him to no purpose, and took leave of him with these words: "You walk too slow for me, worthy sir; I must not lose a moment, for I have to pass the River on the green Snake, and carry this fine present from my husband to the fair Lily." So saying she stepped faster forward; but the fair Youth pushed on with equal speed, and hastened to keep up with her. "You are going to the fair Lily!" cried he; "then our roads are the same. But what present is this you are bringing her?"

"Sir," said the Woman, "it is hardly fair, after so briefly dismissing the questions I put to you, to inquire with such vivacity about my secrets. But if you like to barter, and tell me your adventures, I will not conceal from you how it stands with me and my presents." They soon made a bargain; the dame disclosed her circumstances to him; told the history of the Pug, and let him see the singular gift.

He lifted his natural curiosity from the basket, and took Mops, who seemed as if sleeping softly, into his arms. "Happy beast!" cried he; "thou wilt be touched by her hands, thou wilt be made alive by her; while the living are obliged to fly from her presence to escape a mournful doom. Yet why say I mournful! Is it not far sadder and more frightful to be injured by her look, than it would be to die by her hand? Behold me," said he to the Woman; "at my years, what a miserable fate have I to undergo. This mail which I have honourably borne in war, this purple which I sought to merit by a wise reign, Destiny has left me; the one as a useless burden, the other as an empty ornament. Crown, and sceptre, and sword are gone; and I am as bare and needy as any other son of earth; for so unblessed are her bright eyes, that they take from every living creature they look on all its force, and those whom the touch of her hand does not kill are changed to the state of shadows wandering alive."

Thus did he continue to bewail, nowise contenting the old Woman's curiosity, who wished for information not so much of his internal as of his external situation. She learned neither the name of his father, nor of his kingdom. He stroked the hard Mops, whom the sunbeams and the bosom of the youth had warmed as if he had been living. He inquired narrowly about the man with the Lamp, about the influences of the sacred light, appearing to expect much good from it in his melancholy case.

Amid such conversation, they descried from afar the majestic arch of the Bridge, which extended from the one bank to the other, glittering with the strangest colours in the splendours of the sun. Both were astonished; for until now they had never seen this edifice so grand. "How!" cried the Prince! "was it not beautiful enough, as it stood before our eyes, piled out of jasper and agate? Shall we not fear to tread it, now that it appears combined in graceful complexity, of emerald and chrysopras and chrysolite?" Neither of them knew the alteration that had taken place upon the Snake: for it was indeed the Snake, who every day at noon curved herself over the River, and stood forth in the form of a bold-swelling bridge.* The travellers stepped upon it with a reverential feeling, and passed over it in silence.

No sooner had they reached the other shore, than the bridge began to heave and stir; in a little while, it touched the surface of the water, and the green Snake in her proper form came gliding after the wanderers. They had scarcely thanked her for the privilege of crossing on her back, when they found that, besides them three, there must be other persons in the company, whom their eyes could not discern. They heard a hissing, which the Snake also answered with a hissing; they listened, and at length caught what follows: "We shall first look about us in the fair Lily's Park," said a pair of alternating voices; "and then request you at nightfall, so soon as we are anywise presentable, to introduce us to this paragon of beauty. At the shore of the great Lake, you will find us."—"Be it so," replied the Snake; and a hissing sound died away in the air.

Our three travellers now consulted in what order they should introduce themselves to the fair Lady; for however many people might be in her company, they were obliged to enter and depart singly, under pain of suffering very hard severities.

The Woman with the metamorphosed Pug in the basket first approached the garden, looking round for her Patroness; who was not difficult to find, being just engaged in singing to her harp. The finest tones proceeded from her, first like circles on the surface of the still lake, then like a light breath they set the grass and the bushes in motion. In a green enclosure, under the shadow of a stately group of many diverse trees, was she seated; and again did she enchant the eyes, the ear, and the heart of the woman, who approached with rapture, and swore within herself that since she saw her last, the fair one had grown fairer than ever. With eager gladness from a distance she expressed her reverence and admiration for the lovely maiden. "What a happiness to see you, what a Heaven does your presence spread around you! How charmingly the harp is leaning on your bosom, how softly your arms surround it, how it seems as if longing to be near you, and how it sounds so meekly under the touch of your slim fingers! Thrice happy youth, to whom it were permitted to be there!"

So speaking she approached; the fair Lily raised her eyes: let her hands drop from the harp, and answered: "Trouble me not with untimely praise; I feel my misery but the more deeply. Look here, at my feet lies the poor Canary-bird, which used so beautifully to accompany my singing; it would sit upon my harp, and was trained not to touch me; but today, while I, refreshed by sleep, was raising a peaceful morning hymn, and my little singer was pouring forth his harmonious tones more gaily than ever, a Hawk darts over my head; the poor little creature, in affright, takes refuge in my bosom, and I feel the last palpitations of its departing life. The plundering Hawk indeed was caught by my look, and fluttered fainting down into the water; but what can his punishment avail me? my darling is dead, and his grave will but increase the mournful bushes of my garden."

"Take courage, fairest Lily!" cried the Woman, wiping off a tear, which the story of the hapless maiden had called into her eyes; "compose yourself; my old man bids me tell you to moderate your lamenting, to look upon the greatest misfortune as a forerunner of the greatest happiness, for the time is at hand; and truly," continued she, "the world is going strangely on of late. Do but look at my hand, how black it is! As I live and breathe, it is grown far smaller: I must hasten, before it vanish altogether! Why did I engage to do the Will-o'-wisps a service, why did I meet the Giant's shadow, and dip my hand in the River? Could you not afford me a single cabbage, an artichoke, and an onion? I would give them to the River, and my hand were white as ever, so that I could almost show it with one of yours.

"Cabbages and onions thou mayest still find; but artichokes thou wilt search for in vain. No plant in my garden bears either flowers or fruit; but every twig that I break, and plant upon the grave of a favourite, grows green straightway, and shoots up in fair boughs. All these groups, these bushes, these groves my hard destiny has so raised around me. These pines stretching out like parasols, these obelisks of cypresses, these colossal oaks and beeches, were all little twigs planted by my hand, as mournful memorials in a soil that otherwise is barren."*

To this speech the old Woman had paid little heed; she was looking at her hand, which, in presence of the fair Lily, seemed every moment growing blacker and smaller. She was about to snatch her basket and hasten off, when she noticed that the best part of her errand had been forgotten. She lifted out the onyx Pug, and set him down, not far from the fair one, in the grass. "My husband," said she, "sends you this memorial; you know that you can make a jewel live by touching it. This pretty faithful dog will certainly afford you much enjoyment; and my grief at losing him is brightened only by the thought that he will be in your possession."

The fair Lily viewed the dainty creature with a pleased, and as it seemed, with an astonished look. "Many signs combine," said she, "that breathe some hope into me: but ah! is it not a natural deception which makes us fancy, when misfortunes crowd upon us, that a better day is near?

*If aught can overspan the Time-River, then what but Understanding, but Thought, in its moment of plenitude, in its favourable noon-moment?—D. T.

* In SUPERNATURALISM, truly, what is there either of flower or of fruit? Nothing that will (altogether) content the greedy Time-River. Stupendous, funereal sacred-groves, "in a soil that otherwise is barren!"—D. T.

"What can these many signs avail me,
My Singer's Death, thy coal-black Hand?
This Dog of Onyx, that can never fail me?
And coming at the Lamp's command!

"From human joys removed for ever,
With sorrows compassed round I sit:
Is there a Temple at the River?
Is there a Bridge? Alas, not yet!"

The good old dame had listened with impatience to this singing, which the fair Lily accompanied with her harp, in a way that would have charmed any other. She was on the point of taking leave, when the arrival of the green Snake again detained her. The Snake had caught the last lines of the song, and on this matter forthwith began to speak comfort to the fair Lily.

"The Prophecy of the Bridge is fulfilled!" cried the Snake: "you may ask this worthy dame how royally the arch looks now. What formerly was untransparent jasper, or agate, allowing but a gleam of light to pass about its edges, is now become transparent precious stone. No beryl is so clear, no emerald so beautiful of hue."

"I wish you joy of it," said Lily; "but you will pardon me if I regard the prophecy as yet unaccomplished. The lofty arch of your bridge can still but admit foot-passengers; and it is promised us that horses and carriages and travellers of every sort shall, at the same moment, cross this bridge in both directions. Is there not something said, too, about pillars, which are to arise of themselves from the waters of the River?

The old Woman still kept her eyes fixed on her hand; she here interrupted their dialogue, and was taking leave. "Wait a moment," said the fair Lily, "and carry my little bird with you. Bid the Lamp change it into topaz; I will enliven it by my touch; with your good Mops it shall form my dearest pastime: but hasten, hasten; for, at sunset, intolerable putrefaction will fasten on the hapless bird, and tear asunder the fair combination of its form for ever."

The old Woman laid the little corpse, wrapped in soft leaves, into her basket, and hastened away.

"However it may be," said the Snake, recommencing their interrupted dialogue, "the Temple is built."

"But it is not at the River," said the fair one.

"It is yet resting in the depths of the Earth," said the Snake; "I have seen the Kings and conversed with them."

"But when will they arise?" inquired Lily.

The Snake replied: "I heard resounding in the Temple these deep words, *The time is at hand*."

A pleasing cheerfulness spread over the fair Lily's face: "'Tis the second time," said she, "that I have heard these happy words to-day: when will the day come for me to hear them thrice?"

She rose, and immediately there came a lovely maiden from the grove, and took away her harp. Another followed her, and folded up the fine-carved ivory stool, on which the fair one had been sitting, and put the silvery cushion under her arm. A third then made her appearance, with a large parasol worked with pearls; and looked whether Lily would require her in walking. These three maidens were beyond expression beautiful; and yet their beauty but exalted that of Lily, for it was plain to every one that they could never be compared to her.*

Meanwhile the fair one had been looking, with a satisfied aspect, at the strange onyx Mops. She bent down, and touched him, and that instant he started up. Gaily he looked around, ran hither and thither, and at last, in his kindest manner, hastened to salute his benefactress. She took him in her arms, and pressed him to her. "Cold as thou art," cried she, "and though but a half-life works in thee, thou art welcome to me; tenderly will I love thee, prettily will I play with thee, softly caress thee, and firmly press thee to my bosom." She then let him go, chased him from her, called him back, and played so daintily with him, and ran about so gayly and so innocently with him on the grass, that with new rapture you viewed and participated in her joy, as a little while ago her sorrow had attuned every heart to sympathy.

This cheerfulness, these graceful sports were interrupted by the entrance of the woful Youth. He stepped forward, in his former guise and aspect; save that the heat of the day appeared to have fatigued him still more, and in the presence of his mistress he grew paler every moment. He bore upon his hand a Hawk, which was sitting quiet as a dove, with its body shrunk and its wings drooping.

"It is not kind in thee," cried Lily to him, "to bring that hateful thing before my eyes, the monster, which to-day has killed my little singer."

"Blame not the unhappy bird!" replied the Youth; "rather blame thyself and thy destiny; and leave me to keep beside me the companion of my wo."

Meanwhile Mops ceased not teasing the fair Lily; and she replied to her transparent favourite, with friendly gestures. She clapped her hands to scare him off; then ran, to entice him after her. She tried to get him when he fled, and she chased him away when he attempted to press near her. The Youth looked on in silence, with increasing anger; but at last, when she took the odious beast, which seemed to him unutterably ugly, on her arm, pressed it to her white bosom, and kissed its black snout with her heavenly lips, his patience altogether failed him, and full of desperation he exclaimed: "Must I, who by a baleful fate exist beside thee, perhaps to the end, in an absent presence, who by thee have lost my all, my very self, must I see before my eyes, that so unnatural a monster can charm thee into gladness, can awaken thy attachment, and enjoy thy embrace? Shall I any longer keep wandering to and fro, measuring my dreary course to that side of the River and to

* Who are these three? Faith, Hope, and Charity, or others of that kin?—D. T.—Faith, Hope, and Fiddlestick!—O. Y.

this? No, there is still a spark of the old heroic spirit sleeping in my bosom, let it start this instant into its expiring flame! If stones may rest in thy bosom, let me be changed to stone; if thy touch kills, I will die by thy hands."

So saying he made a violent movement; the Hawk flew from his finger, but he himself rushed towards the fair one; she held out her hands to keep him off, and touched him only the sooner. Consciousness forsook him; and she felt with horror the beloved burden lying on her bosom. With a shriek she started back, and the gentle youth sank lifeless from her arms upon the ground.

The misery had happened! The sweet Lily stood motionless, gazing on the corpse. Her heart seemed to pause in her bosom; and her eyes were without tears. In vain did Mops try to gain from her any kindly gesture; with her friend, the world for her was all dead as the grave. Her silent despair did not look round for help; she knew not of any help.

On the other hand, the Snake bestirred herself the more actively; she seemed to meditate deliverance; and in fact her strange movements served at last to keep away, for a little, the immediate consequences of the mischief. With her limber body, she formed a wide circle round the corpse, and seizing the end of her tail between her teeth, she lay quite still.

Ere long one of Lily's fair waiting-maids appeared; brought the ivory folding-stool, and with friendly beckoning constrained her mistress to sit down on it. Soon afterwards there came a second; she had in her hand a fire-coloured veil, with which she rather decorated than concealed the fair Lily's head. The third handed her the harp, and scarcely had she drawn the gorgeous instrument towards her, and struck some tones from its strings, when the first maid returned with a clear round mirror; took her station opposite the fair one; caught her looks in the glass, and threw back to her the loveliest image that was to be found in nature.* Sorrow heightened her beauty, the veil her charms, the harp her grace; and deeply as you wished to see her mournful situation altered, not less deeply did you wish to keep her image, as she now looked, for ever present with you.

With a still look at the mirror, she touched the harp; now melting tones proceeded from the strings, now her pain seemed to mount, and the music in strong notes responded to her wo; sometimes she opened her lips to sing, but her voice failed her; and ere long her sorrow melted into tears, two maidens caught her helpfully in their arms, the harp sank from her bosom, scarcely could the quick servant snatch the instrument and carry it aside.

"Who gets us the Man with the Lamp, before the sun set?" hissed the Snake, faintly, but audibly: the maids looked at one another, and Lily's tears fell faster. At this moment came the Woman with the Basket, panting and altogether breathless. "I am lost and maimed for life!" cried she; "see how my hand is almost vanished; neither Ferryman nor Giant would take me over, because I am the River's debtor; in vain did I promise hundreds of Cabbages and hundreds of Onions; they will take no more than three; and no Artichoke is now to be found in all this quarter."

"Forget your own care," said the Snake, "and try to bring help here; perhaps it may come to yourself also. Haste with your utmost speed to seek the Will-o'-wisps; it is too light for you to see them, but perhaps you will hear them laughing and hopping to and fro. If they be speedy, they may cross upon the Giant's shadow, and seek the Man with the Lamp and send him to us."

The Woman hurried off at her quickest pace, and the Snake seemed expecting as impatiently as Lily the return of the Flames. Alas! the beam of the sinking Sun was already gilding only the highest summits of the trees in the thicket, and long shadows were stretching over lake and meadow; the Snake hitched up and down impatiently, and Lily dissolved in tears.

In this extreme need, the Snake kept looking round on all sides; for she was afraid every moment that the Sun would set, and corruption penetrate the magic circle, and the fair youth immediately moulder away. At last she noticed sailing high in the air, with purple-red feathers, the Prince's Hawk, whose breast was catching the last beams of the Sun. She shook herself for joy at this good omen; nor was she deceived; for shortly afterwards the Man with the Lamp was seen gliding towards them across the Lake, fast and smoothly, as if he had been travelling on skates.

The Snake did not change her posture; but Lily rose and called to him: "What good spirit sends thee, at the moment when we were desiring thee, and needing thee, so much?"

"The spirit of my Lamp," replied the Man, "has impelled me, and the Hawk has conducted me. My Lamp sparkles when I am needed, and I just look about me in the sky for a signal; some bird or meteor points to the quarter towards which I am to turn. Be calm, fairest Maiden! whether I can help I know not; an individual helps not, but he who combines himself with many at the proper hour. We will postpone the evil, and keep hoping. Hold thy circle fast," continued he, turning to the Snake; then set himself upon a hillock beside her, and illuminated the dead body. "Bring the little Bird* hither too, and lay it in the circle!" The maidens took the little corpse from the basket, which the old Woman had left standing, and did as he directed.

---

* Does not man's soul *rest* by Faith, and look in the *mirror* of Faith? Does not Hope "decorate rather than conceal?" Is not Charity (Love) the beginning of *music*?—Behold, too, how the Serpent, in this great hour, has made herself a Serpent-of-Eternity; and (even as genuine THOUGHT, in our age, has to do for so much) preserves the seeming-dead within her folds, that suspended animation issue not in noisome, horrible, irrevocable dissolution!—D. T.

* What are the Hawk and this Canary-bird, which here prove so destructive to one another? Ministering servants, implements, of these two divided Halves of the Human Soul; name them I will not; more is not written.—D. T.

Meanwhile the Sun had set, and as the darkness increased, not only the Snake and the old Man's Lamp began shining in their fashion, but also Lily's veil gave out a soft light, which gracefully tinged, as with a meek dawning red, her pale cheeks, and her white robe. The party looked at one another, silently reflecting; care and sorrow were mitigated by a sure hope.

It was no unpleasing entrance, therefore, that the woman made, attended by the two gay Flames, which in truth appeared to have been very lavish in the interim, for they had again become extremely meager; yet they only bore themselves the more prettily for that, towards Lily and the other ladies. With great tact, and expressiveness, they said a multitude of rather common things to these fair persons; and declared themselves particularly ravished by the charm which the gleaming veil* spread over Lily and her attendant. The ladies modestly cast down their eyes, and the praise of their beauty made them really beautiful. All were peaceful and calm, except the old Woman. In spite of the assurance of her husband, that her hand could diminish no farther, while the Lamp shone on it, she asserted more than once, that if things went on thus, before midnight this noble member would have utterly vanished.

The Man with the Lamp had listened attentively to the conversation of the Lights; and was gratified that Lily had been cheered, in some measure, and amused by it. And, in truth, midnight had arrived they knew not how. The old Man looked to the stars, and then began speaking: "We are assembled at the propitious hour; let each perform his task, let each do his duty; and a universal happiness will swallow up our individual sorrows, as a universal grief consumes individual joys."

At these words arose a wondrous hubbub;† for all the persons in the party spoke aloud, each for himself, declaring what they had to do; only the three maids were silent; one of them had fallen asleep beside the harp, another near the parasol, the third by the stool; and you could not blame them much, for it was late. The Fiery youths, after some passing compliments which they devoted to the waiting-maids, had turned their sole attention to the Princess, as alone worthy of exclusive homage.

"Take the mirror," said the Man to the Hawk; "and with the first sunbeam illuminate the three sleepers, and awake them, with light reflected from above."

The Snake now began to move; she loosened her circle, and rolled slowly, in large rings, forward to the River. The two Will-o'-wisps followed with a solemn air; you would have taken them for the most serious Flames in nature. The old Woman and her husband seized the Basket, whose mild light they had scarcely observed till now; they lifted it at both sides, and it grew still larger and more luminous; they lifted the body of the Youth into it, laying the Canary-bird upon his breast; the Basket rose into the air and hovered above the old Woman's head, and she followed the Will-o'-wisps on foot. The fair Lily took Mops on her arm, and followed the Woman; the Man with the Lamp concluded the procession, and the scene was curiously illuminated by these many lights.

But it was with no small wonder that the party saw, when they approached the River, a glorious arch mount over it, by which the helpful Snake was affording them a glittering path. If by day they had admired the beautiful transparent precious stones, of which the Bridge seemed formed; by night they were astonished at its gleaming brilliancy. On the upper side the clear circle marked itself sharp against the dark sky, but below, vivid beams were darting to the centre, and exhibiting the airy firmness of the edifice. The procession slowly moved across it; and the Ferryman who saw it from his hut afar off, considered with astonishment the gleaming circle, and the strange lights which were passing over it.*

No sooner had they reached the other shore, than the arch began, in its usual way, to swag up and down, and with a wavy motion to approach the water. The Snake then came on land, the Basket placed itself upon the ground, and the Snake again drew her circle around it. The old Man stooped towards her, and said: "What hast thou resolved on?"

"To sacrifice myself rather than be sacrificed," replied the Snake; "promise me that thou wilt leave no stone on shore."

The old Man promised; then addressing Lily: "Touch the Snake," said he, "with thy left hand, and thy lover with thy right." Lily knelt, and touched the Snake, and the Prince's body. The latter in the instant seemed to come to life; he moved in the basket, nay he raised himself into a sitting posture; Lily was about to clasp him; but the old Man held her back, and himself assisted the youth to rise, and led him forth from the Basket and the circle.

The Prince was standing; the Canary-bird was fluttering on his shoulder; there was life again in both of them, but the spirit had not yet returned; the fair youth's eyes were open, yet he did not see, at least he seemed to look on all without participation. Scarcely had their admiration of this incident a little calmed, when they observed how strangely it had fared in the meanwhile with the Snake. Her fair taper body had crumbled into thousands and thousands of shining jewels: the old Woman reaching at her Basket had chanced to come against the circle; and of the shape or structure of the Snake there was now nothing to be seen, only a bright ring of luminous jewels was lying in the grass.†

---

* Have not your march-of-intellect Literators always expressed themselves particularly ravished with any glitter from a veil of *Hope*; with "progress of the species," and the like?—D. T.

† Too true: dost thou not hear it, Reader? In this our Revolutionary "twelfth hour of the night," all persons speak aloud (some of them by cannon and drums!) "declaring what they have to do;" and Faith, Hope, and Charity (after a few passing compliments from the Belles-Lettres Department,) thou seest, have *fallen asleep!*—D. T.

* Well he might, worthy old man; as Pope Pius, for example, did, when he lived in Fontainbleau!—D. T.—As our Bishops, when voting for the Reform Bill?—O. Y.

† So! Your Logics, mechanical Philosophies, Politics, Sciences, your whole modern System of THOUGHT, is

The old Man forthwith set himself to gather the stones into the basket; a task in which his wife assisted him. They next carried the Basket to an elevated point on the bank; and here the man threw its whole lading, not without contradiction from the fair one and his wife, who would gladly have retained some part of it, down into the River. Like gleaming twinkling stars the stones floated down with the waves; and you could not say whether they lost themselves in the distance, or sank to the bottom.

"Gentlemen," said he with the Lamp, in a respectful tone to the Lights, "I will now show you the way, and open you the passage; but you will do us an essential service, if you please to unbolt the door, by which the Sanctuary must be entered at present, and which none but you can unfasten."

The Lights made a stately bow of assent, and kept their place. The old Man of the Lamp went foremost into the rock, which opened at his presence; the Youth followed him, as if mechanically; silent and uncertain, Lily kept at some distance from him; the old Woman would not be left, and stretched out her hand that the Light of her husband's Lamp might still fall upon it. The rear was closed by the two Will-o'-wisps, who bent the peaks of their flames towards one another, and appeared to be engaged in conversation.

They had not gone far till the procession halted in front of a large brazen door, the leaves of which were bolted with a golden lock. The Man now called upon the Lights to advance; who required small entreaty, and with their pointed flames soon ate both bar and lock.

The brass gave a loud clang, as the doors sprang suddenly asunder; and the stately figures of the Kings appeared within the Sanctuary, illuminated by the entering Lights. All bowed before these dread sovereigns, especially the Flames made a profusion of the daintiest reverences.

After a pause, the gold King asked: "Whence come ye?"—"From the world," said the old Man.—"Whither go ye?" said the silver King. —"Into the world," replied the Man.—"What would ye with us?" cried the brazen King.— "Accompany you," replied the Man.

The composite King was about to speak, when the gold one addressed the Lights, who had got too near him: "Take yourselves away from me, my metal was not made for you." Thereupon they turned to the silver King, and clasped themselves about him; and his robe glittered beautifully in their yellow brightness. "You are welcome," said he, "but I cannot feed you; satisfy yourselves elsewhere, and bring me your light." They removed; and gliding past the brazen King who did not seem to notice them, they fixed on the compounded King. "Who will govern the world?" cried he with a broken voice.—"He who stands upon his feet," replied the old Man.—"I am he," said the mixed King.—"We shall see," replied the Man; "for the time is at hand."

The fair Lily fell upon the old Man's neck, and kissed him cordially. "Holy Sage!" cried she, "a thousand times I thank thee; for I hear that fateful word the third time." She had scarcely spoken, when she clasped the old Man still faster; for the ground began to move beneath them; the Youth and the old Woman also held by one another; the Lights alone did not regard it.

You could feel plainly that the whole Temple was in motion; as a ship that softly glides away from the harbour, when her anchors are lifted; the depths of the Earth seemed to open for the Building as it went along. It struck on nothing; no rock came in its way.

For a few instants, a small rain seemed to drizzle from the opening of the dome; the old Man held the fair Lily fast, and said to her: "We are now beneath the River: we shall soon be at the mark." Ere long they thought the Temple made a halt; but they were in an error; it was mounting upwards.

And now a strange uproar rose above their heads. Planks and beams in disordered combination now came pressing and crashing in, at the opening of the dome. Lily and the Woman started to a side; the Man with the Lamp laid hold of the Youth, and kept standing still. The little cottage of the Ferryman, for it was this which the Temple in ascending had severed from the ground and carried up with it, sank gradually down, and covered the old Man and the Youth.

The women screamed aloud, and the Temple shook, like a ship running unexpectedly aground. In sorrowful perplexity, the Princess and her old attendant wandered round the cottage in the dawn; the door was bolted, and to their knocking, no one answered. They knocked more loudly, and were not a little struck, when at length the wood began to ring. By virtue of the Lamp locked up in it, the hut had been converted from the inside to the outside into solid silver. Ere long too its form changed; for the noble metal shook aside the accidental shapes of planks, posts, and beams, and stretched itself out into a noble case of beaten ornamented workmanship. Thus a fair little temple stood erected in the middle of the large one; or if you will, an Altar worthy of the Temple.*

By a stair which ascended from within, the noble Youth now mounted aloft, lighted by the old man with the Lamp; and, as it seemed, supported by another, who advanced in a white short robe, with a silver rudder in his hand; and was soon recognised as the Ferryman, the former possessor of the cottage.

The fair Lily mounted the outer steps, which led from the floor of the Temple to the Altar; but she was still obliged to keep herself apart from her Lover. The old Woman, whose hand in the absence of the Lamp had grown

to decease; and old ENDEAVOUR, "grasping at her basket," shall "come against" the inanimate remains, and "only a bright ring of luminous jewels" shall be left there! Mark well, however, what next becomes of it.—D. T.

* Good! The old Church, shaken down "in disordered combination," is admitted, in this way, into the new perennial Temple of the Future; and, clarified into enduring silver, by the Lamp, becomes an Altar worthy to stand there. The Ferryman too is not forgotten.—D. T.

still smaller, cried: "Am I then to be unhappy after all? Among so many miracles, can there be nothing done to save my hand?" Her husband pointed to the open door, and said to her: "See, the day is breaking; haste, bathe thyself in the River."—"What an advice!" cried she; "it will make me all black; it will make me vanish altogether; for my debt is not yet paid." "Go," said the man, "and do as I advise thee: all debts are now paid."

The old Woman hastened away; and at that moment appeared the rising sun, upon the rim of the dome. The old Man stept between the Virgin and the Youth, and cried with a loud voice: "There are three which have rule on Earth; Wisdom, Appearance, and Strength." At the first word, the gold King rose, at the second the silver one; and at the third the brass king slowly rose, while the mixed King on a sudden very awkwardly plumped down.*

Whoever noticed him could scarcely keep from laughing, solemn as the moment was; for he was not sitting, he was not lying, he was not leaning, but shapelessly sunk together.†

The Lights,‡ who till now had been employed upon him, drew to a side; they appeared, although pale in the morning radiance, yet once more well-fed, and in good burning condition; with their peaked tongues, they had dexterously licked out the gold veins of the colossal figure to its very heart. The irregular vacuities which this occasioned had continued empty for a time, and the figure had maintained its standing posture. But when at last the very tenderest filaments were eaten out, the image crashed suddenly together; and that, alas, in the very parts which continue unaltered when one sits down; whereas the limbs, which should have bent, sprawled themselves out unbowed and stiff. Whoever *could* not laugh was obliged to turn away his eyes; this miserable shape and no-shape was offensive to behold.

The Man with the Lamp now led the handsome Youth, who still kept gazing vacantly before him, down from the altar, and straight to the brazen King. At the feet of this mighty Potentate, lay a sword in a brazen sheath. The young man girt it around him. "The sword on the left, the right free!" cried the brazen voice. They next proceeded to the silver King; he bent his sceptre to the youth; the latter seized it with his left hand, and the King in a pleasing voice said: "Feed the sheep!" On turning to the golden King, he stooped with gestures of paternal blessing, and pressing his oaken garland on the young man's head, said: "Understand what is highest!"

During this progress, the old Man had carefully observed the Prince. After girding on the sword, his breast swelled, his arms waved, and his feet trod firmer; when he took the sceptre in his hand, his strength appeared to soften, and by an unspeakable charm to become still more subduing; but as the oaken garland came to deck his hair, his features kindled, his eyes gleamed with inexpressible spirit, and the first word of his mouth was "Lily!"

"Dearest Lily!" cried he, hastening up the silver stairs to her, for she had viewed his progress from the pinnacle of the altar: "Dearest Lily! what more precious can a man, equipt with all, desire for himself than innocence and the still affection which thy bosom brings me? O my friend!" continued he, turning to the old Man, and looking at the three statues; glorious and secure is the kingdom of our fathers; but thou hast forgotten the fourth power, which rules the world, earlier, more universally, more certainly—the power of Love." With these words, he fell upon the lovely maiden's neck; she had cast away her veil, and her cheeks were tinged with the fairest, most imperishable red.

Here the old Man said with a smile: "Love does not rule; but it trains,* and that is more."

Amid this solemnity, this happiness and rapture, no one had observed that it was now broad day; and all at once, on looking through the open portal, a crowd of altogether unexpected objects met the eye. A large space surrounded with pillars formed the fore-court, at the end of which was seen a broad and stately Bridge stretching with many arches across the River. It was furnished, on both sides, with commodious and magnificent colonnades for foot-travellers, many thousands of whom were already there, busily passing this way or that. The broad pavement in the centre was thronged with herds and mules, with horsemen and carriages, flowing like two streams, on their several sides, and neither interrupting the other. All admired the splendour and convenience of the structure; and the new King and his Spouse were delighted with the motion and activity of this great people, as they were already happy in their own mutual love.

"Remember the Snake in honour," said the man with the Lamp; "thou owest her thy life, thy people owe her the Bridge, by which these neighbouring banks are now animated and combined into one land. Those swimming and shining jewels, the remains of her sacrificed body, are the piers of this royal bridge; upon these she has built and will maintain herself."†

The party were about to ask some explanation of this strange mystery, when there entered four lovely maidens at the portal of the Temple. By the Harp, the Parasol, and the folding Stool, it was not difficult to recognise the

* Dost thou note this, O Reader; and look back with new clearness on former things? A gold King, a silver, and a brazen King: WISDOM, dignified APPEARANCE, STRENGTH; these three harmoniously united bear rule: *dis*harmoniously cobbled together in sham-union (as in the foolish composite King of our foolish "Transition-era,") they, once the Gold (or wisdom) is *all* out of them, "very awkwardly plump down.—D. T.

† As, for example, does not Charles X. (one of the poor fractional composite Realities emblemed herein) rest, even now, "shapelessly enough sunk together," at Holyrood, in the city of Edinburgh?—D. T.

‡ March-of-intellect Lights were well capable of such a thing.—D. T.

* It fashions (*bildet*,) or educates.—O. Y.

† Honour to her indeed! The Mechanical Philosophy, though dead, has not died and lived in vain; but her works are there: "upon these *she*" (THOUGHT, new-born, in glorified shape) "has built herself and will maintain herself;" and the Natural and Supernatural shall henceforth, thereby, be one.—D. T.

waiting-maids of Lily; but the fourth, more beautiful than any of the rest, was an unknown fair one, and in sisterly sportfulness she hastened with them through the Temple, and mounted the steps of the Altar.*

"Wilt thou have better trust in me another time, good wife!" said the man with the Lamp to the fair one: "Well for thee, and every living thing that bathes this morning in the River!"

The renewed and beautified old Woman, of whose former shape no trace remained, embraced with young eager arms the man with the Lamp, who kindly received her caresses. "If I am too old for thee," said he, smiling, "thou mayest choose another husband to-day; from this hour no marriage is of force, which is not contracted anew."

"Dost thou not know, then," answered she, "that thou too art grown younger?"—"It delights me if to thy young eyes I seem a handsome youth: I take thy hand anew, and am well content to live with thee another thousand years."†

The Queen welcomed her new friend, and went down with her into the interior of the altar, while the King stood between his two men, looking towards the bridge, and attentively contemplating the busy tumult of the people.

But his satisfaction did not last; for ere long he saw an object which excited his displeasure. The great Giant, who appeared not yet to have awoke completely from his morning sleep, came stumbling along the Bridge, producing great confusion all around him. As usual, he had risen stupified with sleep, and had meant to bathe in the well-known bay of the River; instead of which he found firm land, and plunged upon the broad pavement of the Bridge. Yet although he reeled into the midst of men and cattle in the clumsiest way, his presence, wondered at by all, was felt by none; but as the sunshine came into his eyes, and he raised his hands to rub them, the shadows of his monstrous fists moved to and fro behind him with such force and awkwardness, that men and beasts were heaped together in great masses, were hurt by such rude contact, and in danger of being pitched into the River.‡

The King, as he saw this mischief, grasped with an involuntary movement at his sword; but he bethought himself, and looked calmly at his sceptre, then at the Lamp and the Rudder of his attendants. "I guess thy thoughts," said the man with the Lamp; "but we and our gifts are powerless against this powerless monster. Be calm! He is doing hurt for the last time, and happily his shadow is not turned to us."

Meanwhile the Giant was approaching nearer; in astonishment at what he saw with open eyes, he had dropt his hands; he was now doing no injury, and came staring and agape into the fore-court.

He was walking straight to the door of the Temple, when all at once in the middle of the court, he halted, and was fixed to the ground. He stood there like a strong colossal statue, of reddish glittering stone, and his shadow pointed out the hours,* which were marked in a circle on the floor around him, not in numbers, but in noble and expressive emblems.

Much delighted was the King to see the monster's shadow turned to some useful purpose; much astonished was the Queen; who, on mounting from within the Altar, decked in royal pomp with her virgins, first noticed the huge figure, which almost closed the prospect from the Temple to the Bridge.

Meanwhile the people had crowded after the Giant, as he ceased to move; they were walking round him, wondering at his metamorphosis. From him they turned to the Temple, which they now first appeared to notice,† and pressed towards the door.

At this instant the Hawk with the mirror soared aloft above the dome; caught the light of the sun, and reflected it upon the group, which was standing on the altar. The King, the Queen, and their attendants, in the dusky concave of the Temple, seemed illuminated by a heavenly splendour, and the people fell upon their faces. When the crowd had recovered and risen, the King with his followers had descended into the Altar, to proceed by secret passages into his palace; and the multitude dispersed about the Temple to content their curiosity. The three Kings that were standing erect they viewed with astonishment and reverence; but the more eager were they to discover what mass it could be that was hid behind the hangings, in the fourth niche; for by some hand or another, charitable decency had spread over the resting-place of the Fallen King a gorgeous curtain, which no eye can penetrate, and no hand may dare to draw aside.

The people would have found no end to their gazing and their admiration, and the crowding multitude would have even suffocated one another in the Temple, had not their attention been again attracted to the open space.

Unexpectedly some gold-pieces, as if falling from the air, came tinkling down upon the marble flags; the nearest passers-by rushed thither to pick them up; the wonder was repeated several times, now here, now there. It is easy to conceive that the shower proceeded from our two retiring Flames, who wished to have a little sport here once more, and were thus gaily spending, ere they went away, the gold which they had licked from the members of the sunken King. The people still ran eagerly about, pressing and pulling one another, even when the gold had ceased to fall. At length they gradually dispersed, and went their way; and to the present hour the Bridge is swarming with travellers, and the Temple is the most frequented on the whole Earth.‡

* Mark what comes of bathing in the TIME-River, at the entrance of a New Era!—D. T.

† And so REASON and ENDEAVOUR being once more married, and in the honey-moon, need we wish them joy?—D. T.

‡ Thou rememberest the *Catholic Relief Bill*; witnessest the *Irish Education Bill?* Hast heard, five hundred times, that the "Church" was "in Danger," and now at length believest it?—D. T.—Is D. T. of the Fourth Estate, and Popish-Infidel, then?—O. Y.

* Bravo!—D. T.

† Now first; when the beast of a SUPERSTITION-Giant has got his quietus. Right!—D. T.

‡ It is the Temple of the whole civilized earth. Finally, may I take leave to consider this *Mährchen* as the deepest Poem of its sort in existence; as the only true Prophecy emitted for who knows how many centuries?—D. T.—Certainly: England is a free country.—O. Y.

DIDEROT.

[Foreign Quarterly Review, 1833.]

The *Acts* of the *Christian Apostles*, on which, as we may say, the world has now for eighteen centuries had its foundation, are written in so small a compass, that they can be read in one little hour. The *Acts* of the *French Philosophes*, the importance of which is already fast exhausting itself, lie recorded in whole acres of typography, and would furnish reading for a lifetime. Nor is the stock, as we see, yet anywise complete, or within computable distance of completion. Here are Four quite new Octavos, recording the labours, voyages, victories, amours, and indigestions of the Apostle Denis: it is but a year or two since a new contribution on Voltaire came before us; since Jean Jacques had a new *Life* written for him; and then of those *Feuilles de Grimm*, what incalculable masses may yet lie dormant in the Petersburgh Library, waiting only to be awakened and let slip!—Reading for a lifetime? Thomas Parr might begin reading in long-clothes, and stop in his last hundred and fiftieth year without having ended. And then, as to when the process of addition will cease, and the Acts and Epistles of the Parisian Church of Antichrist will have completed themselves; except in so far as the quantity of paper written on, or even manufactured, in those days being finite and not infinite, the business one day or other must cease, and the Antichristian Canon close for the last time,—we yet know nothing.

Meanwhile, let us nowise be understood as lamenting this stupendous copiousness, but rather as viewing it historically with patience, and indeed with satisfaction. Memoirs, so long as they are true, how stupid soever, can hardly be accumulated in excess. The stupider they are, let them simply be the sooner cast into the oven; if true, they will always instruct more or less, were it only in the way of confirmation and repetition; and, what is of vast moment, they do not *mis*-instruct. Day after day looking at the high destinies which yet await Literature, which Literature will ere long address herself with more decisiveness than ever to fulfil, it grows clearer to us that the proper task of Literature lies in the domain of Belief; within which "Poetic Fiction," as it is charitably named, will have to take a quite new figure, if allowed a settlement there. Whereby were it not reasonable to prophesy that this exceeding great multitude of Novel-writers, and such like, must (in a new generation) gradually do one of two things: either retire into nurseries, and work for children, minors, and semi-fatuous persons of both sexes; or else, what were far better, sweep their Novel-fabric into the dust-cart, and betake them with such faculty as they have to understand and record what is *true*,—of which, surely, there is, and will for ever be, a whole Infinitude unknown to us, of infinite importance to us! Poetry, it will more and more come to be understood, is nothing but higher Knowledge; and the only genuine Romance (for grown persons) Reality. The Thinker is the Poet, the Seer: let him who *sees* write down according to his gift of sight; if deep and with inspired vision, then creatively, poetically; if common, and with only uninspired, every-day vision, let him at least be faithful in this and write *Memoirs*.

On us still so near at hand, that Eighteenth century in Paris presenting itself nowise as portion of the magic web of Universal History, but only as the confused and ravelled mass of threads and thrums, ycleped *Memoirs*, in process of *being* woven into such,—imposes a rather complex relation. Of which, however, as of all such, the leading rules may be happily comprised in this very plain one, prescribed by Nature herself: to search in them, so far as they seem worthy, for whatsoever can help us forward on our own path, were it in the shape of intellectual instruction, of moral edification, nay of mere solacement and amusement. The Bourbons, indeed, took a shorter method, (the like of which has been often recommended elsewhere;) they shut up and hid the *graves* of the Philosophes, hoping that their lives and writings might likewise thereby go out of sight, and out of mind; and thus the whole business would be, so to speak, *suppressed*. Foolish Bourbons! These things were not done in a corner, but on high places, before the anxious eyes of all mankind: hidden they can in nowise be: to conquer them, to resist them, our first indispensable preliminary is to see and comprehend them. To us, indeed, as their immediate successors, the right comprehension of them is of prime necessity; for, sent of God or of the Devil, they have plainly enough gone before us, and left us such and such a world: it is on ground of their tillage, with the stubble of their harvest standing on it, that we now have to plough. Before all things then, let us understand what ground it is; what manner of men and husbandmen these were. For which reason, be all authentic Philosophe-Memoirs welcome, each in its kind! For which reason, let us now, without the smallest reluctance, penetrate into this wondrous Gospel according to Denis Diderot, and expatiate there to see whether it will yield us aught.

In any phenomenon, one of the most important moments is the *end*. Now this epoch of the Eighteenth or Philosophe-century was pro-

* 1. *Mémoires, Correspondance, et Ouvrages inédits de Diderot; publiés d'après les manuscrits confiés, en mourant, par l'auteur à Grimm.* 4 tom. 8vo. Paris, 1831.

2. *Œuvres de Denis Diderot; procédées de Mémoires historiques et philosophiques sur sa Vie et ses Ouvrages, par J. A. Naigeon.* 22 tom. 8vo. Paris, 1821.

perly the End; the End of a Social System which for above a thousand years had been building itself together, and, after that, had begun, for some centuries, (as human things all do,) to moulder down. The mouldering down of a Social System is no cheerful business either to form part of, or to look at: however, at length, in the course of it, there comes a time when the mouldering changes into a rushing; active hands drive in their wedges, set to their crowbars; there is a comfortable appearance of work going on. Instead of here and there a stone falling out, here and there a handful of dust, whole masses tumble down, whole clouds and whirlwinds of dust: torches too are applied, and the rotten easily takes fire: so what with flame-whirlwind, what with dust-whirlwind, and the crush of falling towers, the concern grows eminently interesting; and our assiduous craftsmen can encourage one another with *Vivats*, and cries of *Speed the work.* Add to this, that of all labourers, no one can see such rapid extensive fruit of his labour as the Destroyer can and does: it will not seem unreasonable that measuring from effect to cause, he should esteem his labour as the best and greatest: and a Voltaire, for example, be by his guild-brethren and apprentices confidently accounted "not only the greatest man of this age, but of all past ages, and perhaps the greatest that Nature could produce." Worthy old Nature! She goes on producing whatsoever is needful in each season of her course; and produces, with perfect composure, that Encyclopedist opinion, that she can produce no more.

Such a torch-and-crowbar period of quick rushing down and conflagration, was this of the *Siècle de Louis Quinze;* when the Social System having all fallen to rottenness, rain-holes, and noisome decay, the shivering natives resolved to cheer their dull abode by the questionable step of setting it on fire. Questionable we call their Manner of procedure; the thing itself, as all men may now see, was inevitable; one way or other, whether by prior burning or milder methods, the old house must needs be new-built. We behold the business of pulling down, or at least of assorting the rubbish, still go resolutely on, all over Europe: here and there some traces of new foundation, of new building up, may now also, to the eye of Hope, disclose themselves.

To get acquainted with Denis Diderot and his life were to see the significant epitome of all this, as it works on the thinking and acting soul of a man, fashions for him a singular element of existence, gives himself therein a peculiar hue and figure. Unhappily, after all that has been written, the matter still is not luminous: to us strangers, much in that foreign economy, and method of working and living, remains obscure; much in the man himself, and his inward nature and structure. But, indeed, it is several years since the present Reviewer gave up the idea of what could be called *understanding* any Man whatever, even himself. Every Man, within that inconsiderable figure of his, contains a whole spirit-kingdom and Reflex of the ALL; and though to the eye but some six standard feet in size, reaches downwards and upwards, unsurveyable, fading into the regions of Immensity and of Eternity. Life everywhere, as woven on that stupendous ever-marvellous "Loom of Time," may be said to fashion itself of a woof of light indeed, yet on a warp of mystic darkness: only he that created it can understand it. As to this Diderot, had we once got so far that we could, in the faintest degree, personate him; take upon ourselves his character and his environment of circumstances, and act his Life over again in that small Private-Theatre of ours, (under our own Hat,) with moderate Illusiveness and histrionic effect,—*that* were what, in conformity with common speech, we should name *understanding* him, and could be abundantly content with.

In his manner of appearance before the world, Diderot has been, perhaps to an extreme degree, unfortunate. His literary productions were invariably dashed off in hottest haste, and left generally, (on the waste of Accident,) with an ostrich-like indifference. He had to live, in France, in the sour days of a *Journal des Trevoux;* of a suspicious, decaying Sorbonne. He was too poor to set foreign presses, at Kehl, or elsewhere, in motion; too headlong and quick of temper to seek help from those that could: thus must he, if his pen was not to lie idle, write much of which there was no publishing. His Papers accordingly are found flying about, like Sybil's leaves, in all corners of the world: for many years no tolerable collection of his Writings was attempted; to this day there is none that in any sense can be called perfect. Two spurious, surreptitious Amsterdam Editions, "or rather formless, blundering Agglomerations," were all that the world saw during his life. Diderot did not hear of these for several years, and then only, it is said, "with peals of laughter," and no other practical step whatever. Of the four that have since been printed, (or *re*printed, for Naigeon's of 1798, is the great original,) no one so much as pretends either to be complete or selected on any system. Brière's, the latest, of which alone we have much personal knowledge, is a well-printed book, perhaps better worth buying than any of the others; yet without arrangement, without coherence, purport; often lamentably in need of commentary: on the whole, in reference to the wants and specialities of this time, as good as *un*edited. Brière seems, indeed, to have hired some person, or thing, to play the part of Editor; or rather more things than one, for they sign themselves Editors in the plural number; and from time to time, throughout the work, some asterisk attracts us to the bottom of the leaf, and to some printed matter subscribed "EDITS.": but unhappily the journey is for most part in vain; in the course of a volume or two, we learn two well that nothing is to be gained there; that the Note, whatever it professedly treat of, will, in strict logical speech, mean only as much as to say: "Reader! thou perceivest that we Editors, to the number of at least two, are alive, and if we had any information would impart it to thee.—EDITS." For the rest, these "EDITS." are polite people; and with this uncertainty (as to their being persons or things) clearly before them, continue, to all appearance, in moderately good spirits.

One service they, or Brière for them, (if, indeed, Brière is not himself they, as we sometimes surmise,) have accomplished for us: sought out and printed the long-looked-for, long-lost *Life of Diderot* by Naigeon. The lovers of biography had for years sorrowed over this concealed Manuscript, with a wistfulness from which hope had nigh fled. A certain Naigeon, the beloved disciple of Diderot, had (if his own word, in his own editorial Preface, was to be credited) written a Life of him; and, alas! whither was it now vanished? Surely all that was dark in Denis the Fatalist had there been illuminated; nay, was there not, probably, a glorious "Light-street" carried through that whole Literary Eighteenth Century? And was not Diderot, long belauded as "the most encyclopedical head that perhaps ever existed," now to show himself as such in,—the new Practical Encyclopedia, philosophic, economic, speculative, digestive, of LIFE,—in three score and ten Years, or Volumes? Diderot too was known as the vividest, noblest talker of his time: considering all that Boswell, with his slender opportunities, had made of Johnson, what was there we had not a right to expect!

By Brière's endeavour, as we said, the concealed Manuscript of Naigeon now lies, as published Volume, on this desk. Alas! a written *life*, too like many an acted life, where hope is one thing, fulfilment quite another! Perhaps, indeed, of all biographies ever put together by the hand of man, this of Naigeon's is the most uninteresting. Foolish Naigeon! We wanted to see and know how it stood with the bodily man, the clothed, boarded, bedded, working, and warfaring Denis Diderot, in that Paris of his; how he looked and lived, what he did, what he said: had the foolish Biographer so much as told us what colour his stockings were! Of all this, beyond a date or two, not a syllable, not a hint! nothing but a dull, sulky, snuffling, droning, interminable lecture on Atheistic Philosophy; how Diderot came upon Atheism, how he taught it, how true it is, how inexpressibly important. Singular enough, the zeal of *the devil's* house hath eaten Naigeon up. A man of coarse, mechanical, perhaps intrinsically rather feeble intellect; and then, with the vehemence of some pulpit-drumming "Gowkthrapple," or "precious Mr. Jabesh Rentowel,"—only that *his* kirk is of the *other* complexion! Yet must he too see himself in a wholly backsliding world, where much theism and other scandal still rules; and many times Gowkthrapple Naigeon be tempted to weep by the streams of Babel. Withal, however, he is *wooden;* thoroughly mechanical, as if Vaucanson himself had made him; and that singularly tempers his fury.—Let the reader, finally, admire the bounteous produce of this Earth, and how one element bears nothing but the other matches it: here have we not the truest *odium theologicum*, working quite *demonologically*, in a worshipper of the Everlasting Nothing! So much for Naigeon; what we looked for from him, and what we have got.

Must Diderot then be given up to oblivion, or remembered not as Man, but merely as Philosophic-Atheistic Logic-Mill? Did not Diderot live, as well as think? An amateur reporter in some of the Biographical Dictionaries declares that he heard him talk one day, in nightgown and slippers, for the space of two hours, concerning earth, sea, and air, with a fulgorous impetuosity almost beyond human, rising from height to height, and at length finish the climax by "dashing his nightcap against the wall." Most readers will admit this to be biography; we, alas, must say, it comprises nearly all about the Man Diderot that hitherto would abide with us.

Here, however, comes "Paulin, Publishing-Bookseller," with a quite new contribution: a long series of Letters, extending over fifteen years; unhappily only love-letters, and from a married sexagenarian; yet still letters from his own hand. Amid these insipid floods of *tendresse, sensibilité*, and so forth, vapid, like long-decanted small-beer, many a curious biographic trait comes to light; indeed, we can hereby see more of the individual Diderot, and his environment, and method of procedure there, than by all the other books that have yet been published of him. Forgetting or conquering the species of nausea that such a business, on the first announcement of it, may occasion, and in many of the details of it cannot but confirm, the biographic reader will find this well worth looking into. Nay, is it not something of itself, to see that Spectacle of the Philosophe in Love, or, at least, zealously endeavouring to fancy himself so? For scientific purposes a considerable tedium, of "noble sentiment" (and even worse things) can be undergone. How the most encyclopedical head that perhaps ever existed, now on the borders of his grand climacteric, and already, provided with wife and child, comports himself in that trying circumstance of preternuptial (and, indeed, at such age, and with so many "indigestions," almost preternatural) devotion to the queens of this earth, may, by the curious in science, (who have nerves for it,) be here seen. There is besides a lively *Memoir* of him by Mademoiselle Diderot, though too brief, and not very true-looking. Finally, in one large Volume, his *Dream of d'Alembert*, greatly regretted and commented upon by Naigeon; which we could have done without. For its bulk, that little *Memoir* is the best of the whole. Unfortunately, as hinted, Mademoiselle, resolute of all things to be *piquante*, writes, or rather *thinks*, in a smart, antithetic manner, nowise the fittest for clearness or credibility: without suspicion of voluntary falsehood, there is no appearance that this is a camera-lucida picture, or a portrait drawn by legitimate rules of art. Such resolution to be piquant is the besetting sin of innumerable persons of both sexes, and wofully mars any use there might otherwise be in their writing or their speaking. It is, or was, the fault specially imputed to the French: in a woman and Frenchwoman, who besides has much to tell us, it must even be borne with. And now, from these diverse scattered materials, let us try how coherent a figure of Denis Diderot, and his earthly Pilgrimage and Performance, we can piece together.

In the ancient Town of Langres, in the month of October, 1713, it begins. Fancy Langres, aloft on its hill top, amid Roman ruins, nigh the sources of the Saone and of the Marne, with its coarse substantial houses, and fifteen thousand inhabitants, mostly engaged in knife-grinding; and one of the quickest, clearest, most volatile, and susceptive little figures of that century, just landed in the World there. In this French Sheffield, Diderot's Father was a Cutler, master of his craft; a much-respected and respect-worthy man; one of those ancient craftsmen (now, alas! nearly departed from the earth, and sought, with little effect, by idyllists, among the "Scottish peasantry," and elsewhere) who, in the school of practice, have learned not only skill of hand, but the far harder skill of head and of heart; whose whole knowledge and virtue, being by necessity a knowledge and virtue to do somewhat, is true, and has stood trial: humble modern patriarchs, brave, wise, simple; of worth rude, but unperverted, like genuine unwrought silver, native from the mine! Diderot loved his father, as he well might, and regrets on several occasions that he was painted in holiday clothes, and not in the workday costume of his trade, "with apron and grinder's-wheel, and spectacles pushed up,"—even as he lived and laboured, and honestly made good for himself the small section of the Universe he pretended to occupy. A man of strictest veracity and integrity was this ancient master; of great insight and patient discretion, so that he was often chosen as umpire and adviser; of great humanity, so that one day crowds of poor were to "follow him with tears to his long home." An outspoken Langres neighbour gratified the now fatherless Philosopher with this saying—"Ah, Monsieur Diderot, you are a famous man, but you will never be your father's equal." Truly, of all the wonderful illustrious persons that come to view in the biographic part of these six-and-twenty Volumes, it is a question whether this old Langres Cutler is not the worthiest; to us no other suggests himself whose worth can be admitted, without lamentable pollutions and defacements to be deducted from it. The Mother also was a loving-hearted, just woman: so Diderot might account himself well-born: and it is a credit to the man that he always (and sometimes in the circle of kings and empresses) gratefully did so.

The Jesuits were his schoolmasters: at the age of twelve, the encyclopedical head was "tonsured." He was quick in seizing, strong in remembering and arranging; otherwise flighty enough; fond of sport, and from time to time getting into trouble. One grand event, significant of all this, he has himself commemorated: his Daughter records it in these terms.

"He had chanced to have a quarrel with his comrades: it had been serious enough to bring on him a sentence of exclusion from college on some day of public examination and distribution of prizes. The idea of passing this important time at home, and grieving his parents, was intolerable: he proceeded to the college-gate; the porter refused him admittance; he presses in while some crowd is entering, and sets off running at full speed; the porter gets at him with a sort of pike he carried, and wounds him in the side: the boy will not be driven back; arrives, takes the place that belonged to him: prizes of all sorts, for composition, for memory, for poetry, he obtains them all. No doubt he had deserved them; since even the resolution to punish him could not withstand the sense of justice in his superiors. Several volumes, a number of garlands had fallen to his lot; being too weak to carry them all, he put the garlands round his neck, and, with his arms full of books, returned home. His mother was at the door; and saw him coming through the public square in this equipment, and surrounded by his school-fellows: one should be a mother to conceive what she must have felt. He was feasted, he was caressed: but next Sunday, in dressing him for church, a considerable wound was found on him, of which he had not so much as thought of complaining."

"One of the sweetest moments of my life," writes Diderot himself, of this same business, with a slight variation, "was more than thirty years ago, and I remember it like yesterday, when my Father saw me coming home from the college, with my arms full of prizes that I had carried off, and my shoulders with the garlands they had given me, which, being too big for my brow, had let my head slip through them. Noticing me at a distance, he threw down his work, hastened to the door to meet me, and could not help weeping. It is a fine sight, a true man and rigorous falling to weep!"

Mademoiselle, in her quick-sparkling way, informs us, nevertheless, that the school-victor, getting tired of pedagogic admonitions and inflictions, whereof there were many, said "one morning" to his father, "that he meant to give up school!"—"Thou hadst rather be a cutler, then?"—"With all my heart."—They handed him an apron, and he placed himself beside his father. He spoiled whatever he laid hands on, penknives, whittles, blades of all kinds. It went on for four or five days; at the end of which he rose, proceeded to his room, got his books there, and returned to college,—and having, it would appear, in this simple manner sown his college wild-oats, never stirred from it again.

To the Reverend Fathers, it seemed that Denis would make an excellent Jesuit; wherefore they set about coaxing and courting, with intent to crimp him. Here, in some minds, a certain comfortable reflection on the diabolic cunning and assiduity of these Holy Fathers, now happily all dissolved and expelled, will suggest itself. Along with which may another melancholy reflection no less be in place: namely, that these Devil-serving Jesuits should have shown a skill and zeal in their teaching vocation, such as no Heaven-serving body, of what complexion soever, anywhere on our earth now exhibits. To decipher the talent of a young vague Capability, who must one day be a man and a Reality; to take him by the hand, and train him to a spiritual trade, and set him up in it, with tools, shop, and good-will, were doing him in most cases an unspeakable service,—on this one proviso, it is true, that the trade be a just and honest one; in which proviso surely there should lie no hinderance to such servive, but rather a help. Nay, could many a poor Dermody, Hazlitt, Heron, Derrick, and such like, have been trained to be a good Jesuit, were it greatly worse than to have lived painfully as a bad Nothing-at-all? But indeed, as was said, the Jesuits are dissolved; and Corporations of all sorts have perished, (from corpulence;) and now, instead of the seven corporate selfish spirits, we have the one-and-thirty millions of discorporate selfish; and the rule, *Man, mind thyself*, makes a jumble and a scramble, and crushing press (with dead-pressed figures, and dismembered limbs enough;) into whose dark chaotic depths (for human Life is ever unfathomable) one shudders to look. Loneliest of all, weakest and worst-bested, in that world-scramble, is the extraordinary figure known in these times as Man of Letters! It appears to be indubitable that this state of matters will alter and improve itself,—in a century or two. But to return:

"The Jesuits," thus sparkles Mademoiselle, "employed the temptation, which is always so seductive, of travelling and of liberty; they persuaded the youth to quit his home, and set forth with a Jesuit, to whom he was attached. Denis had a friend, a cousin of his own age; he intrusted his secret to him, wishing that he should accompany them. But the cousin, a tamer and discreeter personage, discovered the whole project to the father; the day of departure, the hour, all was betrayed. My grandfather kept the strictest silence; but before going to sleep he carried off the keys of the street door; and at midnight, hearing his son descend, he presented himself before him, with the question, 'Whither bound, at such an hour?' 'To Paris,' replied the young man, 'where I am to join the Jesuits.'—'That will not be tonight; but your desires shall be fulfilled: let us in the first place go to sleep.'

"Next morning his father engaged two places in the public conveyance, and carried him to Paris, to the College d'Harcourt. He settled the terms of his little establishment, and bade his son good-b'ye. But the worthy man loved his child too well to leave him without being quite satisfied about his situation: he had the constancy to stay a fortnight longer, killing the time, and dying of tedium, in an inn, without seeing the sole object he was delaying for. At the end, he proceeded to the College; and my father has often told me that this proof of tenderness would have made him go to the end of the world, if the old man had required it. 'Friend,' said he, 'I am come to know if your health keeps good; if you are content with your superiors, with your diet, with others, and with yourself. If you are not well, if you are not happy, we will go back again to your mother. If you like better to remain here, I have but to speak a word with you, to embrace you, and give you my blessing.' The youth assured him that he was perfectly contented, that he liked his new abode very much. My grandfather then took leave of him, and went to the Principal, to know if he was satisfied with his pupil."

On which side also the answer proving favourable, the worthy father returned home. Denis saw little more of him; never again resided under his roof, though for many years, and to the last, a proper intercourse was kept up; not, as appears, without a visit or two on the son's part, and certainly with the most unwearied, prudent superintendence and assistance on the father's. Indeed, it was a worthy family, that of the Diderots; and a fair degree of natural affection must be numbered among the virtues of our Philosophe. Those scenes about rural Langres, and the old homely way of life there, as delineated fictitiously in the *Entretien d'un Père avec ses Enfans*, and now more fully, as a matter of fact, in this just-published *Correspondance*, are of a most innocent, cheerful, peacefully-secluded character; more pleasing, we might almost say more poetical, than could elsewhere be gathered out of Diderot's whole Writings. Denis was the eldest of the family, and much looked up to, with all his short-comings: there was a Brother, who became a clergyman; and a truehearted, sharp-witted Sister, who remained unmarried, and at times tried to live in partnership with this latter,—rather unsuccessfully. The Clergyman being a conscientious, even straight-laced man, and Denis such as we know, they had, naturally enough, their own difficulties to keep on brotherly terms; and indeed, at length, abandoned the task as hopeless. The Abbé stood rigorous by his Breviary, from time to time addressing solemn monitions to the lost Philosophe, who also went on his way. He is somewhat snarled at by the Denisian side of the house for this; but surely without ground: it was his virtue rather; at lowest his destiny. The true Priest, who could, or should, look peaceably on an *Encyclopédie*, is yet perhaps waited for in the world; and of all false things, is not a false Priest the falsest?

Meanwhile Denis, at the College d'Harcourt, learns additional Greek and Mathematics, and quite loses taste for the Jesuit career. Mad pranks enough he played, we doubt not; followed by reprimands. He made several friends, however; got intimate with the Abbé Bernis, poet at that time; afterwards Cardinal. "They used to dine together, for six sous a-piece, at the neighbouring *Traiteur's;* and I have often heard him vaunt the gayety of these repasts."

"His studies being finished," continues Mademoiselle, "his father wrote to M. Clement de Ris, a Procureur at Paris, and his countryman, to take him as boarder, that he might study Jurisprudence and the Laws. He continued here two years; but the business of *actes* and *inventaires* had few charms for him. All the time he could steal from the office-desk was employed in prosecuting Latin and Greek, in which he thought himself still imperfect; Mathematics, which he to the last continued passionately fond of; Italian, English, &c. In the end he gave himself up so completely to his taste for letters, that M. Clement thought it right to inform his father how ill the youth was employing his time. My grandfather then expressly commissioned M. Clement to urge and constrain him to make choice of some profession, and once for all to become Doctor, Procureur, or Advocate. My father begged time to think of it; time was given. At the end of several months these proposals were again laid before him: he answered that the profession of Doctor did not please him, for he could not think of killing any body; that the Procureur business was too difficult to execute with delicacy; that he would willingly choose the profession of Advocate, were it not that he felt an invincible repugnance to occupy himself all his life with other people's business. 'But,' said M. Clement, 'what *will* you be then?'—'On my word, nothing, nothing whatever, (*Ma foi, rien, mais rien du tout.*) I love study; I am very happy, very content, and want nothing else.'"

Here clearly is a youth of spirit, determined to take the world on the broadside, and eat thereof, and be filled. His decided turn, like that of so many others, is for the trade of sovereign prince, in one shape or other; unhappily, however, the capital and outfit to set it up is wanting. Under which circumstances, nothing remains but to instruct M. Clement de Ris that no more board-wages will henceforth be paid, and the young sovereign may, at his earliest convenience, be turned out of doors.

What Denis, perched aloft in his own-hired attic, may have thought of it now, does not appear. The good old Father, in stopping his allowance, had reasonably enough insisted on one of two things: either that he should betake him to some intelligible method of existence, wherein all help should be furnished him; or else return home within the week. Neither of which could Denis think of doing. A similar demand continued to be reiterated for the next ten years, but always with the like none-effect. King Denis, in his furnished attic, with or without money to pay for it, was now living and reigning, like other kings, "by the grace of God;" and could nowise resolve to abdicate. A sanguineous, vehement, volatile mortal; young, and in so wide an earth, it seemed to him next to impossible but he must find gold-mines there. He lived, while victual was to be got, taking no thought for the morrow. He had books, he had merry company, a whole piping and dancing Paris round him; he could teach Mathematics, he could turn himself so many ways; nay, might not he become a Mathematician one day; a glorified Savant, and strike the stars with his sublime head! Meanwhile he is like to be overtaken by one of the sharpest of human calamities, "cleanness of teeth."

"One Shrove Tuesday morning, he rises, gropes in his pocket; he has not wherewith to dine; will not trouble his friends who have not invited him. This day, which in childhood he had so often passed in the middle of relations who adored him, becomes sadder by remembrance: he cannot work; he hopes to dissipate his melancholy by a walk; goes to the Invalides, to the Courts, to the Bibliothèque du Roi, to the Jardin des Plantes. You may drive away tedium; but you cannot give hunger the slip. He returns to his quarters; on entering he feels unwell; the landlady gives him a little toast and wine; he goes to bed. 'That day,' he has often said to me, 'I swore that, if ever I came to have any thing, I would never in my life refuse a poor man help, never condemn my fellow-creatures to a day as painful.'"

That Diderot, during all this period, escaped starvation, is plain enough by the result: but how he specially accomplished that, and the other business of living, remains mostly left to conjecture. Mademoiselle, confined at any rate within narrow limits, continues as usual too intent on sparkling: is *brillante* and *pétillante*, rather than lucent and illuminating. How inferior, for *seeing* with, is your brightest train of fireworks to the humblest farthing candle! Who Diderot's companions, friends, enemies, patrons were, what his way of life was, what the Paris he lived in and from his garret looked down on was, we learn only in hints, dislocated, enigmatic. It is in general to be impressed on us, that young Denis, as a sort of spiritual swashbuckler, who went about conquering Destiny, in light rapier-fence, by way of amusement; or at lowest, in reverses, gracefully insulting her with mock reverences,—lived and acted like no other man; all which being freely admitted, we ask, with small increase of knowledge, How he did act then?

He gave lessons in Mathematics, we find; but with the princeliest indifference as to payment: "was his scholar lively, and prompt of conception, he sat by him teaching all day; did he chance on a blockhead, he returned not back. They paid him in books, in movables, in linen, in money, or not at all; it was quite the same." Farther, he made Sermons, (to order;) as the Devil is said to quote Scripture: a Missionary bespoke half-a-dozen of him (of Denis, that is) for the Portuguese Colonies, and paid for them very handsomely at fifty crowns each. Once, a family Tutorship came in his way, with tolerable appointments, but likewise with incessant duties: at the end of three months, he waits upon the house-father with this abrupt communication: "I am come, Monsieur, to request you to seek a new tutor; I cannot remain with you any longer."—"But, Monsieur Diderot, what is your grievance? Have you too little salary? I will double it. Are you ill-lodged? Choose your apartment. Is your table ill-served? Order your own dinner. All will be cheap to parting with you." —"Monsieur, look at me: a citron is not so yellow as my face. I am making men of your children; but every day I am becoming a child with them. I feel a hundred times too rich and two well off in your house; yet I must leave it: the object of my wishes is not to live better, but to keep from dying."

Mademoiselle grants that, if sometimes "drunk with gayety," he was often enough plunged in bitterness; but then a Newtonian problem, a fine thought, or any small godsend of that sort, would instantly cheer him again. The "gold mines" had not yet come to light. Meanwhile, between him and starvation we can still discern Langres covertly stretching out its hand. Of any Langres man, coming in his way, Denis frankly borrows; and the good old Father refuses not to pay. The

Mother is still kinder, at least softer: she sends him direct help, as she can; not by the post, but by a serving-maid, who travelled these sixty leagues on foot; delivered him a small sum from his mother; and, without mentioning it, added all her own savings thereto. This Samaritan journey she performed three times. "I saw her some years ago," adds Mademoiselle; "she spoke of my father with tears; her whole desire was to see him again: sixty years' service had impaired neither her sense nor her sensibility."

It is granted also that his company was "sometimes good, sometimes indifferent, not to say bad." Indeed putting all things together, we can easily fancy that the last sort was the preponderating. It seems probable that Denis, during these ten years of probation, walked chiefly in the subterranean shades of Rascaldom; now swilling from full Circe-goblets, now snuffing with haggard expectancy the hungry wind; always "sorely flamed on from the neighbouring hell." In some of his fictitious writings, a most intimate acquaintance with the nether-world of Polissons, Escrocs, Filles de Joye, Maroufles, Maquerelles, and their ways of doing, comes to light: among other things, (as may be seen in *Jacques le Fataliste*, and elsewhere,) a singular theoretic expertness in what is technically named "raising the wind;" which miracle, indeed, Denis himself is expressly (in this *Mémoire*) found once performing, and in a style to require legal cognisance, had not the worthy Father "sneered at the dupe, and paid." The dupe here was a proselytizing Abbé, whom the dog glozed with professions of life-weariness and turning monk; which all evaporated, once the money was in his hands. On other occasions, it might turn out otherwise, and the gudgeon-fisher hook some shark of prey.

Literature, except in the way of Sermons for the Portuguese Colonies, or other the like small private dealings, had not yet opened her hospitable bosom to him. Epistles, precatory and amatory, for such as had more cash than grammar, he may have written; Catalogues also, Indexes, Advertisements, and, in these latter cases, even seen himself in print. But now he ventures forward, with bolder step, towards the interior mysteries, and begins producing Translations from the English. Literature, it is true, was then, as now, the universal free-hospital and Refuge for the Destitute, where all mortals, of what colour and kind soever, had liberty to live, or at least to die: nevertheless, for an enterprising man, its resources at that time were comparatively limited. Newspapers were few; Reporting existed not, still less the inferior branches, with their fixed rate per line: Packwood and Warren, much more Panckoucke, and Ladvocat, and Colburn, as yet slumbered (the last century of their slumber) in the womb of Chaos; Fragmentary Panegyric-literature had not yet come into being, therefore could not be paid for. Talent wanted a free staple and workshop, where wages might be certain; and too often, like virtue, was praised and left starving. Lest the reader overrate the munificence of the literary cornucopia in France at this epoch, let us lead him into a small historical scene, that he may see with his own eyes. Diderot is the historian; the date too is many years later, when times, if any thing, were mended:

"I had given a poor devil a manuscript to copy. The time he had promised it at having expired, and my man not appearing, I grow uneasy; set off to hunt him out. I find him in a hole the size of my hand, almost without daylight, not the wretchedest tatter of serge to cover his walls; two straw-bottom chairs, a flock-bed, the coverlet chiselled with worms, without curtains; a trunk in a corner of the chimney, rags of all sorts hooked above it; a little white-iron lamp, with a bottle for pediment to it; on a deal shelf a dozen of excellent books. I chatted with him three quarters of an hour. My gentleman was naked as a worm," (*nu comme un ver:* it was August;) "lean, dingy, dry, yet serene, complaining of nothing, eating his junk of bread with appetite, and from time to time caressing his beloved, who reclined on that miserable truckle, taking up two-thirds of the room. If I had not known that happiness resides in the soul, my Epictetus of the Rue Hyacinthe might have taught it me."

Notwithstanding all which, Denis, now in his twenty-ninth year, sees himself necessitated to fall desperately, and over head and ears, in love. It was a virtuous, pure attachment: his first of that sort, probably also his last. Readers who would see the business poetically delineated, and what talent Diderot had for such delineations, may read this Scene in the once-noted Drama of the *Père de Famille.* It is known that he drew from the life; and with few embellishments, which too, except in the French Theatre, do not beautify.

"ACT I.—SCENE VII.

Saint-Albin. Father, you shall know all. Alas! how else can I move you?—The first time I ever saw her was at church. She was on her knees at the foot of the altar, beside an aged woman, whom I took for her mother. Ah father! what modesty, what charms!.... Her image followed me by day, haunted me by night, left me rest nowhere. I lost my cheerfulness, my health, my peace. I could not live without seeking to find her..... She has changed me; I am no longer what I was. From the first moment all shameful desires fade away from my soul; respect and admiration succeed them. Without rebuke or restraint on her part, perhaps before she had raised her eyes on me, I became timid; more so from day to day; and soon I felt as little free to attempt her virtue as her life.

The Father. And who are these women? How do they live?

Saint-Albin. Ah! if you knew it, unhappy as they are! Imagine that their toil begins before day, and often they have to continue it through the night. The mother spins on the wheel; hard coarse cloth is between the soft small fingers of Sophie, and wounds them.*

* The real trade appears to have been a "sempstress one in laces and linens;" the poverty is somewhat exaggerated: otherwise the shadow may be faithful enough.

Her eyes, the brightest eyes in this world, are worn at the light of a lamp. She lives in a garret, within four bare walls; a wooden table, a couple of chairs, a truckle-bed, that is their furniture. O Heavens, when ye fashioned such a creature, was this the lot ye destined her!

The Father. And how got you access? Speak me truth.

Saint-Albin. It is incredible what obstacles I had, what I surmounted. Though now lodged there, under the same roof, I at first did not seek to see them: if we met on the stairs, coming up, going down, I saluted them respectfully. At night, when I came home, (for all day I was supposed to be at my work,) I would go knock gently at their door; ask them for the little services usual among neighbours —as water, fire, light. By degrees they grew accustomed to me; rather took to me. I offered to serve them in little things: for instance, they disliked going out at night; I fetched and carried for them."

The real truth here is, "I ordered a set of shirts from them; said I was a Church-licentiate just bound for the Seminary of St. Nicholas,—and, above all, had the tongue of the old serpent." But to skip much, and finish:

"Yesterday I came as usual: Sophie was alone; she was sitting with her elbows on the table, her head leant on her hand; her work had fallen at her feet. I entered without her hearing me: she sighed. Tears escaped from between her fingers, and ran along her arms. For some time, of late, I had seen her sad. Why was she weeping? What was it that grieved her? Want it could no longer be; her labour and my attentions provided against that. Threatened by the only misfortune terrible to me, I did not hesitate: I threw myself at her knees. What was her surprise: Sophie, said I, you weep; what ails you? Do not hide your trouble from me: speak to me; oh speak to me! She spoke not. Her tears continued flowing. Her eyes, where calmness no longer dwelt, but tears and anxiety, bent towards me, then turned away, then turned to me again. She said only, Poor Sergi! unhappy Sophie!—I had laid my face on her knees; I was wetting her apron with my tears."

In a word, there is nothing for it but marriage. Old Diderot, joyous as he was to see his Son once more, started back in indignation and derision from such a proposal; and young Diderot had to return to Paris, and be forbid the beloved house, and fall sick, and come to the point of death, before the fair one's scruples could be subdued. However, she sent to get news of him; "learnt that his room was a perfect dog-kennel, that he lay without nourishment, without attendance, wasted, sad: thereupon she took her resolution: mounted to him, promised to be his wife; and mother and daughter now became his nurses. So soon as he recovered, they went to Saint-Pierre, and were married at midnight, (1744)." It only remains to add, that if the Sophie whom he had wedded fell much short of this Sophie whom he delineates, the fault was less in her qualities, than in his own unstable fancy: as in youth she was "tall. beautiful, pious, and wise," so through a long life she seems to have approved herself a woman of courage, discretion, faithful affection; far too good a wife for such a husband.

"My father was of too jealous a character to let my mother continue a traffic, which obliged her to receive strangers and treat with them: he begged her therefore to give up that business; she was very loath to consent; poverty did not alarm her on her own account, but her mother was old, unlikely to remain with her long, and the fear of not being able to provide for all her wants was afflicting: nevertheless, persuading herself that this sacrifice was necessary for her husband's happiness, she made it. A charwoman looked in daily, to sweep their little lodging, and fetch provisions for the day; my mother managed all the rest. Often when my father dined or supped out, she would dine or sup on bread; and took a great pleasure in the thought that, next day, she could double her little ordinary for him. Coffee was too considerable a luxury for a household of this sort: but she could not think of his wanting it, and every day gave him six sous to go and have his cup, at the Café de la Regence, and see the chess-playing there.

"It was now that he translated the *History of Greece* in three volumes," (by the English Stanyan;) "he sold it for a hundred crowns. This sum brought a sort of supply into the house. * * *

"My mother had been brought to bed of a daughter: she was now big a second time. In spite of her precautions, solitary life, and the pains she had taken to pass off her husband as her brother, his family, in the seclusion of their province, learnt that he was living with two women. Directly the birth, the morals, the character of my mother became objects of the blackest calumny. He foresaw that discussions by letter would be endless; he found it simpler to put his wife into the stage-coach, and send her to his parents. She had just been delivered of a son; he announced this event to his father, and the departure of my mother. 'She set out yesterday,' said he, "she will be with you in three days. You will say to her what shall please you, and send her back when you are tired of her.' Singular as this sort of explanation was, they determined, in any case, on sending my father's sister to receive her. Their first welcome was more than cold: the evening grew less painful to her; but next morning betimes she went in to her father-in-law; treated him as if he had been her own father; her respect and her caresses charmed the good, sensible old man. Coming down stairs, she began working: refused nothing that could please a family whom she was not afraid of, and wished to be loved by. Her conduct was the only excuse she gave for her husband's choice: her appearance had prepossessed them in her favour; her simplicity, her piety, her talents for household economy secured her their tenderness; they promised her that my father's disinheritment should be revoked. They kept her three months; and sent her back loaded with whatever they could think would be useful or agreeable to her."

All this is beautiful, told with a graceful simplicity; the beautiful, real-ideal prose-idyl of a Literary Life: but, alas, in the music of your prose-idyl there lurks ever an accursed dissonance (or the players make one;) where men are, there will be mischief. "This journey," writes Mademoiselle, "cost my mother many tears." What will the reader say, when he finds that Monsieur Diderot has, in the interim, taken up with a certain Madame de Puisieux; and welcomes his brave Wife (worthy to have been a true man's) with a heart and bosom henceforth estranged from her! Madame Diderot "made two journeys to Langres, and both were fatal to her peace." This affair of the Puisieux, for whom he despicably enough not only burned, but toiled and made money, kept him busy for some ten years; till at length, finding that she played false, he gave her up; and minor miscellaneous flirtations seem to have succeeded. But, returning from her *second* journey, the much-enduring House-mother finds him in a meridian glory with one Voland, the *un*-maiden Daughter of a "Financier's Widow;" to whom we owe this present preternuptial *Correspondence;* to whom indeed he mainly devoted himself for the rest of his life, "parting his time between his study and her;" to his own Wife and household giving little save the trouble of cooking for him, and of painfully, with repressed or irrepressible discontent, keeping up some appearance of terms with him. Alas! alas! and his Puisieux seems to have been a hollow Mercenary (to whose scandalous soul he reckons obscenest of Books fit nutriment;) and the Voland an elderly Spinster, with *cœur sensible, cœur honnête, ame tendre et bonne!* And then those old dinings on bread; the six sous spared for his cup of coffee! Foolish Diderot, scarcely pardonable Diderot! A hard saying it is, yet a true one: scoundrelism signifies injustice, and should be left to scoundrels alone. For thy wronged Wife, whom thou hast sworn far other things to, ever in her afflictions (here so hostilely scanned and written of,) a true sympathy will awaken; and sorrow that the patient, or even impatient, endurances of such a woman should be matter of speculation and self-gratulation to such another.

But looking out of doors now, from an indifferently-guided Household, which must have fallen shamefully in pieces, had not a wife been wiser and stronger than her husband,—we find the Philosophe making distinct way with the Bibliopolic world; and, likely, in the end, to pick up a kind of living there. The Stanyan's *History of Greece;* the other English-translated, nameless *Medical Dictionary,* are dropped by all editors as worthless: a like fate might, with little damage, have overtaken the *Essai sur le Merite et la Vertu,* rendered or redacted out of Shaftesbury's *Characteristics.* In which redaction, with its Notes, of anxious Orthodoxy, (and bottomless Falsehood looking through it,) we individually have found nothing, save a confirmation of the old twice-repeated experience, That in Shaftesbury's famed Book there lay, if any meaning, a meaning of such long-windedness, circumvolution, and lubricity, that, like an eel, it must for ever slip through our fingers, and leave us alone among the gravel. One reason may partly be, that Shaftesbury was not only a Skeptic but an Amateur Skeptic; which sort a darker, more earnest, have long since swallowed and abolished. The meaning of a delicate, perfumed, gentlemanly individual standing there, in that war of Titans, (hill meeting hill with all its woods,) and putting out hand to it—with a pair of tweezers?

However, our Denis has now emerged from the intermediate Hades of Translatorship into the Heaven of perfected Authorship; empties his common-place book of *Pensées Philosophiques,* (it is said in the space of four days;) writes his metaphysico-Baconian phantasmagories on the *Interprétation de la Nature,* (an endless business to "interpret;") and casts the money-produce of both into the lap of his Scarlet-woman Puisieux. Then forthwith, for the same object, in a shameful fortnight, puts together the beastliest of all past, present, or future dull Novels; a difficult feat, unhappily not an impossible one. If any mortal creature, even a Reviewer, be again compelled to glance into that Book, let him bathe himself in running water, put on change of raiment, and be unclean until the even. As yet the metaphysico-Atheistic *Lettre sur les Sourds et Muets,* and *Lettre sur les Aveugles,* which brings glory and a three months' lodging in the Castle of Vincennes, are at years' distance in the background. But already by his gilded tongue, growing repute, and sanguineous, projecting temper, he has persuaded Booksellers to pay off the Abbé Gua, with his lean Version of *Chambers's Dictionary of Arts,* and convert it into an *Encyclopédie,* with himself and D'Alembert for Editors; and is henceforth (from the year of grace 1751) a duly dis-indentured *Man of Letters,* an indisputable and more and more conspicuous member of that surprising guild.

Literature, ever since its appearance in our European world, especially since it emerged out of Cloisters into the open Market-place, and endeavoured to make itself room, and gain a subsistence there, has offered the strangest phases, and consciously or unconsciously done the strangest work. Wonderful Ark of the Deluge, where so much that is precious, nay priceless to mankind, floats carelessly onwards through the Chaos of distracted Times,—if so be it may one day find an Ararat to rest on, and see the waters abate! The History of Literature, especially for the last two centuries, is our proper Church History; the other Church, during that time, having more and more decayed from its old functions and influence, and ceased to have a history. And now, to look only at the outside of the matter, think of the Tassos and older or later Racines, struggling to raise their office from its pristine abasement of Court-jester: and teach and elevate the World, in conjunction with that other quite heteroclite task of solacing and glorifying some *Pullus Jovis,* in plush cloak and other gilt or golden king-tackle, that they in the interim might live thereby! Consider the Shakspeares and Molières, plying a like trade, but on a double material: glad of any royal or noble patronage, but eliciting, as their surer stay, some fractional contribution from the thick-skinned, many-pocketed million. Saumaises, now bully-fighting "for a hundred gold Jacobuses," now closeted with Queen Christinas, who blow the fire with their own queenly mouth, to make a pedant's breakfast; anon cast forth (being scouted and confuted,) and dying of heartbreak, coupled with henpeck. Then the Laws of Copyright, the Quarrels of Authors, the Calamities of Authors; the Heynes dining on boiled peasecods, the Jean Pauls on water; the Johnsons bedded and boarded on fourpence-halfpenny a-day. Lastly, the unutterable confusion worse confounded of our present Periodical existence; when, among other phenomena, a young Fourth Estate (whom all the three elder may try if they can hold) is seen sprawling and staggering tumultuously through the world; as yet but a huge, raw-boned, lean *calf;* fast growing, however, to be a Pharaoh's lean cow, —of whom let the fat-kine beware! All this of the mere exterior, or dwelling-place of Literature, not yet glancing at the internal, at the Doctrines emitted or striven after, will the future Eusebius and Mosheim have to record; and (in some small degree) explain to us what it means. Unfathomable is its meaning: Life, mankind's Life, ever from its unfathomable fountains, rolls wondrous on, another though the same; in Literature too, the seeing eye will distinguish Apostles of the Gentiles, Proto and Deutero-martyrs; still less will the Simon Magus, or Apollonius with the golden thigh be wanting. But all now is on an infinitely *wider scale;* the elements of it all swim far scattered, and still only striving towards union;—whereby, indeed, it happens that to the most, under this new figure, they are unrecognisable.

French Literature, in Diderot's time, presents itself in a certain state of culmination, where causes long prepared are rapidly becoming effects; and was doubtless in one of its more notable epochs. Under the Economic aspect, in France, as in England, this was the Age of Booksellers; when, as a Dodsley and Miller could risk capital in an *English Dictionary*, a Lebreton and Briasson could become purveyors and commissariat officers for a French *Encyclopédie.* The world for ever loves Knowledge, and would part its last sixpence in payment thereof: this your Dodsleys and Lebretons well saw; moreover they could act on it, for as yet PUFFERY was not. Alas, offences must come; Puffery from the first was inevitable: wo to them, nevertheless, by whom it did come! Meanwhile, as we said, it slept in Chaos: the Word of man and tradesman was still partially credible to man. Booksellers were therefore a possible, were even a necessary class of mortals, though a strangely anomalous one; had they kept from lying, or lied with any sort of moderation, the anomaly might have lasted still longer. For the present, they managed in Paris as elsewhere: the Timber-headed could perceive that for Thought the world would give money; farther, by mere shopkeeper cunning, that true Thought, as in the end sure to be recognised, and by nature infinitely more durable, was better to deal in than false; farther, by credible tradition of public consent, that such and such had the talent of furnishing true Thought, (say rather *truer*, as the more correct word:) on this hint the Timber-headed spake and bargained. Nay, let us say he bargained, and worked, for most part with industrious assiduity, with patience, suitable prudence; nay, sometimes with touches of generosity and magnanimity, beautifully irradiating the circumambient mass of greed and dulness. For the rest, the two high contracting parties roughed it out as they could; so that if Booksellers, in their back parlour Valhalla, drank wine out of the sculls of Authors, (as they were fabled to do,) Authors, in the front-apartments, from time to time, gave them a Rowland for their Oliver: a Johnson can knock his Osborne on the head, like any other Bull of Bashan; a Diderot commands his corpulent Panckouke to "leave the room and go to the devil;" *allez au diable, sortez de chez moi!*

Under the internal or Doctrinal aspect, again, French Literature, we can see, knew far better what it was about than English. That fable, indeed, first set afloat by some Trevoux Journalist of that period, and which has floated foolishly enough into every European ear since then, of there being an Association specially organized for the destruction of government, religion, society, civility, (not to speak of tithes, rents, life, and property,) all over the world; which hell-serving Association met at the Baron d'Holbach's, there had its blue-light sederunts, and published Transactions legible to all,—was and remains nothing but a fable. Minute-books, president's hammer, ballot-box, punch-bowl of such Pandemonium have not been produced to the world. The sect of Philosophes existed at Paris, but as other sects do; held together by loosest, informal, unrecognised ties; within which every one, no doubt, followed his own natural objects, of proselytism, of glory, of getting a livelihood. Meanwhile, whether in constituted association or not, French Philosophy resided in the persons of the French Philosophes; and, as a mighty deep-struggling force, was at work there. Deep struggling, irrepressible; the subterranean fire, which long heaved unquietly, and shook all things with an ominous motion, was here, we can say, forming itself a decided spiracle;—which, by and by, as French Revolution, became that volcano-crater, world-famous, world-appalling, world-maddening, as yet very far from closed! Fontenelle said, he wished he could live sixty years longer, and see what that universal infidelity, depravity, and dissolution of all ties would turn to. In threescore years Fontenelle might have seen strange things; but not the end of the phenomenon, perhaps in three hundred.

Why France became such a volcano-crater, what specialities there were in the French national character, and political, moral, intellectual condition, by virtue whereof French Philosophy there and not elsewhere, then and not sooner or later, evolved itself,—is an inquiry that has been often put, and cheerfully answered; the true answer of which might lead us far. Still deeper than this *Whence* were the question of *Whither*;—with which, also, we intermeddle not here. Enough for us to understand that there verily a Scene of Universal History is being enacted (a little living TIME-picture in the bosom of ETERNITY)—and with the feeling due in that case, to ask not so much Why it is, as What it is. Leaving priorities and posteriorities aside, and cause-and-effect to adjust itself elsewhere, conceive so many vivid spirits thrown together into Europe, into the Paris of that day, and see how they demean themselves, what they work out and attain there.

As the *mystical* enjoyment of an object goes infinitely farther than the *intellectual*, and we can *look* at a picture with delight and profit, after all that we can be *taught* about it is grown poor and wearisome; so here, and by far stronger reason, these light Letters of Diderot to the Voland, again unveiling and *showing* Parisian Life, are worth more to us than many a heavy tome laboriously struggling to explain it. True, we have seen the picture (that same Parisian life-picture) ten times already; but can look at it an eleventh time; nay this, as we said, is not a canvas-picture, but a life-picture, of whose significance there is no end for us. Grudge not the elderly Spinster her existence, then; say not she has lived in vain. For what of History there is, in this Preternuptial Correspondence, should we not endeavour to forgive and forget all else, the *sensibilité* itself? The curtain which had fallen for almost a century is again drawn up; the scene is alive and busy. Figures grown historical are here seen face to face, and again live before us.

A strange theatre that of French Philosophism; a strange dramatic corps! Such another corps for brilliancy and levity, for gifts and vices, and all manner of sparkling inconsistencies, the world is not like to see again. There is Patriarch Voltaire, of all Frenchmen the most French; he whom the French had, as it were, long waited for, "to produce at once, in a single life, all that French genius most prized and most excelled in;" of him and his wondrous ways, as of one known, we need say little. Instant enough to "crush the Abomination" (*écraser l'Infame,*) he has prosecuted his Jesuit-hunt over many lands and many centuries, in many ways, with an alacrity that has made him dangerous, and endangered him: he now sits at Ferney, withdrawn from the active toils of the chase; cheers on his hunting-dogs mostly from afar: Diderot, a beagle of the first vehemence, he has rather to restrain. That all extant and possible Theology be abolished, will not content the fell Denis, as surely it might have done; the Patriarch must address him a friendly admonition on his Atheism, and make him eat it again.

D'Alembert, too, we may consider as one known; of all the Philosophe fraternity, he who in speech and conduct agrees best with our English notions; an independent, patient, prudent man; of great faculty, especially of great clearness and method; famous in Mathematics; no less so, to the wonder of some, in the intellectual provinces of Literature. A foolish wonder; as if the Thinker could think only on one thing, and not on *any* thing he had a call towards. D'Alembert's *Mélanges*, as the impress of a genuine spirit, in peculiar position and probation, have still instruction for us, both of head and heart. The man lives retired here, in questionable seclusion with his Espinasse; incurs the suspicion of apostasy, because in the *Encyclopédie* he saw no Evangile and celestial Revelation, but only a huge Folio Dictionary; and would not venture life and limb on it, without a "consideration." Sad was it to Diderot to see his fellow-voyager make for port, and disregard signals, when the sea-krakens rose round him! They did not quarrel; were always friendly when they met, but latterly met only at the rate of "once in the two years." D'Alembert died when Diderot was on his death-bed: "My friend," said the latter to the news-bringer, "a great light is gone out."

Hovering in the distance, with wo-struck, minatory air, stern-beckoning, comes Rousseau. Poor Jean Jacques! Alternately deified, and cast to the dogs; a deep-minded, high-minded, even noble, yet wofully misarranged mortal, with all misformations of Nature intensated to the verge of madness by unfavourable Fortune. A lonely man; his life a long soliloquy! The wandering Tiresias of the time;—in whom, however, did lie prophetic meaning, such as none of the others offer. Whereby indeed it might partly be that the world went to such extremes about him; that, long after his departure, we have seen one whole nation worship him, and a Burke, in the name of another, class him with the off-scourings of the earth. His true character, with its lofty aspirings and poor performings; and how the spirit of the man worked so wildly, like celestial fire in a thick dark element of chaos, and shot forth ethereal radiance, all-piercing lightning, yet could not illuminate, was quenched and did not conquer: this, with what lies in it, may now be pretty accurately appreciated. Let his history teach all whom it concerns, to "*harden* themselves against the ills which Mother Nature will try them with;" to seek within their own soul what the world must for ever deny them; and say composedly to the Prince of the Power of this lower Earth and Air: Go thou thy way; I go mine!

Rousseau and Diderot were early friends: who has forgotten how Jean Jacques walked to the Castle of Vincennes, where Denis (for heretical Metaphysics, and irreverence to the Strumpetocracy) languishes in durance; and devised his first Literary Paradox on the road thither? Their Quarrel, which, as a fashionable hero of the time complains, occupied all Paris, is likewise famous enough. The reader recollects that heroical epistle of Diderot to Grimm on that occasion, and the sentence: "Oh, my friend, let us continue virtuous, for the state of those who have ceased to be so makes me shudder." But is the reader aware what the fault of him "who had ceased to be so" was? A series of ravelments and squabbling grudges, "which," says Mademoiselle with much simplicity, "the Devil himself could not understand." Alas, the Devil well understood it, and Tyrant Grimm too did, who had the ear of Diderot, and poured into it his own unjust, almost abominable spleen. Clean paper need not be soiled with a foul story, where the main actor is only "Tyran le Blanc;" enough to know that the "continually virtuous" Tyrant found Diderot "extremely impressionable;" so poor Jean Jacques must go his ways, (with both the scath and the scorn,) and among his many woes bear this also. Diderot is not blamable; pitiable rather; for who would be a pipe, which not Fortune only, but any Sycophant may play tunes on?

Of this same Tyrant Grimm, desiring to speak peaceably, we shall say little. The man himself is less remarkable than his fortune. Changed times indeed, since the thread-bare German Bursch quitted Ratisbon, with the sound of cat-calls in his ears, the condemned "Tragedy, Banise," in his pocket; and fled southward, on a thin travelling-tutorship; —since Rousseau met you, Herr Grimm, "a young man described as seeking a situation, and whose appearance indicated the pressing necessity he was in of soon finding one!" Of a truth, you have flourished since then, Herr Grimm: his introductions of you to Diderot, to Holbach, to the black-locked D'Epinay, where not only you are wormed in, but he is wormed out, have turned to somewhat; the Thread-bare has become well-napped, and got ruffles and jewel-rings, and walks abroad in sword and bag-wig, and lackers his brass countenance with rouge, and so (as *Tyran le Blanc*) recommends himself to the fair; and writes Parisian Philosophe-gossip to the Hyperborean Kings, and his Grimm's Leaves, copied "to the number of twenty," are bread of life to many; and cringes here, and domineers there: and lives at his ease in the Creation, in an effective *tendresse* with the D'Epinay, husband or custom of the country not objecting!—Poor Börne, the new German flying Sansculotte, feels his mouth water, at Paris, over these fleshpots of Grimm; reflecting with what heart he too could write "Leaves," and be fed thereby. Börne, my friend, those days are done! While Northern Courts were a "Lunar Versailles," it was well to have an Uriel stationed in their Sun there; but of all spots in this Universe (hardly excepting Tophet) Paris now is the one we at court could best *dispense* with news from; never more, in these centuries, will a Grimm be missioned thither; never a "Leaf of Börne" be blown court-wards by any wind. As for the Grimm, we can see that he was a man made to rise in the world: a fair, even handsome outfit of talent, wholly marketable; skill in music, and the like, encyclopedical readiness in all ephemera; saloon-wit, a trenchant, unhesitating head; above all, a heart ever in the right place,—in the market-place, namely, and marked "for sale to the highest bidder." Really a methodical, adroit, managing man. By "hero-worship," and the cunning appliance of alternate sweet and sullen, he has brought Diderot to be his patient milch-cow, whom he can milk an Essay from, a Volume from, when he lists. Victorious Grimm! He even escaped those same "horrors of the French Revolution," (with loss of his ruffles;) and was seen at the Court of Gotha, sleek and well to live, within the memory of man.

The world has heard of M. le Chevalier de Saint-Lambert; considerable in Literature, in Love, and War. He is here again, singing the frostiest Pastorals; happily, however, only in the distance, and the jingle of his wires soon dies away. Of another Chevalier, worthy Jancourt, be the name mentioned, and little more: he digs unweariedly, mole-wise, in the Encyclopedic field, catching what he can, and shuns the light. Then there is Helvetius, the well-fed Farmer-general, enlivening his sybaritic life with metaphysic paradoxes. His revelations, *De l'Homme* and *De l'Esprit*, breathe the freest Philosophe-spirit, with Philanthropy and Sensibility enough: the greater is our astonishment to find him here so ardent a Preserver of the Game:

"This Madame de Nocé," writes Diderot, treating of the Bourbonne Hot-springs, "is a neighbour of Helvetius. She told us, the Philosopher was the unhappiest man in the world on his estates. He is surrounded there by neighbours and peasants who detest him. They break the windows of his mansion, plunder his grounds by night, cut his trees, throw down his walls, tear up his spiked paling. He dare not go to shoot a hare, without a train of people to guard him. You will ask me, how it has come to pass? By a boundless zeal for his game. M. Fagon, his predecessor, used to guard the grounds with two keepers and two guns. Helvetius has twenty-four, and cannot do it. These men have a small premium for every poacher they can catch; and there is no sort of mischief they will not cause to get more and more of these. Besides, they are themselves so many hired poachers. Again, the border of his woods was inhabited by a set of poor people, who had got huts there; he has caused all the huts to be swept away. It is these, and such acts of repeated tyranny, that have raised him enemies of all kinds; and the more insolent, says Madame de Nocé, as they have discovered that the worthy Philosopher is a coward. I would not have his fine estate of Voré as a present, had I to live there in these perpetual alarms. What profits he draws from that mode of management I know not: but he is alone there; he is hated,—he is in fear. Ah! how much wiser was our lady Geoffrin, when speaking of a lawsuit that tormented her, she said to me, 'Get done with my lawsuit; they want money? I have it. Give them money. What better use can I make of my money than to buy peace with it?' In Helvetius's place, I would have said, 'They kill me a few hares and rabbits, let them be doing. These poor creatures have no shelter but my forest, let them stay there.' I should have reasoned like M. Fagon, and been adored like him."

Alas! are not Helvetius's preserves, at this hour, all broken up, and lying desecrated? Neither can the others, in what latitude and longitude soever, remain eternally impregnable. But if a Rome was once saved by geese, need we wonder that an England is lost by partridges? We are sons of Eve, who bartered Paradise for an apple.

But to return to Paris and its Philosophe Church militant. Here is a Marmontel, an active subaltern thereof, who fights in a small way, through the *Mercure;* and, in rose-pink romance-pictures, strives to celebrate the "moral sublime." An Abbé Morellet, busy with the Corn Laws, walks in at intervals, stooping, shrunk together, "as if to get nearer himself" (*pour être plus près de lui-même.*) The rogue Galiani alternates between Naples and Paris; Galiani, by good luck, has, "for ever *settled* the question of the Corn Laws;" an idle fellow otherwise; a spiritual Lazzarone; full of frolics, wanton quips, anti-jesuit *gesta*, and wild Italian humour; the sight of his swart, sharp face is the signal for Laughter,—in which indeed, the Man himself has unhappily evaporated, leaving no result behind him.

Of the Baron d'Holbach thus much may be said, that both at Paris and at Grandval he gives good dinners. His two or three score volumes of Atheistic Philosophism, which he published, (at his own expense,) may now be forgotten and even forgiven. A purse open and deep, a heart kindly-disposed, quiet, sociable, or even friendly; these, with excellent wines, gain him a literary elevation, which no thinking faculty he had could have pretended to. An easy, laconic gentleman; of grave politeness; apt to lose temper at play; yet, on the whole, good-humoured, eupeptic, and eupractic: there may he live and let live.

Nor is heaven's last gift to man wanting here; the natural sovereignty of women. Your Châtelets, Epinays, Espinasses, Geoffrins, Deffands, will play their part too; there shall, in all senses, be not only Philosophers, but Philosophesses. Strange enough is the figure these women make: good souls, it was a strange world for them. What with metaphysics and flirtation, system of nature, fashion of dress-caps, vanity, curiosity, jealousy, atheism, rheumatism, *traités, bouts-rimés*, noble-sentiments, and rouge-pots,—the vehement female intellect sees itself sailing on a chaos, where a wiser might have wavered, if not foundered. For the rest, (as an accurate observer has remarked,) they become a sort of Lady-Presidents in that society; attain great influence; and, imparting as well as receiving, communicate to all that is done or said somewhat of their own peculiar tone.

In a world so wide and multifarious, this little band of Philosophes, acting and speaking as they did, had a most various reception to expect; votes divided to the uttermost. The mass of mankind, busy enough with their own work, of course heeded them only when forced to do it; these, meanwhile, form the great neutral element, in which the battle has to fight itself; the two hosts, according to their several success, to recruit themselves. Of the Higher Classes, it appears, the small proportion not wholly occupied in eating and dressing, and therefore open to such a question, are in their favour,—strange as to us it may seem; the spectacle of a Church pulled down is, in stagnant times, amusing, nor do the generality, on either side, yet see whither ulteriorly it is tending. The Reading World, which was then more than now the intelligent, inquiring world, reads eagerly (as it will ever do) whatsoever skilful, sprightly, reasonable-looking word is written for it; enjoying, appropriating the same; perhaps without fixed judgment, or deep care of any kind. Careful enough, fixed enough, on the other hand, is the Jesuit Brotherhood; in these days sick unto death; but only the bitterer and angrier for that. Dangerous are the death-convulsions of an expiring Sorbonne, ever and anon filling Paris with agitation: it behooves your Philosophe to walk warily, and, in many a critical circumstance, to weep with the one cheek, and smile with the other. Nor is Literature itself wholly Philosophe: apart from the Jesuit regulars, in their Trevoux Journals, Sermons, Episcopal Charges, and other camps or casemates, a considerable Guerrilla, or Reviewer force (consisting, as usual, of smugglers, unemployed destitute persons, deserters who have been refused promotion, and other the like broken characters) has organized itself, and maintains a harassing bush-warfare: of these the chieftain is Fréron, once in tolerable repute with the world, had he not, carrying too high a head, struck his foot on stones, and stumbled. By the continual depreciating of talent, grown at length undeniable, he has sunk low enough: Voltaire, in the *Ecossaise*, can bring him on the stage, and have him killed by laughter, under the name, sufficiently recognisable, of *Wasp*, (in French, *Frêlon.*) Another Empecenador, still more hateful, is Palissot, who has written and got acted a Comedy of *Les Philosophes*, at which the Parisians, spite of its dulness, have also laughed. To laugh at *us*! The so meritorious us! Heard mankind ever the like? For poor Palissot, had he fallen into Philosophe hands, serious bodily tar-and-feathering might have been apprehended: as it was, they do what the pen, with its gall and copperas, can; invoke Heaven and Earth to witness the treatment of divine Philosophy;—with which view, in particular, friend Diderot seems to have composed his *Rameau's Nephew*, wherein Palissot and others of his kidney are (figuratively speaking) mauled and mangled, and left not in dog's likeness. So divided was the world, Literary, Courtly, Miscellaneous, on this matter: it was a confused anomalous time.

Among its more notable anomalies may be reckoned the relations of French Philosophism to foreign Crowned Heads. In Prussia there is a Philosophe King; in Russia a Philosophe Empress: the whole North swarms with kinglets and queenlets of the like temper. Nay, as we have seen, they entertain their special ambassador in Philosophedom, their lion's-provider to furnish spiritual Philosophe-provender; and pay him well. The great Frederic, the great Catherine, are as nursing-father and nursing mother to this new Church of Antichrist; in all straits, ready with money, honourable royal asylum, help of every sort,—which, however, except in the money-shape, the wiser of our Philosophes are shy of receiving. Voltaire has tried it in the asylum shape, and found it unsuitable; D'Alembert and Diderot decline repeating the experiment. What miracles are wrought by the arch-magician Time! Could these Frederics, Catherines, Josephs, have looked forward some three-score years; and beheld the Holy Alliance in conference at Laybach! But so goes the world: kings are not seraphic doctors, with gift of prescience, but only men, with common eyesight, participating in the influences of their generation: kings too, like all mortals, have a certain love of knowledge; still more infallibly, a certain desire of applause; a certain delight in mortifying one another. Thus what is persecuted here finds refuge there; and ever, one way or other, the New works itself out full-formed from under the Old; nay the Old, as in this instance, sits sedulously hatching a cockatrice that will one day devour it.

No less anomalous, confused, and contradictory is the relation of the Philosophes to their own Government. How, indeed, could it be otherwise, their relation to Society being still so undecided; and the Government, which might have endeavoured to adjust and preside over this, being itself in a state of anomaly, death-lethargy, and doting decrepitude? The true conduct and position for a French Sovereign towards French Literature, in that country, might have been, though perhaps of all things the most important, one of the most difficult to discover and accomplish. What chance was there that a thick-blooded Louis Quinze, from his *Parc aux Cerfs*, should discover it, should have the faintest inkling of it? His "peaceable soul" was quite otherwise employed: Minister after Minister must consult his own several insight, his own whim, above all his own ease: and so the whole business, now when we look on it, comes out one of the most botched, piebald, inconsistent, lamentable, and even ludicrous objects in the history of Statecraft. Alas, necessity has no *law:* the statesman, without light, perhaps even without eyes, whom Destiny nevertheless constrains to govern (what is still called governing) his nation in a time of World-Downfal, what shall he do, but if so may be, collect the taxes, prevent (in some degree) murder and arson; and for the rest, wriggle hither and thither, return upon his steps, clout up old rents and open new,—and, on the whole, eat his victuals, and let the devil take it? Of the pass to which Statesmanship had come in respect of Philosophism, let this one fact be evidence instead of a thousand. M. de Malesherbes writes to warn Diderot that next day he will give orders to have all his papers seized.—Impossible! answers Diderot: *juste ciel!* how shall I sort them, where shall I hide them, within four-and-twenty hours? *Send them to me*, answers M. de Malesherbes! Thither accordingly they go, under lock and seal; and the hungry catchpoles find nothing but empty drawers.

The *Encyclopédie* was set forth first "with approbation" and *Privilége du Roi;* next, it was stopped by Authority; next, the public murmuring suffered to proceed; then again, positively for the last time, stopped,—and, no whit the less, printed, and written, and circulated, under thin disguises, some hundred and fifty printers working at it with open doors, all Paris knowing of it, only Authority winking hard. Choiseul, in his resolute way, had now shut the eyes of Authority, and kept them shut. Finally, to crown the whole matter, a copy of the prohibited Book lies in the King's private library: and owes favour, and a withdrawal of the prohibition, to the foolishest accident:

"One of Louis Fifteenth's domestics told me," says Voltaire, "that once, the king his master supping, in private circle (*en petite compagnie,*) at Trianon, the conversation turned first on the chase, and from this on gunpowder. Some one said that the best powder was made of sulphur, saltpetre, and charcoal, in equal parts. The Duc de la Vallière, with better knowledge, maintained that for good powder there must be but one part of sulphur, one of charcoal, with five of saltpetre, well filtered, well evaporated, well crystallized.

"'It is pleasant,' said the Duc de Nivernois, 'that we who daily amuse ourselves with killing partridges in the Park of Versailles, and sometimes with killing men, or getting ourselves killed, on the frontiers, should not know what that same work of killing is done with.'

"'Alas! we are in the like case with all things in this world,' answered Madame de Pompadour; 'I know not what the rouge I put upon my cheeks is made of; you would bring me to a nonplus, if you asked how the silk hose I wear are manufactured.' ''Tis a pity,' said the Duc de Vallière, 'that his majesty confiscated our *Dictionnaires Encyclopédiques*, which cost us our hundred pistoles; we should soon find the decision of all our questions there.' The King justified the act of confiscation; he had been informed that these twenty-one folio volumes, to be found lying on all ladies' toilettes, were the most pernicious things in the world for the kingdom of France; he had resolved to look for himself if this were true, before suffering the book to circulate. Towards the end of the repast, he sends three of his valets to bring him a copy; they enter, struggling under seven volumes each. The article *powder* is turned up; the Duc de la Vallière is found to be right: and soon Madame Pompadour learns the difference between the old *rouge d'Espagne* with which the ladies of Madrid coloured their cheeks, and the *rouge des dames* of Paris. She finds that the Greek and Roman ladies painted with a purple extracted from the *murex*, and that consequently our scarlet is the purple of the ancients; that there is more purple in the *rouge d'Espagne*, and more cochineal in that of France. She learns how stockings are woven; the stocking-frame described there fills her with amazement. 'Ah, what a glorious book!' cried she. 'Sire, did you confiscate this magazine of all useful things, that you might have it wholly to yourself, then, and be the one learned man in your kingdom?' Each threw himself on the volumes, like the daughters of Lycomedes on the jewels of Ulysses; each found forthwith whatever he was seeking. Some who had lawsuits were surprised to find the decision of them there. The King reads there all the rights of his crown. 'Well, in truth,' (*mais vraiment*,) said he, 'I know not why they said so much ill of the book.' 'Ah, Sire,' said the Duc de Nivernois, 'does not your majesty see,' &c. &c."

In such a confused world, under such unheard of circumstances, must friend Diderot ply his editorial labours. No sinecure is it! Penetrating into all subjects and sciences; waiting and rummaging in all libraries, laboratories; nay, for many years, fearlessly diving into all manner of workshops, unscrewing stocking looms, and even working thereon, (that the department of *Arts and Trades* might be perfect;) then seeking out contributors, and flattering them; quickening their laziness, getting payment for them; quarrelling with Bookseller and Printer; bearing all miscalculations, misfortunes, misdoings of so many fallible men (for there all at last lands) on his single back: surely this was enough, without having farther to do battle with the beagles of Office, perilously withstand them, expensively sop them, toilsomely elude them! Nevertheless, he perseveres, and will not but persevere;—less, perhaps, with the deliberate courage of a Man, who has compared result and outlay, than with the passionate obstinacy of a Woman who, having made up her mind, will shrink at no ladder of ropes, but ride with her lover, though all the four Elements gainsay it. At every new concussion from the Powers, he roars; say rather, shrieks, for there is a female shrillness in it; proclaiming, Murder! Robbery! Rape! invoking men and angels; meanwhile proceeds unweariedly with the printing. It is a hostile building up (not of the Holy Temple at Jerusalem, but of the Unholy one at Paris:) thus must Diderot, like Ezra, come to strange extremities; and every workman works with his trowel in one hand, in the other his weapon of war; that so, in spite of all Tiglaths, the work go on, and the top-stone of it be brought out with shouting.

Shouting! Ah! what faint broken quaver is that in the shout; as of a man that shouted with the throat only, and inwardly was bowed down with dispiritment? It is Diderot's faint broken quaver: he is sick and heavy of soul. Scandalous enough: the Goth, Lebreton, loving, as he says, his head better even than his profit, has for years gone privily at dead of night, to the finished Encyclopedic proof-sheets, and there with nefarious pen, scratched out whatever to *him* seemed dangerous; filling up the gap as *he* could, or merely letting it fill itself up. Heaven and Earth! Not only are the finer Philosophe sallies mostly cut out,—but hereby has the work become a sunken, hitching, ungainly mass, little better than a monstrosity. Goth! Hun! sacrilegious Attila of the book-trade! Oh, surely for this treason the hottest of Dante's Purgatory were too temperate. Infamous art thou, Lebreton, to all ages,—that read the *Encyclopédie;* and Philosophes not yet in swaddling-clothes shall gnash their teeth over thee, and spit upon thy memory.—Lebreton pockets both the abuse and the cash, and sleeps sound in a whole skin. The able Editor could never be said to get the better of it.

Now, however, it is time that, quitting generalities, we go, in this fine autumn weather, to Holbach's at Grandval, where the hard-worked, but unwearied Encyclopedist, with plenty of ink and writing paper, is sure to be. Ever in the Holbach household, his arrival is a holiday; if a quarrel spring up, it is only because he will not come, or too soon goes away. A man of social talent, with such a tongue as Diderot's, in a mansion where the only want to be guarded against was that of wit, could not be other than welcome. He composes Articles there, and walks, and dines, and plays cards, and talks; languishingly waits letters from his Voland, copiously writes to her. It is in these copious love-despatches that the whole matter is graphically painted: we have an Asmodeus' view of the interior life there, and live it over again with him. The Baroness in red silk, tempered with snow-white gauze, is beauty and grace itself; her old Mother is a perfect romp of fifteen, or younger; the house is lively with company: the Baron, as we said, speaks little, but to the purpose; is seen sometimes with his pipe, in dressing gown and red slippers; otherwise the best of landlords. Remarkable figures drop in: generals disabled at Quebec; fashionable gentlemen rusticating in the neighbourhood; Abbés, such as Galiani, Raynal, Morellet; perhaps Grimm and his Epinay; other Philosophes and Philosophesses. Guests too of less dignity, acting rather as butts than as bowmen: for it is the part of every one either to have wit, or to be the cause of having it.

Among these latter, omitting many, there is one whom, for country's sake, we must particularize; an ancient personage, named Hoop (Hope,) whom they call *Père* Hoop; by birth a Scotchman. Hoop seems to be a sort of fixture at Grandval, not bowman, therefore butt; and is shot at for his lodging. A most shrivelled, wind-dried, dyspeptic, chill-shivering individual; Professor of Life-weariness; sits dozing there,—dozes there, however, with one eye open. He submits to be called *Mummy* without a shrug; cowers over the fire, at the warmest corner. Yet is there a certain sardonic subacidity in Père Hoop; when he slowly unlocks his leathern jaw, we hear him with a sort of pleasure. Hoop has been in various countries and situations; in that croaking metallic voice of his, can tell a distinct story. Diderot apprehended he would one day hang himself: if so, what Museum now holds his remains? The Parent Hoops, it would seem, still dwelt in the city of Edinburgh; he, the second son, as Bourdeaux Merchant, having helped them thither, out of some proud Manor-house no longer weather-tight. Can any ancient person of that city give us trace of such a man? It must be inquired into. One only of Father Hoop's reminiscences we shall report, as the highest instance on record of a national virtue: At the battle of Prestonpans, a kinsman of Hoop, a gentleman with gold rings on his fingers, stands fighting and fencing for life with a rough Highlander; the Highlander, by some clever stroke, whisks the jewelled hand clear off, and then—picks it up from the ground, sticks it in his sporran for future leisure, and fights on! The force of *Virtue** could no further go.

It cannot be uninteresting to the general reader to learn, that in the last days of October, in the year of grace 1770, Denis Diderot overate himself (as he was in the habit of doing,) at Grandval; and had an obstinate "indigestion of bread." He writes to Grimm that it is the worst of all indigestions: to his fair Voland that it lay more than fifteen hours on his stomach, with a weight like to crush the life out of him; would neither *remonter* nor *descendre*; nor indeed stir a hairsbreadth for warm water, *de quelque côté que je la* (the warm water) *prisse.*

Clysterium donare,
Ensuita purgare!

Such things, we grieve to say, are of frequent occurrence: the Holbachian table is all too plenteous; there are cooks too, we know, who boast of their diabolic ability to cause the patient, by successive intensations of their art, to eat with new and ever new appetite, till he explode on the spot. Diderot writes to his fair one, that his clothes will hardly button, that he is thus "stuffed," and thus; and so indigestion succeeds indigestion. Such Narratives fill the heart of sensibility with amazement; nor to the woes that chequer this imperfect, caco-gastric state of existence, is the tear wanting.

The society at Grandval cannot be accounted very dull: nevertheless let no man regretfully compare it with any neighbourhood he may have drawn by lot, in the present day; or even with any no-neighbourhood, if that be his affliction. The gayety at Grandval was of the kind that could not last. Were it not that some Belief is left in Mankind, how could the sport of emitting Unbelief continue? On which ground, indeed, Swift, in his masterly argument "Against abolishing the Christian Religion," urges, not without pathos, that innumerable men of wit, enjoying a comfortable status by virtue of jokes on the Catechism, would hereby be left without pabulum, the staff of life cut away from their hand. The Holbachs were blind to this consideration; and joked away, as if it would last for ever. So too with regard to Obscene Talk: where were the merit of a riotous Mother-in-law, saying and doing, in public, these never-imagined scandals, had not a cunningly-devised fable of Modesty been set afloat; were there not some remnants of Modesty still extant among the unphilosophic classes? The Samoeids (according to Travellers) have few double meanings; among stall cattle the witty effect of such is lost altogether. Be advised, then, foolish old woman! "Burn not thy bed;" the light of it will soon go out, and then?—Apart from the common household topics, which the "daily household epochs" bring with them everywhere, two main elements, we regret to say, come to light in the conversation at Grandval; these, with a spicing of Noble-sentiment, are, unfortunately, Blasphemy and Bawdry. Whereby, at this distance, the whole matter grows to look poor, and effete; and we can honestly rejoice that it all *has* been, and need not be again.

But now, hastening back to Paris, friend Diderot finds proof-sheets enough on his desk and notes, and invitations, and applications from distressed men of letters; nevertheless runs over, in the first place, to seek news from the Voland; will then see what is to be done. He writes much; talks and visits much: besides the Savans, Artists, spiritual Notabilities, domestic or migratory, of the period, he has a liberal allowance of unnotable Associates; especially a whole bevy of young or oldish, mostly rather spiteful Women; in whose gossip he is perfect. We hear the rustling of their silks, the clack of their pretty tongues, tittle-tattle "like their pattens when they walk;" and the sound of it, fresh as yesterday, through this long vista of Time has become significant, almost prophetic. Life could not hang heavy on Diderot's hands: he is a vivid, open, all-embracing creature; could have found occupation anywhere; has occupation here forced on him, enough and to spare. "He had much to do, and did much of his own," says Mademoiselle; "yet three-fourths of his life was employed in helping whomsoever had need of his purse, of his talents, of his management: his study, for the five and twenty years I knew it, was like a well-frequented shop, where, as one customer went, another came." He could not find it in his heart to refuse any one. He has reconciled Brothers, sought out Tutorages, settled Lawsuits; solicited Pensions; advised, and refreshed hungry Authors, instructed ignorant ones: he has written advertisements for incipient helpless Grocers; he once wrote the dedication (to a pious Duc d'Orleans) of a lampoon against himself,—and so raised some five and twenty gold louis, for the famishing lampooner. For all these things, let not the light Diderot want his reward with us! Other reward, except from himself, he got none; but often the reverse; as in his little Drama, *La Pièce et le Prologue*, may be seen humorously and good-humouredly set forth under his own hand. Indeed, his clients, by a vast majority, were of the scoundrel species; in any case, Denis knew well, that to expect gratitude is to deserve ingratitude.—"Rivière, well contented," (hear Mademoiselle,) "now thanks my father, both for his services and his advices; sits chatting another quarter of an hour, and then takes leave; my father shows him down. As they are on the stairs, Rivière stops, turns round, and asks: 'M. Diderot, are you acquainted with Natural History?'—'Why, a little, I know an aloe from a sago; a pigeon from a colibri.'—'Do you know the history of the *Formica-leo?*'—'No.'—'It is a little insect of great industry: it digs a hole in the ground like a reversed funnel; covers the top with fine light sand; entices foolish insects into it; takes them, sucks them, then says to them: M. Diderot, I have the honour to wish you good day.' My father stood laughing like to split at this adventure."

Thus, amid labour and recreation; questionable Literature, unquestionable Loves; eating and digesting, (better or worse;) in gladness and vexation of spirit, in laughter ending in

* *Virtus* (properly *man*liness, the chief duty of man) meant, in old Rome, *power of fighting*; means, in modern Rome, *Connoisseurship*; in Scotland, *Thrift.*—Ed.

sighs, does Diderot pass his days. He has been hard toiled, but then well flattered, and is nothing of a hypochondriac. What little service renown can do him, may now be considered as done: he is in the centre of the literature, science, art, of his nation; not numbered among the Academical Forty; yet, in his heterodox heart, entitled to be almost proud of the exclusion; successful in Criticism, successful in Philosophism, nay, (highest of sublunary glories,) successful in the Theatre; vanity may whisper, if she please, that excepting the unattainable Voltaire alone, he is the first of Frenchmen. High heads are in correspondence with him, the low-born; from Catharine the Empress to Philidor the Chess-player, he is in honoured relation with all manner of men; with scientific Buffons, Eulers, D'Alemberts; with artistic Falconnets, Vanloos, Riccobonis, Garricks. He was ambitious of being a Philosophe; and now the whole fast-growing sect of Philosophes look up to him as their head and mystagogue. To Denis Diderot, when he stept out of the Langres Diligence at the College d'Harcourt; or afterwards, when he walked in the subterranean shades of Rascaldom, with uneasy steps over the burning marle, a much smaller destiny would have seemed desirable. Within doors, again, matters stand rather disjointed, as surely they might well do: however, Madame Diderot is always true and assiduous; if one Daughter talk enthusiastically, and at length (though her father has written the *Religieuse*) die mad in a convent, the other, a quick, intelligent, graceful girl, is waxing into womanhood, and takes after the father's Philosophism, leaving the mother's Piety far enough aside. To which elements of mixed good and evil from without, add this so incalculably favourable one from within, that of all literary men Diderot is the least a self-listener; none of your puzzling, repenting, forecasting, earnest-bilious temperaments, but sanguineous-lymphatic every fibre of him, living lightly from hand to mouth, in a world mostly painted rose-colour.

The *Encyclopédie*, after nigh thirty years of endeavour, (to which only the siege of Troy may offer some faint parallel,) is finished. Scattered Compositions of all sorts, printed or manuscript, making many Volumes, lie also finished; the Philosophe has reaped no golden harvest from them. He is getting old: can live out of debt, but is still poor. Thinking to settle his daughter in marriage, he must resolve to sell his Library; money is not otherwise to be raised. Here, however, the northern Cleopatra steps imperially forward; purchases his Library for its full value; gives him a handsome pension, as librarian to keep it for her; and pays him moreover fifty years thereof by advance in ready money. This we call imperial, (in a world so necessitous as ours,) though the whole munificence, did not (we find) cost above three thousand pounds; a trifle to the Empress of all the Russias. In fact, it is about the sum your first-rate king eats, as board wages, in one day; who, however, has seldom sufficient: not to speak of charitable overplus. In admiration of his Empress, the vivid Philosophe is now louder than ever; he even breaks forth into (rather husky) singing. Who shall blame him? The Northern Cleopatra (whom, in any case, he must regard with other eyes than we) has stretched out a generous, helping hand to him, where otherwise there was no help, but only hindrance and injury: all men will, and should, more or less, obey the proverb, to praise the fair as their own market goes in it.

One of the last great scenes in Diderot's Life, is his personal visit to this Benefactress. There is but one letter from him with Petersburgh for date, and that of ominous brevity. The Philosophe was of open, unheedful, free-and-easy disposition; Prince and Polisson were singularly alike to him; it was "hail fellow well met," with every Son of Adam, be his clothes of one stuff or the other. Such a man could be no court-sycophant, was ill calculated to succeed at court. We can imagine that the Neva-cholic, and the character of the Neva-water were not the only things hurtful to his nerves there. For King Denis, who had dictated such wonderful anti-regalities in the Abbé Raynal's *History*;* and himself, in a moment of sibylism, emitted that surprising announcement (surpassing all yet uttered, or utterable, in the Tyrtæan way) how

Ses mains (the freeman's) *ourderaient les entrailles du prêtre,*
Au défaut d'un cordon, pour étrangler les rois;

for such a one, the climate of the Neva must have had something oppressive in it. The *entrailles du prêtre* were, indeed, much at his service here, (could he get clutch of them;) but only for musical philosophe fiddle-strings; nowise for a *cordon!* Nevertheless, Cleopatra is an uncommon woman, (or rather an uncommon man,) and can put up with many things; and, in a gentle, skilful way, make the crooked straight. As her Philosophe presents himself in common apparel, she sends him a splendid court-suit; and as he can now enter in a civilized manner, she sees him often, confers with him largely: by happy chance, Grimm too at length arrives; and the winter passes without accident. Returning home in triumph, he can express himself contented, charmed with his reception; has mineral specimens, and all manner of hyperborean memorials for friends; unheard-of-things to tell; how he crossed the bottomless, half-thawed Dwina, with the water boiling up round his wheels, the ice bending like leather, yet crackling like

* "But who *dare* stand for this?" would Diderot exclaim. "I will! I!" eagerly responded the Abbé. "Do but proceed." (*A la Mémoire de Diderot*, by De Meister.)—Was the following one of the passages?

"Happily these perverse instructors (of Kings) are chastised, sooner or later, by the ingratitude and contempt of their pupils. Happily, these pupils too, miserable in the bosom of grandeur, are tormented all their life by a deep *ennui*, which they cannot banish from their palaces. Happily, the religious prejudices which have been planted in their souls, return on them to affright them. Happily, the mournful silence of their people teaches them, from time to time, the deep hatred that is borne them. Happily, they are too cowardly to despise that hatred. Happily, (*heureusement*,) after a life which no mortal, not even the meanest of his subjects, would accept, if he knew all its wretchedness, they find black inquietude, terror and despair, seated on the pillow of their death-bed, (*les noires inquiétudes, la terreur et le désespoir assis au chevet de leur lit de mort.*)" Surely, "kings have poor times of it, to be run foul of by the like of thee!"

mere ice,—and shuddered, and got through safe; how he was carried, coach and all, into the ferry-boat at Mittau, on thirty wild men's backs, who floundered in the mud, and nigh broke his shoulder-blade; how he investigated Holland, and had conversed with Empresses, and High Mightinesses, and principalities and powers, and so seen, and conquered (for his own spiritual behoof) several of the Seven Wonders.

But, alas! his health is broken; old age is knocking at the gate, like an importunate creditor, who has warrant for entering. The radiant, lightly-bounding soul is now getting all dim, and stiff, and heavy with sleep; Diderot too must adjust himself, for the hour draws nigh. These last years he passes retired and private, not idle or miserable. Philosophy or Philosophism has nowise lost its charm; whatsoever so much as calls itself Philosopher can interest him. Thus poor Seneca (on occasion of some new Version of his Works) having come before the public, and been roughly dealt with, Diderot, with a long, last, concentrated effort, writes his *Vie de Sénèque;* struggling to make the hollow solid. Which, alas! after all his tinkering still sounds hollow; and notable Seneca, so wistfully desirous to stand well with Truth, and yet not ill with Nero, is and remains only our perhaps niceliest-proportioned Half-and-half, the plausiblest Plausible on record; no great man, no true man, no man at all; yet how much lovelier than such,—as the mild-spoken, tolerating, charity-sermoning, immaculate Bishop Dogbolt, to a rude, self-helping, sharp-tongued Apostle Paul! Under which view, indeed, Seneca (though surely erroneously, for the origin of the thing was different) has been called, in this generation, "the father of all such as wear shovel-hats."

The *Vie de Sénèque*, as we said, was Diderot's last effort. It remains only to be added of him that he too died; a lingering but quiet death, which took place on the 30th of July, 1784. He once quotes from Montaigne the following, as Skeptic's viaticum: "I plunge stupidly, head foremost, into this dumb Deep, which swallows me, and chokes me, in a moment,—full of insipidity and indolence. Death, which is but a quarter of an hour's suffering, without consequence and without injury, does not require peculiar precepts." It was Diderot's allotment to die with all due "stupidity:" he was leaning on his elbows; had eaten an apricot two minutes before, and answered his wife's remonstrances with: *Mais que diable de mal veux-tu que cela me fasse?* (How the deuse can that hurt me?) She spoke again, and he answered not. His House, which the curious will visit when they go to Paris, was in the Rue Taranne, at the intersection thereof with the Rue Saint-Benôit. The dust that was once his Body went to mingle with the common earth, in the church of Saint-Roch; his Life, the wondrous manifold Force that was in him, that was He,—returned to ETERNITY, and *is* there, and continues there!

Two things, as we saw, are celebrated of Diderot. First, that he had the most encyclopedical head ever seen in this world: second that he talked as never man talked;—properly, as never man his admirers had heard, or as no man living in Paris then. That is to say, his was at once the widest, fertilest, and readiest of minds.

With regard to the Encyclopedical Head, suppose it to mean that he was of such vivacity as to admit, and look upon with interest, almost all things which the circle of Existence could offer him; in which sense, this exaggerated laudation, of Encyclopedism, is not without its fraction of meaning. Of extraordinary openness and compass we must grant the mind of Diderot to be; of a susceptibility, quick activity; even naturally of a depth, and in its practical realized shape, of a universality, which bring it into kindred with the highest order of minds. On all forms of this wondrous Creation he can look with loving wonder; whatsoever thing stands there, has some brotherhood with him, some beauty and meaning for him. Neither is the faculty to see and interpret wanting; as, indeed, this faculty to *see* is inseparable from that other faculty to *look*, from that true wish to look; moreover (under another figure,) Intellect is not a *tool*, but a *hand* that can handle any tool. Nay, in Diderot we may discern a far deeper universality than that shown, or showable, in Lebreton's *Encyclopédie;* namely, a poetical; for, in slight gleams, this too manifests itself. A universality less of the head than of the character; such, we say, is traceable in this man, at lowest the power to have acquired such. Your true Encyclopedical is the Homer, the Shakspeare; every genuine Poet is a living embodied, real Encyclopedia,—in more or fewer volumes; were his experience, his insight of details, never so limited, the w[illegible] world lies imaged as a whole withi[illegible], whosoever has not seized the whole cannot yet speak truly (much less can he speak *musically*, which is harmoniously, *concordantly*) of any part, but will perpetually need new guidance, rectification. The fit use of such a man is as hodman; not feeling the plan of the edifice, let him carry stones to it; if he *build* the smallest stone, it is likeliest to be wrong, and cannot continue there.

But the truth is, as regards Diderot, this saying of the encyclopedical head comes mainly from his having edited a Bookseller's Encyclopedia, and can afford us little direction. Looking into the man, and omitting his trade, we find him by nature gifted in a high degree with openness and versatility, yet nowise in the highest degree; alas, in quite another degree than that. Nay, if it be meant further that in practice, as a writer and thinker, he has taken in the Appearances of Life and the World, and images them back with such freedom, clearness, fidelity, as we have not many times witnessed elsewhere, as we have not various times seen infinitely surpassed elsewhere,—this same encyclopedical praise must altogether be denied him. Diderot's habitual world, we must on the contrary say, is a half-world, distorted into looking like a whole; it is properly, a poor, fractional, insignificant world; partial, inaccurate, perverted from end to end. Alas, it was the destiny of the man to live as a Polemic; to be born also in the morning tide and first splendour of the Mechanical Era; not to know, with the smallest assurance or continuance, that in the Universe, other than a mechanical meaning could exist: which force of destiny acting on him through his whole course, we have obtained what now stands before us: no Seer, but only possibilities of a Seer, transient irradiations of a Seer, looking through the organs of a Philosophe.

These two considerations, which indeed are properly but one, (for a thinker, especially of French birth, in the Mechanical Era, could not be other than a Polemic,) must never for a moment be left out of view in judging the works of Diderot. It is a great truth, one side of a great truth, that the Man makes the Circumstances, and spiritually as well as economically, is the artificer of his own fortune. But there is another side of the same truth, that the man's circumstances are the element he is appointed to live and work in; that he by necessity takes his complexion, vesture, imbodyment, from these, and is, in all practical manifestations, modified by them almost without limit; so that in another no less genuine sense, it can be said the Circumstances make the Man. Now, if it continually behoves us to insist on the former truth towards ourselves, it equally behoves us to bear in mind the latter when we judge of other men. The most gifted soul, appearing in France in the Eighteenth Century, can as little imbody himself in the intellectual vesture of an Athenian Plato, as in the grammatical one; his thought can no more be Greek, than his language can. He thinks of the things belonging to the French eighteenth century, and in the dialect he has learned there; in the light, and under the conditions prescribed there. Thus, as the most original, resolute, and self-directing of all the Moderns has written: "Let a man be but born ten years sooner, or ten years later, his whole aspect and performance shall be different." Grant, doubtless, that a certain perennial Spirit, true for all times and all countries, can and must look through the thinking of certain men, be it in what dialect soever: understand, meanwhile, that strictly this holds only of the highest order of men, and cannot be exacted of inferior orders; among whom, if the most sedulous, loving inspection disclose any even secondary symptoms of such a Spirit, it ought to seem enough. Let us remember well that the high-gifted, high-striving Diderot was born in the point of Time and of Space, when of all uses he could turn himself to, of all dialects speak in, this of Polemical Philosophism, and no other, seemed the most promising and fittest. Let us remember too that no earnest Man, in any Time, ever spoke what was wholly meaningless; that, in all human convictions, much more in all human practices, there was a true side, a fraction of truth; which fraction is precisely the thing we want to extract from them, if we want any thing at all to do with them.

Such palliative considerations (which, for the rest, concern not Diderot, now departed, and indifferent to them, but only ourselves who could wish to *see* him, and not to mis-see him) are essential, we say, through our whole survey of his Opinions and Proceedings, generally so alien to our own; but most of all in reference to his head Opinion, properly the source of all the rest, and the more shocking, even horrible, to us than all the rest: we mean his Atheism. David Hume, dining once in company where Diderot was, remarked that he did not think there were any Atheists. "Count us," said a certain Monsieur ——: they were eighteen. "Well," said the Monsieur ——, "it is pretty fair if you have fished out fifteen at the first cast; and three others who know not what to think of it." In fact, the case was common: your Philosophe of the first water had grown to reckon Atheism a necessary accomplishment. Gowkthrapple Naigeon, as we saw, had made himself very perfect therein.

Diderot was an Atheist, then; stranger still, a proselytizing Atheist, who esteemed the creed worth earnest reiterated preaching, and enforcement with all vigour! The unhappy man had "sailed through the Universe of Worlds and found no Maker thereof; had descended to the abysses where Being no longer casts its shadow, and felt only the rain-drops trickle down; and seen only the glimmering rainbow of Creation, which originated from no Sun; and heard only the everlasting storm which no one governs; and looked upwards for the Divine Eye, and beheld only the black, bottomless, glaring Death's Eye-socket:" such, with all his wide voyages, was the philosophic fortune he had realized.

Sad enough, horrible enough: yet instead of shrieking over it, or howling and Ernulphus'-cursing over it, let us, as the more profitable method, keep our composure, and inquire a little, What possibly it may mean? The whole phenomenon, as seems to us, will explain itself from the fact above insisted on, that Diderot was a Polemic of decided character, in the Mechanical Age. With great expenditure of words and froth, in arguments as waste, wild-weltering, delirious-dismal as the chaos they would demonstrate—which arguments one now knows not whether to laugh at or to weep at, and almost does both,—have Diderot and his sect perhaps made this apparent to all who examine it: That in the French System of Thought, (called also the Scotch, and still familiar enough everywhere, which for want of a better title we have named the Mechanical,) there is no room for a Divinity; that to him for whom "*intellect*, or the power of knowing and believing is still synonymous with *logic*, or the mere power of arranging and communicating," there is absolutely no proof discoverable of a Divinity; and such a man has nothing for it but either (if he be of half spirit, as is the frequent case) to trim despicably all his days between two opinions; or else (if he be of whole spirit) to anchor on the rock or quagmire of Atheism,—and further, should he see fit, proclaim to others that there is good riding there. So much may Diderot have demonstrated: a conclusion at which we nowise turn pale. Was it much to know that Metaphysical Speculation, by nature, whirls round in endless Mahlstroms, both "creating and swallowing—itself?" For so wonderful a self-swallowing product of the Spirit of Time, could any result to arrive at be fitter than this of the ETERNAL No? We thank Heaven that the result *is* finally arrived at; and so now we can look out for something other and further. But, above all things, *proof* of a God? A *probable* God! The smallest of Finites struggling to *prove* to itself (that is to say, if we consider it, to picture out and arrange as diagram, and *include* within itself) the Highest Infinite; in *which*, by hypothesis, *it* lives, and moves, and has its being! This, we conjecture, will one day seem a much more miraculous miracle than that negative result it has arrived at,—or any other result a still absurder chance might have led it to. He who, in some singular Time of the World's History, were reduced to wander about, in stooping posture, with painfully constructed sulphur-match and farthing rushlight, (as Gowkthrapple Naigeon,) or smoky tar-link, (as Denis Diderot,) searching for the Sun, and did not find it; were *he* wonderful and his failure; or the singular Time, and its having put him on that search?

Two small consequences, then, we fancy, may have followed, or be following, from poor Diderot's Atheism. First, that all speculations of the sort we call Natural-theology, endeavouring to prove the beginning of all Belief by some Belief earlier than the beginning, are barren, ineffectual, impossible; and may, so soon as otherwise it is profitable, be abandoned. Of final causes, man, by the nature of the case, can *prove* nothing; knows them (if he know any thing of them) not by glimmering flint-sparks of Logic, but by an infinitely higher light of intuition; never long, by Heaven's mercy, wholly eclipsed in the human soul; and (under the name of Faith, as regards this matter) familiar to us now, historically or in conscious possession, for upwards of four thousand years. To all open men it will indeed always be a favourite contemplation, that of watching the ways of Being, how animate adjusts itself to inanimate, rational to irrational; and this, that we name Nature, is not a desolate phantasm of a chaos, but a wondrous existence and reality. If, moreover, in those same "marks of design," as he has called them, the contemplative man find new evidence of a designing Maker, be it well for him: meanwhile, surely, the still clearer evidence lay nearer home, in the contemplative man's own head that *seeks* after such! In which point of view our extant Natural-theologies, as our innumerable Evidences of the Christian Religion, and such like, may, in reference to the strange season they appear in, have an indubitable value and be worth printing and reprinting; only let us understand for whom, and how, they are valuable; and be nowise wroth with the poor Atheist, whom they have not convinced, and could not, and should not convince.

The second consequence seems to be that this whole current hypothesis of the Universe being "a Machine," and then of an Architect, who constructed it, sitting as it were apart, and guiding it, and *seeing* it go,—may turn out an inanity and nonentity; not much longer tenable: with which result likewise we shall, in the quietest manner, reconcile ourselves. "Think ye," says Goethe, "that God made the Universe, and then let it run round his finger (*am Finger laufen liesse?*)" On the whole, that Metaphysical hurly-burly (of our poor, jarring, self-listening Time) ought at length to compose itself: that seeking for a God *there*, and not *here;* everywhere outwardly in physical Nature, and not inwardly in our own Soul, where alone He is to be found by us,—begins to get wearisome. Above all, that "faint possible Theism," which now forms our common English creed, cannot be too soon swept out of the world. What is the nature of that individual, who with hysterical violence theoretically asserts a God, perhaps a revealed Symbol and Worship of God; and for the rest, in thought, word, and conduct, meet with him where you will, is found living as if his theory were some polite figure of speech, and his theoretical God a mere distant Simulacrum, with whom he, for his part, had nothing further to do? Fool! The ETERNAL is no Simulacrum; God is not only There, but Here, or nowhere, in that life-breath of thine, in that act and thought of thine,—and thou wert wise to look to it. If there is no God, as the fool hath said in his heart, then live on with thy decencies, and lip-homages, and inward Greed, and falsehood, and all the hollow cunningly-devised halfness that recommends thee to the Mammon of this world: if there *is* a God, we say, look to it! But in either case, what art thou? The Atheist is false; yet is there, as we see, a fraction of truth in him: he is true compared with thee; thou unhappy mortal, livest wholly in a lie, art wholly a lie.

So that Diderot's Atheism comes, if not to much, yet to something: we learn this from it (and from what it stands connected with, and may represent for us,) that the Mechanical System of Thought is, in its essence, Atheistic; that whosoever will admit no organ of truth but logic, and nothing to exist but what can be argued of, must even content himself with his sad result, as the only solid one he can arrive at; and so with the best grace he can "of the æther make a gas, of God a force, of the second world a coffin;" of man an aimless nondescript, "little better than a kind of vermin." If Diderot, by bringing matters to this parting of the roads, have enabled or helped us to strike into the truer and better road, let him have our thanks for it. As to what remains, be pity our only feeling; was not his creed miserable enough; nay, moreover, did not he bear its miserableness, so to speak, in our stead, so that it need now be no longer borne by any one.

In this same, for him unavoidable circumstance, of the age he lived in, and the system of thought universal then, will be found the key to Diderot's whole spiritual character and procedure; the excuse for much in him that to us is false and perverted. Beyond the meagre "rush-light of closet-logic," Diderot recognised no guidance. That "the Highest cannot be spoken of in words," was a truth he had not dreamt of. Whatsoever thing he cannot debate of, we might almost say measure and weigh, and carry off with him to be eaten and enjoyed, is simply not there for him. He dwelt all his days in the "thin rind of the Conscious;" the deep fathomless domain of the Unconscious, whereon the other rests, and has its meaning, was not, under any shape, surmised by him. Thus must the Sanctuary of Man's Soul stand perennially shut against this man; where his hand ceased to grope, the World ended: within such strait conditions had he to live and labour. And naturally to distort and dislocate, more or less, all things he laboured on: for whosoever, in one way or another, recognises not that "Divine Idea of the World, which lies at the bottom of Appearances," can rightly interpret no Appearance; and whatsoever spiritual thing he does, must do it partially, do it falsely.

Mournful enough, accordingly, is the account which Diderot has given himself of Man's existence; on the duties, relations, possessions whereof he had been a sedulous thinker. In every conclusion we have this fact of his Mechanical culture. Coupled too with another fact honourable to him: that he stuck not at half measures; but resolutely drove on to the result, and held by it. So that we cannot call him a skeptic; he has merited the more decisive name of Denier. He may be said to have denied that there was any the smallest Sacredness in Man, or in the Universe; and to have both speculated and lived on this singular footing. We behold in him the notable extreme of a man guiding himself with the least spiritual Belief that thinking man perhaps ever had. Religion, in all recognisable shapes and senses, he has done what man can do to clear out of him. He believes that pleasure is pleasant; that a lie is unbelievable; and there, his *credo* terminates; nay there, what perhaps makes his case almost unique, his very fancy seems to fall silent.

For a consequent man, all possible spiritual perversions are included under that grossest one of "proselytizing Atheism;" the rest, of what kind and degree soever, cannot any longer astonish us. Diderot has them of all kinds and degrees; indeed, we might say, the French Philosophe (take him at his *word*, for inwardly much that was foreign adhered to him, do what he could) has emitted a Scheme of the World, to which all that Oriental Mullah, Bonze, or Talapoin have done in that kind is poor and feeble. Omitting his whole unparalleled Cosmoganies and Physiologies; coming to his much milder Tables of the Moral Law, we shall glance here but at one minor external item, the relation between man and man; and at only one branch of this, and with all slightness, the relation of covenants; for example, the most important of these, Marriage.

Diderot has convinced himself, and, indeed, as above became plain enough, acts on the conviction, that Marriage, contract it, solemnize it in what way you will, involves a solecism which reduces the amount of it to simple zero. It is a suicidal covenant; annuls itself in the very forming. "Thou makest a vow," says he, twice or thrice, as if the argument were a clencher, "thou makest a vow of eternal constancy under a rock, which is even then crumbling away." True, O Denis! the rock crumbles away: all things are changing; man changes faster than most of them. That, in the meanwhile, an Unchangeable lies under all this, and looks forth, solemn and benign, through the whole destiny and workings of man, is another truth; which no Mechanical Philosophe, in the dust of his logic-mill, can be expected to grind out for himself. Man changes, and will change: the question then arises, Is it wise in him to tumble forth, in headlong obedience to this love of change; is it so much as possible for him? Among the dualisms of man's wholly dualistic nature, this we might fancy was an observable one: that along with his unceasing tendency to change, there is a no less ineradicable tendency to persevere. Were man only here to change, let him, far from marrying, cease even to hedge in fields, and plough them; before the autumn season, he may have lost the whim of reaping them. Let him return to the nomadic state, and set his house on wheels; nay there too a certain restraint must curb his love of change, or his cattle will perish by incessant driving, without grazing in the intervals. O Denis, what things thou babblest in thy sleep! How, in this world of perpetual flux, shall man secure himself the smallest foundation, except hereby alone: that he take pre-assurance of his Fate; that in this and the other high act of life, his Will, with all solemnity, *abdicate* its right to change; voluntarily become involuntary, and say once for all, Be there then no further dubitation on it! Nay, the poor unheroic craftsman; that very stocking-weaver, on whose loom thou now as amateur weavest: must not even he do as much,—when he signed his apprentice-indentures? The fool! who had such a relish in himself for all things, for kingship and emperorship; yet made a vow (under penalty of death by hunger) of eternal constancy to stocking-weaving. Yet otherwise, were no thriving craftsmen possible; only botchers, bunglers, transitory nondescripts; unfed, mostly gallows-feeding. But, on the whole, what feeling it was in the ancient devout deep soul, which of Marriage made *a Sacrament*: this, of all things in the world, is what Denis will think of for æons, without discovering. Unless, perhaps, it were to increase the vestry-fees!

Indeed, it must be granted, nothing yet seen or dreamt of can surpass the liberality of friend Denis as *magister morum*; nay, often our poor Philosophe feels called on, in an age of such Spartan rigor, to step forth into the public Stews, and emit his inspiring *Macte virtute!* there. Whither let the curious in such matters follow him: we, having work elsewhere, wish him "good journey,"—or rather "safe return." Of Diderot's indelicacy and indecency there is for us but little to say. Diderot is not what we call indelicate and indecent; he is utterly unclean, scandalous, shameless, sansculottic-samoedic. To declare with lyric fury that this is wrong; or with historic calmness, that a pig of sensibility would go distracted did you accuse him of it, may (especially in countries where "indecent exposure" is cognised at police-offices) be considered superfluous. The only question is one in Natural History: Whence comes it? What may a man, not otherwise without elevation of mind, of kindly character, of immense professed philanthropy; and doubtless of extraordinary insight, mean thereby? To us it is but another illustration of the fearless, all-for-logic, thoroughly consistent, Mechanical Thinker. It coheres well enough with Diderot's theory of man; that there is nothing of sacred either in man or around man; and that chimeras are chimerical. How shall he for whom nothing, that cannot be jargoned of in debating-clubs, exists, have any faintest forecast of the depth, significance, divineness of SILENCE; of the sacredness of "Secrets known to all?"

Nevertheless, Nature is great; and Denis was among her nobler productions. To a soul of his sort something like what we call Conscience could nowise be wanting: the feeling of Moral Relation, of the Infinite character thereof, (as the essence and soul of all else that can be felt or known,) must assert itself in him. Yet how assert itself? An Infinitude to one, in whose whole Synopsis of the Universe no Infinite stands marked? Wonderful enough is Diderot's method; and yet not wonderful, for we see it, and have always seen it, daily. Since there is nothing sacred in the Universe, whence this sacredness of what you call Virtue? Whence or how comes it that you, Denis Diderot, *must* not do a wrong thing; could not, without some qualm, speak, for example, one Lie, to gain Mohammed's Paradise with all its houris? There is no resource for it, but to get into that interminable ravelment of Reward and Approval, virtue being its own reward; and assert louder and louder,—contrary to the stern experience of all men, from the Divine Man, expiring with agony of bloody sweat on the accursed tree, down to us two, O reader (if we have ever done one Duty)—that Virtue is synonymous with Pleasure. Alas! was Paul, an apostle of the Gentiles, virtuous; and was virtue its own reward, when *his* approving conscience told him that he was "the chief of sinners," and (bounded to this life alone) "of all men the most miserable?" Or has that same so sublime Virtue, at bottom, little to do with Pleasure, if with far other things? Are Eudoxia, and Eusebeia, and Euthanasia, and all the rest of them, of small account to Eubosia and Eupepsia; and the pains of any moderately-paced Career of Vice (Denis himself being judge) as a drop in the bucket to the "Career of Indigestions?" This is what Denis never in this world will grant.

But what then will he do? One of two things: admit, with Grimm, that there are "two justices,"—which may be called by many handsome names, but properly are nothing but the pleasant justice, and the unpleasant; whereof only the former is binding. Herein, however, Nature has been unkind to Denis; he is not a literary court-toad-eater; but a free, genial, even poetic creature. There remains, therefore, nothing but the second expedient, to "assert louder and louder;" in other words, to become a Philosophe-Sentimentalist. Most wearisome, accordingly, is the perpetual clatter kept up here about *vertu, honnêteté, grandeur, sensibilité, ames-nobles;* how unspeakably good it is to be virtuous, how pleasant, how sublime: "In the Devil and his grandmother's name, *be* virtuous; and let us have an end of it!" In such sort (we will nevertheless joyfully recognise) does great Nature in spite of all contradictions, declare her royalty, her divineness; and, for the poor Mechanical Philosophe, has prepared since the substance is hidden from him, a shadow wherewith he can be cheered.

In fine, to our ill-starred Mechanical Philosophe-Sentimentalist, with his loud preaching and rather poor performing, shall we not, in various respects, "thankfully stretch out the hand?" In all ways, "it was necessary that the logical side of things should likewise be made available." On the whole, wondrous higher developments of much, of Morality among the rest, are visible in the course of the world's doings, at this day. A plausible prediction were that the Ascetic System is not to regain its exclusive dominancy. Ever, indeed, must Self-denial, "*Annihilation of Self*, be the beginning of all moral action:" meanwhile, he that looks well, may discern filaments of a nobler System, wherein this lies included as one harmonious element. Who knows what new unfoldings and complex adjustments await us, before, (for example,) the true relation of moral Greatness to moral Correctness, and their proportional value, can be established? How, again, is perfect tolerance for the Wrong to co-exist with ever-present conviction that Right stands related to it, as a God does to a Devil,—an Infinite to an opposite Infinite? How, in a word, through what tumultuous vicissitudes, after how many false partial efforts, deepening the confusion, shall it, at length, be made manifest, and kept continually manifest to the hearts of men, that the Good is not properly the highest, but the Beautiful; that the true Beautiful (differing from the false, as Heaven does from Vauxhall,) comprehends in it the Good?—In some future century, it may be found that Denis Diderot, acting and professing, in wholeness and with full conviction, what the immense multitude act in halfness and without conviction,—has, though by strange inverse methods, forwarded the result. It was long ago written, the Omnipotent "maketh the wrath of the wicked" (the folly of the foolish) "to praise Him." In any case, Diderot acted it, and not we; Diderot bears it, and not we: peace be with Diderot!

The other branch of his renown in excellence as a Talker. Or in wider view, (think his admirers,) his philosophy was not more surpassing than his delivery thereof. What his philosophy amounts to we have been examining: but now, that in this other conversational province he was eminent, is easily believed. A frank, ever-hoping, social character; a mind full of knowledge, full of fervour; of great compass, of great depth, ever on the alert: such a man could not have other than a "mouth of gold." It is still plain, whatsoever thing imaged itself before him, was imaged in the most lucent clearness; was rendered back, with light labour, in corresponding clearness. Whether, at the same time, Diderot's conversation, relatively so superior, deserved the intrinsic character of supreme, may admit of question. The worth of words spoken depends, after all, on the wisdom that resides in them; and in Diderot's words there was often too little of this. Vivacity, far-darting brilliancy, keenness of theoretic vision, paradoxical ingenuity, gayety, even touches of humour; all this must have been here; whosoever had preferred sincerity, earnestness, depth of practical rather than theoretic insight, with not less of impetuosity, of clearness and sureness, with humour, emphasis, or such other melody or rhythm as that utterance demanded,—must have come over to London; and (with forbearant submissiveness) listened to our Johnson. Had we the stronger man, then? Be it rather, as in that Duel of Cœur-de-Leon with the light, nimble, yet also invincible Saladin, that each nation had the strength which most befitted it.

Closely connected with this power of conversation is Diderot's facility of composition. A talent much celebrated; numerous really surprising proofs whereof are on record; how he wrote long works within the week; sometimes within almost the four-and-twenty hours. Unhappily, enough still remains to make such feats credible. Most of Diderot's Works bear the clearest traces of extemporaneousness; *stans pede in uno!* They are much liker printed talk, than the concentrated well-considered utterance, which, from a man of that weight, we expect to see set in types. It is said, "he wrote good pages, but could not write a good book." Substitute *did not* for *could not;* and there is some truth in the saying. Clearness, as has been observed, comprehensibility at a glance, is the character of whatever Diderot wrote: a clearness which, in visual objects, rises into the region of the Artistic, and resembles that of Richardson or Defoe. Yet, grant that he makes his meaning clear, what is the nature of that meaning itself? Alas, for most part, only a hasty, flimsy, superficial meaning, with gleams of a deeper vision peering through. More or less of Disorder reigns in all Works that Diderot wrote; not order, but the plausible appearance of such: the true heart of the matter is not found; "he skips deftly along the radii, and skips over the centre, and misses it."

Thus may Diderot's admired Universality and admired facility have both turned to disadvantage for him. We speak not of his reception by the world: this indeed is the "age of specialities;" yet, owing to other causes, Diderot the Encyclopedist had success enough. But, what is of far more importance, his inward growth was marred: the strong tree shot not up in any one noble stem, (bearing boughs, and fruit, and shade all round;) but spread out horizontally, after a very moderate height, into innumerable branches, not useless, yet of quite secondary use. Diderot could have been an Artist; and he was little better than an Encyclopedic Artisan. No smatterer indeed; a faithful artisan; of really universal equipment, in his sort: he did the work of many men, yet nothing, or little, which many could not have done.

Accordingly, his Literary Works, now lying finished some fifty years, have already, to the most surprising degree, sunk in importance. Perhaps no man so much talked of is so little known; to the great majority he is no longer a Reality, but a Hearsay. Such, indeed, partly, is the natural fate of Works Polemical, which almost all Diderot's are. The Polemic annihilates his opponent; but in so doing annihilates himself too, and both are swept away to make room for something other and farther. Add to this, the slight-textured transitory character of Diderot's style, and the fact is well enough explained. Meanwhile, let him, to whom it applies, consider it; him among whose gifts it was to rise into the Perennial, and who dwelt rather low down in the Ephemeral, and ephemerally fought and scrambled there! Diderot the great has contracted into Diderot the easily-measurable: so must it be with others of the like.

In how many sentences can the net-product of all that tumultuous Atheism, printed over many volumes, be comprised! Nay, the whole *Encyclopédie*, that world's wonder of the eighteenth century, the Belus' Tower of an age of refined Illumination, what has it become! Alas! no stone-tower, that will stand there as our strength and defence through all times: but, at best, a wooden *Helepolis*, (City-taker,) wherein stationed, the Philosophus Policaster has burnt and battered down many an old ruinous Sorbonne; and which now, when that work is pretty well over, may, in turn, be taken asunder, and used as firewood. The famed Encyclopedical Tree itself has proved an artificial one, and borne no fruit. We mean that, in its nature, it is mechanical only; one of those attempts to parcel out the invisible mystical Soul of Man, with its *infinitude* of phases and character, into shop-lists of what are called "faculties," "motives," and such like; which attempts may indeed be made with all degrees of insight, from that of a Doctor Spurzheim to that of Denis Diderot, or Jeremy Bentham; and prove useful for a day, but for a day only.

Nevertheless it were false to regard Diderot as a Mechanist and nothing more; as one working and grinding blindly in the mill of mechanical Logic, joyful with his lot there, and unconscious of any other. Call him one rather who contributed to deliver us therefrom: both by his manful whole spirit as a Mechanist, which drove all things to their ultimatum and crisis; and even by a dim-struggling faculty, which virtually aimed beyond this. Diderot, we said, was gifted by Nature for an Artist: strangely flashing through his mechanical encumbrances, are rays of thought, which belong to the Poet, to the Prophet; which, in other environment, could have revealed the deepest to us. Not to seek far, consider this one little sentence, which he makes the last of the dying Sanderson: *Le temps, la matière, et l'espace ne sont peut-être qu'un point* (Time, Matter, and Space are perhaps but *a point!*)

So too, in Art, both as a speaker and a doer, he is to be reckoned as one of those who pressed forward irresistibly out of the artificial barren sphere of that time, into a truer genial one. His Dramas, the *Fils Naturel*, the *Père de Famille*, have indeed ceased to live; yet is the attempt towards great things visible in them; the attempt remains to us, and seeks otherwise, and has found, and is finding, fulfilment. Not less in his *Salons*, (Judgments of Art-Exhibitions,) written hastily for Grimm, and by ill chance, on artists of quite secondary character, do we find the freest recognition of whatever excellence there is; nay, an impetuous endeavour, not critically but even creatively, towards something more excellent. Indeed, what with their unrivalled clearness, painting the picture over again for us, so that we too *see* it, and can judge it; what with their sunny fervour, inventiveness, real artistic genius, (which only cannot manipulate,) they are, with some few exceptions in the German tongue, the only Pictorial Criticisms we know of worth reading. Here too, as by his own practice in the Dramatic branch of art, Diderot stands forth as the main originator (almost the sole one in his own country) of that many-sided struggle towards what is called Nature, and copying of Nature, and faithfulness to Nature; a deep indispensable truth, subversive of the old error; yet under that figure, only a half-truth, for Art too is Art, as surely as Nature is Nature; which struggle, meanwhile, either as half-truth or working itself into a whole truth, may be seen (in countries that have any Art) still forming the tendency of all artistic endeavour. In which sense, Diderot's *Essay on Painting* has been judged worth translation by the greatest modern Judge of Art, and greatest modern Artist, in the highest kind of Art; and may be read anew, with argumentative commentary and exposition, in *Goethe's Works*.

Nay, let us grant, with pleasure, that for Diderot himself the realms of Art were not wholly unvisited; that he too, so heavily imprisoned, stole Promethean fire. Among these multitudinous, most miscellaneous Writings of his, in great part a manufactured farrago of Philosophism no longer saleable, and now looking melancholy enough,—are two that we can almost call Poems; that have something perennially poetic in them: *Jacques le Fataliste;* in a still higher degree, the *Neveu de Rameau*. The occasional *blueness* of both; even that darkest indigo in some parts of the former, shall not altogether affright us. As it were, a loose straggling sunbeam flies here over Man's Existence in France, now nigh a century behind us: "from the height of luxurious elegance to the depths of shamelessness;" all is here. Slack, careless seems the combination of the picture; wriggling, disjointed, like a bundle of flails; yet strangely united in the painter's inward unconscious feeling. Wearisomely crackling wit gets silent; a grim, taciturn, dare-devil, almost Hogarthian humour, rises in the background. Like this there is nothing that we know of in the whole range of French Literature: La Fontaine is shallow in comparision; the La Bruyère wit-species not to be named. It resembles *Don Quixote*, rather; of somewhat similar stature; yet of complexion altogether different; through the one looks a sunny Elysium, through the other a sulphurous Erebus: both hold of the Infinite. This *Jacques*, perhaps, was not quite so hastily put together: yet there too haste is manifest: the Author finishes it off, not by working out the figures and movements, but by dashing his brush against the canvas; a manœuvre which in this case has not succeeded. The *Rameau's Nephew*, which is the shorter, is also the better; may pass for decidedly the best of all Diderot's Compositions. It looks like a Sibylline utterance from a heart all in fusion: no ephemeral thing (for it was written as a Satire on Palissot) was ever more perennially treated. Strangely enough, too, it lay some fifty years, in German and Russian Libraries; came out first in the masterly version of Goethe, in 1805; and only (after a deceptive *re*-translation by a M. Saur, a courageous mystifier otherwise,) reached the Paris public, in 1821,—when perhaps *all*, for whom, and against whom it was written, were no more!—It is a farce-tragedy; and its fate has corresponded to its purport. One day it must also be translated into English; but will require to be done by *head*; the common steam-machinery will not meet it.

We here (*con la bocca dolce*) take leave of Diderot in his intellectual aspect, as Artist and Thinker: a richly endowed, unfavourably situated nature; whose effort, much marred, yet not without fidelity of aim, can triumph, on rare occasions; is perhaps nowhere utterly fruitless. In the moral aspect, as Man, he makes a somewhat similar figure; as indeed, in all men, in him especially, the Opinion and the Practice stand closely united; and as a wise man has remarked, "the speculative principles are often but a supplement (or excuse) to the practical manner of life." In conduct, Diderot can nowise seem admirable to us; yet neither inexcusable; on the whole, not at all quite worthless. Lavater traced in his physiognomy "something timorous;" which reading his friends admitted to be a correct one. Diderot, in truth, is no hero: the earnest soul, wayfaring and warfaring in the complexities of a World like to overwhelm him, yet wherein he by Heaven's grace will keep faithfully warfaring, prevailing or not, can derive small solacement from this light, fluctuating, not to say flimsy existence of Diderot: no Gospel in that kind has he left us. The man, in fact, with all his high gifts, had rather a female character. Susceptible, sensitive, living by impulses, which at best he had *fashioned* into some show of principles; with vehemence enough, with even a female uncontrollableness; with little of manful steadfastness, considerateness, invincibility. Thus, too, we find him living mostly in the society of women, or of men who, like women, flattered him, and made life easy for him; recoiling with horror from an earnest Jean Jacques, who understood not the science of walking in a vain show; but imagined (poor man) that truth was there as a thing to be told, as a thing to be acted.

We call Diderot, then, not a coward; yet not in any sense a brave man. Neither towards himself, nor towards others, was he brave. All the virtues, says M. de Meister, which require not "a great *suite* (sequency) of ideas," were his: all that do require such a *suite* were not his. In other words, what duties were easy for him, he did: happily Nature had rendered several easy. His spiritual aim, moreover, seemed not so much to be enforcement, exposition of Duty, as discovery of a Duty-made-easy. Natural enough that he should strike into that province of *sentiment, cœur-noble*, and so forth. Alas, to declare that the beauty of virtue is beautiful, costs comparatively little; to win it, and wear it, is quite another enterprise,—wherein the loud braggart, we know, is not the likeliest to succeed. On the whole, peace be with *sentiment*, for that also lies behind us!—For the rest, as hinted, what duties were difficult our Diderot left undone. How should he, the *cœur sensible*, front such a monster as Pain? And now, since misgivings cannot fail in that course, what is to be done but fill up all asperities with floods of *Sensibilité*, and so voyage more or less smoothly along? *Est-il bon? Est-il méchant?* is his own account of himself. At all events, he was no voluntary hypocrite; that great praise can be given him. And thus with Mechanical Philosophism, and *passion vive;* working, flirting; "with more of softness than of true affection, sometimes with the malice and rage of a child, but on the whole an inexhaustible fund of goodnatured simplicity," has he come down to us for better for worse: and what can we do but receive him?

If now we and our reader, reinterpreting for our present want that Life and Performance of Diderot, have brought it clearer before us, be the hour spent thereon, were it even more wearisome, no profitless one! Have we not striven to unite our own brief present moment more and more compactly with the Past and with the Future; have we not done what lay at our hand towards reducing that same Memoirism of the Eighteenth Century into History, and "weaving" a thread or two thereof nearer to the condition of a "web?"

But finally, if we rise with this matter (as we should try to do with all) into the proper region of Universal History, and look on it with the eye not of this time, or of that time, but of Time at large, perhaps the prediction might stand here, that intrinsically, essentially little lies in it; that one day when the net-result of our European way of life comes to be summed up, this whole as yet so boundless concern of French Philosophism will dwindle into the thinnest of fractions, or vanish into nonentity! Alas, while the rude History and Thoughts of those same "*Juifs misérables*," the barbaric War-song of a Deborah and Barak, the rapt prophetic Utterance of an unkempt Isaiah, last now (with deepest significance) say only these three thousand years,—what has the thrice resplendent *Encyclopédie* shrivelled into within these three-score! This is a fact which, explain it, express it, in which way he will, your Encyclopedist should actually consider. *Those* were tones caught from the sacred Melody of the All, and having harmony and meaning for ever; *these* of his are but outer discords, and their jangling dies away without result. "The special, sole, and deepest theme of the World's and Man's History," says the Thinker of our time, "whereto all other themes are subordinated, remains the Conflict of UNBELIEF and BELIEF. All epochs wherein Belief prevails, under what form it may, are splendid, heart-elevating, fruitful for contemporaries and posterity. All epochs, on the contrary, wherein Unbelief, under what form soever, maintains its sorry victory, should they even for a moment glitter with a sham splendour, vanish from the eyes of posterity; because no one chooses to burden himself with study of the unfruitful.

ON HISTORY AGAIN.

[FRASER'S MAGAZINE, 1833.]

[The following singular fragment on *History* forms part, as may be recognised, of the Inaugural Discourse delivered by our assiduous "D. T." at the opening of the *Society for the Diffusion of Common Honesty*. The Discourse, if one may credit the Morning Papers, "touched in the most wonderful manner, didactically, poetically, almost prophetically, on all things in this world and the next, in a strain of sustained or rather of suppressed passionate eloquence rarely witnessed in Parliament or out of it: the chief bursts were received with profound silence,"—interrupted, we fear, by snuff-taking. As will be seen, it is one of the didactic passages that we introduce here. The Editor of this Magazine is responsible for its accuracy, and publishes, if not with leave given, then with leave taken.—O. Y.]

* * * HISTORY recommends itself as the most profitable of all studies: and truly, for such a being as Man, who is born, and has to learn and work, and then after a measured term of years to depart, leaving descendants and performances, and so, in all ways, to vindicate himself as vital portion of a Mankind, no study could be fitter. History is the Letter of Instructions, which the old generations write and posthumously transmit to the new; nay

it may be called, more generally still, the Message, verbal or written, which all Mankind delivers to every man; it is the only *articulate* communication (when the inarticulate and mute, intelligible or not, lie round us and in us, so strangely through every fibre of our being, every step of our activity) which the Past can have with the Present, the Distant with what is Here. All Books, therefore, were they but Song-books or treatises on Mathematics, are in the long run historical documents,—as indeed all Speech itself is: thus might we say, History is not only the fittest study, but the only study, and includes all others whatsoever. The Perfect in History, he who understood, and saw and knew within himself, *all* that the whole Family of Adam had hitherto *been* and hitherto *done*, were perfect in all learning extant or possible; needed not henceforth to *study* any more; and henceforth nothing left but to *be* and to *do* something himself, and others might make History of it, and learn of *him*.

Perfection in any kind is well known not to be the lot of man: but of all supernatural perfect-characters, this of the Perfect in History (so easily conceivable too) were perhaps the most miraculous. Clearly a faultless monster which the world is not to see, not even on paper. Had the Wandering Jew, indeed, begun to wander at Eden, and with a Fortunatus' Hat on his head! Nanac Shah too, we remember, steeped himself three days in some sacred Well; and there learnt enough: Nanac's was a far easier method; but unhappily not practicable,—in this climate. Consider, however, at what immeasurable distance from this Perfect Nanac your highest Imperfect Gibbons play their part? Were there no brave men, thinkest thou, before Agamemnon? Beyond the Thracian Bosphorus, was all dead and void; from Cape Horn to Nova Zembla, round the whole habitable Globe, not a mouse stirring? Or, again, in reference to Time:—the Creation of the World is indeed old, compare it to the Year One; yet young, of yesterday, compare it to Eternity! Alas, all Universal History is but a sort of Parish History; which the "P. P. Clerk of this Parish," member of "our Alehouse Club" (instituted for what "Psalmody" is in request there) puts together,—in such sort as his fellow-members will praise. Of the *thing* now gone silent, named Past, which was once Present, and loud enough, how much do we know? Our "Letter of Instructions" comes to us in the saddest state; falsified, blotted out, torn, lost, and but a shred of it in existence; this too so difficult to read or spell.

Unspeakably precious meanwhile is our shred of a "Letter," is our "written or spoken Message," such as we have it. Only he who understands what has been, can know what should be and will be. It is of the last importance that the individual have ascertained his relation to the whole; "an individual helps not," it has been written; "only he who unites with many at the proper hour." How easy, in a sense for your all-instructed Nanac to work without waste of force, (or what we call fault;) and, in practice, act new History, as perfectly as, in theory, he knew the old! Comprehending what the given world was, what it had and what it wanted, how might his clear effort strike in at the right time and the right point; wholly increasing the true current and tendency, nowhere cancelling itself in opposition thereto! Unhappily, such smooth-running, ever-accelerated course is nowise the one appointed us; cross currents we have, perplexed backfloods; innumerable efforts (every new man is a new effort) consume themselves in aimless eddies: thus is the River of Existence so wild-flowing, wasteful; and whole multitudes, and whole generations, in painful unreason, spend and are spent on what can never profit. Of all which, does not one half originate in this which we have named want of Perfection in History; —the other half, indeed, in another want still deeper, still more irremediable?

Here, however, let us grant that Nature, in regard to such historic want, is nowise blamable: taking up the other face of the matter, let us rather admire the pains she has been at, the truly magnificent provision she has made, that this same Message of Instructions might reach us in boundless plenitude. Endowments, faculties enough we have: it is her wise will too that no faculty imparted to us shall rust from disuse; the miraculous faculty of Speech, once given, becomes not more a gift than a necessity; the Tongue, with or without much meaning, will keep in motion; and only in some La Trappe, by unspeakable self-restraint, forbear wagging. As little can the fingers that have learned the miracle of Writing lie idle; if there is a rage of speaking, we know also there is a rage of writing, perhaps the more furious of the two. It is said, "so eager are men to speak, they will not let one another get to speech;" but, on the other hand, writing is usually transacted in private, and every man has his own desk and inkstand, and sits independent and unrestrainable there. Lastly, multiply this power of the Pen some ten thousand fold: that is to say, invent the Printing-Press, with its Printer's Devils, with its Editors, Contributors, Booksellers, Billstickers, and see what it will do! Such are the means wherewith Nature, and Art the daughter of Nature, have equipped their favourite, man, for publishing himself to man.

Consider now two things: first, that one Tongue, of average velocity, will publish at the rate of a thick octavo volume per day; and then how many nimble enough Tongues may be supposed to be at work on this Planet Earth, in this City London, at this hour! Secondly, that a literary Contributor, if in good heart and urged by hunger, will many times (as we are credibly informed) accomplish his two magazine sheets within the four-and-twenty hours; such Contributors being now numerable not by the thousand, but by the million. Nay, taking History in its narrower, vulgar sense, as the mere chronicle of "occurrences" (of things that can be, as we say, "narrated,") our calculation is still but a little altered. Simple Narrative, it will be observed, is the grand staple of Speech: "the common man," says Jean Paul, "is copious in Narrative, exiguous in Reflection; only with the cultivated man is it otherwise, reverse-wise."

Allow even the thousandth part of human publishing for the emission of Thought, though perhaps the millionth were enough, we have still the nine hundred and ninety-nine employed in History proper, in relating occurrences, or conjecturing probabilities of such; that is to say, either in History or Prophecy, which is a new form of History;—and so the reader can judge with what abundance this life-breath of the human intellect is furnished in our world; whether Nature has been stingy to him or munificent. Courage, reader! Never can the historical inquirer want pabulum, better or worse; are there not forty-eight longitudinal feet of small-printed History in thy Daily Newspaper?

The truth is, if Universal History is such a miserable defective "shred" as we have named it, the fault lies not in our historic organs, but wholly in our misuse of these; say rather, in so many wants and obstructions, varying with the various age, that pervert our right use of them; especially two wants that press heavily in all ages: want of Honesty, want of Understanding. If the thing published is not true, is only a supposition, or even a wilful invention, what can be done with it, except abolish it and annihilate it? But again, Truth, says Horne Tooke, means simply the thing *trowed*, the thing believed; and now, from this to the thing *extant*, what a new fatal deduction have we to suffer! Without Understanding, Belief itself will profit little: and how can your publishing avail, when there was no vision in it, but mere blindness? For us in political appointments, the man you appoint is not he who was ablest to discharge the duty, but only he who was ablest to be appointed; so too, in all historic elections and selections, the maddest work goes on. The even worthiest to be known is perhaps of all others the least spoken of; nay some say, it lies in the very nature of such events to be so. Thus, in those same forty-eight longitudinal feet of History, or even when they have stretched out into forty-eight longitudinal miles, of the like quality, there may not be the forty-eighth part of a hair's-breadth that will turn to any thing. Truly, in these times, the quantity of printed Publication that will need to be consumed with fire, before the smallest permanent advantage can be drawn from it, might fill us with astonishment, almost with apprehension. Where, alas, is the intrepid Herculean Dr. Wagtail, that will reduce all these paper-mountains into tinder, and extract therefrom the three drops of Tinder-water Elixir?

For, indeed, looking at the activity of the historic Pen and Press through this last half-century, and what bulk of History it yields for that period alone, and how it is henceforth like to increase in decimal or vigesimal geometric progression,—one might feel as if a day were not distant, when perceiving that the whole Earth would not now contain those writings of what was done in the Earth, the human memory must needs sink confounded, and cease remembering!—To some the reflection may be new and consolatory, that this state of ours is not so unexampled as it seems; that with memory and things memorable the case was always intrinsically similar. The Life of Nero occupies some diamond pages of our Tacitus: but in the parchment and papyrus archives of Nero's generation how many did it fill? The Author of the *Vie de Sénèque*, at this distance, picking up a few residuary snips, has with ease made two octavos of it. On the other hand, were the contents of the then extant Roman memories, or, going to the utmost length, were all that was then *spoken* on it, put in types, how many "longitudinal feet" of small-pica had we,—in belts that would go round the Globe?

History, then, before it can become Universal History, needs of all things to be compressed. Were there no epitomizing of History, one could not remember beyond a week. Nay, go to that with it, and exclude compression altogether, we could not remember an hour, or at all: for Time, like Space, is *infinitely* divisible; and an hour with its events, with its sensations and emotions, might be diffused to such expansion as should cover the whole field of memory, and push all else over the limits. Habit, however, and the natural constitution of man, do themselves prescribe serviceable rules for remembering; and keep at a safe distance from us all such fantastic possibilities;—into which only some foolish Mohammedan Caliph, ducking his head in a bucket of enchanted water, and so beating out one wet minute into seven long years of servitude and hardship, could fall. The rudest peasant has his complete set of Annual Registers legibly printed in his brain; and, without the smallest training in Mnemonics, the proper pauses, sub-divisions, and subordinations of the little to the great, all introduced there. Memory and Oblivion, like Day and Night, and indeed like all other Contradictions in this strange dualistic Life of ours, are necessary for each other's existence: Oblivion is the dark page, whereon Memory writes her light-beam characters, and makes them legible; were it all light, nothing could be read there, any more than if it were all darkness.

As with man and these autobiographic Annual-Registers of his, so goes it with Mankind and its Universal History, (which also is *its* Autobiography:) a like unconscious talent of remembering and of forgetting again does the work here. The transactions of the day, were they never so noisy, cannot remain loud for ever; the morrow comes with its new noises, claiming also to be registered: in the immeasurable conflict and concert of this chaos of existence, figure after figure sinks, as *all* that has emerged must one day sink: what cannot be kept in mind will even go out of mind; History contracts itself into readable extent; and at last, in the hands of some Bossuet or Müller, the whole printed History of the World, from the Creation downwards, has grown shorter than that of the Ward of Portsoken for one solar day.

Whether such contraction and epitome is always wisely formed, might admit of question; or rather, as we say, admits of no question. Scandalous Cleopatras and Messalinas, Caligulas and Commoduses, in unprofitable proportion, survive for memory; while a scientific

Pancirollus must write his Book of Arts Lost; and a moral Pancirollus (were the vision lent him) might write a still more mournful Book of Virtues Lost; of noble men, doing, and daring, and enduring, whose heroic life, as a new revelation and development of Life itself, were a possession for all, but is now lost and forgotten, History having otherwise filled her page. In fact, here as elsewhere what we call Accident governs much; in any case, History must come together not as it should, but as it can and will.

Remark nevertheless how, by natural tendency alone, and as it were without man's forethought, a certain fitness of selection, and this even to a high degree, becomes inevitable. Wholly worthless the selection could not be, were there no better rule than this to guide it: that men permanently speak only of what is extant and actively alive beside them. Thus do the things that have produced fruit, nay whose fruit still grows, turn out to be the things chosen for record and writing of; which things alone were great, and worth recording. The Battle of Chalons, where Hunland met Rome, and the Earth was played for, at sword-fence, by two earth bestriding giants, the sweep of whose swords cut kingdoms in pieces, hovers dim in the languid remembrance of a few; while the poor police-court Treachery of a wretched Iscariot, transacted in the wretched land of Palestine, centuries earlier, for "thirty pieces of silver," lives clear in the heads, in the hearts of all men. Nay moreover, as only that which bore fruit was great; so of all things, that whose fruit is still here and growing must be the greatest, the best worth remembering; which again, as we see, by the very nature of the case, is mainly the thing remembered. Observe too how this "mainly" tends always to become a "solely," and the approximate continually approaches nearer: for triviality after triviality, as it perishes from the living activity of men, drops away from their speech and memory, and the great and vital more and more exclusively survive there. Thus does Accident correct Accident; and in the wondrous boundless jostle of things, (an aimful POWER presiding over it, say rather, dwelling *in* it,) a result comes out that may be put up with.

Curious, at all events, and worth looking at once in our life, is this same compressure of History, be the process thereof what it may. How the "forty-eight longitudinal feet" have shrunk together after a century, after ten centuries! Look back from end to beginning, over any History; over our own *England*: how, in rapidest law of perspective, it dwindles from the canvas! An unhappy Sybarite, if we stand within two centuries of him and name him Charles Second, shall have twelve times the space of a heroic Alfred; two or three thousand times, if we name him George Fourth. The whole Saxon Heptarchy, though events, to which Magna Charta, and the world-famous Third Reading, are as dust in the balance, took place then (for did not England, to mention nothing else, get itself, if not represented in Parliament, yet converted to Christianity?) is summed up practically in that one sentence of Milton's (the only one succeeding writers have copied, or readers remembered) of the "fighting and flocking of kites and crows." Neither was that an unimportant wassail-night, when the two black-browed Brothers, strong-headed, headstrong, Hengist and Horsa, (*Stallion* and *Horse*,) determined on a man-hunt in Britain, the boar-hunt at home having got over-crowded; and so, of a few hungry Angles, made an English Nation, and planted it here, and—produced *thee*, O Reader! Of Hengist's whole campaignings scarcely half a page of good Narrative can now be written; the *Lord-Mayor's Visit to Oxford* standing, meanwhile, revealed to mankind in a respectable volume. Nay what of this? Does not the Destruction of a Brunswick Theatre take above a million times as much telling as the Creation of a World?

To use a ready-made similitude, we might liken Universal History to a magic web; and consider with astonishment how, by philosophic insight and indolent neglect, the ever-growing fabric wove itself forward, out of that ravelled immeasurable mass of threads and thrums, (which we name *Memoirs*;) nay, at each new lengthening, (at each new epoch,) changed its whole proportions, its hue and structure to the very origin. Thus, do not the records of a Tacitus acquire new meaning, after seventeen hundred years, in the hands of a Montesquieu? Niebuhr must reinterpret for us, at a still greater distance, the writings of a Titus Livius: nay, the religious archaic chronicles of a Hebrew Prophet and Lawgiver escape not the like fortune; and many a ponderous Eichhorn scans, with new-ground philosophic spectacles, the revelation of a Moses, and strives to re-produce for this century what, thirty centuries ago, was of plainly infinite significance to all. Consider History with the beginnings of it stretching dimly into the remote Time; emerging darkly out of the mysterious Eternity: the ends of it enveloping *us* at this hour, whereof we, at this hour, both as actors and relators, form part! In shape we might mathematically name it *Hyperbolic-Asymptotic*; ever of *infinite* breadth around us; soon shrinking within narrow limits: ever narrowing more and more into the infinite depth behind us. In essence and significance it has been called "the true Epic Poem, and universal Divine Scripture, *whose* 'plenary inspiration' no man (out of Bedlam or in it) shall bring in question." * * *

COUNT CAGLIOSTRO.

IN TWO FLIGHTS.

[FRASER'S MAGAZINE, 1833.]

Flight First.

"THE life of every man," says our friend Herr Sauerteig, "the life even of the meanest man, it were good to remember, is a Poem; perfect in all manner of Aristotelean requisites; with beginning, middle, and end; with perplexities, and solutions; with its Will-strength, (*Willenkraft*,) and warfare against Fate, its elegy and battle-singing, courage marred by crime, everywhere the two tragic elements of Pity and Fear; above all, with supernatural machinery enough,—for was not the man *born* out of NONENTITY; did he not *die*, and miraculously vanishing return thither? The most indubitable Poem! Nay, whoso will, may he not name it a Prophecy, or whatever else is highest in his vocabulary; since only in Reality lies the essence and foundation of all that was ever fabled, visioned, sung, spoken, or babbled by the human species; and the actual Life of Man includes in it all Revelations, true and false, that have been, are, or are to be. Man! I say therefore, *reverence thy fellow-man.* He too issued from Above; is mystical and supernatural, (as thou namest it:) this know thou of a truth. Seeing also that we ourselves are of so high Authorship, is not that, in very deed, 'the highest Reverence,' and most needful for us: 'Reverence for oneself?'

"Thus, to my view, is every Life, more properly is every Man that has life to lead, a small strophe, or occasional verse, composed by the Supernal Powers; and published, in such type and shape, with such embellishments, emblematic head-piece and tail-piece as thou seest, to the thinking or unthinking universe. Heroic strophes some few are; full of force and a sacred fire, so that to latest ages the hearts of those that read therein are made to tingle. Jeremiads others seem: mere weeping laments, harmonious or disharmonious Remonstrances against Destiny; whereat we too may sometimes profitably weep. Again have we not (flesh-and-blood) strophes of the idyllic sort,—though in these days rarely, owing to Poor Laws, Game Laws, Population Theories, and the like! Farther, of the comic laughter-loving sort; yet ever with an unfathomable earnestness, as is fit, lying underneath: for, bethink thee, what is the mirthfullest, grinning face of any Grimaldi, but a transitory *mask*, behind which quite otherwise grins—the most indubitable *Death's-head!* However, I say farther, there are strophes of the pastoral sort, (as in Ettrick, Affghaunistan, and elsewhere;) of the farcic-tragic, melodramatic, of all named and a thousand unnameable sorts there are poetic strophes, written, as was said, in Heaven, printed on Earth, and published, (bound in woollen cloth, or *clothes*,) for the use of the studious. Finally, a small number seem utter Pasquils, mere ribald libels on Humanity: these too, however, are at times worth reading.

"In this wise," continues our too obscure friend, "out of all imaginable elements, awakening all imaginable moods of heart and soul, 'barbarous enough to excite, tender enough to assuage,' ever contradictory yet ever coalescing, is that mighty world-old Rhapsodia of Existence, page after page, (generation after generation,) and chapter, (or epoch,) after chapter, poetically put together! This is what some one names 'the grand sacred Epos, or Bible of World-History; infinite in meaning as the Divine Mind it emblems; wherein he is wise that can read here a line and there a line.

"Remark, too, under another aspect, whether it is not in this same Bible of World-History that all men, in all times, with or without clear consciousness, have been unwearied to read, (what we may call *read*;) and again to write, or rather to be *written!* What is all History, and all Poesy, but a deciphering somewhat thereof, (out of that mystic heaven-written Sanscrit,) and rendering it into the speech of men? *Know thyself*, value thyself, is a moralist's commandment, (which I only half approve of;) but *Know others*, value others, is the hest of Nature herself. Or again, *Work while it is called To-day:* is not that also the irreversible law of being for mortal man? And now, what is all working, what is all knowing, but a faint interpreting and a faint showing forth of that same *Mystery of Life*, which ever remains infinite,—heaven-written mystic Sanscrit? View it as we will, to him that lives Life is a divine matter; felt to be of quite sacred significance. Consider the wretchedest 'straddling biped that wears breeches' of thy acquaintance; into whose wool-head, Thought, as thou rashly supposest, never entered; who, in froth-element of business, pleasure, or what else he names it, walks forever in a vain show; asking not Whence, or Why, or Whither; looking up to the Heaven above as if some upholsterer had made it, and down to the Hell beneath as if *he* had neither part nor lot there: yet tell me, does not he too, over and above his five finite senses, acknowledge some sixth *infinite* sense, were it only that of Vanity? For, sate him in the other five as you may, will this sixth sense leave him rest? Does he not rise early and sit late, and study impromptus, and, (in constitutional countries,) parliamentary motions, and bursts of eloquence, and gird himself in whalebone, and pad himself and perk himself, and in all ways painfully take heed of his goings; feeling (if we must admit it) that an altogether infinite endowment has been intrusted him also, namely, a Life to lead? Thus does he too, with his whole force, in his own way, proclaim that the world-old Rhapsodia of

Existence is divine, and an inspired Bible; and, himself a wondrous *verse* therein, (be it heroic, be it pasquillic,) study with his whole soul, as we said, both to *read* and *to be written!*

"Here also I will observe, that the *manner* in which men read this same Bible is, like all else, proportionate to their stage of culture, to the circumstances of their environment. First, and among the earliest Oriental nations, it was read wholly like a Sacred Book; most clearly by the most earnest, those wondrous Hebrew Readers; whose reading accordingly was itself sacred, has meaning for all tribes of mortal men; since ever, to the latest generation of the world, a true utterance from the innermost of man's being will speak significantly to man. But, again, in how different a style was that other Oriental reading of the Magi; of Zerdusht, or whoever it was that first so opened the matter? Gorgeous semi-sensual Grandeurs and Splendours; on infinite darkness brightest-glowing light and fire;—of which, all defaced by Time, and turned mostly into lies, a quite late reflex, in those Arabian Tales and the like, still leads captive every heart. Look thirdly at the earnest West, and that Consecration of the Flesh, which stept forth life-lusty, radiant, smiling-earnest, in immortal grace, from under the chisel and the stylus of old Greece. Here too was the Infinite intelligibly proclaimed as infinite: and the antique man walked between a Tartarus and an Elysium, his brilliant Paphos-islet of existence embraced by boundless oceans of sadness and fatal gloom.—Of which three antique manners of reading, our modern manner, you will remark, has been little more than the imitation; for always, indeed, the West has been rifer of doers than of speakers. The Hebrew manner has had its echo in our Pulpits and choral aisles; the Ethnic Greek and Arabian in numberless mountains of Fiction, rhymed, rhymeless, published by subscription, by puffery, in periodicals, or by money of your own, (*durch eignes Geld.*) Till now at last (by dint of iteration and reiteration through some ten centuries) all these manners have grown obsolete, wearisome, meaningless; listened to only as the monotonous moaning wind, while there is nothing else to listen to;—and so now, well nigh in total oblivion of the Infinitude of Life, (except what small *unconscious* recognition the 'straddling biped' above argued of may have,) we wait, in hope and patience, for some *fourth* manner of anew convincingly announcing it."

These singular sentences from the *Æsthetische Spring-würzel* we have thought right to translate and quote, by way of proem and apology. We are here about to give some critical account of what Herr Sauerteig would call a "flesh-and-blood Poem of the purest Pasquil sort;" in plain words, to examine the biography of the most perfect scoundrel that in these latter ages has marked the world's history. Pasquils too, says Sauerteig, "are at times worth reading." Or quitting that mystic dialect of his, may we not assert in our own way, that the history of an Original Man is always worth knowing? So magnificent a thing is Will, (incarnated in a creature of like fashion with ourselves,) we run to witness *all* manifestations thereof: what man soever has marked out a peculiar path of life for himself, (let it lead this way or that way,) and successfully travelled the same, of him we specially inquire, How he travelled; What befell him on the journey? Though the man were a knave of the first water, this hinders not the question, How he managed his knavery? Nay, it rather encourages such question; for nothing properly is wholly despicable, at once detestable and forgettable, but your half-knave, he who is neither true nor false; who never in his existence once spoke or did any true thing, (for indeed his mind lives in twilight with cat-vision, incapable of *discerning* truth;) and yet had not the manfulness to speak or act any decided lie; but spent his whole life in plastering together the True and the False, and therefrom manufacturing the Plausible. Such a one our Transcendentals have defined as a moral Hybrid and chimera; therefore, under the moral point of view, as an Impossibility, and mere deceptive Nonentity,—put together for commercial purposes. Of which sort, nevertheless, how many millions, through all manner of gradations, from the wielder of king's sceptres to the vender of brimstone matches, at tea-tables, council-tables, behind shop-counters, in priests' pulpits, incessantly and everywhere, do now, in this world of ours, in this isle of ours, offer themselves to view! From such, at least from this intolerable over-proportion of such, might the merciful Heavens one day deliver us. Glorious, heroic, fruitful for his own Time, and for all Time, (and all Eternity) is the constant Speaker and Doer of Truth! If no such again, in the present generation, is to be vouchsafed us, let us have at least the melancholy pleasure of beholding a decided Liar. Wretched mortal, that with a single eye to be "respectable," for ever sittest cobbling together Inconsistencies, which stick not for an hour, but require ever new gluten and labour,—will it, by no length of experience, no bounty of Time or Chance, be revealed to thee that Truth is of Heaven and Falsehood is of Hell; that if thou cast not from thee the one or the other, thy existence is wholly an illusion and optical and tactual Phantasm; that properly thou existest not at all? Respectable! What in the Devil's name, is the use of Respectability, (with never so many gigs and silver spoons,) if thou inwardly art the pitifullest of all men? I would thou wert either cold or hot.

One such desirable second-best, perhaps the chief of all such, we have here found in the Count Alessandro di Cagliostro, Pupil of the Sage Althotas, Foster-child of the Scherif of Mecca, probable Son of the last King of Trebisond; named also Acharat, and unfortunate child of Nature; by profession healer of diseases, abolisher of wrinkles, friend of the poor and impotent, grandmaster of the Egyptian Mason-lodge of High Science, Spirit-summoner, Gold-cook, Grand Cophta, Prophet, Priest, and thaumaturgic morallist and Swindler; really a Liar of the first magnitude, thoroughpaced in all provinces of lying, what one may call the King of Liars. Mendez Pinto, Baron Münchäusen, and others, are celebrated in this art, and not without some colour of justice; yet must it in candour remain doubtful whether any of these comparatively were much more than liars from the teeth onwards: a perfect character of the species in question, who lied not in word only, nor in act and word only, but continually, in thought, word, and act; and, so to speak, lived wholly in an element of lying, and from birth to death did nothing but lie,—was still a desideratum. Of which desideratum Count Alessandro offers, we say, if not the fulfilment, perhaps as near an approach to such as the limited human faculties permit. Not in the modern ages, probably not in the ancient, (though these had their Autolycus, their Apollonius, and enough else,) did any completer figure of this sort issue out of Chaos and Old Night: a sublime kind of figure, presenting himself with "the air of calm strength," of sure perfection in his art; whom the heart opens itself to with wonder and a sort of welcome. "The only vice, I know," says one, "is Inconsistency." At lowest, answered we, he that *does* his work shall have his work judged of. Indeed, if Satan himself has in these days become a poetic hero, why should not Cagliostro, for some short hour, be a prose one? "One first question," says a great Philosopher, "I ask of every man: Has he an aim, which with undivided soul he follows, and advances towards? Whether his aim is a right one or a wrong one, forms but my second question." Here then is a small "human Pasquil," not without poetic interest.

However, be this as it may, we apprehend the eye of science at least cannot view him with indifference. Doubtful, false as much is in Cagliostro's manner of being, of this there is no doubt, that starting from the lowest point of Fortune's wheel, he rose to a height universally notable; that, without external furtherance, money, beauty, bravery, almost without common sense, or any discernible worth whatever, he sumptuously supported, for a long course of years, the wants and digestion of one of the greediest bodies, and one of the greediest minds; outwardly in his five senses, inwardly in his "sixth sense, that of vanity," nothing straitened. Clear enough it is, however much may be supposititious, that this japanned Chariot, rushing through the world, with dust-clouds and loud noise, at the speed of four swift horses, and topheavy with luggage, has an existence. The six Beef-eaters too, that ride prosperously heralding his advent, honourably escorting, menially waiting on him, are they not realities? Ever must the purse open, paying turnpikes, tavern-bills, drink-moneys, and the thousandfold tear and wear of such a team; yet ever, like a horn-of-plenty, does it pour; and after brief rest, the chariot ceases not to roll. Whereupon rather pressingly rises the scientific question: How? Within that wonderful machinery, of horses, wheels, top-luggage, beef-eaters, sits only a gross, thickset individual, evincing dulness enough; and by his side a Seraphina, with a look of doubtful reputation: how comes it that means still meet ends, that the whole Engine (like a steam-coach wanting fuel) does not stagnate, go silent, and fall to pieces in the ditch? Such question did the scientific curiosity of the present writer often put: and for many a day in vain.

Neither, indeed, as Book-readers know, was he peculiar herein. The great Schiller, for example, struck both with the poetic and the scientific phases of the matter, admitted the influences of the former to shape themselves anew within him; and strove with his usual impetuosity to burst (since unlocking was impossible) the secrets of the latter: and so his unfinished Novel, the *Geisterseher*, saw the light. Still more renowned is Goethe's Drama of the *Gross-Kophta;* which, as himself informs us, delivered him from a state of mind that had become alarming to certain friends; so deep was the hold this business, at one of its epochs, had taken of him. A dramatic Fiction, that of his, based on the strictest possible historical study and inquiry; wherein perhaps the faithfullest image of the historical Fact, as yet extant in any shape, lies in artistic miniature curiously unfolded. Nay mere Newspaper-readers, of a certain age, can bethink them of our London Egyptian Lodges of High Science; of the Countess Seraphina's dazzling jewelleries, nocturnal brilliancies, sibyllic ministrations and revelations; of Miss Fry and Milord Scott, and Messrs. Priddle and Shark Bailiff; and Lord Mansfield's judgment-seat; the Comte d'Adhémar, the Diamond Necklace, and Lord George Gordon. For Cagliostro, hovering through unknown space, twice (perhaps thrice) lighted on our London, and did business in the great chaos there.

Unparalleled Cagliostro! Looking at thy so attractively decorated private theatre, wherein thou actedst and livedst, what hand but itches to draw aside thy curtain; overhaul thy paste-boards, paintpots, paper-mantles, stage-lamps, and turning the whole inside out, find *thee* in the middle thereof! For there of a truth wert thou: though the rest was all foam and sham, there sattest *thou,* as large as life, and as esurient; warring against the world, and indeed conquering the world, for it remained thy tributary, and yielded daily rations. Innumerable Sheriff's-officers, Exempts, Sbirri, Alguazils, of every European climate, were prowling on thy traces, their intents hostile enough; thyself wast single against them all; in the whole earth thou hadst no friend. What, say we in the whole earth? In the whole universe thou hadst no friend! Heaven knew nothing of thee (*could* in charity know nothing of thee;) and as for Beelzebub, *his* friendship, as is ascertained, cannot count for much.

But to proceed with business. The present inquirer, in obstinate investigation of a phenomenon so noteworthy, has searched through the whole not inconsiderable circle which his tether (of circumstances, geographical position, trade, health, extent of money capital) enables him to describe: and, sad to say, with the most imperfect results. He has read Books in various languages and jargons; feared not to soil his fingers, hunting through ancient dusty Magazines, to sicken his heart in any labyrinth of iniquity and imbecility;

nay he had not grudged to dive even into the infectious *Mémoirs de Casanova*, for a hint or two,—could he have found that work, which, however, most British Librarians make a point of denying that they possess. A painful search, as through some spiritual pest-house; and then with such issue! The quantity of discoverable Printing about Cagliostro (so much being burnt) is now not great; nevertheless in frightful proportion to the quantity of information given. Except vague Newspaper rumours and surmises, the things found written of this Quack are little more than temporary Manifestoes, by himself, by gulled or gulling disciples of his: not true therefore; at best only certain fractions of what he wished or expected the blinder Public to reckon true; misty, embroiled, for most part highly stupid; perplexing, even provoking; which can only be believed—to be (under such and such conditions) Lies. Of this sort emphatically is the English "*Life of the Count Cagliostro*, price three shillings and sixpence:" a Book indeed which one might hold (so fatuous, inane is it) to be some mere dream-vision and unreal eidolon, did it not now stand palpably there, as "Sold by T. Hookham, Bond Street, 1787;" and bear to be handled, spurned at, and torn into pipe-matches. Some human creature doubtless was at the writing of it; but of what kind, country, trade, character, or gender, you will in vain strive to fancy. Of like fabulous stamp are the *Mémoires pour le Comte de Cagliostro*, emitted with *Requête à joindre*, from the Bastille (during that sorrowful business of the Diamond Necklace) in 1786; no less the *Lettre du Comte de Cagliostro au Peuple Anglais*, which followed shortly after, at London; from which two indeed, that fatuous inexplicable English *Life* has perhaps been mainly manufactured. Next come the *Mémoires authentiques pour servir à l'Histoire du Comte de Cagliostro*, (twice printed in the same year 1786, at Strasburg and at Paris;) a swaggering, lascivious Novellette, without talent, without truth or worth, happily of small size. So fares it with us: alas, all this is but the *outside* decorations of the private theatre, or the sounding of catcalls and applauses from the stupid audience; nowise the interior bare walls and dress-room which we wanted to see! Almost our sole even half-genuine documents are a small barren Pamphlet, *Cagliostro démasqué à Varsovie, en* 1780; and a small barren Volume purporting to be his *Life*, written at Rome, of which latter we have a French version, dated 1791. It is on this *Vie de Joseph Balsamo, connu sous le Nom de Comte Cagliostro*, that our main dependence must be placed; of which Work, meanwhile, whether it is wholly or only half-genuine, the reader may judge by one fact: that it comes to us through the medium of the Roman Inquisition, and the proofs to substantiate it lie in the Holy Office there. Alas, this reporting Familiar of the Inquisition was too probably something of a Liar; and he reports lying Confessions of one who was not so much a Liar as a Lie! In such enigmatic duskiness, and thrice-folded involution, after all inquiries, does the matter yet hang.

Nevertheless, by dint of meditation and comparison, light-points that stand fixed, and abide scrutiny, do here and there disclose themselves; diffusing a fainter light over what otherwise were dark, so that it is no longer invisible, but only dim. Nay, after all, is there not in this same uncertainty a kind of fitness, of poetic congruity? Much that would offend the eye stands discreetly lapped in shade. Here too Destiny has cared for her favourite: that a powder-nimbus of astonishment, mystification, and uncertainty, should still encircle the Quack of Quacks, is right and suitable; such was by Nature and Art his chosen uniform and environment. Thus, as formerly in Life, so now in History, it is in huge fluctuating smoke-whirlwinds, partially illumed (into a most brazen glory,) yet united, coalescing with the region of everlasting Darkness, in miraculous clear-obscure, that he works and rides.

"Stern Accuracy in inquiring, bold Imagination in expounding and filling up; these," says friend Sauerteig, "are the two pinions on which History soars,"—or flutters and wabbles. To which two pinions let us and the readers of this Magazine now daringly commit ourselves. Or chiefly indeed to the *latter* pinion (of Imagination;) which, if it be the *larger*, will make an unequal flight. Meanwhile, the style at least shall if possible be equal to the subject.

Know, then, that in the year 1743, in the city of Palermo, in Sicily, the family of Signor Pietro Balsamo, a shopkeeper, were exhilerated by the birth of a Boy. Such occurrences have now become so frequent that, miraculous as they are, they occasion little astonishment: old Balsamo for a space, indeed, laid down his ell-wands and unjust balances; but for the rest, met the event with equanimity. Of the possettings, junkettings, gossippings, and other ceremonial rejoicings, transacted according to the custom of the country, for welcome to a New-comer, not the faintest tradition has survived; enough, that the small New-comer, hitherto a mere ethnic or heathen, is in a few days made a Christian of, or as we vulgarly say, christened; by the name of Giuseppe. A fat, red, globular kind of fellow, not under nine pounds avoirdupois, the bold Imagination can figure him to be: if not proofs, there are indications that sufficiently betoken as much.

Of his teething and swaddling adventures, of his scaldings, squallings, pukings, purgings, the strictest search into History can discover nothing; not so much as the epoch when he passed out of long-clothes stands noted in the fasti of Sicily. That same "larger pinion," (of Imagination,) nevertheless, conducts him from his native blind-alley, into the adjacent street *casaro;* descries him, with certain contemporaries now unknown, essaying himself in small games of skill; watching what phenomena, of carriage-transits, dog-battles, street-music, or such like, the neighbourhood might offer (intent above all on any windfall of chance *provender;*) now, with incipient scientific spirit, paddling in the gutters; now, as small poet, or maker, baking mud-pies. Thus does he tentatively coast along the outskirts of

Existence, till once he shall be strong enough to land and make a footing there. Neither does it seem doubtful that with the earliest exercise of speech, the gifts of simulation and dissimulation began to manifest themselves: Giuseppe (or Beppo, as he was now called) could indeed speak the truth,—but only when he saw his advantage in it. Hungry also, as above hinted, he too probably often was: a keen faculty of digestion, a meager larder within doors; these two circumstances, so frequently conjoined in this world, reduced him to his inventions. As to the thing called Morals, and knowledge of Right and Wrong, it seems pretty certain that such knowledge (the sad fruit of Man's Fall) had in great part been spared him; if he ever heard the commandment, *Thou shalt not steal*, he most probably could not believe in it, therefore could not obey it. For the rest, though of quick temper, and a ready striker, (where clear prospect of victory showed itself,) we fancy him vociferous rather than bellicose, not prone to violence where stratagem will serve; almost pacific, indeed, had not his many wants necessitated him to many conquests. Above all things, a brazen impudence developes itself; the crowning gift of one born to scoundrelism. In a word, the fat, thickset Beppo, as he skulks about there, plundering, playing dog's-tricks, with his finger in every mischief, already gains character; shrill housewives of the neighbourhood, whose sausages he has filched, whose weaker sons maltreated, name him Beppo Maldetto, and indignantly prophesy that he will be hanged. A prediction which, as will be seen, the issue has signally falsified.

We hinted that the household larder was in a leanish state: in fact, the outlook of the Balsamo family was getting troubled; old Balsamo had, during these things, been called away on his long journey. Poor man! The future eminence and pre-eminence of his Beppo he foresaw not, or what a world's-wonder he had thoughtlessly generated; as indeed, which of us, by much calculating, can sum up the net-total (Utility, or Inutility) of any his most indifferent act,—a seed cast into the seed-field of Time, to grow there, producing fruits or poisons, for ever! Meanwhile Beppo himself gazed heavily into the matter: hung his thick lips, while he saw his mother weeping; and, for the rest, eating what fat or sweet thing he could come at, let Destiny take its course.

The poor widow, (ill-named *Felicita*,) spinning out a painful livelihood by such means as only the poor and forsaken know, could not but many times cast an impatient eye on her brass-faced, voracious Beppo; and ask him, If he never meant to turn himself to any thing! A maternal uncle, of the moneyed sort, (for he has uncles not without influence,) has already placed him in the Seminary of Saint Roch, to gain some tincture of schooling there: but Beppo feels himself misplaced in that sphere; "more than once runs away;" is flogged, snubbed, tyrannically checked on all sides; and finally, with such slender stock of schooling as had pleased to offer itself, returns to the street. The widow, as we said, urges him, the uncles urge: Beppo, wilt thou never turn thyself to any thing? Beppo, with such speculative faculty, from such low watch-tower, as he commands, is in truth, (being forced to it,) from time to time, looking abroad into the world; surveying the conditions of mankind, therewith contrasting his own wishes and capabilities. Alas, his wishes are manifold; a most hot Hunger, (in all kinds,) as above hinted; but on the other hand, his leading capability seemed only the Power to Eat. What profession, or condition, then? Choose; for it is time. Of all the terrestrial professions, that of Gentleman, it seemed to Beppo, had, under these circumstances, been most suited to his feelings: but then the outfit? the apprentice-fee? Failing which, he, with perhaps as much sagacity as one could expect, decides for the Ecclesiastical.

Behold him then, once more by the uncle's management, journeying (a chubby, brass-faced boy of thirteen) beside the Reverend Father General of the Benfratelli, to their neighbouring Convent of Cartegirone, with intent to enter himself novice there. He has donned the novice-habit; is "intrusted to the keeping of the Convent Apothecary," on whose gallipots and crucibles he looks round with wonder. Were it by accident that he found himself Apothecary's Famulus, were it by choice of his own—nay was it not, in either case, by *design*, of Destiny intent on perfecting her work?—enough, in this Cartegirone Laboratory there awaited him, (though as yet he knew it not,) life-guidance and determination; the great want of every genius, even of the scoundrel-genius. He himself confesses that he here learned some (or, as he calls it, *the*) "principles of chemistry and medicine." Natural enough: new books of the Chemists lay here, old books of the Alchymists; distillations, sublimations visibly went on; discussions there were, oral and written, of gold-making, salve-making, treasure-digging, divining-rods, projection, and the alcahest: besides, had he not, among his fingers, calxes, acids, Leyden-jars? Some first elements of medico-chemical conjurorship, so far as phosphorescent mixtures, aqua-toffana, ipecacuanha, cantharides tincture, and such like would go, were now attainable; sufficient (when the hour came) to set up any average Quack, much more the Quack of Quacks. It is here, in this unpromising environment, that the seeds, therapeutic, thaumaturgic, of the Grand Cophta's stupendous workings and renown were sown.

Meanwhile, as observed, the environment looked unpromising enough. Beppo with his two endowments, of Hunger and of Power to Eat, had made the best choice he could; yet, as it soon proved, a rash and disappointing one. To his astonishment, he finds that even here he "is in a conditional world;" and, if he will employ his capability of eating, (or enjoying,) must first, in some measure, work and suffer. Contention enough hereupon: but now dimly arises, or reproduces itself, the question, Whether there were not a *shorter* road, that of stealing! Stealing,—under which, generically taken, you may include the whole art of scoundrelism; for what is Lying itself but a *theft* of my belief?—stealing, we say, is properly the North-West Passage to Enjoyment: while common Navigators sail painfully along torrid shores, laboriously doubling this or the other Cape of Hope, your adroit Thief-Parry, drawn on smooth dog-sledges, is already there and back again. The misfortune is that stealing requires a talent; and failure in that North-West voyage is more fatal than in any other. We hear that Beppo was "often punished:" painful experiences of the fate of genius; for all genius, by its nature, comes to disturb *somebody* in his ease, and your thief-genius more so than most!

Readers can now fancy the sensitive skin of Beppo mortified with prickly cilices, wealed by knotted thongs; his soul afflicted by vigils and forced fasts; no eye turned kindly on him; everywhere the bent of his genius rudely contravened. However, it is the first property of genius to grow in spite of contradiction, and even by means thereof;—as the vital germ pushes itself through the dull soil, and lives by what strove to bury it! Beppo, waxing into strength of bone and character, sets his face stiffly against persecution, and is not a whit disheartened. On *such* chastisements and chastisers he can look with a certain genial disdain. Beyond convent walls, with their sour stupid shavelings, lies Palermo, lies the world; here too is he, still alive,—though worse off than he wished; and feels that the world is his oyster, which he (by chemical or other means) will one day open. Nay, we find there is a touch of grim Humour unfolds itself in the youth; the surest sign (as is often said) of a character naturally great. Witness, for example, how he acts on this to his ardent temperament so trying occasion. While the monks sit at meat, the impetuous voracious Beppo (that stupid Inquisition Biographer records it as a thing of course) is set not to eat with them, not to pick up the crumbs that fall from them, but to stand "reading the Martyrology" for their pastime! The brave adjusts himself to the inevitable. Beppo reads that dullest Martyrology of theirs; but reads out of it not what is printed there, but what his own vivid brain on the spur of the moment devises: instead of the names of Saints, all heartily indifferent to him, he reads out the names of the most notable Palermo "unfortunate-females," now beginning to interest him a little. What a "deep world-irony" (as the Germans call it) lies here! The Monks, of course, felled him to the earth, and flayed him with scourges; but what did it avail? This only became apparent, to himself and them, that he had now outgrown their monk discipline; as the psyche does its chrysalis-shell, and bursts it. Giuseppe Balsamo bids farewell to Cartegirone for ever and a day.

So now, by consent or not of the ghostly Benfratelli (Friars of *Mercy*, as they were named!) our Beppo has again returned to the maternal uncle at Palermo. The uncle naturally asked him, What he next meant to do? Beppo, after stammering and hesitating for some length of weeks, makes answer: Try Painting. Well and good! So Beppo gets him colours, brushes, fit tackle, and addicts himself for some space of time to the study of what is innocently called *Design*. Alas, if we consider Beppo's great Hunger, now that new senses were unfolding in him, how inadequate are the exiguous resources of Design; how necessary to attempt quite another deeper species of Design, of Designs! It is true, he lives with his uncle, has culinary meat; but where is the pocket-money for other costlier sorts of meats to come from? As the Kaiser Joseph was wont to say: From my head alone (*De ma tête seule!*)

The Roman Biographer (though a most wooden man) has incidentally thrown some light on Beppo's position at this juncture: both on his wants and his resources. As to the first, it appears (using the wooden man's phraseology) that he kept the "worst company," led the "loosest life;" was hand in glove with all the swindlers, gamblers, idle apprentices, unfortunate-females, of Palermo: in the study and practice of Scoundrelism diligent beyond most. The genius which has burst asunder convent-walls, and other rubbish of impediments, now flames upward towards its mature splendour. Wheresoever a stroke of mischief is to be done, a slush of so-called vicious enjoyment to be swallowed, there with hand and throat is Beppo Balsamo seen. He will be a Master, one day, in his profession. Not indeed that he has yet quitted Painting, or even purposes so much: for the present, it is useful, indispensable, as a stalking-horse to the maternal uncle and neighbours; nay to himself, for with all the ebullient impulses of scoundrel-genius restlessly seething in him, irrepressibly bursting through, he has the noble unconsciousness of genius; guesses not, dares not guess, that he is a born scoundrel, much less a born world-scoundrel.

But as for the other question, of his resources, these we perceive were several-fold, and continually extending. Not to mention any pictorial exiguities, (existing mostly in Expectance,) there had almost accidentally arisen for him, in the first place, the resource of Pandering. He has a fair cousin living in the house with him, and she again has a lover; Beppo stations himself as go-between; delivers letters; fails not to drop hints that a lady, to be won or kept, must be generously treated; that such and such a pair of ear-rings, watch, necklace, or even sum of money, would work wonders; which valuables (adds the wooden Roman Biographer) "he then appropriated furtively." Like enough! Next, however, as another more lasting resource, he forges; at first in a small way, and trying his apprentice-hand: tickets for the theatre, and such trifles. Ere long, however, we see him fly at higher quarry; by practice he has acquired perfection in the great art of counterfeiting hands; and will exercise it on the large or on the narrow scale, for a consideration. Among his relatives is a Notary, with whom he can insinuate himself; for purpose of study, or even of practice. In the presses of this Notary lies a Will, which Beppo contrives to come at, and falsify "for the benefit of a certain Religious House." Much good may it do them! Many years afterwards, the fraud was detected; but Beppo's benefit in it was spent and safe long before. Thus again the stolid Biographer expresses horror or wonder that he should have forged leave-of-absence for a monk, "counterfeiting the signature of the Superior." Why not? A forger must forge what is wanted of him; the Lion truly preys not on mice; yet shall he refuse such if they jump into his mouth? Enough, the indefatigable Beppo has here opened a quite boundless mine; wherein through his whole life he will, as occasion calls, dig, at his convenience. Finally, he can predict fortunes and show visions; by phosphorus and legerdemain. This however, only as a dilettantism; to take up the earnest profession of Magician does not yet enter into his views. Thus perfecting himself in all branches of his art, does our Balsamo live and grow. Stupid, pudding-faced as he looks and is, there is a vulpine astucity in him; and then a wholeness, a heartiness, a kind of blubbery impetuosity, an oiliness so plausible-looking: give him only length of life, he will rise to the top of his profession.

Consistent enough with such blubbery impetuosity in Beppo is another fact we find recorded of him, that at this time he was found "in most brawls," whether in street or tavern. The way of his business led him into liability to such; neither as yet had he learned prudence by age. Of choleric temper, with all his obesity; a square-built, burly, vociferous fellow; ever ready with his stroke, (if victory seemed sure;) nay, at bottom, not without a certain pig-like defensive-ferocity, perhaps even something more. Thus, when you find him making a point to attack, if possible, "*all* officers of justice," and deforce them; delivering the wretched from their talons: was not this, we say, a kind of dog-faithfulness, and public spirit, either of the mastiff or of the cur species? Perhaps, too, there was a touch of that old Humour and "world-irony" in it. One still more unquestionable feat he is recorded (we fear, on imperfect evidence) to have done: "assassinated a canon."

Remonstrances from growling maternal uncles could not fail; threats, disdains from ill-affected neighbours; tears from an expostulating widowed mother; these he shakes from him like dewdrops from the lion's mane. Still less could the Police neglect him; him the visibly rising Professor of Swindlery; the swashbuckler, to boot, and deforcer of bailiffs: he has often been captured, haled to their bar; yet hitherto, by defect of evidence, by good luck, intercession of friends, been dismissed with admonition. Two things, nevertheless, might now be growing clear: first, that the die was cast with Beppo, and he a scoundrel for life; second, that such a mixed, composite, crypto-scoundrel life could not endure, but must unfold itself into a pure, declared one. The Tree that is planted stands not still; *must* pass through all its stages and phases, from the state of acorn to that of green leafy oak, of withered leafless oak; to the state of felled timber, finally to that of firewood and ashes. Not less (though less visibly to dull eyes) the Act that is done, the Condition that has realized itself; above all things, the Man (with his Fortunes) that has been born. Beppo, every way in vigorous vitality, cannot continue half painting half swindling in Palermo; must develop himself into whole swindler; and, unless hanged there, seek his bread elsewhere. What the proximate cause, or signal, of such crisis and development might be, no man could say; yet most men would have confidently guessed, The Police. Nevertheless it proved otherwise; not by the flaming sword of Justice, but by the rusty dirk of a foolish private individual, is Beppo driven forth.

Walking one day in the fields (as the bold historic Imagination will figure) with a certain ninny of a "Goldsmith named Marano," as they pass one of those rock-chasms frequent in the fair Island of Sicily, Beppo begins, in his oily, voluble way, to hint that Treasures often lay hid; that a Treasure lay hid *there* (as he knew by some pricking of his thumbs, divining rod, or other talismanic monition;) which Treasure might, by aid of science, courage, secrecy, and a small judicious advance of money, be fortunately lifted. The gudgeon takes: advances (by degrees) to the length of "sixty gold Ounces;" sees magic circles drawn in the wane or in the full of the moon, blue (phosphorus) flames arise, split twigs auspiciously quiver; and at length—demands peremptorily that the Treasure be dug. A night is fixed on: the ninny Goldsmith, trembling with rapture and terror, breaks ground; digs, with thick breath and cold sweat, fiercely down, down, Beppo relieving him: the work advances; when, ah! at a certain stage of it (*before* fruition) hideous yells arise, a jingle like the emptying of Birmingham; six Devils pounce upon the poor sheep Goldsmith, and beat him almost to *mutton;* mercifully sparing Balsamo,—who indeed has himself summoned them thither, and as it were created them (with goatskins and burnt cork.) Marano, though a ninny, now knew how it lay; and furthermore that he had a stiletto. One of the grand drawbacks of swindler-genius! You accomplish the Problem; and then—the Elementary Quantities (Algebraic Symbols) you worked on will fly in your face!

Hearing of stilettos, our Algebraist begins to look around him, and view his empire of Palermo in the concrete. An empire now much exhausted; much infested, too, with sorrows of all kinds, and every day the more; nigh ruinous, in short; not worth being stabbed for. There is a world elsewhere. In any case, the young Raven has now shed his pens, and got fledged for flying. Shall he not spurn the whole from him, and soar off? Resolved, performed! Our Beppo quits Palermo; and, as it proved, on a long voyage: or as the Inquisition Biographer has it, "he fled from Palermo, and overran the whole Earth."

Here then ends the First Act of Count Alessandro Cagliostro's Life-drama. Let the curtain drop; and hang unrent, before an audience of mixed feeling, till the First of August.

COUNT CAGLIOSTRO.

IN TWO FLIGHTS.

[FRASER'S MAGAZINE, 1833.]

Flight Last.

BEFORE entering on the second Section of Count Beppo's History, the Editor will indulge in a philosophical reflection.

This Beppic Hegira (Flight from Palermo) we have now arrived at brings us down, in European History, to somewhere about the epoch of the Peace of Paris. Old Feudal Europe (while he flies forth into the whole Earth) has just finished the last of her "tavern brawls," (or wars;) and lain down to doze, and yawn, and disconsolately wear off the headaches, bruises, nervous prostration, and flaccidity consequent thereon: for the brawl had been a long one, (Seven Years long;) and there had been many such, begotten, as is usual, of Intoxication, (from Pride, or other Devil's-drink,) and foul humours in the constitution. Alas, it was not so much a disconsolate doze, after ebriety and quarrel, that poor old Feudal Europe had now to undergo, and then on awakening to drink anew (wine of Abomination,) and quarrel anew: old Feudal Europe has fallen a-dozing to die! Her next awakening will be with no tavern-brawl (at the *King's Head* or *Prime Minister;*) but with the stern Avatar of DEMOCRACY, hymning its world-thrilling birth and battle song in the distant West;—therefrom to go out conquering and to conquer, till it have made the circuit of all the Earth, and old dead Feudal Europe is born again (after infinite pangs!) into a new Industrial one. At Beppo's Hegira, as we said, Europe was in the last languor and stertorous fever-sleep of Dissolution: alas, with us and with our sons, (for a generation or two,) it is almost still worse,—were it not that in Birth-throes there is ever Hope, in Death-throes the final departure of Hope.

Now the philosophic reflection we were to indulge in, was no other than this, most germane to our subject: the portentous extent of Quackery, the multitudinous variety of Quacks that along with our Beppo, and under him each in his degree, overran all Europe during that same period, the latter half of last century. It was the very age of impostors, cut-purses, swindlers, double-gangers, enthusiasts, ambiguous persons; quacks simple, quacks compound; crack-brained, or with deceit prepense; quacks and quackeries of all colours and kinds. How many Mesmerists, Magicians, Cabalists, Swedenborgians, Illuminati, Crucified Nuns, and Devils of Loudun! To which the Inquisition Biographer adds Vampires, Sylphs, Rosicrucians, Free-masons, and an *Et cetera.* Consider your Schröpfers, Cagliostros, Casanovas, Saint-Germains, Dr. Grahams; the Chevalier d'Eon, Psalmanazar, Abbé Paris, and the Ghost of Cock-lane! As if Bedlam had broken loose; as if rather (in that "spiritual Twelfth-hour of the Night") the everlasting Pit had opened itself, and from its still blacker bosom had issued Madness and all manner of shapeless Misbirths, to masquerade and chatter there.

But, indeed, if we consider, how could it be otherwise? In that stertorous last fever-sleep of our European world, must not Phantasms enough (born of the Pit, as all such *are*) flit past, in ghastly masquerading and chattering? A low scarce-audible moan (in Parliamentary Petitions, Meal-mobs, Popish Riots, Treatises on Atheism) struggles from the moribund sleeper; frees him not from his hellish guests and saturnalia: Phantasms these "of a dying brain." So too, when the old Roman world, the measure of its iniquities being full, was to expire, and (in still bitter agonies) be born again, had they not Veneficæ, Mathematici, Apolloniuses with the Golden Thigh, Apollonius' Asses, and False Christs enough,—before a REDEEMER arose!

For, in truth, and altogether apart from such half-figurative language, Putrescence is not more naturally the scene of unclean creatures in the world physical, than Social Decay is of quacks in the world moral. Nay, look at it with the eye of the mere Logician, of the Political Economist. In such periods of Social Decay, what is called an overflowing Population, that is a Population which, under the old Captains of Industry, (named Higher Classes, *Ricos Hombres*, Aristocracies, and the like,) can no longer find work and wages, increases the number of Unprofessionals, Lack-alls, Social Nondescripts; with appetite of utmost keenness, which there is no known method of satisfying. Nay more, and perversely enough, ever as Population augments, your Captains of Industry can and do dwindle more and more into Captains of Idleness; whereby the more and more overflowing Population is worse and worse governed (shown *what to do*, for that is the only government:) thus is the candle lighted at both ends; and the number of social Nondescripts increases in *double*-quick ratio. Whoso is alive, it is said, "must live;" at all events, will live; a task which daily gets harder, reduces to stranger shifts. And now furthermore, with general economic distress, in such a Period, there is usually conjoined the utmost decay of moral principle: indeed, so universal is this conjunction, many men have seen it to be a concatenation and causation; justly enough, except that such have (ever since a certain religious-repentant feeling went out of date) committed one sore mistake: what is vulgarly called putting the cart before the horse. Political-Economical Benefactor of the Species! deceive not thyself with barren sophisms: National suffering *is* (if thou wilt understand the words) verily a "judgment of

God;" has ever been preceded by national crime. "Be it here once more maintained before the world," cries Sauerteig, in one of his *Springwürzel*, "that temporal Distress, that Misery of any kind, is not the *cause* of Immortality, but the effect thereof! Among individuals, it is true, so wide is the empire of Chance, poverty and wealth go all at hap-hazard; a Saint Paul is making tents at Corinth, while a Kaiser Nero fiddles, in ivory palaces over a burning Rome. Nevertheless here too, if nowise wealth and poverty, yet well-being and ill-being, even in the temporal economic sense, go commonly in respective partnership with Wisdom and with Folly: no man can, for a length of time, be wholly wretched, if there is not a disharmony (a folly and wickedness) within himself; neither can the richest Crœsus, and never so eupeptic, (for he too has indigestions and dies at last from surfeit,) be other than discontented, perplexed, unhappy, if he be a Fool."—This we apprehend is true, O Sauerteig, yet not the whole truth: for there is more than days' work and days' wages in this world of ours; which, as thou knowest, is itself quite other than a "Workshop and Fancy-Bazaar," is also a "mystic Temple and Hall of Doom." Thus we have heard of such things as good men struggling with adversity, and offering a spectacle for the very gods.—"But with a nation," continues he, "where the multitude of the chances covers, in great measure, the uncertainty of Chance, it may be said to hold always that general Suffering is the fruit of general Misbehaviour, general Dishonesty. Consider it well; had all men stood faithfully to their posts, the Evil, when it first rose, had been manfully fronted, and abolished, not lazily blinked, and left to grow, with the foul sluggard's comfort: 'It will last my time.' Thou foul sluggard, and even thief (*Faulenzer, ja Dieb!*) For art thou not a thief, to pocket thy day's wages (be they counted in *groschen* or in gold thousands) for this, if it be for any thing, for watching on thy special watch-tower that God's City (which this His World is, where His children dwell) suffer no damage; and, all the while, to watch only that thy own ease be not invaded,—let otherwise hard come to hard as it will and can? Unhappy! It will last thy time: thy worthless sham of an existence, wherein nothing but the Digestion was real, will have evaporated in the interim; it will last thy time: but will it last thy *Eternity?* Or what if it should *not* last thy time, (mark that also, for that also will be the fate of *some* such lying sluggard;) but take fire, and explode, and consume thee like the moth!"

The sum of the matter, in any case, is, that national Poverty and national Dishonesty go together; that continually increasing social Nondescripts get ever the hungrier, ever the falser. Now say, have we not here the very making of Quackery; raw-material, plastic-energy, both in full action? Dishonesty the raw-material, Hunger the plastic-energy: what will not the two realize? Nay observe farther how Dishonesty is the raw-material not of Quacks only, but also, in great part, of Dupes. In Goodness, were it never so simple, there is the surest instinct for the Good; the uneasiest unconquerable repulsion for the False and Bad. The very Devil Mephistopheles cannot deceive poor guileless Margaret: "it stands written on his front that he never loved a living soul." The like too has many a human inferior Quack painfully experienced; the like lies in store for our hero Beppo. But now with such abundant raw-material not only to make Quacks of, but to feed and occupy them on, if the plastic-energy (of Hunger) fail not, what a world shall we have! The wonder is not that the eighteenth century had very numerous Quacks, but rather that they were not innumerable.

In that same French Revolution alone, which burnt up so much, what unmeasured masses of Quackism were set fire to; nay, as foul mephitic fire-damp in that case, were made to flame in a fierce, sublime *splendour;* coruscating, even illuminating! The Count Saint Germain, some twenty years later, had found a quite new element, of Fraternization, Sacred right of Insurrection, Oratorship of the Human Species, wherefrom to body himself forth quite otherwise: Schröpfer needed not now, as Blackguard undeterred, have solemnly shot himself in the *Rosenthal;* might have solemnly sacrificed himself, as Jacobin half-heroic, in the *Place de la Révolution.* For your quack-genius is indeed born, but also made; circumstances shape him or stunt him. Beppo Balsamo, born British in these new days, could have conjured fewer Spirits; yet had found a living and glory, as Castlereagh Spy, Irish Associationist, Blacking-Manufacturer, Book-Publisher, Able Editor. Withal too the reader will observe that Quacks, in every time, are of two sorts: the Declared Quack; and the Undeclared, who, if you question him, will deny stormfully, both to others and to himself; of which two quack-species the proportions vary with the varying capacity of the age. If Beppo's was the age of the Declared, therein, after all French Revolutions, we will grant, lay one of its main distinctions from ours; which is it not yet (and for a generation or two) the age of the Undeclared? Alas, almost a still more detestable age;—yet now (by God's grace) with Prophecy, with irreversible Enactment (registered in Heaven's chancery,—where *thou* too, if thou wilt *look*, mayst read and know) that its death-doom shall not linger. Be it speedy, be it sure!—And so herewith were our philosophical reflection, on the nature, causes, prevalence, decline, and expected (temporary) destruction of Quackery, concluded; and now the Beppic poetic Narrative can once more take its course.

Beppo then, like a Noah's Raven, is out upon that watery waste, (of dissolute, beduped, distracted European Life,) to see if there is any carrion there. One unguided little Raven, in the wide-weltering "Mother of dead Dogs:" will he not come to harm; will he not be snapt up, drowned, starved, and washed to the Devil there? No fear of him,—for a time. His eye, (or scientific judgment,) it is true, as yet takes in only a small section of it; but then his scent (instinct of genius) is prodigious: several endowments (forgery and others) he has unfolded into talents; the two sources of all quack-talent, Cunning and Impudence, are his in richest measure.

As to his immediate course of action and adventure, the foolish Inquisition Biographer, it must be owned, shows himself a fool, and can give us next to no insight. Like enough, Beppo "fled to Messina;" simply as to the nearest city, and to get across to the mainland: but as to this "certain Althotas" whom he met there, and voyaged with to Alexandria in Egypt, and how they made hemp into silk, and realized much money, and came to Malta, and studied in the Laboratory there, and then the certain Althotas died,—of all this what shall be said? The foolish Inquisition Biographer is uncertain whether the certain Althotas was a Greek or a Spaniard: but unhappily the prior question is not settled, whether he *was* at all. Superfluous it seems to put down Beppo's own account of his procedure; he gave multifarious accounts, as the exigencies of the case demanded: this of the "certain Althotas," and hemp made into false silk, is as verisimilar as that other of the "sage Althotas," the heirship-apparent of Trebisond, and the Scherif of Mecca's "Adieu, unfortunate Child of Nature." Nay the guesses of the ignorant world; how Count Cagliostro had been travelling tutor to a Prince, (name not given,) whom he murdered and took the money from; with others of the like,—were perhaps still more absurd. Beppo, we can see, was out and away,—the Devil knew whither. Far, variegated, painful, might his roamings be. A plausible-looking shadow of him shows itself hovering over Naples and Calabria; thither, as to a famed high-school of Laziness and Scoundrelism, he may likely enough have gone to graduate. Of the Malta Laboratory, and Alexandrian hemp-silk, the less we say the better. This only is clear: That Beppo dived deep down into the lugubrious-obscure regions of Rascaldom; like a Knight to the palace of his Fairy; remained unseen there, and returned thence armed at all points.

If we fancy, meanwhile, that Beppo already meditated becoming grand Cophta, and riding at Strasburg in the Cardinal's carriage, we mistake much. Gift of Prophecy has been wisely denied to man. Did a man *foresee* his life, and not merely *hope* it, and grope it, and so, by Necessity and Free-will, make and fabricate it into a reality, he were no *man*, but some other kind of creature, superhuman or subterhuman. No man sees far: the most see no farther than their noses. From the quite dim uncertain mass of the future, ("lying there," says a Scotch Humourist, "uncombed, uncarded, like a mass of *tarry wool* proverbially *ill to spin*,") they spin out, better or worse, their rumply, infirm thread of Existence, (and wind it up, up—till the spool is *full;*) seeing but some little half-yard of it at once; exclaiming, as they look into the betarred, entangled mass of Futurity, We *shall* see!

The first authentic fact with regard to Beppo is, that his swart squat figure becomes visible in the Corso and Campo Vaccino of Rome; that he "lodges at the Sign of the Sun in the Rotunda," and sells pen-drawings there. Properly they are not pen-drawings; but printed engravings or etchings, to which Beppo, with a pen and a little Indian ink, has added the degree of scratching to give them the air of such. Thereby mainly does he realize a thin livelihood. From which we infer that his transactions in Naples and Calabria, with Althotas and hemp-silk, or whatever else, had not turned to much.

Forged pen-drawings are no mine of wealth: neither was Beppo Balsamo any thing of an Adonis; on the contrary, a most dusky, bull-necked, mastiff-faced, sinister-looking individual: nevertheless, on applying for the favour or the hand of Lorenza Feliciani, a beautiful Roman donzella, "dwelling near the Trinity of the Pilgrims," the unfortunate child of Nature prospers beyond our hopes. Authorities differ as to the rank and status of fair Lorenza: one account says, she was the daughter of a Girdle-maker; but adds erroneously that it was in Calabria. The matter must remain suspended. Certain enough, she was a handsome buxom creature, "both pretty and lady-like," (it is presumable;) but having no offer, in a country too prone to celibacy, took up with the bull-necked forger of pen-drawings, whose suit too was doubtless pressed with the most flowing rhetoric. She gave herself in marriage to him; and the parents admitted him to quarter in their house, till it should appear what was next to be done.

Two kitchen-fires, says the Proverb, burn not on one hearth: here, moreover, might be quite special causes of discord. Pen-drawing, at best a hungry concern, has now exhausted itself, and must be given up: but Beppo's household prospects brighten, on the other side; in the charms of his Lorenza he sees before him what the French call "a Future confused and immense." The hint was given; and with reluctance, or without reluctance, (for the evidence leans *both* ways,) was taken and reduced to practice: Signor and Signora Balsamo are forth from the old Girdler's house, into the wide world, seeking and finding adventures.

The foolish Inquisition Biographer, with painful scientific accuracy, furnishes a descriptive catalogue of all the successive Cullies (Italian Counts, French Envoys, Spanish Marquises, Dukes, and Drakes) in various quarters of the known world, whom this accomplished pair took in; with the sums each yielded, and the methods employed to bewitch him. Into which descriptive catalogue, why should we here so much as cast a glance? Cullies, (the easy cushions on which knaves and knavesses repose and fatten,) have at all times existed in considerable profusion: neither can the fact of a "clothed animal," (Marquis or other,) having acted in that capacity to never such lengths, entitle him to mention in History. We pass over these. Beppo (or, as we must now learn to call him, the Count) appears at Venice, at Marseilles, at Madrid, Cadiz, Lisbon, Brussels; makes scientific pilgrimage to Saint-Germain, (in Westphalia,) religious commercial to Saint James in Compostella, to Our Lady in Loretta: south, north, east, west, he shows himself; finds everywhere Lubricity and Stupidity, (better or worse provided with cash,) the two elements on which he thaumaturgically can work and live. Practice makes perfection; Beppo too was an apt scholar. By all methods he can awaken the stagnant imagination; cast maddening powder in the eyes. Already in Rome he has cultivated whiskers, and put on the uniform of a Prussian Colonel: dame Lorenza is fair to look upon; but how much fairer, if by the air of distance and dignity you lend enchantment to her! In other places, the Count appears as real Count; as Marquis Pelligrini, (lately from foreign parts;) as Count this and Count that, Count Proteus-Incognito; finally as Count Alessandro Cagliostro.* Figure him shooting through the world with utmost rapidity; ducking under here, when the sword-fishes (of justice) make a dart at him; ducking up yonder, in new shape, at the distance of a thousand miles; not unprovided with forged vouchers of Respectability; above all, with that best voucher of Respectability, a four-horse carriage, beef-eaters, and open purse, for Count Cagliostro has ready money and pays his way. At some Hotel of the Sun, Hotel of the Angel, Gold Lion, or Green Goose, or whatever Hotel it is, in whatever world famous City, his chariot-wheels have rested; sleep and food have refreshed his live-stock, chiefly the pearl and soul thereof, his indispensable Lorenza, now no longer Dame Lorenza, but Countess Seraphina, looking seraphic enough! Moneyed Donothings, whereof in this vexed Earth there are many, ever lounging about such places, scan and comment on the foreign coat-of-arms; ogle the fair foreign woman; who timidly recoils from their gaze, timidly responds to their reverences, as in halls and passages, they obsequiously throw themselves in her way: ere long one moneyed Donothing (from amid his tags, tassels, sword-belts, fop-tackle, frizzled hair without brains beneath it) is heard speaking to another: "Seen the Countess?—Divine creature that!" and so the game is begun.

Let not the too sanguine reader, meanwhile, fancy that it is all holyday and heyday with his lordship. The course of Scoundrelism, any more than that of true love, never did run smooth. Seasons there may be when Count Proteus-Incognito has his epaulettes torn from his shoulders; his garment-skirts clipt close by the buttocks; and is bid sternly tarry at Jericho till his beard be grown. Harpies of Law defile his solemn feasts; his light burns languid; for a space seems utterly snuffed out, and dead in malodorous vapour. Dead only to blaze up the brighter! There is scoundrel-life in Beppo Cagliostro; cast him among the mud, tread him out of sight there, the miasmata do but stimulate and refresh him, he rises sneezing, is strong and young again.

Behold him, for example, again in Palermo, (after having seen many men and many lands;) and how he again escapes thence. Why did he return to Palermo? Perhaps to astonish old friends by new grandeur; or for temporary shelter, if the Continent were getting hot for him; or perhaps in the mere way of general trade. He is seized there, and clapt in prison, for those foolish old businesses of the treasure-digging Goldsmith, of the forged Will.

"The manner of his escape," says one, whose few words on this obscure matter are so many light-points for us, "deserves to be described. The son of one of the first Sicilian Princes, and great landed Proprietors, (who moreover had filled important stations at the Neapolitan Court,) was a person that united with a strong body and ungovernable temper all the tyrannical caprice, which the rich and great, without cultivation, think themselves entitled to exhibit.

"Donna Lorenza had contrived to gain this man; and on him the fictitious Marchese Pellegrini founded his security. The Prince testified openly that he was the protector of this stranger pair: but what was his fury when Joseph Balsamo, at the instance of those whom he had cheated, was cast into prison! He tried various means to deliver him; and as these would not prosper, he publicly, in the President's antechamber, threatened the plaintiffs' Advocate with the frightfullest misusage if the suit were not dropt, and Balsamo forthwith set at liberty. As the Advocate declined such proposal, he clutched him, beat him, threw him on the floor, trampled him with his feet, and could hardly be restrained from still farther outrages, when the President himself came running out, at the tumult, and commanded peace.

"This latter, a weak, dependent man, made no attempt to punish the injurer; the plaintiffs and their Advocate grew fainthearted; and Balsamo was let go; not so much as a registration in the Court-Books specifying his dismissal, who occasioned it, or how it took place."*

Thus sometimes, "a friend in the court is better than a penny in the purse!" Marchese Pellegrini "quickly thereafter left Palermo, and performed various travels, thereof my author could impart no clear information." Whither, or how far, the Game-chicken Prince went with him is not hinted.

So it might, at times, be quite otherwise than in coach-and-four that our Cagliostro journeyed. Occasionally we find him as outrider journeying on horseback; only Seraphina and her sop (whom she is to suck and eat) lolling on carriage-cushions; the hardy Count glad that hereby he can have the shot paid. Nay sometimes he looks utterly poverty-struck, and must journey one knows not how. Thus one briefest but authentic-looking glimpse of him presents itself in England, in the year 1772: no Count is he here, but mere Signor Balsamo again; engaged in house-painting, for which he has a most peculiar talent. Was it true that he painted the country house of "a Doctor Benemore;" and having not painted, but only smeared it, was refused payment, and got a lawsuit with expenses instead? If Dr. Benemore have left any representatives in this Earth, they are desired to speak out. We add only, that if young Beppo had one of the pret-

* Not altogether an *invention* this last; for his grand-uncle (a bell-founder at Messina?) was actually surnamed *Cagliostro*, as well as named *Giuseppe*.—O. Y.

* Goethe's *Werke*, b. xxviii 132.

tiest wives, old Benemore had one of the ugliest daughters; and so, putting one thing to another, matters might not be so bad.

For it is to be observed, that the Count, on his own side, even in his days of highest splendour, is not idle. Faded dames of quality have many wants: the Count has not studied in the convent Laboratory, or pilgrimed to the Count Saint-Germain, in Westphalia, to no purpose. With loftiest condescension he stoops to impart somewhat of his supernatural secrets,—for a consideration. Rowland's Kalydor is valuable; but what to the Beautifying-water of Count Alessandro! He that will undertake to smooth wrinkles, and make withered green parchment into a fair carnation skin, is he not one whom faded dames of quality will delight to honour? Or again, let the Beautifying-water succeed or not, have not such dames (if calumny may be in aught believed) *another* want? This want too the indefatigable Cagliostro will supply,—for a consideration. For faded gentlemen of quality the Count likewise has help. Not a charming Countess alone; but a "Wine of Egypt," (cantharides not being unknown to him,) sold in drops, more precious than nectar; which what faded gentleman of quality would not purchase with any thing short of life? Consider now what may be done with potions, washes, charms, love-philtres, among a class of mortals, idle from the mother's womb; rejoicing to be taught the Ionic dances, and meditating of love from their tender nails!

Thus waxing, waning, broad-shining, or extinct, an inconstant but unwearied Moon, rides on its course the Cagliostric star. Thus are Count and Countess busy in their vocation; thus do they spend the golden season of their youth,—"for the Greatest Happiness of the greatest number?" Happy enough, had there been no sumptuary or adultery, or swindlery Law-acts; no Heaven above, no Hell beneath; no flight of Time, and gloomy land of Eld and Destitution and Desperation, towards which, by law of Fate, they see themselves at all moments, with frightful regularity, unaidably drifting.

The prudent man provides against the inevitable. Already Count Cagliostro, with his love-philtres, his cantharidic Wine of Egypt; nay far earlier, by his blue-flames and divining-rods, (as with the poor sheep Goldsmith of Palermo;) and ever since, by many a significant hint thrown out where the scene suited,—has dabbled in the Supernatural. As his seraphic Countess gives signs of withering, and one luxuriant branch of industry will die and drop off, others must be pushed into budding. Whether it was in England during what he called his "first visit," in the year 1776, (for the before-first, house-smearing visit was, reason or none, to go for nothing,) that he first thought of Prophecy as a trade, is unknown: certain enough he had begun to practise it then; and this indeed not without a glimpse of insight into the national character. Various, truly, are the pursuits of mankind; whereon they would fain, unfolding the future, take Destiny by surprise; with us however, as a nation of shopkeepers, they may be all said to centre in this one, *Put money in thy purse!* O for a Fortunatus'-Pocket, with its ever-new coined gold;—if, indeed, the true prayer were not rather: O for a Crassus'-Drink, (of *liquid* gold,) that so the accursed throat of Avarice might for once have enough and to spare! Meanwhile whoso should engage, keeping clear of the gallows, to teach men the secret of making money, were not he a Professor sure of audience? Strong were the general Skepticism; still stronger the general Need and Greed. Count Cagliostro, from his residence in Whitcombe street, it is clear, had looked into the mysteries of the Little-go; by occult science knew the lucky number. Bish as yet was not; but Lotteries were; gulls also were. The Count has his Language-master, his Portuguese Jew, his nondescript Ex-Jesuits, whom he puts forth, as antennæ, into coffee-houses, to stir up the minds of men. "Lord" Scott, (a swindler swindled,) and Miss Fry, and many others were they here could tell what it cost them: nay the very Lawbooks, and Lord Mansfield and Mr. Howarth speak of hundreds, and jewel-boxes, and quite handsome booties. Thus can the bustard pluck geese, and (if Law get the carcass) live upon their giblets;—now and then, however, finds a vulture, too tough to pluck.

The attentive reader is no doubt curious to understand all the What and the How of Cagliostro's procedure while England was the scene. As we too are, and have been; but unhappily all in vain. To that English *Life*, (of uncertain gender,) none, as was said, need in their utmost extremity repair. Scarcely the very lodging of Cagliostro can be ascertained; except incidentally that it was once in Whitcombe street; for a few days, in Warwick Court, Holborn: finally, for some space, in the King's Bench Jail. Vain were it meanwhile, for any reverencer of genius to pilgrim thither, seeking memorials of a great man. Cagliostro is clean gone: on the strictest search, no token never so faint discloses itself. He went, and left nothing behind him;—except perhaps a few cast-clothes, and other inevitable exuviæ, long since, not indeed annihilated, (this nothing can be,) yet beaten into mud, and spread as new soil over the general surface of Middlesex and Surrey; floated by the Thames into old Ocean; or flitting (the gaseous parts of them) in the universal Atmosphere, borne thereby to remotest corners of the Earth, or beyond the limits of the Solar System! So fleeting is the track and habitation of man; so wondrous the stuff he builds of; his house, his very house of houses, (what we call his Body,) were he the first of geniuses, will evaporate in the strangest manner, and vanish even whither we have said.

To us on our side, however, it is cheering to discover, for one thing, that Cagliostro found antagonists worthy of him: the bustard plucking geese, and living on their giblets. found not our whole Island peopled with geese, but here and there (as above hinted) with vultures, with hawks of still sharper quality than his. Priddle, Aylett, Saunders, O'Reilly: let these stand forth as the vindicators of English national character. By whom Count Alessandro Cagliostro, as in dim fluctuating outline indubitably appears, was bewritted, arrested, fleeced, hatchelled, bewildered, and bedevilled, till the very Jail of King's Bench seemed a refuge from them. A wholly obscure contest, as was natural; wherein, however, to all candid eyes the vulturous and falconish character of our Isle fully asserts itself; and the foreign Quack of Quacks, with all his thaumaturgic Hemp-silks, Lottery-numbers, Beauty-waters, Seductions, Phosphorus boxes, and Wines of Egypt, is seen matched, and nigh throttled, by the natural unassisted cunning of English Attorneys. Whereupon the bustard, feeling himself so pecked and plucked, takes wing, and flies to foreign parts.

One good thing he has carried with him, notwithstanding: initiation into some primary arcana of Free-masonry. The Quack of Quacks, with his primitive bias towards the supernatural-mystificatory, must long have had his eye on Masonry; which, with its blazonry and mummery, sashes, drawn sabres, brothers Terrible, brothers Venerable, (the whole so imposing by candle-light,) offered the choicest element for him. All men profit by *Union* with men; the quack as much as another; nay in these two words *Sworn Secrecy* alone has he not found a very talisman! Cagliostro then determines on Masonship. It was afterwards urged that the lodge he and his Seraphina got admission to (for she also was made a Mason, or Masoness; and had a riband-garter solemnly bound on, with order to sleep in it for a night) was of low rank in the social scale; numbering not a few of the pastrycook and hairdresser species. To which it could only be replied, that these alone spoke French; that a man and mason, though he cooked pastry, was still a man and mason. Be this as it might, the apt Recipiendary is rapidly promoted through the three grades of Apprentice, Companion, Master; at the cost of five guineas. That of his being first raised into the air, by means of a rope and pulley fixed in the ceiling, "during which the heavy mass of his body must assuredly have caused him a dolorous sensation;" and then being forced blindfold to shoot himself (though with privily *dis*loaded pistol) in sign of courage and obedience: all this we can esteem an apocrypha,—palmed on the Roman Inquisition, otherwise prone to delusion. Five guineas, and some foolish froth-speeches (delivered over liquor, and otherwise) was the cost. If you ask now, In *what* London Lodge was it? Alas, we know not, and shall never know. Certain only that Count Alessandro *is* a master-mason; that having once crossed the threshold, his plastic genius will not stop there. Behold, accordingly, he has bought from a "Bookseller" certain manuscripts belonging to "one George Cofton, a man absolutely unknown to him" (and to us,) which treat of the "Egyptian Masonry!" In other words, Count Alessandro will *blow* with his new five-guinea bellows; having always occasion to raise the wind.

With regard specially to that huge soap-bubble of an Egyptian Masonry which he blew, and as conjuror caught many flies with, it is our painful duty to say a little; not much. The Inquisition Biographer, with deadly fear of heretical and democratical and black-magical Freemasons before his eyes, has gone into the matter to boundless depths: commenting, elucidating, even confuting: a certain expository masonic Order-Book of Cagliostro's, which he has laid hand on, opens the whole mystery to him. The ideas he declares to be Cagliostro's; the composition all a Disciple's, for the Count had no gift that way. What then does the Disciple set forth? or, at lowest, the Inquisition Biographer say that he sets forth? Much, much that is not to the point.

Understand, however, that once inspired, by the absolutely unknown George Cofton, with the notion of Egyptian Masonry, wherein as yet lay much "magic and superstition," Count Alessandro resolves to free it of these impious ingredients, and make it a kind of Last Evangile, or Renovator of the Universe,—which so needed renovation. "As he did not believe any thing in matter of Faith," says our wooden Familiar, "nothing could arrest him." True enough: how did he move along then? to what length did he go?

"In his system he promises his followers to conduct them to *perfection*, by means of a *physical and moral regeneration;* to enable them by the former, (or physical) to find the *prime matter*, or Philosopher's Stone, and the *acacia* which consolidates in man the forces of the most vigorous youth and renders him immortal; and by the latter (or moral) to procure them a Pentagon, which shall restore man to his primitive state of innocence, lost by original sin. The Founder supposes that this Egyptian Masonry was instituted by Enoch and Elias, who propagated it in different parts of the world: however, in time, it lost much of its purity and splendour. And so, by degrees, the Masonry of men had been reduced to pure buffoonery; and that of women been almost entirely destroyed, having now for most part no place in common Masonry. Till at last, the zeal of the *Grand Cophta* (so are the High-priests of Egypt named) had signalized itself by restoring the Masonry of both sexes to its pristine lustre."

With regard to the great question of constructing this invaluable Pentagon, which is to abolish Original Sin: how you have to choose a solitary mountain, and call it Sinai; and build a Pavilion on it to be named Sion, with twelve sides, in every side a window, and three stories, one of which is named Ararat; and with Twelve Masters, each at a window, yourself in the middle of them, go through unspeakable formalities, vigils, removals, fasts, toils, distresses, and hardly get your Pentagon after all,—we shall say nothing. As little concerning the still grander and painfuller process of Physical Regeneration, or growing young again; a thing not to be accomplished without a forty-days' course of medicine, purgations, sweating-baths, fainting-fits, root-diet, phlebotomy, starvation, and desperation, more perhaps than it is all worth. Leaving these interior solemnities, and many high moral precepts of union, virtue, wisdom, and doctrines of Immortality and what not, will the reader care to cast an indifferent glance on certain esoteric ceremonial parts of this Egyptian Masonry,—as the Inquisition Biographer, if we miscellaneously cull from him, may enable us?

"In all these ceremonial parts," huskily avers the wooden Biographer, "you find as much sacrilege, profanation, superstition, and idolatry, as in common Masonry: invocations of the holy Name, prosternations, adorations lavished on the Venerable, or head of the Lodge; aspirations, insufflations, incense-burnings, fumigations, exorcisms of the Candidates and the garments they are to take; emblems of the sacro-sanct Triad, of the Moon, of the Sun, of the Compass, Square, and a thousand thousand other iniquities and ineptitudes, which are now well known in the world."

"We above made mention of the Grand Cophta. By this title has been designated the founder or restorer of Egyptian Masonry. Cagliostro made no difficulty in admitting" (to me the Inquisitor) "that under such name he was himself meant: now in this system the Grand Cophta is compared to the Highest: the most solemn acts of worship are paid him; he has authority over the Angels; he is invoked on all occasions; every thing is done in virtue of his power: which you are assured he derives immediately from God. Nay more: among the various rites observed in this exercise of Masonry, you are ordered to recite the *Veni Creator spiritus*, the *Te Deum*, and some Psalms of David: to such an excess is impudence and audacity carried, that in the Psalm, *Memento, Domine, David et omnis mansuetudinis ejus*, every time the name David occurs, that of the Grand Cophta is to be substituted.

"No Religion is excluded from the Egyptian Society: the Jew, the Calvinist, the Lutheran, can be admitted equally well with the Catholic, if so be they admit the existence of God and the immortality of the soul." "The men elevated to the rank of master take the names of the ancient Prophets; the women those of the Sibyls."

* * "Then the Grand Mistress blows on the face of the female Recipiendary, all along from brow to chin, and says: "I give you this breath, to cause to germinate and become alive in your heart the Truth which we possess; to fortify in you the," &c., &c.—"Guardian of the new Knowledge which we prepare to make you partake of, by the sacred names of *Helios, Mene, Tetragrammaton*."

"In the *Essai sur les Illuminés*, printed at Paris in 1789, I read that these latter words were suggested to Cagliostro as Arabic or Sacred ones by a Sleight-of-hand Man, who said that he was assisted by a spirit, and added that this spirit was the Soul of a Cabalist Jew, who by art-magic had killed his pig before the Christian Advent."

* * "They take a young lad, or a girl who is in the state of innocence: such they call the *Pupil* or the *Columb*; the Venerable communicates to him the power he would have had before the Fall of Man; which power consists mainly in commanding the pure Spirits; these Spirits are to the number of Seven: it is said they surround the Throne; and that they govern the seven Planets: their names are Anael, Michael, Raphael, Gabriel, Uriel, Zobiachel, Anachiel."

Or would the reader wish to see this *Columb* in action? She can act in two ways; either behind a curtain, behind a hieroglyphically-painted Screen with "table and three candles;" or as here "before the Caraffe," and showing face. If the miracle fail, it can only be because she is not "in the state of innocence,"—an accident much to be guarded against. This Scene is at Mittau;—we find, indeed, that it is a *Pupil* affair, not a *Columb* one; but for the rest that is perfectly indifferent:

"Cagliostro accordingly (it is his own story still) brought a little Boy into the Lodge; son of a nobleman there. He placed him on his knees before a table, whereon stood a Bottle of pure water, and behind this some lighted candles: he made an exorcism round the Boy, put his hand on his head; and both, in this attitude, addressed their prayers to God for the happy accomplishment of the work. Having then bid the child look into the Bottle, directly the child cried that he saw a garden. Knowing hereby that Heaven assisted him, Cagliostro took Courage, and bade the child ask of God the grace to see the Angel Michael. At first the child said: 'I see something white; I know not what it is.' Then he began jumping, stamping like a possessed creature, and cried: 'There now! I see a child, like myself, that seems to have something angelical.' All the assembly, and Cagliostro himself, remained speechless with emotion. * * * The child being anew exorcised, with the hands of the Venerable on his head, and the customary prayers addressed to Heaven, he looked into the Bottle, and said, he saw his sister at that moment coming down stairs, and embracing one of her brothers. That appeared impossible, the brother in question being then hundreds of miles off: however, Cagliostro felt not disconcerted; said they might send to the country-house (where the sister was) and see."*

Wonderful enough. Here, however, a fact rather sudden transpires, which (as the Inquisition Biographer well urges) must serve to undeceive all believers in Cagliostro; at least, call a blush into their cheeks. It seems: "The Grand cophta, the restorer, the propagator of Egyptian Masonry, Count Cagliostro himself, testifies, in most part of his System, the profoundest respect for the Patriarch Moses: *and yet* this same Cagliostro affirmed before his judges that he had always felt the insurmountablest antipathy to Moses; and attributes this hatred to his constant opinion, that Moses was a thief for having carried off the Egyptian vessels; which opinion, in spite of all the luminous arguments that were opposed to him to show how erroneous it was, he has continued to hold with an invincible obstinacy!" How reconcile these two inconsistencies? Aye, how?

But to finish off this Egyptian Masonic business, and bring it all to a focus, we shall now, for the first and for the last time, peep one moment through the spyglass of Monsieur de Luchet, in that *Essai sur les Illuminés* of his. The whole matter being so much of a chimera, how

* *Vie de Joseph Balsamo; traduite d'après l'original Italien.* (Paris, 1791.) Ch. ii iii.

can it be painted otherwise than chimerically? Of the following passage one thing is true, that a creature of the seed of Adam believed it to be true. List, list, then; O list!

"The Recipiendary is led by a darksome path, into an immense hall, the ceiling, the walls, the floor of which are covered by a black cloth, sprinkled over with red flames and menacing serpents: three sepulchral lamps emit, from time to time, a dying glimmer; and the eye half distinguishes, in this lugubrious den, certain wrecks of mortality suspended by funereal crapes: a heap of skeletons forms in the centre a sort of altar; on both sides of it are piled books; some contain menaces against the perjured; others the deadly narrative of the vengeances which the Invisible Spirit has exacted; of the infernal evocations for a long time pronounced in vain.

"Eight hours elapse. Then Phantoms, trailing mortuary veils, slowly cross the hall, and sink in caverns, without audible noise of trap-doors or of falling. You notice only that they are gone, by a fetid odour exhaled from them.

"The Novice remains four-and-twenty hours in this gloomy abode, in the midst of a freezing silence. A rigorous fast has already weakened his thinking faculties. Liquors, prepared for the purpose, first weary, and at length wear out his senses. At his feet are placed three cups, filled with a drink of greenish colour. Necessity lifts them towards his lips; involuntarily fear repels them.

"At last appears two men; looked upon as the ministers of death. These gird the pale brow of the Recipiendary with an auroral-coloured riband, dipt in blood, and full of silvered characters mixed with the figure of Our Lady of Loretto. He receives a copper crucifix, of two inches length; to his neck are hung a sort of amulets, wrapped in violet cloth. He is stript of his clothes; which two ministering brethren deposit on a funeral pile, erected at the other end of the hall. With blood, on his naked body, are traced crosses. In this state of suffering and humiliation, he sees approaching with large strides five Phantoms, armed with swords, and clad in garments dropping blood. Their faces are veiled: they spread a velvet carpet on the floor; kneel there; pray; and remain with outstretched hands crossed on their breasts, and face fixed on the ground, in deep silence. An hour passes in this painful attitude. After which fatiguing trial, plaintive cries are heard; the funeral pile takes fire, yet casts only a pale light; the garments are thrown on it and burnt. A colossal and almost transparent Figure rises from the very bosom of the pile. At sight of it, the five prostrated men fall into convulsions insupportable to look on: the too faithful image of those foaming struggles wherein a mortal at handgrips with a sudden pain ends by sinking under it.

"Then a trembling voice pierces the vault, and articulates the formula of those execrable oaths that are to be sworn: my pen falters; I think myself almost guilty to retrace them."

O Luchet, what a taking! Is there no hope left, thinkest thou? Thy brain is all gone to addled albumen; help seems none, if not in that last mother's-bosom of all the ruined: Brandy-and-water!—An unfeeling world may laugh; but ought to recollect that, forty years ago, these things were sad realities,—in the heads of many men.

As to the execrable oaths, this seems the main one: "Honour and respect *Aqua Toffana*, as a sure, prompt, and necessary means of purging the Globe, by the death or the hebetation of such as endeavour to debase the Truth, or snatch it from our hands." And so the catastrophe ends by bathing our poor half-dead Recipiendary first in blood, then, after some genuflections, in water; and "serving him a repast composed of roots,—we grieve to say, mere potatoes-and-point.

Figure now all this boundless cunningly devised Agglomerate of royal-arches, death's-heads, hieroglyphically painted screens, *Columbs* "in the state of innocence;" with spacious masonic halls, dark, or in the favourablest theatrical light-and-dark; Kircher's magic-lantern, Belshazzar hand-writings, (of phosphorus;) "plaintive tones," gong-beatings; hoary beard of a supernatural Grand Cophta emerging from the gloom;—and how it acts not only indirectly through the foolish senses of men, but directly on their Imagination; connecting itself with Enoch and Elias, with Philanthropy, Immortality, Eleutheromania, and Adam Weisshaupt's Illuminati, and so downwards to the infinite Deep: figure all this; and in the centre of it, sitting eager and alert, the skilfullest Panourgos, working the mighty chaos, into a creation—of ready money. In such a wide plastic ocean of sham and foam had the Archquack now happily begun to envelope himself.

Accordingly he goes forth prospering and to prosper. Arrived in any City, he has but by masonic grip to accredit himself with the Venerable of the place; and, not by degrees as formerly, but in a single night, is introduced in Grand Lodge to all that is fattest and foolishest far or near; and in the fittest arena, a gilt-pasteboard Masonic hall. There between the two pillars of Jachin and Boaz, can the great Sheepstealer see his whole flock (of Dupeables) assembled in one penfold; affectionately blatant, licking the hand they are to bleed by. Victorious Acharat-Beppo! The genius of Amazement, moreover, has now shed her glory round him; he is radiant-headed, a supernatural by his very gait. Behold him everywhere welcomed with vivats, or in awe-struck silence: gilt-pasteboard Freemasons receive him under the Steel-Arch (of crossed sabres;) he mounts to the Seat of the Venerable; holds high discourse hours long on Masonry, Morality, Universal Science, Divinity, and Things in general, with "a sublimity, an emphasis, and unction," proceeding, it appears, "from the special inspiration of the Holy Ghost." Then there are Egyptian Lodges to be founded, corresponded with (a thing involving expense;) elementary fractions of many a priceless arcanum (nay, if the place will stand it, of the Pentagon itself) can be given to the purified in life: how gladly would he *give* them, but they have to be brought from the uttermost ends of the world and cost money. Now, too, with what tenfold impetuosity do all the old trades of Egyptian Drops, Beauty-waters, Secret-favours, expand themselves, and rise in price! Life-weary, moneyed Donothing, this seraphic Countess is Grand Priestess of the Egyptian Female Lodges; has a touch of the supramundane Undine in her: among all thy intrigues, hadst thou ever yet Endymion-like an intrigue with the lunar Diana,—called also Hecate? And thou, O antique, much-loving faded Dowager, *this* Squire-of-dames can (it appears probable) command the Seven Angels, Uriel, Anachiel and Company; at lowest, has the eyes of all Europe fixed on him!—The dog pockets money enough, and can seem to despise money.

To us, much meditating on the matter, it seemed perhaps strangest of all, how Count Cagliostro, received under the Steel Arch, could hold Discourses, of from one to three hours long, on Universal Science, of such unction, we do not say as to seem inspired by the Holy Spirit, but as not to get him lugged out of doors, (after his first head of method,) and drowned in whole oceans of salt-and-water. The man could not speak; only babble in long-winded diffusions, chaotic circumvolutions tending nowhither. He had no thought for speaking with; he had not even a language. His Sicilian-Italian, and Laquais-de-Place French, garnished with shreds from all European dialects, was wholly intelligible to no mortal; a Tower-of-Babel jargon, which made many think him a kind of Jew. But indeed, with the language of Greeks, or of Angels, what better were it? The man once for all has no articulate utterance; that tongue of his emits noises enough, but no speech. Let him begin the plainest story, his stream stagnates at the first stage; chafes ("ahem! ahem!"); loses itself in the earth; or, bursting over, flies abroad without bank or channel,—into separate plashes. Not a stream, but a lake, a wide-spread indefinite marsh. His whole thought is confused, inextricable; what thought, what resemblance of thought he has, cannot deliver itself, except in gasps, blustering gushes, spasmodic refluences, which made bad worse. Bubble, bubble, toil and trouble: how thou bubblest, foolish "Bubbly-jock!" Hear him once, (and on a dead-lift occasion,) as the Inquisition Gurney reports it:

"'I mean, and I wish to mean, that even as those who honour their father and mother, and respect the sovereign Pontiff, are blessed of God; even so all that I did, I did it by the order of God, with the power which he vouchsafed me, and to the advantage of God and of Holy Church; and I mean to give the proofs of all that I have done and said, not only physically but morally, by showing that as I have served God for God and by the power of God, he has given me at last the counterpoison to confound and combat Hell; for I know no other enemies than those that are in Hell, and if I am wrong the Holy Father will punish me; if I am right he will reward me, and if the Holy Father could get into his hands to-night these answers of mine, I predict to all brethren, believers and unbelievers, that I should be at liberty to-morrow morning.' Being desired to give these proofs then, he answered: 'To prove that I have been chosen of God as an apostle to defend and propagate religion, I say that as the Holy Church has instituted pastors to demonstrate in face of the world that she is the true Catholic faith, even so, having operated with approbation and by the counsel of pastors of the Holy Church, I am, as I said, fully justified in regard to all my operations; and these pastors have assured me that my Egyptian Order was divine, and deserved to be formed into an Order sanctioned by the Holy Father, as I said in another interrogatory.'"

How then, in the name of wonder, said we, could such a babbling, bubbling Turkey-cock speak "with unction?"

Two things here are to be taken into account. First, the difference between speaking and public speaking; a difference altogether generic. Secondly, the wonderful power of a certain audacity, (often named impudence.) Was it never thy hard fortune, good Reader, to attend any Meeting convened for Public purposes; any Bible Society, Reform, Conservative, Thatched-Tavern, Hogg-Dinner, or other such Meeting? Thou hast seen some full-fed Long-ear, by free determination, or on sweet constraint, start to his legs and give voice. Well aware wert thou that there was not, had not been, could not be, in that entire ass-cranium of his any fraction of an idea: nevertheless mark him. If at first an ominous haze flit round, and nothing, not even nonsense, dwell in his recollection,—heed it not; let him but plunge desperately on, the spell is broken. Common-places enough are at hand; "labour of love," "rights of suffering millions," "throne and altar," "divine gift of song," or what else it may be: the Meeting, by its very *name*, has environed itself in a given element of Common-place. But anon, behold how his talking-organs gets heated, and the friction vanishes; cheers, applauses (with the previous dinner and strong drink) raise him to the height of noblest temper. And now (as for your vociferous Dullard is easiest of all) let him keep on the soft, safe *parallel* course, (parallel to the Truth, or nearly so; for Heaven's sake, not in *contact* with it,) no obstacle will meet him; on the favouring "given element of Common-place" he triumphantly careers. He is as the ass, whom you took and cast headlong into the water: the water at first threatens to swallow him; but he finds, to his astonishment, that he can *swim* therein, that it is buoyant and bears him along. One sole condition is indispensable: audacity, (vulgarly called impudence.) Our ass must *commit* himself to his watery "element;" in free daring, strike forth his four limbs from him: then shall he not drown and sink, but shoot gloriously forward, and swim, to the admiration of bystanders. The ass, safe landed on the other bank, shakes his rough hide, wonderstruck himself at the faculty that lay in him, and waves joyfully his long ears: so too the public speaker. Cagliostro, as we know him of old, is not without a certain blubbery oiliness, (of soul as of body,) with vehemence lying under it; has the volublest, noisiest tongue; and in the audacity vulgarly called impudence is without a fellow. The Common-places of such Steel-Arch Meetings are soon at his finger ends: that same blubbery oiliness and vehemence lying under it (once give them an element and stimulus) are the very gift of a fluent public speaker—to Dupeables.

Here too let us mention a circumstance, not insignificant, if true, which it may readily enough be. In younger years, Beppo Balsamo once, it is recorded, took some pains to procure, "from a country vicar," under quite false pretences, "a bit of cotton steeped in holy oils." What could such bit of cotton steeped in holy oils do for him? An Unbeliever from any basis of conviction the unbelieving Beppo could never be; but solely from stupidity and bad morals. Might there not lie in that chaotic blubbery nature of his, at the bottom of all, a certain musk-grain of real Superstitious Belief? How wonderfully such a musk-grain of Belief will flavour, and impregnate with seductive odour, a whole inward world of Quackery, so that every fibre thereof shall smell *musk*, is well known. No Quack can persuade like him who has himself some persuasion. Nay, so wondrous is the act of Believing, Deception and Self-deception must, rigorously speaking, coexist in all Quacks; and he perhaps were definable as the best Quack, in whom the smallest musk-grain of the latter would sufficiently flavour the largest mass of the former.

But indeed, as we know otherwise, was there not in Cagliostro a certain pinchbeck counterfeit of all that is golden and good in man, of somewhat even that is best? Cheers, and illuminated hieroglyphs, and the ravishment of thronging audiences, can make him maudlin; his very wickedness of practice will render him louder in eloquence of theory; and "philanthropy," "divine science," "depth of unknown worlds," "finer feelings of the heart," and such like shall draw tears from most asses of sensibility. Neither, indeed, is it of moment how *few* his elementary Commonplaces are, how empty his head is, so he but agitate it well; thus a lead drop or two, put into the emptiest dry-bladder, and jingled to and fro, will make noise enough; and even (if skilfully jingled) a kind of martial music.

Such is the Cagliostric palver, that bewitches all manner of believing souls. If the ancient Father was named Chrysostom, or Mouth-of-Gold, be the modern Quack named Pinchbecko-stom, or Mouth-of-Pinchbeck; in an Age of Bronze such metal finds elective affinities. On the whole, too, it is worth considering what element your Quack specially works in: the element of Wonder! The Genuine, be he artist or artisan, works in the finitude of the Known; the Quack in the infinitude of the Unknown. And then how, in rapidest progression, he grows and advances, once start him! "Your name is up," says the adage, "you may lie in bed." A nimbus of Renown and preternatural Astonishment envelopes Cagliostro; enchants the general eye. The few reasoning mortals, scattered here and there, that see through him, deafened in the universal hubbub, shut their lips in sorrowful disdain; confident in the grand remedy, Time The Enchanter meanwhile rolls on his way, what boundless materials of Deceptibility (which are two mainly: first, Ignorance, especially Brute-mindedness, the natural fruit of religious Unbelief; then Greediness) exist over Europe, in this the most deceivable of modern ages, are stirred up, fermenting in his behoof. He careers onward as a Comet; his nucleus (of paying and praising Dupes) embraces, in long radius, what city and province he rests over; his thinner tail (of wondering and curious Dupes) stretches into remotest lands. Good Lavater, from amid his Swiss Mountains, could say of him: "Cagliostro, a man; and a man such as few are; in whom, however, I am not a believer. O that he were simple of heart and humble, like a child; that he had feeling for the simplicity of the Gospel, and the majesty of the Lord (*Hoheit des Herrn!*) Who were so great as he? Cagliostro often tells what is not true, and promises what he does not perform. Yet do I nowise hold his operations as deception, though they are not what he calls them."* If good Lavater could so say of him, what must others have been saying!

Comet-wise, progressing with loud flourish of kettledrums, everywhere under the Steel Arch, evoking spirits, transmuting metals (to such as could stand it,) the Archquack has traversed Saxony; at Leipsic has run athwart the hawser of a brother quack (poor Schröpfer, here scarcely recognisable as "*Scieffert*,") and wrecked him. Through Eastern Germany, Prussian Poland, he progresses; and so now at length (in the spring of 1780) has arrived at Petersburgh. His pavilion is erected here, his flag prosperously hoisted: Mason-lodges have long ears; he is distributing (as has now become his wont) Spagiric Food, medicine for the poor; a train-oil Prince Potemkin (or something like him, for accounts are dubious) feels his chops water over a seraphic Seraphina: all goes merry, and promises the best. But in those despotic countries the Police is so arbitrary! Cagliostro's thaumaturgy must be overhauled by the Empress's Physician (Rogerson, a hard Annandale Scot;) is found naught, the Spagiric Food unfit for a dog: and so, the whole particulars of his Lordship's conduct being put together, the result is that he must leave Petersburgh, in a given brief term of hours. Happy for him that it was so brief: scarcely is he gone, till the Prussian Ambassador appears with a complaint, that he has falsely assumed the Prussian uniform at Rome; the Spanish Ambassador with a still graver complaint, that he has forged bills at Cadiz. However, he is safe over the marches: let them complain their fill.

In Courland and in Poland great things await him; yet not unalloyed by two small reverses. The famed Countess von der Recke, (a born Fair Saint, what the Germans call *Schöne Seele*,) as yet quite young in heart and experience, but broken down with grief for de-

***Lettre du Comte Mirabeau sur Cagliostro et Lavater* (Berlin, 1786 P. 42.)

parted friends, seeks to question the world-famous Spirit-summoner on the secrets of the Invisible Kingdoms; whither, with fond, strained eyes, she is incessantly looking. The *galimathias* of Pinchbecko-stom cannot impose on this pure-minded simple woman: she recognises the Quack in him, (and in a printed Book makes known the same:) Mephisto's mortifying experience with Margaret, as above foretold, renews itself for Cagliostro.* At Warsaw too, though he discourses on Egyptian Masonry, on Medical Philosophy, and the ignorance of Doctors, and performs successfully with *Pupil* and *Columb*, a certain "Count M." cherishes more than doubt; which ends in certainty, in a written *Cagliostro Unmasked.* The Archquack, triumphant, sumptuously feasted in the city, has retired with a chosen set of believers, with whom, however, was this unbelieving "M.," into the country, to transmute metals, to prepare perhaps the Pentagon itself. All that night, before leaving Warsaw, "our dear Master" had spent conversing with spirits. Spirits? cries "M.:" Not he; but melting ducats: he has melted a mass of them in this crucible, which now, by sleight of hand, he would fain substitute for that other, filled as you all saw, with red-lead, carefully luted down, smelted, set to cool, smuggled from among our hands, and now (look at it, ye asses!) —found broken and hidden among these bushes! Neither does the Pentagon, or Elixir of Life, or whatever it was, prosper better. "Our sweet Master enters into expostulation;" "swears by his great God, and his honour, that he will finish the work and make us happy. He carries his modesty so far as to propose that he shall work with chains on his feet; and consents to lose his life, by the hands of his disciples, if before the end of the *fourth passage*, his word be not made good. He lays his hand on the ground, and kisses it; holds it up to Heaven, and again takes God to witness that he speaks true; calls on him to exterminate him if he lies." A vision of the hoary-bearded Grand Cophta himself makes night solemn. In vain! The sherds of that broken red-lead crucible (which pretends to stand here unbroken half-full of silver) lie *there*, before your eyes: that "resemblance of a sleeping child," grown visible in the magic cooking of our Elixir, proves to be an inserted rosemary-leaf: the Grand Cophta cannot be gone too soon.

Count "M." balancing towards the opposite extreme, even thinks him inadequate as a Quack.

"Far from being modest," says this Unmasker, "he brags beyond expression, in anybody's presence, especially in women's, of the grand faculties he possesses. Every word is an exaggeration, or a statement you feel to be improbable. The smallest contradiction puts him in fury: his vanity breaks through on all sides; he lets you give him a festival that sets the whole city a-talking. Most impostors are supple, and endeavour to gain friends. This one, you might say, studies to appear arrogant, to make all men enemies, by his rude injurious speeches, by the squabbles and grudges he introduces among friends." "He quarrels with his coadjutors for trifles; fancies that a simple giving of the lie will persuade the public that they are liars." "Schröpfer at Leipsic was far cleverer." "He should get some ventriloquist for assistant: should read some Books of Chemistry; study the tricks of Philadelphia and Comus."*

Fair advices, good "M.;" but do not you yourself admit that he has a "natural genius for deception;" above all things, "a forehead of brass, (*front d'airain,*) which nothing can disconcert?" To such a genius, and such a brow, Comus and Philadelphia, and all the ventriloquists in Nature, can add little. Give the Archquack his due. These arrogancies of his prove only that he is mounted on his high horse, and has now the world under him.

Such reverses (occurring in the lot of every man) are, for our Cagliostro, but as specks in the blaze of the meridian Sun. With undimmed lustre he is, as heretofore, handed over from this "Prince P." to that "Prince Q." among which high believing potentates, what is an incredulous "Count M.?" His pockets are distended with ducats and diamonds: he is off to Vienna, to Frankfort, to Strasburg, by extra post; and there also will work miracles. "The train he commonly took with him," says the Inquisition Biographer, "corresponded to the rest; he always travelled post, with a considerable suite: couriers, lackeys, body-servants, domestics of all sorts, sumptuously dressed, gave an air of reality to the high birth he vaunted. The very liveries he got made at Paris cost twenty *Louis* each. Apartments furnished in the height of the mode; a magnificent table, open to numerous guests; rich dresses for himself and his wife, corresponded to this luxurious way of life. His feigned generosity likewise made a great noise. Often he gratuitously doctored the poor, and even gave them alms."†

In the inside of all this splendid travelling and lodging economy, are to be seen, as we know, two suspicious-looking rouged or unrouged figures, of a Count and a Countess; lolling on their cushions there, with a jaded, haggard kind of aspect, they eye one another sullenly, in silence, with a scarce-suppressed indignation; for each thinks the other does not work enough and eats too much. Whether Dame Lorenza followed her peculiar side of the business with reluctance or with free alacrity, is a moot-point among Biographers: not so, that, with her choleric adipose Archquack, she had a sour life of it, and brawling abounded. If we look still further inwards, and try to penetrate the inmost self-consciousness (what in another man would be called the conscience) of the Archquack himself, the view gets most uncertain; little or nothing to be seen but a thick fallacious haze. Which indeed *was* the main thing extant there. Much in the Count Front-d'airain remains dubious; yet hardly this: his want of clear insight into any thing, most of all into his own

* *Zeitgenossen*, No. XV. § *Frau von der Recke.*

* *Cagliostro démasqué à Varsovie, en* 1780. (Paris 1786.) P. 35 *et seq.*

† *Vie de Joseph Balsamo*, p. 41.

inner man. Cunning in the supreme degree he has; intellect next to none. Nay, is not cunning (couple it with an esurient character) the natural consequence of *defective* intellect. It is properly the vehement exercise of a short, poor vision; of an intellect sunk, bemired; which can attain to no free vision, otherwise it would lead the esurient man to be honest.

Meanwhile gleams of muddy light will occasionally visit all mortals; every living creature (according to Milton, the very Devil) has some more or less faint resemblance of a Conscience; must make inwardly certain auricular confessions, absolutions, professions of faith, —were it only that he does not yet quite loathe, and so proceed to hang himself. What such a Porcus as Cagliostro might specially feel, and think, and *be*, were difficult in any case to say; much more when contradiction and mystification, designed and unavoidable, so involve the matter. One of the most authentic documents preserved of him is the Picture of his Visage. An Effigies once universally diffused; in oil-paint, aquatint, marble, stucco, and perhaps gingerbread, decorating millions of apartments: of which remarkable Effigies one copy, engraved in the line-manner, happily still lies here. Fittest of visages; worthy to be worn by the Quack of Quacks! A most portentous face of scoundrelism: a fat, snub, abominable face; dew-lapped, flat-nosed, greasy, full of greediness, sensuality, oxlike obstinacy; a forehead impudent, refusing to be ashamed; and then two eyes turned up seraphically languishing, as in divine contemplation and adoration; a touch of quiz too: on the whole, perhaps the most perfect quack-face produced by the eighteenth century. There he sits, and seraphically languishes, with this epigraph:

De l'Ami des Humains reconaissez les traits:
Tous ses jours sont marqués par de nouveaux bienfaits,
Il prolonge la vie, il secourt l'indigence;
Le plaisir d'être utile est seul sa récompense.

A probable conjecture were that this same Theosophy, Theophilanthropy, Solacement of the Poor, to which our Archquack now more and more betook himself, might serve not only as bird-lime for external game, but also half-unconsciously as salve for assuaging his own spiritual sores. Am not I a charitable man? could the Archquack say: if I have erred myself, have I not, by theosophic unctuous discourses, removed much cause of error? The lying, the quackery, what are these but the method of accommodating yourself to the temper of men; of getting their ear, their dull long ear, which Honesty had no chance to catch? Nay, at worst, is not this an unjust world; full of nothing but beasts of prey, four-footed or two-footed? Nature has commanded, saying: Man, help thyself. Ought not the man of my genius, since he was not born a Prince, since in these scandalous times he has not been elected a Prince; to make himself one? If not by open violence, (for which he wants military force;) then surely by superior science,—exercised in a private way. Heal the diseases of the Poor, the far deeper diseases of the ignorant: in a word, found Egyptian Lodges, and get the means of founding them.—By such soliloquies can Count Front-of-brass Pinchbecko-stom, in rare atrabiliar hours of self-questioning, compose himself. For the rest, such hours are rare: the Count is a man of action and digestion, not of self-questioning; usually the day brings its abundant task; there is no time for abstractions,—of the metaphysical sort.

Be this as it may, the Count has arrived at Strasburg; is working higher wonders than ever. At Strasburg, indeed, (in the year 1783,) occurs his apotheosis: what we can call the culmination and Fourth Act of his Life-drama. He was here for a number of months; in full blossom and radiance, the envy and admiration of the world. In large hired hospitals, he with open drug-box, (containing "Extract of Saturn,") and even with open purse, relieves the suffering poor; unfolds himself lamblike, angelic to a believing few, of the rich classes; turns a silent minatory lion-face to unbelievers, were they of the richest. Medical miracles have in all times been common: but what miracle is this of an Oriental or Occidental Serene-Excellence that, "regardless of expense," employs himself not in preserving game, but in curing sickness, in illuminating ignorance? Behold how he dives, at noonday, into the infectious hovels of the mean; and on the equipages, haughtinesses, and even dinner-invitations, turns only his negatory front-of-brass! The Prince Cardinal de Rohan, Archbishop of Strasburg, first-class Peer of France, of the Blood-royal of Brittany, intimates a wish to see him; he answers: "If Monseigneur the Cardinal is sick, let him come, and I will cure him: if he is well, he has no need of me, I none of him."* Heaven, meanwhile, has sent him a few disciples; by a nice tact, he knows his man; to one speaks only of Spagiric Medicine, Downfal of tyranny, and the Egyptian Lodge; to another, of quite high matters, beyond this diurnal sphere; of visits from the Angel of Light, visits from him of Darkness; passing a Statue of Christ, he will pause with a wondrously accented plaintive "Ha!" as of recognition, as of thousand-years remembrance; and when questioned, sink into mysterious silence. *Is* he the Wandering Jew, then? Heaven knows! At Strasburg, in a word, Fortune not only smiles but laughs upon him: as crowning favour, he finds here the richest, inflammablest, most open-handed Dupe ever yet vouchsafed him; no other than this same many-titled Louis de Rohan; strong in whose favour, he can laugh again at Fortune.

Let the curious reader look at him, for an instant or two, through the eyes of two eye-witnesses; the Abbé Georgel, (Prince Louis's diplomatic Factotum,) and Herr Meiners, the Göttingen Professor:

"Admitted at length," says our too-prosing Jesuit Abbé, to the sanctuary of this Æsculapius, Prince Louis saw, according to his own account, in the incommunicative man's physiognomy, something so dignified, so imposing, that he felt penetrated with a religious awe, and reverence dictated his address. Their

* *Mémoires de l'Abbé Georgel*, ii. 48.

interview, which was brief, excited more keenly than ever his desire of farther acquaintance. He attained it at length: and the crafty empiric graduated so cunningly his words and procedure, that he gained, without appearing to court it, the Cardinal's entire confidence, and the greatest ascendency over his will. 'Your soul,' said he one day to the Prince, 'is worthy of mine; you deserve to be made participator of all my secrets.' Such an avowal captivated the whole faculties, intellectual and moral, of a man who at all times had hunted after secrets of alchemy and botany. From this moment their union became intimate and public: Cagliostro went and established himself at Saverne, while his Eminence was residing there; their solitary interviews were long and frequent." * * "I remember once, having learnt, by a sure way, that Baron de Planta (his Eminence's man of affairs) had frequent, most expensive orgies, in the Archiepiscopal Palace, where Tokay wine ran like water, to regale Cagliostro and his pretended wife, I thought it my duty to inform the Cardinal; his answer was, 'I know it; I have even authorized him to commit abuses, if he judge fit.'" * * "He came at last to have no other will than Cagliostro's: and to such a length had it gone, that this sham Egyptian, finding it good to quit Strasburg for a time, and retire into Switzerland, the Cardinal, apprized thereof, despatched his Secretary as well to attend him, as to obtain Predictions from him; such were transmitted in cipher to the Cardinal on every point he needed to consult of."*—

"Before ever I arrived in Strasburg," (hear now the as prosing Protestant Professor,) "I knew almost to a certainty that I should not see Count Cagliostro: at least, not get to speak with him. From many persons I had heard that he, on no account, received visits from curious Travellers, in a state of health; that such as, without being sick, appeared in his audiences were sure to be treated by him, in the brutalest way, as spies." * * "Nevertheless, though I saw not this new god of Physic near at hand and deliberately, but only for a moment as he rolled on in a rapid carriage, I fancy myself to be better acquainted with him than many who have lived in his society for months." "My unavoidable conviction is, that Count Cagliostro, from of old, has been more of a cheat than an enthusiast; and also that he continues a cheat to this day.

"As to his country, I have ascertained nothing. Some make him a Spaniard, others a Jew, or an Italian, or a Ragusan; or even an Arab, who had persuaded some Asiatic Prince to send his son to travel in Europe, and then murdered the youth, and taken possession of his treasures. As the self-styled Count speaks badly all the languages you hear from him, and has most likely spent the greater part of his life under feigned names far from home, it is probable enough no sure trace of his origin may ever be discovered.

"On his first appearance in Strasburg he connected himself with the Freemasons; but only till he felt strong enough to stand by himself: he soon gained the favour of the Prætor and the Cardinal; and through these the favour of the Court, to such a degree that his adversaries cannot so much as think of overthrowing him. With the Prætor and Cardinal he is said to demean himself as with persons who were under boundless obligation to him, to whom he was under none: the equipage of the Cardinal he seems to use as freely as his own. He pretends that he can recognise Atheists or Blasphemers by the smell; that the vapour from such throws him into epileptic fits; into which sacred disorder he, like a true juggler, has the art of falling when he likes. In public he no longer vaunts of rule over spirits, or other magical arts; but I know, even as certainly, that he still pretends to evoke spirits, and by their help and apparition to heal diseases, as I know this other fact, that he understands no more of the human system, or the nature of its diseases, or the use of the commonest therapeutic methods, than any other quack.

"According to the crediblest accounts of persons who have long observed him, he is a man to an inconceivable degree choleric, (*heftig*,) heedless, inconstant; and therefore doubtless it was the happiest idea he ever in his whole life came upon, this of making himself inaccessible; of raising the most obstinate reserve as a bulwark round him; without which precaution he must long ago have been caught at fault.

"For his own labour he takes neither payment nor present; when presents are made him of such sort as cannot without offence be refused, he forthwith returns some counter-present, of equal or still higher value. Nay he not only takes nothing from his patients, but frequently admits them, months long, to his house and his table, and will not consent to the smallest recompense. With all this disinterestedness, (conspicuous enough, as you may suppose,) he lives in an expensive way, plays deep, loses almost constantly to ladies; so that, according to the very lowest estimate, he must require at least 20,000 livres a year. The darkness which Caligostro has, on purpose, spread over the sources of his income and outlay, contributes even more than his munificence and miraculous cures to the notion that he is a divine extraordinary man, who has watched Nature in her deepest operations, and among other secrets stolen that of Gold-making from her." * * "With a mixture of sorrow and indignation over our age, I have to record that this man has found acceptance, not only among the great, who from of old have been the easiest bewitched by such, but also with many of the learned, and even physicians and naturalists."*

Halcyon days; only too good to continue! All glory runs its course; has its culmination, and then its often precipitous decline. Eminence Rohan, with fervid temper and small instruction, perhaps of dissolute, certainly of dishonest manners, in whom the faculty of Wonder had attained such prodigious develop-

* Georgel, *ubi supra.*

* Meiners: *Briefe über die Schweiz,* (as quoted in *Mirabeau.*)

ment, was indeed the very stranded whale for jackals to feed on: unhappily, however, no one jackal could long be left in solitary possession of him. A sharper-toothed she-jackal now strikes in; bites infinitely deeper; stranded whale and he-jackal both are like to become her prey. A young French Mantuamaker, "Countess de La Motte-Valoise, descended from Henry II. by the bastard line," without Extract of Saturn, Egyptian Masonry, or any (verbal) conference with Dark Angels, —has genius enough to get her finger in the Archquack's rich Hermetic Projection, appropriate the golden proceeds, and even finally break the crucible. Prince Cardinal Louis de Rohan is off to Paris, under her guidance, to see the long-invisible Queen, (or Queen's Apparition;) to pick up the Rose in the Garden of Trianon, dropt by her fair sham-royal hand; and then—descend rapidly to the Devil, and drag Cagliostro along with him.

The intelligent reader observes, we have now arrived at that stupendous business of the *Diamond Necklace:* into the dark complexities of which we need not here do more than glance: who knows but, next month, our Historical Chapter, written specially on this subject, may itself see the light? Enough, for the present, if we fancy vividly the poor whale Cardinal, so deep in the adventure that Grand-Cophtic "predictions transmitted in cipher" will no longer illuminate him; but the Grand Cophta must leave all masonic or other business, happily begun in Naples, Bourdeaux, Lyons, and come personally to Paris with predictions at first hand. "The new Calchas," says poor Abbé Georgel, "must have read the entrails of his victim ill; for, on issuing from these communications with the Angel of Light and of Darkness, he prophesied to the Cardinal that this happy correspondence" (with the Queen's Similitude) "would place him at the highest point of favour; that his influence in the Government would soon become paramount; that he would use it for the propagation of good principles, the glory of the Supreme Being, and the happiness of Frenchmen." The new Calchas was ind[illegible] at fault: but how could he be otherwise? Let these high Queen's favours, and all terrestrial shiftings of the wind, turn as they will, *his* reign, he can well see, is appointed to be temporary: in the mean while, Tokay flows like water; prophecies of good, not of evil, are the method to keep it flowing. Thus if, for Circe de La Motte-Valoise, the Egyptian Masonry is but a foolish enchanted cup to turn her fat Cardinal into a quadruped withal, she herself converse-wise, for the Grand Cophta, is one who must ever fodder said quadruped (with Court Hopes,) and stall-feed him fatter and fatter,—it is expected for the knife of *both* parties. They are mutually useful; live in peace, and Tokay festivity, though mutually suspicious, mutually contemptuous. So stand matters, through the spring and summer months of the year 1785.

But fancy next that,—while Tokay is flowing within doors, and abroad Egyptian Lodges are getting founded, and gold and glory, from Paris as from other cities, supernaturally coming in,—the latter end of August has arrived, and with it Commissary Chesnon, to lodge the whole unholy Brotherhood, from Cardinal down to Sham-queen, in separate cells of the Bastille! There, for nine long months, let them howl and wail (in bass or treble;) and emit the falsest of false *Mémoires;* among which that *Mémoire pour le Comte de Cagliostro, en presence des autres Co-Accusés*, with its Trebisond Acharats, Scherifs of Mecca, and Nature's unfortunate Child, all gravely printed with French types in the year 1786, may well bear the palm. Fancy that Necklace or Diamonds will nowhere unearth themselves; that the Tuileries Palace sits struck with astonishment, and speechless chagrin; that Paris, that all Europe, is ringing with the wonder. That Count Front-of-brass Pinchbecko-stom, confronted, at the judgment bar, with a shrill, glib Circe de La Motte, has need of all his eloquence; that nevertheless the Front-of-brass prevails, and exasperated Circe "throws a candlestick at him." Finally, that on the 31st of May, 1786, the assembled Parliament of Paris, "at nine in the evening, after a sitting of eighteen hours," has solemnly pronounced judgment: and now that Cardinal Louis is gone "to his estates;" Countess de La Motte is shaven on the head, branded with red-hot-iron, "V" (*Voleuse*) on both shoulders, and confined for life to the Salpetrière; her Count wandering uncertain, with diamonds for sale, over the British Empire; the Sieur de Villette (for handling a queen's pen) banished for ever; the too queenlike Demoiselle Gay d'Oliva (with her unfathered infant) "put out of Court;"—and Grand Cophta Cagliostro liberated, indeed, but pillaged, and ordered forthwith to take himself away. His disciples illuminate their windows; but what does that avail? Commissary Chesnon, Bastille-Governor Launay cannot recollect the least particular of those priceless effects, those gold-rouleaus, repeating watches of his: he must even retire to Passy that very night; and two days afterwards, sees nothing for it but Boulogne and England. Thus does the miserable pickle-herring tragedy of the Diamond Necklace wind itself up, and wind Cagliostro once more to inhospitable shores.

Arrived here, and lodged tolerably in "Sloane Street, Knightsbridge," by the aid of Mr. (Broken Wine-merchant Apothecary) Swinton, to whom he carries introductions, he can drive a small trade in Egyptian pills, (sold *in Paris* at thirty shillings the dram;) in unctuously discoursing to Egyptian Lodges; in "giving public audiences as at Strasburg,"—if so be any one will bite. At all events, he can, by the aid of amanuensis-disciples, compose and publish his *Lettre au Peuple Anglais;* setting forth his unheard-of generosities, unheard-of injustices suffered (in a world not worthy of him) at the hands of English Lawyers, Bastille Governors, French Counts, and others; his *Lettre aux Français*, singing to the same tune, predicting too (what many inspired Editors had already boded) that "the Bastille would be destroyed" and "a King would come who should govern by States-General." But, alas, the shafts of Criticism are busy with him; so many hostile eyes look towards him: the world, in short, is get ting too hot for him. Mark, nevertheless, how the brow of brass quails not; nay a touch of his old poetic Humour, even in this sad crisis, unexpectedly unfolds itself. One Morande, Editor of a *Courier de l'Europe* published here at that period, has for some time made it his distinction to be the foremost of Cagliostro's enemies. Cagliostro (enduring much in silence) happens once, in some "public audience," to mention a practice he had witnessed in Arabia the Stony: the people there, it seems, are in the habit of fattening a few pigs annually, on provender mixed with arsenic; whereby the whole pig-carcase by and by becomes, so to speak, arsenical; the arsenical pigs are then let loose into the woods; eaten by lions, leopards, and other ferocious creatures; which latter naturally all die in consequence, and so the woods are cleared of them. This adroit practice the Sieur Morande thought a proper subject for banter; and accordingly, in his Seventeenth and two following Numbers, made merry enough with it. Whereupon Count Front-of-brass, whose patience has limits, writes as Advertisement (still to be read in old files of the *Public Advertiser*, under date September 3, 1786) a French Letter, not without causticity and aristocratic disdain; challenging the witty Sieur to breakfast with him, for the 9th of November next, in the face of the world, on an actual Sucking Pig, fattened by Cagliostro, but cooked, carved, and selected from by the Sieur Morande,—under bet of Five Thousand Guineas sterling that next morning thereafter, he the Sieur Morande shall be dead, and Count Cagliostro be alive! The poor Sieur durst not cry, Done; and backed out of the transaction, making wry faces. Thus does a kind of red coppery splendour encircle our Archquack's decline; thus with brow of brass, grim smiling, does he meet his destiny.

But suppose we should now, from these foreign scenes, turn homewards, for a moment, into the native alley in Palermo! Palermo, with its dinginess, its mud or dust; the old black Balsamo House, the very beds and chairs, all are still standing there: and Beppo has altered so strangely, has wandered so far away. Let us look; for happily we have the fairest opportunity.

In April, 1787, Palermo contained a Traveller of a thousand; no other than the great Goethe from Weimar. At his Table-d'hote he heard much of Cagliostro; at length also of a certain Palermo Lawyer, who had been engaged by the French Government to draw up an authentic genealogy and memoir of him. This Lawyer, and even the rude draught of his Memoir, he with little difficulty gets to see; inquires next whether it were not possible to see the actual Balsamo Family, whereof it appears the mother and a widowed sister still survive. For this matter, however, the Lawyer can do nothing; only refer him to his Clerk; who again starts difficulties: To get at those genealogic Documents he has been obliged to invent some story of a Government Pension being in the wind for those poor Balsamos; and now that the whole matter is finished, and the Paper sent off to France, has nothing so much at heart as to keep out of their way:

"So said the Clerk. However, as I could not abandon my purpose, we after some study concerted that I should give myself out for an Englishman, and bring the family news of Cagliostro, who had lately got out of the Bastille, and gone to London.

"At the appointed hour, it might be three in the afternoon, we set forth. The house lay in the corner of an Alley, not far from the main-street named *Il Casaro.* We ascended a miserable stair, and came straight into the kitchen. A woman of middle stature, broad and stout, yet not corpulent, stood busy washing the kitchen dishes. She was decently dressed; and, on our entrance, turned up the one end of her apron, to hide the soiled side from us. She joyfully recognised my conductor, and said: 'Signor Giovanni, do you bring us good news? Have you made out any thing?'

"He answered: 'In our affair, nothing yet: but here is a Stranger that brings a salutation from your Brother, and can tell you how he is at present.'

"The salutation I was to bring stood not in our agreement: meanwhile, one way or other, the introduction was accomplished. 'You know my Brother?' inquired she.—'All Europe knows him,' answered I; 'and I fancied it would gratify you to hear that he is now in safety and well; as, of late, no doubt you have been anxious about him.'—'Step in,' said she, 'I will follow you directly;' and with the Clerk I entered the room.

"It was large and high; and might, with us, have passed for a saloon; it seemed, indeed, to be almost the sole lodging of the family. A single window lighted the large walls, which had once had colour; and on which were black pictures of saints, in gilt frames, hanging round. Two large beds, without curtains, stood at one wall; a brown press, in the form of a writing-desk, at the other. Old rush-bottomed chairs, the backs of which had once been gilt, stood by; and the tiles of the floor were in many places worn deep into hollows. For the rest, all was cleanly; and we approached the family, which sat assembled at the one window, in the other end of the apartment.

"Whilst my guide was explaining, to the old Widow Balsamo, the purpose of our visit, and by reason of her deafness must repeat his words several times aloud, I had time to observe the chamber and the other persons in it. A girl of about sixteen, well formed, whose features had become uncertain by small-pox, stood at the window; beside her a young man, whose disagreeable look, deformed by the same disease, also struck me. In an easy-chair, right before the window, sat or rather lay a sick, much disshapen person, who appeared to labour under a sort of lethargy.

"My guide having made himself understood, we were invited to take seats. The old woman put some questions to me; which, however, I had to get interpreted before I could answer them, the Sicilian dialect not being quite at my command.

"Meanwhile I looked at the aged widow with satisfaction. She was of middle stature, but well-shaped; over her regular features, which age had not deformed, lay that sort of peace usual with people that have lost their hearing; the tone of her voice was soft and agreeable.

"I answered her questions; and my answers also had again to be interpreted for her.

"The slowness of our conversation gave me leisure to measure my words. I told her that her son had been acquitted in France, and was at present in England, where he met with good reception. Her joy, which she testified at these tidings, was mixed with expressions of a heartfelt piety; and as she now spoke a little louder and slower, I could the better understand her.

"In the mean time, the daughter had entered, and taken her seat beside my conductor, who repeated to her faithfully what I had been narrating. She had put on a clean apron; had set her hair in order under the net-cap. The more I looked at her, and compared her with her mother, the more striking became the difference of the two figures. A vivacious, healthy Sensualism (*Sinnlichkeit*) beamed forth from the whole structure of the daughter: she might be a woman of about forty. With brisk blue eyes, she looked sharply round; yet in her look I could trace no suspicion. When she sat, her figure promised more height than it showed when she rose: her posture was determinate, she sat with her body leaned forwards, the hands resting on the knees. For the rest, her physiognomy, more of the snubby than the sharp sort, reminded me of her Brother's Portrait, familiar to us in engravings. She asked me several things about my journey, my purpose to see Sicily; and was convinced I would come back, and celebrate the Feast of Saint Rosalia with them.

"As the grandmother, meanwhile, had again put some questions to me, and I was busy answering her, the daughter kept speaking to my companion half-aloud, yet so that I could take occasion to ask what it was. He answered: Signora Capitummino was telling him that her Brother owed her fourteen gold Ounces; on his sudden departure from Palermo, she had redeemed several things for him that were in pawn; but never since that day had either heard from him, or got money or any other help, though it was said he had great riches, and made a princely outlay. Now would not I perhaps undertake, on my return, to remind him, in a handsome way, of the debt, and procure some assistance for her; nay, would I not carry a Letter with me, or at all events get it carried? I offered to do so. She asked where I lodged, whither she must send the Letter to me? I avoided naming my abode, and offered to call next day towards night, and receive the letter myself.

"She thereupon described to me her untoward situation: how she was a widow with three children, of whom the one girl was getting educated in a convent, the other was here present, and her son just gone out to his lesson. How, beside these three children, she had her mother to maintain; and moreover out of Christian love had taken the unhappy sick person there to her house, whereby the burden was heavier: how all her industry would scarcely suffice to get necessaries for herself and hers. She knew indeed that God did not leave good works unrewarded; yet must sigh very sore under the load she had long borne.

"The young people mixed in the dialogue, and our conversation grew livelier. While speaking with the others, I could hear the good old widow ask her daughter: If I belonged, then, to their holy Religion? I remarked also that the daughter strove, in a prudent way, to avoid an answer; signifying to her mother, so far as I could take it up: that the Stranger seemed to have a kind feeling towards them; and that it was not well-bred to question any one straightway on that point.

"As they heard that I was soon to leave Palermo, they became more pressing, and importuned me to come back; especially vaunting the paradisaic days of the Rosalia Festival, the like of which was not to be seen and tasted in all the world.

"My attendant, who had long been anxious to get off, at last put an end to the interview by his gestures; and I promised to return on the morrow evening, and take the letter. My attendant expressed his joy that all had gone off so well, and we parted mutually content.

"You may fancy the impression this poor and pious, well-dispositioned family had made on me. My curiosity was satisfied; but their natural and worthy bearing had raised an interest in me, which reflection did but increase.

"Forthwith, however, there arose from me anxieties about the following day. It was natural that this appearance of mine, which at the first moment had taken them by surprise, should, after my departure, awaken many reflections. By the Genealogy I knew that several others of the family were in life: it was natural that they should call their friends together, and in the presence of all, get these things repeated which, the day before, they had heard from me with admiration. My object was attained; there remained nothing more than, in some good fashion, to end the adventure. I accordingly repaired next day, directly after dinner, alone to their house. They expressed surprise as I entered. The Letter was not ready yet, they said; and some of their relations wished to make my acquaintance, who towards night would be there.

"I answered that having to set off to-morrow morning, and visits still to pay, and packing to transact, I had thought it better to come early than not at all.

"Meanwhile the son entered, whom yesterday I had not seen. He resembled his sister in size and figure. He brought the Letter they were to give me; he had, as is common in those parts, got it written out of doors, by one of their Notaries that sit publicly to do such things. The young man had a still, melancholy, and modest aspect; inquired after his Uncle, asked about his riches and outlays, and added sorrowfully, Why had he so forgotten his kindred? 'It were our greatest fortune,' continued he, 'should he once return hither, and take notice of us; but,' continued he, 'how came he to let you know that he had relatives in Palermo? It is said, he everywhere denies us, and gives himself out for a man of great birth.' I answered this question, which had now arisen by the imprudence of my Guide at our first entrance, in such sort as to make it seem that the Uncle, though he might have reasons for concealing his birth from the public, did yet, towards his friends and acquaintance, keep it no secret.

"The sister, who had come up during this dialogue, and by the presence of her brother, perhaps also by the absence of her yesterday's friend, had got more courage, began also to speak with much grace and liveliness. They begged me earnestly to recommend them to their Uncle, if I wrote to him; and not less earnestly, when once I should have made this journey through the Island, to come back and pass the Rosalia Festival with them.

"The mother spoke in accordance with her children. 'Sir,' said she, 'though it is not seemly, as I have a grown daughter, to see stranger gentlemen in my house, and one has cause to guard against both danger and evil-speaking, yet shall you ever be welcome to us, when you return to this city.'

"'O yes,' answered the young ones, 'we will lead the Gentleman all round the Festival: we will show him every thing, get a place on the scaffolds, where the grand sights are seen best. What will he say to the great Chariot, and more than all, to the glorious Illumination!'

"Meanwhile the Grandmother had read the letter and again read it. Hearing that I was about to take leave, she arose, and gave me the folded sheet. 'Tell my son,' began she with a noble vivacity, nay, with a sort of inspiration, 'Tell my son how happy the news have made me, which you brought from him! Tell him that I clasp him to my heart'—here she stretched out her arms asunder, and pressed them again together on her breast—'that I daily beseech God and our Holy Virgin for him in prayer; that I give him and his wife my blessing; and that I wish before my end to see him again, with these eyes, which have shed so many tears for him.'

"The peculiar grace of the Italian tongue favoured the choice and noble arrangement of these words, which moreover were accompanied with lively gestures, wherewith that nation can add such a charm to spoken words.

"I took my leave, not without emotion. They all gave me their hands; the children showed me out; and as I went down stairs, they jumped to the balcony of the kitchen window, which projected over the street; called after me, threw me salutes, and repeated, that I must in no wise forget to come back. I saw them still on the balcony, when I turned the corner."*

Poor old Felicita, and must thy pious prayers, thy motherly blessings, and so many tears shed by those old eyes, be all in vain! To thyself, in any case, they were blessed.—As for the Signora Capitummino, with her three fatherless children, we can believe at least, that the fourteen gold Ounces were paid, by a sure hand, and so her heavy burden, for some space, lightened a little.

Count Cagliostro, all this while, is rapidly proceeding with his Fifth Act; the red coppery splendour darkens more and more into final gloom. Some boiling muddle-heads of a dupeable sort there still are in England: Popish-Riot Lord George, for instance, will walk with him to Count Barthélemy's, or d'Adhémar's; and, in bad French and worse rhetoric, abuse the Queen of France: but what does it profit? Lord George must one day (after noise enough) revisit Newgate for it; and in the meanwhile, hard words pay no scores. Apothecary Swinton begins to get wearisome; French spies look ominously in; Egyptian Pills are slack of sale; the old vulturous Attorney-host anew scents carrion, is bestirring itself anew: Count Cagliostro, in the May of 1787, must once more leave England. But whither? Ah, whither! At Bâle, at Bienne, over Switzerland, the game is up. At Aix in Savoy, there are baths, but no gudgeons in them: at Turin, his Majesty of Sardinia meets you with an Order to begone on the instant. A like fate from the Emperor Joseph at Roveredo;—before the *Liber memorialis de Caleostro dum esset Roboretti* could extend to many pages! Count Front-of-brass begins confessing himself to priests: yet "at Trent paints a new hieroglyphic Screen,"—touching last flicker of a light that once burnt so high! He pawns diamond buckles; wanders necessitous hither and thither; repents, unrepents; knows not what to do. For Destiny has her nets round him; they are straitening, straitening; too soon he will be *ginned!*

Driven out from Trent, what shall he make of the new hieroglyphic Screen, what of himself? The way-worn Grand-Cophtess has begun to blab family secrets; she longs to be in Rome, by her mother's hearth, by her mother's grave; in any nook, where so much as the shadow of refuge waits her. To the desperate Count Front-of-brass all places are nearly alike: urged by a female babble, he will go to Rome then; why not? On a May-day, of the year 1789, (when such glorious work had just begun in France, to him all forbidden!) he enters the Eternal City: it was his doom-summons that called him thither. On the 29th of next December, the Holy Inquisition, long watchful enough, detects him founding some feeble (moneyless) ghost of an Egyptian Lodge; "picks him off," (as the military say,) and locks him hard and fast in the Castle of St. Angelo:

Voi ch' intrate lasciat' ogni speranza!

Count Cagliostro did not lose all hope: nevertheless a few words will now suffice for him. In vain, with his mouth of pinchbeck and his front of brass, does he heap chimera on chimera; demand religious Books, (which are freely given him:) demand clean Linen, and an interview with his Wife, (which are refused him;) assert now that the Egyptian Masonry is a divine system, accommodated to erring and gullible men, which the Holy Father, when he

* Goethe's *Werke*, (*Italiænische Reise*,) xxviii. 146.

knows it, will patronize; anon that there are some four millions of Freemasons, spread over Europe, all sworn to exterminate Priest and King, wherever met with: in vain! they will not acquit him, as misunderstood Theophilanthropist; will not emit him, in Pope's pay, as renegade Masonic Spy: "he can't get out." Donna Lorenza languishes, invisible to him, in a neighbouring cell; begins at length to *confess!* Whereupon he too, in torrents, will emit confessions and forestall her: these the Inquisition pocket and sift (whence this *Life of Balsamo*); but will not let him out. In fine, after some eighteen months of the weariest hounding, doubling, worrying, and standing at bay, His Holiness gives sentence: The Manuscript of Egyptian Masonry is to be burnt by hand of the common Hangman, and all that intermeddle with such Masonry are accursed; Giuseppe Balsamo, justly forfeited of life, (for being a Freemason,) shall nevertheless in mercy be forgiven; instructed in the duties of penitence, and even kept safe thenceforth and till death,—in ward of Holy Church. Ill-starred Acharat, must it so end with thee! This was in April, 1791.

He addressed (how vainly!) an appeal to the French Constituent Assembly. As was said, in Heaven, in Earth, or in Hell there was no Assembly that could well take his part. For four years more, spent one knows not how,—most probably in the furor of edacity, with insufficient cookery, and the stupor of indigestion,—the curtain lazily falls. There rotted and gave way the cordage of a tough heart. One summer morning of the year 1795, the Body of Cagliostro is still found in the prison at St. Leo; but Cagliostro's Self has escaped,—*whither* no man yet knows. The brow of brass, behold how it has got all unlackered; these pinchbeck lips can lie no more: Cagliostro's work is ended, and now only his *account* to present. As the Scherif of Mecca said, "Nature's unfortunate child, adieu!"

Such, according to our comprehension thereof, is the rise, progress, grandeur, and decadence of the Quack of Quacks. Does the reader ask, What good was in it, Why occupy his time and hours with the biography of such a miscreant? We answer, It was stated on the very threshold of this matter, in the loftiest terms, by Herr Sauerteig, that the Lives of all Eminent Persons (miscreant or creant) ought to be written. Thus has not the very Devil his *Life*, deservedly written not by Daniel Defoe only, but by quite other hands than Daniel's? For the rest, the Thing represented on these pages is no sham, but a Reality; thou hast it, O reader, as we have it: Nature was pleased to produce even such a man, even so, not otherwise; and the Editor of this Magazine is here mainly to record (in an adequate manner) what *she*, of her thousandfold mysterious richness and greatness, produces.

But the moral lesson? Where is the moral lesson? Foolish reader, in every Reality, nay in every genuine Shadow of a Reality, (what we call Poem,) there lie a hundred such, or a million such, according as thou hast the *eye* to read them! Of which hundred or million lying *here* (in the present Reality,) couldst not thou, for example, be advised to take this one, to thee, worth all the rest: Behold, I too have attained that immeasurable, mysterious glory of being *alive;* to me also a Capability has been intrusted: shall I strive to work it out (manlike) into Faithfulness, and Doing; or (quacklike) into Eatableness, and Similitude of Doing? Or why not rather (gigman-like, and following the "respectable," countless multitude)—into *both?* The decision is of quite *infinite* moment; see thou make it aright.

But in fine, look at this matter of Cagliostro (as at all matters) with thy heart, with thy whole mind; no longer merely squint at it with the poor side-glance of thy calculative faculty Look at it not *logically* only, but *mystically.* Thou shalt in sober truth see it (as Sauerteig asserted) to be a "Pasquillant verse," of most inspired writing in its kind, in that same "Grand Bible of Universal History;" wondrously and even indispensably connected with the "Heroic" portions that stand there; even as the all-showing Light is with the Darkness wherein nothing can be seen; as the hideous taloned *roots* are with the fair *boughs*, and their leaves and flowers and fruit; both of which, and not one of which, make the Tree. Think also whether thou hast known no Public Quacks, on far higher scale than this, whom a Castle of St. Angelo never could get hold of; and how, as Emperors, Chancellors, (having found much fitter machinery,) they could run their Quack-career; and make whole kingdoms, whole continents, into one huge Egyptian Lodge, and squeeze supplies, of money or blood, from it, at discretion? Also, whether thou even now knowest not Private Quacks, innumerable as the sea-sands, toiling *half*-Cagliostrically, of whom Cagliostro is as the ideal type-specimen? Such is the world. Understand it, despise it, love it; cheerfully hold on thy way through it, with thy eye on higher loadstars!

DEATH OF THE REV. EDWARD IRVING.

[Fraser's Magazine, 1835.]

Edward Irving's warfare has closed; if not in victory, yet in invincibility, and faithful endurance to the end. The Spirit of the Time, which could not enlist him as its soldier, must needs, in all ways, fight against him as its enemy: it has done its part, and he has done his. One of the noblest natures—a man of antique heroic nature, in questionable modern garniture, which he could not wear! Around him a distracted society, vacant, prurient; heat and darkness, and what these two may breed: mad extremes of flattery, followed by madder contumely, by indifference and neglect!—these were the conflicting elements; this is the result they have made out among them. The voice of our "son of thunder," with its deep tone of wisdom, (that belonged to all articulate-speaking ages,) never inaudible amid wildest dissonances, (that belonged to this inarticulate age, which slumbers and somnambulates, which cannot *speak*, but only screech and gibber,) has gone silent so soon. Closed are those lips. The large heart, with its large bounty, where wretchedness found solacement, and they that were wandering in darkness the light as of a home, has paused. The strong man can no more: beaten on from without, undermined from within, he must sink overwearied, as at nightfall, when it was yet but the mid-season of day. Irving was forty-two years and some months old: Scotland sent him forth a Herculean man; our mad Babylon wore him and wasted him, with all her engines; and it took her twelve years. He sleeps with his fathers, in that loved birthland: Babylon with its deafening inanity rages on; but to him henceforth innocuous, unheeded—for ever.

Reader, thou hast seen and heard the man (as who has not?) with wise or unwise wonder; thou shalt not see or hear him again. The work, be what it might, is *done;* dark curtains sink over it, enclose it ever deeper into the unchangeable Past.—Think (if thou be one of a thousand, and worthy to do it) that here once more was a genuine man sent into this our *un*genuine phantasmagory of a world, which would go to ruin without such; that here once more, under thy own eyes, in this last decade, was enacted the old Tragedy (and has had its fifth-act now) of *The Messenger of Truth in the Age of Shams,*—and what relation thou thyself mayest have to that. Whether any? Beyond question, thou thyself art *here;* either a dreamer or awake; and one day shalt cease to dream.

This man was appointed a Christian Priest; and strove with the whole force that was in him to *be* it. To be it: in a time of Tithe Controversy, Encyclopedism, Catholic Rent, Philanthropism, and the Revolution of Three Days! He might have been so many things; not a speaker only, but a doer; the leader of hosts of men. For his head (when the Fog-Babylon had not yet obscured it) was of strong far-searching insight; his very enthusiasm was sanguine, not atrabiliar; he was so loving, full of hope, so simple-hearted, and made all that approached him his. A giant force of activity was in the man; speculation was accident, not nature. Chivalry, adventurous field-life of the old Border (and a far nobler sort) ran in his blood. There was in him a courage dauntless, not pugnacious; hardly fierce, by no possibility ferocious: as of the generous war-horse, gentle in its strength, yet that laughs at the shaking of the spear.—But, above all, be what he might, to be a *reality* was indispensable for him. In his simple Scottish circle, the highest form of manhood attainable or known was that of Christian; the highest Christian was the Teacher of such. Irving's lot was cast. For the foray-spears were all rusted into earth there; Annan Castle had become a Town-hall; and Prophetic Knox had sent tidings thither: Prophetic Knox—and, alas, also Skeptic Hume,—and (as the natural consequence) Diplomatic Dundas. In such mixed incongrous element had the young soul to grow.

Grow nevertheless he did (with that strong vitality of his); grow and ripen. What the Scottish uncelebrated Irving was, they that have only seen the London celebrated (and distorted) one can never know. Bodily and spiritually, perhaps there was not (in that November, 1822,) a man more full of genial energetic life in all these Islands.

By a fatal chance, Fashion cast her eye on him, as on some impersonation of Novel-Cameronianism, some wild product of Nature from the wild mountains; Fashion crowded round him, with her meteor lights, and Bacchic dances; breathed her foul incense on him; intoxicating, poisoning. One may say, it was his own nobleness that forwarded such ruin: the excess of his sociability and sympathy, of his value for the suffrages and sympathies of men. Syren songs, as of a new Moral Reformation, (sons of Mammon, and high sons of Belial and Beelzebub, to become sons of God, and the gumflowers of Almack's to be made living roses in a new Eden,) sound in the inexperienced ear and heart. Most seductive, most delusive! Fashion went her idle way, to gaze on Egyptian Crocodiles, Iroquois Hunters, or what else there might be, forgot this man,—who unhappily could not in his turn forget. The intoxicating poison had been swallowed; no force of natural health could cast it out. Unconsciously, for most part in deep unconsciousness, there was now the impossibility to live neglected; to walk on the quiet paths, where alone it is well with us. Singularity must henceforth succeed Singularity. O foulest Circean draught, thou poison of Popular Applause! madness is in thee, and death; thy end is Bedlam and the Grave. For the last seven years, Irving, forsaken by the world, strove either to recall it, or to forsake it; shut himself up in a lesser world of ideas and persons, and lived isolated there. Neither in this was there health: for this man such isolation was not fit; such ideas, such persons.

One light still shone on him; alas, through a medium more and more turbid: the light from Heaven. His Bible was there, wherein must lie healing for all sorrows. To the Bible he more and more exclusively addressed himself. If it is the written Word of God, shall it not be the acted Word too? Is it mere sound, then; black printer's-ink on white rag-paper? A half-man could have passed on without answering; a whole man must answer. Hence Prophecies of Millenniums, Gifts of Tongues,—whereat Orthodoxy prims herself into decent wonder, and waves her Avaunt! Irving clave to his Belief, as to his soul's soul; followed it whithersoever, through earth or air, it might lead him; toiling as never man toiled to spread it, to gain the world's ear for it,—in vain. Ever wilder waxed the confusion without and within. The misguided noble-minded had now nothing left to do but die. He died the death of the true and brave. His last words, they say, were: "In life and in death, I am the Lord's."—Amen! Amen!

One who knew him well, and may with good cause love him, has said: "But for Irving, I had never known what the communion of man with man means. His was the freest, brotherliest, bravest human soul mine ever came in contact with: I call him, on the whole, the best man I have ever (after trial enough) found in this world, or now hope to find.

"The first time I saw Irving was six-and-twenty years ago, in his native town, Annan. He was fresh from Edinburgh, with College prizes, high character, and promise: he had come to see our Schoolmaster, who had also been his. We heard of famed Professors, of high matters classical, mathematical, a whole Wonderland of Knowledge: nothing but joy, health, hopefulness without end, looked out from the blooming young man. The last time I saw him was three months ago, in London. Friendliness still beamed in his eyes, but now from amid unquiet fire; his face was flaccid, wasted, unsound; hoary as with extreme age: he was trembling over the brink of the grave. Adieu, thou first Friend; adieu, while this confused Twilight of Existence lasts! Might we meet where Twilight has become Day!"

THE DIAMOND NECKLACE.

[Fraser's Magazine, 1837.]

CHAPTER I.

AGE OF ROMANCE.

The age of Romance has not ceased; it never ceases; it does not, if we will think of it, so much as very sensibly decline. "The passions are repressed by social forms; great passions no longer show themselves?" Why, there are passions still great enough to replenish Bedlam, for it never wants tenants; to suspend men from bed-posts, from improved-drops at the west end of Newgate. A passion that explosively shivers asunder the Life it took rise in ought to be regarded as considerable: more, no passion, in the highest hey-day of Romance, yet did. The passions, by grace of the Supernal and also of the Infernal Powers, (for both have a hand in it,) can never fail us.

And then as to "social forms," be it granted that they are of the most buckram quality, and bind men up into the pitifullest, straitlaced, common-place Existence,—you ask, Where is the Romance? In the Scotch way one answers, Where is it not? That very spectacle of an Immortal Nature, with faculties and destiny extending through Eternity, hampered and bandaged up, by nurses, pedagogues, posture-masters, and the tongues of innumerable old women, (named "force of public opinion;") by prejudice, custom, want of knowledge, want of money, want of strength, into, say, the meager Pattern-Figure that, in these days, meets you in all thoroughfares; a "god-created Man," all but abnegating the character of Man; forced to exist, automatized, mummy-wise, (scarcely in rare moments audible or visible from amid his wrappages and cerements,) as Gentleman or Gigman;* and so selling his birthright of Eternity, for the three daily meals, poor at best, which time yields:—is not this spectacle itself highly romantic, tragical,—if we had eyes to look at it? The high-born (highest-born, for he came out of Heaven) lies drowning in the despicablest puddles; the priceless gift of Life, which he can have but *once*, for he waited a whole Eternity to be born, and now has a whole Eternity waiting to see what he will do when born,—*this* priceless gift we see strangled slowly out of him by innumerable packthreads; and there

* "I always considered him a respectable man.—What do you mean by respectable? He kept a Gig."—*Thurtell's Trial.*

remains of the glorious Possibility, which we fondly named Man, nothing but an inanimate mass of foul loss and disappointment, which we wrap in shrouds and bury underground,—surely with well-merited tears. To the Thinker here lies Tragedy enough; the epitome and marrow of all Tragedy whatsoever.

But so few are Thinkers? Aye, Reader, so few think; there is the rub! Not one in the thousand has the smallest turn for thinking; only for passive dreaming and hearsaying, and active babbling by rote. Of the eyes that men do glare withal so few can *see*. Thus is the world become such a fearful confused Treadmill; and each man's task has got entangled in his neighbour's and pulls it awry; and the Spirit of Blindness, Falsehood, and Distraction (justly named the Devil) continually maintains himself among us; and even hopes (were it not for the Opposition, which by God's Grace will also maintain itself) to become supreme. Thus, too, among other things, has the Romance of Life gone wholly out of sight: and all History, degenerating into empty invoice-lists of Pitched Battles and Changes of Ministry; or, still worse, into "Constitutional History," or "Philosophy of History, or "Philosophy teaching by Experience," is become dead, as the Almanacs of other years,—to which species of composition, indeed, it bears, in several points of view, no inconsiderable affinity.

"Of all blinds that shut up men's vision," says one, "the worst is self." How true! How doubly true, if self, assuming her cunningest, yet miserablest disguise, come on us in never-ceasing, all-obscuring reflexes from the innumerable selves of others; not as Pride, not even as real Hunger, but only as Vanity, and the shadow of an imaginary Hunger, (for Applause;) under the name of what we call "Respectability!" Alas now for our Historian: to his other spiritual deadness (which, however, so long as he physically breathes cannot be complete) this sad new magic influence is added! Henceforth his Histories must all be screwed up into the "dignity of History." Instead of looking fixedly at the *Thing*, and first of all, and beyond all, endeavouring to *see* it, and fashion a living Picture of it, (not a wretched politico-metaphysical Abstraction of it,) he has now quite other matters to look to. The thing lies shrouded, invisible, in thousand-fold hallucinations, and foreign air-images: what did the Whigs say of it? What did the Tories? The Priests? The Freethinkers? Above all, what will my own listening circle say of *me* for what I say of it? And then his Respectability in general, as a literary gentleman; his not despicable talent for philosophy! Thus is our poor Historian's faculty directed mainly on two objects; the Writing and the Writer, both of which are quite extraneous; and the thing written of fares as we see. Can it be wonderful that Histories (wherein open lying is not permitted) are unromantic? Nay, our very Biographies, how stiff-starched, foisonless, hollow! They stand there respectable; and what more? Dumb idols; with a skin of delusively painted waxwork; and inwardly empty, or full of rags and bran. In our England especially, which in these days is become the chosen land of Respectability, Life-writing has dwindled to the sorrowfullest condition; it requires a man to be some disrespectable, ridiculous Boswell before he can write a tolerable Life. Thus, too, strangely enough, the only Lives worth reading are those of Players, emptiest and poorest of the sons of Adam; who nevertheless were sons of his, and brothers of ours; and by the nature of the case, had already bidden Respectability good-day. Such bounties, in this, as in infinitely deeper matters, does Respectability shower down on us. Sad are thy doings, *O Gig;* sadder than those of Juggernaut's Car: that, with huge wheel, suddenly crushes asunder the bodies of men; thou, in thy light-bobbing Long-Acre springs, gradually winnowest away their souls!

Depend upon it, for one thing, good Reader, no age ever seemed the Age of Romance to itself. Charlemagne, let the Poets talk as they will, had his own provocations in the world: what with selling of his poultry and potherbs, what with wanton daughters carrying secretaries through the snow; and, for instance, that hanging of the Saxons over the Weser-bridge, (thirty thousand of them, they say, at one bout,) it seems to me that the Great Charles had his temper ruffled at times. Roland of Roncesvalles, too, we see well in thinking of it, found rainy weather as well as sunny; knew what it was to have hose need darning; got tough beef to chew, or even went dinnerless; was saddle-sick, calumniated, constipated, (as his madness, too clearly indicates;) and oftenest felt, I doubt not, that this was a very Devil's world, and he (Roland) himself one of the sorriest caitiffs there. Only in long subsequent days, when the tough beef, the constipation, and the calumny, had clean vanished, did it all begin to seem Romantic, and your Turpins and Ariostos found music in it. So, I say, is it *ever!* And the more, as your true hero, your true Roland, is ever *unconscious* that he is a hero: this is a condition of all true greatness.

In our own poor Nineteenth Century, the writer of these lines has been fortunate enough to see not a few glimpses of Romance; he imagines this Nineteenth is hardly a whit less romantic than that Ninth, or any other, since centuries began. Apart from Napoleon, and the Dantons, and Mirabeaus, whose fire-words (of public speaking) and fire-whirlwinds, (of cannon and musquetry,) which for a season darkened the air, are, perhaps, at bottom but superficial phenomena, he has witnessed, in remotest places, much that could be called romantic, even miraculous. He has witnessed overhead the infinite Deep, with greater and lesser lights, bright-rolling, silent-beaming, hurled forth by the Hand of God; around him, and under his feet, the wonderfullest Earth, with her winter snow-storms and her summer spice-airs, and (unaccountablest of all) *himself* standing there. He stood in the lapse of Time; he saw Eternity behind him and before him. The all-encircling mysterious tide of FORCE, thousandfold, (for from force of Thought to force of Gravitation what an interval!) billowed shoreless on; bore him too along with it,—he too was part of it. From its bosom rose and vanished, in perpetual change, the lordliest Real-Phantasmagory, (which was Being;) and ever anew rose and vanished; and ever that lordliest many-coloured scene was full, another yet the same. Oak-trees fell, young acorns sprang: Men too, new-sent from the Unknown, he met, of tiniest size, who waxed into stature, into strength of sinew, passionate fire and light: in other Men the light was growing dim, the sinews all feeble; they sank, motionless, into ashes, into invisibility; returned *back* to the Unknown, beckoning him their mute farewell. He wanders still by the parting-spot; cannot hear *them;* they are far, how far!—It was a sight for angels, and archangels; for, indeed, God himself had made it wholly. One many-glancing asbestos-thread in the Web of Universal-History, spirit-woven, it rustled there, as with the howl of mighty winds, through that "wild roaring Loom of Time." Generation after generation, (hundreds of them, or thousands of them, from the unknown Beginning,) so loud, so stormful busy, rushed torrent-wise, thundering down, down; and fell all silent (only some feeble re-echo, which grew ever feebler, struggling up,) and Oblivion swallowed them *all*. Thousands more, to the unknown Ending, will follow: and *thou* here (of this present one) hangest as a drop, still sungilt, on the giddy edge; one moment, while the Darkness has not yet engulphed thee. O Brother! is *that* what thou callest prosaic; of small interest? Of small interest, and for *thee?* Awake, poor troubled sleeper: shake off thy torpid nightmare-dream; look, see, behold it, the Flame-image; splendours high as Heaven, terrors deep as Hell: this is God's Creation; this is Man's Life!—Such things has the writer of these lines witnessed, in this poor Nineteenth Century of ours; and what are all such to the things he yet hopes to witness? Hopes, with truest assurance. "I have painted so much," said the good Jean Paul, in his old days, "and I have never seen the Ocean; the Ocean of Eternity I shall not fail to see!"

Such being the intrinsic quality of this Time, and of all Time whatsoever, might not the Poet who chanced to walk through it find objects enough to paint? What object soever he fixed on, were it the meanest of the mean, let him but paint it in its actual truth, as it swims there, in such environment; world-old, yet new, and never ending; an indestructible portion of the miraculous All,—his picture of it were a Poem. How much more if the object fixed on were not mean, but one already wonderful; the (mystic) "actual truth" of which, if it lay not on the surface, yet shone through the surface, and invited even Prosaists to search for it!

The present writer, who unhappily belongs to that class, has, nevertheless, a firmer and firmer persuasion of two things: first, as was seen, that Romance exists; secondly, that now, and formerly, and ever more it exists, strictly speaking, in Reality alone. The thing that *is*, what can be *so* wonderful; what, especially to us that *are*, can have such significance? Study Reality, he is ever and anon saying to himself; search out deeper and deeper *its* quite endless mystery: see it, know it; then, whether thou wouldst learn from it, and again teach; or weep over it, or laugh over it, or love it, or despise it or in any way relate thyself to it, thou hast the firmest enduring basis: *that* hieroglyphic page is one thou canst read on for ever, find new meaning in for ever.

Finally, and in a word, do not the critics teach us: "In whatsoever thing thou hast thyself felt interest, in that or in nothing hope to inspire others with interest?"—In partial obedience to all which, and to many other principles, shall the following small Romance of the *Diamond Necklace* begin to come together. A small Romance, let the reader again and again assure himself, which is no brainweb of mine, or of any other foolish man's; but a fraction of that mystic "spirit-woven web," from the "Loom of Time," spoken of above. It is an actual Transaction that happened in this Earth of ours. Wherewith our whole business, as already urged, is to paint it truly.

For the rest, an earnest inspection, faithful endeavour has not been wanting, on our part; nor (singular as it may seem) the strictest regard to chronology, geography, (or rather in this case, topography,) documentary evidence, and what else true historical research would yield. Were there but on the reader's part a kindred openness, a kindred spirit of endeavour! Beshone strongly, on both sides, by such united twofold Philosophy, this poor opaque Intrigue of the *Diamond Necklace* became quite translucent between us; transfigured, lifted up into the serene of Universal History; and might hang there like a smallest Diamond Constellation, visible without telescope,—so long as it could.

CHAPTER II.

THE NECKLACE IS MADE.

Herr, or as he is now called Monsieur, Boehmer, to all appearance wanted not that last infirmity of noble and ignoble minds—a love of fame; he was destined also to be famous more than enough. His outlooks into the world were rather of a smiling character: he has long since exchanged his guttural speech, as far as possible, for a nasal one; his rustic Saxon fatherland for a polished city of Paris, and thriven there. United in partnership with worthy Monsieur Bassange, a sound practical man, skilled in the valuation of all precious stones, in the management of workmen, in the judgment of their work, he already sees himself among the highest of his guild: nay, rather the very highest,—for he has secured (by purchase and hard money paid) the title of King's Jeweller; and can enter the Court itself, leaving all other Jewellers, and even innumerable Gentlemen, Gigmen, and small Nobility, to languish in the vestibule. With the costliest ornaments in his pocket, or borne after him by assiduous shop-boys, the happy Boehmer sees high drawing-rooms and sacred *ruelles* fly open, as with talismanic *Sesame;* and the brightest eyes of the whole world grow brighter: to him alone of men the Unapproachable reveals herself in mysterious *negligée;* taking and giving counsel. Do not, on all gala-days and gala-nights, his works praise him? On the gorgeous robes of State, on Court-dresses and Lords' stars, on the diadem of Royalty; better still, on the swan-neck of Beauty, and her queenly garniture from plume-bearing aigrette to shoe-buckle on fairy-slipper,—that blinding play of colours is Boehmer's doing: he is *Jouaillier-Bijoutier de la Reine.*

Could the man but have been content with it! He could not: Icarus-like, he must mount too high; have his wax-wings melted, and descend prostrate,—amid a cloud of vain goose-quills. One day, a fatal day (of some year, probably, among the *Seventies* of last Century,)* it struck Boehmer: Why should not I, who, as Most Christian King's Jeweller, am properly first Jeweller of the Universe,—make a Jewel which the Universe has not matched? Nothing can prevent thee, Boehmer, if thou have the skill to do it. Skill or no skill, answers he, I have the ambition: my Jewel, if not the beautifullest, shall be the dearest. Thus was the Diamond Necklace determined on.

Did worthy Bassange give a willing or a reluctant consent? In any case he consents; and co-operates. Plans are sketched, consultations held, stucco models made; by money or credit the costliest diamonds come in; cunning craftsmen cut them, set them: proud Boehmer sees the work go prosperously on. Proud man! Behold him on a morning after breakfast: he has stepped down to the innermost workshop, before sallying out; stands there with his laced three-cornered hat, cane under arm; drawing on his gloves: with nod, with nasal-guttural word, he gives judicious confirmation, judicious abnegation, censure, and approval. A still joy is dawning over that bland, blond face of his; he can think (while in many a sacred boudoir he visits the Unapproachable) that an *opus magnum,* of which the world wotteth not, is progressing. At length comes a morning when care has terminated, and joy cannot only dawn but shine; the Necklace, that shall be famous and world-famous, is made.

Made we call it, in conformity with common speech: but properly it was not made; only, with more or less spirit of method, arranged and agglomerated. What "spirit of method" lay in it, might be made; nothing more. But to tell the various Histories of those various Diamonds, from the first making of them; or even (omitting all the rest) from the first digging of them in the far Indian mines! How they lay, for uncounted ages and æons (under the uproar and splashing of such Deucalion Deluges, and Hutton Explosions, with steam enough, and Werner Submersions) silently imbedded in the rock; nevertheless (when their hour came) emerged from it, and first beheld the glorious Sun smile on them, and with their many-coloured glances smiled back on him. How they served next (let us say) as eyes of Heathen Idols, and received worship. How they had then, by fortune of war or theft, been knocked out; and exchanged among camp-suttlers for a little spirituous liquor, and bought by Jews, and worn as signets on the fingers of tawny or white Majesties; and again been lost, with the fingers too, and perhaps life, (as by Charles the Rash, among the mud-ditches of Nancy,) in old-forgotten glorious victories: and so, through innumerable varieties of fortune,—had come at last to the cutting-wheel of Boehmer; to be united in strange fellowship, with comrades also blown together from all ends of the Earth, each with a History of its own! Could these aged stones (the youngest of them Six Thousand years of age, and upwards) but have spoken,—*there* were an Experience for Philosophy to teach by. But now, as was said, by little caps of gold (which gold also has a history,) and daintiest rings of the same, they are all, being so to speak, enlisted under Boehmer's flag,—made to take rank and file, in new order; no Jewel asking his neighbour whence he came; and parade there for a season. For a season only; and then—to disperse, and enlist anew *ad infinitum.* In such inexplicable wise are Jewels, and Men also, and indeed all earthly things, jumbled together and asunder, and shovelled and wafted to and fro, in our inexplicable chaos of a World. This was what Boehmer called *making* his Necklace.

So, in fact, do other men speak, and with even less reason. How many men, for example, hast thou heard talk of making money: of making say a million and a half of money? Of which million and a half, how much, if one were to look into it, had they *made?* The accurate value of their Industry: not a sixpence more. Their making, then, was but, like Boehmer's, a clutching and heaping together;—by-and-by to be followed also by a dispersion. Made? Thou too vain individual! were these towered ashlar edifices; were these fair bounteous leas, with their bosky umbrages and yellow harvests; and the sunshine that lights them from above, and the granite rocks and fire-reservoirs that support them from below, made by *thee?* I think, by another. The very shilling that thou hast was dug (by man's force) in Carinthia and Paraguay; smelted sufficiently; and stamped, as would seem, not without the advice of our late Defender of the Faith, his Majesty George the Fourth. Thou hast it, and holdest it; but whether, or in what sense, thou hast *made* any farthing of it, thyself canst not say. If the courteous reader ask, What things, then, are made by man? I will answer him, Very few indeed. A Heroism, a Wisdom (a god-given Volition that has realized itself) is made now and then: for example, some five or six Books (since the Creation) have been made. Strange that there are not more; for surely every encouragement is held out. Could I, or thou, happy reader, but make one, the world would let us keep it (unstolen) for Fourteen whole years,—and take what we could get for it.

* Except that Madame Campan (*Memoires,* tome ii.) says the Necklace "was intended for Du Barry," one cannot discover, within many years, the date of its manufacture. Du Barry went "into half-pay" on the 10th of May, 1774,—the day when her king died.

But in a word, Monsieur Boehmer has made his Necklace, what he calls made it: happy man is he. From a Drawing as large as reality, kindly furnished by "Taunay, Print-seller, of the Rue d'Enfer;* and again, in late years, by the Abbé Georgel, in the Second Volume of his *Mémoires*, curious readers can still fancy to themselves what a princely Ornament it was. A row of seventeen glorious diamonds, as large almost as filberts, encircle, not too tightly, the neck, a first time. Looser, gracefully fastened thrice to these, a three-wreathed festoon, and pendants enough (simple pear-shaped, multiple star-shaped, or clustering amorphous) encircle it, enwreath it, a second time. Loosest of all, softly flowing round from behind, in priceless catenary, rush down two broad threefold rows; seem to knot themselves (round a very Queen of Diamonds,) on the bosom; then rush on, again separated, as if there were length in plenty; the very tassels of them were a fortune for some men. And now, lastly, two other inexpressible threefold rows, also with their tassels, unite themselves (when the Necklace is on at rest) and into a doubly inexpressible *six*fold row; stream down (together or asunder) over the hind-neck,—we may fancy, like lambent Zodiacal or Aurora-Borealis fire.

All these on a neck of snow slight-tinged with rose-bloom, and within it royal Life: amidst the blaze of lustres; in sylphish movements, espiegleries, coquetteries, and minuet-mazes; with every movement a flash of star-rainbow colours, bright almost as the movements of the fair young soul it emblems! A glorious ornament; fit only for the Sultana of the World. Indeed, only attainable by such; for it is valued at 1,800,000 livres; say in round numbers, and sterling money, between eighty and ninety thousand pounds.

* Frontispiece of the "*Affaire du Collier*, Paris 1785;" where from Georgel's Editor has copied it. This "*Affaire du Collier*, Paris, 1785," is not, properly a Book: but a bound Collection of such Law Papers (*Mémoires pour*, &c.) as were printed and emitted by the various parties in that famed "Necklace Trial." These Law-Papers, bound into Two Volumes quarto: with Portraits, such as the Printshops yielded them at the time; likewise with patches of *MS.*, containing Notes, Pasquinade-songs, and the like, of the most unspeakable character occasionally,—constitute this "*Affaire du Collier*;" which the Paris Dealers in Old Books can still procure there. It is one of the largest collections of Falsehoods that exist in print; and, unfortunately, still, after all the narrating and history there has been on the subject, forms our chief means of getting at the truth of that Transaction. The First Volume contains some Twenty-one *Mémoires pour:* not, of course, Historical statements of truth; but Culprits' and Lawyers' statements of what they wished to be believed; each party *lying* according to his ability to lie. To reach the truth, or even any honest guess at the truth, the immensities of rubbish must be sifted, contrasted, rejected: what grain of historical evidence may lie at the bottom is then attainable. Thus, as this Transaction of the Diamond Necklace has been called the "Largest Lie of the Eighteenth Century," so it comes to us borne, not unfitly, on a whole illimitable dim Chaos of Lies!

Nay, the Second Volume, entitled *Suite de l'Affaire du Collier*, is still stranger. It relates to the Intrigue and Trial of one Bette d'Étienville, who represents himself as a poor lad that had been kidnapped, blindfolded, introduced to beautiful Ladies, and engaged to get husbands for them; as setting out on this task, and gradually getting quite bewitched and bewildered;—most indubitably, going on to bewitch and bewilder other people on all hands of him: the whole *in consequence* of this "Necklace Trial," and the noise it was making! Very curious. The Lawyers did verily busy themselves with this affair of Bette's; there are scarecrow Portraits given, that stood in the Printshops, and no man can know whether the Originals ever so much as existed. It is like the Dream *of* a Dream. The human mind stands stupent; ejaculates the wish that such Gulph of Falsehood would close itself,—before general Delirium supervene, and the Speech of Man become mere incredible, meaningless jargon, like that of choughs and daws. Even from Bette, however, by assiduous sifting, one gathers a particle of truth here and there.

CHAPTER III.

THE NECKLACE CANNOT BE SOLD.

Miscalculating Boehmer! The Sultana of the Earth shall never wear that Necklace of thine; no neck, either royal or vassal, shall ever be the lovelier for it. In the present distressed state of our finances, (with the American War raging round us,) where thinkest thou are eighty thousand pounds to be raised for such a thing? In this hungry world, thou fool, these five hundred and odd Diamonds, good only for looking at, are intrinsically worth less to us than a string of as many dry Irish potatoes, on which a famishing Sansculotte might fill his belly. Little knowest thou, laughing Jouaillier-Bijoutier, great in thy pride of place, in thy pride of *savoir-faire*, what the world has in store for thee. Thou laughest there; by-and-by thou wilt laugh on the wrong side of thy face mainly.

While the Necklace lay in stucco effigy, and the stones of it were still "circulating in Commerce," Du Barry's was the neck it was meant for. Unhappily, as all dogs (male and female) have but their day, her day is gone; and now (so busy has Death been) she sits retired, on mere half-pay, without prospects, at Saint-Cyr. A generous France will buy no more neck-ornaments for *her*:—O Heaven! the Guillotine-axe is already forging (North, in Swedish Dalecarlia, by sledge-hammers and fire; South, too, by taxes and *tailles*) that will sheer her neck in twain!

But, indeed, what of Du Barry! A foul worm; hatched by royal heat, on foul composts, into a flaunting butterfly; now diswinged, and again a worm! Are there not Kings' Daughters and Kings' Consorts: is not Decoration the first wish of a female heart,—often also (if the heart is empty) the last? The Portuguese Ambassador is here, and his rigorous Pombal is no longer Minister: there is an Infanta in Portugal, purposing by Heaven's blessing to wed.—Singular! the Portuguese Ambassador, though without fear of Pombal praises, but will not purchase.

Or why not our own loveliest Marie-Antoinette, once Dauphiness only; now every inch a Queen: what neck in the whole Earth would it beseem better? It is fit only for her. —Alas, Boehmer! King Louis has an eye for diamonds; but, he too, is without overplus of money: his high Queen herself answers queen-like, "We have more need of Seventy-fours than of Necklaces." *Laudatur et alget!*—Not without a qualmish feeling, we apply next to the Queen and King of the Two Sicilies.* In

* See *Mémoires de Campan*, ii 1—26.

vain, O Boehmer! In crowned heads there is no hope for thee. Not a crowned head of them can spare the eighty thousand pounds. The age of Chivalry is gone, and that of Bankruptcy is come. A dull, deep, pressing movement rocks all thrones: Bankruptcy is beating down the gate, and no Chancellor can longer barricade her out. She will enter; and the shoreless fire-lava of DEMOCRACY is at her back! Well may Kings, a second time, "sit still with awful eye," and think of far other things than Necklaces.

Thus for poor Boehmer are the mournfullest days and nights appointed; and this high-promising year (1780, as we laboriously guess and gather) stands blacker than all others in his calendar. In vain shall he, on his sleepless pillow, more and more desperately revolve the problem; it is a problem of the insoluble sort, a true "irreducible case of Cardan:" the Diamond Necklace will not sell.

CHAPTER IV.

AFFINITIES: THE TWO FIXED-IDEAS.

Nevertheless, a man's little Work lies not isolated, stranded; a whole busy World (a whole native-element of mysterious, never-resting Force) environs it; will catch it up; will carry it forward, or else backward: always, infallibly, either as living growth, or at worst as well-rotted manure, the Thing Done will come to use. Often, accordingly, for a man that had finished any little work, this were the most interesting question: In such a boundless whirl of a world, what hook will it be, and what hooks, that shall catch up this little work of mine; and whirl *it* also,—through such a dance? A question, we need not say, which, in the simplest of cases, would bring the whole Royal Society to a nonplus.—Good Corsican Letitia! while thou nursest thy little Napoleon, and he answers thy mother-smile with those deep eyes of his, a world-famous French Revolution, with Federations of the *Champ de Mars*, and September Massacres, and Bakers' Customers *en queue*, is getting ready: many a Danton and Desmoulins; prim-visaged, Tartuffe-looking Robespierre, (as yet all schoolboys;) and Marat weeping (and cursing) bitter rheum, as he pounds horse-drugs,—are preparing the fittest arena for him!

Thus, too, while poor Boehmer is busy with those Diamonds of his, picking them "out of Commerce," and his craftsmen are grinding and setting them; a certain ecclesiastical Coadjutor and Grand Almoner, and prospective Commendator and Cardinal, is in Austria, hunting and giving suppers; for whom mainly it is that Boehmer and his craftsmen so employ themselves. Strange enough, once more! The foolish Jeweller at Paris, making foolish trinkets; the foolish Ambassador at Vienna, making blunders and debaucheries: these Two, all uncommunicating, wide asunder as the Poles, are hourly forging for each other the wonderfullest hook-and-eye; that will hook them together, one day,—into artificial Siamese-Twins, for the astonishment of mankind.

Prince Louis de Rohan is one of those select mortals born to honours, as the sparks fly upwards; and, alas, also (as all men are) to troubles no less. Of his genesis and descent much might be said, by the curious in such matters; yet, perhaps, if we weigh it well, intrinsically little. He can, by diligence and faith, be traced back some hand-breadth or two, (some century or two;) but after that, merges in the mere "blood-royal of Brittany;" long, long on this side of the Northern Immigrations, he is not so much as to be sought for;—and leaves the whole space onwards from that, into the bosom of Eternity, a blank, marked only by one point, the Fall of Man! However, and what alone concerns us, his kindred, in these quite recent times, have been much about the Most Christian Majesty; could there pick up what was going. In particular, they have had a turn of some continuance for Cardinalship and Commendatorship. Safest trades these, of the calm, do-nothing sort: in the do-something line, in Generalship, or such like, (witness poor Cousin Soubise, at Rossbach,*) they might fare not so well. In any case, the actual Prince Louis, Coadjutor at Strasburg, while his uncle, the Cardinal-Archbishop, has not yet deceased, and left him his dignities, but only fallen sick, already takes his place on one grandest occasion: he, thrice-happy Coadjutor, receives the fair, young, trembling Dauphiness, Marie-Antoinette, on her first entrance into France; and can there, as Ceremonial Fugleman, with fit bearing and semblance, (being a tall man, of six-and-thirty,) do the needful. Of his other performances up to this date, a refined History had rather say nothing.

In fact, if the tolerating mind will meditate it with any sympathy, what could poor Rohan perform? Performing needs light, needs strength, and a firm clear footing; all of which had been denied him. Nourished, from birth, with the choicest physical spoon-meat, indeed; yet, also, with no better spiritual Doctrine and Evangel of Life than a French Court of Louis the Well-beloved could yield; gifted, moreover, (and this, too, was but a new perplexity for him,) with shrewdness enough to see through much, with vigour enough to despise much; unhappily, not with vigour enough to spurn it from him, and be for ever enfranchised of it,—he awakes, at man's stature, with man's wild desires, in a World of the merest incoherent Lies and Delirium; himself a nameless Mass of delirious Incoherence,—covered over, at most, (and held in a little,) by

* Here is the Epigram they made against him on occasion of Rossbach,—in that "Despotism tempered by Epigrams," which France was then said to be:—

"Soubise dit, la lanterne à la main,
J'ai beau chercher, où diable est mon armée?
Elle était là pourtant hier matin:
Me l'a-t-on prise, ou l'aurais-je égarée?—
Que vois-je, ô ciel! que mon âme est ravie!
Prodige heureux! la voilà, la voilà!—
Ah, ventrebleu! qu'est-ce donc que cela?
Je me trompais, c'est l'armée ennemie!"

LACRETELLE, ii. 206.

conventional Politesse, and a Cloak of prospective Cardinal's Plush. Are not Intrigues, might Rohan say, the industry of this our Universe; nay, is not the Universe itself, at bottom, properly an Intrigue? A Most Christian Majesty, in the *Parc-aux-cerfs*: he, thou seest, is the god of this lower world; our war-banner (in the fight of Life) and celestial *Entouto-nika* is a Strumpet's Petticoat: these are thy gods, O France!—What, in such singular circumstances, could poor Rohan's creed and world-theory be, that he should "perform" thereby? Atheism? Alas, no; not even Atheism: only Machiavelism; and the indestructible faith that "ginger is hot in the mouth." Get ever new and better *ginger*, therefore; chew it ever the more diligently: 't is all thou hast to look to, and that only for a day.

Ginger enough, poor Louis de Rohan: too much of ginger! Whatsoever of it, for the five senses, money, or money's worth, or back-stairs diplomacy, can buy; nay, for the sixth sense, too, the far spicier ginger: Antecedence of thy fellow-creatures,—merited, at least, by infinitely finer housing than theirs. Coadjutor of Strasburg, Archbishop of Strasburg, Grand Almoner of France, Commander of the Order of the Holy Ghost, Cardinal, Commendator of St. Wast d'Arras (one of the fattest benefices here below): all these shall be housings for Monseigneur: to all these shall his Jesuit Nursing-mother, (our vulpine Abbé Georgel,) through fair court-weather and through foul, triumphantly bear him,—and wrap him with them, fat, somnolent, Nurseling as he is.—By the way, a most assiduous, ever-wakeful Abbé is this Georgel; and wholly Monseigneur's. He has scouts dim-flying, far out, in the great deep of the world's business; has spider-threads that over-net the whole world; himself sits in the centre ready to run. In vain shall King and Queen combine against Monseigneur: "I was at M. de Maurepas' pillow before six," —persuasively wagging my sleek coif, and the sleek reynard-head under it; I managed it all for him. Here, too, on occasion of Reynard Georgel, we could not but reflect what a singular species of creature your Jesuit must have been. Outwardly, you would say, a man; the smooth semblance of a man: inwardly, to the centre, filled with stone! Yet in all breathing things, even in stone Jesuits, are inscrutable sympathies: how else does a Reynard Abbé so loyally give himself, soul and body, to a somnolent Monseigneur;—how else does the poor Tit, to the neglect of its own eggs and interests, nurse up a huge lumbering Cuckoo; and think its pains all paid, if the soot-brown Stupidity will merely grow bigger and bigger!—Enough, by Jesuitic or other means, Prince Louis de Rohan shall be passively kneaded and baked into Commendator of St. Wast and much else; and truly *such* a Commendator as hardly, since King Thierri (first of the *Fainéans*) founded that Establishment, has played his part there.

Such, however, have Nature and Art combined together to make Prince Louis. A figure thrice-clothed with honours; with plush, and civic, and ecclesiastic garniture of all kinds; but in itself little other than an amorphous congeries of contradictions, somnolence and violence, foul passions, and foul habits. It is by his plush cloaks and wrappages mainly, as above hinted, that such a figure sticks together (what we call, "coheres,") in any measure; were it not for these, he would flow out boundlessly on all sides. Conceive him, further, with a kind of radical vigour and fire, (for he can see clearly at times, and speak fiercely;) yet left in this way to stagnate and ferment, and lie overlaid with such floods of fat material,—have we not a true image of the shamefullest Mud-volcano, gurgling and sluttishly simmering, amid continual steamy indistinctness, (except, as was hinted, in wind-*gusts*;) with occasional terrifico-absurd Mud-explosions!

This, garnish it and fringe it never so handsomely, is, alas, the intrinsic character of Prince Louis. A shameful spectacle: such, however, as the world has beheld many times; as it were to be wished (but is not yet to be hoped) the world might behold no more. Nay, are not all possible delirious incoherences, outward and inward, summed up, for poor Rohan, in this one incrediblest incoherence, that *he*, Prince Louis de Rohan, is named Priest, Cardinal of the Church? A debauched, merely libidinous mortal, lying there quite helpless, *dis*-solute, (as we well say;) whom to see Church Cardinal (that is, symbolical *Hinge*, or main Corner, of the Invisible Holy in this World) an Inhabitant of Saturn might split with laughing,—if he did not rather swoon with pity and horror!

Prince Louis, as ceremonial fugleman at Strasburg, might have hoped to make some way with the fair young Dauphiness; but seems not to have made any. Perhaps, in those great days, so trying for a fifteen years' Bride and Dauphiness, the fair Antoinette was too preoccupied: perhaps, in the very face and looks of Prospective-Cardinal Prince Louis, her fair young soul read, all unconsciously, an incoherent *Roué*-ism, (bottomless Mud-volcano-ism,) from which she by instinct rather recoiled.

However, as above hinted, he is now gone, in these years, on Embassy to Vienna: with "four-and-twenty pages," (if our remembrance of Abbé Georgel serve) "of noble birth," all in scarlet breeches; and such a retinue and parade as drowns even his fat revenue in perennial debt. Above all things, his Jesuit Familiar is with him. For so everywhere they must manage: Eminence Rohan is the cloak, Jesuit Georgel the man or automaton within it. Rohan, indeed, sees Poland a-partitioning; or rather Georgel, with his "masked Austrian" traitor, "on the ramparts," sees it for him: but what can he do? He exhibits his four-and-twenty scarlet pages, (who "smuggle" to quite unconscionable lengths;) rides through a Catholic procession, Prospective-Cardinal as he is, because it is too long, and keeps him from an appointment: hunts, gallants; gives suppers, Sardanapalus-wise, the finest ever seen in Vienna. Abbé Georgel (as we fancy it was) writes a Despatch in his name "every fortnight;"—mentions, in one of these, that "Maria Theresa stands, indeed, with the handkerchief in one hand, weeping for the woes of Poland; but with the sword in the other hand, ready to cut Poland in sections, and take her share."* Untimely joke; which proved to Prince Louis the root of unspeakable chagrins! For Minister D'Aiguillon (much against his duty) communicates the Letter to King Louis; Louis to Du Barry, to season her *souper*, and laughs over it: the thing becomes a court-joke; the filially-pious Dauphiness hears it, and remembers it. Accounts go, moreover, that Rohan spake censuringly of the Dauphiness to her Mother: this, probably, is but hearsay and false; the devout Maria Theresa disliked him, and even despised him, and vigorously laboured for his recall.

Thus, in rosy sleep and somnambulism, or awake only to quaff the full wine-cup of the Scarlet Woman, (his mother,) and again sleep and somnambulate, does the Prospective-Cardinal and Commendator pass his days. Unhappy man! This is not a world that was made in sleep; that it is safe to sleep and somnambulate in. In that "loud-roaring Loom of Time" (where above nine hundred millions of hungry Men, for one item, restlessly weave and work,) so many threads fly humming from their "eternal spindles;" and swift invisible shuttles, far darting, to the Ends of the World, —complex enough! At this hour, a miserable Boehmer in Paris (whom thou wottest not of) is spinning, of diamonds and gold, a paltry thrum that will go nigh to strangle the life out of thee.

Meanwhile Louis the well-beloved has left (for ever) his *Parc-aux-cerfs;* and, amid the scarce-suppressed hootings of the world, taken up his last lodging at St. Denis. Feeling that it was all over, (for the small-pox has the victory, and even Du Barry is off,) he, as the Abbé Georgel records, "made the *amende honorable* to God," (these are his Reverence's own words;) had a true repentance of three days' standing; and so, continues the Abbé, "fell asleep in the Lord." Asleep in the Lord, Monsieur l'Abbé! If such a mass of Laziness and Lust fell asleep in the Lord, *who*, fanciest thou, is it that falls asleep—elsewhere? Enough that he did fall asleep; that thick-wrapt in the Blanket of the Night, under what keeping we ask not, *he* never through endless Time can, for his own or our sins, insult the face of the Sun any more;—and so now we go onward, if not to less degrees of beastliness, yet, at least and worst, to cheering varieties of it.

Louis XVI. therefore reigns, (and under the Sieur Gamain, makes locks;) his fair Dauphiness has become a Queen. Eminence Rohan is home from Vienna; to condole and congratulate. He bears a letter from Maria Theresa; hopes the Queen will not forget old Ceremonial Fuglemen, and friends of the Dauphiness. Heaven and Earth! The Dauphiness Queen will not see him; orders the Letter to be *sent* her. The King himself signifies briefly that he "will be asked for when wanted!"

Alas! at Court, our motion is the delicatest, unsurest. We go spinning, as it were, on teetotums, by the edge of bottomless deeps. Rest is fall; so is one false whirl. A moment ago, Eminence Rohan seemed waltzing with the best: but, behold, his teetotum has *carried him over;* there is an inversion of the centre of gravity; and so now, heels uppermost, velocity increasing as the time, space as the square of the time,—he rushes.

On a man of poor Rohan's somnolence and violence, the sympathizing mind can estimate what the effect was. Consternation, stupefaction, the total jumble of blood, brains, and nervous spirits; in ear and heart, only universal hubbub, and louder and louder singing of the agitated air. A fall comparable to that of Satan! Men have, indeed, been driven from Court; and borne it, according to ability. A Choiseul, in these very years, retired Parthian-like, with a smile or scowl; and drew half the Court-host along with him. Our Wolsey, though once an *Ego et Rex meus*, could journey, it is said, without strait-waistcoat, to his monasetry; and there, telling beads, look forward to a still longer journey. The melodious, too soft-strung, Racine, when his King turned his back on him, emitted one meek wail, and submissively—died. But the case of Coadjutor de Rohan differed from all these. No loyalty was in him that he should die; no self-help, that he should live; no faith that he should tell beads. His is a mud-volcanic character; incoherent, mad, from the very foundation of it. Think, too, that his Courtiership (for how could any nobleness enter there?) was properly a gambling speculation: the loss of his trump Queen of Hearts can bring nothing but flat, unredeemed despair. No other game has he, in this world,—or in the next. And then the exasperating *Why?* the *How came it?* For that Rohanic, or Georgelic, sprightliness of the "handkerchief in one hand, and sword in the other," (if indeed, that could have caused it all,) has quite escaped him. In the name of Friar Bacon's Head, *what* was it? Imagination, with Desperation to drive her, may fly to all points of Space;—and return with wearied wings, and no tidings. Behold *me here:* this, which is the first grand certainty for man in general, is the first and last and only one for poor Rohan. And then his *Here!* Alas, looking upwards, he can eye, from his burning marle, the azure realms, once his; Cousin Countess de Marsan, and so many Richelieus, Polignacs, and other happy angels, male and female, all blissfully gyrating there; while he—!

Nevertheless hope, in the human breast, though not in the diabolical, springs eternal The outcast Rohan bends all his thoughts, faculties, prayers, purposes, to one object; one

* *Mémoires de l'Abbé Georgel*, ii. 1—220. Abbé Georgel, who has given, in the place referred to, a long solemn Narrative of the Necklace Business, passes for the grand authority on it: but neither will he, strictly taken up, abide scrutiny. He is vague as may be; writing in what is called the "soaped-pig" fashion: yet sometimes you *do* catch him, and hold him. There are hardly above three dates in his whole Narrative. He mistakes several times; perhaps, once or twice, wilfully misrepresents, a little. The main incident of the business is misdated by him, almost a twelvemonth. It is to be remembered that the poor Abbé wrote in exile; and with cause enough for prepossessions and hostilities.

object he will attain, or go to Bedlam. How many ways he tries; what days and nights of conjecture, consultation; what written unpublished reams of correspondence, protestation, back-stairs diplomacy of every rubric! How many suppers has he eaten; how many given,—in vain! It is his morning song, and his evening prayer. From innumerable falls he rises; only to fall again. Behold him even, with his red stockings, at dusk, in the Garden of Trianon: he has bribed the Concierge; will see her Majesty in spite of Etiquette and Fate; peradventure, pitying his long sad King's-evil, she will touch him, and heal him. In vain, (says the Female Historian, Campan.)* The Chariot of Majesty shoots rapidly by, with high-plumed heads in it; Eminence is known by his red stockings, but not looked at, only laughed at, and left standing like a Pillar of Salt.

Thus through ten long years (of new resolve and new despondency, of flying from Saverne to Paris, and from Paris to Saverne) has it lasted; hope deferred making the heart sick. Reynard Georgel and Cousin de Marsan, by eloquence, by influence, and being "at M. de Maurepas' pillow before six," have secured the Archbishopric, the Grand-Almonership, (by the medium of Poland;) and, lastly, to tinker many rents, and appease the Jew, that fattest Commendatorship, founded by King Thierri the Donothing—perhaps with a view to such cases. All good! languidly croaks Rohan; yet all not the one thing needful; alas, the Queen's eyes do not yet shine on me.

Abbé Georgel admits (in his own polite diplomatic way) that the mud-volcano was much agitated by these trials; and in time quite changed. Monseigneur deviated into cabalistic courses, after elixirs, philtres, and the philosopher's stone; that is, the volcanic stream grew thicker and heavier: at last by Cagliostro's magic, (for Cagliostro and the Cardinal by elective affinity must meet,) it sank into the opacity of perfect London fog! So, too, if Monseigneur grew choleric; wrapped himself up in reserve, spoke roughly to his domestics and dependents,—were not the terrifico-absurd mud explosions becoming more frequent? Alas, what wonder? Some nine-and-forty winters have now fled over his Eminence, (for it is 1783,) and his beard falls white to the shaver; but age for him brings no "benefit of experience." He is possessed by a fixed-idea!

Foolish Eminence! is the Earth grown all barren and of a snuff colour, because one pair of eyes in it look on thee askance? Surely thou hast thy Body there yet; and what of Soul might from the first reside in it. Nay, a warm, snug Body, with not only five senses, (sound still in spite of much tear and wear,) but most eminent clothing besides;—clothed with authority over much, with red Cardinal's cloak, red Cardinal's hat; with Commendatorship, Grand-Almonership (so kind have thy Fripiers been,) and dignities and dominions too tedious to name. The stars rise nightly, with tidings (for thee, too, if thou wilt listen) from the infinite Blue; Sun and Moon bring vicissitudes of season; dressing green, with flower-borderings, and cloth of gold, this ancient ever-young Earth of ours, and filling her breasts, with all-nourishing mother's milk. Wilt thou work? The whole Encyclopedia (not Diderot's only, but the Almighty's) is there for thee to spread thy broad faculty upon. Or, if thou have no faculty, no Sense, hast thou not (as already suggested) Senses, to the number of five. What victuals thou wishest, command; with what wine savoureth thee, be filled. Already thou art a false lascivious Priest; with revenues of, say, a quarter of a million sterling; and no mind to mend. Eat, foolish Eminence; eat with voracity,—leaving the shot till *afterwards!* In all this the eyes of Marie Antoinette can neither help thee nor hinder.

And yet what is the Cardinal, dissolute, mud-volcano though he be, more foolish herein, than all Sons of Adam? Give the wisest of us once a "fixed-idea,"—which, though a temporary madness, who has not had?—and see where his wisdom is! The Chamois-hunter serves his doomed seven years in the Quicksilver Mines; returns salivated to the marrow of the backbone; and next morning,—goes forth to hunt again. Behold Cardalion, King of Urinals; with a woful ballad to his mistress' eyebrow! He blows out, Werter-wise, his foolish existence, because *she* will not have it to keep; heeds not that there are some five hundred millions of other mistresses in this noble Planet; most likely much such as she. O foolish men! They sell their Inheritance, (as their mother did hers,) thought it is Paradise, for a crotchet: will they not, in every age, dare not only grape-shot and gallows-ropes, but Hell-fire itself, for better sauce to their victuals? My friends, beware of fixed-ideas.

Here, accordingly, is poor Boehmer with one in his head too! He has been hawking his "irreducible case of Cardan" (that Necklace of his) these three long years, through all Palaces and Ambassadors' Hotels, over the old "nine Kingdoms," (or more of them that there now are:) searching, sifting Earth, Sea, and Air, for a customer. To take his Necklace in pieces, and so, losing only his manual labour and expected glory, dissolve his fixed-idea, and fixed diamonds, into current ones: this were simply casting out the Devil—from himself; a miracle, and perhaps more! For he too has a Devil or Devils: one mad object that he strives at; that he too will attain, or go to Bedlam. Creditors, snarling, hound him on from without; mocked Hopes, lost Labours, bear-bait him from within: to these torments his fixed-idea keeps him chained. In six-and-thirty weary revolutions of the Moon, was it

* Madame Campan, in her Narrative, and, indeed, in her *Memoirs* generally, does not seem to *intend* falsehood: this, in the Business of the Necklace, is saying a great deal. She rather, perhaps, intends the producing of an impression; which may have appeared to herself to be the right one. But, at all events, she has, here or elsewhere, no notion of historical rigour; she gives hardly any date, or the like; will tell the same thing, in different places, different ways, &c. There is a tradition that Louis XVIII. revised her *Mémoires* before publication. She requires to be read with skepticism everywhere; but yields something in that way.

wonderful the man's brain had got dried a little?

Behold, one day, being Court-Jeweller, he too bursts, almost as Rohan had done, into the Queen's retirement, or apartment; flings herself (as Campan again has recorded) at her Majesty's feet; and there, with clasped, uplifted hands, in passionate nasal-gutturals, with streaming tears and loud sobs, entreats her to do one of two things: Either to buy his Necklace; or else graciously to vouchsafe him her royal permission to drown himself in the River Seine. Her majesty, pitying the distracted, bewildered state of the man, calmly points out the plain third course: *Dépécez votre Collier*, (take your Necklace in pieces;)—adding, withal, in a tone of queenly rebuke, that if he would drown himself, he at all times could, without her furtherance.

Ah, *had* he drowned himself, with the Necklace in his pocket; and Cardinal Commendator at his skirts! Kings, above all, beautiful Queens, as far-radiant Symbols on the pinnacles of the world, are so exposed to madmen. Should these two fixed-ideas that beset this beautifullest Queen, and almost burst through her Palace-walls, one day *unite*, and this *not* to jump into the River Seine;—what maddest result may be looked for!

CHAPTER V.

THE ARTIST.

If the reader has hitherto (in our too figurative language) seen only the figurative hook and the figurative eye, which Boehmer and Rohan, far apart, were respectively fashioning for each other, he shall now see the cunning Milliner (an actual, unmetaphorical Milliner) by whom these two individuals, with their two implements, are brought in contact, and hooked together into stupendous artificial Siamese-Twins;—after which the whole nodus and solution will naturally combine and unfold itself.

Jeanne de St. Remi, by courtesy or otherwise, Countess, styled also *of Valois*, and even *of France*, has now, (in this year of Grace, 1783,) known the world for some seven-and-twenty summers; and had crooks in her lot. She boasts herself descended, by what is called *natural* generation, from the Blood-Royal of France: Henri Second, before that fatal tourney-lance entered his right eye, and ended him, appears to have had, successively or simultaneously, four—unmentionable women: and so, in *vice* of the third of these, came a certain Henri de St. Remi into this world; and, as High and Puissant Lord, ate his victuals and spent his days, on an allotted domain of Fontette, near Bar-sur-Aube, in Champagne. Of High and Puissant Lords, at this Fontette, six other generations followed; and thus ultimately, in a space of some two centuries,—succeeded in realizing this brisk little Jeanne de St. Remi, here in question. But, ah, what a falling off! The Royal Family of France has well-nigh forgotten its left-hand collaterals; the last High and Puissant Lord, (much clipt by his predecessors,) falling into drink, and left by a scandalous world to drink his pitcher *dry*, had to alienate by degrees his whole worldly Possessions, down almost to the indispensable, or inexpressibles; and die at last in the Paris Hôtel-Dieu; glad that it was not on the street. So that he has indeed given a sort of bastard Life-royal to little Jeanne, and her little brother; but not the smallest earthly provender to keep it in. The mother, in her extremity, forms the wonderfullest connections; and little Jeanne, and her little brother, go out into the highways to beg.*

A charitable Countess Boulainvilliers, struck with the little bright-eyed tatterdemalion from the carriage window, picks her up; has her scoured, clothed; and rears her, in her fluctuating, miscellaneous way, to be, about the age of twenty, a nondescript of Mantuamaker, Soubrette, Court-beggar, Fine-lady, Abigail, and Scion-of-Royalty. Sad combination of trades! The Court, after infinite soliciting, puts one off with a hungry dole of little more than thirty pounds a year. Nay, the audacious Count Boulainvilliers dares (with what purposes he knows best) to offer some suspicious presents!† Whereupon his good Countess (especially as Mantuamaking languishes) thinks it could not but be fit to go down to Bar-sur-Aube; and there see whether no fractions of that alienated Fontette Property, held, perhaps, on insecure tenure, may, by terror or cunning, be recoverable. Burning her paper patterns; pocketting her pension, (till more come,) Mademoiselle Jeanne sallies out thither, in her twenty-third year.

Nourished in this singular way, alternating between saloon and kitchen-table, with the loftiest of pretensions, meanest of possessions, our poor High and Puissant Mantuamaker has realized for herself a "face not beautiful, yet with a certain piquancy;" dark hair, blue eyes; and a character, which the present writer, a determined student of human nature, declares to be undecipherable. Let the Psychologists try it! Jeanne de Saint-Remi de Valois de France actually lived, and worked, and was: she has even published, at various times, three considerable Volumes of Autobiography, with loose Leaves (in Courts of Justice) of unknown number;‡ wherein he that runs may

---

* *Vie de Jeanne Comtesse de Lamotte*, (by Herself.) Vol. I.

† He was of Hebrew descent: grandson of the renowned Jew Bernard, whom Louis XV., and even Louis XVI., used to "walk with in the Royal Garden," when they wanted him to lend them money.—See *Souvenirs du Duc de Levis*; *Mémoires de Duclos*, &c.

‡ Four *Mémoires Pour* by her, in this *Affaire du Collier*; like "Lawyers' tongues turned inside out!" Afterwards one Volume, *Mémoires Justificatifs de la Comtesse de*, &c., (London, 1788;) with Appendix of "Documents," so-called. This has also been translated into a kind of English. Then two Volumes, as quoted above: *Vie de Jeanne de*, &c.; printed in London,—by way of extorting money *from Paris*. This latter Lying Autobiography of Lamotte was bought up by French persons in authority. It was the burning of this *Editio Princeps* in the Sevres Potteries, on the 30th of May, 1792, which raised such a smoke, that the Legislative Assembly took alarm; and had an investigation about it, and considerable examining of Potters, &c., till the truth came out. Copies of the Book were speedily reprinted after the Tenth of August. It is in English too; and, except in the Necklace part, is not so entirely distracted as the former.

read,—but not understand. Strange Volumes! more like the screeching of distracted night-birds, (suddenly disturbed by the torch of Police-Fowlers,) than the articulate utterance of a rational unfeathered biped. Cheerfully admitting these statements to be all lies; we ask, How any mortal could, or should, *so* lie?

The Psychologists, however, commit one sore mistake; that of searching, in every character named human, for something like a conscience. Being mere contemplative recluses, for most part, and feeling that Morality is the Heart of Life, they judge that with all the world it is so. Nevertheless, as practical men are aware, Life can go on in excellent vigour, without crotchet of that kind. What is the essence of Life? Volition? Go deeper down, you find a much more universal root and characteristic: Digestion. While Digestion lasts, Life cannot, in philosophical language, be said to be extinct: and Digestion will give rise to Volitions enough, at any rate, to Desires (and attempts) which may pass for such. He who looks neither before nor after, any further than the Larder, and Stateroom, (which is properly the finest compartment of the Larder,) will need no World-theory, (Creed, as it is called,) or Scheme of Duties: lightly leaving the world to wag as it likes with any theory or none, his grand object is a theory (and practice) of ways and means. Not goodness or badness is the type of him; only shiftiness or shiftlessness.

And now, disburdened of this obstruction, let the Psychologists consider it under a bolder view. Consider the brisk Jeanne de Saint-Remi de Saint-Shifty as a Spark of vehement Life (not developed into Will of any kind, yet fully into Desires of all kinds) cast into such a Life-element as we have seen. Vanity and Hunger; a Princess of the Blood, yet whose father had sold his inexpressibles; uncertain whether fosterdaughter of a fond Countess, with hopes sky-high, or supernumerary Soubrette, with not enough of Mantuamaking: in a word, *Gigmanity disgigged;* one of the saddest, pitiable, unpitied predicaments of man! She is of that light unreflecting class, of that light unreflecting sex: *varium semper et mutabile.* And then her Fine-Ladyism, though a purseless one: capricious, coquettish, and with all the finer sensibilities of the heart; now in the rackets, now in the sullens; vivid in contradictory resolves; laughing, weeping without reason,—though these acts are said to be signs of reason. Consider, too, how she has had to work her way, all along, by flattery and cajolery; wheedling, eaves-dropping, and nambypambying: how she needs wages, and knows no other productive trades. Thought can hardly be said to exist in her: only Perception and Device. With an understanding lynx-eyed for the surface of things, but which pierces beyond the surface of nothing; every individual thing (for she has never seized the heart of it) turns up a new face to her every new day, and seems a thing changed, a different thing. Thus sits, or rather vehemently bobs and hovers her vehement mind, in the middle of a boundless many-dancing whirlpool of gilt-shreds, paper clippings, and windfalls,—to which the revolving chaos of my Uncle-Toby's Smoke-jack was solidity and regularity. Reader! thou for thy sins must have met with such fair Irrationals; fascinating, with their lively eyes, with their quick snappish fancies; distinguished in the higher circles, in Fashion, even in Literature: they hum and buzz there, on graceful film wings;—searching, nevertheless, with the wonderfullest skill, for honey: "*un*tamable as flies!"

Wonderfullest skill for honey, we say; and, pray, mark that, as regards this Countess de Saint-Shifty. Her instinct-of-genius is prodigious; her appetite fierce. In any foraging speculation of the private kind, she, unthinking as you call her, will be worth a hundred thinkers. And so of such untamable flies the untamablest, Mademoiselle Jeanne is now buzzing down, in the Bar-sur-Aube Diligence; to inspect the honey-jars of Fontette; and see and smell whether there be any flaws in them.

Alas, at Fontette, we can, with sensibility, behold straw-roofs we were nursed under; farmers courteously offer cooked milk, and other country messes; but no soul will part with his Landed Property, for which (though cheap) he declares hard money was paid. The honey-jars are all close, then?—However, a certain Monsieur de Lamotte, a tall Gendarme, home on furlough from Lunéville, is now at Bar; pays us attentions; becomes quite particular in his attentions,—for we have a face "with a certain piquancy," the liveliest glib-snappish tongue, the liveliest kittenish manner, (not yet hardened into *cat*-hood,) with thirty pounds a-year, and prospects. M. de Lamotte, indeed, is as yet only a private sentinel; but then a private sentinel in the *Gendarmes:* and did not his father die fighting "at the head of his company," at Minden? Why not in virtue of our own Countess-ship dub him too Count; by left-hand collateralism, get him advanced? —Finished before the furlough is done! The untamablest of flies has again buzzed off; in wedlock with M. de Lamotte; if not to get honey, yet to escape spiders; and so lies in garrison at Lunéville, amid coquetries and hysterics, in Gigmanity disgigged—disconsolate enough.

At the end of four long years, (too long,) M. de Lamotte, or call him now *Count* de Lamotte, sees good to lay down his fighting-gear, (unhappily still only the musket,) and become what is by certain moderns called "a Civilian:" not a Civil-Law Doctor; merely a citizen, one who does not live by being killed. Alas! cold eclipse has all along hung over the Lamotte household. Countess Boulainvilliers, it is true, writes in the most feeling manner: but then the Royal Finances are so deranged! Without personal pressing solicitation, on the spot, no Court-Solicitor, were his pension the meagrest, can hope to better it. At Lunéville, the sun indeed shines; and there is a kind of Life; but only an un-Parisian, half or quarter Life; the very tradesmen grow clamorous, and no cunningly devised fable, ready money alone, will appease them. Commandant Marquis d'Autichamp* agrees with Madame Boulain-

* He is the same Marquis d'Autichamp, who was to "relieve Lyons," and raise the Siege of Lyons, in Autumn, 1793, but could not do it.

villiers that a journey to Paris were the project; whither, also, he himself is just going. Perfidious Commandant Marquis! His plan is seen through: he dares to presume to make love to a Scion-of-Royalty; or to hint that he could dare to presume to do it. Whereupon, indignant Count de Lamotte, as we said, throws up his commission, and down his fire-arms; without further delay. The King loses a tall private sentinel; the world has a new blackleg: and Monsieur and Madame de Lamotte take places in the Diligence for Strasburg.

Good Fostermother Boulainvilliers, however, is no longer at Strasburg: she is forward at the Archiepiscopal palace in Saverne; on a visit there, to his Eminence Cardinal Commendator Grand-Almoner Archbishop Prince Louis de Rohan! Thus, then, has Destiny at last brought it about. Thus, after long wanderings, on paths so far separate, has the time come, (in this late year 1783,) when, of all the nine hundred millions of the Earth's denizens, these pre-appointed two beheld each other!

The foolish Cardinal, since no sublunary means, not even bribing of the Trianon Concierge, will serve, has taken to the superlunary: he is here, with his fixed-idea; and volcanic vapourosity, darkening, under Cagliostro's management, into thicker and thicker opaque,—of the Black-Art itself. To the glance of hungry genius Cardinal and Cagliostro could not but have meaning. A flush of astonishment, a sigh over boundless wealth (for the mountains of debt lie invisible) in the hands of boundless Stupidity; some vague looming of indefinite hope: all this one can well fancy. But, alas, what, to a high plush Cardinal, is a now insolvent Scion-of-Royalty,—though with a face of some piquancy? The good Fostermother's visit, in any case, can last but three days; then, amid old nambypambyings, with the effusions of the nobler sensibilities, and tears of pity (at least for oneself,) Countess de Lamotte, and husband, must off with her to Paris, and new possibilities at Court. Only when the sky again darkens, can this vague looming from Saverne look out, by fits, as a cheering weather-sign.

CHAPTER VI.

WILL THE TWO FIXED-IDEAS UNITE?

However, the sky, according to custom, is not long in darkening again. The King's finances, we repeat, are in so distracted a state! No D'Ormesson, no Joly de Fleury, weary of milking the already dry, will increase that scandalous Thirty Pounds of a Scion-of-Royalty by a single doit. Calonne himself, who has a willing ear and encouraging word for all mortals whatsoever, only with difficulty, and by aid of Madame of France,* raises it still to some still miserable Sixty-five. Worst of all, the good Fostermother Boulainvilliers, in few months, suddenly dies: the wretched widower, sitting there, with his white handkerchief, to receive condolences, with closed shutters, mortuary tapestries, and sepulchral cressets burning, (which, however, the instant the condolences are gone, he blows out, to save oil,) has the audacity again, amid crocodile tears, to—drop hints!* Nay, more, he (wretched man in all senses) abridges the Lamotte table; will besiege virtue both in the positive and negative way. The Lamottes, wintery as the world looks, cannot begone too soon.

* Campan.

As to Lamotte the husband, he, for shelter against much, decisively dives down to the "subterranean shades of Rascaldom;" gambles, swindles; can hope to live, miscellaneously, if not by the Grace of God, yet by the Oversight of the Devil,—for a time. Lamotte the wife also makes her packages: and waving the unseductive Count Boulainvilliers Save-all a disdainful farewell, removes to the *Belle Image* in Versailles; there, within wind of Court, in attic apartments, on poor water-gruel board, resolves to await what can betide. So much, in few months of this fateful year 1783, has come and gone.

Poor Jeanne de Saint-Remi de Lamotte Valois, Ex-Mantuamaker, Scion-of-Royalty! What eye, looking into those bare attic apartments, and water-gruel platters of the *Belle Image*, but must, in spite of itself, grow dim with almost a kind of tear for thee! There thou art, with thy quick lively glances, face of a certain piquancy, thy gossamer untamable character, snappish sallies, glib all-managing tongue; thy whole incarnated, garmented, and so sharply appetent "spark of Life;" cast down alive into this World, without vote of thine, (for the Elective Franchises have not yet got that length;) and wouldst so fain live there. Paying scot-and-lot; providing, or fresh-scouring, silk court-dresses; "always keeping a gig!" Thou must hawk and shark to and fro, from anteroom to anteroom; become a kind of terror to all men in place, and women that influence such; dance not light Ionic measures, but attendance merely; have weepings, thanksgiving effusions, aulic, almost forensic, eloquence: perhaps eke out thy thin livelihood by some coquetries, in the small way;—and so, most poverty-stricken, cold-blighted, yet with young keen blood struggling against it, spin forward thy unequal feeble thread, which the Clotho-scissors will soon clip!

Surely, now, if ever, were that vague looming from Saverne welcome, as a weather-sign. How doubly welcome is his plush Eminence's personal arrival;—for with the earliest spring he has come in person, as he periodically does; vaporific, driven by his fixed-idea.

Genius, of the mechanical practical kind, what is it but a bringing together of two Forces that fit each other, that will give birth to a third? Ever, from Tubalcain's time, Iron lay ready hammered; Water, also, was boiling and bursting: nevertheless, for want of a genius, there was as yet no Steam-engine. In his Eminence Prince Louis, in that huge,

* *Vie de Jeanne de Lamotte, &c., écrite par elle-même*, i.

restless, incoherent Being of his, depend on it, brave Countess, there are Forces deep, manifold; nay, a fixed-idea concentrates the whole huge Incoherence as it were into one Force: cannot the eye of genius discover its *fellow?*

Communing much with the Court-*valetaille*, our brave Countess has more than once heard talk of Boehmer, of his Necklace, and threatened death by water; in the course of gossiping and tattling, this topic from time to time emerges; is commented upon with empty laughter,—as if there lay no further meaning in it. To the common eye there is indeed none: but to the eye of genius? In some moment of inspiration, the question rises on our brave Lamotte: were not *this*, of all extant Forces, the cognate one that would unite with Eminence Rohan's? Great moment, light-beaming, fire-flashing; like birth of Minerva; like all moments of Creation! Fancy how pulse and breath flutter, almost stop, in the greatness: the great not Divine Idea, the great Diabolic Idea is too big for her.—Thought (how often must we repeat it?) rules the world; Fire and, in a less degree, Frost; Earth and Sea, (for what is your swiftest ship, or steamship but a *Thought*—imbodied in wood?); Reformed Parliaments, rise and ruin of Nations,—sale of Diamonds: all things obey Thought. Countess de Saint Remi de Lamotte, by power of thought is now made woman. With force of genius she represses, crushes deep down, her Undivine Idea; bends all her faculty to realize it. Prepare thyself, Reader for a series of the most surprising Dramatic Representations ever exhibited on any stage.

We hear tell of Dramatists, and scenic illusion how "natural," how illusive it was: if the spectator, for some half-moment, can half-deceive himself into the belief that it was real, he departs doubly content. With all which, and much more of the like, I have no quarrel. But what must be thought of the Female Dramatist who, for eighteen long months, can exhibit the beautifullest Fata-morgana to a plush Cardinal, wide awake, with fifty years on his head; and so lap him in her scenic illusion that he never doubts but it is all firm earth, and the pasteboard Coulisse-trees are producing Hesperides apples? Could Madame de Lamotte, then have written a *Hamlet?* I conjecture, not. More goes to the writing of a *Hamlet* than completest "imitation" of all characters and things in this Earth; there goes, before and beyond all, the rarest *understanding* of these, insight into their hidden essences and harmonies. Erasmus's Ape, as is known in Literary History, sat by while its Master was shaving, and "imitated" every point of the process; but its own foolish beard grew never the smoother.

As in looking at a finished Drama, it were nowise meet that the spectator first of all got behind the scenes, and saw the burnt-corks, brayed-resin, thunder-barrels, and withered hunger-bitten men and women, of which such heroic work was made: so here with the reader. A peep into the side-scenes shall be granted him, from time to time. But, on the whole, repress, O reader, that too insatiable scientific curiosity of thine; let thy *æsthetic* feeling first have play; and witness what a Prospero's-grotto poor Eminence Rohan is led into, to be pleased he knows not why.

Survey first what we might call the stage-lights, orchestra, general structure of the theatre, mood and condition of the audience. The theatre is the World, with its restless business and madness; near at hand rise the royal Domes of Versailles, mystery around them, and as background the memory of a thousand years. By the side of the River Seine walks, haggard, wasted, a Jouaillier-Bijoutier de la Reine, with necklace in his pocket. The audience is a drunk Christopher Sly in the fittest humour. A fixed-idea, driving him headlong over steep places, like that of the Gadarenes' Swine, has produced a deceptibility, as of desperation, that will clutch at straws. Understand one other word: Cagliostro is prophesying to him! The Quack of Quacks has now for years had him in leading. Transmitting "predictions in cipher;" questioning, before Hieroglyphic Screens, Columbs in a state of Innocence, for elixirs of life, and philosopher's stone; unveiling, in fuliginous, clear-obscure the (sham) majesty of nature; he isolates him more and more from all unpossessed men. Was it not enough that poor Rohan had become a dissolute, somnolent-violent, ever-vapory Mud-volcano; but black Egyptian magic must be laid on him!

If, perhaps, too, our Countess de Lamotte, with her blandishments,—for though not beautiful, she "has a certain piquancy," *et cetera?*—Enough, his poor Eminence sits in the fittest place, in the fittest mood: a newly-awakened Christopher Sly; and with his "small ale," too, beside him. Touch, only, the lights with fire-tipt rod; and let the orchestra soft-warbling strike up their fara-lara fiddle-diddle-dee!

CHAPTER VII.

MARIE-ANTOINETTE.

Such a soft-warbling fara-lara was it to his Eminence, when (in early January of the year 1784) our Countess first, mysteriously, and under seal of sworn secrecy, hinted to him that, with her winning tongue and great talent as Anecdotic Historian, she had worked a passage to the ear of Queen's Majesty itself.* Gods! Dost *thou* bring with thee airs from Heaven? Is thy face yet radiant with some reflex of that Brightness beyond bright!—Men with fixed idea are not as other men. To listen to a plain varnished tale, such as your Dramatist can fashion; to ponder the words; to snuff them up, as Ephraim did the east-wind, and grow flatulent and drunk with them: what else could poor Eminence do? His poor somnolent, so swift-rocked soul feels a new

* Compare Rohan's *Mémoires Pour*, (there are four of them,) in the *Affaire du Collier*, with Lamotte's four. They go on in the way of controversy, of argument, and response.

element infused into it; turbid resinous light, wide-coruscating, glares over the "waste of his imagination." Is he interested in the mysterious tidings? Hope has seized them; there is in the world nothing else that interests him.

The secret friendship of Queens is not a thing to be let sleep: ever new Palace Interviews occur;—yet in deepest privacy; for how should her Majesty awaken so many tongues of Principalities and Nobilities, male and female, that spitefully watch her? Above all, however, "on the 2d of February," that day of "the Procession of blue Ribands,"* much was spoken of; somewhat, too, of Monseigneur de Rohan!—Poor Monseigneur, hadst thou *three* long ears, thou'dst hear her.

But will she not, perhaps, in some future priceless Interview, speak a good word for thee? Thyself shalt speak it, happy Eminence; at least, write it: our tutelary Countess will be the bearer!—On the 21st of March goes off that long exculpatory imploratory Letter: it is the first Letter that went off from Cardinal to Queen; to be followed, in time, by "above two hundred others;" which are graciously answered by verbal Messages, nay, at length by Royal Autographs on gilt paper,—the whole delivered by our tutelary Countess.† The tutelary Countess comes and goes, fetching and carrying; with the gravity of a Roman Augur, inspects those extraordinary chicken-bowels, and draws prognostics from them. Things are in fair train: the Dauphiness took some offence at Monseigneur, but the Queen has nigh forgotten it. No inexorable Queen; ah no! So good, so free, light-hearted; only sore beset with malicious Polignacs and others;—at times, also, short of money.

Marie Antoinette, as the reader well knows, has been much blamed for want of Etiquette. Even now, when the other accusations against her have sunk down to oblivion and the Father of Lies, this of wanting Etiquette survives her;—in the Castle of Ham, at this hour,‡ M. de Polignac and Company may be wringing their hands, not without an oblique glance at *her* for bringing them thither. She indeed discarded Etiquette; once, when her carriage broke down, she even entered a hackney-coach. She would walk, too, at Trianon, in mere straw-hat, and, perhaps, muslin gown! Hence, the Knot of Etiquette being loosed, the Frame of Society broke up; and those astonishing "Horrors of the French Revolution" supervened. On what Damocles' hairs must the judgment-sword hang over this distracted Earth! Thus, however, it was that Tenterden Steeple brought an influx of the Atlantic on us, and so Godwin Sands. Thus, too, might it be that because Father Noah took the liberty of, say, rinsing out his wine-vat, his Ark was floated off, and a World drowned.—Beautiful Highborn that wert so foully hurled low! For, if thy Being came to thee out of old Hapsburgh Dynasties, came it not also (like my own) out of Heaven? *Sunt lachrymæ rerum, et mentem mortalia tangunt.* Oh, is there a man's heart that thinks, without pity, of those long months and years of slow-wasting ignominy;—of thy Birth, soft-cradled in Imperial Schönbrunn, the winds of heaven not to visit thy face too roughly, thy foot to light on softness, thy eye on splendour; and then of thy Death, or hundred Deaths, to which the Guillotine and Fouquier Tinville's judgment-bar was but the merciful end? Look *there*, O man born of woman! The bloom of that fair face is wasted, the hair is gray with care; the brightness of those eyes is quenched, their lids hang drooping, the face is stony, pale, as of one living in death. Mean weeds (which her own hand has mended)* attire the Queen of the World. The death-hurdle, where thou sittest, pale, motionless, which only curses environ, must stop: a people, drunk with vengeance, will drink it again in full draught: far as the eye reaches, a multitudinous sea of maniac heads; the air deaf with their triumph-yell! The Living-dead must shudder with yet one other pang: her startled blood yet again suffuses with the hue of agony that pale face, which she hides with her hands. There is, then, *no* heart to say, God pity thee? O think not of these; think of Him whom thou worshippest, the Crucified,—who, also, treading the wine-press *alone*, fronted sorrow still deeper; and triumphed over it, and made it Holy; and built of it a "Sanctuary of Sorrow," for thee and all the wretched! Thy path of thorns is nigh ended. One long last look at the Tuileries, where thy step was once so light,—where thy children shall not dwell. The head is on the block; the axe rushes—Dumb lies the World; that wild-yelling World, and all its madness, is behind thee.

Beautiful Highborn that wert so foully hurled low! Rest yet in thy innocent gracefully heedless seclusion, (unintruded on by me,) while rude hands have not yet desecrated it. Be the curtains, that shroud in (if for the last time on this Earth) a Royal Life, still sacred to me. *Thy* fault, in the French Revolution, was that thou wert the Symbol of the Sin and Misery of a thousand years; that with Saint-Bartholomews, and Jacqueries, with Gabelles, and Dragonades, and Parcs-aux-cerfs, the heart of mankind was filled full,—and foamed over, into all-involving madness. To no Napoleon, to no Cromwell wert thou wedded: such sit not in the highest rank, of themselves; are raised on high by the shaking and confounding of all the ranks. As poor peasants, how happy, worthy had ye two been! But by evil destiny ye were made a King and Queen of; and so both once more—are become an astonishment and a by-word to all times.

CHAPTER VIII.

THE TWO FIXED-IDEAS WILL UNITE.

"Countess de Lamotte, then, had penetrated into the confidence of the Queen? Those gilt-

* Lamotte's *Mémoires Justificatifs*, (London, 1788.)

† See *Georgel:* see Lamotte's *Mémoires;* in her Appendix of "Documents" to that volume, certain of these Letters are given.

‡ A. D. 1831.

* Weber: *Mémoires concernant Marie-Antoinette*, (London, 1809,) tom. iii., notes, 106.

paper Autographs were actually written by the Queen?" Reader, forget not to repress that too insatiable, scientific curiosity of thine! What I know is that a certain Vilette-de-Rétaux, with military whiskers, denizen of Rascaldom, comrade there of Monsieur le Comte, is skilful in imitating hands. Certain it is, also, that Madame la Comtesse has penetrated to the Trianon —Doorkeeper's. Nay, as Campan herself must admit, she has met, "at a Man-midwife's in Versailles," with worthy Queen's-valet Lesclaux,—or Desclos, for there is no uniformity in it. With these, or the like of these, she in the back-parlor of the Palace itself, (if late enough,) may pick a merry-thought, sip the foam from a glass of Champagne. No further seek her honours to disclose, for the present: or anatomically dissect, as we said, those extraordinary chicken-bowels, from which *she*, and she alone, can read Decrees of Fate, and also realize them.

Skeptic, seest thou his Eminence waiting there, in the moonlight; hovering to and fro on the back terrace, till she come out—from the ineffable Interview?* He is close muffled; walks restlessly observant; shy also, and courting the shade. She comes: up closer with thy capote, O Eminence, down with thy broad-brim; for she has an escort! 'T is but the good Monsieur Queen's-valet Lesclaux: and now he is sent back again, as no longer needful. Mark him, Monseigneur, nevertheless; thou wilt see him yet another time. Monseigneur marks little: his heart is in the ineffable Interview, in the gilt-paper Autograph, alone. —Queen's-valet Lesclaux? Methinks, he has much the stature of Villette, denizen of Rascaldom! Impossible!

How our Countess managed with Cagliostro? Cagliostro, gone from Strasburg, is as yet far distant, winging his way through dim Space; will not be here for months: only his "predictions in cipher" are here. Here or there, however, Cagliostro, to our Countess, can be useful. At a glance, the eye of genius has descried him to be a bottomless slough of falsity, vanity, gulosity, and thick-eyed stupidity: of foulest material, but of fattest;—fit compost for the Plant she is rearing. Him who has deceived all Europe she can undertake to deceive. His Columbs, demonic Masonries, Egyptian Elixirs, what is all this to the light-giggling exclusively practical Lamotte? It runs off from her, as all speculation, good, bad, and indifferent, has always done, "like water from one in wax-cloth dress." With the lips meanwhile she can honour it; Oil of Flattery (the best patent antifriction known) subdues all irregularities whatsoever.

On Cagliostro, again, on his side, a certain uneasy feeling might, for moments intrude itself: the raven loves not ravens. But what can he do? Nay, she is partly playing *his* game: can he not spill her full cup yet, at the right season, and pack her out of doors? Oftenest, in their joyous orgies, this light fascinating Countess,—who perhaps has a design on *his* heart, seems to him but one other of those light *Papiliones*, who have fluttered round him in all climates; whom with grim muzzle he has snapt by the thousand.

Thus, what with light fascinating Countess, what with Quack of Quacks, poor Eminence de Rohan lies safe; his mud-volcano placidly simmering in thick Egyptian haze: withdrawn from all the world. Moving figures, as of men, he sees; takes not the trouble to look at. Court-cousins rally him; are answered in silence; or, if it go too far, in mud-explosions terrifico-absurd. Court-cousins and all mankind are unreal shadows merely; Queen's favour the only substance.

Nevertheless, the World, on its side, too, has an existence; lies not idle in these days. It has got its Versailles Treaty signed, long months ago; and the Plenipotentiaries all home again, for votes of thanks. Paris, London, and other great Cities, and small, are working, intriguing; dying, being born. There, in the Rue Taranne, for instance, the once noisy Denis Diderot has fallen silent enough. Here, also, in Bolt Court, old Samuel Johnson, like an over-wearied Giant, must lie down, and slumber without dream;—the rattling of carriages and wains, and all the world's din and business rolling by, as ever, from of old.—Sieur Boehmer, however, has not yet drowned himself in the Seine; only walks haggard, wasted, purposing to do it.

News (by the merest accident in the world) reach Sieur Boehmer, of Madame's new favour with her Majesty! Men will do much before they drown. Sieur Boehmer's Necklace is on Madame's table, his guttural nasal rhetoric in her ear: he will abate many a pound and penny of the first just price; he will give cheerfully a Thousand Louis-d'or, as *cadeau*, to the generous Scion-of-Royalty that shall persuade her majesty. The man's importunities grow quite annoying to our Countess; who, in her glib way, satirically prattles how she has been bored,—to Monseigneur, among others.

Dozing on down cushions, far inwards, with soft ministering Hebes, and luxurious appliances; with ranked Heyducs, and a *Valetaille* innumerable, that shut out the prose-world and its discord: thus lies Monseigneur, in enchanted dream. Can he, even in sleep, forget his tutelary Countess, and her service? By the delicatest presents he alleviates her distresses, most undeserved. Nay, once or twice, gilt Autographs, from a Queen,—with whom he is evidently rising to unknown heights in favour, —have done Monseigneur the honour to make him *her* Majesty's Grand Almoner, when the case was pressing. Monseigneur, we say, has had the honour to disburse charitable cash, on her Majesty's behalf, to this or the other distressed deserving object: say only to the length of a few thousand pounds, advanced from his own funds;—her majesty being at the moment so poor, and charity a thing that will not wait. Always Madame, good foolish, gadding creature, takes charge of delivering the money.—Madame can descend from her attics, in

* See *Georgel*.

the *Belle Image*; and feel the smiles of Nature and Fortune, a little; so bounteous has the Queen's Majesty been.*

To Monseigneur the power of money over highest female hearts had never been incredible. Presents have, many times, worked wonders. But then, O Heavens, *what* present? Scarcely were the Cloud-Compeller himself, all coined into new Louis-d'or, worthy to alight in such a lap. Loans, charitable disbursements, however, as we see, are premissible; these, by defect of payment, may become presents. In the vortex of his Eminence's day-dreams, lumbering multiform slowly round, this of importunate Boehmer and his Necklace, from time to time, turns up. Is the Queen's Majesty at heart desirous of it; but again, at the moment, too poor? Our tutelary Countess answers vaguely, mysteriously;—confesses, at last, under oath of secrecy, her own private suspicion that the Queen wants this same Necklace, of all things; but dare not, for a stingy husband, buy it. She, the Countess de Lamotte, will look further into the matter; and, if aught serviceable to his Eminence can be suggested, in a good way suggest it, in the proper quarter.

Walk warily, Countess de Lamotte; for now, with thickening breath, thou approachest the moment of moments! Principalities and Powers, *Parlement*, *Grand Chambre*, and *Tournelle*, with all their whips and gibbet-wheels; the very Crack of Doom hangs over thee, if thou trip. Forward, with nerve of iron, on shoes of felt; *like* a Treasure-digger, "in silence; looking neither to the right nor left," where yawn abysses deep as the Pool, and all Pandemonium hovers eager to rend thee into rags!

CHAPTER IX.

PARK OF VERSAILLES.

Or will the reader incline rather taking the other and sunny side of the matter to enter that Lamottic-Circean theatrical establishment of Monseigneur de Rohan; and see there how (under the best of Dramaturgists) Melodrama, with sweeping pall, flits past him; while the enchanted Diamond fruit is gradually ripening, to fall by a shake?

The 28th of July (of this same momentous 1784) has come; and with it the most rapturous tumult into the heart of Monseigneur. Ineffable expectancy stirs up his whole soul, with the much that lies therein, from its lowest foundations: borne on wild seas to Armida Islands, yet (as is fit) through Horror dim-hovering round, he tumultuously rocks. To the Chateau, to the Park! This night the Queen will meet thee, the Queen herself: so far has our tutelary Countess brought it. What can ministerial impediments, Polignac intrigues, avail against the favour, nay (Heaven and Earth!) perhaps the tenderness of a Queen? She vanishes from amid their meshwork of Etiquette and Cabal; descends from her celestial Zodiac to thee, a shepherd of Latmos. Alas, a white-bearded, pursy shepherd, fat and scant of breath! Who can account for the taste of females? But thou, burnish up thy whole faculties of gallantry, thy fifty years' experience of the sex; this night, or never!—In such unutterable meditations, does Monseigneur restlessly spend the day; and long for darkness, yet dread it.

Darkness has at length come. The perpendicular rows of Heyducs, in that Palais or Hotel de Strasbourg, are all cast prostrate in sleep; the very Concierge resupine, with open mouth, audibly drinks in nepenthe; when Monseigneur, "in blue greatcoat, with slouched hat," issues softly, with his henchman, (Planta of the Grisons,) to the Park of Versailles. Planta must loiter invisible in the distance; Slouched-hat will wait here, among the leafy thickets; till our tutelary Countess, "in black domino," announce the moment, which surely must be near.

The night is of the darkest for the season; no Moon; warm, slumbering July, in motionless clouds, drops fatness over the Earth. The very stars from the Zenith see not Monseigneur; see only his cloud-covering, fringed with twilight in the far North. Midnight, telling itself forth from these shadowy Palace Domes? All the steeples of Versailles, the villages around, with metal tongue, and huge Paris itself dull-droning, answer drowsily Yes! Sleep rules this Hemisphere of the World. From Arctic to Antarctic, the Life of our Earth lies all, in long swaths, or rows, (like those rows of Heyducs and snoring Concierge,) successively mown down, from vertical to horizontal, by Sleep! Rather curious to consider.

The flowers are all asleep in Little Trianon, the roses folded in for the night; but the Rose of Roses still wakes. O wondrous Earth! O doubly wondrous Park of Versailles with Little and Great Trianon,—and a scarce-breathing Monseigneur! Ye Hydraulics of Lenotre, that also slumber, with stop-cocks, in your deep leaden chambers, babble not of *him*, when ye arise. Ye odorous balm-shrubs, huge spectral Cedars, thou sacred Boscage of Hornbeam, ye dim Pavilions of the Peerless, whisper not! Moon, lie silent, hidden in thy vacant cave; no star look down: let neither Heaven nor Hell peep through the blanket of the Night, to cry, Hold, Hold!—The Black Domino? Ha! Yes!—With stouter step than might have been expected, Monseigneur is under way; the Black Domino had only to whisper, low and eager: "In the Hornbeam Arbour!" And now, Cardinal, O now!—Yes, there hovers the white Celestial; "in white robe of *linon moucheté*," finer than moonshine; a Juno by her bearing: there in that bosket! Monseigneur, down on thy knees; never can red breeches be better wasted. O he would kiss the royal shoe-tie, or its shadow, (were there one:) not words; only broken gaspings, murmuring prostrations, eloquently speak his meaning. But, ah, behold! Our tutelary Black Domino, in haste, with vehement whisper: "*On vient!*" The white Juno drops a fairest Rose, with these ever-memorable words. "*Vous*

---

* *Georgel.* Rohan's Four *Memoires Pour:* Lamotte's Four.

savez ce que cela veut dire (you know what that means;") vanishes in the thicket, the Black Domino hurrying her with eager whisper of "*Vite, vite,* (away, away!") for the sound of footsteps (doubtless from Madame, and Madame d'Artois, unwelcome sisters that they are!) is approaching fast. Monseigneur picks up his Rose; runs as for the King's plate; almost overturns poor Planta, whose laugh assures him that all is safe.*

O Ixion de Rohan, happiest mortal of this world, since the first Ixion of deathless memory,—who, nevertheless, in that cloud-embrace, begat strange Centaurs! Thou art Prime Minister of France without peradventure: is not this the Rose of Royalty, worthy to become ottar of roses, and yield perfume for ever? How *thou*, of all people, wilt contrive to govern France in these very peculiar times.—But that is little to the matter. There, doubtless, is thy Rose, (which, methinks, it were well to have a Box or Casket made for:) nay, was there not in the dulcet of thy Juno's "*Nous savez*" a kind of trepidation, a quaver,—as of still deeper meanings!

Reader, there is hitherto no item of this miracle that is not historically proved and *true*.—In distracted black-magical phantasmagory, adumbrations of yet higher and highest Dalliances,† hover stupendous in the background: whereof your Georgels and Campans, and other official characters, *can* take no notice! There, in distracted black-magical phantasmagory, let these hover. The truth of them for us is that they do so hover. The truth of them in itself is known only to three persons: Dame (self-styled Countess) de Lamotte; the Devil; and Philippe Egalité,—who furnished money and facts for the Lamotte *Memoires*, and, before guillotinement, begat the present King of the French.

Enough, that Ixion de Rohan, lapsed almost into deliquium, by such sober certainty of waking bliss, is the happiest of all men; and his tutelary Countess the dearest of all women, save one only. On the 25th of August, (so strong still are those villainous Drawing-room cabals,) he goes weeping, but submissive, (by order of a gilt Autograph,) home to Saverne; till further dignities can be matured for him. He carries his Rose, now considerably faded, in a Casket of fit price; may, if he so please, perpetuate it as *pot-pourri*. He names a favourite walk in his Archiepiscopal pleasure-grounds, *Promenade de la Rose;* there let him court digestion, and loyally somnambulate till called for.

I notice it as a coincidence in chronology, that, few days after this date, the Demoiselle (or even, for the last month, Baroness) Gay d'Oliva began to find Countess de Lamotte "not at home," in her fine Paris hotel, in her fine Charonne country-house; and went no more, with Villette, and such pleasant dinner-guests, and her, to see Beaumarchais' *Marriage de Figaro*,* running its hundred nights.

* Compare *Georgel*, Lamotte's *Mémoires Justificatifs*, and the *Mémoires Pour* of the various parties, especially Gay d'Oliva's. Georgel places the scene in the year 1785; quite wrong. Lamotte's "royal Autographs" (as given in the Appendix to *Mémoires Justificatifs*) seem to be misdated as to the day of the month. There is endless confusion of dates.

† Lamotte's *Memoires Justificatifs;* MS. Songs in the *Affaire du Collier*, &c. &c. Nothing can exceed the brutality of these things, (unfit for Print or Pen;) which, nevertheless, found believers; increase of believers, in the public exasperation; and did the Queen (say all her historians) incalculable damage.

* Gay d'Oliva's First *Mémoire Pour*, p. 37.

CHAPTER X.

BEHIND THE SCENES.

"The Queen?" Good reader, *thou* surely art not a Partridge the Schoolmaster, or a Monseigneur de Rohan, to mistake the stage for a reality!—"But who this Demoiselle d'Oliva was?" Reader, let us remark rather how the labours of our Dramaturgic Countess are increasing.

New actors I see on the scene; not one of whom shall guess what the other is doing; or, indeed, know rightly what himself is doing. For example, cannot Messieurs de Lamotte and Villette, of Rascaldom, like Nisus and Euryalus, take a midnight walk of contemplation, with "footsteps of Madame and Madame d'Artois," (since all footsteps are much the same,) without offence to any one? A Queen's Similitude can believe that a Queen's Self (for frolic's sake) is looking at her through the thickets;† a terrestrial Cardinal can kiss with devotion a celestial Queen's slipper, or Queen's Similitude's slipper,—and no one but a Black Domino the wiser. All these shall follow each his precalculated course; for their inward mechanism is known and fit wires hook themselves on this. To Two only is a clear belief vouchsafed: to Monseigneur, (founded on stupidity;) to the great creative Dramaturgist, sitting at the heart of the whole mystery, (founded on completest insight.) Great creative Dramaturgist! How, like Schiller, "by union of the Possible with the Necessarily-existing, she brings out the"—Eighty thousand Pounds! Don Aranda, with his triple-sealed missives and hoodwinked secretaries, bragged justly that he cut down the Jesuits in one day; but here, without ministerial salary, or King's favour, or any help beyond her own black domino, labours a greater than he. How she advances, stealthily, steadfastly, with Argus eye and ever ready-brain; "with nerve of iron, on shoes of felt!" O worthy to have intrigued for Jesuitdom, for Pope's Tiara;—to have been Pope Joan thyself, in those old days; and as Arachne of Arachnes, sat in the centre of that stupendous spider-web, that, reaching from Goa to Acapulco, and from Heaven to Hell, overnetted the thoughts and souls of men!—Of which spider-web stray tatters, in favourable dewy mornings, even yet become visible.

The Demoiselle d'Oliva? She is a Parisian Demoiselle of three-and-twenty, tall, blond, and beautiful;‡ from unjust guardians, and an evil world, she has had somewhat to suffer.

† See *Lamotte;* see *Gay d' Oliva*.

‡ I was then presented "to two Ladies, one of whom was remarkable for the richness of her shape, She had blue eyes and chestnut hair' (Bette d'Etienville's Second *Mémoire Pour;* in the *Suite de l'Affaire du Collier*.)

"In the month of June, 1784," says the Demoiselle herself, in her (judicial) Autobiography, "I occupied a small apartment in the Rue du Jour, Quartier St. Eustache. I was not far from the Garden of the Palais-Royal; I had made it my usual promenade." For, indeed, the real God's-truth is, I was a Parisian unfortunate-female, with moderate custom; and one must go where his market lies. "I frequently passed three or four hours of the afternoon there, with some women of my acquaintance, and a little child of four years old, whom I was fond of, whom his parents willingly trusted with me. I even went thither alone, except for him, when other company failed.

"One afternoon, in the month of July following, I was at the Palais-Royal: my whole company, at the moment, was the child I speak of. A tall young man, walking alone, passes several times before me. He was a man I had never seen. He looks at me; he looks fixedly at me. I observe even that always, as he comes near, he slackens his pace, as if to survey me more at leisure. A chair stood vacant; two or three feet from mine. He seats himself there.

"Till this instant, the sight of the young man, his walks, his approaches, his repeated gazings, had made no impression on me. But now when he was sitting so close by, I could not avoid noticing him. His eyes ceased not to wander over all my person. His air becomes earnest, grave. An unquiet curiosity appears to agitate him. He seems to measure my figure, to seize by turns all parts of my physiognomy."—He finds me (but whispers not a syllable of it) tolerably like, both in person and profile; for even the Abbé Georgel says, I was a *belle courtisane*.

"It is time to name this young man: he was the Sieur de Lamotte, styling himself Comte de Lamotte." Who doubts it? He praises "my feeble charms;" expresses a wish to "pay his addresses to me." I, being a lone spinster, know not what to say; think it best in the meanwhile to retire. Vain precaution! "I see him all on a sudden appear in my apartment!"

On his "ninth visit" (for he was always civility itself) he talks of introducing a great Court-lady, by whose means I may even do her Majesty some little secret-service,—the reward of which will be unspeakable. In the dusk of the evening, silks mysteriously rustle; enter the creative Dramaturgist, Dame, styled Countess, de Lamotte; and so—the too intrusive, scientific reader, has now, for his punishment, *got* on the wrong side of that loveliest Transparency; finds nothing but grease-pots, and vapour of expiring wicks!

The Demoiselle Gay d'Oliva may once more sit, or stand, in the Palais-Royal, with such custom as will come. In due time, she shall again, but with breath of Terror, be blown upon; and blown out of France to Brussels.

This is she whom Bette, and Bette's Advocate, intended the world to take for Gay d'Oliva. "The other is of middle size: dark eyes, chestnut hair, white complexion: the sound of her voice is agreeable; she speaks perfectly well, and with no less facility than vivacity;" this one is meant for Lamotte. Oliva's real name was Essigny; the *Oliva* (OLISVA, anagram of VALOIS) was given her by Lamotte along with the title of *Baroness*, MS. Notes, *Affaire du Collier*.)

CHAPTER XI.

THE NECKLACE IS SOLD.

Autumn, with its gray moaning winds, and coating of red strown leaves, invites Courtiers to enjoy the charms of Nature; and all business of moment stands still. Countess de Lamotte, while everything is so stagnant, and even Boehmer (though with sure hope) has locked up his Necklace for the season, can drive, with her Count and his Euryalus, Villette, down to native Bar-sur-Aube; and there (in virtue of a Queen's bounty) show the envious a Scion-of-royalty *re*-grafted; and make them yellower looking on it. A well-varnished chariot, with the Arms of Valois duly painted in bend-sinister; a house gallantly furnished, bodies gallantly attired,—secure them the favourablest reception from all manner of men. The very Duc de Penthièvre (Egalité's father-in-law) welcomes our Lamotte, with that urbanity characteristic of his high station, and the old school. Worth, indeed, makes the man, or woman; but leather (of gig-straps) and prunella (of gig-lining) first makes it *go*.

The great creative Dramaturgist has thus let down her drop-scene; and only, with a Letter or two to Saverne, or even a visit thither, (for it is but a day's drive from Bar,) keeps up a due modicum of intermediate instrumental music. She needs some pause, in good sooth, to collect herself a little; for the last act and grand Catastrophe is at hand. Two fixed-ideas, (Cardinal's and Jeweller's,) a negative and a positive, have felt each other; stimulated now by new hope, are rapidly revolving round each other, and approximating; like two flames, are stretching out long fire-tongues to join and be one.

Boehmer, on his side, is ready with the readiest; as, indeed, he has been these four long years. The Countess, it is true, will have neither part nor lot in that foolish *Cadeau* of his, or in the whole foolish Necklace business: this she has in plain words (and even not without asperity, due to a bore of such magnitude) given him to know. From her, nevertheless, by cunning inference, and the merest accident in the world, the sly Jouaillier-Bijoutier has gleaned thus much, that Monseigneur de Rohan is the man. Enough! Enough! Madame shall be no more troubled. Rest there, in hope, thou Necklace of the Devil; but, O Monseigneur, be thy return speedy!

Alas, the man lives not that would be speedier than Monseigneur, if he durst. But as yet no gilt Autograph invites him, permits him; the few gilt Autographs are all negatory, procrastinating. Cabals of Court; for ever cabals! Nay, if it be not for some Necklace, or other such crotchet or necessity, who knows but he may *never* be recalled, (so fickle is womankind;) but forgotten, and left to rot here, like his Rose, into *pot-pourri?* Our tutelary Countess, too, is shyer in this matter than we ever saw her. Nevertheless, by intense skilful cross-questioning, he has extorted somewhat; sees partly how it stands. The Queen's Majesty will have her Necklace, (for when, in such case, had not woman her way?); and can even pay for it—by instalments; but then the stingy husband! Once for all, she will not be seen in the business. Now, therefore, were it, or were it not, permissible to mortal to transact it secretly in her stead? That is the question. If to mortal, then to Monseigneur. Our Countess has even ventured to hint afar off at Monseigneur (kind Countess!) in the proper quarter; but his discretion is doubted,—in regard to money matters.—Discretion? And I on the *Promenade de la Rose?*—Explode not, O Eminence! Trust will spring of trial: thy hour is coming.

The Lamottes, meanwhile, have left their farewell card with all the respectable classes of Bar-sur-Aube; our Dramaturgist stands again behind the scenes at Paris. How is it, O Monseigneur, that she is still so shy with thee, in this matter of the Necklace; that she leaves the love-lorn Latmian shepherd to droop, here in lone Saverne, like weeping-ash, in naked winter, on his Promenade of the Rose, with vague commonplace responses that "his hour is coming?"—By Heaven and Earth! at last, in late January, it is *come*. Behold it, this new gilt Autograph: "To Paris, on a small business of delicacy, which our Countess will explain,"—which I already know! To Paris! Horses; Postillions; Beefeaters!—And so his resuscitated Eminence, all wrapt in furs, in the pleasantest frost, (Abbé Georgel says, *un beau froid de Janvier,*) over clear-jingling highways, rolls rapidly,—borne on the bosom of Dreams.

O Dame de Lamotte, has the enchanted Diamond fruit ripened, then? Hast thou *given* it the little shake, big with unutterable fate?—I? can the Dame justly retort: Who saw me in it?—The reader, therefore, has still Three scenic Exhibitions to look at, by our great Dramaturgist; then the Fourth and last,—by another Author.

To us, reflecting how oftenest the true moving force in human things works hidden underground, it seems small marvel that this month of January, (1785,) wherein our Countess so little courts the eye of the vulgar historian, should, nevertheless, have been the busiest of all for her; especially the latter half thereof.

Wisely eschewing matters of business, (which she could never in her life understand,) our Countess will personally take no charge of that bargain-making; leaves it all to her Majesty and the gilt Autographs. Assiduous Boehmer, nevertheless, is in frequent close conference with Monseigneur: the Paris Palais-de-Strasbourg, shut to the rest of men, sees the Jouaillier-Bijoutier, with eager official aspect, come and go. The grand difficulty is —must we say it?—her Majesty's wilful whimsicality, unacquaintance with Business. She positively will not write a gilt Autograph, *authorizing* his Eminence to make the bargain; but writes rather, in a petting manner, that the thing is of no consequence, and can be given up! Thus must the poor Countess dash to and fro, like a weaver's shuttle, between Paris and Versailles; wear her horses and nerves to pieces; nay, sometimes in the hottest haste, wait many hours within call of the Palace, considering what *can* be done, (with none but Villette to bear her company,)—till the Queen's whim pass.

At length, after furious-driving and conferences enough, on the 29th of January, a middle course is hit on. Cautious Boehmer shall write out (on finest paper) his terms; which are really rather fair: Sixteen hundred thousand livres; to be paid in five equal instalments; the first this day six months; the other four from three months to three months; this is what Court-Jewellers, Boehmer and Bassange, on the one part, and Prince Cardinal Commendator Louis de Rohan, on the other part, will stand to; witness their hands. Which written sheet of finest paper our poor Countess must again take charge of, again dash off with to Versailles; and therefrom, after trouble unspeakable, (shared in only by the faithful Villette, of Rascaldom,) return with it, bearing this most precious marginal note,—"*Bon—Marie Antoinette de France,*" in the Autograph hand! Happy Cardinal! this *thou* shalt keep in the innermost of all thy repositories. Boehmer, meanwhile, secret as Death, shall tell no man that he has sold his Necklace; or if much pressed for an actual sight of the same, confess that it is sold to the Favourite Sultana of the Grand Turk for the time being.*

Thus, then, do the smoking Lamotte horses at length get rubbed down, and feel the taste of oats, after midnight; the Lamotte Countess can also gradually sink into needful slumber, perhaps not unbroken by dreams. On the morrow the bargain shall be concluded; next day the Necklace be delivered, on Monseigneur's receipt.

Will the reader, therefore, be pleased to glance at the following two Life-Pictures, Real-Phantasmagories, or whatever we may call them: they are the two first of those Three scenic real-poetic Exhibitions, brought about by our Dramaturgist: short Exhibitions, but essential ones.

CHAPTER XII.

THE NECKLACE VANISHES.

It is the first day of February; that grand day of Delivery. The Sieur Boehmer is in the Court of the Palais de Strasbourg; his look mysterious-official, but (though much emaciated) radiant with enthusiasm. The Seine has missed him: though lean, he will fatten again, and live through new enterprises.

Singular, were we not used to it: the name,

* *Campan.*

Boehmer, as it passes upwards and inwards, lowers all halberts of Heyducs in perpendicular rows: the historical eye beholds him, bowing low, with plenteous smiles, in the plush Saloon of Audience. Will it please Monseigneur, then, to do the *ne-plus-ultra* of Necklaces the honour of looking at it? A piece of Art, which the Universe cannot parallel, shall be parted with (Necessity compels Court-Jewellers) at that ruinously low sum. They, the Court-Jewellers, shall have much ado to weather it; but their work, at least, will find a fit Wearer, and go down to juster posterity. Monseigneur will merely have the condescension to sign this Receipt of Delivery: all the rest, her Highness the Sultana of the Sublime Porte has settled it.—Here the Court-Jeweller, with his joyous, though now much emaciated face, ventures on a faint knowing smile; to which, in the lofty dissolute-serene of Monseigneur's, some twinkle of permission could not but respond.—This is the First of those Three real-poetic Exhibitions, brought about by our Dramaturgist,—with perfect success.

It was said, long afterwards, that Monseigneur should have known, that Boehmer should have known, her Highness the Sultana's marginal-note (that of "*Right—Marie Antoinette of France*") to be a forgery and mockery: the *of France* was fatal to it. Easy talking, easy criticizing! But how are two enchanted men to know; two men with a fixed-idea each, a negative and a positive, rushing together to neutralize each other in rapture?—Enough, Monseigneur has the *ne-plus-ultra* of Necklaces, conquered by man's valour and woman's wit; and rolls off with it, in mysterious speed, to Versailles,—triumphant as a Jason with his Golden Fleece.

The Second grand scenic Exhibition by our Dramaturgic Countess occurs in her own apartment at Versailles, so early as the following night. It is a commodious apartment, with alcove; and the alcove has a glass door.* Monseigneur enters,—with a follower bearing a mysterious Casket; carefully depositing it, and then respectfully withdrawing. It is the Necklace itself in all its glory! Our tutelary Countess, and Monseigneur, and we, can at leisure admire the queenly Talisman; congratulate ourselves that the painful conquest of it is achieved.

But, hist! A knock, mild, but decisive, as from one knocking with authority! Monseigneur and we retire to our alcove; there, from behind our glass screen, observe what passes. Who comes? The door flung open: *de par la Reine!* Behold him, Monseigneur: he enters with grave, respectful, yet official air; worthy Monsieur Queen's-valet Lesclaux, the same who escorted our tutelary Countess, that moonlight night, from the back apartments of Versailles. Said we not, thou wouldst see *him* once more?—Methinks, again, spite of his Queen's-uniform, he has much the features of Villette of Rascaldom!—Rascaldom or Valetdom, (for to the blind all colours are the same,) he has, with his grave, respectful, yet official air, received the Casket, and its priceless contents; with fit injunction, with fit engagements; and retires bowing low.

Thus, softly, silently, like a very Dream, flits away our solid necklace,—through the Horn Gate of Dreams!

* *Georgel*, &c.

CHAPTER XIII.

SCENE THIRD: BY DAME DE LAMOTTE.

Now, too, in these same days (as he can afterwards prove by affidavit of Landlords) arrives Count Cagliostro himself, from Lyons! No longer by predictions in cipher; but by his living voice, (often in wrapt communion with the unseen world, "with Caraffe and four candles;") by his greasy prophetic bulldog face, (said to be the "most perfect quack-face of the eighteenth century,") can we assure ourselves that all is well; that all will turn "to the glory of Monseigneur, to the good of France, and of mankind,"* and Egyptian masonry. "Tokay flows like water;" our charming Countess, with her piquancy of face, is sprightlier than ever; enlivens with the brightest sallies, with the adroitest flatteries to all, those suppers of the gods. O Nights, O Suppers—too good to last! Nay, now also occurs another and Third scenic Exhibition, fitted by its radiance to dispel from Monsiegneur's soul the last trace of care.

Why the Queen does not, even yet, openly receive me at Court? Patience, Monseigneur! Thou little knowest those too intricate cabals; and how she still but works at them silently, with royal suppressed fury, like a royal lioness only *delivering* herself from the hunter's toils. Meanwhile, is not thy work done? The Necklace, she rejoices over it; beholds (many times in secret) her Juno-neck mirrored back the lovelier for it,—as our tutelar Countess can testify. Come to-morrow to the *Œil de Bœuf;* there see with eyes, in high noon, as already in deep midnight thou hast seen, whether in *her* royal heart there were delay.

Let us stand, then, with Monseigneur, in that *Œil de Bœuf*, in the Versailles Palace Gallery; for all well-dressed persons are admitted: there the Loveliest, in pomp of royalty, will walk to mass. The world is all in pelisses and winter furs; cheerful, clear,—with noses tending to blue. A lively many-voiced Hum plays fitful, hither and thither; of sledge parties and Court parties: frosty state of the weather; stability of M. de Calonne; Majesty's looks yesterday;—such Hum as always, in these sacred Court-spaces since Louis le Grand made and consecrated them, has, with more or less impetuosity, agitated our common Atmosphere.

Ah, through that long high Gallery what figures have passed—and vanished! Louvois,—with the Great King, flashing fire-glances on the fugitive; in his red right hand a pair of tongs, which pious Maintenon hardly holds

* *Georgel*, &c.

back: Louvois, where art thou? Ye *Maréchaux de France?* Ye unmentionable-women of past generations? Here also was it that rolled and rushed the "sound, absolutely like thunder,"* of Courtier hosts; in that dark hour when the signal light in Louis the Fifteenth's chamber-window was blown out; and his ghastly infectious Corpse lay alone, forsaken on its tumbled death-lair, "in the hands of some poor women:" and the Courtier-hosts rushed from the Deep-fallen to hail the New-risen! These too rushed, and passed; and their "sound, absolutely like thunder," became silence. Figures? Men? They are fast fleeting Shadows: fast chasing each other: it is not a Palace, but a Caravansera.—Monseigneur, (with thy too much Tokay overnight!) cease puzzling: here *thou* art, this blessed February day:—the Peerless, will she turn lightly that high head of hers, and glance aside into the *Œil de Bœuf*, in passing? Please Heaven, she will. To our tutelary Countess, at least, she promised it;† though, alas, so fickle is womankind!—

Hark! Clang of opening doors! She issues, like the Moon in silver brightness, down the Eastern steeps. *La Reine vient!* What a figure! I (with the aid of glasses) discern *her*. O Fairest, Peerless! Let the hum of minor discoursing hush itself wholly; and only one successive rolling peal of *Vive la Reine* (like the moveable radiance of a train of fire-works) irradiate her path.—Ye Immortals! She does, she beckons, turns her head this way!—"Does she not?" says Countess de Lamotte.—Versailles, the *Œil de Bœuf*, and all men and things, are drowned in a sea of Light; Monseigneur and that high beckoning Head are alone, with each other, in the Universe.

O Eminence, what a beatific vision! Enjoy it, blest as the gods; ruminate and re-enjoy it, with full soul: it is the last provided for thee. Too soon (in the course of these six months) shall thy beatific vision, like Mirza's vision, gradually melt away; and only oxen and sheep be grazing in its place;—and thou, as a doomed Nebuchadnezzar, be grazing with them.

"Does she not?" said the Countess de Lamotte. That it is a habit of hers; that hardly a day passes *without* her doing it: this the Countess de Lamotte did not say.

CHAPTER XIV.

THE NECKLACE CANNOT BE PAID.

Here, then, the specially Dramaturgic labours of Countess de Lamotte may be said to terminate. The rest of her life is Histrionic merely, or Histrionic and Critical; as, indeed, what had all the former part of it been but a *Hypocrisia*, a more or less correct Playing of Parts? O "Mrs. Facing-both-ways, (as old Bunyan said,) what a talent hadst thou! No Proteus ever took so many shapes, no Chameleon so often changed color. One thing thou wert to Monseigneur; another thing to Cagliostro, and Vilette of Rascaldom; a third thing to the World, (in printed *Mémoires*;) a fourth thing to Philippe Egalité: all things to all men!

Let her, however, we say, but manage now to *act* her own parts, with proper Histrionic illusion; and, by Critical glosses, give her past Dramaturgy the fit aspect, to Monsiegneur and others: this henceforth, and not new Dramaturgy, includes her whole task. Dramatic Scenes, in plenty, will follow of themselves; especially that Fourth and final Scene, spoken of above as by another Author,—by Destiny itself.

For in the Lamotte Theatre (so different from our common Pasteboard one) the Play goes on, even when the Machinist has left it. Strange enough: those Air-images, which from her Magic-lantern she hung out on the empty bosom of Night, have clutched hold of this solid-seeming World, (which some call the Material World, as if that made it more a Real one,) and will tumble hither and thither the solidest mass there. Yes, reader, so goes it here below. What thou callest a Brain-web, or mere illusive Nothing, *is* it not a web of the Brain; of the Spirit which inhabits the Brain; and which, in this World, rather, as I think, to be named the spiritual one,) very naturally moves and tumbles hither and thither all things it meets with, in Heaven or in Earth?—So, too, the Necklace, though we saw it vanish through the Horn Gate of Dreams, and in my opinion man shall never more behold it,—yet its activity ceases not, nor will. For no Act of a man, no Thing, (how much less the man himself!) is extinguished when *it* disappears: through considerable times (there are instances of Three Thousand Years) it visibly works; invisibly, unrecognised, it works through endless times. Such a Hyper-magical is this our poor old Real world; which some take upon them to pronounce effete, prosaic! Friend, it is thyself that art all withered up into effete Prose, dead as ashes: know this, (I advise thee;) and seek passionately, with a passion little short of desperation, to have it remedied.

Meanwhile, what will the feeling heart think to learn that Monseigneur de Rohan (as we prophesied) again experiences the fickleness of a Court; that, notwithstanding beatific visions, at noon and midnight, the Queen's Majesty (with the light ingratitude of her sex) flies off at a tangent; and, far from ousting his detested and detesting rival, Minister Breteuil, and openly delighting to honour Monseigneur, will hardly vouchsafe him a few gilt Autographs, and those few of the most capricious, suspicious, soul-confusing tenor? What terrifico-absurd explosions, which scarcely Cagliostro, with Caraffe and four candles, can still; how many deep-weighed Humble Petitions, Explanations, Expostulations, penned with fervidest eloquence, with craftiest diplomacy,—all delivered by our tutelar Countess: in vain!—O Cardinal, with what a huge iron mace, like Guy of Warwick's, thou smitest Phantasms in two (which close again, take shape again;) and only thrashest the air!

One comfort, however, is that the Queen's Majesty has committed herself. The Rose of

---

* *Campan.* † See *Georgel.*

Trianon, and what may pertain thereto, lies it not here? That "*Right—Marie Antoinette of France*," too; and the 30th of July, first-instalment-day, coming? She shall be *brought* to terms, good Eminence! Order horses and beef-eaters for Saverne; there, ceasing all written or oral communication, starve her into capitulating.* It is the bright May month: his Eminence again somnambulates the *Promenade de la Rose;* but now with grim dry eyes; and, from time to time, terrifically stamping.

But who is this that I see mounted on costliest horse and horse-gear; betting at Newmarket Races; though he can speak no English word, and only some Chevalier O'Niel, some Capuchin Macdermot (from Bar-sur Aube) interprets his French into the dialect of the Sister Island? Few days ago I observed him walking in Fleet-street, thoughtfully through Temple-Bar;—in deep treaty with Jeweller Jeffreys, with Jeweller Grey,† for the sale of Diamonds: such a lot as one may boast of. A tall handsome man; with ex-military whiskers; with a look of troubled gayety, and rascalism: you think it is the Sieur (self-styled Count) de Lamotte; nay, the man himself confesses it! The Diamonds were a present to his Countess,—from the still bountiful Queen.

Villette, too, has he completed his sales at Amsterdam? Him I shall by and by behold; not betting at Newmarket, but drinking wine and ardent spirits in the Taverns of Geneva. Ill-gotten wealth endures not; Rascaldom has no strongbox. Countess de Lamotte, for what a set of cormorant scoundrels hast thou laboured; art thou still labouring!

Still labouring, we may say: for as the fatal 30th of July approaches, what is to be looked for but universal Earthquake; Mud-explosion that will blot out the face of Nature? Methinks, stood I in thy pattens, Dame de Lamotte, I would cut and run.—"Run!" exclaims she, with a toss of indignant astonishment: "calumniated Innocence run?" For it is singular how in some minds (that are mere bottomless "chaotic whirlpools of gilt shreds") there is no deliberate Lying whatever; and nothing is either believed or disbelieved, but only (with some transient suitable Histrionic emotion) spoken and heard.

Had Dame de Lamotte a certain greatness of character, then; at least, a strength of transcendant audacity, amounting to the bastard-heroic? Great, indubitably great, is her Dramaturgic and Histrionic talent: but as for the rest, one must answer, with reluctance, No. Mrs. Facing-both-ways is a "Spark of vehement Life," but the furthest in the world from a brave woman: she did not, in any case, show the bravery of a woman; did, in many cases, show the mere screaming trepidation of one. Her grand quality is rather to be reckoned negative: the "untamableness" as of a fly; the "wax-cloth dress" from which so much ran down like water. Small sparrows, as I learn, have been trained to fire cannon; but would make poor Artillery Officers in a Waterloo. Thou dost not call that Cork a strong swimmer? which, nevertheless, shoots, without hurt, the Falls of Niagara; defies the thunderbolt itself to sink it, for more than a moment. Without intellect, imagination, power of attention, or any spiritual faculty, how brave were one,—with fit motive for it, such as hunger! How much might one dare, by the simplest of methods, by not thinking of it, not knowing it!—Besides, is not Cagliostro, foolish blustering Quack, still here? No scapegoat had ever broader back. The Cardinal, too, has he not money? Queen's Majesty, even in effigy, shall not be insulted; the Soubises, De Marsans, and high and puissant Cousins, must huddle the matter up: Calumniated Innocence, in the most universal of Earthquakes, will find *some* crevice to whisk through, as she has so often done.

But all this while how fares it with his Eminence, left somnambulating the *Promenade de la Rose;* and at times truculently stamping? Alas, ill; and ever worse. The starving method, singular as it may seem, brings no capitulation; brings only, after a month's waiting, our tutelary Countess, with a gilt Autograph, indeed, and "all wrapt in silk threads, sealed where they cross,—but which we read with curses.*

We must back again to Paris; there pen new Expostulations; which our unwearied Countess will take charge of, but, alas, can get no answer to. However, is not the 30th of July coming?—Behold (on the 19th of that month,) the shortest, most careless of Autographs with some fifteen hundred pounds of real money in it, to pay the—interest of the first instalment; the principal (of some thirty thousand) not being at the moment perfectly convenient! Hungry Boehmer makes large eyes at this proposal; will accept the money, but only as part of payment; the man is positive: a Court of Justice, if no other means, shall get him the remainder. What now is to be done?

Farmer-general Mons. Saint-James, Cagliostro's disciple, and wet with Tokay, will cheerfully advance the sum needed—for her Majesty's sake; thinks, however (with all his Tokay,) it were good to *speak* with her Majesty first.—I observe, meanwhile, the distracted hungry Boehmer driven hither and thither, not by his fixed-idea; alas, no, but by the far more frightful *ghost* thereof,—since no payment is forthcoming. He stands, one day, speaking with a Queen's waiting-woman (Madam Campan herself,) in "a thunder-shower, which neither of them notice,"—so thunderstruck are they.† What weather-symptoms for his Eminence!

The 30th of July has come, but no money; the 30th is gone, but no money. O Eminence, what a grim farewell of July is this of 1785! The last July went out with airs from Heaven,

* See *Lamotte.*

† Grey lived in No. 13, New Bond Street; Jeffreys in Piccadilly (Rohan's *Mémoire Pour;* see also *Count* de Lamotte's Narrative, in *Mémoires Justificatifs.*) Rohan says, "Jeffreys bought more than 10,000*l.* worth."

* See *Lamotte.* † *Campan.*

and Trianon Roses. *These* August days, are they not worse than dog's days; worthy to be blotted out from all Almanacs? Boehmer and Bassange thou canst still see; but only "return from them swearing."* Nay, what new misery is this? Our tutelary Histrionic Countess enters, distraction in her eyes;† she has just been at Versailles; the Queen's Majesty, with a levity of caprice which we dare not trust ourselves to characterize, declares plainly that she will deny ever having got the Necklace; ever having had, with his Eminence any transaction whatsoever!—Mud-explosion without parallel in volcanic annals. —The Palais de Strasbourg appears to be beset with spies; the Lamottes (for the Count, too, is here) are packing up for Bur-sur-Aube. The Sieur Boehmer, has he fallen insane? Or into communication with Breteuil?—

And so distractedly and distractively, to the sound of all Discords in Nature, opens that Fourth, final Scenic Exhibition, composed by Destiny.

CHAPTER XV.

SCENE FOURTH: BY DESTINY.

It is Assumption-day, the 15th of August. Don thy pontificalia, Grand-Almoner; crush down these hideous temporalities out of sight. In any case, smooth thy countenance into some sort of lofty-dissolute serene: thou hast a thing they call worshipping God to enact, thyself the first actor.

The Grand-Almoner has done it. He is in Versailles *Œil de Bœuf* Gallery; where male and female Peerage, and all Noble France in gala, various and glorious as the rainbow, waits only the signal to begin worshipping: on the serene of his lofty-dissolute countenance, there can nothing be read.‡ By Heaven! he is sent for to the Royal Apartment!

He returns with the old lofty-dissolute look, inscrutably serene: has his turn for favour actually come, then? Those fifteen long years of soul's travail are to be rewarded by a birth?—Monsieur le Baron de Breteuil issues; great in his pride of place, in this the crowning moment of his life. With one radidiant glance, Breteuil summons the Officer on Guard: with another, fixes Monseigneur: "*De par le Roi, Monseigneur:* you are arrested! At *your* risk, Officer!"—Curtains as of pitch-black whirlwind envelope Monseigneur; whirl off with him,—to outer darkness. Versailles Gallery explodes aghast; as if Guy Fawkes's Plot had *burst* under it. "The Queen's Majesty was weeping," whisper some. There will be no Assumption service; or such a one as was never celebrated since Assumption came in fashion.

Europe, then, shall ring with it from side to side!—But why rides that Heyduc as if all the Devils drove him? It is Monseigneur's Heyduc: Monseigneur spoke three words in German to him, at the door of his Versailles Hôtel; even handed him a slip of writing, which (some say, with borrowed Pencil, "in his red square cap") he had managed to prepare on the way hither.* To Paris! To the Palais-Cardinal! The horse dies on reaching the stable; the Heyduc swoons on reaching the cabinet: but his slip of writing fell from his hand; and I (says the Abbé Georgel) was there. The red Portfolio, containing all the gilt Autographs, is burnt utterly, with much else, before Breteuil can arrive for apposition of the seals!—Whereby Europe, in ringing from side to side, must worry itself with guessing: and at this hour (on this paper) sees the matter in such an interesting clear-obscure.

Soon Count Cagliostro and his Seraphic Countess go to join Monseigneur, in State Prison. In few days, follows Dame de Lamotte (from Bar-sur-Aube); Demoiselle d'Oliva by and by (from Brussels); Villette-de-Retaux from his Swiss retirement, in the taverns of Geneva. The Bastille opens its iron bosom to them all.

CHAPTER LAST.

MISSA EST.

Thus, then, the Diamond Necklace having, on the one hand, vanished through the Horn Gate of Dreams, and so (under the pincers of Nisus Lamotte and Euryalus Villette) lost its sublunary individuality and being; and, on the other hand, all that trafficked in it, sitting now safe under lock and key, that justice may take cognisance of them,—our engagement in regard to the matter is on the point of terminating. That extraordinary *Procès du Collier* (Necklace Trial,) spinning itself through Nine other ever-memorable Months, to the astonishment of the hundred and eighty-seven assembled *Parliementiers*, and of all Quiddunes, Journalists, Anecdotists, Satirists, in both Hemispheres, is, in every sense, a "Celebrated Trial," and belongs to Publishers of such. How, by innumerable confrontations and expiscatory questions, through entanglements, doublings, and windings that fatigue eye and soul, this most involute of Lies is finally winded off to the scandalous-ridiculous cinder-heart of it, let others relate.

Meanwhile, during these Nine ever-memorable Months, till they terminate late at night precisely with the May of 1786,† how many "fugitive leaves," quizzical, imaginative, or at least mendacious, were flying about in Newspapers; or stitched together as Pamphlets; and what heaps of others were left creeping in Manuscript, we shall not say;—having, indeed, no complete Collection of them, and, what is more to the purpose, little to

* *Lamotte.* † *Georgel.*

‡ This is Bette d'Enteville's description of him; "A handsome man, of fifty; with high complexion; hair white-gray, and the front of the head bald: of high stature; carriage noble and easy, though burdened with a certain degree of corpulency; who, I never doubted, was Monsieur de Rohan." (First *Mémoire Pour.*)

* *Georgel.*

† On the 31st of May, 1786, sentence was pronounced: about ten at night, the Cardinal got out of the Bastille; large mobs hurrahing round him,—out of spleen to the Court. (See *Georgel.*)

do with such Collection. Nevertheless, searching for some fit Capital of the composite order, to adorn adequately the now finished singular Pillar of our Narrative, what can suit us better than the following, so far as we know, yet unedited,

Occasional Discourse, by Count Alessandro Cagliostro, Thaumaturgist, Prophet, and Arch-Quack; delivered in the Bastille: Year of Lucifer, 5789; *of the Hegira Mohammedan, (from Mecca,)* 1201; *of the Hegira Cagliostric, (from Palermo,)* 24; *of the Vulgar Era*, 1785.

"Fellow Scoundrels,—An unspeakable Intrigue, spun from the soul of that Circe-Megæra, by our voluntary or involuntary help, has assembled us all, if not under one roof-tree, yet within one grim iron-bound ring-wall. For an appointed number of months, in the ever-rolling flow of Time, we, being gathered from the four winds, did by Destiny work together in body corporate; and, joint labourers in a Transaction already famed over the Globe, obtain unity of Name, (like the Argonauts of old,) as *Conquerors of the Diamond Necklace.* Ere long it is done, (for ring-walls hold not captive the free Scoundrel for ever;) and we disperse again, over wide terrestrial Space; some of us, it may be, over the very marches of Space. Our Act hangs indissoluble together; floats wondrous in the older and older memory of men: while we, little band of Scoundrels, who saw each other, now hover so far asunder, to see each other no more, if not once more only on the universal Doomsday, the last of the Days!

"In such interesting moments, while we stand within the verge of parting, and have not yet parted, methinks it were well here, in these sequestered Spaces, to institute a few general reflections. Me, as a public speaker, the Spirit of Masonry, of Philosophy, and Philanthropy, and even of Prophecy (blowing mysterious from the Land of Dreams) impels to do it. Give ear, O Fellow Scoundrels, to what the Spirit utters; treasure it in your hearts, practise it in your lives.

"Sitting here, penned up in this which (with a slight metaphor) I call the Central Cloaca of Nature, where a tyrannical De Launay can forbid the bodily eye free vision, you with the mental eye see but the better. This Central Cloaca, is it not rather a Heart, into which, from all regions, mysterious conduits introduce, and forcibly inject, whatsoever is choicest in the Scoundrelism of the Earth; there to be absorbed, or again (by the other auricle) ejected into new circulation? Let the eye of the mind run along this immeasurable venous-arterial system; and astound itself with the magnificent extent of Scoundreldom; the deep, I may say, unfathomable, significance of Scoundrelism.

"Yes, brethren, wide as the Sun's range is our Empire; wider than old Rome's in its palmiest era. I have in my time been far; in frozen Muscovy, in hot Calabria, east, west, wheresoever the sky overarches civilized man: and never hitherto saw I myself an alien; out of Scoundreldom I never was. Is it not even said, from of old, by the opposite party: '*All* men are liars?' Do they not (and this nowise 'in haste') whimperingly talk of 'one just person,' (as they call him,) and of the remaining thousand save one that take part with us? So decided is our majority."—(Applause.)

"Of the Scarlet Woman,—yes, Monseigneur, without offence,—of the Scarlet Woman that sits on Seven Hills, and her Black Jesuit Militia, out foraging from Pole to Pole, I speak not; for the story is too trite: nay, the Militia itself, as I see, begins to be disbanded, and invalided, for a second treachery; treachery to herself! Nor yet of Governments; for a like reason. Ambassadors, said an English punster, *lie* abroad for their masters. Their masters, we answer, lie, at home, for themselves. Not of all this, nor of Courtship, (with its so universal Lovers' vows,) nor Courtiership, nor Attorneyism, nor Public Oratory, and Selling by Auction, do I speak: I simply ask the gainsayer, Which is the particular trade, profession, mystery, calling, or pursuit of the Sons of Adam that they successfully manage in the other way? He cannot answer!—No: Philosophy itself, both practical and even speculative, has, at length (after shamefullest groping) stumbled on the plain conclusion that Sham is indispensable to Reality, as Lying to Living; that without Lying the whole business of the world, from swaying of senates to selling of tapes, must explode into anarchic discords, and so a speedy conclusion ensue.

"But the grand problem, Fellow Scoundrels, as you well know, is the *marrying* of Truth and Sham; so that they become one flesh, man and wife, and generate these three: Profit, Pudding, and Respectability that always keeps her Gig. Wondrously, indeed, do Truth and Delusion play into one another: Reality rests on Dream. Truth is but the *skin* of the bottomless Untrue: and ever, from time to time, the Untrue *sheds* it; is clear again; and the superannuated True itself becomes a Fable. Thus do all hostile things crumble back into our Empire; and of its increase there is no end.

"O brothers, to think of the Speech without meaning, (which is mostly ours,) and of the Speech with contrary meaning, (which is wholly ours,) manufactured by the organs of Mankind in one solar day! Or call it a day of Jubilee, when public Dinners are given, and Dinner-orations are delivered: or say, a Neighbouring Island in time of General Election! O ye immortal gods! The mind is lost; can only admire great Nature's plenteousness with a kind of sacred wonder.

"For, tell me, What is the chief end of man? 'To glorify God,' said the old Christian Sect, now happily extinct. 'To eat and find eatables by the readiest method,' answers sound Philosophy, discarding whims. If the *readier* method (than this of persuasive-attraction) is discovered,—point it out.—Brethren, I said the old Christian Sect was happily extinct: as, indeed, in Rome itself, there goes the wonderfullest traditionary Prophecy,* of that Nazareth Christ coming back, and being crucified a second time *there;* which truly I see not in the

* Goethe mentions it (*Italiænische Reise.*)

least how he could fail to be. Nevertheless, that old Christian whim, of an actual living and ruling God, and some sacred covenant binding all men in Him, with much other mystic stuff, does, under new or old shape, linger with a few. From these few, keep yourselves for ever far! They must even be left to their whim, which is not like to prove infectious.

"But neither are we, my Fellow Scoundrels, without our Religion, our Worship; which, like the oldest, and all true Worships, is one of Fear. The Christians have their Cross, the Moslem their Cresent: but have not we, too, our—Gallows? Yes, *infinitely* terrible is the Gallows; bestrides, with its patibulary fork, the Pit of bottomless Terror. No Manicheans are we; our God is One. Great, exceeding great, I say, is the Gallows; of old, even from the beginning, in this world; knowing neither variableness nor decadence; for ever, for ever, over the wreck of ages, and all civic and ecclesiastic convulsions, meal-mobs, revolutions, the Gallows with front serenely terrible towers aloft. Fellow Scoundrels, fear the Gallows, and have no other fear! *This* is the Law and the Prophets. Fear every emanation of the Gallows. And what is every buffet, with the fist, or even with the tongue, of one having authority, but some such emanation. And what is Force of Public Opinion but the infinitude of such emanations,—rushing combined on you like a mighty stormwind? Fear the Gallows, I say! O when, with its long black arm, *it* has clutched a man, what avail him all terrestrial things? These pass away, with horrid nameless dinning in his ears; and the ill-starred Scoundrel pendulates between Heaven and Earth, a thing rejected of *both*."—(Profound sensation.)

"Such, so wide in compass, high, gallows-high in dignity, is the Scoundrel Empire; and for depth, it is deeper than the Foundations of the World. For what was Creation itself wholly (according to the best Philosophers) but a Divulsion by the Time-Spirit, (or Devil so-called;) a forceful Interruption, or breaking asunder, of the old Quiescence of Eternity? It was Lucifer that fell, and made this lordly World arise. Deep? It is bottomless-deep; the very Thought, diving, bobs up from it baffled. Is not this that they call Vice of Lying the *Adam-Kadmon*, or primeval Rude-Element, old as Chaos mother's-womb of Death and Hell; whereon their thin film of Virtue, Truth, and the like, poorly wavers—for a day? All Virtue, what is it, even by their own showing, but Vice transformed,—that is, manufactured, rendered artificial? 'Man's Vices are the roots from which his Virtues grow out and see the light,' says one: 'Yes,' add I, 'and thanklessly steal their nourishment!' Were it not for the nine hundred ninety and nine unacknowledged (perhaps martyred and calumniated) Scoundrels, how were their single Just Person (with a murrain on him!) so much as possible?—Oh, it is high, high: these things are too great for me; Intellect, Imagination, flags her tired wings; the soul lost, baffled"—

—Here Dame de Lamotte tittered audibly, and muttered, *Coq-d'-Inde*, (which, being interpreted into the Scottish tongue, signifies *Bubbly-Jock!*) The Arch-Quack, whose eyes were turned inwards as in rapt contemplation, started at the titter and mutter: his eyes flashed outwards with dilated pupil; his nostrils opened wide; his very hair seemed to stir in its long twisted pigtails, (his fashion of curl;) and as Indignation is said to make Poetry, it here made Prophecy, or what sounded as such. With terrible, working features, and gesticulation not recommended in any Book of Gesture, the Arch-Quack, in voice supernally discordant (like Lions worrying Bulls of Bashan) began:

"Sniff not, Dame de Lamotte; tremble, thou foul Circe-Megæra: thy day of desolation is at hand! Behold ye the Sanhedrim of Judges, with their fanners (of written Parchment) loud-rustling, as they winnow all her chaff, and down-plumage, and she stands there naked and mean?—Villette, Oliva, do *ye* blab secrets? Ye have no pity of her extreme need; she none of yours. Is thy light-giggling, untamable heart at last heavy? Hark ye! Shrieks of one cast out; whom they brand on both shoulders with iron stamp; the red hot "V," thou *Voleuse*, hath it entered thy soul? Weep, Circe de Lamotte; wail there in truckle bed, and hysterically gnash thy teeth: nay, do, smother thyself in thy door-mat coverlid; thou hast found thy mates; thou art in the Salpêtrière!—Weep, daughter of the high and puissant Sans-inexpressibles! Buzz of Parisian Gossipry is about thee; but not to help thee: no, to eat before thy time. What shall a King's Court do with thee, thou unclean thing, while thou yet livest? Escape! Flee to utmost countries; hide there, if thou canst, thy mark of Cain!—In the Babylon of Fogland! Ha! is that my London? See I Judas Iscariot Egalité? Print, yea print abundantly the abominations of your two hearts: breath of rattlesnakes can bedim the steel mirror, but only for a time.—And there! Ay, there at last! Tumblest thou from the lofty leads, poverty-stricken, O thriftless daughter of the high and puissant, escaping bailiffs? Descendest thou precipitate, in dead night, from window in the third story: hurled forth by Bacchanals, to whom thy shrill tongue had grown unbearable?* Yea, through the smoke of that new Babylon thou fallest headlong; one long scream of screams makes night hideous: thou liest there, shattered like addle egg, 'nigh to the Temple of Flora!' O Lamotte, has thy *Hypocrisia* ended, then? Thy many characters were all acted. Here at last thou actest not, but art what thou seemest: a mangled squelch of gore, confusion, and abomination; which men huddle underground, with no burial stone. Thou gallows-carrion!"—

—Here the prophet turned up his nose, (the broadest of the eighteenth century,) and opened

* The English Translator of Lamotte's *Life* says, she fell from the leads of her house, nigh the Temple of Flora, endeavouring to escape seizure for debt; and was taken up so much hurt that she died in consequence. Another report runs that she was flung out of window, as in the Cagliostric text. One way or other she did die, on the 23d of August, 1791 (*Biographie Universelle*, xxx. 287.) Where the "Temple of Flora" was, or is, one knows not.

wide his nostrils with such a greatness of disgust, that all the audience, even Lamotte herself, sympathetically imitated him —"O Dame de Lamotte! Dame de Lamotte! Now, when the circle of thy existence lies complete: and my eye glances over these two score and three years that were lent thee, to do evil as thou couldst; and I behold thee a bright-eyed little Tatterdemalion, begging and gathering sticks in the Bois de Boulogne; and also at length a squelched Putrefaction, here on London pavements; with the headdressings and hungerings, the gaddings and hysterical gigglings that came between,—*What* shall I say was the meaning of thee at all?—

"Villette-de-Retaux! Have the catchpoles trepanned thee, by sham of battle, in thy Tavern, from the sacred Republican soil.* It is thou that wert the hired Forger of Handwritings? Thou wilt confess it? Depart, unwhipt, yet accursed.—Ha! The dread Symbol of our Faith? Swings aloft, on the Castle of St. Angelo, a Pendulous Mass, which I think I discern to be the body of Villette! There let him end; the sweet morsel of our Juggernaut.

"Nay, weep not thou, disconsolate Oliva; blear not thy bright blue eyes, daughter of the shady Garden! Thee shall the Sanhedrim not harm: this Cloaca of Nature emits thee; as notablest of unfortunate-females, thou shalt have choice of husbands not without capital; and accept one.† Know this, for the vision of it is true.

"But the Anointed Majesty whom ye profaned? Blow, spirit of Egyptian Masonry, blow aside the thick curtains of Space! Lo you, her eyes are red with their first tears of pure bitterness; not with their last. Tirewoman Campan is choosing, from the Printshops of the Quais, the reputed-best among the hundred likenesses of Circe de Lamotte:‡ a Queen shall consider if the basest of women ever, by any accident, darkened daylight or candle-light for the highest. The Portrait answers: 'Never!'—(Sensation in the audience.)

"—Ha! What is *this?* Angels, Uriel, Anachiel, and the other Five; Pentagon of Rejuvenescene; Power that destroyed Original Sin; Earth, Heaven, and thou Outer Limbo, which men name Hell! Does the Empire of Imposture waver? Burst there, in starry sheen, updarting, Light-rays from out *its* dark foundations; as it rocks and heaves, not in travail-throes, but in death-throes? Yea, Light-rays, piercing, clear, that salute the Heavens,—lo, they *kindle* it; their starry clearness becomes as red Hellfire! Imposture is burnt up; one Red-sea of Fire, wild-billowing enwraps the World; with its fire-tongue licks at the Stars. Thrones are hurled into it, and Dubois Mitres, and Prebendal Stalls that drop fatness, and—ha! what see I?—all the *Gigs* of Creation: all, all! Wo is me! Never since Pharaoh's Chariots, in the Red-sea of water, was there wreck of Wheel-vehicles like this in the Sea of Fire. Desolate, as ashes, as gases, shall they wander in the wind.

"Higher, higher, yet flames the Fire-Sea; crackling with new dislocated timber; hissing with leather and prunella. The metal Images are molten; the marble Images become mortar-lime; the stone Mountains sulkily explode. Respectability, with all her collected Gigs inflamed for funeral pyre, wailing, leaves the Earth,—to return under new Avatar. Imposture, how it burns, through generations: how it is burnt up—for a time. The World is black ashes; which—when will they grow green? The Images all run into amorphous Corinthian brass; all Dwellings of men destroyed; the very mountains peeled and riven, the valleys black and dead: it is an empty World! Wo to them that shall be born then!——A King, a Queen, (ah me!) were hurled in; did rustle once; flew aloft, crackling, like paper-scroll. Oliva's Husband was hurled in; Iscariot Egalité; thou grim De Launay, with thy grim Bastille; whole kindreds and peoples; five millions of mutually destroying Men. For it is the End of the Dominion of Imposture (which is Darkness and opaque Firedamp; and the burning up, with unquenchable fire, of all the Gigs that are in the Earth!"—Here the Prophet paused, fetching a deep sigh; and the Cardinal uttered a kind of faint, tremulous Hem!

"Mourn not, O Monseigneur, spite of thy nephritic cholic, and many infirmities. For thee mercifully it was not unto death.* O Monseigneur, (for thou hadst a touch of goodness,) who would not weep over thee, if he also laughed? Behold! The not too judicious Historian, that long years hence, amid remotest wilderness, writes thy Life, and names thee *Mud-volcano;* even he shall reflect that it *was* thy Life this same; thy *only* chance through whole Eternity; which thou (poor gambler) hast expended *so:* and, even over his hard heart, a breath of dewy pity for thee shall blow.—O Monseigneur, thou wert not all ignoble: thy Mud-volcano was but strength dislocated, fire misapplied. Thou wentest ravening through the world; no Life-elixir or Stone of the Wise could *we* two (for want of funds) discover: a foulest Circe undertook to fatten thee; and thou hadst to fill thy belly with the east wind. And burst? By the Masonry of

* See *Georgel*, and Villette's *Mémoire*.

† *Affaire du Collier* is this MS. Note: "Gay d'Oliva, a common-girl of the Palais-Royal, who was chosen to play a part in this Business, got married, some years afterwards, to one Beausire, an Ex-Noble, formerly attached to the d'Artois Household. In 1790, he was Captain of the National Guard Company of the Temple. He then retired to Choisy, and managed to be named Procureur of that Commune: he finally employed himself in drawing up Lists of Proscription in the Luxembourg Prison, when he played the part of informer, (*mouton.*) See *Tableau des Prisons de Paris sous Robespierre.*" These details are correct. In the *Mémoires sur les Prisons,* (new Title of the Book just referred to,) ii. 171, we find this: "The second Denouncer was Beausire, an Ex-Noble, known under the old government for his intrigues. To give an idea of him, it is enough to say that he married the d'Oliva," &c., as in the MS. Note already given. Finally is added: "He was the main spy of Boyenval; who, however, said that he made use of him; but that Fouquier-Tinville did not like him, and would have him guillotined in good time."

‡ See *Campan*.

* Rohan was elected of the Constituent Assembly; and even got a compliment or two in it, as Court-victim, from here and there a man of weak judgment. He was one of the first who, recalcitrating against "Civil Constitution of the Clergy," &c., took himself across the Rhine.

Enoch. No! Behold has not thy Jesuit Familiar his Scouts dim-flying over the deep of human things? Cleared art thou of crime, save that, of fixed-idea; weepest, a repentant exile, in the Mountains of Auvergne. Neither shall the Red Fire-sea itself consume thee; only consume thy Gig, and, instead of Gig (O rich exchange!) restore thy Self. Safe beyond the Rhine-stream, thou livest peaceful days; savest many from the fire, and anointest their smarting burns. Sleep finally, in thy mother's bosom, in a good old age!"—The Cardinal gave a sort of guttural murmur, or gurgle, which ended in a long sigh.

"O Horrors, as ye shall be called," again burst forth the Quack, "why have ye missed the Sieur de Lamotte; why not of him, too, made gallows-carrion? Will spear, or sword-stick, thrust at him, (or supposed to be thrust,) through window of hackney-coach, in Piccadilly of the Babylon of Fog, where he jolts disconsolate, not let out the imprisoned animal existence? Is he poisoned, too?"* Poison will not kill the Sieur Lamotte; nor steel, nor massacres.† Let him drag his utterly superfluous life to a second and a third generation; and even admit the not too judicious Historian to see his face before he die.

"But, ha!" cried he, and stood wide-staring, horror struck, as if some Cribb's fist had knocked the wind out of him: "O horror of horrors! Is it not Myself I see? Roman Inquisition! Long months of cruel baiting! *Life of Giuseppe Balsamo!* Cagliostro's Body still lying in St. Leo Castle, his *Self* fled—*whither?* By-standers wag their heads, and say; 'The Brow of Brass, behold how it has got all unlackered; these Pinchbeck lips can lie no more!' Eheu! Ohoo!"—and he burst into unstanchable blubbering of tears; and sobbing out the moanfullest broken howl, sank down in swoon; to be put to bed by De Launay and others.

Thus spoke (or thus might have spoken) and prophesied, the Arch-quack Cagliostro; and truly much better than he ever else did: for not a jot or tittle of it (save only that of our promised Interview with Nestor de Lamotte, which looks unlikelier than ever, for we have not heard of him, dead or living, since 1826,) but he has turned out to be literally *true*. As, indeed, in all his History, one jot or title of untruth, that we could render true, is, perhaps, not discoverable; much as the distrustful reader may have disbelieved.

Here, then, our little labour ends. The Necklace was, and is no more: the stones of it again "circulate in commerce" (some of them perhaps, in Rundle's at this hour;) may give rise to what other Histories we know not. The Conquerors of it, every one that trafficked in it, have they not all had their due, which was Death?

This little Business, like a little cloud, bodied itself forth in skies clear to the unobservant: but with such hues of deep-tinted villany, dissoluteness, and general delirium, as to the observant, betokened it electric; and wise men (a Goethe, for example) boded Earthquakes. Has not the Earthquakes come?

MEMOIRS OF MIRABEAU.*

[LONDON AND WESTMINSTER REVIEW, 1837.

A PROVERB says, "The house that is a-building looks not as the house that is built," Environed with rubbish and mortar-heaps with scaffold-poles, hodmen, dust-clouds, some rudiments only of that thing that is to be, can, to the most observant, disclose themselves through the mean tumult of the thing that hitherto is. How true is this same with regard to all works and facts whatsoever in our world; emphatically true in regard to the highest fact and work which our world witnesses,—the Life of what we call an Original Man. Such a man is one not made altogether by the common pattern; one whose phases and goings forth cannot be prophesied of, even approximately; though, indeed, by their very newness and strangeness they most of all provoke prophecy. A man of this kind, while he lives on earth, is "unfolding himself out of nothing into something," surely under very complex conditions:

* See Lamotte's Narrative, (*Mémoires Justificatifs.*)

† Lamotte, after his wife's death, had returned to Paris; and been arrested—*not* for building churches. The Sentence of the old Parlement against him, in regard to the Necklace business, he gets annulled by the new Courts; but is, nevertheless, "retained in confinement," (*Moniteur* Newspaper, 7th August, 1782.) He was still in Prison at the time the September Massacre broke out. From Maton de la Varenne we cite the following grim passage: Maton is in La Force Prison.

"At one in the morning," (of Monday, September 3,) writes Maton, "the grate that led to our quarter was again opened. Four men in uniform, holding each a naked sabre and blazing torch, mounted to our corridor; a turnkey showing the way; and entered a room close on ours, to investigate a box, which they broke open. This done, they halted in the gallery; and began interrogating one Cuissa, to know where Lamotte was; who, they said, under a pretext of finding a treasure, which they should share in, had swindled one of them out of 300 livres, having asked him to dinner for that purpose. The wretched Cuissa, whom they had in their power, and who lost his life that night, answered, all trembling, that he remembered the fact well, but could not say what had become of the prisoner. Resolute to find this Lamotte and confront him with Cuissa, they ascended into other rooms, and made further rummaging there; but apparently without effect, for I heard them say to one another: "Come, search among the corpses, then for, *Nom de Dieu!* we must know what is become of him."' (*Ma Resurrection, par Maton de la Varenne;* reprinted in the *Histoire Parlementaire,* xviii. 142.)—Lamotte lay in the Bicêtre Prison; but had got out, precisely in the nick of time,—and dived beyond soundings.

* *Mémoires biographiques, littéraires, et politiques, de Mirabeau; écrits par lui-même, par son Père Oncle, et son Fils Adoptif* (Memoirs, biographical, literary, and political, of Mirabeau: written by himself, by his Father, his Uncle, and his Adopted Son.) 8 vols. 8vo, Paris, 1834—36.

he is drawing continually towards him, in continual succession and variation, the materials of his structure, nay, his very plan of it, from the whole realm of accident, you may say, and from the whole realm of free-will: he is *building* his life together in this manner; a guess and a problem as yet, not to others only but to himself. Hence such criticism by the bystanders; loud no-knowledge, loud misknowledge! It is like the opening of the Fisherman's Casket in the Arabian Tale, this beginning and growing-up of a life: vague smoke wavering hither and thither; some features of a Genie looming through; of the ultimate shape of which no fisherman or man can judge. And yet, as we say, men do judge, and pass provisional sentence, being forced to it; you can predict with what accuracy! "Look at the audience in a theatre," says one: "the life of a man is there compressed within five hours' duration; is transacted on an open stage, with lighted lamps, and what the fittest words and art of genius can do to make the spirit of it clear; yet listen, when the curtain falls, what a discerning public will say of that! And now, if the drama extended over three-score and ten years; and were enacted, not with a view to clearness, but rather indeed with a view to concealment, often in the deepest attainable involution of obscurity; and your discerning public occupied otherwise, cast its eye on the business now here for a moment, and then there for a moment?" Wo to him, answer we, who has no court of appeal against the world's judgment! He is a doomed man: doomed by conviction to hard penalties; nay, purchasing acquittal (too probably) by a still harder penalty, that of being a trivialty, superficialty, self-advertiser, and partial or total quack, which is the hardest penalty of all.

But suppose farther, that the man, as we said, was an original man; that his life-drama would not and could not be measured by the three unities alone, but partly by a rule of its own too: still farther, that the transactions he had mingled in were great and world-dividing; that of all his judges there were not one who had not something to love him for unduly, to hate him for unduly! Alas! is it not precisely in this case, where the whole world is promptest to judge, that the whole world is likeliest to be wrong: natural opacity being so doubly and trebly darkened by accidental difficulty and perversion? The crabbed moralist had some show of reason who said: "To judge of an original contemporary man, you must, in general, reverse the world's judgment about him; the world is not only wrong on that matter, but cannot on any such matter be right."

One comfort is, that the world is ever working itself righter and righter on such matters; that a continual revisal and rectification of the world's first judgment on them is inevitably going on. For, after all, the world loves its original men, and can in no wise forget them; not till after a long while; sometimes not till after thousands of years. Forgetting *them*, what indeed, should it remember? The world's wealth is its original men; by these and their works it is a world and not a waste: the memory and record of what MEN it bore—this is the sum of its strength, its sacred "property for ever," whereby it upholds itself, and steers forward better or worse, through the yet undiscovered deep of Time. All knowledge, all art, all beautiful or precious possession of existence, is, in the long run, this, or connected with this. Science itself, is it not, under one of its most interesting aspects, Biography; is it not the Record of the *Work* which an original man, still named by us, or not now named, was blessed by the heavens to do? That Sphere-and-cylinder is the monument and abbreviated history of the man Archimedes; not to be forgotten, probably, till the world itself vanish. Of Poets, and what they have done, and how the world loves them, let us, in these days, very singular in respect of that Art, say nothing, or next to nothing. The greatest modern of the poetic guild has already said: "Nay if thou wilt have it, who but the poet first formed gods for us, brought them down to us, raised us up to them?"

Another remark, on a lower scale, not unworthy of notice, is by Jean Paul: that, "as in art, so in conduct, or what we call morals, before there can be an Aristotle, with his critical canons, there must be a Homer, many Homers with their heroic performances." In plainer words, the original man is the true creator (or call him revealer) of Morals too: it is from his example that precepts enough are derived, and written down in books and systems: he properly is the *Thing;* all that follows after is but talk about the thing, better or worse interpretation of it, more or less wearisome and ineffectual discourse of logic on it. A remark, this of Jean Paul's which, well meditated, may seem one of the most pregnant lately written on these matters. If any man had the ambition of building a new system of morals, (not a promising enterprise, at this time of day,) there is no remark known to us which might better serve him as a chief corner-stone, whereon to found, and to build, high enough, nothing doubting;—high, for instance, as the Christian Gospel itself. And to whatever other heights man's destiny may yet carry him! Consider whether it was not, from the first, by example, or say rather by human exemplars, and such reverent imitation or abhorrent aversion and avoidance as these gave rise to, that man's duties were made indubitable to him? Also, if it is not yet, in these last days, by very much the same means, (example, precept, prohibition, "force of public opinion," and other forcings and inducings,) that the like result is brought about; and, from the Woolsack down to the Treadmill, from Almack's to Chalk Farm and the west-end of Newgate, the incongruous whirlpool of life is forced and induced to whirl with some attempt at regularity? The two Mosaic Tables were of simple limited stone; no logic appended to them: we, in our days, are privileged with Logic—Systems of Morals, Professors of Moral Philosophy, Theories of Moral Sentiment, Utilities, Sympathies, Moral Senses, not a few; useful for those that feel comfort in them. But to the observant eye, is it not still plain that the rule of man's life rests not very steadily on logic (rather carries logic unsteadily resting on *it*, as an excuse, an exposition, or ornamental solacement to oneself and others;) that ever, as of old, the thing a man will do is the thing he feels commanded to do; of which command, again, the origin and reasonableness remains often as good as *in*demonstrable by logic; and, indeed, lies mainly in this, that it has been demonstrated otherwise and better by experiment; namely, that an experimental (what we name original) man has already done it, and we have *seen* it to be good and reasonable, and now know it to be so once and for evermore?—Enough of this.

He were a sanguine individual, surely, that should turn to the French Revolution for new rules of conduct and creators or exemplars of morality,—except, indeed, exemplars of the gibbetted, *in-terrorem* sort. A greater work, it is often said, was never done in the world's history by men so small. Twenty-five millions (say these severe critics) are hurled forth out of all their old habitudes, arrangements, harnessings, and garnitures, into the new, quite void arena and career of *Sansculottism;* there to show what originality is in them. Fanfaronading and gesticulation, vehemence, effervescence, heroic desperation, they do show in abundance; but of what one can call originality, invention, natural stuff or character, amazingly little. Their heroic desperation, such as it was, we will honour and even venerate, as a new document (call it rather a renewal of that primeval ineffaceable document and charter) of the manhood of man. But, for the rest, there were Federations; there were Festivals of Fraternity, "the Statute of Nature pouring water from her two *mammelles,*" and the august Deputies all drinking of it from the same iron saucer: Weights and Measures were attempted to be changed; the Months of the Year became Pluviose, Thermidor, Messidor (till Napoleon said, *Il faudra se débarrasser de se Messidor,* One must get this Messidor sent about its business:) also Mrs. Momoro and others rode prosperous, as Goddesses of Reason; and then, these being mostly guillotined, Mahomet Robespierre did, with bouquet in hand, and in new nankeen trowsers, in front of the Tuileries, pronounce the scraggiest of prophetic discourses on the *Etre Suprême,* and set fire to much emblematic pasteboard:—all this, and an immensity of such, the twenty-five millions did devise and accomplish; but (apart from their heroic desperation, which was no miracle either, beside that of the old Dutch, for instance) this, and the like of this, was almost all. Their arena of *Sansculottism* was the most original arena opened to man for above a thousand years; and they, at bottom, were unexpectedly common-place in it. Exaggerated common-place, triviality run distracted, and a kind of universal "Frenzy of John Dennis," is the figure they exhibit. The brave Forster,—sinking slowly of broken heart, in the midst of that volcanic chaos of the Reign of Terror, and clinging still to the cause, which, though now bloody and terrible, he believed to be the highest, and for which he had sacrificed all, country, kindred, fortune, friends, and life,—compares the Revolution, indeed, to "an explosion and new creation of the world;" but the actors in it, that went buzzing about him, to a "*handvoll mücken,* handful of flies."* And yet, one may add, this same explosion of a world was their work; the work of these—flies? The truth is, neither Forster nor any man can see a French Revolution; it is like seeing the ocean: poor Charles Lamb complained that he could not see the multitudinous ocean at all, but only some insignificant fraction of it from the deck of the Margate hoy. It must be owned, however, (urge these severe critics,) that examples of rabid triviality abound, in the French Revolution, to a lamentable extent. Consider Maximilien Robespierre; for the greater part of two years, what one may call Autocrat of France. A poor sea-green (*verdâtre,*) atrabiliar Formula of a man; without head, without heart, or any grace, gift, or even vice beyond common, if it were not vanity, astucity, diseased rigour (which some count strength) as of a cramp: really a most poor sea-green individual in spectacles; meant by Nature for a Methodist parson of the stricter sort, to doom men who departed from the written confession; to chop fruitless shrill logic; to contend, and suspect, and ineffectually wrestle and wriggle; and, on the whole, to love, or to know, or to be (properly speaking) Nothing;—this was he who, the sport of wracking winds, saw himself whirled aloft to command *la première nation de l'univers,* and all men shouting long life to him; one of the most lamentable, tragic, sea-green objects, ever whirled aloft in that manner, in any country, to his own swift destruction, and the world's long wonder!

So argue these severe critics of the French Revolution: with whom we argue not here; but remark rather, what is more to the purpose, that the French Revolution did disclose original men: among the twenty-five millions, at least one or two units. Some reckon, in the present stage of the business, as many as three: Napoleon, Danton, Mirabeau. Whether more will come to light, or of what sort, when the computation is quite liquidated, one cannot say: meanwhile let the world be thankful for these three;—as, indeed, the world is; loving original men, without limit, were they never so questionable, well knowing how rare they are! To us, accordingly, it is rather interesting to observe how on these three also, questionable as they surely are, the old process is repeating itself; how these also are getting known in their true likeness. A second generation, relieved in some measure from the spectral hallucinations, hysterical ophthalmia, and natural panic-delirium of the first contemporary one, is gradually coming to discern and measure what its predecessor could only execrate and shriek over: for, as our Proverb said, the dust is sinking, the rubbish-heaps disappear; the built house, such as it is, and was appointed to be, stands visible, better or worse.

Of Napoleon Bonaparte, what with so many bulletins, and such self-proclamation from artillery and battle-thunder, loud enough to

* Forster's Briefe und Nachlass.

ring through the deafest brain, in the remotest nook of this earth, and now, in consequence, with so many biographies, histories, and historical arguments for and against, it may be said that *he* can now sift for himself; that his true figure is in a fair way of being ascertained. Doubtless it will be found one day what significance was in him; how (we quote from a New England Book) "the man was a divine missionary, though unconscious of it; and preached, through the cannon's throat, that great doctrine, *La carrière ouverte aux talens*, (The tools to him that can handle them,) which is our ultimate Political Evangel, wherein alone can Liberty lie. Madly enough he preached, it is true, as enthusiasts and first missionaries are wont; with imperfect utterance, amid much frothy rant; yet as articulately, perhaps, as the case admitted. Or call him, if you will, an American backwoodsman, who had to fell unpenetrated forests, and battle with innumerable wolves, and did not entirely forbear strong liquor, rioting, and even theft; whom, nevertheless, the peaceful sower will follow, and, as he cuts the boundless harvest, bless."—From "the incarnate Moloch," which the word once was, onwards to this quiet version, there is a considerable progress.

Still more interesting is it, not without a touch almost of pathos, to see how the rugged *Terræ Filius* Danton begins likewise to emerge, from amid the blood-tinted obscurations and shadows of horrid cruelty, into calm light; and seems now not an Anthropophagus, but partly a man. On the whole, the Earth feels it to be something to have a "Son of Earth;" *any* reality, rather than a hypocrisy and formula! With a man that went honestly to work with himself, and said and acted, in any sense, with the whole mind of him, there is always something to be done. Satan himself, according to Dante, was a praiseworthy object, compared with those *juste-milieu* angels (so over-numerous in times like ours) who "were *neither* faithful nor rebellious," but were for their little selves only: trimmers, moderates, plausible persons, who, in the Dantean Hell, are found doomed to this frightful penalty, that "they have not the hope to die, (*non han speranza di morte;*) but sunk in torpid death-life, in mud and the plague of flies, they are to doze and dree for ever,—"hateful to God and to the Enemies of God:"

"*Non ragionum di lor, ma guarda e passa!*"

If Bonaparte were the "armed Soldier of Democracy," invincible while he continued true to that, then let us call this Danton the *Enfant Perdu*, and *un*enlisted Revolter and Titan of Democracy, which could not yet have soldiers or discipline, but was by the nature of it lawless. An Earthborn, we say, yet honestly born of Earth! In the *Memoirs of Garat*, and elsewhere, one sees these fire-eyes beam with earnest insight, fill with the water of tears; the huge rude features speak withal of wild human sympathies; that Antæus' bosom also held a heart. "It is not the alarm-cannon that you hear," cries he to the terror-struck, when the Prussians were already at Verdun: "it is the *pas de charge* against our enemies. *De l'audace, et encore de l'audace, et toujours de l'audacc:* to dare, and again to dare, and without limit to dare!"—there is nothing left but that. Poor "Mirabeau of the Sansculottes," what a mission! And it could not be but done,—and it was done! But, indeed, may there not be, if well considered, more virtue in this feeling itself, once bursting earnest from the wild heart, than in whole lives of immaculate Pharisees and Respectabilities, with their eye ever set on "character," and the letter of the law: "*Que mon nom soit flétri*, Let my name be blighted, then; let the Cause be glorious, and have victory!" By and by, as we predict, the Friend of Humanity, since so many Knife-grinders have no story to tell him, will find some sort of story in this Danton. A rough-hewn giant of a man, (not anthropophagous entirely;) whose "figures of speech" (and also of action) "are all gigantic;" whose "voice reverberates from the domes,"—and dashes Brunswick across the marches in a very wrecked condition. Always his total freedom from cant is one thing; even in his briberies, and sins as to money, there is a frankness, a kind of broad greatness. Sincerity, a great rude sincerity, (of insight and of purpose,) dwelt in the man, which quality is the root of all: a man who could see through many things, and would stop at very few things; who marched impetuously, where to march was almost certainly to fall; and now bears the penalty, in a "name" blighted, yet, as we say, visibly clearing itself. Once cleared, why should not this name, too, have significance for men? The wild history is a tragedy, as all human histories are. Brawny Dantons, still to the present hour, "rend the glebe," as simple brawny Farmers, and reap peaceable harvests, at Arcis-sur-Aube; and *this* Danton—! It is an *un*rhymed tragedy; very bloody, fuliginous, (after the manner of the *elder* dramatists;) yet full of tragic elements; not undeserving natural pity and fear. In quiet times, perhaps still at a great distance, the happier onlooker may stretch out the hand, across dim centuries, to him, and say: "Ill-starred brother, how thou foughtest with wild lion-strength, and yet not with strength *enough*, and flamedst aloft, and wert trodden down of sin and misery;—behold, thou also wert a man!" It is said there lies a Biography of Danton written, in Paris, at this moment; but the editor waits till the "force of public opinion" ebb a little. Let him publish, with utmost convenient despatch, and say what he knows, if he do know it: the lives of remarkable men are always worth understanding instead of misunderstanding; and public opinion must positively adjust itself the best way it can.

But without doubt the far most interesting, best-gifted of this questionable trio is not the Mirabeau of the Sansculottes, but the Mirabeau himself: a man of much finer nature than either of the others; of a genius equal in strength (we will say) to Napoleon's; but a much humaner genius, almost a poetic one. With wider sympathies of his own, he appeals far more persuasively to the sympathies of men.

Of him, too, it is interesting to notice the progressive dawning, out of calumny, misrepresentation, and confused darkness, into visibility and light; and how the world manifests its continued curiosity about him; and as book after book comes forth with new evidence, the matter is again taken up, the old judgment on it revised and anew revised;—whereby, in fine, we can hope the right, or approximately right, sentence will be found; and so the question be left settled. It would seem this Mirabeau also is one whose memory the world will not, for a long while, let die. Very different from many a high memory, dead and deep buried long since then! In his lifetime, even in the final effulgent part of it, this Mirabeau took upon him to write, with a sort of awe-struck feeling, to our Mr. Wilberforce; and did not, that we can find, get the benefit of any answer. Pitt was prime minister, and then Fox, then again Pitt, and again Fox, in sweet vicissitude; and the noise of them, reverberating through Brookes's and the club-rooms, through tavern dinners, electioneering hustings, leading articles, filled all the earth; and it seemed as if those two (though which might be *which*, you could not say) were the Ormuzd and Ahriman of political nature;—and now! Such difference is there (once more) between an original man, of never such questionable sort, and the most dexterous, cunningly-devised parliamentary mill. The difference is great; and one of those on which the future time makes largest contrast with the present. Nothing can be more important than the mill while it continues and grinds; important above all to those who have sacks about the hopper. But the grinding once done, how can the memory of it endure? It is important now to no individual, not even to the individual with a sack. So that, this tumult well over, the memory of the original man, and of what small revelation he, as Son of Nature and brother-man, could make, does naturally rise on us: his memorable sayings, actings, and sufferings, the very vices and crimes he fell into, are a kind of pabulum which all mortals claim their right to.

Concerning *Peuchet*, *Chaussard*, *Gassicourt*, and, indeed, all the former Biographers of Mirabeau, there can little be said here, except that they abound with errors: the present ultimate *Fils Adoptif*, has never done picking faults with them. Not as memorials of Mirabeau, but as memorials of the world's relation to him, of the world's treatment of him, they may, a little longer, have some perceptible significance. From poor Peuchet (he was known in the *Moniteur* once,) and other the like labourers in the vineyard, you can justly demand thus much; and not justly much more.

Etienne Dumont's *Souvenirs sur Mirabeau* might not, at first sight, seem an advance towards true knowledge, but a movement the other way, and yet it was really an advance. The book, for one thing, was hailed by a universal choral blast from all manner of reviews and periodical literatures that Europe, in all its spellable dialects, had: whereby, at least, the minds of men were again drawn to the subject; and so, amid whatever hallucination, ancient or new-devised, some increase of insight was unavoidable. Besides, the book itself did somewhat. Numerous specialities about the great Frenchman, as read by the eyes of the little Genevese, were conveyed there; and could be deciphered, making allowances. Dumont is faithful, veridical; within his own limits he has even a certain freedom, a picturesqueness and light clearness. It is true, the whim he had of looking at the great Mirabeau as a thing set in motion mainly by him (M. Dumont) and such as he, was one of the most wonderful to be met with in psychology. Nay, more wonderful still, how the reviewers, pretty generally, some from whom better was expected, took up the same with aggravations; and it seemed settled on all sides, that here again a pretender had been stripped, and the great made as little as the rest of us (much to our comfort); that, in fact, figuratively speaking, this enormous Mirabeau, the sound of whom went forth to all lands, was no other than an enormous trumpet, or coach-horn, (of japanned tin,) through which a dexterous little M. Dumont was blowing all the while, and making the noise! Some men and reviewers have strange theories of man. Let any son of Adam, the shallowest now living, try honestly to scheme out, within his head, an existence of this kind; and say how verisimilar it looks! A life and business actually conducted on such coach-horn principle,—we say not the life and business of a statesman and world-leader, but say of the poorest laceman and tape-seller,—were one of the chief miracles hitherto on record. Oh, M. Dumont! But thus, too, when old Sir Christopher struck down the last stone in the Dome of St. Paul's, was it he that carried up the stone? No; it was a certain strong-backed man, never mentioned, (covered with envious or unenvious oblivion,)—probably of the Sister Island.

Let us add, however, more plainly, that M. Dumont was less to blame here than his reviewers were. The good Dumont accurately records what ingenious journey-work and fetching and carrying he did for his Mirabeau; interspersing many an anecdote, which the world is very glad of; extenuating nothing we do hope, nor exaggerating any thing: this is what he did, and had a clear right and call to do. And what if it failed, not altogether, yet in some measure if it did fail, to strike him, that he still properly was but a Dumont? Nay, that the gift this Mirabeau had of enlisting such respectable Dumonts to do hod-work and even skilful handiwork for him; and of ruling them and bidding them by the look of his eye; and of making them cheerfully fetch and carry for him, and serve him as loyal subjects, with a kind of chivalry and willingness,—that this gift was precisely the kinghood of the man, and did itself stamp him as a leader among men! Let no man blame M. Dumont (as some have too harshly done); his error is of oversight, and venial; his worth to us is indisputable. On the other hand, let all men blame such public instructors and periodical individuals as drew that inference and life-theory for him, and brayed it forth in that loud manner; or rather, on the whole, do not blame, but pardon, and pass by on the other side. Such things are an ordained trial of public patience, which perhaps is the better for discipline; and seldom, or rather never, do any lasting injury.

Close following on Dumont's "Reminiscences" came this Biography by M. Lucas Montigny, "Adopted Son;" the first volume in 1834, the rest at short intervals; and lies complete now in Eight considerable Volumes octavo: concerning which we are now to speak,—unhappily, in the disparaging sense. In fact it is impossible for any man to say unmixed good of M. Lucas's work. That he, as Adopted Son, has lent himself so resolutely to the washing of his hero white, and even to the white-washing of him where the natural colour was black, be this no blame to him; or even, if you will, be it praise. If a man's Adopted Son may not write the best book he can for him, then who may? But the fatal circumstance is, that M. Lucas Montigny has not written a book at all; but has merely clipped and cut out, and cast together the materials for a book, which other men are still wanted to write. On the whole M. Montigny rather surprises one. For the reader probably knows, what all the world whispers to itself, that when "Mirabeau, in 1783, adopted this infant born the year before," he had the best of all conceivable obligations to adopt him; having, by his own act, (*non*-notarial,) summoned him to appear in this World. And now consider both what Shakspeare's Edmund, what Poet Savage, and such like, have bragged; and also that the Mirabeaus, from time immemorial, had (like a certain British kindred known to us) "produced many a blackguard, but not one blockhead!" We almost discredit that statement, which all the world whispers to itself; or, if crediting it, pause over the ruins of families. The Haarlem canal is not flatter than M. Montigny's genius. He wants the talent which seems born with all Frenchmen, that of presenting what knowledge he has in the most knowable form. One of the solidest men, too: doubtless a valuable man; whom it were so pleasant for us to praise, if we could. May he be happy in a private station, and never write more;—except for the Bureaux de Préfecture, with tolerably handsome official appointments, which is far better!

His biographical work is a monstrous quarry, or mound of shot-rubbish, in eight strata, hiding valuable matter, which he that seeks will find. Valuable, we say; for the Adopted Son having access, nay welcome and friendly entreaty, to family papers, to all manner of archives, secret records; and working therein long years, with a filial unweariedness, has made himself piously at home in all corners of the matter. He might, with the same spirit, (as we always upbraidingly think,) so easily have made us at home too! But no: he brings to light things new and old; now precious illustrative private documents, now the poorest public heaps of mere pamphleteer and parliamentary matter, so attainable elsewhere, often so omissible were it not to be attained; and jumbles and tumbles the whole together with such reckless clumsiness, with such endless copiousness (having wagons enough) as gives the reader many a pang. The very pains bestowed on it are often perverse; the whole is become so hard, heavy; unworkable, except in the sweat of one's brow! Or call it a mine,—artificial-natural silver mine. Threads of beautiful silver ore lie scattered, which you must dig for, and sift: suddenly, when your thread or vein is at the richest, it vanishes (as is the way with mines) in thick masses of agglomerate and pudding-stone, no man can guess whither. This is not as it should be; and yet unfortunately it could be no other. The long bad book is so much easier to do than the brief good one; and a poor bookseller has no way of measuring and paying but by the ell, cubic or superficial. The very weaver comes and says, not "I have woven so many ells of stuff," but "so many ells of *such* stuff:" satin and Cashmere-shawl stuff,—or, if it be so, duffle and coal-sacking, and even cobweb stuff.

Undoubtedly the Adopted Son's will was good. Ought we not to rejoice greatly in the possession of these same silver-veins; and take them in the buried mineral state, or in any state; too thankful to have them now indestructible, now that they are printed? Let the world, we say, be thankful to M. Montigny, and yet know what it is they are thanking him for. No *Life of Mirabeau* is to be found in these Volumes, but the amplest materials for writing a *Life*. Were the Eight Volumes well riddled and smelted down into One Volume, such as might be made, that one were the volume! Nay it seems an enterprise of such uses, and withal so feasible, that some day it is as good as sure to be done, and again done, and finally well done.

The present reviewer, restricted to a mere article, purposes, nevertheless, to sift and extract somewhat. He has bored (so to speak) and run mine-shafts through the book in various directions, and knows pretty well what is in it, though indeed not so well where to find the same, having unfortunately (as reviewers are wont) "mislaid our paper of references!" Wherefore, if the best extracts be not presented, let not M. Lucas suffer. By one means and another, some sketch of Mirabeau's history; what befel him successively in this World, and what steps he successively took in consequence; and how he and it, working together, made the thing we call Mirabeau's Life,—may be brought out; extremely imperfect, yet truer, one can hope, than the Biographical Dictionaries and ordinary voice of rumour give it. Whether, and if so, where and how, the current estimate of Mirabeau is to be rectified, fortified, or in any important point overset and expunged, will hereby come to light, almost of itself, as we proceed. Indeed, it is very singular, considering the emphatic judgments daily uttered, in print and speech, about this man, what Egyptian obscurity rests over the mere facts of his external history; the right knowledge of which, one would fancy, must be the preliminary of any judgment, however faint. But thus, as we always urge, are such judgments generally passed: vague *plebiscita*, (decrees of the common people;) made up of innumerable loud empty ayes and loud empty noes; which are without meaning, and have only sound and currency: *plebiscita* needing so much revisal!—To the work, however.

One of the most valuable elements in these eight chaotic volumes of M. Montigny is the knowledge he communicates of Mirabeau's father; of his kindred and family, contemporary and anterior. The father, we in general knew, was Victor Riquetti, Marquis de Mirabeau, called and calling himself the *Friend of Men;* a title, for the rest, which bodes him no good, in these days of ours. Accordingly one heard it added with little surprise, that this Friend of Men was the enemy of almost every man he had to do with; beginning at his own hearth, ending at the utmost circle of his acquaintance; and only beyond that, feeling himself free to love men. "The old hypocrite!" cry many,—not we. Alas, it is so much easier to love men while they exist only on paper, or quite flexible and compliant in your imagination, than to love Jack and Kit who stand there in the body, hungry, untoward; jostling you, barring you, with angular elbows, with appetites, irascibilities, and a stupid will of their own! There is no doubt but old Marquis Mirabeau found it extremely difficult to get on with his brethren of mankind; and proved a crabbed, sulphurous, choleric old gentleman, many a sad time: nevertheless, there is much to be set right in that matter; and M. Lucas, if one can carefully follow him, has managed to do it. Had M. Lucas but seen good to print these private letters, family documents, and more of them, (for he "could make thirty octavo volumes,") in a separate state; in mere chronological order, with some small commentary of annotation; and to leave all the rest alone!—As it is, one must search and sift. Happily the old Marquis himself, in periods of leisure, or forced leisure, whereof he had many, drew up certain "unpublished memoirs" of his father and progenitors; out of which memoirs young Mirabeau also in forced leisure (still more forced, in the Castle of If!) redacted one Memoir, of a very readable sort: by the light of this latter, so far as it will last, we walk with convenience.

The Mirabeaus were Riquettis by surname, which is a slight corruption of the Italian *Arrighetti.* They came from Florence: cast out of it in some Guelph-Ghibelline quarrel, such as were common there and then, in the year 1267. Stormy times then, as now! The chronologist can remark that Dante Alighieri was a little boy of some four years that morning the Arrighettis had to go, and men had to say, "They are gone, these villains! They are gone, these martyrs!" the little boy listening with interest. Let the boy become a man, and he too shall have to go; and prove *come è duro calle,* and what a world this is; and have his poet-nature not killed, for it would not kill, but darkened into Old-Hebrew sternness, and sent onwards to Hades and Eternity for a home to itself. As Dame Quickly said in the Dream—"Those were rare times, Mr. Rigmarole!—Pretty much like our own," answered he.—In this manner did the Arrighettis (doubtless in grim Longobardic ire) scale the Alps; and become Tramontane French Riquettis; and produce,—among other things, the present article in this Review.

It was hinted above that these Riquettis were a notable kindred; as indeed there is great likelihood, if we knew it rightly, the kindred and fathers of most notable men are. The Vaucluse fountain, that gushes out as a river, may well have run some space under ground in that character, before it found vent. Nay perhaps it is not always, or often, the intrinsically greatest of a family-line that becomes the noted one, but only the best favoured of fortune. So rich here, as elsewhere, is Nature, the mighty Mother; and scatters from a single Oak-tree, as provender for pigs, what would plant the whole Planet into an oak-forest! For truly, if there were not a *mute* force in her, where were she with the speaking and exhibiting one? If under that frothy superficies of braggarts, babblers, and high-sounding, richly-decorated personages, that strut and fret, and preach in all times *Quam parvâ sapientiâ regatur,* there lay not some substratum of silently heroic men; working as men; with man's energy, enduring and endeavouring; invincible, who whisper not even to themselves how energetic they are?—The Riquetti family was, in some measure, defined already by analogy to that British one; as a family totally exempt from blockheads, but a little liable to produce blackguards. It took root in Provence, and bore strong southern fruit there: a restless, stormy line of men; with the wild blood running in them, and as if there had been a doom hung over them ("like the line of Atreus," Mirabeau used to say,) which really there was, the wild blood itself being doom enough. How long they had stormed in Florence and elsewhere, these Riquettis, history knows not; but for the space of those five centuries, in Provence, they were never without a man to stand Riquetti-like on the earth. Men sharp of speech, prompt of stroke; men quick to discern, fierce to resolve; headlong, headstrong, strong every way; who often found the civic race-course too strait for them, and kicked against the pricks; doing this thing or the other, which the world had to animadvert upon, in various dialects, and find "clean against rule."

One Riquetti (in performance of some vow at sea, as the tradition goes) chained two mountains together: "the iron chain is still to be seen at Moustier;—it stretches from one mountain to the other, and in the middle of it there is a large star with five rays;" the supposed date is 1390. Fancy the Smiths at work on *this* business! The town of Moustier is in the Basses-Alpes of Provence: whether the Riquetti chain creaks there to this hour, and lazily swags in the winds, with its "star of five rays" in the centre, and offers an uncertain perch to the sparrow, we know not. Or perhaps it was cut down in the Revolution time, when there rose such a hatred of noblesse, such a famine for iron; and made into pikes? The Adopted Son, so minute generally, ought to have mentioned, but does not.—That there was building of hospitals, endowing of convents, Chartreux, Récollets, down even to Jesuits; still more, that there was harrying and fighting, needs not be mentioned: except only that all this went on with uncommon emphasis among the Riquettis. What quarrel could there be and a Riquetti not in it? They fought much: with an eye to profit, to redress of disprofit; probably too for the art's sake.

What proved still more rational, they got footing in Marseilles as trading nobles, (a kind of French Venice in those days,) and took with great diligence to commerce. The family biographers are careful to say that it was in the Venetian style, however, and not ignoble. In which sense, indeed, one of their sharp-spoken ancestors, on a certain bishop's unceremoniously styling him "Jean de Riquetti, Merchant of Marseilles," made ready answer, "I am, or was, merchant of police here," (first consul, an office for nobles only,) "as my Lord Bishop is merchant of holy-water:" let his Reverence take that. At all events, the ready-spoken proved first-rate traders; acquired their *bastide*, or mansion, (white, on one of those green hills behind Marseilles,) endless warehouses: acquired the lands first of this, then of that; the lands, Village, and Castle of Mirabeau on the banks of the Durance; respectable Castle of Mirabeau, "standing on its scarped rock, in the gorge of two valleys, swept by the north wind,"—very brown and melancholy-looking now! What is extremely advantageous, the old Marquis says, they had a singular talent for choosing wives; and always chose discreet, valiant women; whereby the lineage was the better kept up. One grandmother, whom the Marquis himself might all but remember, was wont to say, alluding to the degeneracy of the age: "You are men? You are but mannikins (*sias houmachomes*, in Provençal;) we women, in our time, carried pistols in our girdles, and could use them too." Or fancy the Dame Mirabeau sailing stately towards the church-font; another dame striking in to take precedence of her; the Dame Mirabeau despatching this latter with a box on the ear (*soufflet*) and these words: "Here, as in the army, the baggage goes last!" Thus did the Riquettis grow, and were strong; and did exploits in their narrow arena, waiting for a wider one.

When it came to courtiership, and your field of preferment was the Versailles Œil-de-Bœuf, and a Grand Monarque walking encircled with scarlet women and adulators there, the course of the Mirabeaus grew still more complicated. They had the career of arms open, better or worse: but that was not the only one, not the main one; gold apples seemed to rain on other careers,—on that career lead bullets mostly. Observe how a Bruno, Count de Mirabeau, comports himself:—like a rhinoceros yoked in carriage-gear; his fierce forest-horn set to dangle a plume of *fleurs-de-lis*. "One day he had chased a *blue man* (it is a sort of troublesome usher, at Versailles) into the very cabinet of the king, who thereupon ordered the Duke de la Feuillade to 'put Mirabeau under arrest.' Mirabeau refused to obey; 'he would not be punished for chastising the insolence of a valet; for the rest, would go to the *diner du roi*, (king's dinner,) who might then give his order himself.' He came accordingly; the king asked the duke why he had not executed the order? The duke was obliged to say how it stood; the king, with a goodness equal to his greatness, then said, 'It is not of to-day that we know him to be mad; one must not ruin him,'"—and rhinoceros Bruno journeyed on. But again, on the day when they were "inaugurating the pedestrian statue of King Louis in the Place des Victoires," (a masterpiece of adulation,) the same Mirabeau, "passing along the Pont Neuf with the Guards, raised his spontoon to his shoulder before Henry the Fourth's statue, and saluting first, bawled out, 'Friends, we will salute this one; he deserves it as well as some:'" (*Mes amis, saluons celui-ci; il en vaut bien un autre.*)—Thus do they, the wild Riquettis, in a state of courtiership. Not otherwise, according to the proverb, do wild bulls, unexpectedly finding themselves in crockery-shops. O Riquetti kindred, into what centuries and circumstances art thou come down!

Directly prior to our old Marquis himself, the Riquetti kindred had as near as possible gone out. Jean Antoine, afterwards named Silverstock, (*Col de Argent*,) had, in the earlier part of his life, been what he used to call *killed*,—of seven-and-twenty wounds in one hour. Haughtier, juster, more choleric man need not be sought for in biography. He flung gabellemen and excisemen into the river Durance (though otherwise a most dignified, methodic man) when their claims were not clear; he ejected, by the like brief process, all manner of attorneys from his villages and properties; he planted vineyards, solaced peasants. He rode through France repeatedly, (as the old men still remembered,) with the gallantest train of outriders, on return from the wars; intimidating innkeepers and all the world, into mute prostration, into unerring promptitude, by the mere light of his eye;—withal drinking rather deep, yet never seen affected by it. He was a tall, straight man (of six feet and upwards) in mind as in body; Vendôme's "right arm" in all campaigns. Vendôme once presented him to Louis the Great, with compliments to that effect, which the splenetic Riquetti quite spoiled. Erecting his *killed* head (which needed the silver stock now to keep it straight,) he said: "Yes, Sire; and had I left my fighting, and come up to court, and bribed some *catin* (scarlet-woman!) I might have had my promotion and fewer wounds to-day!" The Grand King, every inch a king, instantaneously spoke of something else.

But the reader should have first seen that same killing; how twenty-seven of those unprofitable wounds were come by in one fell lot. The *Battle of Casano* has grown very obscure to most of us; and indeed Prince Eugene and Vendôme themselves grow dimmer and dimmer, as men and battles must; but, curiously enough, this small fraction of it has brightened up again to a point of history for the time being:—

"My grandfather had forseen that manœuvre" (it is Mirabeau, the Count, not the Marquis, that reports: Prince Eugene has carried a certain bridge which the grandfather had charge of;) "but he did not, as has since happened at Malplaquet and Fontenoy, commit the blunder of attacking right in the teeth a column of such weight as that. He lets them advance, hurried on by their own impetuosity and by the pressure of their rearward; and now, seeing them pretty well engaged, he raised his troop, (it was lying flat on the ground,) and rushing on, himself at the head of them, takes the enemy in flank, cuts them in two, dashes them back, chases them over the bridge again, which they had to repass in great disorder and haste. Things brought to their old state, he resumes his post on the crown of the bridge, shelters his troop as before, which, having performed all this service under the sure deadly fire of the enemy's double lines from over the stream, had suffered a good deal. M. de Vendôme coming up, full gallop, to the attack, finds it already finished, the whole line flat on the earth, only the tall figure of the colonel standing erect! He orders him to do like the rest, not to have himself shot till the time came. His faithful servant cries to him, 'Never would I expose myself without need; I am bound to be here, but you, Monseigneur, are bound not. I answer to you for the post; but take yourself out of it, or I give it up.' The Prince (Vendôme) then orders him, in the king's name, to come down. 'Go to, the king and you: I am at my work; go you and do yours.' The good generous Prince yielded. The post was entirely untenable.

"A little afterwards my grandfather had his right arm shattered. He formed a sort of sling for it of his pocket handkerchief, and kept his place; for there was a new attack getting ready. The right moment once come, he seizes an axe in his left hand; repeats the same manœuvre as before; again repulses the enemy, again drives him back over the bridge. But it was here that ill fortune lay in wait for him. At the very moment while he was recalling and ranging his troop, a bullet struck him in the throat; cut asunder the tendons, the jugular vein. He sank on the bridge; the troop broke and fled. M. de Montolieu, Knight of Malta, his relative, was wounded beside him: he tore up his own shirt, and those of several others, to staunch the blood, but fainted himself by his own hurt. An old serjeant, named Laprairie, begged the aide-major of the regiment, one Guadin, a Gascon, to help and carry him off the bridge. Guadin refused, saying he was dead. The good Laprairie could only cast a camp-kettle over his colonel's head, and then run. The enemy trampled over him in torrents to profit by the disorder; the cavalry at full speed, close in the rear of the foot. M. de Vendôme, seeing his line broken, the enemy forming on this side the stream, and consequently the bridge lost, exclaimed, 'Ah! Mirabeau *is dead* then;' a eulogy for ever dear and memorable to us."

How nearly, at this moment, it was all over with the Mirabeaus; how, but for the cast of an insignificant camp-kettle, there had not only been no Article *Mirabeau* in this Review, but no French Revolution, or a very different one; and all Europe had found itself in far other latitudes at this hour, any one who has a turn for such things may easily reflect. Nay, without great difficulty, he may reflect farther, that not only the French Revolution and this Article, but all revolutions, articles, and achievements whatsoever, the greatest and the smallest, which this world ever beheld, have not once but often, in their course of genesis, depended on the veriest trifles, castings of camp-kettles, turnings of straws; except only that we do not *see* that course of theirs. So inscrutable is genetic history; impracticable the theory of causation, and transcends all calculus of man's devising! Thou, thyself, O Reader, (who art an achievement of importance,) over what hair breadth bridges of Accident, through yawning perils, and the man-devouring gulf of Centuries, hast thou got safe hither,—from Adam all the way!

Be this as it can, *Col d' Argent* came alive again, by "miracle of surgery:" and, holding his head up by means of a silver stock, walked this earth many long days, with respectability, with fiery intrepidity and spleen; did many notable things: among others, produced, in dignified wedlock, Mirabeau the Friend of Men; who, again produced Mirabeau the Swallower of Formulas; from which latter, and the wondrous blazing funeral-pyre he made for himself, there finally goes forth a light, whereby those old Riquetti destinies, and many a strange old hidden thing, become noticeable.

But perhaps in the whole Riquetti kindred there is not a stranger figure than this very Friend of Men; at whom, in the order of time, we have now arrived. That Riquetti who chained the mountains together, and hung up the star with five rays to sway and bob there, was but a type of him. Strong, tough as the oak-root, and as gnarled and unwedgeable; no fibre of him running straight with the other: a block for Destiny to beat on, for the world to gaze at, with ineffectual wonder! Really a most notable, questionable, hateable, loveable old Marquis. How little, amid such jingling triviality of Literature, *Philosophie*, and the pretentious cackle of innumerable Baron Grimms, with their correspondence and self-proclamation, one could fancy that France held in it such a Nature-product as the Friend of Men! Why, there is substance enough in this one Marquis to fit out whole armies of *Philosophes*, were it properly attenuated. So many poor Thomases perorate and have *éloges*, poor Morellets speculate, Marmontels moralize in rose-pink manner, Diderots become possessed of encyclopedical heads, and lean Barons de Beaumarchais fly abroad on the wings of *Figaros;* and this brave old Marquis has been hid under a bushel! He was a Writer, too; and had talents for it, (certain of the talents,) such as few Frenchmen have had since the days of Montaigne. It skilled not: he, being unwedgeable, has remained in antiquarian cabinets; the others, splitting up so readily, are the ware you find on all market-stalls, much prized (say, as brimstone Lucifers, "*light bringers*," so called) by the generality. Such is the world's way. And yet complain not;

this rich, unwedgeable old Marquis, have we not him too at last, and can keep him all the longer than the Thomases?

The great Mirabeau used to say always that his father had the greater gifts of the two; which surely is saying something. Not that you can subscribe to it in the full sense, but that in a very wide sense you can. So far as mere speculative head goes, Mirabeau is probably right. Looking at the old Marquis as a speculative thinker and utterer of his thought, and with what rich colouring of originality he gives it forth, you pronounce him to be superior, or even say supreme in his time; for the genius of him almost rises to the poetic. Do our readers know the German Jean Paul, and his style of thought? Singular to say, the old Marquis has a quality in him resembling afar off that of Paul; and actually works it out in his French manner, far as the French manner can. Nevertheless intellect is not of the speculative head only; the great end of intellect surely is, that it makes one *see* something: for which latter result the whole man must co-operate. In the old Marquis there dwells withal a crabbedness, stiff, cross-grained humour, a latent fury and fuliginosity, very perverting; which stiff crabbedness, with its pride, obstinacy, affectation, what else is it at bottom but *want* of strength? The real quantity of our insight—how justly and how thoroughly we shall comprehend the nature of a thing, especially of a human thing—depends on our patience, our fairness, lovingness, what strength soever we have: intellect comes from the whole man, as it is the light that enlightens the whole man. In this true sense, the younger Mirabeau, with that great flashing eyesight of his, that broad, fearless freedom of nature he had, was very clearly the superior man.

At bottom, perhaps, the main definition you could give of old Marquis Mirabeau is, that he was of the Pedant species. Stiff as brass, in all senses; unsympathizing, uncomplying; of an endless, unfathomable pride, which cloaks but does nowise extinguish an endless vanity and need of shining: stately, euphuistic mannerism enveloping the thought, the morality, the whole being of the man. A solemn, high-stalking man; with such a fund of indignation in him, or of latent indignation; of contumacity, irrefragability;—who (after long experiment) accordingly looks forth on mankind and this world of theirs with some dull-snuffling word of forgiveness, of contemptuous acquittal; or oftenest with clenched lips, (nostrils slightly dilated,) in expressive silence. Here is pedantry; but then pedantry under the most interesting new circumstances; and withal carried to such a pitch as becomes sublime, one might almost say, transcendental. Consider indeed whether Marquis Mirabeau could be a pedant, as your common Scaligers and Scioppiuses are! His arena is not a closet with Greek manuscripts, but the wide world and Friendship to Humanity. Does not the blood of all the Mirabeaus circulate in his honorable veins? He too would do somewhat to raise higher that high house; and yet, alas, it is plain to him that the house is sinking: that much is sinking. The Mirabeaus, and above all others, this Mirabeau, are fallen on evil times. It has not escaped the old Marquis how nobility is now decayed, nearly ruinous; based no longer on heroic nobleness of conduct and effort, but on sycophancy, formality, adroitness; on Parchments, Tailors' trimmings, Prunello, and Coach-leather: on which latter basis, unless his whole insight into Heaven's ways with Earth have misled him, no institution in this God-governed world can pretend to continue. Alas, and the priest "has now no tongue but for plate-licking;" and the tax-gatherer squeezes; and the strumpetocracy sits at its ease, in high-cushioned lordliness, under baldachins and cloth of gold: till now at last, what with one fiction, what with another, (and veridical Nature dishonouring all manner of fictions and refusing to pay realities for them,) it has come so far that the Twenty-five millions, long scarce of knowledge, of virtue, happiness, cash, are now fallen scarce of food to eat; and do not, with that natural ferocity of theirs which Nature has still left them, feel the disposition to die starved; and all things are nodding towards chaos, and no man layeth it to heart! One man exists who might perhaps stay or avert the catastrophe, were he called to the helm: the Marquis Mirabeau. His high, ancient blood, his heroic love of truth, his strength of heart, his loyalty and profound insight, (for you cannot hear him speak without detecting the man of genius,) this, with the appalling predicament things have come to, might give him claims. From time to time, at long intervals, such a thought does flit, portentous, through the brain of the Marquis. But ah! in these scandalous days, how shall the proudest of the Mirabeaus fall prostrate before a Pompadour? Can the Friend of Men hoist, with good hope, as his battle-standard, the furbelow of an unmentionable woman? No; not hanging by the apron-strings of such a one will this Mirabeau rise to the premiership; but summoned by France in her day of need, in her day of vision, or else not at all. France does not summon; the *else* goes its road.

Marquis Mirabeau tried Literature, too, as we said; and with no inconsiderable talent; nay, with first-rate talents in some sort: but neither did this prosper. His *Ecce signum*, in such era of downfall and all-darkening ruin, was Political Economy; and a certain man, whom he called "the Master,"—that is, Dr. Quesnay. Round this master (whom the Marquis succeeded as master himself) he and some other idolaters did idolatrously gather: to publish books and tracts, periodical literature, proclamation by word and deed—if so were, the world's dull ear might be opened to salvation. The world's dull ear continued shut. In vain preached this apostle and that other, simultaneously or in Melibœan sequence, in literature, periodical and stationary; in vain preached the Friend of Men, (*L'Ami des Hommes*,) number after number, through long volumes,—though really in a most eloquent manner. Marquis Mirabeau had the indisputablest ideas; but then his style! In very truth, it is the strangest of styles, though one of the richest;

a style full of originality, picturesqueness, sunny vigour; but all cased and slated over, threefold, in metaphor and trope; distorted into tortuosities, dislocations; starting out into crotchets, cramp turns, quaintnesses, and hidden satire; which the French head had no ear for. Strong meat, too tough for babes! The Friend of Men found warm partisans, widely scattered over this Earth; and had censer-fumes transmitted him from Marquises, nay, from Kings and principalities, over seas and alpine chains of mountains; whereby the pride and latent indignation of the man were only fostered; but at home, with the million all jigging each after its suitable scrannel-pipe, he could see himself make no way,—if it were not way towards being a monstrosity and thing men wanted "to see;" not the right thing! Neither through the press, then, is there progress towards the premiership? The staggering state of French statesmen must even stagger whither it is bound. A light public froths itself into tempest about Palissot and his comedy of "*Les Philosophes*,"—about Glück-Piccini Music; neglecting the call of Ruin; and hard must come to hard. Thou, O Friend of Men, clench thy lips together; and wait, silent as the old rocks. Our Friend of Men did so, or better; not wanting to himself, the lion-hearted old Marquis! For his latent indignation has a certain devoutness in it; is a kind of holy indignation. The Marquis, though he knows the *Encyclopédie*, has not forgotten the higher Sacred Books, or that there is a God in this world, (very different from the French *Etre Suprême*.) He even professes, or tries to profess, a kind of diluted Catholicism, in his own way, and thus turns an eye towards heaven: very singular in his attitude here too. Thus it would appear this world is a mad imbroglio which no Friend of Men can set right: it shall go wrong then, in God's name: and the staggering state of all things stagger whither it can. To deep, fearful depths,—not to bottomless ones!

But in the Family Circle? There surely a man, and Friend of Men, is supreme; and ruling with wise autocracy, may make something of it. Alas, in the family circle it went not better, but worse? The Mirabeaus had once a talent for choosing wives: had it deserted them in this instance, then, when most needed? We say not so: we say only that Madame la Marquise had human freewill in her too; that all the young Mirabeaus were likely to have human freewill, (in great plenty;) that within doors as without, the Devil is busy. Most unsuccessful is the Marquis as ruler of men: his family kingdom, for the most part, little otherwise than in a state of mutiny. A sceptre as of Rhadamanthus will sway and drill that household into perfection of Harrison Clockwork; and cannot do it. The royal ukase goes forth in its calm, irrefragable justice! meets hesitation, disobedience open or concealed. Reprimand is followed by remonstrance; harsh coming thunder mutters, growl answering growl. With unaffectedly astonished eye the Marquis appeals to destiny and Heaven; explodes, since he needs must then, in red lightning of paternal authority. How it went, or who by forethought might be to blame, one knows not; for the *Fils Adoptif*, hemmed in by still extant relations, is extremely reticent on these points: a certain Dame de Pailly, "from Switzerland, very beautiful and very artful," glides half-seen through the Mirabeau household, (the Marquis's Orthodoxy, as we said, being but of the diluted kind:) there are evesdroppers, confidential servants; there are Pride, Anger, Uncharitableness, Sublime Pedantry and the Devil always busy. Such a figure as Pailly, of herself, bodes good to no one. Enough, there are Lawsuits, *Lettres de Cachet;* on all hands, *peine forte et dure.* Lawsuits, long drawn out, before gaping *Parlements*, between man and wife; to the scandal of an unrighteous world; how much more of a righteous Marquis, minded once to be an example to it! *Lettres de Cachet*, to the number (as some count) of fifty-four, first and last, for the use of a single Marquis: at times the whole Mirabeau fire-side is seen empty, (except Pailly and Marquis;) each individual sitting in his separate Strong-house, there to bethink himself. Stiff are your tempers, ye young Mirabeaus; not stiffer than mine the old one's! What pangs it has cost the fond paternal heart to go through all this Brutus duty, the Marquis knows and Heaven. In a less degree, what pangs it may cost the filial heart to go *under* (or undergo) the same! The former set of pangs he crushes down into his soul (aided by Heaven) suppressively, as beseems a man and Mirabeau: the latter set,—are they not self-sought pangs; medicinal; that will cease of their own accord, when the unparalleled filial impiety pleases to cease? For the rest, looking at such a world and such a family, at these prison-houses, mountains of divorce-papers, and the staggering state of French statesmen, a Friend of Men may pretty naturally ask himself, Am not I a strong old Marquis, then, whom all this has not driven into Bedlam,—not into Hypochondria, dyspepsia even? The Heavens are bounteous, and make the back equal to the burden.

Out of all which circumstances, and of such struggle against them, there has come forth this Marquis de Mirabeau, shaped (it was the shape *he* could arrive at) into one of the most singular Sublime Pedants that ever stepped the soil of France. Solemn moral rigour, as of some antique Presbyterian Ruling Elder: heavy breadth, dull heat, choler and pride as of an old "Bozzy of Auchinleck;" then a high flown euphuistic courtesy, the airiest mincing ways, suitable to your French Seigneur! How the two divine missions (for both seem to him divine) of Riquetti and Man of Genius (or World-schoolmaster) blend themselves; and philosophism, chivalrous euphuism, presbyterian ruling-elderism, all in such strength, have met, to give the world assurance of a man! There never entered the brain of Hogarth, or of rare old Ben, such a piece of Humour (high meeting with low, and laughter with tears) as, in this brave old Riquetti, Nature has presented us ready-made. For withal there is such genius in him; rich depth of character; indestructible cheerfulness and health breaking out (in spite of these divorce-papers) ever and anon,—like strong sunlight in thundery weather. We have heard of the "strife of Fate with Freewill" producing Greek Tragedies, but never heard it till now produce such astonishing comico-tragical French Farces. Blessed old Marquis,—or else accursed! He is there, with his broad bull-brow; with the huge cheek bones; those deep eyes, glazed as in weariness; the lower visage puckered into a simpering graciosity, which would pass itself off for a kind of smile. What to do with him? Welcome, thou tough old Marquis, with thy better and thy worse! There is stuff in thee, (very different from moonshine and formula;) and stuff is stuff, were it never so crabbed.

Besides the old Marquis de Mirabeau, there is a Brother, the Bailli de Mirabeau: a man who, serving as Knight of Malta, governing in Guadaloupe, fighting and doing hard sea-duty, has sown his wild oats long since; and settled down here, in the old "Castle of Mirabeau on its sheer rock," (for the Marquis usually lives at Bignon, another estate within reach of Paris,) into one of the worthiest quiet uncles and house-friends. It is very beautiful, this mild strength, mild clearness and justice of the brave Bailli, in contrast with his brother's nodosity; whom he comforts, defends, admonishes, even rebukes; and on the whole reverences (both as head Riquetti and as World-schoolmaster) beyond all living men. The frank true love of these two brothers is the fairest feature in Mirabeaudom; indeed the only feature which is always fair. Letters pass continually: in letter and extract we here, from time to time, witness (in these Eight chaotic Volumes) the various personages speak their dialogue, unfold their farce-tragedy. The *Fils Adoptif* admits mankind into this strange household, though stingily, uncomfortably, and all in darkness, save for his own capricious dark-lantern. Seen or half seen, it is a stage; as the whole world is. What with personages, what with destinies, no stranger house-drama was enacting on the Earth at that time.

Under such auspices, which were not yet ripened into events and fatalities, but yet were inevitably ripening towards such, did Gabriel Honoré, at the Mansion of Bignon, between Sens and Nemours, on the 9th day of March, 1749, first see the light. He was the fifth child; the second male child; yet born heir, the first having died in the cradle. A magnificent "enormous" fellow, as the gossips had to admit, almost with terror: the head especially great; "two grinders" in it, already shot!—Rough-hewn, truly, yet with bulk, with limbs, vigour bidding fair to do honour to the line. The paternal Marquis (to whom they said, "*N'ayez pas peur*," Don't be frightened) gazed joyful, we can fancy, and not fearful, on this product of his; the stiff pedant features relaxing into a veritable smile. Smile, O paternal Marquis: the future indeed "veils sorrow and joy," one knows not in what proportion; but here is a new Riquetti, whom the gods send; with the rudiments in him, thou wouldst guess, of a very Hercules, fit for Twelve Labours, which surely are themselves the best joys. Look at the oaf, how he sprawls. No stranger Riquetti ever sprawled under our Sun: it is as if, in this thy man-child, Destiny had swept together all the wildnesses and strengths of the Riquetti lineage, and flung him forth as her finale in that kind. Not without a vocation! He is the last of the Riquettis; and shall do work long memorable among mortals.

Truly, looking now into the matter, we might say, in spite of the gossips, that on this whole Planet, in those years, there was hardly born such a man-child as this same, in the "Mansion-house of Bignon, not far from Paris," whom they named Gabriel Honoré. Nowhere, we say, came there a stouter or braver into this Earth; whither they come marching by the legion and the myriad, out of Eternity and Night!—Except, indeed, what is notable enough, one other that arrived some few months later, at the town of Frankfort on the Maine, and got christened *Johann Wolfgang Goethe*. Then, again, in some ten years more, there came another still liker Gabriel Honoré in his brawny ways. It was into a mean hut that this one came, an infirm hut, (which the wind blew down at the time,) in the shire of Ayre, in Scotland: him they named *Robert Burns*. These, in that epoch, were the Well-born of the World; by whom the world's history was to be carried on. Ah! could the well-born of the world be always rightly bred, rightly entreated there, what a world were it? But it is not so; it is the reverse of so. And then few (like that Frankfort one) can peaceably vanquish the world, with its black imbroglios; and shine above it, in serene help to it, like a sun! The most can but *Titanically* vanquish it, or be vanquished by it: hence, instead of light, (stillest and strongest of things,) we have but lightning; red fire, and oftentimes conflagrations, which are very woful.

Be that as it might, Marquis Mirabeau determined to give his son, and heir of all the Riquettis, such an education as no Riquetti had yet been privileged with. Being a world-schoolmaster, (and indeed a *Martinus Scriblerus*, as we here find, more ways than one,) this was not strange in him; but the results were very lamentable. Considering the matter now, at this impartial distance, you are lost in wonder at the good Marquis; know not whether to laugh at him, or weep over him; and on the whole are bound to do both. A more sufficient product of Nature than this "enormous Gabriel," as we said, need not have been wished for: "beating his nurse," but then loving her, and loving the whole world; of large desire, truly, but desire towards *all* things, the highest and the lowest: in other words, a large mass of *life* in him, a large man waiting there! Does he not rummage (the rough cub, now tenfold rougher by the effect of small-pox) in all places, seeking something to know: dive down to the most unheard-of recesses for papers to read? Does he not, spontaneously, give his hat to a peasant-boy whose head-gear was defective? He writes the most sagacious things, in his fifth year, extempore, at table; setting forth what "*Monsieur Moi*" (Mr. Me) is bound to do. A rough strong genuine soul, of the frankest open temper; full of loving fire and strength; looking out so brisk with his clear hazel eyes, with his brisk sturdy bulk, what might not fair breeding have done for him! On so many occasions, one feels as if he needed nothing in the world but to be well let alone.

But no; the scientific paternal hand must interfere, at every turn, to assist Nature: the young lion's whelp has to grow up all bestrapped, bemuzzled in the most extraordinary manner: shall wax and unfold himself by theory of education, by square and rule,—going punctual, all the way, like Harrison Clockwork, according to the theoretic program; or *else*—! O Marquis, world-schoolmaster, what theory of education is this? No lion's whelp or young Mirabeau will go like clockwork, but far otherwise. "He that spareth the rod hateth the child;" that on its side is true: and yet Nature, too, is strong: "Nature will come running back, though thou expel her with a fork!" In one point of view there is nothing more Hogarthian comic than this long Peter Peeble's *ganging plea* of "Marquis Mirabeau *versus* Nature and others:" yet in a deeper point of view it is but too serious. Candid history will say that whatsoever of worst it was in the power of art to do, against this young Gabriel Honoré, was done. Not with unkind intentions; nay, with intentions which, at least, began in kindness. How much better was Burns's education, (though this, too, went on under the grimmest pressures,) on the wild hill-side, by the brave peasant's hearth, with no theory of education at all, but poverty, toil, tempest, and the handles of the plough!

At bottom, the Marquis's wish and purpose was not complex, but simple. That Gabriel Honoré de Riquetti shall become the very same man that Victor de Riquetti is; perfect as he is perfect: this will satisfy the fond father's heart, and nothing short of this. Better exemplar, truly, were hard to find; and yet, O Victor de Riquetti, poor Gabriel, on his side, wishes to be Gabriel and not Victor! Stiffer loving Pedant never had a more elastic loving Pupil. Offences (of mere *elasticity*, mere natural springing-up, for most part) accumulate by addition: Madame Pailly and the confidential servants, on this as on all matters, are busy. The household itself is darkening, the mistress of it gone; the Lawsuits (and by-and-by Divorce-Lawsuits) have begun. Worse will grow worse, and ever worse, till Rhadamanthus-Scriblerus Marquis de Mirabeau, swaying vainly the sceptre of order, see himself environed by a waste chaos as of Bedlam. Stiff is he; elastic (and yet still loving, reverent) is his son and pupil. Thus cruelty, and yearnings that must be suppressed; indignant revolt, and hot tears of penitence, alternate, in the strangest way, between the two; and for long years our young Alcides has (by Destiny, his own Demon, and Juno de Pailly) Labours enough imposed on him.

But, to judge what a task was set this poor paternal Marquis, let us listen to the following successive utterances from him; which he emits, in letter after letter, mostly into the ear of his Brother the good Bailli. Cluck, cluck,—is it not as the sound of an agitated parent-fowl, now in terror, now in anger, at the brood it has brought out?

"'This creature promises to be a very pretty subject.' 'Talent in plenty, and cleverness, but more faults still inherent in the substance of him.' 'Only just come into life, and the extravasation (*extravasement*) of the thing already visible! A spirit cross-grained, fantastic, iracund, incompatible, tending towards evil before knowing it, or being capable of it.' 'A high heart under the jacket of a boy; it has a strange instinct of pride this creature; noble withal; the embryo of a shaggy-headed bully and killcow, that would swallow all the world, and is not twelve years old yet.' 'A type, profoundly inconceivable, of baseness, sheer dull grossness, (*platitude absolue*,) and the quality of your dirty, rough-crusted caterpillar, that will uncrust itself or fly.' 'An intelligence, a memory, a capacity, that strike you, that astonish, that frighten you.' 'A nothing bedizened with crotchets. May fling dust in the eyes of silly women, but will never be the fourth part a man, if by good luck he be any thing.' 'One whom you may call ill-born, this elder lad of mine; who bodes, at least hitherto, as if he could become nothing but a madman: almost invincibly maniac, with all the vile qualities of the maternal stock over and above. As he has a great many masters, and all, from the confessor to the comrade, are so many reporters for me, I see the nature of the beast, and don't think we shall ever do any good with him.'"

In a word, offences (of elasticity or expansivity) have accumulated to such height, in the lad's fifteenth year, that there is a determination taken, on the part of Rhadamanthus-Scriblerus, to pack him out of doors, one way or the other. After various plannings, the plan of one Abbé Choquenard's Boarding-school is fallen upon: the rebellious Expansive shall to Paris; there, under ferula and short-commons, contract himself and consider. Farther, as the name Mirabeau is honourable and right honourable, he shall not have the honour of it; never again, but be called *Pierre Buffière*, till his ways decidedly alter. This *Pierre Buffière* was the name of an estate of his mother's in the Limousin: sad fuel of those smoking lawsuits which at length blazed out as divorce-lawsuits. Wearing this melancholy nick-name of Peter Buffière, as a perpetual badge, had poor Gabriel Honoré to go about for a number of years; like a misbehaved soldier with his eyebrows shaven off; alas, only a fifteen-years' recruit yet, too young for that!

Nevertheless, named or shorn of his name, Peter or Gabriel, the youth himself was still there. At Choquenard's Boarding-school, as always afterwards in life, he carries with him, he unfolds and employs, the qualities which Nature gave, which no shearing or shaving of art and mistreatment could take away. The *Fils Adoptif* gives a grand list of studies followed, acquisitions made: ancient languages, ("and we have a thousand proofs of his indefatigable tenacity in this respect;") modern languages, English, Italian, German, Spanish; then "passionate study of mathematics;" design pictorial and geometrical; music, so as to read it at sight, nay, to compose in it; singing, to a high degree; "equitation, fencing, dancing, swimming, and tennis:" if only the half of which were true, can we say that Pierre Buffière spent his time ill? What is more precisely certain, the disgraced Buffière worked his way very soon into the good affections of all and sundry, in this House of Dicipline, who came in contact with him; schoolfellows, teachers, the Abbé Choquenard himself. For, said the paternal Marquis, he has the tongue of the old Serpent! In fact, it is very notable how poor Buffière, Comte de Mirabeau, revolutionary King Riquetti, or whatever else they might call him, let him come, under what discommendation he might, into any circle of men, was sure to make them his ere long. To the last, no man could look into him with his own eyes, and continue to hate him. He could talk men *over*, then? Yes, O Reader: and he could *act* men over: for at bottom, that was it. The large open soul of the man, purposing deliberately no paltry, unkindly, or dishonest thing towards any creature, was felt to be withal a *brother's* soul. Defaced by black drossy obscurations very many; but yet shining out, lustrous, warm; in its troublous effulgence, great! That a man be loved the better by men the nearer they come to him: is not this the fact of all facts? To know what extent of prudential diplomacy (good, indifferent, and even bad) a man has, ask public opinion, journalistic rumour, or at most the persons he dines with: to know what of real worth is in him, ask infinitely deeper and farther; ask, first of all, those who have tried by experiment; who, were they the foolishest people, can answer pertinently here if anywhere. "Those at a distance esteem of me a little worse than I; those near at hand a little better than I:" so said the good Sir Thomas Browne; so will all men say who have much to say on that.

The Choquenard Military Boarding-School having, if not fulfilled its functions, yet ceased to be a house of penance, and failed of its function, Marquis Mirabeau determinded to try the Army. Nay, it would seem, the wicked mother has been privily sending him money; which he, the traitor, has accepted! To the army therefore. And so Pierre Buffière has a basnet on his big head; the shaggy pock-pitted visage looks martially from under horse-hair and clear metal; he dresses rank, with tight bridle-hand and drawn falchion, in the town of Saintes, as a bold volunteer dragoon. His age was but eighteen as yet, and some months.

The people of Saintes grew to like him amazingly; would even "have lent him money to any extent." His Colonel, one De Lambert, proved to be a martinet, of sharp sour temper: the shaggy visage of Buffière, radiant through its seaminess with several things, had not altogether the happiness to content him. Furthermore there was an *Archer* (Bailiff) at Saintes, who had a daughter: she, foolish minx, liked the Buffière visage *better* even than the Colonel's! For one can fancy what a pleader Buffière was, in this great cause; with the tongue of the old serpent. It was his first *amourette;* plainly triumphant: the beginning of a quite unheard-of career in that kind. The aggrieved Colonel emitted "satires," through the mess-rooms; this bold volunteer dragoon was not the man to give him worse than he brought: matters fell into a very unsatisfactory state between them. To crown the whole, Buffière went one evening (contrary to wont, now and always) to the gaming-table, and lost four *louis.* Insubordination, Gambling, Archer's daughter: Rhadamanthus thunder from Bignon: Buffière doffs his basnet, flies covertly to Paris. Negotiation there now was; confidential spy to Saintes; correspondence, fulmination: Dupont de Nemours as daysman between a Colonel and a Marquis, both in high wrath,—Buffière to pay the piper! Confidential spy takes evidence; the whole atrocity comes to light: what wilt thou do, O Marquis, with this devil's child of thine? Send him to Surinam; let the tropical heats and rain tame the hot liver of him!—so whispered paternal Brutus-justice and Pailly; but milder thoughts prevailed. *Lettre de Cachet* and the Isle of Rhé shall be tried first. Thither fares poor Buffière; not with Archers' daughters, but with Archers; amid the dull rustle and autumnal brown of the falling leaves of 1768, his nineteenth autumn. It is his second Hercules' Labour; the Choquenard Boarding-house was the first. Bemoaned by the loud Atlantic he shall sit there, in winter season, under ward of a Bailli d'Aulan, governor of the place, and said to be a very Cerberus.

At Rhé the old game is played: in few weeks, the Cerberus Bailli is Buffière's; baying, out of all his throats, in Buffière's behalf! What "sorcery" is this that the rebellious prodigy has in him, O Marquis? Hypocrisy, cozenage which no governor of strong places can resist? Nothing short of the hot swamps of Surinam will hold him quiet, then? Happily there is fighting in Corsica; Paoli fighting on his last legs there; and Baron de Vaux wants fresh troops against him. Buffière, though he likes not the cause, will go thither gladly; and fight his very best: how happy if, by any fighting, he can conquer back his baptismal name, and some gleam of paternal tolerance! After much soliciting, his prayer is acceded to: Buffière, with the rank now of "Sub-lieutenant of Foot, in the Legion of Lorraine," gets across the country to Toulon, in the month of April; and enters "on the plain which furrows itself without plough" (euphuistic for *ocean:*) "God grant he may not have to row there one day," —in red cap, as convict galley-slave! Such is the paternal benediction and prayer; which was realized. Nay, Buffière, it would seem, before quitting Rochelle, indeed "hardly yet two hours out of the fortress of Rhé," had fallen into a new atrocity,—his first duel; a certain quondam messmate (discharged for swindling) having claimed acquaintance with him on the streets; which claim Buffière saw good to refuse; and even to resist, when demanded at the sword's point! The "Corsican Buccaneer" (*flibustier Corse*) that he is!

The Corsican Buccaneer did, as usual, a giant's or two giants' work in Corsica; fighting, writing, loving; "eight hours a day of study;" and gained golden opinions from all manner of men and women. It was his own notion that Nature had meant him for a soldier; he felt so equable and at home in that business,—the wreck of discordant death-tumult, and roar of cannon serving as a fine regulatory marching-music for him. Doubtless Nature meant him for a Man of Action; as she means all great souls that have a strong body to dwell in: but Nature will adjust herself to much. In the course of twelve months, (in May, 1770,) Buffière gets back to Toulon; with much manuscript in his pocket; his head full of military and all other lore, "like a library turned topsy-turvy;" his character much risen, as we said, with every one. The brave Bailli Mirabeau, though almost against principle, cannot refuse to see a chief nephew, as he passes so near the old Castle on the Durance: the good uncle is charmed with him; finds, "under features terribly seamed and altered from what they were," (bodily and mentally,) all that is royal and strong, nay, an "expression of something refined, something gracious;" declares him, after several days of incessant talk, to be the best fellow on earth, (if well dealt with,) who will shape into statesman, generalissimo, pope, what thou pleasest to desire! Or, shall we give poor Buffière's testimonial in mess-room dialect; in its native twanging vociferosity, and garnished with old oaths,—which, alas, have become for us almost old prayers now,—the vociferous Moustachio-figures, whom they twanged through, having all vanished so long since: "*Morbleu, Monsieur, l'Abbé; c'est un garçon, diablement vif; mais c'est un bon garçon, qui a de l'esprit comme trois cent mille diables; et parbleu, un hommo très brave.*"

Moved by all manner of testimonials and entreaties from uncle and family, the rigid Marquis consents, not without difficulty, to see this anomalous Peter Buffière of his; and then, after solemn deliberation, even, to un-Peter him, and give him back his name. It was in September that they met; at Aiguesperse, in the Limousin near the *lands* of *Pierre Bouffière*. Soft ruth comes stealing through the Rhadamanthine heart; tremblings of faint hope even, which, however, must veil itself in austerity and rigidity. The Marquis writes: "I perorate him very much;" observe "my man, how he droops his nose, and looks fixedly, a sign that he is reflecting; or whirls away his head, hiding a tear: serious, now mild, now severe, we give it him alternately; it is thus I manage the mouth of this fiery animal." Had he but read the *Ephémérides*, the *Economiques*, the *Précis des Elémens* ("the most laboured book I have done, though I wrote it in such health:") had he but got grounded in my Political Economy! Which, however, he does not take to with any heart. On the contrary, he unhappily finds it hollow, pragmatical, a barren jingle of formulas; pedantic even; unnutritive as the east wind. Blasphemous words; which (or the like of them) any eavesdropper has but to report to "the Master!"—And yet, after all, is it not a brave Gabriel this rough-built young Hercules; and has finished handsomely his Second Labour? The head of the fellow is 'a wind-mill and fire-mill of ideas." The War-office makes him captain, and he is passionate for following soldiership: but then, unluckily, your Alexander needs such tools;—a whole world for workshop! "Where are the armies and herring-shoals of men to come from? Does he think I have money," snuffles the old Marquis, "to get him up battles like Harlequin and Scaramouch?" The fool! he shall settle down into rurality; first, however, though it is a risk, see a little of Paris.

At Paris, through winter, the brave Gabriel carries all before him; shines in saloons, in the Versailles Œil-de-Bœuf; dines with your Duke of Orleans, (young Chartres, not yet become *Egalité*, hob-nobbing with him;) dines with your Guéménés, Broglies, and mere Grandeurs; and is invited to hunt. Even the old women are charmed with him, and rustle in their satins: such a light has not risen in the Œil-de-Bœuf for some while. Grant, O Marquis, that there are worse sad-dogs than this. The Marquis grants partially; and yet, and yet! Few things are notabler than these successive surveys by the old Marquis, critically scanning his young Count:—

"'I am on my guard; remembering how vivacity of head may deceive you as to a character of morass (*de tourbe:*) but, all considered one must give him store of exercise; what the devil else to do with such exuberance, intellectual and sanguineous? I know no woman but the Empress of Russia with whom this man were good to marry yet.' 'Hard to find a dog (*drôle*) that had more talent and action in the head of him than this; he would reduce the devil to terms.' 'Thy nephew Whirlwind (*l'Ouragan*) assists me; yesterday the valet Luce, who is a sort of privileged simpleton, said pleasantly, "Confess, M. le Comte, a man's body is very unhappy to carry a head like that."' 'The *terrible gift of familiarity* (as Pope Gregory called it!) He turns the great people here round his finger.' Or again, though all this is some years afterwards: 'They have never done telling me that he is easy to set a-rearing; that you cannot speak to him reproachfully but his eyes, his lips, his colour testify that all is *giving way;* on the other hand, the smallest word of tenderness will make him burst into tears, and he would fling himself into the fire for you.' 'I pass my life in cramming him (*à le bourrer*) with principles, with all that I know; for this man, ever the same as to his fundamental properties, has done nothing by these long and solid studies but augment the rubbish-heap in his head, which is a library turned topsy-turvy; and then his talent for dazzling by superficials, for he has *swallowed all formulas*, and cannot substantiate any thing.' 'A wicker-basket, that lets all through; disorder born; credulous as a nurse; indiscreet; a liar' (kind of white liar) 'by exaggeration, affirmation, effrontery, without need, and merely to tell histories; a confidence that dazzles you on every thing; cleverness and talent without limit. For the rest, the vices have infinitely less root in him than the virtues; all is facility, impetuosity, ineffectuality, (not for want of fire, but of plan;) wrong-spun, ravelled (*défaufilé*) in character: a mind that meditates in the vague, and builds of soap-bells.' 'Spite of the bitter ugliness, the intercadent step, the trenchant breathless blown-up precipitation, and the look, or, to say better, the atrocious eyebrow of this man when he listens and reflects, something told me that it was all but a scarecrow of old cloth, this ferocious outward garniture of his; that, at bottom, here was perhaps the man in all France least capable of deliberate wickedness.' 'Pie and jay by instinct.' 'Wholly reflex and reverberance (*tout de reflet et de réverbère*); drawn to the right by his heart, to the left by his head, which he carries four paces from him.' 'May become the Coryphæus of the Time.' 'A blinkard (*myope*) precipitancy, born with him, which makes him take the quagmire for firm earth—'"

Cluck, cluck,—in the name of all the gods, what prodigy is this I have hatched? Web-footed, broad-billed; which will run and drown itself, if Mercy and the parent-fowl prevent not!

How inexpressibly true, meanwhile, is this that the old Marquis says: "He has swallowed all formulas" (*il a humé, toutes les formules*) and made away with them! Formulas, indeed, if we think of it, Formulas and Gabriel Honoré had been, and were to be, at death-feud from first to last. What formulas of this formalized (established) world had been a kind one to Gabriel? His soul could find no shelter in them, they were unbelievable; his body no solacement, they were tyrannical, unfair. If there were not *pabulum* and substance beyond formulas, and in spite of them, then wo to him! To this man formulas would yield no existence or habitation, if it were not in the Isle of Rhé and such places; but threatened to choke the life out of him: either formulas or he must go the wall; and so, after a tough fight, *they*, as it proves, will go. So cunningly thrifty is Destiny; and is quietly shaping her tools for the work they are to do, while she seems but spoiling and breaking them! For, consider, O Marquis, whether France herself will not, by-and-by, have to swallow a formula or two? This sight thou lookest on from the baths of Mount d'Or, does it not bode something of that kind? A summer day in the year 1777:—

"'O Madame! the narrations I would give you if I had not a score of letters to answer, on dull sad business! I would paint to you the votive feast of this town, which took place on the 14th. The savages descending in torrents from the Mountains,—our people ordered not to stir out. The curate with surplice and stole; public justice in periwig; *Maréchaussé*, sabre in hand, guarding the place, before the bagpipes were permitted to begin. The dance interrupted, a quarter of an hour after, by battle; the cries and fierce hissings of the children, of the infirm, and other onlookers, ogling it, tarring it on, as the mob does when dogs fight. Frightful men, or rather wild creatures of the forest, in coarse woollen jupes and broad girths of leather, studded with copper nails; of gigantic stature, heightened by the high sabots; rising still higher on tip-toe, to look at the battle; beating time to it; rubbing their sides with their elbows: their face haggard, covered with their long greasy hair; top of the visage waxing pale, bottom of it twisting itself into the rudiments of a cruel laugh, a ferocious impatience.—And these people pay the *taille!* And you want to take from them their salt too! And you know not what you strip bare, or, as you call it, govern; what, with the heedless, cowardly squirt of your pen, you will think you can continue stripping with impunity for ever, till the Catastrophe come! Such sights recall deep thoughts to one. 'Poor Jean-Jacques!' I said to myself; 'they that sent thee, and thy System, to copy music among such a People as these same, have confuted thy System but ill!' But, on the other hand, these thoughts were consolatory for a man who has all his life preached the necessity of solacing the poor, of universal instruction; who has tried to show what such instruction and such solacement ought to be, if it would form a barrier (the sole possible barrier) between oppression and revolt; the sole but the infallible treaty of peace between the high and the low! Ah, Madame! this government by blind-man's-buff, stumbling along too far, will end by the GENERAL OVERTURN.'"

Prophetic Marquis!—Might other nations listen to thee better than France did: for it concerns them *all!* But now is it not curious to think how the whole world might have gone so differently, but for this very prophet? Had the young Mirabeau had a father as other men have; or even no father at all! Consider him, in that case, rising by natural gradation, by the rank, the opportunity, the irrepressible buoyant faculties he had, step after step, to official place,—to the chief official place; as in a time when Turgots, Neckers, and men of ability, were grown indispensable, he was sure to have done. By natural witchery he bewitches Marie Antoinette; her most of all, with her quick susceptive instincts, her quick sense for whatever was great and noble, her quick hatred for whatever was pedantic, Neckerish, Fayettish, and pretending to be great. King Louis is a nullity; happily then reduced to be one: there would then have been at the summit of France the one French man who could have grappled with that great question; who, yielding and refusing, managing, guiding, and, in short, *seeing* and daring what was to be done, had perhaps saved France her Revolution; remaking her by peaceabler methods! But to the Supreme Powers it seemed not so. Once after a thousand years all nations were to see the great Conflagration and Self-combustion of a Nation,—and learn from it if they could. And now, for a Swallower of Formulas, was there a better schoolmaster on earth than this very Friend of Men; a better education conceivable than this which Alcides-Mirabeau had? Trust in heaven, good reader, for the fate of nations, for the fall of a sparrow.

Gabriel Honoré has acquitted himself so well in Paris, turning the great people round his thumb, with that "*fond gaillard,*" (basis of gayety,) with that *terrible don de la familiarité;* with those ways he has. Neither, in the quite opposite Man-of-business department, when summer comes and rurality with it, is he found wanting. In the summer of the year, the old

Friend of Men despatches him to the Limousin, to his own estate of Pierre Buffière, or his wife's own estate, (under the law-balance about this time;) to see whether any thing can be done for men there. Much is to be done there; the Peasants, short of all things, even of victuals, here as everywhere, wear "a settled *souffre-douleur* (pain-stricken) look, as if they reckoned that the pillage of men was an inevitable ordinance of Heaven, to be put up with like the wind and the hail." Here, in the solitude of the Limousin, Gabriel is still Gabriel: he rides, he writes, and runs; eats out of the poor people's pots; speaks to them, redresses them; institutes a court of Villager *Prudhommes* (good men and true),—once more carries all before him. Confess, O Rhadamanthine Marquis, we say again, that there are worse sad-dogs than this! "He is," confesses the Marquis, "the Demon of the Impossible," (*le démon de la chose impossible.*) Most true this also: *impossible* is a word not in his dictionary. Thus the same Gabriel Honoré, long afterwards, (as Dumont will witness,) orders his secretary to do some miracle or other, miraculous within the time. The secretary answers, "Monsieur, it is impossible," "Impossible?" answers Gabriel: "*Ne me dites jamais ce bête de mot,*" (Never name to me that blockhead of a word!) Really, one would say, a good fellow, were he well dealt with,—though still broad-billed, and with latent tendencies to take the water. The following otherwise insignificant Letter, addressed to the Bailli, seems to us worth copying. Is not his young Lordship, if still in the dandy-state and style-of-mockery, very handsome in it; standing there in the snow? It is of date December, 1771, and far onwards on the road towards Mirabeau Castle:

"*Fracti bello satisque repulsi ductores Danaûm:* here, dear uncle, is a beginning in good Latin, which means that I am broken with fatigue, not having, this whole week, slept more than sentinels do; and sounding, at the same time, with the wheels of my vehicle, most of the ruts and jolts that lie between Paris and Marseilles. Ruts deep and numerous. Moreover, my axle broke between Mucreau, Romané, Chambertin, and Beaune; the centre of four wine districts; what a geographical point, if I had had the wit to be a drunkard! The mischief happened towards five in the evening; my lackey had gone on before. There fell nothing at the time but melted snow; happily it afterwards took some consistency. The neighbourhood of Beaune made me hope to find genius in the natives of the country: I had need of good counsel; the devil counselled me at first to swear, but that whim passed, and I fell by preference into the temptation of laughing; for a holy priest came jogging up, wrapt to the chin; against the blessed visage of whom the sleet was beating, which made him cut so singular a face, that I think this was the thing drove me from swearing. The holy man inquired, seeing my chaise on its beam-ends, and one of the wheels wanting, whether any thing had befallen me? I answered, 'there was nothing falling here but snow.' 'Ah,' said he, ingeniously, 'it is your chaise, then, that is broken.' I admired the sagacity of the man, and begged him to double his pace, with his horse's permission, (who was also making a pleasant expression of countenance, as the snow beat on his nose,) and to be so good as give notice at Chaigny that I was there. He assured me he would tell it to the post-mistress herself, she being his cousin; that she was a very amiable woman, married three years ago to one of the honestest men of the place, nephew to the king's procureur at ——: in fine, after giving me all the outs and ins of himself, the curate, of his cousin, his cousin's husband, and I know not whom more, he was pleased to give his spurs to his horse, which thereupon gave a grunt, and went on. I forgot to tell you that I had sent the postilion off to Mucreau, which he knew the road to, for he went thither daily, he said, to have a glass; a thing I c uld well believe, or even two glasses. The man was but tipsified when he went; happily when he returned, which was very late, he was drunk. I walked sentry: several Beaune men passed, all of whom asked me, if any thing had befallen? I answered one of them, that it was an experiment; that I had been sent from Paris to see whether a chaise would run with one wheel; mine had come so far, but I was going to write that two wheels were preferable. At this moment my worthy friend struck his shin against the other wheel; clapped his hand on the hurt place; swore, as I had near done; and then said, smiling, 'Ah, Monsieur, there is the other wheel!' 'The devil there is!' said I, as if astonished. Another, after examining long, with a very capable air, informed me, '*Ma foi*, Monsieur! it is your *essi*' (meaning *essieu*, or axle) 'that is broken.'"

Mirabeau's errand to Provence, in this winter season, was several-fold. To look after the Mirabeau estates; to domesticate himself among his people and peers in that region;—perhaps to choose a wife. Lately, as we saw, the old Marquis could think of none suitable, if it were not the Empress Catharine. But Gabriel has ripened astonishingly since that, under this sunshine of paternal favour,—the first gleam of such weather he has ever had. Short of the Empress, it were very well to marry, the Marquis now thinks, provided your bride had money. A bride, not with money, yet with connections, expectations, is found; and by stormy eloquence (Marquis seconding) is carried: wo worth the hour! Her portrait, by the seconding Marquis himself, is not very captivating: "Marie-Emilie de Covet, only daughter of the Marquis de Marignane, in her eighteenth year then; she had a very ordinary face, even a vulgar one at the first glance; brown, nay, almost tawny (*mauricaud*); fine eyes, fine hair; teeth not good, but a prettyish continual smile; figure small, but agreeable, though leaning a little to one side: showed great sprightliness of mind, ingenuous, adroit, delicate, lively, sportful; one of the most essentially pretty characters." This brown, almost tawny, little woman (much of a fool too) Mirabeau gets to wife (on the 22d of June, 1772:) with her, and with a pension of 3,000 francs from his father-in-law, and one of 6,000 from his own father, (say 500*l.* in all,) and rich expectancies, he shall sit down, in the bottom of Provence, by his own hired hearth, in the town of Aix, and bless Heaven.

Candour will admit that this young Alexander (just beginning his twenty-fourth year) might grumble a little, seeing only one such world to conquer. However, he had his books, he had his hopes; health, faculty; a Universe (whereof even the town of Aix formed part) all rich with fruit and forbidden-fruit round him; the unspeakable "seed-field of Time" wherein to sow: he said to himself, "Go to, I will be wise." And yet human nature is frail. One can judge, too, whether the old Marquis, now coming into decided lawsuit with his wife, was of a humour to forgive peccadilloes. The terrible, hoarsely calm, Rhadamanthine way in which he expresses himself on this matter of the lawsuit to his Brother, and enjoins silence from all mortals but him, might affect weak nerves; wherefore, contrary to purpose, we omit it. O, just Marquis? In fact, the Riquetti household, at this time, can do little for frail human nature; except, perhaps, make it fall faster. The Riquetti household is getting scattered; not always led asunder, but driven and hurled asunder: the tornado times for it have begun. One daughter is Madame du Saillant, (still living,) a judicious sister: another is Madame de Cabris, not so judicious; for, indeed, her husband has lawsuits, (owing to "defamatory couplets" proceeding from him;) she gets "insulted on the public promenade of Grasse," by a certain Baron de Villeneuve-Moans, whom some defamatory couplet had touched upon;—all the parties in the business being fools. Nay, poor woman, she, by-and-by, we find, takes up with preternuptial persons; with a certain Brainson in epaulettes, described candidly, by the *Fils Adoptif*, as "a man who"—is not fit to be described.

A young heir-apparent of all the Mirabeaus is required to make some figure; especially in marrying himself. The present young heir-apparent has nothing to make a figure with but bare 500*l.* a year, and very considerable debts. Old Mirabeau is hard as the Mosaic rock, and no wand proves miraculous on him; for *trousseaus, cadeaus,* foot-washings, festivities, and house-heatings, he does simply not yield one sous. The heir must himself yield them. He does so, and handsomely: but, alas, the 500*l.* a year, and very considerable debts? Quit Aix and dinner-giving; retire to the old Chateau in the gorge of two valleys! Devised and done. But now, a young wife used to the delicacies of life, ought she not to have some suite of rooms done up for her? Upholsterers hammer and furbish; with effect; not without bills. Then the very considerable Jew-debts! Poor Mirabeau sees nothing for it, but to run to the father-in-law with tears in his eyes; and conjure him to make those "rich expectations" in some measure fruitions. Forty thousand francs; to such length will the father-in-law, moved by these tears, by this fire-eloquence, table ready money; provided old Marquis Mirabeau, who has some provisional reversionary interest in the thing, will grant quittance. Old Marquis Mirabeau, written to in the most impassioned, persuasive manner, answers by a letter, of the sort they call *Sealed* Letter, (*lettre de cachet,*) ordering the impassioned Persuasive, under his Majesty's hand and seal, to bundle into Coventry, as we should say; into Manosque, as the Sealed Letter says! —Farewell, thou old Chateau, with thy upholstered rooms, on thy sheer rock, by the angry-flowing Durance: welcome, thou miserable little borough of Manosque, since hither Fate drives us! In Manosque, too, a man can live, and read; can write an *Essai sur le Despotisme,* (and have it printed in Switzerland, 1774;) full of fire and rough vigour, and still worth reading.

The *Essay on Despotism,* with so little of the *Ephémérides* and Quesnay in it, could find but a hard critic in the old Marquis; snuffling out something (one fancies) about "Reflex and reverberance;" formulas getting swallowed; rash hairbrain treating matters that require age and gravity;—however, let it pass. Unhappily there came other offences. A certain gawk, named Chevalier de Gassaud, accustomed to visit in the house at Manosque, sees good to commence a kind of theoretic flirtation with the little brown Wife, which she theoretically sees good to return. Billet meets billet; glance follows glance, *crescendo allegro;*—till the husband opens his lips, volcano-like, with a proposal to kick Chevalier de Gassaud out of doors. Chevalier de Gassaud goes unkicked, but not without some explosion or *éclat.* there is like to be a duel; only that Gassaud, knowing what a sword this Riquetti wears, will not fight; and his father has to plead and beg. Generous Count, kill not my poor son: alas, already this most lamentable explosion itself has broken off the finest marriage settlement, and now the family will not hear of him! The generous Count, so pleaded with, not only flings the duel to the winds, but gallops off, (forgetful of the *lettre de cachet,*) half desperate, to plead with the marriage-family; to preach with them, and pray, till they have taken poor Gassaud into favour again. Prosperous in this, (for what can resist such pleading?) he may now ride home more leisurely, with the consciousness of a right action for once.

As we said, this ride of his lies beyond the limits fixed in the royal Sealed Letter; but no one surely will mind it, no one will report it. A beautiful summer evening: O, poor Gabriel, it is the last peaceably prosperous ride thou shalt have for long,—perhaps almost ever in the world! For lo! who is this that comes curricling through the level yellow sun-light like one of Respectability, keeping his gig? By Day and Night! it is that base Baron, de Villeneuve-Moans, who insulted sister Cabris in the Promenade of Grasse! Human nature, without time for reflection, is liable to err. The swift-rolling gig is already in contact with one, the horse rearing against your horse; and you dismount, almost without knowing. Satisfaction which gentlemen expect, Monsieur! No? Do I hear rightly No? In that case, Monsieur,—and this wild Gabriel, (*horresco referens!*) clutches the respectable Villeneuve Moans; and horsewhips him there, not emblematically only, but practically, on the king's highway: seen of some peasants! Here is a message for Rumour to blow abroad.

Rumour blows,—to Paris as elsewhither: for answer, (on the 26th of June, 1774,) there arrives a fresh Sealed Letter, of more emphasis; there arrive with it grim catchpoles and their chaise: the Swallower of Formulas, snatched away from wife, child, (then dying,) and last shadow of a home even in exile, is trundling towards Marseilles; towards the Castle of If, which frowns out among the waters in the roadstead there! Girt with the blue Mediterranean; within iron stanchions; cut off from pen, paper, and friends, and men, except the Cerberus of the place, who is charged to be very sharp with him, there shall he sit: such virtue is in a Sealed Letter; so has the grim old Marquis ordered it. Our gleam of sunshine, then, is darkening miserably down? Down, O thou poor Mirabeau, to thick midnight! Surely Formulas are all too cruel on thee: thou art getting really into war with formulas, (terriblest of wars;) and thou, by God's help and the devil's, wilt make away with them,—in the terriblest manner! From this hour, we say, thick and thicker darkness settles round poor Gabriel; his life-path growing ever painfuller; alas, growing ever more devious, beset by *ignes fatui*, and lights not of heaven. Such Alcides' Labours have seldom been allotted to any man.

Check thy hot frenzy, thy hot tears, poor Mirabeau; adjust thyself as it may be; for there is no help. Autumn becomes loud winter, revives into gentle spring: the waves beat round this Castle of If, at the mouth of Marseilles harbour; girdling in the unhappiest man. No, not the unhappiest: poor Gabriel has such a "*fond gaillard*," (basis of joy and gayety;) there is a deep fiery life in him, which no blackness of destiny can quench. The Cerberus of If, M. Dallègre, relents, as all Cerberuses do with him; gives paper; gives sympathy and counsel. Nay, letters have already been introduced; "buttoned in some scoundrel's gaiters," the old Marquis says! On Sister du Saillant's kind letter there fall "tears;" nevertheless you do not always weep. You do better; write a brave *Col de Argent's* Memoirs (quoted from above;) occupy yourself with projects and efforts. Sometimes, alas, you do worse, though in the other direction,—where Canteen-keepers have pretty wives! A mere peccadillo this of the frail fair *Cantinière*, (according to the *Fils Adoptif;*) of which too much was made at the time.—Nor are juster consolations wanting; sisters and brothers bidding you be of hope. Our readers have heard Count Mirabeau designated "as the elder of my lads:" what if we now exhibited the younger for one moment? The Maltese Chevalier de Mirabeau, a rough son of the sea in those days: he also is a sad dog, but has the advantage of not being the elder. He has started from Malta, from a sick bed, and got hither to Marseilles, in the dead of winter; the link of Nature drawing him, shaggy sea-monster as he is.

"It was a rough wind; none of the boatmen would leave the quay with me: I induced two of them, more by bullying than by money; for thou knowest I have no money, and am well furnished, thank God, with the gift of speaking or stuttering. I reach the Castle of If: gates closed; and the Lieutenant, as M. Dallègre was not there, tells me quite sweetly that I must return as I came. 'Not, if you please, till I have seen Gabriel.'—'It is not allowed.'—'I will write to him.'—'Not that either.'—'Then I will wait for M. Dallègre.'—'Just so; but for four-and-twenty hours, not more.' Whereupon I take my resolution; go to la Mouret," (canteen-keeper's pretty wife;) "we agree that so soon as the tattoo is beat, I shall see this poor devil. I get to him, in fact; not like a *paladin*, but like a pickpocket or a gallant, which thou wilt; and we unbosom ourselves. They had been afraid that he would heat my head to the temperature of his own: Sister Cabris, they do him little justice; I can assure thee that while he was telling me his story, and when my rage broke out in these words: 'Though still weakly, I have two arms, strong enough to break M. Villeneuve-Moans's, or his cowardly persecuting brother's at least,' he said to me, '*Mon ami*, thou wilt ruin us both.' And, I confess, this consideration alone, perhaps, hindered the execution of a project, which could not have profited, which nothing but the fermentation of a head such as mine could excuse."—Vol. ii. p. 43.

Reader, this tarry young Maltese chevalier is the Vicomte de Mirabeau, or Younger Mirabeau; whom all men heard of in the Revolution time,—oftenest by the more familiar name of *Mirabeau-Tonneau*, or Barrel Mirabeau, from his bulk, and the quantity of drink he usually held. It is the same Barrel Mirabeau who, in the States-General, broke his sword, because the Noblesse gave in, and chivalry was now ended: for in politics he was directly the opposite of his elder brother; and spoke considerably as a public man, making men laugh, (for he was a wild surly fellow, with much wit in him and much liquor;)—then went indignantly across the Rhine, and drilled Emigrant Regiments; but as he sat one morning in his tent, sour of stomach doubtless and of heart, meditating in Tartarean humour on the turn things took, a certain captain or subaltern demands admittance on business; is refused; again demands, and then again, till the Colonel Viscount Barrel Mirabeau, blazing up into a mere burning brandy-barrel, clutches his sword, and tumbles out on this *canaille* of an intruder,—alas, on the *canaille* of an intruder's sword's point, (who drew with swift dexterity,) and dies, and it is all done with him! That was the fifth act of Barrel Mirabeau's life-tragedy, (unlike, and yet like, this first act in the Castle of If;) and so the curtain fell, the Newspapers calling it "apoplexy" and "alarming accident."

Brother and sisters, the little brown Wife, the Cerberus of If, all solicit for a penitent unfortunate sinner. The old Marquis's ear is deaf as that of Destiny. Solely, by way of variation, not of alleviation, (especially as the If Cerberus too has been bewitched,) he has this sinner removed, in May next, after some nine months' space, to the Castle of Joux; an "old Owl's nest, with a few invalids," among the Jura Mountains. Instead of melancholy main, let him now try the melancholy granites, (still capped with snow at this season,) with their mists and owlets; and on the whole adjust himself as if for permanence or continuance there; on a pension of 1,200 francs, fifty pounds a year, since he could not do with five hundred! Poor Mirabeau;—and poor Mirabeau's Wife? Reader, the foolish little brown woman tires of soliciting; her child being buried, her husband buried alive, and her little brown self being still above ground and under twenty, she takes to recreation, theoretic flirtation; ceases soliciting, begins successful forgetting. The marriage, cut asunder that day the catchpole chaise drew up at Manosque, will never come together again, in spite of efforts; but flow onwards in two separate streams, to lose itself in the frightfullest sand-deserts. Husband and wife never more saw each other with eyes.

Not far from the melancholy Castle of Joux lies the little melancholy borough of Pontarlier; whither our Prisoner has leave, on his parole, to walk when he chooses. A melancholy little borough; yet in it is a certain Monnier Household; whereby hangs, and will hang, a tale. Of old M. Monnier, respectable legal President, now in his seventy-fifth year, we shall say less than of his wife, Sophie Monnier, (once de Ruffey, from Dijon, sprung from legal Presidents there,) who is still but short way out of her teens. Yet she has been married (or seemed to be married) four years: one of the loveliest sad-heroic women of this or any district of country. What accursed freak of Fate brought January and May together here once again? Alas, it is a custom there, good reader! Thus the old Naturalist Buffon, who, at the age of sixty-three, (what is called "the St. Martin's summer of incipient dotage and new myrtle garlands," which visits some men,) went ransacking the country for a young wife, had very nearly got this identical Sophie; but did get another, known as Madame de Buffon, well known to Philip Egalité, having turned out ill. Sophie de Ruffey loved wise men, but not at that extremely advanced period of life. However, the question for her is: Does she love a Convent better? Her mother and father are rigidly devout, and rigidly vain and poor: the poor girl, sad-heroic, is probably a kind of freethinker. And now, old President Monnier "quarrelling with his daughter; and then coming over to Pontarlier with gold-bags, marriage-settlements, and the prospect of dying soon?" It is that same miserable tale, often sung against, often spoken against; very miserable indeed.—But fancy what an effect the fiery eloquence of a Mirabeau produced in this sombre Household: one's young girl-dreams incarnated, most unexpectedly, in this wild glowing mass of manhood, (though rather ugly;) old Monnier himself gleaming up into a kind of vitality to hear him! Or fancy whether a sad-heroic face, glancing on you with a thankfulness like to become glad-heroic, were not ——? Mirabeau felt, by known symptoms, that the sweetest, fatalest incantation was stealing over him, which could lead only to the devil, for all parties interested. He wrote to his wife, entreating, in the name of Heaven, that she would come to him: thereby might the "sight of his duties" fortify him; he meanwhile would at least forbear Pontarlier. The wife "answered by a few icy lines, indicating, in a covert way, that she thought me not in my wits." He ceases forbearing Pontarlier; sweeter is it than the Owl's nest: he returns thither, with sweeter and ever sweeter welcome; and so ——!

Old Monnier saw nothing, or winked hard;—not so our old foolish Commandant of the Castle of Joux. He, though kind to his prisoner formerly, "had been making some pretensions to Sophie himself; he was but forty or five-and-forty years older than I; my ugliness was not greater than his; and I had the advantage of being an honest man." Green-eyed Jealousy, in the shape of this old ugly Commandant, warns Monnier by letter; also, on some thin pretext, restricts Mirabeau henceforth to the four walls of Joux. Mirabeau flings back such restriction in an indignant Letter to this green-eyed Commandant; indignantly steps over into Switzerland, which is but a few miles off;—returns, however, in a day or two, (it is dark January, 1776,) covertly to Pontarlier. There is an explosion, what they call *éclat*. Sophie Monnier, sharply dealt with, resists; avows her love for Gabriel Honoré; asserts her right to love him, her purpose to continue doing it. She is sent home to Dijon; Gabriel Honoré covertly follows her thither. Explosions: what a continued series of explosions,—through winter, spring, summer! There are tears, devotional exercises, threatenings to commit suicide; there are stolen interviews, perils, proud avowals, and lowly concealments. He on his part, "voluntarily constitutes himself prisoner;" and does other haughty, vehement things; some Commandants behaving honourably, and some not: one Commandant (old Marquis Mirabeau of the Château of Bignon) getting ready his thunderbolts in the distance! "I have been lucky enough to obtain Mont St. Michel, in Normandy," says the old Marquis: "I think that prison good, because there is first the castle itself, then a ring-work all round the mountain; and, after that, a pretty long passage among the sands, where you need guides, to avoid being drowned in the quicksands." Yes, it rises there, that Mountain of St. Michel, and Mountain of Misery; towering sheer up, like a bleak Pisgah with outlooks only into Desolation, sand, salt-water, and Despair.* Fly, thou poor Gabriel Honoré! Thou poor Sophie, return to Pontarlier; for Convent-walls too are cruel!

Gabriel flies; and indeed there fly with him sister Cabris and her preternuptial epauletted Brianson, who are already in flight for their own behoof: into deep thickets and covered ways, wide over the South-west of France. Marquis Mirabeau, thinking with a fond sorrow of Mont St. Michel and its quicksands, chooses the two best bloodhounds the Police of Paris has, (Inspector Brugnière and another), and, unmuzzling them, cries: Hunt!—"Monsieur, we have done all that the human mind

* See Mémoires de Madame de Genlis, iii. 201.

(*l'esprit humain*) can imagine, and this when the heats are so excessive, and we are worn out with fatigue, and our legs swoln."

No: all that the human mind can imagine is ineffectual. On the twenty-third night of August, (1776,) Sophie de Monnier, in man's clothes, is scaling the Monnier garden-wall at Pontarlier; is crossing the Swiss marches, wrapped in a cloak of darkness, borne on the wings of love and despair. Gabriel Honoré, wrapped in the like cloak, borne on the like vehicle, is gone with her to Holland,—thenceforth a broken man.

"Crime for ever lamentable," ejaculates the *Fils Adoptif;* "of which the world has so spoken, and must for ever speak!" There are, indeed, many things easy to be spoken of it; and also some things not easy to be spoken. Why, for example, thou virtuous *Fils Adoptif*, was that of the Canteen-keeper's wife at If such a peccadillo, and this of the legal President's wife such a crime, lamentable to that late date of "for ever?" The present reviewer fancies them to be the same crime. Again, might not the first grand criminal and sinner in this business be legal President Monnier, the distracted, spleen-stricken, moon-stricken old man;—liable to trial, with non-acquittal or difficult acquittal, at the great Bar of Nature herself? And then the second sinner in it? and the third and the fourth? "He that is *without* sin among you!"—One thing, therefore, the present reviewer will speak, in the words of old Samuel Johnson: My dear *Fils Adoptif*, my dear brethren of Mankind, "endeavour to clear your mind of Cant!" It is positively the prime necessity for all men, and all women and children, in these days, who would have their souls live, (were it even feebly,) and not die of the detestablest asphyxia; as in carbonic vapour, the more horrible (for breathing of) the more clean it looks.

That the *Parlement* of Besançon indicted Mirabeau for *rapt et vol*, abduction and robbery; that they condemned him "in contumacious absence," and went the length of beheading a Paper Effigy of him, was perhaps extremely suitable;—but not to be dwelt on here. Neither do we pry curiously into the garret-life in Holland and Amsterdam; being straitened for room. The wild man and his beautiful sad-heroic woman lived out their romance of reality, as well as was expected. Hot tempers go not always softly together; neither did the course of true love, either in wedlock or in elopement, ever run smooth. Yet it did run, in this instance, copious, if not smooth; with quarrel and reconcilement, tears and heart-effusion; sharp tropical squalls, and also the gorgeous effulgence and exuberance of general tropical weather. It was like a little Paphos islet in the middle of blackness; the very danger and despair that environed it made the islet blissful;—even as in virtue of death, life to the fretfullest becomes tolerable, becomes sweet, death being so nigh. At any hour, might not king's exempt or other dread alguazil knock at our garret establishment, (here "in the *Kalbestrand*, at Lequesne the tailor's,") and dissolve it? Gabriel toils for Dutch booksellers; bearing their heavy load; translating *Watson's Philip Second;* doing endless Gibeonite work: earning, however, his gold louis a day. Sophie sews and scours beside him, with her soft fingers, not grudging it: in hard toils, in trembling joys begirt with terrors, with one terror, that of being parted,—their days roll swiftly on. For eight tropical months!—Ah, at the end of some eight months, (14th May, 1777,) enter the alguazil! He is in the shape of Brugnière, our old slot-hound of the South-west; the swelling of his legs is fallen now; this time the human mind has been able to manage it. He carries Kings orders, High Mightiness' sanctions; sealed parchments. Gabriel Honoré shall be carried this way, Sophie that; Sophie, like to be a mother, shall behold him no more. Desperation, even in the female character, can go no farther: she will kill herself that hour, as even the slot-hound believes,—had not the very slot-hound, in mercy, undertaken that they should have some means of correspondence; that hope should not utterly be cut away. With embracings and interjections, sobbings that cannot be uttered, they tear themselves asunder, stony Paris now nigh: Mirabeau towards his prison of Vincennes; Sophie to some milder Convent-parlour relegation, there to await what Fate, very minatory at this time, will see good to bring.

Conceive the giant Mirabeau locked fast, then, in Doubting-castle of Vincennes; his hot soul surging up, wildly breaking itself against cold obstruction; the voice of his despair reverberated on him by dead stone walls. Fallen in the eyes of the world, the ambitious haughty man; his fair life-hopes from without all spoiled and become foul ashes: and from within,—what he has done, what he has parted with and *un*done! Deaf as Destiny is a Rhadamanthine father; inaccessible even to the attempt at pleading. Heavy doors have slammed to; their bolts growling *Wo to thee!* Great Paris sends eastward its daily multitudinous hum; in the evening sun thou seest its weathercocks glitter, its old grim towers and fuliginous life-breath all gilded: and thou?—Neither evening nor morning, nor change of day nor season, brings deliverance. Forgotten of Earth; not too hopefully remembered of Heaven! No passionate *Pater-Peccavi* can move an old Marquis; deaf he as Destiny. Thou must sit there.—For forty-two months, by the great Zodiacal Horologe! The heir of the Riquettis, sinful, and yet more sinned against, has worn out his wardrobe; complaints that his clothes get looped and windowed, insufficient against the weather. His eyesight is failing; the family disorder, *nephritis*, afflicts him; the doctors declare horse-exercise essential to preserve life. Within the walls then! answers the old Marquis. Count de Mirabeau "rides in the garden of forty paces;" with quick turns, hamperedly, overlooked by donjons and high stone barriers.

And yet fancy not Mirabeau spent his time in mere wailing and raging. Far from that!—

> To whine, put finger i' the eye, and sob,
> Because he had ne'er another tub,

was in no case Mirabeau's method, more than Diogenes's. Other such wild-glowing Mass of Life, which you might beat with Cyclops' hammers, (and, alas, not beat the dross *out* of,) was not in Europe at that time. Call him not the strongest man then living; for light, as we said, and not fire, is the strong thing; yet call him strong too, very strong; and for toughness, tenacity, vivaciousness, and a *fond gaillard*, call him toughest of all. Raging passions, ill-governed; reckless tumult from within, merciless oppression from without; ten men might have died of what this Gabriel Honoré did not yet die of. Police-captain Lenoir allowed him, in mercy and according to engagement, to correspond with Sophie; the condition was that the letters should be seen by Lenoir, and be returned into his keeping. Mirabeau corresponded; in fire and tears, copiously, not Werter-like, but Mirabeau-like. Then he had penitential petitions, *Pater-Peccavis* to write, to get presented and enforced; for which end all manner of friends must be urged: correspondence enough. Besides, he could read, though very limitedly: he could even compose or compile; extracting, *not* in the manner of the bee, from the very Bible and Dom Calmet, a *Biblion Eroticon*, which can be recommended to no woman or man. The pious *Fils Adoptif* drops a veil over his face at this scandal; and says lamentably that there is nothing to be said. As for Correspondence with Sophie, it lay in Lenoir's desk forgotten; but was found there by Manuel, Procureur of the Commune in 1792, when so many desks flew open; and by him given to the world. A book which fair sensibility (rather in a private way) loves to weep over: not this reviewer, to any considerable extent; not at all here, in his present strait for room. Good love-letters of their kind notwithstanding. But if any thing can swell farther the tears of fair sensibility over Mirabeau's "*Correspondence of Vincennes*," it must be this: the issue it ended in. After a space of years these two lovers, wrenched asunder in Holland, and allowed to correspond that they might not poison themselves, met again: it was under cloud of night; in Sophie's apartment, in the country; Mirabeau, "disguised as a porter," had come thither from a considerable distance. And they flew into each other's arms; to weep their child dead, their long unspeakable woes? Not at all. They stood, arms stretched oratorically, calling one another to account for causes of jealousy; grew always louder, arms set a-kimbo; and parted quite loud, never to meet more on earth. In September, 1789, Mirabeau had risen to be a world's wonder: and Sophie, far from him, had sunk out of the world's sight, respected only in the little town of Gien. On the 9th night of September, Mirabeau might be thundering in the Versailles *Salle des Menus*, to be reported of all Journals on the morrow; and Sophie, twice disappointed of new marriage, the sad-heroic temper darkened now into perfect black, was reclining, self-tied to her sofa, with a pan of charcoal burning near; to die as the unhappy die. Said we not, "the course of true love never did run smooth?"

However, after two-and-forty months, and negotiations, and more intercessions than in Catholic countries will free a soul out of purgatory, Mirabeau is once more delivered from the strong place: not into his own home, (home, wife, and the whole Past are far parted from him;) not into his father's home; but forth;—hurled forth, to seek his fortune Ishmael-like in the wide hunting-field of the world. Consider him, O Reader; thou wilt find him very notable. A disgraced man, not a broken one; ruined outwardly, not ruined inwardly; not yet, for there is no ruining of him on that side. Such a buoyancy of radical fire and *fond gaillard* he has; with his dignity and vanity, levity, solidity, with his virtues and his vices,—what a front he shows! You would say, he bates not a jot, in these sad circumstances, of what he claimed from Fortune, but rather enlarges it: his proud soul, so galled, deformed by manacles and bondage, flings away its prison-gear, bounds forth to the fight again, as if victory, after all, were certain. Post-horses to Pontarlier and the Besançon Parlement; that that "sentence by contumacy" be annulled, and the Paper Effigy have its Head stuck on again! The wild giant, said to be "absent by contumacy," sits voluntarily in the Pontarlier Jail; thunders in pleadings which make Parlementeers quake, and all France listen; and the Head reunites itself to the Paper Effigy with apologies. Monnier and the De Ruffeys know who is the most impudent man alive: the world with astonishment, who is one of the ablest. Even the old Marquis snuffles approval, though with qualification. Tough old Man, he has lost his own world-famous Lawsuit and other lawsuits, with ruinous expenses; has seen his fortune and projects fail, and even *lettres de cachet* turn out not always satisfactory or sanatory; wherefore he summons his children about him; and, really in a very serene way, declares himself invalided, fit only for the chimney-nook now; to sit patching his old mind together again, (*à rebouter sa tête, à se recoudre pièce à pièce:*) advice and countenance they, the deserving part of them, shall always enjoy; but *lettres de cachet*, or other the like benefit and guidance, not any more. Right so, thou best of old Marquises! There he rests then, like the still evening of a thundery day; thunders no more; but rays forth many a curiously-tinted lightbeam and remark on life; serene to the last. Among Mirabeau's small catalogue of virtues, (very small of formulary and conventional virtues,) let it not be forgotten that he loved this old father warmly to the end; and forgave his cruelties, or forgot them in kind interpretation of them.

For the Pontarlier paper effigy, therefore, it is well: and yet a man lives not comfortably without money. Ah, were one's marriage not disrupted; for the old father-in-law will soon die; those rich expectations were then fruitions! The ablest, not the most shame-faced man in France, is off, next spring (1783,) to Aix; stirring Parlement and Heaven and Earth there, to have his wife back. How he worked; with what nobleness and courage, (according to the *Fils Adoptif;*) giant's work! The sound of him is spread over France and over the world; English travellers (high foreign lordships) turning aside to Aix; and "multitudes gathered even on the roofs" to hear him, the Court-house being crammed to bursting! Demosthenic fire and pathos; penitent husband calling for forgiveness and restitution:—"*ce n'est qu'un claque-dents et un fol,*" rays forth the old Marquis from the chimney-nook: "a chatter-teeth and madman?" The world and Parlement thought not that; knew not what to think, if not that this was the questionablest able man they had ever heard; and, alas, still farther,—that his cause was *untenable*. No wife then; and no money! From this second attack on Fortune, Mirabeau returns foiled, and worse than before; resourceless, for now the old Marquis, too, again eyes him askance. He must hunt Ishmael-like, as we said. Whatsoever of wit or strength he has within himself will stand true to him; on that he can count; unfortunately on almost nothing but that.

Mirabeau's life for the next five years, which creeps troublous, obscure, through several of these Eight Volumes, will probably, in the One right Volume which they hold imprisoned, be delineated briefly. It is the long-drawn practical improvement of the sermon already preached in Rhé, in If, in Joux, in Holland, in Vincennes, and elsewhere. A giant man in the flower of his years, in the winter of his prospects, has to see how he will reconcile these two contradictions. With giant energies and talents, with giant virtues even, he, burning to unfold himself, has got put into his hands, for implements and means to do it with, disgrace, contumely, obstruction; character elevated only as Haman was; purse full only of debt-summonses; household, home, and possessions, as it were, sown with salt; Ruin's plough-share furrowing too deeply himself and all that was his. Under these, and not under other conditions, shall this man now live and struggle. Well might he "weep" long afterwards, (though not given to the melting mood,) thinking over, with Dumont, how his life had been blasted, by himself, by others; and was now so defaced and thunder-riven, no glory could make it whole again. Truly, as we often say, a weaker, and yet very strong man, might have died,—by hypochondria, by brandy, or by arsenic: but Mirabeau did not die. The world is not his friend, nor the world's law and formula? It will be his enemy then; his conqueror and master not altogether. There are strong men who can, in case of necessity, make way with formulas, (*humer les formules,*) and yet find a habitation behind them: these are the very strong; and Mirabeau was of these. The world's esteem having gone quite against him, and most circles of society, with their codes and regulations, pronouncing little but anathema on him, he is nevertheless not lost; he does not sink to desperation; not to dishonesty, or pusillanimity, or splenetic aridity. Nowise! In spite of the world, he is a living strong man there: the world cannot take from him his just consciousness of himself, his warm open-hearted feeling towards others; there are still limits, on all sides, to which the world and the devil cannot drive him. The giant, we say! How he stands, like a mountain; thunder-riven, but broad-based, rooted in the Earth's (in Nature's) own rocks; and will not tumble prostrate! So true is it what a moralist has said: "One could not wish any man to fall into a fault; yet is it often precisely after a fault, or a crime even, that the morality which is in a man first unfolds itself, and what of strength he as a man possesses, now when all else is gone from him."

Mirabeau, through these dim years, is seen wandering from place to place; in France, Germany, Holland, England; finding no rest for the sole of his foot. It is a life of shifts and expedients, *au jour le jour*. Extravagant in his expenses, thriftless, swimming in a welter of debts and difficulties; for which he has to provide by fierce industry; by skill in financiership. The man's revenue is his wits; he has a pen and a head; and, happily for him, "is the demon of the impossible." At no time is he without some blazing project or other, which shall warm and illuminate far and wide; which too often blazes out ineffectual; which in that case he replaces and renews, for his hope is inexhaustible. He writes pamphlets unweariedly as a steam-engine: *On the Opening of the Scheldt*, and Kaiser Joseph: *On the Order of Cincinnatus* and Washington: *on Count Cagliostro*, and the Diamond Necklace. Innumerable are the helpers and journeymen (respectable Mauvillons, respectable Dumonts) whom he can set working for him on such matters; it is a gift he has. He writes Books, in as many as eight volumes, which are properly only a larger kind of Pamphlets. He has polemics with Caron Beaumarchais on the water-company of Paris; lean Caron shooting sharp arrows into him, which he responds to demoniacally, "flinging hills with all their woods." He is intimate with many men; his "terrible gift of familiarty," his joyous courtiership and faculty of pleasing, do not forsake him: but it is a questionable intimacy, granted to the man's talents, in spite of his character: a relation which the proud Riquetti, not the humbler that he is poor and ruined, correctly feels. With still more women is he intimate; girt with a whole system of intrigues, in that sort, wherever he abide; seldom travelling without a—wife (let us call her) engaged by the year, or during mutual satisfaction. On this large department of Mirabeau's history, what can you say, except that his incontinence was great, enormous, entirely indefensible? If any one please (which we do not) to be present, with the *Fils Adoptif*, at "the *autopsie*," and *post-mortem* examination, he will see curious documents on this head; and to what depths of penalty Nature, in her just self-vindication, can sometimes doom men. The *Fils Adoptif* is very sorry. To the kind called unfortunate-females, it would seem, nevertheless, this unfortunate-male had an aversion amounting to complete *nolo-tangere*.

The old Marquis sits apart in the chimney-nook, observant: what this roaming, unresting, rebellious Titan of a Count may ever prove of use for? If it be not, O Marquis, for the general Overturn, *Culbute Générale?* He is swallowing Formulas; getting endless acquaintance with the Realities of things and men: in audacity, in recklessness, he will not, it is like, be wanting. The old Marquis rays out curious observations on life;—yields no effectual assistance of money.

Ministries change and shift; but never, in the new deal, does there turn up a good card for Mirabeau. Necker he does not love, nor is love lost between them. Plausible Calonne hears him Stentor-like denouncing stock-jobbing, (*Denonciation de l'Agiotage:*) communes with him, corresponds with him; is glad to get him sent, in some semi-ostensible or spy-diplomatist character, to Berlin; in any way to have him sopped and quieted. The Great Frederic was still on the scene, though now very near the side-scenes: the wiry thin Drill-serjeant of the World, and the broad burly Mutineer of the World, glanced into one another with amazement; the one making entrance, the other making exit. To this Berlin business we owe pamphlets; we owe *Correspondences*, ("surreptitiously published"—with consent;) we owe (brave Major Mauvillon serving as hodman) the *Monarchie Prussienne*, a Pamphlet in some eight octavo Volumes, portions of which are still well worth reading.

Generally, on first making personal acquaintance with Mirabeau as a writer or speaker, one is not a little surprised. Instead of Irish oratory, with tropes and declamatory fervid feeling, such as the rumour one has heard gives prospect of, you are astonished to meet a certain hard angular distinctness, a totally unornamented force and massiveness: clear perspicuity, strong perspicacity, conviction that wishes to convince,—this beyond all things, and instead of all things. You would say the primary character of those utterances, nay, of the man himself, is sincerity and insight; strength, and the honest use of strength. Which, indeed, it is, O Reader! Mirabeau's spiritual gift will be found on examination to be verily an honest and a great one; far the strongest, best practical intellect of that time; entitled to rank among the strong of all times. These books of his ought to be riddled, like this book of the *Fils Adoptif*. There is precious matter in them; too good to lie hidden among shot rubbish. Hear this man on any subject, you will find him worth considering. He has words in him, rough deliverances; such as men do not forget. As thus: "I know but three ways of living in this world: by wages for work; by begging; thirdly, by stealing, (so named, or not so named.)" Again: "Malebranche saw all things in God; and M. Necker sees all things in Necker!" There are nicknames of Mirabeau's worth whole treatises. "Grandison-Cromwell Lafayette:" write a volume on the man, as many volumes have been written, and try to say more! It is the best likeness yet drawn of him,—by a flourish and two dots. Of such inexpressible advantage is it that a man have "an eye, instead of a pair of spectacles merely;" that, seeing through the formulas of things, and even "making away" with many a formula, he sees into the thing itself, and so know it and be master of it!

As the years roll on, and that portentous decade of the Eighties (or "Era of Hope") draws towards completion, and it becomes ever more evident to Mirabeau that great things are in the wind, we find his wanderings, as it were, quicken. Suddenly emerging out of Night and Cimmeria, he dashes down on the Paris world, time after time; flashes into it with that fire-glance of his; discerns that the time is not yet come; and then merges back again. Occasionally his pamphlets provoke a fulmination and order of arrest, wherefore he must merge the faster. Nay, your Calonne is good enough to signify it beforehand: On such and such a day I shall order you to be arrested; pray make speed therefore. When the Notables meet, in the spring of 1787, Mirabeau spreads his pinions, alights on Paris and Versailles; it seems to him he ought to be secretary of those Notables. No! friend Dupont de Nemours gets it: the time is not yet come. It is still but the time of "Crispin-Catiline" d'Espréménil, and other such animal-magnetic persons. Nevertheless, the Reverend Talleyrand, judicious Dukes, liberal noble friends not a few, are sure that the time will come. Abide thy time.

Hark! On the 27th of December, 1788, here finally is the long-expected announcing itself: royal Proclamation definitively convoking the States-General for May next! Need we ask whether Mirabeau bestirs himself now; whether or not he is off to Provence, to the Assembly of Noblesse there, with all his faculties screwed to the sticking-place? One strong dead-lift pull, thou Titan; and perhaps thou carriest it! How Mirabeau wrestled and strove under these auspices; speaking and contending all day, writing pamphlets, paragraphs, all night; also suffering much, gathering his wild soul together, motionless under reproaches, under drawn swords even, lest his enemies throw him off his guard; how he agitates and represses, unerringly dexterous, sleeplessly unwearied, and is a "demon of the impossible," let all readers fancy. With "a body of Noblesse more ignorant, greedier, more insolent than any I have ever seen," the Swallower of Formulas was like to have rough work. We must give his celebrated flinging up of the handful of dust, when they drove him out by overwhelming majority:—

"What have I done that was so criminal? I have wished that my Order were wise enough to give to-day what will infallibly be wrested from it to-morrow; that it should receive the merits and glory of sanctioning the assemblage of the Three Orders, which all Provence loudly demands. This is the crime of your 'enemy of peace!' Or rather I have ventured to believe that the people might be in the right. Ah, doubtless, a patrician soiled with such a thought deserves vengeance! But I am still guiltier than you think; for it is my belief that the people which complains is always in the right; that its indefatigable patience invariably waits the uttermost excesses of oppression, before it can determine on resisting; that it never resists long enough to obtain complete redress; and does not sufficiently know that to strike its enemies into terror and submission, it has only to stand still, that the most innocent as the most invincible of all powers is the power of refusing to do. I believe after this manner: punish the enemy of peace!

"But you, ministers of a God of peace, who are ordained to bless and not to curse, and yet have launched your anathema on me, without even the attempt at enlightening me, at reasoning with me! And you, 'friends of peace,' who denounce to the people, with all vehemence of hatred, the one defender it has yet found, out of its own ranks;—who, to bring about concord, are filling capital and province with placards calculated to arm the rural districts against the towns, if your deeds did not refute your writings;—who, to prepare ways of conciliation, protest against the royal Regulation for convoking the States-General, because it grants the people as many deputies as both the other orders, and against all that the coming National Assembly shall do, unless its laws secure the triumph of your pretensions, the eternity of your privileges! Disinterested 'friends of peace!' I have appealed to your honour, and summon you to state what expressions of mine have offended against either the respect we owe to the royal authority or to the nation's right? Nobles of Provence, Europe is attentive; weigh well your answer. Men of God, beware; God hears you!

"And if you do not answer, but keep silence, shutting yourselves up in the vague declamations you have hurled at me, then allow me to add one word.

"In all countries, in all times, aristocrats have implacably persecuted the people's friends; and if, by some singular combination of fortune, there chanced to arise such a one in their own circle, it was he above all whom they struck at, eager to inspire wider terror by the elevation of their victim. Thus perished the last of the Gracchi by the hands of the patricians; but, being struck with the mortal stab, he flung dust towards Heaven, and called on the Avenging Deities; and from this dust sprang Marius,—Marius not so illustrious for exterminating the Cimbri as for overturning in Rome the tyranny of the Noblesse!"

There goes some foolish story of Mirabeau having now opened a cloth-shop in Marseilles, to ingratiate himself with the Third Estate; whereat we have often laughed. The image of Mirabeau measuring out drapery to mankind, and deftly snipping at tailors' measures, has something pleasant for the mind. So, that though there is not a shadow of truth in this story, the very lie may justly sustain itself for a while, in the character of lie. Far otherwise was the reality there: "voluntary guard of a hundred men;" Provence crowding by the ten thousand round his chariot wheels; explosions of rejoicing musketry, heaven-rending acclamation; "people paying two louis for a place at the window!" Hunger itself (very considerable in those days) he can pacify by speech. Violent meal mobs at Marseilles and at Aix, unmanageable by fire-arms and governors, he smooths down by the word of his mouth; the governor soliciting him, though unloved. It is as a Roman Triumph, and more. He is chosen deputy for two places; has to decline Marseilles, and honour Aix. Let his enemies look and wonder, and sigh forgotten by him. For this Mirabeau too the career at last opens.

At last! Does not the benevolent Reader, though never so unambitious, sympathize a little with this poor brother mortal in such a case? Victory is always joyful; but to think of such a man, in the hour when, after twelve Hercules' Labours, he does finally triumph! So long he fought with the many-headed coil of Lernean serpents; and, panting, wrestled and wrang with it for life or death,—forty long stern years; and now he has it under his heel! The mountain tops are scaled, are scaled; where the man climbed, on sharp flinty precipices, slippery, abysmal; in darkness, seen by no kind eye,—amid the brood of dragons; and the heart, many times, was like to fail within him, in his loneliness, in his extreme need: yet he climbed, and climbed, glueing his footsteps in his blood; and now, behold, Hyperion-like he has scaled it, and on the summit shakes his glittering shafts of war! What a scene and new kingdom for him; all bathed in auroral radiance of Hope; far-stretching, solemn, joyful: what wild Memnon's music, from the depths of Nature, comes toning through the soul raised suddenly out of strangling death into victory and life! The very bystander, we think, might weep, with this Mirabeau, tears of joy.

Which, alas, will become tears of sorrow! For know, O Son of Adam, (and Son of Lucifer, with that accursed ambition of thine,) that they are all a delusion and piece of demonic necromancy, these same auroral splendours, enchantments and Memnon's tones! The thing thou as mortal wantest is equilibrium, (what is called *rest* or *peace;*) which, God knows, thou wilt never get *so.* Happy they that find it without such searching. But in some twenty-three months more, of blazing solar splendour and conflagration, this Mirabeau will be ashes; and lie opaque, in the Pantheon of great men (or say, French-Pantheon of considerable, or even of considered, and small-noisy men,)—at rest nowhere, save on the lap of his mother earth. There are to whom the gods, in their bounty, give glory: but far oftener it is given in wrath, as a curse and a poison; disturbing the whole inner health and industry of the man; leading onward through dizzy staggerings and tarantula jiggings,—towards no saint's shrine. Truly, if Death did not intervene; or still more happily, if Life and the Public were not a blockhead, and sudden unreasonable oblivion were not to follow that sudden unreasonable glory, and beneficently, though most painfully, damp it down,—one sees not where many a poor glorious man, still more many a poor glorious woman, (for it falls harder on the distinguished-female,) could terminate,—far short of Bedlam.

On the 4th day of May, 1789, Madame de Staël, looking from a window in the main street of Versailles, amid an assembled world, as the Deputies walked in procession from the church of Nôtre-Dame to that of Saint Louis, to hear High Mass, and be constituted *States-General,* saw this: "Among these Nobles who had been deputed to the Third Estate, above all others, the Comte de Mirabeau. The opinion men had of his genius was singularly augmented by the fear entertained of his immorality; and yet it was this very immorality which straitened the influence his astonishing faculties were to secure him. You could not but look long at this man, when once you had noticed him: his immense black head of hair distinguished him among them all; you would have said his force depended on it, like that of Samson: his face borrowed new expression from its very ugliness; his whole person gave you the idea of an irregular power, but a power such as you would figure in a Tribune of the People." Mirabeau's history through the first twenty-three months of the Revolution falls not to be written here: yet it is well worth writing somewhere. The Constituent Assembly, when his name was first read out, received it with murmurs; not knowing what they murmured at! This honourable member they were murmuring over was the member of all members; the august Constituent, without him, were no Constituent at all. Very notable, truly, is his procedure in this section of world-history: by far the notablest single element there: none like to him, or second to him. Once he is seen visibly to have saved, as with his own force, the existence of the Constituent Assembly; to have turned the whole tide of things: in one of those moments which are cardinal; decisive for centuries. The royal Declaration of the *Twenty-third of June* is promulgated: there is military force enough; there is then the king's express order to disperse, to meet as separate Third Estate on the morrow. Bastilles and scaffolds may be the penalty for disobeying. Mirabeau disobeys; lifts his voice to encourage others, all pallid, panic-stricken, to disobey. Supreme Usher De Brézé enters, with the king's renewed order to depart. "Messieurs," said De Brézé, "you heard the king's order?" The Swallower of Formulas bellows out these words, that have become memorable: "Yes, Monsieur, we heard what the king was advised to say; and you, who cannot be interpreter of his meaning to the States-General; you, who have neither vote nor seat, nor right of speech here, you are not the man to remind us of it. Go, Monsieur, tell those who sent you that we are here by will of the Nation; and that nothing but the force of bayonets can drive us hence!" And poor De Brézé vanishes,—back foremost, the *Fils Adoptif* says.

But this, cardinal moment though it be, is perhaps intrinsically among his smaller feats. In general, we would say once more with emphasis, He has "*humé toutes les formules*." He goes through the Revolution like a substance and a force, not like a formula of one. While innumerable barren Sièyeses and Constitution-pedants are building, with such hammering and troweling, their august paper constitution, (which endured eleven months,) this man looks not at cobwebs and *Social-Contracts*, but at things and men; discerning what is to be done,—proceeding straight to do it. He shivers out Usher De Brézé, back foremost, when that is the problem. "Marie Antoinette is charmed with him," when it comes to that. He is the man of the Revolution, while he lives; king of it; and only with life, as we compute, would have quitted his kingship of it. Alone of all these Twelve Hundred, there is in him the faculty of a king. For, indeed, have we not seen how assiduously Destiny had shaped him all along, as with an express eye to the work now in hand? O crabbed old Friend of Men, whilst thou wert bolting this man into Isles of Rhé, Castles of If, and training him so sharply to be *thy*self, not *him*self,—how little knewest thou *what* thou wert doing! Let us add, that the brave old Marquis lived to see his son's victory over Fate and men, and rejoiced in it; and rebuked Barrel Mirabeau for controverting such a Brother Gabriel. In the invalid chimney-nook at Argenteuil, near Paris, he sat raying out curious observations to the last; and died three days before the Bastille fell, precisely when the *Culbute Générale* was bursting out.

But finally, the twenty-three allotted months are over. Madame de Staël, on the 4th of May, 1789, saw the Roman Tribune of the People, and Samson with his long black hair: and on the 4th of April, 1791, there is a Funeral Procession extending four miles: king's ministers, senators, national guards, and all Paris,—torchlight, wail of trombones and music, and the tears of men; mourning of a whole people,—such mourning as no modern people ever saw for one man. This Mirabeau's work then is done. He sleeps with the primeval giants. He has gone over to the majority: *Abiit aa plures.*

In the way of eulogy and dyslogy, and summing up of character, there many doubtless be a great many things set forth concerning this Mirabeau; as already there has been much discussion and arguing about him, better and worse: which is proper surely; as about all manner of new things, were they much less questionable than this new giant is. The present reviewer, meanwhile, finds it suitabler to restrict himself and his exhausted readers to the three following moral reflections.

Moral reflection *first*,—that, in these centuries men are not born demi-gods and perfect characters, but imperfect ones, and mere blamable men, namely, environed with such short-coming and confusion of their own, and then with such adscititious scandal and misjudgment, (got in the work they did,) that they resemble less demi-gods than a sort of god-devils,—very imperfect characters indeed. The demi-god arrangement were the one which, at first sight, this reviewer might be inclined to prefer.

Moral reflection *second*,—however, that probably men were never born demi-gods in any century, but precisely god-devils as we see; certain of whom do become a kind of demi-gods! How many are the men, not censured, misjudged, calumniated only, but tortured, crucified, hung on gibbets,—not as god-devils even, but as devils proper; who have nevertheless grown to seem respectable, or infinitely respectable! For the thing which was *not* they, which was not any thing, has fallen away piecemeal; and become avowedly babble and confused shadow, and no-thing: the thing, which was they, remains. Depend on it, Harmodius and Aristogiton, as clear as they now look, had illegal plottings, conclaves at the Jacobins' Church (of Athens); and very intemperate things were spoken, and also done. Thus too, Marcus Brutus and the elder Junius, are they not palpable Heroes? Their praise is in all Debating Societies; but didst thou read what the Morning Papers said of those transactions of theirs, the week after? Nay, Old Noll, whose bones were dug up and hung in chains, here at home, as the just emblem of himself and his deserts, (the offal of Creation, at that time,) has not he too got to be a very respectable grim bronze-figure, though it is yet only a century and half since; of whom England seems proud rather than otherwise?

Moral reflection *third*, and last,—that neither thou nor we, good Reader, had any hand in the making of this Mirabeau;—else who knows but we had objected, in *our* wisdom? But it was the Upper Powers that made him, without once consulting us; they and not we, so and not otherwise! To endeavour to understand a little what manner of Mirabeau he, so made, might be: this we, according to opportunity, have done; and therefore do now, with a lively satisfaction, take farewell of him, and leave him to fare as he can.

PARLIAMENTARY HISTORY OF THE FRENCH REVOLUTION.*

[LONDON AND WESTMINSTER REVIEW, 1837.]

It appears to be, if not stated in words, yet tacitly felt and understood everywhere, that the event of these modern ages is the French Revolution. A huge explosion bursting through all formulas and customs; confounding into wreck and chaos the ordered arrangements of earthly life; blotting out, one may say, the very firmament and skyey load-stars,—though only for a season. Once in the fifteen hundred years such a thing was ordained to come. To those who stood present in the actual midst of that smoke and thunder, the effect might well be too violent: blinding and deafening, into confused exasperation, almost into madness. These on-lookers have played their part, were it with the printing-press or with the battle-cannon, and are departed: their work, such as it was, remaining behind them;—where the French Revolution also remains. And now, for us who have receded to the distance of some half-century, the explosion becomes a thing visible, surveyable: we see its flame and sulphur-smoke blend with the clear air, (far *under* the stars;) and hear its uproar as part of the sick noise of life,—loud indeed, yet imbosomed too, as all noise is, in the infinite of silence. It is an event which can be looked on; which may still be execrated, still be celebrated and psalmodied; but which it were better now to begin understanding. Really there are innumerable reasons why we ought to know this same French Revolution as it was: of which reasons (apart altogether from that of "Philosophy teaching by Experience," and so forth) is there not the best summary in this one reason, that we so *wish* to know it? Considering the qualities of the matter, one may perhaps reasonably feel that since the time of the Crusades, or earlier, there is no chapter of history so well worth studying.

Stated or not, we say, this persuasion is tacitly admitted, and acted upon. In these days everywhere you find it one of the most pressing duties for the writing guild, to produce history on history of the French Revolution. In France it would almost seem as if the young author felt that he must make this his proof-shot, and evidence of craftsmanship: accordingly they do fire off *Histoires, Précis of Histoires, Annales, Fastes,* (to say nothing of Historical Novels, *Gil Blasses, Dantons, Barnaves, Grangeneuves,*) in rapid succession, with or without effect. At all events it is curious to look upon: curious to contrast the picturing of the same fact by the men of this generation and position with the picturing of it by the men of the last. From Barruel and Fantin Desodoards to Thiers and Mignet there is a distance! Each individual takes up the Phenomenon according to his own point of vision, to the structure of his optic organs;—gives, consciously, some poor crotchetty picture of several things; unconsciously some picture of himself at least. And the Phenomenon, for its part, subsists there, all the while, unaltered; waiting to be pictured as often as you like, its entire meaning not to be compressed into any picture drawn by man.

---

* *Histoire Parlementaire de la Révolution Française, ou Journal des Assemblées Nationales depuis* 1789 *jusqu'en* 1815; *contenant la Narration des Evénemens, les Débats, &c. &c.* (Parliamentary History of the French Revolution, or Journal of the National Assemblies from 1789 to 1815: containing a Narrative of the Occurrences; Debates of the Assemblies; Discussions in the chief Popular Societies, especially in that of the Jacobins; Records of the Commune of Paris; Sessions of the Revolutionary Tribunal; Reports of the leading Political Trials; Detail of the Annual Budgets; Picture of the Moral Movement, extracted from the Newspapers, Pamphlets, &c., of each Period; preceded by an Introduction on the History of France till the Convocation of the States-General.) By P. J. B. Buchez and P. C. Roux. (Tomes 1er—23me et seq.—Paris, 1833—1836.)

Thiers's *History*, in ten volumes foolscap-octavo, contains, if we remember rightly, one reference; and that to a book, not the page or chapter of a book. It has, for these last seven or eight years, a wide or even high reputation; which latter it is as far as possible from meriting. A superficial air of order, of clearness, calm candour, is spread over the work; but inwardly, it is waste, inorganic: no human head that honestly tries can conceive the French Revolution *so*. A critic of our acquaintance undertook, by way of bet, to find four errors per hour in Thiers: he won amply on the first trial or two.* And yet, readers (we must add) taking all this along with them, may peruse Thiers with comfort in certain circumstances, nay, even with profit; for he is a brisk man of his sort; and does tell you much, if you knew nothing.

Mignet's, again, is a much more honestly written book; yet also an eminently unsatisfactory one. His two volumes contain far more meditation and investigation in them than Thiers's ten: their degree of preferability therefore is very high; for it has been said, "Call a book diffuse, and you call it in all senses bad; the writer could not find the right word to say, and so said many more or less wrong ones; did not hit the nail on the head, only smote and bungled about it and about it." Mignet's book has a compactness, a rigour, as if rivetted with iron rods: this also is an image of what symmetry it has;—symmetry, if not of a living earth-born Tree, yet of a firm well-manufactured Gridiron. Without life, without colour or verdure: that is to say, Mignet's genius is heartily *prosaic;* you are too happy that he is not a *quack* as well! It is very mortifying also to study his philosophical reflections: how he jingles and rumbles a quantity of mere abstractions and dead logical formulas, and calls it Thinking;—rumbles and rumbles, till he judges there may be enough; then begins again narrating. As thus:—

"The Constitution of 1791 was made on such principles as had resulted from the ideas and the situation of France. It was the work of the middle class, which chanced to be the strongest then; for, as is well known, whatever force has the lead will fashion the institutions according to its own aims. Now this force, when it belongs to one, is despotism; when to several, it is privilege; when to all, it is right: which latter state is the ultimatum of society, as it was its beginning. France had finally arrived thither, after passing through feudalism, which is the aristocratic institution; and then through absolutism, which is the monarchic one.

"The work of the Constituent Assembly perished not so much by its own defects as by the assaults of factions. Standing between the aristocracy and the multitude, it was attacked by the former, and stormed and won by the latter. The multitude would never have become supreme, had not civil war and the coalition of foreign states rendered its intervention and help indispensable. To defend the country the multitude required to have the governing of it: thereupon (*alors*) it made *its* revolution, as the middle class had made its. The multitude too had its *Fourteenth of July,* which was the *Tenth of August;* its Constituent, which was the Convention; its Government, which was the Committee of *Salut Public;* but, as we shall see," &c. (Chap. iv., vol. I., p. 271.)

Or thus; for there is the like at the end of every chapter:—

"But royalty had virtually fallen, on the Tenth of August; that day was the insurrection of the multitude against the middle class and constitutional throne, as the Fourteenth of July had been the insurrection of the middle classes against the privileged classes and an absolute throne. The Tenth of August witnessed the commencement of the dictatorial and arbitrary epoch of the Revolution. Circumstances becoming more and more difficult, there arose a vast war, which required increased energy; and this energy, unregulated, inasmuch as it was popular, rendered the sway of the lower class an unquiet, oppressive, and cruel sway." "It was not any way possible that the *Bourgeoisie,* (middle class,) which had been strong enough to strike down the old government and the privileged classes, but which had taken to repose after this victory, could repulse the Emigration and united Europe. There was needed for that a new shock, a new faith; there was needed for that a new Class, numerous, ardent, not yet fatigued, and which loved its Tenth of August, as the Burgherhood loved its Fourteenth of," &c., &c. (Ch. v., vol. I., p. 371.)

So uncommonly *lively* are these Abstractions (at bottom only occurrences, similitudes, days of the months, and such like) as rumble here in the historical head! Abstractions really of the most lively, insurrectionary character; nay, which produce offspring, and indeed are oftenest parricidally devoured thereby: such is the jingling and rumbling which calls itself Thinking. Nearly so, though with greater effect, might algebraical *x*'s go rumbling in some Pascal's or Babbage's mill. Just so, indeed, do the Kalmuck people pray: quantities of written prayers are put in some rotary pipkin or calabash, (hung on a tree, or going like the small barrel-churn of agricultural districts;) this the devotee has only to whirl and churn; so long as he whirls, it is prayer; when he ceases whirling, the prayer is done. Alas! this is a sore error, very generally, among French thinkers of the present time. One ought to add that Mignet takes his place at the head of that brotherhood of his; that his little book, though abounding too in errors of detail, better deserves what place it has than any other of recent date.

The older Desodoards, Barruels, Lacretelles, and such like, exist, but will hardly profit much. Toulongeon, a man of talent and integrity, is very vague; often incorrect for an eyewitness: his military details used to be

* "'Notables consented with eagerness,' (Vol. I., p. 10;) whereas they properly did not consent at all; 'Parliament recalled on the 10th of September,' (for the 15th;) and then 'Seance Royale took place on the 20th of the same month, (19th of quite a different month, not the same, nor next to the same;) 'D'Espremenil, a young Counsellor' (of forty and odd;) 'Duport, a young man,' (turned of sixty,) &c., &c.

reckoned valuable; but, we suppose, Jomini has eclipsed them now. The Abbé Montgaillard has shrewdness, decision, insight; abounds in anecdotes, strange facts and reports of facts: his book, being written in the form of Annals, is convenient for consulting. For the rest, he is acrid, exaggerated, occasionally altogether perverse; and, with his hastes and his hatreds, falls into the strangest hallucination;—as, for example, when he coolly records that "Madame de Staël, Necker's daughter, was seen (*on vit*) distributing brandy to the *Gardes Françaises* in their barracks;" that D'Orleans Egalitè had "a pair of *man*-skin breeches,"—leather breeches, of human skin, such as they did prepare in the tannery of Meudon, but *too late* for D'Orleans. The history by *Deux Amis de Liberté* (if the reader secure the original edition) is, perhaps, worth all the others, and offers (at least till 1792, after which it becomes convulsive, semi-fatuous, in the remaining dozen volumes) the best, correctest, most picturesque narrative yet published. It is very correct, very picturesque; wants only *fore-shortening*, shadow, and compression; a work of decided merit: the authors of it, what is singular, appear not to be known.

Finally, our English histories do likewise abound: copious if not in facts, yet in reflections on facts. They will prove to the most incredulous that this French Revolution was, as Chamfort said, no "rose-water Revolution;" that the universal insurrectionary abrogation of law and custom was managed in a most unlawful, uncustomary manner. He who wishes to know how a solid *Custos rotulorum*, speculating over his port after dinner, interprets the phenomena of contemporary universal history, may look in these books: he who does not wish that, need not look.

On the whole, after all these writings and printings, the weight of which would sink an Indiaman, there are, perhaps, only some three publications hitherto that can be considered as forwarding essentially a right knowledge of this matter. The *first* of these is the "Analyse du Moniteur," (complete expository Index, and Syllabus of the Moniteur newspaper from 1789 to 1799;) a work carrying its significance in its title;—provided it be faithfully executed; which it is well known to be. Along with this we may mention the series of portraits, a hundred in number, published with the original edition of it: many of them understood to be accurate likenesses. The natural face of a man is often worth more than several biographies of him, as biographies are written. These hundred portraits have been copied into a book called "Scènes de la Revolution," (which contains other pictures, of small value, and some not useless writing by Chamfort;) and are often to be found in libraries. A republication of Vernet's Caricatures* would be a most acceptable service, but has not been thought of hitherto. The *second work* to be counted here is the "Choix des Rapports, Opinions, et Discours," in some twenty volumes, with an excellent index: parliamentary speeches, reports, &c., are furnished in abundance; complete illustration of all that this Senatorial province (rather a wearisome one) can illustrate. *Thirdly*, we have to name the "Collection of Memoirs," completed several years ago, in above a hundred volumes. Booksellers Baudouin, Editors Berville and Barrière, have done their utmost; adding notes, explanations, rectifications, with portraits also if you like: Louvet, Riouffe, and the two volumes of "Memoirs on the Prisons" are the most attractive pieces. This Baudouin Collection, therefore, joins itself to that of Petitot, as a natural sequel.

* See Mercier's Nouveau Paris, vol. iv. p. 254.

And now a *fourth* work, which follows in the train of these, and deserves to be reckoned along with them, is this "Histoire Parlementaire" of Messieurs Buchez and Roux. The authors are men of ability and repute: Buchez, if we mistake not, is Dr. Buchez, and practises medicine with acceptance; Roux is known as an essayist and journalist: they once listened a little to Saint Simon, but it was before Saint Simonism called itself "a religion," and vanished in Bedlam. We have understood there is a certain bibliomaniac military gentleman in Paris, who in the course of years has amassed the most astonishing collection of revolutionary ware: books, pamphlets, newspapers, even sheets and handbills, ephemeral printings and paintings, such as the day brought them forth, lie there without end.* Into this warehouse (as into all manner of other repositories) Messrs. Buchez and Roux have happily found access: the "Histoire Parlementaire" is the fruit of their labours there. A number (two forming a volume) is published every fortnight: we have the first twenty-two volumes before us, which bring down the narrative to January, 1793; there must be several other volumes out, which we have not yet seen. Conceive a judicious compilation with such resources. Parliamentary Debates, in summary, or (where the occasion warrants it) given at large; this is by no means the most interesting part of the matter: we have excerpts, notices, hints of all imaginable sorts; of newspapers, of pamphlets, of Sectionary and Municipal records, of the Jacobins' club, of placard-journals, nay, of placards and caricatures. No livelier emblem of the time, in its actual movement and tumult, could be presented. The editors connect these fragments by expositions such as are needful; so that a reader coming unprepared to the work can still know what he is about. Their expositions, as we can testify, are handsomely done: but altogether apart from these, the excerpts themselves are the valuable thing. The scissors, in such a

* It is generally known that a similar collection, perhaps still larger and more curious, lies (buried) in the British Museum here—inaccessible for want of a proper catalogue. Some eighteen months ago, the respectable sub-librarian seemed to be working at such a thing: by respectful application to him, you could gain access to his room, and have the satisfaction of mounting on ladders, and reading the outside titles of his books, which was a great help. Otherwise you could not in many weeks ascertain so much as the table of contents of this repository; and, after days of weary waiting, dusty rummaging, and sickness of hope deferred, gave up the enterprise as a "game not worth the candle."

case, are independent of the pen. One of the most interesting English biographies we have is that long thin folio on Oliver Cromwell, published some five-and-twenty years ago, where the editor has merely clipt out from the contemporary newspapers whatsoever article, paragraph, or sentence he found to contain the name of Old Noll, and printed them in the order of their dates. It is surprising that the like has not been attempted in other cases. Had seven of the eight translators of Faust, and seventy times seven of the four hundred four-score and ten Imaginative Authors, but thrown down the writing instrument, and turned to the old newspaper files judiciously with the cutting one!

We can testify, after not a little examination, that the editors of the "Histoire Parlementaire" are men of fidelity, of diligence; that their accuracy in regard to facts, dates, and so forth, is far beyond the average. Of course they have their own opinions, prepossessions even: but these are honest prepossessions, which they do not hide; which one can estimate the force of, allow for the result of. Wilful falsification, did the possibility of it lie in their character, is otherwise out of the question. But, indeed, our editors are men of earnestness, of strict principle; of a faith, were it only in the republican Tricolor. Their democratic faith, truly, is palpable, thorough-going; as it has a right to be, in these days, since it likes. The thing you have to praise, however, is that it is a quiet faith, never an hysterical one; never expresses itself otherwise than with a becoming calmness, especially with a becoming brevity. The hoarse deep croak of Marat, the brilliant sharp-cutting gayety of Desmoulins, the dull bluster of Prudhomme, the cackling garrulity of Brissot, all is welcomed with a cold gravity and brevity; all is illustrative, if not of one thing then of another. Nor are the Royalists Royous, Suleaus, Peltiers, forgotten; "Acts of the Apostles," "King's Friend," nor "Crowing of the Cock:" these, indeed, are more sparingly administered; but at the right time, as is promised, we shall have more. In a word, it may be said of this "Histoire Parlementaire," that the wide promise held out in its title page is really, in some respectable measure, fulfilled. With a fit index to wind it up, (which index ought to be not good only but excellent, so much depends on it here,) this work bids fair to be one of the most important yet published on the History of the Revolution. No library, that professes to have a collection in this sort, can dispense with it.

A "Histoire Parlementaire" is precisely the house, or say, rather, the unbuilt city, of which the single brick *can* form a specimen. In so rich a variety the only difficulty is where to choose. We have scenes of tragedy, of comedy, of farce, of farce-tragedy, oftenest of all; there is eloquence, gravity; there is bluster, bombast, and absurdity: scenes tender, scenes barbarous, spirit-stirring, and then flatly wearisome: a thing waste, incoherent, wild to look upon; but great with the greatness of reality; for the thing exhibited is no vision but a fact. Let us, as the first excerpt, give this tragedy of old Foulon, which all the world has heard of, perhaps not very accurately. Foulon's life-drama, with its hasty cruel sayings and mean doings, with its thousandfold intrigues, and "the people eating grass if they like," ends in this miserable manner. It is the editors themselves who speak; compiling from various resources:—

"Towards five in the morning, (Paris, 22d July, 1789,) M. Foulon was brought in; he had been arrested at Vitry, near Fountainbleau, by the peasants of the place. Doubtless this man thought himself very guilty towards the people," (say, very hateful;) "for he had spread abroad a report of his death; and had even buried one of his servants, who happened to die then, under his own name. He had afterwards hidden himself in an estate of M. de Sartines;" where he was detected and seized.

"M. Foulon was taken to the Hotel de Ville, where they made him wait. Towards nine o'clock the assembled Committee had decided that he should be sent to the Abbaye prison. M. de Lafayette was sent for, that he might execute this order; he was abroad over the Districts: he could not be found. During this time a crowd collected in the square; and required to see Foulon. It was noon: M. Bailly came down; the people listened to him; but still persisted. In the end they penetrated into the great hall of the Hotel de Ville; would see Foulon, 'whom,' say, they, 'you are wanting to smuggle off from justice.' Foulon was presented to them. Then began this remarkable dialogue. M. de la Poize, an Elector:—'Messieurs, every guilty person should be judged.' 'Yes, judged directly, and then hanged.' M. Osselin:—'To judge, one must have judges; let us send M. Foulon to the tribunals.' 'No, no,' replied the people, 'judge him just now.' 'Since you will not have the common judges,' said M. Osselin, 'it is indispensable to appoint others.' 'Well, judge him yourselves.' 'We have no right either to judge or to create judges; name them yourselves.' 'Well,' cried the people, 'M. le Cure of Saint Etienne then, and M. le Cure of Saint-Andre.' Osselin:—'Two judges are not enough; there needs seven.' Thereupon the people named Messrs. Quatremere, Varangue, &c. 'Here are seven judges indeed,' said Osselin, 'but we still want a clerk.' 'Be you clerk.' 'A king's Attorney.' 'Let it be M. Duveyrier.' 'Of what crime is M. Foulon accused?' asked Duveyrier. 'He wished to harass the people; he said he would make them eat grass; he was in the plot; he was for national bankruptcy; he bought up corn.' The two curates then rose, and declared that they refused to judge; the laws of the church not permitting them. 'They are right,' said some; 'they are cozening us,' said others, 'and the prisoner all the while is making his escape.' At these words there rose a frightful tumult in the Hall. 'Messieurs,' said an Elector, 'name four of yourselves to guard him.' Four men accordingly were chosen; sent into the neighbouring apartment, where Foulon was. 'But will you judge then?' cried the crowd. 'Messieurs, you see there are two judges wanting.' 'We name M. Bailly and M. Lafayette.' 'But M.

Lafayette is absent; one must either wait for him, or name some other.' 'Well, then, name directly, and do it yourself.'

"At length the Electors agreed to proceed to judgment; Foulon was again brought in. The foremost part of the crowd joined hands, and formed a chain several ranks deep, in the middle of which he was received. At this moment M. Lafayette came in; went and took his place at the board among the electors, and then addressed to the people a discourse, of which the *Ami du Roi* and the Records of the Town-hall, the two authorities we borrow from here, give different reports."

Lafayette's speech, according to both versions, is to the effect that Foulon is guilty: but that he doubtless has accomplices; that he must be taken to the Abbaye prison, and investigated there. "Yes, yes, to prison! Off with him, off!" cried the crowd. The *Deux Amis* add another not insignificant circumstance, that poor Foulon himself, hearing this conclusion of Lafayette's, clapped hands; whereupon the crowd said, "See! they are both in a story!" Our editors continue and conclude:—

"At this moment there rose a great clamour in the square. 'It is the Palais Royal coming,' said one; 'It is the Faubourg Saint Antoine,' said another. Then a well dressed person (*homme bien mis*) advanced towards the board, and said, '*Vouz vous moquez:* what is the use of judging a man who has been judged these thirty years?' At this word, Foulon was clutched; hurled out to the square; and finally tied to the fatal rope, which hung from the *Lanterne* at the corner of the Rue de la Vannerie. The rope was afterwards cut; the head was put on a pike, and paraded,"—with "grass" in the mouth of it, they might have added!—Vol. ii. p. 148.

From the "Revolution de France et de Brabant," Camille Desmoulin's newspaper furnishes numerous extracts, in the earlier volumes; always of a remarkable kind. This *Procureur Général de la Lanterne* has a place of his own in the history of the Revolution; there are not many notabler persons in it than he. A light, harmless creature, as he says of himself; "a man born to write verses," but whom destiny had directed to overthrow bastilles, and go to the guillotine for doing that. How such a man will comport himself in a French Revolution, as he from time to time turns up there, is worth seeing. Of loose, headlong character; a man stuttering in speech; stuttering, infirm, in conduct too, till one huge idea laid hold of him: a man for whom art, fortune, or himself, would never do much, but to whom Nature had been very kind! One meets him always with a sort of forgiveness, almost of underhand love, as for a prodigal son. He has good gifts, and even acquirements: elegant law-scholarship, quick sense, the freest joyful heart: a fellow of endless wit, clearness, soft lambent brilliancy; on any subject you can listen to him, if without approving, yet without yawning. As a writer, in fact, there is nothing French that we have heard of superior or equal to him for these fifty years. Probably some French editor, some day or other, will *sift* that journalistic rubbish and produce out of it, in small neat compass, a "Life and Remains" of this poor Camille. We pick up three light fractions, illustrative of him and of the things he moved in; they relate to the famous Fifth of October, (1789,) when the women rose in insurrection The Palais Royal and Marquis Saint-Huruge have been busy on the King's *veto*, and Lally Tollendall's proposal of an upper house:—

"Was the Palais Royal so far wrong," says Camille, "to cry out against such things? I know that the Palais Royal promenade is strangely miscellaneous; that pickpockets frequently employ the *liberty of the press* there, and many a zealous patriot has lost his handkerchief in the fire of debate. But for all that I must bear honourable testimony to the promenaders in this Lyceum and Stoa. The Palais Royal garden is the focus of patriotism: there do the chosen patriots rendezvous, who have left their hearths and their provinces to witness this magnificent spectacle of the Revolution of 1789, and not to witness without aiding in it. They are Frenchmen; they have an interest in the Constitution, and a right to concur in it. How many Parisians too, instead of going to their Districts, find it shorter to come at once to the Palais Royal. Here you have no need to ask a President if you may speak, and wait two hours till your turn comes. You propose your motion; if it find supporters, they set you on a chair: if you are applauded, you proceed to the redaction: if you are hissed, you go your ways. It is very much the mode the Romans followed; their Forum and our Palais Royal resemble one another."—Vol. ii. p. 414.

Then a few days further on—the celebrated military dinner at Versailles, with the white cockades, black cockades, and "*O Richard! O mon Roi!*" having been transacted:—

"*Paris, Sunday, 4th October*. The king's wife had been so gratified with it, that this *brotherly repast* of Thursday must needs be repeated. It was so on the Saturday, and with aggravations. Our patience was worn out: you may suppose whatever patriot observers there were at Versailles hastened to Paris with the news, or at least sent off despatches containing them. That same day (Saturday evening) all Paris set itself astir. It was a lady, first, who, seeing that her husband was not listened to at his District, came to the bar of the Cafe de Foi, to denounce the anti-national cockades. M. Marat flies to Versailles; returns like lightning; makes a noise like the four blasts of doom, crying to us—Awake, ye Dead! Danton, on his side, sounds the alarm in the *Cordeliers*. On Sunday this immortal Cordeliers' District posts its manifesto; and that very day they would have gone to Versailles, had not M. Crevecœur, their commandant, stood in the way. People seek out their arms however; sally out to the streets in chase of anti-national cockades. The law of reprisals is in force; these cockades are torn off, trampled under foot, with menace of the *Lanterne* in case of relapse. A military gentleman, picking up his cockade, is for fastening it on again; a hundred canes start into the air, saying *veto*. The whole Sunday passes in hunting down the white and the black cockades; in holding council at the Palais Royal, over the Faubourg Saint Antoine, at the end of bridges, on the quais. At the doors of the coffee houses there arise free conferences between the Upper House, of the coats that are within, and the Lower House, of jackets and wool-caps, assembled *extra muros.* It is agreed upon that the audacity of the aristocrats increases rapidly; that Madame Villepatour and the queen's women are distributing enormous white cockades to all comers in the Œil-de-Bœuf; that M. Lecointre, having refused to take one from their hands, has all but been assassinated. It is agreed upon that we have not a moment to lose; that the boat which used to bring us flour from Corbeil, morning and evening, now comes only once in two days:—do they plan to make their attack at the moment when they have kept us for eight-and-forty hours in a fasting state? It is agreed upon," &c.—Vol. iii. p. 63.

We hasten to the catastrophe, which arrives on the morrow. It is related elsewhere, in another leading article:—

"At break of day the women rush towards the Hotel de Ville. All the way, they recruit fresh hands, among their own sex, to march with them; as sailors are recruited at London: there is an active press of women. The Quai de la Ferraille is covered with female crimps. The robust kitchen-maid, the slim mantua-maker, all must go to swell the phalanx; the ancient devotee, tripping to mass in the dawn, sees herself for the first time carried off, and shrieks *help!* whilst more than one of the younger sort secretly is not so sorry at going without mother or mistress to Versailles to pay her respects to the august Assembly. At the same time, for the accuracy of this narrative, I must remark that these women, at least the battalion of them which encamped that night in the Assembly Hall, and had marched under the flag of M. Maillard, had among themselves a Presidentess and Staff; and that every woman, on being borrowed from her mother or husband, was presented to the Presidentess or some of her aids-de-camp, who engaged to watch over her morality, and insure her honour for this day!

"Once arrived on the Place de Grêve, these women piously begin letting down the *Lanterne;* as, in great calamities, you let down the shrine of Saint Genevieve. Next they are for mounting into the Hotel de Ville. The Commandant had been forewarned of this movement: he knew that all insurrections have begun by women, whose maternal bosom the bayonet of the satellites of despotism respects. Four thousand soldiers presented a front bristling with bayonets; kept them back from the step: but behind these women there rose and grew every moment a nucleus of men, armed with pikes, axes, bills; blood is about to flow on the place; the presence of these Sabine women hindered it. The National Guard, which is not purely a machine, as the Minister of War would have the soldier be, makes use of its reason. It discerns that these women, now for Versailles, are going to the root of the mischief. The four thousand Guards, already getting saluted with stones, think it reasonablest to open a passage; and, like waters through a broken dike, the floods of the multitude inundate the Hotel de Ville.

"It is a picture interesting to paint, and one of the greatest in the Revolution, this same army of ten thousand Judiths setting forth to cut off the head of Holofernes; forcing the Hotel de Ville; arming themselves with whatever they can lay hands on; some tying ropes to the cannon-trains, arresting carts, loading them with artillery, with powder and balls for the Versailles National Guard, which is left without ammunition; others driving on the horses, or seated on cannon, holding the redoubtable match; seeking for their generalissimo, not aristocrats with epaulettes, but Conquerors of the Bastille!"—Vol. iii. p. 110.

So far Camille on veto, scarcity, and the Insurrection of Women, in the end of 1789.

We terminate with a scene of a very different complexion, being some three years farther on, that is to say, in *September,* 1792! *Félémhesi,* (anagram for *Méhée Fils,*) in his "Vérité toute entière," a pamphlet really more veracious than most, thus testifies, after a good deal of preambling:—

"I was going to my post about half past two," (Sunday, the 2d of September, tocsins all ringing, and Brunswick just at hand;) "I was passing along the Rue Dauphine; suddenly I hear hisses. I look, I observe four hackney-coaches, coming in a train, escorted by the Fédéré's of the departments.

"Each of these coaches contained four persons: they were individuals" (priests) "arrested in the preceding domiciliary visits. Billaud-Varennes, Procureur-Substitute of the Commune, had just been interrogating them at the Hotel de Ville; and now they were proceeding towards the Abbaye, to be provisionally detained there. A crowd is gathering; the cries and hisses redouble: one of the prisoners, doubtless out of his senses, takes fire at these murmurs, puts his arm over the coach-door, gives one of the Fédéré's a stroke over the head with his cane. The Fédéré, in a rage, draws his sabre, springs on the carriage-steps, and plunges it thrice over into the heart of his aggressor. I saw the blood come out in great jets. 'Kill every one of them; they are scoundrels, aristocrats!' cry the people. The Fédéré's all draw their sabres, and instantly kill the three companions of the one who had just perished. I saw, at this moment, a young man in a white nightgown stretch himself out of that same carriage: his countenance, expressive, but pale and worn, indicated that he was very sick; he had gathered his staggering strength, and, though already wounded, was crying still, '*Grace, grace, pardon!*' but in vain —a mortal stroke united him to the lot of the others.

"This coach, which was the hindmost, now held nothing but corses; it had not stopped during the carnage, which lasted about the space of two minutes. The crowd increases, *crescit eundo;* the yells redouble. The coaches are at the Abbaye. The corpses are hurled into the court; the twelve living prisoners dismount to enter the committee-room. Tw are sacrificed on alighting; ten succeed in entering. The committee had not had time to put the slightest question, when a multitude, armed with pikes, sabres, swords, and bayonets, dashes in; seizes the accused, and kills them. One prisoner, already much wounded, kept hanging by the skirts of a Committee-member, and still struggled against death.

"Three yet remained; one of whom was the Abbé Sicard, teacher of the deaf and dumb. The sabres were already over his head, when Monnot, the watchmaker, flung himself before them, crying, 'Kill me rather, and not this man, who is useful to our country!' These words, uttered with the fire and impetuosity of a generous soul, suspended death. Profiting by this moment of calm, Abbé Sicard and the other two were got conveyed into the back part of the room."

Abbé Sicard, as is well known, survived; and the narrative which he also published exists—sufficient to prove, among other things, that "Félémhesi" had but two eyes, and his own share of sagacity and heart; that he has *mis*-seen, miscounted, and, knowingly or unknowingly, misstated not a little,—as one poor man, in these circumstances, might. Félémhesi continues,—we only inverting his arrangement somewhat:—

"Twelve scoundrels, presided by Maillard, with whom they had probably combined this project beforehand, find themselves 'by chance' among the crowd; and now, being well-known one to another, they unite themselves 'in the name of the sovereign people,' whether it were of their own private audacity, or that they had secretly received superior orders. They lay hold of the prison registers, and turn them over; the turnkeys fall a-trembling; the jailer's wife and the jailer faint; the prison is surrounded by furious men; there is shouting, clamouring: the door is assaulted, like to be forced; when one of the Committee-members presents himself at the outer gate, and begs audience: his signs obtain a moment's silence; the doors open, he advances, gets a chair, mounts on it, and speaks:—'Comrades, friends,' said he, 'you are good patriots; your resentment is just. Open war to the enemies of the common good; neither truce nor mercy; it is a war to the death! I feel like you that they must all perish; and yet, if you are good citizens, you must love justice. There is not one of you but would shudder at the notion of shedding innocent blood.' 'Yes, yes!' reply the people. 'Well, then, I ask of you if, without inquiry or investigation, you fling yourselves like mad tigers on your fellow-men——?' Here the speaker was interrupted by one of the crowd, who, with a bloody sabre in his hand, his eyes glancing with rage, cleaves the press, and refutes him in these terms: 'Tell us, Monsieur le Citoyen, explain to us then, would the *sacres gueux* of Prussians and Austrians, if they were at Paris, investigate for the guilty? Would they not cut right and left, as the Swiss on the Tenth of August did? Well, I am no speaker, I can stuff the ears of no one; but I tell you I have a wife and five children, whom I leave with my section here while I go and fight the enemy: but it is not my bargain that the villains in this prison, whom other villains outside will open the doors to, shall go and kill my wife and children in the meanwhile! I have three boys, who I hope will be usefuller to their country one day than these rascals you want to save. Any way you have but to send them out; we will give them arms, and fight them number for number. Die here or die on the frontiers, I am sure enough to be killed by these villains, but I mean to sell them my life; and, be it I, be it others, the prison shall be purged of these *sacres gueux la*.' 'He is right!' responds the general cry."—And so the frightful "purgation" proceeds.

"At five in the afternoon, Billaud Varennes, Procureur-Substitut, arrives; he had on his sash, and the small puce coat and black wig we are used to see on him: walking over carcasses, he makes a short harangue to the people, and ends thus: 'People, thou art sacrificing thy enemies; thou art in thy duty.' This cannibal speech lends them new animation. The killers blaze up, cry louder than ever for new victims:—how to staunch this new thirst of blood? A voice speaks from beside Billaud; it was Maillard's voice: 'There is nothing more to do here; let us to the *Carmes!*' They run thither: in five minutes more I saw them trailing corpses by the heels. A killer, (I cannot say a man,) in very coarse clothes, had, as it would seem, been specially commissioned to dispatch the Abbé Lenfant; for, apprehensive lest the prey might be missed, he takes water, flings it on the corpses, washes their blood-smeared faces, turns them over, and seems at last to ascertain that the Abbé Lenfant is among them."—Vol. xviii. p. 169.

This is the September massacre, the last scene we can give as a specimen. Thus, in these curious records of the "Histoire Parlementaire," as in some Ezekiel vision become real, does scene after scene disclose itself, now in rose-light, now in sulphurous black, and grow ever more fitful, dream-like,—till the Vendémiaire scene come, and Napoleon blow forth his grape-shot, and Sansculottism be no more!

Touching the political and metaphysical speculations of our two editors, we shall say little. They are of the sort we lamented in Mignet, and generally in Frenchmen of this day—a jingling of formulas; unfruitful as that Kalmuck prayer! Perhaps the strangest-looking particular doctrine we have noticed is this: that the French Revolution was at bottom an attempt to realize Christianity, and fairly put it in action, in our world. For eighteen centuries (it is not denied) men had been doing more or less that way; but they set their shoulder rightly to the wheel, and gave a dead-lift, for the first time *then*. Good M. Roux! and yet the good Roux does mean something by this; and even something true. But a marginal annotator has written on our copy—"For the love of Heaven, Messieurs, *humez vos formules:*" make away with your formulas; take off your facetted spectacles; open your eyes a little and look! There is, indeed, here and there, considerable rumbling of the rotatory calabash, which rattles and rumbles concerning Progress of the Species, *Doc-*

trine du Progrès, Exploitations, le Christ, the *Verbe*, and what not; written in a vein of deep, even of intense seriousness; but profitable, one would think, to no man or woman. In this style M. Roux (for it is he, we understand) painfully composes a preface to each volume, and has even given a whole introductory history of France: we read some seven or eight of his first prefaces, hoping always to get some nourishment; but seldom or never cut him open now. Fighting in that way, behind cover, he is comparatively harmless; merely wasting you so many pence per number: happily the space he takes is small. Whoever wants to form for himself an image of the actual state of French Meditation, and under what surprising shackles a French thinking man of these days finds himself gyved, and mechanized, and reduced to the verge of *zero*, may open M. Roux's Prefaces, and see it as in an expressive summary.

We wish our two French friends all speed in their business; and do again honestly recommend this "Histoire Parlementaire" to any and all of our English friends who take interest in that subject.

MEMOIRS OF THE LIFE OF SCOTT.*

[LONDON AND WESTMINSTER REVIEW, 1838.]

AMERICAN Cooper asserts, in one of his books, that there is "an instinctive tendency in men to look at any man who has become distinguished." True, surely; as all observation and survey of mankind, from China to Peru, from Nebuchadnezzar to Old Hickory, will testify! Why do men crowd towards the improved drop at Newgate, eager to catch a sight? The man about to be hanged is in a distinguished situation. Men crowd to such extent, that Greenacre's is not the only life choked out there. Again, ask of these leathern vehicles, cabriolets, neat-flies, with blue men and women in them, that scour all thoroughfares, Whither so fast? To see dear Mrs. Rigmarole, the distinguished female! Great Mr. Rigmarole, the distinguished male. Or, consider the crowning phenomenon, and summary of modern civilization, a *soirée* of lions. Glittering are the rooms, well-lighted, thronged; bright flows their undulatory flood of blonde gowns and dress-coats, a soft smile dwelling on all faces; for behold there also flow the lions, hovering distinguished: oracles of the age, of one sort or another. Oracles really pleasant to see; whom it is worth while to go and see: look at them, but inquire not of them, depart rather and be thankful. For your lion-*soirée* admits not of speech; there lies the speciality of it. A meeting together of human creatures; and yet (so high has civilization gone) the primary aim of human meeting, that soul might in some articulate utterance unfold itself to soul, can be dispensed with in it. Utterance there is not: nay, there is a certain grinning play of tongue-fence, and make-believe of utterance, considerably worse than none. For which reason it has been suggested, with an eye to sincerity and silence in such lion-*soirées*, Might not each lion be, for example, ticketed, as wine-decanters are? Let him carry, slung round him, in such ornamental manner as seemed good, his silver label with name engraved; you lift his label, and read it, with what farther ocular survey you find useful, and speech is not needed at all. O Fenimore Cooper, it is most true there is "an instinctive tendency in men to look at at any man that has become distinguished;" and, moreover, an instinctive desire in men to become distinguished and be looked at!

For the rest, we will call it a most valuable tendency this; indispensable to mankind. Without it where were star-and-garter, and significance of rank; where were all ambition, money-getting, respectability of gig or no gig; and, in a word, the main impetus by which society moves, the main force by which it hangs together? A tendency, we say, of manifold results: of manifold origin, not ridiculous only, but sublime;—which some incline to deduce from the mere gregarious purblind nature of man, prompting him to run, "as dim-eyed animals do, towards any glittering object, were it but a scoured tankard, and mistake it for a solar luminary," or even, "sheep-like, to run and crowd because many *have* already run!" It is, indeed, curious to consider how men do make the gods that themselves worship. For the most famed man, round whom all the world rapturously huzzahs, and venerates as if his like were not, is the same man whom all the world was wont to jostle into the kennels; not a changed man, but in every fibre of him the same man. Foolish world, what went ye out to see? A tankard scoured bright; and do there not lie, of the self-same pewter, whole barrowfuls of tankards, though by worse fortune all still in the dim state?

And yet, at bottom, it is not merely our gregarious sheep-like quality, but something better, and indeed best; what has been called "the perpetual fact of hero-worship;" our inborn sincere love of great men! Not the gilt farthing, for its own sake, do even fools covet, but the gold guinea which they mistake it for. Veneration of great men is perennial in the nature of man; this, in all times, especially in these, is one of the blessedest facts predicable of him. In all times, even in these seemingly so disobedient times, "it remains a blessed

---

* *Memoirs of the Life of Sir Walter Scott, Baronet.* Vol. i.—vi. Cadell. Edinburgh, 1837.

fact, so cunningly has nature ordered it, *that whatsoever man ought to obey he cannot but obey.* Show the dullest clodpole, show the haughtiest featherhead, that a soul higher than himself is actually here; were his knees stiffened into brass, he must down and worship." So it has been written; and may be cited and repeated till known to all. Understand it well, this of "hero-worship" was the primary creed, and has intrinsically been the secondary and ternary, and will be the ultimate and final creed of mankind; indestructible, changing in shape, but in essence unchangeable; whereon politics, religions, loyalties, and all highest human interests have been and can be built, as on a rock that will endure while man endures. Such is hero-worship; so much lies in that our inborn sincere love of great men!—In favour of which unspeakable benefits of the reality, what can we do but cheerfully pardon the multiplex ineptitudes of the semblance,—cheerfully wish even lion-*soirées*, with labels for their lions or without that improvement, all manner of prosperity? Let hero-worship flourish, say we; and the more and more assiduous chase after gilt farthings while guineas are not yet forthcoming. Herein, at lowest, is proof that guineas exist, that they are believed to exist, and valued. Find great men if you can; if you cannot, still quit not the search; in defect of great men, let there be noted men, men, in such number, to such degree of intensity as the public appetite can tolerate.

Whether Sir Walter Scott was a great man, is still a question with some; but there can be no question with any one that he was a most noted and even notable man. In this generation there was no literary man with such a popularity in any country; there have only been a few with such, taking in all generations and all countries. Nay, it is farther to be admitted that Sir Walter Scott's popularity was of a select sort rather; not a popularity of the populace. His admirers were at one time almost all the intelligent of civilised countries; and to the last, included and do still include a great portion of that sort. Such fortune he had, and has continued to maintain for a space of some twenty or thirty years. So long the observed of all observers; a great man, or only a considerable man; here surely, if ever, is a singularly circumstanced, is a "distinguished" man! In regard to whom, therefore, the "instinctive tendency" on other men's part cannot be wanting. Let men look, where the world has already so long looked. And now, while the new, earnestly expected "Life by his Son-in-law and literary executor" again summons the whole world's attention round him, probably for the last time it will ever be so summoned; and men are in some sort taking leave of a notability, and about to go their way, and commit him to his fortune on the flood of things,—why should not this periodical publication likewise publish its thought about him? Readers of miscellaneous aspect, of unknown quantity and quality, are waiting to hear it done. With small inward vocation, but cheerfully obedient to destiny and necessity, the present reviewer will follow a multitude to do evil or to do no evil; will depend not on the multitude, but on himself. One thing he did decidedly wish; at least to wait till the work were finished: for the six promised volumes, as the world knows, have flowed over into a seventh, which will not for some weeks yet see the light. But the editorial powers, wearied with waiting, have become peremptory; and declare that, finished or not finished, they will have their hands washed of it at this opening of the year. Perhaps it is best. The physiognomy of Scott will not be much altered for us by the seventh volume; the prior six have altered it but little;—as, indeed, a man who has written some two hundred volumes of his own, and lived for thirty years amid the universal speech of friends, must have already left some likeness of himself. Be it as the peremptory editorial powers require.

First, therefore, a word on the "Life" itself. Mr. Lockhart's known powers justify strict requisition in his case. Our verdict in general would be, that he has accomplished the work he schemed for himself in a creditable workmanlike manner. It is true, his notion of what the work was does not seem to have been very elevated. To picture forth the life of Scott according to any rules of art or composition, so that a reader, on adequately examining it, might say to himself, "There is Scott, there is the physiognomy and meaning of Scott's appearance and transit on this earth; such was he by nature, so did the world act on him, so he on the world, with such result and significance for himself and us:" this was by no manner of means Mr. Lockhart's plan. A plan which, it is rashly said, should preside over every biography! It might have been fulfilled with all degrees of perfection from that of the "Odyssey" down to "Thomas Ellwood" or lower. For there is no heroic poem in the world but is at bottom a biography, the life of a man: also, it may be said, there is no life of a man, faithfully recorded, but is a heroic poem of its sort, rhymed or unrhymed. It is a plan one would prefer, did it otherwise suit; which it does not in these days. Seven volumes sell so much dearer than one; are so much easier to write than one. The "Odyssey," for instance, what were the value of the "Odyssey," sold per sheet? One paper of "Pickwick;" or say, the inconsiderable fraction of one. This, in commercial algebra, were the equation: "Odyssey" equal to "Pickwick" divided by an unknown integer.

There is a great discovery still to be made in literature, that of paying literary men by the quantity they *do not* write. Nay, in sober truth, is not this actually the rule in all writing; and, moreover, in all conduct and acting? Not what stands above ground, but what lies unseen *under* it, as the root and subterrene element it sprang from and emblemed forth, determines value. Under all speech that is good for any thing there lies a silence that is better. Silence is deep as eternity; speech is shallow as time. Paradoxical does it seem? Wo for the age, wo for the man, quack-ridden, bespeeched, bespouted, blown about like barren Sahara, to whom this world-old truth were altogether strange!—Such we say is the rule, acted on or not, recognised or not; and he who departs from it, what can he do but spread himself into breadth and length, into superficiality and saleability; and, except as filigree, become comparatively useless? One thinks, had but the hogshead of thin wash, which sours in a week ready for the kennels, been *distilled*, been concentrated! Our dear Fenimore Cooper, whom we started with, might, in that way, have given us one *Natty Leatherstocking*, one melodious synopsis of man and nature in the West, (for it lay in him to do it,) almost as a Saint Pierre did for the islands of the East; and the hundred incoherences, cobbled hastily together by order of Colburn and Company, had slumbered in Chaos, as all incoherences ought if possible to do. Verily this same genius of diffuse-writing, of diffuse-acting, is a Moloch; and souls pass through the fire to him more than enough. Surely if ever discovery was valuable and needful, it were that above indicated, of paying by the work *not* visibly done!—Which needful discovery we will give the whole projecting, railwaying, knowledge-diffusing, march-of-intellect, and otherwise promotive and locomotive societies in the Old and New World, any required length of centuries to make. Once made, such discovery once made, we too will fling cap into the air, and shout *Io Pæan*, the Devil *is* conquered; and in the *mean*while study to think it nothing miraculous that seven biographical volumes are given where one had been better; and that several other things happen, very much as they from of old were known to do, and are like to continue doing.

Mr. Lockhart's aim, we take it, was not that of producing any such highflown work of art as we hint at: or indeed to do much other than to print, intelligibly bound together by order of time, and some requisite intercalary exposition, all such letters, documents, and notices about Scott as he found lying suitable, and as it seemed likely the world would undertake to read. His work, accordingly, is not so much a composition, as what we may call a compilation well done. Neither is this a task of no difficulty; this too is a task that may be performed with extremely various degrees of talent: from the "Life and Correspondence of Hannah More," for instance, up to this "Life of Scott," there is a wide range indeed! Let us take the seven volumes, and be thankful that they are genuine in their kind. Nay, as to that of their being seven and not one, it is right to say that the public so required it. To have done other would have shown little policy in an author. Had Mr. Lockhart laboriously compressed himself, and instead of well-done compilation, brought out the well-done composition in one volume instead of seven, which not many men in England are better qualified to do, there can be no doubt that his readers for the time had been immeasurably fewer. If the praise of magnanimity be denied him, that of prudence must be conceded, which perhaps he values more.

The truth is, the work, done in this manner, too, was good to have: Scott's Biography, if uncomposed, lies printed and indestructible here, in the elementary state, and can at any time be composed, if necessary, by whosoever has call to that. As it is, as it was meant to be, we repeat, the work is vigorously done. Sagacity, decision, candour, diligence, good sense: these qualities are throughout observable. The dates, calculations, statements, we suppose to be accurate; much laborious inquiry, some of it impossible for another man, has been gone into, the results of which are imparted with due brevity. Scott's letters, not interesting generally, yet never absolutely without interest, are copiously given; copiously, but with selection; the answers to them still more select. Narrative, delineation, and at length personal reminiscences, occasionly of much merit, of a certain rough force, sincerity, and picturesqueness, duly intervene. The scattered members of Scott's Life do lie here, and could be disentangled. In a word, this compilation is the work of a manful, clear-seeing, conclusive man, and has been executed with the faculty and combination of faculties the public had a right to expect from the name attached to it.

One thing we hear greatly blamed in Mr. Lockhart: that he has been too communicative, indiscreet, and has recorded much that ought to have lain suppressed. Persons are mentioned, and circumstances, not always of an ornamental sort. It would appear there is far less reticence than was looked for! Various persons, name and surname, have "received pain:" nay, the very hero of the biography is rendered unheroic; unornamental facts of him, and of those he had to do with, being set forth in plain English: hence "personality," "indiscretion," or worse, "sanctities of private life," &c. &c. How delicate, decent is English biography, bless its mealy mouth! A Damocles' sword of *Respectability* hangs for ever over the poor English life-writer, (as it does over poor English life in general,) and reduces him to the verge of paralysis. Thus it has been said, "there are no English lives worth reading except those of Players, who by the nature of the case have bidden Respectability good day." The English biographer has long felt that if in writing his Man's Biography, he wrote down any thing that could by possibility offend any man, he had written wrong. The plain consequence was that, properly speaking, no biography whatever could be produced. The poor biographer, having the fear *not* of God before his eyes, was obliged to retire as it were into vacuum; and write in the most melancholy, straitened manner, with only vacuum for a result. Vain that he wrote, and that we kept reading volume on volume; there was no biography, but some vague ghost of a biography, white, stainless; without feature or substance; *vacuum*, as we say, and wind and shadow,—which indeed the material of it was.

No man lives without jostling and being jostled; in all ways he has to *elbow* himself through the world, giving and receiving offence. His life is a battle, in so far as it is an entity at all. The very oyster, we suppose, comes in collision with oysters: undoubtedly enough it does come in collision with Necessity and Difficulty; and helps itself through, not as a perfect ideal oyster, but as an imperfect real one. Some kind of remorse must be known to the oyster; certain hatreds, certain pusillanimities. But as for man, his conflict is continual with the spirit of contradiction, that is without and within; with the evil spirit, (or call it with the weak, most necessitous, pitiable spirit,) that is in others and in himself. His walk, like all walking, (say the mechanicians,) is a series of *falls*. To paint man's life is to represent these things. Let them be represented, fitly, with dignity and measure; but above all, let them be represented. No tragedy of *Hamlet*, with the part of Hamlet omitted by particular desire! No ghost of a Biography, let the Damocles' sword of Respectability (which after all is but a pasteboard one) threaten as it will! One hopes that the public taste is much mended in this matter! that vacuum-biographies, with a good many other vacuities related to them, are withdrawn or withdrawing into vacuum. Probably it was Mr. Lockhart's feeling of what the great public would approve that led him, open-eyed, into this offence against the small criticising public; we joyfully accept the omen.

Perhaps then, of all the praises copiously bestowed on his work, there is none in reality so creditable to him as this same censure, which has also been pretty copious. It is a censure better than a good many praises. He is found guilty of having said this and that, calculated not to be entirely pleasant to this man and that; in other words, calculated to give him the thing he worked in a living set of features, not leave him vague, in the white beatified ghost condition. Several men, as we hear, cry out, "See, there is something written not entirely pleasant to me! Good friend, it is pity: but who can help it? They that will crowd about bonfires may, sometimes very fairly, get their beards singed; it is the price they pay for such illumination; natural twilight is safe and free to all. For our part, we hope all manner of biographies that are written in England will henceforth be written so. If it is fit that they be written otherwise, then it is still fitter that they be not written at all: to produce not things, but ghosts of things, can never be the duty of man. The biographer has this problem set before him: to delineate a likeness of the earthly pilgrimage of a man. He will compute well what profit is in it, and what disprofit; under which latter head this of offending any of his fellow-creatures will surely not be forgotten. Nay, this may so swell the disprofit side of his account, that many an enterprise of biography, otherwise promising, shall require to be renounced. But once taken up, the rule above all rules is to do *it*, not to do the ghost of it. In speaking of the man and men he has to deal with, he will of course keep all his charities about him, but also all his eyes open. Far be it from him to set down aught *untrue*; nay, not to abstain from, and leave in oblivion, much that is true. But having found a thing or things essential for his subject, and well computed the for and against, he will in very deed set down such thing or things, nothing doubting,—*having*, we may say, the fear of God before his eyes, and no other fear whatever Censure the biographer's prudence; dissent from the computation he made, or agree with it; be all malice of his, be all falsehood, nay, be all offensive avoidable inaccuracy, condemned and consumed; but know that by this plan only, executed as was possible, could the biographer hope to make a biography: and blame him not that he did what it had been the worst fault not to do.

As to the accuracy or error of these statements about the Ballantynes and other persons aggrieved, which are questions much mooted at present in some places, we know nothing at all. If they are inaccurate, let them be corrected; if the inaccuracy was avoidable, let the author bear rebuke and punishment for it. We can only say, these things carry no look of inaccuracy on the face of them; neither is anywhere the smallest trace of ill-will or unjust feeling discernible. Decidedly the probabilities are, and till better evidence arise, the fair conclusion is, that the matter stands very much as it ought to do. Let the clatter of censure, therefore, propagate itself as far as it can. For Mr. Lockhart it virtually amounts to this very considerable praise, that, standing full in the face of the public, he has set at naught, and been among the first to do it, a public piece of cant; one of the commonest we have, and closely allied to many others of the fellest sort, as smooth as it looks.

The other censure, of Scott being made unheroic, springs from the same stem; and is, perhaps, a still more wonderful flower of it. Your true hero must have no features, but be white, stainless, an impersonal ghost-hero! But connected with this, there is a hypothesis now current, due probably to some man of name, for its own force would not carry it far; That Mr. Lockhart at heart has a dislike to Scott, and has done his best in an underhand treacherous manner to dishero him! Such hypothesis is actually current: he that has ears may hear it now and then. On which astonishing hypothesis, if a word must be said, it can only be an apology for silence, "that there are things at which one stands struck silent, as at first sight of the Infinite." For if Mr. Lockhart is fairly chargeable with any radical defect, if on any side his insight entirely fails him, it seems even to be in this, that Scott is altogether lovely to him; that Scott's greatness spreads out for him on all hands beyond reach of eye; that his very faults become beautiful, his vulgar worldlinesses are solid prudences, proprieties; and of his worth there is no measure. Does not the patient biographer dwell on his *Abbots*, *Pirates*, and hasty theatrical scene-paintings; affectionately analyzing them, as if they were Raphael pictures, time-defying *Hamlets, Othellos?* The novel-manufactory, with his £15,000 a year, is sacred to him as creation of a genius, which carries the noble victor up to heaven. Scott is to Lockhart the unparalleled of the time; an object spreading out before him like a sea without shore. Of *that* astonishing hypothesis, let expressive silence be the only answer.

And so in sum, with regard to "Lockhart's

Life of Scott," readers that believe in us shall read it with the feeling that a man of talent, decision, and insight wrote it; wrote it in seven volumes, not in one, because the public would pay for it better in that state; but wrote it with courage, with frankness, sincerity; on the whole, in a very readable, recommendable manner, as things go. Whosoever needs it can purchase it, or the loan of it, with assurance more than usual that he has ware for his money. And now enough of the written life; we will glance a little at the man and his acted life.

Into the question whether Scott was a great man or not, we do not propose to enter deeply. It is, as too usual, a question about words. There can be no doubt but many men have been named and printed *great* who were vastly smaller than he: as little doubt moreover that of the specially *good* a very large portion, according to any genuine standard of man's worth, were worthless in comparison to him. He for whom Scott is great may most innocently name him so; may with advantage admire his great qualities, and ought with sincere heart to emulate them. At the same time, it is good that there be a certain degree of precision in our epithets. It is good to understand, for one thing, that no popularity, and open-mouthed wonder of all the world, continued even for a long series of years, can make a man great. Such popularity is a remarkable fortune; indicates a great adaptation of the man to his element of circumstances; but may or may not indicate any thing great in the man. To our imagination, as above hinted, there is a certain apotheosis in it; but in the reality no apotheosis at all. Popularity is as a blaze of illumination, or alas, of conflagration kindled round a man; *showing* what is in him; not putting the smallest item more into him; often abstracting much from him; conflagrating the poor man himself into ashes and *caput mortuum!* And then, by the nature of it, such popularity is transient; your "series of years," quite unexpectedly, sometimes almost all on a sudden, terminates! For the stupidity of men, especially of men congregated in masses round any object, is extreme. What illuminations and conflagrations have kindled themselves, as if new heavenly suns had risen, which proved only to be tar-barrels, and terrestrial locks of straw! Profane princesses cried out, "One God, one Farinelli!"—and whither now have they and Farinelli danced? In literature, too, there have been seen popularities greater even than Scott's, and nothing perennial in the interior of them. Lope de Vega, whom all the world swore by, and made a proverb of; who could make an acceptable five-act tragedy in almost as many hours; the greatest of all popularities past or present, and perhaps one of the greatest men that ever ranked among popularities: Lope himself, so radiant, far-shining, has not proved to be a sun or star of the firmament; but is as good as lost and gone out, or plays at best, in the eyes of some few, as a vague aurora-borealis, and brilliant ineffectuality. The great man of Spain sat obscure at the time, all dark and poor, a maimed soldier; writing his Don Quixote in prison. And Lope's fate withal was sad, his popularity perhaps a curse to him; for in this man there was something ethereal too, a divine particle traceable in few other popular men; and such far shining diffusion of himself, though all the world swore by it, would do nothing for the true life of him even while he lived: he had to creep into a convent, into a monk's cowl, and learn, with infinite sorrow, that his blessedness had lain elsewhere; that when a man's life feels itself to be sick and an error, no voting of by-standers can make it well and a truth again. Or coming down to our own times, was not August Kotzebue popular? Kotzebue, not so many years since, saw himself, if rumour and hand-clapping could be credited, the greatest man going; saw visibly his Thoughts, dressed out in plush and pasteboard, permeating and perambulating civilized Europe; the most iron visages weeping with him, in all theatres from Cadiz to Kamschatka; his own "astonishing genius," meanwhile, producing two tragedies or so per month: he on the whole blazed high enough: he too has gone out into Night and *Orcus*, and already is not. We will omit this of popularity altogether, and account it as making simply nothing towards Scott's greatness or non-greatness, as an accident, not a quality.

Shorn of this falsifying *nimbus*, and reduced to his own natural dimensions, there remains the reality, Walter Scott, and what we can find in him: to be accounted great, or not great, according to the dialects of men. Friends to precision of epithet will probably deny his title to the name "great." It seems to us there goes other stuff to the making of great men than can be detected here. One knows not what idea worthy of the name of great, what purpose, instinct, or tendency, that could be called great, Scott ever was inspired with. His life was worldly; his ambitions were worldly. There is nothing spiritual in him; all is economical, material, of the earth earthy. A love of picturesque, of beautiful, vigorous, and graceful things; a genuine love, yet not more genuine than has dwelt in hundreds of men named minor poets: this is the highest quality to be discerned in him. His power of representing these things too, his poetic power, like his moral power, was a genius *in extenso*, as we may say, not *in intenso*. In action, in speculation, *broad* as he was, he rose nowhere high; productive without measure as to quantity, in quality he for the most part transcended but a little way the region of commonplace. It has been said, "no man has written as many volumes with so few sentences that can be quoted." Winged words were not his vocation; nothing urged him that way: the great mystery of existence was not great to him; did not drive him into rocky solitudes to wrestle with it for an answer, to be answered or to perish. He had nothing of the martyr; into no "dark region to slay monsters for us," did he, either led or driven, venture down: his conquests were for his own behoof mainly, conquests over common market labour, and reckonable in good metallic coin of the realm. The thing he had faith in, except power, power of what sort soever, and even of the rudest sort, would be difficult to point out. One sees not that he believed in any thing; nay, he did not even disbelieve; but quietly acquiesced, and made himself at home in a world of conventionalities: the false, the semi-false, and the true were alike true in this, that they were there, and had power in their hands more or less. It was well to feel so; and yet not well! We find it written, "Wo to them that are at ease in Zion;" but surely it is a double wo to them that are at ease in Babel, in Domdaniel. On the other hand he wrote many volumes, amusing many thousands of men. Shall we call this great? It seems to us there dwells and struggles another sort of spirit in the inward parts of great men!

Brother Ringletub, the missionary, inquired of Ram-Dass, a Hindoo man-god, who had set up for godhood lately, What he meant to do, then, with the sins of mankind? To which Ram-Dass at once answered, he had *fire enough in his belly* to burn up all the sins in the world. Ram-Dass was right so far, and had a spice of sense in him; for surely it is the test of every divine man this same, and without it he is not divine or great,—that he *have* fire in him to burn up somewhat of the sins of the world, of the miseries and errors of the world: why else is he there? Far be it from us to say that a great man must needs, with benevolence prepense, become a "friend of humanity;" nay, that such professional self-conscious friends of humanity are not the fatalest kind of persons to be met with in our day. All greatness is unconscious, or it is little and naught. And yet a great man without *such* fire in him, burning dim or developed as a divine behest in his heart of hearts, never resting till it be fulfilled, were a solecism in nature. A great man is ever, as the Transcendentalists speak, possessed with an *idea*. Napoleon himself, not the superfinest of great men, and ballasted sufficiently with prudences and egoisms, had nevertheless, as is clear enough, an idea to start with: the idea that Democracy was the Cause of Man, the right and infinite Cause. Accordingly he made himself "the armed soldier of Democracy;" and did vindicate it in a rather great manner. Nay, to the very last, he had a kind of idea, that, namely, of "*la carrière ouverte aux talens*, the tools to him that can handle them;" really one of the best ideas yet promulgated on that matter, or rather the one true central idea, towards which all the others, if they tend anywhither, must tend. Unhappily it was in the military province only that Napoleon could realize this idea of his, being forced to fight for himself the while: before he got it tried to any extent in the civil province of things, his head by much victory grew light, (no head can stand more than its quantity;) and he lost head, as they say, and became a selfish ambitionist and quack, and was hurled out, leaving his idea to be realized, in the civil province of things, by others! Thus was Napoleon; thus are all great men: children of the idea; or, in Ram-Dass's phraseology, furnished with fire to burn up the miseries of men. Conscious or unconscious, latent or unfolded, there is small vestige of any such fire being extant in the inner-man of Scott.

Yet on the other hand, the surliest critic must allow that Scott was a genuine man, which itself is a great matter. No affectation, fantasticality, or distortion, dwelt in him; no shadow of cant. Nay, withal, was he not a right brave and strong man, according to his kind? What a load of toil, what a measure of felicity, he quietly bore along with him; with what quiet strength he both worked on this earth, and enjoyed in it; invincible to evil fortune and to good! A most composed invincible man; in difficulty and distress, knowing no discouragement, Samson-like, carrying off on his strong Samson-shoulders the gates that would imprison him; in danger and menace, laughing at the whisper of fear. And then, with such a sunny current of true humour and humanity, a free joyful sympathy with so many things; what of fire he had, all lying so beautifully *latent*, as radical latent heat, as fruitful internal warmth of life; a most robust, healthy man! The truth is, our best definition of Scott were perhaps even this, that he was, if no great man, then something much pleasanter to be, a robust, thoroughly healthy, and withal, very prosperous and victorious man. An eminently well-conditioned man, healthy in body, healthy in soul; we will call him one of the *healthiest* of men. Neither is this a small matter: health is a great matter, both to the possessor of it and to others. On the whole, that humourist in the Moral Essay was not so far out, who determined on honouring health only; and so instead of humbling himself to the highborn, to the rich and well-dressed, insisted on doffing hat to the healthy: coronetted carriages with pale faces in them passed by as failures miserable and lamentable; trucks with ruddy-cheeked strength dragging at them were greeted as successful and venerable. For does not health mean harmony, the synonym of all that is true, justly-ordered, good; is it not, in some sense, the net-total, as shown by experiment, of whatever worth is in us? The healthy man is a most meritorious product of nature, so far as he goes. A healthy body is good; but a soul in right health,—it is the thing beyond all others to be prayed for; the blessedest thing this earth receives of Heaven. Without artificial medicament of philosophy, or tight-lacing of creeds, (always very questionable,) the healthy soul discerns what is good, and adheres to it, and retains it; discerns what is bad, and spontaneously casts it off. An instinct from nature herself, like that which guides the wild animals of the forest to their food, shows him what he shall do, what he shall abstain from. The false and foreign will not adhere to him; cant and all fantastic, diseased incrustations are impossible—as Walker the *Original*, in such eminence of health was *he* for his part, *could* not by much abstinence from soap and water, attain to a dirty face! This thing thou canst work with and profit by, this thing is substantial and worthy; that other thing thou canst not work with, it is trivial and inapt: so speaks unerringly the inward monition of the man's whole nature. No need of logic to prove the most argumentative absurdity absurd; as Goethe says of himself, "all this ran down from me like water from a man in wax-cloth dress." Blessed is the healthy nature; it is the coherent, sweetly co-operative, not incoherent, self-distracting, self-destructive one! In the harmonious adjustment and play of all the faculties, the just balance of oneself gives a just feeling towards all men and all things. Glad light from within radiates outwards, and enlightens and embellishes.

Now all this can be predicated of Walter Scott, and of no British literary man that we remember in these days, to any such extent,—if it be not perhaps of one, the most opposite imaginable to Scott, but his equal in this quality and what holds of it: William Cobbett! Nay, there are other similarities, widely different as they two look; nor be the comparison disparaging to Scott: for Cobbett also, as the pattern John Bull of his century, strong as the rhinoceros, and with singular humanities and genialities shining through his thick skin, is a most brave phenomenon. So bounteous was Nature to us; in the sickliest of recorded ages, when British literature lay all puking and sprawling in Werterism, Byronism, and other sentimentalism, tearful or spasmodic, (fruit of internal *wind*,) Nature was kind enough to send us two healthy Men, of whom she might still say, not without pride, "These also were made in England; such limbs I still make there!" It is one of the cheerfullest sights, let the question of its greatness be settled as you will. A healthy nature may or may not be great; but there is no great nature that is not healthy.—Or, on the whole, might we not say, Scott, in the new vesture of the nineteenth century, was intrinsically very much the old fighting Borderer of prior centuries; the kind of man Nature did of old make in that birthland of his? In the saddle, with the foray-spear, he would have acquitted himself as he did at the desk with his pen. One fancies how in stout *Beardie* of Harden's time, he could have played Beardie's part; and *been* the stalwart buff-belted *terræ filius* he in this late time could only delight to draw. The same stout self-help was in him; the same oak and triple brass round his heart. He too could have fought at Redswire, cracking crowns with the fiercest, if that had been the task; could have harried cattle in Tynedale, repaying injury with compound interest; a right sufficient captain of men. A man without qualms or fantasticalities; a hard-headed, sound-hearted man, of joyous robust temper, looking to the main chance, and fighting direct thitherward: *valde stalwartus homo!*—How much in that case had slumbered in him, and passed away without sign. But indeed, who knows how much slumbers in many men. Perhaps our greatest poets are the *mute* Miltons; the vocal are those whom by happy accident we lay hold of, one here, one there, as it chances, and *make* vocal. It is even a question, whether, had not want, discomfort, and distress-warrants been busy at Stratford-on-Avon, Shakspeare himself had not lived killing calves or combing wool! Had the Edial Boarding-school turned out well, we had never heard of Samuel Johnson; Samuel Johnson had been a fat schoolmaster and dogmatic gerundgrinder, and never know that he was more. Nature is rich: those two eggs thou art eating carelessly to breakfast, could they not have been hatched into a pair of fowls, and have covered the whole world with poultry?

But it was not harrying of cattle in Tynedale, or cracking of crowns at Redswire, that this stout Border chief was appointed to perform. Far other work. To be the song-singer and pleasant tale-teller to Britain and Europe, in the beginning of the artificial nineteenth century; here, and not there, lay his business. Beardie of Harden would have found it very amazing. How he shapes himself to this new element; how he helps himself along in it, makes it too do for him, lives sound and victorious in it, and leads over the marches such a spoil as all the cattle-droves the Hardens ever took were poor in comparison to: this is the history of the life and achievements of *our* Sir Walter Scott, Baronet;—whereat we are now to glance for a little! It is a thing remarkable; a thing substantial; of joyful, victorious sort; not unworthy to be glanced at. Withal, however, a glance here and there will suffice. Our limits are narrow; the thing, were it never so victorious, is not of the sublime sort, nor extremely edifying; there is nothing in it to censure vehemently, nor love vehemently: there is more to wonder at than admire; and the whole secret is not an abstruse one.

Till towards the age of thirty, Scott's life has nothing in it decisively pointing towards literature, or indeed towards distinction of any kind; he is wedded, settled, and has gone through all his preliminary steps, without symptoms of renown as yet. It is the life of every other Edinburgh youth of his station and time. Fortunate we must name it, in many ways. Parents in easy or wealthy circumstances, yet unencumbered with the cares and perversions of aristocracy: nothing eminent in place, in faculty, or culture, yet nothing deficient; all around is methodic regulation, prudence, prosperity, kind-heartedness; an element of warmth and light of affection, industry, and burgherly comfort, heightened into elegance; in which the young heart can wholesomely grow. A vigorous health seems to have been given by Nature; yet, as if Nature had said withal, "Let it be a health to express itself by mind, not by body," a lameness is added in childhood; the brave little boy, instead of romping and bickering, must learn to think; or at lowest, what is a great matter, to sit still. No rackets and trundling-hoops for this young Walter; but ballads, history-books, and a world of legendary stuff, which his mother and those near him are copiously able to furnish. Disease, which is but superficial, and issues in outward lameness, does not cloud the young existence, rather forwards it towards the expansion it is fitted for. The miserable disease had been one of the internal nobler parts, marring the general organization; under which no Walter Scott could have been forwarded, or with all his other endowments could have been producible or possible. "Nature gives healthy children much: how much! Wise education is a wise unfolding of this; often it unfolds itself better of its own accord."

Add one other circumstance: the place where; namely, Presbyterian Scotland. The influences of this are felt incessantly, they stream in at every pore. "There is a country accent," says La Rochefoucault, "not in speech only, but in thought, conduct, character, and manner of existing, which never forsakes a man." Scott, we believe, was all his days an Episcopalean Dissenter in Scotland; but that makes little to the matter. Nobody who knows Scotland and Scott can doubt but Presbyterianism, too, had a vast share in the forming of him. A country where the entire people is, or even once has been, laid hold of, filled to the heart with an infinite religious idea, has "made a step from which it cannot retrograde." Thought, conscience, the sense that man is denizen of a universe, creature of an eternity, has penetrated to the remotest cottage, to the simplest heart. Beautiful and awful, the feeling of a heavenly behest, of duty god-commanded, overcanopies all life. There is an inspiration in such a people: one may say in a more special sense, "the inspiration of the Almighty giveth them understanding." Honour to all the brave and true; everlasting honour to brave old Knox, one of the truest of the true! That, in the moment while he and his cause, amid civil broils, in convulsion and confusion, were still but struggling for life, he sent the schoolmaster forth to all corners, and said, "Let the people be taught:" this is but one, and indeed an inevitable and comparatively inconsiderable item in his great message to men. His message, in its true compass, was, "Let men know that they are men; created by God, responsible to God; who work in any meanest moment of time what will last through eternity." It is verily a great message. Not ploughing and hammering machines, not patent digesters (never so ornamental) to digest the produce of these: no, in no wise; born slaves neither of their fellowmen, nor of their own appetites; but men! This great message Knox did deliver, with a man's voice and strength; and found a people to believe him.

Of such an achievement, we say, were it to be made once only, the results are immense. Thought, in such a country, may change its form, but cannot go out; the country has attained *majority;* thought, and a certain spiritual manhood, ready for all work that man can do, endures there. It may take many forms: the form of hard-fisted, money-getting industry, as in the vulgar Scotchman, in the vulgar New Englander; but as compact developed force and alertness of faculty, it is still there; it may utter itself, one day, as the colossal skepticism of a Hume, (beneficent this too, though painful, wrestling, Titan-like, through doubt and inquiry towards new belief;) and again, some better day, it may utter itself as the inspired melody of a Burns: in a word, it is and continues in the voice and the work of a nation of hardy, endeavouring, considering men, with whatever that may bear in it, or unfold from it. The Scotch national character originates in many circumstances; first of all, in the Saxon stuff there was to work on; but next, and beyond all else except that, in the Presbyterian Gospel of John Knox. It seems a good national character; and, on some sides, not so good. Let Scott thank John Knox, for he owed him much, little as he dreamed of debt in that quarter! No Scotchman of his time was more entirely Scotch than Walter Scott: the good and the not so good, which all Scotchmen inherit, ran through every fibre of him.

Scott's childhood, school-days, college-days, are pleasant to read of, though they differ not from those of others in his place and time. The memory of him may probably enough last till this record of them become far more curious than it now is. "So lived an Edinburgh Writer to the Signet's son in the end of the eighteenth century," may some future Scotch novelist say to himself in the end of the twenty-first! The following little fragment of infancy is all we can extract. It is from an autobiography which he had begun, which one cannot but regret he did not finish. Scott's best qualities never shone out more freely than when he went upon anecdote and reminiscence. Such a master of narrative and of himself could have done personal narrative well. Here, if any where, his knowledge was complete, and all his humour and good-humour had free scope:

"An odd incident is worth recording. It seems my mother had sent a maid to take charge of me, at this farm of Sandy-Knowe, that I might be no inconvenience to the family. But the damsel sent on that important mission had left her heart behind her, in the keeping of some wild fellow, it is likely, who had done and said more to her than he was like to make good. She became extremely desirous to return to Edinburgh; and, as my mother made a point of her remaining where she was, she contracted a sort of hatred at poor me, as the cause of her being detained at Sandy-Knowe. This rose, I suppose, to a sort of delirious affection, for she confessed to old Alison Wilson, the housekeeper, that she had carried me up to the craigs under a strong temptation of the Devil to cut my throat with her scissors, and bury me in the moss. Alison instantly took possession of my person, and took care that her confidant should not be subject to any further temptation, at least so far as I was concerned. She was dismissed, of course, and I have heard afterwards became a lunatic.

"It is here, at Sandy-Knowe, in the residence of my paternal grandfather, already mentioned, that I have the first consciousness of existence; and I recollect distinctly that my situation and appearance were a little whimsical. Among the odd remedies recurred to, to aid my lameness, some one had recommended that so often as a sheep was killed for the use of the family, I should be stripped, and swathed up in the skin warm as it was flayed from the carcass of the animal. In this Tartar-like habiliment I well remember lying upon the floor of the little parlour in the farm-house, while my grandfather, a venerable old man with white hair, used every excitement to make me try to crawl. I also distinctly remember the late Sir George M'Dougal of Mackerstown, father of the present Sir Henry Hay M'Dougal, joining in the attempt. He was, God knows how, a relation of ours; and I still recollect him in his old-fashioned military habit, (he had been Colonel of the Greys,) with a small cocked-hat deeply laced, an embroidered scarlet waistcoat, and a light-coloured coat, with milk-white locks tied in a military fashion, kneeling on the ground before me, and dragging his watch along the carpet to induce me to follow it. The benevolent old soldier, and the infant wrapped in his sheep-skin, would have afforded an odd group to uninterested spectators. This must have happened about my third year, (1774,) for Sir George M'Dougal and my grandfather both died shortly after that period. —Vol. i. pp. 15—17.

We will glance next into the "*Liddesdale raids.*" Scott has grown up to be a brisk-hearted jovial young man and advocate: in vacation time he makes excursions to the Highlands, to the Border Cheviots and Northumberland; rides free and far, on his stout galloway, through bog and brake, over the dim moory debatable land,—over Flodden and other fields and places, where, though he yet knew it not, his work lay. No land, however dim and moory, but either has had or will have its poet, and so become not unknown in song. Liddesdale, which was once as prosaic as most dales, having now attained illustration, let us glance thither-ward: Liddesdale too is on this ancient Earth of ours under this eternal Sky; and gives and takes, in the most incalculable manner, with the Universe at large! Scott's experiences there are rather of the rustic Arcadian sort; the element of whiskey not wanting. We should premise that here and there a feature has perhaps been aggravated for effects' sake:

"During seven successive years," writes Mr. Lockhart, (for the autobiography has long since left us,) "Scott made a *raid*, as he called it, into Liddesdale with Mr. Shortreed, sheriff-substitute of Roxburgh, for his guide; exploring every rivulet to its source, and every ruined *peel* from foundation to battlement. 'At this time no wheel carriage had ever been seen in the district—the first, indeed, was a gig, driven by Scott himself for a part of his way, when on the last of these seven excursions. There was no inn or public-house of any kind in the whole valley; the travellers passed from the shepherd's hut to the minister's manse, and again from the cheerful hospitality of the manse to the rough and jolly welcome of the homestead: gathering, wherever they went, songs and tunes, and occasionally more tangible relics of antiquity—even such a 'rowth of auld knicknackets' as Burns ascribes to Captain Grose. To these rambles Scott owed much of the materials of his 'Minstrelsy of the Scottish Border;' and not less of that intimate acquaintance with the living manners of these unsophisticated regions, which constitutes the chief charm of one of the most charming of his prose works. But how soon he had any definite object before him in his researches, seems very doubtful. 'He was *makin' himsell* a' the time,' said Mr. Shortreed; 'but he didna ken maybe what he was about till years had passed: at first he thought o' little, I dare say, but the queerness and the fun.'

"'In those days,' says the Memorandum before me, 'advocates were not so plenty—at least about Liddesdale;' and the worthy Sheriff-substitute goes on to describe the sort of bustle, not unmixed with alarm, produced at the first farm-house they visited, (Willie Elliot's at Millburnholm,) when the honest man was informed of the quality of one of his guests. When they dismounted, accordingly, he received Mr. Scott with great ceremony, and insisted upon himself leading his horse to the stable. Shortreed accompanied Willie, however, and the latter, after taking a deliberate peep at Scott, 'out by the edge of the door cheek,' whispered, 'Weel, Robin, I say, de'il hae me if I's be a bit feared for him now; he's just a chield like ourselves, I think.' Half-a-dozen dogs of all degrees had already gathered round the 'advocate,' and his way of returning their compliments had set Willie Elliot at once at his ease.

"According to Mr. Shortreed, this good man of Millburnholm was the great original of Dandie Dinmont." * * "They dined at Millburnholm; and, after having lingered over Willie Elliot's punch-bowl, until, in Mr. Shortreed's phrase, they were 'half-glowrin,' mounted their steeds again, and proceeded to Dr. Elliot's at Cleughhead where ('for,' says my Memorandum, 'folk were na very nice in those days,') the two travellers slept in one and the same bed—as, indeed, seems to have been the case with them throughout most of their excursions in this primitive district. Dr. Elliot (a clergyman) had already a large MS. collection of the ballads Scott was in quest of." * * * "Next morning they seem to have ridden a long way for the purpose of visiting one 'auld Thomas o' Tuzzilehope,' another Elliot, I suppose, who was celebrated for his skill on the Border pipe, and in particular for being in possession of the real *lill** of *Dick o' the Cow.* Before starting, that is, at six o'clock, the ballad hunters had, 'just to lay the stomach, a devilled duck or twae, and some *London* porter.' Auld Thomas found them, nevertheless, well disposed for 'breakfast' on their arrival at Tuzzilehope; and this being over, he delighted them with one of the most hideous and unearthly of all specimens of 'riding music,' and, moreover, with considerable libations of whisky-punch, manufactured in a certain wooden vessel, resembling a very small milk-pail, which he called 'Wisdom,' because it 'made' only a few spoonfuls of spirits—though he had the art of replenishing it so adroitly, that it had been celebrated for fifty years as more fatal to sobriety than any bowl in the parish. Having done due honour to 'Wisdom,' they again mounted, and proceeded

* Loud tune: German. *lullen.*

over moss and moor to some other equally hospitable master of the pipe. 'Ah me,' says Shortreed, 'sic an endless fund o' humour and drollery as he then had wi' him! Never ten yards but we were either laughing or roaring and singing. Wherever we stopped, how brawlie he suited himsell to every body! He aye did as the lave did; never made himsell the great man, or took ony airs in the company. I've seen him in a' moods in these jaunts, grave and gay, daft and serious, sober and drunk—(this, however, even in our wildest rambles, was rare)—but, drunk or sober, he was aye the gentleman. He lookit excessively heavy and stupid when he was *fou*, but he was never out o' gude-humour.'"

These are questionable doings, questionably narrated; but what shall we say of the following, wherein the element of whisky plays an extremely prominent part? We will say that it *is* questionable, and not exemplary, whisky mounting clearly beyond its level; that indeed charity hopes and conjectures, here may be some aggravating of features for effect's sake!

"On reaching, one evening, some *Charlies-hope* or other (I forget the name) among those wildernesses, they found a kindly reception, as usual; but, to their agreeable surprise after some days of hard living, a measured and orderly hospitality as respected liquor. Soon after supper, at which a bottle of elderberry wine alone had been produced, a young student of divinity, who happened to be in the house, was called upon to take the 'big ha' Bible,' in the good old fashion of 'Burns's Saturday Night;' and some progress had been already made in the service, when the good man of the farm, whose 'tendency,' as Mr. Mitchell says, 'was soporific,' scandalized his wife and the dominie by starting suddenly from his knees, and, rubbing his eyes, with a stentorian exclamation of 'By ——, here's the keg at last!' and in tumbled, as he spoke the word, a couple of sturdy herdsmen, whom, on hearing a day before of the advocate's approaching visit, he had despatched to a certain smuggler's haunt, at some considerable distance, in quest of a supply of *run* brandy from the Solway Frith. The pious 'exercise' of the household was hopelessly interrupted. With a thousand apologies for his hitherto shabby entertainment, this jolly Elliot, or Armstrong, had the welcome *keg* mounted on the table without a moment's delay, and gentle and simple, not forgetting the dominie, continued carousing about it until daylight streamed in upon the party. Sir Walter Scott seldom failed, when I saw him in company with his Liddesdale companion, to mimic with infinite humour the sudden outburst of his old host on hearing the clatter of horses' feet, which he knew to indicate the arrival of the keg—the consternation of the dame—and the rueful despair with which the young clergyman closed the book."—Vol. i. pp. 195—199.

From which Liddesdale *raids*, which we here, like the young clergyman, close not without a certain rueful despair, let the reader draw what nourishment he can. They evince satisfactorily, though in a rude manner, that in those days young advocates, and Scott, like the rest of them, were *alive* and alert,—whisky sometimes preponderating. But let us now fancy that the jovial young advocate has pleaded his first cause; has served in yeomanry drills; been wedded, been promoted sheriff, without romance in either case; dabbling a little the while, under guidance of Monk Lewis, in translations from the German, in translation of "Goethe's Götz with the Iron Hand;"—and we have arrived at the threshold of the "Minstrelsy of the Scottish Border," and the opening of a new century.

Hitherto, therefore, there has been made out, by nature and circumstance working together, nothing unusually remarkable, yet still something very valuable; a stout effectual man of thirty, full of broad sagacity and good humour, with faculties in him fit for any burden of business, hospitality, and duty, legal or civic:—with what other faculties in him no one could yet say. As indeed, who, after life-long inspection, can say what is in any man? The uttered part of a man's life, let us always repeat, bears to the unuttered, unconscious part a small unknown proportion; he himself never knows it, much less do others. Give him room, give him *impulse;* he reaches down to the infinite with that so straitly-imprisoned soul of his; and *can* do miracles if need be! It is one of the comfortablest truths that great men abound, though in the unknown state. Nay as above hinted, our greatest, being also by nature our *quietest*, are perhaps those that remain unknown! Philosopher Fichte took comfort in this belief, when from all pulpits and editorial desks, and publications, periodical and stationary, he could hear nothing but the infinite chattering and twittering of commonplace become ambitious; and in the infinite stir of motion nowhither, and of din which should have been silence, all seemed churned into one tempestuous yesty froth, and the stern Fichte almost desired "taxes on knowledge" to allay it a little;—he comforted himself, we say, by the unshaken belief that Thought did still exist in Germany; that thinking men, each in his own corner, were verily doing their work, though in a silent latent manner.* Walter Scott, as a latent Walter, had never amused all men for a score of years in the course of centuries and eternities, or gained and lost, say a hundred thousand pounds stirling by literature; but he might have been a happy and by no means a useless,—nay, who knows at bottom whether not a still usefuller Walter! However that was not his fortune. The Genius of rather a singular age,—an age at once destitute of faith and terrified at skepticism, with little knowledge of its whereabout, with many sorrows to bear or front, and on the whole with a life to lead in these new circumstances,—had said to himself: What man shall be the temporary comforter, or were it but the spiritual comfit-maker, of this my poor singular age, to solace its dead tedium and manifold sorrows a little? So had the Genius said, looking over all the world, what man? and found him walking the dusty outer parliament-house of Edinburgh,

*Fichte, *Ueber das Wesen des Gelehrten.*

with his advocate-gown on his back; and exclaimed, That is he!

The "Minstrelsy of the Scottish Border" proved to be a well, from which flowed one of the broadest rivers. Metrical romances, (which in due time pass into prose romances;) the old life of men resuscitated for us; it is a mighty word! Not as dead tradition, but as a palpable presence, the past stood before us. There they were, the rugged old fighting men; in their doughty simplicity and strength, with their heartiness, their healthiness, their stout self-help, in their iron basnets, leather jerkins, jack-boots, in their quaintness of manner and costume; there as they looked and lived; it was like a new discovered continent in literature; for the new century, a bright El Dorado,—or else some fat beatific land of Cockaigne, and Paradise of Donothings. To the opening nineteenth century, it is languor and paralysis; nothing could have been welcomer. Most unexpected, most refreshing, and exhilarating; behold our new El Dorado; our fat beatific Lubberland, where one can enjoy and do nothing! It was the time for such a new literature; and this Walter Scott was the man for it. The *Lays*, the *Marmions*, the *Ladys* and *Lords* of Lake and Isles, followed in quick succession, with ever-widening profit and praise. How many thousands of guineas were paid down for each new Lay; how many thousands of copies (fifty and more sometimes) were printed off then and subsequently; what complimenting, reviewing, renown, and apotheosis there was; all is recorded in these seven volumes, which will be valuable in literary statistics. It is a history, brilliant, remarkable; the outlines of which are known to all. The reader shall recall it, or conceive it. No blaze in his fancy is likely to mount higher than the reality did.

At this middle period of his life, therefore, Scott, enriched with copyrights, with new official incomes and promotions, rich in money, rich in repute, presents himself as a man in the full career of success. "Health, wealth, and wit to guide them," (as his vernacular proverb says,) all these three are his. The field is open for him, and victory there: his own faculty, his own self, unshackled, victoriously unfolds itself,—the highest blessedness that can befall a man. Wide circle of friends, personal loving admirers: warmth of domestic joys, vouchsafed to all that can true-heartedly nestle down among them; light of radiance and renown given only to a few: who would not call Scott happy? But the happiest circumstance of all is, as we said above, that Scott had in himself a right healthy soul, rendering him little dependent on outward circumstances. Things showed themselves to him not in distortion or borrowed light or gloom, but as they were. Endeavour lay in him and endurance, in due measure; and clear vision of what was to be endeavoured after. Were one to preach a Sermon on Health, as really were worth doing, Scott ought to be the text. Theories are demonstrably true in the way of logic; and then in the way of practice, they prove true or else not true: but here is the grand experiment, Do they turn out well? What boots it that a man's creed is the wisest, that his system of principles is the superfinest, if, when set to work, the life of him does nothing but jar, and fret itself into *holes?* They are untrue in that, were it in nothing else, these principles of his; openly convicted of untruth;—fit only, shall we say, to be rejected as counterfeits, and flung to the dogs? We say not that; but we do say that ill-health, of body or of mind, is *defeat*, is battle (in a good or in a bad cause) with bad success; that health alone is victory. Let all men, if they can manage it, contrive to be healthy! He who in what cause soever sinks into pain and disease, let him take thought of it; let him know well that it is not good *he* has arrived at yet, but surely evil,—may, or may not be, on the way towards good.

Scott's healthiness showed itself decisively in all things, and nowhere more decisively than in this: the way in which he took his fame; the estimate he from the first formed of fame. Money will buy money's worth; but the thing men call fame what is it? A gaudy emblazonry, not good for much,—except indeed as it too may turn to money. To Scott it was a profitable pleasing superfluity, no necessary of life. Not necessary, now or ever? Seemingly without much effort, but taught by nature, and the instinct which instructs the sound heart what is good for it and what is not, he felt that he could always do without this same emblazonry of reputation; that he ought to put no trust in it; but be ready at any time to see it pass away from him, and to hold on his way as before. It is incalculable, as we conjecture, what evil he escaped in this manner; what perversions, irritations, mean agonies without a name, he lived wholly apart from, knew nothing of. Happily before fame arrived, he had reached the mature age at which all this was easier to him. What a strange Nemesis lurks in the felicities of men! In thy mouth it shall be sweet as honey, in thy belly it shall be bitter as gall? Some weakly-organized individual, we will say at the age of five-and-twenty, whose main or whole talent rests on some prurient susceptivity, and nothing under it but shallowness and vacuum, is clutched hold of by the general imagination, is whirled aloft to the giddy height; and taught to believe the divine-seeming message that he is a great man: such individual seems the luckiest of men: and is he not the unluckiest? Swallow not the Circe-drought, O weakly-organized individual; it is fell poison; it will dry up the fountains of thy whole existence, and all will grow withered and parched; thou shalt be wretched under the sun! Is there, for example, a sadder book than that "Life of Byron," by Moore? To omit mere prurient susceptivities that rest on vacuum, look at poor Byron, who really had much substance in him. Sitting there in his self-exile, with a proud heart striving to persuade itself that it despises the entire created universe; and afar off, in foggy Babylon, let any pitifullest whipster draw pen on him, your proud Byron writhes in torture,—as if the pitiful whipster were a magician, or his pen a galvanic wire struck into the Byron's spinal marrow?

Lamentable, despicable,—one had rather be a kitten and cry mew! O, son of Adam, great or little, according as thou art loveable, those thou livest with will love thee. Those thou livest *not* with, is it of moment that they have the alphabetic letters of thy name engraved on their memory with some signpost likeness of thee (as like as I to Hercules) appended to them? It is not of moment; in sober truth, not of any moment at all! And yet, behold, there is no soul now whom thou canst love freely,—from *one* soul only art thou always sure of reverence enough; in presence of no soul is it rightly well with thee! How is thy world become desert; and thou, for the sake of a little babblement of tongues, art poor, bankrupt, insolvent not in purse, but in heart and mind. "The golden calf of self-love," says Jean Paul, "has grown into a burning Phalaris' bull, to consume its owner and worshipper." Ambition, the desire of shining and outshining, was the beginning of sin in this world. The man of letters who founds upon his fame, does he not thereby alone declare himself a follower of Lucifer (named *Satan*, the Enemy,) and member of the Satanic school?——

It was in this poetic period that Scott formed his connection with the Ballantynes; and embarked, though under cover, largely in trade. To those who regard him in the heroic light, and will have *vates* to signify prophet as well as poet, this portion of his biography seems somewhat incoherent. Viewed as it stood in the reality, as he was and as it was, the enterprise, since it proved so unfortunate, may be called lamentable, but cannot be called unnatural. The practical Scott, looking towards practical issues in all things, could not but find hard cash one of the most practical. If, by any means, cash could be honestly produced, were it by writing poems, were it by printing them, why not? Great things might be done ultimately; great difficulties were at once got rid of,—manifold higglings of booksellers, and contradictions of sinners hereby fell away. A printing and bookselling speculation was not so alien for a maker of books. Voltaire, who indeed got no copyrights, made much money by the war commissariat, in his time; we believe by the victualling branch of it. Saint George himself, they say, was a dealer in bacon in Cappadocia. A thrifty man will help himself towards his object by such steps as lead to it. Station in society, solid power over the good things of this world, was Scott's avowed object; towards which the precept of precepts is that of Iago: Put money in thy purse.

Here, indeed, it is to be remarked, that, perhaps, no literary man of any generation has less value than Scott for the immaterial part of his mission in any sense; not only for the fantasy called fame, with the fantastic miseries attendant thereon; but also for the spiritual purport of his work, whether it tended hitherward or thitherward, or had any tendency whatever; and indeed for all purports and results of his working, except such, we may say, as offered themselves to the eye, and could, in one sense or the other be handled, looked at, and buttoned into the breeches-pocket. Somewhat too little of a fantast, this *vates* of ours! But so it was: in this nineteenth century, our highest literary man, who immeasurably beyond all others commanded the world's ear, had, as it were, no message whatever to deliver to the world; wished not the world to elevate itself, to amend itself, to do this or to do that, except simply pay him for the books he kept writing. Very remarkable; fittest, perhaps, for an age fallen languid, destitute of faith and terrified at skepticism? Or, perhaps, for quite another sort of age, an age all in peaceable triumphant motion? But, indeed, since Shakspeare's time there has been no greater speaker so unconscious of an aim in speaking. Equally unconscious these two utterances; equally the sincere complete products of the minds they came from: and now if they were equally *deep?* Or, if the one was living fire, and the other was futile phosphorescence and mere resinous firework? It will depend on the relative worth of the minds; for both were equally spontaneous themselves, unencumbered by an ulterior aim. Beyond drawing audiences to the Globe Theatre, Shakspeare contemplated no result in those plays of his. Yet they have had results! Utter with free heart what thy own *dæmon* gives thee: if fire from heaven it shall be well; if resinous firework, it shall be—as well as it could be, or better than otherwise! The candid judge will, in general, require that a speaker, in so extremely serious a universe as this of ours, have something to speak about. In the heart of the speaker there ought to be some kind of gospel-tidings burning till it be uttered; otherwise it were better for him that he altogether held his peace. A gospel somewhat more decisive than this of Scott's,—except to an age altogether languid, without either skepticism or faith? These things the candid judge will demand of literary men; yet withal will recognise the great worth there is in Scott's honesty, if in nothing more, in his being the thing he was with such entire good faith. Here is a something not a nothing. If no skyborn messenger, heaven looking through his eyes; then neither is it a chimera with his systems, crotchets, cants, fanaticisms, and "last infirmity of noble minds,"—full of misery, unrest, and ill-will; but a substantial, peaceable, terrestrial man. Far as the Earth is under the Heaven, does Scott stand below the former sort of character; but high as the cheerful flowery Earth is above waste Tartarus does he stand above the latter. Let him live in his own fashion, and do honour to him in that.

It were late in the day to write criticisms on those Metrical Romances: at the same time, the great popularity they had seems natural enough. In the first place, there was the indisputable impress of worth, of genuine human force, in them. This, which lies in some degree, or is thought to lie, at the bottom of all popularity, did to an unusual degree, disclose itself in these rhymed romances of Scott's. Pictures were actually painted and presented; human emotions conceived and sympathized with. Considering that wretched Della-Cruscan and other vamping-up of old worn-out tatters was the staple article then, it may be granted that Scott's excellence was superior and supreme. When a Hayley was the main singer, a Scott might well be hailed with warm welcome. Consider whether the *Loves of the Plants*, and even the *Loves of the triangles*, could be worth the loves and hates of men and women! Scott was as preferable to what he displaced, as the substance is to wearisomely repeated shadow of a substance. But, in the second place, we may say that the *kind* of worth which Scott manifested was fitted especially for the then temper of men. We have called it an age fallen into spiritual languor, destitute of belief, yet terrified at skepticism; reduced to live a stinted half-life, under strange new circumstances. Now vigorous whole-life, this was what of all things these delineations offered. The reader was carried back to rough strong times, wherein those maladies of ours had not yet arisen. Brawny fighters, all cased in buff and iron, their hearts too sheathed in oak and triple brass, caprioled their huge war-horses, shook their death-doing spears; and went forth in the most determined manner, nothing doubting. The reader sighed, yet not without a reflex solacement: "O, that I could have lived in those times, had never known these logic-cobwebs, this doubt, this sickliness; and been and felt myself alive among men alive!" Add lastly, that in this new-found poetic world there was no call for effort on the reader's part; what excellence they had, exhibited itself at a glance. It was for the reader, not the El Dorado only, but a beatific land of a Cockaigne and Paradise of Donothings! The reader, what the vast majority of readers so long to do, was allowed to lie down at his ease, and be ministered to. What the Turkish bath-keeper is said to aim at with his frictions, and shampooings, and fomentings, more or less effectually, that the patient in total idleness may have the delights of activity,—was here to a considerable extent realized. The languid imagination fell back into its rest; an artist was there who could supply it with high-painted scenes, with sequences of stirring action, and whisper to it, Be at ease, and let thy tepid element be comfortable to thee. "The rude man," says the critic, "requires only to see something going on. The man of more refinement must be made to feel. The man of complete refinement must be made to reflect."

We named the "Minstrelsy of the Scottish Border" the fountain from which flowed this great river of Metrical Romances; but according to some they can be traced to a still higher, obscurer spring; to Goethe's "Götz von Berlichingen with the Iron Hand;" of which, as we have seen, Scott in his earlier days executed a translation. Dated a good many years ago, the following words in a criticism on Goethe are found written; which probably are still new to most readers of this Review:

"The works just mentioned, *Götz* and *Werter*, though noble specimens of youthful talent, are still not so much distinguished by their intrinsic merits as by their splendid fortune. It would be difficult to name two books which have exercised a deeper influence on the subsequent literature of Europe than these two performances of a young author; his first-fruits, the produce of his twenty-fourth year. *Werter* appeared to seize the hearts of men in all quarters of the world, and to utter for them the word which they had long been waiting to hear. As usually happens, too, this same word, once uttered, was soon abundantly repeated; spoken in all dialects, and chaunted through all notes of the gamut, till the sound of it had grown a weariness rather than a pleasure. Skeptical sentimentality, view-hunting, love, friendship, suicide, and desperation, became the staple of literary ware; and though the epidemic, after a long course of years, subsided in Germany, it reappeared with various modifications in other countries, and everywhere abundant traces of its good and bad effects are still to be discerned. The fortune of *Berlichingen with the Iron Hand*, though less sudden, was by no means less exalted. In his own country, *Götz*, though he now stands solitary and childless, became the parent of an innumerable progeny of chivalry plays, feudal delineations, and poetico-antiquarian performances: which, though long ago deceased, made noise enough in their day and generation: and with ourselves his influence has been perhaps still more remarkable. Sir Walter Scott's first literary enterprise was a translation of *Götz von Berlichingen*: and, if genius could be communicated like instruction, we might call this work of Goethe's the prime cause of *Marmion* and the *Lady of the Lake*, with all that has followed from the same creative hand. Truly, a grain of seed that has lighted in the right soil! For if not firmer and fairer, it has grown to be taller and broader than any other tree; and all the nations of the earth are still yearly gathering of its fruit."

How far "Götz von Berlichingen" actually affected Scott's literary destination, and whether without it the rhymed romances, and then the prose romances of the Author of Waverly, would not have followed as they did, must remain a very obscure question; obscure, and not important. Of the fact, however, there is no doubt but these two tendencies, which may be named *Götzism* and *Werterism*, of the former of which Scott was representative with us, have made, and are still in some quarters making the tour of all Europe. In Germany, too, there was this affectionate half-regretful looking back into the past; Germany had its buff belted watch-tower period in literature, and had even got done with it, before Scott began. Then, as to *Werterism*, had not we English our Byron and his genius? No form of Werterism in any other country had half the potency: as our Scott carried chivalry literature to the ends of the world, so did our Byron Werterism. France, busy with its Revolution and Napoleon, had little leisure at the moment for Götzism or Werterism; but it has had them both since, in a shape of its own: witness the whole "Literature of Desperation" in our own days, the beggarliest form of Werterism yet seen, probably its expiring final form: witness also, at the other extremity of the scale, a noble-gifted Chateaubriand, Götz and Werter, both in one.—Curious: how all Europe is but like a set of parishes of the same county: participant of the self-same influences, ever since the Crusades, and earlier;—and these glorious wars of ours are but like parish-brawls, which begin in mutual ignorance, intoxication, and boastful speech: which end in broken windows, damage, waste, and bloody noses; and which one hopes the general good sense is now in the way towards putting down, in some measure!

But, however, leaving this to be as it can, what it concerned us here to remark was, that British Werterism, in the shape of those Byron Poems, so potent and poignant, produced on the languid appetite of men a mighty effect. This too was a "class of feelings deeply important to modern minds; feelings which arise from *passion incapable of being converted into action*, which belong to an age as indolent, cultivated, and unbelieving as our own!" The "languid age without either faith or skepticism" turned towards Byronism with an interest altogether peculiar: here, if no cure for its miserable paralysis and languor, was at least an indignant statement of the misery; an indignant Ernulphus' curse read over it,—which all men felt to be something. Half-regretful lookings into the Past gave place, in many quarters, to Ernulphus' cursings of the Present. Scott was among the first to perceive that the day of Metrical Chivalry Romances was declining. He had held the sovereignty for some half-score of years, a comparatively long lease of it; and now the time seemed come for dethronement, for abdication; an unpleasant business· which however he held himself ready, as a brave man will, to transact with composure and in silence. After all, Poetry was not his staff of life; Poetry had already yielded him much money; *this* at least it would not take back from him. Busy always with editing, with compiling, with multiplex official, commercial business, and solid interests, he beheld the coming change with unmoved eye.

Resignation he was prepared to exhibit in this matter;—and now behold there proved to be no need of resignation. Let the Metrical Romance become a Prose one; shake off its rhyme-fetters, and try a wider sweep! In the spring of 1814 appeared "Waverly;" an event memorable in the annals of British literature; in the annals of British book-selling thrice and four times memorable. Byron sang, but Scott narrated; and when the song had sung itself out through all variations onwards to the "Don-Juan" one, Scott was still found narrating, and carrying the whole world along with him. All bygone popularity of chivalry lays was swallowed up in a far greater. What "series" followed out of "Waverly," and how and with what result, is known to all men; was witnessed and watched with a kind of rapt astonishment by all. Hardly any literary reputation ever rose so high in our Island; no reputation at all ever spread so wide. Walter Scott became Sir Walter Scott, Baronet, of Abbotsford; on whom fortune seemed to pour her whole cornucopia of wealth, honour, and worldly good; the favourite of Princes and of Peasants, and all intermediate men. His "Waverly series," swift-following one on the other apparently without end, was the universal reading, looked for like an annual harvest, by all ranks in all European countries. A curious circumstance superadded itself, that the author though known was unknown. From the first, most people suspected, and soon after the first few intelligent persons much doubted, that the Author of "Waverly" was Walter Scott. Yet a certain mystery was still kept up; rather piquant to the public; doubtless very pleasant to the author, who saw it all; who probably had not to listen, as other hapless individuals often had, to this or the other long-drawn "clear proof at last," that the author was not Walter Scott, but a certain astonishing Mr. So-and-so;—one of the standing miseries of human life in that time. But for the privileged author, it was like a king travelling incognito. All men know that he is a high king, chivalrous Gustaf or Kaiser Joseph; but he mingles in their meetings without cumber of etiquette or lonesome ceremony, as Chevalier du Nord, or Count of Lorraine: he has none of the weariness of royalty, and yet all the praise, and the satisfaction of hearing it with his own ears. In a word, the Waverly Novels circulated and reigned triumphant; to the general imagination the "'Author of Waverly'" was like some living mythological personage, and ranked among the chief wonders of the world.

How a man lived and demeaned himself in such unwonted circumstances is worth seeing. We would gladly quote from Scott's correspondence of this period; but that does not much illustrate the matter. His letters, as above stated, are never without interest, yet also seldom or never very interesting. They are full of cheerfulness, of wit, and ingenuity; but they do not treat of aught intimate; without impeaching their sincerity, what is called sincerity, one may say they do not, in any case whatever, proceed from the innermost parts of the mind. Conventional forms, due considerations of your own and your correspondent's pretensions and vanities, are at no moment left out of view. The epistolary stream runs on, lucid, free, glad-flowing; but always, as it were *parallel* to the real substance of the matter, never coincident with it. One feels it hollowish under foot. Letters they are of a most humane man of the world, even exemplary in that kind! but with the man of the world always visible to them;—as indeed it was little in Scott's way to speak perhaps even with himself in any other fashion. We select rather some glimpses of him from Mr. Lockhart's record The first is of dining with Royalty or Prince-Regentship itself; an almost official matter:

"On hearing from Mr. Croker (then Secretary to the Admirality) that Scott was to be in town by the middle of March, (1815,) the Prince said—'Let me know when he comes, and I'll get up a snug little dinner that will suit him;' and, after he had been presented and graciously received at the *levee*, he was invited to dinner accordingly, through his excellent friend Mr. Adam, (now Lord Chief Commissioner of the

Jury Court in Scotland,) who at that time held a confidential office in the royal household. The Regent had consulted with Mr. Adam also as to the composition of the party. 'Let us have,' said he, 'just a few friends of his own, and the more Scotch the better;' and both the Commissioner and Mr. Croker assure me that the party was the most interesting and agreeable one in their recollection. It comprised, I believe, the Duke of York—the Duke of Gordon (then Marquess of Huntly)—the Marquess of Hertford (then Lord Yarmouth)—the Earl of Fife—and Scott's early friend Lord Melville. 'The Prince and Scott,' says Mr. Croker, 'were the two most brilliant story-tellers, in their several ways, that I have ever happened to meet; they were both aware of their *forte*, and both exerted themselves that evening with delightful effect. On going home, I really could not decide which of them had shone the most.(!) The Regent was enchanted with Scott, as Scott was with him; and on all his subsequent visits to London, he was a frequent guest at the royal table.' The Lord Chief Commissioner remembers that the Prince was particularly delighted with the poet's anecdotes of the old Scotch judges and lawyers, which his Royal Highness sometimes *capped* by ludicrous traits of certain ermined sages of his own acquaintance. Scott told, among others, a story, which he was fond of telling, of his old friend the Lord Justice-Clerk Braxfield; and the commentary of his Royal Highness on hearing it amused Scott, who often mentioned it afterwards. The anecdote is this:—Braxfield, whenever he went on a particular circuit, was in the habit of visiting a gentleman of good fortune in the neighbourhood of one of the assize towns, and staying at least one night, which, being both of them ardent chess-players, they usually concluded with their favourite game. One Spring circuit the battle was not decided at daybreak; so the Justice-Clerk said,—'Weel, Donald, I must e'en come back this gate, and let the game lie ower for the present;' and back he came in October, but not to his old friend's hospitable house; for that gentleman had in the interim been apprehended on a capital charge, (of forgery,) and his name stood on the *Porteous Roll*, or list of those who were about to be tried under his former guest's auspices. The laird was indicted and tried accordingly, and the jury returned a verdict of *guilty*. Braxfield forthwith put on his cocked hat, (which answers to the black cap in England,) and pronounced the sentence of the law in the usual terms—'To be hanged by the neck until you be dead; and may the Lord have mercy upon your unhappy soul!' Having concluded this awful formula in his most sonorous cadence, Braxfield, dismounting his formidable beaver, gave a familiar nod to his unfortunate acquaintance, and said to him in a sort of chuckling whisper—'And now Donald, my man, I think I've checkmated you for ance.' The Regent laughed heartily at this specimen of Macqueen's brutal humour; and 'I'faith, Walter,' said he, 'this old big-wig seems to have taken things as coolly as my tyrannical self. Don't you remember Tom Moore's description of me at breakfast—

"'The table spread with tea and toast,
Death-warrants and the Morning Post?'

"Towards midnight, the Prince called for 'a bumper, with all the honours, to the Author of Waverley;' and looked significantly, as he was charging his own glass, to Scott. Scott seemed somewhat puzzled for a moment, but instantly recovering himself, and filling his glass to the brim, said, 'Your Royal Highness looks as if you thought I had some claim to the honours of this toast. I have no such pretensions, but shall take good care that the real Simon Pure hears of the high compliment that has now been paid him.' He then drank off his claret; and joined with a stentorian voice in the cheering, which the Prince himself timed. But before the company could resume their seats his Royal Highness, 'Another of the same, if you please, to the Author of Marmion,—and now, Walter, my man, I have checkmated you for *ance*.' The second bumper was followed by cheers still more prolonged: and Scott then rose, and returned thanks in a short address, which struck the Lord Chief Commissioner as 'alike grave and graceful.' This story has been circulated in a very perverted shape." * * * "Before he left town he again dined at Carlton House, when the party was a still smaller one than before, and the merriment if possible still more free. That nothing might be wanting, the Prince sang several capital songs."—Vol. iii. pp. 340—343.

Or take, at a very great interval in many senses, this glimpse of another dinner, altogether *un*officially and much better described. It is James Ballantyne the printer and publisher's dinner, in Saint-John Street, Canongate, Edinburgh, on the birtheve of a Waverley Novel:

"The feast was, to use one of James's own favorite epithets, *gorgeous;* an aldermanic display of turtle and venison, with the suitable accompaniments of iced punch, potent ale, and generous Madeira. When the cloth was drawn, the burly præses arose, with all he could muster of the port of John Kemble, and spouted with a sonorous voice the formula of Macbeth—

'Fill full!
I drink to the general joy of the whole table!'

This was followed by 'The King, God bless him!' and second came—'Gentlemen, there is another toast which never has been nor shall be omitted in this house of mine: I give you the health of Mr. Walter Scott, with three times three!' All honour having been done to this health, and Scott having briefly thanked the company, with some expressions of warm affection to their host, Mrs. Ballantyne retired;—the bottles passed round twice or thrice in the usual way; and then James rose once more, every vein on his brow distended: his eyes solemnly fixed on vacancy, to propose, not as before in his stentorian key, but with ''bated breath,' in the sort of whisper by which a stage conspirator thrills the gallery—'*Gentlemen, a bumper to the immortal Author of Waverley!*'—The uproar of cheering, in which Scott made a fashion of joining, was succeeded by deep silence; and then Ballantyne proceeded—

'In his Lord-Burleigh look, serene and serious,
A something of imposing and mysterious'—

to lament the obscurity in which his illustrious but too modest correspondent still chose to conceal himself from the plaudits of the world; to thank the company for the manner in which the *nominis umbra* had been received; and to assure them that the Author of 'Waverley' would, when informed of the circumstance, feel highly delighted—'the proudest hour of his life,' &c. &c. The cool, demure fun of Scott's features during all this mummery was perfect; and Erskine's attempt at a gay *nonchalance* was still more ludicrously meritorious. Aldiborontiphoscophornio, however, bursting as he was, knew too well to allow the new Novel to be made the subject of discussion. Its name was announced, and success to it crowned another cup; but after that, no more of Jedediah. To cut the thread, he rolled out unbidden some one of his many theatrical songs, in a style that would have done no dishonour to almost any orchestra—*The Maid of Lodi*, or perhaps *The Bay of Biscay, oh!*—or *The sweet little cherub that sits up aloft*. Other toasts followed, interspersed with ditties from other performers; old George Thomson, the friend of Burns, was ready, for one, with *The Moorland Wedding*, or *Willie brew'd a peck o' maut*;—and so it went on, until Scott and Erskine, with any clerical or very staid personage that had chanced to be admitted, saw fit to withdraw. Then the scene was changed. The claret and olives made way for broiled bones and a mighty bowl of punch; and when a few glasses of the hot beverage had restored his powers, James opened *ore rotundo* on the merits of the forthcoming romance. 'One chapter—one chapter only!' was the cry. After '*Nay, by'r Lady, nay!*' and a few more coy shifts, the proof-sheets were at length produced, and James, with many a prefatory hem, read aloud what he considered as the most striking dialogue they contained.

"The first I heard so read was the interview between Jeanie Deans, the Duke of Argyle, and Queen Caroline, in Richmond Park; and, notwithstanding some spice of the pompous tricks to which he was addicted, I must say he did the inimitable scene great justice. At all events, the effect it produced was deep and memorable; and no wonder that the exulting typographer's *one bumper more to Jedediah Cleishbotham* preceded his parting-stave, which was uniformly *The Last Words of Marmion*, executed certainly with no contemptible rivalry of Braham."—Vol. iv. pp. 166—168.

Over at Abbotsford, things wear a still more prosperous aspect. Scott is building there, by the pleasant banks of the Tweed; he has bought and is buying land there; fast as the new gold comes in for a new Waverly Novel, or even faster, it changes itself into moory acres, into stone, and hewn or planted wood:

"About the middle of February" (1820)—says Mr. Lockhart, "it having been ere that time arranged that I should marry his eldest daughter in the course of the spring—I accompanied him and part of his family on one of those flying visits to Abbotsford, with which he often indulged himself on a Saturday during term. Upon such occasions, Scott appeared at the usual hour in Court, but wearing, instead of the official suit of black, his country morning-dress, green jacket, and so forth, under the clerk's gown."—"At noon, when the Court broke up, Peter Mathieson was sure to be in attendance in the Parliament Close; and, five minutes after, the gown had been tossed off; and Scott, rubbing his hands for glee, was under weigh for Tweedside. As we proceeded," &c.

"Next morning there appeared at breakfast John Ballantyne, who had at this time a shooting or hunting-box a few miles off, in the vale of the Leader, and with him Mr. Constable, his guest; and it being a fine clear day, as soon as Scott had read the church service and one of Jeremy Taylor's sermons, we all sallied out before noon on a perambulation of his upland territories; Maida (the hound) and the rest of the favourites accompanying our march. At starting we were joined by the constant henchman, Tom Purdie,—and I may save myself the trouble of any attempt to describe his appearance, for his master has given us an inimitably true one in introducing a certain personage of his Redgauntlet:—'He was, perhaps, sixty years old; yet his brow was not much furrowed, and his jet-black hair was only grizzled, not whitened, by the advance of age. All his motions spoke strength unabated; and, though rather under-sized, he had very broad shoulders, was square made, thin-flanked, and apparently combined in his frame muscular strength and activity; the last somewhat impaired, perhaps, by years, but the first remaining in full vigour. A hard and harsh countenance; eyes far sunk under projecting eyebrows, which were grizzled like his hair; a wide mouth, furnished from ear to ear with a range of unimpaired teeth of uncommon whiteness, and a size and breadth which might have become the jaws of an ogre, completed this delightful portrait.' Equip this figure in Scott's cast-off green jacket, white hat, and drab trousers; and imagine that years of kind treatment, comfort, and the honest consequence of a confidential *grieve** had softened away much of the hardness and harshness originally impressed on the visage by anxious penury, and the sinister habits of a *black-fisher*;—and the Tom Purdie of 1820 stands before us.

"We were all delighted to see how completely Scott had recovered his bodily vigour, and none more so than Constable, who, as he puffed and panted after him, up one ravine and down another, often stopped to wipe his forehead, and remarked, that 'it was not every author who should lead him such a dance.' But Purdie's face shone with rapture as he observed how severely the swagbellied bookseller's activity was tasked. Scott exclaimed exultingly, though, perhaps, for the tenth time, 'This will be a glorious spring for our trees, Tom!'—'You may say that, Sheriff,' quoth Tom,—and then lingering a moment for Constable—'My certy,' he added, scratching his head, 'and I think it will be a grand

* Overseer; German, *graf*.

season for *our buiks* too.' But indeed Tom always talked of *our buiks* as if they had been as regular products of the soil as *our aits* and *our birks*. Having threaded first the Hexilcleugh and then the Rhymer's Glen, we arrived at Huntly Burn, where the hospitality of the kind *Weird sisters*, as Scott called the Miss Fergusons, reanimated our exhausted bibliopoles, and gave them courage to extend their walk a little further down the same famous brook. Here there was a small cottage in a very sequestered situation," (named Chiefswood,) "by making some little additions to which Scott thought it might be converted into a suitable summer residence for his daughter and future son-in-law." * * "As we walked homeward, Scott, being a little fatigued, laid his left hand on Tom's shoulder, and leaned heavily for support, chatting to his 'Sunday pony,' as he called the affectionate fellow, just as freely as with the rest of the party; and Tom put in his word shrewdly and manfully, and grinned and grunted whenever the joke chanced to be within his apprehension. It was easy to see that his heart swelled within him from the moment the Sheriff got his collar in his gripe." —Vol. iv. p. 349, 353.

That Abbotsford became infested to a great degree with tourists, wonder-hunters, and all that fatal species of people, may be supposed. Solitary Ettrick saw itself populous: all paths were beaten with the feet and hoofs of an endless miscellany of pilgrims. As many as "sixteen parties" have arrived at Abbotsford in one day; male and female; peers, Socinian preachers, whatsoever was distinguished, whatsoever had love of distinction in it! Mr. Lockhart thinks there was no literary shrine ever so bepilgrimed, except Ferney in Voltaire's time, who, however, was not half so accessible. A fatal species! These are what Schiller calls "the flesh-flies;" buzzing swarms of bluebottles, who never fail where any taint of human glory or other corruptibility is in the wind. So has Nature decreed. Scott's *healthiness*, bodily and mental, his massive solidity of character, nowhere showed itself more decisively than in his manner of encountering this part of his fate. That his bluebottles were blue, and of the usual tone and quality, may be judged. Hear Captain Basil Hall, (in a very compressed state:)

"We arrived in good time, and found several other guests at dinner. The public rooms are lighted with oil-gas, in a style of extraordinary splendour. The," &c.—"Had I a hundred pens, each of which at the same time should separately write down an anecdote, I could not hope to record one-half of those which our host, to use Spenser's expression, 'welled out alway.'"—"Entertained us all the way with an endless string of anecdotes;"—"came like a stream of poetry from his lips;"—"path muddy and scarcely passable, yet I do not remember ever to have seen any place so interesting as the skill of this mighty magician had rendered this narrow ravine."—"Impossible to touch on any theme, but straightway he has an anecdote to fit it."—"Thus we strolled along, borne, as it were, on the stream of song and story."—"In the evening we had a great feast indeed. Sir Walter asked us if we had ever read Christabel."—"Interspersed with these various readings, were some hundreds of stories, some quaint, some pathetical."—"At breakfast today we had, as usual, some 150 stories—God knows how they came in."—"In any man so gifted—so qualified to take the loftiest, proudest line at the head of the literature, the taste, the imagination of the whole world!"—"For instance, he never sits at any particular place at table, but takes," &c., &c.—Vol. v. p. 375—402.

Among such worshippers, arriving in "sixteen parties a-day," an ordinary man might have grown buoyant; have felt the god, begun to nod, and seemed to shake the spheres. A slightly splenetic man, possessed of Scott's sense, would have swept his premises clear of them: Let no bluebottle approach here, to disturb a man in his work,—under pain of sugared *squash* (called quassia) and king's yellow! The good Sir Walter, like a quiet brave man, did neither. He let the matter take its course; enjoyed what was enjoyable in it: endured what could not well be helped; persisted meanwhile in writing his daily portion of romance-*copy*, in preserving his composure of heart;—in a word, accommodated himself to this loud-buzzing environment, and made it serve him, as he would have done (perhaps with more ease) to a silent, poor, and solitary one. No doubt it affected him too, and in the lamentablest way fevered his internal life,—though he kept it well down; but it affected him *less* than it would have done almost any other man. For his guests were not all of the bluebottle sort; far from that. Mr. Lockhart shall furnish us with the brightest aspect a British Ferney ever yielded, or is like to yield: and therewith we will quit Abbotsford and the dominant and culminant period of Scott's life:

"It was a clear, bright, September morning, with a sharpness in the air that doubled the animating influence of the sunshine, and all was in readiness for a grand coursing match on Newark Hill. The only guest who had chalked out other sport for himself was the stanchest of anglers, Mr. Rose; but he, too, was there on his *shelty*, armed with his salmon-rod and landing-net, and attended by his Hinves, and Charlie Purdie, a brother of Tom, in those days the most celebrated fisherman of the district. This little group of Waltonians, bound for Lord Somerville's preserve, remained lounging about to witness the start of the main cavalcade. Sir Walter, mounted on Sibyl, was marshalling the order of procession with a huge hunting-whip; and among a dozen frolicsome youths and maidens, who seemed disposed to laugh at all discipline, appeared, each on horseback, each as eager as the youngest sportsman in the troop, Sir Humphry Davy, Dr. Wollaston, and the patriarch of Scottish belles-lettres, Henry Mackenzie. The Man of Feeling, however, was persuaded with some difficulty to resign his steed for the present to his faithful negro follower, and to join Lady Scott in the sociable, until we should reach the ground of our *battue*. Laidlaw, on a long-tailed wiry Highlander, yclept *Hoddin Grey*, which carried him nimbly and stoutly, although his feet almost touched the ground as he sat, was the adjutant. But the most picturesque figure was the illustrious inventor of the safety-lamp. He had come for his favourite sport of angling, and had been practising it successfully with Rose, his travelling companion, for two or three days preceding this; but he had not prepared for coursing fields, or had left Charlie Purdie's troop for Sir Walter's on a sudden thought, and his fisherman's costume—a brown hat with flexible brim, surrounded with line upon line of catgut, and innumerable fly-hooks—jack-boots worthy of a Dutch smuggler, and a fustian surtout dabbled with the blood of salmon, made a fine contrast with the smart jackets, white-cord breeches, and well polished jockey-boots of the less distinguished cavaliers about him. Dr. Wollaston was in black, and, with his noble serene dignity of countenance, might have passed for a sporting archbishop. Mr. Mackenzie, at this time in the 76th year of his age, with a white hat turned up with green, green spectacles, green jacket, and long brown leathern gaiters buttoned upon his nether anatomy, wore a dog-whistle round his neck, and had, all over, the air of as resolute a devotee as the gay captain of Huntly Burn. Tom Purdie and his subalterns had preceded us by a few hours with all the greyhounds that could be collected at Abbotsford, Darnick, and Melrose; but the giant Maida had remained as his master's orderly, and now gambolled about Sibyl Grey, barking for mere joy like a spaniel puppy.

"The order of march had been all settled, and the sociable was just getting under weigh, when *the Lady Anne* broke from the line, screaming with laughter, and exclaimed, 'Papa, papa, I knew you could never think of going without your pet.' Scott looked round, and I rather think there was a blush as well as a smile upon his face, when he perceived a little black pig frisking about his pony, and evidently a self-elected addition to the party of the day. He tried to look stern, and cracked his whip at the creature, but was in a moment obliged to join in the general cheers. Poor piggy soon found a strap round its neck, and was dragged into the background;—Scott, watching the retreat, repeated with mock pathos the first verse of an old pastoral song—

> 'What will I do gin my hoggie die ?
> My joy, my pride, my hoggie !
> My only beast, I had na mae,
> And wow ! but I was vogie !'

—the cheers were redoubled—and the squadron moved on.

"This pig had taken, nobody could tell how, a most sentimental attachment to Scott, and was constantly urging its pretensions to be admitted a regular member of his *tail* along with the greyhounds and terriers; but, indeed, I remember him suffering another summer under the same sort of pertinacity on the part of an affectionate hen. I leave the explanation for philosophers—but such were the facts. I have too much respect for the vulgarly calumniated donkey, to name him in the same category of pets with the pig and the hen; but a year or two after this time, my wife used to drive a couple of these animals in a little garden chair, and whenever her father appeared at the door of our cottage, we were sure to see Hannah More and Lady Morgan (as Anne Scott had wickedly christened them) trotting from their pasture, to lay their noses over the paling, and, as Washington Irving says of the old white-haired hedger with the Parisian snuff-box, 'to have a pleasant crack wi' the laird.'"—Vol. v. p. 7—10.*

"There (at Chiefswood) my wife and I spent this summer and autumn of 1821—the first of several seasons which will ever dwell on my memory as the happiest of my life. We were near enough Abbotsford to partake as often as we liked of its brilliant and constantly varying society; yet could do so without being exposed to the worry and exhaustion of spirit which the daily reception of new comers entailed upon all the family, except Sir Walter himself. But, in truth, even he was not always proof against the annoyances connected with such a style of open house-keeping. Even his temper sank sometimes under the solemn applauses of learned dulness, the vapid raptures of painted and perriwigged dowagers, the horseleech avidity with which underbred fo-

* On this subject let us report an anecdote furnished by a correspondent of our own, whose accuracy we can depend on:—"I myself was acquainted with a little Blenheim cocker, one of the smallest, beautifullest, and wisest of lapdogs, or dogs, which, though Sir Walter knew it not, was very singular in its behaviour towards him. *Shandy*, so hight this remarkable cocker, was extremely shy of strangers: promenading on Prince's street, which in fine weather used to be crowded in those days, he seemed to live in perpetual fear of being stolen; if any one but looked at him admiringly, he would draw back with angry timidity, and crouch towards his own lady-mistress. One day a tall, irregular, busy-looking man came halting by; the little dog ran towards him, began fawning, frisking, licking at his feet: it was Sir Walter Scott! Had Shandy been the most extensive reader of Reviews, he could not have done better. Every time he saw Sir Walter afterwards, which was some three or four times in the course of visiting Edinburgh, he repeated his demonstrations, ran leaping, frisking, licking the Author of 'Waverly's' feet. The good Sir Walter endured it with good-humour; looked down at the little wise face, at the silky shag-coat of snow-white and chestnut-brown; smiled, and avoided hitting him as they went on,—till a new division of streets or some other obstacles put an end to the interview. In fact he was a strange little fellow, this Shandy. He has been known to sit for hours looking out at the summer moon, with the saddest wistfullest expression of countenance; altogether like a Wertereau Poet. He would have been a Poet, I dare say, if he could have found a *publisher*. But his moral tact was the most amazing. Without reason shown, without word spoken or act done, he took his likings and dislikings; unalterable; really almost unerring. His chief aversion, I should say, was to the genus *quack*, above all to the genus *acrid-quack;* these, though never so clear-starched, bland-smiling, and beneficent, he absolutely would have no trade with. Their very sugar-cake was unavailing. He said with emphasis, as clearly as barking could say it: 'Acrid-quack, avaunt!' Would to Heaven many a prime minister and high person in authority had such an invaluable talent! On the whole, there is more in this universe than our philosophy has dreamt of. A dog's instinct is a voice of Nature too; and farther, *it* has never babbled itself away in idle jargon and hypothesis, but always adhered to the practical, and grown in silence by continual communion with fact. We do the animals injustice. Their body resembles our body, Buffon says; with its four limbs, with its spinal marrow, main organs in the head, and so forth: but have they not a kind of soul, equally the rude draught and imperfect imitation of ours? It is a strange, an almost solemn and pathetic thing to see an intelligence imprisoned in that dumb rude form; struggling to express itself out of that;—even as we do out of our imprisonment; and succeed very imperfectly!"

reigners urged their questions, and the pompous simpers of condescending magnates. When sore beset at home in this way, he would every now and then discover that he had some very particular business to attend to on an outlying part of his estate; and, craving the indulgence of his guests over night, appear at the cabin in the glen before its inhabitants were astir in the morning. The clatter of Sibyl Grey's hoofs, the yelping of Mustard and Spice, and his own joyous shout of *reveillée* under our windows, were the signal that he had burst his toils, and meant for that day to 'take his ease in his inn.' On descending, he was to be found seated with all his dogs and ours about him, under a spreading ash that overshadowed half the bank between the cottage and the brook, pointing the edge of his woodman's-axe, and listening to Tom Purdie's lecture touching the plantation that most needed thinning. After breakfast he would take possession of a dressing-room up stairs, and write a chapter of *The Pirate;* and then, having made up and despatched his packet for Mr. Ballantyne, away to join Purdie wherever the foresters were at work—and sometimes to labour among them as strenuously as John Swanston,—until it was time either to rejoin his own party at Abbotsford, or the quiet circle of the cottage. When his guests were few and friendly, he often made them come over and meet him at Chiefswood in a body towards evening; and surely he never appeared to more amiable advantage than when helping his young people with their little arrangements upon such occasions. He was ready with all sorts of devices to supply the wants of a narrow establishment; he used to delight particularly in sinking the wine in a well under the *brae* ere he went out, and hauling up the basket just before dinner was announced—this primitive device being, he said, what he had always practised when a young housekeeper, and in his opinion far superior in its results to any application of ice; and in the same spirit, whenever the weather was sufficiently genial, he voted for dining out of doors altogether, which at once got rid of the inconvenience of very small rooms, and made it natural and easy for the gentlemen to help the ladies, so that the paucity of servants went for nothing."—Vol. v. pp. 123, 124.

Surely all this is very beautiful; like a picture of Boccaccio: the ideal of a country life in our time. Why could it not last? Income was not wanting: Scott's official permanent income was amply adequate to meet the expense of all that was valuable in it; nay, of all that was not harassing, senseless, and despicable. Scott had some £2,000 a year without writing books at all. Why should he manufacture and not create, to make more money; and rear mass on mass for a dwelling to himself, till the pile toppled, sank, crashing, and buried him in its ruins, when he had a safe pleasant dwelling ready of its own accord? Alas, Scott, with all his health, was *infected;* sick of the fearfullest malady, that of Ambition! To such length had the King's baronetcy, the world's favour, and "sixteen parties a-day," brought it with him. So the inane racket must be kept up, and rise ever higher. So masons labour, ditchers delve; and there is endless, altogether deplorable correspondence about marble-slabs for tables, wainscotting of rooms, curtains with the trimmings of curtains, orange-coloured or fawn-coloured: Walter Scott, one of the gifted of the world, whom his admirers called the most gifted, must kill himself that he may be a country gentleman, the founder of a race of Scottish lairds. It is one of the strangest, most tragical histories ever enacted under this sun. So poor a passion can lead so strong a man into such mad extremes. Surely, were not man a fool always, one might say there was something eminently distracted in this, *end* as it would, of a Walter Scott writing daily with the ardour of a steam-engine, that he might make £15,000 a year, and buy upholstery with it. To cover the walls of a stone house in Selkirkshire with knicknacks, ancient armour, and genealogical shields, what can we name it but a being bit with delirium of a kind? That tract after tract of moorland in the shire of Selkirk should be joined together on parchment and by ring-fence, and named after one's name,—why, it is a shabby small-type edition of your vulgar Napoleons, Alexanders, and conquering heroes, not counted venerable by any teacher of men!—

"The whole world was not half so wide
To Alexander when he cried
Because he had but one to subdue,
As was a narrow paltry tub to
Diogenes; who ne'er was said,
For aught that ever I could read,
To whine, put finger i' the eye and sob,
Because he had ne'er another tub."

Not he! And if, "looked at from the Moon, which itself is far from Infinitude," Napoleon's dominions were as small as mine, *what*, by any chance of possibility, could Abbotsford landed-property ever have become? As the Arabs say, there is a black speck, were it no bigger than a bean's eye, in every soul; which once set it a-working, will overcloud the whole man into darkness and quasi-madness, and hurry him balefully into Night!

With respect to the literary character of these "Waverly Novels," so extraordinary in their commercial character, there remains, after so much reviewing, good and bad, little that it were profitable at present to say. The great fact about them is, that they were faster written and better paid for than any other books in the world. It must be granted, moreover, that they have a worth far surpassing what is usual in such cases; nay, that if literature had no task but that of harmlessly amusing indolent, languid men, here was the very perfection of literature; that a man, here more emphatically than ever elsewhere, might fling himself back, exclaiming, "Be mine to lie on this sofa, and read everlasting Novels of Walter Scott!" The composition, slight as it often is, usually hangs together in some measure, and *is* a composition. There is a free flow of narrative, of incident and sentiment; an easy master-like coherence throughout, as if it were the free dash of a master's hand, "round as the O of Giotto."* It is the perfection of

* "Venne a Firenze, (il cortigiano del Papa,) e andato una mattina in bottega di Giotto, che lavorava, gli

extemporaneous writing. Farthermore, surely he was a blind critic who did not recognise here a certain genial sunshiny freshness and picturesqueness; paintings both of scenery and figures, very graceful, brilliant, occasionally full of grace and glowing brightness, blended in the softest composure; in fact, a deep sincere love of the beautiful in nature and man, and the readiest faculty of expressing this by imagination and by word. No fresher paintings of nature can be found than Scott's; hardly anywhere a wider sympathy with man. From Davie Deans up to Richard Cœur-de-Lion; from Meg Merrilies to Die Vernon and Queen Elizabeth! It is the utterance of a man of open soul; of a brave, large, free-seeing man, who has a true brotherhood with all men. In joyous picturesqueness and fellow-feeling, freedom of eye and heart; or to say it in a word, in general *healthiness* of mind, these novels prove Scott to have been amongst the foremost writers.

Neither in the higher and highest excellence, of drawing character, is he at any time altogether deficient; though at no time can we call him, in the best sense, successful. His Bailie Jarvies, Dinmonts, Dalgettys (for their name is legion) do look and talk like what they give themselves out for; they are, if not *created* and made poetically alive, yet deceptively *enacted* as a good player might do them. What more is wanted then? For the reader lying on a sofa, nothing more; yet for another sort of reader, much. It were a long chapter to unfold the difference in drawing a character between a Scott, a Shakspeare, and a Goethe? Yet it is a difference literally immense: they are of different species; the value of the one is not to be counted in the coin of the other. We might say in a short word, which means a long matter, that your Shakspeare fashions his characters from the heart outwards; your Scott fashions them from the skin inwards, never getting near the heart of them! The one set became living men and women; the other amount to little more than mechanical cases, deceptively painted automatons. Compare Fenella with Goethe's Mignon, which, it was once said, Scott had "done Goethe the honour" to borrow. He has borrowed what he could of Mignon. The small stature, the climbing talent, the trickiness, the *mechanical case*, as we say, he has borrowed; but the soul of Mignon is left behind. Fenella is an unfavourable specimen for Scott; but it illustrates, in the aggravated state, what is traceable in all the characters he drew. To the same purport, indeed, we are to say that these famed books are altogether addressed to the everyday mind; that for any other mind, there is next to no nourishment in them. Opinions, emotions, principles, doubts, beliefs, beyond what the intelligent country gentleman can carry along with him, are not to be found. It is orderly, customary, it is prudent, decent; nothing more. One would say, it lay not in Scott to give much more; getting out of the ordinary range, and attempting the heroic, which is but seldom the case, he falls almost at once into the rose-pink sentimental,—descries the Minerva Press from afar, and hastily quits that course; for none better than he knew it to lead nowhither. On the whole, contrasting Waverly, which was carefully written, with most of its followers, which were written extempore, one may regret the extempore method. Something very perfect in its kind might have come from Scott; nor was it a low kind: nay, who knows how high, with studious self-concentration, he might have gone; what wealth nature had implanted in him, which his circumstances, most unkind while seeming to be kindest, had never impelled him to unfold?

But after all, in the loudest blaring and trumpeting of popularity, it is ever to be held in mind, as a truth remaining true for ever, that literature *has* other aims than that of harmlessly amusing indolent, languid men: or if literature have them not, then literature is a very poor affair; and something else must have them, and must accomplish them, with thanks or without thanks; the thankful or thankless world were not long a world otherwise! Under this head there is little to be sought or found in the "Waverley Novels." Not profitable for doctrine, for reproof, for edification, for building up or elevating, in any shape! The sick heart will find no healing here, the darkly struggling heart no guidance: the Heroic that is in all men no divine awakening voice. We say, therefore, that they do not found themselves on deep interests, but on comparatively trivial ones; not on the perennial, perhaps not even on the lasting. In fact, much of the interest of these novels results from what may be called contrasts of costume. The phraseology, fashion of arms, of dress and life, belonging to one age, is brought suddenly, with singular vividness, before the eyes of another. A great effect this; yet, by the very nature of it, an altogether temporary one. Consider, brethren, shall not we too one day be antiques, and grow to have as quaint a costume as the rest? The stuffed dandy, only give him *time*, will become one of the wonderfullest mummies. In antiquarian museums, only two centuries hence, the steeple-hat will hang on the next peg to Franks and Company's patent, antiquarians deciding which is uglier: and the Stultz swallow-tail, one may hope, will seem as incredible as any garment that ever made ridiculous the respectable back of man. Not by slashed breeches, steeple-hats, buff-belts, or antiquated speech, can romance heroes continue to interest us; but simply and solely, in the long run, by being men. Buff-belts and all manner of jerkins and costumes are transitory; man alone is perennial. He that has gone deeper into this than other men, will be remembered longer than they; he that has not,

chiese un poco di disegno per mandarlo a sua Santità. Giotto, che garbatissimo era, prese un foglio, ed in quello con un pennello tinto di rosso, fermato il braccio al financo per farne compasso, e girato la mano fece un tondo sì pari di sesto e di profilo, che fu a vederlo una maraviglia. Ciò fatto ghignando disse al cortigiano, Eccovi il disegno." . . . . "Onde il Papa, e molti cortigiani intendenti conobbero perciò, quanto Giotto avanzasse d'eccelenza tutti gli altri pittori del suo tempo. Divolgatasi poi questa cosa, ne nacque il proverbio, che ancora è in uso dirsi a gli nomini di grossa pasta: *Tu sei più tondo che l' O di Giotto.*"—Vasari, *Vite* (Roma, 1759), i. 46.

not. Tried under this category, Scott with his clear practical insight, joyous temper, and other sound faculties, is not to be accounted little, —among the ordinary circulating library heroes he might well pass for a demi-god. Not little; yet neither is he great; there were greater, more than one or two in his own age: among the great of all ages, one sees no likelihood of a place for him.

What then is the result of these Waverley romances? Are they to amuse one generation only? One or more. As many generations as they can, but not all generations: ah no, when our swallow-tail has become fantastic as trunk-hose, they will cease to amuse!—Meanwhile, as we can discern, their results have been several-fold. First of all, and certainly not least of all, have they not perhaps had this result: that a considerable portion of mankind has hereby been sated with mere amusement, and set on seeking something better? Amusement in the way of reading can go no farther, can do nothing better, by the power of man; and men ask, Is this what it can do? Scott, we reckon, carried several things to their ultimatum and crisis, so that change became inevitable: a great service, though an indirect one. Secondly, however, we may say, these historical novels have taught all men this truth, which looks like a truism, and yet was as good as unknown to writers of history and others, till so taught: that the by-gone ages of the world were actually filled by living men, not by protocols, state-papers, controversies, and abstractions of men. Not abstractions were they, not diagrams and theorems; but men, in buff or other coats and breeches, with colour in their cheeks, with passions in their stomach, and the idioms, features, and vitalities of very men. It is a little word this; inclusive of great meaning! History will henceforth have to take thought of it. Her faint hearsays of "philosophy teaching by experience" will have to exchange themselves everywhere for direct inspection and imbodyment: this, and this only, will be counted experience; and till once experience have got in, philosophy will reconcile herself to wait at the door. It is a great service, fertile in consequences, this that Scott has done; a great truth laid open by him;—correspondent indeed to the substantial nature of the man; to his solidity and veracity even of imagination, which, with all his lively discursiveness, was the characteristic of him.

A word here as to the extempore style of writing, which is getting much celebrated in these days. Scott seems to have been a high proficient in it. His rapidity was extreme, and the matter produced was excellent considering that: the circumstances under which some of his novels, when he could not himself write, were dictated, are justly considered wonderful. It is a valuable faculty this of ready writing; nay farther, for Scott's purpose it was clearly the only good mode. By much labour he could not have added one guinea to his copy-right; nor could the reader on the sofa have lain a whit more at ease. It was in all ways necessary that these works should be produced rapidly; and, round or not, be thrown off like Giotto's O. But indeed, in all things, writing or other, which a man engages in, there is the indispensablest beauty in knowing *how to get done.* A man frets himself to no purpose; he has not the sleight of the trade; he is not a craftsman, but an unfortunate borer and bungler, if he know not when to have done. Perfection is unattainable: no carpenter ever made a mathematically accurate right-angle in the world; yet all carpenters know when it is right enough, and do not botch it, and lose their wages by making it too right. Too much pains-taking speaks disease in one's mind, as well as too little. The adroit sound-minded man will endeavour to spend on each business approximately what of pains it deserves; and with a conscience void of remorse will dismiss it then. All this in favour of easy writing shall be granted, and, if need were, enforced and inculcated. And yet, on the other hand, it shall not less but more strenuously be inculcated, that in the way of writing no great thing was ever, or will ever be done with ease, but with difficulty! Let ready writers, with any faculty in them, lay this to heart. Is it with ease, or not with ease, that a man shall *do his best,* in any shape; above all, in this shape, justly named of "soul's travail," working in the deep places of thought, imbodying the true out of the obscure and possible, environed on all sides with the uncreated false? Not so, now or at any time. The experience of all men belies it; the nature of things contradicts it. Virgil and Tacitus, were they ready writers? The whole *Prophecies of Isaiah* are not equal in extent to this cobweb of a review article. Shakspeare, we may fancy, wrote with rapidity; but not till he had thought with intensity: long and sore had this man thought, as the seeing eye may discern well, and had dwelt and wrestled amid dark pains and throes, —though his great soul is silent about all that. It was for him to write rapidly at fit intervals, being ready to do it. And herein truly lies the secret of the matter: such swiftness of mere writing, after due energy of preparation, is doubtless the right method; the hot furnace having long worked and simmered, let the pure gold flow out at one gush. It was Shakspeare's plan; no easy writer he, or he had never been a Shakspeare. Neither was Milton one of the mob of gentlemen that write with ease; he did not attain Shakspeare's faculty, one perceives, of even writing fast *after* long preparation. but struggled while he wrote. Goethe also tells us he "had nothing sent him in his sleep;" no page of his but he knew well how it came there. It is reckoned to be the best prose, accordingly, that has been written by any modern. Schiller, as an unfortunate and unhealthy man, "*könnte nie fertig werden,* never could get done;" the noble genius of him struggled not wisely but too well, and wore his life itself heroically out. Or did Petrarch write easily? Dante sees himself "growing gray" over his *Divine Comedy;* in stern solitary death-wrestle with it, to prevail over it, and do it, if his uttermost faculty may: hence, too, it is done and prevailed over, and the fiery life of it endures for evermore among men. No: creation, one would think, cannot be easy;

your Jove has severe pains and fire-flames in the head, out of which an armed Pallas is struggling! As for manufacture, that is a different matter, and may become easy or not easy, according as it is taken up. Yet of manufacture, too, the general truth is that, given the manufacturer, it will be worthy in direct proportion to the pains bestowed upon it; and worthless always, or nearly so, with no pains. Cease, therefore, O ready-writer, to brag openly of thy rapidity and facility; to thee (if thou be in the manufacturing line) it is a benefit, an increase of wages; but to me it is sheer loss, worsening of my pennyworth: why wilt thou brag of it to me? Write easily, by steam if thou canst contrive it, and canst sell it; but hide it like virtue! "Easy writing," said Sheridan, "is sometimes d——d hard reading." Sometimes; and always it is sure to be rather useless reading, which indeed (to a creature of few years and much work) may be reckoned the hardest of all.

Scott's productive facility amazed everybody; and set Captain Hall, for one, upon a very strange method of accounting for it without miracle;—for which see his "journal," above quoted from. The Captain, on counting line for line, found that he himself had written in that journal of his almost as much as Scott, at odd hours in a given number of days; "and as for the invention," says he, "it is known that this costs Scott nothing, but comes to him of its own accord." Convenient indeed!—But for us too Scott's rapidity is great, is a proof and consequence of the solid health of the man, bodily and spiritual; great, but unmiraculous; not greater than that of many others besides Captain Hall. Admire it, yet with measure. For observe always, there are two conditions in work: let me fix the quality, and *you* shall fix the quantity! Any man may get through work rapidly who easily satisfies himself about it. Print the *talk* of any man, there will be a thick octavo volume daily; make his writing three times as good as his talk, there will be the third part of a volume daily, which still is good work. To write with never such rapidity in a passable manner, is indicative, not of a man's genius, but of his habits; it will prove his soundness of nervous system, his practicability of mind, and in fine, that he has the knack of his trade. In the most flattering view, rapidity will betoken health of mind: much also, perhaps most of all, will depend on health of body. Doubt it not, a faculty of easy writing is attainable by man! The human genius, once fairly set in this direction, will carry it far. William Cobbett, one of the healthiest of men, was a greater improviser even than Walter Scott: his writing, considered as to quality and quantity, of Rural Rides, Registers, Grammars, Sermons, Peter Porcupines, Histories of Reformation, ever-fresh denouncements of Potatoes and Papermoney,—seems to us still more wonderful. Pierre Bayle wrote enormous folios, one sees not on what motive-principle; he flowed on for ever, a mighty tide of ditch-water; and even died flowing, with the pen in his hand. But indeed the most unaccountable ready-writer of all is, probably, the common Editor of a Daily Newspaper. Consider his leading-articles; what they treat of, how passably they are done. Straw that has been thrashed a hundred times without wheat; ephemeral sound of a sound; such portent of the hour as all men have seen a hundred times turn out inane; how a man, with merely human faculty, buckles himself nightly with new vigour and interest to this thrashed straw, nightly thrashes it anew, nightly gets up new thunder about it; and so goes on thrashing and thundering for a considerable series of years; this is a fact remaining still to be accounted for, in human physiology. The vitality of man is great.

Or shall we say, Scott, among the many things he carried towards their ultimatum and crisis, carried this of ready-writing too, that so all men might better see what was in it? It is a valuable consummation. Not without results;—results, at some of which Scott as a Tory politician would have greatly shuddered. For if once Printing have grown to be as Talk, then DEMOCRACY (if we look into the roots of things) is not a bugbear and probability, but a certainty, and event as good as come! "Inevitable seems it me." But leaving this, sure enough the triumph of ready-writing appears to be even now; everywhere the ready-writer is found bragging strangely of his readiness. In a late translated "Don Carlos," one of the most indifferent translations ever done with any sign of ability, a hitherto unknown individual is found assuring his reader, "The reader will possibly think it an excuse, when I assure him that the whole piece was completed within the space of ten weeks, that is to say, between the sixth of January and the eighteenth of March of this year, (inclusive of a fortnight's interruption from over exertion;) that I often translated twenty pages a-day, and that the fifth act was the work of five days."* O hitherto unknown individual, what is it to me what time it was the work of, whether five days or five decades of years? The only question is, How hast thou done it?—So, however, it stands: the genius of Extempore irresistibly lording it, advancing on us like ocean-tides, like Noah's deluges—of ditch-water! The prospect seems one of the lamentablest. To have all Literature swum away from us in watery Extempore, and a spiritual time of Noah supervene? That surely is an awful reflection, worthy of dyspeptic Matthew Bramble in a London fog! Be of comfort, O splenetic Matthew; it is not Literature they are swimming away; it is only Book-publishing and Book-selling. Was there not a Literature *before* Printing or Faust of Mentz, and yet men wrote extempore? Nay, before Writing or Cadmus of Thebes, and yet men spoke extempore? Literature is the Thought of thinking Souls; this, by the blessing of God, can in no generation be swum away, but remains with us to the end.

Scott's career, of writing impromptu novels to buy farms with, was not of a kind to terminate voluntarily, but to accelerate itself more

* "Don Carlos," a Dramatic Poem, from the German of Schiller, Mannheim and London, 1837.

and more; and one sees not to what wise goal it could, in any case, have led him. Bookseller Constable's bankruptcy was not the ruin of Scott; his ruin was that ambition, and even false ambition, had laid hold of him; that his way of life was not wise. Whither could it lead? Where could it stop? New farms there remained ever to be bought, while new novels could pay for them. More and more success but gave more and more appetite, more and more audacity. The impromptu writing must have waxed even thinner; declined faster and faster into the questionable category, into the condemnable, into the general condemned. Already there existed, in secret, everywhere a considerable opposition party; witnesses of the Waverley miracles, but unable to believe in them, forced silently to protest against them. Such opposition party was in the sure case to grow; and even, with the impromptu process ever going on, ever waxing thinner, to draw the world over to it. Silent protest must at length come to words; harsh truths, backed by harsher facts of a world-popularity overwrought and worn out, behoved to have been spoken;—such as can be spoken now without reluctance when they can pain the brave man's heart no more. Who knows? Perhaps it was better ordered to be all *otherwise*. Otherwise, at any rate, it was. One day the Constable mountain, which seemed to stand strong like the other rock mountains, gave suddenly, as the ice-bergs do, a loud-sounding crack; suddenly, with huge clangor, shivered itself into ice-dust; and sank, carrying much along with it. In one day Scott's high-heaped money-wages became fairy-money and nonentity; in one day the rich man and lord of land saw himself penniless, landless, a bankrupt among creditors.

It was a hard trial. He met it proudly, bravely,—like a brave proud man of the world. Perhaps there had been a prouder way still; to have owned honestly that he *was* unsuccessful then, all bankrupt, broken, in the world's good's and repute; and to have turned elsewhither for some refuge. Refuge did lie elsewhere; but it was not Scott's course, or fashion of mind, to seek it there. To say, Hitherto I have been all in the wrong, and this my fame and pride, now broken, was an empty delusion and spell of accursed witchcraft! It was difficult for flesh and blood! He said, I will retrieve myself, and make my point good yet, or die for it. Silently, like a proud strong man, he girt himself to the Hercules' task, of removing rubbish-mountains, since that was it; of paying large ransoms by what he could still write and sell. In his declining years too; misfortune is doubly and trebly unfortunate that befalls us then. Scott fell to his Hercules' task like a very man, and went on with it unweariedly; with a noble cheerfulness, while his lifestrings were cracking, he grappled with it, and wrestled with it, years long, in death-grips, strength to strength;—and *it* proved the stronger; and his life and heart did crack and break: the cordage of a most strong heart! Over these last writings of Scott, his *Napoleons, Demonologies, Scotch Histories*, and the rest, criticism, finding still much to wonder at, much to commend, will utter no word of blame; this one word only, Wo is me! The noble warhorse that once laughed at the shaking of the spear, how is he doomed to toil himself dead, dragging ignoble wheels! Scott's descent was like that of a spent projectile; rapid, straight down;—perhaps mercifully so. It is a tragedy, as all life is; one proof more that Fortune stands on a restless *globe;* that Ambition, literary, warlike, politic, pecuniary, never yet profited any man.

Our last extract shall be from Volume Sixth; a very tragical one. Tragical, yet still beautiful; waste Ruin's havoc borrowing a kind of sacredness from a yet sterner visitation, that of Death! Scott has withdrawn into a solitary lodging-house in Edinburgh, to do daily the day's work there; and had to leave his wife at Abbotsford in the last stage of disease. He went away silently; looked silently at the sleeping face he scarcely hoped ever to see again. We quote from a Diary he had begun to keep in those months, on hint from Byron's *Ravenna Journal:* copious sections of it render this sixth volume more interesting than any of the former ones:—

"*Abbotsford, May* 11, (1826.)— * * * It withers my heart to think of it, and to recollect that I can hardly hope again to seek confidence and counsel from that ear, to which all might be safely confided. But in her present lethargic state, what would my attendance have availed? —and Anne has promised close and constant intelligence. I must dine with James Ballantyne to-day *en famille*. I cannot help it; but would rather be at home and alone. However, I can go out too. I will not yield to the barren sense of hopelessness which struggles to invade me."

"*Edinburgh,—Mrs. Brown's lodgings, North St. David Street—May* 12.—I passed a pleasant day with kind J. B., which was a great relief from the black dog, which would have worried me at home. He was quite alone.

"Well, here I am in Arden. And I may say with Touchstone, 'When I was in a better place;' I must, when there is occasion, draw to my own Baillie Nicol Jarvie's consolation —'One cannot carry the comforts of the Saut-Market about with one.' Were I at ease in mind, I think the body is very well cared for. Only one other lodger in the house, a Mr. Shandy—a clergyman; and, despite his name, said to be a quiet one."

"*May* 14.—A fair good-morrow to you, Mr. Sun, who are shining so brightly on these dull walls. Methinks you look as if you were looking as bright on the banks of the Tweed; but look where you will, Sir Sun, you look upon sorrow and suffering.—Hogg was here yesterday in danger, from having obtained an accommodation of £100 from James Ballantyne, which he is now obliged to repay. I am unable to help the poor fellow, being obliged to borrow myself."

"*May* 15.—Received the melancholy intelligence that all is over at Abbotsford."

"*Abbotsford, May* 16.—She died at nine in the morning, after being very ill for two days —easy at last. I arrived here late last night. Anne is worn out, and has had hysterics, which returned on my arrival. Her broken accents were like those of a child, the language as well as the tones broken, but in the most gentle voice of submission. "Poor mamma—never return again—gone for ever—a better place." Then, when she came to herself, she spoke with sense, freedom, and strength of mind, till her weakness returned. It would have been inexpressibly moving to me as a stranger—what was it then to the father and the husband? For myself, I scarce know how I feel; sometimes as firm as the Bass Rock, sometimes as weak as the water that breaks on it. I am as alert at thinking and deciding as I ever was in my life. Yet, when I contrast what this place now is, with what it has been not long since, I think my heart will break. Lonely, aged, deprived of my family—all but poor Anne; an impoverished, an embarrassed man, deprived of the sharer of my thoughts and counsels, who could always talk down my sense of the calamitous apprehensions which break the heart that must bear them alone.—Even her foibles were of service to me, by giving me things to think of beyond my weary self-reflections.

"I have seen her. The figure I beheld is, and is not my Charlotte—my thirty years' companion. There is the same symmetry of form, though those limbs are rigid which were once so gracefully elastic—but that yellow mask, with pinched features, which seems to mock life rather than emulate it, can it be the face that was once so full of lively expression? I will not look on it again. Anne thinks her little changed, because the latest idea she had formed of her mother is as she appeared under circumstances of extreme pain. Mine go back to a period of comparative ease. If I write long in this way, I shall write down my resolution, which I should rather write up, if I could."

"*May* 18.— * * Cerements of lead and of wood already hold her; cold earth must have her soon. But it is not my Charlotte, it is not the bride of my youth, the mother of my children, that will be laid among the ruins of Dryburgh, which we have so often visited in gayety and pastime. No, no."

"*May* 22.— * * Well, I am not apt to shrink from that w. ich is my duty, merely because it is painful; but I wish this funeral-day over. A kind of cloud of stupidity hangs about me, as if all were unreal that men seem to be doing and talking."

"*May* 26.— * * Were an enemy coming upon my house, would I not do my best to fight, although oppressed in spirits; and shall a similar despondency prevent me from mental exertion? It shall not, by Heaven!"

"*Edinburgh, May* 30.—Returned to town last night with Charles. This morning resume ordinary habits of rising early, working in the morning, and attending the Court." * * "I finished correcting the proofs for the Quarterly; it is but a flimsy article, but then the circumstances were most untoward.—This has been a melancholy day—most melancholy. I am afraid poor Charles found me weeping. I do not know what other folks feel, but with me the hysterical passion that impels tears is a terrible violence—a sort of throttling sensation—then succeeded by a state of dreaming stupidity, in which I ask if my poor Charlotte can actually be dead."—Vol. vi. pp. 297, 307.

This is beautiful as well as tragical. Other scenes, in that Seventh Volume, must come, which will have no beauty, but be tragical only. It is better that we are to end here.

And so the curtain falls; and the strong Walter Scott is with us no more. A possession from him does remain; widely scattered; yet attainable; not inconsiderable. It can be said of him, "when he departed he took a Man's life along with him." No sounder piece of British manhood was put together in that eighteenth century of time. Alas, his fine Scotch face, with its shaggy honesty, sagacity, and goodness, when we saw it latterly on the Edinburgh streets, was all worn with care, the joy all fled from it;—ploughed deep with labour and sorrow. We shall never forget it; we shall never see it again. Adieu, Sir Walter, pride of all Scotchmen, take our proud and sad farewell.

VARNHAGEN VON ENSE'S MEMOIRS.*

[London and Westminster Review, 1838.]

The Lady *Rahel*, or Rachel, surnamed *Levin* in her maiden days, who died some five years ago as Madam Varnhagen von Ense, seems to be still memorable and notable, or to have become more than ever so, among our German friends. The widower, long known in Berlin and Germany for an intelligent and estimable man, has here published successively, as author, or as editor and annotator, so many volumes, nine in all, about her, about himself, and the things that occupied and environed them. Nine volumes, properly, of German Memoirs; of letters, of miscellanies, biographical and autobiographical; which we have read not without zeal and diligence, and in part with great pleasure. It seems to us that such of our readers as take interest in things German, ought to be apprized of this publication; and withal that there are in it enough of things European and universal to furnish out a few pages for readers not specially of that class.

One may hope, Germany is no longer to any person that vacant land, of gray vapour and chimeras, which it was to most Englishmen, not many years ago. One may hope that, as readers of German have increased a hundredfold, some partial intelligence of Germany, some interest in things German, may have increased in a proportionably higher ratio. At all events, Memoirs of men, German or other, will find listeners among men. Sure enough, Berlin city, on the sandy banks of the Spree, is a living city, even as London is, on the muddy banks of Thames. Daily, with every rising of the blessed heavenly light, Berlin sends up the smoke of a hundred thousand kindled hearths, the fret and stir of five hundred thousand new-awakened human souls;—marking or defacing with *such* smoke-cloud, material or spiritual, the serene of our common all-embracing Heaven. One Heaven, the same for all, embraces that smoke-cloud too, adopts it, absorbs it, like the rest. Are there not dinner-parties, "æsthetic teas;" scandal-mongeries, changes of ministry, police cases, literary gazettes? The clack of tongues, the sound of hammers, mount up in that corner of the planet too, for certain centuries of time. Berlin has its royalties and diplomacies, its traffickings, travailings; literatures, sculptures, cultivated heads, male and female; and boasts itself to be "the intellectual capital of Germany." Nine volumes of Memoirs out of Berlin will surely contain something for us.

Samuel Johnson, or perhaps another, used to say, there was no man on the streets whose biography he would not like to be acquainted with. No rudest mortal walking there who has not seen and known experimentally something, which, could he tell it, the wisest would hear willingly from him! Nay, after all that can be said and celebrated about poetry, eloquence, and the higher forms of composition and utterance; is not the primary use of speech itself this same, to utter *memoirs*, that is, memorable experiences to our fellow-creatures? A fact is a fact; man is for ever the brother of man. That thou, Oh my brother, impart to me truly how it stands with thee in that inner man of thine, what lively images of things passed thy memory has painted there; what hopes, what thoughts, affections, knowledges, do now dwell there: for this and for no other object that I can see, was the gift of speech and of hearing bestowed on us two. I say not how thou feignest. Thy fictions, and thousand and one Arabian Nights, promulgated as fictions, what are they also at bottom but this, things that *are* in thee, though only images of things? But to bewilder me with *falsehoods*, indeed; to ray out error and darkness,—misintelligence, which means misattainment, otherwise failure and sorrow; to go about confusing worse our poor world's confusion, and, as a son of Nox and Chaos, propagate delirium on earth: not surely with *this* view, but with a far different one, was that miraculous tongue suspended in thy head, and set vibrating there! In a word, do not two things, *veracity* and *memoir-writing*, seem to be prescribed by Nature herself and the very constitution of man? Let us read, therefore, according to opportunity,—and, with judicious audacity, review!

Our nine printed volumes we called German Memoirs. They agree in this general character, but are otherwise to be distinguished into kinds, and differ very much in their worth for us. The first book on our list, entitled "Rahel," is a book of private letters; three thick volumes of Letters written by that lady: selected from her wide correspondence; with a short introduction, with here and there a short note, and that on Varnhagen's part all. Then follows, in two volumes, the work named "Gallery of Portraits;" consisting principally of Letters *to* Rahel, by various persons, mostly persons of note; to which Varnhagen, as editor, has joined some slight commentary, some short biographical sketch of each. Of these five volumes of German Letters we will say, for the present, that they seem to be calculated for Germany, and even for some special circle there, rather than for England or us. A glance

*1. *Rahel. Ein Buch des Andenkens für ihre Freunde.* (Rahel. A Book of Memorial for her Friends.) 3 vols. Berlin, 1834.

2. *Gallerie von Bildnissen aus Rahel's Umgang und Briefwechsel.* (Gallery of Portraits from Rahel's Circle of Society and Correspondence.) Edited by K. A. Varnhagen von Ense. 2 vols. Leipsic, 1836.

3. *Denkwürdigkeiten und vermischte Schriften.* (Memoirs and Miscellaneous Writings.) By K. A. Varnhagen von Ense. 4 vols. Mannheim, 1837–38.

at them afterwards, we hope, will be possible. But the third work, that of Varnhagen himself, is the one we must chiefly depend on here; the four volumes of "Memoirs and Miscellanies;" lively pieces; which can be safely recommended as altogether pleasant reading to every one. They are "Miscellaneous Writings," as their title indicates; in part collected and reprinted out of periodicals, or wherever they lay scattered; in part sent forth now for the first time. There are criticisms, notices literary or didactic; always of a praiseworthy sort, generally of small extent. There are narrations; there is a long personal narrative, as it might be called, of service in the "Liberation War," of 1814, wherein Varnhagen did duty, as a volunteer officer, in Tettenborn's corps, among the Cossacks: this is the longest piece, by no means the best. There is farther a curious narrative of Lafayette's escape (brief escape with recapture) from the Prison of Olmütz. Then also there is a curious biography of Doctor Bollmann, the brave young Hanoverian, who aided Lafayette in that adventure. Then other biographies not so curious; on the whole, there are many biographies: Biography, we might say, is the staple article; an article in which Varnhagen has long been known to excel. Lastly, as basis for the whole, there are presented, fitfully, now here, now there, and with long intervals, considerable sections of Autobiography;—not confessions, indeed, or questionable work of the Rousseau sort, but discreet reminiscences, personal and other, of a man who having looked on much, may be sure of willing audience in reporting it well. These are the four volumes written by Varnhagen von Ense; those are the five edited by him. We shall regard his autobiographic memorials as a general substratum, upholding and uniting into a certain coherence the multifarious contents of these publications: it is Varnhagen von Ense's passage through life; this is what it yielded him; these are the things and persons he took note of, and had to do with, in travelling thus far.

Beyond ascertaining for ourselves what manner of eyesight and way of judgment this our memoir-writer has, it is not necessary to insist much on Varnhagen's qualities or literary character here. He seems to us a man peculiarly fitted, both by natural endowment and by position and opportunity, for writing memoirs. In the space of half a century that he has lived in this world, his course has been what we might call erratic in a high degree: from the student's garret in Halle or Tübingen to the Tuileries hall of audience and the Wagram battle-field, from Chamisso the poet to Napoleon the Emperor, his path has intersected all manner of paths of men. He has a fine intellectual gift; and what is the foundation of that and of all, an honest, sympathizing, manfully patient, manfully courageous heart. His way of life, too erratic we should fear for happiness or ease, and singularly checkered by vicissitude, has had this considerable advantage, if no other, that it has trained him, and could not but train him, to a certain Catholicism of mind. He has been a student of literature, an author, a student of medicine, a soldier, a secretary, a diplomatist. A man withal of modest, affectionate nature; courteous and yet truthful; of quick apprehension, precise in utterance; of just, extensive, occasionally of deep and fine insight,—this is a man qualified beyond most to write memoirs. We should call him one of the best memoir-writers we have met with; decidedly the best we know of in these days. For clearness, grace of method, easy comprehensibility, he is worthy to be ranked among the French, who have a natural turn for memoir-writing; and in respect of honesty, valourous gentleness, and simplicity of heart, his character is German, not French.

Such a man, conducting us in the spirit of cheerful friendliness, along his course of life, and delineating what he has found most memorable in it, produces one of the pleasantest books. Brave old Germany, in this and the other living phasis, now here, now there, from Rhineland to the East-sea, from Hamburg and Berlin to Deutsch-Wagram and the Marchfield, paints itself in the colours of reality; with notable persons, with notable events For consider withal in what a time this man's life has lain: in the thick of European things, while the Nineteenth Century was opening itself. Amid convulsions and revolutions, outward and inward,—with Napoleons, Goethes, Fichtes; while prodigies and battle-thunder shook the world, and, "amid the glare of conflagrations, and the noise of falling towns and kingdoms," a new era of thought was also evolving itself: one of the wonderfullest times! On the whole, if men like Varnhagen were to be met with, why have we not innumerable Memoirs? Alas, it is because the men like Varnhagen are *not* to be met with; men with the clear eye and the open heart. Without such qualities, memoir-writers are but a nuisance; which so often as they show themselves, a judicious world is obliged to sweep into the cesspool, with loudest possible prohibition of the like. If a man is not open-minded, if he is ignorant, perverse, egoistic, splenetic; on the whole, if he is false and stupid, how shall he write memoirs?—

From Varnhagen's young years, especially from his college years, we could extract many a lively little sketch, of figures partially known to the reader; of Chamisso, La Motte Fouqué, Raumer, and other the like; of Platonic Schleiermacher, sharp, crabbed, shrunken, with his wire-drawn logic, his sarcasms, his sly malicious ways; of Homeric Wolf, with his biting wit, with his grim earnestness and inextinguishable Homeric laugh, the irascible great-hearted man. Or of La Fontaine, the sentimental novelist, over whose rose-coloured moral-sublime what fair eye has not wept? Varnhagen found him "in a pleasant house near the Saale-gate" of Halle, with an ugly good-tempered wife, with a pretty niece, which latter he would not allow to read a word of his romance stuff, but "kept it locked from her like poison;" a man jovial as Boniface, swollen out on booksellers' profit, church, preferments, and fat things, "to the size of a hogshead;" for the rest, writing with such velocity (he did some hundred and fifty weeping volumes in his time) that he was obliged to hold in, and "write only two days in the week;" this was La Fontaine, the sentimental novelist. But omitting all these, let us pick out a family-picture of one far better worth looking at, Jean Paul in his little home at Baireuth,—"little city of my habitation, which I belong to on this side the grave!" It is Sunday, the 23d of October, 1808, according to Varnhagen's note-book. The ingenious youth of four-and-twenty, as a rambling student, passes the day of rest there, and luckily for us has kept memorandums:

"*Visit to Jean Paul Friedrich Richter.*—This forenoon I went to Jean Paul's. Friend Harscher was out of humour, and would not go, say what I would. I too, for that matter, am but a poor, nameless student: but what of that?

"A pleasant, kindly, inquisitive, woman, who had opened the door to me, I at once recognised for Jean Paul's wife by her likeness to her sister. A child was sent off to call its father. He came directly: he had been forwarned of my visit by letters from Berlin and Leipsic; and received me with great kindness. As he seated himself beside me on the sofa, I had almost laughed in his face, for in bending down somewhat he had the very look our Neumann, in his 'Versuchen und Hindernissen,' has jestingly given him, and his speaking and what he spoke confirmed that impression. Jean Paul is of stout figure; has a full, well-ordered face; the eyes small, gleaming out on you with lambent fire, then again veiled in soft dimness; the mouth friendly, and with some slight motion in it even when silent. His speech is rapid, almost hasty, even stuttering somewhat here and there; not without a certain degree of dialect, difficult to designate, but which probably is some mixture of Frankish and Saxon, and of course is altogether kept down within the rules of cultivated language.

"First of all I had to tell him what I was charged with in the shape of messages, then whatsoever I could tell in any way, about his Berlin friends. He willingly remembered the time he had lived in Berlin, as Marcus Herz's neighbour, in Leder's house where I, seven years before, had first seen him in the garden by the Spree, with papers in his hand, which it was privately whispered were leaves of 'Hesperus.' This talk about persons, and then still more about Literature growing out of that, set him fairly underway, and soon he had more to impart than to inquire. His conversation was throughout amiable and good-natured, always full of meaning, but in quite simple tone and expression. Though I knew beforehand that his wit and humour belonged only to his pen, that he could hardly write the shortest note without these introducing themselves, while on the contrary his oral utterance seldom showed the like,—yet it struck me much that, in this continual movement and vivacity of mood to which he yielded himself, I observed no trace of these qualities. His demeanour otherwise was like his speaking; nothing forced, nothing studied, nothing that went beyond the burgher tone. His courtesy was the free expression of a kind heart; his way and bearing were patriarchal, considerate of the stranger, yet for himself too altogether unconstrained. Neither in the animation to which some word or topic would excite him, was this fundamental temper ever altered; nowhere did severity appear, nowhere any exhibiting of himself, any watching or spying of his hearer; everywhere kindheartedness, free movement of his somewhat loose-flowing nature, open course for him, with a hundred transitions from one course to the other, howsoever or whithersoever it seemed good to him to go. At first he praised every thing that was named of our new appearances in Literature; and then when we came a little closer to the matter, there was blame enough and to spare. So of Adam Müller's Lectures, of Friedrich Schlegel, of Tieck and others. He said, German writers ought to hold by the people, not by the upper classes, among whom all was already dead and gone; and yet he had just been praising Adam Müller, that he had the gift of speaking a deep word to cultivated people of the world. He is convinced that, from the opening of the old Indian world, nothing is to be got for us, except the adding of one other mode of poetry to the many modes we have already, but no increase of ideas: and yet he had just been celebrating Friedrich Schlegel's labours with the Sanscrit, as if a new salvation were to issue out of that. He was free to confess that a right Christian in these days, if not a Protestant one, was inconceivable to him; that changing from Protestantism to Catholicism seemed a monstrous perversion; and with this opinion great hope had been expressed, a few minutes before, that the Catholic spirit in Friedrich Schlegel, combined with the Indian, would produce much good! Of Schleiermacher he spoke with respect; signified, however, that he did not relish his 'Plato' greatly; that in Jacobi's, in Herder's soaring flight of soul he traced far more of those divine old sages than in the learned acumen of Schleiermacher; a deliverance which I could not let pass without protest. Fichte, of whose 'Addresses to the German Nation,' held in Berlin under the sound of French drums, I had much to say, was not a favourite of his; the decisiveness of that energy gave him uneasiness; he said he could only read Fichte as an exercise, 'gymnastically,' and that with the purport of his Philosophy he had now nothing more to do.

"Jean Paul was called out, and I staid awhile alone with his wife. I had now to answer many new questions about Berlin; her interest in persons and things of her native town was by no means sated with what she had already heard. The lady pleased me exceedingly; soft, refined, acute, she united with the loveliest expression of household goodness an air of higher breeding and freer management than Jean Paul seemed to manifest. Yet, in this respect too, she willingly held herself inferior, and looked up to her gifted husband. It was apparent every way that their life together was a right happy one. Their three children, a boy and two girls, are beautiful, healthy, well-conditioned creatures. I had a hearty pleasure in them; they recalled other dear children to my thoughts, whom I had lately been beside! * * *

"With continual copiousness and in the best humour, Jean Paul (we were now at table) expatiated on all manner of objects. Among the rest, I had been charged with a salutation from Rahel Levin to him, and the modest question, 'Whether he remembered her still?' His face beamed with joyful satisfaction: 'How could one forget such a person?' cried he impressively. 'That is a woman alone of her kind: I liked her heartily well, and more now than ever, as I gain in sense an apprehension to do it; she is the only woman in whom I have found genuine humour, the one woman of this world who had humour!' He called me a lucky fellow to have such a friend; and asked, as if proving me and measuring my value, 'How I had deserved that?'

"*Monday, 24th October.*—Being invited, I went a second time to dine. Jean Paul had just returned from a walk; his wife, with one of the children, was still out. We came upon his writings; that questionable string with most authors, which the one will not have you touch, which another will have you keep jingling continually. He was here what I expected him to be; free, unconstrained, good-natured, and sincere with his whole heart. His 'Dream of a Madman,' just published by Cotta, was what had led us upon this. He said he could write such things at any time; the mood for it, when he was in health, lay in his own power; he did but seat himself at the harpsichord, and fantasying for a while on it, in the wildest way, deliver himself over to the feeling of the moment, and then write his imaginings,—according to a certain predetermined course, indeed, which however he would often alter as he went on. In this kind he had once undertaken to write a 'Hell,' such as mortal never heard of; and a great deal of it is actually done, but not fit for print. Speaking of descriptive composition, he also started as in fright when I ventured to say that Goethe was less complete in this province; he reminded me of two passages in 'Werter,' which are indeed among the finest descriptions. He said that to describe any scene well the poet must make the bosom of a man his *camera obscura*, and look at it through *this*, then would he see it poetically. * *

"The conversation turned on public occurrences, on the condition of Germany, and the oppressive rule of the French. To me discussions of that sort are usually disagreeable; but it was delightful to hear Jean Paul express, on such occasion, his noble patriotic sentiments; and for the sake of this rock-island I willingly swam through the empty tide of uncertain news and wavering suppositions which environed it. What he said was deep, considerate, hearty, valiant, German to the marrow of the bone. I had to tell him much; of Napoleon, whom he knew only by portraits; of Johannes von Müller; of Fichte, whom he now as a patriot admired cordially; of the Marquez de la Romana and his Spaniards, whom I had seen in Hamburgh. Jean Paul said he at no moment doubted, but the Germans, like the Spaniards, would one day rise, and Prussia would avenge its disgrace, and free the country; he hoped his son would live to see it, and did not deny that he was bringing him up for a soldier. * * *

"*October 25th.*—I staid to supper, contrary to my purpose, having to set out next morning early. The lady was so kind, and Jean Paul himself so trustful and blithe, I could not withstand their entreaties. At the neat and well-furnished table (reminding you that South Germany was now near) the best humour reigned. Among other things we had a good laugh at this, that Jean Paul offered me an introduction to one of, what he called his dearest friends in Stuttgart,—and then was obliged to give it up, having irrevocably forgotten his name! Of a more serious sort again was our conversation about Tieck, Friedrich and Wilhelm Schlegel, and others of the romantic school. He seemed in ill humour with Tieck at the moment. Of Goethe he said: 'Goethe is a consecrated head; he has a place of his own, high above us all.' We spoke of Goethe afterwards for some time: Jean Paul, with more and more admiration, nay, with a sort of fear and awe-struck reverence.

"Some beautiful fruit was brought in for dessert. On a sudden, Jean Paul started up, gave me his hand, and said: 'Forgive me, I must go to bed! Stay you here in God's name, for it is still early, and chat with my wife; there is much to say, between you, which my talking has kept back. I am a *Spiessburger*,' (of the Club of Odd Fellows,) 'and my hour is come for sleep.' He took a candle, and said, good night. We parted with great cordiality, and the wish expressed on both sides, that I might stay at Baireuth another time."

These biographic phenomena; Jean Paul's loose-flowing talk, his careless variable judgments of men and things; the prosaic basis of the free-and-easy in domestic life with the poetic Shandean, Shakspearean, and even Dantesque, that grew from it as its public outcome; all this Varnhagen had to rhyme and reconcile for himself as he best could. The loose-flowing talk and variable judgments, the fact that Richter went along, "looking only right before him as with blinders on," seemed to Varnhagen a pardonable, nay, an amiable peculiarity, the mark of a trustful, spontaneous, artless nature; connected with whatever was best in Jean Paul. He found him on the whole (what we at a distance have always done) "a genuine and noble man: no deception or impunity exists in his life; he is altogether as he writes, loveable, hearty, robust, and brave. A valiant man I do believe: did the cause summon, I fancy he would be readier with his sword too than the most." And so we quit our loved Jean Paul, and his simple little Baireuth home. The lights are blown out there, the fruit platters swept away, a dozen years ago, and all is dark now,—swallowed in the long night. Thanks to Varnhagen that he has, though imperfectly, rescued any glimpse of it, one scene of it, still visible to eyes, by the magic of pen and ink.

The next picture that strikes us is not a family-piece, but a battle-piece: Deutsch-Wagram, in the hot weather of 1809; whither Varnhagen, with a great change of place and plan, has wended, proposing now to be a soldier, and rise by fighting the tyrannous French. It is a fine picture; with the author's best talent in it. Deutsch-Wagram village is filled with soldiers of every uniform and grade; in all manner of movements and employments; Archduke Karl is heard "fantasying for an hour on the piano-forte," before his serious generalissimo duties begin. The Marchfeld has its camp, the Marchfeld is one great camp of many nations—Germans, Hungarians, Italians, Madshars; advanced sentinels walk steadily, drill serjeants bustle, drums beat; Austrian generals gallop, "in blue-gray coat and red breeches"—combining "simplicity with conspicuousness." Faint on our south-western horizon appears the *Stephans-thurm* (St. Stephen's Steeple) of Vienna; south, over the Danube, are seen endless French hosts defiling towards us, with dust and glitter, along the hill-roads; one may hope, though with misgivings, there will be work soon.

Meanwhile, in every regiment there is but one tent, a chapel, used also for shelter to the chief officers; you, a subaltern, have to lie on the ground, in your own dug trench, to which, if you can contrive it, some roofing of branches and rushes may be added. It is burning sun and dust, occasionally it is thunder-storm and water-spouts; a volunteer, if it were not for the hope of speedy battle, has a poor time of it: your soldiers speak little, except unintelligible Bohemian Sclavonic; your brother ensigns know nothing of Xenophon, Jean Paul, of patriotism, or the higher philosophies; hope only to be soon back at Prague, where are billiards and things suitable. "The following days were heavy and void: the great summer-heat had withered the grass and grove; the willows of the Russbach were long since leafless, in part barkless; on the endless plain fell nowhere a shadow; only dim dust-clouds, driven up by sudden whirlblasts, veiled for a moment the glaring sky, and sprinkled all things with a hot rain of sand. We gave up drilling as impossible, and crept into our earth-holes." It is feared, too, there will be no battle: Varnhagen has thoughts of making off to the fighting Duke of Brunswick-Oels, or some other that will fight. "However," it would seem, "the worst trial was already over. After a hot, wearying, wasting day, which promised nothing but a morrow like it, there arose on the 30th of June, from beyond the Danube, a sound of cannon-thunder; a solacing refreshment to the languid soul! A party of French, as we soon learned, had got across from the Lobau, by boats, to a little island named Mühleninsel, divided only by a small arm from our side of the river; they had then thrown a bridge over this too, with defences; our batteries at Esslingen were for hindering the enemy's passing there, and his nearest cannons about the Lobau made answer." On the fourth day after,

"Archduke John got orders to advance again as far as Marcheck; that, in the event of a battle on the morrow, he might act on the enemy's right flank. With us too a resolute engagement was arranged. On the 4th of July, in the evening, we were ordered, if there was cannonading in the night, to remain quiet till daybreak; but at daybreak to be under arms. Accordingly, so soon as it was dark, there began before us, on the Danube, a violent fire of artillery; the sky glowed ever and anon with the cannon flashes, with the courses of bombs and grenadoes: for nearly two hours this thunder-game lasted on both sides; for the French had begun their attack almost at the same time with ours, and while we were striving to ruin their works on the Lobau, they strove to burn Enzersdorf town, and ruin ours. The Austrian cannon could do little against the strong works on the Lobau. On the other hand, the enemy's attack began to tell; in his object was a wider scope, more decisive energy; his guns were more numerous, more effectual: in a short time Enzersdorf burst out in flames, and our artillery struggled without effect against their superiority of force. The region round had been illuminated for some time with the conflagration of that little town, when the sky grew black with heavy thunder: the rain poured down, the flames dwindled, the artillery fired seldomer, and at length fell silent altogether. A frightful thunder-storm, such as no one thought he had ever seen, now raged over the broad Marchfeld, which shook with the crashing of the thunder, and, in the pour of rain-floods and howl of winds, was in such a roar, that even the artillery could not have been heard in it."

On the morrow morning, in spite of Austria and the war of elements, Napoleon, with his endless hosts, and "six hundred pieces of artillery" in front of them, is across, advancing like a conflagration, and soon the whole Marchfeld, far and wide, is in a blaze.

"Ever stronger batteries advanced, ever larger masses of troops came into action; the whole line blazed with fire, and moved forward and forward. We, from our higher position, had hitherto looked at the evolutions and fightings before us, as at a show; but now the battle had got nigher; the air over us sang with cannon-balls, which were lavishly hurled at us, and soon our batteries began to bellow in answer. The infantry got orders to lie flat on the ground, and the enemy's balls at first did little execution; however, as they kept incessantly advancing, the regiments ere long stood to their arms. The Archduke Generalissimo, with his staff, came galloping along, drew bridle in front of us; he gave his commands; looked down into the plain, where the French still kept advancing. You saw by his face that he heeded not danger or death, that he lived altogether in his work; his whole bearing had got a more impressive aspect, a loftier determination, full of joyous courage, which he seemed to diffuse round him; the soldiers looked at him with pride and trust, many voices saluted him. He had ridden a little towards Baumersdorf, when an adjutant came galloping back, and cried: "Volunteers forward!" In an instant, almost the whole company of Captain Marais stept out as volunteers: we fancied it was to storm the enemy's nearest battery, which was advancing through the corn-fields in front; and so, cheering with loud shout, we hastened down the declivity, when a second adjutant came in with the order that we were but to occupy the Russbach, defend the passage of it, and not to fire till the enemy was quite close. Scattering ourselves into skirmishing order, behind willow-trunks, and high corn, we waited with firelocks ready; covered against cannon-balls, but hit by musket shots and howitzer grenades, which the enemy sent in great numbers to our quarter. About an hour we waited here, in the incessant roar of the artillery, which shot both ways over our heads; with regret we soon remarked that the enemy's were superior, at least, in number, and delivered twice as many shots as ours, which, however, was far better served; the more did we admire the active zeal and valorous endurance by which the unequal match was nevertheless maintained.

"The Emperor Napoleon meanwhile saw, with impatience, the day passing on without a decisive result; he had calculated on striking the blow at once, and his great accumulated force was not to have directed itself all hitherward in vain. Rapidly he arranged his troops for storming. Marshal Bernadotte got orders to press forward, over Atterkla, towards Wagram; and, by taking this place, break the middle of the Austrian line. Two deep storming columns were at the same time to advance, on the right and left, from Baumersdorf over the Russbach; to scale the heights of the Austrian position, and sweep away the troops there. French infantry had, in the mean while, got up close to where we stood; we skirmishers were called back from the Russbach, and again went into the general line; along the whole extent of which a dreadful fire of musketry now began. This monstrous noise of the universal, never-ceasing crack of shots, and still more, that of the infinite jingle of iron, in handling more than twenty thousand muskets, all crowded together here, was the only new and entirely strange impression that I, in these my first experiences in war, could say I had got; all the rest was in part conformable to my preconceived notion, in part even below it: but every thing, the thunder of artillery never so numerous, every noise, I had heard or figured, was trifling, in comparison with this continuous storm-tumult of the small arms, as we call them—that weapon by which indeed our modern battles do chiefly become deadly."

What boots it? Ensign Varnhagen and Generalissimo Archduke Karl are beaten; have to retreat in the best possible order.—The sun of Wagram sets as that of Austerlitz had done; the war has to end in submission and marriage; and, as the great Atlantic tide-stream rushes into every creek and alters the current there, so for our Varnhagen too a new chapter opens—the diplomatic one, in Paris first of all. Varnhagen's experiences "At the Court of Napoleon," as one of his sections is headed, are extremely entertaining. They are tragical, comical, of mixed character; always dramatic, and vividly given. We have a grand Schwartzenberg Festival, and the Emperor himself, and all high persons present in grand gala, with music, light, and crowned goblets, in a wooden pavilion, with upholstery and draperies: a rag of drapery flutters the wrong way athwart some wax-light, shrivels itself up in quick fire, kindles the other draperies, kindles the gums and woods, and all blazes into swift choking ruin; a beautiful Princess Schwartzenberg, lost in the mad tumult, is found on the morrow as ashes amid the ashes! Then also there are *soirees* of Imperial notabilities; "the gentlemen walking about in varied talk, wherein you detect a certain cautiousness; the ladies all solemnly ranged in their chairs, rather silent for ladies." Berthier is a "man of composure," *not* without higher capabilities. Denon, in spite of his kind speeches, produces an ill effect on one; and in his *habit habile*, with court-rapier and lace-cuffs, "looks like a dizened ape." Cardinal Maury in red stockings, he that was once Abbe Maury, "pet son of the scarlet woman," whispers diplomatically in your ear, in passing, *Nous avons beaucoup de joie de vous voir ici.* But the thing that will best of all suit us here, is the presentation to Napoleon himself:

"On Sunday, the 22d of July, (1810,) was to be the Emperor's first levee after that fatal occurrence of the fire; and we were told it would be uncommonly fine and grand. In Berlin I had often accidentally seen Napoleon, and afterwards at Vienna and Schönbrunn; but always too far off for a right impression of him. At Prince Schwartzenberg's festival, the look of the man, in that whirl of horrible occurrences, had effaced itself again. I assume, therefore, that I saw him for the first time now, when I saw him *rightly*, near at hand, with convenience, and a sufficient length of time. The frequent opportunities I afterwards had, in the Tuileries and at St. Cloud, (in the latter place especially, at the brilliant theatre, open only to the Emperor and his guests, where Talma, Fleury, and La Raucourt figured,) did but confirm, and, as it were, complete that first impression.

"We had driven to the Tuileries, and arrived through a great press of guards and people at a chamber, of which I had already heard, under the name of *Salle des Ambassadeurs.* The way in which, here in this narrow ill-furnished pen, so many high personages stood jammed together, had something ludicrous and insulting in it, and was indeed the material of many a Paris jest.—The richest uniforms and court dresses were, with difficulty and anxiety, struggling hitherward and thitherward; intermixed with Imperial liveries of men handing refreshments, who always, by the near peril, suspended every motion of those about them. The talk was loud and vivacious on all sides; people seeking acquaintances, seeking more room, seeking better light. Seriousness of mood, and dignified concentration of oneself, seemed foreign to all; and what a man could not bring with him, there was nothing here to produce. The whole matter had a distressful, offensive air; you found yourself ill off, and waited out of humour. My look, however, dwelt with especial pleasure on the members of our Austrian Embassy, whose bearing and demeanour did not discredit the dignity of the old Imperial house.—Prince Schwartzenberg, in particular, had a stately aspect; ease without negligence, gravity without assumption, and over all an honest goodness of expression; beautifully contrasted with the smirking saloon-activity, the perked up courtierism and pretentious nullity of many here. * * *

"At last the time came for going up to audience. On the first announcement of it, all rushed without order towards the door; you squeezed along, you pushed and shoved your neighbour without ceremony. Chamberlains, pages, and guards, filled the passages and ante-chamber; restless, overdone officiousness struck you here too; the soldiers seemed the only figures that knew how to behave in their business,—and this, truly, they had learned, not at Court, but from their drill-sergeants.

"We had formed ourselves into a half-circle in the Audience Hall, and got placed in several crowded ranks, when the cry of '*L'Empereur!*' announced the appearance of Napoleon, who entered from the lower side of the apartment. In simple blue uniform, his little hat under his arm, he walked heavily towards us. His bearing seemed to me to express the contradiction between a will that would attain something, and a contempt for those by whom it was to be attained. An imposing appearance he would undoubtedly have liked to have; and yet it seemed to him not worth the trouble of acquiring; acquiring, I may say, for by nature he certainly had it not. Thus there alternated in his manner a negligence and a studiedness, which combined themselves only in unrest and dissatisfaction. He turned first to the Austrian Embassy, which occupied one extremity of the half-circle. The consequences of the unlucky festival gave occasion to various questions and remarks. The Emperor sought to appear sympathetic, he even used words of emotion; but this tone by no means succeeded with him, and accordingly he soon let it drop. To the Russian Ambassador, Kurakin, who stood next, his manner had already changed into a rougher; and in his farther progress some face or some thought must have stung him, for he got into violent anger; broke stormfully out on some one or other, not of the most important there, whose name has now escaped me; could be pacified with no answer, but demanded always new; rated and threatened, and held the poor man, for a good space, in tormenting annihilation. Those who stood nearer, and were looking at this scene, not without anxieties of their own, declared afterwards that there was no cause at all for such fury; that the Emperor had merely been seeking an opportunity to vent his ill humour, and had done so even intentionally on this poor wight, that all the rest might be thrown into due terror, and every opposition beforehand beaten down.

"As he walked on, he again endeavoured to speak more mildly; but his jarred humour still sounded through. His words were short, hasty, as if shot from him, and on the most indifferent matters had a passionate rapidity; nay, when he wished to be kindly, it still sounded as if he were in anger. Such a raspy, untamed voice as that of his I have hardly heard.

"His eyes were dark, overclouded, fixed on the ground before him; and only glanced backwards in side-looks now and then, swift and sharp, on the persons there. When he smiled, it was but the mouth and a part of the cheeks that smiled; brow and eyes remained gloomily motionless. If he constrained these also, as I have subsequently seen him do, his countenance took a still more distorted expression. This union of gloom and smile had something frightfully repulsive in it. I know not what to think of the people who have called this countenance gracious, and its kindliness attractive. Were not his features, though undeniably beautiful in the plastic sense, yet hard and rigourous like marble; foreign to all trust, incapable of any heartiness?

"What he said, whenever I heard him speaking, was always trivial both in purport and phraseology; without spirit, without wit, without force, nay, at times, quite poor and ridiculous. Faber, in his 'Notices sur l'Interieur de la France,' has spoken expressly of his questions, those questions which Napoleon was wont to prepare before-hand for certain persons and occasions, to gain credit thereby for acuteness and special knowledge. This is literally true of a visit he had made a short while before to the great Library: all the way on the stairs he kept calling out about that passage in Josephus where Jesus is made mention of; and seemed to have no other task here but that of showing off this bit of learning; it had altogether the air of a question got by heart. * * * His gift lay in saying things sharp, or at least unpleasant; nay, when he wanted to speak in another sort, he often made no more of it than insignificance: thus it befel once, as I myself witnessed in Saint-Cloud, he went through a whole row of ladies, and repeated twenty times merely these three words, "*Il fait chaud.*" * * *

"At this time there circulated a song on his second marriage; a piece composed in the lowest popular tone, but which doubtless had originated in the higher classes. Napoleon saw his power and splendour stained by a ballad, and breathed revenge; but the police could no more detect the author than they could the circulators. To me among others a copy, written in a bad hand and without name, had been sent by the city post; I had privately with friends amused myself over the burlesque, and knew it by heart. Altogether at the wrong time, exactly as the Emperor, gloomy and sour of humour, was now passing me, the words and tune of that song came into my head; and the more I strove to drive them back, the more decidedly they forced themselves forward; so that my imagination, excited by the very frightfulness of the thing, was getting giddy, and seemed on the point of breaking forth into the deadliest offence,—

when happily the audience came to an end; and deep repeated bows accompanied the exit of Napoleon; who to me had addressed none of his words, but did, as he passed, turn on me one searching glance of the eye, with the departure of which it seemed as if a real danger had vanished.

"The Emperor gone, all breathed free, as if disloaded from a heavy burden. By degrees the company again grew loud, and then went over altogether into the noisy disorder and haste which had ruled at the commencement. The French courtiers especially took pains to redeem their late downbent and terrified bearing by a free jocularity now; and even in descending the stairs there arose laughter and quizzing at the levee, the solemnity of which had ended here."

Such was Varnhagen von Ense's presentation to Napoleon Bonaparte in the Palace of the Tuileries. What Varnhagen saw remains a possession for him and for us. The judgment he formed on what he saw will—depend upon circumstances. For the eye of the intellect "sees in all objects what it brought with it the means of seeing." Napoleon is a man of the sort which Varnhagen elsewhere calls *daimonisch*, a "demonic man;" whose meaning or magnitude is not very measurable by men; who, with his *ownness* of impulse and insight, with his mystery and strength, in a word, with his *originality*, (if we will understand that,) reaches down into the region of the perennial and primeval, of the inarticulate and unspeakable; concerning whom innumerable things may be said, and the right thing not said for a long while, or at all. We will leave him standing on his own basis, at present; bullying the hapless, obscure functionary there; declaring to all the world the meteorological fact, *Il fait chaud.*

Varnhagen, as we see, has many things to write about; but the thing which beyond all others he rejoices to write about, and would gladly sacrifice all the rest to, is the memory of Rahel, his deceased wife. Mysterious indications have of late years flitted round us, concerning a certain Rahel, a kind of spiritual queen in Germany, who seems to have lived in familiar relation to most of the distinguished persons of that country in her time. Travellers to Germany, now a numerous sect with us, ask you as they return from æsthetic capitals and circles, "Do you know Rahel?" Marquis Custine, in the "Revue de Paris," (treating of this book of "Rahel's Letters,") says, by experience: "She was a woman as extraordinary as Madame de Staël, for her faculties of mind, for her abundance of ideas, her light of soul, and her goodness of heart: she had, moreover, what the author of Corinne' did not pretend to, a disdain for oratory; she did not write. The silence of minds like hers is a force too. With more vanity, a person so superior would have sought to make a public for herself: but Rahel desired only friends. She spoke to communicate the life that was in her; never did she speak to be admired." Goethe testifies that she is a "right woman; with the strongest feelings I have ever seen, and the completest mastery of them." Richter addresses her by the title *geflügelte*, "winged one." Such a Rahel might be worth knowing.

We find, on practical inquiry, that Rahel was of Berlin; by birth a Jewess, in easy not affluent circumstances; who lived, mostly there, from 1771 to 1833. That her youth passed in studies, struggles, disappointed passions, sicknesses, and other sufferings and vivacities to which one of her excitable organization was liable. That she was deep in many spiritual provinces, in poetry, in art, in philosophy;—the first, for instance, or one of the first to recognise the significance of Goethe, and teach the Schlegels to do it. That she wrote nothing; but thought, did, and spoke, many things, which attracted notice, admiration spreading wider and wider. That in 1814 she became the wife of Varnhagen; the loved wife, though her age was forty-three, exceeding his by some twelve years or more, and she could never boast of beauty. That without beauty, without wealth, foreign celebrity, or any artificial nimbus whatsoever, she had grown in her silently progressive way to be the most distinguished woman in Berlin; admired, partly worshipped by all manner of high persons, from Prince Louis of Prussia downwards; making her mother's, and then her husband's house the centre of an altogether brilliant circle there. This is the "social phenomenon of Rahel." What farther could be readily done to understand such a social phenomenon we have endeavoured to do; with what success the reader shall see.

First of all, we have looked at the Portrait of Rahel given in these volumes. It is a face full of thought, of affection, and energy; with no pretensions to beauty, yet loveable and attractive in a singular degree. The strong high brow and still eyes are full of contemplation; the long upper lip (sign of genius, some say) protrudes itself to fashion a curved mouth, condemnable in academies, yet beautifully expressive of laughter and affection, of strong endurance, of noble silent scorn; the whole countenance looking as with cheerful clearness through a world of great pain and disappointment; one of those faces which the lady meant when she said, "But are not all beautiful faces ugly, then, to begin with?" In the next place, we have read diligently whatsoever we could anywhere find written about Rahel; and have to remark here that the things written about her, unlike some things written by her, are generally easy to read. Varnhagen's account of their intercourse; of his first young feelings towards her, his long waiting, and final meeting of her in snowy weather under the Lindens, in company with a lady whom he knew, his tremulous speaking to her there, the rapid progress of their intimacy; and so onwards, to love, to marriage: all this is touching and beautiful; a Petrarcan romance, and yet a reality withal.

Finally, we have read in these three thick volumes of Letters,—till in the second thick volume, the reading faculty unhappily broke down, and had to skip largely thenceforth, only diving here and there at a venture with considerable intervals! Such is the melancholy fact. It must be urged in defence that these volumes are of the toughest reading; calculated, as we said for Germany, rather than for England or us. To be written with such indisputable marks of ability, nay of genius, of depth and sincerity, they are the heaviest business we perhaps ever met with. The truth is, they do not suit us at all. They are *subjective* letters, what the metaphysicians call subjective, not *objective;* the grand material of them is endless depicturing of moods, sensations, miseries, joys, and lyrical conditions of the writer; no definite picture drawn, or rarely any, of persons, transactions, or events which the writer stood amidst; a wrong material, as it seems to us. To what end? To what end? we always ask. Not by looking at itself, but by looking at things out of itself, and ascertaining and ruling these, shall the mind become known. "One thing above all other," says Goethe once, "I have never *thought about thinking*." What a thrift almost of itself equal to a fortune in these days: "*habe nie ans Denken gedacht!*" But how much wastefuller still it is to *feel about Feeling!* One is wearied of that; the healthy soul avoids that. Thou shalt look outward, not inward. Gazing inward on one's own self,—why, this can drive one mad, like the monks of Athos, if at last too long. Unprofitable writing this *subjective* sort does seem; —at all events, to the present reviewer, no reading is so insupportable. Nay, we ask, might not the world be entirely deluged by it, unless prohibited? Every mortal is a microcosm; to himself a *macro*cosm, or universe large as nature; universal nature would barely hold what he *could* say about himself. Not a dyspeptic tailor on any shopboard of this city but could furnish all England, the year through, with reading about himself, about his emotions, and internal mysteries of wo and sensibility, if England would read him. It is a course which leads nowhither; a course which should be avoided.

Add to all this, that such self-utterance on the part of Rahel, in these letters, is in the highest degree vapourous, vague. Her very mode of writing is complex, nay, is careless, incondite; with dashes and splashes, with notes of admiration, of interrogation, (nay, both together sometimes,) with involutions, abruptness, whirls, and tortuosities; so that even the grammatical meaning is altogether burdensome to seize. And then when seized, alas, it is as we say, of due likeness to the phraseology; a thing crude, not articulated into propositions, but flowing out as in bursts of interjection and exclamation. No wonder the reading faculty breaks down! And yet we do gather gold grains and precious thought here and there; though out of large wastes of sand and quicksand. In fine, it becomes clear, beyond doubting, both that this Rahel was a woman of rare gifts and worth, a woman of true genius; and also that her genius has passed away, and left no impress of itself there for us. These printed volumes produce the effect not of speech, but of multifarious, confused wind-music. It seems to require the aid of pantomime, to tell us what it means. But after all, we can understand how *talk* of that kind, in an expressive mouth, with bright deep eyes, and the vivacity of social movement, of question and response, may have been delightful; and moreover that, for those to whom they vividly recall such talk, these letters may still be delightful. Hear Marquis de Custine a little farther:

"You could not speak with her a quarter of an hour without drawing from that fountain of light a shower of sparkles. The comic was at her command equally with the highest degree of the sublime. The proof that she was natural is, that she understood laughter as she did grief; she took it as a readier means of showing truth; all had its resonance in her, and her manner of receiving the impressions which you wished to communicate to her modified them in yourself: you loved her at first because she had admirable gifts; and then, what prevailed over every thing, because she was entertaining. She was nothing for you, or she was all; and she could be all to several at a time without exciting jealousy, so much did her noble nature participate in the source of all life, of all clearness. When one has lost in youth such friend," &c., &c. . . . "It seems to me you might define her in one word: she had the head of a sage and the heart of an apostle, and in spite of that, she was a child and a woman as much as any one can be. Her mind penetrated into the obscurest depths of nature; she was a thinker of as much and more clearness than our Theosophist Saint Martin, whom she comprehended and admired; and she felt like an artist. Her perceptions were always double; she attained the sublimest truths by two faculties which are incompatible in ordinary men, by feeling and by reflection. Her friends asked of themselves,—Whence came these flashes of genius which she threw from her in conversation? Was it the effect of long studies? Was it the effect of sudden inspirations? It was the intuition granted as recompense by Heaven to souls that are true. These martyr souls wrestle for the truth, which they have a forecast of; they suffer for the God whom they love, and their whole life is the school of eternity."*

This enthusiastic testimony of the clever sentimental marquis is not at all incredible to us, in its way: yet from these letters we have nothing whatever to produce that were adequate to make it good. As was said already, it is not to be made good by excerpts and written documents; its proof rests in the memory of living witnesses. Meanwhile, from these same wastes of sand, and even of quicksand dangerous to linger in, we will try to gather a few grains the most like gold, that it may be guessed, by the charitable, whether or not a Pactolus once flowed there:

"If there be miracles, they are those that are in our breast; what we do not know, we call by that name. How astonished, almost how ashamed are we, when the inspired moment comes, and we get to know them!"

"One is late in learning to lie: and late in learning to speak the truth."—"I cannot, be-

* "Revue de Paris," Novembre, 1837.

cause I cannot lie. Fancy not that I take credit for it: I cannot, just as one cannot play upon the flute."

"In the meanest hut is a romance, if you knew the hearts there."

"So long as we do not take even the injustice which is done us, and which forces the burning tears from us; so long as we do not take even this for just and right, we are in the thickest darkness, without dawn."

"Manure with despair,—but let it be genuine; and you will have a noble harvest."

"True misery is ashamed of itself: hides itself, and does not complain. You may know it by that."

"What a commonplace man! If he did not live in the same time with us, no mortal would mention him."

"Have you remarked that Homer, whenever he speaks of the water, is always great; as Goethe is, when he speaks of the stars."

"If one were to say, 'You think it easy to be original: but no, it is difficult; it costs a whole life of labour and exertion,'—you would think him mad, and ask no more questions of him. And yet his opinion would be altogether true, and plain enough withal. Original, I grant, every man might be, and must be, if men did not almost always admit mere undigested hearsays into their head, and fling them out again undigested. Whoever honestly questions himself, and faithfully answers, is busied continually with all that presents itself in life; and is incessantly inventing, had the thing been invented never so long before. Honesty belongs as a first condition to good thinking; and there are almost as few absolute dunces as geniuses. Genuine dunces would always be original; but there are none of them genuine: they have almost always understanding enough to be dishonest."

"He (the blockhead) tumbled out on me his definition of genius; the trivial old distinctions of intellect and heart; as if there ever was, or could be, a great intellect with a mean heart!"

"Goethe? When I think of *him*, tears come into my eyes: all other men I love with my own strength; he teaches me to love with his. My Poet!"

"Slave-trade, war, marriage, working-classes:—and they are astonished, and keep clouting and remending?"

"The whole world is, properly speaking, a tragic *embarras*."

". . . . I here, Rahel the Jewess, feel that I am as unique as the greatest appearance in this earth. The greatest artist, philosopher or poet, is not above me. We are of the same element; in the same rank, and stand together. Whichever would exclude the other, excludes only himself. But to me it was appointed not to write, or act, but *to live:* I lay in embryo till my century; and then was, in outward respects, so *flung away*.—It is for this reason that I tell you. But pain, as I know it, is a life too: and I think with myself, I am one of those figures which Humanity was fated to evolve, and then never to use more, never to have more: Me no one can comfort."—"Why *not* be beside oneself, dear friend? There are beautiful parentheses in life, which belong neither to us nor to others: beautiful I name them, because they give us a freedom we could not get by sound sense. Who would volunteer to have a nervous fever? And yet it may save one's life. I love rage; I use it, and patronize it."—"Be not alarmed; I am commonly calmer. But when I write to a *friend's heart*, it comes to pass that the sultry laden horizon of my soul breaks out in lightning. Heavenly men *love* lightning."

"*To Varnhagen.* . . One thing I must write to thee; what I thought of last night in bed, and for the first time in my life. That I, as a relative and pupil of Shakspeare, have, from my childhood upwards, occupied myself much with death, thou mayest believe. But never did my own death affect me; nay, I did not even think of this fact, that I was affected by it. Now, last night there was something I had to write; I said Varnhagen must know this thing, if he is to think of me after I am dead. And it seemed to me as if I must die; as if my heart were flitting away over this earth, and I must follow it; and my death gave me pity: for never before, as I now saw, had I thought that it would give anybody pity: of thee I knew it would do so, and yet it was the first time in my life I had seen this, or known that I had never seen it. In such solitude have I lived: comprehend it! I thought, when I am dead, then first will Varnhagen know what sufferings I had; and all his lamenting will be in vain; the figure of me meets him again through all eternity no more; swept away am I *then*, as our poor Prince Louis is. And no one can be kind to me then; with the strongest will, with the exertion of despair, no one: and this thought of thee about me was what at last affected me. I must write of this, though it afflict thee never so." * * *

"*To Rose, a younger sister, on her marriage in Amsterdam.*—Paris, 1801. . . . . Since thy last letter I am sore downcast. Gone art thou! No Rose comes stepping in to me with true foot and heart, who knows me altogether, knows all my sorrows *altogether*. When I am sick of body or soul, alone, alone thou comest not to me any more; thy room empty, quite empty, for ever empty. Thou art away, to try thy fortune. O Heaven! and to me not even *trying* is permitted. Am not *I* in luck! The garden in the Lindenstrasse where we used to be with Hanne and Feu—was it not beautiful? I will call it *Rose* now; with Hanne and Hanse will I go often thither, and none shall know of it. Dost thou recollect that night when I was to set out with Fink the time before last? How thou hadst to sleep up stairs, and then to stay with me? O my sister, I might be as ill again—though not for that cause: and thou too, what may not lie before thee! But, no, thy name is Rose; thou hast *blue* eyes, and a far other life than I with my stars and black ones. * * * Salute mamma a million times; tell her I congratulate her from the heart; the more so as *I* can never give her such a pleasure! God willed it not. But I, in her place, would have great pity for a child so circumstanced. Yet let her not lament for me. I know all her goodness, and thank her with my soul. Tell her I have the fate of nations and of the greatest men before my eyes here: they too go tumbling even so on the great sea of Existence, mounting, sinking, swallowed up. From of *old* all men have seemed to me like spring blossoms, which the wind blows off and whirls; none knows where they fall, and the fewest come to fruit."

Poor Rahel! The Frenchman said above she was an artist and apostle, yet had not ceased to be a child and woman. But we must stop short. One other little scene, a scene from her death-bed by Varnhagen, must end the tragedy:

". . . . She said to me one morning, after a dreadful night, with the penetrating tone of that lovely voice of hers: 'O, I am *still* happy; I am God's creature still; He knows of me; I shall come to see how it was good and needful for me to suffer: of a surety I had something to learn by it. And am I not already happy in this trust, and in all the love that I feel and meet with?'

"In this manner she spoke, one day, among other things, with joyful heartiness, of a dream which always from childhood she had remembered and taken comfort from. 'In my seventh year,' said she, 'I dreamt that I saw God quite near me; he stood expanded above me, and his mantle was the whole sky; on a corner of this mantle I had leave to rest, and lay there in peaceable felicity till I awoke. Ever since, through my whole life, this dream has returned on me, and in the worst times was present also in my waking moments, and a heavenly comfort to me. I had leave to throw myself at God's feet, on a corner of his mantle, and he screened me from all sorrow there: He permitted it.' * * * The following words, which I felt called to write down exactly as she spoke them on the 2d of March, are also remarkable: 'What a history!' cried she with deep emotion: 'A fugitive from Egypt and Palestine am I here; and find help, love, and kind care among you. To thee, dear August, was I sent by this guiding of God, and thou to me; from afar, from the old times, of Jacob and the Patriarchs! With a sacred joy I think of this my origin, of all this wide web of pre-arrangement. How the oldest remembrances of mankind are united with the newest reality of things, and the most distant times and places are brought together. What for so long a period of my life I considered as the worst ignominy, the sorest sorrow and misfortune, that I was born a Jewess, this I would not part with now for any price. Will it not be even so with these pains of sickness? Shall I not one day mount joyfully aloft on them, too; feel that I could not want them for any price? O August, this is just, this is true; we will try to go on thus!' Thereupon she said, with many tears, 'Dear August, my heart is refreshed to its inmost; I have thought of Jesus, and wept over his sorrows; I have felt, for the first time felt, that he is my Brother. And Mary, what must she have suffered! She saw her beloved Son in agony, and did not sink; she *stood* at the Cross. That I could not have done; I am not strong enough for that. Forgive me, God, I confess how weak I am.' * * *

"At nightfall, on the 6th of March, Rahel felt herself easier than for long before, and expressed an irresistible desire to be new dressed. As she could not be persuaded from it, this was done, though with the utmost precaution. She herself was busily helpful in it, and signified great contentment that she had got it accomplished. She felt so well she expected to sleep. She wished me good-night, and bade me also go and sleep. Even the maid, Dora, was to go and sleep; however, she did not.

"It might be about midnight, and I was still awake, when Dora called me: 'I was to come, she was much worse.' Instead of sleep, Rahel had found only suffering, one distress added to another; and now all had combined into decided spasm of the breast. I found her in a state little short of that she had passed six days ago. The medicines left for such an occurrence (regarded as possible, not probable) were tried; but this time with little effect. The frightful struggle continued; and the beloved sufferer, writhing in Dora's arms, cried, several times, 'This pressure against her breast was not to be borne, was pushing her heart out:' the breathing, too, was painfully difficult. She complained that 'it was getting into her head now, that she felt like a cloud there;' she leaned back with that. A deceptive hope of some alleviation gleamed on us for a moment, and then went out for ever; the eyes were dimmed, the mouth distorted, the limbs lamed! In this state the doctors found her; their remedies were all bootless. An unconscious hour and half, during which the breast still occasionally struggled in spasmodic efforts—and this noble life breathed out its last. The look I got then, kneeling almost lifeless at her bed, stamped itself, glowing, for ever into my heart."

So died Rahel Varnhagen von Ense, born Levin, a singular biographic phenomenon of this century; a woman of genius, of true depth and worth, whose secluded life, as one cannot but see, had in it a greatness far beyond what has many times fixed the public admiration of the whole world; a woman equal to the highest thoughts of her century; in whom it was not arrogance, we do believe, but a just self-consciousness, to feel that "the highest philosopher, or poet, or artist was not above her, but of a like element and rank with her." That such a woman should have lived unknown and, as it were, silent to the world, is peculiar in this time.

We say not that she was equal to De Staël, nor the contrary; neither that she might have written De Staël's books, nor even that she might not have written far better books. She has ideas unequalled in De Staël; a sincerity, a pure tenderness and genuineness which that celebrated person had not, or had lost. But what then? The subjunctive, the optative are vague moods: there is no tense one can found on but the preterite of the indicative. Enough for us, Rahel did not write. She sat imprisoned, or it might be sheltered and fosteringly embowered, in those circumstances of hers; she "was not appointed to write or to act, but only to live." Call her not unhappy on that account, call her not useless; nay, perhaps, call her happier and usefuller. Blessed are the humble, are they that are *not* known. It is written, "Seekest thou great things, seek them not;" live where thou art, only live wisely, live diligently. Rahel's life was not an idle one for herself or for others: how many souls may "the sparkles showering from that light-fountain" have kindled and illuminated; whose new virtue goes on propagating itself, increasing itself, under incalculable combinations, and will be found in far places, after many days! She left no stamp of herself on paper; but in other ways, doubt it not, the virtue of her working in this world will survive all paper. For the working of the good and brave, seen or unseen, endures literally for ever, and cannot die. Is a thing nothing because the morning papers have not mentioned it? Or can a nothing be made something, by ever so much babbling of it there? Far better, probably, that no morning or evening paper mentioned it; that the right hand knew not what the left was doing! Rahel might have written books, celebrated books. And yet, what of books? Hast thou not already a bible to write, and publish in print, that is eternal; namely, a Life to lead? Silence, too, is great; there should be great silent ones, too.

Beautiful it is to see and understand that no worth, known or unknown, *can* die even in this earth. The work an unknown good man has done is like a vein of water flowing hidden under ground, secretly making the ground green; it flows and flows, it joins itself with other veins and veinlets; one day it will start forth as a visible perennial well. Ten dumb centuries had made the speaking Dante; a well he of many veinlets. William Burnes, or Burns, was a poor peasant; could not prosper in his "seven acres of nursery-ground," nor any enterprise of trade and toil; had to "thole a factor's snash," and read attorney letters, in his poor hut, "which threw us all into tears;" a man of no money-capital at all, of no account at all; yet a brave man, a wise and just, in evil fortune faithful, unconquerable to the death. And there wept withal among the others a boy named *Robert*, with a heart of melting pity, of greatness and fiery wrath; and *his* voice, fashioned here by this poor father, does it not already reach, like a great elegy, like a stern prophecy, to the ends of the world? "Let me make the songs, and you shall make the laws!" What chancellor, king, senator, begirt with never such sumptuosity, dyed velvet, blaring, and celebrity, could you have named in England that was so momentous as that William Burns? Courage!—

We take leave of Varnhagen with true goodwill, and heartily thank him for the pleasure and instruction he has given us.

PETITION ON THE COPY-RIGHT BILL.

[THE (LONDON) EXAMINER, 1839.]

To the Honourable the Commons of England in Parliament assembled, the Petition of Thomas Carlyle, a Writer of Books,

Humbly showeth,

That your petitioner has written certain books, being incited thereto by various innocent or laudable considerations, chiefly by the thought that said books might in the end be found to be worth something.

That your petitioner had not the happiness to receive from Mr. Thomas Tegg, or any Publisher, Republisher, Printer, Bookseller, Bookbuyer, or other the like man or body of men, any encouragement or countenance in writing of said books, or to discern any chance of receiving such; but wrote them by effort of his own and the favour of Heaven.

That all useful labour is worthy of recompense; that all honest labour is worthy of the chance of recompense; that the giving and assuring to each man what recompense his labour has actually merited, may be said to be the business of all Legislation, Polity, Government, and Social Arrangement whatsoever among men;—a business indispensable to attempt, impossible to accomplish accurately, difficult to accomplish without inaccuracies that become enormous, unsupportable, and the parent of Social Confusions which never altogether end.

That your petitioner does not undertake to say what recompense in money this labour of his may deserve; whether it deserve any recompense in money, or whether money in any quantity could hire him to do the like.

That this his labour has found hitherto, in money or money's worth, small recompense or none; that he is by no means sure of its ever finding recompense, but thinks, that, if so, it will be at a distant time, when he, the laborer, will probably no longer be in need of money, and those dear to him will still be in need of it.

That the law does at least protect all persons in selling the production of their labour at what they can get for it, in all market places, to all lengths of time. Much more than this the law does to many, but so much it does to all, and less than this to none.

That your petitioner cannot discover himself to have done unlawfully in this his said labour of writing books, or to have become criminal, or have forfeited the law's protection thereby. Contrariwise your petitioner believes firmly that he is innocent in said labour; that if he be found in the long run to have written a genuine enduring book, his merit therein, and desert towards England and English and other men, will be considerable, not easily estimable in money; that on the other hand, if his book prove false and ephemeral, he and it will be abolished and forgotten, and no harm done.

That, in this manner, your petitioner plays no unfair game against the world; his stake being life itself, so to speak, (for the penalty is death by starvation,) and the world's stake nothing till once it see the dice thrown; so that in any case the world cannot lose.

That in the happy and long-doubtful event of the game's going in his favour, your petitioner submits that the small winnings thereof do belong to him or his, and that no other mortal has justly either part or lot in them at all, now, henceforth, or for ever.

May it therefore please your Honourable House to protect him in said happy and long-doubtful event; and (by passing your Copy-Right Bill) forbid all Thomas Teggs and other extraneous persons, entirely unconcerned in this adventure of his, to steal from him his small winnings, for a space of sixty years at the shortest. After sixty years, unless your Honourable House provide otherwise, they may begin to steal.

And your petitioner will ever pray.

THOMAS CARLYLE.

DR. FRANCIA.*

[FOREIGN QUARTERLY REVIEW.]

THE confused South American revolution, and set of revolutions, like the South American continent itself, is doubtless a great confused phenomenon; worthy of better knowledge than men yet have of it. Several books, of which we here name a few known to us, have been written on the subject; but bad books mostly, and productive of almost no effect. The heroes of South America have not yet succeeded in picturing any image of themselves, much less any true image of themselves, in the Cis-Atlantic mind or memory.

Iturbide, "the Napoleon of Mexico," a great man in that narrow country, who was he? He made the thrice-celebrated "Plan of Iguala:" a constitution of no continuance. He became Emperor of Mexico, most serene "Augustin I.:" was deposed, banished to Leghorn, to London; decided on returning;—landed on the shore at Tampico, and was there met, and shot: this, in a vague sort, is what the world knows of the Napoleon of Mexico, most serene Augustin the First, most unfortunate Augustin the Last. He did himself publish memoirs or memorials,† but few can read them. Oblivion, and the deserts of Panama, have swallowed this brave Don Augustin: *vate caruit sacro.*

And Bolivar, "the Washington of Columbia," Liberator Bolivar, he too is gone without his fame. Melancholy lithographs represent to us a long-faced, square-browed man; of stern, considerate, *consciously* considerate aspect, mildly aquiline form of nose; with terrible angularity of jaw; and dark deep eyes, somewhat too close together, (for which latter circumstance we earnestly hope the lithograph alone is to blame:) this is Liberator Bolivar:—a man of much hard fighting, hard riding, of manifold achievements, distresses, heroisms and histrionisms in this world; a many-counselled, much-enduring man; now dead and gone:—of whom, except that melancholy lithograph, the cultivated European public knows as good as nothing. Yet did he not fly hither and thither, often in the most desperate manner, with wild cavalry clad in blankets, with War of Liberation, "to the death?" Clad in blankets, *ponchos* the South Americans call them: it is a square blanket, with a short slit in the centre, which you draw over your head, and so leave hanging: many a liberative cavalier has ridden, in those hot climates, without further dress at all; and fought handsomely too, wrapping the blanket round his arm, when it came to the charge.

With such cavalry, and artillery and infantry to match, Bolivar has ridden, fighting all the way, through torrid deserts, hot mud swamps, through ice-chasms beyond the curve of perpetual frost,—more miles than Ulysses ever sailed: let the coming Homers take note of it. He has marched over the Andes more than once; a feat analogous to Hannibal's; and seemed to think little of it. Often beaten, banished from the firm land, he always returned again, truculently fought again. He gained in the Cumana regions the "immortal victory" of Carababo and several others; under him was gained the finishing "immortal victory" of Ayacucho in Peru, where Old Spain, for the last time, burnt powder in those latitudes, and then fled without return. He was Dictator, Liberator, almost emperor, if he had lived. Some three times over did he, in solemn Columbian parliament, lay down his Dictatorship with Washington eloquence; and as often,

---

* 1. *Funeral Discourse delivered on occasion of celebrating the obsequies of his late Excellency the Perpetual Dictator of the Republic of Paraguay, the Citizen Dr. José Gaspar Francia, by Citizen the Rev. Manuel Antonia Perez, of the Church of the Incarnation, on the 20th of October*, 1840. In the "British Packet and Argentine News," No. 813. Buenos Ayres: March 19, 1842.

2. *Essai Historique sur la Révolution de Paraguay, et le Gouvernement Dictatorial du Docteur Francia. Par* MM. Rengger et Longchamp. 2de édition. Paris, 1827.

3. *Letters on Paraguay.* By J. P. and W. P. Robertson. 2 vols. Second edition. London, 1839.

4. *Francia's Reign of Terror.* By the same. London, 1829.

5. *Letters on South America.* By the same. 3 vols. London, 1843.

6. *Travels in Chile and La Plata.* By John Miers. 2 vols. London, 1826.

7. *Memoirs of General Miller, in the Service of the Republic of Peru.* 2 vols. 2d edition. London, 1829.

† A Statement of some of the principal Events in the Public Life of Augustin de Iturbide: written by Himself. London, 1843.

on pressing request, take it up again, being a man indispensable. Thrice, or at least twice, did he, in different places, painfully construct a Free Constitution; consisting of "two chambers, and a supreme governor for life with liberty to name his successor," the reasonablest democratic constitution you could well construct; and twice, or at least once, did the people, on trial, declare it disagreeable. He was of old, well known in Paris; in the dissolute, the philosophico-political and other circles there. He has shone in many a gay Parisian *soirée*, this Simon Bolivar; and he, in his later years, in autumn, 1825, rode triumphant into Potosi and the fabulous Inca Cities, with clouds of feathered Indians somersetting and warwhopping round him*—and "as the famed *Cerro*, metalliferous Mountain, came in sight, the bells all pealed out, and there was a thunder of artillery," says General Miller! If this is not a Ulysses, Polytlas and Polymetis, a much enduring and many counselled man; where was there one? Truly a Ulysses whose history were worth its ink,—had the Homer that could do it, made his appearance!

Of General San Martin, too, there will be something to be said. General San Martin, when we last saw him, twenty years ago or more,—through the organs of the authentic steadfast Mr. Miers,—had a handsome house in Mendoza, and "his own portrait, as I remarked, hung up between those of Napoleon and the Duke of Wellington." In Mendoza, cheerful, mudbuilt, whitewashed Town, seated at the eastern base of the Andes, "with its shady public walk well paved and swept;" looking out pleasantly, on this hand, over wide horizons of Pampa wilderness; pleasantly on that, to the Rocky-chain, *Cordillera* they call it, of the sky-piercing Mountains, capt in snow, or with volcanic fumes issuing from them: there dwelt General *Ex*-Generalissimo San Martin, ruminating past adventures over half the world; and had his portrait hung up between Napoleon's and the Duke of Wellington's.

Did the reader ever hear of San Martin's march over the Andes in Chile? It is a feat worth looking at; comparable, most likely, to Hannibal's march over the Alps, while there was yet no Simplon or Mont-Cénis highway; and *it* transacted itself in the year 1817. South American armies think little of picking their way through the gullies of the Andes; so the Buenos-Ayres people, having driven out their own Spaniards, and established the reign of freedom, though in a precarious manner, thought it were now good to drive the Spaniards out of Chile, and establish the reign of freedom there also instead: whereupon San Martin, commander at Mendoza, was appointed to do it. By way of preparation, for he began from afar, San Martin, while an army is getting ready at Mendoza, assembles "at the fort of San Carlos by the Aguanda river," some days' journey to the south, all attainable tribes of the Pehuenche Indians, to a solemn *Palaver*, so they name it, and civic entertainment, on the esplanade there. The ceremonies and deliberations, as described by General Miller, are somewhat surprising; still more the concluding civic feast, which lasts for three days, which consists of horses' flesh for the solid part, and horses' blood with ardent spirits *ad libitum* for the liquid, consumed with such alacrity, with such results as one may fancy. However, the women had prudently removed all the arms beforehand; nay, "five or six of these poor women, taking it by turns, were always found in a sober state, watching over the rest;" so that comparatively little mischief was done, and only "one or two" deaths by quarrel took place.

The Pehuenches having drunk their ardent-water and horses' blood in this manner, and sworn eternal friendship to San Martin, went home, and—communicated to his enemies, across the Andes, the road he meant to take. This was what San Martin had foreseen and meant, the knowing man! He hastened his preparations, got his artillery slung on poles, his men equipt with knapsacks and haversacks, his mules in readiness; and, in all stillness, set forth from Mendoza by *another* road. Few things in late war, according to General Miller, have been more noteworthy than this march. The long straggling line of soldiers, six thousand and odd, with their quadrupeds and baggage, winding through the heart of the Andes, breaking for a brief moment the old abysmal solitudes!—For you farre along, on some narrow roadway, through stony labyrinths; huge rock-mountains hanging over your head, on this hand; and under your feet, on that, the roar of mountain-cataracts, horror of bottomless chasms;—the very winds and echoes howling on you in an almost preternatural manner. Towering rock-barriers rise sky-high before you, and behind you, and around you; intricate the outgate! The roadway is narrow; footing none of the best. Sharp turns there are, where it will behove you to mind your paces; one false step, and you will need no second; in the gloomy jaws of the abyss you vanish, and the spectral winds howl requiem. Somewhat better are the suspension bridges, made of bamboo and leather, though they swing like see-saws: men are stationed with lassos, to gin you dexterously, and fish you up from the torrent, if you trip there.

Through this kind of country did San Martin march; straight towards San Iago, to fight the Spaniards and deliver Chile. For ammunition wagons he had *sorras*, sledges, canoe-shaped boxes, made of dried bull's-hide. His cannons were carried on the back of mules, each cannon on two mules judiciously harnessed: on the packsaddle of your foremost mule, there rested with firm girths a long strong pole; the other end of which (*forked* end, we suppose) rested, with like girths, on the packsaddle of the hindmost mule; your cannon was slung with leathern straps on this pole, and so travelled, swaying and dangling, yet moderately secure. In the knapsack of each soldier was eight days' provender, dried beef ground into snuff-powder, with a modicum of pepper, and a slight seasoning of biscuit or

* Memoirs of General Miller.

maizemeal; "store of onions, of garlic," was not wanting: Paraguay tea could be boiled at eventide, by fire of scrub-bushes, or almost of rock-lichens or dried mule-dung. No further baggage was permitted: each soldier lay, at night, wrapt in his *poncho*, with his knapsack for pillow, under the canopy of heaven; lullabied by hard travail: and sank soon enough into steady nose-melody, into the foolishest rough colt-dance of unimaginable Dreams. Had he not left much behind him in the Pampas,—mother, mistress, what not; and was like to find somewhat, if he ever got across to Chile living? What an entity, one of those night-leaguers of San Martin; all steadily snoring there, in the heart of the Andes, under the eternal stars! Wayworn sentries with difficulty keep themselves awake: tired mules chew barley rations, or doze on three legs; the feeble watchfire will hardly kindle a cigar; Canopus and the Southern Cross glitter down; and all snores steadily, begirt by granite deserts, looked on by the constellations in that manner! San Martin's improvident soldiers ate out their week's rations almost in half the time; and for the last three days, had to rush on, spurred by hunger: this also the knowing San Martin had foreseen; and knew that they could bear it, these rugged *Guachos* of his; nay, that they would march all the faster for it. On the eighth day, hungry as wolves, swift and sudden as a torrent from the mountains, they disembogued; straight towards San Iago, to the astonishment of men;—struck the doubly astonished Spaniards into dire misgivings; and then, in pitched fight, after due manœuvres, into total defeat on the "Plains of Maypo," and again, positively for the last time, on the Plains or Heights of "Chacabuco;" and completed the "deliverance of Chile," as was thought, for ever and a day.

Alas, the "deliverance of Chile was but commenced; very far from completed. Chile, after many more deliverances, up to this hour, is always but "delivered," from one set of evil doers to another set! San Martin's Manœuvres to liberate Peru, to unite Peru and Chile, and become some Washington-Napoleon of the same, did not prosper so well. The suspicion of mankind had to rouse itself; Liberator Bolivar had to be called in; and some revolution or two to take place in the interim. San Martin sees himself peremptorily, though with courtesy, complimented over the Andes again; and in due leisure, at Mendoza, hangs his portrait between Napoleon's and Wellington's. Mr. Miers considered him a fairspoken, obliging, if somewhat artful man. Might not the Chilenos as well have *taken* him for their Napoleon? They have gone farther, and, as yet, fared little better!

The world-famous General O'Higgins, for example, he, after some revolution or two, became Director of Chile; but so terribly hampered by "class-legislation," and the like, what could he make of it? Almost nothing! O'Higgins is clearly of Irish breed; and, though a Chileno born, and "natural son of Don Ambrosio O'Higgins, formerly the Spanish Viceroy of Chile," carries his Hibernianism in his very face. A most cheery, jovial, buxom countenance, radiant with pepticity, good humour, and manifold effectuality in peace and war! Of his battles and adventures let some luckier epic writer sing or speak. One thing we Foreign Reviewers will always remember: his father's immense merits towards Chile in the matter of highways. Till Don Ambrosio arrived to govern Chile, some half century ago, there probably was not a made road of ten miles long from Panama to Cape Horn. Indeed, except his roads, we fear there is hardly any yet. One omits the old Inca causeways, as too narrow (being only three feet broad) and altogether unfrequented in the actual ages. Don Ambrosia made, with incredible industry and perseverance and skill, in every direction, roads. From San Iago to Valparaiso, where only sure-footed mules with their packsaddles carried goods, there can now wooden-axled cars, loud-sounding, or any kind of vehicle, commodiously roll. It was he that shaped these passes, through the Andes, for most part; hewed them out from mule-tracks into roads, certain of them. And think of his *casuchas*. Always on the higher inhospitable solitudes, at every few miles' distance, stands a trim brick cottage, or *cashucha*, into which the forlorn traveller, introducing himself, finds covert and grateful safety; nay food and refection,—for there are "iron boxes" of pounded beef or other provender, iron boxes of charcoal; to all which the traveller, having bargained with the Post-office authorities, carries a key.* Steel and tinder are not wanting to him, nor due iron skillet, with water from the stream: there he, striking a light, cooks hoarded victuals at eventide, amid the lonely pinnacles of the world, and blesses Governor O'Higgins. With "both hands," it may be hoped,—if there is vivacity of mind in him:

> Had you seen this road before it was made,
> You would lift both your hands and bless General Wade.

It affects one with real pain to hear from Mr. Miers, that the war of liberty has half ruined these O'Higgins *casuchas*. Patriot soldiers, in want of more warmth than the charcoal box could yield, have not scrupled to tear down the door, doorcase, or whatever wooden thing could be come at, and burn it, on the spur of the moment. The storm-stayed traveller, who sometimes, in threatening weather, has to linger here for days, "for fifteen days together," does not lift both his hands, and bless the Patriot soldier!

Nay, it appears, the O'Higgins roads, even in the plain country, have not, of late years, been repaired, or in the least attended to, so distressed was the finance department; and are now fast verging towards impassability and the condition of mule-tracks again. What a set of animals are men and Chilenos! If an O'Higgins did not now and then appear among them, what would become of the unfortunates? Can you wonder that an O'Higgins sometimes loses temper with them; *shuts* the persuasive outspread hand, clutching some sharpest hide whip, some terrible sword of justice or gallows

* Miers.

lasso therewith, instead,—and becomes a Dr. Francia now and then! Both the O'Higgins and Francia, it seems probable, are phases of the same character; both, one begins to fear, are indispensable from time to time, in a world inhabited by men and Chilenos!

As to O'Higgins the Second, Patriot, Natural son O'Higgins, he, as we said, had almost no success whatever as a governor; being hampered by class-legislation. Alas, a governor in Chile cannot succeed. A governor there has to resign himself to the want of success; and should say, in cheerful interrogative tone, like that Pope elect, who, showing himself on the balcony, was greeted with mere howls, "*Non piacemmo al popolo?*"—and thereupon proceed cheerfully to the *next* fact. Governing is a rude business everywhere; but in South America it is of quite primitive rudeness; they have no parliamentary way of changing ministries as yet; nothing but the rude primitive way of hanging the old ministry on gibbets, that the new may be installed! Their government has altered its name, says the sturdy Mr. Miers, rendered sulky by what he saw there: altered its name, but its nature continues as before. Shameless peculation, malversation, that is their government: oppression formerly by Spanish officials, now by native hacendados, land-proprietors,—the thing called justice still at a great distance from them, says the sulky Mr. Miers!—Yes, but coming always, answer we; every new gibbeting of an old ineffectual ministry bringing justice somewhat nearer! Nay, as Miers himself has to admit, certain improvements are already indisputable. Trade everywhere, in spite of multiplex confusions, has increased, is increasing: the days of somnolent monopoly and the old Acapulco ship are gone, quite over the horizon. Two good, or partially good measures, the very necessity of things has everywhere brought about in those poor countries: clipping of the enormous bat-wings of the clergy, and emancipating of the slaves. Bat-wings, we say; for truly the South American clergy had grown to be as a kind of bat-vampires:—readers have heard of that huge South American blood-sucker, which fixes its bill in your circulating vital-fluid as you lie *asleep*, and there sucks; waving you with the motion of its detestable leather wings into ever deeper sleep; and so drinking till *it* is satisfied, and you—do not awaken any more! The South American governments, all in natural feud with the old church-dignitaries, and likewise all in great straits for cash, have everywhere confiscated the monasteries, cashiered the disobedient dignitaries, melted the superfluous church-plate into piasters; and, on the whole, shorn the *wings* of their vampire; so that if it still suck, you will at least have a chance of awakening before death!—Then again, the very want of soldiers of liberty led to the emancipating of blacks, yellows, and other coloured persons; your mulatto, nay your negro, if well drilled, will stand fire as well as another.

Poor South American emancipators; they began with Volney, Raynal and Company, at that gospel of Social Contract and the Rights of Man; under the most unpropitious circumstances; and have hitherto got only to the length we see! Nay now, it seems, they do possess "universities," which are at least schools with other than monk teachers: they have got libraries, though as yet almost nobody reads them, and our friend Miers, repeatedly knocking at all doors of the Grand Chile National Library, could never to this hour discover where the key lay, and had to content himself with looking in through the windows.* Miers, as already hinted, desiderates unspeakable improvements in Chile;—desiderates, indeed, as the basis of all, an immense increase of soap-and-water. Yes, thou sturdy Miers, dirt is decidedly to be removed, whatever improvements, temporal or spiritual, may be intended next? According to Miers, the open, still more the secret personal nastiness of those remote populations, rises almost towards the sublime. Finest silks, gold brocades, pearl necklaces, and diamond ear-drops, are no security against it: alas, all is not gold that glitters; somewhat that glitters is mere putrid fish-skin! Decided, enormously increased appliance of soap-and-water, in all its branches, with all its adjuncts; this, according to Miers, would be an improvement. He says also ("in his haste," as is probable, like the Hebrew Psalmist) that all Chileno men are liars; all, or in appearance, all! A people that uses almost no soap, and speaks almost no truth, but goes about in that fashion, in a state of personal nastiness, and also of spiritual nastiness, approaching the sublime; such people is not easy to govern well!—

But undoubtedly by far the notablest of all these South American phenomena is Dr. Francia and his Dictatorship in Paraguay; concerning whom and which we have now more particularly to speak. Francia and his "reign of terror" have excited some interest, much vague wonder in this country; and especially given a great shock to constitutional feeling. One would rather wish to know Dr. Francia;—but unhappily one cannot! Out of such a murk of distracted shadows and rumours, in the other hemisphere of the world, who would pretend at present to decipher the real portraiture of Dr. Francia and his Life? None of us can. A few credible features, wonderful enough, original enough in our constitutional time, will perhaps to the impartial eye disclose themselves; these, with some endeavour to interpret these, may lead certain readers into various reflections, constitutional and other, not entirely without benefit.

Certainly, as we say, nothing could well shock the constitutional feeling of mankind, as Dr. Francia has done. Dionysius the tyrant of Syracuse, and indeed the whole breed of tyrants, one hoped, had gone many hundred years ago, with their reward; and here, under our very nose, rises a new "tyrant," claiming also *his* reward from us! Precisely when constitutional liberty was beginning to be understood a little, and we flattered ourselves that by due ballot-boxes, by due registration

* Travels in Chile.

courts, and bursts of parliamentary eloquence, something like a real National Palaver would be got up in those countries,—arises this tawny-visaged, lean, inexorable Dr. Francia; claps you an embargo on all that; says to constitutional liberty, in the most tyrannous manner, Hitherto, and no farther! It is an undeniable, though an almost incredible fact, that Francia, a lean private individual, Practitioner of Law, and Doctor of Divinity, did, for twenty or near thirty years, stretch out his rod over the foreign commerce of Paraguay, saying to it, Cease! The ships lay high and dry, their pitchless seams all yawning on the clay banks of the Parana; and no man could trade but by Francia's license. If any person entered Paraguay, and the Doctor did not like his papers, his talk, conduct, or even the cut of his face,—it might be the worse for such person! Nobody could leave Paraguay on any pretext whatever. It mattered not that you were man of science, astronomer, geologer, astrologer, wizard of the north; Francia heeded none of these things. The whole world knows of M. Aimé Bonpland; how Francia seized him, descending on his tea-establishment in Entre Rios, like an obscene vulture, and carried him into the interior, contrary even to the law of nations; how the great Humboldt and other high persons expressly applied to Dr. Francia, calling on him, in the name of human science, and as it were under penalty of reprobation, to liberate M. Bonpland; and how Dr. Francia made no answer, and M. Bonpland did not return to Europe, and indeed has never yet returned. It is also admitted that Dr. Francia had a gallows, had jailers, law-fiscals, officials; and executed, in his time, "upwards of forty persons," some of them in a very summary manner. Liberty of private judgment, unless it kept its mouth shut, was at an end in Paraguay. Paraguay lay under interdict, cut off for above twenty years from the rest of the world, by a new Dionysius of Paraguay. All foreign commerce had ceased; how much more all domestic constitution-building! These are strange facts. Dr. Francia, we may conclude at least, was not a common man but an uncommon.

How unfortunate that there is almost no knowledge of him procurable at present! Next to none. The Paraguenos can in many cases spell and read, but they are not a literary people; and, indeed, this Doctor was, perhaps, too awful a practical phenomenon to be calmly treated of in the literary way. Your Breughel paints his sea-storm, not while the ship is labouring and cracking, but after he has got to shore, and is safe under cover! Our Buenos-Ayres friends, again, who are not without habits of printing, lay at a great distance from Francia, under great obscurations of quarrel and controversy with him; their constitutional feeling shocked to an extreme degree by the things he did. To them, there could little intelligence float down, on those long muddy waters, through those vast distracted countries, that was not more or less of a distracted nature; and then from Buenos-Ayres over into Europe, there is another long tract of distance, liable to new distractions. Francia, Dictator of Paraguay, is, at present, to the European mind, little other than a chimera; at best, the statement of a puzzle, to which the solution is still to seek. As the Paraguenos, though not a literary people, can many of them spell and write, and are not without a discriminating sense of true and untrue, why should not some real "Life of Francia," from those parts, be still possible? If a writer of genius arise there, he is hereby invited to the enterprise. Surely in all places your writing genius ought to rejoice over an acting genius, when he falls in with such; and say to himself: "Here or nowhere is the thing for me to write of! Why do I keep pen and ink at all, if not to apprize men of this singular acting genius and the like of him? My fine-arts and æsthetics, my epics, literatures, poetics, if I will think of it, do all at bottom mean either that or else nothing whatever!"

Hitherto our chief source of information as to Francia is a little book, the second on our list, set forth in French some sixteen years ago, by the Messrs. Rengger and Longchamp. Translations into various languages were executed; of that into English it is our painful duty to say that no man, except in the case of extreme necessity, shall use it as reading. The translator, having little fear of human detection, and seemingly none at all of divine or diabolic, has done his work even unusually ill; with ignorance, with carelessness, with dishonesty prepénse; coolly *omitting* whatsoever he *saw* that he did not understand:—poor man, if he yet survive, let him reform in time! He has made a French book, which was itself but lean and dry, into the most wooden of English false books; doing evil as he could in that matter;—and claimed wages for it, as if the feat deserved *wages* first of all! Reformation, even on the small scale, is highly necessary.

The Messrs. Rengger and Longchamp were, and we hope still are, two Swiss Surgeons; who in the year 1819 resolved on carrying their talents into South America, into Paraguay, with views towards "natural history," among other things. After long towing and struggling in those Parana floods, and distracted provinces, after much detention by stress of weather and of war, they arrived accordingly in Francia's country; but found that without Francia's leave they could not quit it again. Francia was now a Dionysius of Paraguay. Paraguay had grown to be, like some mousetraps and other contrivances of art and nature, easy to enter, impossible to get out of. Our brave Surgeons, our brave Rengger (for it is he alone of the two that speaks and writes) reconciled themselves; were set to doctoring of Francia's soldiery, of Francia's self; collected plants and beetles; and, for six years, endured their lot rather handsomely: at length, in 1825, the embargo was for a time lifted, and they got home. This book was the consequence. It is not a good book, but at that date there was, on the subject, no other book at all; nor is there yet any other better, or as good. We consider it to be authentic, veracious, moderately accurate; though lean and dry, it is intelligible, rational; in the French original, not unreadable. We may say it embraces up to this date, the present date, all of importance that is yet known in Europe about the Doctor Despot; add to this its indisputable *brevity;* the fact that it can be read sooner by several hours than any other *Dr. Francia:* these are its excellences,—considerable, though wholly of a comparative sort.

After all, brevity is the soul of wit! There is an endless merit in a man's knowing when to have done. The stupidest man, if he will be brief in proportion, may fairly claim some hearing from us: he too, the stupidest man, has seen something, heard something, which is his own, distinctly peculiar, never seen or heard by any man in this world before; let him tell us that,—he, brief in proportion, shall be welcome!

The Messrs. Robertson, with their "Francia's Reign of Terror," and other books on South America, have been much before the world of late; and failed not of a perusal from this reviewer; whose next sad duty it now is to say a word about them. The Messrs. Robertson, some thirty or five-and-thirty years ago, were two young Scotchmen, from the neighbourhood of Edinburgh, as would seem: who, under fair auspices, set out for Buenos-Ayres, thence for Paraguay, and other quarters of that remote continent, in the way of commercial adventure. Being young men of vivacity and open eyesight, they surveyed with attentive view those convulsed regions of the world; wherein it was evident that revolution raged not a little; but also that precious metals, cowhides, Jesuits' bark, and multiplex commodities, were nevertheless extant; and iron or brazen implements, ornaments, cotton and woollen clothing, and British manufactures not a few, were objects of desire to mankind. The brothers Robertson, acting on these facts, appear to have prospered, to have extensively flourished in their commerce; which they gradually extended up the river Plate, to the city of the Seven Streams or Currents, (*Corrientes* so called,) and higher even to Assumpcion, metropolis of Paraguay; in which latter place, so extensive did the commercial interests grow, it seemed at last expedient that one or both of the prosperous brothers should take up his personal residence. Personal residence accordingly they did take up, one or both of them, and maintain, in a fluctuating way, now in this city, now in that, of the De la Plata, Parana or Paraguay country, for a considerable space of years; how many years, in precise arithmetic, it is impossible, from these inextricably complicated documents now before us, to ascertain. In Paraguay itself, in Assumpcion city itself, it is very clear, the brothers Robertson did, successively or simultaneously, in a fluctuating inextricable manner, live for certain years; and occasionally saw Dr. Francia with their own eyes,—though to them or others, he had not yet become notable.

Mountains of cow and other hides, it would appear quitted those countries by movement of the brothers Robertson, to be worn out in Europe as tanned boots and horse-harness, with more or less satisfaction,—not without due profit to the merchants, we shall hope. About the time of Dr. Francia's beginning his "reign of terror," or earlier it may be, (for there are no dates in these inextricable documents,) the Messrs. Robertson were lucky enough to take final farewell of Paraguay, and carry their commercial enterprises into other quarters of that vast continent, where the reign was not of terror. Their voyagings, counter-voyagings, comings and goings, seem to have been extensive, frequent, inextricably complex; to Europe, to Tucuman, to Glasgow, to Chile, to Laswade and elsewhither; too complex for a succinct intelligence, as that of our readers has to be at present. Sufficient for us to know, that the Messrs. Robertson did bodily, and for good, return to their own country some few years since; with what net result of cash is but dimly adumbrated in these documents; certainly with some increase of knowledge—had the unfolding of it but been brief in proportion! Indisputably the Messrs. Robertson had somewhat to tell: their eyes had seen some new things, of which their hearts and understandings had taken hold more or less. In which circumstances the Messrs. Robertson decided on publishing a book. Arrangements being made, two volumes of "Letters on Paraguay" came out, with due welcome from the world, in 1839.

We have read these "Letters" for the first time lately: a book of somewhat *aqueous* structure: immeasurably thinner than one could have wished; otherwise not without merit. It is written in an off-hand, free-glowing, very artless, very incorrect style of language, of thought, and of conception; breathes a cheerful, eupeptic, social spirit, as of adventurous South-American Britons, worthy to succeed in business; gives one, here and there, some visible concrete feature, some lively glimpse of those remote sun-burnt countries; and has throughout a kind of bantering humour or quasi-humour, a joviality and healthiness of heart, which is comfortable to the reader, in some measure. A book not to be despised in these dull times: one of that extensive class of books which a reader can peruse, so to speak, "with one eye shut and the other not open;" a considerable luxury for some readers. These "Letters on Paraguay" meeting, as would seem, a unanimous approval, it was now determined by the Messrs. Robertson that they would add a third volume, and entitle it "Dr. Francia's Reign of Terror." They did so, and this likewise the present reviewer has read. Unluckily the authors had, as it were, nothing more whatever to say about Dr. Francia, or next to nothing; and under this condition, it must be owned they have done their book with what success was well possible. Given a cubic inch of respectable Castile soap, To lather it up in water so as to fill one puncheon wine-measure: this is the problem; let a man have credit (of its kind) for doing his problem! The Messrs. Robertson have picked almost every fact of significance from "Rengger and Longchamp," adding some not very significant reminiscences of their own; this is the square inch of soap; you lather it up in Robertsonian loquacity, joviality, Commercial-Inn banter, Leading-Article philosophy, or other aqueous vehicles, till it fills the puncheon, the volume of four hundred pages, and say "There!" The public, it would seem, did not fling even this in the face of the venders, but bought it as a puncheon filled; and the consequences are already here: Three volumes more on "South America," from the same assiduous Messrs Robertson! These also, in his eagerness, this present reviewer has read; and has, alas, to say that they are simply the old volumes in new vocables, under a new figure. Intrinsically all that we did not already know of these three volumes,—there are craftsmen of no great eminence who will undertake to write it in one sheet! Yet there they stand, three solid-looking volumes, a thousand printed pages and upwards; three puncheons *more* lathered out of the old square inch of Castile soap! It is too bad. A necessitous ready-witted Irishman sells you an indifferent grey-horse; steals it overnight, paints it black, and sells it to you again on the morrow; *he* is haled before judges, sharply cross-questioned, tried and almost executed, for such adroitness in horse-flesh: but there is no law yet as to books!

M. de la Condamine, about a century ago, was one of a world-famous company that went into those equinoctial countries, and for the space of nine or ten years did exploits there. From Quito to Cuença he measured you degrees of the meridian, climbed mountains, took observations, had adventures; wild Creoles opposing Spanish nescience to human science; wild Indians throwing down your whole cargo of instruments occasionally in the heart of remote deserts, and striking work there.* M. de la Condamine saw bull-fights at Cuença, five days running; and, on the fifth day, saw his unfortunate too audacious surgeon massacred by popular tumult there. He sailed the entire length of the Amazons River, in Indian canoes; over narrow Pongo rapids, over infinite mud-waters, the infinite tangled wilderness with its reeking desolation on the right hand of him and on the left;—and had mischances, adventures, and took celestial observations all the way, and made remarks! Apart altogether from his meridian degrees, which belong in a very strict sense to world-history and the advancement of all Adam's sinful posterity, this man and his party saw and suffered many hundred times as much of mere romance adventure as the Messrs. Robertson did:—Madame Godin's passage down the Amazons, and frightful life-in-death amid the howling forest-labyrinths, and wrecks of her dear friends, amounts to more adventure of itself than was ever dreamt of in the Robertsonian world. And of all this M. de la Condamine gives pertinent, lucid, and conclusively intelligible and credible account in one very small octavo volume; not quite the eighth part of what Messrs. Robertson have already written, in a not pertinent, not lucid, or conclusively intelligible and credible manner. And the Messrs. Robertson talk repeatedly, in their last volumes, of writing still other volumes on Chile "if the public will encourage." The Public will be a monstrous fool if it do. The Public ought to stipulate first that the real new knowledge forthcoming there about Chile be separated from the knowledge or ignorance already known; that the preliminary question be rigorously put, Are several volumes the space to hold it, or a small fraction of one volume?

On the whole, it is a sin, good reader, though there is no Act of Parliament against it; an indubitable *male*faction or crime. No mortal has a right to wag his tongue, much less to wag his pen, without saying something: he knows not what mischief he does, past computation; scattering words without meaning,—to afflict the whole world yet, before they cease! For thistle-down flies abroad on all winds and airs of wind: idle thistles, idle dandelions, and other idle products of Nature or the human mind, propagate themselves in that way; like to cover the face of the earth, did not man's indignant providence with reap-hook, with rake, with autumnal steel-and-tinder, intervene. It is frightful to think how every idle volume flies abroad like an idle globular down-beard, embryo of new millions; every word of it a potential seed of infinite new downbeards and volumes; for the mind of man is feracious, is voracious; germinative, above all things, of the downbeard species! Why, the author corps in Great Britain, every soul of them *inclined* to grow mere dandelions if permitted, is now supposed to be about ten thousand strong; and the reading corps, who read merely to escape from themselves, with one eye shut and the other not open, and will put up with almost any dandelion or thing which they can read *without* opening both their eyes, amounts to twenty-seven millions all but a few! O could the Messrs. Robertson, spirited, articulate-speaking men, once know well in what a comparatively blessed mood you close your brief, intelligent, conclusive M. de la Condamine, and feel that you have passed your evening well and nobly, as in a temple of wisdom,—not ill and disgracefully, as in brawling tavern supper-rooms, with fools and noisy persons,—ah, in that case, perhaps the Messrs. Robertson would write their new work on Chile in *part* of a volume!

But enough of this Robertsonian department; which we must leave to the Fates and Supreme Providences. These spirited, articulate-speaking Robertsons are far from the worst of their kind; nay, among the best, if you will;—only unlucky in this case, in coming across the autumnal steel and tinder! Let it cease to rain angry sparks on them: enough now, and more than enough. To cure that unfortunate department by philosophical criticism—the attempt is most vain. Who will dismount on a hasty journey, with the day declining, to attack musquito-swarms with the horsewhip? Spur swiftly through them; breathing perhaps some pious prayer to heaven. By the horse whip they cannot be killed. Drain out the swamps where they are bred,—Ah, couldst thou do something towards that! And in the mean while: How to get on with this of Dr Francia.

The materials, as our reader sees, are of the miserablest: mere intricate inanity (if we except poor wooden *Rengger*,) and little more; not facts, but broken shadows of facts; clouds of confused bluster and jargon;—the whole still more bewildered in the *Robertsons*, by what

* Condamine: Relation d'un Voyage dans l'Intérieur de l'Amérique méridionale.

we may call a running shriek of constitutional denunciation, "sanguinary tyrant," and so forth. How is any picture of Francia to be fabricated out of that? Certainly, first of all, by *omission* of the running shriek! This latter we shall totally omit. Francia, the sanguinary tyrant, was not bound to look at the world through Rengger's eyes, through Parish Robertson's eyes, but faithfully through his own eyes. We are to consider that, in all human likelihood, this Dionysius of Paraguay did mean something; and then ask in quietness, What? The running shriek once hushed, perhaps many things will compose themselves, and straggling fractions of information, almost infinitessimally small, may become unexpectedly luminous!

An unscientific cattle-breeder and tiller of the earth, in some nameless *chacra* not far from the city of Assumpcion, was the father of this remarkable human individual; and seems to have evoked him into being some time in the year 1757. The man's name is not known to us; his very nation is a point of controversy: Francia himself gave him out for an immigrant of French extraction; the popular belief was, that he had wandered over from Brazil. Portuguese or French, or both in one, he produced this human individual, and had him christened by the name of José Gaspar Rodriguez Francia, in the year above mentioned. Rodriguez no doubt had a mother too; but her name also, nowhere found mentioned, must be omitted in this delineation. Her name, and all her fond maternities, and workings, and sufferings, good brown lady, are sunk in dumb forgetfulness; and buried there along with her, under the twenty-fifth parallel of Southern Latitude; and no British reader is required to interfere with them! José Rodriguez must have been a loose-made tawny creature, much given to taciturn reflection; probably to crying humours, with fits of vehement ill-nature: such a subject, it seemed to the parent Francia cautiously reflecting on it, would, of all attainable trades, be suitablest for preaching the gospel, and doing the divine offices, in a country like Paraguay. There were other young Francias; at least one sister and one brother in addition; of whom the latter by and by went mad. The Francias, with their adust character, and vehement French-Portuguese blood, had perhaps all a kind of aptitude for madness. The Dictator himself was subject to the terriblest fits of hypochondria, as your adust "men of genius" too frequently are! The lean Rodriguez, we fancy, may have been of a devotional turn withal; born half a century earlier, he had infallibly been so. Devotional or not, he shall be a priest, and *do* the divine offices in Paraguay, perhaps in a very unexpected way.

Rodriguez having learned his hornbooks and elementary branches at Assumpcion, was accordingly despatched to the University of Cordova in Tucuman, to pursue his curriculum in that seminary. So far we know, but almost no farther. What kind of curriculum it was, what lessons, spiritual spoonmeat, the poor lank sallow boy was crammed with, in Cordova High Seminary; and how he took to it, and pined or throve on it, is entirely uncertain. Lank sallow boys in the Tucuman and other high Seminaries are often dreadfully ill-dealt with, in respect to their spiritual spoonmeat, as the times go! Spoon-poison you might often call it rather: as if the object were to make them Mithridateses, able to live on poison! Which may be a useful art, too, in its kind! Nay, in fact, if we consider it, these high seminaries and establishments exist there, in Tucuman and elsewhere, not for that lank sallow boy's special purposes, but for their own wise purposes; they were made and put together, a long while since, without taking the smallest counsel of the sallow boy! Frequently they seem to say to him, all along: "This precious thing that lies in thee, O sallow boy, of 'genius,' so called, it may to thee and to eternal Nature, be precious; but to us and to temporary Tucuman, it is not precious, but pernicious, deadly: we require thee to quit this, or expect penalties!" And yet the poor boy, how can he quit it; eternal Nature herself, from the depths of the Universe, ordering him to go on with it? From the depths of the Universe, and of his own Soul, latest revelation of the Universe, he is, in a silent, imperceptible, but irrefragable manner, directed to go on with it,—and has to go, though under penalties. Penalties of very death, or worse! Alas, the poor boy, so willing to obey temporary Tucumans, and yet unable to disobey eternal Nature, is truly to be pitied. Thou shalt be Rodriguez Francia! cries Nature, and the poor boy to himself. Thou shalt be Ignatius Loyola, Friar Ponderoso, Don Fatpauncho Usandwonto! cries Tucuman. The poor creature's whole boyhood is one long lawsuit: Rodriguez Francia against All Persons in general. It is so in Tucuman, so in most places. You cannot advise effectually into what high seminary he had best be sent; the only safe way is to bargain beforehand, that he have force born with him sufficient to make itself good against all persons in general!

Be this as it may, the lean Francia prosecutes his studies at Cordova, waxes gradually taller towards new destinies. Rodriguez Francia, in some kind of Jesuit scullcap, and black college serge gown, a lank rawboned creature, stalking with a down-look through the irregular public streets of Cordova in those years, with an infinitude of painful unspeakabilities in the interior of him, is an interesting object to the historical mind. So much is unspeakable, O Rodriguez; and it is a most strange Universe this we are born into; and the theorem of Ignatius Loyola and Don Fatpauncho Usandwonto seems to me to hobble somewhat! Much is unspeakable; lying within one like a dark lake of doubt, of Acherontic dread leading down to Chaos itself. Much is unspeakable, answers Francia; but somewhat also is speakable,—this for example: That I will not be a priest in Tucuman in these circumstances; that I should like decidedly to be a secular person rather, were it even a lawyer! Francia, arrived at man's years, changes from Divinity to Law. Some say it was in Divinity that he graduated, and got his Doctor's hat;

Rengger says, Divinity; the Robertsons, likelier to be incorrect, call him Doctor of Laws. To our present readers it is all one, or nearly so. Rodriguez quitted the Tucuman *Alma Mater*, with some beard on his chin, and reappeared in Assumpcion to look out for practice at the bar.

What had Rodriguez contrived to learn, or grow to, under this his *Alma Mater* in Cordova, when he quitted her? The answer is a mere guess; his curriculum, we again say, is not yet known. Some faint smattering of Arithmetic, or the everlasting laws of numbers; faint smattering of Geometry, everlasting laws of Shapes; these things we guess, not altogether in the dark, Rodriguez did learn, and found extremely remarkable. Curious enough: That round Globe put into that round Drum, to touch it at the ends and all round, it is precisely as if you clapt 2 into the inside of 3, not a jot more, not a jot less: wonder at it, O Francia; for in fact it is a thing to make one pause! Old Greek Archimedeses, Pythagorases, dusky Indians, old nearly as the hills, detected such things; and they have got across into Paraguay, into this brain of thine, thou happy Francia. How is it, too, that the Almighty Maker's planets run in those heavenly spaces, in paths which are conceivable in thy poor human head as Sections of a cone? The thing thou conceivest as an Ellipse, the Almighty Maker has set his Planets to roll in that. Clear proof, which neither Loyola nor Usandwonto can contravene, that *Thou* too art denizen of this universe; that thou too, in some inconceivable manner, wert present at the Council of the Gods!—Faint smatterings of such things Francia did learn in Tucuman. Endless heavy fodderings of Jesuit theology, poured on him and round him by the wagonload, incessantly, and year after year, he did not learn; but left lying there as shot rubbish. On the other hand, some slight inkling of human grammatical vocables, especially of French vocables, seems probable. French vocables; bodily garments of the "Encyclopedie" and Gospel according to Volney, Jean Jacques and Company; of infinite import to Francia!

Nay, is it not in some sort beautiful to see the sacred flame of ingenuous human curiosity, love of knowledge, awakened, amid the damp somnolent vapours, real and metaphorical, the damp tropical poison-jungles, and fat Lethean stupefactions and entanglements, even in the heart of a poor Paraguay Creole? Sacred flame, no bigger yet than that of a farthing rushlight, and with nothing but second-hand French class-books in science, and in politics and morals nothing but the Raynals and Rousseaus, to feed it: an *ill*-fed, lank-quavering, most blue-coloured, almost ghastly-looking flame; but a needful one, a kind of sacred one even that! Thou shalt love knowledge, search what *is* the *truth* of this God's Universe; thou art privileged and bound to love it, to search for it, in Jesuit Tucuman, in all places that the sky covers; and shall try even Volneys for help, if there be no other help! This poor blue-coloured inextinguishable flame in the soul of Rodriguez Francia, there as it burns better or worse, in many figures, through the whole life of him, is very notable to me. Blue flame though it be, it has to burn up considerable quantities of poisonous lumber from the general face of Paraguay; and singe the profound impenetrable forest-jungle, spite of all its brambles and lianas, into a very black condition,—intimating that there shall be disease and removal on the part of said forest-jungle; peremptory removal; that the blessed Sunlight shall again look in upon his cousin Earth, tyrannously hidden from him, for so many centuries now! Courage, Rodriguez!

Rodriguez, indifferent to such remote considerations, successfully addicts himself to law-pleadings, and general private studies, in the city of Assumpcion. We have always understood he was one of the best advocates, perhaps the very best, and, what is still more, the justest that ever took briefs in that country. This the Robertsonian "Reign of Terror" itself is willing to admit, nay repeatedly asserts, and impresses on us. He was so just and true, while a young man; gave such divine prognostics of a life of nobleness; and then, in his riper years, so belied all that! Shameful to think of; he bade fair, at one time, to be a friend of humanity of the first water; and then gradually, hardened by political success, and love of power, he became a mere ravenous goul, or solitary thief in the night; stealing the constitutional palladiums from their parliament houses—and executed upward of forty persons! Sad to consider what men and friends of humanity will come to!

For the rest it is not given to this or as yet to any editor, till a Biography arrive from Paraguay, to shape out, with the smallest clearness, a representation of Francia's existence as an Assumpcion Advocate; the scene is so distant, the conditions of it so unknown. Assumpcion city, near three hundred years old now, lies in free-and-easy fashion, on the left bank of the Parana River, embosomed among fruit-forests, rich tropical umbrage; thick wood round it everywhere,—which serves for defence too against the Indians. Approach by which of the various roads you will, it is through miles of solitary shady avenue, shutting out the sun's glare; over-canopying, as with grateful green awning, the loose sand-highway,—where, in the early part of this century, (date undiscoverable in those intricate volumes,) Mr. Parish Robertson, advancing on horseback, met one cart driven by a smart brown girl, in red bodice, with long black hair, not unattractive to look upon; and for a space of twelve miles, no other articulate-speaking thing whatever.*

The people of that profuse climate live in a careless abundance, troubling themselves about few things; build what wooden carts, hide-beds, mud-brick houses, are indispensable; import what of ornamental lies handiest abroad; exchanging it for Paraguay tea in sewed goatskins. Riding through the town of Santa Fé, with Parish Robertson at three in the afternoon, you will find the entire population just risen from its siesta; slipshod, half-

* Letters on Paraguay.

buttoned; sitting in its front verandahs open to the street, eating pumpkins with voracity,—sunk to the ears in pumpkins; imbibing the grateful saccharine juices, in a free and easy way. They look up at the sound of your hoofs, not without good humour. Frondent trees parasol the streets,—thanks to Nature and the Virgin. You will be welcome at their *tertulias*,—a kind of "*swarrie*," as the flunkey says, "consisting of flirtation and the usual trimmings: *swarrie* on the table about seven o'clock." Before this, the whole population, it is like, has gone to bathe promiscuously, and cool and purify itself in the Parana: promiscuously, but you have all got linen bathing-garments and can swash about with some decency; a great relief to the human tabernacle in those climates. At your *tertulia*, it is said, the Andalusian eyes, still bright to the tenth or twelfth generation, are distractive, seductive enough, and argue a soul that would repay cultivating. The beautiful half-savages; full of wild sheet-lightning, which might be made continuously luminous! Tertulia well over, you sleep on hide stretchers, perhaps here and there on a civilized mattrass, within doors or on the housetops.

In the damp flat country parts, where the mosquitoes abound, you sleep on high stages, mounted on four poles, forty feet above the ground, attained by ladders; so high, blessed be the Virgin, no mosquito can follow to sting, —it is a blessing of the Virgin or some other. You sleep there, in an indiscriminate arrangement, each in his several *poncho* or blanket-cloak; with some saddle, deal-box, wooden log, or the like, under your head. For bed-tester is the canopy of everlasting blue: for night-lamp burns Canopus in his infinite spaces; mosquitoes cannot reach you, if it please the Powers. And rosy-fingered Morn, suffusing the east with sudden red and gold, and other flame-heraldry of swift-advancing Day, attenuates all dreams; and the sun's first level light-volley sheers away sleep from living creatures everywhere; and living men do then awaken on their four-post stage there, in the Pampas,—and might begin with prayer if they liked, one fancies! There is an altar decked on the horizon's edge yonder, is there not; and a cathedral wide enough?—How, over night, you have defended yourselves against vampires, is unknown to this editor.

The Guacho population, it must be owned, is not yet fit for constitutional liberty. They are a rude people; lead a drowsy life, of ease and sluttish abundance,—one shade, and but one, above a dog's life, which is defined as "ease and scarcity." The arts are in their infancy; and not less the virtues. For equipment, clothing, bedding, household furniture, and general outfit of every kind, those simple populations depend much on the skin of the cow; making of it most things wanted, lasso, bolas, ship-cordage, rimmings of cart-wheels, spatterdashes, beds, and house-doors. In country places they sit on the skull of the cow: General Artigas was seen, and spoken with, by one of the Robertsons, sitting among field-officers, all on cow-skulls, toasting stripes of beef, and "dictating to three secretaries at once."* They sit on the skull of the cow in country places; nay they heat themselves, and even burn lime, by igniting the carcass of the cow.

One art they seem to have perfected, and one only—that of riding. Astleys and Ducrows must hide their head, all glories of Newmarket and Epsom dwindle to extinction, in comparison of Guacho horsemanship. Certainly if ever Centaurs lived upon the earth, these are of them. They stick on their horses as if both were one flesh; galloping where there seems hardly path for an ibex; leaping like kangaroos, and flourishing their nooses and bolases the while. They can whirl themselves round under the belly of the horse, in cases of war-stratagem, and stick fast, hanging on by the mere great toe and heel. You think it is a drove of wild horses galloping up: on a sudden, with wild scream, it becomes a troop of Centaurs with pikes in their hands. Nay, they have the skill, which most of all transcends Newmarket, of riding on horses that are *not* fed; and can bring fresh speed and alacrity out of a horse which, with you, was on the point of lying down. To ride on three horses with Ducrow they would esteem a small feat: to ride on the broken-winded fractional part of one horse, that is the feat!

Their huts abound in beef, in reek also, and rubbish; excelling in dirt most places that human nature has anywhere inhabited. Poor Guachos! They drink Paraguay tea, sucking it up in succession, through the same tin pipe, from one common skillet. They are hospitable, sooty, leathery, lying, laughing fellows; of excellent talent in their sphere. They have stoicism, though ignorant of Zeno; nay stoicism coupled with real gayety of heart. Amidst their reek, they laugh loud, in rough jolly banter; they twang, in a plaintive manner, rough love-melodies on a kind of guitar; smoke infinite tobacco; and delight in gambling and ardent spirits, ordinary refuge of voracious empty souls. For the same reason, and a better, they delight also in Corpus-Christi ceremonies, mass-chantings, and devotional performances. These men are fit to be drilled into something! Their lives stand there like empty capacious bottles, calling to the heavens and the earth, and all Dr. Francias who may pass that way: "Is there nothing to put into us, then? Nothing but nomadic idleness, Jesuit superstition, rubbish, reek, and dry stripes of tough beef?" Ye unhappy Guachos, —yes, there is something other, there are several things other, to put into you! But withal, you will observe, the seven devils have first to be put out of you: Idleness, lawless Brutalness, Darkness, Falseness—seven devils or more. And the way to put something into you is, alas, not so plain at present! Is it,—alas, on the whole, is it not perhaps to lay good horse-whips lustily *upon* you, and cast out these seven devils as a preliminary?

How Francia passed his days in such a region, where philosophy, as is too clear, was at the lowest ebb? Francia, like Quintus Fixlein, had "perennial fire-proof joys, namely

* Letters on Paraguay.

employments." He had much law-business, a great and ever-increasing reputation as a man at once skilful and faithful in the management of causes for men. Then, in his leisure hours, he had his Volneys, Raynals; he had second-hand scientific treatises in French; he loved to "interrogate Nature," as they say; to possess theodolites, telescopes, star-glasses,—any kind of glass or book, or gazing implement whatever, through which he might try to catch a glimpse of Fact in this strange Universe: poor Francia! Nay, it is said, his hard heart was not without inflammability; was sensible to those Andalusian eyes still bright in the tenth or twelfth generation. In such case, too, it may have burnt, one would think, like anthracite, in a somewhat ardent manner. Rumours to this effect are afloat; not at once incredible. Pity there had not been some Andalusian pair of eyes, with speculation, depth and soul enough in the rear of them to fetter Dr. Francia permanently, and make a house-father of him. It had been better; but it befell not. As for that light-headed, smart, brown girl whom, twenty years afterwards, you saw selling flowers on the streets of Assumpcion, and leading a light life, is there any certainty that she was Dr. Francia's daughter? Any certainty that, even if so, he could and should have done something considerable for her?* Poor Francia, poor light-headed, smart, brown girl,—this present reviewer cannot say!

Francia is a somewhat lonesome, down-looking man, apt to be solitary even in the press of men; wears a face not unvisited by laughter, yet tending habitually towards the sorrowful, the stern. He passes everywhere for a man of veracity, punctuality, of iron methodic rigour; of iron rectitude, above all. "The skilful lawyer," "the learned lawyer," these are reputations; but the "honest lawyer!" This law-case was reported by the Robertsons before they thought of writing a "Francia's Reign of Terror," with that running shriek, which so confuses us. We love to believe the anecdote, even in its present loose state, as significant of many things in Francia:

"It has been already observed that Francia's reputation, as a lawyer, was not only unsullied by venality, but conspicuous for rectitude.

"He had a friend in Assumpcion of the name of Domingo Rodriguez. This man had cast a covetous eye upon a Naboth's vineyard, and this Naboth, of whom Francia was the open enemy, was called Estanislao Machain. Never doubting that the young doctor, like other lawyers, would undertake his unrighteous cause, Rodriguez opened to him his case, and requested, with a handsome retainer, his advocacy of it. Francia saw at once that his friend's pretensions were founded in fraud and injustice; and he not only refused to act as his counsel, but plainly told him, that much as he hated his antagonist Machain, yet if he (Rodriguez) persisted in his iniquitous suit, that antagonist should have his (Francia's) most zealous support. But covetousness, as Ahab's story shows us, is not so easily driven from its pretensions; and in spite of Francia's warning, Rodriguez persisted. As he was a potent man in point of fortune, all was going against Machain and his devoted vineyard.

"At this stage of the question, Francia wrapped himself one night in his cloak, and walked to the house of his inveterate enemy, Machain. The slave who opened the door, knowing that his master and the doctor, like the houses of Montagu and Capulet, were smoke in each other's eyes, refused the lawyer admittance, and ran to inform his master of the strange and unexpected visit. Machain, no less struck by the circumstance than his slave, for some time hesitated; but at length determined to admit Francia. In walked the silent doctor to Machain's chamber. All the papers connected with the law-plea—voluminous enough I have been assured—were outspread upon the defendant's escritoire.

"'Machain,' said the lawyer, addressing him, 'you know I am your enemy. But I know that my friend Rodriguez meditates, and will certainly, unless I interfere, carry against you an act of gross and lawless aggression; I have come to offer my services in your defence.'

"The astonished Machain could scarcely credit his senses; but poured forth the ebullition of his gratitude in terms of thankful acquiescence.

"The first 'escrito,' or writing, sent in by Francia to the Juez de Alzada, or Judge of the Court of Appeal, confounded the adverse advocates, and staggered the judge, who was in their interest. 'My friend,' said the judge to the leading counsel, 'I cannot go forward in this matter, unless you bribe Dr. Francia to be silent.' 'I will try,' replied the advocate, and he went to Naboth's counsel with a hundred doubloons, (about three hundred and fifty guineas,) which he offered him as a bribe to let the cause take its iniquitous course. Considering, too, that his best introduction would be a hint that his douceur was offered with the judge's concurrence, the knavish lawyer hinted to the upright one that such was the fact.

"'*Salga Usted*,' said Francia, '*con sus viles pensamientos, y vilisimo oro de mi casa.*' 'Out with your vile insinuations and dross of gold from my house.'

"Off marched the venal drudge of the unjust judge; and in a moment putting on his capoté, the offended advocate went to the residence of the Juez de Alzada. Shortly relating what had passed between himself and the myrmidon,—'Sir,' continued Francia, 'you are a disgrace to law, and a blot upon justice. You are, moreover, completely in my power; and unless to-morrow I have a decision in favour of my client, I will make your seat upon the bench too hot for you, and the insignia of your judicial office shall become the emblems of your shame.'

"The morrow *did* bring a decision in favour of Francia's client. Naboth retained his vineyard; the judge lost his reputation; and the young doctor's fame extended far and wide."

On the other hand, it is admitted that he quarrelled with his father, in those days; and, as is reported, never spoke to him more. The

* Robertson.

subject of the quarrel is vaguely supposed to have been "money matters." Francia is not accused of avarice; nay, is expressly acquitted of loving money, even by Rengger. But he did hate injustice;—and probably was not indisposed to allow *himself*, among others, "the height of fair play!" A rigorous, correct man, that will have a spade be a spade; a man of much learning in Creole law, and occult French sciences, of great talent, energy, fidelity:—a man of some temper withal: unhappily subject to private "hypochondria; black private thunder-clouds, whence probably the origin of these *lightnings*, when you poke into him! He leads a lonesome self-secluded life; "interrogating nature" through mere star-glasses, and Abbé-Raynal philosophies—who in that way will yield no very exuberant response. Mere law-papers, advocate fees, civic officialities, renowns, and the wonder of Assumpcion Guachos;—not so much as a pair of Andalusian eyes that can *lasso* him, except in a temporary way: this man seems to have got but a lean lease of nature, and may end in a rather shrunk condition! A century ago, with this attrabiliar earnestness of his, and such a reverberatory furnace of passions, inquiries, unspeakabilities burning in him, deep under cover, he might have made an excellent monk of St. Dominic, fit almost for canonization; nay, an excellent Superior of the Jesuits, Grand Inquisitor, or the like, had you developed him in that way. But, for all this, he is now a day too late. Monks of St. Dominic that might have been, do now, instead of devotional raptures and miraculous suspensions in prayer, produce,—brown accidental female infants, to sell flowers, in an indigent state, on the streets of Assumpcion! It is grown really a most barren time; and this Francia with his grim unspeakabilities, with his fiery splenetic humours, kept close under lock and key, what has he to look for in it? A post on the bench, in the municipal *Cabildo*,—nay, he has already a post in the Cabildo; he has already been Alcalde, Lord-Mayor of Assumpcion, and ridden in such gilt coach as they had. He can look for little, one would say, but barren moneys, barren Guacho world-celebrities; Abbé-Raynal philosophisms also very barren; wholly a barren life-voyage of it, ending—in *zero*, thinks the Abbé-Raynal?

But no; the world wags not that way in those days. Far over the waters there have been federations of the Champ de Mars; guillotines, portable-guillotines, and a French people risen against tyrants; there has been a *Sansculottism*, speaking at last in canon-volleys and the crash of towns and nations over half the world. Sleek Fatpauncho Usandwonto, sleek aristocratic Donothingism, sunk as in death-sleep in its well-stuffed easy chair, or staggering in somnambulism on the house-tops, seemed to itself to hear a voice say, Sleep no more, Donothingism; Donothingism doth murder sleep! It was indeed a terrible explosion, that of Sansculottism; commingling very Tartarus with the old-established stars;—fit, such a tumult was it, to awaken all but the dead. And out of it there had come Napoleonisms, Tamerlanisms; and then as a branch of these, conventions of Aranjuez, soon followed by Spanish Juntas, Spanish Cortes; and, on the whole, a smiting broad awake of poor old Spain itself, much to its amazement. And naturally of New Spain next,—*its* double amazement, seeing itself awake! And so, in the new hemisphere too, arise wild projects, angry arguings; arise armed gatherings in Santa Marguerita Island with Bolivars and Invasions of Cumana; revolts of La Plata, revolts of this and then of that; the subterranean electric element, shock on shock, shaking and exploding, in the new hemisphere too, from sea to sea. Very astonishing to witness, from the year 1810 and onwards. Had Dr. Rodriguez Francia three ears, he would hear; as many eyes as Argus, he would gaze! He is all eye, he is all ear. A new, entirely different figure of existence is cut out for Dr. Rodriguez.

The Paraguay people as a body, lying far inland, with little speculation in their heads, were in no haste to adopt the new republican gospel; but looked first how it would succeed in shaping itself into facts. Buenos Ayres, Tucuman, most of the La Plata provinces, had made their revolutions, brought in the reign of liberty, and unluckily driven out the reign of law and regularity; before the Paraguenos could resolve on such an enterprise. Perhaps they are afraid? General Belgrano, with a force of a thousand men, missioned by Buenos Ayres, came up the river to countenance them, in the end of 1810; but was met on their frontier in array of war; was attacked, or at least was terrified, in the night watches, so that his men all fled;—and on the morrow, poor General Belgrano found himself not a countenancer, but one needing countenance; and was in a polite way sent down the river again!* Not till a year after did the Paraguenos, by spontaneous movement, resolve on a career of freedom;—resolve on getting some kind of Congress assembled, and the old government sent its ways. Francia, it is presumable, was active at once in exciting and restraining them: the fruit was now drop-ripe, we may say, and fell by a shake. Our old royal governor went aside, worthy man, with some slight grimace, when ordered to do so; National Congress introduced itself: secretaries read papers, compiled chiefly out of Rollin's Ancient History, and we became a Republic: with Don Fulgencio Yegros, one of the richest Guachos and best horsemen of the province, for *President*, and two assessors with him, called also *Vocales*, or Vowels, whose names escape us; Francia, as *Secretary*, being naturally the Consonant, or motive soul of the combination. This, as we grope out the date, was in 1811. The Paraguay Congress, having completed this constitution, went home again to its field-labours, hoping a good issue.

Feebler light hardly ever dawned for the historical mind, than this which is shed for us by Rengger, Robertsons, and Company, on the birth, cradling, baptismal processes, and early fortunes of the new Paraguay Republic. Through long vague, and, indeed, intrinsically

* Rengger.

vacant pages of their books, it lies gray, undecipherable, without form and void. Francia was secretary, and a republic did take place; this, as one small clear-burning fact, shedding far a comfortable visibility, conceivability over the universal darkness, and making it into conceivable dusk with one rushlight fact in the centre of it,—this we do know; and, cheerfully yielding to necessity, decide that this shall suffice us to know. What more is there? Absurd somnolent persons, struck broad awake by the subterranean concussion of civil and religious liberty all over the world, meeting together to establish a republican career of freedom, and compile official papers out of Rollin,—are not a subject on which the historical mind *can* be enlightened. The historical mind, thank Heaven, forgets such persons and their papers, as fast as you repeat them. Besides, these Guacho populations are greedy, superstitious, vain; and, as Miers said in his haste, mendacious every soul of them! Within the confines of Paraguay, we know for certain but of one man who would do himself an injury to do a just or true thing under the sun; one man who understands in his heart that this Universe is an eternal Fact,—and not some huge temporary Pumpkin, saccharine, absinthian; the rest of its significance chimerical merely! Such men cannot have a history, though a Thucydides came to write it.—Enough for us to understand that Don This was a vapouring blockhead, who followed his pleasures, his peculations, and Don That another of the same; that there occurred fatuities, mismanagements innumerable; then discontents, open grumblings, and, as a running accompaniment, intriguings, caballings, outings, innings; till the Government House, fouler than when the Jesuits had it, became a bottomless, pestilent inanity, insupportable to any articulate-speaking soul; till Secretary Francia should feel that he, for one, could not be Consonant to such a set of Vowels; till Secretary Francia, one day, flinging down his papers, rising to his feet, should jerk out with oratorical vivacity his lean right hand, and say, with knit brows, in a low swift tone, "Adieu, Senhores; God preserve you many years!"

Francia withdrew to his *chacra*, a pleasant country-house in the woods of Ytapúa not far off; there to interrogate Nature, and live in a private manner. Parish Robertson, much about this date, which we grope and guess to have been perhaps in 1812, was boarded with a certain ancient Donna Juanna, in that same region; had *tertulias* of unimaginable brilliancy; and often went shooting of an evening. On one of those—but he shall himself report:

"On one of those lovely evenings in Paraguay, after the south-west wind has both cleared and cooled the air, I was drawn, in my pursuit of game, into a peaceful valley, not far from Donna Juanna's, and remarkable for its combination of all the striking features of the scenery of the country. Suddenly I came upon a neat and unpretending cottage. Up rose a partridge; I fired, and the bird came to the ground A voice from behind called out, '*Buen tiro*' 'a good shot.' I turned round, and beheld a gentleman of about fifty years of age, dressed in a suit of black, with a large scarlet *capote*, or cloak, thrown over his shoulders. He had a *maté*-cup in one hand, a cigar in the other; and a little urchin of a negro, with his arms crossed, was in attendance by the gentleman's side. This gentleman's countenance was dark, and his black eyes were very penetrating, while his jet hair, combed back from a bold forehead, and hanging in natural ringlets over his shoulders, gave him a dignified and striking air. He wore on his shoes large golden buckles, and at the knees of his breeches the same."

"In exercise of the primitive and simple hospitality common in the country, I was invited to sit down under the corridor, and to take a cigar and *maté* (cup of Paraguay tea.) A celestial globe, a large telescope, and a theodolite were under the little portico; and I immediately inferred that the personage before me was no other than Doctor Francia."

Yes, here for the first time in authentic history, a remarkable hearsay becomes a remarkable visuality; through a pair of clear human eyes, you look face to face on the very figure of the man. Is not this verily the exact record of those clear Robertsonian eyes, and seven senses; entered accurately, then and not afterwards, on the ledger of the memory? We will hope so; who can but hope so? The figure of the man will, at all events, be exact. Here too is the figure of his library;—the conversation, if any, was of the last degree of insignificance, and may be left out, or supplied *ad libitum*:

"He introduced me to his library, in a confined room, with a very small window, and that so shaded by the roof of the corridor, as to admit the least portion of light necessary for study. The library was arranged on three rows of shelves, extending across the room, and might have consisted of three hundred volumes. There were many ponderous books on law; a few on the inductive sciences; some in French and some in Latin upon subjects of general literature, with Euclid's Elements, and some school-boy treatises on algebra. On a large table were heaps of law-papers and processes. Several folios bound in vellum were outspread upon it; a lighted candle (though placed there solely with a view to light cigars) lent its feeble aid to illumine the room; while a maté-cup and inkstand, both of silver, stood on another part of the table. There was neither carpet nor mat on the brick floor; and the chairs were of such ancient fashion, size, and weight, that it required a considerable effort to move them from one spot to another."

Peculation, malversation, the various forms of imbecility and voracious dishonesty, went their due course in the government offices of Assumpcion, unrestrained by Francia, and unrestrainable:—till, as we may say, it reached a height; and, like other suppurations and diseased concretions in the living system, had to burst, and take itself away. To the eyes of Paraguay in general, it had become clear that such a reign of liberty was unendurable;—that some new revolution, or change of ministry, was indispensable.

Rengger says that Francia withdrew "more

than once" to his *chacra*, disgusted with his colleagues; who always, by unlimited promises and protestations, had to flatter him back again: and then anew disgusted him. Francia is the Consonant of these absurd "Vowels;" no business can go on without Francia! And the finances are deranged, insolvent; and the military, unpaid, ineffective, cannot so much as keep out the Indians; and there comes trouble and rumour of war from Buenos Ayres;—alas, from what quarter of the great continent come there other than troubles and rumours of war? Patriot generals become traitor generals; get themselves "shot in market-places:" revolution follows revolution. Artigas, close on our borders, has begun harrying the Banda Oriental with fire and sword; "dictating despatches from cow-skulls." Like clouds of wolves,—only feller, being mounted on horseback, with pikes,—the Indians dart in on us; carrying conflagration and dismay. Paraguay must get itself governed, or it will be worse for Paraguay! The eyes of Paraguay, we can well fancy, turn to the one man of talent they have, the one man of veracity they have.

In 1813 a second Congress is got together: we fancy it was Francia's last advice to the Government suppuration, when it flattered him back for the last time, to ask his advice. That such suppuration do now dissolve itself, and a new Congress be summoned! In the new Congress, the *Vocales* are voted out; Francia and Fulgencio are named joint *Consuls*: with Francia for Consul, and Don Fulgencio Yegros for *Consul's*-cloak, it may be better. Don Fulgencio rides about in gorgeous sash and epaulettes, a rich man and horse-subduer; good as a Consul's cloak;—but why should the real Consul have a *cloak?* Next year in the third Congress, Francia, "by insidious manœuvring," by "favour of the military," and, indeed, also in some sort, we may say, by law of Nature,—gets himself declared *Dictator:* "three years," or for life, may in these circumstances mean much the same. This was in 1814. Francia never assembled any Congress more; having stolen the constitutional palladiums, and insidiously got his wicked will! Of a Congress that compiled constitutions out of Rollin, who would not lament such destiny? This Congress should have met again! It was indeed, say Rengger and the Robertsons themselves, such a Congress as never met before in the world; a Congress which knew not its right hand from its left; which drank infinite rum in the taverns; and had one wish, that of getting on horseback, home to its field-husbandry and partridge-shooting. The military mostly favoured Francia; being gained over by him,—the thief of constitutional palladiums.

With Francia's entrance on the government as Consul, still more as Dictator, a great improvement, it is granted even by Rengger, did in all quarters forthwith show itself. The finances were husbanded, were accurately gathered; every official person in Paraguay had to bethink him, and begin doing his work, instead of merely seeming to do it. The soldiers Francia took care to see paid and drilled; to see march, with real death-shot and service, when the Indians or other enemies showed themselves. *Guardias*, guardhouses, at short distances, were established along the river's bank and all round the dangerous frontiers; wherever the Indian centaur-troop showed face, an alarm-cannon went off, and soldiers, quickly assembling, with actual death-shot and service, were upon them. These wolf-hordes had to vanish into the heart of their deserts again. The land had peace. Neither Artigas, nor any of the fire-brands and war-plagues which were distracting South America from side to side, could get across the border. All negotiation or intercommuning with Buenos Ayres, or with any of these war-distracted countries, was peremptorily waived. To no Congress of Lima, General Congress of Panama, or other general or particular congress would Francia, by deputy or message, offer the smallest recognition. All South America raging and ravening like one huge dog-kennel gone rabid, we here in Paraguay have peace, and cultivate our tea-trees: why should we not let well alone? By degrees, one thing acting on another, and this ring of frontier "guard-houses" being already erected there, a rigorous *sanitary line*, impregnable as brass, was drawn round all Paraguay; no communication, import or export trade allowed, except by the Dictator's license,—given on payment of the due moneys, when the political horizon seemed innocuous; refused when otherwise. The Dictator's trade-licenses were a considerable branch of his revenues; his entrance dues, somewhat onerous to the foreign merchant, (think the Messrs. Robertson,) were another. Paraguay stood isolated; the rabid dog-kennel raging round it, wide as South America, but kept out as by lock and key.

These were vigorous measures, gradually coming on the somnolent Guacho population! It seems, meanwhile, that, even after the perpetual dictatorship, and onwards to the fifth or the sixth year of Francia's government, there was, though the constitutional palladiums were stolen, nothing very special to complain of. Paraguay had peace; sat under its tea-tree, the rabid dog-kennel, Indians, Artigueno and other war-firebrands, all shut out from it. But in that year 1819, the second year of the perpetual dictatorship, there arose, not for the first time, dim indications of "plots," even dangerous plots! In that year the firebrand Artigas was finally quenched; obliged to beg a lodging even of Francia, his enemy;—and got it, hospitably though contemptuously. And now straightway there advanced, from Artigas's lost, wasted country, a certain General Ramirez, his rival and victor, and fellow-bandit and firebrand. This General Ramirez advanced up to our very frontier; first, with offers of alliance: failing that, with offers of war; on which latter offer he was closed with, was cut to pieces; and—a letter was found about him, addressed to Don Fulgencio Yegros, the rich Guacho horseman and Ex-Consul; which arrested all the faculties of Dr. Francia's most intense intelligence, there and then! A conspiracy, with Don Fulgencio at the head of it; conspiracy which seems the wide-spread the farther one investigates it; which has been brewing itself these "two years," and now "on Good-Friday next" is to be burst out; starting with the massacre of Dr. Francia and others, whatever it may close with!* Francia was not a man to be trifled with in plots! He looked, watched, investigated, till he got the exact extent, position, nature, and structure of this plot fully in his eye; and then—why, then he pounced on it like a glede-falcon, like a fierce condor, suddenly from the invisible blue; struck beak and claws into the very heart of it, tore it into small fragments, and consumed it on the spot. It is Francia's way! This was the last plot, though not the first plot, Francia ever heard of during his perpetual dictatorship.

It is, as we find, over these three or these two years, while the Fulgencio plot is getting itself pounced upon and torn in pieces, that the "reign of terror," properly so called, extends. Over these three or these two years only,—though the "running shriek" of it confuses all things to the end of the chapter. It was in this stern period that Francia executed above forty persons. Not entirely inexplicable! "*Par Dios*, ye shall not conspire against me; I will not allow it. The career of freedom, be it known to all men, and Guachos, is not yet begun in this country; I am still only casting out the Seven Devils. My lease of Paraguay, a harder one than your stupidities suppose, is for life; the contract is, Thou must die if thy lease be taken from thee. Aim not at my life, ye constitutional Guachos,—or let it be a diviner man than Don Fulgencio, the horse-subduer, that does it. By heaven, if you aim at my life, I will bid you have a care of your own!" He executed upwards of forty persons. How many he arrested, flogged, cross-questioned—for he is an inexorable man! If you are guilty, or suspected of guilt, it will go ill with you here. Francia's arrest, carried by a grenadier, arrives; you are in strait prison; you are in Francia's bodily presence; those sharp St. Dominic eyes, that diabolic intellect, prying into you, probing, cross-questioning you, till the secret cannot be hid: till the "three ball cartridges" are handed to a sentry;—and your doom is Rhadamanthine!

But the plots, as we say, having ceased by this rough surgery, it would appear that there was, for the next twenty years, little or no more of it, little or no use for more. The "reign of terror," one begins to find, was properly a reign of rigour; which would become "terrible" enough if you infringed the rules of it, but which was peaceable otherwise, regular otherwise. Let this, amid the "running shriek," which will and should run its full length in such circumstances, be well kept in mind.

It happened too, as Rengger tells us, in the same year, (1820, as we grope and gather,) that a visitation of locusts, as sometimes occurs, destroyed all the crops of Paraguay; and there was no prospect but of universal dearth or famine. The crops are done; eaten by locusts; the summer at an end! We have no foreign trade, or next to none, and never had almost any; what will become of Paraguay and its Guachos? In Guachos is no hope, no help: but in a Dionysius of the Guachos? Dictator Francia, led by occult French sciences and natural sagacity, nay, driven by necessity itself, peremptorily commands the farmers throughout all Paraguay to sow a certain portion of their lands anew; with or without hope, under penalties! The result was a moderately good harvest still: the result was a discovery that two harvests were, every year, possible in Paraguay; that agriculture, a rigorous Dictator presiding over it, could be infinitely improved there.* As Paraguay has about 100,000 square miles of territory mostly fertile, and only some two souls planted on each square mile thereof, it seemed to the Dictator that this, and not foreign trade, might be a good course for his Paraguenos. This accordingly, and not foreign trade, in the present state of the political horizon, was the course resolved on; the course persisted in, "with evident advantages," says Rengger. Thus, one thing acting on another,—domestic plot, hanging on Artigas's country from without; and locust swarms with improvement of husbandry in the interior; and those guard-houses all already there, along the frontier,—Paraguay came more and more to be hermetically closed; and Francia reigned over it, for the rest of his life, as a rigorous Dionysius of Paraguay, without foreign intercourse, or with such only as seemed good to Francia.

How the Dictator, now secure in possession, did manage this huge Paraguay, which, by strange "insidious" and other means, had fallen in life-lease to him, and was his to do the best he could with, it were interesting to know. What the meaning of him, the result of him actually was? One desiderates some Biography of Francia by a native!—Meanwhile, in the "*Æsthetische Briefwechsel*" of Herr Professor Sauerteig, a work not yet known in England, nor treating specially of this subject, we find, scattered at distant intervals, a remark or two which may be worth translating. Professor Sauerteig, an open soul, looking with clear eye and large recognizing heart over all accessible quarters of the world, has cast a sharp sun-glance here and there into Dr. Francia too. These few philosophical remarks of his, and then a few anecdotes gleaned elsewhere, such as the barren ground yields, must comprise what more we have to say of Francia.

"Pity," exclaims Sauerteig once, "that a nation cannot reform itself, as the English are now trying to do, by what their newspapers call 'tremendous cheers!' Alas, it cannot be done. Reform is not joyous but grievous: no single man can reform himself without stern suffering and stern working; how much less can a nation of men? The serpent sheds not his old skin without rusty disconsolateness: he is not happy but miserable! In the *Water-cure* itself, do you not sit steeped for months, washed to the heart in elemental drenchings: and like Job, are made to curse your day?

* Rengger.

* Rengger, 67, &c.

Reforming of a nation is a terrible business! Thus, too, Medea, when she made men young again, was wont (*du Himmel!*) to hew them in pieces, with meat-axes; cast them into caldrons, and boil them for a length of time. How much handier could they but have done it by 'tremendous cheers' alone!"

—

"Like a drop of surgical antiseptic liquid, poured (by the benign Powers, as I fancy!) into boundless brutal corruptions; very sharp, very caustic, corrosive enough, this tawny tyrannous Dr. Francia, in the interior of the South American continent,—he, too, is one of the elements of the grand phenomenon there. A monstrous moulting process taking place; —monstrous gluttonous *boa-constrictor* (he is of length from Panama to Patagonia) shedding his old skin; whole continent getting itself chopped to pieces, and boiled in the Medea caldron, to become young again,—unable to manage it by 'tremendous cheers' alone!"

—

"What they say about 'love of power' amounts to little. Power? Love of 'power' merely to make flunkies come and go for you is a 'love,' I should think, which enters only into the minds of persons in a very infantine state! A grown man, like this Dr. Francia, who wants nothing, as I am assured, but three cigars daily, a cup of *maté*, and four ounces of butchers' meat with brown bread; the whole world and its united flunkies, taking constant thought of the matter, can do nothing for him but that only. That he already has, and has had always; why should he, not being a minor, love flunkey 'power?' He loves to see *you* about him, with your flunkey promptitudes, with your grimaces, adulations, and sham-loyalty. You are so beautiful, a daily and hourly feast to the eye and soul? Ye unfortunates, from his heart rises one prayer, That the last created flunkey had vanished from this universe, never to appear more!

"And yet truly a man does tend, and must under frightful penalties perpetually tend, to be king of his world; to stand in his world as what he is, a centre of light and order, not of darkness and confusion. A man loves power: yes, if he sees disorder his eternal enemy rampant about him, he does love to see said enemy in the way of being conquered; he can have no rest till that come to pass! Your Mohammed can bear a rent cloak, but clouts it with his own hands, how much more a rent country, a rent world. He has to imprint the image of his own veracity upon the world, and shall, and must, and will do it, more or less: it is at his peril if he neglect any great or any small possibility he may have of this. Francia's inner flame is but a meager, blue-burning one: let him irradiate midnight Paraguay with it, such as it is."

—

"Nay, on the whole, how cunning is Nature in getting *her* farms leased! Is it not a blessing this Paraguay can get the one veracious man it has, to take lease of it, in these sad circumstances? His farm profits, and whole wages, it would seem, amount only to what is called 'Nothing and find yourself!' Spartan food and lodging, solitude, two cigars, and a cup of *maté* daily, he already had."

Truly, it would seem, as Sauerteig remarks, Dictator Francia had not a very joyous existence of it, in this his life-lease of Paraguay! Casting out of Seven Devils from a Guacho population is not joyous at all; both exorcist and exorcised find it sorrowful! Meanwhile, it does appear, there was some improvement made; no veritable labour, not even a Dr. Francia's, is in vain.

Of Francia's improvements there might as much be said of his cruelties or rigours; for indeed, at bottom, the one was in proportion to the other. He improved agriculture:—not two ears of corn where only one grew, but two harvests of corn, as we have seen! He introduced schools, "boarding-schools," "elementary schools," and others, on which Rengger has a chapter; everywhere he promoted education, as he could; repressed superstition as he could. Strict justice between man was enforced in his law-courts: he himself would accept no gift, not even a trifle, in any case whatever. Rengger, on packing up for departure, had left in his hands, not from forgetfulness, a Print of Napoleon; worth some shillings in Europe, but invaluable in Paraguay, where Francia, who admired this hero much, had hitherto seen no likeness of him but a Nürnberg caricature. Francia sent an express after Rengger, to ask what the value of the Print was. No value; M. Rengger could not sell Prints; it was much, at his Excellency's service. His Excellency straightway returned it. An exact, decisive man! Peculation, idleness, ineffectuality, had to cease in all the public offices of Paraguay. So far as lay in Francia, no public and private man in Paraguay was allowed to slur his work; all public and all private men, so far as lay in Francia, were forced to do their work or die! We might define him as the born enemy of quacks; one who has from Nature a heart-hatred of *un*veracity in man or in thing, wheresoever he sees it. Of persons who do not speak the truth, and do not act the truth, he has a kind of diabolic-divine impatience; they had better disappear out of his neighbourhood. Poor Francia: his light was but a very sulphurous, meager, blue-burning one; but he irradiated Paraguay with it (as our Professor says) the best he could.

That he had to maintain himself *alive* all the while, and would suffer no man to glance contradiction at him, but instantaneously repressed all such: this too we need no ghost to tell us; this lay in the very nature of the case. His lease of Paraguay was a *life*-lease. He had his "three ball cartridges" ready for whatever man he found aiming at *his* life. He had frightful prisons. He had *Tevego* far up among the wastes, a kind of Paraguay Siberia, to which unruly persons, not yet got the length of shooting, were relegated. The main exiles, Rengger says, were drunken mulattoes and the class called unfortunate-females. They lived miserably there; became a sadder, and perhaps a wiser, body of mulattoes and unfortunate-females.

But let us listen for a moment to the Reverend Manuel Perez as he preaches, "in the Church of the Incarnation at Assumpcion, on the 20th October, 1840," in a tone somewhat nasal, yet trustworthy withal. His Funeral Discourse, translated into a kind of English, presents itself still audible in the "Argentine News" of Buenos Ayres, No. 813. We select some passages; studying to abate the nasal tone a little; to reduce, if possible, the Argentine English under the law of grammar. It is the worst translation in the world, and does poor Manuel Perez one knows not what injustice. This Funeral Discourse has "much surprised" the Able Editor, it seems;—has led him perhaps to ask, or be readier for asking, Whether all that confused loud litanying about "reign of terror," and so forth, was not possibly of a rather long-eared nature?

"Amid the convulsions of revolution," says the Reverend Manuel, "The Lord, looking down with pity on Paraguay, raised up Don José Gaspar Francia for its deliverance. *And when*, in the words of my text, *the children of Israel cried unto the Lord, the Lord raised up a deliverer to the children of Israel, who delivered them.*"

"What measures did not his Excellency devise, what labours undergo, to preserve peace in the Republic at home, and place it in an attitude to command respect from abroad! His first care was directed to obtain supplies of arms, and to discipline soldiers. To all that would import arms he held out the inducement of exemption from duty, and the permission to export in return whatever produce they preferred. An abundant supply of excellent arms was, by these means, obtained. I am lost in wonder to think how this great man could attend to such a multiplicity of things! He applied himself to study of the military art; and, in a short time, taught the exercise, and directed military evolutions like the skilfullest veteran. Often have I seen his Excellency go up to a recruit, and show him by example how to take aim at the target. Could any Parágueno think it other than honourable to carry a musket, when his Dictator taught him how to manage it? The cavalry-exercise too, though it seems to require a man at once robust and experienced in horsemanship, his Excellency as you know did himself superintend: at the head of his squadrons he charged and manœuvred, as if bred to it: and directed them with an energy and vigour which infused his own martial spirit into these troops."

"What evils do not the people suffer from highwaymen!" exclaims his Reverence, a little farther on; "violence, plunder, murder, are crimes familiar to these malefactors. The inaccessible mountains and wide deserts in this Republic seemed to offer impunity to such men. Our Dictator succeeded in striking such a terror into them that they entirely disappeared, seeking safety in a change of life. His Excellency saw that the manner of inflicting the punishment was more efficacious than even the punishment itself; and on this principle he acted. Whenever a robber could be seized, he was led to the nearest guardhouse (*Guardia*); a summary trial took place; and, straightway, so soon as he had made confession, he was shot. These means proved effectual. Ere long the Republic was in such security, that, we may say, a child might have travelled from the Uruguay to the Parana without other protection than the dread which the Supreme Dictator inspired."—This is saying something, your Reverence!

"But what is all this compared to the demon of anarchy. Oh!" exclaims his simple Reverence, "Oh, my friends, would I had the talent to paint to you the miseries of a people that fall into anarchy? And was not our Republic on the very eve of this? Yes, brethren."—"It behoved his Excellency to be prompt; to smother the enemy in his cradle! He did so. He seized the leaders; brought to summary trial, they were convicted of high treason against the country. What a struggle now, for his Excellency, between the law of duty and the voice of feeling"—if feeling to any extent there were! "I," exclaimed his Reverence, "am confident that had the doom of imprisonment on those persons seemed sufficient for the state's peace, his Excellency never would have ordered their execution." It was unavoidable; nor was it avoided; it was done! "Brethren, should not I hesitate, lest it be a profanation of the sacred place I now occupy, if I seem to approve sanguinary measures in opposition to the mildness of the Gospel? Brethren, no. God himself approved the conduct of Solomon in putting Joab and Adonijah to death." Life is sacred, thinks his Reverence, but there is something more sacred still: wo to him who does not know that withal!

Alas, your Reverence, Paraguay has not yet succeeded in abolishing capital punishment, then? But indeed neither has Nature, anywhere that I hear of, yet succeeded in abolishing it. Act with the due degree of perversity, you are sure enough of being violently put to death, in hospital or highway—by dyspepsia, delirium tremens, or stuck through by the kindled rage of your fellow-men! What can the friend of humanity do? Twaddle in Exeter-hall or elsewhere, "till he become a bore to us," and perhaps worse! An advocate in Arras once gave up a good judicial appointment, and retired into frugality and privacy, rather than doom one culprit to die by law. The name of this advocate, let us mark it well, was Maximilien Robespierre. There are sweet kinds of twaddle that have a deadly virulence of poison concealed in them; like the sweetness of sugar of lead. Were it not better to make *just* laws, think you, and then execute them strictly,—as the gods still do?

"His Excellency next directed his attention to purging the state from another class of enemies," says Perez in the Incarnation Church; "the peculating tax-gatherers, namely. Vigilantly detecting their frauds, he made them refund for what was past, and took precautions against the like in future; all their accounts were to be handed in, for his examination, once every year."

"The habit of his Excellency when he delivered out articles for the supply of the public; that prolix and minute counting of things apparently unworthy of his attention—had its origin in the same motive. I believe that he did so, less from a want of confidence in the individuals lately appointed for this purpose, than from a desire to show them with what delicacy they should proceed. Hence likewise his ways, in scrupulously examining every piece of artisans' workmanship."

"Republic of Paraguay, how art thou indebted to the toils, the vigils and cares of our Perpetual Dictator! It seemed as if this extraordinary man were endowed with ubiquity, to attend to all thy wants and exigences. Whilst in his closet, he was traversing thy frontiers to place thee in an attitude of security. What devastation did not those inroads of Indians from the Chaco occasion to the inhabitants of Rio-Abajo? Ever and anon there reached Assumpcion, tidings of the terror and affliction caused by their incursions. Which of us hoped that evils so wide-spread, ravages so appalling, could be counteracted? Our Dictator, nevertheless, did devise effectual ways of securing that part of the Republic.

"Four respectable fortresses with competent garrisons have been the impregnable barrier which has restrained the irruptions of those ferocious Savages. Inhabitants of Rio-Abajo! rest tranquil in your homes: you are a portion of the people whom the Lord confided to the care of our Dictator; you are safe."

"The precautions and wise measures he adopted to repel force, and drive back the Savages to the north of the Republic; the fortresses of Climpo, of San Carlos de Apa, placed on the best footing for defence; the orders and instructions furnished to the Villa de la Concepcion,—secured that quarter of the republic under attack from all.

"The great wall, ditch, and fortress on the opposite bank of the river Paraná; the force and judicious arrangement of the troops distributed over the interior in the south of our Republic, have commanded the respect of its enemies in that quarter."

"The beauty, the symmetry and good taste displayed in the building of cities convey an advantageous idea of their inhabitants," continues Perez: "Thus thought Caractacus, King of the Angles,"—thus think most persons! "His Excellency, glancing at the condition of the capital of the republic, saw a city in disorder and without police; streets without regularity, houses built according to the caprice of their owners."

But enough, O Perez; for it becomes too nasal! Perez, with a confident face, asks, in fine, Whether all these things do not clearly prove to men and Guachos of sense, that Dictator Francia *was* "the deliverer whom the Lord raised up to deliver Paraguay from its enemies?"—Truly, O Perez, the benefits of him seem to have been considerable. Undoubtedly a man "sent by Heaven,"—as all of us are! Nay, it may be, the benefit of him is not even yet exhausted, even yet entirely become visible. Who knows but, in unborn centuries, Paragueno men will look back to their lean iron Francia, as men do, in such cases, to the one veracious person, and institute considerations! Oliver Cromwell, dead two hundred years, does yet speak; nay, perhaps, now first begins to speak. The meaning and meanings of the one true man, never so lean and limited, starting up direct from Nature's heat, in this bewildered Guacho world, gone far away from Nature, are endless!

The Messrs. Robertson are very merry on this attempt of Francia's to rebuild on a better plan the City of Assumpcion. The City of Assumpcion, full of tropical vegetation and "permanent hedges, the deposits of nuisance and vermin,"* has no pavement, no straightness of streets; the sandy thoroughfare, in some quarters, is torn by the rain into gullies, impassable with convenience to any animal but a kangaroo. Francia, after meditation, decides on having it remodelled, paved, straightened—irradiated with the image of the one regular man. Robertson laughs to see a Dictator, sovereign ruler, straddling about, "taking observations with his theodolite," and so forth: O Robertson, if there was no other man that *could* observe with a theodolite? Nay, it seems further, the improvement of Assumpcion was attended, once more, with the dreadfullest tyrannies: peaceable citizens dreaming no harm, no active harm to any soul, but mere peaceable passive dirt and irregularity to all souls, were ordered to pull down their houses which happened to stand in the middle of streets; forced (under rustle of the gallows) to draw their purses, and rebuild them elsewhere! It is horrible. Nay, they said Francia's true aim in these improvements, in this cutting down of the luxuriant "cross hedges" and architectural monstrosities, was merely to save himself from being shot, from under cover, as he rode through the place. It may be so: but Assumpcion is now an improved, paved city, much squarer in the corners (and with the planned capacity, it seems, of growing ever squarer;*) passable with convenience, not to kangaroos only, but to wooden bullock-carts and all vehicles and animals.

Indeed our Messrs. Robertson find something comic as well as tragic in Dictator Francia; and enliven their running shriek, all through this "Reign of Terror," with a pleasant vein of conventional satire. One evening, for example, a Robertson being about to leave Paraguay for England, and having waited upon Francia to make the parting compliments, Francia, to the Robertson's extreme astonishment, orders in a large bale of goods, orders them to be opened on the table there: Tobacco, poncho-cloth, and other produce of the country, all of first-rate quality, and with the prices ticketed. These goods this astonished Robertson is to carry to the "Bar of the House of Commons," and there to say, in such fashion and phraseology as a native may know to be suitable: "Mr. Speaker—Dr. Francia is Dictator of Paraguay, a country of tropical fertility, and 100,000 square miles in extent, producing these commodities at these prices. With nearly all foreign nations he declines altogether to trade; but with the English, such is his notion of them, he is willing and desirous to trade. These are his commodities, in endless quantity; of this quality, at these prices. He wants arms for his part.

* Perez.

What say you, Mr. Speaker?"—Sure enough, our Robertson, arriving at the "Bar of the House of Commons" with such a message, would have cut an original figure! Not to the "House of Commons," was this message properly addressed; but to the English Nation; which Francia, idiot-like, supposed to be somehow represented, and made accessible and addressable in the House of Commons. It was a strange imbecility in any Dictator!—The Robertson, we find accordingly, did *not* take this bale of goods to the bar of the House of Commons; nay, what was far worse, he did not, owing to accidents, go to England at all, or bring any arms back to Francia at all: hence, indeed, Francia's unreasonable detestation of him, hardly to be restrained within the bounds of common politeness! A man who said he would do, and then did not do, was at no time a kind of man admirable to Francia. Large sections of this "Reign of Terror" are a sort of unmusical sonata, or free duet with variations, to this text: "How unadmirable a hide-merchant that does not keep his word!"—"How censurable, not to say ridiculous and imbecile, the want of common politeness in a Dictator!"

Francia was a man that liked performance: and sham-performance, in Paraguay as elsewhere, was a thing too universal. What a time of it had this strict man with *un*real performers, imaginary workmen, public and private, cleric and laic! Ye Guachos,—it is no child's play, casting out those Seven Devils from you!

Monastic or other entirely slumberous church-establishments could expect no great favour from Francia. Such of them as seemed incurable, entirely slumberous, he somewhat roughly shook awake, somewhat sternly ordered to begone. *Débout canaille fainéante*, as his prophet Raynal says; *Débout: aux champs, aux ateliers!* Can I have you sit here, droning old metre through your nose; your heart asleep in mere gluttony, the while; and all Paraguay a wilderness or nearly so,—the Heaven's blessed sunshine growing mere tangles, lianas, yellow-fevers, rattlesnakes, and jaguars on it? Up, swift, to work,—or mark this governmental horsewhip, what the crack of it is, what the cut of it is like to be!—Incurable, for one class, seemed archbishops, bishops, and such like; given merely to a sham-warfare against extinct devils. At the crack of Francia's terrible whip they went, dreading what the cut of it might be. A cheap worship in Paraguay, according to the humour of the people, Francia left; on condition that it did no mischief. Wooden saints and the like ware, he also left sitting in their niches: no new ones, even on solicitation, would he give a doit to buy. Being petitioned to provide a new patron saint for one of his new fortifications once, he made this answer: "O people of Paraguay, how long will you continue idiots? While I was a Catholic I thought as you do; but I now see there are no saints but good cannons that will guard our frontiers!"* This also is noteworthy. He inquired of the two Swiss surgeons, what their religion was; and then added, "Be of what religion you like, here: Christians, Jews, Mussulmans,—but don't be Atheists."

Equal trouble had Francia with his laic workers, and indeed with all manner of workers; for it is in Paraguay as elsewhere, like priest like people. Francia had extensive barrack-buildings, nay city-buildings, (as we have seen,) arm-furnishings; immensities of work going on, and his workmen had in general a tendency to be imaginary. He could get no work out of them; only a more or less deceptive similitude of work! Masons, so-called, builders of houses did not build, but merely seemed to build; their walls would not bear weather; stand on their bases in high winds. Hodge-razors, in all conceivable kinds, were openly marketed, "which were never meant to shave, but only to be sold!" For a length of time Francia's righteous soul struggled sore, yet unexplosively, with the propensities of these unfortunate men. By rebuke, by remonstrance, encouragement, offers of reward, and every vigilance and effort, he strove to convince them that it was unfortunate for a Son of Adam to be an imaginary workman; that every Son of Adam had better make razors which *were* meant to shave. In vain, all in vain! At length Francia lost patience with them. "Thou wretched Fraction, wilt thou be the ninth part even of a tailor? Does it beseem thee to weave cloth of devil's dust instead of true wool; and cut and sew it as if thou wert not a tailor, but the fraction of a very tailor! I cannot endure every thing!" Francia, in despair, erected his "Workman's Gallows." Yes, that institution of the country did actually exist in Paraguay; men and workmen saw it with eyes. A most remarkable, and on the whole, not unbeneficial institution of society there. Robertson gives us the following scene with the Belt-maker of Assumpcion; which, be it literal, or in part poetic, does, no doubt of it, hold the mirror up to Nature in an altogether true, and surely in a surprising manner:

"In came, one afternoon, a poor shoemaker, with a couple of grenadiers' belts, neither according to the fancy of the Dictator. 'Sentinel,'—said he,—and in came the Sentinel; when the following conversation ensued:

"Dictator:—'Take this *bribonazo* (a very favourite word of the Dictator's, and which being interpreted, means 'most impertinent scoundrel')—'take this *bribonazo* to the gibbet over the way; walk him under it half-a-dozen times: and now,' said he, turning to the trembling shoemaker, 'bring me such another pair of belts, and instead of *walking* under the gallows, we shall try how you can *swing* upon it.'

"Shoemaker:—'Please your excellency I have done my best.'

"Dictator:—'Well, *bribon*, if this *be* your best, I shall do *my* best to see that you never again mar a bit of the state's leather. The belts are of no use to me; but they will do very well to hang you upon the little framework which the grenadier will show you.'

"Shoemaker:—'God bless your excellency, the Lord forbid! I am your vassal, your

* Rengger.

slave: day and night have I served, and will serve my lord; only give me two days more to prepare the belts; *y por el alma de un triste zapatéro*, (by the soul of a poor shoemaker,) I will make them to your excellency's liking.'

"Dictator:—'Off with him, sentinel!'

"Sentinel:—'*Venga, bribon:* come along, you rascal.'

"Shoemaker:—'Senor Excelentisimo: *This very night* I will make the belts according to your excellency's pattern.'

"Dictator:—'Well, you shall have till the morning; but still you must pass under the gibbet: it is a salutary process, and may at once quicken the work and improve the workmanship.'

"Sentinel:—'*Vamonos, bribon;* the supreme commands it.'

"Off was the shoemaker marched: he was, according to orders, passed and repassed under the gibbet, and then allowed to retire to his stall."

He worked there with such an alacrity and sibylline enthusiasm, all night, that his belts on the morrow were without parallel in South America; and he is now, if still in this life, Belt-maker general to Paraguay, a prosperous man; grateful to Francia and the gallows, we may hope, for casting certain of the seven devils out of him!

Such an institution of society would evidently not be introducable, under that simple form, in our old-constituted European countries. Yet it may be asked of constitutional persons in these times, By what succedaneum they mean to supply the want of it, then? In a community of imaginary workmen, how can you pretend to have any government, or social thing whatever, that were real? Certain ten-pound franchisers, with their "tremendous cheers," are invited to reflect on this. With a community of quack workmen, it is by the law of Nature impossible that other than a quack government can be got to exist. Constitutional or other, with ballot-boxes or with none, your society in all its phases, administration, legislation, teaching, preaching, praying, and writing periodicals per sheet, will be a quack society; terrible to live in, disastrous to look upon. Such an institution of society, adapted to our European ways, seems pressingly desirable. O Guachos, South-American and European, what a business is it, casting out your seven devils!—

But perhaps the reader would like to take a view of Dr. Francia in the concrete, there as he looks and lives; managing that thousand-sided business for his Paraguenos, in the time of Surgeon Rengger? It is our last extract, or last view of the Dictator, who must hang no longer on our horizon here:

"I have already said that Doctor Francia, so soon as he found himself at the head of affairs took up his residence in the habitation of the former Governors of Paraguay. This edifice, which is one of the largest in Assumpcion, was erected by the Jesuits, a short time before their expulsion, as a house of retreat for laymen, who devoted themselves to certain spiritual exercises instituted by Saint Ignatius. This structure the Dictator repaired and embellished; he has detached it from the other houses in the city, by interposing wide streets. Here he lives, with four slaves, a little negro, one male and two female mulattoes, whom he treats with great mildness. The two males perform the functions of valet-de-chambre and groom. One of the two mulatto women is his cook, and the other takes care of his wardrobe. He leads a very regular life. The first rays of the sun very rarely find him in bed. So soon as he rises, the negro brings a chafing-dish, a kettle, and a pitcher of water; the water is made to boil there. The Dictator then prepares, with the greatest possible care, his *maté*, or Paraguay tea. Having taken this, he walks under the interior colonnade that looks upon the court, and smokes a cigar, which he first takes care to unroll, in order to ascertain that there is nothing dangerous in it, though it is his own sister who makes up his cigars for him. At six o'clock comes the barber, an ill-washed, ill-clad mulatto, given to drink too; but the only member of the faculty whom he trusts in. If the Dictator is in good humour, he chats with the barber; and often in this manner makes use of him to prepare the public for his projects; this barber may be said to be his Official Gazette. He then steps out, in his dressing-gown of printed calico, to the outer colonnade, an open space with pillars, which ranges all round the building: here he walks about, receiving at the same time such persons as are admitted to an audience. Towards seven, he withdraws to his room, where he remains till nine; the officers and other functionaries then come to make their reports, and receive his orders. At eleven o'clock, the *fiel del fecho* (principal secretary) brings the papers which are to be inspected by him, and writes from his dictation till noon. At noon all the officers retire, and Dr. Francia sits down to table. His dinner, which is extremely frugal, he always himself orders. When the cook returns from market, she deposits her provisions at the door of her master's room; the Doctor then comes out, and selects what he wishes for himself. After dinner he takes his *siesta*. On awakening, he drinks his *maté*, and smokes a cigar, with the same precautions as in the morning. From this till four or five, he occupies himself with business, when the escort to attend him on his promenade arrives. The barber then enters and dresses his hair, while his horse is getting ready. During his ride, the Doctor inspects the public works, and the barracks, particularly those of the cavalry, where he has had a set of apartments prepared for his own use. While riding, though surrounded by his escort, he is armed with a sabre, and a pair of double-barrelled pocket-pistols. He returns home about nightfall, and sits down to study till nine; then he goes to supper, which consists of a roast pigeon and a glass of wine. If the weather be fine, he again walks in the outer colonnade, where he often remains till a very late hour. At ten o'clock he gives the watchword. On returning into the house, he fastens all the doors himself."

Francia's brother was already mad. Francia banished this sister by-and-by, because she had employed one of his grenadiers, one of the public government's soldiers, on some errand of her own.* Thou lonely Francia!

Francia's escort of cavalry used to "strike men with the flat of their swords," much more assault them with angry epithets, if they neglected to salute the Dictator as he rode out. Both he and they, moreover, kept a sharp eye for assassins; but never found any, thanks perhaps to their watchfulness.* Had Francia been in Paris!—At one time, also, there arose annoyance in the Dictatorial mind from idle crowds gazing about his Government House, and his proceedings there! Orders were given that all people were to move on, about their affairs, straight across this government esplanade; instructions to the sentry, that if any person paused to gaze, he was to be peremptorily bidden, Move on!—and if he still did not move, to be shot with ball-cartridge. All Paraguay men moved on, looking to the ground, swift as possible, straight as possible, through those precarious spaces; and the affluence of crowds thinned itself almost to the verge of solitude. One day, after many weeks or months, a human figure did loiter, did gaze in the forbidden ground: "Move on!" cried the sentry, sharply; —no effect: "Move on!" and again none. Alas, the unfortunate human figure was an Indian, did not understand human speech, stood merely gaping interrogatively,—whereupon a shot belches forth at him, the whewing of winged lead; which luckily only whewed, and did not hit! The astonishment of the Indian must have been great, his retreat-pace rapid. As for Francia he summoned the sentry with hardly suppressed rage, "What news, *Amigo?*" The sentry quoted "your Excellency's order;" Francia cannot recollect such an order; commands now, that at all events such order cease.

It remains still that we say a word, not in excuse, which might be difficult, but in explanation, which is possible enough, of Francia's unforgivable insult to human science in the person of M. Aimé Bonpland. M. Aimé Bonpland, friend of Humboldt, after much botanical wandering, did, as all men know, settle himself in Entre Rios, an Indian or Jesuit country close on Francia, now burnt to ashes by Artigas; and there set up a considerable establishment for the improved culture of Paraguay tea. Botany? Why, yes,—and perhaps commerce still more. "Botany!" exclaims Francia: "It is shop-keeping agriculture, and tends to prove fatal to my shop. Who is this extraneous individual? Artigas could not give him right to Entre Rios; Entre Rios is at least as much mine as Artigas's! Bring him to me!" Next night, or next, Paraguay soldiers surround M. Bonpland's tea establishment; gallop M. Bonpland over the frontiers, to his appointed village in the interior; root out his tea-plants; scatter his four hundred Indians, and—we know the rest! Hard-hearted Monopoly refusing to listen to the charmings of Public Opinion or Royal-Society presidents, charm they never so wisely! M. Bonpland, at full liberty some time since, resides still in South America,—and is expected by the Robertsons, not altogether by this Editor, to publish his Narrative, with a due running shriek.

* Rengger.

Francia's treatment of Artigas, his old enemy, the bandit and firebrand, reduced now to beg shelter of him, was good; humane, even dignified. Francia refused to see or treat with such a person, as he had ever done; but readily granted him a place of residence in the interior, and "thirty piastres a month till he died." The bandit cultivated fields, did charitable deeds, and passed a life of penitence, for his few remaining years. His bandit followers, who took to plundering again, says M. Rengger, "were instantly seized and shot."

On the other hand, that anecdote of Francia's dying father—requires to be confirmed! It seems, the old man, who, as we saw, had long since quarrelled with his son, was dying, and wished to be reconciled. Francia "was busy; —what was in it?—could not come." A second still more pressing message arrives: "The old father dare not die unless he sees his son; fears he shall never enter heaven, if they be not reconciled."—"Then let him enter ——!" said Francia; "I will not come!"* If this anecdote be true, it is certainly, of all that are in circulation about Dr. Francia, by far the worst. If Francia, in that death-hour, could not forgive his poor old father, whatsoever he had, or could in the murkiest, sultriest imagination be conceived to have done against him, then let no man forgive Dr. Francia! But the accuracy of public rumour, in regard to a Dictator who has executed forty persons, is also a thing that can be guessed at. To whom was it, by name and surname, that Francia delivered this extraordinary response? Did the man make, or can he now be got to make, affidavit of it, to credible articulate-speaking persons resident on this earth? If so, let him do it—for the sake of the psychological sciences.

One last fact more. Our lonesome Dictator, living among Guachos, had the greatest pleasure, it would seem, in rational conversation, —with Robertson, with Rengger, with any kind of intelligent human creature, when such could be fallen in with, which was rarely. He would question you with eagerness about the ways of men in foreign places, the properties of things unknown to him; all human interest and insight was interesting to him. Only persons of no understanding being near him for most part, he had to content himself with silence, a meditative cigar and cup of *maté*. O Francia, though thou hadst to execute forty persons, I am not without some pity for thee!

In this manner, all being yet dark and void for European eyes, have we to imagine that the man Rodriguez Francia passed, in a remote, but highly remarkable, not unquestionable or inquestioned manner, across the confused theatre of this world. For some thirty years, he was all the government his native Paraguay could be said to have. For some six-and-twenty years he was express Sovereign of it; for some three, or some two years, a Sovereign with bared sword, stern as Rhadamanthus: through all his years, and

* Robertson.

through all his days, since the beginning of him, a Man or Sovereign of iron energy and industry, of great and severe labour. So lived Dictator Francia, and had no rest; and only in Eternity any prospect of rest. A life of terrible labour;—but for the last twenty years, the Fulgencio plot being once torn in pieces and all now quiet under him, it was a more equable labour: severe but equable, as that of a hardy draught-steed fitted in his harness; no longer plunging and champing; but pulling steadily,—till he do all his rough miles, and get to his still *home*.

So dark were the Messrs. Robertson concerning Francia, they had not been able to learn in the least whether, when their book came out, he was living or dead. He was living then, he is dead now. He is dead, this remarkable Francia; there is no doubt about it: have not we and our readers heard pieces of his Funeral Sermon? He died on the 20th of September, 1840, as the Rev. Perez informs us; the People crowding round his Government House with much emotion, nay, "with tears," as Perez will have it. Three Excellencies succeeded him, as some "Directorate," "*Junta Gubernativa*," or whatever the name of it is, before whom this reverend Perez preaches. God preserve them many years.

THE END.

www.ingramcontent.com/pod-product-compliance
Lightning Source LLC
LaVergne TN
LVHW021232110826
845150LV00002B/314

* 9 7 8 1 4 2 5 5 6 2 1 4 4 *